MAP
SOUTHEAST ASIA

TURNING POINTS AND TRANSITIONS

The **ISEAS – Yusof Ishak Institute** (formerly Institute of Southeast Asian Studies) is an autonomous organization established in 1968. It is a regional centre dedicated to the study of socio-political, security, and economic trends and developments in Southeast Asia and its wider geostrategic and economic environment. The Institute's research programmes are grouped under Regional Economic Studies (RES), Regional Strategic and Political Studies (RSPS), and Regional Social and Cultural Studies (RSCS). The Institute is also home to the ASEAN Studies Centre (ASC), the Nalanda-Sriwijaya Centre (NSC) and the Singapore APEC Study Centre.

ISEAS Publishing, an established academic press, has issued more than 2,000 books and journals. It is the largest scholarly publisher of research about Southeast Asia from within the region. ISEAS Publishing works with many other academic and trade publishers and distributors to disseminate important research and analyses from and about Southeast Asia to the rest of the world.

TURNING POINTS AND TRANSITIONS

Selections from *Southeast Asian Affairs*
1974–2018

Edited by **Daljit Singh • Malcolm Cook**

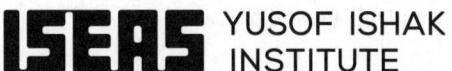

First published in Singapore in 2018 by
ISEAS Publishing
30 Heng Mui Keng Terrace
Singapore 119614

E-mail: publish@iseas.edu.sg
Website: http://bookshop.iseas.edu.sg

All rights reserved. No part of this publication may be reproduced, stored in a retrieval system, or transmitted in any form or by any means, electronic, mechanical, photocopying, recording or otherwise, without the prior permission of the ISEAS – Yusof Ishak Institute.

© 2018 ISEAS – Yusof Ishak Institute

The responsibility for facts and opinions in this publication rests exclusively with the authors and their interpretations do not necessarily reflect the views or the policy of the publisher or its supporters.

ISEAS Library Cataloguing-in-Publication Data

Southeast Asian Affairs. Selection. 1974–2018.
   Turning Points and Transitions : Selections from Southeast Asian Affairs 1974–2018 / edited by Daljit Singh and Malcolm Cook.
   1. Southeast Asia—Politics and government.
   2. Southeast Asia—Foreign relations.
   3. Southeast Asia—Strategic aspects.
   4. Southeast Asia—Economic policy.
   5. ASEAN.
   6. Regionalism—Southeast Asia.
   7. Southeast Asia—Foreign relations—China.
   8. China—Foreign relations—Southeast Asia.
   I. Daljit Singh, editor.
   II. Cook, Malcolm, editor.
DS526.7 S726   2018

ISBN 978-981-4843-07-2 (hard cover)
ISBN 978-981-4843-08-9 (e-book, PDF)

Typeset by Superskill Graphics Pte Ltd
Printed in Singapore by Mainland Press Pte Ltd

Contents

Message from the Director	xi
Foreword by Hal Hill	xii
Foreword by A.B. Shamsul	xiv
Introduction *Daljit Singh*	xvi

THE REGION

The Diplomatic Emergence of China and Its Implications for Southeast Asia (1975*) *Victor C. Funnell*	3
Stability and Security in the Region after ANZUK (1975) *George G. Thomson*	9
The Question of the "Overseas Chinese" (1976) *Wang Gungwu*	20
Southeast Asia 1976: The Handling of Contradictions (1977) *Chan Heng Chee*	32
The "Fukuda Doctrine" and Its Implications for Southeast Asia (1978) *Toru Yano*	54
Expanding Horizons in Southeast Asia? (1994) *Michael Leifer*	60
AFTA in the Light of New Economic Developments (1995) *Florian A. Alburo*	67
The ASEAN Economic Miracle Unravels (1999) *Manuel F. Montes*	79
Southeast Asia in 1999: A False Dawn? (2000) *Daljit Singh*	91
East Timor's Future: Southeast Asian or South Pacific? (2001) *Hal Hill*	101
Southeast Asia in 2002: From Bali to Iraq — Co-operating for Security (2003) *Chin Kin Wah*	112

The Year in ASEAN: The Charter, Trade Agreements, and the
Global Economic Crisis (2010)   126
Rodolfo C. Severino

Seeking Stability in Turbulent Times: Southeast Asia's New Normal? (2015)   133
See Seng Tan and Oleg Korovin

China's Two Silk Roads Initiative: What It Means for Southeast Asia (2015)   150
David Arase

China's International Strategy and Its Implications for Southeast Asia (2016)   166
Zhang Zhexin

BRUNEI

Negara Brunei Darussalam: "A New Nation but an Ancient Country" (1985)   179
Sharon Siddique

Brunei Darussalam: Challenging Stability (2016)   190
Christopher B. Roberts and Malcolm Cook

CAMBODIA

Cambodia and Regional Diplomacy (1982)   201
Sheldon W. Simon

Kampuchea 1979–81: National Rehabilitation in the Eye of an
International Storm (1982)   215
Ben Kiernan

Cambodia 1991: Lasting Peace or Decent Interval? (1992)   227
Mike Yeong

Hun Sen's Pre-emptive Coup: Causes and Consequences (1998)   244
Sorpong Peou

Cambodia in 2017: *Plus ça change…* (2018)   260
Khatharya Um

INDONESIA

Indonesia's Armed Forces: Rejuvenation and Regeneration (1982)   275
Donald E. Weatherbee

Indonesia: The Pancasila State (1985)   283
Donald E. Weatherbee

Contents

The Indonesian Economy Facing the 1990s: Structural Transformation and
Economic Deregulation (1990) 296
Sjahrir

A Year of Upheaval and Uncertainty: The Fall of Soeharto and
Rise of Habibie (1999) 310
Leo Suryadinata

Indonesia: The Regional Autonomy Laws, Two Years Later (2003) 326
Gary F. Bell

The Impact of Domestic and Asian Regional Changes on Indonesian
Foreign Policy (2010) 340
Dewi Fortuna Anwar

ISIS in Indonesia (2015) 353
Sidney Jones and Solahudin

LAOS

Laos: Coping with Confinement (1982) 363
Joseph J. Zasloff and MacAlister Brown

Laos: The Chinese Connection (2009) 384
Martin Stuart-Fox

MALAYSIA

The Security "Gap" in Peninsula Malaysia (1976) 401
Chandran Jeshurun

The 'Battle Royal' – The UMNO Elections of 1987 (1988) 411
A.B. Shamsul

Malaysia: A Fateful September (1999) 431
John Funston

Tears and Fears: Tun Mahathir's Last Hurrah (2004) 444
Bridget Welsh

Malaysia: Political Transformation and Intrigue in an Election Year (2009) 460
Johan Saravanamuttu

MYANMAR

Burma in 1988: *Perestroika* with a Military Face (1989) 477
James F. Guyot

Myanmar 1990: New Era or Old (1991) 494
R.H. Taylor

Myanmar: No Turning Back (2012) 507
Moe Thuzar

Myanmar's General Election 2015: Change was the Name of the Game (2016) 520
Tin Maung Maung Than

THE PHILIPPINES
An Overview of the Philippines (1974) 543
Lim Yoon Lin

Unfinished Revolution: The Philippines in 1986 (1987) 548
David G. Timberman

Terrorism: Evolving Regional Alliances and State Failure in Mindanao (2006) 572
Kit Collier

SINGAPORE
Singapore's Foreign Policy in the Seventies: The Reconciliation of Global
and Regional Interests (1974) 585
Kawin Wilairat

The Downturn in the Singapore Economy: Problems, Prospects and Possibilities
for Recovery (1986) 601
Cheah Hock Beng

A Return to Normal Politics: Singapore General Elections 2011 (2012) 622
Terence Chong

THAILAND
The Revolutionary Situation in Thailand (1975) 637
Boonsanong Punyodyana

American Military Withdrawal from Thailand (1976) 644
Thanat Khoman

The Thai Economy: From Boom to Gloom? (1997) 649
Peter G. Warr

Thailand: A Year of Diminishing Expectations (1999) 665
Naruemon Thabchumpon

Thailand: A Reckoning with History Begins (2007) 678
Michael J. Montesano

What Went Wrong with the Thai Democracy? (2015) 702
Suchit Bunbongkarn

VIETNAM
Vietnam in Perspective (1975) 713
Ng Shui Meng

Year One of Postcolonial Vietnam (1977) 723
Huynh Kim Khanh

Vietnam, ASEAN and the Indochina Refugee Crisis (1980) 738
Frank Frost

Vietnam and ASEAN: A First Anniversary Assessment (1997) 762
Carlyle A. Thayer

Vietnam: In Search of a New Growth Model (2016) 772
Jonathan Pincus

*The year refers to the date of original publication.

Message from the Director

It is a great pleasure for me to write this message for *Turning Points and Transitions: Selections from Southeast Asian Affairs 1974–2018*. This volume is one of the major projects that the ISEAS – Yusof Ishak Institute has undertaken this year to commemorate the fiftieth anniversary of the Institute.

Southeast Asian Affairs is an annual review of the politics, international relations and economics of Southeast Asia. Started in 1974, it was the first major publication series undertaken by ISEAS, commencing six years after its birth. It is still the only publication on Southeast Asia of its kind anywhere in the world today.

A glance at the table of contents of *Turning Points and Transitions* will show chapters on many of the key political, diplomatic and economic developments in the region over the forty-five years covered by the series. Many are authored by prominent scholars and intellectuals of the time, both Asian and Western, with their own individual perspectives.

Needless to say, the editors faced a difficult task selecting 57 chapters out of the 960 in the series. As observed in the Introduction to this volume, they have strived to capture the most important turning points and trends in the rich and eventful history of the region. I think they have succeeded admirably in doing so.

Turning Points and Transitions should be of interest to scholars, students and all others who are curious about the recent history of this region. In a way, it serves as a memory bank for those of us who have lived through those times, to be drawn upon for reflection on how the region came to be what it is today. For the younger generation, it can provide a valuable window into the region's most recent half century of history, which is salient to their understanding of the present.

I thank the editors, Daljit Singh and Malcolm Cook, as well as others who worked with them, for compiling this remarkable volume.

Choi Shing Kwok
Director
ISEAS – Yusof Ishak Institute

Foreword

Hal Hill

For anybody working on Southeast Asia, the ISEAS – Yusof Ishak Institute (hereafter ISEAS) has been a "light on the hill", a beacon of warm hospitality and serious scholarship for fifty years. ISEAS has quickly established itself as unquestionably the leading institution in the field, a great testimony to the vision of its founders and to the wonderful work of its staff, past and present.

In what is arguably its flagship publication, *Southeast Asian Affairs* (hereafter *SEAA*) has been published annually since 1974. Each year, the Southeast Asian community, both within and beyond the region, and from the academic, policy, media and NGO worlds, eagerly awaits the arrival of this volume.

The series has generally followed a winning formula that has clearly stood the test of time. There are general overviews of politics, international relations, economics and social affairs. Then follows detailed country surveys highlighting, interpreting and assessing recent developments. The guiding principle has been to invite scholars with a deep knowledge of the subject matter to write analytical yet accessible and concise papers looking backwards and forward.

Perusing the pages of the present volume — *Turning Points and Transitions: Selections from Southeast Asian Affairs 1974–2018* — the reader is introduced to a veritable "who's who" of Southeast Asian Studies since the 1970s: Wang Gungwu, Chan Heng Chee, Michael Leifer, Rodolfo Severino, Sharon Siddique, Sjahrir, Suchit Bunbongkarn, and many, many others.

Appropriately, the editors have selected papers that call attention to key turning points and trends in the region. These are well reflected in some of the chapter titles: "the handling of contradictions", "the ASEAN economic miracle unravels", "from Bali to Iraq", "Kampuchea 1979–81", "the fall of Soeharto and the rise of Habibie", "what went wrong with the Thai democracy?", among many other arresting titles.

The timing of this volume is propitious. It is an opportunity to celebrate ISEAS's fiftieth birthday, to showcase its unrivalled network of scholars and to reflect on the "journey" that the region has taken since 1974. Few if any regions of the world can match Southeast Asia for its dynamism, its diversity, its rising economic and political coherence, and its effective international engagement. All these dimensions are evident in this wide-ranging volume.

An older generation clearly recalls the great challenges these new nation states faced as they began to make their way in an uncertain world. It needs to be remembered that the region's prospects in the 1960s were highly uncertain. *South-*

east Asia in Turmoil by Brian Crozier (1965) was a widely read volume at the time. This was the era of the "Peking-Pyongyang-Hanoi-Phnom Penh-Jakarta axis of newly emerging forces". Indonesia was "confronting" Malaysia. Malaysia and Singapore separated after a brief union. In the Cold War era, the countries in the region were seen as "dominoes" in some quarters, likely to fall to communism's southern thrust.

How wrong were these gloomy prognostications! ASEAN has emerged as the most durable and influential regional grouping in the developing world. The World Bank labelled several of the countries "miracle economies". Poverty has fallen more rapidly in this region than any other in the world.

But history doesn't stand still. New challenges abound throughout Southeast Asia. Composed of small and medium-sized states, the region has to juggle great power rivalry and its unpredictable effects. The democratic forces in the region are fragile. Some of the former economic stars appear to have lost their dynamism. There is rising inequality between and within nation states. The "ASEAN Way" has both strengths and limitations. Profound environmental challenges are on the horizon. We will look to future editions of *SEAA* to help us anticipate, interpret and understand these and many other issues.

Daljit Singh and Malcolm Cook have achieved the herculean task of judiciously selecting these 57 papers from the 960 published since 1974, and condensing the original versions where relevant. I congratulate them for this magnificent volume, and for expertly piloting the *SEAA* series over many years.

I also wish to congratulate ISEAS on its uniquely important, perceptive and durable contributions to understanding this fascinating region over the past fifty years. In an era of instant communications and "fake news", the work of the Institute is as important and as relevant now as the day it was established.

Hal Hill
H.W. Arndt Professor Emeritus of
Southeast Asian Economies
Arndt Corden Department of Economics
Crawford School
College of Asia and the Pacific
Australian National University

Foreword

Shamsul, A.B.

The region now known as Southeast Asia has been called the Malay World, Malay Archipelago, Nusantara, East Indies, the Far East, and Southeast Asia or the ASEAN region. All these terms are still in use in various contexts for different purposes, quite often interchangeably, for instance, in books on the history of Southeast Asia available for undergraduate teaching across the globe.

The region physically includes mainland and maritime components. The "Malay World" is being used by a number of academic institutions and publications in Malaysia, Indonesia and the United Kingdom. Others prefer to use Nusantara, instead, the old Javanese terminology for "archipelago". It refers to the maritime area of Southeast Asia. When British naturalists, explorers and biological scientists analysed the flora and fauna of the maritime region, they preferred to use the term "Malay Archipelago". The French, German, Austrian and British orientalists of the nineteenth century refer to this maritime geophysical space as part of the Far East.

The term "Southeast Asia" that refers to the present mainland and maritime parts of the region was first used by American priest and educator Howard Malcom in 1837. During the Second World War, a century later, the Allied forces established a South-East Asia Command (SEAC) in 1943 that covered the areas previously known as the Dutch East Indies; British Burma, Malaya and Borneo; French Indochina; and Thailand. In 1944, the Washington D.C.–based National Geographic Society published the first map of Southeast Asia as we know it today, based on SEAC's military concept.

What is significant is that each of these names or labels for the region was constructed with different sets of knowledge content serving the specific purposes of whoever its originators were — imperialists, colonialists, researchers or academicians. The knowledge produced, based on empirical evidence derived from this region, often enriched the global discourse on a particular theory or concept.

For instance, the contribution of Alfred Russel Wallace (1858) was instrumental in establishing the "natural selection theory", based on his eight-year research in the Malay Archipelago that was accepted and recognized by Charles Darwin himself. Similarly, the internationally well-known theory of "plural society" by J.S. Furnivall (1948), that was well received and applied widely in Africa and Latin America, was based on his research in Indonesia and Burma, which formed the empirical core of his theory. In 1983, Ben Anderson published his *Imagined Communities* based on field research conducted mainly in Indonesia, introducing his theory of nationalism and the origin of a nation.

Foreword

ISEAS, founded in 1968, and its annual *Southeast Asian Affairs*, produced since 1974, have been among the pioneers in helping to dissolve the mental barriers between Southeast Asian scholars and thinkers shaped by long periods of colonial rule by different colonial masters, in the process contributing to better understandings and the gradual evolution of a regional identity.

They have also remained at the core of the construction of knowledge, the making of narratives, analyses and debate about Southeast Asian studies. More than that, much conceptualizing and theorizing within the global study of international relations and security studies, such as the debate between realism and constructivism or neo-realism versus constructivism, have often referred to Southeast Asia for empirical evidence and case studies. The corpus of knowledge provided by ISEAS and annually by *Southeast Asian Affairs* has helped to shape such theoretical discourses.

Both the regional section of *Southeast Asian Affairs* and the essays on individual countries of Southeast Asia have in the last four decades provided researchers, academics, policymakers, political analysts, risk studies specialists and others from all over the world a window to the region and the happenings within it. This will continue to be so into the future.

I congratulate ISEAS for bringing out *Turning Points and Transitions: Selections from Southeast Asian Affairs 1974–2018*. It is an impressive collection of essays from the annual *Southeast Asian Affairs* over a period of forty-five years.

Shamsul, A.B.
Distinguished Professor &
Founding Director
National Institute of Ethnic Studies
Universiti Kebangsaan Malaysia

Member
International Advisory Panel
ISEAS – Yusof Ishak Institute

Introduction

Daljit Singh

Southeast Asian Affairs, the annual publication of the ISEAS – Yusof Ishak Institute, was launched in 1974 as an annual review of the politics, economies and international relations of Southeast Asia and its individual states. It is the only publication of its kind and is used by scholars, think tanks, universities and others interested in contemporary Southeast Asia.

As Professor Donald Weatherbee said in his short commemorative essay in *Southeast Asian Affairs 2013* to mark the fortieth anniversary of the publication, "the collected volumes of *Southeast Asian Affairs* have become a compendium documenting the dynamic evolution of regional and national developments in Southeast Asia from the end of the 'second' Vietnam War to the alarms and struggles of today." The chapters in the publication are written by experts and analysts both from within Southeast Asia and abroad in Australia, Northeast Asia, North America, Europe and India. As Weatherbee put it in the same essay, "A full list of contributors … reads like a kind of who's who in Southeast Asian studies."

The present publication, *Turning Points and Transitions*, is produced to commemorate the fiftieth anniversary of the founding of ISEAS in 1968. It comprises a selection of 57 chapters from the 45 issues of *Southeast Asian Affairs* from 1974, the first year of its publication, to 2018.

The Twists and Turns of International Relations

During these years, Southeast Asia went through major political and economic transformations.

Consider the international relations of the region. The communist victories in South Vietnam, Laos and Cambodia in 1975 crystallized the region's division into two blocs — one communist and the other non-communist. There were alarms then over the intentions of a victorious Hanoi regime with a seemingly invincible "million-man" army supplied by the Soviet Union and China. The nervousness was not unwarranted, given Hanoi's hostile propaganda against ASEAN and its self-characterization as the "beachhead" or "vanguard" of socialism in Southeast Asia, which was interpreted in the region as implying that it was only a matter of time before other countries would be "liberated". With the withdrawal of U.S. military power from the mainland of Southeast Asia, the field seemed open for communism to advance into a strategic vacuum. Sino-Soviet rivalry brought no real comfort to the ASEAN states; rather, they feared that it would increase the threat through competitive bidding by the two giant communist states for influence with the communist movements in Thailand, Malaysia, the Philippines and Burma which were already engaged in insurgency warfare against the governments of these countries.

But then, within a few years, something largely unexpected happened. A growing Sino-Vietnamese schism erupted into open conflict after Vietnam invaded Cambodia in 1978. At the root of this rift was the Chinese belief that Vietnam had become a tool for the expansion of Soviet influence in Southeast Asia, a region China viewed as its hinterland and traditional sphere of influence. So, in a rapid turn of the geopolitical kaleidoscope, Southeast Asia found China becoming a balancer against the Vietnam-Soviet alliance in Southeast Asia. With the backing of China, ASEAN gave political support to resisting Vietnam in Cambodia, and Thailand became a platform for material assistance to the resistance forces. With the Vietnamese army on its border, Thailand felt the most threatened. In 1982, Thanat Khoman, the former Thai foreign minister, described Vietnam as a "tiger squatting" on Thailand's doorstep. In 1983, a senior Thai Foreign Ministry official said, "With us it is not an academic question, it is a matter of survival. China is on our side and that is all that matters."[1]

From sanctuaries and bases in Thailand, China armed the Khmer Rouge insurgents operating in Cambodia against the government that Hanoi had installed in Phnom Penh. This was part of the Chinese strategy to bleed Vietnam militarily and economically. When President Gorbachev of the Soviet Union cut Moscow's massive aid to Vietnam in the late 1980s, Hanoi could not sustain its occupation of Cambodia in the face of an intractable Khmer Rouge insurgency and a hostile China. The end of the Cambodian conflict through the Paris Peace Accords of 1991 was another significant turning point in recent Southeast Asian history.

The second half of the 1970s and the 1980s also saw a major reordering of international relations in the region following the U.S.-China détente. It is now easy to forget how bitter the U.S.-China enmity was in the 1950s and 1960s. But by the late 1970s and in the 1980s the United States and China were working together to check the common foe, the Soviet Union, in Asia. This realignment led the states of ASEAN to move to develop diplomatic and economic relations with China, with Malaysia being the first to do so in 1974 and Indonesia and Singapore the last in 1990. In 1978, Chinese leader Deng Xiaoping announced the opening up of China, and a few years later Beijing ended support for the communist parties engaged in insurgencies and subversion against the governments of non-communist Southeast Asia, which had been a major factor in their deep mistrust of China.

China needed to cultivate friends in its confrontation with the Soviet Union, and it also needed investments from abroad as it opened up its economy. In 1993 it became a Dialogue Partner of ASEAN and participated actively in the ASEAN Regional Forum and, later, in other multilateral fora established under the ASEAN umbrella. It soon became a major diplomatic player in the region and, within the first decade of the new century, also the largest or second-largest trading partner of ASEAN countries.

In the second decade of the new century, however, China became much more assertive in pursuing its interests. Developments in the South China Sea, including China's rejection of the ruling of the Permanent Court of Arbitration in the case brought against it under the UNCLOS by the Philippines, its militarization of land features in the South China Sea, and its pressures on ASEAN and ASEAN states are cases in point. Meanwhile, the Obama administration in the United States had announced its "pivot" to Asia, later renamed "rebalance". U.S.-China competition for influence in the region seemed set to intensify.

ASEAN Matures and Faces New Challenges

ASEAN itself matured as a diplomatic and political consultative body during the forty-five years covered by this volume. The 1976 ASEAN Summit in Bali was a turning point, resulting in the ASEAN Concorde and the Treaty of Amity and Cooperation. ASEAN enhanced its international standing in the 1980s when it functioned as a single diplomatic community at the United Nations and other international forums to oppose Vietnam's invasion and occupation of Cambodia and to find a diplomatic solution to the crisis. In 1992, soon after the end of the Cold War, it boldly decided to create a regional architecture stretching well beyond the confines of Southeast Asia. This was the ASEAN Regional Forum (ARF), which first met in 1994 and included all the major powers of the Asia-Pacific. The purpose was to manage major power dynamics in order to maximize Southeast Asian regional autonomy. Other Asia-Pacific-wide forums under the ASEAN umbrella were to follow in subsequent years. In 1992 the Association also signed the ASEAN Free Trade Agreement, which marked the first significant step towards economic integration and was to lead to the ASEAN Economic Community in the second decade of the twenty-first century.

Arguably ASEAN was at the peak of its international standing between the end of the Cold War and the Asian Financial Crisis of 1997. It began to take in the other countries of Southeast Asia as new members so that by 1999 all the ten Southeast Asian countries were members of the Association.

But ASEAN soon began to encounter some difficult challenges. The first was the financial crisis which damaged the economies of key countries like Indonesia, Malaysia and Thailand and also had political reverberations within them. In particular, the downfall of the Soeharto regime and the emergence of a democratic Indonesia that was preoccupied with domestic affairs meant reduced interest on the part of Jakarta in exercising its soft leadership role in ASEAN, which had been an important factor in the Association's successes heretofore. The new members from the Indochina countries and Myanmar were much less developed and had different political histories and outlooks, which tested ASEAN's cohesiveness. Perhaps the biggest, and ongoing, challenge to confront ASEAN was the shifting balance of power that became apparent after the 2010s in China's more assertive posture in the South China Sea, which damaged ASEAN unity.

Still, ASEAN has remained an indispensable organization for the ten member countries for intra–Southeast Asian affairs, while the ASEAN-based security and economic architectures remain important components of the East Asian order.

The Individual States of Southeast Asia

Developments within some of the individual countries of Southeast Asia during the period 1973 to 2017 were no less dramatic than the international relations of the region. Brunei became a sovereign independent state and the sixth member of ASEAN in 1984. Myanmar saw long periods of military rule and finally, in the second decade of the twenty-first century, major reforms initiated by the military itself which led to the establishment of a democratically elected civilian government, though the military still dominated the security sector. Cambodia arguably witnessed the most upheavals: the turmoil and destruction caused by the spillover of the Vietnam war into its territory in 1973–75; the brutalities of Khmer Rouge rule; Vietnamese invasion and occupation; a new democratic constitutional system set up under the Paris Peace Agreement; and the emergence of Prime Minister Hun Sen as the dominant strong man. Indonesia went through the military-based authoritarian Soeharto rule for over twenty years; a severe economic crisis in 1998 that also resulted in Soeharto's downfall; and the emergence of a rumbustious democracy.

In Malaysia there was accelerated implementation of preferential policies for the Malay community to raise their socio-economic status; more Islamization; the split between Prime Minister Mahathir Mohammad and his deputy Anwar Ibrahim which set in motion political tides contributing to the eventual loss in 2008 of the ruling coalition's critical two-thirds majority in Parliament. The Philippines had President Marcos's martial law regime and then the EDSA People's Power uprising. Thailand experienced major domestic upheavals and bloodshed in the 1970s and a number of military coups throughout the period 1973 to 2017.

The Selection Process

Needless to say the selection of 57 chapters for this volume out of 960 was a challenging task. The main criterion was to capture as well as possible the important turning points and trends in the Southeast Asian region's political, security and economic history from 1973 — from both the Southeast Asian and international perspectives. Examples of turning points for the regional section of this volume are the diplomatic emergence of China after a decade of self-isolation during the years of the Cultural Revolution, the victories in 1975 of revolutionary communism in the states of Indochina, ASEAN's first summit meeting in Bali, the establishment of the ARF, and the Asian Financial Crisis, among others.

Examples of turning points for individual countries are Vietnam's invasion and occupation of Cambodia in 1978, the 1991 Paris Peace Accords on Cambodia, Burma's election and imposition of military rule in 1991, Myanmar's political reforms in 2011, Malaysia's general election of 2008 which saw the ruling coalition lose its two-thirds majority — and many more.

Some chapters have been selected because they reflect important trends of the times. On the regional plane these include Southeast Asia's changing relations with China over the years. Likewise, with respect to the individual countries of the region, there are chapters on the effects of Khmer Rouge rule on Cambodian society, the character of Pancasila rule in Soeharto's Indonesia, and the communist insurgency in Malaysia in the mid-1970s, to name just a few.

Inevitably, some excellent chapters could not be included because they did not meet the editors' criteria of turning points or important trends. Further, for a number of the original chapters we had to use only relevant excerpts. For example, in Ben Kiernan's long chapter on Cambodia in *Southeast Asian Affairs 1982* we were interested only in the sections on the effects of Khmer Rouge rule on Cambodia's economy and society. We were also mindful of the need to manage length.

Note

1. Cited in Robert O. Tilman, *Southeast Asia and the Enemy Beyond* (Westview Press, 1987), pp. 1 and 84, respectively.

The Region

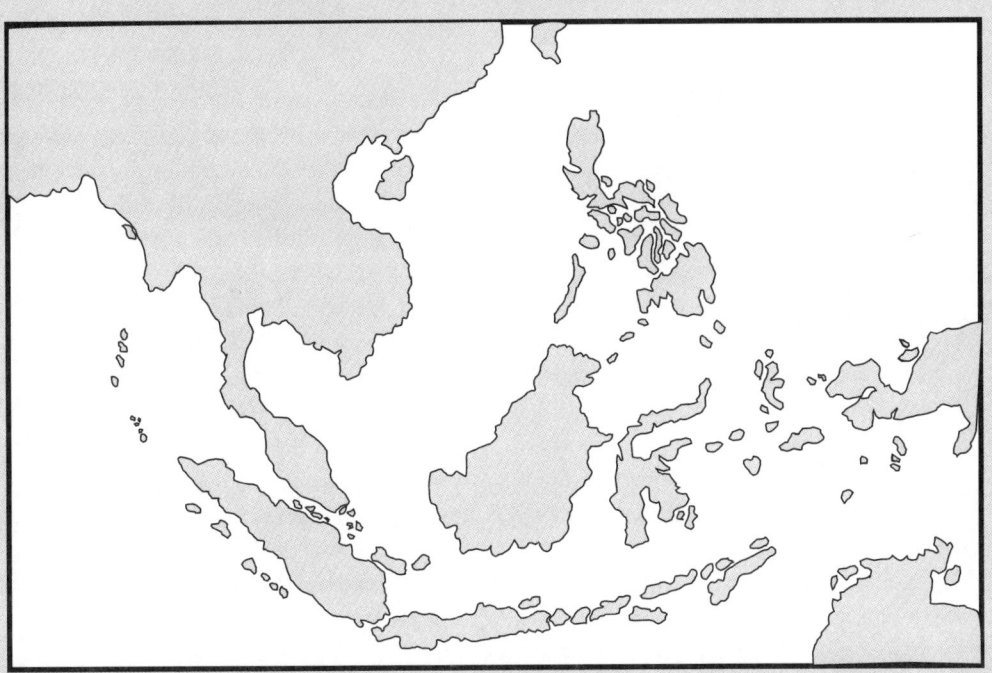

THE DIPLOMATIC EMERGENCE OF CHINA AND ITS IMPLICATIONS FOR SOUTHEAST ASIA

Victor C. Funnell

China's startling and still recent emergence from isolation into world diplomacy has left other countries rather breathless. There seems to be a high degree of coincidence between several developments that have contributed to this unexpected change in policy. Firstly, there was the ending of the turmoil of the Cultural Revolution in China itself, and a return to greater normality in internal and external policies. Secondly, there was the strenuous attempt of the Nixon Administration to end American involvement in Vietnam and place U.S. policy in Asia, including China, on a new footing. Thirdly, there was the inevitable but much delayed admission of China to the United Nations in September 1971, where she took her place as a permanent member of the Security Council. These three developments, occurring in rapid succession, undoubtedly heightened the impact of the arrival of China on the world stage. In the subsequent period, other countries have been engaged in readjusting, in their several ways, to the new circumstances.

By far the most important of these developments, in terms of its implications for the future shape of international relations and the strategic balance in Southeast Asia, has been the *rapprochement* between Peking and Washington. This factor alone has contributed immensely to the new and alarming (or exciting, depending on the point of view) fluidity in Southeast Asian affairs today. The old guidelines and the old alliances are rapidly being replaced by as yet largely untried experiments in regional diplomacy. New assessments are still being made of what really constitutes the national interest, based on new analyses of Chinese and American intentions in the area. China's role in the United Nations and her own internal stability are still relevant

---

Reprinted from *Southeast Asian Affairs 1975* (Singapore: Institute of Southeast Asian Studies, 1975), pp. 15–19. At the time of original publication, Victor C. Funnell was a Lecturer in Politics and Fellow in Southeast Asian Studies at the University of Hull, United Kingdom.

factors to be taken into consideration, but when it comes to a realistic political appraisal, these things pale beside the American withdrawal from the Asian mainland and the consequent looming of China's economic and military potential. No longer is the dividing line simply between two opponents, communist and non-communist. There is the now familiar element of Sino-Soviet rivalry, and the chrysalis of Japanese power, to be used in a way that may not continue to be confined simply to the economic sphere. It is in this quadrilateral situation that the countries of Southeast Asia now have to find their way. Their response has been twofold. First, they have sought to find each other in a regional embrace; and second, they have scanned the signposts pointing to a new approach to China, some by one route, some by another. A feature of ASEAN, and one reason for its present vitality, is the confidence it has engendered in its members through the practice of pooling information over a wide field, of co-ordinating policies that have moved beyond the economic to the political, and of confiding bilateral initiatives where these occur (as in the case of China). Here is a regional grouping that is not too constricted by a common approach, but which can heal divisions and tolerate individual ventures by member countries. Though in no way constituting a fifth power to match the four sides of the quadrilateral, ASEAN obviously strengthens the voice of smaller countries in dealing with the giants, if they can speak unitedly and with authority about matters affecting the region.

Nevertheless, it would not do to claim too much. In the whole sequence of events leading to the present expansive diplomatic phase, the countries of Southeast Asia have played almost no part at all. It is still true to say that they react, rather than act, in world affairs, and there is very little that can change this in the forseeable future. Recognition of this basic relationship to the great powers can only be beneficial in working out realistic and feasible policies for the region as a whole or for individual countries. Indeed, the concept of the "neutralization" of Southeast Asia, which some criticize as hopelessly idealistic and impractical, at least recognizes the necessity for great power guarantees if it is to stand any chance at all. This involves self-denial by the mighty rather than deterrence by the weak. Still, such restraint seems unlikely, especially in view of great power rivalry and the strategic situation of Southeast Asia. The idea also implies agreement among regional countries themselves on its general value and validity, and this is by no means forthcoming. The attitude of North Vietnam, for one, is uncompromising. Much depends on the definition of "neutralization". It may not be the same as "neutrality". It may refer simply to the elimination of foreign military bases, and it is sometimes so conceived, particularly in Malaysia. At this level, the idea is not impossible of fulfilment. But assuming that the Soviet Union, the United States, Japan, and China all see some advantage in respecting the desire for "neutralization", however defined, who then would be the beneficiary? In the long term, with Southeast Asia proclaimed a "zone of peace", the major profit would surely lie with that huge and populous country that is itself in Asia, that has contiguous borders with several Southeast Asian countries, that has exported several millions of its population to those same countries, and that has had long historical and cultural ties with the area, namely, China. The tendency of neutralization, then, would be to substitute Chinese for American or

Russian or Japanese dominance. Possibly this thought has already occurred to the policy-makers in Peking, which may explain China's apparent ready acceptance of the "neutralization" idea, as well as that of the control of the Malacca Straits by neighbouring countries.

Whichever way it goes, China's very proximity, as well as her entry into the world community, imposes on her near neighbours in Southeast Asia the necessity for reaching some kind of accommodation with her. Relations already exist with the other great powers, but for a variety of reasons China is, perhaps, the least well represented in the diplomatic sense. Only Burma, Laos, and North Vietnam have resident Chinese missions. Malaysia and China have agreed to exchange ambassadors (as of November 1974). The rest of the countries are mostly at the stage of preliminary contacts, often secret, leading possibly to a broadening of exchanges step by step. To some extent, the whole traditional formula of "recognition" is outmoded, since, in practice, a variety of contacts are occurring daily at the United Nations, and through trade and sports. Still, there is much to be done, with many problems to be ironed out, before Southeast Asia as a whole has full diplomatic relations with its powerful and enigmatic neighbour.

Such a step at once raises a host of domestic problems for the countries concerned. In this respect, China, and relations with China, are surely unique. The China issue reaches directly into some of their most vexing national preoccupations. What is apparent now has been apparent since, at least, the Bandung Conference in 1955. The indigenous nationalism of newly independent, ex-colonial territories raises, in an acute form, the question of the loyalty of the ethnic Chinese among their populations, especially when joined to the emergence of a strong communist régime in Peking after 1949. There is the fear of subversion, whether ideological or nationalistic in origin, that could be exercised among such groups by a China that is seen to be unified and effective and, in present circumstances, evincing a new respectability. Furthermore, the economic power wielded by local Chinese in Southeast Asia, the merchants and bankers of the region, coupled with the Chinese penchant for education, makes their role crucial to the development of the new states, thus exciting and exacerbating, all the more, indigenous nationalism and political misgivings. There is a tangle here that is very difficult to unloose, as recent history shows. A further factor has been the attitude of China herself to the ethnic Chinese in Southeast Asia, and the relationships between local communists and the Chinese Communist Party. Thus, relations with China are perceived to be at several levels simultaneously, as between States, between Communist Parties, and between individuals. At the present time, however, one has the strong impression that the major problem for Southeast Asia is not China, but the local Chinese, not one of rebellion so much as deep-seated loyalties. With expanded contacts with China in the offing, a race is on to achieve national integration and create a distinct national identity. The pressure is now on the ethnic Chinese to conform to local customs and languages, and to seek complete assimilation into the local community. Indonesia has banned the use of Chinese surnames and abolished Chinese schools. Singapore has universal conscription and National Day parades. Malaysia has sought and obtained Peking's approval for her nationality policies, as an extra admonition to local Chinese to conform. The approach to China is measured by domestic progress towards full integration. Left to themselves, possibly, the countries of Southeast Asia would not yet be contemplating the opening to Peking. For some, as Singapore's Prime Minister is quoted as saying, "Ping-pong diplomacy has come too soon." Indeed, there is an evident measure of reluctance on the whole. Recognition of Communist China may be postponed for one year, two years, or ten. The trend, nevertheless, is unmistakable, and is due in large measure to the changes in policy initiated in Peking and Washington. Everything, really, has flowed from that. A new world order is being created, and Southeast Asia is not excluded.

If these are the wide perspectives opened up by the diplomatic emergence of China, it can hardly be surprising that, however reluctantly, the countries of Southeast Asia have put their best foot forward in seeking ways of sounding out the Chinese on their mutual approach to a new relationship. It would be true to say that most of the running has come from Southeast Asia. China, however, has certainly proved receptive. This is a joint enterprise, and much will depend on China's own attitude and the impression this makes on other Asian governments. Their estimate of the relative internal stability of the Peking regime is important. What sort of China are they dealing with? The Cultural Revolution spilled across frontiers to embroil relations with other countries. The struggle within the leadership continues, in sporadic campaigns against Confucius or Lin Piao, which increases speculation as to the predictability of China's actions; and this bears unfavourably on the notion of closer contact. Mao is now eighty and Chou En-lai, seventy-six. Both have been at the helm for a long time, neither is fully fit, yet no emerging pattern of leadership in Party and State is apparent. There is no means of knowing how long present policies will last, or whether assurances received today will prove valid tomorrow. China has undergone some rapid changes of course in the past, and may do so again. All these are factors that must enter into any calculations by other Asian states of the timely moment at which to enter serious negotiations on bilateral relations.

Against this must be set the present indications of China's desire to open a fresh dialogue with Southeast Asia. This is revealed not only by invitations to sporting teams to participate in tournaments in Peking. There is little doubt in Kuala Lumpur, for instance, that China is anxious to extend her friendship to other Southeast Asian governments in the way that she has done with Malaysia. In winning friends and influence, China could repeat the Malaysian precedent in meeting conditions and damping down fears by giving assurances on such matters as subversion and citizenship where required; and, in all cases, seem to adhere to a thoroughly correct stance of dealing only with governments. Malaysia will become the focus for many curious and anxious eyes in Southeast Asia after the new Chinese Ambassador takes up residence in Kuala Lumpur. Meanwhile, by hints and gestures, China can encourage others and reassure the doubters. A case in point is the open Chinese support, already mentioned, for neutralization and the Malacca Straits proposal. Another more direct signal was given to the Indonesians in mid-1974, when the Chinese waived regulations to allow the plane carrying the Indonesian Foreign Minister, Adam Malik, to fly across China on its way from Pyongyang to Ulan Bator without making the usual obligatory stop in Peking. Such courtesies are no more than straws in the wind, perhaps, yet they contain a clear diplomatic message which is certainly understood by the recipients. They are, in any case, backed up by much more substantial communication between the two sides, in direct talks between representatives at international conferences or inside embassies in foreign capitals. The Indonesians, for example, profited from the occasion of the international conference on Vietnam in Paris in early 1973 to hold talks with the Chinese representatives present, including the Foreign Minister, Chi Peng-fei. Over the past two years, the Thais have utilized their sporting contacts with China, involving half a dozen visits to China and two Chinese teams to Thailand, as well as the forum provided by the United Nations and various embassies around the world, in the same quest. In 1973, Malaysia was able to initiate the eventually successful talks with the Chinese at the common meeting ground of the United Nations. It is note-worthy that the initial Chinese reluctance to give the assurances demanded by the Malaysians on subversion and relations with local communists was later modified to the suggestion that this could be postponed until after recognition had taken place, and finally fully conceded in the final communiqué normalizing relations. Whether this represents a real and historic turning-point in relations with China, as the Malaysians like to believe, or whether it is a restatement of the old Bandung principles, based on *pancasila*, may be disputed, but what it does illustrate, particularly in that part of the communiqué where China explicitly rejects the concept of dual nationality for ethnic Chinese living abroad, is the current Chinese desire to reach agreement with Southeast Asian countries and conciliate their known susceptibilities by going a long way to meet them. The test, of course, will be in action and not in words alone, and it is here that different degrees of optimism or pessimism can be found between Malaysia and her Southeast Asian neighbours.

These attitudes directly relate to a government's sense of internal security, and this domestic aspect cannot be too much emphasized. It is this that will govern the pace of a country's approach to China, and which must remain the first priority. Security is not only concerned with invasions, but also the right ordering of social and economic problems. The attraction of China could grow or diminish according to whether local disaffection or frustration is met and remedied, particularly among the ethnic Chinese. Local communists are not necessarily linked organizationally with the Chinese, but they could be used by China, or both could use each other, as levers in a political struggle in a situation of unrest, resulting from whatever cause. This is a possibility that a country like Singapore, whose population is so heavily Chinese, cannot afford to ignore. In the murky world of international intrigue and in great power rivalries evident in Southeast Asia, and increasingly so in the Indian Ocean, which involve China quite as fully as Russia or any of the others, who can say that this is an extra weapon that Peking would virtuously refuse to employ in any circumstances? To realists like the present leaders of Singapore, there are some chances that are not worth taking. A similar attitude can be found in Indonesia. Indonesian leaders have their own particular reason, in the liaison that sprang up between the Chinese and the PKI before 1965, for being cautious now. If internal problems including that of the full assimilation of the Chinese population, can be settled, and the designs of residual PKI elements defeated, then the resulting degree of stability will enable the government to contemplate the resumption of relations with China, sooner rather than later. This is the perspective of Thailand and the Philippines as well. It certainly does not betray any great disposition to take China on trust, since the existing domestic conditions do not appear to preclude relations with the Soviet Union, East Germany, and other communist powers. The truth, put bluntly, that these countries do not have millions of their expatriates living in Southeast Asia, must be faced. That is the essential difference, and not one of ideology. The greatest disadvantage that China labours under in Southeast Asia today is the "overseas Chinese" communities. This may be unjust, but it remains a political fact.

These, then, are some of the implications for Southeast Asia of the diplomatic emergence of China. They are not new, nor are they wholly confined to Southeast Asia. Many countries of the East and West, communist and non-communist, are perplexed by the unfamiliar panorama now unfolding. This broader perspective suggests one further point, in conclusion. The full impact of China on the world has yet to be felt. This is a sobering thought, since the preliminaries have already created such a stir. China, now, disclaims great power status, and professes to resent the "collusion" of the superpowers in ordering the world to their advantage. It is unlikely that this self-identification with the "Third World" really makes many converts in Africa, Asia, and South America, though it may reflect a realistic estimate of China's present economic and technological level. Yet China is a nuclear power, and her military forces have immense deterrent value, if not yet fully contemporary striking power. This fact is not lost on her smaller, weaker neighbours. Nor are they unaware of her status at the United Nations as one of the "Big Five", with the right of veto. China certainly does not fit easily into the categories usually associated with the "Third World". This is a stance that she will find increasingly difficult to maintain. As the development of economic and social forces in China gathers momentum and the irresistible movement to modernization proceeds, with or without Mao, leading to the definitive emergence of a bureaucratic, nationalist *status quo* power that we already see in fledgling form, with all the pretensions to world influence that such powers commonly acquire, then it will become harder to deny her a pre-eminent role in the continent of Asia, similar to that now enjoyed by the United States in the western hemisphere and by the Soviet Union in Eastern Europe. In these conditions, Southeast Asia would seem to be marked out as the proper sphere for the exercise of a predominant Chinese influence. Someone will have to move over. Whether or not this comes to pass, and there are many qualifications that could be made, whether they be eventual modifications in China's internal political structure, or the effect of concurrent development by other Asian nations, such as Japan and India, as a counter-weight, there is a potential here that is calculated to cause many heads of government in Southeast Asia to rest uneasy.

STABILITY AND SECURITY IN THE REGION AFTER ANZUK

George G. Thomson

Implicit in the Five Power Defence Arrangements (FPDA) of 16 April 1971 is an assessment, generally agreed upon by the participating states, of the contemporary situation in Southeast Asia. Explicit in ANZUK, established in November 1971, is the action which Australia, New Zealand, and the United Kingdom agreed at the time was required in the circumstances by their national interests, and which was acceptable to Malaysia and Singapore, the other two partners. But in the changed circumstances of 1974 their assessments of the regional situation have diverged, and priorities in the pursuit of national interests have been changed by political choices and economic pressures. ANZUK (an integrated command of the three services set up by Australia, New Zealand, and the United Kingdom independently of the FPDA on the grounds of efficiency and economy), a *modus operandi* of the FPDA, was neither its purpose nor its prescription. With the end of the process of dismantling ANZUK on 1 January 1975, the FPDA remains intact as a convention of consultation on what is still agreed to be an area of common concern, though not necessarily of common diagnosis in description, or common direction of action. The strategic baby has not been thrown out with the tactical or political bath-water. Whether it will be more or less effective as a pentagonal pattern of power without ANZUK can only be assessed in the light of the new circumstances as reflected in the five facets of the national interests of the members.

Reprinted with minor revisions from *Southeast Asian Affairs 1975* (Singapore: Institute of Southeast Asian Studies, 1975), pp. 151–59. At the time of original publication, George G. Thomson was a Visiting Professor, Department of Politics and Public Administration, Nanyang University, Singapore.

Changed Circumstances

What were the circumstances out of which grew both the Five Power Defence Arrangements and the ANZUK Force? The precipitating issue was the announcement by the British in 1968 of the accelerated and specific timetable of their withdrawal from their base in Singapore, and from their commitments under the Anglo-Malayan Defence Agreement. The robust image of Mountbatten of SEAC (Southeast Asia Command) in 1945 and of Mountbatten of India in 1947 had faded in the eyes of the world and in the esteem of the British people. Dilatory, if not dillettante, strategic thinking was caught up by the urgencies of political party change and economic stringency which set the background and the pace of the Labour Government's announcement in 1968 of complete British withdrawal before the end of 1971, thus setting the terminal date by which alternative arrangements were required to be made. The tensions of Singapore's abrupt, unplanned, and complete separation from Malaysia in 1965 continued; and the Kuala Lumpur riots of April 1969 at first sight seemed to strengthen the same groups as those which had inspired separation. Meanwhile Singapore had not yet proved her capacity, militarily and economically, for national survival. In 1968, Suharto took over the full power of the Indonesian Presidency from Sukarno, and the abrasive aftermath of Confrontation had not yet yielded to the lubrication of ASEAN. Meanwhile, in a still tense and turbulent Pacific area, the Nixon Doctrine, announced by the President in Guam in 1969, gave warning of U.S. disinclination towards fuller involvement and of US. abandonment of hopes of a peace in Vietnam by domination; while actual military disinvolvement from Vietnam, though in secret process, appeared as unlikely as U.S. defeat. The fever of Vietnam still raged infectiously high and neither *détentiste* Russia nor post-Cultural Revolution China appeared to be, or to wish to be, moderators in Southeast Asia. The feeling of a common threat of China appeared as the only rationale for regional unity in East Asia, Southeast Asia, and Australasia, while Russian influence was growing in India and the Indian Ocean.

The final decision of the British Government to withdraw permanently based forces from Singapore by 1971 ended the pattern of power set out in the Anglo-Malayan Defence Agreement (AMDA) with the newly independent Federation of Malaya in 1957, by which, in return for the right to continued use of her forces and facilities in Malaya for the fulfilment of her Commonwealth and international obligations, the United Kingdom gave an unqualified guarantee of the security of Malaya and Singapore. Australia and New Zealand "associated" themselves with the Agreement without accepting the full obligations. The establishment of Singapore as a sovereign state in 1965 did not affect her status within the AMDA. The agreement of the Conservative Government, elected to power in the United Kingdom in 1970, to a continued temporary resident military presence in Singapore was not a change in the strategy of retreat, but a tactical adjustment of the same order of magnitude and significance as the Labour Government's declared readiness, after withdrawal, to take part in joint exercises, or to deploy U.K.-based troops to the area, in appropriate circumstances; and successive British Governments have repeated in essence a statement made in 1968 by Mr Healey, then British Minister for Defence, that the United Kingdom was not "turning its back on an area in which we have appreciable economic interests, as well as deep historic ties".

The Birth of FPDA and ANZUK

The consequent dangerous vacuum of power in a crucial sector of the still turbulent Southeast Asia required an alternative filling. The first conference to discuss the problem involved the Five Powers. Held in Kuala Lumpur in June 1968 at the invitation of the Malaysian Prime Minister, the conference established two axioms for the future: firstly, that it was not a problem for a Southeast Asian, Commonwealth, or United Nations agenda, but for an *ad hoc* agreement among the five powers directly concerned; and secondly, that the fact and shape and size of any successor forces must be agreed upon by Malaysia and Singapore. A third axiom was established in the first point of the joint communiqué of the conference that the Malaysian and Singapore Governments regarded their defence as "indivisible, requiring close and constant co-operation between them". This implied declaration of non-hostility answered any post-separation doubts as to whether external troops would be involved in inter-territorial or intra-territorial hostilities. Finally, the Australian and New Zealand Governments committed themselves to continue to maintain forces in the area, pending final decisions, and to assist in the development of the Malaysian and Singapore military forces.

After a second meeting of Ministers of the five governments in London on 11 April 1971, a communiqué was issued to announce their agreement to set up a consultative and cooperative partnership on the pattern of ANZUS, to fill the vacuum. Formal confirmation followed in the separate and simultaneous exchange of parallel bilateral notes between each of the ANZUK governments, individually with the Singapore and Malaysian Governments, in Singapore and Kuala Lumpur on 1 December 1971. The essence of the arrangement is set out in Clause 5 of the communiqué which promises that "in the event of any form of armed attack, externally organized or supported, or the threat of such an attack, against Malaysia or Singapore", the five governments would "immediately consult together for the purpose of deciding what measures should be taken, jointly or separately, in relation to such threat or attack". There were no specific or hypothetical commitments to action. The only commitment — and one which required no treaty — was the responsibility of Malaysia and Singapore for their own defence, and for their existent and growing capacity to carry that responsibility. Side by side with the diplomatic discussions went the military discussions of the three ANZUK powers among themselves, and each bilaterally with the Governments of Malaysia and Singapore for the setting up of a resident force of 7,100 men, which on grounds of effectiveness and economy was put under a joint, predominantly Australian, command and logistics structure. Therefore, when the AMDA lapsed on 1 November 1971, the FPDA and ANZUK came into being on the same day. There was, hence, neither a policy-making nor a military vacuum.

The appearance of continuity obscured the deliberate and decisive discontinuity of policies, and ANZUK, the military emblem of policy and extent of the changes, obscured the essence. The 26,000 British servicemen remaining in 1971 were replaced by a three-nation force of 7,200 — 3,400 Australians, 2,600

British, and 1,200 New Zealanders. But ANZUK was not a miniaturized answer to the same macrocosmic problem faced by the British at the end of the imperial phase of their history. Nor was the United Kingdom only liquidating a past. The FPDA was a pause for the *national Britain* to discover, for *a yet indeterminate future, a global non-imperial* role which was economically possible and politically acceptable. Australia and New Zealand were not pulling dead British chestnuts out of a dying imperial fire. While their troops had gone to Vietnam in part to encourage, in an ANZUS context, U.S. troop activity in the Western Pacific, their troops were in Malaysia only marginally, if at all, to encourage the British to linger on. The new and real problem was not the departure of the British, the last of the colonial powers, but the phasing of the departure and the effect of the final departure on the stability and prosperity of the region as a vital concern for Malaysia and Singapore; for the region; for the adjacent island-states of Australia and New Zealand; and for the great powers, who were showing their active interest. Moreover, Malaysia and Singapore were not *the* regional problem but *one* facet of the regional problem, as Southeast Asia was one facet of the Western Pacific problem.

Moreover, the continuity of military action masked the change of motive and stature between an Expeditionary Force fulfilling a London-focused Commonwealth policy, and independent and autonomous forces, equal in status, reflecting the new, pragmatic, permanent, and general Pacific orientation of Australia and New Zealand, nationally responding to their geography, their indigenous history, and to new and nearer, and no less massive, economic appeals. Their presence in Southeast Asia would continue only as long as they were wanted by the countries to which they were posted. Their role of training and assistance, and of contributing to a sense of indivisible defence was specific, active, and direct. And this was essentially a transitional and temporary role, lasting as long as, and no longer than, there was agreed need. ANZUK, then, is to be judged not as a further retreat from the past, but as the first of a growing number of deliberate steps towards the future of the region. Again, the military unity of ANZUK seemed solid in contrast to the contingent consultations of the FPDA. But the FPDA reflected the situation better because it was consultative, not through indecisiveness but from flexibility in exploring a new and developing situation, and in establishing a continuous and evolving relationship. And, in fact, ANZUK was the outcome of individual agreements between its three constituent members, and between Malaysia and Singapore separately. Finally, the judgement of the value of ANZUK has been clouded by the exaggerated political party differences over the issue in the United Kingdom and in Australia which have obscured the degree of agreement in these two countries on a fundamental change in national policy.

Dismantling of ANZUK

In the three years from the establishment of ANZUK in 1971 to its dismantling on 1 January 1975, the international situation in the Western Pacific, as well as the political outlooks of the three governments, with the election of Labour Governments in Australia and New Zealand in 1972, and of a Labour Government in the United Kingdom in February 1974, has changed.

The basic changes were the accommodation of attitudes between Washington and Peking and the ending of direct U.S. military involvement in Vietnam in January 1973. This ended the polarization and proliferation of anti-Peking groupings and the dominance of ideology in diplomacy and strategy, and changed U.S. policy from one of assertion to one of accommodation. In the climate of American opinion and policy after Vietnam and Watergate, the five powers each must adjust their strategy to their separate assessments of what U.S. policy is likely to be.

But there is not likely to be a defined U.S. policy, definitely underwritten by military action. The element of indeterminacy will be a problem for her friends and adversaries. It will be a policy not of action but of reaction, using her power to forestall any revolutionary change, to her disadvantage, of the pattern of power in the Pacific. As near the definitive as any is the statement made by the U.S. Ambassador to the Philippines, William Sullivan, on 14 September 1973: "We think it is essential for the United States to retain its military presence precisely as it can be seen that we are not abandoning our friends in the area. Our task is to maintain an equilibrium of great powers ... as a great canopy so that other countries of Asia will not have to look over their shoulders at the menace of attack from the mainland." Until the countries in the region can defend themselves, "for the United States, it's going to involve a continued limited military presence and a continued economic presence".

In the new setting, Australia and New Zealand are seeking security and prosperity in the Pacific area, particularly in the South Pacific and Southeast Asia, by establishing more direct, intimate, and active relationships over a wider range of interests, with their Asian-Pacific neighbours.

The tactical change over ANZUK was precipitated by the Australian Labour Government which came to power in December 1972 with a firm electoral commitment to withdraw its ground forces from Singapore; it decided to reduce the total number of its forces to 150 and take them outside the ANZUK Command by April 1975. By that terminal date, the future of the two Mirage Squadrons which are part of the Integrated Air Defence Command, the one joint Five Power Command, would be reconsidered. As Australia had provided the first Commander and the logistics and supplies systems of ANZUK, the impact of their withdrawal could not have been more decisive. The 6th Battalion Royal Australian Regiment, the Artillery Battery, and the Signals Unit began to withdraw in September 1973. Australians should not be surprised if their decision appeared to be in response to a change in ideology rather than to a change in regional circumstance, a party rather than a national decision, and based on a confusion between conscripts in Vietnam and regulars in Singapore, or if *a readjustment of policy was seen as a revolution in policy*. Mr Whitlam, in a speech in Parliament on 24 May 1973, emphasized that the change was from one of "containment, forward defence, and ideological confrontation", which was no longer relevant and had become "counter-productive", to one of "ideological co-existence and strategic interdependence between great and small powers alike". But in assessing long term trends and seeking continuities amid change, national interests prevail over partisan politics.

While withdrawing Australian troops, Mr Whitlam underlined that "in no way do we repudiate or downgrade the Five Power

Arrangements"; nor was "isolationism an option for Australia or for any Australian Government". The new policy was one of "defence co-operation" which "looks to the development of relations in the defence field through co-operation in such areas as technical aid, training assistance, joint exercises, and continuing consultation". Co-operation would be arranged bilaterally and "on an informal basis without the need for fixed and formal military pacts". Mr Whitlam predicted that in two years, Australian forces would be more effective and efficient than could have been achieved by maintaining forces overseas. "The desire and the need for co-operation has not changed; all that has changed is the view of the Australian Government about the best way of achieving that co-operation and making it more valuable for all of us. Some components of Australian forces are going home but Australia is not going away." In line with this policy, Australia would provide "highly professional, highly mobile, finely equipped forces capable of, and experienced in, prompt co-operation with friendly forces".

In New Zealand, a contemporary Labour Government reacting to the same situation chose a different course of action. Mr Kirk, when he became Prime Minister, said that his country's policy would be independent, self-reliant, sensitive, and responsive to the needs of other peoples, "eschewing an excessive loudness or stridency, ill-suited to the New Zealand size and national character". New Zealand, too, desired defence co-operation.

In his 1973 Review of Foreign Policy, Mr Kirk said, "It is in our interest that countries in the area should maintain their independence and freedom of action — this naturally helps us to maintain ours — and we believe that by entering actively into cooperative defence arrangements as part of an overall nexus of relationships, we can make our contribution towards developing the confidence and sense of security which the Asia-Pacific region needs at this time of change and flux in the world power scene." New Zealand, too, established diplomatic relations with Peking and withdrew her troops from Vietnam. "*Détente,*" Mr Kirk told the Indonesian Parliament on 14 December 1973, "has given us new scope. The superpowers have stood back from their confrontation in Asia and the Pacific, and left those of us who live there more breathing space and a chance to decide for ourselves the shape we will build in the region, to enlarge our common interests, and to expand regional co-operation." In the climate of *détente*, policies based on confrontation no longer applied. To the Indonesians, Mr Kirk described the FPDA as a "pledge of involvement in the region", a "gesture of readiness to stand by our friends in a time of rapid change".

To Mr Kirk, the FPDA, while military in form, was mainly a "political device to foster stability, preserve national integrity, and develop independence". In April 1973 the Minister of Defence, Mr Faulkner, announced his government's decision to keep its forces in the area even if the U.K. forces withdrew, "as long as they are wanted by the governments concerned while building up their defence potentialities". Their value "lay not in the military forces eventually being employed in some violent capacity, but that the presence of military force helps create the climate in which no violent conflict can emerge". He believed that the countries of Southeast Asia "see our willingness to maintain forces in the area as evidence that we understand their problems, that we are serious in our desire to help them, and that we are willing to pay a price in terms of public criticism which makes them readier to listen...." An example of this understanding was the decision to remain in SEATO because of the importance Thailand attached to it. Finally, the army would be used for other than military purposes. "Unused machinery rusts and it is essential both for the morale of the armed forces and for their public image that they should be seen to be engaged in constructive and useful activities in time of peace." They had already built a road in Thailand, a harbour in Samoa, and run a hospital in Vietnam.

Following the Australian decision, the then Conservative British Government, after consultation with its four partners, decided to continue its ANZUK contribution while it was still the wish of their partners; although quite apart from the Ulster commitment, it would not add to it. The re-elected Labour Government in 1974 was limited by its previous commitment to withdraw, although the issue was recessive during the election. It "recalled" the decision of 1968, but there was no unqualified endorsement or announcement of intention of immediate implementation. The statements made by Mr Mason, the Defence Secretary, on 21 March 1974, and by Mr Healey in his budget speech on 22 April were identical. "Outside Europe we shall examine the contribution made by our military presence to the maintenance of peace and stability, recalling the decision made by Her Majesty's Government in 1968 that our forces shall be withdrawn from Southeast Asia. There will be full consultation with our allies wherever their interests are involved." The strategic thinking of 1968 which presumably is still the basis for military decision, though economic pressures have increased, was summarized in the Supplementary Statement on Defence Policy 1967, presented to Parliament in July 1967.

> First, as our friends and allies outside Europe build up their own forces, the most valuable contribution we can make is the sophisticated elements which they may find it difficult to provide for themselves. Second ... while the visible presence of even small forces — not necessarily dependent on large and expensive base facilities — may be a good deterrent, it will be more economical to rely mainly on sending forces from Britain in a crisis.

The long promised definitive statement of British defence policy was made in the House of Commons on 3 December 1974 by Mr Roy Mason, the Secretary of State for Defence, after a remarkable display of reticence by Ministers and backbenchers alike. "We propose," he said, "to withdraw our forces stationed under the Five Power Defence Arrangements in South East Asia, with the exception of a small group which we will continue to contribute to the integrated air defence system. The consultative provisions of the Five Power Defence Arrangements would, however, remain in force, and it would certainly be our intention to maintain close links with the armed forces and defence authorities of our partners. We would, of course, maintain our membership of CENTO and SEATO, but without declaring specific forces to either."

Related decisions which made up the pattern of commitments in the relevant region, were the reduction of forces in Hong Kong, the withdrawal of forces from Brunei, Gan, and Mauritius, the termination of the Simonstown Agreement with South Africa, and "given the effects of these decisions in the Indian Ocean area and the

Soviet naval presence there", agreement with U.S. proposals for a "relatively modest expansion of the facilities on the island of Diego Garcia which they enjoy jointly with us, under an existing agreement with Her Majesty's Government". In the nine months of what Mr Mason described as "the most extensive and thorough review of our system of defence ever undertaken by a British Government in peace time", the prime considerations had been NATO as the "lynch-pin of British security" and Britain's economic situation. The economic aim was a reduction over ten years of the defence proportion of the gross national product from 5½% to 4½%.

After four years, ANZUK ceases, not through any error in conception or failure of purpose, but because of the changed strategic and diplomatic climate of the region in general, and the independent changes of policy particularly by the Australian and British Governments. Militarily and administratively, it had worked well. An Australian public relations statement which posed the question of the degree to which it had contributed to the stability of the region gave the unexceptionable answer that "the brief period during which the presence of ANZUK existed has been one of peace and continued economic growth for Singapore and Malaysia". During the period, too, the military strength of the two territories had grown.

But the benefits had not been one-sided. ANZUK was part of a pattern of mutual assistance and advantage. Although the immediate emphasis on its formation was to see Singapore and Malaysia through a major and unexpectedly early transformation of defence attitudes and activities, a successful and peaceful transformation was no less in the interest of the ANZUK powers in an area of international and not merely local importance; and as the area will continue to be of concern to the five powers involved in the FPDA, it is in this climate of interdependence which continues, that future military dispositions will require to be discussed.

FPDA Continues

The dismantling of ANZUK in no way affects the FPDA which, being primarily military in focus, can only continue in order to concern itself with military matters; and in the military field it is only one, and not the dominant one, of the many regional security links. Nor will there cease to be military interest or involvement or assistance in the military problems of the Southeast Asian region in general. The U.K. commitment to Hong Kong, though reduced, and interest in the Indian Ocean; the New Zealand continued military presence in Southeast Asia, and continued commitment to SEATO; the Australian policy of defence co-operation with Indonesia, Singapore, and Malaysia; and the Australian and New Zealand commitments to their adjacent area of the South Pacific, whose common links with Southeast Asia will grow — these will continue by bilateral agreements after the end of ANZUK. And even in its own limited area, ANZUK was an adjunct in aid of the Malaysian and Singapore forces, which always carried the prime responsibility for their defence, and which now, from their own internal development and from external assistance, have become the better able to carry that responsibility for the general advantage.

Military advice and assistance will continue in the form of advice and training, equipment, and joint exercises to enhance the effectiveness of these forces.

Tun Abdul Razak, Prime Minister of Malaysia, said on 30 January 1974 after a visit to the Butterworth Air Base that Malaysia still needed Australia's advice and assistance in the development of her defence programmes. Up to 150 Australians will remain in Singapore to assist, and maintain close contact with, the Singapore forces. The Australian Government has announced increases in its military aid; to Indonesia by A$1,000,000 to a total of A$6,200,000; to Malaysia by A$315,000 to a total of A$6,300,000; and to Singapore by A$242,000 to a total of A$5,100,000. The New Zealand force in Southeast Asia will remain in Singapore and her troop training facilities will continue to be made available; and specialist officer training in all three ANZUK countries, as in other countries, will continue to be used. The United Kingdom has not yet announced her specific commitments.

The Integrated Air Defence Command with its headquarters in Butterworth, Malaysia, and an operational base in Tengah, Singapore, will continue. It includes two Australian Mirage Squadrons, one New Zealand Transport Squadron, and a visiting Skyhawk Squadron, as well as a small U.K. Technical Unit. Because of the importance of air defence both as an arm of defence and as a combined operation difficult to unscramble; because of the longer time it takes to build up an effective air force in modern terms; and because of its value in giving continuous tropical training; this form of assistance by Australia and New Zealand will be continued as long as the Malaysian and Singapore Governments wish it to continue. In naval terms, the three ANZUK powers are separately and nationally interested in the security of Southeast Asian waters for their merchant ships — the United Kingdom as operating 10% of the world's mercantile marine, and as responsible for the defence of Hong Kong; Australia and New Zealand as vulnerable from the sea and dependent on seaborne commerce, and not wishing that their adjacent Southeast Asian waters should be dominated by a major force with a naval offensive potential, using the pretext of moving in to fill a vacuum of naval power. Therefore, apart from ANZUK, the naval ships of the three countries, surface or submarine, would, as long as they are welcome, wish to use the fuelling, berthing, and repair facilities of Singapore, and gain the experience of individual navigation and joint exercises in the waters of the region. Under the FPDA, an Australian unit of a destroyer, a frigate, and a submarine, and a New Zealand frigate will continue to be stationed in Singapore.

The problem which is isolated is that of ground troops. Their presence is supplementary but they demonstrate a more than ordinary degree of joint interest. They establish a pattern of joint discussion at the technical and operational level; by creating confidence, they enhance security and stability; they facilitate regular training and assistance. They contribute to a climate and habit of co-operation. In no sense are they a garrison or an imperial hangover. They cannot be discussed in terms of forward defence because of their small numbers; and the concept, like that of fortress defence, expresses an out-of-date pattern of defence. Nor is a military presence antagonistic when the soldier has taken his normal place as part of the apparatus of independence. The soldier is — and looks — no more and no less antagonistic than the foreign businessman. Rather, the troops are a present and continuing gesture of co-operation with the state to which they are posted by invitation. They are socially and physically acclimatized and operationally trained in the area. They express a different and broader concept of the place of the soldier in the scheme of things, as the New Zealanders understand in their readiness to use their troops for civilian reconstruction. These are positive advantages for both sides.

On the other hand, to bring in soldiers is an immediate danger signal, quite apart from problems of air-bases and overflight routes on the way. The troops' acceptability based on the familiarity of continuity of presence has been lost. They come, and appear to come in their own interest. The costs of overseas maintenance above the costs of maintenance in a home base, are not high, while the recruiting appeal is high. A soldier in the area is worth two out of the area, just as a gift means more than a promise, however genuinely made. But if economic pressure or the priority of other interests precludes a presence, other avenues and opportunities of help remain.

ANZUK has served its transitional purpose, and there is no question of the revival of the three-nation, three-service force. It succeeded in the international climate of *détente* and the regional climate of ASEAN. Its existence helped to establish, in the partners' minds and in the mind of the world, that Australian and New Zealand national interests are directly and irrevocably involved in the security of the region. For the United Kingdom, the ending of ANZUK is a further step in disinvolvement — Hong Kong becoming more of a political and less of a military problem. The FPDA now becomes an arrangement for assistance on the initiative of the Malaysian and Singapore Governments and not an exclusive one. No future *casus belli* has been defined, and no promise of action in such contingencies have been made; when, if at all, they are made they will be bilateral. Action or pressure by the former ANZUK powers to reduce regional tensions will be secondary and supplementary to those in the region. Action against internal subversion will be in the form of co-operation in policies to build economic stability in the resource-rich region, assistance in building up the military effectiveness of the national governments of the region, and advice on counter-insurgency methods, if needed and available. The extent to which these issues will be discussed and policies defined by formal conference consultations by the five powers, or by informal diplomatic contacts, remains to be seen; but the second is the more likely, because the more unobtrusive.

Conclusion

The future could take two extreme shapes. The first suggested in the speech by Tun Abdul Razak already quoted that "all foreign bases in the region would have to be phased out when the neutrality concept for Southeast Asia is implemented". The other extreme is a deliberate thrust into the region by a great power as part of a major growth of world tension and involving either the waters or the territories of the region. In either circumstance, a predominantly military FPDA would count for little. But neither extreme is immediately foreseeable. *Détente* will continue in different degrees of "de-tension" (if one may coin the phrase), the great powers manoeuvring for position well away from the brink of action; and within the region, the turbulence of transition will continue under the shadows but under neither the control nor the domain of the great powers — unless the unresolved and unpredictable continuing struggle in Vietnam creates an explosive situation. But if the transition is controlled and moderate in pace, economically for the better, and undistorted by dominant and collectively irresistible external pressures, the FPDA which has never been, can never be, and was never planned to be, a dominant force, can acceptably and positively contribute to the climate and structure of the regional security which is essential to regional self-development.

THE QUESTION OF THE "OVERSEAS CHINESE"

Wang Gungwu

During the years which saw maximum Chinese withdrawal from international affairs together with maximum United States military commitment to Southeast Asia, the years 1965–71, there was very little journalistic or scholarly interest in the Chinese communities living in Southeast Asia. It was not until after June 1971, when President Nixon announced that he was going to visit Peking, that anxious questions once more began to be regularly asked about the future role of the "Overseas Chinese". All the fears of the 1950s concerning these Chinese were quickly revived and a large variety of questions were asked. Most of them centred on two related problems with wide ramifications. Firstly, will the Chinese in Southeast Asia be the targets of subversion? Secondly, will they be encouraged to resist assimilation and reassert their Chineseness?

On both these, opinions were divided. There were many who felt strongly that the diplomatic reemergence of China necessarily meant trouble for Southeast Asian countries with Chinese minorities, although some concentrated more on the consequences of American military withdrawal than on what the Chinese planned to do. Others were confident that the time for such fears was over. Most of the Chinese had settled down and made their peace with the new nationalist governments that had emerged since 1945. Most of them were economically well-off and too committed to the more or less *laissez faire* economics of the region to want to destroy them. Where there was danger, it would come from the growing discontent among the indigenous poor and the political awakening of the indigenous young. Thus one view concentrates on the intentions of

---

Reprinted from Lim Joo-Jock and S.B.D. de Silva, eds., *Southeast Asian Affairs 1976* (Singapore: Institute of Southeast Asian Studies, 1976), pp. 103–10. At the time of original publication, Wang Gungwu was Professor of Far Eastern History, Research School of Pacific Studies, Australian National University.

China and the other on the effectiveness of Southeast Asian governments. There should also be a third which looks more closely at the reactions of the local Chinese. Although no great threat need be expected from them, there will be changes among them in some specific ways, for example, regarding citizenship among those who have been nationals of the Republic of China in Taiwan and regarding the new perspectives on issues of loyalty and assimilation. These changes will depend on the current policies of Southeast Asian governments, the numbers of Chinese and the degree of assimilation already achieved in each country, and not least on the attitudes of individual Chinese about their countries of adoption.

By May 1974, China's own policies towards Southeast Asia became clearer. They emphasized the acceptance of the existing international system and the desire for a new start with governments so far hostile to China. The main events of the three years since the Nixon announcement confirm this. The People's Republic of China was admitted into the United Nations in October 1971. Over forty countries which had previously recognized Taiwan or refrained from recognizing either of the Chinas, had established full diplomatic relations. Changes within China, too, confirmed a desire for stability and development. Lin Piao had fallen in September 1971, the Chinese Communist Party had been restructured in the provinces, and a new Central Committee was elected at its Tenth Party Congress in August 1973. Although a fierce political campaign against Lin Piao and against Confucius continued in 1974, the trends were towards firm control within and a steady policy without. In particular, foreign policy statements concerning the United States, Japan and the Third World, even when laced with violent anti-Soviet sentiments, could be described as reassuring to Southeast Asian governments. Also, in the treatment of visitors to China, the scrupulous distinction made between foreigners of Chinese descent and "Overseas Chinese" with Chinese passports has been widely noted. Taken together with other assurances the Chinese Government were giving at the protracted negotiations with Malaysia's representatives through 1972 and 1973, the key developments did assuage old fears. When Tun Razak agreed to visit Peking in May 1974, his decision suggested that he saw more advantages than risks in taking Chinese assurances at their face value. A year later, both President Marcos of the Philippines and Premier Kukrit of Thailand were to accept the need for change for similar reasons. It now appears that the Singapore Government will also follow the same path, especially if Indonesia indicates its willingness to restore relations with China.

Now that China has largely achieved its aim of conciliation with the ASEAN countries, it remains to be seen if China might now act differently towards people of Chinese origin who have settled in the region and begin to urge them to act on China's behalf in any way and whether the local citizens of Chinese descent themselves might now rediscover their Chineseness and slow down, if not stop, the process of assimilation altogether. For the past year and a half since Malaysia's recognition of China, a number of developments have been relevant to the problem of the "Overseas Chinese", especially to the need to clarify further what the term "Overseas Chinese" really means now.

The three most important developments have been: (a) the political changes in the pivotal state of Thailand; (b) the transformation of Indochina and its impact on United States policies towards the ASEAN countries and ASEAN policies towards China and the Soviet Union; and (c) the consequences of world-wide inflation and recession on the economic conditions of the noncommunist states in the region. Related to these three are a number of other events also important for those of Chinese origin. These include the growing strength of insurgency forces in Thailand and Thai efforts to prevent its eastern neighbours, Laos and Cambodia, from supporting these insurgents, the residual United States support for Thailand as the new line of defence against the spread of communism and the Thai-Malaysia border campaigns against a combination of Malaysian Chinese, Thai and Thai-Malay insurgent forces. Also notable are the rise of *bumiputra* (Malay and other indigenous) discontent in Malaysia and Singapore's concern with noncommunist subversion: both have long-term implications for those of Chinese origin, especially if the more crucial developments in Thailand are not resolved and its security problems endanger the whole length of the Malay Peninsula.

With each development, it becomes more imperative to question the use of the term "Overseas Chinese". It has been used in its broadest sense to cover all people of Chinese descent resident abroad and it roughly translates the Chinese term *Hua-ch'iao* (Chinese sojourners). For Southeast Asia, the more specialized *Nanyang Hua-Chi'ao* or Nanyang Chinese has been widely used until the 1960s. This is a term which has implied a single community with a considerable solidarity. It is a term I have questioned for some twenty years, but it still survives largely because the government in Taiwan has retained it in its official publications. The People's Republic became more wary of the term after the Bandung Conference in 1955 but were not always consistent until the 1960s. Since then, it has distinguished between "Foreign Chinese" and "Overseas Chinese", that is, the large majority of those who are foreign nationals but of Chinese descent and the small minority of Chinese nationals who more or less permanently reside abroad. The fact that the two governments use *Hua-ch'iao* with different meanings has not helped clarify the term for Southeast Asian governments. Specially confusing has been the way the government in Taipei has encouraged the view that all those of Chinese descent are Chinese first and foreign citizens second. This has often made China's position very difficult. On the one hand, foreign governments doubt its sincerity when it declares that all Chinese should become loyal citizens of their respective adopted countries. On the other, some foreign nationals of Chinese descent retain the hope that, at the crunch, China will offer them refuge and help, if not full protection. The classic example of how awkward the problem can be for the two Chinese governments, for the Southeast Asian governments and for various types of Chinese abroad alike, is that of Indonesia. For the past twenty years, there have been: (a) Indonesians of Chinese descent; (b) Chinese who are citizens of the People's Republic; (c) Chinese who are citizens of the Republic of China (Taiwan) whom the Indonesians treat as "stateless"; (d) stateless Chinese waiting for Indonesian citizenship, willing to be protected by the People's Republic (before 1966) and by the Republic in Taiwan (since 1967) while waiting; and (e) stateless Chinese awaiting citizenship who want to have nothing to do with either government.

Within Southeast Asia, the term "Overseas Chinese" or *Hua-ch'iao* is now less widely used. In government publications and in the media, including those in Chinese, the trend is to avoid any reference to Chinese except, when necessary, as *Ma-Hua, Yin-Hua, T'ai-Hua* and *Fei-Hua* (Malaysian, Indonesian, Thai and Filipino Chinese). Those of Chinese descent sometimes refer to themselves as *Hua-jen* (Chinese person) or *Hua-yi* (descendant of Chinese), self-consciously dropping the *ch'iao* in *Hua-ch'iao* which had emphasized that they were merely sojourners always intending to return to China. It is still not certain whether this marks simply a formal and artificial avoidance of *Hua-ch'iao* for most of those of Chinese descent. Nor is it certain that the various governments take the formal change in terminology as a real indication that their subjects have really changed their attitudes towards their new homes. But it is an important step to drop the term *Hua-ch'iao* for all but those who are citizens of China or Taiwan if we are to reduce the confusion and encourage more accurate understanding of a complex situation.

To return to the case of Indonesia, it is obviously unscientific, and verging on racism, to refer to all five categories as Chinese or Overseas Chinese. Categories (a) and (e) should normally be called Indonesians except when circumstances make it necessary to call them Indonesian Chinese. Category (d) should also be called Indonesian Chinese, although there might be times when (Overseas) Chinese would be more appropriate. Categories (b) and (c) are clearly (Overseas) Chinese. A slightly less complex situation existed in Cambodia (until April) and Laos (until July) where relations with China had undergone various changes. Categories similar to the five found in Indonesia have existed since about 1955, but the picture had become much simplified by 1971 when Prince Sihanouk was overthrown and Lon Nol seized power. And since the middle of 1975, only two categories remain: Cambodians and Laotians (of Chinese descent) and (Overseas) Chinese. Such a development has already occurred in Burma where relations with China since 1950 have been relatively steady. There are Burmese (including Sino-Burman, Sino-Shan, etc., if local identifications are pursued further) and there are (Overseas) Chinese. Another curious but aberrant development occurred in Vietnam. In North Vietnam, the question of being of Chinese descent had long been meaningless and Chinese is used only for those who have come from China or carry Chinese passports. In South Vietnam where the numbers of Chinese had been much larger since the nineteenth century and where the government in Taiwan was recognized as China until April 1975, most Chinese were forced to take Vietnamese nationality by the government of Ngo Dinh Diem (1955–63). While this did not reconcile such Chinese to Vietnamese aspirations, it did make the position simpler for the new government of the Republic of Socialist Vietnam when it took over power in May 1975. It would be interesting to see if the Vietnamese of Chinese descent who had not escaped from the country have been given a choice of becoming (Overseas) Chinese again or have been treated as Vietnamese in every respect.

Obviously, the question of which government is recognized has been an important factor in determining who is or is not Chinese. Where a Southeast Asian government has consistently dealt only with China, the definition of "Chinese" has steadily narrowed and only those who are citizens of the People's Republic are Overseas Chinese or *Hua-ch'iao*. This has not been so clear when diplomatic relations were with the Republic in Taiwan, or when neither China nor Taiwan was officially recognized. In such cases, as with Thailand and the Philippines and with Malaysia and Singapore, a new stage in definition is now due. On 31 May, 1974, Malaysia established diplomatic relations with the People's Republic, recognized it as the sole legal government of China and decided to close down its consulate in Taipei. On 9 June 1975, the Philippines followed suit and announced that it would remove all its official representatives from Taiwan and ask Taiwan to withdraw its representatives within one month. On 1 July 1975, Thailand also agreed to do the same. For all three countries, the implications for its citizens of Chinese origin, for its Chinese and for those who may be stateless, are great.

The official and legal position is relatively simple. Despite the variations in the three joint communiqués signed, they all agreed that those of Chinese descent who adopted the nationality of any of the three countries automatically forfeited Chinese nationality. Dual nationality was therefore untenable. It was also understood that China did not recognize "stateless" Chinese and by this, China hoped to encourage the three governments to facilitate the acquisition of local citizenship by those of Chinese origin. No exact figures of those involved have been published officially, but it has been generally assumed that, for Malaysia, some 120,000 noncitizens are involved and, for Thailand and the Philippines, about 300,000 and 100,000 "Taiwan citizens" respectively are being asked to choose between local and Chinese citizenship. The Chinese Government has repeatedly emphasized that those who choose to be Chinese should abide by the laws of the land, respect local customs and live in friendship with the people of the three countries. For such Chinese, China will protect their rights and interests in accordance with international practice.

From the point of view of the three Southeast Asian governments, the question is also a political one. The "Taiwan Chinese" in Thailand and the Philippines had never worked against the local governments before, and therefore may expect some consideration on their position. Will they now acquiesce easily with their changed status? As for Malaysia, with its history of suspicion of the loyalties of those of Chinese origin, how sure is it of the loyalty of another 100,000 more if most of those who had not previously qualified are now given the local citizenship they want? Malaysia has the additional problem of associating the Communist Party of Malaya (CPM) with the Chinese and with those of Chinese descent. In this way, communist opposition has always been linked with external intervention. If there should be virtually no more Chinese but only Malaysians (Chinese) who might or might not support the CPM, would this now be a largely internal matter which cannot so easily be blamed on others? The problems for each of the three Southeast Asian countries are obviously different, but so far the governments have been assured loudly and clearly by the Chinese Government that the *Hua-ch'iao* of the past are almost extinct, that "foreign Chinese" are not China's concern and not the target of subversion by China and that such Chinese are not encouraged to resist local assimilation and assert what is left of their Chineseness. It seems to me that China has not been ambiguous about these problems. The ambiguity stems more from the attitudes and the experiences of those descendants of Chinese who have made their homes in the region.

The rest of this survey will concentrate on the *Ma-Hua*, *T'ai-Hua* and *Fei-Hua*, that is, the *Hua-jen* or *Hua-yi* of Malaysia, Thailand and the Philippines. The first and most obvious point to note is that "Chinese" has been defined differently in each country. The Filipino definition has been the most clear-cut: only those who are aliens are counted as Chinese, and both local and foreign demographers respect this form of counting. For Thailand, the definition has been less consistent. Officially, the Thai definition is the same as that of the Philippines, but demographers and political commentators consistently blur the picture by making rough estimates of all Thai nationals who are part-Chinese or of Chinese descent together with alien Chinese and using figures of Chinese ranging from two-and-a-half to four million. As for Malaysia, the official definition is itself confusing. Apart from a few part-Chinese who are unequivocally Malay and have been acknowledged as such, everyone of Chinese descent, whether he is a Malaysian citizen or not, has been counted as Chinese. There are understandable historical reasons for this method of counting, but its retention in the official census and other publications makes it difficult to get rid of the residual sense of all such Chinese being in some ways *Hua-ch'iao* whether they are citizens or not. It emphasizes that they are culturally unassimilated and that this is more important than their protestations of loyalty to Malaysia. This encourages a feeling of separateness that keeps alive the idea of being discriminated against and makes some Malaysian Chinese adopt a negative attitude towards the country. This in turn sustains the doubts about their political loyalty.

Another critical point to note is the attitude towards China of all those who may be counted as Chinese in one way or another, whether they are aliens or local citizens of part-Chinese or Chinese descent. It has become clear for more than a decade that very few such Chinese are interested in returning to China to live. This is only partly because of the fact that returning to China is almost always an irreversible act. More important is the fact that China does not welcome them back. It may still want them to remit funds to assist relatives in China, but it recognizes that Chinese who have lived abroad all or most of their lives are unlikely to settle easily in China. Equally important is the realization among most of those who have settled in countries which are more or less capitalist, that they could not do well in a planned socialist society. They may or may not believe that the political and economic system in China is the best possible for the people in China, but they know that they would not be able to adjust unless they rejected their present way of life altogether and became committed to the new Chinese ideals. But then those few who are ideologically committed to the Marxism-Leninism of China may well feel that their contribution to the historical process can be better made by fighting social injustice and economic exploitation in their adopted countries where the need for revolution is greater. They may be inspired by Marxist ideals, but they would be far more effective if they identified with local grievances and supported indigenous movements and played down their own Chinese origins. The choice may be more difficult if the indigenous revolution itself succeeds, as in the Indochina states. Those who did not leave Saigon-Cholon and Phnom Penh in April 1975, may wish to choose whether to live in a Vietnamese/Cambodian socialist society or to return as Chinese to live in a Chinese form of it. It would be interesting to observe what decisions will be made in the next few years.

All this is not to say that there is no residual nostalgia for "the old country" or no sympathy at all for the goals of the Chinese revolution. The important thing is to set this beside a general suspicion of, if not hostility towards, the spread of communism into their adopted country. This is not only among traditionalists, capitalists and pro-Taiwan loyalists but also among the petty bourgeois traders and artisans who form the majority of *Hua-jen* or *Hua-yi* in every country in the region except in Malaysia and Singapore. Such a situation may not remain constant. It could change radically if government policies fail to give them a firm stake in their adopted countries and win their loyalties. But there is little doubt that fewer and fewer of them are tempted to identify with China unless they are pushed or forced to do so. Nor are they happy to contemplate their fate if local communists should seize power and declare them to be among the exploiters of the indigenous peoples.

More specifically, what are the attitudes of *Ma-Hua*, *T'ai-Hua* and *Fei-Hua* towards Malaysia, Thailand and the Philippines respectively since the establishment of diplomatic relations with China? Although all three countries are members of ASEAN, their security problems are quite different and these problems influence directly their views about China, communism, and their present and future citizens of Chinese descent. And the attitudes of these *Hua-yi* would also depend on the nature of these security problems and their respective governments' policies towards them as trustworthy citizens. As mentioned earlier, the most critical developments since the Vietnamese and Cambodian victories in April 1975 concern the politics of Thailand and the insurgent forces in Thailand and Malaysia. Of more general concern for all ASEAN countries is the question of United States policy in Asia and the duration and impact of economic uncertainty in Japan and the United States on the region.

Let me begin with the Philippines where the problem is simplest and where the numbers of Chinese are comparable to those in Indonesia, Burma, Cambodia, Laos, Vietnam, the "outer ring" of the region. Here part-Chinese (mestizos) are almost wholly assimilated and barely distinguishable from Filipinos. Some of them may be specially enthusiastic about close trading relations with China, but there is no problem of subversion from this group at all. As for the 100,000 (96,308 in 1972) alien Chinese, there had been a degree of alienation because most of them who had been born in the country felt that they were discriminated against and had been prevented from becoming naturalized Filipino citizens by the simple operation of law. But in anticipation of diplomatic relations with the People's Republic of China, President Marcos' Letter of instruction No. 270 relaxed the conditions for citizenship and encouraged those who still wished to become Filipinos to fill in the new application forms provided. The first closing date for such new applications, 31 May 1975, gave very little time for the aliens to respond. This was extended to 30 June, by which date about 19,500 applications had been submitted covering about 60,000 individuals (including children who are still minors). This means that about 60% of the alien Chinese are seeking naturalization and submitting themselves to scrutiny by the National Bureau of Investigation and the National Intelligence and Security Authority. Even if all of them are granted Filipino citizenship, there remain about 40,000 who for various reasons have not applied. Some were unable to find the 6–10,000 pesos needed to submit their applications, some may wish to become citizens of China and others may wish to retain their Taiwan passports even if it means that they would be "stateless" while they live in the Philippines.

There is no reason to doubt that those seeking naturalization would eventually identify with the larger Filipino community, especially if they are Christians, speak the national language or local dialects and had begun to be active in local political and cultural affairs. Their assimilation will be assisted by organizations like the Pagkakaisa sa Pag-unlad, which has for the past five years prepared the ground for just such a situation. As for the remaining 40,000 (including children), it is not clear how many will eventually become Chinese citizens or be treated as such by the Chinese and Filipino Governments. At this stage, it does not appear that there will be more than 20,000 adult Chinese citizens in the country for the next decade. This does appear to be a figure both governments can live with, without serious difficulty. The detailed arrangements for each individual and his family may take time to sort out and there may be considerable dislocations to begin with. But there should be no threat to good relations between China and the Philippines from this source, and it may be expected that, after a short period of uncertainty, this aspect of the Chinese problem in the Philippines will be essentially settled. Only one area of concern remains, If Taiwan does become part of the People's Republic and the Philippines-China boundary is drawn along the Luzon Strait (Bashi Channel), is a dispute likely? One could speculate for years about this, but there is nothing to suggest that these questions would involve the Chinese citizens or the Filipino citizens of Chinese descent.

A more complex problem faces the government of Thailand and the Chinese in Thailand. There are three major reasons for this. Firstly, the legal and the social definitions of "Chinese" have not coincided as clearly as in the Philippines. Secondly, Thailand has been deeply involved in the wars in Indochina in which China has invariably supported the opposite side. Thirdly, the problem of insurgency is serious and the insurgents have been receiving encouragement and help from the Chinese Communist Party, if not from the government itself.

The question of how Chinese are counted in Thailand has already been mentioned. The position of the 310,000 alien Chinese is similar to that in the Philippines. The Thai Government will speed up the granting of Thai nationality to those who want it, but it expects the majority to seek Chinese nationality or try to retain their Taiwan passports under special arrangements. Unlike in the Philippines, the proportion of those seeking Thai nationality is likely to be fewer because Thai nationality had always been easier to obtain and most of those who wanted it would have got it before 1975. Should large numbers, say some 200,000 become Chinese nationals, the government may be a little anxious, But the real anxiety may stem from another source. A large number or those who had acquired Thai nationality since the 1930s may still not be fully assimilated into Thai society. This has not previously troubled the Thai Government because it had never placed great store on the artificial "conversion principle" of naturalization, but depended on the more natural but time-consuming "continuum method of cultural assimilation," a method whereby the Sino-Thai assimilated in the nineteenth century drew other Thai Chinese gradually across the bridge they provided into Thai society. Given time and patience, the policy has been remarkably successful. Today the large majority of Thai Chinese are Sino-Thai and their fierce loyalty to the social structure in which they have a large stake is not doubted. Their numbers, their cohesion and their determination to persist with the assimilationist policy may overcome any fear that this process may now be arrested. But the continuum picture never looks complete and there have always been questions about whether the method could not work both ways and whether there might not be pressure to have the process reversed. The persistent doubts about this have led to the loose way all writers refer to "Chinese" in Thailand and count all those who are of Chinese ancestry, adding to the alarming figures often used of two-and-a-half to four million "Chinese". This kind of counting reflects an underlying suspicion that many Thai Chinese may be willing to revive their Chinese connections, if not actually identify themselves as Chinese, if the circumstances were different and it was expedient or profitable to do so.

Another facet of the question is the composition of this large more or less "Chinese" population. If indeed Thais of Chinese or part-Chinese origin number some 8% of the total population and are largely living in urban centres, it would mean that a large proportion of them are petty bourgeoisie and proletariat, as they certainly are in Bangkok. Such urban centres produced the restless reformist intelligentsia that have shaken the political structure since October 1973, and these certainly include many of Chinese or part-Chinese origin. There is still no doubt that these Thai Chinese would act as Thais rather than as "Chinese". But in the present context of the new communist-dominated states east and north of the country and renewed speculation about direct Chinese support for the insurgents within Thailand and on the Thai-Malaysian border, any Thai Chinese political activity against the status quo could be seen as a security problem for the government. It could again create the doubt as to how many of these Thai Chinese could stand to have their loyalty tested. But it would be tragic if this should lead the Thai leaders to forget that, although many Thai Chinese have maintained kinship links with towns and villages in South China, most of them have done well in the traditionalist, conservative and capitalist system of Thailand and very few have ever identified with the government and dominant ideology of China, whether militarist, nationalist or communist.

As for Malaysia, the Chinese problem is much more obvious and Tun Razak took the greatest risk of his career to go to Peking, normalize relations between Malaysia and China and show that he is not anti-Chinese. The chief reason for the bold step was his concern to move Southeast Asia towards a "zone of peace, freedom and neutrality". Considerations of trade with China, channelled through government agencies wherever possible, were also important. At the same time, an acknowledgement by China of his government's legitimacy, China's official assurance of noninterference in Malaysia's internal affairs, its firm confirmation that Malaysians of Chinese origin can expect nothing from China while those who choose to be Chinese must abide by the laws of Malaysia could improve Tun Razak's position as a wise and clear-sighted national leader. The risk has been worth taking because it has finally taken the ambiguity out of the nationality problem for the Malaysian Chinese. If many of them are still not satisfied with the Razak Government, they will have to seek a Malaysian solution. Their attitudes towards their adopted country is likely to be better focused and they are more likely to seek common cause with those equally dissatisfied of whatever ethnic origins, and seek to right injustices as Malaysians. Thus, although the developments of the past eighteen years of independence have shown that Malaysian Chinese must learn to accept a subordinate political position, that their communal economic power is limited in an economy tied to a larger global system, and that full cultural assimilation with the *bumiputra* is almost impossible, the same period has confirmed that such citizens of Chinese origin are capable of making a political commitment to Malaysia and of adapting to the change from an Anglo-Malayan framework of the 1950s to an emerging Southeast Asian state of the 1970s.

There has, of course, been a resumption of violence by the Communist Party of Malaya since May 1974, and the CPM continues to be dominated by Malaysians of Chinese origin, although many of the original leaders had never been citizens of independent Malaya or Malaysia and are now either aliens or "stateless". Also, there has been a resorting to urban violence by groups unknown, notably around Merdeka Day 1975, most likely by Malaysians of Chinese origin. These represent at least two sources of possible danger to the political stability of the country. But neither of them is a straightforward matter of good versus evil or Chinese versus Malay, as still being represented by some observers and analysts. The CPM violence stems from a view of history that sees revolution as inevitable, that sees the country, and the region as a whole, as ready for radical change. It has been encouraged by the diplomatic successes of China and the communist victories in Indochina, but it is no longer specifically Chinese in origin. In fact, the CPM's capacity to make political gains depends more on its fraternal relations with Thai and Malay rebels on both sides of the Thai-Malaysia border than on overt Malaysian Chinese support. As for the urban violence, if it arises, as it appears to, from the increasing discontent of some Malaysians of Chinese origin, it would be primarily the product of an ongoing complex historical process. This is the process of transforming a postcolonial plural society into a nation-state founded on *bumiputra* sovereignty. However just may be the efforts at economic redistribution and however necessary the "melting-pot" philosophy is to the cause of nation-building, it must be recognized that the process will be painful and divisive. And should the process be poorly managed, it could be far more disruptive to the country than a Marxist-Leninist-Maoist world view so alien still to most Malaysians.

In short, the government of Malaysia has good reason to be anxious about a sizeable urban proletariat of Chinese origin, but the operative word need not be "Chinese" but "proletariat". There has never been any serious threat to political stability from the middle class professionals and the successful traders, whatever their origins; the main threat which had failed in the 1950s had been abstractly ideological and revolutionary, but it has now begun to be reshaped in terms of reduced opportunities, aborted expectations and actual downward social mobility. Here the nature of the newly settled communities of migrant background needs to be taken into account. Immigrants are notoriously restless. They long for upward mobility, at least for the promise of future upward mobility. In the new nation-state where those of Chinese origin form some 35% of the population, mobility upwards for all is obviously impossible. Thus the majority over a time would have to accept a levelling and stabilizing of certain classes which all settled peoples are forced to recognize as the norm. For most, therefore, their proletariat class will grow and persist, and as they seek and find protection in the defensiveness of their class, they will be more and more Malaysian in their use of legitimate local institutions to enhance their standard of living and reduce their social grievances. A secure, firmly established proletariat is rarely revolutionary, and if it does gain class solidarity, rarely racist. The time seems to have come for much less emphasis on ethnic origins and much less fear of the proletariat. This is not to say that there is no revolutionary potential in the countryside. In Southeast Asia, it is still agrarian unrest that threatens the residual traditional political structures. But this is not a Malaysian Chinese threat, it is not a force that can benefit either the Malaysian Chinese bourgeois or proletariat. The recent developments suggest that Malaysian Chinese have little to gain from political instability and it is not too late for their leaders to hammer this home to their supporters, to other Malaysians and to the government alike.

It would be difficult to summarize the "Overseas Chinese" problem for Southeast Asia as a whole. The following should serve merely as a framework for a better understanding of the more general aspects of the problem.

A. From the point of view of the Southeast Asian governments:
  (1) The suspicion remains that their own citizens of Chinese descent are likely to be Chinese first and loyal citizens second. On the assumption that the Chinese are inclined to act on behalf of China, the distrust of revolutionary China encourages the distrust of all Chinese, even their own citizens.
  (2) The political and cultural assimilation of Chinese is regarded as being only skin-deep, hence assimilation is no guarantee against subversion. Only racial mixture over a long period of time can eliminate "the Chinese problem".
  (3) The economic power of "Overseas Chinese" and their own citizens of Chinese descent is a long-term threat. It has so far been contained by the Western-dominated "neocolonial" or multinational trading system. If Western power withdraws, more draconian measures will be needed to keep this "Chinese" power down.
B. From the point of view of China:
  (4) Southeast Asia, like the rest of the Third World, is ready for independence, liberation and revolution. China can help by using the right tactics. The key strategy lies in the success of China and the socialist camp. Those of Chinese origin in the region are largely unrevolutionary and must not be allowed to stand in the way of that success.
  (5) Not only will the revolution be

ultimately victorious, Chinese influence in the neighbourhood must inevitably grow. Time is on its side. China can afford to ignore the "Overseas Chinese"; they are now dispensable. In any case, when Chinese influence is overwhelming, those who still wish to do so may identify with China again.

C. From the point of view of the Chinese settled in Southeast Asia:

(6) The majority owe no loyalty to China, but the habit of sojourning is being kept alive by discrimination, by insecurity, by cultural arrogance, by irrational hopes about China's ultimate protection and by false ideas about greener pastures elsewhere.

(7) Where those who are identifiably Chinese are numerous enough, there is the defence and withdrawal into ghettos. This phenomenon is already noticeable in the major cities, especially in those of the "outer ring" of countries like Indonesia, Burma, the Philippines and the Indochina states.

(8) Only in the core countries of Thailand, Malaysia and Singapore can the citizens of Chinese descent still play a positive, meaningful and worthwhile role. This could, in theory, be in the name of the world revolution, but is more likely to be on behalf of their respective nation-states if their stakes — which vary considerably between these three countries — in them can be better defined.

SOUTHEAST ASIA 1976
The Handling of Contradictions

Chan Heng Chee

The main variable of Southeast Asian politics in 1976 was the emergence and institutionalization of the communist governments in Indochina. International politics in the region was primarily responses arising from this fact, involving mutual assessment, diplomatic fencing and a series of attempts by the various governments adhering to basically two ideologically contradictory political systems to formulate a working relationship. For the non-communist governments of Indonesia, Malaysia, the Philippines, Singapore and Thailand, even the anticipation of an eventual communist takeover in South Vietnam did not prepare them for the swiftness and the completeness of the communist victories throughout 1975. The Cambodian proclamation of a revolutionary government on 17 April was followed by the entry of North Vietnamese troops into Saigon on 30 April and, only a few months later, a bloodless transition of power took place within the coalition government in Laos, leaving the Pathet Lao in total control of the country by the end of November. Domestic politics in the noncommunist states was not solely a function of the external threat of communism, but political issues were recognizably forced or attenuated by the considerations of internal subversion, the weakening of the political will of leaderships and the need to build up national resilience, particularly in states which are the nearest neighbours of Indochina. In the new communist states the concern, domestically, was to create an administrative infrastructure to facilitate economic development and reconstruction and the protection of their territorial borders and newly gained sovereignty.

For the student of politics interested in unravelling the meaning behind the packed events and developments in the area a

---

Reprinted from Huynh Kim Khanh, ed., *Southeast Asian Affairs 1977* (Singapore: Institute of Southeast Asian Studies, 1977), pp. 3–21. At the time of original publication, Chan Heng Chee was Senior Lecturer at the Department of Political Science of the University of Singapore and Visiting Fellow at the Institute of Southeast Asian Studies.

year after the establishment of the three communist regimes in Southeast Asia, it may be efficient to utilize the theme of the confrontation of contradictions, for without any question the noncommunist governments in the region have to deal with the presence of a fundamentally different, if not opposed, political force — communist governments which have emerged as a regional power very suddenly. This article will explore the handling of this contradiction from the stand point of the noncommunist states of ASEAN and that of communist Vietnam, Laos and Cambodia. It proposes to examine first, the perceptions of the ASEAN states of the political situation and their policies; secondly, the perceptions, priorities and policies of the communist states; and thirdly, the dialogue and interaction between the ASEAN and the Indochinese states.

The Response from ASEAN States

By the time the stage was set for the communist takeover in Indochina, the political perception and political analysis of the Association of Southeast Asian Nations (ASEAN) Governments had undergone major transformations (though not every one at the same pace nor in the same details) accelerated by the sudden changes in the international influences at work in the region. By 1975 the withdrawal of the British military commitment was a fact. American military disengagement was set in motion by the Nixon Doctrine and reaffirmed by the Ford Pacific Doctrine. The South-East Asia Treaty Organization (SEATO) was gradually being phased out. For the first time in several decades Southeast Asia faces a markedly reduced military presence of Western military powers. What this means is that those accustomed to a protective security umbrella provided by an external ally would have to restructure their defence arrangements to meet this new contingency. The bipolar international system dominated by the U.S. and the Soviet Union had given way to a multipolar system in which the new players were the United States, the Soviet Union, the People's Republic of China (PRC) and the economically powerful Japan, and of whom the U.S. and USSR related to each other in ambiguous and still unpredictable ways. All were likely to affect developments in Southeast Asia in the seventies and eighties.

The most significant development in international politics was the U.S. *rapprochement* with its traditional adversaries, the PRC and the USSR, which hastened the normalization of relations between many of the Southeast Asian Governments and the communist powers. This changing scenario however underlined one ironical development: whereas Cold War tensions between the longstanding adversaries were lessening, on another front an ideological confrontation had all the potentiality of building up in post-Vietnam Southeast Asia.

The Soviet Union manifesting its interests in the region managed from 1969 onwards to be remarkably successful in its diplomacy, eliciting responses to its overtures of friendship from previously pro-Western and resistant governments. Southeast Asian Governments noted the Sino-Soviet rivalry and hoped to use it to their own advantage. A decisive revision had taken place in their thinking so that now political leaders in the region no longer accepted Cold War tenets. Their perceptions of security problems had immensely sharpened, seeing them in their particularities linked to the socio-economic imperatives rather than as a vague generalized threat born of a conspiracy of an ideological monolithic force. The most obvious signal of this transformation was the proposal of Malaysia in 1970 to declare Southeast Asia a zone of peace, freedom and neutrality under big power guarantee for in many ways Malaysia, solidly anticommunist and pro-West, was the least expected innovator in this field of foreign policy.

The actual determining factors of the respective roles of the major powers would depend on the acquiescence of the Southeast Asian Governments, the capacity and the willingness of the external powers to intervene and the political rivalry between the powers.

In the early reaction to the communist victories all ASEAN leaders expressed a self-confidence in their capacity to deal with the new political situation. None believed that the communist armies would begin their march through neighbouring borders but they anticipated increased communist activities in their countries and feared the spillover of surplus and captured arms. Recognition was offered at once to Cambodia on 18 April 1975 but it was not a case, as Thai Foreign Minister Chartchai Chunhawan claimed, a question of ASEAN countries "conducting their affairs jointly", although he called a meeting of the ambassadors of ASEAN countries in Bangkok to discuss this matter. Closer co-ordination of ASEAN policies was much more apparent only a year later; Indonesia expressed a difference of opinion here, and only eleven days after the fall of Phnom Penh and ten days after the other ASEAN Governments did it recognize the new government. In the case of the Provisional Revolutionary Government of South Vietnam (PRGSV), the initial reaction of Malaysia was more welcoming than Indonesia's or Singapore's. It was the first ASEAN country to recognize the Vietcong Government and Tun Razak immediately declared that ASEAN was prepared to co-operate with the new governments in Indochina and assist in the reconstruction of the country whilst Indonesia and Singapore took a little more time to evaluate the situation. At the May 1975 ASEAN Foreign Ministers' meeting the respective governments worked out a common position, accepted the *fait accompli* and reiterated support for the five principles of co-existence whereby states with different political and social systems could live together in harmony. By August 1976 every ASEAN Government had established diplomatic relations with Vietnam. Cambodia was recognized by all ASEAN states and had diplomatic relations with Thailand, Malaysia, the Philippines and Singapore. All the ASEAN Governments had maintained diplomatic ties with the coalition government of Laos and did not break them after the communist takeover but relations are best characterized as inactive.

The Bali Summit

Emergent Indochina had one major effect upon ASEAN. It pumped new unity and purpose, adding political will into the flaccid organization. The strengthening of ASEAN was seen by all the Southeast Asian leaders as a means to increase regional resilience and assist in the economic development of the member countries thereby undercutting insurgency and the appeal of communism internally. A few statements of certain Indonesian leaders indicate that they were also lobbying for military strengthening, a view not shared by all the ASEAN members, nor significantly by General Panggabean, the Minister of Defence and Security of the country.

Even before the scheduled ASEAN summit meeting, noticeable increased contacts took place on a bilateral basis between ASEAN leaders. In July 1975 Kukrit Pramoj of Thailand paid a visit to all the ASEAN capitals. The Prime Minister of Singapore went to Thailand on a scheduled visit in January, in turn was visited by President and Mrs. Marcos later the same month in Singapore. Hussein Onn, the newly made Prime Minister of Malaysia, after two weeks in power, paid an official visit to Singapore, Jakarta and Bangkok, whilst Marcos after Tun Razak's funeral stopped to see President Suharto for quick discussions.

The Bali summit, the first meeting of the five ASEAN Heads of Government was held on 23–25 February 1976, eight years after the inauguration of the Association. The historic meeting produced two documents — the Treaty of Amity and Co-operation and the Declaration of ASEAN Concord — and the establishment of an ASEAN Secretariat in Jakarta. The commitment to economic co-operation was underlined along with other objectives among which were the resolution "to eliminate threats posed by the subversion to its stability", the "early establishment of a Zone of Peace, Freedom and Neutrality" and the commitment to rely "exclusively on peaceful processes in the settlement of intraregional differences." The Bali Declaration was important as a tangible response of noncommunist Southeast Asia to the changing balance of power in the region and whilst most of the analysis of ASEAN up till then highlighted conflicts more than commonality, the Bali meeting proclaimed a new unity underlying the differences. That the declared objective of economic co-operation could not be realized in the establishment of a free trade zone was a major drawback but not sufficiently fatal to the desire to fashion closer regional ties. Ultimately, what is important in the long run is the establishment of an overarching machinery encouraging bi and multilateral meetings, promoting in incremental ways, activities and a dependency network which constitute the sinews of regional integration. The final communiqué also expressed a readiness to develop fruitful relations with mutually beneficial co-operation with other countries in the region and invited other countries to adhere to the Treaty of Amity and Co-operation. This gesture was a generalized way of testing the response of the new communist regimes.

In the wake of the Bali meeting, the Economic Ministers discussed the development of four projects — a diesel engine plant (Singapore), a urea plant (Indonesia and Malaysia), a superphosphates plant (the Philippines), and a soda ash plant (Thailand), backed by the allocation of S$250–$300 million (US$1 = S$2.45) investment in each of the industrial projects. Since February there seems to be a growing determination to present an ASEAN position on major world bodies. The ASEAN Labour Ministers' meeting in Baguio City in May discussed the common stand to be presented at the World Labour Conference in Geneva later that June, touching on the role of foreign investors and multinationals. Throughout the year, several bi and multilateral meetings were conducted between officials of ASEAN Governments on tax agreements and extradition accords, and other working groups such as the Federation of ASEAN Chambers of Commerce also met.

The ASEAN summit did not produce a military pact but an understanding of low profile bilateral collaboration in security matters between individual member countries, outside of the purview of the regional framework. Besides Indonesia, none of the other leaders were willing to entertain the idea of a military pact though inevitably the meeting concerned itself with national and regional security. It was also in security that differences between some ASEAN members were still outstanding for not every ASEAN member had worked out in tandem the balance between national interest and regional interest.

The case of the border talks focused this problem. The Seventh Border Committee Meeting between Indonesia and Malaysia proceeded with both sides in agreement on border security issues which is the need to hunt down some 500 guerillas active along the common border. The two countries promised to co-operate in training, communications and intelligence. In addition, less directly security matters such as sea-water pollution, an antidrug campaign and search and rescue operations were also brought up. The Indonesians also decorated the Malaysian Inspector-General of Police Tan Sri Mohamed Haniff bin Omar with the *Bintang Bhayang-Kara Utama*, the highest Indonesian police award as an indication of the good relations between the two police forces. The border relations between Thailand and Malaysia, by contrast, reached a low point in the middle of 1976. Between 6–7 June, Malaysia was forced to withdraw 410 members of its Fourth Battalion Police Field Force (BPP) in face of a demonstration by 10,000 Thais against the counter-insurgency forces which for decades had been stationed at the border town. Thai BPP and paramilitary forces replaced them. Bangkok reiterated previous requests of reviewing the twelve-year-old border treaty between the two countries. Underlying the conflict is a clash of interests of the two sides. Thai authorities would wish to extend the co-operation to cover the pursuit of Muslim separatists as well as communists, a condition the predominantly Malay Government in Kuala Lumpur cannot acquiesce to. The meeting between Seni Pramoj and Hussein Onn was unable to produce a solution to this problem. There were indications that the Seni Government did not view the communist threat to be as imminent or serious as the control of Muslim nationalists and some reports suggest that Thai border police had reached a *modus vivendi* with the Malaysian Communists seeking sanctuary on the Thai side of the border.

Whatever the differences, a *coup* by right-wing military leaders in Bangkok on 6 October dramatically altered this relationship. Shortly after the *coup* General Kriangsak Chamanand, Secretary General of the National Reform Advisory Council (NARC), dropped the embarrassing demand that Malaysia should co-operate with Thailand in the suppression of Muslim separatists in the joint operation in both territories, and the General Border Committee Meeting was scheduled to be held in Thailand in 1977.

This *coup* had other far-reaching implications for the policies and responses of the ASEAN Governments as the year was drawing to an end and will be discussed in its proper context in this paper.

Malaysia

Individually, each of the ASEAN Governments took measures to adjust to the new regional situation through increased "national resilience". Malaysia and Singapore did this by emphasizing internal vigilance as most pertinent to security. For Malaysia, heavy concern was placed on mobilizing effort at all levels to generate economic growth and distribution through the Third Malaysia Plan (TMP). The Prime Minister of Malaysia adopted a two-pronged attack. He took action against corrupt officials in government which inevitably involved also dealing with dissidents in the party ranks. Concurrently, he intensified security operations throughout the country.

In an attempt to strengthen the legitimacy of the political leadership, the Mentri Besar of Selangor, Datuk Harun Idris, was investigated for his alleged corruption and charged in court amid veiled threats of social and political upheaval. The prosecution of the powerful grassroots leader weakened the unity of the ruling Malay party and raised the question of whether the iota of legitimacy added to government, if at all, were more important than the unity of the party at this juncture of development and security problems. Hussein Onn's determination to cleanse government leadership was diverted by the power struggle that followed Tun Razak's death as the succession order was fought out.

Hussein Onn's position in mid-1976 was steadily undermined by the charge of the United Malays' National Organization (UMNO) right-wing and pro-Harun supporters that communist elements held positions of power in government and exercised considerable influence. The implication was that this was by dint of the Prime Minister's patronage and also represented, by implication, criticism of Tun Razak's leadership and recruitment policy. To meet this challenge and recoup his position a week before the UMNO General Assembly, Onn's only option lay in the detention of two Malay editors named in a confession of two detained Singapore Malay editors as the masterminds of a "Communist plot" to subvert the Malay community. The detention in Kuala Lumpur of Abdul Samad Ismail, the literary doyen of the Malay intellectual circles and the Managing Editor of the Straits Times Group, culminated a series of arrests of suspected communist agents, up till then, mainly ethnic Chinese. The significance of the Samad Ismail arrest was not only the implication that communism as a threat to the national security was creeping into the Malay community in subtle ways, but that a leadership struggle in UMNO was cast in terms of legitimacy based on willingness to be tough on communism and subversion.

The establishment of the communist régimes in Indochina had heightened concern to the extent that in Malaysian domestic politics the fear of subversion had intruded symbolically and seriously into the arena of politics to become an emotive and legitimate weapon with which to strike at political opponents. By November this anticommunist crusade resulted in the removal and detention of two Malay Deputy Ministers and the detention of three opposition party politicians as well as a Malaysian Chinese Association (MCA) leader. If Tun Razak had hoped for a deescalation of communist guerilla warfare with the establishment of diplomatic relations with the PRC, he was mistaken. The incidence of activities in fact increased both in the urban areas and in the rural, partly because of the split in the Malaysian communist movement.

Thus, on the more conventional security front, the Malaysian Government continued its operations against subversion throughout the country in the New Villages which were suspect. Villagers were screened, documents captured, curfew hours imposed and several people detained. The pace intensified and in one New Village in Taiping, Perak, it was reported that 12,000 villagers were screened. In March, it was announced that the decision was made to train wives and children of policemen in the use of firearms. The increased concern with stability might have alarmed investors with the result that the Deputy Prime Minister Dr. Mohamed Mahathir in July was pushed to state that all the references to security did not mean that the situation was serious but were necessary if they were to overcome the situation to increase the people's awareness of this problem.

Singapore

The Singapore Government throughout the year took successive repressive measures against the left-wing movement, detaining communist and subversive suspects. The government dramatically made two exposés of communist activities in Singapore. The first sketched out an elaborate network of communist agents radiating from Kuala Lumpur to Singapore involving a cadre-training camp in Johore, a guerilla camp in Southern Thailand, contact points in Bangkok, Hong Kong, and recruitment, propaganda and fund-raising in Sydney. The agents involved significantly were members of the upper strata of society and, disturbingly for the government, a member of the armed forces as well. The second exposé alleged communist infiltration among students of the technical colleges to recruit the skilled and the "brains". The two notable features of both the Malaysian and Singaporean political actions were first, the apparent co-operation and joint action between the two governments, and that they were directed to counter the infiltration of communist influence into the ranks of the middle class intellectuals, professionals, businessmen and students.

Whilst the tough action against the left-wing movement may have been a response to the criticism of the Socialist International and the Dutch Party move to expel the republic from the international socialist movement (the rationale here is that the Singapore leadership wished to demonstrate domestically and internationally that preventive detention is utterly necessary of governments threatened with the reality of underground subversion), there is little doubt that the post-Vietnam situation in Singapore would not have been followed by tougher measures against the radical movement to control the expected upsurge and spread of united front activities.

Indonesia

There were indications that some military leaders sought to strengthen Indonesia against the communist threat by increasing its military capacity. President Suharto successfully obtained military assistance from the United States to the tune of S$45 million, a figure twice the previous year's. But the pressure in Indonesia to combat the communist threat does not seem to be very intense. With the crushing of the Partai Komunis Indonesia (PKI) and the relative distance from Indochina, cut off as it is from land contact with the contiguous continental and peninsular Southeast Asia, it must sense a modicum of security.

It is easy to read the invasion of Portuguese Timor by Indonesia in 7 December 1975 as a clear cut reflex on its part to the changing regional balance of power and an attempt to forestall the struggle of the Revolutionary Front for an Independent East Timor (Fretilin) to gain control of the country. Yet reading Indonesian history and the policy over West Irian, the Indochinese events were only incidental to the thrust at Timor.

In an attempt to arrest the emergence of an independent left-wing regime at its doorstep, the Indonesian leadership moved with alacrity and impunity against UN pressure to establish through the use of force its claim over what it regarded as its sphere of interest. Initially Suharto and his advisers had probably hoped to influence political developments through the pro-Indonesian parties of the Timorese Democratic Union (UDT) and the Timorese Popular Democratic Association (Apodeti) without the need for direct intervention. When the civil war broke out, its participation was less covert. On 17 July 1976, President Suharto promulgated the law on the integration of East Timor as the twenty-seventh province of Indonesia. Residual resistance by Fretilin guerillas has been reported in the interior of the country and Suharto admitted before an audience of university students in Bandung in August that in some areas the guerillas possess some strength and are still a force to be reckoned with.

The Philippines

The most striking aspect of the Philippines' response to the changed circumstances of regional politics was not in its domestic policy but in the dramatic remodelling of foreign policy. Since the establishment of martial law the close U.S.-Filipino alignment has been rapidly diminished as Marcos belatedly weaned his country from the American orbit. From 1962, there has been a progressive emphasis on regionalism, the development of trade and diplomatic relations with communist countries, closer identification with Third World countries including, perhaps expediently, support for the Arab countries' struggle in the Middle East and a desire to reestablish a new relationship with the U.S. compatible with the changing realities of Southeast Asia. In 1976, the Philippines applied to the credentials committee of the nonaligned summit for observer status, a recognition formerly denied it because of its close ties with the U.S. Marcos has by now officially visited the two leading communist powers in the world and established full diplomatic relations with both. He has also established diplomatic relations with the new communist régimes that were responsive — namely, Vietnam and Cambodia.

In the current negotiations with the United States on the renewing of the three military agreements — the Military Bases Agreement of 1947, the Mutual Defence Assistance Pact of 1947, and the Mutual Defence Treaty of 1952 — the Philippines has sought to introduce new terms for the continued U.S. presence in the two major bases, Clark Air Force Base and Subic Bay Naval Base and the maintenance of forces numbering some 14,000 men. The Philippines in the current negotiations has indicated a readiness to continue the arrangement but on condition that Filipino sovereignty is established over the bases thereby terminating U.S. extraterritoriality rights, increased compensation rates for the use of the base and the determination of the period of use.

The Thailand-Vietnam-Laos-Cambodia Quadrille

Of the ASEAN States, Thailand alone shares common borders with Cambodia and Laos. The implication of this fact is that inadvertently it will be the testing ground of the uneasy relationship between the communist and the noncommunist countries in the region. For Thailand, the major question will be whether Vietnam and Laos and perhaps Cambodia will be able to resist aid and interference in the revolutionary process in that country. Its *rapprochement* with the PRC was pressured by a very immediate imperative; it was counting on Chinese backing to counteract future Vietnamese ambition. From the perspective of the communist regimes, they would be equally concerned with the security policy of the Thais and the association of Thailand with the major powers in the control and containment of communist movements and communism. Thus Thailand's course of actions with regards to Vietnam, Laos and Cambodia was more complicated, subtle and provocatively managed than any of the ASEAN countries and will receive far lengthier treatment in this essay.

The capacity of Thailand to respond and choose between policies was greatly affected by four salient facts about Thai politics. First Thailand, during the period of civilian rule between October 1973 and October 1976, was characterized by a highly fluid and volatile political process where the conflicting demands from extreme right to extreme left were organized and articulated with equal passion. Furthermore new social groups such as students, labour, intellectuals and professionals sought to share power in the political system to put an end to the military-bureaucratic polity of the past. Government in these circumstances was frequently paralyzed in the attempt to reconcile the interests of all. Between January 1974 and April 1976 after elections to parliament were reinstituted, the multiparty parliament had changed hands from Seni Pramoj's coalition cabinet to Kukrit's and back to Seni again. The left-right confrontation in Thailand is definitely heightened by the proximity of communist victories in time and space. Secondly, though the military dictatorship was overthrown in October 1973, military men were still in positions of power not necessarily confined to the military administrative structures. They entered government via political parties and the civilian bureaucracy and have never ceased to be a powerful element in Thai politics. Events in later 1976 precipitated the seizure of power by the military. A third factor, related to the second, is the entrenchment of American interests in Thailand and the American presence in terms of economic interests and military equipment installations and, possibly even more enduring, the ties between military individuals of both sides. To the extent that the last two factors are institutionalized they must circumscribe the range of policy options for the Thai Government. Fourthly, Thai authorities are engaged in the process of fighting a very real insurgency movement in the North and Northeast led by the Communist Party of Thailand which is home-grown, though ethnically more heavily non-Thai. This situation is now complicated by the presence of several thousand Vietnamese and Laotian refugees from the war who, together with the resident Vietnamese, have become a source of worry to the Thais. Whatever role that the neighbouring communist powers will opt for is of immediate concern to them.

The importance of a sound Thai relationship has been acknowledged by Vietnam in its willingness to open up direct talks, a position it had steadfastly refused during the war because of the presence of U.S. military bases in Thailand. As early as January 1975, Foreign Minister

Nguyen Duy Trinh sent letters to his Thai counterpart stating that the DRV was interested in normalizing relations between the two countries. Right after the victory against the U.S. a delegation from the PRGSV visited Thailand and negotiated unsuccessfully for the return of the airplanes and ships brought to Thailand by fleeing military personnel from Saigon. This delegation was followed by the visit of Deputy Foreign Minister Phan Hien to Bangkok, lasting almost a week from 21–26 May. Significantly, no final communiqué was issued although the door for further negotiations was left open. According to *Nhan Dan* the Vietnamese demanded as conditions for the restoration of diplomatic relations the following four conditions — "the abandonment of the Thai policy of collusion with the U.S.", the return of all ships, airplanes and other American supplied equipment moved to Thailand prior to the fall of the Saigon regime, a definite end to the presence of American troops and military bases in Thailand and the complete respect for fundamental national rights and integrity of the peoples of Vietnam, Laos and Cambodia. But the stiffness of Vietnamese demands was met by an equally stiff opposition from the Thai military circle to reconciliation with Vietnam.

Kukrit, moved perhaps by the desire to make peace with Vietnam but certainly by the need to placate strident left-wing criticism, set 31 January 1976 as the date for the closure of American facilities at the airbases, the pullout of combat planes and American service personnel. This dateline was subsequently extended to 20 March and finally to 20 July when total pullout except for 270 military advisers of the Joint Military Advisory group and the equipment and installations was to take effect. Throughout the negotiations Hanoi kept a close watch and maintained the pace of verbal attack and pressure on Thailand in its broadcasts and official papers. On the whole it was pleased with the overall withdrawal development, calling it "a victory in the struggle of the Thai people for national independence and democracy", but warned that Thai rightists were "still harbouring insidious schemes", so when news of the delivery of a squadron of fighter bombers to Thailand by the U.S. broke out, Hanoi bitterly charged Washington with playing a "game of mock withdrawal". After July Hanoi's rhetoric against Thailand was markedly reduced. The removal of the bases, though not as total as Vietnam would have wished, none the less paved the way for the normalization of relations. Under Seni's Government, full diplomatic relations were established on 6 August 1976 followed by the improvement of relations with Laos and the opening of parts of the border closed since December 1975.

Seni's attempt to adopt a policy of conciliation with Vietnam and greater Thai neutrality did not receive the support of the Thai right-wing and military factions who disagreed with appeasement. The *rapprochement* did not have time to prove productive. On 6 October 1976 military leaders, using the opportunity of severe unrest generated by the return of former Prime Minister Thanom Kittikachorn, seized power. The early indications are that the new leadership, the National Administrative Reform Council (composed of solidly conservative elements) will wish to orientate Thai foreign policy and develop a new warmth in relations with the U.S. The three senior officials including the chief negotiator with the U.S. that led to the American withdrawal have been removed from office. A chilling in relations with Vietnam and Laos was apparent with Hanoi and Vientiane's daily denouncements of Thailand.

The Vietnamese accused the military leaders of being U.S. paid agents inviting U.S. imperialism back. Hostility was unavoidable given the Thai policy of a domestic hardline against left-wing radical groups and any communist suspects, particularly the arrests and harassment of Vietnamese residents in the Northeast. Thai newspapers which have resumed publication after the *coup* have escalated reports on clashes with communist infiltrators.

Thailand's relations with the new Laotian régime got off on a bad start when Laotian gunboats fired on Thai patrol boats in the Mekong River Incident in November 1975, Thailand recalled its ambassador and promptly closed the Mekong border. Thai-Lao relations in the past at best were fraught with tension. Thailand — the richer, culturally more established nation — had looked with condescension on its poorer neighbour as something approximating a satellite, for as landlocked Laos' sole supplier of imported goods, it dominated the country economically. The economic blockade that followed was lifted in January when the Thais opened two points in Nong Khai Province. Attempts to resume talks for the normalization of relations were unsuccessful for Laos wanted the entire border opened as a condition for holding talks. Thailand feared such a move would increase the routes of infiltration of men and equipment and increase the opportunities of training for the insurgents. For most of the year Laos joined Vietnam in bitterly denouncing Thailand for the presence of the military bases and the closure of the border.

Only in mid-June were conditions favourable for the creation of better relations. In the wake of a general thaw in Vietnamese-ASEAN relations, particularly in Vietnamese-Thai relations and the failure of U.S.-Thai military talks, certain elements of the Thai parliamentary élite visited Vientiane and informed the Laotians that Thailand was prepared to drop its previous condition that bilateral talks must precede the opening of the Mekong. Possibly, the Thais were also feeling the consequences of the border closure. The Foreign Minister Pichai Rattakul visited Laos on 10 August. His reasons for the new policy were couched in security terms. First, he argued, if Thailand exerted too much pressure on Laos it would be forcing the latter to look to other friends, implying a Thai role in preventing the overly close identification between Laos and Vietnam or any other socialist country by offering Laos an economic option; secondly, the closing of the border was in fact only on paper as the smuggling of goods and weapons and illegal entry still continued. By opening the borders at certain crossing points the government hoped to exercise some control. Finally, it was at least as important to security to maintain a dialogue with both Vietnam and Laos if they were going to confront the very sensitive and thorny problem of infiltration and interference. The talks settled some important issues for Thailand. It exacted an agreement from Laos to release all Thais detained in Laos and to accept the return of the refugees from Thailand. Laos also promised not to interfere in the internal affairs of Thailand nor would it allow any foreign country to use its territory as a base for aggression or intervention of other countries. The agreements however were never properly implemented and a month later Vientiane was denouncing Thai ultrarightists for unilaterally restricting the relations and contacts between the two countries. With the return of the right-wing military dictatorship it is likely the relations will deteriorate even further.

Thailand's interests with Cambodia centre round trade and security along their lengthy common border. In spelling out a policy towards Cambodia, it has been influenced by the position and stance of Cambodia itself. Unlike Laos, the Cambodians were less closely identified with the Vietnamese and seemed determined not to depend on any one communist power, in particular Vietnam. Furthermore Cambodia seemed from the outset to be too engrossed with its internal problems to be seriously active beyond its borders. Much more of a protégé of the PRC than the Soviet Union, the Cambodians, on the encouragement of the Chinese, arrived in Bangkok in October 1975 to achieve an economic and diplomatic *rapprochement*. The two countries agreed to exchange ambassadors at a later specified date. The limited relationship was sometimes strained by the fire exchanges between Thai fishing vessels and Cambodian patrol boats. In February, the Cambodians launched a somewhat mysterious charge against the U.S. who were accused together with the Thais of conducting a bombing raid on Siem Reap from Thai territory. No major break however ensued. On 16 June a party of Thai officials led by the Foreign Minister paid a surprise secret visit to Cambodia and held talks "in a friendly atmosphere". The joint communiqué indicated that there were four main concerns — the opening of diplomatic relations, the agreement to demarcate the common border, the settlement and repatriation of the Cambodian refugees and the release of the arrested Thai fishermen who had strayed into Cambodian waters.

The Response of Vietnam, Laos and Cambodia

It is not possible to discuss the perceptions, priorities and policies of the Indochinese states with regard to regional politics without recognizing that all three states, especially Vietnam, went through a bitter and long struggle against the United States to win the war. Consequently their world view is dominated by a deep-rooted suspicion of American intentions and they feel constantly threatened. At the same time, paradoxically, the emergence of the communist regimes in Southeast Asia has taken place at a time when ASEAN political leaders are far more flexible in their policy responses and have discarded orthodox Cold War views. Thus the three régimes in the unfolding postwar situation are critically evaluating the sincerity in the noncommunist pronouncements as much as noncommunist governments fear the intransigence and duplicity on the part of the communists. The depth of this suspicion can only be appreciated if one remembers that one of the ASEAN states sent troops and mercenaries to fight on the side of the U.S. forces and anticommunist regimes in Saigon and Phnom Penh whilst those who did not either sold or serviced food and war weapons and equipment to their enemy.

Whilst these two factors substantially shape the overall perception of the political context, the policies each will adopt will be an interaction between perception and goal priorities which each of the separate leaderships of Vietnam, Laos and Cambodia will take. Would they choose to take advantage of the favourable conditions of regional co-operation to assist their development or would they fall back to rely on traditional allies such as the Soviet Union and the PRC remained one of the more interesting questions a year after the war ended. To choose a wider co-operation would not only mean greater independence from the larger communist powers but also perhaps a more stable and fruitful exchange in the region. What is still ambiguous is the extent to which the Indochinese states intend to fulfill their ideological role in the promotion of revolutionary movements in the area, and on this score the attention is primarily directed on Vietnam, as the most war-experienced, militarily powerful and ideologically tested regional communist power. What were some of the policies adopted by the communist states in terms of their interests?

As expected, Vietnam, Laos and Cambodia lost no time to declare their "militant solidarity" and establish ties with each other but this did not result in any move to form an Indochina Federation at all as some quarters had anticipated. In the newfound solidarity the two less powerful nations have insisted on and frequently asserted their independence and separate identity. In the case of Cambodia, it was quite clear from the start, there was, as the Singapore Prime Minister noted, "greater People's Republic of China influence which may not see eye-to-eye with Vietnam". Although a delegation led by Le Duan, the first Secretary of the Vietnamese Workers' Party, visited Phnom Penh in August 1975, nothing came of the visit and the Cambodians visited Vietnam in September on the occasion of the thirtieth Anniversary of the Democratic Republic of Vietnam (DRV). A Very real lack of trust seems to exist between Cambodia and Vietnam with the Cambodians fearing Vietnamese encroachment. During the war, Vietnamese communist forces occupied some areas of Cambodia in 1970–73 and since the war there have been reports of clashes between Vietnam and Khmer communist forces along the borders. Cambodia's foreign policy appears to be designed to check Vietnamese dominance by developing good relations with the Chinese and neighbouring Thailand. The first international treaty Democratic Cambodia signed was an economic, cultural co-operation agreement with the PRC in August 1975, the result of a visit by a delegation led by Khieu Samphan. A return visit was made by the Chinese Minister of Foreign Trade Li Chang to Cambodia's capital in March 1976 where another economic agreement, the precursor it would appear of many more to come, was signed.

If the Cambodians have remained somewhat aloof from Vietnam, Laos rapidly moved so close to the latter that it has been viewed by Southeast Asian leaders as a Vietnamese pawn. In February 1976, Laos paid its first official visit to Hanoi and agreed to co-operate in many areas including economics, health, culture, civil aviation, postal communications and press information services. Perhaps the most crucial concession to the Laotians was the Vietnamese agreement to cede a small stretch of dockside territory to Laotian sovereignty to allow goods to pass directly into Laotian control to counteract the effects of the closure of the Thai border. Of concern to the noncommunist Southeast Asian leaders, who were vigilantly looking for signs of militant communism, was the fact that throughout the visit, the statements of the leaders and the propaganda organs of the two countries were highly political and militant, couched in strong revolutionary terms. Le Duan in the welcoming reception saw the victories of Laos, Cambodia and Vietnam as signalling a new era, "altering the balance of power in the world and strengthening and consolidating the offensive position of the revolutionary currents." The final communiqué reaffirmed their support for revolutionary movements and warned Southeast Asian Governments that "...Laos and Vietnam will participate in making Southeast Asian countries independent, peaceful and truly neutral."

Laotians, however have steadfastly denied the "satellite" or "pawn" theory. In an interview with the Japanese newspaper *Manichi Shimbun* in July 1976 Kaysone Phoumvihane, the Prime Minister of the Lao People's Democratic Republic, described the relationship thus: "The relationship between Vietnam and us is based on friendship, solidarity and co-operation to build our countries according to their own ways" and he emphasized that their co-operation was based on the agreement

> to respect equality between the two countries, respect each other's independence, sovereignty and territorial integrity, respect each other's legitimate interest, not to interfere in each other's internal affairs, constantly enhance mutual confidence and develop co-operation between the two countries in the economic, cultural, scientific and technical fields on the basis of mutual benefit and mutual assistance.

In spite of the denials a co-ordination of the two countries' foreign policies was however apparent throughout the year. In July on the last leg of his Southeast Asian tour Phan Hien, the Minister of Foreign Affairs of the Socialist Republic of Vietnam, visited Laos for discussions. *Radio Hanoi* reported that the two sides saw "eye-to-eye" in all matters and worked out concrete measures to further strengthen the "unshakeable fraternal friendship" and to speed up their close co-operation in all fields. Significantly, it also mentioned that the two sides declared they would do their best to work for the success of the nonaligned summit in Colombo. It is possible, even probable, that a joint position on ASEAN had been worked out during this visit.

Laos has also developed close relations with the Soviet Union. The basis was as much ideological affinity as the practical desire to increase options and aid for development. When Kaysone Phoumvihane visited Moscow in April 1976, the Russians pledged "cultural, scientific and economic co-operation on the basis of complete equality and mutual benefit" with the signing of agreements. It has been estimated that some 500 to 1,500 Soviet advisers are currently in Laos, mainly in the technical areas, and batches of Laotian students are sent on Russian scholarships to study in Moscow. Laos also signed an agreement with Peking for economic and technical co-operation and interest-free loans. In September, a Lao party and government delegation paid official visits to Cuba, Czechoslovakia, Rumania, Hungary, Poland and Mongolia, completing the establishment of close links with all the comradely nations but hopefully to increase the sources of assistance. Indeed, the Laotians have indicated that far from "leaning to one side", they are ready to receive aid from all countries without any conditions attached. President Souphanuvong has said in an interview with the editor of the *Journal of Contemporary Asia* that Laos was prepared to receive foreign investment provided that economic co-operation would be carried out along the principles of equality and mutual benefit. Laos has already borrowed US$3.2 million from the International Monetary Fund to service the country's foreign debt as well as in buying essential commodities.

It also chose to remain a member of the Mekong Project.

Reading Vietnam's policies to probe its real intentions has become the main preoccupation of Southeast Asian political leaders and analysts since it is quite clear it will be the main pace-setter of relations for the communist regimes vis-à-vis the other countries. In an important statement on the Thirtieth Anniversary of the Foundation of the Democratic Republic of Vietnam in September 1975 concerning the nation's new tasks during peacetime, Premier Pham Van Dong asserted that for Vietnam, the glorious period had begun — the period of peaceful construction. The new phase required the Vietnamese to first strengthen their friendship with

> the socialist countries which are bound to us by the common ideal of building socialism and communism [read USSR and PRC and other communist countries], secondly, the relations with the fraternal neighbouring countries, relations which have become still closer in the new situation [read Laos and Cambodia], thirdly to expand relations in many aspects with other countries in Southeast Asia, fourthly, the non-aligned countries and fifthly in economic, cultural, scientific and technical relations with all other countries on the principle of mutual respect for each other's independence, sovereignty, non-interference in each other's internal affairs, equality and mutual benefit.

Finally, Premier Pham also stated that Vietnam would be prepared to establish normal relations with the United States on the basis of the Paris Agreement. It is quite clear Southeast Asia looms large in Vietnamese priority and comes after the logical ideological relationships and even before the traditional nonaligned allies. In this respect, Vietnam and, for that matter, Laos and Cambodia are quite different from the Russians and the Chinese after the two emerged from their revolutions. Ideologically, the Indochinese communists do no seem as orthodox in their political views, refraining from dividing the world into simply black and white. This could be the result of being late in their revolutionary success. They are revolutionaries who have the benefit of improving on the early experience and policy choices of the USSR and the PRC. The pressure to maintain ideological purity is absent at a time when the world is accustomed to and has accepted communist ideology as a fact of life and polycentrism is an established condition within the socialist camp. Certainly, the subsequent behaviour of both Vietnam and Laos reveal a strand of pragmatism when it comes to the question of trade and aid. What we may be witnessing is in fact the very important difference between third generation communists and their predecessors (the Russians being the first, the Chinese the second to establish political power through a long armed struggle), which is their ability to come to terms with reality and development relatively free of ideological dogmatism. This once again affirms what is already so clear to the rest of the world — that the impulses of nationalism rather than proletarian internationalism are far stronger and more fundamentally dictate the policies of communist leaderships. That said, it is not denied that militant dogmatic factions do exist and can gain ascendance at particular periods of history or that even third generation communists in the long run want to see revolutionary régimes established elsewhere. Whether they wish to promote revolution as a major and clear aspect of their foreign policy is a less conclusive issue.

In immediate postwar statements, Vietnam jubilantly pronounced that a new era had dawned in Southeast Asia, a position to be expected in the flush of victory. *Nhan Dan* declared in its editorial on "Irreversible Trends of Southeast Asian Nations" in May 1975 that

> Southeast Asia has entered a new situation and is facing a very brilliant perspective. The people of this region are having very favourable conditions for breaking away from their dependence on the imperialists, chasing the U.S. imperialists out of their country with their hangers-on and are building a happy life and establishing relations of friendly co-operation among themselves.

Revolution was at this stage only obliquely referred to, but U.S. imperialism was consistently the target of its attacks. If Southeast Asians were exhorted in any way it was to develop as independent, peaceful and nonaligned nations rather than to be "hitched to the ruinous waggon [*sic*] of U.S. imperialism". However, in one deviation, its rhetoric sharply escalated during the Bali summit when open calls to revolution were made. What Vietnam meant by independent, peaceful and nonaligned was spelt out in April 1976 in "Southeast Asia after Vietnam", an important article published in *Vietnam Courier*, the English language official organ for foreign reading. Its definition would call for

> cutting off the relations of political, military, economic and cultural dependence on the U.S. Only by so doing can these countries realise their full potential in the service of their own people and at the same time contribute to regional and international co-operation.

Arising from its own security fears and deep hostility towards the United States, it has consistently attacked those ASEAN countries which have retained military bases on their soil and has made the removal of the military bases a condition for the establishment of relations. In calling for the establishment of economic and cultural independence, Vietnam has made this a major thrust of its foreign policy in its approach to nonaligned countries. It has made a strong stand of calling developing countries to form a struggle front in the sphere of raw materials to break the imperialist hold on the world economic order.

Yet the emergence of peaceful, independent nonaligned nations seemed not the only development the Vietnamese hoped for. In openly declaring its sympathy with the aspirations of the peoples of Southeast Asia for independence and freedom and in its assertion that the "principal policy of the Vietnamese people and government is resolutely to support the national cause of the Southeast Asian peoples", that the Vietnamese people "strongly believe that like themselves the peoples of Southeast Asia will bring their glorious struggle to victory", Southeast Asian Governments can only conclude that the policy is also to support revolutionary struggles, and it is little wonder that they anxiously probe to see if support has extended beyond rhetoric.

In consolidating its ties with communist countries, the Vietnamese have become much closer to the Russians than the Chinese. Apart from the fact that the PRC was in a weaker position to grant aid, the Chinese détente with the U.S. in 1972 was viewed unfavourably by the Vietnamese, but the most thorny problem in the relations could prove to be the dispute brewing over the Paracel and Spratly Islands, both believed to be oil-rich. The Vietnamese have already marked them on their map under the names of Truong Sa and Hoang Sa. On the other hand, they have signed two economic agreements in 1975 with the USSR for aid and trade during 1976 and a long term pact for assistance in Hanoi's five-year plan.

Little is known of Cambodia's internal development and adjustment to the assumption of power, state-building and internal economic development since it has chosen to remain a closed society. It is quite apparent it has settled for harsh mobilization, thoroughly nationalistic and emphatically self-reliant policies to set the country in order.

Since the new régime has come into being, the Laotians have endeavoured to build and consolidate an administrative system from "the center to the grassroots". At the same time the leaders have a task of simply getting its population to work, step up production to achieve self-sufficiency in food, resume operations in the factories and enterprises, repair roads and develop communications, all of which were neglected during the civil war. The new leadership seeks to establish a new culture and correct old habits of the population. Long hair and high heels have become targets of recent campaigns, and film and the school curriculum are some of the means through which the Laotian leadership hope to change the people. The present leadership face a small but very real resistance to the new order from General Vang Pao, an ex-Laotian army officer, who is known to be gathering all the dissidents of the regime to overthrow the communist government in a guerilla-styled revolt. The counter-revolutionaries are counting on the Meo and Lao Theung tribesmen who are not really integrated with the majority Lao population to increase their base. The Lao Democratic People's Republic (LDPR) Government is presently directing efforts at the Meo tribesmen (who had fought against the Pathet Lao and consequently feared harsh retribution after the Pathet Lao victory and who now formed the bulk of the refugees in Thailand) to induce their return to the country; otherwise the threat that they may be trained and used by right-wing Thais and the CIA to undermine the security of the new regime will constantly hound the government.

The leadership in divided Vietnam moved quickly to prepare for the re-unification of the country. Following elections in the North and South in April 1976 the first step towards consolidation, the two halves of Vietnam were reunified as one state known as the Socialist Republic of Vietnam on 2 July. The transition took place smoothly, an event long since anticipated and planned for. In his Political Report to the National Assembly, Le Duan addressed himself to the problems of the transformation of the economy and the propagation of a socialist ideology and culture and the new type of socialist man. The party targetted the transformation of private ownership and capitalism to socialist ownership to be achieved in the next fifteen to twenty years. In domestic reconstruction, the Vietnamese face an enormous physical task and the need to find a fantastic amount of money and technology. One estimate by a UN research team of the overall financial need for the restoration of transport and a return to the prewar level in agricultural production was US$432 million. The Vietnamese have displayed nonideological instincts on this matter. So far aid has been received from the USSR, Algeria, the PRC, Iraq, Libya and Sweden and in April 1976, Nguyen Co Thach, the Vice-Minister for Foreign Ministry of the DRV, paid a week-long visit to the United Arab

Emirates, obviously exploring new avenues for assistance whilst diplomatic relations at the ambassadorial level was established with Kuwait. Vietnam has also successfully sought membership in the World Bank, the International Monetary Fund and the Asian Development Bank and trade links have been forged with France, Japan, Singapore, Britain and other capitalist countries.

The problems of development are not all monetary. On the Thirty-First Anniversary of the Foundation Day of the Socialist Republic of Vietnam (SRV) in 1976, Vice-President Nguyen Huu Tho, reviewing the achievements since liberation admitted that the government had displayed many weaknesses and shortcomings in face of the new and complex tasks. Greater efforts were called to improve economic and market management and the distribution of goods and materials to support rehabilitation, development of production and stabilization. The administrative apparatus needed strengthening at all levels and it was recognized that the problem of speculation and hoarding existed. The Vietnamese leadership is also expressly concerned with the creeping corruption among its high level cadres in the south which it has to control if the revolution is to succeed in the long term. Differences in the leadership over the strategy of development were hinted at during the year with the army leaders, Vo Nguyen Giap and Van Tien Dung, the Chief of the Vietnam People's Army (VPA) General Staff, pressing for a militarist line on a strong national defence based on the building of national defence industries, an enlarged militia, the need to build a modem battle-tested regular modern army and international solidarity with other communist states and parties against the more moderate line of Premier Pham Van Dong and other State leaders. If the schism reaches serious proportions Southeast Asian Governments may witness frequent vacillations in policy between the hardline and the moderate, and most probably never a totally committed effort either way.

Indochina and ASEAN

Although initially at least two ASEAN Government leaders have indicated their preparedness to accept the Indochinese states as members of ASEAN in the distant future, not withstanding the differences in ideology and social systems, and a conciliatory stance has been adopted by all the ASEAN member countries, Vietnam, Laos and Cambodia remained cool to the regional organization. The real feelings of the Vietnamese were clarified on the eve of the Bali summit when it launched by far the most bitter attack on the ASEAN Governments. *Quan Doi Nhan Dan's* commentary charged the ASEAN meeting as being U.S. inspired and declared that the U.S. was using ASEAN "to carry out U.S. neo-Colonialist policy to oppose the patriotic and progressive movements in Southeast Asia." In this statement the Vietnamese paper linked members of the ASEAN countries with U.S. military power in the war effort. It is likely that suspicions that ASEAN might be turned into a military organization at this summit meeting prompted the Vietnamese to react thus sharply. Possibly Vietnamese leaders chose to connect President Ford's visit at the end of 1975 to Indonesia and the Philippines (two places he included on his visit to the PRC) with the subsequent declaration of the Pacific Doctrine, wherein, a new U.S. defence line was discernibly drawn from Korea to Guam including Japan, Okinawa,

Taiwan, Indonesia and the Philippines. In their analysis a sinister understanding must have been reached to rely on Indonesia and using ASEAN to uphold the defence interests of the U.S. and the suppression of revolutionary governments in the Southeast Asian region. On occasion they have charged the U.S. with promoting Indonesia as the regional policemen and they were aware of the U.S. Congress programme of military assistance to all the ASEAN countries except Singapore. At the same time it is conceivable that this attack was also made as a reminder to Thailand, who was in the process of negotiating with the U.S. over the military withdrawal, of its condition for future relations. Even at the end of the Bali meeting, they maintained their hostile stance and *Nhan Dan* issued an article entitled, "Time has never been so good to Southeast Asians," a piece which encouraged the peoples of Southeast Asia to struggle against the reactionary pro-West Governments.

The Laotian stand on ASEAN is similar to Vietnam's. Premier Kaysone Phoumvihane has described it as "an organization set up by the U.S. imperialists following the dismantlement of the SEATO" whose real nature is to "defend the interests of U.S. neo-colonialism". The Laotian Government, he stressed, would never participate in it. However the Premier drew a distinction between the regional organization and the individual ASEAN countries. Laos was "prepared to have good relations separately with each ASEAN country on the basis of peaceful co-existence." On the issue of ASEAN, the Vietnamese and the Laotian position is markedly different from that of the Russians and the Chinese who have spoken positively of the summit.

Hostility was decelerated with an abrupt switch in policy from Vietnam in the middle of the year. With reunification achieved and the problems of economic transformation foremost in the minds of the leadership, Vietnamese pragmatism prevailed. The SRV, patently interested in trade and technical exchange with Southeast Asia in the reconstruction and rehabilitation phase, opted for a warming of relations with the region's governments. Several factors made this possible. By this time it was clear that ASEAN was not to be transformed into a security organization, the American withdrawal from Thailand was definitely fixed at 20 July and signs pointed to a strenuous attempt by the Philippines to regain sovereignty over its bases. Thus on 6 July, Phan Hien, the Vice-Minister for Foreign Affairs, led a goodwill mission to several Southeast Asian capitals. The itinerary was carefully planned to avoid the implication that Vietnam in any way recognized ASEAN. Phan's trip included Laos and Burma, both non-ASEAN members, and excluded Thailand, an ASEAN state. On the eve of his departure, Nguyen Duy Trinh, the Vice-Premier and Minister of Foreign Affairs of the SRV, outlined the four points of his country's foreign policy towards Southeast Asia. They were proclaimed to be respect for each other's independence, sovereignty and territorial integrity, nonaggression, noninterference in each other's internal affairs, equality, mutual benefit and peaceful co-existence; a determination not to allow any foreign country to use one's territory as a base for direct and indirect aggression and intervention against the other country and other countries in the region; the establishment of friendly and good neighbourly relations, economic co-operation and cultural exchanges on the basis of equality, and mutual benefit and the settlement of disputes among the countries in the region, through negotiations in a spirit of equality, mutual understanding and respect and the development of co-operation among the countries in the region for the building of prosperity in keeping with each country's specific peace and genuine neutrality in Southeast Asia, thereby contributing to peace in the world. Two new points were major modifications of their former firm stand. One related to the peaceful settlement of disputes by negotiations, never emphasized in previous foreign policy statements, and the other was the fourth point which recognizes the building of prosperity in keeping with each other's specific conditions, implying a compromised acceptance of the separate ideological approaches to development, at least for the moment.

If the Vietnamese were using this as a testing trip to determine the sincerity of the ASEAN leaders, Phan Hien found the Malaysians to be, as anticipated, very warm; President Marcos was profuse with praise for Hanoi's role in having taught the whole world one of the most important lessons of history. Singapore alone of the ASEAN countries displayed a coolness that betold wariness of Vietnamese intentions. The real gains were not particularly spectacular. Full diplomatic relations were established with the Philippines whilst Malaysia offered to help them rehabilitate the damaged rubber plantations and develop the oil palm industry; some cement, plywood, galvanized iron and nails for construction were obtained from the Philippines, together with a promise of an exchange of technical delegations with Singapore and further development of the trade and economic relations and technical assistance from Indonesia.

Trust did not grow from the latest normalization of relations between Vietnam and the ASEAN states. Shortly after Phan Hien's trip, the Fifth Non-Aligned Summit Conference held at Sri Lanka on 18–19 August became the *cause célébre* in diplomatic relations between the Indochinese communists and the governments of ASEAN countries, reawakening the barely subsided fears about Indochinese attitudes towards peace and stability in the region. Laos, supported by Vietnam, succeeded in blocking any reference in the political declaration of the summit conference to the Kuala Lumpur Declaration on a Southeast Asian Zone of Peace, Freedom and Neutrality. The Malaysian delegation, which sought a reaffirmation of the declaration accepted at the 1971 Non-Aligned Conference, encountered strong Laotian objection and a counter-proposal amendment in which Laos called for a recognition that the recent revolutionary victories had modified the balance of forces in Southeast Asia favouring the forces of peace, national independence, democracy and progress. The Laotians also called the conference to support "the struggle of the people of Southeast Asia against neo-colonialism" and demanded the renunciation of all military alliances with the U.S. in the region so that the countries could become "truly independent, pacific and neutral". This confrontation nullified whatever thaw was introduced in the political dialogue, although the reactions of the ASEAN Governments were not uniform. The Prime Minister of Singapore, Lee Kuan Yew, probably expressed the similar doubts of the governments when he said,

It makes me wonder which countries of Southeast Asia are not "genuine" in their independence and should be helped to become "genuine". Is this the precursor of the kind of double definition of independence which will classify a Marxist state as genuinely independent and the others as not being genuine, and so their peoples are to be supported to overthrow by violence established democratic government?

The Singapore position has been consistently much tougher than the other Southeast Asian countries. Malaysia's reactions were noticeably far less angry, nor did it play up the conference confrontation in its press as heavily as Singapore. This however should be due to the desire not to heighten the embarrassment of the Malaysian Government especially since Hussein Onn himself went to the conference and had lobbied some neutral countries such as Burma enroute to the meeting. Relations with the Indonesians seemed least upset and Adam Malik, the Foreign Minister, invited Pham Van Dong to visit Indonesia at the Colombo meeting. Although the rancour has abated, reciprocal trust has not returned.

In retrospect, the fact is that Laos and Vietnam have been consistent in their position towards the nonrecognition of ASEAN and hence the statement issued and backed by the regional organization must ideologically be unacceptable to them. Laos explained in a *Siang Pasason* [Voice of the People] commentary announced over Radio Vientiane its objection: "The Kuala Lumpur Declaration was issued during that period 1971 when the U.S. was intensifying their war of aggression in Indochina in order to cover up the participation of the ASEAN countries in the U.S. war of aggression in Laos, Vietnam and Cambodia and to fool world public opinion into thinking that ASEAN countries had good intentions." The Vietnamese had indicated even during their tour of Malaysia, the Philippines, Singapore and Indonesia that they did not accept the Malaysian version of the zone of peace, freedom and neutrality.

The issue has been raised of manipulation by an external power but it is likely to have been a Vietnamese-Laotian move when Phan Hien visited Laos in July and some agreement on strategy was worked out. Yet tactically the Vietnamese and Laotian stand at Colombo was taken at very high cost. Subsequent events showed that this meeting alienated the Malaysians who were till then Vietnam's best ally among the ASEAN states and confirmed the hardline position of the others. The result seems to be that after the right-wing leaders assumed power in Thailand, ASEAN leaders as a group were more predisposed to move towards closer security arrangements, obviously against the perceived communist threat. In November and December a series of visits took place initially with the Singapore Defence Minister's visit to Bangkok, followed by the Malaysian Home Minister. The new Thai Premier, Thanin Kraivichien, made a tour of the ASEAN countries in early December. He called for tighter co-operation among ASEAN countries to prevent the "threat of communism". In the Singapore stopover the two countries came out with a joint statement declaring that "every ASEAN member country should endeavour to enhance its self-confidence and self-reliance as well as eliminate threats posed by subversion to its stability, thus strengthening national and ASEAN resilience." On the Indonesian leg of his tour the Thai Premier included several top-ranking military men such as the Defence Minister Admiral Sangad Charolyu and the Deputy Supreme Commander of the Armed Forces, General

Kriangsak Chamanand. President Suharto had meanwhile made an informal one-day visit to Singapore ostensibly to discuss the development of Bantam and to conclude the agreement on preferential trading arrangements, investment guarantees and avoidance of double taxation. It is likely that security was also on the agenda. Two weeks later the Singapore Prime Minister paid a two-day unofficial visit to Kuala Lumpur at the invitation of the Malaysian Prime Minister.

It is unlikely a formal military pact will be arrived at in the immediate future. The advantages are not so clearly obvious at this point in time whereas the polarization and tensions likely to ensue in the region are certain. The communist states would be forced to react to the confrontation in equal terms. Closer bilateral agreements on security co-operation with a high degree of co-ordination among the ASEAN states are however bound to take place.

Conclusion

In the postwar relations of Southeast Asia the political leadership of polar political systems have moved uncertainly in new directions and returned to predictable paths. Tension and mistrust, which are to be expected, have marked the relationship. The anticommunist ASEAN countries believe that two ideologically opposed systems can co-exist and on that basis they have sought limited reconciliation with Vietnam, Laos and Cambodia. But the logic of equivocal language and the dogma of an expansionist ideology have not always been easy to follow and far more complex to interpret. The signs are that Vietnam, Laos and Cambodia have shown an inclination to pursue pragmatic policies in the pursuit of national interests; notwithstanding the militant slogans, there has been no increased evidence of support for subversion and infiltration substantial enough to signify a definite aggressive policy. The Indochinese states have one immediate goal which is the removal of all U.S. military bases in the region and, in the middle term, the end of U.S. hegemony in the politics and economics of the region. Ultimately, as communists they must wish to see the success of other revolutionary movements but it is doubtful they will promote these at the cost of their particular interests and at high risk, putting in jeopardy their efforts to rebuild their nation.

Thus the obvious hardening of position by the ASEAN leaders towards the communist regimes, especially in the case of Thailand whose policies and reactions towards Vietnam and Laos since the *coup* have been highly provocative, may set in train a whole series of destabilizing factors pushing their adversaries into an aggressive response. Some of the leaderships of the ASEAN states have yet to show they comprehend the full import of the social and political pressures for, unless they match their rhetoric with serious policies for social change, they cannot eliminate unrest nor diminish the appeals of communism among sections of their people.

THE "FUKUDA DOCTRINE" AND ITS IMPLICATIONS FOR SOUTHEAST ASIA
A Japanese Perspective

Toru Yano

The "Fukuda Doctrine"

Manila was the last stop on Prime Minister Takeo Fukuda's tour of Southeast Asia. There, on 18 August, he delivered his noteworthy speech on Japan's policy towards that region. Japanese news media have billed the event as an epoch-making unveiling of what they call the "Fukuda Doctrine", finding deep significance in the very fact that such a speech was made. While I would not go so far as to call the contents of the Manila address a "doctrine", it is certainly the first time since the Second World War that a Japanese Prime Minister has made such a systematic presentation of views on relations with Southeast Asia.

The main points of the speech were as follows: first, Japan is committed to peace and to the role of an economic power; it will not become a military power. Secondly, as "an especially close friend" of ASEAN (Association of Southeast Asian Nations), Japan will co-operate in efforts to strengthen the solidarity of that organization. Thirdly, Japan will emphasize "heart-to-heart" contacts, building stronger ties as an equal partner not only economically, but in the social, political, and cultural realms as well. Fourthly, Japan will forge particularly close economic and trade relations with the countries of Southeast Asia and continue to deal with them in the context of the world economy. Fifthly, Japan will also attempt to foster relations based on mutual understanding with the nations of Indochina. Prime Minister Fukuda phrased these points as the "pillars" of Japan's Southeast Asian policy.

No doubt the real intentions behind the Prime Minister's speech will be interpreted variously as time goes on, but my immediate impression is that his approach

---

Reprinted from Leo Suryadinata, ed., *Southeast Asian Affairs 1978* (Singapore: Institute of Southeast Asian Studies, 1978), pp. 60–64. At the time of original publication, Toru Yano was Professor of Political Science at the Center for Southeast Asian Studies, Kyoto University.

came out of a compromise between an aggressive Japanese stance advocating active, full-scale involvement in Southeast Asia, and a passive view similar to the Meiji period's "dissociation from Asia" thesis, which holds that Japan must avoid deep involvement in that region. Be that as it may, the very fact that Japan should publicly announce any sort of a "doctrine" at all on this subject is fraught with significance.

Role of Japan and the U.S. in Southeast Asia

A broad historical background underlies these events; the force of its logic has pushed Japan into the stage centre of Asian regional politics, irrespective of the will of the Japanese people. We did not actively seek to expand Japan's role in Southeast Asia. In our view, Japan's present position is the inevitable consequence of history.

The Indochina War ended in April 1975, concluding a protracted and unhappy historical sequence, and at the same time inaugurating a new "season of diplomacy" in Asia. As the international environment surrounding Japan continues to change rapidly, it is necessary to reconsider what sort of international order, or disorder, is in the process of construction, partly as a result of Japan's own diplomatic participation.

It is an ironic possibility that the "loss" of Vietnam may have had more historical significance for Japan than for the U.S. That is to say, no matter how affirmative an attitude the U.S. might display towards nationalism in China and Southeast Asia, the U.S. remains essentially passive with regard to the maintenance of order in Asia. Japan, on the other hand, with its important interests in the region, has been driven into taking on a major share of the responsibility in the construction of a new order. Moreover, there is a strong possibility that the U.S. may decide to assign Japan a central role in its new Asian strategy.

Even as the relative importance of Southeast Asia in U.S. foreign policy seems to have dropped virtually to zero in the wake of historical developments, its importance for Japan has increased proportionately. This turnabout will no doubt pose new questions and problems which have to be worked out in the context of the Japan-U.S. relationship. The psychological impact on Japan has been subtle but profound. It has been somewhat of a revelation for the Japanese to discover that there is a region from which the U.S. can withdraw at will, but from which Japan cannot.

It appears that the "joint communiqué" issued at the close of Prime Minister Fukuda's meeting with President Jimmy Carter during his March visit to Washington, D.C. drew different reactions in the two countries concerned. Paragraph five of the communiqué included the confirmation that both the U.S. and Japan are "prepared to continue providing co-operation and assistance in support of the efforts of the ASEAN countries towards regional cohesion and development." This attracted far more serious public attention in Japan than in the U.S. In Japan, this provision was interpreted as public admission that U.S. responsibility in Southeast Asia had been transferred to Japan. It is unclear whether this interpretation is merely excessively cynical, or eminently realistic. The concern for Southeast Asian affairs now evinced by the U.S. is very modest compared to the zeal shown by Japan. Moreover, there is very little evidence that the Japanese Government has made active efforts to bolster American concern. It appears, in other words, that in the same manner as Europe has Africa, and the U.S. has Latin America, Japan is presently acquiring its own "hinterland" in Southeast Asia.

Japan is now at the point where it must decide whether to be content with that situation or make renewed efforts to resist the tide of history. It seems, however, that the inability of the Japanese to fully comprehend the overall schema of the American Asian policy is causing considerable irritation to the U.S. An analysis of present Japanese images of U.S. policy towards Asia may be useful at this juncture.

Japan's recent *démarche* in the realm of Southeast Asian policy was not necessarily a response to American desires. Rather, it resulted from the convergence of a number of historical circumstances. Japan's foreign policy line began to change in 1973 when preparations were being made for former Prime Minister Kakuei Tanaka's January 1974 visit to the ASEAN nations. Hence, it is evident that even before the conclusion of the Vietnam War, the Japanese Government had begun to anticipate the courses of history. In fact, negotiations towards the establishment of diplomatic relations were initiated at about that time with the Hanoi Government. That burst of "independent diplomacy" was further reinforced by the oil crisis that took the world by surprise in the autumn of 1973. Following that event, Tanaka's visit to Southeast Asia provided an occasion for the people of that region to retaliate bitterly against Japan whom they perceived as interested only in a flashy brand of resource diplomacy. Rather than dampen Japan's concern for that region, however, the riots that greeted Tanaka in Jakarta served to encourage a stance that was more refined and receptive than ever before.

Japan and ASEAN

The fall of Vietnam in April 1975 precipitated an overall reassessment of the conditions under which Japan could enjoy greater freedom of action. Hence that event confirmed and reinforced an approach that had already begun to emerge — an independent search for "freedom of action" instead of total reliance on an international order constructed by the U.S.

The final and decisive element in the development of an active Japanese policy towards Southeast Asia was the first ASEAN summit conference of February 1976. That conference created a situation in which Japan, regardless of past difficulties, needed to have an articulate policy towards ASEAN. The Japanese understood the historical significance of the first ASEAN summit conference in a dual sense. In the first place, the meeting "legitimized" the ASEAN organization itself and the efforts it had made up to that time. Moreover, by giving substance to ASEAN as a noncommunist regional bloc, the conference granted credibility for the view that Southeast Asia would divide into two opposing camps. Additionally, Japan was forced to take another look not only at the ASEAN member states but also the other nations of the area, particularly the three Indochinese nations and Burma. In effect, Japan began to formulate a systematic approach to the Southeast Asian region as a whole.

ASEAN itself began to take great strides after the February 1976 summit conference. Several points should be noted as characteristic of the changes that organization has experienced in the past year or so. One is that its member nations have recovered from the psychological shock resulting from the fall of Vietnam and have developed the confidence to preserve a system that is different from that adopted by the Indochinese nations. Then, ASEAN has increasingly become an economic as opposed to a political entity. Prior to the summit conference, and partly as a result of the Vietnam War, ASEAN had often spoken out in a political vein, for example, in advancing concepts of neutrality, and so on. Since last February, however, concern for trade has been increasingly conspicuous. Henceforth, it may be more apt when discussing issues relating to ASEAN to treat it as an organization primarily concerned with economic policy-making.

Another point is that the ASEAN countries now have greater expectations with regard to the role of Japan in the region. Behind this development is the increasing crystallization of the U.S. withdrawal from Asia under the Carter Administration, and the request for Japanese participation and know-how made by the ASEAN countries as they embark on industrialization projects. Nevertheless, the change in attitude since the visit of former Prime Minister Tanaka three years ago is a very welcome development from the Japanese point of view. Although Japan has not completed its formulation of systematic policy towards Southeast Asia, the decision has already been made that Japan should respond actively to the changes that have taken and are taking place within the region. There remains a sharp divergence of views among the Japanese on the subject of Southeast Asian policy; but Japan's postwar Asian policy has never been based on a national consensus. The time certainly has come for Japan to act positively with regard to the Southeast Asian region.

Prime Minister Fukuda's recent tour of Southeast Asia, and the "Fukuda Doctrine" he presented in Manila, reflect in concentrated form the changes that have taken place in Japanese attitudes towards Southeast Asia. Japan first sought to respond idealistically and philosophically to the new Southeast Asia, taking up concrete policy alternatives only secondarily. The "philosophy of accommodation" which Japan currently has in mind is composed of various elements. The following list might seem somewhat visionary, but its components can all be found in the 7 August "Japan-ASEAN Joint Communiqué."

In the first place, ASEAN will have to be seen in a global context. It must be considered as one element in Japan's overall policy approach to relations with developing nations, or the north-south problem. Last year's United Nations Conference on Trade and Development (UNCTAD) convention provided an opportunity for ASEAN economic policy to be integrated with the philosophy of a new international economic order. That organization's approach to the issue of a common fund for primary products is particularly forceful. Nine of the ten "hardcore items" included therein are relevant to the ASEAN countries, and a couple of them, copper and rubber, are for ASEAN alone. Hence it is assumed that ASEAN has become avidly concerned with the north-south problem.

Secondly, vast changes have taken place in the expectations levied on Japan by the Southeast Asian nations, and Japan finds it necessary to be receptive. The common demands of all ASEAN countries may be listed as follows, with the emphasis on the first three: (1) co-operation in joint ASEAN industrialization projects; (2) provision of access to the Japanese market for ASEAN products, both primary and manufactured; (3) introduction of an export indemnity system in order to stabilize the prices of primary products; and (4) granting of favourable treatment with regard to accumulated debts.

When economic relations between Japan and ASEAN are considered in the context of the new stance of that organization, and especially when the Japanese and ASEAN standpoints are juxtaposed against one another, what might be called a "perspective gap" emerges in bold relief. An important aspect of that gap, of course, is the spectacular size of the Japanese economy in comparison with that of the ASEAN countries. From the perspective of Japan, ASEAN member states are of relatively little consequence but, conversely, from the viewpoint of the ASEAN nations, Japan is of critical importance, particularly with regard to Southeast Asian products and industry. Trade figures provide an apt illustration of this disparity. ASEAN nations account for about 10% of total Japanese imports and exports, 15% of resource imports, and 20% of private investment. From the ASEAN viewpoint, however, Japan absorbs 30% of the total import and export trade that ASEAN nations carry on with many different countries, and 100% of specific export-oriented resources.

A second important aspect of the "perspective gap" has to do with Japanese preconceptions. When expansion of trade between Japan and the ASEAN nations is considered as a way to respond to charges concerning excess exports and one-sided trade, the assumption has tended to be that, if Japan co-operates in the development of natural resources for later importation, the trade imbalances will be rectified. However, the error of this preconception has finally been realized. Japan already maintains an unfavourable trade balance with resource-exporting countries such as Indonesia and Malaysia, and so when development and import of resources are further accelerated, the result in the case of those countries is merely to enhance the excess of their exports to Japan over imports. Conversely, Japan then tends to compensate by further exacerbating its favourable trade balance vis-à-vis those nations in the region that lack resources. Japan must remain sensitive to the difference between those ASEAN nations which have resources and those which do not, and carefully consider economic co-operation and aid policy towards them bearing that distinction in mind.

Additionally, in the interest of peace and stability in the Southeast Asian region, relations of peaceful co-existence must be established between the ASEAN nations and the Indochinese states despite accumulated antagonism and the differing political and social systems. At present, Indochina is still quite hostile towards ASEAN. The establishment of peaceful relations between the two blocs would not only play an extremely significant role in the maintenance of stability in the region, but it would also affect the degree of independence the three Indochinese nations are able to manifest in their relations with the Soviet Union and China. Peace is eminently desirable as an impetus towards a healthy degree of autonomy in the region as a whole. Japan has a useful function in that regard by utilizing every available opportunity to convey the peaceful intentions of the ASEAN countries to the Indochinese side. It can also keep ASEAN apprised of the true intentions and inward-looking tendencies of the Indochinese nations, thereby allaying needless tension in both blocs.

Steps Towards Stability in Southeast Asia

It is likely that Japan will face a number of collateral problems in the process of playing the role of facilitator in bringing about a new "open" Southeast Asia. Aside from domestic public opinion, Japan's diplomacy could be upset by unpredictable factors such as political instability in the region, developments in the Sino-Soviet dispute, and so on. Among those factors is the direction that U.S. diplomatic interests will take in Southeast Asia. That factor, which has a direct bearing on the conditions for Japan's "freedom of action" must be watched closely. Of particular concern is the U.S. approach to the three nations of Indochina. Japan must continue to call upon the U.S. to play a constructive role throughout Southeast Asia.

The first step towards a constructive role for the U.S. in Southeast Asia is the establishment of stable relations with the Vietnam Government. Japan would unconditionally welcome the development of a more intimate dialogue between Washington and Hanoi. One hopes that the U.S. will become a little more sensitive to historical changes.

Japan and the U.S. must achieve a common understanding with regard to Southeast Asia. That understanding should incorporate the following elements. In the first place, the exercise of hegemony by any great power in the region is perceived by the ASEAN and Indochinese nations as inimical to their interests. Secondly, all the nations of Southeast Asia, including those of Indochina, require economic cooperation from the West. Thirdly, while Sino-Soviet rivalry persists, the nations of Indochina will most likely escape domination by either China or the Soviet Union and be able to proceed along independent lines. Further, they will probably become socialist countries with a higher degree of freedom than is evident in the Eastern European bloc. On these points, at least, it should be possible for Japan and the U.S. to agree and to follow similar policies with regard to Southeast Asia.

EXPANDING HORIZONS IN SOUTHEAST ASIA?

Michael Leifer

Southeast Asian states revised their strategic horizons during 1993 through an ASEAN-inspired initiative arising from the impact of the end of the Cold War. That development occurred, however, without a corresponding revision in economic horizons; nor was there any evident reconsideration of domestic political orders, which were in general strengthened.

During the Cold War, Southeast Asia and Indochina in particular had been coupled to international contention, which was inherent in the global balance of power. It was for this reason that Southeast Asia was described at one time as the Balkans of the Orient in an analogy with the condition of southeast Europe before the outbreak of World War I. With the end of the Cold War, global rivalry has ceased to exist in the same way as a point of reference for regional relations. This has been demonstrated with the end of the Cambodian conflict as a major international problem.

The states of Southeast Asia now inhabit a different strategic environment but not a fundamentally different international society, which is distinguished still by the absence of a common government able to enforce law and order. Furthermore, as a result of the end of the Cold War, Southeast Asia has begun to be called into question as a coherent category through which to address problems of regional security. A growing interdependence in security matters between Southeast and East Asia in particular has been perceived and registered by regional states. At issue, however, is the significance of a novel development in extended multilateral security dialogue joining Southeast and East Asia, inspired during the year by the Association of Southeast Asian Nations

---

Reprinted in abridged format from Daljit Singh, ed., *Southeast Asian Affairs 1994* (Singapore: Institute of Southeast Asian Studies, 1994), pp. 3–21. At the time of original publication, Michael Leifer was Professor of International Relations at the London School of Economics and Political Science.

(ASEAN). Does that development indicate a genuine structural adjustment to a new strategic horizon or is it little more than a tinkering with the form of existing regional security arrangements?

Apart from involvement in vestigial security arrangements, which are both a legacy of colonialism and the Cold War, provision for either collective defence or collective security has not been undertaken on an exclusive basis by regional states. ASEAN, which repudiated military pacts from the outset, has established a limited regional security system based on a formula of conflict avoidance and management. The scope of that undertaking was extended within Southeast Asia in July 1992 but without augmenting its corporate membership. Vietnam and Laos acceded to ASEAN's Treaty of Amity and Co-operation so that only Cambodia and Myanmar within the region do not have a formal relationship with the Association. During 1993, however, the horizon of such security arrangements was extended beyond the region, with ASEAN taking the initiative to invite East Asian and Pacific states to inaugurate a multilateral security dialogue.

In July 1993, at the annual meeting of its foreign ministers held in Singapore, ASEAN convened a wider regional forum in an attempt to cope with the post-Cold War regional pattern of power. A prime concern was with the strategic latitude enjoyed by an increasingly powerful China in the wake of the disintegration of the Soviet Union and America's withdrawal from military bases in the Philippines. It had become apparent, especially as a result of contention over sovereign jurisdiction in the South China Sea, that the security of Southeast Asia could not be insulated and addressed separately from adjoining East Asia and the Pacific. ASEAN's initiative, which was encouraged by Japan and the United States, constituted an attempt to subsume East and Southeast Asia within the same structure of regional confidence-building. The initiative took the form of an initial meeting of foreign ministers who agreed to convene again in Bangkok in 1994 but without any indication of a commitment to institutional underpinning.

By contrast with ASEAN's own intricate and substantial network of intramural ties built up over the years, the new ASEAN Regional Forum stands as a mere shell, at least for the time being. Nonetheless, the willingness of ASEAN's members to contemplate a wider strategic horizon for security arrangements beyond the conventional geographic bounds of Southeast Asia needs to be noted. That willingness to be less proprietorial about arrangements for regional security stands in contrast to the misgivings expressed by ASEAN's heads of government about the regional plans of President Clinton. He convened an informal meeting of Asian-Pacific leaders in Seattle immediately after the annual ministerial meeting of Asia-Pacific Economic Co-operation (APEC) in that city in November 1993. ASEAN had made a formal commitment to establish its own free trade area in January 1992 and great resistance was displayed to suggestions for expanding the framework of formal trade liberalization beyond the bounds of the Association.

The changing bounds of regional security stand in contrast also to the resilience of the post-colonial successor state in Southeast Asia, which has been reinforced in its territorial domain during 1993. For example, the ability of the United Nations Transitional Authority in Cambodia (UNTAC) to fulfil its mandate against all expectations has served, at least for the time being, to uphold the integrity of the Khmer state. Accordingly, the concept of an Indochina, inherited by Vietnam from France, which has long been part of the strategic architecture of post-colonial Southeast Asia has become moribund. Elsewhere within the region, governments have more effectively overcome challenges to central power and have resisted Western exhortations over human rights, which have been perceived as intended to assist such challenges. For example, the military government in Myanmar may be an international pariah but it has been increasingly successful in containing separatist challenge from ethnic minorities, which have tested the Myanmar state from independence.

Orderly political succession within Indonesia still remains to be addressed but President Soeharto has reasserted his political authority without difficulty through re-election for a further five-year term of office and in determining the leadership of Golkar, the government's electoral vehicle. In Malaysia the manner of Ghafar Baba's displacement by Anwar Ibrahim as Deputy President of the United Malays National Organization (UMNO) almost certainly caused consternation to its President, Prime Minister Dr Mahathir Mohamad. But that episode was not an augury of disorderly political change but rather an indication of political institutionalization and of forthcoming orderly succession. Even the Philippines, for long depicted as the sick man of ASEAN, has begun to show signs of political cohesion under the presidency of Fidel Ramos. Elsewhere in the region, Laos has weathered the death of its veteran leader Kaysone Phoumvihan in November 1992, while Brunei continues to maintain the only ruling monarchy some ten years after reluctantly achieving full independence from Britain. In choosing a new President, Singapore's electorate demonstrated its political ambivalence in seeking a balance between strong and accountable government. Structural political tensions may abound within the states of Southeast Asia but they have not been registered robustly during 1993.

Regional Security beyond ASEAN

At their fourth summit in Singapore in January 1992, ASEAN's heads of government sanctioned the use of the annual Post-Ministerial Conference (PMC) for promoting external dialogues on enhancing regional security. This forum for discussion with so-called dialogue partners among industrialized states, which has followed on the meeting held every year by ASEAN's foreign ministers, had been inaugurated in limited form after its second summit in Kuala Lumpur in August 1977. In July 1992 the subject of regional security was addressed in meetings with dialogue partners in Manila after the foreign ministers had held their annual gathering. Those discussions took place on a serial and not a multilateral basis.

The momentum of this departure from established practice was sustained through Japanese initiative and the withdrawal of long-standing American objections, especially as Washington's encouragement was presented as complementary to a continuing regional military deployment. In January 1993, in a speech in Bangkok, Japan's Prime Minister, Kiichi Miyazawa, exhorted Asian and Pacific nations to "develop a long-term vision regarding the future of peace and security for their region". He called for a political and security dialogue in which Japan would be prepared to play an active part but without any intention of rearming or giving up its long-standing security relationship with the United States.

ASEAN responded in May by convening in Singapore the first-ever meeting of senior officials of the PMC in order to prepare the agenda for the next PMC in July. It was attended by officials from the six ASEAN states and by counterparts from the Association's seven dialogue partners, Australia, Canada, the European Community (now Union), Japan, New Zealand, South Korea, and the United States. During the meeting, the post-Cold War political and security landscape in the Asia-Pacific region was addressed with collective measures such as preventive diplomacy and confidence-building in mind. There was no attempt to discuss multilateral defence co-operation as a way of coping with a changing balance of power. The main outcome was an agreement to extend the structure of dialogue even further so as to include other regional states in order "to evolve a predictable and constructive pattern of relationships in the Asia-Pacific". In practice, this meant inviting China and Russia to participate as full parties in multilateral security consultations in late July as well as Vietnam, Laos, and Papua New Guinea, all three of which enjoyed observer status at the annual meetings of ASEAN's foreign ministers. The rapid growth of China's economic and military power dominated the discussions with a consensus emerging on the need to engage the People's Republic in an expanded security dialogue.[1] Just prior to the Association's annual meeting, Singapore's Foreign Minister, Wong Kan Seng, the chairman for the occasion, offered the complementary comment that he saw multilateral security dialogues "as another means of helping the US stay engaged in this dynamic and economically important region".[2]

ASEAN's foreign ministers held their annual meeting in Singapore on 23–24 July and in their communiqué agreed to continue an intra-mural dialogue on security co-operation involving foreign ministry and defence officials that had begun at a special senior officials' meeting in Manila in June 1992. They also welcomed the outcome of the first meeting of senior officials of the ASEAN PMC in the previous May and endorsed the proposal to invite China, Laos, Papua New Guinea, Russia, and Vietnam to meet formally with ASEAN members and their dialogue partners at the "ASEAN Regional Forum" in Bangkok in 1994. The communiqué reiterated how important it was for ASEAN to work with its dialogue partners and other regional states to evolve a more predictable and constructive pattern of political security relationships in the Asia-Pacific. In an example of a different kind of shared interest, the foreign ministers welcomed the human rights consensus attained at the World Conference on Human Rights in Vienna in June. They pointedly affirmed, however, that

> They [human rights] should be addressed in a balanced and integrated manner and protected and promoted with due regard for specific cultural, social, economic and political circumstances.

In the evening of 25 July, prior to the regular PMC, the eighteen foreign ministers from the members of the prospective ASEAN Regional Forum sat down to an informal dinner with the object of registering their common intent. The ASEAN Regional Forum was described as a consultative body to discuss security issues without any indication of how it would function except that its first meeting proper in Bangkok would be preceded by one of senior officials from all eighteen members. In effect, the ASEAN security model of conflict management and avoidance was being extended in geographic scope to create a wider but embryonic framework without concrete measures immediately in mind for regional problem-solving. Whether the Forum will evolve into more than a dining club and so lend substance to its declaratory expression remains to be seen. The significance of the embryonic undertaking is that the ASEAN states and its candidate members have been obliged to expand their strategic horizons in the interest of addressing the problem of common security. An attendant danger is that Southeast Asian states may find themselves drawn into the conflicts of Northeast Asia without fully comprehending their nature and complexity.[3]

ASEAN in APEC

All the governments of ASEAN had been parties to APEC from its formation in 1989 as a loose consultative forum established as the result of an Australian initiative. In early July, at the meeting in Tokyo of the Group of Seven (G-7) industrialized countries, President Clinton called for a summit of Asian-Pacific leaders in Seattle in November to follow the ministerial meeting of APEC scheduled to take place in that city. When the foreign ministers of ASEAN met in Singapore later in the month, they were not of one mind over how their governments should respond to this invitation. President Clinton, moved by domestic economic difficulties popularly identified with his country's trading deficit with Asia, had signalled an intention to transform the consultative body into the prime vehicle for creating a so-called "New Pacific Community". That initiative gave rise to suspicions of American domination. Malaysia's Prime Minister, Dr Mahathir Mohamad, had already stated that he would not be attending, while Indonesia's President Soeharto had commented that APEC should not dilute the identity of existing regional groups.

ASEAN's heads of government had already committed the Association to establishing a free trade area at their summit in Singapore in January 1992 with a timetable of fifteen years for progressive tariff reductions to begin from January 1993. When the six foreign ministers met in Singapore in July 1993, the implementation of the ASEAN Free Trade Area (AFTA) had stalled because of a lack of co-operation from Indonesia, the Philippines, and Thailand. Nonetheless, they reaffirmed the importance of implementing the Common Effective Preferential Tariff (CEPT) scheme within the agreed time-frame but without indicating a revised timetable. It was only at the ASEAN Economic Ministers' Meeting in early October that it was found possible to "kick-start" AFTA with a revised agreement to begin tariff cuts from January 1994.

An additional economic issue that was addressed at the meeting of foreign ministers in July was that of the East Asian Economic Caucus (EAEC); a proposal for an exclusive regional forum without the United States, Australia, New Zealand, and Canada — all Western members of APEC — which had been put forward by Dr Mahathir in 1990. This proposal had been greeted with equivocation within ASEAN as well as generating resistance beyond its walls. Dr Mahathir had peremptorily rejected President Clinton's invitation to Seattle out of resentment that his own proposal for an EAEC was being diminished by America's enthusiasm for transforming APEC beyond its original consultative role. In the event, ASEAN worked out a compromise formula to accommodate Dr Mahathir's proposal, which was accepted grudgingly by Malaysia. It was decided that

> the ASEAN Economic Ministers' Meeting (AEM) would be the appropriate body to provide support and direction for the EAEC, taking into account that prospective members of EAEC are also members of APEC. Pursuant to this, the foreign ministers agreed that the EAEC is a caucus within APEC.

That exercise in creative ambiguity did not provide any indication of how the agreed formula might work in practice.

In the event, all of ASEAN's heads of government, except that of Malaysia, attended the informal summit in Seattle in late November after APEC's ministerial meeting. There was mixed enthusiasm for the occasion because of concern that ASEAN might find itself dragooned into a liberal trading arrangement, for which its economies were not ready, linked also to monitored performance in human rights. Additional concern was expressed that its regional role, including the initiative for an ASEAN Regional Forum, might be made subordinate to a new overarching design dictated by the United States. Such misgivings were set aside up to a point because of a common interest in the United States continuing its engagement in the security of the region and also because the American market has played an important part in the export-led growth of ASEAN economies. Moreover, the prospective attendance of Chinese and Japanese heads of government gave the meeting a unique significance beyond regional economic relationships that could not be ignored.

Prior to the meeting, senior officials of the Association consulted closely and adopted the common position that ASEAN would oppose APEC evolving into a trade-negotiating body that could weaken the global trading system. Strong opposition was expressed to the proposal in a report from an "Eminent Persons Group" commissioned by APEC that an Asia-Pacific Economic Community be established by 1996. In the event, prior suspicions were not confirmed. APEC was not subjected to structural change but a new network of extended regional contacts at the highest level was established. A declaratory commitment was made to foster freer trade but the original consultative role of APEC was upheld. The measure of assurance on ASEAN's part over the future direction of APEC was indicated by President Soeharto's willingness to host a second informal summit in Jakarta in 1994 after the next scheduled ministerial meeting. Moreover, he made the point of remarking on his return to Jakarta from Seattle that "We hope that Mahathir will attend in the spirit of ASEAN cooperation".

The only sour note to arise from APEC was a revival of tension between Malaysia and Australia after Prime Minister Paul Keating had described Dr Mahathir as a recalcitrant for having boycotted the Seattle gathering. A letter from Mr Keating to Dr Mahathir, which stopped short of the full apology expected in Kuala Lumpur, served to keep the issue alive until the Malaysian Cabinet decided to put relations "back on track" on 11 December. For his part, Dr Mahathir remained unrepentant in his advocacy of the EAEC, which he insisted "must be firmed up further" to balance regional groupings elsewhere.[4]

Indonesia's willingness to host a second meeting of APEC leaders in Jakarta in 1994 provided an indication of a continuing search by the republic for an international role beyond the limiting confines of ASEAN. That search had been fulfilled in part by assuming the chair of the Non-Aligned Movement in September 1992. A measure of frustration had been experienced in early July in Tokyo, however, when President Soeharto had to be satisfied with separate audiences with President Clinton and Prime Minister Miyazawa instead of addressing all the members of the G-7 on behalf of the Non-Aligned Movement, as he had requested. He did not allow any sense of pique at having been lectured on his government's human rights failings by the American President in Tokyo to cloud his judgement over attending the meeting in Seattle in November. A further indication of Indonesia's assumption of a more assertive diplomatic role was the surprise visit to Jakarta by Israel's Prime Minister, Yitzhak Rabin. He paid an unannounced three-hour "courtesy call" on 15 October flying in from China to be received without protocol by President Soeharto in his capacity as chair of the Non-Aligned Movement. A month before, President Soeharto had received Yasser Arafat to be briefed about the accord reached between the Palestine Liberation Organization and Israel. Prime Minister Rabin's visit was depicted as a logical corollary as well as providing an example of the continuing ability of Indonesia's President to spring surprises and to dictate his country's political agenda.[5]

Notes

1. *Straits Times*, 22 May 1993.
2. *International Herald Tribune*, 19 July 1993.
3. For a recent analysis of the changing architecture of regional security, see Amitav Acharya, *A New Regional Order in South-East Asia: ASEAN in the Post-Cold War Era*, Adelphi Papers no. 279 (London: International Institute of Strategic Studies/Brasseys, 1993).
4. *International Herald Tribune*, 9 December 1993.
5. See the editorial comments in the *Jakarta Post*, 16 October 1993 and in *Kompas*, 18 October 1993.

AFTA IN THE LIGHT OF NEW ECONOMIC DEVELOPMENTS

Florian A. Alburo

1. Introduction

It was at the 1992 Association of Southeast Asian Nations (ASEAN) Summit that the six states made a stronger commitment to a liberal trade regime through the instrument of the Common Effective Preferential Tariff (CEPT). They decided to establish an ASEAN Free Trade Area (AFTA).

Coming on the heels of the North American Free Trade Agreement (NAFTA) and Europe 1992, AFTA did not evolve from a comprehensive and detailed programme of liberalization complete with rules and procedures. In fact the agreement incorporating AFTA was less than 10 pages. Compare this with the NAFTA document exceeding 2,000 pages. Yet AFTA stands out among all attempts in ASEAN at economic co-operation in several ways. First, this was the first time that ASEAN described free trade as its eventual goal, a break from its previous mind-set of cautious liberalization. Second, the Heads of Governments in ASEAN identified 15 product groups for accelerated liberalization, thus avoiding a lengthy process of negotiations among bureaucrats to identify product groups, Third, there was a definite timetable within which free trade would be achieved, that is in 15 years. Finally, the CEPT was a vast improvement over an earlier (1987) programme for enhanced Preferential Trading Arrangements (PTA), which allowed for more automatic liberalization of items, deeper margins of preferences, and more product coverage than under PTA. This latter programme did not really progress substantially, suffered from delays in submission of items for liberalization, and some members were behind schedule for as much as two years.

As shown in Figure 1, the CEPT has two tracks: fast and normal. In the fast

---

Reprinted from Daljit Singh and Liak Teng Kiat, eds., *Southeast Asian Affairs 1995* (Singapore: Institute of Southeast Asian Studies, 1995), pp. 61–73. At the time of original publication, Florian A. Alburo was Professor of Economics at the School of Economics, University of the Philippines.

FIGURE 1
General Formula of Original CEPT Tariff Reduction Schedule

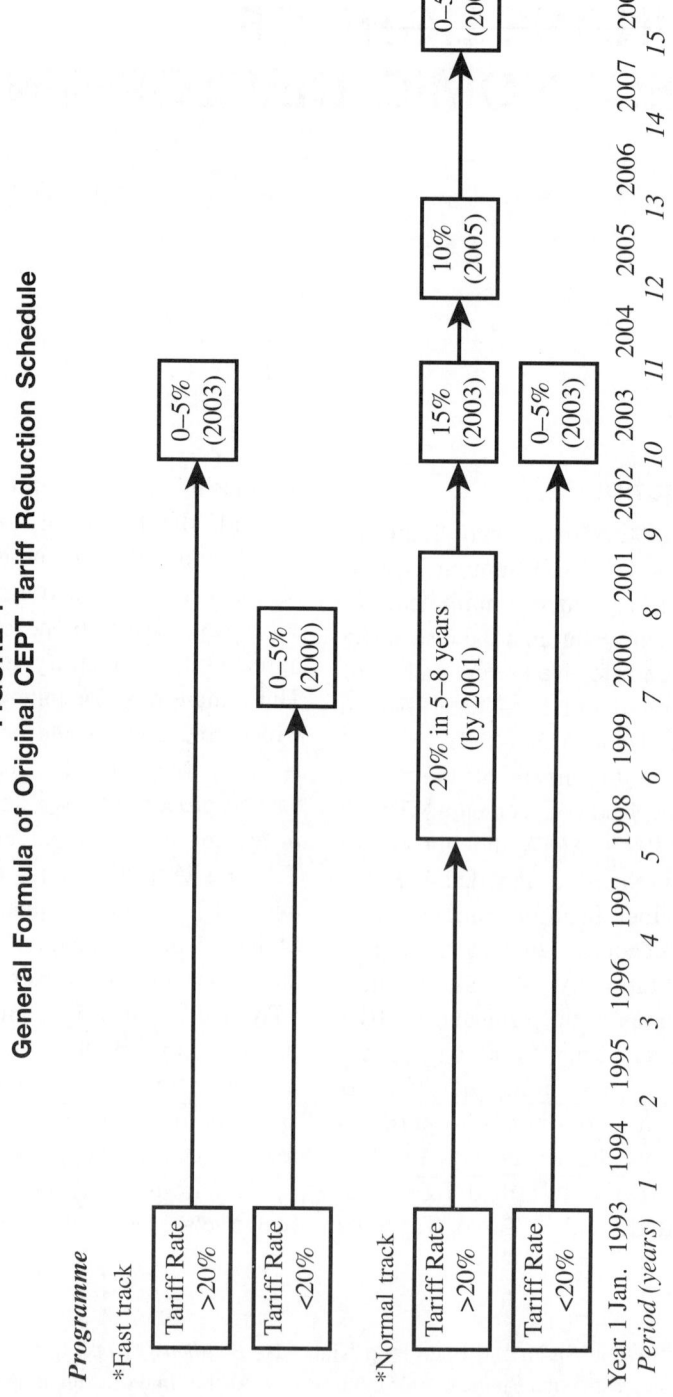

track, according to the 1992 agreements, the achievement of free trade was to take place in 10 years, that is by 2003. For items with base tariff rates exceeding 20 per cent, reductions were to be spread over 10 years till 2003. For items with rates below 20 per cent, reductions were to be completed by the year 2000.

In the normal track, tariffs of more than 20 per cent were to be reduced in three stages: to 20 per cent by 2001, 15 per cent by 2003, 10 per cent by 2005 and free trade (0–5 per cent) in 2008. For items with tariff rates less than 20 per cent, reductions were to be completed by 2003.

The coverage of CEPT included all manufactures, processed agricultural products, and capital goods at the HS 6-digit level. However, agricultural products were excluded from the CEPT. In addition, exclusions were also allowed at the HS 8/9-digit levels for manufactured products member states may consider as sensitive.

While the CEPT is the major instrument for achieving AFTA, it is by no means the only one. There are others as well. One is the commitment to remove quantitative restrictions after products are included in the CEPT. Another is the elimination of non-tariff barriers within five years from CEPT's start. Then there are the harmonization of standards, reciprocal recognition of tests, removal of barriers to foreign investments etc.

AFTA was decided upon in response to the uncertainties of the global economic environment in the early nineties. The Uruguay Round of Multilateral Trade Agreement was not progressing enough by the time of the Mid-Term Review, and in relation to the targeted completion by 1992. The European Community was consolidating into what was perceived as a "Fortress Europe". The United States was pushing for the early completion of NAFTA. The world economy was in danger of becoming a tri-polar environment of Europe, the United States and Japan. And AFTA was seen as a minor insurance in this context. These uncertainties also explain ASEAN's reluctant agreement to join the Asia-Pacific Economic Co-operation (APEC) forum in the hope that a global trade accord will materialize, avoiding the danger of tri-polarity or a return to bilateralism.

The firm resolve by world economic leaders to see an orderly global trade environment led to a successful conclusion of the Uruguay Round (UR) by April 1994. The ratification processes were in full swing thereafter and a critical mass was achieved to start a more comprehensive multilateral framework under the aegis of a World Trade Organization (WTO) in 1995.

In a sense, the conclusion of the GATT-UR Agreement has diminished the uncertainty of the economic environment that gave impetus to the decision to form AFTA in the first place. Whether AFTA has lost its significance or relevance is another matter given that the UR is still to be implemented and many of its components still to be assessed in each individual ASEAN state and regionally. Add to this the continuing discussions in Europe (the Maastricht Treaty) and NAFTA on trade liberalization that imply, if not the same uncertainty that faced the global economy before, adjustments may have to be made to assure harmony and consistency in the world economic order.

The purpose of this article is to review AFTA in the light of the new economic developments. The next section briefly describes some of the elements of the globalization phenomenon taking place today and how tariffs, the main instrument in AFTA, fit into the picture. The third section summarizes the new global trade environment illustrated and dictated by the GATT-UR. The summary will focus on those aspects that matter to AFTA. In the fourth section, a review is made of the recently agreed acceleration of AFTA and the other measures adopted to accompany the acceleration. The fifth section examines the relevance of AFTA in the light of all these developments. In particular its relevance is viewed in the context of the recent Ministerial pronouncements for its acceleration.

The concluding section then considers the prospects for AFTA especially in view of the changes in the emerging new international economic environment. It is argued that AFTA may acquire a new dimension not only of relevance but importance to the region, depending on how fast it can adjust, alter the pace, content, and timing of its implementation, and recognize some of the underlying changes in economic structures taking place globally and especially in Asia.

2. Globalization and Tariffs

The use of tariffs for protection, for revenue or both has had a long history in ASEAN, with the exception perhaps of Brunei Darussalam, for tariffs have been instrumental in the industrialization process of ASEAN. Of course there have been wide variations in their use. Early departure from the import-substitution strategy (driven by cascading tariffs) has been important to successful outward orientation. On the other hand continued inward looking strategies have deterred respectable export levels from being attained.

Prominent tariff regimes have not prevented international firms from jumping tariff walls and penetrating domestic markets. The impact on the economy of tariffs and foreign investment operating within protective tariff walls — and there is substantial documentation to show this — is not quite positive. Domestic firms are not exposed to the frontiers of technology and management practices. International firms operating in the domestic market do not bring in state-of-the-art technology and management since they enjoy protection from the world markets (including their own parent firms) provided by high tariffs. In short, the tariff regimes define the behaviour of local firms and foreign firms in the domestic markets. This characterization of protected economies has applied to most ASEAN members in varying degrees and during transition from import substitution to export orientation. In today's economic environment, how relevant are tariffs, and attention to them?

The last few years have seen the phenomenon of globalization in the world economy. Although it is not across all trade sectors, and indeed is confined to a few sectors such as electronics and consumer products, it may be illustrative of what will happen in the future on a broader scale. The globalization of production has been driven by a combination of more openness, liberal trade regimes, greater mobility of factors, and the encompassing infrastructure of telecommunications, transportation and information technology. Globalization is synonymous with a "borderless world". There is also a globalization of consumption taking place as the reach of satellite television expands choices and makes tastes more homogeneous.

From globalization has emerged the global firm. This firm is unlike the transnational corporation of the recent past that is usually large, concentrated in resources and even integrated. Now both a small firm and a large firm can actively transact in the global market-place whether horizontally or vertically. Economies of scale are not as important as certain other critical properties.

First, the global firm is really a network firm, that is one whose production processes along with their components are spread out globally and any one of the firms along the chain does the product completion. There is therefore a larger interdependence among the network firms. Second, there are now other forms of firm arrangements than the traditional equity investments. They include licensing, supply contracts, procurement arrangements, joint ventures, etc. They constitute new mechanisms through which firms operate so that even companies considered "closed" are capable of being network firms. Third, and related to the first two properties, in the global firm the emphasis is more on co-ordination and less on control. This is consistent with newer forms of firm relationships and the network basis of production. Indeed one result of these properties is that a global firm may not have a physical factory and yet produce a volume of output. Fourth, there is now mutuality of relationships among firms based on the presumption that all parties to the globalization process have something to contribute to production. This is unlike before when the host firm receiving foreign investments absorbed technology, management capacities and skills but provided only marginal contribution such as unskilled labour. In a global set-up relationships are two-way. Finally, while all firm sizes take part in the globalization process, firms also form groups or enter into alliances to take advantage of joint services, joint marketing, and other similar economies without necessarily entering into joint ownership. In fact, competition may become more acute among groups of firms than among firms.

Although globalization is not proceeding uniformly across all industries, it is expanding from the confines of electronics and consumer products into other industries (for example telecommunications, airlines). More interestingly, as technology catches up in other industries arising, for example, from globalized electronics and telecommunication industries, the globalization process will tend to become extensive as well.

One major implication of this globalization and the emergence of the network firm is the declining importance and relevance of tariffs to trading economies. Whereas previously tariffs were essential for promoting industrial processes, it seems that with a globalized firm network, processes may be broadly scattered yet final outputs are accessed via trade. Whereas previously tariffs provided protection to products in domestic markets, it seems that with globalization tariffs no longer matter since markets are global and production takes place everywhere. Tariffs have lost their relevance especially for certain types of industries or products that are part of globalization.

Some of the ASEAN states are now integral to the globalization processes taking place in the world economy. The range of participation appears wide: from hosting international procurement offices and producing specific components to the assembly of products with inputs from the rest of the world. For example, Singapore is host to procurement offices, assembles a wide range of electronic and consumer products, as well as produces specific items for assembly elsewhere. Malaysia is now headquarters for global production of room air-conditioners. The Philippines produces computer components for Japanese multinationals yet the firms are not controlled by the multinationals.

There are similar arrangements in Thailand and Indonesia.

There is no doubt that ASEAN's integration into the global economy renders attention to tariffs (and their reduction) redundant. It makes sense to see their unilateral reduction to minimal rates although one can argue that this will hold true only for that narrow set of industries that is globalized. Nevertheless, the central focus on tariff reduction in AFTA remains questionable in this light.

3. The New Global Trade Environment

With the implementation of the GATT-UR Agreement by members of the newly-established (1995) World Trade Organization, dramatic changes in the global trade environment can be expected. The overall landscape of AFTA will likewise change. The aim of this section is not to discuss the new agreement in detail, but to highlight those aspects that would alter the environment for AFTA.

The UR Agreement is perhaps the most comprehensive set of trade rules so far. It covers almost all trading sectors: those which heretofore were excluded from the multilateral framework and those which, though administered by GATT, were actually GATT-inconsistent. In addition the agreement sets new rules for new sectors, tightens disciplines, and removes or reduces grey areas which threatened the stability of the global trading system. Agricultural trade, which was not in the GATT rules, will now be subject to transparency and liberalization in stages, and trade in textiles and clothing, which was bound by the Multi-Fibre Agreement (MFA), will now be integrated into the overall trading rules over a specified period of time.

The available estimates of the macroeconomic impact of the UR show that, overall, the world stands to gain from the accord mainly because of the increased trade and the increased incomes it will generate. The boost to trade comes not only from more liberalized trade but also from conversion of non-tariff barriers to tariffs.

The impact of the UR on the Asia-Pacific region will be considerable. Although there has been some increase in trade within Asia (and within ASEAN), this is considered to be the result of the region's participation in global trade rather than regionalization *per se*. In short the region's openness to the rest of the world has reduced potential trade diversion from any regionalization attempt.

In order to appreciate how this new economic regime arising from the UR will impinge on ASEAN, it will be useful to focus on a number of aspects of the UR Agreement: (1) the period of adjustment; (2) the substance of the UR Agreement; (3) the tariff cuts agreed upon for industrial products; and (4) the agreements on quantitative restrictions. ASEAN also needs to see AFTA in the light of the multilateral nature of the UR Agreement. In addition, though the Agreement has barely touched on the proliferation of free trade areas and procedures for their review, it is important to see how ASEAN fits in this.

The period for the completion of the Agreement's implementation is at most 10 years for developing, and six years for developed, countries for most of the components. The timetable is even more meaningful because products are identified by specific tariff line, measured milestones are indicated, and procedures for dealing with deviations from the set time path are spelled out.

Although the AFTA timetable has now been reduced from 15 years to 10, it is not strictly comparable with the UR Agreement because ASEAN's aim is free trade at the target date. Yet there are interesting but subtle points to note. For one, in AFTA most of the products for liberalization come later in the timetable and can be back-loaded (for example in terms of trade value) to the later part; this does not seem to be the case with the UR. For another, while AFTA makes a distinction in the timetable between products whose base tariffs are high (greater than 20 per cent) or those with low base tariffs, in the UR the magnitude of the reduction is the operating guideline. In any case, a timetable of 10 years for full adjustment seemed a stronger commitment to liberalization than AFTA's original 15 years.

The coverage of the UR is clearly across the board and not just confined to manufactured goods as in AFTA. In agricultural trade, both unprocessed and processed products are covered though the liberalization is in two stages. It is also inclusive for textiles and clothing. Though integration from MFA into WTO begins with four categories of products, the manner of how the rest are to be integrated is clearly specified. In the case of services, the scope is defined and the principles laid out. Though liberalization of this sector still has some way to go, the annexes indicate that at least two areas, financial and telecommunications services, will lead the way in the inclusion of services in the multilateral trade framework.

Although a number of items in the UR are not discussed here, it is clear that AFTA's coverage has been more limited than the UR. (Changes in AFTA are discussed in the next section). AFTA specifically excluded agriculture but included processed agricultural goods. It did not cover trade in services.

On industrial products, though the average tariff rates in the pre-UR period varied considerably, the commitment under the UR Agreement is towards significant declines over six- or 10-year periods. The tariff rates of industrial products of the developed countries are to fall by 38 per cent. Of course their averages are already low; hence the absolute reductions may not be large.

A number of points in the agreement on reduction of tariffs of industrial products is interesting. One is that the offered tariff rates for most product categories of developed countries will turn out to be within the 0–5 per cent rates aimed at by AFTA. Another is that these reductions are to be made in five steps or by the year 2000 — earlier than the original AFTA completion schedule in 2008. It is also interesting that the ASEAN states themselves had offered tariff reductions that are to take place by 2005.

Cutting across agricultural and non-agricultural trade is the programme to replace or remove non-tariff barriers (NTB). This has taken three forms: (1) conversion of NTBs on agricultural imports into tariff equivalents, and then subsequent liberalization; (2) phase out of the MFA; and (3) phase out of grey area measures. Moreover the reduction of subsidies would also remove one more significant distortion to world trade.

Many of the means used by agricultural producers to distort agricultural trade have been addressed in the agreement. The steps taken in transforming NTBs to tariffs are also indicated. Distinctions are made between government support that is non-distortive and that which involves transfers from consumers to producers, stipulating that the latter is to be phased out. Once the process of conversion to tariffs is completed there is overall agreement to lower these by 36 per cent for developed, and 24 per cent for developing, countries over six and 10 years respectively.

The MFA, another persistent NTB, is also to be phased out over 10 years according to a schedule. The schedule not only allows existing bilateral arrangements to be "outgrown" but also allows progressive participation by new producers.

The other NTBs are to be phased out over four years. These include measures such as voluntary export restraints (VER), orderly marketing arrangements, etc. While the agreement allows the retention of one grey-area measure until the year 2000, it is quite clear that the rest will have to go and conform to GATT rules.

It is to be noted again that ASEAN countries had likewise participated in the conclusion of the UR and are bound by the Agreements. Thus ASEAN's agricultural sector will see the reduction of NTBs and their conversion into tariffs, for example in Indonesia, Philippines and Thailand. For some of the ASEAN countries, the phase out of the MFA may be threatening but may also provide long term benefits. There is no exception to growing out of MFA. In the grey areas, ASEAN does not have concrete participation but illustrates what cannot be admitted as new measures.

In AFTA, there are elements that are similar to the UR Agreements. There is the removal of quantitative restrictions which members commit to after inclusion of products with the CEPT. Members are to eliminate non-tariff barriers within five years from the start of the CEPT concessions. And of course tariffs are scheduled for eventual reduction to 0–5 per cent for those included in the CEPT.

However, these similarities hide important differences. The first is that in the UR Agreement, the details of what products are to be liberalized and how are spelled out including the entire time path of the programme. This minimizes any alterations along the way and gives a clear signal of certainty. Contrast this with AFTA where, with the exception of the 15 product groups for accelerated reduction, ASEAN reached agreement first, and left the specific items for the programme for the tariff reductions for later negotiations. Second, the time frame for global liberalization is shorter under the UR, although its goal is not free trade, than under the original AFTA schedule, but the magnitude (in percentage terms) of the tariff reduction is quite significant for developed countries (6.3 per cent per year). In AFTA the reduction on average was to be between two per cent per year (for products with 20 per cent base rate) and 7.5 per cent per year (for products with base rates greater than 20 per cent).

Article XXIV of GATT relating to customs union and free trade areas (FTA) has not been substantially modified in the UR. However since the article specifies that the overall or common external tariffs of the FTA must not be more restrictive than was the case before the area was formed, the UR points to an assessment based on its tariff offers. The other provisions under this article remain the same. Apart from this condition that the common area tariffs be not more restrictive than before is the condition that the FTA must have substantial trade within the area liberalized.

4. Accelerating AFTA

Although calls to accelerate AFTA were made even at the start, it was not until after the UR was concluded that there was some official recognition of the need. Hence at the ASEAN Economic Ministers Meeting in late 1994 there was an agreement to realize AFTA more rapidly.

The acceleration is in the implementation of the CEPT. As can be seen from Figure 1, the normal track was originally aimed for completion by 2008 and the fast track by 2003. In the revised CEPT the normal track was to be completed by 2003 in two steps: (1) the reduction in tariff rates in excess of 20 per cent to 20 per cent by January 1998, and (2) reduction from 20 per cent to 0–5 per cent by January 2003. For the fast track products, the liberalization was to take place by the year 2000 instead of 2003. Similarly, there were to be two steps: (1) tariffs in excess of 20 per cent were to be reduced to 0–5 per cent by January 2000, and (2) tariffs rates below 20 per cent were to be reduced to 0–5 per cent by 1998. These revisions of AFTA really constitute a timetable adjustment for achieving free trade status in 10 years instead of the original 15 years. Moreover, for fast track products the completion time is seven years instead of the original 10 years.

Apart from the change in timetable, ASEAN also expanded the components of AFTA beyond those under the CEPT. Among these are (1) the inclusion of the agriculture sector in the CEPT; (2) the placing of services on the agenda for consideration for eventual liberalization; and (3) the possible extension of the programme to include new ASEAN members.

The coverage of agriculture in the CEPT is itself a recognition of the breakthrough in agricultural trade liberalization in the UR. Yet the decision in ASEAN has been to set up a mechanism to address sensitive agricultural products. One wonders whether these have not all been identified in the offers made at the UR. However, the ASEAN Economic Ministers agreed that agricultural products that are not sensitive will immediately be included in the AFTA liberalization scheme.

Following the UR Agreement on services, that is the General Agreement on Trade in Services (GATS), ASEAN has agreed to the establishment of an ASEAN Framework for Co-operation in Services. A Working Group in Services, chaired by the Philippines, will complete a draft Agreement by June 1995. Unlike the UR, however, ASEAN's emphasis on services trade is co-operation in services sectors where ASEAN's competitiveness can be enhanced, such as mutual recognition of licences and certification systems of specified service providers.

At the same time as AFTA is being accelerated, the entry of Vietnam into ASEAN will extend the CEPT. Vietnam is meanwhile applying to join the WTO and has submitted the necessary information and documentation on its trade policies which form the basis for assessing membership. This will also become the basis for its participation in the CEPT. There may be adjustments for Vietnam on the scope and length of time of the CEPT process but the point is that the size of AFTA will be larger.

In all, the declaration to accelerate AFTA merits several observations. First, the CEPT acceleration is more of a time phase reduction than a structural change in the scope of the liberalization process. If the scope remains the same, then the accelerated CEPT does not change the fact that most of the items fall under the normal track. Table 1 shows that for all ASEAN states more than half of tariff lines are scheduled for reduction to the 0–5 per cent rates under the normal track. Even in the case of the Philippines the proportion

TABLE 1
Proportion of Tariff Lines in AFTA's Normal Track

	Total Tariff Lines	Ratio (%)
Brunei Darussalam	6,079	60.2
Indonesia	7,355	61.7
Malaysia	8,777	63.9
Philippines	4,451	76.8
Singapore	5,722	61.5
Thailand	8,763	60.0

Source: Basic data from ASEAN Secretariat.

of 77 per cent remains. Thus the trade structure originally implicit in the menu of tariff lines for liberalization has not been altered with this time acceleration. Second, although agriculture has been included in the acceleration of AFTA, its contents are basically still subject to negotiations. This does not help to provide a clear signal for a rapid actualization of AFTA. It would have been understandable if the consideration of agricultural trade was starting from scratch, but this is not the case. Most ASEAN countries had already made specific offers in the UR. Indeed one alternative could have been to begin from those offers and then demonstrate their accelerated implementation under AFTA. This of course could still be the end result of the mechanisms set-up.

Third, the other parts of the Accelerated AFTA are important items that fit well into an AFTA Plus programme more consistent with a real regional grouping. These other measures include the harmonization of tariff and customs nomenclature and procedure, an ASEAN plan on infrastructure development, the eventual elimination of the temporary exclusion list in the CEPT, and the elimination of NTBs.

Finally, the original AFTA (that is before the decision to accelerate) may have already triggered private sector investments based on the assumption of protection over 15 years, and an accelerated pace may disturb these private sector calculations. In fact, because of the strong signals given out by AFTA at the start, this is not an unlikely scenario. Given this, the acceleration of AFTA can meet some resistance among ASEAN members from specific industries and tariff lines. This need not change the direction but will create some sticky points along the way.

5. The Relevance of AFTA

What will be the implications for AFTA of the rapid changes taking place in the global economic environment and the changes that are occurring in the global behaviour of firms? These new developments will have a bearing on how AFTA will be seen, and how it will proceed along its path. In fact, as pointed out before, the accelerated AFTA is in part a response to these changes.

Instead of AFTA losing relevance or diminishing in importance, one can argue, on the basis of these new changes, that AFTA may acquire a new significance in the context of the new global environment. Several factors can dictate the way in which a new AFTA, assuming it goes beyond the accelerated programme outlined in the previous section, evolves.

The tariff reduction programme CEPT (both normal and fast track) is still the major component of AFTA despite the completed multilateral negotiations of the UR. How this will shape up beyond the 0–5 per cent target tariff rates in the context of the WTO hinges on two interrelated developments. One is that free trade areas may have a role in demonstrating how the process of further rounds of tariff reductions can be achieved and in this context ASEAN can potentially be an example for the WTO. Indeed given the very large number of countries in the international community, a new tariff reduction round can be fruitful initially only in the regional groupings around the world. The other is that the outcome of AFTA, that is what has been liberalized *within* ASEAN, can become a basis for multilateralization of tariff liberalization. Under these two circumstances AFTA can play a significant and important role.

How the WTO will eventually conduct a new round of tariff liberalization is not yet known. As a new institution it may be responsive to new ways of carrying out liberalization. There is no reason why negotiations cannot be conducted on a regional level whether based on groupings or actual "request and offer" list by individual economies in the region. The process of further tariff reduction in AFTA can facilitate a new round.

Services is another dimension that can alter the relevance of AFTA. If ASEAN can move the liberalization of trade in services at a pace faster than the UR Agreements, the region can demonstrate how services trade should develop globally. Put differently, the ASEAN region can serve as a model for the implementation of some of the basic principles agreed upon in the UR, and this will then also strengthen AFTA. Even the earlier stages of negotiations can be illuminating for a multilateral setting. After all, the ASEAN states display the diversity in services trade that is a microcosm of the issues surrounding the UR Agreement on services.

As the number of member states in ASEAN expands, AFTA will gain added stature especially if new members immediately participate in the trade liberalization scheme. Eventually ASEAN is expected to become ASEAN-10, with Vietnam clearly the next candidate. An expanded ASEAN will not only reflect wider markets but also some regional solidarity that can be a basis for regionally-based liberalization efforts. Even if ASEAN sets different speeds for trade liberalization for new members, trade creation will still receive a boost. With the conclusion of the UR Agreements, one would think groupings would lose their appeal. In the case of ASEAN, however, expanded membership will widen liberalization in the "small" before venturing into a larger setting.

If the collective vision of AFTA and ASEAN's common political, economic and social infrastructure goals are successfully carried out, the new global firms will find a receptive host in ASEAN. This is not to say that the process of globalization is not already taking place in ASEAN. Indeed both Singapore and Malaysia are active locations of highly integrated network firms. Although the ASEAN plan of Action on Infrastructure Development, for example, is specifically catered to subregional arrangements in ASEAN, the more infrastructurally-linked ASEAN is, the more enhanced will be the globalization network in each of the member countries. Both the plan of Action on Infrastructure and on Transportation and Communications will contribute to this enhancement.

In the end changes in how AFTA is seen may have a bearing on the relevance of overall ASEAN economic co-operation. In particular, the increasing importance of intra-industry trade as a significant basis of AFTA will strengthen its relevance.

There are indeed mutual benefits to be derived from trade among economies which are similar in endowments, industrial structure, and even consumption patterns. That would seem to be what AFTA is all about.

6. Conclusion

A fundamental transformation is taking place in the global economy among ASEAN's major trading partners and in the global economic environment. A new global trading institution, the WTO, is to start functioning. All these will alter the shape of ASEAN in general and question the relevance of AFTA in particular.

Although AFTA was a bold step at trade liberalization in the region when it was started, it was really born in the midst of uncertainty in the global trading environment. Fortunately the success of the UR Agreement diminished the need for regionalism and called for a new relevance for AFTA consistent with breakthroughs in the global trading framework.

Indeed this new global framework has recognized the fundamental changes taking place among trading agents, the advances in global infrastructure, and the new arrangements among firms in certain industries that seem to pave the way for a changed world economy.

The ASEAN governments were quick to recognize how these fundamental changes would affect the region and AFTA. ASEAN in fact moved towards not only shortening the timetable of AFTA but also expanding and intensifying liberalization to keep pace with new changes. Thus, AFTA appears to be taking on a new meaning. It has encompassed more than trade in goods and more than tariff reductions. There is the reality of adding new participants to the scheme as ASEAN expands its membership. And the ASEAN governments seem determined on collective action on infrastructure development for more integrated economies.

AFTA therefore remains relevant in the light not only of new economic structures but also of the dynamic behavioural changes taking place among firms. ASEAN seems to have made the right pronouncements.

What is unclear at this point is whether the right pronouncements that ASEAN has been making will be translated into concrete measures in terms of procedures, trade regulations, and bureaucratic processes. More pointedly, it is unclear whether the accelerated AFTA (or AFTA-Plus) will come about within its stated time frame. It will spell the difference between a relevant AFTA and an irrelevant AFTA.

THE ASEAN ECONOMIC MIRACLE UNRAVELS

Manuel F. Montes

In 1998, the Asian economic miracle seemed like a distant dream for the economies of Southeast Asia, with the string of bad news being blamed on excesses committed during the years of strong growth. The countries reeled from the continued withdrawal of capital from the region, the disintegration and collapse of confidence in domestic financial sectors, policy- and psychology-induced demand contractions, the interdependent weaknesses in the international value of their currencies, and political conflict and a significant erosion of the social consensus over economic policy.

The Southeast Asian economies faced these problems in common, but the impact varied according to the level of development, specific features in their financial systems, the nature of the governments' responses to the crisis, and the impact of the crisis on political stability.

The withdrawal of capital from the region in 1998 constituted the biggest shared factor among the Southeast Asian economies. The level of capital outflow, initiated by the Thai economic crisis of July 1997, increased in 1998 for the four most severely affected ASEAN economies — Indonesia, Malaysia, the Philippines, and Thailand — plus South Korea, with net capital outflows accelerating from US$1 billion in 1997 to $28 billion in 1998. In 1996, there had actually been net inflows of $103 billion.

The fickle nature of short-term portfolio investments was much in evidence during 1998.[1] There was a brief slowdown of capital outflow from the region in the first quarter of 1998, but the levels accelerated as evidence of a deep recession in Japan became inescapable and the yen weakened, Russia's teetering economy saw the offering of interest rates on short-

---

Reprinted from Daljit Singh and John Funston, eds., *Southeast Asian Affairs 1999* (Singapore: Institute of Southeast Asian Studies, 1999), pp. 20–31. At the time of original publication, Manuel F. Montes was Senior Fellow and Co-ordinator of Economic Studies at the East-West Center, Hawaii.

term Russian bonds reach 80 to 100 per cent, and Indonesia's thirty-year political arrangements disintegrated with President Soeharto's resignation in May.

In August, the Russian economic programme collapsed and a general retreat from portfolio investments in all emerging markets ensued.[2] The premium on developing country debt shot up to unprecedented levels of 10 to 15 percentage points by October 1998. Brazil lost at least US$20 billion dollars in international reserves between the Russian collapse and the start of an International Monetary Fund (IMF) economic rescue package in November 1998; this package collapsed in mid-January 1999. Between 1997 and 1998, private capital flows to the emerging economies fell from US$260 billion to US$152 billion in favour of industrial country equity markets.

Southeast Asian currencies fell to their lowest level in January 1998, but then started to firm. The first two data columns of Table 1 indicate the substantial declines in the nominal exchange rates of the Southeast Asian currencies and the Korean won from their pre-crisis values. The last column suggests that since the first quarter of 1998, these values have actually appreciated.

In 1998, Indonesia's economy, Southeast Asia's largest, plunged, with real output shrinking by 15.3 per cent, inflation soaring 72 per cent, and the dollar value of the rupiah tumbling by as much as 80 per cent from its pre-crisis level (Table 2). In 1998, investments fell by 42 per cent, exports by 9 per cent, and consumption by 15 per cent from their 1997 levels (Table 3). The loss in these key elements of macroeconomic demand underline the disintegration of macroeconomic stability that had been an Indonesian achievement in the previous three decades.

Two Indonesian IMF programmes failed before the May resignation of President Soeharto. Private currency markets greeted the IMF programme of early January 1998 (a redesign of the October 1997 IMF programme) with such great incredulity that its exchange rate assumptions were made obsolete the morning after its announcement. Unrest and violence in May, sparked

TABLE 1
Rates of Depreciation of East Asian Currencies
(Exchange Rates to the U.S. Dollar)

	Level of Local Currency Unit/US$			Rates of Depreciation		
				Since 1 July '97		24 Jan '98
	1 Jul '98	24 Jan '98	3 Feb '99	to 24 Jan '98	to 3 Feb '99	to 3 Feb '98
Indonesia	2,432.00	14,800.00	8,425.00	–83.6	–71.1	75.7
Malaysia	2.52	4.58	3.80	–44.9	–33.7	20.5
Philippines	26.37	43.50	38.50	–39.4	–31.5	13.0
Singapore	1.43	1.76	1.69	–18.8	–15.4	4.1
Thailand	24.53	54.00	36.80	–54.6	–33.3	46.7
Korea	888.00	1,744.00	1,170.00	–49.1	–24.1	49.1

Source: Manuel F. Montes, *The Currency Crisis in Southeast Asia* (ISEAS, 1998), p. xv; United Nations Project Link, New York.

TABLE 2
GDP Growth Rates
(In per cent)

	1997	1998e	1998f
Indonesia	4.6	−15.3	−3.4
Malaysia	7.7	−7.5	−2.0
Philippines	5.3	0.2	2.5
Singapore	7.8	1.5	−0.8
Thailand	−0.4	−8.0	1.0
Vietnam	8.8	3.5	3.5

Notes: "1998e" denotes 1998 estimates by United Nations Project Link, New York. "1998f" denotes 1999 forecasts by author.

by the rapid implementation of IMF provisions requiring the removal of fuel and food subsidies, soon led to the President's resignation.

A third 1998 IMF programme, designed under the new B.J. Habibie government, was expansionary, in contrast with the earlier and more standard IMF contractionary programmes. It permitted generous fiscal deficits — an almost unprecedented 8.3 per cent of gross domestic product (GDP) for 1998 — and allowed more realistic time schedules for reform actions. The new government, however, presided over a nation undergoing profound social change, as it tried to establish more credible processes for determining political leadership. That process will be carried forward by new elections for a National Assembly in June 1999, and the Assembly will in turn elect a new President by December 1999.

While the Habibie government did an acceptable job of hewing to the IMF programme targets and keeping to the reform schedule, macroeconomic stability and investment confidence depend very much on the reinstatement of political stability. The uncertainty over the outcomes of the electoral processes of 1999 originates not only in the outcome itself (and thus the nature of the economic programme of the winning coalition) but also in the question of whether the winning coalition, whoever it may include, will garner a sufficient measure of political legitimacy.

In the meantime, the economic dislocation has seen an increase in the incidence of poverty, from 11 per cent to at least 14 per cent, and a scramble by the current government to institute

TABLE 3
Growth Rates of Key Demand Variables and Inflation
(In per cent)

	Exports		Investments		Private Consumption		CPI Inflation	
	1998e	1999f	1998e	1999f	1998e	1999f	1998e	1999f
Indonesia	−8.9	1.2	−41.6	1.0	−15.1	−4.0	71.7	11.4
Malaysia	−15.3	6.9	−8.5	−1.2	−3.1	−0.5	8.2	1.7
Philippines	10.0	13.2	−6.1	6.2	2.8	3.6	9.3	8.3
Singapore	−12.7	0.8	2.2	2.0	1.0	2.3	1.8	1.9
Thailand	7.2	4.4	−27.4	−1.7	−10.5	−0.2	8.4	4.1

Notes: "1998e" denotes 1998 estimates by United Nations Project Links, New York. "1999f" denotes 1999 forecasts by the author.

social programmes to assist those losing employment or unable to cope with the price increases in basic goods. The impact of the Indonesian crisis on human welfare will also be felt in long-term ways. For example, the incidence of school drop-out of young children will be felt in the future. Ethnic violence, especially against Chinese shopowners, has also poisoned business confidence, at least for the medium-term.

The Indonesian economy hit bottom in 1998 and the economic decline, measured in terms of the negative rate of growth of the Indonesia economy, will be about 3 to 4 per cent in 1999. The restructuring and rehabilitation of the banking system and the restoration of credit facilities to the Indonesian corporate sector are being addressed under the IMF-sponsored programme and through international negotiations. These processes are by nature time-consuming since they must deal with specific banks, companies, loan projects, and collateral assets. The context of overall macroeconomic uncertainty makes all parties to these operations unsympathetic to rapid disclosure and compromise, and asset stripping under bankruptcy procedures has become endemic.

Indonesia's medium to long-term prospects depend heavily on the restoration of political stability and the completion of economic restructuring. Positive economic growth in 2000 is highly likely if the 1999 electoral processes do not result in uncontrolled violence. The real question is whether the high and steady rates of economic growth of the past can be reinstated soon. Given the enormous obstacles facing Indonesia, high rates of growth are not in prospect for the next four years.

Macroeconomic instability also hobbled the Malaysian economy in 1998, when its GDP contracted about 7.5 per cent. As in Indonesia, the main macroeconomic demand elements fell precipitously in 1998; exports declined by 15.3 per cent from 1997 levels, and investment fell by 9 per cent (Table 3). The fall in exports to Asia and the softness in international commodity prices, both induced by the East Asian economic recession, explain the export decline. On the other hand, the impact of the withdrawal of private capital and the burgeoning credit problems in the financial sector induced the investment decline.

As in all of Southeast Asia, the crisis saw investment overconfidence replaced by private pessimism and public policy conflicts. When the Asian economic crisis began in 1997, the Malaysian financial sector had seen almost half a decade of credit expansion. In 1994, bank credits grew by 14.4 per cent from the previous year, then by 30.5 per cent in 1995, and by 24.5 per cent in 1996. As a proportion of GDP, these credits hovered at around 103 per cent, and then began to increase markedly in 1995 and 1996. Commercial bank credit as a percentage of GDP increased from 70.6 per cent in 1994 to 80.0 per cent in 1995. After 1995, finance companies credit as a proportion of GDP also increased markedly.

The vulnerability of Malaysia's domestic credit expansion to external developments stemmed from the fact that shares of stock in the domestic equity market had been pledged as collateral during the expansion. Foreign investment in domestic equities underpinned these prices. When the Asian crisis abetted foreign withdrawals from the stock market (a process that was magnified by potential gains that could be made from currency speculation and margin trading) Malaysian equity prices collapsed taking with them the viability of the loans in the financial system. While Malaysian prudential regulation had been generally sound before the Asian crisis, the loss of collateral values was systemic and the full-blown financial crisis itself further fomented macroeconomic and currency instability.

The government initially responded to the crisis by implementing IMF-style contractionary policies meant to assure private actors that currency values would be stable and stave off capital withdrawals. Contractionary policy, of course, reduced the growth rate and the prospects for growth and profits and weakened the financial system even further. The alternative, expansionary policy, while it would have been the appropriate remedy to private sector pessimism, would have also been counterproductive since it would have fed currency speculation and could have accelerated the ringgit's rate of depreciation.

In July 1998, Malaysia instituted a recovery plan that began to sidle away from the contractionary approach. It had two elements: first, a financial restructuring programme, and secondly, targetted expansionary policies especially in social spending. Malaysia created an asset management company that would take over poor loans and set aside funds for the recapitalization of the banking system.

Even as its leaders pointed out the problems inherent in unstable international capital markets, Malaysia maintained a friendly, consultative relationship with the IMF. It enjoyed international support from public agencies for its recovery programme and quickly obtained a loan from the World Bank to fund the initial social spending objectives. However, private international markets remained sceptical and Malaysia had to postpone an international debt flotation meant to finance its bank restructuring programmes because the markets were requiring high interest rates.

On 1 September 1998, Malaysia took the Draconian step of announcing the imposition of capital controls. This move anticipated the breaking out into the open of the political conflict between Prime Minister Mahathir Mohamad and Finance Minister Anwar Ibrahim, which, given Anwar's reputation as the standard-bearer of conventional, rational economic policy, would certainly have sparked massive private capital flight and a meltdown in the international value of the ringgit. By providing Malaysia with the means to undertake more extensive expansionary policy without undermining the ringgit and financial stability, instituting capital controls cut the Gordian knot and resolved the Malaysian policy dilemma.

The impact of the imposition of the controls provided the economy the respite that has laid the basis for a Malaysian economic recovery. Stock market values stabilized and the dire predictions that capital controls could only exacerbate capital flight proved unfounded. Malaysia instituted the policy just at the moment when the fall in the value of the Japanese yen was arrested, helping to firm up the currency values in the region. However, these positive trends were counteracted by Malaysia's burgeoning domestic political conflict and the seizing up of the international capital markets after the Russian debt default in August 1998.

The overall trends in Asian recovery permitted Malaysia to begin to replace the administrative controls with taxes in February 1999 (about the time when, internationally, the Brazilian rescue package disintegrated). Private markets responded positively to Malaysia's softening of capital regulation.

Even though the economy will either shrink by one per cent or grow marginally in 1999, it can be said that Malaysia has weathered the Asian economic storm. The rehabilitation of the credit system, as elsewhere, is time-consuming and will dampen domestic investment. The political adjustments have not worked themselves out fully and could have economic impact in the future. It remains to be seen whether Malaysia, which endured the storm with its policy independence intact and with some reputation of success in policy innovation, will be forced to reconsider key elements of its development strategy.

In comparative terms, the Philippines has been spared the worst of the East Asian crisis. In fact, with the expected slowdown in the Singaporean economy, the Philippines will manage in 1999 to enjoy a higher growth rate than Singapore and will have the highest growth rate in the region, except for Vietnam. Unlike the other Southeast Asian economies, only investment demand slackened (by 6.1 per cent) in 1998 for the Philippines. Exports grew by 10 per cent, and consumption spending by 2.8 per cent (Table 3).

Domestically, however, the crisis has been felt painfully. The economy was only beginning to shake away the series of economic crises that had begun in 1981. The Philippines had been the only Asian economy in the last twenty years where the numbers of people below the poverty line had increased and needed continued growth to make a dent on the problem. The Philippines managed to attain GDP growth rates in the order of 5 per cent only in 1996 and 1997; while respectable, these growth rates missed the 8 per cent that had been anticipated in 1992, and were still well below rates that had been achieved by other ASEAN countries in the 1990s. The onset of the crisis knocked the economic growth rate to a barely positive 0.2 per cent in 1998.

The collapse of the peso along with the other regional currencies and the drastic raising of interest rates had the familiar feel of the country's previous balance of payments crises. The Ramos administration in its waning months instituted a contractionary response to the crisis, requiring all government departments to cut spending by 25 per cent. The Estrada administration essentially maintained the contractionary stance and has only in the beginning of 1999 begun to discuss reversing this.

In contrast to its Southeast Asian neighbours, the Philippines must live down a reputation of suffering from Latin American-style structural weaknesses in its savings rate and fiscal finances. Living with this reputation essentially means that the impact of rising fiscal deficits on the renewal of short-term credit lines, and consequently on currency instability, is more immediate and greater in magnitude than would be the case for other economies with higher savings rates and healthier fiscal balances. Before the crisis, the Philippines had achieved great success in placing its fiscal finances on a firmer footing. In the two years prior to the East Asian crisis, the country had an unprecedented near fiscal surplus. It is ironic that the growth slowdown has once again weakened the fiscal situation and Philippine policy-makers are caught in a bind.

As the country with the densest economic links with other economies in the region, it was only a matter of time before Singapore's economy would slow down in response to the economic difficulties of its trade and investment partners. Singapore's slowdown began in 1998 and will worsen in 1999; in 1998, economic growth was 1.5 per cent, down from 7.8 per cent in 1997. In 1999, the economy is expected to shrink by about 1 per cent. In 1998, exports declined by 12.7 per cent as demand from regional partners collapsed (while demand from the United States and European markets remained strong), investment grew by only 2.2 per cent, and private consumption grew by only 1 per cent.

Unemployment has doubled from its historical average to about 4 per cent. Job losses in the electronics sector, the financial sector and from the slump in the retail trade were the most conspicuous. The government has devoted some of its crisis response resources to expanding the job retraining programme.

The most immediate threat to the Singapore economy was collapsing external demand (which would have been difficult to overcome with domestic policies). The government's response has cautiously emphasized efforts to enhance international competitiveness and to ride out the regional recession. It has cut taxes and fees and reduced the size of mandated wage benefits. It has also accepted a moderate deterioration in public sector surplus. The Singapore dollar has been permitted to depreciate moderately in nominal terms but the emphasis has been on reducing domestic costs.

The next most serious threat to Singapore was the deterioration in bank portfolios, which were heavily exposed to the regional economies, especially Malaysia and Indonesia. The Singapore financial system has been well-regulated, perhaps even tending towards over-regulation. But even a well-supervised system cannot guarantee against widespread losses in adverse times. In the course of the crisis, special efforts to make public estimates of the non-performing loans helped to stave off private pessimism over the soundness of the financial system. Singapore continued to take small but significant steps to reduce regulatory oversight in the financial system to enhance Singapore's potential as an international financial centre.

Thailand's 8 per cent loss in GDP in 1998 was unprecedented and was due directly to a 27.8 per cent fall in investment spending and 10.5 per cent fall in consumption (Tables 2 and 3). Thailand's crisis triggered the East Asian crisis and embodied all the key elements in the other crisis countries: the abrupt reversal of capital flows to an economy with a financial sector weakened by an over-investment binge that had been fed by external borrowing. Its post-crisis experience also reflects many of the elements that are being retraced in the other crisis economies.

Thailand's initial IMF programme depended on a contractionary public policy which intensified the demand contraction emanating from the private sector. The size of the actual economic contraction in 1998 contrasted with the original IMF projection of positive growth. The severe investment contraction emanated from the loss of business confidence and the severe credit crunch in the financial sector. The credit crunch had basically two sources: the high interest rate policy that characterized the initial IMF-sponsored response to the crisis, and the melt-down in the financial sector itself (fed by the accompanying bankruptcies in the corporate sector).

At the onset of the crisis, Thailand moved to liberalize foreign participation in the financial sector. Heavy reliance on public-sector-led rehabilitation increased claims on domestic savings and crowded out investment required for recovery. As in other countries, foreign participation has raised concerns about the "fire sale" of Thai assets and the eventual loss of national control over the country's development destiny. The problem hinges on the proper valuation of distressed assets and the search for a balance between the interests of buyers who want to buy cheaply and restart operations, and private owners who want to wait for an improvement in the overall economy to raise their selling price. This means that the public sector will have to bear a heavier burden in sustaining demand, and will find itself with ownership control of many distressed companies.

Thailand's exports have remained relatively immune from the crisis. If anything, the more favourable exchange rate has boosted output from Thailand's competitive agricultural sector. Exports grew by 7.2 per cent in 1998.

Vietnam's economy, which grew by 8.8 per cent in 1997, decelerated significantly to a growth of 3.5 per cent in 1998 (Table 2). The same lower growth rate is expected in 1999. Vietnam devalued its currency moderately in 1998. More critical has been the loss of interest on the part of foreign investors, which is partly due to the regional crisis but also has much to do with increasing investor frustration at bureaucratic and social obstacles to expanding investment.

The other Southeast Asian economies also experienced significant difficulties in 1998. The fall in world oil prices, and the collapse of Amedeo, a major conglomerate owned by a brother of the Sultan — both related at least indirectly to the Asian crisis — ruffled the traditional calm of petroleum-rich Brunei. Falling demand for their exports and the sudden collapse of investment flows, especially from the region, inflicted plummeting currency values and output growth in the region's transitional economies — Cambodia, Laos, and Myanmar.

Debating Economic Development

The economic crisis started an extensive discussion about development strategy in Southeast Asia, whose key economies had been deemed by the World Bank as "miracle economies" in their development efforts. The experience of the crisis raises the following issues for these economies.

External Openness

Openness to the external economy had been touted as a key ingredient in the past economic success of the Southeast Asian economies. They have steadily increased their share of world trade and have also increased their share of trade with each other. Because investors brought their access to the world market with them, this openness to foreign investment played a key role in winning international markets. Foreign investors also brought with them technology, information about international market trends, and modern managerial practices.

Southeast Asia's success in this type of openness had provided the region with the confidence to liberalize imports more quickly and to remove restrictions on a whole range of types of capital inflows. This latter liberalization effectively permitted foreign investors to lend domestically in more diverse ways, including purchasing domestic bonds, buying shares of equity, and simply opening fixed deposit accounts in local banks.

The East Asian crisis is, therefore, a crisis among successful globalizers and the question of drawing the appropriate lessons arises. This, however, depends very much on one's analysis of the causes of the crisis.

Trade openness had a limited role in sparking the capital withdrawals that set off the crisis in 1997. Because of a cyclical downturn in the electronics industry and the increasing competitiveness of China, many Southeast Asian economies did experience a significant downturn in exports in 1996. But the current account deficits that might have justified a widespread fall in currency values, were not uniform among the Southeast Asian economies and in the case of Malaysia, even though large, the deficits were showing a downward trend.

Trade openness is certainly more demanding with regard to exchange rate management in protecting a country's competitiveness. The region's currencies tended to be very strong prior to the crisis because of the enormous offers of capital from external sources and high domestic interest rates. This suggests that sustainable trade openness requires greater caution with capital inflows as these inflows restrict the scope of domestic authorities to reconcile exchange rate outcomes to real sector and development objectives, if the latter objectives are indeed paramount.[3] The alternative would be to accept that openness to all types of capital inflows is consistent only with fully flexible exchange rates. The exchange rate would then have little role to play in real sector or current account objectives.

The effect of increased intra-regional trade has meant that both demand contractions and currency collapses of individual economies will have immediate regional implications. The crisis solicits the prompt recognition that economic openness also means greater regional interdependence and the need for institutions that facilitate regional co-operation in macroeconomic management. Weaknesses and policy mistakes in individual economies will affect other economies in the region, even if they do not partake of the same weaknesses. Imperfections in international capital markets should also encourage the search for coordinated responses in crisis situations.

In a series of ASEAN meetings after the crisis member countries have clearly stated their intention to maintain open trade regimes and to persevere in efforts to remove trade barriers. In the area of international finance, the ASEAN finance ministers have called for a regional surveillance and monitoring mechanism to be located in the ASEAN Secretariat. The initial work on the proposal is being carried out at the Asian Development Bank.

Asian Governance

One of the touted advantages of the East Asian approach to development had been the close coordination between business and government. The crisis has exposed innumerable examples of loan projects that partook of collusion and corruption. Such stories have also characterized other systemic episodes of financial collapse, such as the savings-and-loan association in the United States and the banking failures in the Scandanavian economies in the late 1980s and early 1990s.

Domestic political rhetoric increasingly highlight objections to "corruption, collusion, and nepotism". Economic reform programmes, almost all of which are sponsored by some international agency, are inspired by the objectives of instituting transparency and accountability in economic decision-making. The crisis has brought conflicts over these issues into the open and the international community into the equation.

These modernizing pressures had been well in train in the Southeast Asian economies before the crisis, impelled in no small part by the steady rise in per capita incomes. It is increasingly becoming a matter of conventional wisdom to say that these safeguards and norms should have been instituted even before the countries permitted the private sector access to the practically unlimited capital resources from overseas.

Structural reform programmes and political change can accelerate the introduction of these norms into the legal and administrative rules. But it is only the actual practice of these norms that will identify which of these modern, mostly imported, practices can actually prevent the kinds of abuses that occurred before the crisis, and how they can be adapted to Southeast Asian societies. Family-dominated business groups will not disappear overnight, and took a long time to lose their influence in Western capitalist economies. The emergence of genuinely independent judiciaries, effective media oversight, and vibrant opposition parties cannot be achieved through legislation. It took the West at least a century to establish relatively reliable bankruptcy procedures and traditions, and even in the West these procedures are severely tested in episodes of large failures.

There is also the danger that the Asian economies will lose some of the advantages in development decision-making that they used to enjoy before the crisis if the reforms are carried out slavishly to Western norms. Relocating responsibility from the family to market responsibility, or from public regulation to market discipline, is not advantageous in those instances where the market is susceptible to speculative bubbles and instability, and where markets are dominated by a few private participants. Financial markets are a case in point. In Europe, the most successful transition from a planned economy to a market economy has been secured by countries that have implemented controlled privatization and resisted a drastic disintegration of state capacity.

Sources of Growth

Throughout most of the period of its development success, the Southeast Asian economies had relied distinctly on certain sources of growth. Capturing export markets had always been a priority, and, therefore, export demand had traditionally been an indispensable source of growth and a key determinant of short-term economic performance. Investment as a means to improve productivity and achieve structural transformation had also been emphasized. This had been sustained by relatively high savings rates in most of the Southeast Asian economies, and society in turn supported policies in favour of higher savings rates.

In the wake of the crisis, there are indications that the emphases on export and investment demand will be moderated, and there are considerations that suggest that perhaps Southeast Asian economies might find such a development to their own advantage. The moderating pressures emanate from the democratizing tendencies in most of the Southeast Asian societies and from the kinds of structural changes that are occurring as a result of the East Asian crisis.

The export drive, while it pulled a significant portion of the population out of poverty, had tended to be insensitive to issues of labour and civil rights and environmental sustainability. The social pressures that the crisis has unleashed in domestic political life will make it more difficult to use export competitiveness as the reason for ignoring these concerns. Paying greater attention to these issues is not necessarily a recipe for the loss of export competitiveness. Steady productivity growth and moving up the technological ladder are more decisive in the medium-term, especially with the proliferation of competitors in the world market. While it will require much wisdom and forebearance among domestic parties, changes such as enhanced civil and labour rights, more control over local resources by local communities, and protecting future income earning ability by protecting the environment, may actually sustain productivity growth.

The investment drive has raised questions about government encouragement and subsidy for development projects, and the ongoing reform processes will likely reduce government capacities in this regard in the future. The crisis has exposed numerous sectors where "over-investment" in productive capacity has occurred, whether or not impelled by government subsidy or private-sector speculation. It also indicates that financial-savings-driven growth in the early 1990s was poured disproportionately into unsustainable property development, underwritten by rising collateral values.

The investment drive has also tended to emphasize investment in physical and financial assets, to the relative neglect of human investment, which is more difficult to finance from domestic savings, and a significant portion of which tends to be counted as consumption expenditure. In the years immediately preceding the crisis, high savings rates in Southeast Asia were invested in the region and augmented by foreign savings. As the quality of these investment projects slid, the falling marginal efficiency of investment schedule in the context of high domestic investment rates, and the viability of the domestic credit system foundered.

To avoid poor domestic investments in the future, the Southeast Asian economies will need to invest more of their high domestic savings externally. It is also natural to suggest that Southeast Asian countries should permit faster consumption growth, encourage investment in education, and improve the living standards of the poorer members of society. This will also imply greater reliance on domestic, as opposed to export, demand to propel growth.

Conclusion

The next few years promise to be singularly challenging ones for the economies of Southeast Asia. Economic recovery will install a changed economic landscape and must be pursued in the context of possibly profound political change. Managing the recovery process in the interest of long-term development will severely test the wisdom and national cohesion of the societies in Southeast Asia.

It remains to be seen whether the Southeast Asian economies can recover the same type of dynamic growth that moved the rest of the world to tag them as "miracle economies". The latter might also be moved to take a more nuanced view of the nature of the Asian miracle in Southeast Asia. Before 1992 or thereabouts, the region's key economies grew based on steady and solid achievements in progressive trade integration into the world economy. In the years immediately leading to the crisis, these economies relied too heavily on credit expansion fed by asset price inflation and foreign borrowing. The dynamic of the last few years proved unsustainable. Rehabilitating the financial sector is necessary to restore growth, and this arduous task is now under way. Recovering the older, more sustainable dynamic is necessary to restore the Asian miracle.

Notes

1. Michael Howell, "Asia's 'Victorian' Financial Crisis" (Paper presented at the Conference on the East Asian Economic Crisis, Institute for Development Studies at the University of Sussex, 13–14 July 1998), p. 59.
2. Manuel F. Montes, and Vladimir V. Popov, *The Asian Crisis Turns Global* (Singapore: Institute of Southeast Asian Studies, 1999), p. 3.
3. Manuel F. Montes, *The Currency Crisis in Southeast Asia (Updated Edition)* (Singapore: Institute of Southeast Asian Studies, 1998), pp. 20–21.

SOUTHEAST ASIA IN 1999
A False Dawn?

Daljit Singh

If 1998 was the year of economic crisis, 1999 was the year of recovery. The pervasive gloom of 1998 receded somewhat, but Southeast Asia still, at best, presented a mixed picture. Economic recovery among the older members of the Association of Southeast Asian Nations (ASEAN) generated a palpable sense of optimism. Even Indonesia, with its battered economy, could inspire some hope after it held a relatively peaceful and fair parliamentary election, followed by a presidential election which resulted in the establishment of a democratic government with the moral and political legitimacy to govern. But there was also tragedy, followed by humanitarian intervention, in East Timor and, for Indonesia, enormous uncertainties remained. Elsewhere, the reforms needed to deal with the weaknesses in state and corporate governance which the crisis had highlighted were only partially addressed, raising doubts about the sustainability of the recoveries. Conditions in Laos, Myanmar, and Vietnam were worse than in 1998. The durability of the new democracy in Indonesia was not assured, while in the rest of Southeast Asia, progress towards more tolerant, enlightened, and democratic societies was patchy, mixed with stasis, even regression.

ASEAN sought to overcome a crisis of credibility. The broader Asia-Pacific strategic environment remained relatively benign. There were, however, more signs of Sino-American competition. China's claims and posture in the South China Sea remained a troubling long-term strategic lever against Southeast Asia.

The Association of Southeast Asian Nations

A Question of Credibility

ASEAN has become a feeble managing vehicle [of the Southeast Asian regional

---

Reprinted in abridged format from Daljit Singh, ed., *Southeast Asian Affairs 2000* (Singapore: Institute of Southeast Asian Studies, 2000), pp. 3–24. At the time of original publication, Daljit Singh was a Senior Research Fellow at the Institute of Southeast Asian Studies, Singapore.

order] ... ASEAN has been diminished in international standing and, in important respects, is not the same entity that was set up in 1967 based on a set of common understandings about reconciliation among governments of convergent political outlooks. (Michael Leifer)[1]

ASEAN has overextended itself — with members so vastly different as Myanmar and Singapore it has lost credibility, and its ability to provide any semblance of security across maritime Southeast Asia has been undermined. (Paul Dibb)[2]

ASEAN's inability to deal with the challenges posed by intransigent regimes in Myanmar and Cambodia was mirrored by its ineffectiveness in dealing with transnational issues ... ASEAN disarray throughout the year was the product of many factors ... (Carlyle A. Thayer)[3]

The above are but three examples of sceptical assessments of ASEAN. Regional governments, or at least some of them, did acknowledge that the Association had a credibility problem. At the ASEAN Ministerial Meeting (AMM) in Singapore in July, Prime Minister Goh Chok Tong stated:

> ... whether or not criticisms that have been levelled at ASEAN are deserved, they exist. This is a fact we must deal with, because perceptions, even inaccurate perceptions, can define political reality.

Foreign Minister Jayakumar said: "... the essential challenge that ASEAN faces is one of credibility. But I can state with confidence that we have taken a firm step forward in beginning a process of renewal." Earlier, at the Hanoi summit in December 1998, Thai Prime Minister Chuan Leekpai had observed that the crisis had "raised doubts and questions about whether ASEAN can regain its vibrancy and vitality. Some have gone so far as to write us off", while Malaysian Prime Minister Mahathir had noted that the crisis had "created the impression of an ASEAN in disarray".

Critics have pointed to a number of events or ASEAN's response to them which diminished ASEAN's credibility. They include the admission of Myanmar into the Association in 1996; the haze over Indonesia, Malaysia, Brunei, and Singapore in 1997 caused by fires in Indonesia; Hun Sen's coup in Cambodia in 1997 which overturned the power-sharing arrangements in the coalition government sanctioned earlier by the United Nations Transitional Authority in Cambodia (UNTAC); the regional economic crisis; the deterioration of bilateral relations between some ASEAN member countries in 1998; and developments in East Timor in 1999.

However, a blanket censure of ASEAN's behaviour in relation to these developments would be unfair because ASEAN's performance was in fact a mixed one. It would have been unrealistic, for instance, to expect ASEAN to prevent or resolve the regional economic crisis. It was caused by a combination of external factors like massive short-term capital flows and domestic weaknesses in individual ASEAN countries, in relation to both of which there was little that ASEAN as an organization could do. As ASEAN Secretary-General Rudolfo Severino has said, blaming ASEAN for failure to deal with the crisis is "something akin to blaming the OAS [Organization of American States] for the financial crisis in Mexico some years ago, or for the forest fires in Brazil, or the OAU [Organization of African Unity] for Africa's recent sorrows".[4] Yet, just as in the past the economic success of its members had boosted ASEAN's credibility, now the economic crisis, by exposing the many shortcomings in state and corporate governance, hurt the Association's image. It also weakened ASEAN by weakening its member countries, especially Indonesia which had been regarded as "the first among equals" in the Association.

On the haze and on Cambodia, ASEAN did more than what it is credited for. The solution to the regional haze problem depended very much on Indonesia's capacity and willingness to stop the clearance of plantation and forest land by burning. Still, ASEAN had a Co-operation Plan on Transboundary Pollution since 1995. The 1997 haze led to much more frequent consultations on measures to address the problem. In frank discussions, officials have touched on sensitive areas like Indonesia's land and forestry use policies.

In response to the 1997 coup in Cambodia engineered by Hun Sen, ASEAN postponed Cambodia's admission into the Association, originally scheduled for July 1997, and established a task force of three ASEAN foreign ministers to help achieve a settlement of the problem. ASEAN urged Hun Sen to return to the power-sharing arrangements stipulated under the 1991 Paris Accords and the ASEAN Post-Ministerial Conference (PMC) supported ASEAN's position. Thus, although Japan played an important role, ASEAN was pro-active in seeking a solution.

ASEAN's credibility in the West and among civil society groups in ASEAN countries was undoubtedly affected by the admission of Myanmar into the Association in 1996. ASEAN may have underestimated how this event would affect perceptions of the Association, especially when it was followed in quick order by the economic crisis and its political fall-out, both of which weakened ASEAN. By 1999, ASEAN's policy of "constructive engagement" with Yangon had not produced any significant result. The coming of the economic crisis seemed to make the prospect of change even more remote. It made the generals in Myanmar feel more insecure because of the significant indirect economic impact of the crisis on Myanmar and the dark political lessons they would have likely drawn from the fate of the Soeharto regime.

The importance of bilateral relations between ASEAN members for the Association's strength and credibility tended to be obscured by bigger and more dramatic events like the regional crisis. Yet in 1998 their deterioration between several states was as important a factor as any other in weakening ASEAN and contributing to an impression of disarray. The difficulties in bilateral relations were brought about partly by the political aftershocks of the Asian crisis. Indonesian President Habibie's and Philippine President Estrada's support for former Deputy Prime Minister Anwar Ibrahim soured these two countries' relations with Malaysia. A number of issues in Singapore-Malaysia relations in 1998 brought the relationship to a low point not seen for many years. They included the relocation of Malaysian CIQ (Customs, Immigration, and Quarantine) facilities in Singapore for railway services, alleged violations of Malaysian airspace by Singapore military aircraft and the publication of Senior Minister Lee's memoirs. Relations between Singapore and the Habibie administration in Jakarta were also testy.

In 1999, bilateral relations between the older members improved from the lows of 1998, but they remained problematic. The CLOB (Central Limit Order Book) International issue continued to contribute to Singapore-Malaysia tensions while other outstanding issues like the relocation of Malaysian CIQ facilities remained unresolved. Relations between Malaysia and the Philippines were adversely affected again by Malaysia's occupation of Investigator Shoal in the Spratlys, also claimed by the Philippines. Myanmar-Thailand relations deteriorated seriously over the hostage crisis involving the Myanmar embassy in Bangkok.

Finally, ASEAN could not have wagered for a more difficult test for its principle of non-intervention in the internal affairs of a member state than the unleashing of death and destruction in East Timor by Indonesia-backed militias.[5] Indonesia's actions in East Timor had always been a sensitive matter in ASEAN, and whatever each country privately felt about the events of 1999, it proved difficult, if not impossible, at least initially, for ASEAN as an organization or for individual members to express public outrage or to urge humanitarian intervention (though some civil society groups did). After Indonesia yielded to international pressure for humanitarian intervention, Philippines, Thailand, Singapore, and Malaysia contributed to the Australian-led International Force for East Timor (INTERFET) and later to the U.N. Transitional Authority in East Timor (UNTAET). ASEAN's image was not helped by Dr Mahathir's public remarks questioning the validity of the referendum in East Timor well after its outcome.

"Enhanced Interaction"

The principle of non-intervention became a focus of some attention when Thai Foreign Minister Surin Pitsuwan said in an address in June 1998 that ASEAN countries should be prepared to "intervene" in domestic affairs "in the form of peer pressure or friendly advice, when a matter of domestic concern poses a threat to regional stability".[6] He dubbed this "constructive intervention". However, a month later, at the AMM in Singapore, to remove the impression that he was suggesting a modification of the principle of non-intervention, he renamed the idea "flexible engagement". In the same speech he made it clear that ASEAN must adhere to the principle of non-intervention but at the same time find a way to deal with new problems and challenges which damage ASEAN's credibility if left unaddressed: "The principle of non-intervention is not the real issue ... the real issue is how we can work together in dealing with the new challenges of a new millennium." "Flexible engagement" was discussed at the 1998 AMM in Manila. It met opposition from most members, with only the Philippines siding Thailand. The international media publicity to this division added to the impression of an ASEAN in disarray.

However, the Meeting decided, as a compromise, to have "enhanced interaction" in the future. "Enhanced interaction" was not defined, but presumably it meant more frank and frequent exchanges of views in private. It was tried at the next Ministerial Meeting in Singapore in July 1999, at the "Sentosa Retreat", out of sight of the media. The Joint Communiqué at the end of the AMM stated that at the Retreat the foreign ministers held "frank and wide-ranging discussions" and described the Retreat as "part of a continuous process of serious re-examination of the longer term issues facing ASEAN". The chairman of the meeting, Singapore Foreign Minister

S. Jayakumar, described the session as "heart-to-heart brainstorming". He added:

> I have never come across discussions with such candour. The Foreign Ministers spoke of views which they told me they would not have expressed, if not for the retreat.[7]

Subjects discussed ranged from civil society, human rights, democracy, to the future of ASEAN and of the ARF. A frank exchange of views in private at annual retreats on domestic issues which can have adverse impact on neighbours or on the credibility of ASEAN would constitute progress in the quality of ASEAN discussions, but critics doubted it would have any effect on policies.

All members regard the retention of the principle of non-intervention as essential. What is at issue is the need for some adjustments to take account of changed circumstances. Non-intervention has after all been a governing principle in relations between states since Westphalia in the seventeenth century. However, it has been under review internationally in recent years so that it can be made relevant to changes in international society.

Yet it would be wrong to assume that ASEAN countries have never at all "interfered" in each other's affairs. Various instances can be cited of such "intervention" in the past — leaders, usually in private, took up domestic issues in other member countries, especially when such issues could have adverse effects on neighbours or on the region, and there have also been attempts to mediate or mitigate strained bilateral relations between members.[8] Such "interventions", made in the "ASEAN Way" have sometimes been successful. On the other hand, there is no way of compelling a country to change its behaviour if it does not want to. There is no prior political price for membership of the Association nor political or economic sanctions for unacceptable behaviour.

———

One effect of the economic crisis was a keener appreciation among policy élites of ASEAN member states, or at least of those member states that have been the principal drivers of the Association, of ASEAN's limitations. The crisis had also demonstrated that the IMF, based in Washington, did not react as fast in dealing with the Asian crisis as it did with the Mexican crisis in 1994. One reason for this was that the latter impinged much more directly and urgently on the national interests of the United States than the Thai crisis of July 1997 did. Yet a Japanese-ASEAN proposal made in September 1997 for an Asian Monetary Fund which could respond more speedily, and with more capital, to Asian crises was torpedoed by the United States. Furthermore, any reform of the international financial system, including some monitoring of the activities of hedge funds, a topic which aroused much favourable interest in Southeast Asia in the wake of the crisis, was seen to be unlikely to be implemented because it was not in the interests of the leading Western powers, especially the United States, to do so.

ASEAN+3

It was such realities that gave push to the idea of an East Asian regionalism based upon the ASEAN+3 forum which first met at the second ASEAN Informal Summit in Kuala Lumpur in 1997 soon after the financial cyclone hit the region, although it had already constituted the Asian half (but without Cambodia, Myanmar, and Laos) of the ASEM process from a few years earlier.

If ASEAN by itself was not seen as having the necessary critical mass to achieve better financial and economic security in a world of huge daily transcontinental flows of speculative funds, why not team up with the larger economies of Northeast Asia? East Asian regionalism, if one went by the actions and rhetoric of its proponents, was more than just an idea by 1999. ASEAN Secretary-General Rudolf C. Severino described the third ASEAN+3 summit in Manila in late November 1999 as "part of a general convergence of purpose in East Asia, a process that has been building up". He went on to say:

> ... the developing forum may serve to diffuse any potential rivalries among the stronger countries of East Asia ... synergies in the economies may strengthen the economic muscle of the region. Closer financial cooperation ... could give the region a greater voice in international financial decisions that is not possible for ASEAN alone.[9]

There was talk of expanding AFTA to an East Asian Free Trade Area to be established through a bilateral building block approach, for example, a Japan–South Korea free trade area, a Japan-Singapore one, and so forth.[10]

The finance ministers of the thirteen countries met for the first time in Manila in April 1999. Their deputies and heads of central banks had already been meeting to discuss co-operation in relation to economic recovery and prevention of future crises and to develop Asia's thinking on the reform of the international financial system. Just before the summit in Manila, senior officials of the thirteen countries met for the first time, and this was expected to be repeated at future summits. Foreign ministers were to meet in the margins of the ASEAN-PMC meetings in Bangkok in the year 2000 to review progress in the implementation of the Joint Statement on East Asia Co-operation issued at the end of the ASEAN+3 meeting in Manila. And trade ministers of the ten East Asian countries were to meet for consultations in May 2000 in Myanmar, immediately following the annual retreat of the ASEAN economic ministers. An East Asian Vision Group, headed by former South Korean Foreign Minister Han Sung Joo, will present its recommendations on East Asian co-operation at the 7th ASEAN Summit in Brunei in 2001.

A joint statement on East Asia Co-operation issued at the Manila Summit mentions co-operation not just in economic and social fields but also in "the political-security area" in relation to which the heads of state/government agreed to "continuing dialogue, coordination, and cooperation to increase mutual understanding and trust towards forging lasting peace and stability in East Asia". The leaders also agreed to "intensify coordination and cooperation" in various international and regional fora such as the United Nations, the World Trade Organization (WTO), APEC, ASEM, and the ARF as well as in regional and international financial institutions.

Elections and Political Change

If assessed by the quality of governance, institution-building, and management of political change, Southeast Asia presented at best a mixed picture in 1999. And all the states were under challenge to varying degrees by forces unleashed by the economic crisis, the dynamics of globalization, or because of failure to carry out domestic reforms.

The Older ASEAN Members

Political change came to Indonesia in 1998–99, almost with a vengeance, after over thirty years of the authoritarian Soeharto regime. In 1999 the country at last had a democratically elected government which enjoyed the support of the main political groups. However, the durability of Southeast Asia's newest democracy remained a question mark.

The new government under President Abdurrahman Wahid faced enormous economic and political problems, including the challenge of bringing a wayward military under civilian control. And, given the fact that the President had had two strokes before, his health was a matter of serious concern. His passage from the political scene is likely to bring to power his vice-president who may not enjoy the confidence of the major forces across the country's political and religious divide.

If 1999 showed a fragile democracy in Indonesia struggling painfully to build the institutions for better governance, in Malaysia, which had been blessed with sounder institutional moorings and capacity, there was a less dramatic but unmistakeable deterioration of some important institutions,[11] though the economy did show a strong turn around. There was a sense of coming political change, but the confrontations spawning it still had to run their course. That a historical transformation of the political landscape could be taking place seemed confirmed by the general elections of November 1999 in which the United Malays National Organisation (UMNO), the core political force of the Barisan Nasional ruling coalition, saw significant erosion of its support among ethnic Malays, increasing numbers of whom voted for the opposition Barisan Alternatif (BA), particularly Islamic party PAS (Parti Islam SeMalaysia). It was not clear at the end of 1999 whether the final denouement would lead to greater Islamicization, a healthy two-(coalition) party system, or a return to status quo ante under a revitalized UMNO and National Front.

In the general election, the Barisan Nasional still won a comfortable two-thirds majority in parliament. Yet the desertion by Malay voters of the party which has symbolized Malay political power since independence in 1957 was highly significant, because it could threaten the legitimacy of UMNO as the guardian of Malay political power. The causes of UMNO's decline and PAS' resurgence were not difficult to divine: a perception among many Malays that Anwar Ibrahim's treatment at the hands of the authorities has been unfair and cruel, and the effectiveness of the Islamic party's message in the northern states that in contrast to UMNO it stood for a clean, non-corrupt government.

A suitable *political* response was needed from the top UMNO leaders to these challenges. Yet it was difficult to see it coming, given the way Malaysia Inc. has been constructed over the past two decades and given the sad spectacle of Dr Mahathir and Anwar Ibrahim each finding himself in a political box after burning all bridges with the other. Rather, the indications at the end of 1999 were that administrative and repressive means would be used to thwart the BA and PAS. These carry the risk of being counterproductive in the long run.

Emerging slowly from the economic crisis, Thailand was struggling to put in place the necessary reforms that would improve state and corporate governance whose weaknesses had been shown up by the economic crisis. Economic and political reforms have moved in tandem. New economic legislation to address economic problems — passed or under debate — covered areas such as bankruptcy, competition policy, money laundering, reform of financial institutions, privatization, and educational reform. On the political side implementation of the new (1997) reform constitution and acts such as the Official Information Act (1997) led to greater transparency and more public political participation. Entrenched vested interests were sometimes able to resist change, but overall the Chuan government and an increasingly strong civil society were able to maintain the reform momentum.

In the Philippines, the Estrada administration compared increasingly unfavourably with its predecessor, the Ramos administration, because of poor judgement in the selection of people to key advisory positions to the President, and ill-considered snap decisions springing more from emotion than reason. The consequential decline in credibility weakened the political clout to push ahead with the reforms started by his predecessor, contributing to a sense of stagnation, if not backsliding. Although the Philippines was not seriously affected by the Asian crisis, post-crisis growth is not as robust as that of its neighbours. The economy grew by 3.2 per cent in 1999 after declining 0.5 per cent in 1998. The Asian Development Bank projects a growth of 3.8 per cent for 2000.

Indochina and Myanmar

Vietnam, Myanmar, and Laos, fearful of change, were either marking time or sliding back. In Vietnam the regime continued to be in a survivalist mode. Growth rates were down to less than half of what they were a few years ago. A new phase of bold reforms, a *doi moi* II, was overdue in order to galvanize the economy to faster growth and more efficiency but was unlikely to be coming any time soon. A lack of consensus within the Communist Party, the fear of the political consequences of change, and genuine confusion over how and which way to move after seeing the effects of the Asian crisis on the more open economies, seem to have sapped the desire for reforms of the order needed. It is left to be seen if the Ninth Party Congress, presently scheduled for 2001, will result in any bold decisions.

The economic recovery in the older ASEAN member states may not help Vietnam as much as it hopes. It will not be status quo ante. For one thing, the other regional countries, more directly affected by the Asian crisis, have undertaken reforms and are likely to be more attractive destinations for foreign investments at a time when there has been increasing disenchantment with Vietnam for its bureaucratic obstacle course and other disincentives. Also, the significant slowdown in growth rates in Vietnam has not been due wholly to the indirect effects of the Asian crisis; it has also been the result of diminishing returns from the first phase of reforms in the late 1980s and early 1990s.

There are about 2 million new entrants to the work-force each year and a population growth rate of about 2 per cent. In terms of average national per capita income growth, Vietnam needs an economic growth rate of 2 per cent to just stand still. Given the World Bank's estimates of GDP growth of 3.5 per cent for 2000 and 3 per cent for 2001, it will do only slightly better.

(It receives over US$2 billion in external aid and about US$3 billion in remittances from Vietnamese living or working abroad). But this would be a far cry from the optimism the country inspired in the early 1990s as the next Asian tiger.

In Myanmar the political stasis seemed set to continue. Three years after admission into ASEAN, there was no sign of political evolution. The continuing deterioration of the economy is likely to make the regime more insecure and repressive. An indication of how far Myanmar continues to fall behind the rest of the region is the condition of higher education. Universities are closed down if and when there is student unrest. They were closed in 1996 and were beginning to be slowly reopened only in 1999. About 100,000 students who did not take their final examinations in 1996 were still waiting to do so. Another 300,000 to 400,000 who had passed their entrance examinations are waiting to enter the universities.

In Laos a combination of mismanagement and severe effects of the Asian crisis has sent the economy reeling. Inflation is 140 per cent a year and over the two years 1998 and 1999 its currency, the kip, has fallen 900 per cent against the U.S. dollar.[12] The economic meltdown has produced inevitable strains on the small urban population in an otherwise rural country with the majority of people living on subsistence agriculture. On 26 October 1999 there was a small demonstration of students and teachers calling for freedom of expression, multi-party democracy, and release of political prisoners, which was quickly squelched by the security police and many of those involved arrested. There has been increased militarization of the regime, with seven of the eight politburo members now military men.

Out of the four new members of ASEAN, Cambodia was the only one where the situation was better in 1999, compared with 1998 and the years before. This was due to the achievement, at last, of relative political stability because of the accommodation between Hun Sen and Prince Ranariddh (and the consequent emergence of Hun Sen as the undisputed leader) and the end of the long-drawn Khmer Rouge insurgency. With political stability and pursuit of economic reforms, the economy was set to stabilize and improve. However, the country was starting from a very low base and still faces massive problems of poverty, environmental degradation, and an HIV (human immunodeficiency virus) epidemic.

Notes

1. Michael Leifer, *Political and Security Outlook for Southeast Asia*, Trends in Southeast Asia series no. 2 (Singapore: Institute of Southeast Asian Studies, January 2000).
2. Paul Dibb, "Asia's Insecurity", *Survival*, Autumn 1999.
3. Carlyle Thayer, "Southeast Asia: Challenge to Unity and Regime Legitimacy", in *Southeast Asian Affairs 1999* (Singapore: Institute of Southeast Asian Studies, 1999).
4. Rudolfo Severino, Secretary-General of ASEAN, "Asia Policy Lecture: What ASEAN Is and What It Stands For" (Speech given at the Research Institute for Asia and the Pacific, University of Sydney, Australia, 22 October 1998).
5. Any assessment of ASEAN must of course take into account the limitations which the Association originally set for itself. These were that ASEAN would not be a supranational organization and that members would refrain from interference

in each other's internal affairs. Were it not for these preconditions, ASEAN would not have been set up in the first place nor achieved the progress it subsequently made, given the history of conflict and suspicion among the original five members. Thirty years on, the four new members on the mainland of Southeast Asia found it easy to join the organization precisely because of these principles. The critics of ASEAN, however, would contend that whatever its built-in limitations, the international community would expect a regional organization, especially one like ASEAN which has been touted as the most successful example of regionalism in the Third World, to do more to manage or mitigate crises in its own backyard.

6. Surin Pitsuwan, "Thailand's Foreign Policy during the Economic and Social Crisis" (Paper presented at a seminar in the Faculty of Political Science, Thammasat University, 12 June 1998).
7. *Sunday Times* (Singapore), 25 July 1999.
8. For a more detailed examination, see John Funston, *ASEAN and the Principle of Non-Intervention — Practice and Prospects*, Trends in Southeast Asia no. 5 (Singapore: Institute of Southeast Asian Studies, 2000).
9. *Far Eastern Economic Review*, 23 December 1999, p. 27.
10. Tommy Koh, Executive Director of the Asia-Europe Foundation in Singapore, "Progress toward an East Asian Free Trade Area", *International Herald Tribune*, 14 December 1999, p. 8.
11. See Khoo Boo Teik, "Unfinished Crises: Malaysian Politics in 1999", in this volume.
12. *Asiaweek*, 24 December 1999.

EAST TIMOR'S FUTURE
Southeast Asian or South Pacific?[1]

Hal Hill

Introduction

Following on from the tragic events of September 1999, East Timor will shortly become the world's newest nation. Presumably, in time it will also become a member of the Association of Southeast Asian Nations (ASEAN). As it charts its way forward, one of the key challenges it faces will be to define its international economic orientation. Indonesia and Australia will always be East Timor's major trading partners and diplomatic focus, in addition to its membership of the Portuguese-speaking world.

However, there is a broader question of whether its world-view, and its political, economic and social institutions, will be predominantly "Southeast Asian" or "South Pacific". This is meant not simply in a geographic sense, since a case could be made for the fact that it belongs to either region. Nor is it addressing the issue of whether an independent East Timor will join both ASEAN and the Pacific Islands Forum (or whether it might even be forced to choose between them). Rather, it is the more fundamental question of whether its economic performance will more closely resemble that of its neighbours to its northwest or east. That is, will it be an outward-looking, growing and increasingly prosperous country, or a mendicant, aid-dependent state, with a bloated public sector and stagnant living standards. The latter, unfortunately, characterizes many of the Pacific Islands.[2]

In many respects, after the immediate task of rehabilitation is completed, East Timor will resemble a typical Pacific Island economy, albeit at the poorest end

---

Reprinted from Daljit Singh and Anthony Smith, eds., *Southeast Asian Affairs 2001* (Singapore: Institute of Southeast Asian Studies, 2001), pp. 82–92. At the time of original publication, Hal Hill was Professor in the Division of Economics, Research School of Pacific and Asian Studies, The Australian National University.

of the spectrum. It will be a large aid recipient, dependent also on remittances. Its institutions are weak, and its human capital resources rather limited. It is small, both in a geographic and a demographic sense, and rather isolated.

With its history of neglect and oppression, it is difficult to be optimistic about the future. The challenges might appear insuperable. Much of its physical infrastructure is shattered, while the supply of public utilities is most inadequate.

More than 80,000 of its people are still located in squalid refugee camps across the border in West Timor, and in other parts of Indonesia. It does not possess a constitution, a political system, or a functioning bureaucracy. Much of its commercial expertise has fled the country — for example, its small ethnic Chinese community in 1975–76, and the Bugis traders from South Sulawesi in 1999. Many of its teachers and senior civil servants returned hastily to Indonesia in the second half of 1999, never to return. More than half the urban population does not have regular employment. The 22 per cent of the population who voted for autonomy (that is, against independence) still harbour deep resentment and fear. Some of these people, the so-called militia in particular, combined with disaffected elements of the Indonesian armed forces, threaten to disrupt peace and order.

However, there are some rays of hope. Unlike Portugal's former colonies in Africa, there are at least some prospects for stability and peace, both internal and external. Although pressures will emerge as political activity intensifies in the run-up to the inaugural general election (especially with more than ten political parties across the political spectrum vying for votes), the key elements of the East Timorese leadership appear to be reasonably united around the three major figures associated with the achievement of independence. They are its likely inaugural president, Xanana Gusmaõ, a long-time guerrilla leader and head of the National Council for Timorese Resistance (CNRT); the likely prime minister and foreign minister, José Ramos Horta, the movement's principal international spokesman for the past quarter century; and the spiritual leader and head of the Catholic Church (East Timor is about 95 per cent Catholic), Bishop Carlos Belo. Notwithstanding widespread bitterness in Indonesia, the administration of Abdurrahman Wahid, which came to power two months after the referendum and signalled a major break with the Soeharto era, has indicated a desire to develop a co-operative relationship with the new nation. Owing to its tragic history, the world is well disposed towards East Timor, and in consequence, international aid flows are large. As a new nation, there is much to learn from the mistakes of others in the realm of economic policy and public administration. Moreover, unlike other countries obtaining their independence in the wake of bitter conflict, East Timor's recent economic history and its resource base are fairly well documented. Finally, there is a substantial East Timorese diaspora abroad, many of whom have much to offer by way of expertise and investment.

The country is also not without commercial potential. A mini resource boom is in prospect, offering considerable medium-term revenue flows. Oil and gas could loom very large, and within a decade government revenues could be equivalent to as much as 50 per cent of current gross domestic product (GDP). The exact magnitude of these revenues will depend on negotiations with Australia concerning the demarcation of the Timor Gap, international oil prices, the Timorese's oil tax regime, and future explorations. Coffee also has good prospects, with annual exports of US$50 million or more considered feasible. The East Timor product commands a price premium in international markets, owing to its quality and the fact that it is certified to be free of pesticides. Already the U.S. coffee chain, Starbucks, features East Timorese coffee in some of its outlets. Tourism is another sector of great potential. East Timor is a region of great scenic beauty and superb beaches. Air services between Dili and the two major adjacent cities, Denpasar (Bali) and Darwin (Australia), have already resumed, and as the infrastructure is rebuilt, tourism can be expected to develop into a significant export industry. An obvious prerequisite for its expansion is the restoration of peace in the border regions with West Timor. Public health programmes, particularly malaria eradication, are also crucial.

It is important to emphasize just how low East Timor's starting point is. Its per capita income of about US$300 is one of the lowest in the world. Even if rapid economic growth of, say, 5 per cent per capita is achieved (approximately comparable to the record under the "normalization period" of Indonesian rule), it would take about twelve years to catch up with Indonesia's *current* income level. Slower growth, of 2 per cent per capita, would extend this period to fifty-five years.

Recent Developments

It is impossible to estimate with any precision the economic cost of the massive dislocation which occurred in September–October 1999. Some 70–80 per cent of buildings were destroyed, modern-sector commerce came to a halt, for several months there was no functioning government, and agricultural cycles were disrupted.

By late 1999, following pacification, an international rescue effort was mounted under the auspices of the United Nations, which established the United Nations Transitional Administration in East Timor (UNTAET). Initially, the relief effort focused on ensuring adequate food supplies, basic humanitarian assistance, and the most urgent infrastructure rehabilitation priorities. By early 2000, and with independence looming, the focus began to shift to medium-term issues associated with the foundation of a new state, including establishing a functioning bureaucracy, adopting monetary and exchange rate arrangements, and a fiscal policy framework.

Table 1 provides some rough indicators of economic activity and external support during the transition period. Growth in the last two full years of Indonesian rule slowed down as a consequence of the country's economic crisis, although the deceleration was not as marked as in other parts of Indonesia. There was then a calamitous decline in 1999, followed by economic recovery. It will take several years for a return to 1997 levels of economic activity. Per capita GDP estimates are impossible in the absence of reliable population figures. The data also indicate that living standards did not fall as sharply as GDP, since the share of consumption in GDP rose by about 50 per cent between 1999 and 2001. This in turn was facilitated by a large increase in external savings, to over 50 per cent of GDP. Both fiscal and current account deficits were very large during the Indonesian period; they continue to be as international donors have quickly replaced the aid flows from Jakarta.

TABLE 1
East Timor: Short-Term Economic Indicators

	1997	1998	1999	2000	2001
GDP ($ million)	383	375	228	263	303
GDP growth (real, %)	4	–2	–38	15	15
Consumption (% of GDP)	72	74	93	114	111
External savings (% of GDP)	25	21	21	52	55
Fiscal balance (% of GDP)	–67	–29	–36	–55	–35
Current account I (% of GDP)	–33	–29	–23	–52	–55
Current account II (% of GDP)	–6	–4	–2	–52	–55

Notes: All figures are very approximate. Those for 2000 are estimated projections, while for 2001 they are simply projections. The data on fiscal balances refer to fiscal years 1997 to 1997–98, etc. Current account "I" and "II" refer to estimates excluding and including official transfers respectively.
Sources: Data provided by the East Timorese authorities.

The civil service during Indonesian rule numbered approximately 33,000 persons. Initial estimates of the minimum requirements by the joint UN/World Bank Assessment mission in late 1999 suggested a total of about 12,000. With the imposition of a fiscal framework, including defined expenditure targets, and the CNRT's belief that the proposed civil service wages were too low, this number was reduced further to around 10,000. Whether such a figure, just 30 per cent of the pre-independence total, can be sustained in the face of international commitments and the powerful pressures for public sector employment — motivated by a desire for much-needed public programmes or simply patronage — remains to be seen. More recently, there are indications that the size of the civil service will expand.

The budget deficit initially proposed for FY 2000/01 was about 54 per cent of GDP, similar to that in the late (pre-crisis) Indonesian period and, likewise, entirely grant financed. This deficit will fall quickly as short-term humanitarian assistance begins to taper off. Revenue is projected to be about 6 per cent of GDP in 2000/01. In the first half of 2000, a number of revenue measures had already been introduced, or announced. These included a 5 per cent across-the-board import duty, various excise taxes, a 5 per cent sales tax, a 5 per cent tax on hotels, restaurants, accommodation, and vehicle rentals, a 5 per cent presumptive tax on coffee sales, and a 10 per cent wage tax.

Major Development Challenges

The task of nation-building is complicated at the best of times, but East Timor has to grapple with daunting challenges of physical reconstruction, reconciliation, the development of political institutions, and virtually every conceivable development policy issue. The focus of this section is the latter, but it is impossible to ignore the political and social backdrop — that is, a constitution has to be drafted, political parties are in the process of being established, peace in the country-side (and especially along the border with West

Timor) has to be restored, and an inaugural general election has to be conducted.

A national language policy has to be decided. This is proving to be a particularly complex issue, with four languages being considered. There is Tetum, the *lingua franca* of East Timor, but considered to be insufficiently "scientific" for formal education and legal purposes. Secondly, there is Portuguese, which is spoken by just 5 per cent of the population, but it is preferred by much of the political élite, which has strong emotional ties to Portugal, viewing it as the only significant nation-state which sustained their struggle against Indonesian rule. The Portuguese-speaking world is making a determined effort to support the introduction of the language, including an offer to place a teacher in every secondary school. The nascent national university in Dili has a programme which plans to use Portuguese entirely as the language of instruction within a decade. The major international language is actually Bahasa Indonesia (diplomatically referred to as "Malay" in some circles), which is spoken by practically everybody under the age of 40 years, since universal primary education was introduced to the then province from the late 1970s. However, for obvious reasons, there is widespread political resistance to its adoption as an official national language. Finally, there is English, which is now quite widely spoken in Dili, given the large international presence, and also the returning East Timorese diaspora (the majority of whom lived in Australia in the period 1975–99).

Free of political constraints, a national language policy might recognize Tetum (and various regional dialects) as an informal social language, Indonesian/Malay as the national language, and English for the small educated élite and the international connections it confers. However, it appears that the pressure to adopt Portuguese as the official language may well be unstoppable. For a country with such limited educational and commercial resources, such a strategy may be costly.

Returning to development policy, the following are among the key challenges that the new nation is grappling with.

Macroeconomic Policy

This is obviously a critical policy area. Unless macroeconomic stability can be achieved, and "institutionalized", there is little prospect of rapid economic development. Here at least, there are some promising signs. In the case of monetary and exchange rate policy, it makes little sense for a tiny economy lacking basic financial institutions to attempt to run an independent policy regime. UNTAET has adopted the U.S. dollar as the Territory's legal tender during the interim period. Beyond this, there are reasonable prospects that a similar arrangement will be adopted by an independent East Timor, perhaps in the form of a currency board (CB) system, under which the local currency will be pegged to a foreign currency, or basket of currencies.

The case of fiscal policy is more complicated and challenging. How quickly should East Timor aim for fiscal autonomy? How should it manage potentially large oil and gas revenues? And how should it fund its civil service, and what size should it be?

As the International Monetary Fund (IMF) and donors correctly emphasize, it is crucially important to develop a framework for expenditure and revenue flows, to educate the community not to expect across-the-board subsidies (especially to better-off urban dwellers), and to inculcate the expectation that taxes are necessary and have to be paid. This is especially so since, first, subsidies were a part of life during the Indonesian period; secondly, donor fatigue could — and probably will — set in quickly; and thirdly, the framework needs to be intact before the large oil revenue flows commence.

Conversely, within a coherent fiscal framework, there is a case for running a very large short-term (for example, in this and the next two or three financial years) fiscal deficit, and a significant one for the medium-term (the three or so financial years beyond this). This is provided the deficit can be aid-financed and relies minimally (if at all) on oil, and any subsidies are transparent and earmarked as short-term.

The rationale for such a strategy includes the following:

- There is a large task of national reconstruction, especially the stock of dwellings. Moreover, up to 80,000 refugees across the border may have to be re-absorbed into East Timorese society and its economy.
- It takes time to adjust from a period of large subsidies, of the type applicable during the Indonesian period. Moreover, while one would want to avoid as much as possible aid dependence à la the Pacific Islands, it is a reality that tiny, very poor countries do receive considerable long-term aid flows.
- There is a massive public sector adjustment to be made. The civil service has been cut by almost two-thirds from 1997 (about 33,000 persons down to 12,000; this figure includes also teachers and police). This group now has to run an entire nation, rather than function as a sort of distant "post office", as was more or less the case during the period of highly centralized rule from Jakarta. Ninety per cent of public servants are in the low-pay categories, but they are now expected to work a full working week, in contrast to the widespread moonlighting prevalent during the Indonesian period.
- In the transition period, major policy and institutional challenges have to be sorted out, and national institutions established. These include, for example: defining the legal system, including land and property ownership; developing institutions to deal with the rest of the world (not least a diplomatic corps); and setting up a national statistical agency. There is also the major problem of dealing with so many aid agencies and programmes. (Donors are cooperating in principle, and no doubt substantially in practice, but they all want to have their own programmes recognized. They all have a tendency to favour capital works over maintenance, and they all want access to the top echelons of the overstretched, tiny, internationally-educated East Timorese élite.) These will all involve much expense.
- In a country with a particularly traumatic recent history, deficiencies in core areas such as basic education and health need to be addressed more quickly than is usually the case, as the basis for constructing a viable civil society and achieving sustainable economic development.
- It takes time to establish effective tax collection procedures.

It is therefore not surprising that fiscal policy issues are among the most difficult and hotly debated. The general principles of fiscal prudence and caution, user-pays for most public services, a lean civil service remunerated at market levels, and as broad a tax net as possible are critical. However, much revolves around the question of how long the transition period can and should last, and how large the subsidies and hence the deficit should be in the next three to five years. This in turn requires some assessment of the capacity of the emerging political system to get off the "subsidy drip" after the transition period. The more pessimistic the assessment of this issue, the stronger is the case for pushing quickly for a tough fiscal stance to be in place by independence.

On the horizon, as noted, oil and gas are likely to loom large in the East Timorese economy, with revenue flows perhaps equivalent to as much as 50 per cent of government revenue within a decade. It is impossible to overstate the importance of effective management of these resources. They provide undreamed of wealth, and if used wisely could provide the basis for rapid and sustained development. However, the experience with resource booms in so many countries has been disastrous — that is, widespread corruption, enrichment of a tiny, politically connected élite, government waste and inefficiency, and the familiar "Dutch disease" impact on the non-oil tradeable sectors. It will be imperative to keep most of the oil revenue outside the government's routine budget. Placing them in some sort of offshore escrow account would appear to be the best solution.

Trade and Openness

East Timor has very little choice other than to maintain an open trade regime. Its sea and land boundaries with the rest of eastern Indonesia are so porous that high trade barriers would almost certainly be circumvented by smuggling. By late 2000, it was already clearly evident that there was extensive, unofficially sanctioned trade across the East–West Timor land boundary, even though in principle this boundary was officially sealed off.

International transport networks have been restored, as noted, though there may be problems with monopolies. Informal small-scale shipping networks are thought to be developing again. Domestically, there is the question of whether the extensive road network constructed during the Indonesian period can be maintained by an Independent East Timor. There is also the question of how to re-establish shipping networks to the isolated enclave of Oecussi.

The trade regime thus far is clear and open — that is, a 5 per cent across-the-board import duty, plus a fairly widespread 5 per cent surcharge. Customs procedures are now simple and straightforward. As with tax policy, it is important to keep duty exemptions to an absolute minimum. *Yayasan* (non-governmental organizations or NGOs) loom as a potential problem in both cases. Understandably, an administration in urgent need of revenue has turned to these duties as a quick and simple source of funds. However, notwithstanding the difficulties, it would seem desirable to shift towards some sort of turnover tax as quickly as possible, so as to avoid the temptation of using duties as protective devices.

Property Rights and the Legal System

Land titling is a complex issue in all societies in which there is an ill-defined blend of traditional and modern commercial legal systems. However, there is evidence to suggest that, owing to East Timor's turbulent history, the problem is particularly daunting there. Currently, land in East Timor can be claimed under four bases: underlying traditional interests, Portuguese-era titles, Indonesia-era titles, or occupation since the 1999 vote for independence. Most land title offices were apparently destroyed by the departing militias and troops in 1999, and in the process most records were lost. Before that, during the Indonesian period, land under Portuguese control or in Fretilin-sympathetic areas was apparently appropriated by the military. In addition, the sizeable population exodus of 1975 and 1999 have meant that there is an international East Timorese community with outstanding land title claims. Resolving these claims will be a protracted and complex issue, but one which deserves the highest priority. Land disputes and illegal squatting are already widespread. Since a functioning judiciary is barely in place, it may make sense to adopt a lease system in the transitional period, under which land subject to dispute — or likely to be — can be leased for a specified time period (perhaps 5–20 years, depending on the activity), subject to a clear medium-term resolution.

Competitiveness

A major problem of competitiveness seems to be emerging in East Timor. As would be expected, the "expatriate economy" operates on the basis of Darwin (North Australia) plus prices. However, the East Timorese economy is also expensive, partly the result of cost-push pressures resulting from the international presence. Even for East Timorese markets, goods are highly priced. Dili was always expensive in Indonesian times (with at least a 20–40 per cent differential compared to Java). Impressionistic evidence suggests that this differential may now be as much as 100 per cent for many simple consumer goods. This is obviously serious, and will build in a high cost structure. Already, minimum daily wages in the public sector are at least US$4, and these set the benchmark for the tiny "formal" private sector. In the coffee estates, apparently daily wages are about US$3, which is two to three times those in Indonesia.

Related to this is the challenge of public sector wage policy. Wage scales are compressed, with maximum monthly wages of US$800, and approximately a 5:1 differential between top and bottom (excluding the five East Timorese Cabinet members who each receive US$2,000 per month). For a US$300 per capita economy, the minimum is rather high. However, conversely, wages at the top are too low to attract the necessary skills, a problem especially complicated since the "supply price" among the qualified pool — mainly the "diaspora", since the higher echelon Indonesians have returned home — is more or less what they were earning or at least could earn abroad (most now have foreign passports). Some in addition have commitments abroad (for example, children's education) which effectively rule them out from the civil service.

There is, in addition, a general problem of acute skill shortages. This may become less serious when the United Nations departs, but it will certainly remain. To avoid relying on the expensive North Australian labour market, East Timor will need to tap into more competitive East Asian labour markets. Barring Indonesia, the Philippines is the most likely alternative (as has occurred, for example, in neighbouring Papua New Guinea).

Perhaps these are transitional problems, and as expatriates depart, transport networks and commercial relations with Indonesia improve, prices will fall. Meanwhile, a regular shipping service between Surabaya and Dili has been operating for several months, and the impact has not yet been felt. There may be a broader problem of international transport networks, in that all the providers are monopolists, although in principle the markets should be contestable. For example, in the case of air transport, the operators are Merpati (Denpasar-Dili) and Air North, an Ansett subsidiary (Darwin-Dili). Tickets for both are very expensive by international standards. For sea transport, there is one shipping line each from Surabaya and Darwin. In addition, and perhaps partly eroding monopoly rents, there is, as noted, considerable cross-border (that is, East–West Timor) illegal trade.

These cost issues raise the broader question of who will want to invest in the country. The potential should be considerable, especially from among the approximately 80,000 East Timorese diaspora abroad. Currently, not surprisingly, most investments are going into the quick-yielding construction, hotel, and restaurant sectors. Among the problems investors face are:

- Highly insecure ownership arrangements, especially for land.
- Higher cost structures than potential competitors (that is, competitors for footloose investment), such as Indonesia and Vietnam. Wages are much higher in East Timor, as are utilities charges.
- While the use of the U.S. dollar is sensible as a means of securing macroeconomic policy objectives, East Timor is linked to a strong currency, and will most likely have a fairly rigid labour market. Thus, the option of boosting competitiveness via a nominal depreciation which "sticks" (that is, a real effective depreciation) is not available.

- Acute shortages of skilled and semi-skilled labour (for example, electricians, mechanics) for which Darwin prices (which are in turn high by Australian standards) apply.
- Poor infrastructure, including uncertain power supplies (generator back-up is essential). Most businesses use the (expensive) Telstra mobile telephone network.
- Inevitable uncertainty about post-independence policy directions.
- The absence of a modern financial sector. The foreign banks now present — BNU from Portugal, and Australia's Westpac — are obviously reluctant to accept any local collateral in connection with loan applications.
- The absence of a legal code, and any effective form of legal protection.

Social Policy and Urban Bias

East Timor's social indicators are understandably very poor, notwithstanding considerable educational advances during the Indonesian period. Here, priorities matter enormously. Resources allocated to one activity represent forgone opportunities elsewhere. Already, there is the danger of an emerging urban bias, particularly around the capital, Dili, fostered by labour market and social policies, and in consequence of very large aid flows (and oil revenue in prospect).

In education, for example, on both equity and efficiency grounds, it makes sense to concentrate subsidies at primary and junior secondary levels (as was broadly the case under Indonesian rule). For higher levels, it makes sense to invoke the user-pays principle since the gap between the social and private returns to education narrows. However, fear of student protests, and a view that a national university is an important symbol of nation-building, has already begun to result in a reallocation of resources from the primary to the tertiary sectors.

Similarly, in the case of public health expenditures, the highest social returns are likely to be achieved through, for example, public programmes of disease eradication, the provision of potable water supplies, the provision of basic community health services throughout the country, and mass inoculation campaigns, rather than in investments in expensive, high-tech public hospitals. There appears to be an emerging — and probably inevitable — "Dili bias". This refers not just to the expatriate presence, but more fundamentally to key elements of the emerging policy regime, elements which are supported as much by East Timorese as U.N. officials. Examples include: (a) a relatively high minimum wage in the public sector, pushed up in part by high prices, as noted above; (b) the danger that some public utilities will be subsidized; and (c) the provision of middle-class social subsidies.

Conclusion

East Timor is a new nation quite literally being reconstructed "out of the ashes".[3] In more normal circumstances, this would be an exciting challenge — writing a constitution, developing political, legal and educational institutions, and charting the way forward on economic policy.

However, times are anything but normal. The East Timorese people are very poor, and they have lived under very harsh conditions in the last two years. Before that, they experienced a quarter century of troubled rule from Jakarta, and centuries of neglect from Lisbon. Everything is urgent, from holding an election to rebuilding schools and ensuring adequate food supplies. Aid supplies and international commitments are currently plentiful, but this window of opportunity may be fleeting. There will be other crises around the world which will divert international attention, and donor fatigue is a problem everywhere, especially when the inevitable domestic (East Timorese) political squabbles erupt, and tales of corruption and waste in government surface. The Portuguese world is currently very supportive, but it is distant, small, and unlikely to have the resources available to make a durable commitment to East Timor's development.

Against this backdrop, these are crucial times in East Timor. If it is able to lay the foundations for political cohesion and stability, social harmony, and good economic policy, it could in time emerge as a prosperous state, at peace — and integrated — with its neighbourhood, in which its citizens enjoy steadily rising living standards. That is what most of the people of Southeast Asia have come to expect, at least prior to the recent crisis. The alternative scenario is the "South Pacific" one, of socio-economic stagnation, political division, and regional instability. The next few years will give us important clues as to which path East Timor is likely to travel.

Notes

1. This chapter draws on the author's ongoing collaborative research on East Timor with members of the East Timor Study Group, which included fieldwork in November 2000 and January 2001. Some of the issues mentioned here are examined in more detail in the author's forthcoming paper, "Tiny, Poor and War-torn: Development Policy Challenges for East Timor", *World Development*, July 2001. See also Helder Da Costa, "Building East Timor's Economy: The Roles of Foreign Aid, Trade and Investment" (Ph.D. dissertation, University of Adelaide, Adelaide, 2000).

2. For a detailed recent analysis of South Pacific development issues, see R.S. Duncan, S. Cuthbertson, and M. Bosworth, *Pursuing Economic Reform in the Pacific*, Pacific Studies Series No. 18 (Manila: Asian Development Bank, 1999).

3. This borrows the phrase from J.J. Fox and D.B. Soares, eds., *Out of the Ashes: Destruction and Reconstruction of East Timor* (Adelaide: Crawford House Publishing, 2000).

SOUTHEAST ASIA IN 2002
From Bali to Iraq —
Co-operating for Security

Chin Kin Wah

Introduction

The region's recovery from the destabilizing effects of the 1997/98 Asian economic/financial crisis had been patchy, and although by 2002 most gross domestic product (GDP) levels had edged back to pre-crisis levels, per capita incomes had not and unemployment was on the rise. The 3.5 per cent growth in Indonesia was achieved over a low baseline. Its path towards economic restructuring, sustained economic recovery, and political stability remained tortuous.

On the road to economic recovery two developments set back confidence and fuelled uncertainties. The Al-Qaeda terrorist attacks on the United States on 11 September 2001 (commonly referred to as "9/11") opened a new phase of international insecurity. How the United States would pursue the war against global terrorism and with what impacts on the Muslim world fuelled uncertainty. The more open regional economies focussed on the consequences for global travel, business confidence, and the international economy. In retrospect neither the United States nor the most open regional economy, Singapore, was too seriously affected. Within a year both economies had rebounded with Singapore in the third quarter of 2002 seemingly headed for a 4 per cent growth.[1] In 2002 the Malaysian economy grew by 4.2 per cent while the fastest regional growth rate of 7 per cent was recorded by Vietnam. However, the terrorist bombings in Bali on 12 October 2002, which killed 202 people, many of them foreign tourists including 88 Australians, dampened expectations of a re-

---

Reprinted in abridged format from Daljit Singh and Chin Kin Wah, eds., *Southeast Asian Affairs 2003* (Singapore: Institute of Southeast Asian Studies, 2003), pp. 3–23. At the time of original publication, Chin Kin Wah was a Senior Fellow, Institute of Southeast Asian Studies, Singapore.

bound as Southeast Asia initially acquired an undifferentiated image in the minds of foreign investors and in travel advisories as an insecure region.

American concerns that parts of maritime Southeast Asia with their local history of Muslim militancy and rebellion against central authority were vulnerable to penetration by the Al-Qaeda network in search of a "second front" resurfaced following the Afghanistan campaign which commenced in October 2001 and resulted subsequently in the destruction of the Taliban regime and disruption of the Al-Qaeda network. The year 2002 began with regional anticipation of the political fallout of the war against international terrorism and ended with nervous tension over the imminence of war in Iraq. However, it was the October Bali bombings that reignited attention on the connections between regional and global networks of terror through the Jemaah Islamiah (JI) and persuaded those in denial mode to re-examine the threat. While not all regional governments necessarily shared the same domestic concern with Muslim militancy or radicalism (not all of which manifested in terrorism), the challenge of resurgent political Islam and the intensified religiosity among Muslim populations in the region had to be reckoned with, particularly in the political calculus of Muslim-dominant multi-ethnic states. While the vast majority of Muslim populations in the region are overwhelmingly moderate, globalization has sharpened their sensitivities towards and awareness of discontents in the Muslim world and resentments of America. It is the work of the radical few operating in the sea of the moderates that proved most destructive.

Fortuitously the external security environment of Southeast Asia continued to remain relatively stable during this time. The Sino-American turbulence of the previous April faded into the background with the new global challenge posed by terrorism after 9/11 resulting in a positive shift in relations among the major external powers — most notably the improving Sino-American relationship which remains the most important underpin to a stable external security environment of the region.

The threat of international terrorism soon became a point of converging major power security interests. The American-led war against the Al-Qaeda resonated with China's concern with the threat posed by Muslim separatists in Xinjiang and Russia's military preoccupation with Chechen separatists whose challenge to Moscow was most dramatically highlighted by their hostage taking in a Moscow concert hall in October 2002. The spectre of international terrorism especially after the Bali bombings also tempered somewhat regional differences towards security co-operation with the United States. However, new controversies in subsequent months over America's growing assertive, unilateralist drive towards war in Iraq opened new fault lines within the region and threatened to detract from a coherent response to the terrorist challenge.

The External Security Environment

While China saw good tactical sense in avoiding external complications with its impending entry into the World Trade Organization (WTO) and anticipated major domestic leadership transition, awareness that America's global security preoccupation after 9/11 had shifted away from the so-called "China threat" also made for an easier adjustment. Their heightened though separate concerns with international terrorism were reflected in their intelligence sharing, in China's unprecedented albeit cautious support for American military action in a third country (i.e., Afghanistan) and muted acceptance of a new American presence in Central Asia as well as the re-emergence of a limited American military profile in the Philippines. The United States for its part sought to restrain Taiwan President Chen Shui-bian's independence rhetoric, refrained from opposing China's bid for the 2008 Olympics, and in concession to China's security interests added the Eastern Turkistan Islamic Movement in Xinjiang to its list of terrorist organizations. China in turn tightened controls on dual-use missile technology export and further regulated exports of dual-use chemical and biological materials. A high point in a year of warming Sino-American relations was Chinese President Jiang Zemin's visit in late October to the United States, which included the honour of his being the first Asian leader to be received at President George W. Bush's Texas ranch at Crawford. More substantively Bush announced for the first time that he would not support Taiwan's independence.[2] Resumption of Sino-American military contacts and dialogues soon followed.

Chinese leaders were nevertheless careful to emphasize to the United States, the importance not only of restraint in the use of force but also for a multilateral approach in the war against terrorism. China was also reluctant to openly back the expected American-led war against Iraq. Still, for some Southeast Asian governments previously discomforted by volatility in Sino-American relations, the return to a more stable relationship between Beijing and Washington was a welcome development moderating likely dilemmas in their growing security ties with the United States.

For Japan, 9/11 carried reminders of its own vulnerability to urban terrorism most notably the 1995 poison gas attacks by the Aum Shinrikyo group. More importantly it provided an opportunity for consolidation of the security relationship with the United States beyond the old Japanese resort to "cheque-book diplomacy". Growing concern as the year unfolded, over an unpredictable, recalcitrant regime in Pyongyang harbouring a nuclear weapons programme besides posing a missile threat to South Korea and Japan, further underlined the importance of closer co-operation with the United States. Under the hurriedly passed Anti-Terrorism Special Measures Act, which came into effect the previous November, Japan provided unprecedented rear-guard assistance by deploying three destroyers and two naval supply ships to the Indian Ocean to support allied forces engaged in combat in Afghanistan. By December 2002 Tokyo further signalled tacit support for an impending American-led war in Iraq by dispatching an advanced Aegis-class destroyer to replace one of its three destroyers in the Indian Ocean.[3]

Despite deep suspicions of the strengthening U.S.–Japan alliance, China underplayed its public responses. With reference to the latest Japanese deployment, the Chinese Foreign Ministry hoped that Japan would "strictly abide by its exclusively defensive defence policy ... and exercise prudence over these matters".[4] Closer to its heartstrings, China was less inhibited in expressing consternation over Koizumi's April visit to the Yasukuni shrine which commemorates Japan's war dead and is popularly associated with right-wing militarism.[5]

Expressions of Chinese displeasure were to lead Koizumi to put off a visit to China in September to commemorate the thirtieth anniversary of the normalization of Sino-Japanese relations.

The post-9/11 climate of improving external power relations, owed as much to Russia's attempts to work co-operatively with the United States and the North Atlantic Treaty Organization (NATO) while strengthening links with China. In the immediate aftermath of 9/11, President Vladimir Putin sought to reset the framework of co-operation with the United States while hoping to carve out some role for Russia in world affairs. As Russia and the United States found common cause in their respective wars against terrorism and with Russian interest changing towards a new positive relationship with an expanded NATO, they were able to sideline the hitherto contentious issue of national and theatre missile defence systems to focus instead on nuclear force reductions. The Bush-Putin summit in Moscow in May, culminated in a nuclear disarmament agreement to accelerate cuts in long-range nuclear warheads. They also proclaimed a new strategic relationship between them.

Despite Putin's *Westpolitik* he mindfully reaffirmed a partnership with China as the year progressed and it became clearer that the United States might lead a war against Iraq without U.N. backing. Having to cope with a hegemonic America in a unipolar world pointed to the usefulness of a closer Sino-Russian strategic and economic partnership as reflected in Putin's visit to China in December 2002 on the heels of China's leadership transition. In their joint declaration, both veto-wielding members of the U.N. Security Council reiterated that the Iraq question could only be resolved through political-diplomatic means, as well as in keeping to U.N. Security Council resolutions.[6] They also urged the international community to consider separatists operating within their borders as terrorists.

On the region's western flank, India's strategic footprint is understandably most pronounced in South Asia and on the littoral states of the Indian Ocean including Indonesia, Myanmar, Thailand, and Malaysia. However, India's membership in the ARF gives India a strategic "voice" in Southeast Asia and indeed, the wider Asia-Pacific. In the post-9/11 era India moved much closer towards security co-operation with the United States on the back of the anti-terrorism campaign while at the same time demonstrating a capacity to project naval power beyond the Indian Ocean to the outer limits of the South China Sea (which bears the clear "strategic footprint" of China) and well within the strategic environment of ASEAN. In April, India began deploying its navy to escort commercial shipping carrying "high value cargo" (fuel, ammunition, food, and other supplies) through the Straits of Malacca, to U.S. forces operating in the Arabian Sea and Persian Gulf.[7] The following month it conducted for the first time in thirty-nine years joint exercises with the United States involving Indian paratroopers and Special Forces from the U.S. Pacific Command. However, India's value to ASEAN in terms of broader security building with the region should also be seen in terms of how successfully it manages stable relations with China, which is perceived as a competitor, and Pakistan, which is regarded as a source of threat.

The U.S.-led war against terrorism could be said to serve overlapping but not congruent major power security interests. Undoubtedly stable relations among them did not necessarily mean the absence of underlying competitive dynamics. However, these were not necessarily destructive. Considering how overt great power rivalries and contestations of the Cold War had fuelled regional instability by their conjunction with intra-regional conflicts, the stable climate of major power relations which continued through 2002 was an opportune development for the region.

Regional Security Concerns

Stable major power relations in 2002 spared one layer of Southeast Asia's security environment from turbulence. However, the year also witnessed clearer signs of conjuncture between global destabilization generated by a non-state, transnational terrorist movement (the Al-Qaeda) and local insecurity stemming from extremist Islamic movements. While the threat of terrorism loomed over security discourses in Southeast Asia after 9/11, the Al-Qaeda's links with the region predated that defining moment by several years. Militant Muslim operatives in the region have been receiving training in Afghanistan and the southern Philippines. Southeast Asia too has a long history of encounters with terrorism — from militant communist movements to ethnic rebellions and Muslim separatists in southern Thailand and the southern Philippines. The end of the Soeharto regime opened the lid to a democratizing process, which allowed the hitherto repressed political Islam to flourish. However, the decompression of the political process also led to more political disorder at Indonesia's centre and ethno-religious and/or separatist violence in the periphery — East Timor, Maluku, Central Sulawesi, and Aceh. In the Philippines, a surge of Abu Sayyaf terrorist activities was also registered in the two years preceding 9/11, at a time of leadership drift and political transition.

However, globalization of terrorism and the extended reach of the Al-Qaeda network — likened to "a franchising agency that functions through religious internationalism and stateless networks"[8] — reminded the region of the vulnerability to penetration where local conditions and resentments fuelled by economic grievances, corruption, and repression invited exploitation. Threats to American interests everywhere also threatened the locations of such interests. Furthermore international terrorism sharpened attention on a broad spectrum of related transnational, non-conventional security threats, such as money laundering, arms and drug trafficking, piracy, illegal movement of people across borders, and disruption of commercial shipping and maritime trade — issues that ASEAN was increasingly impelled to address as part of a comprehensive war against terrorism albiet with varying results.

In December 2001 Singapore disclosed a terrorist plot against American and Western targets on the island. The plot involved local members of the Jemaah Islamiah (JI), meaning "Islamic community" — a network of operatives straddling Malaysia, Singapore, and Indonesia and with links to the Al-Qaeda which was said to have connections also with the Abu Sayyaf and the Moro Islamic Liberation Front (MILF) in the Philippines, and what the Malaysian government has labelled as the Kumpulan Militan Malaysia (KMM).[9] Following a second round of arrests of JI members in Singapore in August 2002, the Singapore Government affirmed that the JI had not only targeted foreign interests in Singapore but also local assets and installations. It was claimed that among the JI's aims was the establishment of a pan-Islamic caliphate in the region linking Malaysia, Indonesia, Brunei, southern Thailand, and southern Philippines. Their agenda allegedly included actions (such as sabotaging the water supply to Singapore) meant to sow discord between the Malaysian and Singapore governments.

The JI's putative leader was an Indonesian Muslim cleric Abu Bakar Bashir, who operated in Malaysia as a religious teacher in the 1980s and was wanted by the Malaysian police on suspicion of involvement with terrorists. Abu Bakar, by then back in his hometown in Solo, consistently denied links with Osama bin Laden (who he described as a "true Islamic warrior") and the Al-Qaeda although he praised Osama's fight against the United States and its allies.[10]

Initially Indonesia was in denial mode and dismissed external warnings. There was public resentment at pressures from neighbouring governments[11] and the United States to take action against Muslim extremists and clerics like Abu Bakar. Hard evidence of their complicity was demanded. Irresolute government response has been attributed to weak political leadership, weak security apparatus, absence of anti-terrorist legislation, to the transformed psyche of the Indonesian public and leaders after 9/11, which added to distrust of Western powers.[12] Furthermore President Megawati Sukarnoputri needed to tread cautiously to avoid weakening support of the Muslim parties in her coalition government. Vice-President Hamzah Haz who headed the largest Islamic political party even suggested after Megawati's visit to the United States shortly after 9/11 that the attacks were a response to America's sins. In May 2002 he also visited Jafar Umar Thalib, the detained leader of the Laskar Jihad, which was involved in sectarian violence against Christians in Maluku. It can be surmised that with direct presidential elections pending in 2004, Megawati could even less afford to ignore sentiments and political pressures from the "Muslim street".

The Bali bombings whose perpetrators were subsequently linked to the JI, and the resultant outrage made inaction untenable. That incident and a spate of terrorist attacks in the southern Philippines in the same month also generated a heightened sense of regional vulnerability and exposure. The Bali bombings effected a change in public posture on the part of Indonesian officials. Both Defence Minister Matori Abdul Djalil and Foreign Minister Hassan Wirayuda soon publicly conceded to the terrorist threat, and Hamzah Haz himself was obliged to declaim that Indonesia had to go on the offensive against terrorism. Indonesia joined Singapore, Malaysia, the Philippines, and other countries in calling for the JI's inclusion in the U.N. list of terrorist groups and moved towards the detention of Abu Bakar. Following Bali, the Indonesian President speedily issued two anti-terrorism decrees.

Unlike Indonesia, Malaysia displayed more firmness in dealing with the terrorist threat. Indeed Prime Minister Datuk Seri Dr Mahathir Mohamad seeking to be even-handed in dealing with terrorism, was the first Muslim leader to describe Palestinian suicide bombers, among others, as terrorists. In early January 2002 shortly after the Singapore arrests of JI members, he declared support for Singapore's action[13] and announced a second round of arrests of KMM members, promising to hunt down all militant activists and extremist elements in the country. Both Malaysia and Singapore have similar tough internal security laws (inherited from the British colonial government during the period of communist insurgency) that provided for detention without trial. There was also a long tradition of effective co-operation between their respective internal security agencies that has endured the tribulations in their bilateral relations.

In some respects 9/11 gave Mahathir some opportunity to undercut the Parti Islam SeMalaysia (PAS), which has been making inroads to the Muslim electorate at the expense of his political party, United Malays National Organization (UMNO), anchor of the ruling multi-racial Barisan Nasional coalition. Non-Malay opposition parties that had previously reached out towards partnership with PAS were also put off by its Islamic stridency and call for *jihad* against the United States for its actions in Afghanistan. The Mahathir government also sought to link PAS to the KMM and JI. The government won by larger than expected margins in two by-elections in Mahathir's home state of Kedah in July 2002 although the results showed that PAS still had sizeable support among the Malay electorate. Such consideration weighed heavily in an UMNO which in June was rocked by Mahathir's decision to step down from his government and party positions — a decision which he was persuaded subsequently to delay by a year to provide for a more orderly leadership transition. Nevertheless in the post-9/11 political context, Mahathir, in the eyes of his critics, has been able to move against the political opposition with fewer constraints. However, the intensified contestation within political Islam in Malaysia also meant that Mahathir could not ignore the sentiments of the "Muslim street" on Middle East issues and with respect to the U.S. role in Afghanistan and Iraq.

Security Relations with the United States

For most of the year the issue of the war on terror hung heavily over America's relations with the region. However, regional states differed not only in their conventional power relations with the United States, they also reflected differences in their handling of Islamic militancy which may manifest itself in political and social opposition though not necessarily terrorism — a distinction which was not always fully appreciated in Bush's "with us or against us" rhetoric.[14] Those (such as Indonesia, Brunei, and Malaysia) with sizeable Muslim constituencies also sought to balance their condemnations of and response to terrorism in all its forms, with circumspection in their support for any American-led war against the Al-Qaeda and, over the horizon, Iraq — lest they came across to their domestic Muslim publics as being embroiled in a "crusade" against the Islamic world. Even those such as Singapore, the Philippines, and Thailand, which have more evident defence ties with the United States were not unmindful of possible Muslim–non-Muslim fault lines within their respective societies and the strains that could be exerted on these fault lines by a prolonged war in Iraq. America's determination to rely primarily on military means to fight terrorism rather than address the conditions that nurture it also caused unease.

Nevertheless the sense of imminent, inter-penetrating threat brought on by the Bali bombings created new urgency among these regional states to work closer together with the United States and, even up to a point, Australia (with its long-held security interest in the region to its north) despite souring atmospherics over Prime Minister John Howard's overly effusive analogy of "deputy sheriff" to characterize Australia's special relationship with America and his subsequent talk of pre-emptive strikes abroad if there were no alternative means of saving Australia from terrorist attacks.[15]

Since 9/11 the Bush Administration had pressed Jakarta to take tougher measures against Muslim militants. After Bali, the U.S. Ambassador to Indonesia noted a more serious Indonesian effort to deal with the terrorists who, he stressed represented "only a tiny fraction" that might be linked to the Al-Qaeda.[16] However, there was no joint investigation with the United States into the Al-Qaeda's links in Indonesia, given local anti-American feelings. Unlike in the Philippines, the American approach in Indonesia emphasized law-enforcement efforts rather than military action. In taking measures against the extremist groups Megawati, for her part, has been cautious not to alienate the Muslim ground or be seen as acting on the behest of the United States and its allies.

Malaysia's tough stance against terrorism won praise from the United States despite Mahathir's objections to the war in Afghanistan and rhetoric against American unilateralism and role in the Middle East. Economic fundamentals also pointed to the importance of the United States as its biggest foreign investor and trading partner. Reflecting pragmatism, Malaysia agreed to host an anti-terrorism centre (open to all ASEAN members) first broached by President Bush on the sidelines of the 2001 Asia-Pacific Economic Co-operation (APEC) summit. It dismissed suggestions that the centre would involve the deployment of U.S. troops in Malaysia — U.S. involvement would be limited to provision of expertise, training, and equipment. In May, Defence Minister Datuk Seri Najib Tun Razak disclosed the extent of Malaysia's security links with the United States: in the past two years the U.S. navy made more than seventy-five port calls in Malaysia; U.S. Navy Seals conducted training in Malaysia twice a year; the U.S. army held field exercises with its Malaysian counterpart and Malaysia extended jungle warfare training facilities to the United States.[17] Mahathir's Washington visit later that month indicated that despite differences in outlook, sufficient common ground existed between the two countries.[18]

In the centre of a predominantly Muslim neighbourhood Singapore has been acutely conscious of ethno-religious turbulence in the region and any likely impact on its own multi-racial society, which includes a small but by no means inconsequential Malay-Muslim component. The island-state's economic survival depends on being plugged into and staying open in an increasingly globalized world. Yet that very porosity also enhances its vulnerability to transnational security threats of the kind posed by the JI. In both traditional balance-of-power calculus (which points to the need to keep the United States strategically engaged in the region) and in the fight against international terrorism, it has placed itself alongside the United States, which since 1990 has been granted access to vital air and naval facilities on the strategically located island. Such facilities have been drawn upon in America's military campaigns in the Gulf War, in Afghanistan, and most likely again in an impending war against Saddam Hussein. Although the United States wanted more regional navies to escort commercial shipping through regional waters, Singapore, claiming it had a modest navy, contributed by patrolling the Singapore Straits.[19] It granted the U.S. Customs permission to station its inspectors at its major port to screen U.S.-bound cargo. In rendering assistance to the United States, Singapore was well aware of attendant risks to itself and how it might come across as a client state of America. Prime Minister Goh Chok Tong emphasized that Singapore co-operated with the United States on its own terms and as a friend whose interests coincided.[20] The critical importance of the United States to Singapore in other areas (economic security) was well underscored by an impending FTA with the United States that would make the republic the first Asian country to have such a trading arrangement with Washington.

The Philippines had sought to strengthen military ties with the United States since bilateral co-operation was resumed in 1999 after a ten-year hiatus. President Gloria Arroyo was one of the first to pledge support for the American anti-terror campaign and the only regional leader to invite U.S. ground forces to assist the anti-terrorism war. During the Afghanistan War, Manila granted U.S. warplanes landing, refuelling, and over-flight rights. Following 9/11 the United States stepped up training and satellite reconnaissance support in anti-terrorist operations against the Abu Sayyaf — a band of Muslim radicals who gained notoriety for kidnapping local residents and foreigners, including Americans, and which both Manila and Washington claimed had links with the Al-Qaeda. In 2002 Washington pledged to the Philippines US$100 million in development aid and US$55 million to counter terrorism. The beginning of the year saw the deployment of more than 600 U.S. troops including 160 Special Forces personnel in a six-month joint training exercise codenamed "Balikatan" in an area where the Abu Sayyaf was known to operate. In April the Philippines approved additional deployment of U.S. troops to train, exercise with, and assist local forces hunting the Abu Sayyaf. When the exercises ended in July several hundred U.S. troops remained in the Philippines. With respect to the future disposition of American forces — issues that beckon include the constitutional and legal framework for and possible combat roles of these forces — issues that can be controversial with left-wing and nationalist groups in the Philippines.

The Abu Sayyaf was not the only militant group that posed security threats to the Philippine Government. The much larger MILF force is a more formidable challenge. However, the Philippine Government was reluctant to blacklist the MILF (despite its being reportedly linked to the Abu Sayyaf and the Al-Qaeda) so as not to jeopardize ongoing though tenuous peace negotiations with the Front following a ceasefire agreement in September 2001. On the other hand, another insurgent group, the Communist Party of the Philippines (CPP), which had pursued a long-running Maoist rebellion through its military arm, the New People's Army, was blacklisted as a terrorist organization by the United States. In August it suspended peace talks with the Philippine Government and vowed to resume activities to disrupt the Philippine economy.

Thailand's initial hesitancy in declaring support for the U.S. war against terrorism belies its image as a long-time ally of the United States and may have reflected domestic aversion towards the provision of base facilities to the United States as well as concern with the sentiments of the Muslim minorities in the south where Muslim separatists continue to operate. A government attempt in November to deploy 100,000 troops in southern Thailand triggered a public furore.[21] Thailand chose to publicly spotlight intelligence exchange with the United States in the war on terrorism although it also gave U.S. aircraft the right of transit to the Gulf during the Afghan campaign. Anti-terrorism training was incorporated into the annual large-scale Cobra Gold combined military exercises that Thailand conducted with the United States and Singapore in May 2002.[22]

After Bali, Thailand appeared to be in some denial mode with respect to the threat of terrorist attacks on popular tourist spots despite reports that a group of Al-Qaeda operatives had met in Thailand to plan attacks on soft targets in the region months before the Bali bombings.[23] It was not till December 2002 that Thai officials began to acknowledge that a senior Al-Qaeda pointman had previously passed through the country and narrowly avoided arrest. There is little hard evidence linking the Al-Qaeda to the Pattani United Liberation Organization (PULO), a separatist movement operating in the predominantly Muslim southern Thai provinces. PULO is not considered an "Islamist movement" although it has received support from Islamist movements on the Malaysian side of the border.[24]

Shortly after the United States concluded an anti-terrorism pact with ASEAN in August, Myanmar, an ASEAN member, announced that it had broken up a militant separatist group of Rohingya minorities (the Arakan Rohingya National Organization), which had received training in Afghanistan and the Middle East.[25] It has been said that Yangon's action was intended to win U.S. friendship at a time when its bilateral relations with Washington remained largely frozen on account of its poor human rights record and lack of democratic change.

Regional Co-operation at Countering Terrorism

The anti-terror campaign was a major point of American security engagement with the region. Several regional governments received Washington's assistance in disrupting JI activities. The United States had interest in being involved with anti-terrorism initiatives agreed to by the ASEAN Summit of November 2001. In May 2002 the United States signed a joint anti-terrorism declaration with Malaysia that provided a framework for co-operation in the prevention and disruption of and fight against international terrorism — co-operation in which information and intelligence exchange were crucial. According to the Malaysian Foreign Minister this joint declaration provided the basis for the subsequent U.S.–ASEAN Joint Declaration for Co-operation to Combat International Terrorism signed by the ASEAN Foreign Ministers and Colin Powell at Bandar Seri Begawan in late July.[26] Co-operation included intelligence exchange, the blocking of terrorist funds, and tightening of border controls. However, Powell, mindful of some regional sensitivities especially in Indonesia and Vietnam, reassured that the declaration was not a prelude to increased American military presence in the region. At the same venue members of the ARF (meeting back-to-back with the ASEAN meeting with dialogue partners) also agreed to block terrorist financing. Closely following the signing of the ASEAN–U.S. declaration, China not to be left out, proposed a similar arrangement for the "ASEAN+3" gathering which informally links ASEAN to China, Japan, and Korea.[27]

Regional networks of terror could not be unravelled unless regional governments co-operated meaningfully. However, such co-operation could not ignore diversities in regional conditions, political realities, and outlooks. The ASEAN summit of the previous November in Bandar Seri Begawan recognized terrorism as a direct challenge and committed the regional association to "countering, preventing and suppressing all terrorist acts in accordance with the (U.N. Charter)... especially taking into account the importance of all relevant U.N. resolutions". While the declaration unequivocally condemned the 9/11 attacks, it omitted mentioning the war in Afghanistan — an indication of differences in national positions. It noted the framework already established and measures taken to fight transnational crime. Additional measures and capacity-building to combat terrorism were announced but significantly the summit recognized the need to take account of "specific circumstances in the region and in each member country" in considering joint action.[28]

The "specific circumstances of the region" also complicated attempts to extend the trilateral anti-terrorism agreement signed by Malaysia, Indonesia, and the Philippines in Kuala Lumpur in May 2002 to other ASEAN partners although Thailand and Cambodia indicated interest in joining. Its very broad coverage beyond targeting potential terrorist threats and the politically and legally contentious aspects of the other areas covered — such as, information-sharing on money laundering, piracy, hijacking, intrusions, illegal entry, drug trafficking, theft of marine resources, marine pollution, and illicit arms trade — created reticence on the part of other ASEAN members. Absence of a region-wide extradition treaty, lack of standard definitions for crimes, and difficulty in harmonizing national laws were other impediments. ASEAN members also had differences over Malaysia's attempts to seek a definition of terrorism. In May a special meeting of ASEAN Home Affairs and Interior Ministers failed to arrive at a common definition and instead reiterated the need to respect and uphold "the sovereignty, territorial integrity and domestic laws of each ASEAN Member Country" in the fight against terrorism.[29] Intra-ASEAN debate reflected controversies in other international forums including the United Nations that centred on the problem of distinguishing terrorists from freedom fighters. However, the absence of a clear definition did not preclude attempts at co-operating on measures to address specific acts of terrorism including bilateral co-operation between law enforcement agencies.

Expectations of War in Iraq

Towards the year's end the prospect of war over Iraq began to cast a pall of pessimism over Southeast Asia. Concerns focussed on the possible repercussions on those plural societies in the region, which also contain substantial Islamic constituencies.

An America-led pre-emptive war in Iraq without U.N. Security Council authorization, and especially if it became protracted, could also heighten tensions within Southeast Asia where radical groups were portraying the war against terrorism as a war against Islam. Even in the Philippines, the most openly identifiable regional ally of the United States, there were some early signs of unease over the American rush to war with Iraq. In September the Philippine Foreign Secretary Blas Ople said that his country would extend to aircraft and naval vessels overflight and docking rights as well as landing and refuelling facilities if requested. However, he added the proviso that the United States would have to convince the international community that the war was connected with the anti-terrorism campaign.[30] Later President Arroyo's office sought to qualify the Philippine support by saying that such assistance in any war with Iraq would have to be dependent on a U.N. resolution for action.[31] These early nuances in statements stemming from America's staunch regional ally echoed regional dilemmas as well. Differences in ASEAN member's outlooks would make it difficult to achieve a consensual statement of support for the United States just as there was no regional consensual statement on the Afghanistan War, despite wide support for a global partnership in dealing with the threat of international terrorism. In effect a distinction was being drawn between war against terrorism and war against Saddam Hussein, however much the United States sought to link the two. Sensing these fault-lines Iraqi diplomats in the region reportedly tried to lobby regional governments during August with special attention on Thailand and the Philippines to pre-empt their support of the United States. The Iraqis were said to be confident of warmer responses from Muslim-majority Indonesia, Malaysia, and Brunei and perhaps Vietnam and Laos, which generally opposed foreign intervention.[32]

Singapore echoed regional concern that a lengthy war over Iraq leading to excessive loss of Muslim lives could upset the Islamic world — a situation that could be exploited by terrorists to mount attacks on American interests not only within the United States but also worldwide including Southeast Asia. Such an eventuality would heighten the sense of shared vulnerability across Southeast Asia.

Conclusion

The war on terrorism cast a long shadow over the agenda of co-operation between regional states and between them and the major powers, especially the United States, during the course of the year. The challenge of terrorism also brought about a more co-operative climate in the relations among the external powers. The consequent stability in major power relations made for a calmer external security environment for ASEAN. However, the Bali bombings highlighted a conjuncture between destabilization generated by a global network of terror and local instability. But a coherent regional response was not easy to achieve given the complexity of local political interests posed by political Islam. Existing regional fault-lines and divergent perspectives towards an assertive United States in a post-9/11 world were exacerbated by the approach to war in Iraq — increasingly likely to be an American-led campaign without a mandate from the United Nations. Regional efforts to co-operate in the war against international terrorism were also complicated by the diversity of local political conditions and interests.

While the war on terrorism could well have distracted regional efforts at recovering economic growth and development, external economic interests helped to bolster ASEAN's image as a region still being courted with offers of free trade pacts. Such overtures meant, however, that ASEAN itself would need to get its act together to enhance integration and competitiveness. In the final analysis, sustained economic recovery and economic growth will feed back towards enhancing the kind of resilience needed to meet soft-security challenges in a more comprehensive way even as more concerted regional efforts to counter terrorism are worked at. It remains whether the region can demonstrate that it has the political will to grasp these opportunities.

Notes

1. *Straits Times*, 10 September 2002. As it turned out, for the whole of 2002 Singapore's economy grew by 2.2 per cent — less than a third of the average annual rate between 1985 and 2001. Singapore's unemployment rate in 2002 hit a sixteen-year high. One out of every twenty persons in the labour force became unemployed.
2. Pei Minxin, "Symbolic Summit Provides Several Surprises", *Straits Times*, 28 October 2002, p. A3.
3. CNN.com, "Japanese Warship heads for Indian Ocean", 16 December 2002, <http://cnn.worldnews.printthis.clickability.com>.
4. *Straits Times*, 6 December 2002.
5. In the following month it was the turn of the Japanese public to feel anger over the "intrusion" of Chinese police into the Japanese consulate in Shenyang to arrest five North Korean asylum seekers.
6. "China, Russia issue joint statement", Xinhua News Agency, 3 December 2002, <http://fpmews.xinhuanet.com/english/2002-12/03/content_647230.htm>.
7. *Straits Tines*, 8 August 2002.
8. Christopher Coker, *Globalisation and Insecurity in the Twenty-first Century: NATO and the Management of Risk*, Adelphi Paper 345, Oxford University Press for IISS, 2002, p. 39.
9. For an extensive detailing of the Al-Qaeda's links in Southeast Asia, see Rohan Gunaratna, *Inside Al-Qaeda: Global Network of Terror* (London: Hurst, 2002), pp. 174–204.
10. *International Herald Tribune*, 23 January 2002.
11. In February the Indonesian public, legislators, and officials reacted strongly to Singapore Senior Minister's remarks that terrorist leaders were at large in Indonesia.
12. See Irman G. Lanti, "Nationalism behind Jakarta's passivity towards militants", *Straits Times*, 25 January 2002, p. 32.
13. President Megawati herself made no official comment but the Nadhlatul Ulama and the Muhammadiyah as well as the Indonesian Ulema Council criticized the detentions and said the Indonesian authorities should not be swayed by these developments. (*Straits Times*, 8 January 2002.)
14. See Barry Wain, "Unfriendly Fire", *Far Eastern Economic Review*, 12 September 2002, pp. 15–17, 20, 22.
15. In February Indonesia signed an anti-terrorism agreement with Australia. It was essentially an accord, which formalized an ongoing co-operation in intelligence sharing.
16. *Straits Times*, 9 October 2002.
17. *Straits Times*, 3 May 2002.
18. See Munir Majid, "Common ground in Malaysia–US relations", *New Straits Times*, 19 May 2002, p. 11, and Karim Raslan, "US sees Malaysia in new light", *Sunday Star*, 19 May 2002, p. 34.
19. *Straits Times*, 9 August 2002.
20. *Straits Times*, 28 November 2002.
21. *Straits Times*, 7 November 2002.
22. "Enhancing Cooperation in Cobra Gold", *Asia-Pacific Defense Forum*, Winter 2002–03, p. 6.
23. Raymond Bonner, "Qaeda meeting in Thailand planned attacks on tourists", *International Herald Tribune*, 9–10 November 2002. See also Shawn W. Crispin, "In Denial", *Far Eastern Economic Review*, 14 November 2002, p. 24.
24. Rohan Gunaratna, *Inside Al-Qaeda*, p. 203.
25. *Straits Times*, 9 August 2002. Gunaratna noted that Rohingya Muslims from

Myanmar have joined the Al-Qaeda. See his *Inside Al-Qaeda*, p. 204.
26. "ASEAN-United States of America Joint Declaration for Co-operation to Combat International Terrorism", Bandar Seri Begawan, 1 August 2002, <http://www.aseansec.org/7424.htm>.
27. Catherine E. Dalpino, "Making the anti-terrorism pact work", *Straits Times*, 13 August 2002, p. 12.
28. "2001 ASEAN Declaration on Joint Action to Counter Terrorism", <http://www.aseansec.org/5620.htm>.
29. Joint Communique of the Special ASEAN Ministerial Meeting on Terrorism, Kuala Lumpur, 20–21 May 2002, <http://www.aseansec.org/5618.htm>.
30. *Straits Times*, 10 September 2002.
31. *Straits Times*, 16 September 2002.
32. *Bangkok Post*, 16 September 2002.

THE YEAR IN ASEAN
The Charter, Trade Agreements, and the Global Economic Crisis

Rodolfo C. Severino

In the past year, the mass media have highlighted three developments in Southeast Asia, which thus became the subjects of public attention. One was the start of the implementation of the new Charter of the Association of Southeast Asian Nations (ASEAN), particularly the establishment of the ASEAN Inter-governmental Commission on Human Rights (AICHR). Another was the scheduled elimination on 1 January 2010 of tariffs on most goods traded among China and the six older, and more advanced and heavily trading, ASEAN members — Brunei Darussalam, Indonesia, Malaysia, the Philippines, Singapore, and Thailand (the other ASEAN members are Cambodia, Laos, Myanmar, and Vietnam). The third was the response of Southeast Asian countries to the regional impact of the global economic crisis.

The media spotlight on these developments has led the public to expect some dramatic, overnight changes in the region because of them. As an academic, I have sought to dampen such expectations, called for caution, and urged the media and the public to refrain from rash predictions and speculation. As the Americans say, "the jury is still out" on these three questions.

The ASEAN Charter

The drafting of the ASEAN Charter by a task force of senior ASEAN officials, its signing by the ASEAN leaders in November 2007, and its entry into force in December 2008 were significant for six reasons. For the first time, after forty years of existence, ASEAN has adopted a charter for itself, comprehensively placing it more firmly on a rules-based path.

If one looks closely at the Charter's contents, this is more than a matter of form. For the first time, the ASEAN

Reprinted from Daljit Singh, ed., *Southeast Asian Affairs 2010* (Singapore: Institute of Southeast Asian Studies, 2010), pp. 60–67. At the time of original publication, Rodolfo C. Severino was Head, ASEAN Studies Centre at the Institute of Southeast Asian Studies, Singapore.

countries have committed themselves in a formal document to norms having to do with the internal behaviour of states. As first enshrined in the 1976 Treaty of Amity and Cooperation in Southeast Asia, norms for inter-state conduct had guided ASEAN and other countries related to it — the peaceful settlement of disputes, the rejection of the threat or use of force, and non-interference in the internal affairs of nations. This is important in itself, but the Charter goes beyond that. In it, the ASEAN countries have declared their aspiration for such goals as democracy, human rights and fundamental freedoms, the rule of law, good governance, constitutional government, and social justice.

The Charter seeks to expedite decision making in the association, more clearly defining responsibilities for it. It lays squarely on the shoulders of the ASEAN leaders the responsibility for arriving at decisions, including voting if necessary, to resolve issues on which consensus cannot be reached at lower levels. It has established a Committee of Permanent Representatives resident in Jakarta to accelerate the process of decision making on many issues requiring member-states' agreement.

At the same time, and this is the fourth reason, the Charter seeks to cultivate among its members a "culture of compliance". It assigns to the ASEAN National Secretariats at the ministries of foreign affairs the tasks of coordinating the implementation of ASEAN decisions and agreements as well as promoting knowledge and awareness of ASEAN at home. It calls upon the Secretary-General to submit regular reports on compliance and non-compliance with ASEAN agreements and decisions to the leaders, who would be expected to act on them. The Charter calls for the inclusion of dispute-settlement mechanisms in all ASEAN agreements in addition to the one already in place for the economic agreements. It reiterates the aim of the ASEAN Economic Community as the creation of a "single market and production base", re-affirming ASEAN's commitment to regional economic integration.

It seeks to clarify the diplomatic privileges and immunities of ASEAN Secretariat officials and of the permanent representatives and their staffs in Indonesia and in other ASEAN countries in accordance with the 1961 Vienna Convention on Diplomatic Relations or the national law of the ASEAN country concerned.

Lastly, the Charter confers legal personality on ASEAN. What this means exactly is still being worked out. In any case, it enables ASEAN to receive ambassadors from non-ASEAN states and other intergovernmental organizations.

In the one year in which it has been in force, implementation of the Charter has been surprisingly rapid. The Committee of Permanent Representatives is busily functioning in Jakarta. An additional two Deputy Secretaries-General have been appointed, raising the total to four. The ASEAN leaders now meet twice a year, as called for by the Charter, once to make decisions on moving ASEAN forward and the other time to conduct summit-level meetings with their counterparts from outside the region. The ASEAN chairmanship now coincides with the calendar year, with a single chairmanship for most ASEAN bodies. The economic ministers have devised a "scorecard" to keep track of compliance with ASEAN agreements and decisions.

A High-level Legal Experts Group is hard at work on the meaning and implications of ASEAN's legal personality, on the details of the dispute-settlement mechanisms, and on the question of privileges and immunities.

According to the ASEAN Secretariat, twenty-five ambassadors have been accredited to ASEAN (as of 4 January 2010) — those of Australia, Austria, Bulgaria, Canada, China, the Czech Republic, Denmark, the European Union, Finland, France, Greece, India, Italy, Japan, the Republic of Korea, Libya, Luxembourg, Norway, Peru, Portugal, Romania, Russia, Spain, the United Kingdom, and the United States. Of these, those of Australia, China, India, Japan, the Republic of Korea, and the United States are separate from their ambassadors to Indonesia. The United States has announced its desire to establish a resident embassy to ASEAN in Jakarta this year.

Not least, pursuant to the Charter, the terms of reference of the AICHR, something not envisioned even by the bold-thinking Eminent Persons Group on the ASEAN Charter, have been adopted and its members appointed. The members are:

- Brunei Darussalam — Pehin Dato Hamid Bakal, former Syar'ie Chief Judge, State Judiciary Department, formerly with the Ministry of Religious Affairs;
- Cambodia — Om Yentieng, Senior Minister, President of the Cambodian Human Rights Commission and of the Anti-Corruption Unit at the Council of Ministers;
- Indonesia — Rafendi Djamin, prominent human-rights advocate and activist;
- Lao PDR — Bounkeut Sangsomsak, former career diplomat and Vice Minister of Foreign Affairs, former member of the National Assembly;
- Malaysia — Dato' Sri Muhammad Shafee Abdullah, practicing lawyer arguing human rights cases among others and legal adviser to Malaysian prime ministers and the leading political party, the United Malays National Organisation;
- Myanmar — U Kyaw Tint Swe, career diplomat, former Permanent Representative to the United Nations, New York;
- Philippines — Rosario Gonzalez Manalo, retired career diplomat, member of the faculties of several prominent Philippine universities, Philippine representative to the task forces that drafted the ASEAN Charter and the terms of reference of the AICHR;
- Singapore — Richard R. Magnus, retired senior district judge, Chairman of the Casino Regulatory Authority, the Political Films Advisory Panel, the Public Guardian Board, and Temasek Cares TLG Ltd.;
- Thailand — Sriprapha Petcharamesree, Center for Human Rights Studies and Social Development, Mahidol University, of which she is a former Director; and
- Vietnam — Do Ngoc Son, career diplomat, Ambassador to Spain.

The diverse backgrounds of these members, their varied personalities, and the different degrees of their links with and independence from their governments place a question mark on how precisely the commission will function. Having been negotiated by governments, the commission's terms of reference are a product of many compromises.

Several things are clear, however. As noted above, the Charter and the Commission on Human Rights to which it gave rise place human rights, for the first time, on the ASEAN agenda. The commission is to meet twice a year, once at the ASEAN Secretariat and the other time at the country of the ASEAN chair. It cannot but discuss human rights and expose itself to the human rights situations in member countries. These may not necessarily give the commission the independence and "teeth" that some advocates and activists wish. However, it is a significant step forward.

At the same time, it is also clear that, in the continuing absence of a strong and authoritative regional institution, whether and how the provisions of the Charter will be carried out depend on the collective will of the member states and on their perception of how implementing those provisions will serve the interests of the nation, the regime, or even, politically or personally, the leaders themselves. In this sense, the Charter remains like other regional associations of sovereign states, except only for the European Union.

Nevertheless, the Charter does move ASEAN closer to being rules-based and institutionalized, although to what extent remains to be seen.

ASEAN Free Trade Agreements

The second ASEAN-related focus of media and public attention in the past year has been the "effectivity" of ASEAN-China "free trade", supposedly on 1 January 2010. What exactly happened at the beginning of this year? In the Framework Agreement on Comprehensive Economic Cooperation (CEC) that they signed in November 2002, the leaders of ASEAN and China committed themselves to the phased reduction of tariffs on goods traded among China and ASEAN's six older members so as to create a "free trade area (FTA)" among them by 2010. In November 2004, China's Commerce Minister and the Economic Ministers of the ten ASEAN countries signed the trade-in-goods component of the CEC agreement which set 1 January 2010 as the date for the elimination of all tariffs on trade among China and the ASEAN Six. However, up to 150 tariff lines could still be protected by tariffs up to 2012.

Even on the basis of these paper commitments, nothing really dramatic took place at the beginning of 2010. The process of tariff reductions was supposed to have begun in the middle of 2005, with tariffs dropping to no more than five per cent by 2009 on trade among China and the ASEAN Six. Moreover, it remains to be seen whether traders will actually undertake the expense and effort to apply for the preferential — or zero — tariff rates provided for in the CEC and trade-in-goods agreements. Those same traders will say — if they are honest — that what really matters is the ease of doing business in a particular country rather than the tariff rates, that tariff rates are less important than factors like product standards, customs procedures, the state of infrastructure, transportation links, and their cost, taxation, the time it takes for goods to be released from customs or for businesses to be registered, and, of course, corruption. On these things, the ASEAN-China trade-in-goods agreement has nothing to say. In other words, there is nothing to get excited about on ASEAN-China trade simply because of the advent of 2010.

It is probably for this reason that the Indonesian Government, through its Industry and Trade Minister, Mari Elka Pangestu, announced in January 2010 that it had no intention of seeking a re-negotiation of the ASEAN-China agreement. Minister Pangestu correctly pointed out that Indonesia had enough tools to wield against unfair trade practices, like anti-dumping measures. She might have added that the Indonesian business sectors that were so vocal — the most vocal in ASEAN — in denouncing the ASEAN-China agreement as placing Indonesian firms at a competitive disadvantage had had five to seven years to make their views known. Presumably, the Indonesian Government conducted extensive consultations with the business community before sending its negotiators to the conference table with China and the rest of ASEAN. Indeed, Indonesia designated 263 product groups, the most in ASEAN, for the postponement of zero tariffs from 2010 to 2012.

In the case of trade with China, the cause for legitimate complaint is not competition, which is what trade is all about, but the Chinese Government's possible or actual use of state power to support Chinese trading firms, many of which are state-owned. Possible tools are the manipulation of exchange rates, access to credit, and other forms of direct or indirect subsidy to exporting firms. If so, defensive measures ought to be targeted at these instruments and practices rather than at trade and competition themselves.

The broad purpose of FTAs is not only the liberalization and facilitation of trade and investments but to affirm to the world the parties' good relations with one another and their determination to improve and strengthen those relations. It is also to send a signal to the business community that their markets are full of opportunities for one another. In the case of ASEAN and China, this process began long ago. The 2002 CEC framework agreement and the 2004 trade-in-goods agreement were merely steps, albeit important ones, in the process. In this respect, there is nothing magical about 1 January 2010.

Similarly, the trade-in-goods agreement among South Korea and the ASEAN countries, signed in August 2006 (except by Thailand, which acceded to it two and a half years later), called for the abolition of tariffs on trade among South Korea and the ASEAN Six by 1 January 2010. This deadline, however, came and went without attracting the media's attention.

ASEAN signed its trade-in-goods agreement with India in August 2009. The agreement provided for the start of the reduction of tariffs on 1 January 2010 with a view to their eventual elimination. Again, the media took no note of the start of this process.

In the meantime, Japan had signed a "comprehensive partnership agreement" with ASEAN as a group in April 2008, having concluded individual free trade area or comprehensive economic partnership agreements, which differed in their provisions, with the ASEAN Six over the 2000–7 period. Tokyo subsequently signed such an agreement with Vietnam.

ASEAN's free trade area agreement with Australia and New Zealand, negotiated off and on since 2000 and signed in February 2009, is the most comprehensive of the lot, covering not only tariff cutting and elimination, rules of origin, and customs procedures, but also sanitary and phytosanitary measures, product standards and technical regulations, trade in services, the movement of people, electronic commerce, investments, intellectual property, competition, and dispute settlement.

Although the ASEAN-Australia–New Zealand agreement is the broadest and most comprehensive that ASEAN has concluded with external partners, it has received meager public attention, if any. Only the scheduled elimination of tariffs on ASEAN-China trade has attracted attention.

The Global Economic Crisis

The third ASEAN-related question that has been frequently asked over the past year or so has to do with the impact on Southeast Asia of the global economic crisis and what Southeast Asia as a region and as individual countries are doing about it.

Because of the lessons learned from the Asian financial crisis of 1997–98 and for other reasons, Southeast Asia's major financial institutions were, relatively speaking, cushioned from the impact of the global economic crisis that still has to play itself out. However, because market demand in the developed economies has shrunk, many Southeast Asian — and East Asian — countries, their economies dependent on exports and foreign direct investment, have been hit by the contraction of their major export markets and the reduction in investments and tourism. How hard the ASEAN economies have been hit has been, ironically, in direct proportion to the extent of their openness to and reliance on the international economy.

In addition to what Asian governments are already doing — lowering interest rates, fiscal stimulus packages, social safety nets — the usual response from economists both Asian and Western has been to call for a re-structuring of international economic relations, principally between Asia and the West, with Asia increasing its domestic and/or regional consumption and reducing its exports and the West reducing its consumption, especially of imported goods, and its private and public debt.

There are two things to be said about this proposal. The first is that East Asian countries' imports from one another are already increasing, leading to the growing integration of the East Asian economy in terms of regional trade. Trade within East Asia including Japan, that is, ASEAN Plus Three, is now more than fifty-five per cent of total trade, which approaches the equivalent figure for intra-EU trade and exceeds that for the parties to the North American Free Trade Agreement. China's share in East Asian trade is rapidly expanding. There are indications that Southeast Asia's exports to China are increasingly less for assembly in China and re-export to the developed countries than for ultimate consumption in the Chinese market. However, much of East Asia's intra-regional trade is largely accounted for by the growing trade among the three Northeast Asian economies.

The second is that, nevertheless, the proposal's realization and effectiveness, including the economic re-structuring that it entails on both sides, will take time, despite their steady march. New niches have to be found, factories have to be re-tooled, fresh markets have to be cultivated, training in new skills has to be conducted, investment decisions have to be made. We must keep in mind that, in the early stages of their development, North America, Western Europe, and Japan engaged in massive investments in the construction of infrastructure, the extraction of natural resources, and the education and training of human resources, and then went on from there to mass consumption, including eventually of imported goods.

China and India, on the other hand, are currently largely at the investment phase. Although an expanding middle class is at the same time raising somewhat the capacity and propensity of these countries to consume end products, commodities, food, energy, construction materials, and services of many kinds, rather than a broader range of finished goods for direct consumption, are expected to continue to dominate Southeast Asian countries' exports to the two large Asian economies for some time. Thus, to shift from the developed-country to regional, emerging-economy markets would take time and single-minded effort. To take an extreme example, Cambodia's manufactured exports are almost entirely accounted for by garments bound for the European Union. How long will it take Cambodia to find new markets and develop new products? Those markets will certainly not be in Cambodia itself, which the United Nations categorizes as one of the world's least-developed countries. Nor can the Chinese, Indian, or ASEAN markets completely take the place of the old developed-country markets for Southeast Asian exports anytime soon.

One thing is clear. The global economic crisis is no reason for a retreat into national protectionism and other nationalistic political gestures. Rather, it is a reason for accelerated regional economic integration in Southeast Asia and East Asia, as well as the closer regulation of financial institutions. Regional economic integration would both enlarge the "domestic" market and, in the long run, reduce dependence on developed markets. However, the run is long, although it has begun.

Conclusion

The implementation of the ASEAN Charter, the abolition of tariffs on ASEAN's trade with China or other countries, and the response of Southeast Asia to the impact on it of the global economic crisis should not be expected to lead to quick, overnight, and dramatic changes in ASEAN or Southeast Asia. Rather, they should be viewed in perspective, as part of a long-term trend whose effectiveness or ultimate outcome remains uncertain and unpredictable. They may be important, but, like all products of human decision or governmental agreement, should not be the subject of rash predictions or self-confident speculation.

SEEKING STABILITY IN TURBULENT TIMES
Southeast Asia's New Normal?

See Seng Tan and Oleg Korovin

Political and security developments in Southeast Asia in 2014 reflect efforts on the part of Southeast Asian countries as well as ASEAN (the Association of Southeast Asian Nations) to adjust and adapt to the conditions and circumstances of a "new normal" in the wider Asia-Pacific region: a rapidly changing regional strategic environment where emerging powers display greater assertiveness and assurance of their newfound status, whilst established powers experience relative decline and seek to rebalance against the growing power and influence of their rivals. China's rising power and influence appears to have grown from strength to strength, notwithstanding putative efforts by the United States, Japan and others to balance against it partly through rallying Southeast Asian partners in support of their cause. Adding to the growing prospect of regional instability and turbulence was Russia's annexation of Crimea in March, which raised fears among some Southeast Asians over the prospective emulation of Russia's action by more powerful claimant states over the South China Sea region.

At the same time within Southeast Asia, a number of states and societies underwent political transition. Indonesia conducted a successful presidential election in July which saw a popular non-establishment figure, the then Jakarta Governor Joko Widodo (or "Jokowi"), win the presidency. It remains unclear at this point what Jokowi's foreign policy will look like. However, there are early hints that Indonesia might not be as fixated with ASEAN as in the past. Going beyond the "Indo-Pacific" idea advanced by the Yudhoyono

---

Reprinted from Daljit Singh, ed., *Southeast Asian Affairs 2015* (Singapore: Institute of Southeast Asian Studies, 2015), pp. 3–24. At the time of original publication, See Seng Tan was Associate Professor and Deputy Director of the Institute of Defence and Strategic Studies at the S. Rajaratnam School of International Studies (RSIS), Nanyang Technological University, Singapore and Oleg Korovin was an independent scholar.

administration, the Jokowi administration's vision for Indonesia is as a global maritime fulcrum connecting the Indian and Pacific Oceans.[1] Known as "PACINDO", the area of engagement envisioned here is ostensibly geographically more extensive than the Indo-Pacific region the Yudhoyono administration had in mind. To that end, India and the Gulf states have been identified as countries with whom Jokowi would engage more deeply. As a foreign policy adviser to Jokowi has declared: "We used to say ASEAN is *the* cornerstone of our foreign policy. Now we change it to *a* cornerstone of our foreign policy."[2]

After considerable unrest in Thailand caused by the rift between the so-called "Red Shirts" and their "Yellow" rivals, senior officers of the Thai military launched a bloodless coup in May which brought temporary relief but left many questions unanswered. The coup appeared to sour relations between the new military regime and the Thai royalists that supported the coup, on one hand, and the United States on the other. With this downturn in Thai-U.S. relations and its potential ramifications for their security alliance — including the U.S. decision to scale back the Cobra Gold 2015 military exercise — there is growing concern over whether Thailand may seek to deepen further its already substantial ties with China — a step likely to worry Thailand's ASEAN neighbours given their apprehensions over China's actions in the South China Sea.[3] On the other hand, Washington would presumably repair its ties with Bangkok so as not to push the latter into Beijing's embrace.[4]

To be sure, post-colonial Southeast Asia is no stranger to turbulence, not least for a region born out of the Pacific War and forged in the furnace of great power collapse, war and political upheaval.[5]

That said, the current regional situation is unprecedented in that at no time in the region's annals has there ever been the concomitant (albeit uneven) rise of three regional powers, China, Japan and India, and the complications that has posed to the post-World War Two hegemony long enjoyed by a United States. Of these, India remained the odd man out in 2014 in terms of involvement, although Indian Prime Minister Narendra Modi took advantage of the East Asia Summit (EAS) in November to signal his intent to recast India's decades-long "Look East" policy, defined mostly by missed opportunities, to an "Act East" policy under his premiership.[6] The growing strategic competition and alignments among the great powers have engendered uncertainty among Southeast Asian states, whose dedicated project of regional community formation has been confounded by the temptation to break ranks and undermine ASEAN cohesion through unilaterally siding with a particular great power so as to advance their own interests.

At least three noteworthy trends defined Southeast Asia's new normal in 2014. Firstly, China was the outstanding performer among the big powers in the regional diplomatic and economic stakes. A generation removed from the "keeping a low profile" approach that had dominated Chinese foreign policy since the time of Deng Xiaoping, the People's Republic appeared sufficiently self-assured to assert itself on the regional and global stages. Secondly, notwithstanding the presence of multiple players in the South China Sea, China remained the key without which there would be no progress in the maritime disputes among the claimant states. Finally, Southeast Asia and ASEAN continued to labour, frustratingly so in the light of a self-imposed 2015 deadline, for the formation of the ASEAN Community that is unlikely to be achieved in terms of depth of regional cooperation and integration that would satisfy the collective needs of the region.

The Great Game in 2014

The region has been marked by the growing rivalry between emerging and established powers, whose complex interactions threaten to muddy the distinction between what constitutes revisionist actions and what constitutes status quo. For a long time and as a consequence of its role as a strategic guarantor, the United States has occupied a privileged place in the security calculi of East Asian countries in general. The rise of China, the focus of considerable analysis among Asia watchers throughout the post-Cold War period, has often been discussed in terms of its "potential" to rival the United States — an as yet unrealized prospect further deferred by the relative alignment of interests between Beijing and Washington over the global war on terrorism. Two major dynamics are now changing that. The first involves the perceived relative decline of the United States, whose post-Afghanistan strategic "pivot" or "rebalance" to Asia — seen by many Chinese as a containment effort directed against China, even though U.S. officials have strenuously denied that — appeared to be a half-hearted proposition following the global financial crisis of 2007–08 and severe cuts to the U.S. defence budget. The second involves the considerably more recent development of Russia's annexation of Crimea and its ongoing support of the armed rebellion in eastern Ukraine. The chief beneficiary of both these trends, at least in 2014, has arguably been China.

America's Rebalance on Track?

It has been argued that East Asia's security order is undergoing transition from the Cold War-era great power bargains, namely the U.S.-Japan alliance, which made Japan dependent on America for its security and indirectly assured China its security through the restraining impact of the alliance on Japan's strategic ambitions and, the 1972 U.S.-China rapprochement, which paved the way to a tacit coalition against Soviet influence. However, the transition is as yet unformed or at best incomplete great power bargains.[7] The post-Cold War rise of China and the ongoing military "normalization" of Japan — the expectation for a more active and enhanced military role for Japan within the context of its alliance with the United States[8] — led to the dissolution of the older great power bargains. While it could conceivably be argued that the broad-based legitimacy enjoyed by the United States as the region's strategic guarantor constituted a bargain of sorts, its hegemony was at best incomplete given the potential challenge to its leadership posed by China. As the former head of Council for Security Cooperation in the Asia-Pacific (CSCAP) China, Ambassador Shi Chun-Lai, once declared at a CSCAP meeting, China does not accept America's preponderance in the region as much as it "tolerates" it for the time being.[9]

Against this backdrop, America's pivot or rebalance towards Asia, formally announced by President Barack Obama before the Australian Parliament in late 2011,[10] has elicited as many questions from, as it has furnished answers to, security allies and partners who wonder aloud whether their American friends have the stomach to see their commitment to

Asia through in the face of serious fiscal constraints, political uncertainties and diplomatic distractions dogging the United States. In April, Obama undertook a four-nation visit to the region reassuring that the pivot "is real", while his then Defence Secretary — Chuck Hagel, who resigned in late November reportedly because the White House felt he was not the right man to handle shifting priorities like the rise of the Islamic State-led insurgency in Iraq and Syria and the Ebola pandemic in Africa[11] — argued that America "is a Pacific Power for many years. We've looked forward to a continuation of building those relationships and those partnerships [in the region] as we go forward".[12]

Obama's attendance at the Asia-Pacific Economic Cooperation (APEC) summit and the East Asia Summit (EAS) constituted a success in themselves, given his no-shows at both summits in 2013. On the sidelines of APEC 2014, a landmark climate change agreement with China that specifies a timetable for emission reduction was announced. However, Obama's international reputation appeared diminished among the Chinese; for example, a conservative Chinese periodical dismissed the U.S. president's leadership as "insipid" — a far cry from 2009 during Obama's first presidential visit to China where he reportedly dazzled a student audience at a town hall-style meeting in Shanghai.[13]

Russia Leans towards China

On the other hand, Ukraine, where a new pro-Western government came to power after a coup in February 2014, has become the locus of the trans-Atlantic stand-off. Sanctions and diplomatic pressure by the European Union (EU) and the United States have effectively forced Russia to gravitate towards China. Presumably, the Chinese are not particularly enthused by Russia's annexation of Crimea but, at the same time, they worry over the implications the February ouster of Ukrainian President Victor Yanukovich could have had on the region.[14] Moscow has concluded deals, unprecedented in scale, with Beijing to supply China with Russian oil and gas through projects totalling US$400 billion, and has opened the Russian market for Chinese strategic investments.[15] The original plan for Russia was to have two geopolitical support pillars on both ends of the Eurasian continent: China in the East, and Germany in the West. But with the scrapping of its EU-bound South Stream gas pipeline project, it appears Russia's ties with the EU — more specifically with Germany — are now in disrepair.[16] Although the Kremlin has undertaken steps to regroup *vis-à-vis* the EU, its heavy dependence on China is now undeniable, providing Beijing a putative strategic advantage against Washington.

Fairly or otherwise, some Southeast Asians view the Crimean annexation with concern in that it might embolden China to adopt a similarly aggressive approach towards its territorial claims in the South China Sea[17] — a view shared by some Americans.[18] However, on the whole, Southeast Asians are ambivalent over what the Ukraine question might mean for their region. Against those who worry over the prospect of enhanced Chinese assertiveness, there are others who believe U.S. inaction in fact indirectly mollifies China towards self-restraint over Ukraine. Whichever case, the perception cultivated has been that of a United States incapable and/or unwilling to do anything to prevent the belligerence of others despite being the world's sole global power. Arguably, America's troubled pivot and Russia's act of aggression and resulting isolation by the West has been to China's benefit.

China Gains

In many ways, 2014 marked China's emergence as an active and assertive global power. Nowhere has this been more apparent than in Chinese achievements garnered at international meetings, both those chaired by China and those in which it participated. At the APEC Summit in Beijing in November, China demonstrated economic leadership in calling for the creation of a Free Trade Area of the Asia-Pacific (FTAAP) and its "one belt, one road" plan — to which the Chinese have committed a Silk Road fund worth US$40 billion for infrastructure-related investments in addition to its Asian Infrastructure Investment Bank (AIIB) proposal that twenty-one countries have already joined.[19] Beijing's successful conclusion of free trade pacts with Australia and South Korea has only added to China's standing. China will reportedly invest US$1.25 trillion abroad over the next ten years, and import more than US$10 trillion in goods in the next five years.[20] "As its overall national strength grows", as China President Xi Jinping noted in his address to the APEC CEO Summit in November, "China will be both capable and willing to provide more public goods for the Asia-Pacific and the world, especially new initiatives and visions for enhancing regional cooperation." In language reminiscent of his so-called "Chinese dream",[21] Xi told his audience in Beijing, "We are duty-bound to create and fulfil an Asia-Pacific dream for our people."[22] That said, according to Alan Bollard, executive director of the APEC secretariat, "None of the economies want to start negotiating on the FTAAP. It is far too early to do that."[23]

Secondly, China demonstrated diplomatic finesse in improving its troubled ties with Japan. While much was made of the frostiness Chinese President Xi exhibited towards his Japanese counterpart Shinzo Abe at their bilateral exchange on the side of the APEC meeting, the exchange — the first in two years between the two leaders — was an affirmation of the agreement reached in early November between Chinese State Councillor Yang Jiechi and Japanese National Security chief Shotaro Yachi on a four-point consensus on improving Sino-Japanese ties.[24] Chinese nationalistic sentiment over the disputed islands and waters aside, greater stability in its relationship with Japan — particularly in the light of Abe's continued leadership following his successful re-election in mid-December — benefits China more than the prolongation of toxic ties. Thirdly, as noted, the landmark agreement with the United States on climate change is another feather in the Chinese cap.

Finally, China, arguably with less success, has persisted in its efforts to promote a vision for regional security that some see as exclusivist towards the United States. At the Conference on Interaction and Confidence-Building Measures in Asia (CICA) held in Shanghai in May 2014, Xi pledged that China would stick to peaceful methods to resolve its disputes over territory.[25] Echoing his predecessors, Xi has claimed that China would never seek "hegemony or expansion" in the Asia-Pacific, even as it strengthens its diplomatic and military footprint in the region.[26] The logic undergirding Xi's pledge, according to analysts, is a "new security paradigm" that

China wishes to promote, where elements such as mutual respect and understanding and the search for common ground while shelving differences would provide the basis for Asian security to "be handled in the Asian way".[27] In much the same way during the Jiang and Hu presidencies, China consistently advanced its principles of peaceful coexistence and promoted a "new security concept" — first introduced in 1997 and subsequently reintroduced each time with slight modifications — that emphasizes equality, mutual trust, respect and cooperation, consensus through consultation and the peaceful settlement of disputes.[28]

Beyond 2014, whether the aforementioned developments point to a new Chinese charm offensive in the foreseeable future — or, at the least, a restrained version of the "tailored coercion" that Beijing's East and South China Seas policy has been called — remains to be seen, however.[29] At the CICA gathering referred to above, Xi issued a veiled threat against unnamed Southeast Asian countries over their alleged efforts at strengthening military alliances to counter China, reflecting Beijing's inherent suspicions. It raises the possibility that China feels that the United States — presumably having encouraged, if only indirectly, its allies Japan and the Philippines and even a former foe, Vietnam, to harden their stances on their respective islands disputes with China — has not shown it the respect it feels it rightfully deserves. At the Sunnylands summit between Xi and Obama in June 2013, the former outlined China's two key wishes: one, respect from the United States, and two, for "a new relationship among major powers" to be forged between the two countries. Although Obama acknowledged the need for a "new model of cooperation" at the time, others have nonetheless noted his studious avoidance of the Chinese phraseology of a "new model of major country relationships",[30] which perhaps hinted that Washington neither viewed Beijing as responsible nor major — at least not yet. Be that as it may, Southeast Asian countries have by and large taken care to eschew fostering the impression that they are bandwagoning with the Americans to contain China. The influential international relations scholar John Mearsheimer predicted in 2013 that:

> [I]f China continues to grow economically, it will attempt to dominate Asia the way the United States dominates the Western Hemisphere. The United States, however, will go to enormous lengths to prevent China from achieving regional hegemony. Most of Beijing's neighbours, including India, Japan, Singapore, South Korea, Russia, and Vietnam, will join with the United States to contain Chinese power.[31]

However, there has been no obvious taking of sides with the United States to contain China, although the actions of many Southeast Asian countries imply that they continue to subscribe to strategic hedging, institutional engagement through the ASEAN-based regional architecture, and maintaining a balance of the major powers in the region. In an interview with Yoichi Funabashi, the editor-in-chief of the Japanese news daily, *Asahi Shimbun*, Singapore's founding leader, Lee Kuan Yew, once complained about the unfortunate predilection of the conservative Chinese press to translate the phrase "to balance" (*pingheng*) as "to conscribe" (*zhiheng*), hence connoting containment.[32] Such mistakes arouse Chinese anger unnecessarily.

The South China Sea: Choppy as Ever?

As expected, the issue of territorial disputes in the South China Sea dominated the ASEAN Regional Forum (ARF) in Naypidaw in August. The divergence in perceptions and narratives on the South China Sea (hereafter SCS) was noticeably acute. On the one hand, the U.S. Secretary of State, John Kerry, noting the "provocative steps" taken by claimant states "aimed at changing the status quo" (to use Kerry's words), indirectly fingered China as the main culprit whose actions, according to Kerry, have purportedly caused regional trade to suffer and regional relations to deteriorate.[33] The provocations in question presumably included China's controversial placement of its Haiyang Shiyou-981 oil rig — owned by the China National Offshore Oil Corporation (CNOOC) — near the Vietnamese coastline in May, which elicited anti-Chinese violence in Vietnam and the forced evacuation of thousands of Chinese citizens. The Vietnamese Foreign Ministry claimed that Chinese ships "intentionally rammed" two Vietnamese Coast Guard vessels near the oil rig.[34] It has been argued that China's deployment of the oil rig was no strategic mistake but a considered decision to advance its economic interests.[35] That the placement of the oil rig took place a mere few months after the establishment of a wide-ranging agreement between China and Vietnam on trade, infrastructure, energy and maritime affairs in October 2013 suggests however that Beijing likely did not anticipate the extent of Vietnamese anger in reaction. The Chinese subsequently removed the oil rig in July, one month ahead of the previously announced schedule.[36] This left room for speculation whether China sought to mollify its counterpart after a provocation, or if it achieved what it wanted anyway.

Going further, Kerry proposed a moratorium on provocative actions in the SCS, which his Chinese counterpart, Foreign Minister Wang Yi, roundly rejected as "premature".[37] Challenging Kerry's assessment, Wang insisted that the "situation in the SCS is generally stable, and the freedom of navigation there has never seen any problems", and "countries out of the region can have their legitimate concerns, but if they come here for finger-pointing, then we are opposed to that".[38] China similarly rejected calls by the Philippines and other ASEAN countries for disputes to be resolved through arbitration within the framework of the United Nations Convention on the Law of the Sea (UNCLOS).[39] Although China insisted that it would resolutely safeguard its sovereignty and maritime rights in the South China Sea, it nonetheless reiterated its commitment to a "dual track" policy — bilateral consultations and negotiations between claimant states, on the one hand, and between China and ASEAN in their joint pursuit of a binding code of conduct for the South China Sea on the other[40] — to resolve the situation in the South China Sea.

Hitherto, little progress has been achieved on the proposed code of conduct other than member countries of ASEAN reaching a consensus at the ASEAN Summit's leaders retreat in Naypidaw in November over "the need to expeditiously work towards early conclusion" of the code of conduct without specifying its possible contents much less a timeline for completion.[41] That ASEAN foreign ministers had affirmed as far back in August 2013 that the ASEAN states would from henceforth speak with "one voice" in their effort to press China for a speedier conclusion to the code is a stark reminder to the Southeast Asians that the progress in the negotiations is more or less determined by the Chinese.⁴² Yet the process has not been without accomplishments like the establishment of "early harvest" measures, such as hotlines for maritime emergencies to enhance communication.⁴³

ASEAN: Still More Neighbourhood than Community?

With the 2015 deadline for the official début of the ASEAN Community — with its economic, political-security and socio-cultural "pillars" — looming, ASEAN foreign ministers concurred at their leaders retreat in November on the need for their countries to speed up community building and ASEAN integration and to move forward to the realization of the "master plan" for the ASEAN connectivity. In practically every conceivable domain — economic, political, security — the regionalism project has encountered considerable challenges and constraints, many of which ASEAN and its member countries have yet to surmount.

Not Quite There Yet

Supporters and critics of the Association alike are agreed that the anticipated ASEAN Economic Community (AEC) is unlikely to be realized in terms of its envisaged targets, by the end of 2015. In response, ASEAN officials have insisted that the AEC will be pushed through as planned and that it has addressed 80 per cent of the required action lines — or as official reports have it, "ASEAN has implemented 82.1 per cent of the 229 AEC key deliverables targeted for completion by 2013"⁴⁴ — largely in areas such as tariff reduction and the facilitation of trade and investment liberalization.⁴⁵ Many are sceptical about the ability of the member states to complete the remaining and arguably more intractable issues — eliminating non-tariff barriers, creating the ASEAN Single Window, increasing cross-regional mobility of skilled labour and the like — in time for the launch of the AEC.⁴⁶

Ironically, the delay comes at a time when the need for integration is greater than ever before as many Southeast Asian countries, once over-dependent on export-led growth, are now rebalancing their economies and shifting their development strategies toward growing domestic demand. ASEAN states will need to manage their capital flows better and foster deeper economic integration not only to reduce developmental gaps among member countries but also — particularly for Indonesia, Malaysia, the Philippines, Thailand and Vietnam — to overcome the "middle-income trap" as their pace of growth falters.⁴⁷ Sundram Pushpanathan, the former ASEAN Deputy Secretary General responsible for implementing the AEC, has urged the leaders of ASEAN countries to move beyond the "process-based regionalism" that had historically served their national needs but has become a bane in the way of regional progress. Calling for a new regionalism that emphasizes concrete results and outcomes based on a structured and rules-based regime, Pushpanathan argued that for the AEC to be ready by 2015, "it is imperative that ASEAN shifts aggressively towards 'results-based regionalism'. We must act now."⁴⁸ Likewise, Surin Pitsuwan, the Secretary General of ASEAN from 2008 to 2012, has declared that it is time for ASEAN to move beyond the provision of "the centrality of goodwill" to "the centrality of substance".⁴⁹

Nagging Constraints

Nor, for that matter, would the ASEAN Political-Security Community (APSC), which has received considerably less attention from regional policymakers relative to the AEC, be ready by 2015. In the wake of challenges such as the Burmese junta's crackdown on the Buddhist clergy-led demonstrations in Yangon in 2007 (the so-called "Saffron Revolution"), ASEAN leaders amended their initial plan for the "ASEAN Security Community" — as originally stipulated in the 2003 Bali Concord II[50] — to the APSC in an apparent effort to scale back expectations. Recent developments have underscored the wisdom of that decision. They include border disputes among members like that between Cambodia and Thailand over the Preah Vihear promontory — which the International Court of Justice eventually ruled in Cambodia's favour in November 2013[51] — or intramural discord at the ASEAN Ministerial Meeting in Phnom Penh in July 2012 over the organization's position on the South China Sea disputes. The latter led to the ignominy of failing, for the first time in the Association's history, to produce an end-of-meeting communiqué. Subsequently, Indonesia exercised its *de facto* leadership in the Association to cobble together the so-called "six point agreement" as a compromise.[52]

While the ASEAN Coordinating Centre for Humanitarian Assistance on disaster management (AHA Centre) has deployed an Emergency Rapid Assessment Team (ERAT) to the Philippines ahead of Typhoon Hagupit in early December, many worry whether the region has successfully digested the lessons from last year's Typhoon Haiyan, which devastated wide swathes of the Philippines in November 2013. Although some ASEAN states furnished crisis relief in response to Haiyan, they did so on their own national accords rather than under the Association's aegis. Then, the conspicuous lack of an ASEAN-led response was equally revealing about the extent or dearth of collective capability and will,[53] notwithstanding the availability of the AHA Centre and protocols like the ASEAN Agreement on Disaster Management and Emergency Response (AADMER), as well as the participation by the respective militaries of ASEAN members in joint humanitarian assistance and disaster relief (HADR) exercises. The need for concerted and coordinated action among member states is equally true of all areas of intramural collaboration in general; the leader of a member nation has argued that ASEAN ought to respond in a decisive and coordinated fashion to geopolitical developments such as maritime disputes in the South China Sea and security issues like the rise of the Islamic State.[54]

Looking Outward, Not In

When Xi Jinping urged for Asia's security issues to be handled by Asians alone at the CICA meeting in Shanghai in May, few made the connection at the time that the Chinese leader's appeal implicitly recalled the Indonesian mantra of "regional solutions for regional problems".[55] The notion that Southeast Asians are best placed to manage their own security challenges has long captivated the regional imagination and, together with the Cold War concern against "interference" in Southeast Asia by outside powers, has served as a basis for ASEAN treaties and protocols like the 1971 Zone of Peace, Freedom and Neutrality (ZOPFAN) and the 1995 Southeast Asia Nuclear Weapons Free Zone (SEANWFZ). On the other hand, the emergence of ASEAN in the post-Cold War period as the region's leading facilitator of "open" and "inclusive" regionalism[56] — through its participation in the APEC and its formation of a suite of regional arrangements like the ARF, ASEAN+3, East Asia Summit (EAS) and the ASEAN Defence Ministers Meeting-Plus (ADMM-Plus) — has underscored a growing reliance on external powers, rather than their rejection, in the management of regional security.

In the case of the ADMM-Plus, for instance, ASEAN countries look to eight dialogue partners (America, Australia, China, India, Japan, Korea, New Zealand, and Russia) for assistance to develop their national and regional capacities in HADR, nuclear counter-proliferation, ensuring safety and security in the maritime domain, counter-terrorism, and the like. And as noted, despite the focus paid to the development of ASEAN's capabilities in HADR, the organization's relative inaction in response to Typhoon Haiyan — the efforts by individual ASEAN states were obviously nowhere near what America and Britain contributed — only served to underscore the extent and depth of their dependence. However, the aspiration for regional solutions still matters to the extent that the Association's members persist to ensure that the norm of ASEAN centrality in Asian regionalism continues to enjoy the support of all stakeholders, especially the non-ASEAN countries.

One Step Forward, Two Steps Back

The region's democratic transition, uneven at best, had mixed results in 2014. Promising to bring "true democracy" to Thailand, the coup leaders, led by General Prayuth Chan-ocha who had installed himself as prime minister, have formed a Cabinet made up of the junta and former officers — former army chief, Prawit Wongsuwan, is a deputy prime minister; Anupong Paochinda, another former army chief, is interior minister; and Tanasak Patimapragorn, the chief of Thai Defence Forces, is the new foreign minister — plus a few senior bureaucrats — including Pridiyathorn Devakula, a former central banker, as a deputy prime minister with special responsibility for overseeing economic strategy.[57] While most Bangkok residents are relieved that the bloodless military putsch engendered a return to normalcy, a host of problems remain, not least the poor performance of the Thai economy and uncertainty over how the junta will deal with the restive south and with former premier Yingluck Shinawatra and her supporters.[58]

In Indonesia, Joko Widodo defeated the controversial ex-general Prabowo Subianto in the July presidential election and became the first outsider to clinch the Indonesian presidency. Having campaigned on a reformist agenda, Widodo, popularly known as "Jokowi", raised expectations among many Indonesians regarding the prospect of much needed reforms to the nation's infrastructure, social welfare and level of corruption, among other things — a challenging task in the light of the odds stacked against him.[59] However, Jokowi's picks for his Cabinet marked the triumph of what one noted analyst has termed "realpolitik over reform", where requisite compromises to political parties and forces of patronage which backed his candidature had to be made.[60] The surprise, however, was in the extent to which he chose to go in making those compromises. A key example was the inclusion of Ryamizard Ryacudu, a former army chief often criticized by human rights groups, as defence minister; Ryacudu is an ally of former Indonesian President Megawati Sukarnoputri, on whose patronage Jokowi relied heavily. Be that as it may, the new President's decision to make good on his electoral promise to reduce state energy subsidies in an effort to free up funds for development plans is viewed by many economists as a good start.[61]

Myanmar's Chairmanship: Better Than Expected?

The year 2014 marked the first time that Myanmar became chair of ASEAN. The country joined the Association in 1997, but was denied its right to assume chairmanship in 2006 due to the international emphasis on Myanmar's poor track record in the area of human rights and the rule of law which resulted in pressure against the country's assumption of the chairmanship for the year. The decision against Myanmar in 2006 was unpleasant for ASEAN as a whole as it went against the members' general commitment to non-interference in each other's domestic affairs. But it also highlighted the Association's incremental shift towards that which it has termed "enhanced interaction" where particular instances of intramural interference if not interventionism are rationalized and justified.[62]

Notwithstanding the country's ongoing ethno-religious problems, the economic, social and political transformation that Myanmar has undergone under the leadership of President U Thein Sein has been nothing short of remarkable. There remain significant constraints against further change, to be sure. For example, for dissident turned parliamentarian Aung San Suu Kyi to become president — constitutionally she is barred because her late British husband was a foreigner, as are her children — her political party, the National League for Democracy (NLD), would have to win nearly three-quarters of all the seats contested in the upcoming election due (putatively) in late 2015.[63] But the positives achieved have not been insignificant. Freedom of information reforms, including the abolition of media censorship, facilitated in part the public outcry that led to Naypidaw's abrupt *volte face* in September 2011 over the construction of the Myitsone Dam, a Chinese-sponsored project which, when completed, would have supplied generated energy to China and likely caused adverse environmental damage to Burmese soil.[64] In 2013, Myanmar passed Cambodia on Transparency International's Corruption Perceptions Index, making Cambodia the lowest-ranking ASEAN member.[65] Myanmar was placed 157th in the Berlin-based group's 2013 study, an impressive climb of fifteen spots from its rank of 172nd of 176 countries in the 2012 study, while Cambodia tied for 160th place.[66] As ASEAN Secretary-General Le Luong Minh has noted, "Myanmar's chairmanship comes amidst the country's ongoing democratisation and reform process which has been enjoying strong support from ASEAN Member States and the international community at large."[67]

Myanmar came to the chairmanship mindful of the damage to ASEAN's reputation under Cambodia's chairmanship in 2012. "The lesson for Myanmar here is to respect ASEAN tradition, which is to take tiny little diplomatic steps without creating political friction among other ASEAN members, and to know its strategic limits", according to Peter Tan

Keo, an independent analyst who focuses on ASEAN. "It would behove the country to understand its role in stewarding issues, not to stifle them for its own strategic gains or interests, as was clearly the case with Cambodia."[68] In that respect, Myanmar performed remarkably well for a first-timer. The most significant testament to Myanmar's diplomatic prowess in 2014 was the non-escalation of the dispute over South China Sea issues, which returned to the tentative status quo by the end of August. Considering how upset Vietnam, the Philippines, and the United States had been with China's behaviour, what the Burmese accomplished was no small feat. Furthermore, Myanmar managed to avoid antagonizing any of the parties involved. Beijing seemed sufficiently placated that ASEAN's joint statement on the matter did not contain any direct references to China.[69] On their part, Hanoi and Manila, the members most affected in the debacle in Phnom Penh in 2012, managed to get a dedicated ASEAN statement that addressed the South China Sea disputes.[70]

Finally, as ASEAN has increasingly done over the past few years, the organization has used its summits to stress the importance of upholding the principle of "ASEAN centrality" in East Asian regionalism and its supporting architecture. Under Myanmar's leadership, the 2014 ASEAN Summit was no different.[71] The centrality of ASEAN has come under challenge from within and without in the past few years. Crucially, the absence of new great power bargains in the immediate post-Cold War period, allowed ASEAN, from the early 1990s onward, to step into the breach as the region's convenor by providing a regional architecture and convention which brought together regional countries, including the big powers, and institutionalized regular dialogues on political and security issues among them. Put differently, ASEAN's centrality in East Asia's regional architecture has principally been dependent on the regional consensus concerning the Association's relevance to regional order and security. If anything, it is the regional grouping's professed neutrality and relative weakness that great powers, unable to form bargains among themselves, find most attractive because ASEAN threatens no one. However, as events in the Association's recent past suggest, the regional grouping's ability to persuade the external powers to maintain that consensus in a rapidly shifting regional strategic environment has been eroded.[72] Nevertheless Myanmar did what it could to ensure that ASEAN centrality meant something more than mere rhetoric.

Looking Ahead to 2015

It is the contention of this chapter, firstly, that 2014 has effectively been China's year in terms of its accomplishments amid an evolving regional strategic environment characterized by rising and rebalancing powers, and secondly, that ASEAN has lagged in delivering on its regional goals. With the United States likely to look increasingly inward as its polity gradually gears up to vote for a new president in 2016, China will presumably seize the opportunity furnished by a distracted America to cultivate and deepen its ties to Southeast Asia. With Malaysia assuming the chairmanship of ASEAN in 2015, the emphasis will be on mobilizing member countries to complete the task of delivering the AEC by the end of the year; concluding the negotiations for the Regional Comprehensive Economic Partnership (RCEP) comprising the ASEAN states and six of its dialogue partners (Australia,

China, India, Japan, New Zealand and South Korea); and strengthening ASEAN and its suite of institutions by urging ASEAN members to agree to increase their contributions to the organization.⁷³ On the other hand, it remains to be seen what role Indonesia, which has long treated ASEAN as the cornerstone of its foreign policy, would want to play under its new president. Given that Indonesian intellectuals known for their advocacy of a "post-ASEAN foreign policy" for Indonesia are reportedly advising the new President on foreign policy raises the possibility that Indonesia's ties to ASEAN might not be as robust as before.⁷⁴

Notes

1. Rendi A. Witular, "Jokowi Launches Maritime Doctrine to the World", *Jakarta Post*, 13 November 2014.
2. Rizal Sukma at a public conference in Washington in December 2014, emphasis added. Cited in Prashanth Parameswaran, "Is Indonesia Turning Away From ASEAN Under Jokowi?", *The Diplomat*, 18 December 2014, available at <http://thediplomat.com/2014/12/is-indonesia-turning-away-from-asean-under-jokowi/>.
3. Patrick Jory, "China is a Big Winner from Thailand's Coup", *The Diplomat*, 18 June 2014, available at <http://www.eastasiaforum.org/2014/06/18/china-is-a-big-winner-from-thailands-coup/>.
4. Achara Ashayagachat, "Irritation as Thailand Loses Its Charm", *Bangkok Post*, 1 February 2015, available at <http://www.bangkokpost.com/opinion/opinion/463130/irritation-as-thailand-loses-its-charm>.
5. Milton Osborne, *Region of Revolt: Focus on Southeast Asia* (London: Elsevier, 2013).
6. Ankit Panda, "Modi 'Acts East' at East Asia Summit", *The Diplomat*, 14 November 2014, available at <http://thediplomat.com/2014/11/modi-acts-east-at-east-asia-summit/>.
7. Evelyn Goh, *Japan, China, and the Great Power Bargain in East Asia*, EAI Fellows Program Working Paper Series No. 32 (Seoul: East Asia Institute, November 2011), pp. 3–5.
8. Christopher W. Hughes, *Japan's Re-emergence as a "Normal" Military Power*, Adelphi Series 368–9 (Abingdon, Oxon: Routledge, 2007).
9. See Seng Tan, *The Making of the Asia Pacific: Knowledge Brokers and the Politics of Representation* (Amsterdam: Amsterdam University Press, 2013), p. 131.
10. Lenore Taylor, "Changing Fortunes Dictate Another Presidential Pivot", *Sydney Morning Herald*, 17 November 2011, available at <http://www.smh.com.au/federal-politics/political-opinion/changing-fortunes-dictate-another-presidential-pivot-20111117-1nk3t.html>.
11. Perry Bacon, Jr., "A Shifting Battleground: Why Chuck Hagel Resigned", *NBC News*, 24 November 2014, available at <http://www.nbcnews.com/politics/first-read/shifting-battleground-why-chuck-hagel-resigned-n255056>.
12. U.S. Secretary of Defence Chuck Hagel in April 2014, cited in Zachary Keck, "US Swears Asia Pivot Isn't Dead", *The Diplomat*, 2 April 2014, available at <http://thediplomat.com/2014/04/us-swears-asia-pivot-isnt-dead/>.
13. Matt Shiavenza, "The 'Insipid' Mr. Obama Goes to China", *The Atlantic*, 6 November 2014, available at <http://www.theatlantic.com/international/archive/2014/11/obama-visits-china-global-times/382435/>. The Chinese commentary in question is from "Midterm Result Will Further Thwart Obama", *Global Times*, 5 November 2014, available at <http://www.globaltimes.cn/content/890056.shtml>.
14. Author's discussion with members of

the China Institutes of Contemporary International Relations (CICIR) in Singapore on 19 December 2014.
15. Lucy Hornby, "Putin Snubs Europe with Siberian Gas Deal that Bolsters China Ties", *Financial Times*, 10 November 2014, available at <http://www.ft.com/cms/s/0/79eeabb0-6888-11e4-acc0-00144feabdc0.html#axzz3MQEmduSj>.
16. "Putin: Russia Cannot Continue South Stream Construction in Current Situation", *Sputnik*, 1 December 2014, available at <http://sputniknews.com/business/20141201/1015368062.html>.
17. Euan Graham, "Russia's Crimean Annexation: What It Means for East Asia", *RSIS Commentaries*, 25 March 2014; Zachery Keck, "Overseas Chinese and the Crimea Crisis", *The Diplomat*, 10 April 2014, available at <http://thediplomat.com/2014/04/overseas-chinese-and-the-crimea-crisis/>; Parameswaran Ponnudurai, "Will China Use Russian-Style Tactics to Settle Territorial Disputes in Asia?", *Radio Free Asia*, 20 April 2014, available at <http://www.rfa.org/english/commentaries/east-asia-beat/ukraine-04202014053612.html>.
18. David Brunnstrom, "U.S. Warns China not to Try Crimea-style Action in Asia", *Reuters*, 4 April 2014, available at <http://www.reuters.com/article/2014/04/04/us-usa-china-crimea-asia-id USBREA322DA20140404>.
19. Dingding Chen, "China's 'Marshall Plan' is Much More", *The Diplomat*, 10 November 2014, available at <http://thediplomat.com/2014/11/chinas-marshall-plan-is-much-more/>.
20. Dexter Roberts, "Obama and Xi Spar Over Rival Free-Trade Pacts at APEC Forum", *Bloomberg Businessweek*, 10 November 2014, available at <http://www.businessweek.com/articles/2014-11-10/obama-and-xi-spar-over-rival-free-trade-pacts-at-apec-forum>.
21. "Chasing the Chinese Dream", *The Economist*, 4 May 2013, available at <http://www.economist.com/news/briefing/21577063-chinas-new-leader-has-been-quick-consolidate-his-power-what-does-he-now-want-his>.
22. "Chinese President Proposes Asia-Pacific Dream", *China Daily*, 9 November 2014, available at <http://www.chinadaily.com.cn/china/2014-11/09/content_18889698.htm>.
23. Shannon Tiezzi, "China's Push for an Asia-Pacific Free Trade Agreement", *The Diplomat*, 30 October 2014, available at <http://thediplomat.com/2014/10/chinas-push-for-an-asia-pacific-free-trade-agreement/>.
24. The two countries agreed to the following: (1) continue to develop a mutually beneficial relationship based on common strategic interests; (2) agree to overcome political difficulties by "facing history squarely and looking forward to the future"; (3) mutually address the Senkaku/Diaoyu Islands; and (4) agree to gradually resume political, diplomatic and security dialogues through various multilateral and bilateral channels. Shannon Tiezzi, "A China-Japan Breakthrough: A Primer on Their 4 Point Consensus", *The Diplomat*, 7 November 2014, available at <http://thediplomat.com/2014/11/a-china-japan-breakthrough-a-primer-on-their-4-point-consensus/>.
25. John Ruwitch, "China's Xi Issues Veiled Warning to Asia over Military Alliances", *Reuters*, 21 May 2014, available at <http://news.yahoo.com/chinas-xi-says-committed-peacefully-resolving-territorial-disputes-024633860.html>.
26. Jeremy Blum, "Former Foreign Minister Says 'China will Never Seek to become a Hegemonic Power'", *South China Morning Post*, 18 September 2013, available at <http://www.scmp.com/news/china-insider/article/1312346/former-foreign-minister-says-china-will-never-seek-become>; Patrick Donahue and Brian Parkin, "Xi

Says China's Military Expansion Not Aimed at Asian Hegemony", *Bloomberg News*, 29 March 2014, available at <http://www.bloomberg.com/news/2014-03-28/xi-says-china-s-military-expansion-not-aimed-at-asian-hegemony.html>.

27. Kor Kian Beng, "China Puts Low-key Summit in Spotlight", *Straits Times*, 10 May 2014, p. A18.

28. David Capie and Paul Evans, *The Asia-Pacific Security Lexicon*, 2nd ed. (Singapore: Institute of Southeast Asian Studies, 2007), pp. 169–72.

29. Patrick M. Cronin, Ely Ratner, Elbridge Coby, Zachary M. Hosford, and Alexander Sullivan, *Tailored Coercion: Competition and Risk in Maritime Asia* (Washington, D.C.: Center for New American Security, 2014); Robert Haddick, "Salami Slicing in the South China Sea", *Foreign Policy*, 3 August 2012, available at <http://www.foreignpolicy.com/category/section/small_wars>.

30. Elizabeth Economy, "The Xi-Obama Summit: As Good as Expected — and Maybe Even Better", *The Atlantic*, 11 June 2013, available at <http://www.theatlantic.com/china/archive/2013/06/the-xi-obama-summit-as-good-as-expected-and-maybe-even-better/276733/>.

31. John J. Mearsheimer, "Can China Rise Peacefully?", *The National Interest*, 25 October 2014, available at <http://nationalinterest.org/commentary/can-china-rise-peacefully-10204>.

32. "On Power and Stabilising Forces", *Straits Times*, 17 May 2010, available at <http://xinkaishi.typepad.com/a_new_start/asia/page/14/>.

33. John Kerry, "Opening Remarks at ASEAN Regional Forum", *United States Mission to ASEAN*, 10 August 2014, available at <http://asean.usmission.gov/remarks08102014-02.html>.

34. Nguyen Phuong Linh and Michael Martina, "South China Sea Tensions Rise as Vietnam says China Rammed Ships", *Reuters*, 7 May 2014, available at <http://www.reuters.com/article/2014/05/07/us-china-seas-fishermen-idUSBREA4603C20140507>.

35. Dingding Chen, "China's Deployment of Oil Rig is Not a Strategic Mistake", *The Diplomat*, 20 May 2014, available at <http://thediplomat.com/2014/05/chinas-deployment-of-oil-rig-is-not-a-strategic-mistake/>.

36. "Spotlight: China Rebuffs U.S. 'Freeze' Proposal on South China Sea, Raising 'Dual-track' Approach", *Shanghai Daily*, 10 August 2014, available at <http://www.shanghaidaily.com/article/article_xinhua.aspx?id=234543>.

37. "Beijing Hits Out at US South China Sea Proposal", *Straits Times*, 12 August 2014, available at <http://www.straitstimes.com/news/asia/east-asia/story/beijing-hits-out-us-south-china-sea-proposal-20140812>.

38. Thuc D. Pham, "Implications of the US-China Split at the ARF", *The Diplomat*, 5 September 2014, available at <http://thediplomat.com/2014/09/implications-of-the-us-china-split-at-the-arf/>.

39. David Tweed and Sangwon Yoon, "China Rejects Push at Asean to Curb South China Sea Activity", *Bloomberg*, 10 August 2014, available at <http://www.bloomberg.com/news/2014-08-09/south-china-sea-tension-seen-dominating-asean-ministers-meeting.html>.

40. "China Supports 'Dual-track' Approach to Resolve Dispute", *Xinhua*, 10 August 2014, available at <http://usa.chinadaily.com.cn/china/2014-08/10/content_18280191.htm>.

41. "Press Release by the Chairman of the ASEAN Foreign Ministers' Retreat (AMM Retreat)", <http://asean-summit-2014.tumblr.com/post/73949814893/press-release-by-the-chairman-of-the-asean-foreign>.

42. "ASEAN Vows Unity on South China Sea", *Yahoo! News*, 14 August 2013, available at <https://sg.news.yahoo.com/asean-vows-unity-south-china-sea-142838507.html>.

43. Dylan Loh, "ASEAN Must Respond in

Decisive, Coordinated Way to Regional Issues: PM Lee", *Channel NewsAsia*, 12 November 2014, available at <http://www.channelnewsasia.com/news/singapore/asean-must-respond-in/1468054.html>.

44. "The 46th ASEAN Economic Ministers' (AEM) Meeting Joint Media Statement", 25 August 2014, p. 2, available at <http://www.asean.org/images/Statement/2014/aug/JMS%20AEM%2046%20_Final.pdf>.

45. "Myanmar Hosts ASEAN Summit for the First Time", *ASEAN Secretariat News*, 9 May 2014, available at <http://www.asean.org/news/asean-secretariat-news/item/myanmar-hosts-asean-summit-for-the-first-time>.

46. Dario Agnote, "Talks to Build ASEAN Economic Community Slows, ADB Says", *Kyodo News*, 25 September 2014, available at <http://english.kyodonews.jp/news/2014/09/313608.html>; Jayant Menon, "An ASEAN Economic Community by 2015?", *Vox*, 27 September 2014, available at <http://www.voxeu.org/article/asean-economic-community-2015>.

47. *Economic Outlook for Southeast Asia, China and India 2014: Beyond the Middle-Income Trap* (Paris: OECD Development Centre, 2013), available at <http://dx.doi.org/10.1787/saeo-2014-en>.

48. Sundram Pushpanathan, "Opinion: No Place for Passive Regionalism in ASEAN", *Jakarta Post*, 7 April 2010, available at <http://www.thejakartapost.com/news/2010/04/07/no-place-passive-regionalism-asean.html>.

49. Cited in Malminderjit Singh, "Asean Must Do More to Boost Competitiveness: Surin", *Business Times*, 2 June 2011, available at <lkyspp.nus.edu.sg/aci/.../20110602_ACR_Launch-Business_Times.pdf>.

50. "Declaration of ASEAN Concord II (Bali Concord II)", 7 October 2003, available at <http://www.asean.org/news/item/declaration-of-asean-concord-ii-bali-concord-ii>.

51. "UN Court Awards Disputed Preah Vihear Temple Area to Cambodia, Orders Thai Security Forces to Leave", *Australian Broadcasting Corporation (ABC) News*, 12 November 2013, available at <http://www.abc.net.au/news/2013-11-11/un-court-awards-flashpoint-border-temple-area-to-cambodia/5084504>.

52. Donald K. Emmerson, "Beyond the Six Points: How Far Will Indonesia Go?", *East Asia Forum*, 29 July 2012, available at <http://www.eastasiaforum.org/2012/07/29/beyond-the-six-points-how-far-will-indonesia-go/>.

53. Euan Graham, "Super-typhoon Haiyan: ASEAN's Katrina Moment?", *PacNet*, no. 82, 20 November 2013.

54. Dylan Loh, "ASEAN Must Respond in Decisive, Coordinated Way to Regional Issues: PM Lee", *Today*, 12 November 2014.

55. Michael Leifer, "Regional Solutions to Regional Problems?", in *Towards Recovery in Pacific Asia*, edited by Gerald Segal and David S.G. Goodman (London: Routledge, 2000), pp. 108–18.

56. Amitav Acharya, "Ideas, Identity and Institution-Building: From the 'ASEAN Way' to the 'Asia-Pacific Way'?", *The Pacific Review* 10, no. 3 (1997): 319–46.

57. James Hookway, "Veterans of Thai Military Government Take Key Posts in New Cabinet", *The Wall Street Journal*, 1 September 2014, available at <http://www.wsj.com/articles/thai-leaders-name-cabinet-1409488985>.

58. "Uniform Reaction: The Generals Introduce 'True Democracy', Thai-style", *The Economist*, 13 September 2014, available at <http://www.economist.com/news/asia/21616970-generals-introduce-true-democracy-thai-style-uniform-reaction>.

59. "Jokowi Should Act Swiftly on Reform Agenda", *FT View (Financial*

Times), 2 November 2014, available at <http://www.ft.com/intl/cms/s/0/a1251a90-611f-11e4-b935-00144feabdc0.html#axzz3LfMAgE5t>.

60. Edward Aspinall, "Jokowi Fails His First Test", *New Mandala*, 27 October 2014, available at <http://asiapacific.anu.edu.au/newmandala/2014/10/27/jokowi-fails-first-test/>.

61. Rieka Rahadiana, Agus Suhana, and Herdaru Purnomo, "Bank Indonesia Raises Key Rate After Fuel-Price Increase", *Bloomberg*, 18 November 2014, available at <http://www.bloomberg.com/news/2014-11-17/indonesia-s-widodo-increases-subsidized-gasoline-diesel-prices.html>.

62. Jurgen Haacke, "'Enhanced Interaction' with Myanmar and the Project of a Security Community: Is ASEAN Refining or Breaking with Its Diplomatic and Security Culture?", *Contemporary Southeast Asia* 27, no. 2 (August 2005): 188–216; See Seng Tan, "Herding Cats: The Role of Persuasion in Political Change and Continuity in the Association of Southeast Asian Nations (ASEAN)", *International Relations of the Asia-Pacific*, vol. 13, no. 2 (2013), pp. 233–65.

63. "A Choice of Sorts: Myanmar Gets Ready for Elections", *The Economist*, 20 November 2014, available at <http://www.economist.com/news/21631852-myanmar-gets-ready-elections-choice-sorts?zid=309&ah=80dcf288b8561b012f603b9fd9577f0e>.

64. Peter Chalk, *On the Path of Change: Political, Economic and Social Challenges for Myanmar*, ASPI Special Report (Barton, ACT: Australian Strategic Policy Institute, December 2013), pp. 6–7.

65. Justine Drennan, "Myanmar's ASEAN Chairmanship: Lessons from Cambodia", *The Diplomat*, 13 January 2014, available at <http://thediplomat.com/2014/01/myanmars-asean-chairmanship-lessons-from-cambodia/>.

66. Simon Lewis, "Reforming Burma Moves Up Global Corruption Rankings", *The Irrawaddy*, 3 December 2013, available at <http://www.irrawaddy.org/burma/reforming-burma-moves-global-corruption-rankings.html>.

67. Cited in "Myanmar Hosts ASEAN Summit for the First Time".

68. Justine Drennan, "Myanmar's ASEAN Chairmanship: Lessons from Cambodia".

69. "Joint Communiqué 47th ASEAN Foreign Ministers' Meeting", 8 August 2014, p. 48, available at <http://www.asean.org/images/documents/47thAMMandRelatedMeetings/Joint%20Communique%20of%2047th%20AMM%20as%20of%209-8-14%2010%20pm.pdf>.

70. "ASEAN Foreign Ministers' Statement on the Current Developments in the South China Sea", 10 May 2014, available at <http://www.asean.org/news/asean-statement-communiques/item/asean-foreign-ministers-statement-on-the-current-developments-in-the-south-china-sea?category_id=26>.

71. "Press Release by the Chairman of the ASEAN Foreign Ministers' Retreat (AMM Retreat)", 17 January 2014, available at <http://asean-summit-2014.tumblr.com/>.

72. Evelyn Goh, "ASEAN-led Multilateralism and Regional Order: The Great Power Bargain Deficit", *The Asan Forum* (*Special Forum*), 23 May 2014, available at <http://www.theasanforum.org/asean-led-multilateralism-and-regional-order-the-great-power-bargain-deficit/>.

73. Prashanth Parameswaran, "Malaysia as ASEAN Chair in 2015: What To Expect", *The Diplomat*, 22 November 2014, available at <http://thediplomat.com/2014/11/malaysia-as-asean-chair-in-2015-what-to-expect/>.

74. Rizal Sukma, "Indonesia Needs a Post-ASEAN Foreign Policy", *Jakarta Post*, 30 June 2009; Rizal Sukma, "A Post-ASEAN Foreign Policy for a Post-G8 World", *Jakarta Post*, 5 October 2009.

CHINA'S TWO SILK ROADS INITIATIVE
What It Means for Southeast Asia

David Arase

Introduction

In 2013, Chinese President Xi Jinping announced a pair of initiatives that aims to restructure the economy and geopolitics of Eurasia. The Silk Road Economic Belt announced by Xi Jinping in September 2013 during a tour of Central Asian neighbours is a programme to build land transportation corridors that connect China to Europe and all other major Eurasian subregions, including Indochina, South Asia, and Southwest Asia.[1] Then in October 2013, Xi visited Indonesia and announced the 21st Century Maritime Silk Road, which is a port development initiative to broaden Chinese trade channels targetting the maritime regions of Southeast Asia, South Asia, the Middle East, East Africa, and the Mediterranean. Xi Jinping's two Silk Road programmes are a package called the "One Belt — One Road" [*yidai — yilu*] initiative.[2]

Both Xi Jinping and Premier Li Keqiang spent great effort in the year 2014 launching concrete measures to advance the silk roads agenda of Eurasian connectivity and regional cooperation. They hope to build a comprehensive trans-Eurasian network of economic corridors that could sustain China's economic growth and strengthen China's political leverage for decades to come. The consequence would be to draw the countries of Eurasia into China's economic orbit to form what Xi Jinping calls a "community of shared destiny". Members' fortunes would rise as China's own rise continued. A culturally and politically diverse but economically

---

Reprinted from Daljit Singh, ed., *Southeast Asian Affairs 2015* (Singapore: Institute of Southeast Asian Studies, 2015), pp. 25–45. At the time of original publication, David Arase was Visiting Senior Fellow at the Institute of Southeast Asian Studies, Singapore. He was also Resident Professor of International Politics at The Hopkins-Nanjing Centre at Nanjing University, The John Hopkins University — School of Advanced International Studies.

integrated division of labour harmoniously organized by China's trade and financial interests is what China promises. If this vision is fully realized, China's silk roads vision will help realize "the great rejuvenation of the Chinese nation" and the "China Dream" of a wealthy society grounded on Chinese values.

It should be noted that this *yidai — yilu* agenda is a work in progress rather than a fully drawn up master plan. That is, as previous Chinese leaders have done, Xi Jinping is providing a grand strategic vision or agenda for China. The Chinese Communist Party and government must work to realize this agenda to the best of their ability. So, for the rest of Xi Jinping's years in power — expected to last until 2022 — we will hear about the two Silk Roads at every meeting that Xi Jinping or Li Keqiang attends in Europe, Africa, the Middle East and Asia.

The Year of the Silk Roads

Even the briefest summary of high-profile Chinese initiatives that advanced the Silk Roads agenda in 2014 amounts to a long list. Premier Li Keqiang made five overseas tours that highlighted this agenda. In May, Li made a four-nation African tour. In Kenya, he signed a US$3.8 billion agreement to use Chinese high-speed railway technology to connect Nairobi to Mombasa, the largest port in East Africa.

In June, he visited Greece to discuss purchase of both the Greek port Thessaloniki and the Greek state-owned railway. He also negotiated to purchase full ownership of the massive new Piraeus Container Terminal, which is already half-owned and managed by Chinese state-owned shipping giant COSCO.[3] In all, Li signed new deals with Greece valued at US$5 billion.

In October, Li visited Germany, Russia, and Italy, and attended the Asia-Europe Summit (ASEM). China and Germany's signed agreements on bilateral trade, mutual investment and technological cooperation are valued at US$18.1 billion; in Russia, Li Keqiang witnessed the signing of thirty-nine bilateral cooperation agreements and contracts, including a high-speed rail project connecting Moscow and Kazan via the Volga River (to be extended through Kazakhstan to Beijing by 2018 providing another trans-Eurasian rail link from China to Western Europe via Moscow), worth US$10 billion; in Italy, he witnessed Chinese and Italian corporations signing more than ten agreements totaling more than US$10 billion.[4]

In November, Li went to Myanmar to attend the annual ASEAN Summit meetings. During his visit, China signed US$8 billion in agreements with Myanmar and pledged US$10 billion for China-ASEAN infrastructure investment.

In December, Li visited Kazakhstan, Serbia, and Thailand. In Kazakhstan Li attended the Shanghai Cooperation Organisation Summit and witnessed the signing of US$18 billion worth of economic cooperation and infrastructure construction agreements with Kazakhstan. Li then attended the third China–Central and Eastern European Leaders' Meeting in Serbia and announced a US$10 billion Chinese credit line for infrastructure development as well as a US$3 billion Chinese equity investment fund. He also signed an agreement to finance 85 per cent of a new Chinese-built railway linking Budapest to the Greek port of Piraeus on the Mediterranean Sea with intervening stops in Belgrade and Skopje. This deal is worth almost US$3 billion and will open Western, Central, and Eastern Europe to cheap container traffic with China.⁵ Li Keqiang then departed for Thailand where he signed a US$10.6 billion financing deal to build a railway segment between Bangkok and the Chinese border that is part of a planned larger north-south railway network that runs from Kunming down the western, middle, and eastern axes of Indochina. Li also pledged US$3 billion at the Greater Mekong Subregion Economic Cooperation Summit to finance infrastructure connectivity, Chinese machinery exports, and Indochina poverty reduction efforts.

In the course of his five overseas tours, Li Keqiang signed bilateral and multilateral cooperation agreements worth some US$140 billion to advance China's interest in exporting railway and port infrastructure construction and management services that boost Chinese industrial exports and create transportation access to export markets, natural resources, and investment opportunities across and around Eurasia.⁶

The year 2014 also saw landmark initiatives by Xi Jinping that begin to provide an institutional and normative foundation for China's vision of a Eurasian community.

On 21 May 2014, Xi Jinping proposed the New Asian Security Concept to the twenty-six member states of the Conference on Interaction and Confidence Building Measures in Asia (CICA). This organization was originally founded by Kazakhstan and its membership mainly consists of continental rather than maritime Eurasian countries.⁷ He stated, "To beef up and entrench a military alliance targeted at a third party is not conducive to maintaining common security." Rather than traditional security, he asked members to focus on cooperative Asian development as the core security concern for Eurasia. He also asserted that, "it is for the people of Asia to run the affairs of Asia, solve the problems of Asia, and uphold the security of Asia."⁸

In September, Xi Jinping visited India and pledged to invest US$20 billion in upgrading India's infrastructure, especially its railways. China subsequently offered — at no cost to India — to do a feasibility study for a 1,750 km high-speed railway between Delhi and Chennai, a port city on the Bay of Bengal.⁹ Xi also pledged to support India's full membership in the Shanghai Cooperation Organisation.

In October, Xi Jinping and twenty other national representatives signed a Memorandum of Understanding (MOU) to establish the Asian Infrastructure Investment Bank (AIIB) with an initial capitalization of US$50 billion and authorized capitalization of US$100 billion. Xi had announced plans to establish such a bank a year earlier in a visit to Indonesia. The AIIB is expected to emphasize ASEAN infrastructure development.

At the November APEC Summit Meeting, Xi Jinping announced the Silk Road Development Fund to finance infrastructure and trade creation, for which he pledged US$40 billion in funding, of which 65 per cent will come from China's foreign currency reserves, and the rest from China's sovereign wealth fund, the Export-Import Bank of China, and the China Development Bank.¹⁰ The Silk Road Development Fund seems destined to help finance the overland Silk Road Economic Belt.

China's Search for Great Power Status Leads to the Silk Roads

To understand China's Eurasian Silk Roads initiative, one needs to put it into a larger geo-strategic and historical context. China's rise to great power status causes a transition from a unipolar situation of U.S. "hyper-power" to structural bipolarity in the international system. The defining characteristic of a great power is the ability to determine the nature of international order. That is, it has an ability to determine the kinds of principles, norms, and institutions that smaller states will follow, and it begins to exercise this power first of all in its home region. As China figures out how and why it will use its power to restructure the world around it, it must first of all consider the adjustment of relations with the existing great power that has created the present international order, that is, the United States.

The 2008–09 financial crisis seemed to signal the end of U.S. global predominance and greatly accelerated the speed at which China would overtake the U.S. in GDP terms.[11] The Chinese foreign policy stance that emerged in 2009 continued the basic line of peaceful development, but it became much more independent and assertive in demanding certain changes in global and regional governance.[12] By the time leadership passed from Hu Jintao to Xi Jinping in 2012, the emphasis was on the need to establish a "new type of great power relationship" with the U.S. The critical element was gaining U.S. recognition of China's core interests in East Asia while avoiding armed conflict, especially with the U.S. and its allies.

To expand its control of strategic space in East Asian waters, China pursued what the Pentagon called an "Anti-Access/Area Denial" (A2/AD)[13] offshore maritime control strategy. At the same time, it loudly argued a historical case for its exclusive right to maritime territorial jurisdictions that neighbouring states claimed on the basis of rights uniformly accorded to all coastal states by the U.N. Convention on the Law of the Sea (UNCLOS). Simultaneously, China paraded new types of naval, air force, and space capabilities. Maritime skirmishes and incidents began in 2009, and in 2012 China launched paramilitary campaigns to establish civilian maritime occupation and patrol around Scarborough Shoal (Huangyandao) in the South China Sea and the Senkaku (Diaoyu) islets in the East China Sea. The months-long and controlled use of civilian coercive force successfully overcame resistance and established Chinese control (partial in the Senkaku/Diaoyu case but total in the Scarborough/Huangyandao case), while remaining below the threshold that could lead to a military confrontation with the United States.

China continues to use this formula in the East China Sea and the South China Sea to expand its sphere of maritime control against the opposing jurisdictional claims of neighbouring coastal states. In November 2013, China added a new dimension to this formula by declaring a militarily enforceable air defence identification zone (ADIZ) over the Senkaku/Diaoyudao islets in the East China Sea. It appears to be preparing to establish an ADIZ over the South China Sea, if the construction of artificial islands with landing strips is any indication.

Having established a formula for incremental strategic expansion that avoided direct conflict with the U.S., China turned to the reshaping of the Asian regional order to ensure its continuing economic rise and eventual political leadership.

The Economic and Political Agenda in Asia: Community of Shared Destiny

Xi Jinping's announcement of the *yidai — yilu* initiative in September–October 2013 marked a turn of attention toward the restructuring relations with Asia to secure China's future as a great power. Speaking in Indonesia in October, Xi Jinping chose the term 命运共同体 (*mingyun gongtongti*), which translates as "community of common destiny" or "community of shared fate", to express his vision of a China-centred regional community.[14] He then presided over the 23–24 October 2013 Chinese Communist Party Central Leadership Work Forum on Diplomacy Toward the Periphery, which was attended by the entire Standing Committee of the Politburo. Xi Jinping used the occasion to explain the kind of regional order that China aspired to create, and the role that the *yidai — yilu* initiative would play in it.

Xi explained the core idea is that neighbours must link their economic future to the "China Dream", that is, China's continuing rise, especially in economic terms. He then laid out the following framework:

- The use of China's advantages in economy, trade, technology, and finance to build "win-win" cooperation with neighbours;
- Construction of the two Silk Roads;
- The use of trade and investment to create a new kind of regional economic integration;
- An Asian Infrastructure Investment Bank, internationalization of the Chinese currency, renminbi (RMB), and regional financial stability;
- The development of Chinese border areas as gateways to neighbouring countries;
- A new concept of security, based on mutual trust, reciprocity, equality, and coordination through enhanced cooperation mechanisms.
- Public diplomacy and people-to-people exchanges including tourism, technology, education, and provincial level cooperation.[15]

The Silk Roads Agenda

The infrastructure that constitutes the two Silk Roads is both hard and soft. Hard infrastructure is the steel, concrete, computers, and equipment that go into building railways, highways, ports, energy pipelines, industrial parks, border customs facilities, and special trade zones. Soft infrastructure refers to the social and institutional foundations of trade and investment promotion such as diplomacy, development finance institutions, economic cooperation agreements, multilateral cooperation forums, academic research, cultural exchange, tourism, etc.

The Eurasian countries along the Silk Road routes number over sixty, and over fifty have already signed Silk Road cooperation endorsements with China — with notable exceptions such as India. China expects these countries to link their development strategies to China's growing trade and investment. This will lead them to ongoing policy dialogue and coordination, and membership in the China-centred community of shared destiny.

China has a number of reasons to invest in the two Silk Roads. It has become a net importer of energy, industrial commodities, and food, so it needs to secure access to new sources. Moreover, China can now export higher value-added goods and services, including electronic parts, consumer durables, heavy equipment, and construction and engineering services, but it needs to break into export markets. Ports and railway lines not only promote Chinese exports of advanced machinery and engineering services, but also open the way for Chinese trade and investment in as yet unfamiliar markets.

The *yidai — yilu* agenda also addresses the problem of geographically imbalanced development inside China. Inland border provinces have lagged behind the coastal provinces. The Silk Roads give them a chance at prosperity and a better quality of life as outward-looking Eurasian trade hubs. Beijing has designated the following provinces as Eurasian gateways: Jilin facing Mongolia, the Russian Far East, and the Japan Sea sub-region of Northeast Asia (via Russian and North Korean ports);[16] Guangxi working with Hainan and Guangdong facing maritime Southeast Asia; Yunnan facing the Mekong River sub region as well as the Bay of Bengal rim of the Indian Ocean (via Myanmar); and Xinjiang facing Central Asia with onward linkages to the Caspian Sea region, the Arabian Sea region, the Black Sea region, the Mediterranean Sea region, and Eastern and Northern Europe. Each of these Chinese gateway provinces has begun hosting an annual international Expo and a wide range of other regular events to develop trade and investment with foreign partners.

Financing the Silk Roads Agenda

The current tidal wave of Chinese state-guided overseas capital investment began at the end of the 1990s when China articulated a "going out" policy. The idea was to channel surplus savings abroad to secure energy and raw materials.[17] As will be noted below, the size of China's savings surplus and the reasons to invest overseas have only multiplied since then. The result today is a new era of Chinese "South-South cooperation", which means that China as a developing country gives economic aid to meet China's own development needs while also serving the development needs of recipients. This "win-win" economic cooperation formula fits the two Silk Roads agenda because countries along the routes tend to be lower and middle-income developing countries that lack adequate infrastructure. The Asian Development Bank has estimated that developing Asia will need US$8 trillion in infrastructure development from 2010–20 just to keep up with anticipated demand. Economic infrastructure is not a high priority among Western aid donors, and so China has found a special role to play in shaping the economic integration of Eurasia.

China's foreign exchange reserves have grown to US$3.9 trillion, and there is a desire to invest it in more than just U.S. Treasury bills. Growing doubts about the future of the U.S. dollar motivated China to diversify the investment of its foreign exchange reserves and to plan for the internationalization of the RMB. The accumulation of domestic debt has grown so quickly since 2008 that the marginal productivity of domestic investment in the macro-economy is such that it takes RMB5.0 of investment to produce RMB1.0 of GDP growth. This makes attractive the investment of foreign exchange reserves in overseas projects and export finance that not only yields decent financial returns but also stimulates domestic production and promotes higher value-added industrial export-substitution. Multi-billion dollar Silk Road infrastructure projects also allow the promotion of RMB trade invoicing, trade settlement, and project financing across Eurasia. Sustainability of this investment agenda seems feasible if domestic growth can be maintained. The national savings rate is around 40 per cent of GDP, and China runs a chronic current account surplus at around 2 per cent of GDP. China's banking system and international financial flows remain mostly under state control, so the central bank can provide liquidity or bailouts in the case of a crisis. China's Development and Reform Council is considering investing as much as US$800 billion over the next ten years in the two Silk Roads. This seems doable. In 2014, Premier Li Keqiang alone committed at least US$94 billion in new government financing to specific Silk Road projects and programmes at leadership meetings in Silk Road countries.[18]

Governance of the Community of Shared Destiny

The difference in economic scale between China and its neighbours means that deepening economic interdependence gives China more bilateral leverage, and military superiority gives China additional leverage. As a newly risen great power, Beijing is laying out a vision of regional order that fits its unique set of cultural norms, political values, and core interests. How is it likely to govern a China-centred international community?

The West's favoured approach to regional integration (for example, NAFTA and the EU) is economic liberalization. This uses multilateral treaties to remove legal and institutional barriers to trade and investment, and it creates legally binding rules, standards, and dispute resolution mechanisms that states must follow to create a free open space for private sector activity. It does not focus on the provision of physical infrastructure or the channelling of trade in any particular direction; this is left to the free market.

In contrast, China's approach to regional integration centres on policy-led trade facilitation. This features the improvement of trade connectivity by building more efficient transportation linkages, providing more trade and investment finance, streamlining trade and investment approvals, and multiplying human exchange opportunities. It requires policy dialogue between states to shape the direction of development rather than the negotiation of a multilateral trade liberalization agreement that sets uniform and legally binding rules for states to follow and enforce.

China's Silk Roads agenda is to create railways and ports that connect China to points across the Eurasian land mass (the Silk Road Economic Belt) and along the maritime rim of Eurasia (the 21st Century Maritime Silk Road). The result will be to channel Eurasian economic transactions toward China to deepen interdependence between individual countries of Eurasia on the one hand, and the massive Chinese economy on the other. This economic interdependence will give China superior leverage over any other Eurasian country in a one-on-one negotiation, and will give China a leadership position in any Eurasian multilateral economic policy setting.

Advancement of this agenda does not require multilateral treaty negotiations or supranational bureaucratic authority. It merely requires China to supply leadership in the form of initiating discussion, advancing cooperation proposals, lowering information and transaction costs for cooperation partners, and providing them with material incentives such as new infrastructure, credit, investment, and trade opportunities. The allocation of resources is done on an individual, case-by-case basis by Chinese authorities. Other things being equal, this should induce potential partners to voluntarily cooperate with China's Eurasian integration project.

What are some of the key principles that will guide China's governance of the new Eurasian order? Besides the aforementioned South-South mode of economic cooperation, we can point to at least three other principles.

First, there is the practice of bilateralism with reciprocity in Chinese diplomacy. In any matter that affects important Chinese interests, China strongly prefers reliance on bilateral negotiation. In China's view, if others respect China's interests, this respect will be paid back; but if others do not respect China, it will find ways to punish them. Countries that reject Chinese interpretations of history and territorial sovereignty, criticize Chinese human rights practices, or welcome visits of the Dalai Lama may suffer various forms of Chinese punishment such as reduced market access, Chinese obstructionism in international organizations, and diplomatic snubs.

Second, "the principled bottom line" (原则底线 *yuanze dixian*) corollary in China's commitment to peaceful development means that China will fight before it sacrifices its "core interests".[19] These core interests include the preservation of absolute power in the hands of the Chinese Communist Party and the state apparatus; the sovereignty and territorial integrity of the Chinese state; and the continuing stability and development of China's economy.[20] This means that China will not tolerate criticism for lacking liberal democracy and human rights principles; making illegitimate territorial sovereignty claims; or threatening disruption of China's continuing economic development. It reserves the right to use any means at its disposal if anyone challenges these core interests.

Finally, the international rule of law is meant to act as a brake on the arbitrary exercise of state power, and to establish an international community of states with agreed norms and procedures for managing relations. However, in explaining China's concept of the international rule of law, Foreign Minister Wang Yi stated: "Such principles as respect for sovereignty and territorial integrity, peaceful settlement of international disputes and non-interference in the internal affairs of others, as enshrined in the UN Charter, are the foundation stones upon which modern international law and conduct of international relations are built."[21] This definition omits core legal norms in the UN Charter such as state accountability to law, respect for human rights, and the resort to independent adjudication of disputes.[22]

With respect to international judicial institutions, Wang Yi warned: "[they] should avoid overstepping their authority… Still less should they encroach on the rights and interests of other countries under the pretext of 'the rule of law' in total disregard of objectivity and fairness." This begs the question, who will apply international law with objectivity and fairness when China's interests conflict with those of its neighbours?

The answer is found in China's diplomatic practice. China does not turn to international tribunals to resolve sovereignty disputes. Instead, it insists on direct bilateral negotiations with individual disputants, holding in reserve "the principled bottom line". This maximizes China's leverage and minimizes the procedural and substantive normative constraints on international dispute resolution.

The implication of reciprocity in Chinese bilateral diplomacy, the principled bottom line, and China's insistence on the sovereign interpretation of legal rights beyond the reach of international adjudication is that smaller countries will lack the protection of the full range of international legal norms and institutions when disputing with China. They will need to accommodate themselves to the values and interests of China in order to avoid the loss of rights and privileges in the community of common destiny.

This approach to regional community is different from ASEAN-style community in important respects. China promises prosperity in association with its continuing growth and development. But the core-periphery structure of connectivity, governance, and member status in China's community of shared destiny differs from the kind of non-coercive, equal, and impartial multilateralism that ASEAN has developed.

The Silk Roads Agenda in Southeast Asia

At the 2013 China-ASEAN Summit, Premier Li Keqiang introduced China's 2+7 Initiative. China's two fundamental principles of engagement with ASEAN are mutual security and economic cooperation. Based on these principles, China proposes seven ideas: a new China-ASEAN treaty of good neighbourliness and cooperation; an annual China-ASEAN defence ministers' meeting; a goal of US$1 trillion in trade by 2020; the Asian Infrastructure Investment Bank; more reliance on the RMB in central bank reserves, trade invoicing, and bank finance; maritime cooperation in the South China Sea; and cultural exchange. This framework strengthens Chinese influence over Southeast Asia.

On his trip to Malaysia and Indonesia in October 2013, Xi Jinping announced the 21st Century Maritime Silk Road initiative. Though the nearest target is maritime Southeast Asia, the agenda of expanding port access to support maritime trade extends across the Indian Ocean to the Persian Gulf, East Africa, and through the Red Sea into the Mediterranean.

Guangxi as a Maritime Silk Road Hub

In geo-economic terms, Guangxi has a 637km land border with Vietnam and three deep seaports on the South China Sea that can be a main terminus for the Maritime Silk Road. Together with Hainan and Guangdong provinces, Guangxi supports the Pan-Beibu Gulf Economic Cooperation Forum and it hosts the annual China-ASEAN Exposition in Nanning. Guangxi's main cooperation partners are Vietnam, Malaysia, Singapore, the Philippines, Indonesia and Brunei. Talk of a high-speed railway from Guangxi along the Vietnam coastline leading all the way to Singapore is eye-catching, but the Maritime Silk Road focus is investment by Chinese firms such as China Merchant Holdings, COSCO, CITIC, and China Communication Construction Company in port development and operation to develop maritime trade in Southeast Asia, South Asia, East Africa, the Middle East, and the Mediterranean. Table 1 summarizes recent Maritime Silk Road port projects in these subregions, using media reports available in January 2015.

Yunnan as a Silk Road Hub

Landlocked Yunnan has always been a remote and backward border province of China. But the Silk Road Economic Belt agenda now makes Yunnan China's "strategic bridgehead" into Indochina. It borders on Vietnam, Laos, and Myanmar, and the province is a member of the Greater Mekong Sub-region (GMS) Economic

TABLE 1
Maritime Silk Road Port Investments

Port	Country	Investment Value (US$ billion)
Kuantan	Malaysia	2.0
Batam	Indonesia	2.0
Kyaukpyu	Myanmar	2.4
Chittagong	Bangladesh	8.7
Colombo	Sri Lanka	1.3
Hanbantota	Sri Lanka	1.0
Gwadar	Pakistan	1.6
Djibouti	Ethiopia	0.185
Port Bashir	Sudan	0.215
Lamu	Kenya	0.480
Bagamoyo	Tanzania	10.0
Suez Canal corridor	Egypt	1.8
Piraeus	Greece	0.880

Cooperation Programme. The GMS programme brings Yunnan into cooperation with Myanmar, Thailand, Vietnam, Laos, and Cambodia to manage a variety of Mekong River watershed issues. Kunming, the capital of Yunnan, is the hub of land transport corridors. An all-weather highway leads to Bangkok, and another leads to Hanoi. Planned electrified railways will link Kunming to Vientiane, Bangkok, Hanoi, Ho Chi Minh City, Kuala Lumpur, and Singapore.

Yunnan also serves as China's bridgehead to the Bay of Bengal and the wider Indian Ocean region. Myanmar is an indispensable partner in this plan. A high-speed rail link between Yunnan and Yangon is planned. More land corridors will link Kunming to Kyaukpyu on Myanmar's coastline. This is a deep-sea port developed by Chinese firms. Oil and gas pipelines from Kyaukpyu to Kunming are roughly 1,000km long and can carry more than 22 million tons (20 million tonnes) of oil and more than 420 billion cubic feet (11.89 million cubic metres) of natural gas per year. The pipelines bring China energy from the Middle East and Africa that bypasses the long route through the Malacca Strait and South China Sea. In addition, an 868km railway is to be built between Kunming and Kyaukpyu, as well as a highway.

Yunnan is looking beyond Myanmar to link up with Bangladesh and India. Planning to implement the Bangladesh-China-India-Myanmar Economic Corridor began in December 2013. The core element is a 2,800km highway linking Kunming to Kolkata in India. Special customs, trade, and industrial zones along the route are intended to develop industry and build supply chains across China, Myanmar, Bangladesh, and India. The ASEAN Free Trade Area, the ASEAN-China Free Trade Area, and the ASEAN-India Free Trade Area agreements, as well as India's own Bay of Bengal initiatives, have created a low tariff environment for the BCIM corridor. This paves the way for, and will leverage the benefits of, Chinese investment through better connectivity.

Xinjiang-Greater Eurasia

Xinjiang Province borders Mongolia, Russia, Kazakhstan, Kyrgyzstan, Tajikistan, Afghanistan, Pakistan, and India. China's trade with Central Asian countries reportedly climbed 13 per cent to reach US$40 billion in 2013.[23] The province hosted the third annual China-Eurasia Exposition and the China-Eurasia Economic Development and Cooperation Forum in Urumqi on 2–7 September 2013 with ministers and officials from the Ministry of Agriculture, Central Bank, Ministry of Tourism, Ministry of Science and Technology, Department of Public Information, Department of Customs organizing a variety of forums and seminar, and representatives from over twenty countries attending them.[24]

China's Central Asia diplomacy goes back to the mid-1990s when it settled border disputes with newly independent neighbours. In 1996 China hosted the first Shanghai Five Summit involving China, Russia, Kazakhstan, Tajikistan, and Kyrgyzstan to develop strategic trust and cooperation. In 2001, this group added Uzbekistan and became the Shanghai Cooperation Organisation. Subsequently, a number of countries have joined as observers (Afghanistan, India, Iran, Mongolia, and Pakistan), and China has used the SCO to combat the "3 evils" (terrorism, religious extremism, and separatism) and to advance its economic interests in Eurasia.

Xi Jinping used his historic tour of Central Asia in September 2013 to launch the Silk Road Economic Belt from China through Central Asia to reach Europe.[25] The Ministry of Commerce is working out ways to promote cargo transportation, personnel exchange, e-commerce, RMB trade settlement and new cross-border economic cooperation zones. Other ministries are working out ways to promote trade and development in agriculture, tourism, and culture. In November 2013, some twenty-four cities from eight countries signed an agreement to cooperate in building this trans-Eurasian economic belt. During his tour, Xi also proposed the creation of a SCO development bank and signed new investment deals worth US$56 billion, on top of some US$30 billion in existing Chinese FDI in Central Asia.

Central Asian Energy Pipelines

The Turkmenistan-China gas pipeline and the Kazakhstan-China oil pipeline are the two major examples of trans-continental scale infrastructure projects spanning Central Asia. The West-East Gas Pipeline Project (WEPP) connects the eastern markets of China with sources in the Tarim Basin, Uzbekistan, Kazakhstan, and Turkmenistan. With the completion of Phase II, it measures 8,704 kilometres and travels through fifteen provinces. Two additional phases are planned or under construction. The 298km-long Kazakhstan-China oil pipeline transports crude oil from oil fields located in western Kazakhstan to the Dushanzi refinery in Xinjiang. It met its design capacity in 2011.[26]

Trans-Eurasian Railways

With respect to land transportation, which will be the backbone of the New Silk Road Economic Corridor, in December 2012 the Second Eurasian Land Bridge running from Lianyungang on the East China Sea through Urumqi to Rotterdam on the Atlantic, Riga on the Baltic, and the Mediterranean region via Istanbul was completed. A German firm using it today needs only sixteen days to ship a container from a Chongqing factory to Germany. Trans-Eurasian high-speed rail development is also contemplated now that Urumqi is linked to China's domestic network.

Xinjiang-Gwadar (Arabian Sea) Economic Corridor

The Xinjiang-Gwadar Port road and rail construction project now underway runs from Kashgar to the Arabian Sea near the Persian Gulf.[27] It parallels the already widened and improved Karakorum Highway linking China to Pakistan. This is to be the backbone of a China-Pakistan (Arabian Sea) economic corridor, in view of the unsettled conditions in Afghanistan that prevent secure investment in pipelines and railways through that country.

Security Implications

When Xi Jinping explained China's New Asian Security Concept at the May 2014 Conference on Interaction and Confidence Building in Asia (CICA) Summit in Shanghai, he did not offer military alliances or security guarantees to other CICA members. In fact, he urged members to turn away from military alliances altogether. Instead, he offered to develop CICA into a multilateral security forum for Eurasian countries to discuss mainly their economic developmental needs. The notion is that economic interdependence, cooperation, and development brings peace and stability, and that China's continuing growth will enhance the security of any countries linked to it. There is a hint that if any of China's neighbours are troubled by China's military rise and assertiveness, they would do better to put aside their fears in order to benefit from closer economic association with China. However, given the well-known weaknesses of informal multilateral cooperation forums, CICA would not be the first place anyone facing a threat of armed aggression would go to seek help. However, for China the point would be to lead an informal Eurasian security community devoted to common, cooperative, and comprehensive non-traditional security and economic development — without incurring any military obligations or international security commitments.

It would be naïve to believe that China's great power identity, which requires a massive and well-publicized build-up of advanced warfare capabilities, fails to consider traditional security and geopolitical interests. With the construction of Chinese connectivity to the whole of Eurasia's inland regions and maritime rim lands, the consequence of organizing Eurasian security solely as soft cooperation in non-traditional security, is to leave an unconstrained and massively armed China facing no other Eurasian state or alliance of states able to resist its will — unless it possessed a nuclear deterrent capability. Before conceiving of Eurasian security cooperation purely in terms of non-military commitments, it would be advisable that China and every other member limits the legitimate exercise of military power and commits to peaceful dispute resolution by impartially administered justice based on the international rule of law.

The connection of China's *yidai — yilu* programme to geopolitical theories of world domination is also worth noting. The geopolitical theories of Halford Mackinder and Nicolas Spykman focus on the pivotal role of Eurasia.[28] The basic idea is that Eurasia is divided into two macro-strategic zones: the heartland or pivot area of continental power roughly corresponding to the former Soviet Union, and the inner crescent or rimland that is divided into sections and oriented toward the surrounding seas. If any single state were to establish hegemony over the whole of the Eurasian land mass, the scale of resources and the geo-strategic advantages available to that state would allow it to dominate the entire world. The implication of this way of thinking is that, Great Britain before World War I, and the U.S. after World War II played the role of an offshore balancer to Tsarist Russia or the Soviet Union to prevent the consolidation of Eurasian hegemony under a single state. Today there are only two Eurasian states that might have the capacity and will to seek Eurasian hegemony: Russia and China. As explained above, the *yidai — yilu* agenda extends China's economic presence across the Eurasian heartland and around the Eurasian rimlands. This penetration of Chinese economic interests may motivate China to build a Eurasian political association and military presence.[29] Perhaps in a sign of things to come, the Chinese Navy is already patrolling off the coast of East Africa to control pirates, and China has deployed a battalion of armed soldiers to join U.N. forces in South Sudan where China's oil interests have been affected by instability.[30]

Complicating Factors

China's effort to become the Eurasian great power fits the Chinese style of realism, but it confronts certain challenges. First, soft power — the ability to cause others to admire, respect, and emulate — is critically important when trying to build a new kind of international order. Without it, a would-be hegemon has only carrots, sticks, and deception with which to manage the behaviour of others. Does the way Beijing governs its own citizens and national minorities indicate how Beijing would treat other peoples? What one sees is China deploying its growing military and civilian power in intimidating ways to get neighbours to cede their maritime territorial rights granted under the U.N. Convention of the Law of the Sea (UNCLOS) — which China has signed. It is possible that China may decide to embrace the international rule of law and rely on UNCLOS dispute resolution provisions at some point in future, but if it does not, neighbours both large and small will face difficult choices. It is already apparent that few, if any, of China's neighbours are willing to see China govern the region single-handedly.

Second, China may assume that the U.S. will recognize the primacy of China's interests in Asia and cede to it a "sphere of influence". However, the U.S. sees a vital interest at stake in maintaining a strategic defensive perimeter in the Western Pacific and naval supremacy in the world's oceans. Other powers, such as Russia, India, and Japan, may also prudently wish to prevent the kind of Eurasian predominance that China may eventually seek, especially if China continues to demonstrate the "great power autism" of bullying smaller neighbours for marginal territorial gains.[31]

Third, given China's endemic environmental crisis, systemic financial risks, institutional corruption, labour unrest, aging population, and civil society pressures for democratization, it is far from certain that there will be no "black swan" event in China's future that will derail its rapid upward trajectory.

Conclusion

China's Eurasian geo-strategic vision is plausible if one assumes that China's fast-paced economic growth and development can be maintained, and if China's continuing rise does not call forth counter-balancing coalitions of states. Based on a successful programme of Silk Road development, China may command the markets and resources of Eurasia and neighbouring Africa. China's community of shared destiny is simple and easy to manage — for China. It relies on the ability to finance the construction of economic corridors and to incentivize economic cooperation with China, and it puts China at the centre of a Eurasian hub-and-spoke structure of power relations with few legal and strategic constraints on its exercise of sovereign power. A look at what China has done so far shows that it is quickly advancing this agenda both across the heartland and around the margins of the Eurasian land mass.[32] Though China faces many daunting obstacles and uncertainties, the impact of its Eurasian strategy could be lasting, and is today certainly changing the existing Eurasian order.

Notes

1. Map of Yuxinou Railway connecting China with Europe, available at <http://www.therakyatpost.com/wp-content/uploads/2014/03/rail_M.jpg>.
2. Map comparing the Silk Road Economic Belt and the 21st Century Maritime Silk Road, available at <http://www.chinadaily.com.cn/china/images/attachement/jpg/site1/20140411/00221917e13e14b179190f.jpg>.
3. "Chinese Carrier Cosco is Transforming Piraeus — and Has Eyes on Thessaloniki", *The Guardian*, 19 June 2014, available at <http://www.theguardian.com/world/2014/jun/19/china-piraeus-greece-cosco-thessaloniki-railways>; "China's 21st Century 'Maritime Silk Road' Ambitions", *Seatradeglobal.com*, 19 December 2014, available at <http://www.seatrade-global.com/news/asia/chinas-21st-century-maritime-silk-road-ambitions.html>.
4. "China on Track in Russia", *Chinadaily.com*, 14 October 2014, available at <http://www.chinadaily.com.cn/world/2014livisitgrl/2014-10/14/content_18735207.htm>.
5. "China is Planning to Build a Bullet-train that Connects Eastern and Western Europe", *Business Insider*, 16 December 2014, available at <http://www.businessinsider.com/afp-china-steps-up-plan-for-new-export-corridor-into-europe-2014-12>; Press Release: "Five Containers Already Arrived from the Port of Piraeus", Rail Cargo Hungaria, 16 June 2014, available at <http://www.railcargo.hu/en/press-room/press-releases/1962-press-release-five-containers-already-arrived-to-hungary-from-the-port-of-piraeus.html>.
6. "中国'超极推销员'签约1,400亿美元" [China's Super Salesman Closes Deals Worth US$140 Billion], [*Guangzhou Daily*], 29 December 2014, available at <news.xinhuanet.com/world/2014-12/29/c_1113804346.htm>.
7. CICA website, available at <http://www.s-cica.org/index.html>.
8. Statement by H.E. Mr Xi Jinping, "Conference on Interaction and Confidence Building Measures in Asia", 21 May 2014, available at <http://www.s-cica.org/page.php?page_id=711&lang=1>.
9. "China to Offer India Aid for High Speed Rail Study", *Reuters*, 25 November 2014, available at <http://in.reuters.com/article/2014/11/25/china-india-railway-idINKCN0J90EF20141125>.
10. "With New Funds, China Hits a Silk Road Stride", *Caixin*, 3 December 2014, available at <http://english.caixin.com/2014-12-03/100758419.html>.
11. Wu Xinbo, "Understanding the Geopolitical Implications of the Global Financial

Crisis", *The Washington Quarterly* 33, no. 4 (October 2010): 155–63.

12. Elizabeth C. Economy, "The Game Changer: Coping with China's Foreign Policy Revolution", *Foreign Affairs* 89, no. 6 (November/December 2010), available at <http://www.foreignaffairs.com/articles/66865/elizabeth-c-economy/the-game-changer>.

13. Andrew F. Krepinevich, et al., *Meeting the Anti-Access and Area Denial Challenge*, Center for Strategic and Budgetary Assessments, 2003, available at <http://csbaonline.org/publications/2003/05/a2ad-anti-access-area-denial/>.

14. "China Vows to Build Community of Common Destiny with ASEAN", *Xinhua*, 3 October 2013, available at <http://news.xinhuanet.com/english/china/2013-10/03/c_132770494.htm> (accessed 21 March 2014).

15. "Xi Jinping: Let the Sense of Community of Common Destiny Take Deep Root in Neighbouring Countries", Ministry of Foreign Affairs of the People's Republic of China, 25 October 2013, available at <http://www.fmprc.gov.cn/mfa_chn/zyxw_602251/t1093113.shtml>. This agenda was reaffirmed in a broader and more confident vision of Chinese great power leadership at a Central Work Meeting on Foreign Affairs in November 2014. See "习近平出席中央外事工作会议并发表重要讲话" [Xi Jinping attends the Central Work Meeting on Foreign Affairs to make an important speech], *Xinhua Online*, 29 November 2014, available at <http://news.xinhuanet.com/politics/2014-11/29/c_1113457723.htm>.

16. Zarubino port on the Japan Sea will be jointly developed by China and Russia into a 60 million ton/year port linked by road and rail to Jilin Province at the border city of Hunchun. "Russia Port Has Big Regional Goals, Especially for Northeast Asia", *Global Times*, 18 September 2014, available at <http://en.people.cn/business/n/2014/0918/c90778-8784185.html>. Jilin already has road and rail links to the North Korean port of Rajin where it has a long-term lease on pier facilities.

17. Charles Wolf, Jr., Xiao Wang, and Eric Warner, *China's Foreign Aid and Government-sponsored Investment Activities: Scale, Content, Destinations, and Implications* (Santa Monica, CA: RAND National Defense Research Institute, 2013), available at <http://www.rand.org/content/dam/rand/pubs/research_reports/RR100/RR118/RAND_RR118.pdf>.

18. "The Chinese Premier's US$140 Billion Trips Abroad", *China Development Gateway*, 26 December 2014, available at <http://en.chinagate.cn/2014-12/26/content_34416924.htm>.

19. "习近平阐明中国和平发展原则底线" [Xi Jinping Explains the Principled Bottom Line in China's Peaceful Development], *Xinhua Online*, 30 January 2013, available at <http://www.chinanews.com/gn/2013/01-31/4535125.shtml>. Timothy Heath, "Diplomacy Work Forum: Xi Steps Up Efforts to Shape a China-Centered Regional Order", *China Brief*, vol. 13, issue 22 (7 November 2013), available at <http://www.jamestown.org/single/?tx_ttnews[tt_news]=41594&no_cache=1#.VJGRfqbdVRA>.

20. In 2009, speaking at the U.S.-China Strategic and Economic Dialogue, State Councilor Dai Bingguo defined China's core interests in the following way: "中国的核心利益第一是维护基本制度和国家安全，其次是国家主权和领土完整，第三是经济社会的持续稳定发展" [First Round of the U.S.-China Economic Dialogue: Other Important Issues Discussed Besides the Moon], 首轮中美经济对话：除上月球外主要问题均已谈及，中国新闻网，[*China News Online*], 29 July 2009, 9:29 a.m., available at <http://www.chinanews.com.cn/gn/news/2009/07-29/1794984.shtml>.

21. "Full Text of Chinese FM's Signed Article on Int'l Rule of Law", *Xinhua*, 24 October 2014, available at <http://en.people.cn/n/2014/1024/c90883-8799769-2.html>.
22. The U.N.'s definition of the international rule of law starts off this way: "a principle of governance in which all persons, institutions and entities, public and private, *including the State itself*, are accountable to laws that are publicly promulgated, equally enforced and *independently adjudicated*, and which are consistent with *international human rights norms and standards....*" (italics added). "What is the Rule of Law?", United Nations Rule of Law website, available at <http://www.unrol.org/article.aspx?article_id=3>.
23. "China-Central Asia Trade Seeing Fast Growth", *Xinhua*, 13 February 2014, available at <http://news.xinhuanet.com/english/china/2014-02/13/c_133112941.htm> (accessed 21 March 2014).
24. "China-Eurasia Expo, Urumqi, Xinjiang, China-Britain Business Council", China-Britain Business Council, available at <http://www.cbbc.org/cbbc_calendar/event/view?id=610> (accessed 21 March 2014).
25. "China Proposes New Silk Road Free Trade Zone", *China Briefing*, 17 September 2013, available at <http://www.china-briefing.com/news/2013/09/17/china-proposes-new-silk-road-free-trade-zone.html> (accessed 21 March 2014); Aleksandra Jarosiewicz, "A Chinese *Tour de force* in Central Asia", *OSW*, 18 September 2013, available at <http://www.osw.waw.pl/en/publikacje/analyses/2013-09-18/a-chinese-tour-de-force-central-asia> (accessed 21 March 2014).
26. "The World's Longest Oil and Gas Pipelines", *hydrocarbons-technology.com*, 18 October 2012, available at <http://www.hydrocarbons-technology.com/features/featureworlds-longest-oil-gas-pipelines-imports/> (accessed 21 March 2014).
27. Martin W. Lewis, "Balochistan and the New 'Great Game' in Central Asia?", *Geo-Currents*, 20 May 2012, available at <http://www.geocurrents.info/geopolitics/balochistan-and-a-new-great-game-in-central-asia> (accessed 21 March 2014); Shabaz Rana, "Building on Ties: New Premier Indicates Plan to Link Gwadar with China", *The Express-Tribune*, 6 June 2013, available at <http://tribune.com.pk/story/559370/building-on-ties-new-premier-indicates-plan-to-link-gwadar-with-china/> (accessed 21 March 2014).
28. Halford J. Mackinder, "The Round World and the Winning of the Peace", *Foreign Affairs* 21 (1943): 595–605. Nicolas J. Spykman, *America's Strategy in World Politics: The United States and the Balance of Power* (New York: Harcourt, Brace and Company, 1942). See also, Zbigniew Brzezinski, *The Grand Chessboard: American Primacy and Its Geostrategic Imperatives* (New York: Basic Books, 1998).
29. Shannon Tiezzi, "The Maritime Silk Road vs. the String of Pearls", *The Diplomat*, 13 February 2014, available at <http://thediplomat.com/2014/02/the-maritime-silk-road-vs-the-string-of-pearls/>.
30. "Chinese Troops Ready to Join South Sudan UN Force", *BBC News*, 22 December 2014, available at <http://www.bbc.com/news/world-africa-30577294>; "China Oil Fears Over South Sudan Fighting", *BBC News*, 8 January 2014, available at <http://www.bbc.com/news/world-africa-25654155>.
31. Edward N. Luttwak, *The Rise of China vs. the Logic of Strategy* (U.S.: Harvard University Press, 2012).
32. Map of China's proposed Silk Road Routes, available at <http://www.wsj.com/articles/chinas-new-trade-routes-center-it-on-geopolitical-map-1415559290>.

CHINA'S INTERNATIONAL STRATEGY AND ITS IMPLICATIONS FOR SOUTHEAST ASIA

Zhang Zhexin

Amid worldwide salutes and suspicion, China's international strategy took full shape in 2015. While many observers find increasing opportunities in China's multiple initiatives to enhance regional and global development as well as economic cooperation, others see an ever more assertive China, projecting might with its growing wealth. Especially for Southeast Asian nations, the most susceptible to China's moves due to their proximity to and close economic ties with China, the many new Chinese initiatives have brought both hope and challenges. Now that three years have passed since President Xi Jinping took office and the basic framework of China's international strategy has been established, it is time to examine the new features of China's international endeavours and draw salient implications for the future trends of its political, security and economic relations with the world, and in particular with its closest neighbour, ASEAN.

From the author's perspective, despite its widely perceived image as a revisionist, hegemony-seeking power, China has maintained its course of peaceful rise, and its new international strategy features more continuity than change. Nevertheless, with the evolving geopolitical environment of the world and bigger stakes in regional stability and global economic well-being, China has made many adjustments to its international strategy under the new leadership. If effectively implemented and well understood by other nations, this strategy will not only help achieve the grand "Chinese Dream", but also boost global peace and development as well as regional stability and integration.

Reprinted from Malcolm Cook and Daljit Singh, eds., *Southeast Asian Affairs 2016* (Singapore: ISEAS – Yusof Ishak Institute), pp. 55–66. At the time of original publication, Zhang Zhexin was Research Fellow at the Shanghai Institutes for International Studies (SIIS) and a Non-Resident Fellow at the Charhar Institute.

Old Ambition, New Approach: Five Changes to China's International Strategy

The peaceful and inward-focused nature of China's rise was reaffirmed when President Xi put forward China's strategic goal to achieve the "Chinese Dream", a new name for the century-long ambition for "the great rejuvenation of the Chinese nation", on 29 November 2012, only two weeks after he was elected as General Secretary of the Communist Party of China (CPC). Despite occasional headstrong behaviour since then, China has in general demonstrated a peaceful and constructive stance in the international arena, and domestic reform and development have remained its first and foremost strategic targets. Facing the new global political, security and economic realities, however, the Chinese leadership is taking a new approach to achieve this old ambition, mainly reflected in the following five aspects:

Peaceful Rise: From Peace Maintenance to Peace Promotion

In view of its deficient security infrastructure and acknowledging the United States' fundamentally stabilizing role in the Asia-Pacific, China had kept a low profile in the global and regional security realms from the late 1970s to early 2010s, and endeavoured to maintain a peaceful environment for its rise by working closely with its security partners like Russia, the United States and ASEAN, as well as by enhancing regional community building in all directions. However, as the U.S. rebalancing moves since 2010 triggered growing tensions between China and its Pacific neighbours,[1] China has come to realize that, with its growing power, its quiescent peace-maintaining stance is neither convincing to its neighbours nor sufficient for protecting its expanding overseas interests. Thus, it has adopted many proactive measures to consolidate regional peace and stability as well as to foster its global image as a peace-promoting responsible power.

Indeed, the past three years have witnessed much more active Chinese engagement in addressing salient regional security issues, including maintaining stability on the Korean Peninsula, nuclear non-proliferation, building security infrastructure in Afghanistan and Africa, and working with related countries mainly in areas such as peacekeeping, counterterrorism and anti-piracy. For instance, to strengthen its strategic trust with ASEAN, China proposed to institutionalize an informal meeting mechanism for Chinese and ASEAN defence ministers, set up the China–ASEAN defence hotline, and establish a law-enforcement institute for training ASEAN personnel.[2] For another example, despite the criticism from many international observers that China was trying to "block progress" in the Iranian nuclear talks,[3] China's positive role in generating a final deal between Iran and the P5+1 — the United States, Russia, China, the United Kingdom and France, plus Germany — was well appreciated by President Obama.[4]

China's peace-promoting efforts have not been confined to regional security issues. In his speech at the 70th UN General Assembly on 26 September 2015, President Xi announced that China would commit $1 billion for a UN peace fund, and build a peacekeeping standby force of 8,000 troops. Together with Xi's surprising declaration on 3 September of cutting 300,000 Chinese troops, China has increasingly presented itself as a confident and responsible great power in promoting world peace.

New Type Major-Power Relations: From Vague Idealism to Pragmatism

The Chinese leadership was still hopeful about maintaining the strategic congruity between China and other major powers, especially the United States, when President Xi first proposed in February 2012 the notion of a "new-type major-power relationship" that features mutual respect and win-win cooperation. However, as tensions kept growing between China and Japan over the Diaoyu (Senkaku) Islands, and between China and the United States on much wider fronts, the Chinese strategic community has begun to acknowledge the fact that not only has China's relationship with the United States entered a new era of strategic competition, but its relations with other major powers — Russia, the European Union, Japan and India, in particular — are undergoing profound changes as well.[5] Hence, China is adopting a much more pragmatic approach towards other major powers.

First, China is making efforts to avoid any acute conflict with the United States, the only superpower today. Keen observers find that "no conflict and no confrontation" replaced the past emphasis on "win-win cooperation" as the key tone of President Xi's exchange with President Obama on his formal visit to the United States in late September 2015. The reiteration of both leaders on every occasion that "the Pacific Ocean is big enough for all of us" also highlights the fact that China–U.S. strategic trust is so inadequate that both sides have to keep reassuring each other about a concept deemed almost self-evident but a few years ago.

Second, China is seeking to strengthen ties with other major powers by expanding realms of cooperation, sometimes in tacit concession of short-term interests. Its comprehensive strategic partnership with the European Union is a case in point. To weigh against the U.S. rebalancing in the Asia-Pacific, China has extended various trade and investment terms to key EU members and managed to win their support for its "Belt and Road" initiative, the establishment of the Asian Infrastructure Investment Bank (AIIB) and other financial or cultural initiatives.[6] With regards to Japan, the second-largest Asian economy and a major U.S. ally, China has also withdrawn from its past insistence on "no high-level dialogue unless Japan openly admits its war crimes", and thus the China, Japan and South Korea summit reconvened on 1 November 2015, three and a half years after the previous one was held.

Finally, worried about being encircled by a U.S.-led coalition, China is more actively engaged in strategic cooperation with Russia and Central Asian nations. Though a China–Russia alliance is still a remote possibility, both countries will apparently work more closely together in the face of growing pressure from the United States. That President Xi proposed the New Asian Security Concept calling for "people of Asia to run the affairs of Asia" at the Conference on Interaction and Confidence Building Measures in Asia (CICA)[7] also indicates a shift of China's strategic basis from the West Pacific to central Eurasia.

Peripheral Diplomacy: From Marginal to Central Concern

Despite its rhetoric on maintaining good relations with its neighbours, China's strategic focus had been until recently on relations with such key powers as the

United States, Japan and Russia. It was widely believed that China's relations with Southeast Asian nations, even those in territorial disputes with China, could be well managed given a sound China–U.S. relationship. Hence, China has tended to seek settlement of regional security problems with the United States rather than with regional countries directly. Recognizing that China–U.S. relations are no longer a guarantee of good neighbourly relations, however, China is placing much more emphasis on developing its peripheral diplomacy independent of major power factors.

Compared with its efforts to consolidate relations with South and Central Asian neighbours, China has put more resources into fostering closer ties with Southeast Asia, not only because such relations are more difficult to manage due to the varied conditions of the ten ASEAN members, but also because a good China–ASEAN relationship is key to the realization of China's security and economic blueprints. Since the first CPC Central Meeting on China's Peripheral Diplomacy was held on 24 October 2013, President Xi and Premier Li Keqiang have visited nearly all ASEAN countries, and the "2+7 Cooperation Framework" has been implemented with great enthusiasm and fruitful results,[8] advancing China–ASEAN relations to new levels year after year.

To minimize the impact of South China Sea disputes on the general trends of China–ASEAN relations, China has refrained from rabid actions, even in time of crises, as showcased in its sober settlement with Vietnam on the "Oil Rig HD-981 Incident" in July 2014. It has also engaged more closely with other claimants in maintaining regional stability, culminating in President's Xi's visits to Vietnam and the Philippines in mid-November 2015. Such endeavours, together with the Chinese leadership's repeated emphasis on developing a "community of common destiny", as well as the many new Chinese initiatives to enhance economic, social and infrastructure ties with ASEAN and other neighbouring countries, imply that peripheral diplomacy has become one of China's central concerns.

International Contribution: From Reciprocity to More Public Goods

As a developing nation, China had long held the principle of matched reciprocity in international relations — with its repeated advocating for "mutual benefit" a clear example. Yet, in recent years the Chinese strategic community has realized that it is the commitment to global responsibility and a greater willingness to provide public goods that make a power great. Therefore, China has been trying to contribute more internationally in line with its growing national strength.

During his meeting with President Obama at Sunnylands in early June 2013, President Xi extended the grand vision of the "Chinese Dream" from "the rejuvenation of the Chinese nation and accomplishment of the vast public's happiness" to "the realisation of the common dream for peace and prosperity through win-win cooperation with other nations of the world". Meanwhile, the Chinese leadership has expressed on many occasions China's welcome of "more free riders with its sustained growth".[9] From China's announcement of reducing or exempting official debts of other developing nations once every few years, to its strong support for the UN's post-2015 development agenda, and to the vital role it has been playing in global arenas for tackling climate change, one can find China increasingly ready to provide global public goods rather than seeking immediate reciprocity for its contributions.[10]

Besides those tangible public goods for the world, China is also more active and confident in offering new thoughts and alternatives in promoting world peace and development. For one thing, China has put forward many new initiatives like the AIIB and the Belt and Road initiative aimed at enhancing regional development and economic integration. For another, China is taking great efforts to amend the global political system (such as the UN) and the financial system, like the IMF, so as to help shape a more equitable, sustainable and auspicious global order.

Safeguarding Core Interests: From Deference to Assertiveness

Up to the early 2010s China had more often than not adopted a conciliatory stance towards external challenges to its interests, not only to follow the strategic guideline of *tao guang yang hui* (keeping a low profile while developing its capabilities) over the previous three decades, but also to minimize any negative effect on burgeoning regional economic integration. Hence, its de facto acquiescence to Japan's temporary jurisdiction over the Diaoyu Islands, as well as the exploration and exploitation of oil and other resources by some Southeast Asian nations in disputed waters in the South China Sea.[11] Yet, facing ever more open challenges from those "transgressors" and their potential coalition with extra-regional powers like the United States, China has changed its past deferential attitude to one of more assertiveness.

Declaring that China "would not back off when its core interests are challenged", President Xi has on many occasions emphasized "bottom-line thinking"; meaning that while trying to settle disputes through consultation and enhanced co-operation, the Chinese should always make preparations for the potential worst-case scenario.[12] With such thinking, China keeps upgrading its military and has become bold enough to demonstrate its strength to the world, as exemplified by its impressive military parade on 3 September 2015 in commemoration of the seventieth anniversary of the anti-fascist war. Likewise, China is taking proactive measures to forestall further challenges to its core interests, such as the announcement of the Air Defence Identification Zone in the East China Sea in November 2013 and the accelerated land reclamation in the South China Sea over the past few years, which some believe will give China better leverage in dealing with the United States and in shaping a new environment for better maritime cooperation.[13]

In sum, although China still keeps to the track of peaceful rise under the new Chinese leadership, it has become a more confident — sometimes even assertive — power trying to attain rights and global prestige commensurate to its ever growing responsibilities. The following will address what impact such changes may have on ASEAN nations as well as on their future relationship with China.

Implications of China's International Strategy to ASEAN

At first sight, a stronger and more assertive China is no blessing for ASEAN countries, its closest yet much smaller neighbours.

Consequently, some ASEAN nations — in particular, the Philippines — are beginning to adopt the "Aquino way", which, unlike the previous "ASEAN way" that features consensus among ASEAN members and seeks to settle disputes by friendly consultation, marks a tougher posture towards China even at the price of ASEAN integrity.[14] Moreover, many analysts in ASEAN as well as in the United States advocate strengthening security and economic ties between ASEAN and the United States in order to hedge against China's role in the West Pacific.[15] Such trends, however, tend to exaggerate China's potential threat and thus may harm regional stability, cooperation and sustainable development.

First, China's strategic blueprint is basically set and clear. Contrary to international concerns as to what other bold steps China will take after so many strong moves during the first three years of Xi's presidency, those who are familiar with modern Chinese history would contend that any new Chinese leadership would spend the first few years of its tenure (usually two consecutive five-year terms) designing a general framework for China's international endeavours, including the basic goals, principles and approaches, while focusing on implementing them for the remaining years before its tenure ends. China's reform and opening-up strategy was deliberated within a year and a half of Deng Xiaoping resuming power in the CPC; Jiang Zemin declared in November 1994 that China's strategic goal was to "integrate into an interdependent world",[16] twenty months after he was elected President of China; and Hu Jintao proposed the strategy of speeding up domestic reform and development by exploiting the "strategic opportunity" (of the United States focusing on counterterrorism rather than containing China's rise) shortly after he became CPC General Secretary.

Similarly, many observers find that the basic framework of China's international strategy under President Xi has been established, with the core objective to "create a favourable environment for realising the Chinese Dream".[17] Insisting on balanced development of both hard power and soft power, China's strategic approach for the next five years is "developing through more opening-up and win-win cooperation, more actively engaged in global economic governance, and trying to provide more global public goods".[18] In other words, China maintains that peace, stability and regional cooperation are in its best interest, and thus may very likely refrain from making any major changes or springing "surprises" on the international or regional arenas in the years to follow.

Second, trying to build a strategic bloc against an ever-stronger China is both senseless and risky. While China is fumbling its way towards becoming a more responsible regional power, it would be wise for Southeast Asian nations to adapt to that reality rather than confront it. Any strategic moves against China, especially when perceived by the Chinese as being backed by other majors powers like the United States or Japan, would reinforce the largely prevalent impression that China is being circumscribed by a hostile coalition, and that to seek breakthroughs China may need to either coalesce with other major powers like Russia or take the initiative by "giving a lesson to smaller culprits" as a warning to others.[19] That would certainly be a nightmare for Southeast Asian nations, whose trade with China accounts for nearly seventeen per cent of their total GDP and whose total military spending was less than one-fifth of China's in 2014.[20]

As the ASEAN Community was formally established at the end of 2015, this terrifying scenario is not completely illusory. Although security cooperation among ASEAN members has been focused on non-traditional issues such as counterterrorism, anti-drug smuggling and natural disaster relief, with the need for closer integration, ASEAN will find itself under increasing pressure to take sides: to yield to the "Aquino way" or sacrifice ASEAN integrity; to join a "coalition for freedom of navigation" or to remain in its neutral position as a whole; to be more committed to the already signed Trans-Pacific Partnership (TPP) or to the emerging Regional Comprehensive Economic Partnership (RCEP). Whichever alternative ASEAN takes, it is of vital importance to make sure that it should not be perceived by China as a collective scheme against it.

Third, China–U.S. relations are expected to remain stable, though confrontation may rise over tensions triggered by third parties. As mentioned before, China has made every effort to avoid confrontation with the United States, and both sides keep reassuring each other of their common wish to preserve the stability of their bilateral relationship and of the Asia-Pacific region. Following President Xi's state visit in September 2015, China–U.S. relations will most likely remain stable at least until the end of President Obama's term in early 2017. Even on the most sensitive issues like cyber security and U.S. naval patrols in the disputed waters of the South China Sea, both countries are very likely to stay low key and jointly prevent any escalation. Meanwhile, they will try to enhance their basic strategic trust by conducting more military exchanges, extending prior notice of major manoeuvres in the West Pacific, and securing new codes of conduct for unexpected encounters in the air and at sea.

Nevertheless, given the U.S. security commitments to its Pacific allies, especially the Philippines, if China and the Philippines happen to be engaged in an acute conflict over disputed land features in the South China Sea, the United States would have no other choice but to confront China, at least in military and diplomatic postures. Though not likely to escalate into a major confrontation between China and the United States or ASEAN, any such tensions triggered by a third party would undoubtedly exert a lasting impact on regional stability and economic integration. Thus, not only should major powers like China and the United States exercise more self-restraint and strategic patience, but smaller nations in the region must also refrain from challenging China's core interests — minimizing any potential destabilizing factors — in the South China Sea.

Fourth, regional economic integration is gathering new momentum after a five-year recess. In our rapidly changing times, people are often oblivious to the fact that regionalism was still a catchword for East Asian nations five years ago — China, Japan and South Korea were ardently exploring ways to construct a trilateral free trade zone (FTZ); the ASEAN-plus model of regional economic integration was on a rapid track as well. Worried about being marginalized by such trends, the United States began its rebalancing efforts, first by increasing its military deployment in Northeast Asia after the alleged North Korean sinking of a South Korean naval ship in May 2010, then by enhancing its security partnerships with West Pacific nations to "safeguard freedom of navigation" in the South China Sea; and, in the meantime, by accelerating the TPP negotiation process, thus reaffirming its political, security and economic leadership in the Asia-Pacific.[21] With enduring tensions between China and Japan over the Diaoyu Islands and interpretations of Second World War history, as well as some ASEAN members' prioritization of the TPP, neither the China–Japan–South Korea FTZ nor the ASEAN-plus mechanism has achieved any substantial results over the past five years.

Today, however, regional economic integration is gaining new momentum, which will hopefully culminate in an agreed RCEP framework in the next year or two. Above all, it has already developed a good foundation after eight rounds of negotiation since the first was held in May 2013. Much agreement has been reached on the seven major areas of commodity trade, service trade, investment, technological cooperation, intellectual property rights, policies on competition, and related legal institutions. Next, with four ASEAN members as TPP members, ASEAN as a whole faces the growing need to reach an extensive economic integration pact so as to maintain balanced development among its members and facilitate ASEAN Community-building. Considering its own need for closer engagement with the regional economy and its good relationship with all RCEP members, Laos, the 2016 ASEAN chair, is expected to do its best to push forward RCEP negotiations. Furthermore, the resumed trilateral summit between China, Japan and South Korea in November 2015 has removed one of the biggest barriers for RCEP,[22] and Premier Li Keqiang's announcement in November 2015 of "striving to conclude RCEP negotiation by 2016" further consolidated the political basis of the RCEP process.[23] Finally, an upgraded China–ASEAN partnership, especially in the six key areas of cooperation proposed by Premier Li in Kuala Lumpur, serves as a strong incentive for other nations to follow suit, and thus will generate more momentum for regional economic integration.

Lastly, China's "Belt and Road" initiative is an "express train" that regional nations cannot afford to miss. The initiative will not only advance China's strategic influence, but it is also aimed at boosting development of related nations and strengthening ties among themselves, which will give them more leverage in helping shape China's behaviour in the international arena. Now that the Belt and Road initiative is growing to become China's predominant strategy of international cooperation,[24] the real issue for regional countries is not whether to embrace the initiative, but how to make the best use of the opportunities it creates, while preventing potential side effects on their own strategic designs.

As suggested by Premier Li in November 2015, China intends to link the Belt and Road initiative to the development strategies of regional countries by providing more public goods like the AIIB, "Silk Road Fund", and the "China–ASEAN Investment Cooperation Fund", apart from offering another US$10 billion for infrastructure interconnectivity between ASEAN and China.[25] Towards such proposals many ASEAN members like Malaysia and Indonesia have demonstrated due respect and interest, yet a few others still hold a hesitant or even doubtful stance. Although the Belt and Road initiative is expected ultimately to be built into a complete network across the region, to miss its first key steps may lead to greater delay in the future, which would be regretful both for the development of individual countries and for the general trend of ASEAN integration.

At the present time, the key to sustainable regional stability and development is how to enhance regional economic and cultural integration in a period of profound power transition, rather than simply how to manage the potential threats of a rising China. Towards that goal the new Chinese leadership has come up with a clear road map — to provide more driving force and public goods for regional development and integration; and to promote regional stability by fostering a sense of "community of common destiny" that is built on mutual trust, win-win cooperation and collective actions to tackle common challenges. Certainly, such a vision entails understanding, restraint and the joint effort of all nations in the region.

Notes

1. This is a belief held by most Chinese scholars and strategic planners. For instance, see "'Disturbance' Only Harms China, Japan: Fu Ying", *China Daily*, 26 October 2015 <http://www.china.org.cn/world/2015-10/26/content_36890075.htm>.
2. Li Keqiang's remarks at the 18th ASEAN–China Summit, Kuala Lumpur, 21 November 2015.
3. Jin Liangxiang, "Is China Blocking Iranian Nuclear Negotiations?", *China.org.cn*, 28 December 2014 <http://www.china.org.cn/opinion/2014-12/28/content_34426531.htm>.
4. "Obama Thanks Xi for China's Role in Iran N-accord", *MSN News*, 21 July 2015 <http://www.msn.com/en-in/news/other/obama-thanks-xi-for-chinas-role-in-iran-n-accord/ar-AAdiSkK>.
5. Li Wei and Zhang Zhexin, "New Type China–U.S. Relations in an Era of Strategic Competition", *Quarterly Journal of International Politics*, 2015, no. 1, pp. 25–53.
6. For a brief review of current China–EU relations, see "Op-Ed: China, EU to strengthen strategic cooperation", *Xinhua News*, 4 July 2015 <http://news.xinhuanet.com/english/2015-07/04/c_134380713.htm>.
7. Xi Jinping's Remarks at the Fourth Summit of the Conference on Interaction and Confidence Building Measures in Asia, Shanghai, 21 May 2014.
8. The "2+7 Cooperation Framework" is a blueprint of cooperation proposed by Premier Li Keqiang at the 16th ASEAN–China Summit, Bandar Seri Begawan, on 9 October 2013. The "2" political consensuses are enhancing mutual strategic trust and promoting win-win economic cooperation. The "7" key areas of cooperation include political affairs, economy and trade, interconnectivity, finance, maritime cooperation, security, and people-to-people exchanges.
9. "China Voice: Beijing Welcomes More 'Free Riders' with Its Sustained Growth", *Xinhua News*, 12 November 2014 <http://news.xinhuanet.com/english/china/2014-11/12/c_133785010.htm>.
10. For a comprehensive review of China's role in the global climate governance system and the passing of the UN's post-2015 agenda, see Yu Hongyuan, "Evolution of the Global Climate Governance System and Its Implications"; and Zhang Chun, "Common but Differentiated Commitments: China's Engagement with the 2030 Agenda Global Partnership", both published in *China Quarterly of International Strategic Studies* 1, no. 3 (2015).
11. It is still disputable as to whether rights and interests within the "nine-dash line" are China's pronounced core interests. Although the Chinese government insists on the "inviolability of all islands and reefs within the 'nine-dash line'" — for safeguarding territorial integrity is undoubtedly one of its six core interests

— many Chinese scholars would argue that China's core interest in the South China Sea lies in settling disputes in a peaceful and consultative way. See the Chinese State Council: *White Book on China's Peaceful Development*, 6 September 2011; and "zhongguo 'hexin liyi' buyi kuodahua" [China should be cautious to expand application of "core interests"], *International Herald Leader*, 10 January 2011 <http://news.xinhuanet.com/herald/2011-01/10/c_13683711.htm>.

12. President Xi's remarks at the Plenary Session of the PLA Delegation at the 2nd Conference of the 12th National People's Congress, Beijing, 11 March 2014; and *Xijinpingzongshuji qiangdiao de liudasiweifangfa* [Six principles of thinking emphasized by CPC General Secretary Xi Jinping], CRI.cn news, 11 September 2014 <http://gb.cri.cn/42071/2014/09/11/5951s4687655_1.htm>.

13. Nong Hong, "The Post-Reclamation Scenario in the South China Sea: The Role of China and the United States", *CSIS Asia Maritime Transparency Initiative*, 23 March 2015 <http://amti.csis.org/the-post-reclamation-scenario-in-the-south-china-sea-the-role-of-china-and-the-united-states/>.

14. Aileen San Pablo-Baviera, "South China Sea Disputes: Is Aquino Way the 'ASEAN Way'?", *Eurasia Review*, 9 January 2012 <http://www.eurasiareview.com/09012012-south-china-sea-disputes-is-aquino-way-the-asean-way-analysis/>.

15. Benny Teh Cheng Guan, "Time for a Reevaluation of ASEAN's Role", *The Diplomat*, 1 September 2015 <http://thediplomat.com/2015/09/time-for-a-reevaluation-of-aseans-role/>.

16. Jiang Zemin's remarks at the 2nd APEC Economic Leaders' Meeting, Bogor, Indonesia, 15 November 1994.

17. "Ma Zhengang: Xijinpingzhuxi waijiao zhanlue xintedian" [Ma Zhengang: New features of President Xi Jinping's diplomatic strategy], *People's Forum*, 18 February 2014.

18. Xi Jinping's remarks at the 5th Plenary Meeting of the 18th CPC National Assembly, Beijing, 29 October 2015.

19. See, for example, Yan Xuetong, *Inertia of History: Chinese and the World in the Next Ten Years* (Beijing: CITIC Publishing, 2013), chaps. 1 and 5; and China's quasi-public opinion polls on whether China will "teach the Philippines a lesson", April 2012, available at <http://www.chinaiiss.com/conference/index/51>.

20. SIPRI Military Expenditure Database: 1988–2014.

21. For a popular Chinese view on the U.S. rebalancing scheme, see Li Wei and Zhang Zhexin, "New Type China–U.S. Relations".

22. "S. Korea, Japan Agree to Make Efforts at RCEP, Trilateral FTA with China", *Xinhua News*, 2 November 2015 <http://news.xinhuanet.com/english/2015-11/02/c_134775605.htm>.

23. Li Keqiang's remarks on the 18th ASEAN–China–Japan–South Korea (10+3) Summit, Kuala Lumpur, 21 November 2015.

24. At the time of writing, the Belt and Road initiative remains a "proposal" in China's official rhetoric, but in regard to the fact that it is emphasized at every public address made by Chinese leaders to international audiences and that it is an important part of China's 13th Five-year plan (2016–20), it has developed as China's de facto international strategy. See "yidaiyillu zheng zhubushouhuo zaoqichengguo [The "Belt and Road" initiative is reaping early harvests], *Xinhua Daily Telegraph*, 16 October 2015 <http://news.xinhuanet.com/mrdx/2015-10/16/c_134719858.htm>.

25. Li Keqiang's remarks at the 18th ASEAN–China Summit, Kuala Lumpur, 21 November 2015.

Brunei Darussalam

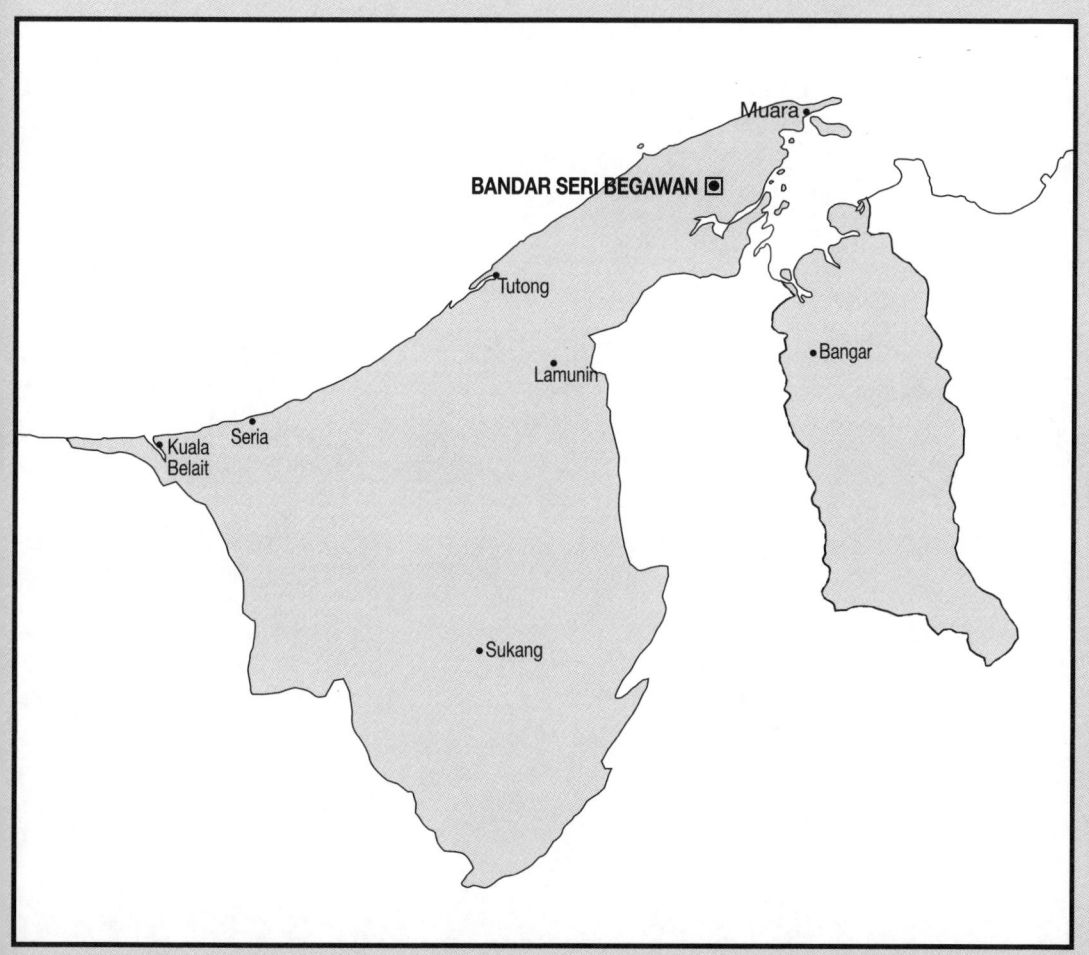

NEGARA BRUNEI DARUSSALAM
"A New Nation but an Ancient Country"

Sharon Siddique

Just before midnight on 31 December 1983, His Majesty the Sultan and Yang Dipertuan Sir Muda Hassanal Bolkiah, 29th ruler of Brunei, began reading the Proclamation of Independence to a crowd of 30,000 gathered at the Taman Haji Sir Omar Ali Saifuddien, Bandar Seri Begawan. He declared Negara Brunei Darussalam (Brunei, Abode of Peace) — "which has never been a colony" — "an independent, sovereign and democratic Malay Muslim monarchy based on Islamic teachings". A 21-gun salute heralded the New Year, and also marked a new era in the long history of this ancient country.

The proclamation outlined the special treaty relationship between Britain and Brunei which dated from 1847. In 1888, Britain assumed responsibility for Brunei's defence and external affairs. Brunei achieved internal self-government under its 1959 constitution which remains in force. The 1959 constitution was promulgated during the reign of His Majesty's father, His Royal Highness the Paduka Seri Begawan Sultan Jeneral Haji Sir Muda Omar Ali Saifuddien, the 28th Sultan, who abdicated in 1967 in favour of his son.[1] The 1979 Treaty of Friendship and Co-operation with Britain led to Brunei's full independence on 1 January 1984. With the reading of the proclamation, Britain relinquished its last responsibilities for the state's defence and foreign affairs.

Immediately following the proclamation ceremony, His Majesty the Sultan and Yang Dipertuan unveiled his new cabinet. The Sultan's personalized rule continues with his holding the offices of Prime Minister, Minister of Finance and Minister of Home Affairs. He named six other ministers, including his father, His Royal

---

Reprinted from Lim Joo-Jock, ed., *Southeast Asian Affairs 1985* (Singapore: Institute of Southeast Asian Studies, 1985), pp. 99–105. At the time of original publication, Sharon Siddique was Senior Research Fellow at the Institute of Southeast Asian Studies.

Highness the Paduka Seri Begawan Sultan (Minister of Defence), and two of his younger brothers, the Perdana Wazir Prince Mohamed Bolkiah (Minister of Foreign Affairs) and the Pengiran Digadong Prince Jefri (Minister of Culture, Youth and Sports cum Deputy Minister of Finance).

In addition, His Majesty named three cabinet ministers who are not members of the immediate royal family. Pengiran Bahrin bin Pengiran Haji Ahas was named Minister of Law and concurrently Minister of Communication. Pengiran Bahrin is a law graduate of Birmingham University. He also obtained his Master of Law from London University and is a barrister of Gray's Inn in London.[2] Pehin Dato Haji Abdul Aziz was named Minister of Education and Health. Pehin Dato Haji Abdul Aziz, who also graduated from a British university, was State Secretary before being appointed Acting Menteri Besar in September 1981. Pehin Dato Abdul Rahman was named Minister of Development. Pehin Dato Abdul Rahman was Acting State Secretary before the attainment of full independence. After naming the cabinet, the Sultan announced the abolition of the posts of Menteri Besar and State Secretary.

In contrast to the rather austere New Year's Eve proclamation ceremony and subsequent cabinet announcement which heralded Negara Brunei Darussalam's full independence, festivities surrounding the 23 February National Day celebrations were lavish.

The official independence celebrations began on 23 February 1984, with a mass rally at the Hassanal Bolkiah National Stadium. In the afternoon, His Royal Highness the Paduka Seri Begawan Sultan opened an exhibition on constitutional development in Brunei. That evening a dinner was held at the new Istana.

Amongst the 4,000 guests were Great Britain's Prince Charles; Singapore's Prime Minister Lee Kuan Yew; Thai Prime Minister General Prem Tinsulanond; the Prime Minister of Malaysia, Datuk Seri Dr Mahathir Mohamed; President Marcos of the Philippines; Indonesia's President Soeharto; President Zia-Ul-Haq of Pakistan; the Agong of Malaysia; President Sir Hammer Roberts of Nauru; Raja Taufahu Tupau IV of Tonga; Taja Malitua Tanu Mafili II of Western Samoa; Syed Faisal Ali of Oman and Governor General Sir Kingford Dibella of Papua New Guinea.

The ten-day celebration, from 23 February to 4 March 1984, also included such events as fireworks displays, cultural and drama shows, parades and displays by the Royal Brunei Armed Forces.

The security arrangements necessary to protect the many VIPs who attended the festivities as well as the protocol necessary to receive them, underscored the responsibilities which full independence had thrust upon the Bruneian leadership in the key areas of defence and diplomacy.

The Polity

It is significant that the birth of Brunei Darussalam was commemorated at two such different celebrations. At the proclamation ceremony, and immediately before at the special thanksgiving prayers held at the Sir Omar Ali Saifuddien Mosque, Bruneians gathered with members of their royal family to focus inward, highlighting their long political tradition, and drawing sustenance from their faith. It was during the proclamation address that His Majesty the Sultan and Yang Dipertuan announced that, in entering this new era of nationhood, Negara Brunei Darussalam would be known as a Negara Melayu Islam Beraja (a Malay

Muslim monarchy). On 23 February in contrast, Bruneians focused outward, highlighting their new status as a fully independent member of the international community of nations. Both foci require elaboration if we are to understand the significance of the year 1984 for the people and leaders of Brunei Darussalam.

The new nation seems firmly grounded on a perception of continuity with the past. His Majesty the Sultan and Yang Dipertuan, in his acceptance speech to the General Assembly on the occasion of Brunei Darussalam's admittance to the United Nations, spoke of this continuity.

> We are a new nation, but an ancient country: one of Asia's oldest. Visitors to Brunei many centuries ago found an established social system with a rich and flourishing culture. Five hundred years ago, under the leadership of my ancestor Sultan Bolkiah, the fifth Islamic Sultan, Brunei played an important role in the spread of the Islamic faith in Southeast Asia.
>
> So we have known pride and glory. But we have also experienced much pain: for three hundred years, from the sixteenth through the nineteenth centuries, our land and our region were wracked by rampant piracy; a series of wars; the violence of those who call themselves explorers, but whom we knew as exploiters.
>
> In this century, we have lived under the protection of an imperial power, albeit a benevolent one — Great Britain — and for a time during World War II, under military occupation by Japan.[3]

There has been a concerted effort during 1984 on the part of the Bruneian leadership to inculcate an understanding of the meaning of the proclamation phrase "an independent, sovereign and democratic Malay Muslim monarchy based on Islamic teachings" amongst Bruneians. His Majesty the Sultan and Yang Dipertuan raised this point in an address to the Chinese community (about 40,000 out of the total population of 200,000), which had gathered to honour him on the occasion of his 38th birthday. He reminded the Chinese and other communities in the country of the necessity of adjusting themselves to the necessities and aspirations of life in a "democratic Malay Muslim monarchy".[4]

A teacher's training course on MIB (Melayu Islam Beraja — Malay Muslim monarchy) was organized in October for about 400 teachers. Lectures were given in three areas — national education (*pendidikan negara*), Islam, and custom (*adat istiadat*).[5] Pehin Dato Haji Abdul Aziz, Minister of Education and Health, in an address at a seminar held for uniformed youth groups, emphasized the importance of inculcating at all levels of society the meaning and aspirations contained in the proclamation phrase.[6]

During the year there has been repeated reference to the role of Islam as the official state religion. Muslim holidays are strictly observed. His Majesty the Sultan and Yang Dipertuan is the Head of Islam, while the Religious Council is the supreme policymaking body on all matters concerning Islam. The Religious Department, which comes under the Prime Minister's office, regulates all official Muslim activities.

The State Mufti, Pehin Dato Haji Ismail bin Omar Abdul Aziz recently made headlines when he accused three international societies with branches registered in Brunei — the Lions Club, Rotary Club and a masonic lodge — of being anti-Islamic and funding and furthering Zionist causes. A senior government official said that the Mufti's editorials in the *Pelita Brunei* were his personal views and not a ruling, but nevertheless, Muslims would be expected to heed his advice.[7]

The sale of liquor in the country is permitted only at selected premises. Muslims are prohibited from entering such places. Restaurants are required by law to put up "non-halal" notices prominently if they serve food not meant for Muslims. There is strict censorship of all films, videos, imported radio and television programmes, books and magazines.

In an address to the Muslim Youth Conference for Southeast Asia and the Pacific of 1984, hosted by Brunei in March, the Sultan reiterated the importance of Islam in Negara Brunei Darussalam:

> I am thankful to Allah, the all pure and the most exalted, for destining Negara Brunei Darussalam to be an Islamic country since the fourteenth century as the result of which it was able to absorb Islamic influences up to the present time, through the efforts of previous Sultans of this country. It is my intention as well as that of my Government to continue preserving the Islamic teachings in accordance with Ahli Sunnah Wal Jamaah as a way of life and foundation in the administration of the Government of Negara Brunei Darussalam — in line with the position of Islam as the official religion of the country.[8]

The cabinet-style government announced by His Majesty the Sultan and Yang Dipertuan seems in keeping with the move to establish a tradition-oriented, Malay Muslim monarchy. A Bruneian senior official echoed this view when he stated, in an interview, that: "The system has served us well for centuries. We should not change for the sake of change or to please others."[9]

Another senior official, the Law Minister, Pengiran Bahrin explained in an interview that the cabinet-style government would provide a streamlined administration suitable to the country's needs. He is quoted as saying that "whereas before department heads had to report to and obtain decisions from the Menteri Besar through the State Secretary, they can now go straight to their respective ministers".[10]

Thus "traditional" does not necessarily connote "reactionary". In the Bruneian context at least, it seems that given the small population (200,000) and physical size (5765 sq. kms.) of the country, such a personalized concentration of administrative power in the hands of a few has the advantage of being a relatively flexible and efficient system of government.

The assumption of full independence means that for the first time since 1888 Bruneian defence and diplomacy are no longer under British management. In both areas 1984 has shown the Brunei Government capable of dealing with the new problems and pressures which have confronted them.

In a series of well-timed moves, the Bruneian leadership began smoothly establishing diplomatic priorities. Just seven days after the Proclamation of Independence on 1 January, Negara Brunei Darussalam became the sixth member of ASEAN.

The foreign ministers of the founder members of ASEAN — Indonesia, Malaysia, the Philippines, Singapore and Thailand — and the Foreign Minister of Brunei signed the declaration of the admission of Brunei Darussalam into ASEAN at the conference room of the ASEAN Secretariat building in Jakarta on 7 January 1984.

In an interview with the *Straits Times* (Singapore) on the eve of Brunei's admission to ASEAN, Brunei's first Foreign Minister, Prince Mohamed Bolkiah, said that Brunei's membership is the logical consequence of a number of factors. "The first and most obvious of these is the geographical one. Then there are also historical and cultural considerations. Most ASEAN nations have, at one time or another, been under the domination of foreign powers. The cultures of the six nations also overlap in a large measure."[11]

Brunei followed ASEAN's lead on the Kampuchea question, the organization's main foreign policy concern. On other issues important to ASEAN, such as trade flows, development aid and the North-South dialogue, Brunei did not appear to take an active role probably because its robust economy is largely based on oil and natural gas.

Eight days later, on 15 January 1984, Brunei became a member of the Organization of the Islamic Conference (OIC). His Majesty the Sultan and Yang Dipertuan Sir Muda Hassanal Bolkiah flew to Casablanca, Morocco, to attend the OIC meeting, thus underlining the significance of the event for Brunei.

In early October 1984, Negara Darussalam Brunei was admitted as the 159th member of the United Nations. In his acceptance speech, His Majesty the Sultan and Yang Dipertuan highlighted world events of concern to Brunei as a member of both ASEAN and the OIC. His Majesty referred to the Vietnamese invasion of Kampuchea, and their disregard for the principle of non-interference in the internal affairs of other states. The Sultan also mentioned the Palestinian cause:

> In the Middle East, the continued denial of the legitimate rights of the Palestinian people constitutes the core of the problems of that region. Brunei Darussalam remains steadfast in her conviction that a just, lasting and comprehensive solution must take into account the legitimate rights of the Palestinian people to self-determination in their own State of Palestine. We also support the Palestine Liberation Organization as the sole representative of the Palestinian people.[12]

Other points which he touched upon in his speech, were to express opposition to the continued Israeli occupation of Arab lands including southern Lebanon, to express concern at continuing conflict between Iran and Iraq, to call for the withdrawal of foreign forces from Afghanistan and to express support for the people of Namibia in their struggle for liberation from South African colonialism.[13]

Another aspect of Bruneian diplomacy were the state visits undertaken by His Majesty the Sultan and Yang Dipertuan. Malaysia was the first country to which the Sultan paid an official state visit after independence. This was followed in April by official state visits to Japan and the Republic of Korea, Indonesia in October and an official trip to Oman, Jordan and Egypt in December.

The visit to Japan signified the importance of Brunei-Japan relations. Japan is Brunei's leading trade partner. Commenting on the importance of the Sultan's visit to Korea, the *Korea Times* carried the following editorial message:

> What makes the Sultan's visit here noteworthy is that it is more a working trip than a mere ceremonial visit paid by a monarch. In addition to being a Head of State, the visiting Sultan is the country's chief executive.... Thus the talks his Majesty will have with President Chun and other Korean leaders are expected to get down to substantive matters and have a realistic and effective impact on future development of bilateral relations.[14]

In 1984 Brunei established high commissions and embassies in London, New York and the ASEAN capitals, Cairo and Washington. Missions are expected to be opened in other countries as trained staff become available. Cairo is an important capital for Brunei because of the number of Bruneian students studying in Egypt. Jeddah is also important because of students, and also because of the large numbers of Bruneians who perform the pilgrimage annually.

Bilateral relations between Brunei and each of its ASEAN partners were cordial in 1984. Significantly, Malaysia was the first country to which His Majesty the Sultan and Yang Dipertuan paid a state visit following Brunei's independence.[15] Co-operation with Indonesia was strengthened by the October state visit by His Majesty. Also visitors from ASEAN countries to Brunei increased after April, when they were allowed to enter for a two-week stay without visas. This reciprocal arrangement is operative amongst all ASEAN member countries.

The Royal Brunei Malay Regiment was renamed the Royal Brunei Armed Forces (RBAF) after independence. In making the name-change announcement, the Deputy Commander of the Armed Forces, Colonel Pehin Dato Haji Mohammad Daud, said that Brunei's entry into ASEAN will enlarge the existing field of co-operation between Brunei's armed forces (some 4,000 strong) and those of some ASEAN countries.[16]

In 1983 the Singapore Armed Forces joined Brunei troops for the first time in battalion exercises. The Singapore Armed Forces runs a jungle training camp for its servicemen in Brunei's Temburong district. Brunei's naval fleet has also held joint exercises with ships of Malaysia and Singapore.

According to a regional news magazine, the RBAF arsenal boasts 12 Scorpion tanks, a battery of field artillery and a battery of Rapier surface-to-air missiles. It also reportedly has six fast patrol craft, equipped with French-made Exocet missiles and Bell helicopter gunships. The RBAF is one of the costlier items in the nation's budget — B$340 million.[17]

In an agreement concluded between Brunei and Great Britain in September 1983, a Gurkha Battalion of the British Army, and certain British personnel on loan to the Royal Brunei Armed Forces, remained in Brunei after independence. Post-independence arrangements for them, as well as for the use by British forces of training facilities in Brunei Darussalam, continue essentially unaltered.

The Economy

Brunei's oil production is managed by Brunei Shell Petroleum Co. Ltd. which came into existence in 1957. In 1973, the government agreed to take up 25 per cent of the total equity. Since 1975, the Brunei Government has had a 50-50 share holding with the Royal Dutch/Shell. Brunei Shell Petroleum is responsible for the exploration and production of oil and natural gas, oil refining and crude oil trading. It employs about 3,000 people.[18]

Dato Everett, former managing director of Brunei Shell, said in an interview in the *Borneo Bulletin* that he believes Brunei's oil will last another 30 to 50 years. According to Dato Everett, Brunei Shell pumped up 180,000 barrels per day (bpd) in 1983, and will average 175,000 bpd in 1984. He said that plans call for a steady cutback to 150,000 bpd by the end of the 1980s and then the maintenance of that level into the next century.[19]

More recently Brunei Shell has announced a cutback in oil production following a world wide fall in demand. Output in December 1984 was down to 110,000 bpd from the average of 175,000 bpd which had been maintained for most of the year.[20]

Although Brunei did not join the Organization of Petroleum Exporting Countries (OPEC) during 1984, Brunei attended the December meeting of OPEC in Geneva as an observer. The invitation came from Indonesia's Mining and Energy Minister, Dr Subroto.

Japan is Brunei's leading trade partner, with exports to Japan exceeding B$4.5 billion for the first 11 months of 1983. Nearly all of Brunei's export of liquefied natural gas (LNG) is to Japan, making up nearly a third of Japan's domestic requirements. Brunei ships about five million tonnes of LNG a year to Japan under a 20-year contract signed in 1973. This accounts for 97 per cent of Brunei's LNG production. Three per cent is retained for internal use. Brunei is the ninth-largest supplier of crude oil to Japan. Japan imports more than half of the crude oil produced by Brunei, accounting for about 2.3 per cent of Japanese total crude oil imports for 1982.[21]

Brunei Shell Petroleum had a change of top management in 1984 when the managing director, Dato Peter Everett, who had held the position since 1979, returned to London to become managing director of Shell U.K. Exploration and Production. The new managing director is Dutchman, Nico Johan van Dijk.

Reminiscing about his long association with Brunei Shell, the departing managing director, Dato Peter Everett, recalled:

> Brunei was already rich then (in 1979) — but the real peak came in 1980–81 during the Iran crisis when oil prices skyrocketed. That was when Brunei was able to build up its foreign reserves.[22]

The management of these large foreign reserves made the headlines in July 1983 when Brunei decided to withdraw its reported B$10 billion-plus investment account from the British Crown Agents. The Brunei Government transferred its entire investment portfolio to the newly-created Brunei Investment Agency. Two U.S. banks (Morgan Guaranty Trust and Citibank), two Japanese securities firms (Nomura and Daiwa), and two British firms have reportedly been appointed as advisers to the Brunei Investment Agency.

In his National Day address, the Sultan reiterated that the Brunei Investment Agency is a key Bruneian institution. He referred to the fact that, although it was set up only shortly before full independence, its return on investments was already better than from the previous arrangement through the British Crown Agents.[23]

Total revenue for the fiscal year 1982 was B$5.8 billion, with a surplus of B$4.2 billion. In 1983 total revenue was B$6.1 billion, with a surplus of B$3.9 billion. Revenue for the year 1984 is expected to exceed B$6.5 billion. B$2.6 billion has been slated for the budget, leaving a surplus of about B$3.9 billion.

With a population of about 200,000, this B$2.6 billion budget figure means an expenditure of more than B$13,000 per person. More than a third of the budget has been allocated for the Development Fund. The Royal Brunei Armed Forces has been allocated 12 per cent of the budget. More than eight per cent has been earmarked for public works, with another eight per cent for education. The diplomatic service has been allocated slightly more than one per cent.[24]

Brunei residents receive free education, free health care, and low interest loans for cars and houses. There is no personal income tax. Of the total workforce of about 65,000, 40 per cent is imported foreign labour engaged in development projects.[25]

In the coming years, Brunei will attempt to decrease its dependence on the oil and gas industry by promoting agriculture and other types of industrial development.

The government has given top priority to agricultural development. In particular, four areas are being pushed by the Agriculture Department — rice, meat, vegetables and fruits. Although Brunei's rice production is increasing, most of the annual demand is supplied from Thailand. Brunei is almost self-sufficient in fresh poultry meat.

About 40 per cent of Bruneian beef needs is supplied from the 1.45 million acre Bruneian-owned Willeroo cattle ranch in Northern Australia. The remaining 60 per cent is shipped live from other Australian exporters. Halal slaughtering will become more sophisticated with a B$8.5 million poultry and beef slaughterhouse complex due to be completed in mid-1985. Goat meat is supplied locally.[26]

Brunei is almost self-sufficient in vegetables, except for potatoes and carrots which cannot be grown locally. Fruits, being seasonal, continue to be imported. The Agriculture Department, however, is experimenting with extending the seasons through the introduction of Thai and Filipino varieties.

Brunei has also moved to modernize and expand its fishing industry. Until recently, 40 per cent of the fish consumed in Brunei was imported. In June three modern fishing trawlers, fitted with the latest electronic fish detection equipment and costing about US$100,000 began local operations from Muara.

Brunei's wealth attracted many potential foreign investors in 1984. This was exemplified by the overwhelming participation response to the trade fair organized at the Hassanal Bolkiah National Stadium on 20 June 1984. Ninety-six companies from 15 countries participated, and a further 20 countries had to be placed on the waiting list. The Malay Chamber of Commerce, which sponsored the event, is planning a bigger fair for 1986.

There was a boom in the early 1980s in the construction industry in preparation for independence. Building tapered off as major projects were rushed to completion before the February Independence celebrations. The construction industry seemed poised for a revival in late 1984, however, with the awarding of a B$47 million contract to construct a new airport terminal. The Brunei Government awarded the contract to Ted Private and Leighton Contractors Asia Ltd., a Brunei-Australian joint venture. One of the biggest problems faced by the construction industry is the shortage of labour. Work on the airport terminal, it was announced, will eventually involve some 200 immigrant workers, mainly Thais and Peninsular Malaysians.[27] Another big development project is the electricity plant to be built in Lumut.

Manpower Management

The biggest problem which Brunei faces in its development programme is a lack of trained manpower in all fields. At the moment, Brunei relies on foreign labour, primarily from neighbouring ASEAN countries. Labour recruitment is strictly controlled. The *Borneo Bulletin* recently carried a news item to the effect that Brunei's boundless wealth and job opportunities is causing high-level diplomatic chaos in the Middle East and North Africa. British and Brunei missions overseas and Brunei's Immigration Department have been swamped with visa applications from foreign workers seeking a new life in the new nation.

In early October, Brunei's Acting Immigration Controller, Awang Julaihi bin Haji Abdul Kadir made a Brunei television appeal to defuse the situation. He blamed what he called "unknown and irresponsible" people for spreading "exaggerated and misleading reports". He said that the government had never made reports or advertised for large-scale recruitment of manpower from these countries as the supply from traditional areas — neighbouring countries — was already sufficient to meet local demands for development projects in the country.[28]

The manpower shortage has also been exacerbated by the "Bruneisation" policy followed by government and foreign firms. Brunei Shell, for example, has become increasingly committed to "Bruneisation", and in 1982 adopted a policy of employing local citizens. They now make up almost half the work force. Recruitment of citizens into the senior staff has been progressing, albeit more slowly. There are today 130 Bruneians among the 900 member senior staff, where there were none 12 years ago.

Also contributing to the achievement of these educational goals was the announcement in October that the former Sultan Hassanal Bolkiah Teacher's Training College would be upgraded to the Sultan Hassanal Bolkiah Institute of Education from January 1985. The new Institute of Education will offer a degree course leading to a Bachelor of Education.

In April Bruneian Education and Health Minister Pehin Dato Haji Abdul Aziz announced that Brunei would begin implementing a bilingual (English and Malay) education system from January 1985. The then Acting Education Director, Awang Razak bin Haji Mohammad said in an interview that the aim of the policy would be "to make every child in Brunei speak Malay and English equally well". Maths, history, geography, science and health science would be taught in English. The director stressed that the bilingual system would enable Bruneians to communicate more with the rest of the world, particularly in technical and commercial fields.[29]

Efforts are also being made by government, and private industry, to provide and upgrade skills. As of February 1984, there were 2,000 students overseas, and the total number of graduates in the country exceeds 600.[30]

The Jefri Bolkiah Engineering Trade School in Kuala Belait provides training for local technicians. The school has been running craftsman courses for 11 years, but it was only in March 1982 that higher level engineering courses began, based on what is known as the British system of Ordinary National Certificates. From an initial 14 students in 1982, the 1984 intake was 57. Of the three-year course, one year is spent working in local industry, sandwiched between classroom and workshop lessons.[31]

Brunei Shell has recently introduced a new education programme to give older employees who missed out on education earlier in life a chance to catch up. The course is known as TEAME (Training Exercise Aimed at Mature Employees). It is aimed at the 30–45 age group who left school without qualifications and now find themselves left behind by younger employees with secondary education. The courses concentrate on English, mathematics and science.[32]

The First Year

In 1984 Brunei Darussalam has been the focus of some world attention. Unaccustomed to "star treatment", the Brunei Government has reacted negatively to some of this (particularly Western) media coverage. At a seminar held recently in Jakarta on ASEAN-EEC relations, the Brunei Director of Information, Awang Haji Badaruddin bin Pengarah Haji Othman presented the view that the Western mass media sometimes tended to misunderstand the positions of the governments and peoples of the ASEAN region. As one example he cited the fact that a certain ASEAN member country was often described as an "absolute monarchy". He took issue with this description, pointing out that the term "absolute monarchy" had negative connotations in the West because it implied a system of government in which the ruler symbolized the arbitrary use of power, sometimes even wielding it against the interests of his people.[33]

The Brunei Government also took exception to certain statements reported in the latest edition of the *Guinness Book of Records* to the effect that Brunei's annual oil revenue of some £2,700 million (B$7.020 million) and its £10,000 million (B$26,000 million) foreign reserves are "effectually at his [the Sultan's] personal disposal", making him the wealthiest man in the world. News reports also carried the story that the new Istana Nurul Iman, completed early this year, was cited in the book as having the world's biggest chandeliers — 12 weighing two tonnes each. In addition, the Singapore *Straits Times* and the *Borneo Bulletin* reported that the Istana, with 1,788 rooms boasts 388 more rooms than the Vatican in Rome, which is listed as the world's largest residential palace.[34]

Referring specifically to the reports, the Brunei Government issued an official denial. "The Government points out that the figures mentioned as Brunei's annual oil revenue and its foreign reserves are inaccurate and the Government categorically denies that the country's foreign reserves are effectually at the personal disposal of the Sultan.... With regard to the Istana which the reports alleged has the world's biggest chandeliers and has the largest number of rooms, these reports are untrue, inaccurate and misleading."[35]

The first year of full independence was a year of quiet triumph for Brunei Darussalam — the new nation which emerged out of the ancient country. The formulation and inculcation of Bruneian concept of nationalism (Melayu Islam Beraja/MIB) proceeded smoothly. Brunei Darussalam became a member of ASEAN, the Commonwealth, the OIC and the United Nations — thus ensuring herself secure regional and international diplomatic vantage points from which to view the world events. The country's economy remained buoyant, and indications are that stable oil and gas revenues would continue in the decades to come.

What then, one might ask, are the problems faced by Brunei Darussalam? The crucial problem could be formulated thus: how to educate manpower in order to manage development. In the short term, manual and skilled labour can continue to be imported from neighbouring countries. Expertise can be purchased from abroad. In the long run, however, it is the task of the government (and one it takes seriously) to ensure that Bruneians do not become back-seat drivers in their own economic development. To avoid this the pace of development must be controlled. More difficult even than pacing, is to establish a basis for directional control of development. Here the governmental yardstick seems to be an unshakeable faith in the official state religion, Islam. His Majesty the Sultan and Yang Dipertuan expressed this when he concluded his acceptance speech at the U.N. General Assembly by reiterating Brunei Darussalam's determination to "continue to modernize our country while keeping faith with the principles of our ancient faith — Islam".[36]

Notes

1. For a detailed version of British-Brunei relations, see D.S. Ranjit Singh, *Brunei 1839–1983: The Problems of Political Survival* (Singapore: Oxford University Press, 1984). For an alternative perspective on events preceeding and subsequent to the 1967 abdication, see Haji Zaini Haji Ahmad, *Brunei Kearah Kemerdekaan 1984* (Kuala Lumpur: Haji Zaini Haji Ahmad, 1984.)
2. *Borneo Bulletin*, 7 January 1984.
3. *Pelita Brunei*, 10 October 1984.
4. *Pelita Brunei*, 5 September 1984.
5. *Pelita Brunei*, 10 October 1984.
6. *Pelita Brunei*, 12 December 1984.
7. *Borneo Bulletin*, 3 November 1984.
8. *Pelita Brunei*, 28 March 1984.
9. *Borneo Bulletin*, 23 February 1984.
10. *Borneo Bulletin*, 7 January 1984.
11. *Straits Times*, 17 January 1984.
12. *Pelita Brunei*, 10 October 1984.
13. *Pelita Brunei*, 10 October 1984.
14. *Borneo Bulletin*, 14 July 1984.
15. For detailed information on Brunei-Malaysia relations, which were particularly strained by events relating to the 1962 uprising, see D.S. Ranjit Singh, op. cit., especially Chapter Eight.
16. *Borneo Bulletin*, 7 January 1984.
17. *Far East Economic Review*, 26 January 1984.
18. *ASEAN Forecast* (Singapore: Executive Publishers Singapore), January 1984, and *Perlita Brunei*, 14 November 1984.
19. *Borneo Bulletin*, 5 September 1984.
20. *Borneo Bulletin*, 1 December 1984.
21. *Straits Times*, 5 April 1984.
22. *Borneo Bulletin*, 15 September 1984.
23. *Borneo Bulletin*, 23 February 1984.
24. *Straits Times*, 2 January 1984.
25. *ASEAN Forecast* (Singapore: Executive Publishers), January 1984.
26. *Borneo Bulletin*, 4 February 1984.
27. *Borneo Bulletin*, 8 December 1984.
28. *Borneo Bulletin*, 13 October 1984.
29. *Borneo Bulletin*, 24 April 1984.
30. *Borneo Bulletin*, 23 February 1984.
31. *Borneo Bulletin*, 23 September 1984.
32. *Borneo Bulletin*, 29 September 1984.
33. *Pelita Brunei*, 18 April 1984.
34. *Straits Times*, 30 November 1984; *Borneo Bulletin*, 8 December 1984.
35. *Pelita Brunei*, 5 December 1984.
36. *Pelita Brunei*, 10 October 1984.

BRUNEI DARUSSALAM
Challenging Stability

Christopher B. Roberts and Malcolm Cook

For Brunei Darussalam, 2015 was primarily about the dilemma of maintaining domestic stability in the face of significant regional and global instability in areas of particular vulnerability for Southeast Asia's smallest country. Plummeting global energy prices saw the country's once extremely large current account surplus reverse into a large deficit. At the same time, as the smallest and weakest claimant in the South China Sea, Brunei has the fewest means to counter the effects of growing Chinese assertiveness, U.S.–China rivalry, and ASEAN ineffectiveness in relation to these disputed waters that lap on to the shores of the Sultanate. Aided by significant long-standing financial, political and diplomatic reserves, Brunei Darussalam was able to maintain an impressive level of social, political and diplomatic stability in these challenging times. On the economic and diplomatic fronts, Bandar Seri Begawan responded by enhancing existing relations and assets and seeking greater diversification. On the social and political fronts, the response was one of greater conservatism and centralization. As Brunei Darussalam's economic problems are significant and structural, the responses will have to pass the test of time for the country to overcome them.

More than Headwinds

Even a cursory glance at Table 1 shows how dramatically the Brunei economy was affected by falling energy prices. And yet, the growth estimates for 2015 are based on inflated price assumptions for both oil and liquefied natural gas, so the reality will

---

Reprinted from Malcolm Cook and Daljit Singh, eds., *Southeast Asian Affairs 2016* (Singapore: ISEAS – Yusof Ishak Institute), pp. 95–105. At the time of original publication, Christopher Roberts was Associate Professor and Director of Executive Education at the Australian Defence Force Academy campus of the University of New South Wales and Malcolm Cook was Senior Fellow at the ISEAS – Yusof Ishak Institute, Singapore.

TABLE 1
Brunei Darussalam — Selected Economic Indicators, 2013–17

	2013	2014 Est.	2015 Proj.	2016 Proj.	2017 Proj.
Nominal GDP (BND million)	20,158	19,066	15,178	16,897	18,318
Nominal Non-Energy GDP (BND million)	7,414	7,698	8,015	8,405	8,862
Real GDP (% change)	–1.8	–1.5	–0.5	2.9	3.4
Energy Sector GDP	–7.2	–6.2	–2.4	4.0	4.4
Non-Energy GDP	2.7	1.9	0.8	2.2	2.7
Average Oil Price (USD per barrel)	115.0	104.4	63.7	71.5	76.1
Average Gas Price (USD per million Btu)	16.9	16.9	10.3	11.5	12.3
Exports (USD million)	11,834	11,124	6,586	7,628	8,464
Of which: Oil and Gas	11,048	10,307	5,729	6,725	7,510
Imports (USD million)	3,617	5,296	5,411	6,263	6,661

Source: International Monetary Fund, June 2015.

likely be even worse. Likewise, current market movements suggest that the IMF price assumptions going forward err on the side of optimism.

The Sultan, His Majesty Haji Hassanal Bolkiah, is well aware that the country's hydrocarbon resources will eventually expire, possibly as early as 2025, and has tried to extend their life in recent years by capping production. The volume of oil production reportedly is now a full 40 per cent less than in 2006.[1] In 2015 the scheduled and unscheduled maintenance of some of the most important energy projects has further hit production. However, the short-term costs of the policy have been exacerbated by the global collapse in the value of hydrocarbons with the price of crude oil having fallen from above US$100 in mid-2014 to less than US$30 per barrel by January 2016 and the value of natural gas per million Btu (British Thermal Unit) having fallen from over US$6 to nearly US$2 during the same period.[2]

Reflecting this vulnerability of concentration, despite the non-energy portion of Brunei's economy growing by 8 per cent in nominal terms from 2013 to 2015, the economy as a whole shrank by a quarter.

In 2015 alone due to restraints on oil production and sharply lower prices, the value of Brunei's exports fell by 36 per cent year-on-year in January–September to 6.77 billion Brunei dollars.[3] Energy exports account for over 95 per cent of Brunei's total exports, though this sector accounts for only 5 per cent of local employment. Back in 2010, Brunei enjoyed a current account surplus the equivalent of 50 per cent of GDP, but this is expected to have transitioned to a current account deficit of 5.6 per cent in 2015 that may widen to as much as 13.8 per cent in 2016. Brunei is moving towards a trade deficit as well.

Fiscal Woes

As greater than 90 per cent of government revenue comes from the export of hydrocarbons, government sector employment and social welfare may be adversely affected in the future. While the energy sector crisis has expanded Brunei's recession to a third year with an anticipated contraction in 2015 GDP of 1.2 per cent, the government appears to be relying on a rebound in hydrocarbon revenue to resolve these financial difficulties rather than undertaking tough fiscal policies to address budgetary shortfalls. Since 2013, government revenue as a share of GDP has fallen dramatically, yet government expenditure as a share of GDP continues to rise. In 2013 the Brunei government enjoyed a 14.1 per cent surplus between government revenue and expenditure as a share of GDP. By the end of 2015, projections suggest this may have fallen to a 15.7 per cent deficit. Nonetheless, extensive overseas investments do mean that Brunei can call on these foreign assets in a worst-case scenario.[4] In 2011 the country's sovereign wealth fund, the Brunei Investment Agency, was estimated to control about US$40 billion.[5]

Diversification and Reform

Facing maturing energy assets, diplomatic difficulties in developing new energy blocks, and a growing population, the Brunei government is focused on diversifying its economic structure and attracting more foreign direct investment in non-energy sectors that account for up to 40 per cent of the total economy. The Sultanate's policies and directives have contributed to the emergence of a few nascent export industries in recent years, including pharmaceuticals, the production

TABLE 2
Brunei Darussalam — Selected Fiscal Indicators, 2013–17
(% of GDP)

	2013	2014 Est.	2015 Proj.	2016 Proj.	2017 Proj.
Total Revenue	51.8	41.8	31.6	37.1	38.9
Oil and Gas	44.6	39.3	28.9	34.6	36.4
Other	7.2	2.5	2.7	2.6	2.5
Total Expenditure	37.7	38.5	47.3	44.1	41.8
Overall Primary Balance	14.1	3.3	–15.7	–6.9	–2.9

Source: International Monetary Fund, June 2015.

of methanol, information and communications technology, halal food, and tourism.⁶ By 2016 Brunei aims to boost tourist arrivals to 400,000, up from 242,000 in 2011. The World Travel and Tourism Council estimates that 2015 arrivals would hit 263,000.⁷ Through significant Chinese investment, Brunei has also started the construction of the Pulau Muara Besar port, a US$2.5 billion petrochemical plant, and a major bridge to the island. These developments are scheduled for completion between 2017 and 2018.⁸

Another key policy of the government is to develop self-sufficiency in staple foods. Since the turn of the century, Brunei has been largely self-sufficient in the production of eggs and poultry and the Sultanate is close to being self-sufficient in a broad range of vegetable crops. The government has also invested heavily in rice production, including more efficient hybrid varieties, but continues to remain heavily reliant on imports for this major commodity.⁹

To aid these goals, the government has pursued economic policy reforms focused on improving the business environment. In the latest *Doing Business* report by the World Bank, Brunei was a star performer. The country jumped 21 positions from 105th to 84th out of 189 economies surveyed, overtaking both Vietnam and the Philippines.¹⁰ In terms of starting a business, Brunei improved 107 levels from 181st in 2015 to 74th in 2016. In September, new tougher anti-corruption laws were introduced that expanded the coverage of government bodies to include government-linked corporations and statutory bodies, and the classification of acts deemed corrupt, to include giving undue preferential treatment and the use of public funds for private purposes.¹¹

The completion of the Trans-Pacific Partnership (TPP) trade negotiations in late 2015, should the deal be ratified, will likely bring new external pressure with the threat of sanctions to Brunei's labour laws. Under the TPP, all twelve parties agree to enforce labour rights recognized in the 1998 International Labour Organization Declaration, while the labour provisions of the TPP are subject to its dispute settlement mechanism. The American union movement has identified Brunei Darussalam as one of four TPP parties of particular concern given the prohibition of strikes, among other identified problems. In November, President Obama, during his visit to the ASEAN Summit in Malaysia, noted that the United States and Brunei Darussalam had reached a bilateral labour agreement under the TPP.¹²

Efforts at diversification have met with limited success so far and the Brunei economy faces particular challenges to diversification and liberalization beyond its very small population base. As one of the wealthiest economies in the world, Brunei has a high cost structure. Recently, this cost structure has been aggravated by the long-standing agreement to keep the Brunei dollar pegged to the Singapore dollar. Recent estimates suggest that the Brunei dollar is significantly overvalued.¹³ With upwards of three-quarters of working-age citizens employed by the state, Brunei's private sector is heavily dependent on imported labour with an estimated 100,000 foreign workers already residing in the country. Troublingly, there are limited professional opportunities outside the public sector. A simultaneous lack of enthusiasm for more labour-intensive roles means that the country's 6.9 per cent unemployment rate (2014) would actually be lower if the figure was restricted to those actively seeking work.[14]

Conservative Continuity

Brunei enjoys a relatively low level of crime and is, alongside Singapore, the safest country in Southeast Asia in terms of violence against the person. Nevertheless, the government has highlighted certain issues of concern. In particular, Sultan Hassanal Bolkiah has lamented what he has referred to as declining social values among the nation's youth. Theft — including items such as cars, mobile phones and other electronic devices — is one of the most common complaints, with the most recent figures revealing a rise in incidents from 3,152 cases in 2012 to 3,854 in 2014.[15] Illicit narcotics offences are another frequent cause of arrest, including charges for recreational usage and trafficking.

In some cases Brunei has been exploited as a transit country from regions such as the Golden Triangle, with destination countries including Malaysia, Singapore and Australia. At the close of 2014, Brunei's Narcotics Control Bureau had arrested 610 drug abusers; however, this represents a 10 per cent decline from the previous year.[16] In April 2015 the Brunei Internal Security Department also detained a Superintendent from the Royal Brunei Police Force for reported "involvement in abetting criminals with known links to criminal groups within and outside the country".[17] Furthermore, intelligence reports from Malaysia and Singapore have stated that Brunei was increasingly vulnerable as a transit point for human trafficking and, more recently, radicalized individuals involved in terrorist plots.[18] In 2015, local authorities detained a sixty-three-year-old Indonesian national at the Brunei International Airport after ammunition and an Islamic State flag were discovered among his possessions.[19]

In the face of these concerns, and at the same time as the economy began to be battered by falling energy prices, the long-serving Sultan has begun to emphasize the need to more strongly enforce the state's official ideology of *Melayu Islam Beraja* (Malay Islamic Monarchy). According to the Brunei Government, this ideology is "a blend of Malay language, culture and Malay customs, the teaching of Islamic laws and values, and the monarchy system, which must be esteemed and practised by all".[20] In line with this campaign, in 2014 the Sultanate ordered that restrictions be placed on Christmas celebrations, limiting them to private settings. Up to 10 per cent of the Brunei population is Christian. In 2015, restrictions were also placed on Chinese Lunar New Year festivities.[21] Brunei has had a local ethnic Chinese community for centuries, which now accounts for 10 to 15 per cent of the population.

The latest religious restrictions build on the October 2013 announcement by the Sultan that the country would be the first in East Asia to introduce a *syariah* (sharia) Islamic penal code. This would be implemented in three phases, with the first in 2014. A complicating factor for the ethnically diverse nation is the fact that some sentences under the *syariah* law will apply to non-Muslims, including "offences" such as disrespecting the fasting month of Ramadan, insulting the Prophet Muhammad, and the option of the death penalty for anyone who commits the "offence" of adultery with a Muslim.[22]

The expected rollout of the second and third phases did not occur in 2015 and no timetable or details of these remaining phases have been publicly disseminated.

Rather, 2015 saw few changes on this front. In May 2015 the government mandated that all shops and restaurants must close by midnight. In August 2015 it implemented a ban against restaurants being open in the daytime during Ramadan. Both of these policies led to a rare display of public criticism in the print media.[23] Brunei's move to enact *syariah* law became entangled with Congressional politics and the TPP. During the Congressional debates about providing the U.S. executive with fast-track Trade Promotion Authority, legislators and TPP opponents brought up concerns about Brunei's *syariah* law and the country's overall human rights record.[24]

Centralization

The Sultan maintains significant powers, including that of the regulation of Islam, the prerogative of mercy in the judiciary, and the ability to rule by decree. The Sultan is the Prime Minister while concurrently holding the Finance and Defence portfolios. In October 2015 this impressive range of powers was expanded further. On 22 October 2015 a Cabinet reshuffle was announced that had the effect of further concentrating power with the Sultan by, among other things, retiring his brother, Prince Mohammad Bolkiah, and taking over his former portfolio of Minister of Foreign Affairs and Trade.[25] The only other remaining political party in the country is the Parti Pembangunan (National Development Party), but it has only a few hundred members and plays no significant role in Bruneian society.[26] The country's structural economic problems, combined with the Sultanate's patchy record of economic and political reform, may have contributed to a degree of insecurity about the long-term future of the monarchy and thereby qualify some of the motives behind the recent imposition of fundamentalist laws and policies and the centralization of political power.

Enhancement and Diversification

As the smallest and weakest state in maritime Southeast Asia and as a South China Sea claimant, Brunei Darussalam has the strongest interest in (i) ASEAN playing an effective role in managing regional security, (ii) in Southeast Asia being insulated from major-power intervention and rivalry, and (iii) in maintaining good relations with all neighbours and major powers. In 2015 the first two were called into greater question, making the latter more difficult to maintain.

On the domestic front, much of the Sultanate's defence policy has focused on professionalization programmes for its armed forces. Such programmes are likely to reinforce a professional ethos, or *esprit de corps*, that will further institutionalize an aversion to involvement in political affairs.[27] The Sultanate has also sought to strengthen its military's information and communications technology. The U.S.-based security company, Northrup Grumman Corporation, has been developing a joint operations centre for command-and-control capability, while the armed forces have also announced their intention to develop a Defence Technology Centre. However, the focus in these two areas has been at the expense of larger weapons systems. While Brunei Darussalam has acquired several patrol vessels in recent years — including two eighty-metre German-built ships — the country's armed forces remain undermanned and too ill-equipped to be of any real deterrent value to regional rivals.[28] In 2015 this situation was aggravated by the country's fiscal woes, with the defence budget being slashed by more than a quarter from the year before.[29]

Enhancement

In 2015, strategic relations with three of the Sultanate's most important and long-standing partners deepened and consolidated. While Brunei's military acquisitions have become far more diversified compared to the immediate years after independence from the United Kingdom in 1984, in February 2015 the two countries entered into a confidential agreement to continue to maintain the 1,100-strong army garrison primarily consisting of a Gurkha infantry battalion.[30] The visit by Michael Fallon in November 2015 was the first by a UK Defence Secretary in eighteen years.

Singapore is also a critical partner, but its importance extends to both the defence and economic domains. Singapore maintains a permanent presence of a hundred personnel from its Armed Forces in Brunei, supported by five UH-1 military helicopters and up to a further 600 Singaporean soldiers at certain times of the year. In the economic sphere, the two countries' currencies are interchangeable, as they have been pegged at parity since 1967. In 2014, 20.4 per cent of Brunei's imports came from Singapore, but in the same year Malaysia surpassed Singapore through the supply of 20.6 per cent of total imports.[31] In May, Singapore and Brunei held the inaugural meeting between the Singapore Ministry of Home Affairs and the Prime Minister's Office of Brunei after the 2014 agreement to cooperate more closely on security issues. The first joint training exercise under this new bilateral mechanism was planned for late 2015.[32]

Since the 1962 revolt, relations with Malaysia have at times been strained. For example, in 2003 there was a brief stand-off between the two countries' navies over the discovery of significant oil reserves in Limpang's offshore Exclusive Economic Zone — the provincial area of Sarawak that splits Brunei into two separate portions of land. However, in 2008 the two countries took a significant step towards the consolidation of cordial relations through a tentative agreement to resolve their territorial disputes concerning both sea and land boundaries. This led, in March 2009, to the signing of "letters of exchange" where Malaysia conceded that Brunei was the rightful owner of blocks L and M (which are directly tangent to Brunei's coast) but that the extraction of any hydrocarbons would be jointly developed. Nonetheless, it was not until August 2015 that the two countries resolved a disagreement over some ambiguous wording in the "letters". Joint development efforts should be able to proceed from 2016.[33] As a possible quid pro quo arrangement, Malaysia then agreed to cooperate in the construction of a new bridge that will strengthen transportation links between Limbang and Temburong. Brunei has, in turn, relinquished its territorial claim to the Limbang district.[34]

Diversification

Despite its small size and limited military capabilities, in the last couple of years Brunei has become a much more active participant in the region's expanding plethora of bilateral, minilateral and multilateral naval exercises. Moving beyond its traditional bilateral exercises with Malaysia, Singapore, Australia and the United States, in 2014 Brunei participated in the Multilateral Maritime Exercise in Qingdao

China held in conjunction with the Western Pacific Naval Symposium. In 2014 Brunei also participated for the first time in the region's largest multilateral naval exercise, the U.S.-led RIMPAC exercises. In 2016 Brunei and Russia plan to participate in their first ever bilateral naval exercise to take place off Brunei.[35] On the Russian side, this could well be organized in conjunction with the planned Russia–China naval exercises in the South China Sea.

Greater defence engagement with the United States, China and Russia reflects Brunei's long-standing policy of pursuing deepening relations with all major powers, a "multi-directional balancing" approach it shares with many of its fellow Southeast Asian states. In 2015 Brunei also strengthened strategic relations with Vietnam and the Philippines, the two Southeast Asian claimants in the South China Sea that have taken the firmest positions against Chinese claims and actions in these disputed waters. In June, a Royal Brunei Armed Forces' delegation visited Vietnam to seek ways of strengthening ties.[36] In September, the heads of the Philippine Army and the Royal Brunei Land Forces agreed to expand joint training.[37]

Looking Ahead

Most of the challenges that the government in Brunei faced in 2015 were the same as those in 2014. What changed was that these challenges intensified and their impact on the Brunei budget, economy and broader strategic situation became more manifest. These challenges will continue in 2016 and for the foreseeable future. It is too early to proclaim this challenging situation as the "new normal" for Brunei Darussalam. Yet, these tougher times are far from being a momentary blip and there are powerful structural, not just cyclical, dimensions to Brunei's present difficulties. Stability, a cherished goal, can quickly become stagnation, an undesirable outcome, if government policies fail to respond to changed circumstances.

Notes

1. "Brunei Feels the Heat of Prolonged Low Oil Prices", *Syrian Arab News Agency*, 7 December 2015.
2. "Petroleum and Other Liquids: Data", U.S. Energy Information Administration, n.d. <http://www.eia.gov/petroleum/data.cfm>.
3. "Brunei Economy: Excessively Dependent on Oil and Gas", *Economist Intelligence Unit*, 7 December 2015.
4. Ibid.; "Brunei: Country Economic Forecast", *Oxford Economics*, January 2016.
5. "The Largest Sovereign Wealth Funds by Assets under Management", *sovereignwealthfundsnews.com*, 16 September 2011.
6. "The Report Brunei Darussalam 2013: Brunei Well Poised to Push Forward with Regional and Domestic Expansions", *BusinessWire*, 12 June 2013.
7. *Travel and Tourism Economic Impact 2015 Brunei* (London: World Travel and Tourism Council, 2015).
8. "Brunei, China Sign Agreement on Construction of Pulau Muara Besar Bridge", Xinhua's China Economic Information Service, 7 May 2015; *Brunei: Country Report* (Economist Intelligence Unit, 2015), p. 13.
9. Nuri Sufri, "New Paddy Variety to Boost Domestic Rice Supply", *Borneo Bulletin*, 3 July 2015.
10. Prime Sarmiento, "Brunei Rises to 84th in WB's Doing Business Rankings", *Brunei Times*, 29 October 2015.
11. Zheng Jie, "New Anti-Corruption Laws

Adopted in Brunei to Tackle Power Abuse", Xinhua, 30 September 2015.
12. Leo Kasim, "Brunei Committed to Labour Reforms under TPP: Obama", *Brunei Times*, 23 November 2015.
13. Syrian Arab News Agency.
14. Koo Jin Shen, "Brunei Unemployment Rate in 2014 at 6.9%", *Brunei Times*, 1 July 2015.
15. "Brunei: Executive Summary", *IHS Jane's Intelligence*, 16 December 2015.
16. Rachel Thien, "Drug-Related Arrests Down Last Year", *Brunei Times*, 6 February 2015.
17. Fadley Faisal, "Senior Cop Held over Links to Crime Rings", *Borneo Bulletin*, 5 April 2015.
18. "Brunei Remains Committed to Fighting Human Trafficking", *Borneo Bulletin*, 3 April 2013; "Asean Ministerial Meeting on Drug Issues in Brunei", *Vietnam News Summary*, 5 September 2013; "The Threat of ISIS and Radicalism in Singapore and the Region", *Straits Times*, 27 May 2015.
19. "Brunei Arrests Indonesian with 'ISIS Flag, Bullets'", *Rappler*, 8 May 2015.
20. Gary D. Bouma, Douglas Pratt, and Rod Ling, "Brunei Darussalm", in *Religious Diversity in Southeast Asia and the Pacific*, edited by Gary D. Bouma, Rod Ling, and Douglas Pratt (Springer, 2009), pp. 47–51.
21. "Brunei Has Made Celebrating Christmas a Criminal Offence", *Daily Tribune*, 23 December 2015.
22. Richard Lloyd Parry, "Fear of Sharia Stalks Opulent Sultanate of Brunei", *The Australian*, 6 June 2015.
23. *Brunei: Country Report*, p. 9; "Brunei Continues 'Daytime Dining' Ban in Restaurants During Ramadan", Channel News Asia, 18 June 2015.
24. Rui Hao Puah, "Brunei's Shariah Dilemma", *cogitASIA*, 25 September 2015.
25. "Brunei Politics: Quick View — A Rare Cabinet Reshuffle", *Economist Intelligence Unit Views Wire*, 4 November 2015; "Brunei Sultan Removes Brother from Cabinet", *Bangkok Post*, 22 October 2015.
26. "Internal Affairs, Brunei", *Jane's Sentinel Security Assessment*, 16 December 2015.
27. "Defence Studies Contract with Brunei Army Secured", *Scoop*, 19 July 2010.
28. "Procurement, Brunei", *Jane's Sentinel Security Assessment*, 4 October 2015.
29. "Drop in Brunei Defence Budget", *Borneo Bulletin*, 10 March 2015.
30. "PM Meeting with the Sultan of Brunei", *M2 Press Wire*, 16 February 2015.
31. "Brunei Fact Sheet", 2015.
32. "Singapore, Brunei Seek to Strengthen Cooperation in Law Enforcement, Security", *Singapore Government News*, 14 May 2015.
33. "Brunei Darussalam, Malaysia: Malaysia Inks a Deal on Overlapping Blocks with Brunei", *Sudan Times*, 13 August 2015.
34. Zukiman Ahmad Zain, "Brunei Sets Investment Sights on Malaysian Economic Corridors", Bernama, 21 December 2010.
35. Rabiatul Kamit, "Russia, Brunei Plan 1st Naval Drill Next Year", *Brunei Times*, 3 June 2015.
36. "Vietnam, Brunei Enhance Defense Ties amid East Sea Tensions", *Vietnam News Brief Service*, 8 June 2015.
37. "Philippines, Brunei to Enhance Defence Ties", *BBC Monitoring Asia Pacific*, 3 September 2015.

Cambodia

CAMBODIA AND REGIONAL DIPLOMACY

Sheldon W. Simon

At bottom, resolution of the seemingly intractable Cambodian conflict depends on responses to a series of difficult politico-military questions:

(1) Is Vietnam's military control of Cambodia a harbinger of additional aggressive intent against Thailand, including possible annexation of the latter's sixteen northeastern provinces heavily populated by ethnic Lao?[1] Worrisome is the fact that Hanoi's most stunning political successes since 1954 have been achieved through military victories, namely, the First and Second Indochina Wars and the more recent invasion of Cambodia and successful defence against China's 1979 border assault.

(2) Has the Soviet relationship to Vietnam embodied in the 1978 Friendship Treaty and actualized through Moscow's subsidation of both the Socialist Republic of Vietnam's (SRV) economy and occupation of Cambodia (and Laos) led to Hanoi's political subordination? Noteworthy in this regard is the regular use of Vietnamese air and naval bases by Soviet Pacific Fleet components as they steam from the Sea of Okhotsk through the South China Sea and Indian Ocean. While Vietnamese spokesmen insisted through 1979 that the Soviets had not received base rights, Hanoi has had virtually nothing to say on this subject for over a year.

(3) Is China's continued military aid to the Khmer Rouge (through Thailand) part of a policy to re-establish a Cambodian client state presumably after the Vietnamese are forced out? The maintenance of PRC military pressure on Vietnam's northern border combined with a growing Khmer

---

Reprinted from Huynh Kim Khanh, ed., *Southeast Asian Affairs 1982* (Singapore: Institute of Southeast Asian Studies, 1982), pp. 196–207. At the time of original publication, Sheldon W. Simon was Professor of Political Science and Director of Arizona State University's Center for Asian Studies.

Rouge guerrilla force of about 35,000 in western Cambodia appears calculated to "bleed" Vietnam and sap its ability to counter China's dominant position on the Asian mainland. On the other hand, Beijing's policy also serves to drive Hanoi into even closer security arrangements with the Soviet Union.

(4) How does the Sino-Soviet/Vietnam confrontation over Cambodia's future affect ASEAN's long-term hopes for a Zone of Peace, Freedom, and Neutrality (ZOPFAN) in Southeast Asia? Does China's *de facto* deterrent threat on Thailand's behalf threaten to split ASEAN's diplomatic unity over the region's preferred future, pitting those states which perceive Beijing to be the major long-term threat to stability (Malaysia and Indonesia) against those who fear a Soviet-Vietnamese *entente* (Singapore and Thailand)?

While these four series of questions may be analytically separate, efforts to answer them must be synthesized if the dynamics of Cambodia's future in the region's diplomacy are to be understood. In essence each major actor (ASEAN states, China, Vietnam, the USSR, the United States, and the components of the Cambodian resistance) possesses a number of options. Varying combinations of options can lead to very different outcomes. It is the task of this paper to explore some of the prominent politico-diplomatic alternatives available to the actors and assess their implications for regional stability.

Major Actors and Options

Vietnam

A key to understanding Cambodia's importance to Vietnam is Hanoi's conviction that a friendly regime in Phnom Penh is vital for Vietnamese security. Therefore, Cambodia is a legitimate Vietnamese sphere of influence. Negotiations over the type of government in Cambodia and the eventual withdrawal of Vietnamese forces are possible as long as all parties understand that whatever the political complexion of the regime in Phnom Penh, it must be subservient to Vietnam's perceived security needs.

Since its occupation in 1979, Hanoi has trained future Cambodian cadre in Vietnamese language schools, encouraged intermarriage between Vietnamese men and Cambodian women, and in 1981 announced the creation of a ruling People's Revolutionary Party of Kampuchea (PRPK) which explicitly traces its origin to the Vietnam-initiated Indochina Communist Party.[2]

Vietnam's primary concern is to obtain a diplomatic endorsement of its dominant position in Indochina. International acceptance of the Heng Samrin/Pen Sovan regime in Cambodia is the last link in Hanoi's chain of control. Hanoi has offered non-aggression pacts to ASEAN members (in 1980) in exchange for their acceptance of the Indochinese status quo. ASEAN's rejection of this initiative was followed by still another gambit to obtain the Association's acceptance of Vietnamese hegemony. A meeting of the Indochinese Foreign Ministers held in Ho Chi Minh City (27–28 January 1981) proposed a regional security conference between Indochina and ASEAN which could then be followed by a broader international conclave, attended by such major powers as China, the USSR, and the United States. Through these meetings Hanoi (and Moscow) hoped to effect a bargain by which the ASEAN states would accept Hanoi's dominance (as well as Soviet base rights) in exchange for a Soviet "guarantee" against further Vietnamese expansion.[3] This gambit proved equally unsuccessful for Vietnam, in part because earlier Soviet assurances against forces of the Vietnam People's Army (VPA) crossing into Thailand had been broken when Vietnamese troops crossed the Thai frontier in late June 1980 to break up Khmer Rouge camps and push refugees clustered near the border further into Thailand's interior.

Hanoi has also attempted to shift the focus of any future negotiations away from its occupation of Cambodia by insisting that the immediate threat to regional stability is centred on the Thai-Khmer border. If the authorities in Bangkok and Phnom Penh could agree on a demilitarized zone on the Thai side of the border, Hanoi stipulates that Vietnam might also agree to remove its forces from the Cambodian frontier region (though not from the rest of Cambodia). The SRV hoped, then, both to obtain ASEAN recognition of the People's Republic of Kampuchea as a regime with which international agreements could be reached and to convince Bangkok to move the Khmer resistance camps inland away from the frontier.[4] This proposition failed too, as the ASEAN states steadfastly adhered to the U.N. resolutions of 1979 and 1980, insisting on a total Vietnamese withdrawal from Cambodia and a broad international conference which would include both the Soviet Union and China as parties to the conflict.

In reality, of course, the Sino-Vietnam relationship is a vital component of Hanoi's Cambodian diplomacy. Vietnamese officials have stated on a number of occasions that VPA forces would not completely withdraw from Cambodia until Beijing accepted the status quo through diplomatic recognition and/or non-aggression pacts with the three Indochinese countries. Thus, it is clear that even Vietnam's call for a regional conference need not lead to a Vietnamese troop withdrawal. China's acceptance of the Cambodian situation is the means to that end (Nayan Chanda, "Hanoi Tightens Up", *Far Eastern Economic Review* [hereafter cited as *FEER*], 17 April 1981, p. 12).

Hanoi insists that as long as China sustains Pol Pot's forces, Vietnam will counter with "fraternal assistance" to Phnom Penh. In all likelihood Vietnam views the Khmer resistance, led by Pol Pot's 35,000 or more guerrillas, as a net political advantage. While Khmer Rouge harassment continues to terrify the Cambodian population with the possibility of a restoration of the Pol Pot regime, Vietnam's occupation is tolerated as a lesser evil. Thus, Hanoi is provided additional time to organize the new PRPK, thoroughly indoctrinate its members, and forge a new Khmer army. Vietnam is using the occupation to create a client state and bureaucracy. (See *Indochina Issues* [Washington, D.C.] [16] May 1981, p. 2.) The SRV's underlying assumption is that time is on its side. By putting the paraphernalia of a national government in place — including a presidency, national assembly, ruling party, and cabinet — Hanoi believes the world community will eventually accept the Heng Samrin/Pen Sovan regime as a reality. These developments may take a few years; but Vietnamese leaders foresee no military or political pressure with which they cannot cope as long as the Soviets sustain their commitment and China does not launch a full-scale war.

Soviet Union

In the wake of the Second Indochina War (1965–75) the USSR hoped to create a new *modus vivendi* between Indochina and ASEAN. For the Soviets, ASEAN constituted a generally praiseworthy effort at regional political and economic co-operation which would resist American efforts to recreate SEATO. To become a truly regional institution, however, ASEAN was urged to open its membership to the states of Indochina.

As tension between Vietnam and China grew in 1978 and as China assiduously courted ASEAN's favour in the new regional conflict, Moscow perceived the need to co-ordinate its own Southeast Asian diplomacy more closely with Vietnam. At minimum it was deemed essential to insure ASEAN's neutrality in the Sino-Soviet/Vietnam imbroglio. Overcoming its antipathy to ASEAN — whose members had opposed Vietnam during the Indochina War — Hanoi offered to negotiate new regional security arrangements with the five upon Soviet urging. Bilateral friendship treaties were proffered to the ASEAN states in 1977 by Foreign Minister Nguyen Duy Trinh and in 1978 by Prime Minister Pham van Dong.

Indeed, Moscow's leverage on Hanoi seemed to increase markedly after the Chinese border incursion into Vietnam in early 1979. Western estimates showed that by mid-1979, about 60% of Vietnam's development budget came from the USSR and nearly one-third of its rice needs were met by Soviet-funded imports. The number of Soviet technical advisers in Vietnam grew from 2,700 in 1977 to 8,000 in mid-1979. Interestingly, however, only about 60% of Soviet aid funds available have actually been drawn by Hanoi.[5] Nevertheless, new aid agreements signed in July 1981 portend even greater dependence on the USSR. The volume of Soviet aid will almost double in the 1981–86 period to be repaid through a virtual monopoly on Vietnamese exports. Specifically, SRV cash crops will be grown to exchange for Soviet capital goods.[6] In effect, SRV access to convertible currency markets will virtually disappear.

Soviet investment in Indochina, estimated at more than US$7 million per day, is probably tolerable.[7] For the first time in history, Moscow has one of the region's most important states as an exclusive client. Soviet ships and aircraft use facilities in both Vietnam and Cambodia to monitor Chinese and American military movements. Vietnam has become, then, an indispensable link in the Soviet Asian security system. If the Soviets and Vietnamese can entice ASEAN to make the concessions necessary to accept Hanoi's dominance in Indochina, then a new regional balance will be legitimated in which the Soviets are guaranteed a major security role by virtue of their treaty with Vietnam and their military presence.

The case for diplomatic co-operation between Hanoi and Moscow should not be interpreted to mean that there are no differences between them. Exclusive dependence on the USSR cannot be a comfortable situation for Vietnamese leaders who have spent decades fighting for independence and heretofore had always managed to balance external mentors. Moreover, there may well be some Vietnamese concern over longer-term Soviet intentions in Indochina. It is not at all certain that the USSR accepts Hanoi's hegemony, particularly if that status could mean a future veto over Soviet military deployments from Indochinese bases. Therefore, reports in 1981 of independent Soviet efforts to establish influence in Phnom Penh with weapons supplies, technical aid, and training could be the first steps in establishing a separate Soviet influence network with the Pen Sovan regime. Particularly noteworthy in this regard has been the presence of thirty Soviet experts in the port of Kompong Som since late 1980 (Nayan Chanda, "The Bigger Brother", *FEER*, 5 June 1981, pp. 24–26). If the Vietnamese reduce their aid and personnel in Cambodia over the next few years, additional opportunities for Soviet influence will develop.

A note of caution is warranted, however; continued Soviet influence in Southeast Asia depends on the maintenance of Moscow's alliance with Vietnam. There are, therefore, limits to how far the Russians will go in developing independent ties to the Phnom Penh regime. At bottom, the Soviets will do nothing to jeopardize their Hanoi connection, although they will test the limits of that relationship in order to expand their strategic position as the Pacific Fleet grows.

China

The People's Republic of China (PRC) is a key player in any resolution of the Cambodian dilemma. China views its conflict with Vietnam as a regional theatre in the global struggle with the USSR. Thus, as long as Hanoi and Moscow are linked and as long as Vietnamese forces remain in Cambodia — presumably providing the Soviets access as well — China will continue to supply the Khmer resistance. A vigorous Khmer insurgency ties down 200,000 Vietnamese troops far from China's border, exacerbates Hanoi's economic problems, and isolates the regime internationally. Chinese leaders have argued that forcing the SRV to be totally dependent on the Soviet Union will actually hasten Vietnam's disillusion with its mentor. The USSR will be unwilling to mitigate Vietnam's economic difficulties; and, over time, internal pressures will compel Hanoi to change its position on Cambodia.

By contrast, were China to accept Vietnam's hegemony over Indochina, the Soviets would have emplaced much of Brezhnev's Asian collective security system. That system would be buttressed on the west by a Soviet-occupied Afghanistan and an India under Mrs Gandhi, which has recognized the Heng Samrin government and favours a strong Soviet position in Southeast Asia in exchange for economic and military assistance as well as diplomatic support in its territorial disputes with China. Beijing fears a possible linkage among the USSR's Afghan-Indian-Indochinese relationships. A prime goal of China's diplomacy, then, is to convince ASEAN not to compromise with Hanoi (and Moscow) so that Southeast Asia will not be added to what China perceives to be a growing Soviet bloc of Asian Third World states.

China has displayed tactical flexibility. In December 1980, Deputy Foreign Minister Han Nian Long altered China's position by no longer demanding a complete withdrawal of Vietnamese forces from Cambodia as a precondition for Beijing's participation in an international conference on Cambodia's future. Thus, the PRC participated in the July 1981 United Nations special conference on the topic. China has also agreed on the necessity of a united front for the Khmer resistance which would dilute Khmer Rouge leadership in exchange for broader international legitimacy and enhanced prospects for maintaining a United Nations seat for Democratic Kampuchea over the next several years of guerrilla struggle.

Specifically, the PRC has recommended both Prince Sihanouk and former Prime

Minister Son Sann as leaders with whom the Khmer Rouge should co-operate. Going beyond issues of cosmetic leadership changes, the PRC has also offered arms to Son Sann and Sihanouk supporters as long as nothing is done to weaken the Khmer Rouge. ASEAN leaders in a May 1981 conclave, however, decided against providing military aid to the resistance themselves at the same time China delivered its initial shipment of weapons to Son Sann's forces. China is also opposed to an ASEAN position worked out in the Association's June 1981 Manila meeting calling for the disarmament of all armed forces in Cambodia as soon as Vietnamese troops leave. It appears, then, that China will insist on a prominent Khmer Rouge role in any post-Vietnam regime.

Beijing's antipathy toward weakening the Khmer Rouge has fuelled suspicions among ASEAN members that China still hopes to re-establish a sphere of influence in Cambodia after the Vietnamese withdraw. The PRC opposes the Malaysia-Indonesia 1980 proposal at Kuantan which would acknowledge Vietnam's domination of Indochina if Hanoi severs its military ties to the USSR. PRC commentators argue that acceptance of Hanoi's hegemony in Indochina would reward aggression and do nothing to break the Soviet connection. Furthermore, any ASEAN interest in a united Indochina under Vietnamese control is based on a false strategic premise: "China wishes neither to set up any sphere of influence in Kampuchea nor to undermine Vietnam; she is only opposing the policies of aggression and expansion pursued by the Vietnamese authorities. She has always sincerely hoped that Vietnam will become an independent and prosperous country and a factor of stability in Southeast Asia." (*Xinhua Commentator*, 11 July 1981, in *FBIS: People's Republic of China [PRC], Daily Report*, 13 July 1981, p. E3.)

Counselling against acquiescence to Hanoi's domination of Indochina, Beijing insists that SRV forces can be rolled back by a combination of political and military pressure. Unification of the Khmer resistance is the political key to blocking international recognition of the Cambodian puppet regime. However, a unified resistance must also be supported with military aid.[8] Beijing has implemented this strategy by both continuing to supply the Khmer Rouge and Son Sann forces and maintaining military pressure on Hanoi's northern border, thus tying down several hundred thousand of the VPA's first line battalions.

In talks with Thai officials during his August 1981 visit to the ASEAN states, Chinese Prime Minister Zhao Ziyang reassured the five that Beijing did not seek to reinstall the Pol Pot regime but would support a non-aligned Cambodia whose government would be formed under U.N.-supervised elections after Vietnamese forces withdraw.[9] While Prime Minister Zhao's disclaimers of any Chinese interest in a regional sphere of influence were generally well received in Southeast Asia, residual suspicions remained over the nature of the PRC's continuing ties to local communist parties. China has insisted for several years that it no longer provides material assistance to regional insurgencies; but Beijing adamantly refuses to sever political ties with sympathetic communist parties. The most Prime Minister Zhao has been willing to state publicly is that China's relations with regional communist parties are "moral and political" and that these parties' activities "in various countries are purely internal matters.... In the past few years China has done its utmost to resolve ... problems left over from history so that they will not become obstacles affecting the development of relations between China and the ASEAN countries" (*Xinhua*, 9 August 1981, in *FBIS: PRC*, 10 August 1981, pp. E5–E6).

ASEAN

The most interesting features of ASEAN diplomacy in the course of the Cambodian confrontation are the five's willingness to defer to the preferences of their most threatened member (Thailand) and the Association's policy of joint consultation before adopting any ASEAN-wide public posture. Efforts by the USSR, SRV, and even China (toward Thailand) to disrupt this united front have been for the most part unavailing. Nevertheless, altruism is not the primary explanation. Rather, ASEAN states feared that unless they coalesced behind Thailand, Bangkok would be tempted to turn to China, thus splitting ASEAN or forcing the Association to align in the Sino-Soviet/Vietnam conflict. ASEAN backs Thailand in large part as a means of retaining the Association's overall independence from great power interference in Southeast Asia.[10] The ASEAN states, then, wish to restore Cambodia's neutrality as a way of excluding outside powers from the region's security politics.

Similarly, the Kuantan Principle enunciated by Malaysia and Indonesia but rejected by Thailand and Singapore, would accept a Vietnamese sphere of influence only if Hanoi's security ties to the USSR are severed. From an ASEAN perspective, implementation of the Kuantan solution could also relieve Sino-Vietnam tensions. China would presumably be less apprehensive of Vietnam as a regional power if it had no ties to the Soviet Union.

ASEAN clearly does not benefit from an indefinite continuation of the status quo: (1) China "bleeding" Vietnam through military pressure on its northern border and the provision of military aid to the Cambodian resistance, countered by (2) Moscow-supported VPA forces fighting along the Thai-Cambodian border. In effect, the status quo enhances both Chinese and Soviet opportunities for further intrusions into Southeast Asian affairs, rendering ASEAN hopes for regional neutrality even more remote. Disengaging from the status quo, however, is a difficult task. China versus a Vietnam/Soviet combination constitutes something of a political stalemate, meaning neither can dominate the region. Should one capitulate, however, ASEAN states foresee the other(s) manoeuvring to assert dominance. Hence, the necessity from ASEAN's perspective of finding a solution for Cambodia that would install a regime which would be viewed as threatening neither China, Vietnam, nor ASEAN. Assuming the concerns of these three sets of actors are essentially defensive, this outcome might be acceptable (whether *feasible* is a different question). However, if China and/or Vietnam are primarily concerned with establishing hegemony, then a solution designed to meet defensive security needs will be insufficient.

Through a diplomatic united front, ASEAN has successfully passed a number of resolutions in the United Nations in 1979, 1980, and 1981 as well as the 1981 New Delhi meeting of non-aligned states calling for the withdrawal of Vietnamese forces from Cambodia. Nevertheless, ASEAN spokesmen have been careful to emphasize that opposition to Vietnam's military occupation does not mean that the five back China. Singapore Deputy

Prime Minister Rajaratnam has forthrightly presented ASEAN's strategic view:

> We want an independent Vietnam. It is in our interests. If Vietnam fell under the domination of China, which remains the chief threat in our view, the whole of Indochina would be under the Chinese thumb. We do not want such a situation. I have told the Vietnamese: "We want a prosperous Vietnam for which we will create no problems. All we ask of you is to leave Kampuchea. Then Singapore and its four ASEAN partners will be able to help you rebuild your country and obtain the assistance of the Western world."

Nevertheless, Rajaratnam continued, if Vietnam remains adamant, then "resorting to guerrilla tactics against the Phnom Penh regime is one of the elements likely to lead to a political solution, in five or six years, say" (Interview in *Le Figaro* [Paris], 12 March 1981, as carried in *FBIS:AP*, 16 March 1981, pp. 4–5).

Indonesian media have also expressed understanding for Vietnam's concern that Cambodia not be controlled by a pro-Chinese regime. Why, then, ASEAN publicists ask, will Hanoi not be satisfied with a neutral Khmer government which threatens neither Vietnam nor Thailand? (*OANA* [Jakarta], 24 March 1981, in *FBIS:AP*, 26 March 1981, p. N1.) ASEAN states have begun to increase their military expenditures significantly in the 1980s in direct response to what they see as a protracted Soviet-supported Vietnamese threat. As Indonesian strategist Jusuf Wanandi puts it: "Hanoi's stubbornness gives China a free hand to implement its policy of destroying Vietnam..." (*FEER*, 15 May 1981, pp. 20–21).

The June 1981 ASEAN Foreign Ministers conference in Manila proffered positive incentives to Hanoi for co-operation on Cambodia. If a neutral Cambodia could be created, the five held out the prospect of joint ASEAN-Indochinese efforts to create a zone of peace, freedom, and neutrality. ASEAN also offered to assist Vietnam's development programme directly and to create a new regional grouping which "could work together to prevent intervention by major powers and meet external threats".[11] While striking in their potential for creating new political relationships between the antagonists, the ASEAN incentives to Hanoi raised more questions than they answered, including how the Association could co-operate with Indochina to prevent external intervention when two of its members (Thailand and the Philippines) possessed formal security ties to the United States. Hanoi's skepticism regarding these ASEAN gambits was understandable.

United States

The United States functions as a secondary, if not peripheral, actor in the Cambodian drama. Washington has not maintained a military presence on the Southeast Asian mainland since 1976; and its aid to Thailand, though important symbolically subsequent to the June 1980 border confrontation with VPA forces, is quite modest. In general the United States has followed ASEAN's lead on Cambodia, although Washington has tended at times to lean toward the harder Chinese line of putting economic and political pressure on Vietnam rather than offering positive incentives for co-operation. Neither the Carter nor Reagan Administrations has been enthusiastic about the Khmer Rouge, however; and China's shift in late 1980 away from insistence on the restoration of an exclusively Khmer

Rouge regime may have resulted from combined ASEAN-U.S. persuasion.

Nevertheless, the Reagan Administration appears more adamantly anti-Vietnam than its predecessor and, therefore, closer to China's perception of how best to resolve the conflict. Secretary of State Haig reportedly urged his hosts to increase arms deliveries to anti-Vietnamese forces in Cambodia during his June 1981 discussions in Beijing. The same report stated that Haig concurred with China's analysis that Vietnam would compromise on Cambodia only after protracted military and economic pressures forced it to realize that the Soviet Union would not provide sufficient assistance (Nayan Chanda, "Haig Turns the Screw", *FEER*, 26 June 1981, pp. 10–12).

Haig's get-tough posture was not well received in ASEAN. The lifting of blanket U.S. restrictions on arms sales to the PRC was censured, for example, by Indonesian Foreign Minister Mochtar Kusumaatmadja who feared that closer Sino-U.S. military ties would further polarize regional politics and move Hanoi more rapidly into Moscow's embrace (ibid.). Moreover, a Sino-American security relationship would continue to erode ASEAN hopes for prohibiting great power military activities in Southeast Asia. These apprehensions appear warranted as increased Chinese and ASEAN pressures on Hanoi have led to a growing number of Soviet advisers in both Vietnam and Cambodia during 1981 (Derek Davies, "Time to Encourage Vietnamese Titoists", *FEER*, 17 July 1981, pp. 30–31).

Some State Department analysts seemed not to agree with U.S. policy, however. An alternative approach stressed that Washington should combine with ASEAN and Japan to offer positive inducements to Vietnam in exchange for the latter's agreement to withdraw its forces from Cambodia and accept a non-aligned coalition government. This line of reasoning pointed out that the United States, ASEAN, and Japan could offer an unequalled package of aid for Vietnam's reconstruction. Because Vietnam's natural economic partners are the Western industrial states and Asia, the USSR has little to offer Hanoi over the long run other than commodities. After the SRV rebuilds its shattered economy, it could produce these itself or trade for all the commodities currently being supplied by the USSR on a barter basis, thus mortgaging Vietnam's small export sector for years to come.[12]

This more positive approach to Vietnam appears to be out of favour in the Reagan Administration where a hard anti-Soviet line dominates foreign policy. A case in point was the September 1981 allegation by Secretary Haig that the USSR was supplying toxic gas to Vietnamese forces for use in Laos and Cambodia. If borne out in further investigations, these revelations could undermine ASEAN's tendency to seek accommodation with Hanoi and move the Association closer to the Washington-Beijing line that Hanoi is serving as an instrument of Soviet expansionism in Southeast Asia.

The Prospects of the Cambodian Resistance

The combined Cambodian resistance consists of a maximum of 40,000 guerrillas of whom almost 35,000 belong to the Khmer Rouge, 5,000 to Son Sann's Khmer People's National Liberation Front (KPNLF) — an umbrella organization of several Khmer Serei resistance groups operating from both sides of the Thai-Cambodian border, and finally a small group of perhaps 500 men loyal to Prince Sihanouk. Although small and fractious, the KPNLF represents the only alternative to both the return of the much larger Khmer Rouge and the continuation of Hanoi's Heng Samrin/ Pen Sovan regime. None of the three groups would survive as a viable military opposition without access to Thai sanctuary, food supplies, and Chinese military aid.

As of late 1980, the Khmer Rouge have stated publicly that they are willing to share power in a broad anti-Vietnamese coalition specifically urging Son Sann and Sihanouk to ally openly with Pol Pot's forces. From the Khmer Rouge perspective, a coalition would enhance its international acceptability while not really threatening its military dominance. Both Son Sann and Sihanouk, by contrast, have severe misgivings about association with their barbarous erstwhile partner. Both fear that a working arrangement could discredit them among non-communist refugees in Thailand and among the general Cambodian population who dread Pol Pot's return.

Since 1980, Son Sann has travelled widely in Europe, Asia, and the United States to solicit support for his third force, claiming that the majority of Cambodians would affiliate if the international community provided the military and political support to permit operations to remain independent of Khmer Rouge control. Son Sann also expressed confidence that any U.N.-supervised election in Cambodia would result both in the loss of authority for the Heng Samrin group and the repudiation of Khmer Rouge control.

Khmer Rouge guerrilla operations have apparently had an impact on local security. In the spring of 1981 Phnom Penh authorities refused to allow correspondents access to large areas of the country. In addition to the traditional trouble zones of east and northeast Cambodia, the provinces of Kompong Tham, Kratie, Kompong Chan, as well as Takeo and Kampot in the south toward the Vietnam frontier were all declared off limits for "security reasons" (*Agence France Presse* [AFP] [Hong Kong], 26 March 1981, in *FBIS:AP*, 26 March 1981, p. H3).

Also in March 1981, ASEAN diplomats initiated an exercise in quiet diplomacy to convince the three resistance groups to form a coalition. As an incentive to Sihanouk, they offered to sponsor his proposal that all Khmer factions be disarmed following a Vietnamese withdrawal at the special July United Nations conference on Cambodia. Subsequently, the Prince also agreed to ASEAN's request to drop his insistence that Democratic Kampuchea be removed from the United Nations pending favourable political changes in Cambodia itself. At the same time Thai officials put considerable pressure on Son Sann to meet with Sihanouk and Khmer Rouge representatives. On threat of losing Thai supply lines, Son Sann reluctantly agreed (Nayan Chanda, "The Road to Singapore", *FEER*, 11 September 1981, pp. 9–10).

Son Sann insists that he be given sufficient military equipment to insure the KPNLF's independent survival in the event of a resistance victory. As he put it, no cooperation with Pol Pot's forces could occur until he had a big enough "stick" when he entered the "tiger's cage".[13] Currently, his fighting forces are outnumbered by Pol Pot's by more than ten to one. There are reports that the United States backs Son Sann's requests for greater military and economic support and would be willing to provide economic aid through Thai distribution points if China gives the KPNLF military aid.[14]

While Sihanouk's small coterie and Son Sann's KPNLF both seek to reduce any Khmer Rouge political role in a united front coalition to a minority of the cabinet portfolios, the two anti-communist leaders are still rivals themselves. Son Sann wants all important government posts for himself, including the Foreign Affairs, Defence, Finance, and Interior Ministries. At most he is willing to grant Sihanouk a titular head-of-state position — outside of politics.[15] Sihanouk dismisses the prospect of a military victory for the resistance as a pipe-dream. Therefore, there need be no concern over a return to power of the discredited Pol Pot regime. At best, a protracted guerrilla war may lead to a negotiated change in the Phnom Penh government. Even if Hanoi agreed to such negotiations, the Vietnamese would never permit the return of Khmer Rouge leaders to positions of authority, claims the Prince.

The greatest achievement of the 2–4 September 1981 Singapore tripartite meeting of Khieu Samphan, Son Sann, and Sihanouk was to present the *illusion* of progress toward a united front sufficient to retain Democratic Kampuchea's U.N. seat for another year by a slightly larger margin than the previous two, 77 to 37 with 31 abstentions. No time limit was placed on a working level committee of the three groups created to form a coalition government.[16] Progress toward the coalition will probably move exceedingly slowly, for Pol Pot's forces have little to gain by compromising. They have already acquired added legitimacy through the ostensible formation of a united front and are stronger on the ground than ever before. The most Son Sann and Sihanouk can expect is that Western states supporting the coalition will provide political and material support directly to them. Thus, Malaysian Foreign Minister Ghazali Shafie has argued that — based on Malaysian intelligence — support for Son Sann's forces is growing inside Cambodia, while the Khmer Rouge remain unable to generate popular enthusiasm. He concludes that over the long run, political power within the resistance will shift to the anti-Khmer Rouge forces. If groups led by Sann and Sihanouk were given real teeth, the possibility of a negotiated solution would be enhanced for Hanoi would not have to fear a Pol Pot comeback and the reinstallation of a pro-Chinese regime (John McBeth, "The Coalition Blues", *FEER*, 18 September 1981, pp. 12–13).

Manoeuvres over Cambodia in the United Nations

ASEAN's global political stature is symbolized by the large margin with which it has maintained the Khmer Rouge seat in the United Nations since 1979 and the convocation of a special U.N. conference on Cambodia over the strenuous objections of Hanoi and Moscow. The conference served, of course, as a forum to condemn Vietnam's occupation and called for a withdrawal of VPA forces, leaving the country temporarily under some kind of undefined United Nations supervision pending free elections. The subsequent freely elected Cambodian Government would adopt a non-aligned policy with unspecified international guarantees. Should these developments come to pass, ASEAN then promised actively to support programmes for the reconstruction of Indochina.

Aside from the propaganda victory against Vietnam, the U.N. special conference seemed to achieve little. Moscow and Hanoi proposed a Southeast Asian regional conference as an alternative which was designed to obtain ASEAN's acceptance of the Indochina status quo.

The Soviets offered to follow this regional meeting with a broader international conference, presumably to ratify and guarantee Vietnam's dominant position in Indochina.

ASEAN states are sensitive to the necessity of offering Vietnam positive incentives for withdrawal but have little in their inventory to overcome the SRV's politico-military control of Cambodia underwritten by Russian military and economic aid. Nevertheless, ASEAN proceeded to insert points in the July 1981 U.N. special conference declaration which could eventually form the basis for new negotiations with Vietnam. Two of these points were opposed by China: one, calling for the disarmament of all factions in Cambodia prior to elections would weaken the Khmer Rouge position; the other, calling for a provisional government prior to general elections could undermine Democratic Kampuchea's legal claim to the Cambodian seat in the United Nations.[17]

ASEAN argued, in contrast, that the disarming of Cambodian factions and U.N. supervision of the transition process during a Vietnamese troop withdrawal would insure that Pol Pot forces would not return to power. Therefore, Vietnam need not fear the return of a Chinese sphere of influence if the VPA left Cambodia. However, Beijing insisted that questions concerning Cambodia's alignment could not be predetermined at an international conference but must be the sole responsibility of whatever government the Cambodian people choose after a Vietnamese withdrawal. Even the procedure of arranging elections, according to Beijing, should be led by the incumbent Democratic Kampuchean Government.[18] China's adamance and the U.N. Conference Declaration compromise, which excised the provision calling for disarmament of Cambodian factions, could hardly have been reassuring to Vietnam. ASEAN's hope of sending positive signals to Hanoi at the U.N. conference was probably deflected by Beijing's manoeuvre.

Conclusion

Although ASEAN deeply desires a negotiated settlement in Cambodia, the five cannot effect that end by themselves. Several other intervening conditions must be met, including alternative sources of economic and military aid to the Soviet Union and Chinese acceptance of some kind of Vietnamese influence in a Cambodian successor government. Both conditions would also require some form of American commitment, which, in turn, would go against ASEAN's goal of an exclusively regional solution.

The USSR is essentially uninterested in any change. It probably prefers to see the continuation of a low-level conflict since that would maintain Hanoi's dependence and permit the Soviets to consolidate their naval and air bases in Vietnam and Cambodia.

In this analyst's view, there is only one possible scenario for a *peaceful* resolution of the Cambodian confrontation. The probability of its realization is not high. It would require ASEAN to negotiate directly with Hanoi over conditions for a complete troop withdrawal with the understanding that ASEAN would not be concerned about the political alignment of the Cambodian regime after Vietnamese forces leave. In effect, ASEAN would be trading an acceptance of a Vietnamese client in Cambodia for the withdrawal of a Vietnamese military threat to Thailand's border provinces. China would have to agree to this arrangement since the Vietnamese have stated they would leave Cambodia only if China lifted its threat of war. There are potential benefits for Beijing in these negotiations too. The PRC could require Vietnam to reduce its economic and military ties to the USSR as a condition for the easing of military pressure on Vietnam's northern border.

Unhappily, although the above scenario appears to meet the security requirements of the major actors, its realization is improbable. To argue that the SRV cut its ties to the USSR in exchange for ASEAN and China's acceptance of Cambodia as a Vietnamese client is unrealistic for it is precisely Hanoi's ties to the Soviet Union which permit the SRV to maintain its dominance.

The Cambodian situation, then, appears unamenable to formal negotiations. ASEAN understands that a political solution is premised on a Cambodian regime acceptable to both Hanoi and Bangkok. At present, there is none. Hanoi believes time is on its side. Over the next several years ASEAN's resolve will weaken as differences over China's regional role are exacerbated. The West will gradually lose interest as its attention moves to political and economic crises elsewhere.

At bottom, the Cambodian conflict demonstrates that Southeast Asian security still cannot be based on indigenous arrangements. As long as regional actors are willing to call on outside great power allies, the region will remain a component of larger rivalries.

Notes

Research for this study was supported by travel grants from the U.S. International Communication Agency, the Earhart Foundation, and a sabbatical leave grant from Arizona State University.

1. The author encountered this concern in interviews with members of Thailand's political elite in 1979 and 1981.
2. See the discussion in Marjorie Niehaus, *Kampuchea: Issues for U.S. Policy* (Washington, D.C.: Congressional Research Service, Library of Congress, 25 June 1981), pp. 5, 11.
3. This argument is made in Les Buszynski, "The Soviet Union and Southeast Asia Since the Fall of Saigon", *Asian Survey* 21, no. 5 (May 1981): 548.
4. Address by Vietnamese Foreign Minister Nguyen Co Thach to the Non-Aligned Conference in New Delhi as carried by the *Vietnam News Agency* (*VNA*), 11 February 1981, in *Foreign Broadcast Information Service: Asia and Pacific, Daily Report* (hereafter cited as *FBIS:AP*), 12 February 1981, pp. K12–K13. And the 14 June 1981 statement of the Indochinese Foreign Ministers Conference as carried by Hanoi Radio, 14 June 1981 in ibid., 15 June 1981, pp. A3–A5.
5. These figures are cited in Justus van der Kroef, "From Phnom Penh to Kabul: The Soviets New Asian Gambit", *International Security Review* 6, no. 1 (Spring 1981), p. 14. See also Francois Nivolon, "Debt Shackles Vietnam", *FEER*, 22 May 1981, p. 59.
6. The aid agreements are assessed in Ton Long, "An Embrace for the Bear", *FEER*, 21 August 1981, p. 48.
7. Dollar estimates of the cost of Soviet aid to Vietnam vary with the rate of international inflation. Singapore Deputy Prime Minister Rajaratnam has estimated US$6 million per day in 1981. The author's view is that by 1982 the same amount of support will be worth approximately US$7 million per day.
8. James Sterba, "China Urges Force in

Cambodia Against Vietnam", *New York Times*, 12 July 1981.
9. Zhao is quoted by Thai Foreign Minister Sitthi Sawatsila in the *Bangkok Post*, 14 August 1981.
10. For a thorough discussion of ASEAN's view of non-alignment, see Sheldon W. Simon, *The ASEAN States and Regional Security* (Stanford: The Hoover Institution Press, forthcoming).
11. These points were reported in the *Bangkok Post*, 19 June 1981, in *FBIS:AP*, 19 June 1981, pp. A1–A2.
12. Author's interviews with U.S. officials in Southeast Asia, June 1981.
13. AFP (Paris), 16 June 1981, in *FBIS:AP*, 18 June 1981, p. A7.
14. Richard Nations, "When Old Friends Meet", *FEER*, 8 May 1981, p. 12; and Mike Chinoy, "Hostility Among Partners...", *Christian Science Monitor*, 18 June 1981.
15. Typical is a report in the *Bangkok Post*, 24 August 1981. Also see Henry Kamm, "Sihanouk Plans to Meet Pol Pot Leader", *New York Times*, 28 August 1981.
16. The text of the short joint statement and a report of the subsequent news conference is printed in *FBIS:AP*, 4 September 1981, pp. H9–H10.
17. Subsequently, the September 1981 tripartite agreement among Khieu Samphan, Son Sann, and Sihanouk superseded the second point. Formation of a coalition did not become an obstacle to Democratic Kampuchea's retention of its U.N. seat for another year.
18. *Xinhua Commentator*, 17 July 1981, in *FBIS:PRC*, 17 July 1981, pp. E1–E2.

KAMPUCHEA 1979–81
National Rehabilitation in the Eye of an International Storm

Ben Kiernan

On 25 March 1979, Jean-Pierre Gallois of the Agence France Presse (AFP), the first Western journalist admitted to Kampuchea after the overthrow of the Pol Pot regime, filed this report from Phnom Penh:

> The Cambodia that survived Pol Pot is like a dismembered body that is trying to come back to life. Its economy is shattered, its communications severed. Millions of hectares of rice paddies have been temporarily abandoned. A population of refugees is returning home along pitted roads and highways or assembling in the suburbs of empty and dilapidated cities.
>
> Phnom Penh, which two non-communist journalists have been allowed to visit for the first time since January 7, is in the image of the rest of the country. There is no drinking water, no telephone, no mail service, no transport, no registry office, no money, no markets, hardly any electricity, hardly any schools, hardly any medical dispensaries. The city is so quiet that bird-song has a sinister ring to it. Its residents survive like nomads by eating roots, wild fruit, leaves and fish, and sometimes rice and flour distributed by the authorities.
>
> The new government has no effective political control of the country and cannot guarantee the security of its citizens throughout the territory. Phnom Penh unofficially admits that all the southwest of the country lies beyond its administration, and that the situation is only secure in the capital itself and in the provinces east of the Mekong. The region bordering Thailand lies completely outside its control.
>
> In Phnom Penh itself, there are three Vietnamese advisers for every Cambodian official, ten Vietnamese soldiers for every Cambodian one.
>
> City dwellers returning home, particularly workers, are still grouped outside the towns waiting... Neither the new Cambodian government nor their Vietnamese allies seem at present willing to give these returning

---

Reprinted in abridged format from Huynh Kim Khanh, ed., *Southeast Asian Affairs 1982* (Singapore: Institute of Southeast Asian Studies, 1982), pp. 167–95. At the time of original publication, Ben Kiernan was a PhD candidate at Monash University (Australia).

refugees a responsibility in the running of the country's affairs...

Cambodia cut in two, with a non-existent economy and a phantom government still presents a picture of darkness. Only faith and hope can save the Cambodian people from extinction.

About one and a half million people, of a population of seven million or more, had perished in the Pol Pot period from 1975 to early 1979, including up to 500,000 deaths by execution and the rest from starvation, disease, and overwork. Inside the country the change of government was welcome, but many international observers felt that the new Vietnamese occupying force, also acting in the name of communism, would be just as brutal. It was even feared that Kampuchea would finally disappear from the map of Southeast Asia, its inhabitants sharing a fate perhaps similar to that of the Australian aborigines.

On 7 January 1982, the People's Republic of Kampuchea (PRK) was three years old. After three drastic changes of regime in a decade, Kampuchea had entered another phase of its history, ushered in by the invasion and continuing occupation of 150,000 Vietnamese troops. Perhaps ironically, this massive foreign presence had provided the military shield for an ambitious project of national recovery launched by the PRK regime headed by Pen Sovan, Sae Phuthang, and Heng Samrin. The means used for this end were careful planning (on the part of the leadership) and hard work (on the part of the population) — factors apparently evident to Jean-Pierre Gallois as merely "faith and hope" — plus a good deal of international "charity". By the end of 1981, considerable success had been achieved in rehabilitation, but the country remained at the centre of a high-pitched international controversy over the role and continued presence of the Vietnamese Army on its territory. This article reviews developments in Kampuchea since the PRK's foundation; I will attempt to bring together personal observations inside the country in 1980 and 1981, and evidence from a variety of secondary sources.

Agriculture

Perhaps the greatest success of the Pol Pot regime was the post-war recovery of the agricultural economy. By 1977 Kampuchea was producing enough rice to feed its population, a real achievement against the background of rural destruction and dislocation caused by the 1970–75 war and in particular by U.S. saturation bombardment of the major rice-producing areas up to 1973.

However, malnutrition and starvation persisted in Kampuchea through 1977 and 1978, because of the Democratic Kampuchea regime's policy of hoarding and even exporting rice (to China in most cases, in exchange for military equipment), while keeping to a bare minimum the rations distributed to the people. This was made possible by the nation-wide organization of "Co-operatives" comprising the inhabitants of a village or a subdistrict (many of whom had been forcibly transferred from elsewhere), in which meals were eaten communally in specially-built canteens. Rations usually consisted of thin rice gruel rather than rice, and vegetables — meat and condiments were rarely provided. At the same time, freedom of movement was limited (even private foraging was prohibited in most places), working hours numbered ten to twelve or even more per day, and the penalty for complaints, laziness, and real or suspected disloyalty was increasingly that of death.

It was not surprising, then, that when the Vietnamese invasion dissolved the Pol Pot administration in early 1979, the co-operative system simply collapsed. Despite the raising of production levels between 1975 and 1978 (on an absolute basis, rather than concomitant with the labour input in man-hours), the Kampucheans had received little benefit from the economic advances and in fact tended to regard the co-operatives as prison camps. So in most places local cadre of the Democratic Kampuchea regime, conscious of their inability to mount a classic guerrilla resistance to the Vietnamese by remaining among the population "like fish in water", simply disappeared into the hills and forests; the inhabitants then seized their personal belongings such as pots, pans, farm tools and draught animals, which had been confiscated and communalized, and headed off. People roamed the country either searching for relatives and family or, in the case of many hundreds of thousands of people evacuated during the Pol Pot period from the east of the country to the west or from the cities to the countryside, returning to their homes and villages. Because people were still able to harvest the 1978–79 rice crop, there was little starvation during this period, except among the half a million or so people who accompanied or were driven by the Pol Pot forces into the hills and forests (the remnants of whom began to appear on the Thai border as walking skeletons in September 1979).

However, with continuing fighting and as many as half a million other people still on the road in the areas controlled by the PRK as late as August 1979, the agricultural system was severely dislocated. The amount of land planted for the 1979–80 crop was minimal, probably only a third of the area sown in a normal year. Further, the draft animal population had fallen to about 800,000 (compared to 2.5 million in 1970) as a result of the many years of war. A major rice shortage, and the threat of mass starvation, was easily predictable, at least for the second quarter of 1980 and beyond. Fearing this, and also taking advantage of the freedom of movement offered (or tolerated) by the new PRK regime to escape from the country or make contact with relatives abroad, and engage in the burgeoning lucrative border trade, about 300,000 Kampucheans from the PRK/Vietnamese-controlled populated plains headed for the Thai border in the last quarter of 1979. (In the first three months after the overthrow of Pol Pot, only 5,000 Kampucheans had taken refuge in Thailand.)

In view of the looming threat (but not yet reality) of disaster, in June 1979 the PRK requested large-scale international aid, but imposed strict conditions in ensuing negotiations with relief agencies, in particular demanding that no aid be given to the "Pol Pot forces along the Thai border" where they had found sanctuary and military manoeuvrability. This led to an outcry in the West, and especially when Hanoi's Deputy Foreign Minister Phan Hien stated in September that there was no starvation in Kampuchea but only "pockets of famine", there were widespread denunciations of Vietnam and the PRK for deliberately presiding over the final extinction of the Khmer people, through "subtle and systematic genocide", in the words of Francois Ponchaud. In retrospect, however, such fears were unwarranted; the refugees who arrived at the Thai border in deplorable physical condition were almost exclusively from Pol Pot-held enclaves (and in one case from a base held by the anti-communist KPNLF[1]), whereas people coming from PRK areas, and those who remained there, were in nowhere near such a state. Nevertheless the potential for a nation-wide calamity remained, because of the poor harvest that was about to be brought in in December and January. Vietnam had shipped in 120,000 tonnes of food by the end of October (*Keesings Contemporary Archives*, 23 January 1981, p. 3067), and 30,000 tonnes of Soviet food aid arrived in Kompong Som by mid-October (*Observer*, 21 October 1979); but before 12 October, when 1,500 tonnes of aid donated by the British-based agency Oxfam arrived, the total Western relief contribution was only 200 tonnes.

Fortunately, on 26 September negotiations had been concluded between relief agencies, led by the UNICEF/ICRC (International Committee of the Red Cross) joint programme, and Phnom Penh, which dropped most of its conditions. The delivery of aid began several weeks later, peaking at 1,000 tonnes per day in December 1979. From October 1979 to December 1980, 400,000 tonnes of rice were sent to Kampuchea — 235,000 tonnes by UNICEF/ICRC and Western agencies, 140,000 tonnes by the Soviet Union, and 25,000 tonnes from Eastern Europe and Vietnam. The Soviet Union further provided 24,000 tonnes of wheat and flour,[2] bringing its total aid to Kampuchea to the value of US$134 million by April 1980 (*FEER*, 6 June 1980).

If the Kampuchean population at the time was estimated at around 5.5 million, this would if evenly distributed have provided an average of 73 kg of rice per person for the fourteen-month period, or about 5 kg per person per month. In fact, because of the tremendous transportation problems, an inexperienced administration (to which the government assigned priority in rationing, along with other employees unable to grow food or search for food during working hours), corruption, and sporadic delivery, rations distributed to peasants averaged only 1 to 2 kg per person per month (varying from one-quarter of a kilogram to 7 kg). Nevertheless, large-scale starvation was averted: peasants supplemented their meagre rations with the produce of the small 1979–80 crop, and by living off the rich Kampuchean countryside, eating fruit, vegetables, secondary crops such as corn and potatoes, crabs and fish. It was a tough year; in the countryside between July and October, peasants usually reported a lack of rice, but very little actual starvation.

Government priority was effectively given to the delivery to the peasants of 70,000 tonnes of seed rice (60,000 tonnes provided by UNICEF/ICRC and Western agencies, and 10,000 tonnes by Vietnam) for use in the 1980 planting season. As a result, the December 1980 rice harvest was a successful one, at least twice as big as the previous year's — approximately 1,000,000 tonnes of paddy (yielding 700,000 tonnes of rice compared to the 1979 figure of 300,000). Further, like the previous year, the PRK imposed no taxation on agricultural producers, a policy made possible by the international aid rice which was rationed to the administration (such as the 15,000 members of the Ministry of Agriculture) and other state employees and factory workers. The *Economist* described the 1980 crop as evidence of an "excellent recovery in food output... [In the] long term it is likely that Cambodia may re-emerge as a food exporter". (*Economist Intelligence Unit, Quarterly Economic Review of Indochina*, Third Quarter 1981 [hereafter cited as

Economist Intelligence Unit, Indochina, Third Quarter 1981].) It was clear that despite a rice shortfall of over 100,000 tonnes, the United Nations' (principally UNICEF) contribution to Kampuchean (internal) relief and rehabilitation, worth a total of more than US$200 million up to December 1980, had been relatively well spent. The price of rice on the free market in Phnom Penh fell from three riels per kilogram to one and one half in January 1981.

By February, at least 185,000 refugees had returned from the Thai border to their villages inside Kampuchea (as had 115,000 Kampucheans who had fled to Vietnam, and 20,000 who had fled to Laos, in the Pol Pot period) (*Age*, 21 January 1981). In December 1980, the "land bridge", the U.N. and Western-sponsored emergency relief operation at the Thai border, was brought to an end.

By the end of 1981, the total value of aid provided under the UNICEF/ICRC umbrella reached $338 million, of which the United States provided $85 million.[3] (An additional $303 million in aid was sent to the refugee camps on the Thai border, with a population of 300,000. Much of this aid went into the hands of the Pol Pot army, the effects of which will be discussed below.) However, during 1981 there was a much reduced need for food aid. UNICEF sent over $100 million worth of supplies into Kampuchea, including a targeted 75,000 tonnes of rice through the World Food Program, all but 12,000 tonnes of which had arrived by September (*FEER*, 25 September 1981). For its part the Soviet Union provided 55,000 tonnes of rice, wheat flour, and corn (its target was 80,000), and was expected to deliver 13,000 tonnes of fertilizer, 200 trucks, over 200 other vehicles (and two passenger aeroplanes), and 130,000 tonnes of fuel, as part of a bilateral aid programme valued at over $100 million for the year.[4] India also donated $3.2 million worth of food and medicine (*Economist Intelligence Unit*, Indochina, Third Quarter 1981).

Education

Schools were closed under the Democratic Kampuchea regime, and its attempts to teach children to read and write after they had completed daily production tasks were notoriously unsuccessful, contributing to a serious illiteracy problem. In 1979 the new PRK government estimated the number of illiterates at one and a half million. By June of that year, however, 50,000 children were already claimed to be attending daily primary school in makeshift buildings or under trees, and by December UNICEF agreed the figure had reached as high as 900,000. The majority of experienced teachers perished in the Pol Pot period, and others fled abroad; only 4,500 of the 20,000 teachers practising in late 1979 were qualified. The rest were simply high-school graduates, or worse, given rough training courses in politics, teaching techniques, and psychology before and after they commenced teaching. By late 1980 the number of children in primary school had risen to 1,300,000, with 30,000 teachers, and a year later the figures were 1,503,000 (in May 1981 UNICEF had predicted 1.5 million)[5] and 37,000 respectively.[6] Despite the low quality of the teaching staff, most children in Kampuchea now have the opportunity to achieve basic literacy. At a press conference in Phnom Penh on 22 September 1981, Education Minister Pen Navuth even claimed that "there are now more children in school than in the days of peace under Sihanouk". Further, according to PRK Ministry of Education statistics, by late 1981 over 140,000 illiterates had completed part-time adult education courses (for which factory workers, among others, were allowed time off work to attend), and another 250,000 were enrolled in them.

Secondary education remains much more limited, but is also expanding. The number of middle schools open in 1979 was 14; by late 1981 the figure was 97, catering for 40,000 pupils. Senior high schools increased in number from one to five over the same period, and enrolment reached 1,800.[7]

Such expansion was largely possible because of the reopening of the Ecole Normale Supérieure and the École de Pedagogie in the capital, where 3,000 teachers were trained, and the creation of twenty provincial training centres which produced a total of 12,000 teachers over the 1979–81 period.

According to the Director of Education for Kompong Cham province, a former philosophy professor, the developing new education system "will be a good one ... because it will be free". Students, he said, will not have to depend on poorly stocked libraries if they cannot afford the expensive textbooks imported from France, as was the case in the past. Books written in Khmer, which for the first time has become the sole medium of instruction, are distributed free. The first of these were printed in 1980, one for each of a dozen subjects, including History, Literature, Mathematics, Social Deportment, and Folk Tales. By September 1981, thirty-nine different titles had been printed for primary education, a total of 3,019,000 volumes, nearly all of which had been distributed. For secondary schools, fourteen titles had been mimeographed, in 8,000 copies, and another thirty-one were ready for printing.[8] The national weekly newspaper, *Kampuchea*, has also been distributed to schools for use in reading and, most probably, political lessons.

Finally, it is noteworthy that because of the acute shortage of teachers, the state has authorized Buddhist monks to open schools in a number of rural areas. Visiting journalists in 1981 came across monastery schools in Takeo and Kompong Cham provinces.[9] In Phnom Penh, several courses of evening classes in English and French were offered by teachers on a private basis, with the backing of the government; however, in September 1981 these were ordered to close, for reasons that remain unclear. At the same time, the state-run Institute of Languages was established, teaching English, French, Vietnamese, Russian, and Spanish to those students in Phnom Penh who wish to take up extra studies. (The school system does not offer foreign language courses.)

At the tertiary level, the Faculty of Medicine was reopened in 1979; two young doctors, whose studies had been interrupted by Pol Pot's 1975 victory, graduated a year later, followed by another seventeen in 1981. (There were then 89 students in medicine and 139 in pharmacy.) The School of Agronomy at Chamcar Daung has run three-month courses in tractor maintenance, water management, and veterinary science for several hundred students,[10] and the Tuk Tla Vocational School is also functioning in Phnom Penh. In September 1981, the former Khmero-Soviet Higher Technical Institute reopened in the capital, with a normal first-year intake of 220 students, half of them in the engineering field. The Institute has four faculties — construction, agricultural hydrology, electrical engineering, and geology — and plans to offer twenty-one different subjects. A Soviet professor who taught there from 1966 to 1969 has returned as an adviser; much of the teaching and the textbooks will be in the Russian language. Further, by November 1981 a total of 944 Khmers had been sent for prolonged courses of study in the Soviet Union (614), Eastern Europe (217), Vietnam (83), and Cuba (25).[11] Three others were sent to India in 1981 for training in archaeology, presumably with a view to the restoration of Angkor Wat and other Kampuchean historical monuments.

Religion

Buddhism has undergone a visible if limited revival since 1979, after a three-year period in which organized religion was abolished and many monks executed. Nearly all Khmers still consider themselves at least nominal Buddhists; monks in their saffron robes can now be seen in every district; and on holy days large groups of people can be seen taking offerings to newly-reopened monasteries in rural areas. But it would seem that the country is not yet productive enough to support large numbers of monks living from alms donated by the population, as 70,000 to 100,000 did in former years. Also, the socialist PRK regime probably keeps a close watch on religion and intends to limit the monks to smaller numbers than before. Since mid-1980 no one under 50 years old has been allowed to become a monk, although one often sees young novices who presumably entered the monkhood during 1979.

Most reopened monasteries had three to six monks by the end of 1981; in Phnom Penh's prestigious Wat Unnalom the numbers increased from twenty in 1980 to twenty-eight in 1981. For the capital as a whole the figure was 170 monks. According to the country's Buddhist Patriarch, the Venerable Tep Vong, there were 3,000 in the country in mid-1981 (and 700 pagodas under reconstruction).[12] The number of monks is still low, but their reappearance and daily activities in the towns and villages gives the population confidence that the assault on their life-style launched by the Pol Pot regime is not about to be repeated, even if the new regime is also a communist one. This confidence was no doubt reinforced by the government's sponsorship of an ordination ceremony for 1,500 monks in Phnom Penh in mid-1980. But the same ceremony also raised another point — the close links between state and religion. Tep Vong is himself a Vice-Chairman of the National Assembly, a position which he owes to his loyalty to the regime. The new politicized role of the Buddhist hierarchy was highlighted when 400 monks representing all provinces gathered in Phnom Penh from April to June 1981. According to Tep Vong, they were given a course of lectures on two subjects: a) Buddhism, and b) "the historic victory of 7 January and the revival of Buddhism". According to Pen Sovan:

> As far as monks are concerned, our Front has a well-defined political line: to respect the traditions, mores and customs of our people. *All monks who have direct relations with the people are members of the Front* (emphasis added). The Front has helped and does help the monks to properly understand current events, to grasp the principles of the political line and to strengthen Buddhist discipline and laws in accordance with the beliefs of the Kampuchean people. (*Rapport politique*.)

The other organized religions in Kampuchea are Islam and Christianity. The Muslims, an ethnic group known as the Chams, suffered from executions, starvation, and disease even more than the Khmer population, largely because of Pol Pot's racialist policies. Their numbers apparently fell from as many as 200,000 to as few as 50,000. But wherever there are Cham communities in Kampuchea today, there are newly-reopened mosques, with turbanned holy men in checked sarongs and serious young boys studying the Koran and even the Arabic as well as the Khmer script.

Ibrahim, a Muslim dignitary who studied for four years in Cairo and in 1980 became one of the seventy-odd members of the Ministry of Religious Affairs in Phnom Penh, insists that the Chams once again have the freedom to organize their religious activities and that the former Muslim "networks" throughout the country have been re-established. At the time I interviewed Ibrahim, Yos Por, Secretary-General of the Salvation Front and then in charge of the Ministry, was leading a delegation of Muslims to visit Cham communities in Kampot province.

By late 1980 six mosques had been opened in the Phnom Penh area, and a good number in the provinces, but Muslim dignitaries were thinly stretched: only 20 of the previous 113 in Kampuchea survived the Pol Pot period.

Kampuchean Christians are very few in number (perhaps several thousand) and are therefore less politically significant and more vulnerable. They are also seen by some, probably incorrectly, as less "national" than other religious communities, and therefore suffer from discrimination. Until June 1980 there were five weekly Protestant services being performed again in Phnom Penh, by a Khmer pastor, but at that point several Protestants were arrested and interrogated by the police; others then became afraid to attend services, and now there is only one each week. Little information is available about Kampuchea's remaining Catholics.

Culture

Traditional Khmer culture, theatre, and dance were suppressed and largely destroyed during the Pol Pot period, and one of the most striking features of Kampuchea in 1980–81 was their revival and increasingly wide diffusion, with state backing.

At the National Theatre in Phnom Penh, for example, performances had reached a high artistic standard by mid-1980. They covered a range: classical royal ballet, usually based on the Khmer version of the Ramayana, and performed in elaborate, colourful, silk costumes, masks and head-dress; folk dances (for example, *angre*, *rook trei*) using more simple rural costumes and masks, bamboo sticks and fishing baskets; and several ethnic minority dances such as the seductive Cham "Love Handkerchief" and a hill-tribe ceremonial called "Kill the buffalo, drink the wine".

The theatre also performs overtly political scenes, such as Kampuchea-Vietnam-Laos solidarity dances, and one called "Peace in Indochina" which is more like a war dance, however defensive. And then there is "Blood and Tears", a shocking re-enactment of the final stages of a Pol Pot massacre; the semi-darkness and slow-motion violence are punctuated by a moving lament of the suffering sung with tremendous sadness and beauty by a woman. In the end Heng Samrin's Salvation Front troops arrive and apprehend the Pol Pot executioners. Their victims wake up and stand in a chorus as fists go up, all eyes turn to the massive PRK flag suddenly projected at the back of the stage, and then hands are religiously outstretched towards it. The scene ends with a eulogy of the new revolution. Despite the agonizing memories it recalls, and the ceremonial ending, "Blood and Tears" is a popular scene in Phnom Penh, no doubt because of the degree of realism. The Kampuchean tragedy has not lacked melodrama. One thing is missing, however: the overwhelming role played by Vietnamese troops in abolishing the killer regime.

One noticeable feature of the new political theatre is a rather ironic mixture of traditional Khmer intellectual and social imagery with that of contemporary Marxism-Leninism. "Peace in Indochina", for instance, features three women in classical Kampuchean, Lao, and Vietnamese costumes standing firmly side by side, swaying in unison as a mustachioed, black-clad caricature of an old-fashioned Chinese sorcerer attempts to draw them towards him with an invisible magic rope. Even more startling was a scene performed after the declaration of the People's Revolutionary Party of Kampuchea in May 1981, called "Salute the Party Flag": thirty teenagers with tonsured heads and silken *samput* tucked between their legs — costumes recalling the atmosphere of the nineteenth-century Khmer court — paraded on the stage under an enormous emblem of the hammer-and-sickle. With typical dramatic mastery, this political scene was immediately followed by the "Love Handkerchief".

Comedy scenes include "The Shameless Enemy", a hilarious half-hour in which three clowns jump around the stage in and out of each other's arms, terrified out of their wits by the ghost of a man who has just died. At the very end the inevitable Front troops burst in, unmasking the ghost who just as inevitably turns out to be a Pol Pot figure. As he is led away the leading clown, an experienced actor who is now the political cadre of the theatre group, explains to the audience that they should not allow the enemy who seems to have disappeared to keep manipulating and haunting them. It is a thoughtful scene of social relevance, and its cathartic impact is effected with some subtlety.

What is more interesting and significant than these events in the capital is the extent to which the 1979–80 revival of Khmer culture penetrated to the rural districts and villages. As always, the classical royal ballet was not to be found in the countryside, but other performing troupes were proliferating. By late 1980, every province had its professional theatre and performing group, and the PRK was well on the way to achieving Keo Chenda's aim of a cultural group for each of the country's 100-odd districts, besides children's theatre groups set up in many urban and rural orphanages.

In 1980 Takeo province, for instance, had a professional theatre group of about thirty people, who performed every Saturday evening in the province capital, and in various districts on other days. In Kampot there was a similar troupe, as well as a performing group of children from the provincial orphanage. Both were newly-established but surprisingly entertaining, having been trained by a talented young English-speaking producer who had been transferred from Kompong Thom province after building up similar groups there during 1979. The results of this man's work include an uproarious comedy entitled "Pol Pot Runs out of Food". Ravenous guerrillas in black pyjamas hide behind bushes, licking their chops frenetically as a peasant laden with all the goodies of the Kampuchean countryside (rice and bean cakes wrapped in banana leaves, rice wine, sugar palm juice in bamboo cylinders, fruit, and a stick of sugar cane) proceeds to spend a leisurely afternoon getting drunk and fishing in a pond, oblivious of the suffering antics of his former oppressors. There was also a long and thoughtful skit on the dangers of illiteracy for the poor, performed in the framework of a *yike*, a traditional Khmer dramatic form.

At the district level in 1980, Santuk district of Kompong Thom had an orchestra of nine (a female singer, six elderly men on traditional instruments, and two boys on drums and guitar), each member of which received a salary of 90 riels per month, about the same as that of a junior official. Staung district had a much bigger cultural group of fifty, and Baray a much smaller one. On the other side of the country in Prey Veng province, Kompong Trabek district had a theatre group of over thirty. In mid-1981 however, the financial strain on the government apparently began to tell, funding was withdrawn for district-level troupes, and their members returned to their villages. Instead, province-level troupes were built up to over fifty people each, and two small teams were established in every province to screen movie films in rural areas. Similar expansion has taken place at the national level. When the best forty performers of the National Theatre left in September 1981 for a tour of the Soviet Union and Eastern Europe, it was clearly shown that artistic standards did not noticeably decline. The first performance for many years of the Tum Teav, a traditional love story with a muted anti-royalist theme, in Phnom Penh in early 1981, drew large crowds, as did two Khmer-language films about the horrors of the Pol Pot period.

At the Fourth Party Congress in May 1981, Keo Chenda, no longer Minister of Culture but present as Party Secretary for Phnom Penh, claimed that the Party Municipal Committee "will strive to make the city not only an administrative capital but a political, cultural and economic centre of the country" (*FBIS*, 28 May 1981, p. H7).

The Limits of Independence

Despite the increased guerrilla activity, by 1981 Kampuchea was recovering steadily from destruction, war, and decimation of its population. The Khmer race is not about to disappear; rather, reports that Kampuchea is experiencing a "birth explosion reminiscent of Europe's post-war baby boom", were confirmed by Kampuchean officials and foreign aid workers (*Age*, 16 May 1981). Further, extensive travels along the Vietnamese-Kampuchean border in 1980 revealed no evidence of Vietnamese citizens coming to settle on Kampuchean land. And the revival and reinvigoration of traditional Khmer culture, along with the reappearance of the Buddhist religion and the establishment of a national education system once again should ensure that Kampuchean society retains much of its distinctive character.

What is a possible danger for the Kampuchean nation is simply a loss of political independence. The key here is not the small number of Soviet personnel in Phnom Penh, nor the Vietnamese military presence (since, while Democratic Kampuchea remains a potential threat, most Khmers are clearly prepared to tolerate the foreign occupation), but the Vietnamese advisers in the Kampuchean government ministries: there is general suspicion among lower-ranking Khmer officials in Phnom Penh that these advisers wield too much power. Interestingly, it is already clear that a large number of them are packing their bags. In 1979, Takeo province had forty Vietnamese advisers, while in 1980 Khmer officials there said there were none; minor officials in Prey Veng told me privately that their Vietnamese advisers were fewer than in 1979; two officials in Kompong Cham told me in separate private conversations that the advisers to their province had been reduced in number from twenty to eight over the same period; a minor official in Kandal told me his province had had twenty advisers in 1979, but that in 1980 there were twelve, and only five attached to the administration. In Phnom Penh's Ministry of Foreign Affairs, there were twelve in 1979, two in 1980, and one in 1981. By 1980, all Vietnamese advisers were apparently gone from the Ministry of Education. Also in 1980, the Vietnamese ambassador to Kampuchea, Ngo Dien, told me that all the advisers at the district level were in the process of being withdrawn. I found this to be largely the case; in Kong Pisei district of Kompong Speu, for instance, all three had returned home by 1980, according to local Khmer officials. In January 1981, journalist Barry Wain found that "Vietnamese advisers have withdrawn from all 99 subdistricts and five of the 11 districts" in Siemreap province: "'At the district level, we can run the business ourselves', says Keo Han, a Kampuchean province spokesman, indicating it won't be long before the six others pull out" (*Asian Wall Street Journal*; 30 January 1981). By August 1981, it was generally agreed that the number of advisers had been reduced to 50% of the 1979 level.[13]

A similar pattern seems discernible in the PRK Armed Forces, although information about them is much more difficult to gather. According to journalist Michael Richardson, during 1980 a decision was made "to limit direct involvement of Vietnamese in training" (*Age*, 31 January 1981). Further, in March 1981, Vietnamese garrisons withdrew from outlying areas close to Kampuchea's border with Thailand. Although this provided an opportunity for increased activity on the part of Democratic Kampuchea forces, it also allowed PRK troops to play a much more significant role in confronting them. From April 1981, there was a substantial build-up in the PRK Armed Forces in Western Kampuchea, according to a reliable diplomatic source in Bangkok. While there was still no sign of a reduction in the total number of Vietnamese troops in Kampuchea before a breakthrough in the international deadlock was achieved, this was nevertheless another encouraging indication of the reconstitution of the Kampuchean state. But particularly in the administration, the withdrawal of the advisers must continue steadily if the political aspirations of a large number of Kampucheans are ever to be fulfilled.

Economically, socially, and politically, Kampuchea had come a long way since 1979, although apprehension still remained about its future status. Hun Sen's view of the international storm over Kampuchea, as he expressed it in a September 1981 interview, was that Kampuchea is "a small country" which needed foreign protection at this point in its history: "Our people have opted for defence by the Vietnamese, who are better than the Chinese, the Thai or the Americans," he said. Other Kampucheans of different political backgrounds acknowledge the need for this foreign protection also, but do so sadly, in the knowledge that powers more attractive to them than Vietnam remain hostile to the PRK. In the words of one former supporter of the Lon Nol regime:

The US left Kampuchea without saying goodbye, and then Pol Pot took power. During the Pol Pot period I hoped constantly that the Americans would come to save us, but they didn't. And when the Vietnamese came to save us, they criticised Vietnam. The Americans would have been preferable, but they didn't come. At least the Vietnamese did come. And now the Americans vote for Pol Pot in the United Nations.

Notes

1. In this period nearly 4,000 civilians died, of a total of 6,000 held hostage by anti-communist guerrillas loyal to Son Sann's Khmer Peoples National Liberation Front. See the report by Roland-Pierre Paringaux in *Le Monde*, 21 December 1979. See below for more discussion of the KPNLF.
2. *FEER*, 19 December 1980.
3. Interagency Working Group on Kampuchea, "Humanitarian Operations Arising out of Developments in Kampuchea", New York, 1 September 1981.
4. Ibid., 7 May 1981.
5. Interagency Working Group, op. cit., 7 May 1981.
6. "*Statistique scolaire*", Ministry of Education, Phnom Penh, September 1981.
7. Ibid.
8. "*Situation des manuels scolaires jusqu'en 19/9/81*", Ministry of Education, Phnom Penh, September 1981.
9. Victoria Butler, personal communication.
10. Joel Charny, "More Troubles Ahead for Kampuchea's Economy", *Indochina Issues*, Washington, no. 20 (October 1981), p. 6.
11. "*État récapitulatif de l'envoi des étudiants dans les pays socialistes frères*", Ministry of Education, Phnom Penh, September 1981.
12. Interview with Victoria Butler, of the *Toronto Globe and Mail*, September 1981.
13. See for instance the testimony of Stephen Heder at a U.S. Congressional Hearing on Indochina, 23 October 1981.

CAMBODIA 1991
Lasting Peace or Decent Interval?

Mike Yeong

On 23 October 1991 Cambodia took a tentative step towards lasting peace when the four Khmer factions and 19 countries signed a UN-brokered peace accord in Paris which ended the 13-year-old war in Cambodia. It is at best a fragile peace as indicated by the series of violent events — the mob attack on Khmer Rouge leaders and demonstrations against corruption — that took place in Phnom Penh after the signing of the peace accord.

To understand how "peace" finally returned to Cambodia, it is necessary to examine the events that led to the first "breakthrough" in June which in turn led to the signing of the peace accord on 23 October. Before doing that, it may be useful to understand what the peace accord actually entails.

The UN Peace Accord: Main Features

Under the accord, the United Nations Transitional Authority in Cambodia (UNTAC) will, on the advice of the 12-member Supreme National Council (SNC) headed by Prince Norodom Sihanouk, run the country until UN-supervised free elections are held, probably in April 1993. The day-to-day administration will continue to be in the hands of the State of Cambodia (SOC), the regime installed by Vietnamese forces in January 1979, while UNTAC will oversee the running of five key ministries — defence, finance, foreign affairs, interior and information.

During this period, a 10,000-member UN peace-keeping force will be deployed inside Cambodia to enforce the ceasefire

---

Reprinted from Daljit Singh, ed., *Southeast Asian Affairs 1992* (Singapore: Institute of Southeast Asian Studies, 1992), pp. 103–19. At the time of original publication, Mike Yeong was a Fellow at the Institute of Southeast Asian Studies, Singapore.

— in place since 1 May 1991 — and to demobilize the four Khmer factions. Under a compromise agreement, 70 per cent of each of the four rival armies will be demobilized by UNTAC — which is expected in Cambodia in April or May 1992 — with the remaining 30 per cent to be held in UNTAC-controlled cantonments until just before the elections when they are expected to be totally demobilized or absorbed into a new Cambodian national army under the new government.

About four million out of the 8.5 million Cambodians are eligible to vote, and they will choose a 120-member national assembly, based on the electoral system of proportional representation. Political parties with a minimum of 5,000 members will be eligible to contest the elections. The presidential election is expected to be held immediately after the elections for the national assembly.

The Position in Early 1991

When 1991 began, the Khmer resistance, especially the Khmer Rouge, were occupying the propaganda high ground because of their commitment to full and immediate implementation of the UN peace plan whereas Phnom Penh and Hanoi found themselves on the defensive, having to explain why they raised a number of objections to it.

The UN peace plan was drafted by Indonesia and France, the two co-chairmen of the 1989 Paris International Conference on Cambodia (PICC), on the basis of the 28 August 1990 framework document prepared by the five permanent members of the UN Security Council (Perm Five). The Phnom Penh regime — and Hanoi — had accepted the Perm Five framework document, but in November, when the UN peace plan was drawn up, they opposed certain elements in it. In essence, the Phnom Penh regime had two major objections to the UN peace plan. First, it demanded that the "political and military status quo" be maintained. In other words, it was against the total dissolution of the SOC government and its army pending the holding of free elections. Second, it wanted a reference to "genocide" in the peace plan. The regime argued that since the SNC was only an embodiment of Cambodian sovereignty and not a government, the SOC should continue to administer the country until a new government was elected. It also contended that it was easier to demobilize the regime's army as it was a conventional force than the resistance which was largely a guerrilla force, which made it easier for the resistance to disguise their fighters and hide their weapons. The regime further contended that since the UN peace plan did not provide sufficient guarantees to prevent Pol Pot from seizing power, its army should not be dismantled as it was the only force that could take on the Khmer Rouge.

Sihanouk denounced Phnom Penh and Hanoi for reneging on their agreement to accept the UN peace plan in full. Relations between him and the Phnom Penh regime deteriorated as accusations were exchanged. Matters were not helped by the decision of a French court early in the year to fine Prince Sihanouk 20,000 francs for slandering Hor Nam Hong, the SOC's foreign minister.

The task of the Perm Five at the beginning of 1991 was therefore to persuade Hanoi and Phnom Penh to accept the UN peace plan in full. The account below will attempt to show that the turning point in this regard probably came during visits by Vietnamese and SOC leaders to Moscow in May 1991. However, these visits would not have produced the desired flexibility over the UN peace plan if Hanoi and Phnom Penh had not already realized that there was no other viable option after the impending drastic curtailment in Soviet support. In particular, it must have been clear to them by then that the United States would not lift the economic embargo nor would China normalize relations without a peace settlement first in Cambodia.

The Soviet Connection

With the collapse of communist regimes in Eastern Europe and the mounting economic problems in the Soviet Union, Hanoi and Phnom Penh, in the beginning of the year, were bracing themselves for a drastic cut in aid from the socialist bloc, a possibility of which they already had been forewarned. In January, a visiting Soviet state planning commission delegation told its Vietnamese counterpart that from 1991 trade between the two countries would be based on a "new mechanism", namely, payment would be in hard currency at world prices. Vietnam was probably also asked to repay the estimated US$10 billion debt it owes Moscow.

There was more bad news. In early 1991, Hanoi was told that several members of Comecon, the Soviet-dominated socialist trading bloc, were calling for its dissolution. Hanoi had wanted to use the February meeting in Budapest to urge that Comecon be reformed instead of dismantled, but the meeting was cancelled. In June, Hanoi was told Comecon had ceased to function. As 80 per cent of Vietnam's imports came from Comecon countries, Hanoi's concern about the bloc's dissolution was indeed real. In better times, East European members had absorbed large numbers of Vietnamese workers which helped to alleviate the chronic unemployment problem in Vietnam. With the collapse of the communist regimes in Eastern Europe, many Vietnamese workers were forced to return home, adding to Hanoi's economic and social woes.

In March, Vietnamese Foreign Minister Nguyen Co Thach declared that Vietnam could no longer look to the Soviet Union for economic survival and that it had to seek closer ties with Southeast Asia and Europe. Prince Ranariddh, leader of the group loyal to Prince Sihanouk, disclosed that Richard Solomon, U.S. Assistant Secretary of State for East Asia and the Pacific, had assessed in March that Vietnam could not remain intransigent indefinitely because of the economic difficulties caused by the reduction in Soviet and East European aid.

Though not a member of Comecon, the Phnom Penh regime had been receiving considerable aid from Comecon countries in the past 12 years. In February, a Soviet official said in Phnom Penh that Soviet aid to Cambodia, particularly oil supply, would be reduced in 1991.[1] *Liberation*, a French newspaper, reported that Phnom Penh needed 250,000 tonnes of oil for 1991 but the Soviet Union was prepared to supply only 5,000 tonnes. And in contrast to the previous practice of concluding five-year economic agreements with Phnom Penh, Moscow would agree only to a one-year agreement. On 24 March, a Soviet official announced that Soviet technicians working in key sectors in Cambodia, such as water and electricity utilities, would be withdrawn.[2] A Phnom Penh official earlier revealed that Soviet aid to Cambodia had been cut by about 80 per cent, or 40 million riels.[3] Hardest hit were the state budget and the industrial and labour sectors. By year end, it was reported that civil servants, policemen and soldiers had not been paid salaries for periods ranging from a few months to a year, which no doubt helped fuel the anger at the anti-corruption demonstrations in the Cambodian capital in December.

By March, the Phnom Penh regime was facing serious economic difficulties. Resistance officials reported that the capital was running out of food and other daily necessities, and that the riel had become worthless because the regime was printing more paper money to keep pace with spiralling prices. Social order was also breaking down as theft, burglary and robbery were reportedly on the rise. That month, the regime issued an appeal to non-governmental organizations and international institutions for food aid, claiming that the country was facing a serious food shortage — about one million tonnes — due to a poor harvest caused by insufficient supply of chemical fertilizer and a long spell of drought. The situation was compounded by large-scale flooding in June.

In contrast, the Khmer Rouge were profiting from logging and mining of gemstones in areas under their control in western Cambodia. Thai and Western intelligence sources estimated that the Khmer Rouge were reaping in as much as US$5 million a month by granting licences to Thai businessmen for logging and gem mining near the strategic town of Pailin, which they had captured shortly after the Vietnamese withdrawal in September 1989. (In March, presumably in an attempt to deny the Khmer Rouge access to an important source of revenue, Phnom Penh forces, backed by Vietnamese troops as well as MiG-21 fighter planes and helicopter gunships, launched fierce attacks on Khmer Rouge positions near Pailin. They were, however, unable to dislodge the Khmer Rouge.) Hun Sen later acknowledged that the Khmer Rouge had lots of money which they could use to buy political influence during the election.

The U.S. Connection

While Nguyen Co Thach was urging his government to look to Southeast Asia and Europe for trade and investment, Hanoi was feverishly courting the United States and China. In July 1990, Congressional pressures had forced the Bush Administration to withdraw recognition for the Cambodian coalition government headed by Prince Sihanouk.

Pressures continued to mount in 1991. In the beginning of the year, the administration was forced to freeze millions of dollars of non-lethal aid earmarked for the non-communist Cambodian resistance. At the second U.S.-Vietnam dialogue in mid-February, Vietnamese Justice Minister Phan Hien urged American legislators, journalists and businessmen to pressure the Bush Administration to lift the trade embargo on Vietnam and to normalize relations with Hanoi. The Democrats were not the only ones pressurizing the administration. In April, Republican Senator Richard Lugar, a senior member of the Senate foreign relations committee, argued in an article in the *Christian Science Monitor* that it was time to change U.S. policy towards Vietnam.

A steady stream of U.S. delegations — mainly Congressmen — meanwhile was heading towards Hanoi and Phnom Penh. The common argument made by these delegations was that the U.S. embargo had put American companies at a disadvantage as they could not compete with the Japanese and the Europeans who were capturing the Indochinese markets by default.

The administration countered with a strategy of its own. In April, Richard

Solomon met the Vietnamese ambassador to the UN in New York and presented the Vietnamese Government with a plan — the so-called "road map" — which detailed a step-by-step approach to normalization of U.S.-Vietnamese relations. In essence, the plan was that for every step Hanoi made to resolve the issues that were of concern to Washington, the United States would match it by lifting certain restrictions. (Indeed, following the signing of the Cambodian peace accord in October 1991, the United States lifted travel restrictions on U.S. citizens visiting Vietnam and announced that the trade embargo on Cambodia would soon be lifted.) The rationale behind the plan is that while the servicemen who are missing in action and prisoners of war (MIA-POW) issue is still Washington's top priority, the administration also wanted Hanoi to honour the letter and spirit of the Cambodian peace accord to the end, that is, until free elections are held. While calling the administration's "road map" plan "constructive", Hanoi reiterated that it had always considered the MIA-POW problem a humanitarian issue, and as such, it should not be linked to the Cambodian problem.

President Bush's special envoy on the MIA-POW issue, General John Vessey, visited Hanoi in April, and at the end of the visit announced the establishment — in June — of a temporary U.S. MIA-POW office in Hanoi. The administration later announced that it was providing Hanoi with US$1 million in humanitarian aid. The money was to be used for manufacturing artificial limbs for Vietnamese crippled during the Vietnam war. In October, General Vessey returned to Hanoi and urged the Vietnamese leadership to resolve the MIA-POW issue quickly. To underline its seriousness in implementing the "road map", in August President Bush renewed the trade embargo by a year.

By offering the "road map", the Bush Administration had denied Hanoi a quick way out of its predicament. Under pressure from various directions, Vietnam was compelled to review its "reservations" over the UN peace plan.

The Chinese Connection

While holding out hope of an early lifting of the U.S. trade embargo, Hanoi was also making overtures to Beijing for normalization of their relations, estranged since 1979. In January 1991, a Vietnamese delegation led by Vu Oanh, the party secretary in charge of economic affairs, visited Beijing to study China's economic reforms. He extended an invitation to the Chinese Government to send a team to Hanoi to study Vietnam's own economic reforms or *doi moi*. It is not known if the Chinese accepted the invitation. Oanh, who was promoted to the Politburo in June, had also proposed the setting up of a committee to discuss security issues but apparently received no reply from the Chinese.[4] Reports on the border trade — mainly barter — between the two countries meanwhile began appearing in the Vietnamese media, with one report claiming that Vo Van Kiet, who replaced Do Muoi as prime minister in June, had taken a personal interest in this area.

Hanoi's overtures were, however, rebuffed by Beijing. Presumably this was because the Vietnamese had refused to accept the November 1990 UN peace plan in full. The Chinese regarded this as breach of an understanding which the two sides had presumably reached at the secret meeting of Chinese and Vietnamese party chiefs in Chengdu in September 1990.[5]

The Sino-Vietnamese thaw resumed shortly after the seventh congress of the Communist Party of Vietnam (CPV) in June where three members who were considered anti-China hardliners — Nguyen Co Thach, Mai Chi Tho, and Nguyen Duc Tam — were dropped from the Politburo. It coincided with the first major breakthrough at the SNC meeting in Pattaya on 26–28 June. Indications that the thaw was indeed under way came in a Radio Hanoi report which said that Chinese party chief Jiang Zemin had sent a message to Do Muoi congratulating the latter on his election as Secretary-General of the CPV. A measure of the importance Beijing had attached to Hanoi's full acceptance of the UN peace plan was the fact that within a month of the signing of the Cambodian peace accord, Sino-Vietnamese relations were completely normalized.

Domestic and Battlefield Pressures

While members of the Perm Five — notably the Soviet Union, China and the United States — were applying subtle pressures on Hanoi and Phnom Penh to accept the UN peace plan, pressures were also building up on the ground, and in places that really mattered.

The resistance had responded to Prince Sihanouk's call in the beginning of the year by stepping up their military activities on the battlefield. By late February, there were reports of fierce fighting in western Cambodia, with each side accusing the other of trying to expand its area of control. The seriousness of the ground situation was reflected in reports that some Vietnamese troops had returned to Cambodia to bolster the Phnom Penh army, a fact confirmed by Richard Solomon when he appeared before Congress in April. Heng Samrin, the regime's president, later acknowledged that the resistance had launched "a remarkable offensive". The Khmer Rouge, however, contended that their intention was not to win a military victory but to force Hanoi and Phnom Penh to accept the UN peace plan.

It is not clear if the intention of both sides was to capture more territory before getting down to serious negotiations. Whatever the motive, it must have been clear to Hanoi and Phnom Penh that in the new international situation, they could not afford the political and economic costs of a protracted war requiring the re-introduction of Vietnamese troops into Cambodia. There was also considerable discontent in Vietnam over the direction the country was heading, in particular the poor state of the economy. This was reflected, among other things, in the serious disagreement among the party's central committee members over the political report that was to be considered by the seventh party congress. As a result, the congress was postponed from May to June.

Significance of the Thai *Coup*

The significance of the *coup* was not lost on Hanoi and Phnom Penh. Their initial reaction was cautious, calling it an internal Thai matter. Indeed, it was Chatichai's initiative — opening direct contact with the SOC — that broke the unity of the Association of South East Asian Nations (ASEAN) on the Cambodian conflict and strengthened Phnom Penh's bargaining position, thus delaying a political settlement.

With the military back in control, Hanoi and Phnom Penh were concerned that Thai policy on Cambodia might harden. Indeed, in one of his first press conferences after the *coup*, General Suchinda Kraprayoon, the Thai army commander, said that peace in Cambodia would not be possible without the participation of the Khmer Rouge. This was the most explicit statement from Thailand calling for the inclusion of the Khmer Rouge in any political settlement.

The Turning Point?

To increase the isolation felt by Hanoi and Phnom Penh, the three resistance leaders — Son Sann, Khieu Samphan and Prince Ranariddh — met Prince Sihanouk in Beijing on 13 March, at the same time that Richard Solomon and Soviet Deputy Foreign Minister Igor Rogachev were holding talks on Cambodia with Chinese officials in the Chinese capital. Top Khmer Rouge officials were also reported to have met at the Thai-Cambodian border to plan a large offensive targeted at the capital Phnom Penh. Amidst the war cries, the PICC co-chairmen and the UN Secretary-General issued a joint statement on 22 April appealing to the Khmer factions to observe a voluntary ceasefire, starting on 1 May until the conclusion of the next SNC meeting. The appeal was immediately welcomed by the Khmer People's National Liberation Front (KPNLF) and the United Front for an Independent, Neutral and Peaceful Cambodia (Funcinpec). On the same day, resistance radio in a commentary said that Vietnam had softened its stance and was likely to relinquish its policy of aggression towards Cambodia. It cited as reason the cut-off of Soviet aid. That same day, the Soviet ambassador to Hanoi disclosed that Vietnamese party chief Nguyen Van Linh and Prime Minister Do Muoi would be making separate visits to Moscow in May for "major talks". Hanoi and Phnom Penh welcomed the ceasefire appeal the following day. The Khmer Rouge were, however, the last to agree to the ceasefire. The acceptance came on 26 April after Khieu Samphan had met with the other resistance leaders and the interim Thai Prime Minister, Anand Panyarachun.

The day after the ceasefire appeal, Hor Nam Hong left for Moscow on a "working visit" on the invitation of his Soviet counterpart, Alexander Bessmertnykh. He also held talks with Igor Rogachev. The discussions no doubt centred on Cambodia. Hor later revealed that Moscow had agreed to extend Phnom Penh a credit line of US$21 million. Presumably this was in exchange for the SOC showing flexibility on the UN peace plan.

Not long after Hor left Moscow, Do Muoi arrived in the Soviet capital, also for a "working visit". He was accompanied by officials from the trade and finance ministries and the state planning commission, which suggested that the talks were mainly on economic matters. The Vietnamese media indeed reported that among the issues discussed by the two sides were implementation of the "new mechanism", Vietnam's relations with the individual Soviet republics, servicing of the Vietnamese debt, and supply of food to the Soviet Union. While Do Muoi was still in Moscow, party chief Nguyen Van Linh arrived and met with Soviet President Mikhail Gorbachev. Linh's visit preceded that of Chinese party leader Jiang Zemin. Presumably Linh briefed Gorbachev on the changes that would take place at the Vietnamese party's congress in June and might have asked the Soviet leader to impress on Jiang Hanoi's interest in normalizing relations with Beijing.

The visits to Moscow by Vietnamese and Phnom Penh officials might well be the critical turning point of the long-drawn out Cambodian peace process. There were suggestions that Moscow had offered Hanoi and Phnom Penh temporary aid relief in exchange for flexibility on the UN peace plan. Much bargaining was, however, still to come as negotiations began in earnest.

Start of Negotiations

Apart from occasional skirmishes, Thai and Western intelligence officials were in general agreement that the ceasefire was being observed by all the Khmer factions. Four days after the ceasefire came into effect, Hun Sen wrote to the PICC co-chairmen proposing that neutral observers be dispatched to Cambodia to observe the ceasefire. A UN team led by Ghanaian general Timothy Dibuama was indeed sent to Cambodia from 11–17 May. The team visited the various camps, including those of the Khmer Rouge.

In anticipation of the bargaining ahead, both sides began intensive public posturing and brinkmanship. Indeed, in response to Hor Nam Hong's call for the ceasefire to be extended till after the signing of the peace accord, the Khmer Rouge threatened to resume fighting if Hanoi and Phnom Penh refused to accept the UN peace plan by 5 June. A Phnom Penh official responded by calling the Khmer Rouge's ultimatum "arrogant". On his part, Hun Sen acknowledged that the reduction of Soviet aid had caused some difficulty but asserted that the situation was not hopeless. He said the Khmer Rouge had lost the chance of a military victory and the only way they could come back to power was through political means. He added that he would be making "fresh proposals" in Jakarta aimed at preventing the Khmer Rouge from returning to power.

The Jakarta Meeting, 2–4 June

The PICC co-chairmen and the UN Secretary-General's special representative, Rafeeuddin Ahmed, had apparently agreed that the only way to push the peace process forward was for Sihanouk to accede to Hun Sen's request that he (Hun Sen) be made Vice-Chairman of the SNC with Sihanouk as the chairman. They persuaded Sihanouk to accept this compromise formula.[6]

When Sihanouk and Hun Sen met on 2 June, they immediately agreed to this arrangement which also entailed increasing the number of SNC members from the existing 12 to 14. They also agreed that if Sihanouk was unable to chair the SNC meeting he could appoint any person from the resistance who would become joint Vice-Chairmen with Hun Sen, and the two Vice-Chairmen would take turns functioning as acting SNC Chairman.

While Son Sann and Prince Ranariddh accepted this formula, it was rejected by Khieu Samphan who felt that the three of them together with Hun Sen should be made joint Vice-Chairmen. With the Khmer Rouge's objection, Sihanouk announced that he would just be an "ordinary" SNC member and that he would act as a "bridge" between Phnom Penh and the Khmer Rouge. He would replace the Funcinpec representative on the SNC, Chausen Kosal, who was stepping down because of old age.

According to Hun Sen, at the Jakarta meeting the KPNLF and Funcinpec had agreed to his proposals to extend the ceasefire and to place a moratorium on foreign arms deliveries, but the Khmer Rouge did not give any commitment.[7] He claimed to have also obtained Sihanouk's agreement on these two points.

Hun Sen also claimed that Sihanouk had agreed with him that the peace process should not be "held hostage" by the Khmer Rouge. Sihanouk therefore accepted his invitation to visit Phnom Penh in November, after which he (Hun Sen) would visit the Prince in Pyongyang where he would present a scenario for ending the conflict. Away from the Khmer Rouge, he and Sihanouk would discuss and finalize what they had agreed on in Jakarta.

Prince Ranariddh, on his part, revealed that in addition to the ceasefire and moratorium on foreign arms, the Jakarta meeting also discussed three issues — Cambodian sovereignty *vis-à-vis* UNTAC, the role of UNTAC, and genocide — which were raised by Hun Sen. The PICC co-chairmen tried to reconcile the various parties on these items, but succeeded only on the genocide issue. Hun Sen apparently agreed to withdraw some words relating to genocide, leaving some which were in accordance with the UN resolutions on genocide. He also agreed to drop his proposal to set up a tribunal to try the "Pol Pot clique". Prince Ranariddh said he and Hun Sen accepted the compromise on the genocide issue proposed by the PICC co-chairmen but Son Sann's side was not clear on the issue while the Khmer Rouge did not accept it.

French Deputy Foreign Minister Alain Vivien, who co-chaired the meeting with Ali Alatas, later accused Khieu Samphan of being obstructive in Jakarta. Giving his own version of the proceedings, Samphan said that Hun Sen had proposed too many amendments, some of which were clearly aimed at changing the fundamental civilian and military tasks of UNTAC. He said the Khmer Rouge could not allow Phnom Penh and Hanoi to destroy the UN peace framework.

Commenting on the failure of the Jakarta meeting, Chinese Foreign Minister Qian Qichen, who was accompanying President Yang Shangkun on a visit to Indonesia shortly after the SNC meeting, said the Cambodians had "better things to do" than fight among themselves. This was widely interpreted as an indirect Chinese criticism of the Khmer Rouge's stance in Jakarta.

Pattaya I, 24-26 June

On 11 June, Prince Sihanouk announced that the 12-member SNC would meet in Pattaya later that month. The four Khmer parties had agreed that he chair a conclave — a private meeting among the Khmer factions — instead of letting the PICC co-chairmen preside as was done previously. The PICC co-chairmen and the UN Secretary-General were, however, asked to send observers to the meeting. On the same day, Hanoi congratulated Sihanouk for showing goodwill towards Hun Sen in Jakarta. Vietnam's ambassador to China, Dang Nghiem Hoanh, attended a reception at Prince Sihanouk's residence in Beijing to celebrate Princess Monique's birthday. The next day, Sihanouk reaffirmed his decision to visit Phnom Penh in November. These were seen as indications that Hun Sen and the Prince might indeed have established some form of understanding if not an alliance.

To what extent this worried the Khmer Rouge and was a factor behind a new expression of flexibility on their part is not known. Following a meeting with General Suchinda in Bangkok on 21 June, Khieu Samphan reportedly said that the Khmer Rouge would "soften" their demands at Pattaya. The Thai army-controlled television reported that Suchinda had told Khieu Samphan that the Khmer Rouge should be more compromising in dealing with the other factions, namely, the Phnom Penh regime. Thai Foreign Minister Asa Sarasin reportedly had also asked Hanoi to persuade Hun Sen not to raise conditions on Prince Sihanouk's appointment as SNC chairman.

On 22 June, Sihanouk met with Son Sann, Khieu Samphan and Prince Ranariddh in Bangkok and announced afterwards that the resistance leaders had given their approval to his five-point proposal to break the impasse. The Thai Foreign Ministry apparently had also sounded out Hun Sen on the proposal, while the PICC co-chairmen and Rafeeuddin Ahmed had endorsed it.

The five points were: first, the SNC to consider itself a "collegial presidency" of a sovereign and united Cambodia and appoint a secretary-general who could be Prince Sihanouk. The secretary-general would not "dominate" the SNC but serve as a "bridge" between the Khmer factions; second, after becoming operational, the SNC would occupy the Cambodian seat at the UN and at all international organizations and conferences; third, while awaiting elections, the two governments — Phnom Penh and the resistance — would function each in its own zone, with its administration, flag, "national" anthem, constitution, laws, etc., and an unlimited ceasefire would be declared on the first day of the SNC meeting in Pattaya; fourth, the headquarters of the SNC could be located in Phnom Penh, Siem Reap-Angkor Wat or Kirirom, a former mountain resort during the time of the Kingdom of Cambodia, which was uninhabited; fifth, the embassies accredited to the SNC would be in the same location as the SNC headquarters.

The next day, 23 June, after an informal meeting of the four Khmer factions at a hotel in Bangkok and a private lunch between Sihanouk and Hun Sen, the five-point proposal was released to the press. Although Sihanouk and Hun Sen expressed optimism about the outcome of the Pattaya meeting, with the former even declaring that the 13-year-old war in Cambodia was over at least on paper, there was much hard bargaining when the SNC met formally on 24 June.

At the end of the first day, the factions agreed to a permanent ceasefire and a moratorium on foreign arms supply. They also agreed that Sihanouk would chair future SNC meetings, even though Hun Sen continued to insist that he be appointed vice-chairman. The meeting also discussed the siting of the SNC headquarters, with Hun Sen arguing that it be located in Phnom Penh while the Khmer Rouge contended that for the safety of their officials it should be established in a liberated zone or at Pailin. The Khmer Rouge finally conceded the point to Hun Sen, but only after the latter had agreed to the following conditions: first, the UN would have a permanent mission attached to the SNC (this was to ensure that future talks would continue to be held under UN auspices); second, the Perm Five and participants of the PICC would establish missions in Phnom Penh; third, the factions would have their own bodyguards to protect their officials inside their own compounds. The Phnom Penh regime would provide protection outside the compound.

On UN verification of the ceasefire and cessation of foreign military aid, the Khmer Rouge proposed that a UN observer team of 500–700 personnel be sent to Cambodia to carry out the two tasks. Hun Sen counter-proposed that a Cambodian military committee, comprising Phnom

Penh and resistance representatives, be established to oversee the implementation of the agreement. He said this was to test the goodwill of the factions. No agreement was reached on this issue. After the meeting, Rafeeuddin Ahmed advised Prince Sihanouk to write to the UN Secretary-General to ask for a UN observer team to be sent to Cambodia. He said the UN could not despatch a peace-keeping force without a signed peace agreement.

While the Pattaya meeting did achieve some success, the thorny issues had yet to be resolved. These were: the relationship between the SNC and UNTAC; demobilization and disarming of the factions; and guarantee that the Khmer Rouge would not return to power. Beneath the goodwill and reconciliation, there was considerable horse-trading in Pattaya. According to one account, in exchange for Phnom Penh not questioning Sihanouk's appointment as SNC chairman and refraining from any mention of "genocide", the Khmer Rouge agreed to accept a permanent ceasefire and the establishment of the SNC headquarters in Phnom Penh.[8] But according to another account, the Phnom Penh regime had agreed not to mention "genocide" if the Khmer Rouge did not mention Vietnamese settlers and Vietnamese annexation of Cambodian territory in eastern Cambodia.

Shortly after the Pattaya meeting was adjourned, Prince Sihanouk reportedly discussed with the PICC co-chairmen and Rafeeuddin Ahmed a proposal to hold the next SNC meeting in Beijing in mid-July. The French news agency, AFP, reported that a "highly reliable source" had disclosed that Sihanouk would visit Hanoi after the meeting in Beijing. This was quickly denied by Prince Sihanouk's office.

Observers noted that compared to previous meetings, members of the Phnom Penh regime and the Khmer Rouge were extraordinarily civil to each other in Pattaya. Hun Sen was heard greeting Khieu Samphan as "my beloved excellency". The Phnom Penh leader subsequently said he would try to be more friendly to the Khmer Rouge members of the SNC and acknowledged that the Khmer Rouge could not be left out of the political efforts to end the war.

The Beijing Meeting, 16–17 July

Prince Sihanouk's proposal to hold the next SNC meeting in Beijing was apparently to pressure the Phnom Penh regime and the Khmer Rouge into "softening" their respective positions. Indeed, even before the meeting, Phnom Penh leaders began making conciliatory remarks. On his part, Hun Sen acknowledged that the Khmer Rouge had observed the ceasefire although there were small-scale violations, and that he would make "utmost efforts" during the visits to Beijing to find a common position on a solution to the Cambodian conflict. Apparently, Hun Sen had been informed by Prince Sihanouk that the Chinese Government had invited him (Hun Sen) to return to Beijing for a second visit after his trip to Pyongyang.

However, on the eve of the Beijing meeting, resistance radio reported that a Chinese foreign ministry spokesman had said that China was allowing Hun Sen to visit Beijing to attend the SNC meeting as an SNC member and at Prince Sihanouk's request. His second visit to Beijing would not be an official visit at the invitation of the Chinese Government, but was meant to facilitate his transit back to Phnom Penh, and was also agreed to at the Prince's request.

The SNC meeting was held in the Diaoyutai state guesthouse on 16 July without a fixed agenda. That everyone wanted the Beijing meeting to appear to be a success — by not discussing the controversial issues — was reflected in the fact that even before the end of the first session, Sihanouk had announced that the next SNC meeting would be held in Bangkok on 26–28 August. Also, of the eight agreements reached in Beijing the only significant one was that Prince Sihanouk was appointed SNC Chairman while Hun Sen agreed to drop his demand to be made Vice-Chairman. (Under the agreement, Sihanouk would resign all positions in the resistance and assume the role of a "neutral" chairman.) In their statement, the Perm Five stated that the appointment of Prince Sihanouk as SNC Chairman had created a "new situation" and a "new opportunity" to bring lasting peace to Cambodia, and the "now operational" SNC should accelerate efforts to overcome the "remaining difficulties".

In not challenging Sihanouk's appointment as SNC Chairman, Hun Sen was rewarded by China's recognition of his regime as a legitimate party in the Cambodian conflict. Indeed, he later told Phnom Penh radio that it was the first time the Chinese Government treated his regime as "one party among the parties", and that Beijing had promised to deal with them on an equal basis.

Shortly after he returned to Phnom Penh, Kyodo News Agency quoted Vietnamese sources in Hanoi as saying that Chea Sim, Chairman of the National Assembly, had staged a *coup* against Hun Sen. This was immediately denied by the regime, and Western sources reported that there were no signs in the capital to suggest that a *coup* had taken place. Chea Sim — considered a hardliner — was said to be unhappy that Hun Sen had made too many concessions in Beijing.

In an indication that there were indeed differences within the regime, on 6 September a Phnom Penh radio commentary reiterated the demand that a reference on genocide be made in the UN document because Pol Pot's return was "still everyone's concern". Hor Nam Hong promptly issued a public clarification, saying that it was not a reversal of the regime's agreement made at the second Pattaya meeting in August where Hun Sen had agreed not to mention genocide in the peace plan. Hor said the commentary was the radio's view, not the official view.

And after the SNC Pattaya meeting on 26–28 August — where the majority of the issues were resolved — Sihanouk warned that if the international community did not support Hun Sen, he could be ousted by hardliners. Sihanouk's warning was made in response to reports that the United States and Britain were unhappy with the "breakthrough" in the SNC talks as it deviated from the Perm Five peace plan.

Fear of a "Red Solution"

On 1 August, Uch Borit, Phnom Penh's ambassador in Hanoi, expressed concern that the United States could impede Cambodian peace efforts by insisting that the UN peace plan be followed to the letter. The United States was apparently uncomfortable with the "new direction" that the peace process had taken since June. This was a reference to the sudden "mad dash" for peace by the Cambodian factions, which was pushed along by Prince Sihanouk.

Washington — and at least one ASEAN leader — had indeed expressed concern about a possible "red solution". Presumably to allay U.S. concern, Prince Sihanouk issued a statement on 2 August — a follow-up to his earlier interview with the Voice of America — which outlined the kind of political and economic system he wanted for Cambodia. He said the majority of the Cambodian people favoured a liberal democratic and free market system, with all the freedom that is now enjoyed by the French people. Expressing keenness in wanting to be president or head of state, Sihanouk said he wanted only limited powers, and that the national assembly should be given the power and responsibility to establish and oust a government, but not the head of state who should be answerable only to the people.

The Phnom Penh regime also tried to play down the fear of a "red solution". In an interview with *Canberra Times* on 6 August, Hor Nam Hong said he did not believe China and Vietnam would try to solve the Cambodian problem outside the SNC framework because the problem must be settled among the Cambodians themselves. Phnom Penh radio also quoted Vietnamese Prime Minister Vo Van Kiet as having rejected reports of a Sino-Vietnamese deal that would deviate from the UN peace plan. The radio said that as a permanent member of the UN Security Council, there was no reason why China would want to discard the UN peace plan.

On 8–10 August, Vietnamese and Chinese deputy foreign ministers met in Beijing to discuss normalization of Sino-Vietnamese relations. Chinese officials reportedly said that while Beijing felt that Vietnam was more co-operative on the Cambodian problem, it was not fully satisfied with the level of co-operation from Hanoi. Resistance radio later reported that Hanoi had agreed at that meeting to send a "high-ranking" official (Deputy Foreign Minister Nguyen Dy Nien) to the SNC meeting in Pattaya on 26–28 August to "observe and smooth out" the meeting. And on the eve of the meeting, Son Sann disclosed that China had told Hanoi that if it wanted to normalize relations with Beijing it would have to help bring about a solution that would be in line with the UN peace plan.

The Pattaya II Meeting, 26–28 August

Not surprisingly, in his opening speech on 26 August Prince Sihanouk said the UN peace plan was the best document to help the Cambodian people restore democracy and justice to the country and urged that it be accepted in full. Before substantive issues were discussed, the meeting agreed that Sihanouk should write to the UN Secretary-General to request the despatch of 200 UN personnel to Cambodia in September to monitor the ceasefire.

Chinese Vice Foreign Minister Xu Dunxin reportedly met with Hun Sen to discuss his amendments — some 200 of them, according to one source — to the UN peace plan and said that Chinese Foreign Minister Qian Qichen's visit to Phnom Penh would depend on the "progress" of the Pattaya meeting.[9] Getting nowhere, Xu met with Nien, the Vietnamese Deputy Foreign Minister, on the first night and they agreed to a deal — in exchange for Hun Sen not raising the issue of genocide, the Khmer Rouge would not mention Vietnamese settlers in Cambodia and Vietnam's annexation of Cambodian territory.

With the presence of the Chinese and Vietnamese deputy foreign ministers to prod the negotiations, the second Pattaya meeting ended more successfully than previous meetings in Pattaya and Beijing.

On disarming, the factions agreed that 70 per cent of their forces would be dissolved immediately, with the remaining 30 per cent regrouped — and disarmed — in cantonments supervised by UNTAC. The 30 per cent would be dissolved just before the election or incorporated into the new Cambodian army under the new government. Representatives of the Perm Five, who met after the SNC meeting, accepted the compromise but urged the SNC to reflect further on the question of total demobilization.

On SNC's relationship with UNTAC, the meeting agreed that the SNC would advise UNTAC on matters pertaining to the role it was designated to perform and if there was no consensus among the SNC members Prince Sihanouk would make the final decision after taking into consideration all the views. The Perm Five's original proposal was that if there was no consensus, the UN Secretary-General's special representative would make the final decision. This was rejected by Hun Sen who felt that it would violate Cambodian sovereignty. (This agreement was modified by the SNC in New York in September. The new formulation is that if the SNC chairman was absent or did not wish to decide on a matter, the UN special representative would make the final decision.)

On genocide, Hun Sen said it was "vigorously discussed" and he and Khieu Samphan agreed that the word would not be mentioned in the peace accord. The meeting also agreed that only political parties with a minimum of 5,000 members would be eligible to contest the elections. This was a compromise figure suggested by Prince Ranariddh. The Khmer Rouge had proposed a minimum of 2,000 members while the KPNLF wanted a higher number — 10,000.

The meeting also agreed to request the UN and the international community to provide aid for the reconstruction of Cambodia, a proposal broached by Hun Sen at previous SNC meetings but rejected by the resistance.

The issue where there was no agreement was on the electoral system. Hun Sen preferred the system of direct election or first-past-the-post, whereas Son Sann, supported by the United States, was in favour of the system proposed by the Perm Five, namely, proportional representation (PR). Hun Sen claimed that Prince Sihanouk was in favour of his proposal while Khieu Samphan and Prince Ranariddh did not express preference for either system.

Hun Sen's arguments were that Cambodia had no experience of the PR system, whereas the direct system had been in use in Cambodia since 1947. Furthermore, the Cambodian people wanted their own local representatives in Parliament whereas the PR system called for voting for parties rather than individuals. He said some people may like a particular party but not the candidates proposed by the party. Son Sann, on the other hand, argued that in the current situation where the Phnom Penh regime and the resistance controlled different parts of Cambodia it was not possible to establish clear electoral constituencies. The PR system would enable political parties to select competent persons to represent them in Parliament. It would also prevent individual candidates from being threatened during the election.

The issue was resolved at the SNC meeting in New York on 19 September when all the parties accepted Rafeeuddin Ahmed's proposal that the PR system be adopted at the provincial level. At that meeting, the SNC also agreed that the national assembly would have 120 seats, the new constitution would be adopted by a two-thirds majority, and elections should be held not later than six months from the first day of electoral registration.

The "Red Solution" Re-examined

Was a "red solution", namely, an understanding between China and Vietnam to maintain a communist regime in Phnom Penh, seriously considered? Probably not, although Beijing and Hanoi did work behind the scenes — occasionally in tandem — to persuade their respective clients to accept the UN peace plan. There was no secret Sino-Vietnamese deal to get Phnom Penh to agree to share power with the Khmer Rouge and do away with UN-supervised free elections. Indeed, having helped draft the UN peace plan, China wanted the full implementation of the plan.

Like China, the other Perm Five members were prepared to employ pressure — including the Soviet Union which had put political pressure on Phnom Penh and Hanoi — to force the Khmer parties to comply with the UN peace plan. On this, there is some evidence to suggest that there had been some co-ordination among the Perm Five.

The Next Battle: Winning Hearts and Minds

With the signing of the peace accord, the fight has moved from the battlefield to the ballot box. Even before the accord was signed, the Phnom Penh regime had begun gearing itself for the elections. It had embarked on a two-prong approach. One was to change the image of the party and the other was to identify itself with the still popular Prince Sihanouk. At the sixth party congress on 17 October — a week before the signing of the peace accord — the party's name was changed from the People's Revolutionary Party of Kampuchea to the Pracheachon (People's) Party. It also adopted a liberal democratic platform, making Cambodia the first government in Indochina to allow opposition parties. The party — which had 30,000 members — pledged that it would respect human rights, adopt a free market system, recognize private landownership and allow independent trade unions and other organizations. On foreign policy, Cambodia would be "permanently neutral", would respect the five principles of peaceful coexistence, be friendly to all countries and support ASEAN's zone of peace, freedom and neutrality. A draft political report — prepared by Chea Sim — which was submitted to the congress said these measures were necessary for the party's own "self-preservation".

In late August, the regime introduced new measures aimed at refurbishing its image such as removing pictures and statues of Karl Marx, Lenin, Ho Chi Minh and two local heroes, Son Ngoc Minh and Tu Samut, from government buildings and public places. The words communism, Marxism-Leninism and socialism were deleted from party documents, and even the colour red — which is commonly associated with communism — was done away with.

Shortly before the Cambodian peace accord was signed, the regime released some of the 2,000 political prisoners it had been holding. It also assured the people in the capital that they would not be evicted from the houses they were occupying. In other words, the properties would not be returned to the original owners, many of whom had abandoned them and left the cities or fled the country in 1975.

In his speech at the party congress, Hun Sen proposed that the party endorse Prince

Sihanouk as its candidate for president in place of Heng Samrin because it was necessary to have a Cambodian personality capable of playing the role of "moderator". Five days after his return to Phnom Penh, the regime reinstated Prince Sihanouk as head of state, after declaring the *coup* that had ousted him from power on 18 March 1970 was illegal. Hun Sen had flown to Beijing to accompany Prince Sihanouk on his historic flight back to Cambodia on 14 November. Hun Sen later asked the Prince to adopt him as his "son", while Chea Sim asked to be Sihanouk's "brother". Phnom Penh leaders also accompanied the Prince on his tour of the country.

On 16 November, Prince Sihanouk disclosed that Hun Sen and Prince Ranariddh had agreed to form a political alliance — apparently suggested by Hun Sen — and that Prince Ranariddh and some members of the royal family would be given Cabinet or sub-Cabinet positions. The two "sons" made public their alliance on 20 November, with Prince Ranariddh giving an assurance that the move was not meant to exclude the other factions. He also revealed that the two sides had signed a military accord whereby troops from both sides could have free travel in each other's zones. While the Khmer Rouge said they were not opposed to the alliance, Son Sann — despite Sihanouk's denial that he was behind the alliance — appealed to the Prince to maintain his neutrality. The Thai military also criticized the alliance.

Indeed, since his return Prince Sihanouk had been heaping praises on Hun Sen — calling him a "remarkable leader" — while criticizing the Khmer Rouge. On 9 December, Prince Ranariddh disclosed that the Chinese had scuttled the "alliance" plan because of the mob attack on Khieu Samphan on his return to Phnom Penh on 27 November. Because of the incident, Sihanouk called off his visits to Hanoi on 20–23 December and to Laos on 24–25 December. The visit of the Chinese Foreign Minister to Cambodia was also postponed. The emergency SNC meeting in Pattaya on 3 December agreed that to prevent a recurrence of the 27 November incident, Khmer Rouge representatives on the SNC would be housed in the same building to be occupied by UNTAC. In their own statement, the Perm Five said they did not want the Khmer factions to deviate from the UN peace plan and expressed regret over the attack on Khieu Samphan. They maintained that the permanent functioning of the SNC in Phnom Penh was vital for the success of the peace process.

While Phnom Penh leaders were ingratiating themselves with Prince Sihanouk, the Khmer Rouge were consolidating their own position in the countryside. They had reportedly been telling the peasants that the SNC had replaced the Phnom Penh regime as the Cambodian Government and that the SNC would be established at village and provincial levels. Shortly after the signing of the peace accord, the Khmer Rouge reportedly tried to force the estimated 340,000 Cambodian refugees and displaced Khmers at the Thai border — especially those in camps controlled by them — to move into "liberated zones" inside Cambodia. The Khmer Rouge are said to have started preparing the ground for the "next battle" — the election — even before there was any movement in the peace process. With their nationalist credentials and reputation for tight discipline and incorruptibility, some observers believed that the Khmer Rouge could win a respectable percentage of the popular votes.

The least prepared and determined of the Khmer factions seemed to be the non-communist groups led by Son Sann and Prince Ranariddh, despite being advised by Western governments to start their campaign of winning the hearts and minds of the Cambodian people early. None the less, Son Sann took the first step in putting his own house in order by settling his differences with General Sak Sutsakhan, the Commander-in-Chief of the KPNLF forces who broke away in 1985, after the Pattaya meeting in June. Prince Ranariddh was reported to be considering some changes to Funcinpec, including the party's name, which he hoped could draw on the popularity of his father, Prince Norodom Sihanouk.

Conclusion

As the new year began, peace in Cambodia is delicately poised. The positive factor is that the major powers that were involved in the conflict are fully committed to the UN peace plan. The series of violent events that took place in Phnom Penh following the signing of the peace accord has shown that the Khmers themselves are their own worst enemy. The deployment of UNTAC in Cambodia will only prevent an early unravelling of the accord. Ultimately whether it is to be lasting peace or a decent interval will depend on the Khmer factions themselves. The record of faithful implementation of peace treaties involving Indochinese countries is unfortunately rather dismal. There is still hope yet that the present Cambodian peace accord will not go the same way as previous Indochinese peace treaties. After all, this one was concluded in the new spirit of the post-Cold War era.

Notes

1. AFP, 4 February 1991.
2. AFP, 24 March 1991.
3. AFP, 12 March 1991.
4. *The Nation*, 5 July 1991.
5. According to research notes taken in Hanoi by a visiting Western scholar in November 1991 after discussions with knowledgeable Western sources as well as Vietnamese officials, and made available to the author, at the Chengdu meeting the Chinese and Vietnamese party leaders reached an agreement on Cambodia — presumably on Hanoi's acceptance of the UN peace plan — but Vietnam could not deliver the Phnom Penh regime and instead received a strong negative reaction from Heng Samrin and Hun Sen when it applied pressure.
6. Voice of the Khmer Radio, 15 June 1991, cited in Foreign Broadcast Information Service (*FBIS*), Daily Report, East Asia, 17 June 1991, p. 43.
7. AFP, 7 June 1991.
8. *The Nation*, 2 July 1991.
9. Voice of the Khmer Radio, 30 August 1991, cited in *FBIS* Daily Report, East Asia, 30 August 1991, p. 46.

HUN SEN'S PRE-EMPTIVE COUP
Causes and Consequences

Sorpong Peou

On 5–6 July 1997, troops loyal to Second Prime Minister Hun Sen (of the Cambodian People's Party, or CPP) and those of First Prime Minister Norodom Ranariddh (leader of the royalist party known as FUNCINPEC, or the National United Front for an Independent, Neutral, Peaceful, and Co-operative Cambodia) engaged in a fierce street battle in Phnom Penh. The fighting stunned the Cambodian people and the world. Within two days, the CPP force defeated its enemy, and then pushed the remnants against the northern Thai-Cambodian border into a tiny strategic area called O Smach. At year's end, Hun Sen still held high the trophy of victory.

This article seeks to explore the events of July 1997. At issue is whether or not what took place constitutes a coup; and, if it is a coup, what kind? I argue that the overthrow of Ranariddh was a coup, not a social revolution or *putsch*. Unlike coups in many other countries, however, it was not caused by factors such as ethnic or ideological antagonisms, socio-political turmoil, or military dominance. I take a structural approach, arguing that Hun Sen's actions must be explained in terms of his struggle for hegemonic preservation, as his party and adversaries braced themselves for the next election scheduled for 1998. (In this study, the term "hegemon" means "leader", and struggle for hegemony simply means struggle for political leadership.) Although the Second Prime Minister has now achieved political dominance, preventing bipolarity from emerging, he has also recreated Cambodia's old power structure, prone to coups, violence, and war.

Reprinted from Derek da Cunha and John Funston, eds., *Southeast Asian Affairs 1998* (Singapore: Institute of Southeast Asian Studies, 1998), pp. 86–102. At the time of original publication, Sorpong Peou was Fellow at the Institute of Southeast Asian Studies, Singapore.

Prelude to a Pre-Emptive Coup

In the debate over whether Hun Sen's actions were or were not a coup, those who supported or sympathized with the Second Prime Minister viewed them as preventing Prince Ranariddh from staging a coup against the government. Those who put the blame on Hun Sen considered his actions a coup. It may be worth describing politico-military developments leading to the July events and then examining the two opposing perspectives more closely.

In May 1993, elections were organized by the United Nations Transitional Authority in Cambodia (UNTAC), which intervened in the country following the Paris Agreement in October 1991. This resulted in a coalition among four elected parties: FUNCINPEC; the CPP; the Khmer People's National Liberation Front (KPNLF) turned Buddhist Liberal Democratic Party (BLDP); and Molinaka, a Sihanouk-aligned group that fought against the State of Cambodia (as the CPP was previously known) in the 1980s, but did not participate in the signing of the Paris Agreement. FUNCINPEC and the CPP emerged as the dominant parties, receiving respectively fifty-eight and fifty-one seats in a 120-member Constituent Assembly, which was transformed into the National Assembly in September 1993. Prince Ranariddh became First Prime Minister, and CPP leader Hun Sen Second Prime Minister.

The coalition was a strange one from the outset. All factions retained their own military forces, and each controlled discrete sections of the bureaucracy. Relations between the the CPP and FUNCINPEC were difficult, and soon became much worse. Tensions between the two prime ministers emerged publicly when Ranariddh held his party's twiced-delayed Congress on 21–22 March 1996. As FUNCINPEC President, Ranariddh took a tough line *vis-à-vis* the CPP, threatening to leave the coalition if FUNCINPEC were not given greater powers at the local level. He was quoted as saying the following: "Being First puppet prime minister, puppet vice-prime minister, puppet ministers, puppet governors and deputy governors and soon-to-be puppet chiefs of districts ... being a puppet is not so good."[1] He preferred to lead an opposition party against the CPP in the National Assembly.

The CPP reacted strongly to Ranariddh's challenge. On 26 March it issued a statement condemning the FUNCINPEC threat to abandon the coalition, claiming that it sapped the spirit of national reconciliation. Although the leaders were seen together for the first time since March at the inauguration of a renovated temple in Phnom Penh on 1 June, Hun Sen still came hard on FUNCINPEC, blaming the latter for the armed forces' failure to capture a Khmer Rouge stronghold in Pailin in late April and criticizing FUNCINPEC Minister of Education Tol Loah for having failed to resolve the shortage of teachers. In June, Hun Sen attacked the FUNCINPEC Minister of Public Works, Ieng Kieth, calling the latter the "worst Minister of Public Works in the last 17 years".[2]

The two prime ministers had no more joint meetings until August, after a Khmer Rouge faction led by Ieng Sary (formerly known as Brother number two in the Khmer Rouge leadership) broke away from the so-called hardliners led by Pol Pot (Brother number one). It was the Khmer Rouge breakaway announced by Hun Sen on 8 August that brought the two dominant parties back together again. On 23 August, they issued a joint statement seeking King

Sihanouk's royal pardon for Ieng Sary. Despite their joint effort to get amnesty for Ieng Sary from the King, the two prime ministers soon began to take unilateral action to win Khmer Rouge defectors over to their own side. The tension between them worsened when their factional troops fought each other in Battambang province. FUNCINPEC Deputy Governor Serey Kosal, who had quarrelled with the CPP Governor Ung Samy, threatened to cut off the province from Phnom Penh. A top CPP leader, Heng Samrin, said on 18 November that the two coalition partners "cannot be allies".[3]

Tensions between the two prime ministers continued to deteriorate in the first half of 1997. Early in the year Ranariddh moved to build a new political front known as the National United Front (NUF), comprising FUNCINPEC, the BLDP, the Khmer Nation Party (KNP) led by the former Finance Minister and senior FUNCINPEC leader Sam Rainsy, and the small Khmer Neutral Party. Amongst its declared policies was the objective of having only one prime minister after the next elections.[4] Hun Sen immediately responded to the NUF by taking steps to build his own political alliance. In February, he signed agreements with the Liberal Democratic Party and a BLDP faction led by Information Minister Ieng Mouley (who had broken away from Son Sann in 1996).

The two prime ministers' political animosities intensified when a number of royalist members of parliament challenged Ranariddh's leadership in mid-April. Hun Sen was quick to extend his support for the renegades, thus upsetting the Prince. The National Assembly did not reconvene as the members of parliament refused to meet. Desperate, Ranariddh agreed to nominal Khmer Rouge leader Khieu Samphan's plan to join the NUF when the latter declared that he wanted to form a new party called the Khmer Solidarity Party, which would break away from the notorious Pol Pot. In late May, troops loyal to Hun Sen seized an arms shipment intended for Ranariddh's use to build up his bodyguard unit. The Prince's top military man Nhek Bun Chhay (Deputy Chief of General Staff of the Armed Forces) apparently continued negotiations with the Khmer Rouge remnants, which may have contributed to the breakup of the Khmer Rouge leadership (as evident in Pol Pot ordering his "defence minister", Son Sen, and his family members executed). On 17 June the Khmer Rouge radio denounced Pol Pot. In Phnom Penh, on the evening of that day, fighting between the bodyguards of Ranariddh and Hun Sen resulted in deaths of two royalist soldiers and one of Hun Sen's.

After the fighting in July, Hun Sen also made no attempt to turn the country back to the past by abolishing the parliamentary system and taking over the position of First Prime Minister from the FUNCINPEC. He instead encouraged the royalist remnants to choose a new leader to replace the deposed Prince as First Prime Minister. Royalist Foreign Minister Ung Huot was then "elected". Hun Sen also recognized, at least in principle and on paper, that FUNCINPEC was still his major coalition partner and made no move to turn Cambodia back into a socialist state, as his People's Republic of Kampuchea (PRK) regime did in the 1980s.

The "Ranariddh Coup" Thesis

The CPP insisted that Hun Sen's action could not be considered a coup. If it were a coup, it was Ranariddh's. The official "Ranariddh Coup" version can be found in official documents issued by the post-coup leadership in Phnom Penh. In their joint letter to Ambassador Thomas Hammarberg (Special Representative of the U.N. Secretary-General on Human Rights in Cambodia), dated 18 November 1997, new First Prime Minister Ung Huot and Second Prime Minister Hun Sen objected to Hammarberg's "mischaracterization" of the 5–6 July events as a *coup d'état*. The letter stated: "You continue to refer to the events in a way that clearly indicates a bias toward the position of the former first Prime Minister and against that of the duly constituted Government in Phnom Penh." It added: "The facts demonstrate that the Royal Government saved the country from a coup; it did not lead one."[5]

Both Ung Huot and Hun Sen reminded Hammarberg of the two major public documents issued by the Ministry of Foreign Affairs and International Co-operation: *White Paper Background on the July 1997 Crisis: Prince Ranariddh's Strategy of Provocation* (9 July 1997), and *Crisis in July Report on the Armed Insurrection: Its Origins, History, and Aftermath* (22 September 1997). The documents provide detailed accounts from Hun Sen's perspective, but fall short of characterizing the overthrow of Prince Ranariddh as a coup. The *White Paper* argues that it was Ranariddh who was at fault because of his "reckless strategy of provocation, which has only served to destabilize Cambodia".[6] It provided a brief background to FUNCINPEC's failure to build itself as a political party, while claiming that the CPP "was sure to win the next election" because "it was active in every province of the country". Consequently, "Prince Ranariddh ... knew that something drastic had to be done in order to bolster flagging fortunes" and since early 1996 his senior advisers "followed a strategy of confrontation and provocation". According to the *White Paper*, the strategy of provocation emerged at the royalist party congress in March 1996, when Ranariddh "openly broke with the CPP" by attacking the coalition government. Ranariddh's claim that the CPP refused to share power with FUNCINPEC is dimissed as a "phony issue".

Moreover, the *White Paper* characterized Ranariddh's attempts to rebuild his power base as part of his strategy to undermine the CPP. His new "political alliance" (the NUF); his "military build-up" policy, aimed at including Khmer Rouge soldiers in the royalist army; his "illegal importation of weapons" in May; his army's "use of violence and intimidation"; and his attempt to destabilize the government by "embracing the Khmer Rouge hardliners" — these were all part of Ranariddh's provocative strategy. Secret and unilateral negotiations with the "remnant Khmer Rouge hardliners" are described as "the most dangerous tactic of all", an "action tantamount to announcing that the coalition government was being terminated. The military build-up and the alliance with the Khmer Rouge was virtually a declaration of war".[7]

The *Crisis in July* provided more evidence to substantiate the argument that Ranariddh was the one who attempted a coup. Ranariddh acted, it argued, when Hun Sen and his family were still in Vietnam. Hun Sen had informed the government that "he would be on vacation from 1 July 1997 until 7 July 1997". Ranariddh, however, changed his plan to visit France, leaving Phnom Penh on 4 July instead of waiting until 9 July as previously scheduled. While Ranariddh was aware of the pending coup one day before his departure, Hun Sen was still unaware of what was going on in the country until after the crisis had already erupted on 5 July. Thus, the paper stated, "if it had been Hun Sen's intention to stage the coup, he hardly would have been on vacation abroad". Ranariddh had started the fight while he was inside the country and Hun Sen outside.[8] Hun Sen had not returned to Phnom Penh until mid-morning of 5 July. Upon his arrival, he appealed for calm. It was not until 1.30 a.m. on 6 July that

> it was decided that a general "mopping up" operation should be carried out that day, starting at 5.30 a.m. The targets included the Tang Krasaing Barracks, Pochentong area and the houses of General Nhiek Bun Chhay and General Chao Sambath.[9]

What Hun Sen had brought about was not a coup, but a "mopping-up operation" aimed at preventing Ranariddh's coup and restoring "law and order" in the country.

Hun Sen's Pre-Emptive Coup

There is no logical and empirical foundation for the "Ranariddh Coup" thesis. The fact that Hun Sen ordered the "mopping-up operation" to deal with the problem of anarchy, as the official documents claimed, proves that what he had brought about was indeed a coup. The fact that he had stayed outside the country before the crisis occurred is irrelevant. Like many coup leaders before him, Hun Sen justified his actions by claiming he would stabilize the political system through a "mopping-up operation".

It may be helpful to discuss what a coup is and what it is not. Often the term is confused with a *putsch* or social revolution. A *putsch* may be defined as an action directed at overthrowing a political leader by a small group of leaders from outside the existing power establishment, but with some degree of mass following. "Revolution" generally means a deliberate, intentional, and potentially violent overthrow of a ruling class by a social group which lead the mobilized masses against the existing political system with the aim of drastically altering the distribution of power within society as well as making major changes in the entire social structure. Political scientists define a coup as a "sudden and violent overthrow of a government, almost invariably by the military or with the help of the military".[10] Power is seized by a group within the system, who make no attempt to change society as a whole, but are only interested in removing political leaders from power.

It should be recalled that Prince Ranariddh was the legitimate leader of FUNCINPEC, which garnered the most seats in the Constituent Assembly and was internationally as well as domestically recognized as the winner of the May 1993 elections. In any mature liberal democracy, Hun Sen would never have been appointed as prime minister at all. At best he would have been deputy prime minister, or receive a ministerial portfolio. Thus, the claim that Hun Sen's action was to prevent Ranariddh's imminent coup is illogical, since the Prince as First Prime Minister could not overthrow himself as leader of the government.

It is also unclear as to who provoked whom. The *Crisis in July* sheds light on some of the CPP's own provocative measures. It describes how two royalist generals (Nhek Bun Chhay, Deputy Chief of General Staff of the Cambodian Armed Forces, and Chao Sambath) refused to co-operate with the CPP's top general Keo Kim Yan (Chief of the General Staff of the Cambodian Armed Forces). Keo Kim Yan asked Nhek Bun Chhay to close down a

FUNCINPEC military post at Wat Phniet. This was hardly a reasonable request, and the latter refused to obey. Then, according to the paper,

> General Keo Kim Yan ordered that Wat Phniet be surrounded, and at 6:30 [on 5 July] the RCAF [Royal Cambodian Armed Forces] entered the camp and met no resistance. The RCAF forces began disarming the illegal soldiers. They arrested 154 illegal troops and seized 236 firearms and two armoured personnel carriers.[11]

The paper also confirmed that before the fighting broke out at Chao Sambath's residence, CPP First Deputy Governor of Phnom Penh Chea Sophara (one of Hun Sen's close allies) called on the Military Police (MP) to negotiate "a surrender of illegal weapons" with the royalist general. This led to the MP approaching Chao Sambath's residence at about 3.00 p.m. on 5 July. The paper does not tell how many MP officers were there, but only describes how they were fired on by Chao Sambath's troops. If this violent incident can be juxtaposed with the one at What Phniet early that morning, Chao Sambath and his troops may have had reason to question the MP's political motives and to start reacting violently to the latter's move. This again raises the question of who provoked whom and who had the right to define what was legal or illegal; after all, the royalist troops still belonged to the First Prime Minister, not to any illegitimate faction.

While the CPP may have had legitimate concerns for its own security, it is clear that Hun Sen was not innocent either. The fact that Ranariddh launched the NUF and then negotiated with the Khmer Rouge in Anlong Veng can be explained by the fact that he had grown vulnerable to Hun Sen. In March 1997, a top royalist leader said a large number of FUNCINPEC members of parliament were afraid to sleep at home and chose to stay at the party headquarters at night. Royalists felt vulnerable to the CPP's growing intimidation. As elections scheduled for 1998 approached, FUNCINPEC leaders recalled their bitter experiences with the CPP in the last elections: until May 1993, around 450 royalist party members in forty-six places died at the hands of CPP loyalists.[12] The CPP's violence against opposition party members is confirmed in the works of former UNTAC officials. Judy Ledgerwood wrote: "The CPP's efforts to win the elections included several tactics that involved the use of coercive state power."[13] She also wrote:

> The violence against FUNCINPEC and other legitimate opposition parties was accompanied, whipped up, justified, explained, and covered up by a highly orchestrated propaganda campaign carried out in CPP/SOC media.[14]

David Ashley also confirmed that "[from] November 1992 to January 1993 there were repeated attacks against opposition party offices (primarily those of FUNCINPEC) ... in virtually every district of Battambang".[15]

Further evidence suggests that the royalist military build-up and the attempt to strike a peace deal with the Khmer Rouge was in all probability defensive or balancing in nature. According to a document alleged to have belonged to General Nhek Bun Chhay and included in one of the two official documents discussed earlier, the CPP provoked FUNCINPEC.[16] FUNCINPEC's fear was further reinforced by the royalist party's internal crisis in mid-April, when a number of its parliamentarians rebelled against the political leadership of Prince Ranariddh and Hun Sen was quick to lend his helping hand to the renegades. This new development was seen by Ranariddh as the Second Prime Minister's unwanted interference in his party's "internal affairs". A Western diplomat also believed that the royalist army's move on 5 July to take over Pochentong international airport was only aimed at capturing half of Phnom Penh and forcing Hun Sen to negotiate with FUNCINPEC.[17]

Hun Sen's decision to launch a "mopping-up operation" was not inconsistent with what he had wanted to do long before the crisis. Apparently, Hun Sen had seriously contemplated a coup around June 1997. According to a well-placed CPP source, Hun Sen had asked CPP Minister of Interior Sar Kheng if the latter would go along with his plan to remove Ranariddh from power by force. Sar Kheng did not support the idea and refused to get involved.[18] Since 1 July, a few days before the fighting on 5–6 July broke out, CPP troops began to round up opposition party members in eastern provinces and shot anyone found resisting.[19] This evidence confirms a U.N. report that summary executions started on 2 July — three days before the coup. According to a U.N. report, "[most] of the 41–60 instances ... occurred between 2 [and] 6 July 1997 or in the following two weeks".[20] This again suggests that the royalists only reacted to the CPP's onslaught before the 5–6 July coup.[21] The U.N. report presents concrete evidence of summary executions, torture, and missing persons after 2–7 July 1997, confirms the incineration of a large number of corpses. Those hastily cremated were not even part of the 41–60 cases of execution in custody.

Hun Sen's swift, decisive seizure of power from Prince Ranariddh at a time when the latter (who had been democratically elected) was no longer in office, therefore, does not theoretically satisfy that action as "coup prevention". It was Hun Sen's pre-emptive coup: he did not act against Ranariddh because the latter had attempted a coup against him, but because the Prince fought back to keep himself in power.

How is all this to be explained? This article does not place emphasis on the role of ideology as the main cause of the July coup. It would also be too simplistic for anyone to make the case that Hun Sen was ruthless simply because he was a "communist dictator". General Lon Nol, who ousted Prince Sihanouk in 1970, was anti-communist, but was no less a dictator. Nor do Hun Sen's actions justify anyone who may be tempted to argue that he was a democrat at heart. Even defenders of communist regimes in Indochina like Michael Vickery recognizes Hun Sen's violent behaviour: "[whatever] Hun Sen's personal qualities ... at worst he is no more murderous than his enemies".[22] Neither of the ideological arguments, therefore, explains his pre-emptive violence. The explanation lies in Cambodia's fragile hegemonic power structure.

Factionalized Armies and the Imbalance of Military Power

The factionalization of the armed forces is a variable that can help explain the coup, though military forces were not leading actors in the July events. Military leaders did not act independently. The CPP's military leaders helped Hun Sen drive Prince Ranariddh out of power, but did not aim at grabbing power for themselves. Military leaders remained loyal to their faction heads.

Before the May 1993 elections, the four major factional armies — FUNCINPEC, the CPP, the Khmer Rouge and the BLDP — were unequal in strength. The non-CPP factions had formed the Coalition Government of Democratic Kampuchea (CGDK) in the early 1980s. Although the exact figures may never be known, the CPP was said to have 131,000 troops, compared with 27,000 for the Khmer Rouge, 27,800 for the BLDP, and 17,500 for FUNCINPEC. Together, the combined resistance force had only about 72,300 men. In terms of police, the CPP numbered around 47,000, compared with 9,000 Khmer Rouge, 400 KPNLF, and 150 FUNCINPEC officers.[23] The CPP thus far outnumbered the resistance groups both individually and collectively. However, while the resistance coalition was not in a position to topple the CPP, neither did it face imminent extinction. What these figures also foreshadowed was that the CPP would continue to enjoy military preponderance after the elections.

Although it may not have been intended to enhance the CPP's dominant status, the Paris Agreement signed in October 1991 widened the imbalance of military power between the resistance forces and the CPP. This was brought about by the CGDK's disintegration into three political parties competing for seats in the Constituent Assembly. UNTAC failed to create a truly neutral political environment, giving further advantages to the CPP. Two major UNTAC failures were its inability to disarm each of the factional armies by 70 per cent, as agreed to by the four Cambodian signatories in Paris, and its ineffective control over Cambodian civil administration. Violations of the ceasefire, particularly by the Khmer Rouge, and UNTAC's inability to get the peace process back on track, resulted in the U.N. decision to allow the non–Khmer Rouge factions to keep their own remaining troops for self-defence. In terms of civil administration, "[what] UNTAC supposedly controlled, it did not" and the CPP "simply administered around UNTAC". In subsequent dealings with the CPP after the Khmer Rouge's defection from the peace plan, UNTAC became "too much" dependent on the CPP's co-operation, "which ruled 80 percent of the country".[24]

After the elections, the CPP continued to enjoy military advantages. Reintegration of the factional armed forces by four parties (FUNCINPEC, CPP, BLDP, and Moulinaka) that had competed in the 1993 elections was attempted after they agreed to form a coalition government. On 2 July 1993, the Co-Commander-in-Chief of the National Armed Forces was appointed, followed by the creation of the Ministry of Defence and the General Staff of the National Armed Forces of Cambodia, and the General Staff Headquarters of the National Armed Forces on 14 July, and by the appointment of two co-defence ministers from the CPP and FUNCINPEC on 24 September. The government also adopted a policy of reforming the armed forces. In reality, these integration and reform initiatives failed as factional troops later clashed in provinces, particularly in Battambang. By late 1996, top military officers belonging to the CPP and FUNCINPEC engaged in verbal attacks. In late December, they clashed during press conferences, accusing each other of assassination plots as both tried to woo Khmer Rouge defectors into joining their own force. Armed clashes spilled into 1997. By April, as the situation worsened, Hun Sen threatened publicly to assassinate three royalist leaders. Nhek Bun Chhay was a target. (The other two were apparently General Ho Sok, executed in custody during the coup, and General Serey Kosal, former

Deputy Governor of Battambang). In short, then, failure in military reintegration efforts resulted in the continued factionalization of the armed forces and the military preponderance enjoyed by the CPP.

Hun Sen versus Ranariddh, and Their Struggle for Hegemony

Factionalized armies and the growing imbalance of military power alone might not have led to the coup. But as top dog, the Second Prime Minister sought further to solidify his control over the government and the National Assembly, apparently in the hope that Prince Ranariddh would be unable to challenge him in the next elections. Growing tensions between the royalist and the CPP armies resulted from growing hostilities between Hun Sen and Ranariddh. Hun Sen was not wrong when he put the blame on his rival co-premier for launching the NUF and for dealing with the Khmer Rouge, who had agreed to join the Front. But the Second Prime Minister forgot or chose to ignore the fact that his bid for political hegemony forced the Prince to adopt these desperate measures. Although FUNCINPEC emerged the winner in the 1993 elections, the CPP refused to accept anything less than an even distribution of political power. In Cambodia's seventeen provinces the number of royalist and CPP governors and deputies was equal, each with thirty-six. Immediately after the elections, the twenty-seven cabinet ministries were made up of thirty-four royalist co-ministers, ministers, and vice-ministers, and thirty-three from the CPP, with Prince Ranariddh and Hun Sen being co–prime ministers.

The balance of political power between the two dominant parties later tilted in favour of the CPP. FUNCINPEC became internally divided and allowed the CPP to take advantage of the divisions. The royalist party was weakened after its Minister of Finance, Sam Rainsy, was expelled from the Cabinet in 1994 and from the National Assembly in 1995, and after Prince Norodom Sirivudh (King Sihanouk's half-brother and Ranariddh's uncle) resigned from his post as minister of foreign affairs. While Sirivudh was replaced by another royalist, Ung Hout, Sam Rainsy was replaced by a CPP member, Keat Chhon. FUNCINPEC was further debilitated by the arrest of Prince Sirivudh, for allegedly plotting to assassinate Hun Sen in late 1995. He was then expelled from the country and went to live in France. Hun Sen even threatened to shoot down the plane that would carry Sirivudh when the latter announced that he would return to Cambodia in late 1996.

Hun Sen also sought to weaken the NUF. On 30 March 1997 a vicious grenade attack was unleashed on a peaceful demonstration led by a major NUF alliance member, the Khmer Nation Party (KNP) headed by Sam Rainsy. Hun Sen's bodyguards were implicated. According to a U.N. report, the KNP had received written authorization for the demonstration from the Ministry of Interior on the morning of 29 March. Copies of the authorization letter were also sent to the Municipal Police, the Royal Gendarmerie, the District Police, and the Office of the Protection Police. While no protection was given to the demonstrators,

> there were heavily armed soldiers in battle-dress positioned since early that morning [30 March] at about two hundred metres from where the demonstrators were to assemble.

The report adds that

> [these] soldiers, who were armed with AK-47s and B-40 rocket launchers, belonged to the Second Prime Minister's personal bodyguard unit, as he himself later confirmed

and that "this was the first time ever that these soldiers were dispatched to a demonstration". Ironically, these soldiers provided no protection to the demonstrators after the grenade attack. Instead of coming to the victims' rescue, they "took battle position and beat injured demonstrators who were fleeing towards them". According to eyewitnesses, the soldiers "made no attempt to arrest any of those who were seen throwing the grenades" but "protected the escape of two perpetrators".[25]

Another blow to Ranariddh occurred in mid-April 1997, when a number of royalist party members rebelled against his party presidency and when Hun Sen lent support to these royalist revisionists, who were unhappy with the power status quo within the party. While Hun Sen had conspired with Ranariddh to expel Sam Rainsy and Sirivudh, respectively, from the National Assembly and from Cambodia, Hun Sen refused to let Ranariddh expel royalist party members who challenged his party leadership. This shows clearly that Hun Sen was mainly interested in weakening FUNCINPEC internally — and he succeeded in doing so. His actions had nothing to do with legality. While he publicly threatened to assassinate three top royalist leaders in April 1997, FUNCINPEC's Sirivudh was arrested in late 1995 and finally exiled to France simply because a Cambodian journalist reported that the Prince was talking (or joking) about killing Hun Sen.

Renewed Challenges and Rational Expectations

Still, even the overall imbalance of politico-military power between Hun Sen and Ranariddh does not by itself explain the coup. One has to look beyond power as the only explanatory variable and examine the timing of the coup. If power were the only relevant factor, a coup could have been executed earlier because Hun Sen had already achieved politico-military preponderance well before July 1997. Late May and June have to be seen as a turning point and early July as a breaking point.

Beginning in mid-May and continuing throughout the month of June, peace negotiations between royalist military officials and the Khmer Rouge remnants in Anlong Veng (the only Khmer Rouge stronghold left) were under way. By 1 June, progress had been made; Khmer Rouge leader Khieu Samphan and Prince Ranariddh met at a site near the Thai border and agreed to meet again on 10 June. At this time, however, the Khmer Rouge began to disintegrate as Pol Pot ordered his own "defence minister", Son Sen, and his family slaughtered. Arriving in Anlong Veng on 12 June, Nhek Bun Chhay found the Khmer Rouge at war with itself, an event that led to the arrest of Pol Pot on 19 June. The royalist–Khmer Rouge negotiations continued after that. But it was not until 22 June that the Khmer Rouge leadership agreed to stop calling itself a "provisional government" and join Ranariddh's NUF.[26]

Early July was the decisive moment. According to Thayer, by 3 July, "both sides had hammered out all details and signed the final agreements". He goes on to say:

> [Negotiators] flew to Phnom Penh to tell [Ranariddh] that everything was done. Ranariddh signed a statement that would

be announced first by radio and then read by Khieu Samphan at a July 6 press conference. Negotiators returned to Anlong Veng on July 4 to inform the Khmer Rouge to proceed with the ceremony.[27]

The 5–6 July coup was in part to pre-empt a politico-military alliance between the royalists and the Khmer Rouge that might help Ranariddh to rebound and would pose a new challenge to Hun Sen's hegemony.

The international circumstances were also favourable to Hun Sen's move. Just before the coup, the anti–Khmer Rouge donor community also put pressure on the Cambodian Government to get its house in order and to restore political stability for economic development. On 1 and 2 July, at the second Consulative Group Meeting (CGM) in Paris, donors presented their views on what Cambodia needed to do to improve the political environment for economic development. The two U.N. Special Representatives to Cambodia jointly supported "Cambodia's own efforts to establish the Rule of Law, respect for human rights and a free market economy".[28] The push for political stability necessary for economic development was echoed by the major donors who expressed disappointment at the lack of Cambodia's progress towards political stability. Germany warned:

> serious down-side risks, stemming mainly from political instability, internal insecurity, weak institutions and other deficiencies ... are threatening the achievements reached and the prospects for further improvements.[29]

Australia argued that what was lacking in Cambodia was, among other things, a "stable political framework".[30] Japan, Cambodia's largest donor, also said it was deeply concerned about the public peace getting worse even in Phnom Penh.[31] The U.S. representative, while calling for free, fair, and peaceful elections, warned:

> we cannot move forward with effective assistance programs ... in the face of political polarization, fears of a return to violence and the reduction in government effectiveness that results.[32]

International financial institutions also raised similar concerns about Cambodia's domestic political instability and wanted to see more action directed at restoring law and order.[33]

This is not to suggest that the donors had a direct interest in seeing Hun Sen remove Ranariddh from power. Nonetheless, the donors' strong demand for law and order may have encouraged Hun Sen to act. At the CGM meeting, CPP Minister of Economy and Finance Keat Chhon simply conceded that there had been "some violent incidents in the last few months" and that

> some criminal elements can and do exploit ... freedom in order to destabilize law and order or to discredit one group or another. Regrettably, certain self-serving and politically motivated sections use such events to malign the country and vilify the leadership.[34]

In his review of the donors' pressing demand, the minister wrote: "The issues of security and political stability remain as the main prerequisites for the development of Cambodia."[35] Hun Sen perhaps had not expected the world to react to his violence against Ranariddh as negatively as it did because he was working to restore political stability.[36]

In short, then, Hun Sen's concern about his political vulnerability led him to view the emerging royalist–Khmer Rouge politico-military alliance as a challenge to his hegemonic standing. He may also have believed that the action he would take against Ranariddh would not upset the world too much: after all, he laid claim to preventing Khmer Rouge remnants returning to power, and thus restoring political stability for the country's economic development.

The Coup's Consequences and the Country's Commotions

The coup that ousted Prince Sihanouk in March 1970 plunged the country into civil war. After that, the Khmer Rouge regime began its reign of terror. A Vietnamese invasion and a U.N.-sponsored election failed to break the vicious cycle. Is the victorious Second Prime Minister now in a position to do what his predecessors had not been able to, namely, achieve political stability? His success in executing the coup may help to keep him in power for a long while, but he may still be vulnerable to coup plots and attempts in the future because of the structural fragility of the state.

Immediately after the coup Hun Sen ordered his troops to push the royalist remnants north towards the Thai-Cambodian border. He sent 800 troops to the new front lines west of Siem Reap province and then mobilized another 1,600 troops, of whom 1,400 came from Kampong Thom and Kampong Cham provinces. By late July the royalists found themselves barely holding on to the key town of Samrong, approximately 330 kilometres northwest of Phnom Penh and 30 kilometres from the Thai border.

By August the royalists were making a quick retreat, and found themselves desperately defending their last stronghold in O Smach on the northern Thai-Cambodian border. The battle for the royalists' last bastion began on 13 August. In the following weeks, there were many conflicting reports on who controlled the area. As the CPP troops closed in on O Smach, more than 40,000 Cambodians took refuge in Thailand. Resistance leaders admitted that O Smach might fall at any time, but claimed that their 3,000 troops were resolved to fight back. At year's end, however, the CPP troops had still failed to capture the area. The royalist force's ability to withstand the CPP's onslaught depended heavily on the Khmer Rouge troops from Anglong Veng, who came to areas in O Smach.

Will the Cambodian adversaries be willing to reach a ceasefire? Definitely, as the inferior forces, the royalists and the Khmer Rouge may not find it too difficult to accept any agreement that would prevent them from being slaughtered by the CPP army. But the CPP cannot be expected to accept any conditions from the resistance groups unless the latter agree to disarm and voluntarily subject themselves to government control. Hun Sen has succeeded in punishing his rivals and pushing them against the Thai border. He would not, in all probability, demand anything less than the latter's total surrender. This kind of condition will in all likelihood keep the conflict protracted.

CPP officials now claim that their party rules unchallenged. And according to one top CPP official, "no one can challenge Hun Sen. The only way to keep Hun Sen down is for those inside the party to soften him up from within."[37] The CPP is apparently divided: Chea Sim (CPP President) and Sar Kheng (CPP Minister of Interior), and former party President Heng Samrin now belong to one faction; Hun Sen and his supporters belong to the other. However, Hun Sen has emerged as the undisputed leader despite the apparent schism. Chea Sim was said to fear Hun Sen as he feared a tiger.[38] Sar Kheng could not do anything against Chief of the National Police Hok Lundy (one of Hun Sen's reliable allies) despite the fact that the latter was under his authority. After the coup, Sar Kheng urged U.N. Representative Hammarberg to put more pressure on Hun Sen.[39]

Unlike the CPP, whose political alliance with other small parties remained intact, the NUF automatically disappeared after the coup. FUNCINPEC as a political party has also disintegrated past the point of no return. Most of its members chose to bandwagon with Hun Sen for short-term security or for rewards. After being "elected" as first prime minister, Ung Huot joined Hun Sen in calling for legal action against Ranariddh and Pol Pot for their crimes against humanity. Other royalist leaders not only competed to take over the job of the overthrown Prince Ranariddh, they also moved to form their own political parties.

The anti-CPP Union of Cambodian Democrats (UCD), formed in Thailand after the coup, seems to be growing weaker and weaker as its members became fragmented. The internal weaknesses were exposed by Son Chhay, a member of parliament (the BLDP Son Sann faction), who said that exiled politicians disliked Ranariddh's management style and even blamed him for creating the events in July. Son Chhay himself had fundamental differences with other members of the UCD.[40]

Seeds of Decline?

Despite a superficially impregnable position, Hun Sen's "unipolar world" might collapse one day if he does not adopt a strategy of benign hegemony. Compared with previous leaders, such as Sihanouk, the Second Prime Minister does not enjoy widespread legitimacy. Hun Sen is not a prince as Sihanouk was. In Cambodian society, popularity still irrationally rests on traditional thinking that "without a king, the kingdom will be shattered". Hun Sen was a peasant, a former Khmer Rouge fighter, and came to power after the Vietnamese invasion of Cambodia in late 1978. Unlike Sihanouk, who had driven the French out of Cambodia, Hun Sen is viewed by his enemies as someone who invited Vietnam into the country. The fact that the CPP lost the 1993 elections further reveals that Hun Sen was not highly popular despite his military preponderance and his party's use of violence. If Prince Sihanouk could be ousted in early 1970, Hun Sen cannot be invincible.

Besides his lack of traditional legitimacy, Hun Sen has failed to gain a clear sense of performance legitimacy. He still presides over a weak state and a relatively strong society. The bureaucracy is incompetent and corrupt, and administrative reform has so far failed. The government's commitment to an initial 20 per cent reduction in the 144,000-strong civil service by the end of 1997 failed to meet its goal; by the end of 1996 the public sector had increased to 163,206.[41] Even with large budgetary support from foreign donors — about half the state budget — the government remained cash-strapped.

With meagre financial resources and a grossly inefficient bureaucratic structure,

Hun Sen's preponderance has depended on, and will continue to rely on, the military and security establishment. Will his generals fight for him? As long as he continues to indulge their corruption, he will certainly obtain their loyalty. Such indulgence, however, will frustrate his reform efforts and jeopardize his attempts to build the state. Cambodian history has shown that a corrupt military leadership is ultimately self-destructive. President Lon Nol (who led the country from 1970 to 1975) was defeated at the hands of the Khmer Rouge because he had turned a blind eye to his generals' rampant corruption. If Hun Sen is unwilling to discipline his generals, for the purpose of maintaining their loyalty to him, he will jeopardize his own efforts to reform the public administration. Moreover, if Hun Sen does not have adequate financial means to meet the military and security apparatus needs — a situation becoming more difficult because of reduced foreign aid — they would rebel against him. Growing military dissatisfaction during the second half of the 1960s, rooted in the termination of U.S. aid to Cambodia, contributed to Sihanouk's eventual demise.

While he may now enjoy the absence of subversive foreign interference, he does not have a foreign patron who is willing and able to lend massive financial and military support as the Soviet Union and Vietnam did for the PRK/SOC during the 1980s. Donors continued to give humanitarian aid to Cambodia, but Hun Sen no longer receives military aid from Western states such as Australia and the United States. Cambodia also failed to gain admission into ASEAN in July, and the United Nations left the Cambodian seat vacant in September.

Growing poverty and potential military dissatisfaction are a recipe for coup plots and attempts.[42] Hun Sen might be able to beat back his challengers a few more times, but he would not have the capability to win all the time. A future coup, however, will not be of a pre-emptive nature, but will be a "rear-end collusion" kind of coup. That is, those who have now chosen to remain silent or bandwagoned with Hun Sen — either out of fear or for short-term rewards and security gains — may one day decide to bring him down because they feel threatened by his unchecked power.

Conclusion

This article contends that what happened in early July was Hun Sen's pre-emptive coup. The coup arose from a situation where Hun Sen wished to enforce his hegemonic position by preventing enfeebled challengers bouncing back.

Although Hun Sen seems to have achieved a degree of political stability, what he has done still keeps Cambodia highly vulnerable to coup plots and attempts, largely because his successes resulted from the use of force that temporarily drove his opponents out of power and frightened others into bandwagoning with him for short-term protection and rewards. Hun Sen and his rivals still operate within an environment where the "politics of survival" prevails over concern for morality and justice. Unless Hun Sen and other Cambodian leaders learn that a violent struggle for hegemony at all costs will not pay in the long run, but will only keep them in a state of perpetual war, they will never agree to compete for legitimate power through the ballot-box in a free and fair manner.

Notes

1. *Phnom Penh Post*, 5–18 April 1996, p. 10.
2. Ibid., 26 July–8 August 1996, p. 1.
3. *Cambodia Daily*, 19 November 1996, p. 8.
4. "The National United Front's Political Beliefs and Objectives" (Unpublished official document, undated).
5. Ung Huot and Hun Sen's letter to Thomas Hammaberg, 18 November 1997, p. 4.
6. Ministry of Foreign Affairs and International Co-operation, the *White Paper Background on the July 1997 Crisis: Prince Ranariddh's Strategy of Provocation* (9 July 1997).
7. Ibid., p. 1.
8. Ministry of Foreign Affairs and International Co-operation, *Crisis in July Report on the Armed Insurrection: Its Origins, History, and Aftermath* (22 September 1997), p. 7.
9. Ibid., p. 10.
10. David Robertson, *The Penguin Dictionary of Politics* (New York: Penguin Books, 1993), p. 118.
11. Ministry of Foreign Affairs and International Co-operation, *Crisis in July Report on the Armed Insurrection: Its Origins, History, and Aftermath*, p. 8.
12. Interviews, March 1997.
13. Ministry of Foreign Affairs and International Co-operation, *Crisis in July Report on the Armed Insurrection: Its Origins, History, and Aftermath*, p. 117.
14. p. 122.
15. p. 170.
16. Annex P, Ministry of Foreign Affairs and International Co-operation, *Crisis in July Report on the Armed Insurrection: Its Origins, History, and Aftermath*.
17. Interview, December 1997.
18. Ibid.
19. Ibid.
20. U.N. Centre for Human Rights, "Evidence of Summary Executions, Torture and Missing Persons since 5–7 July 1997", p. 4.
21. It may be worth noting that both Hun Sen and Ung Huot [... footnote is incomplete in the original article].
22. Michael Vickery's personal remarks on Southeast Asia Discussion List, 29 July 1997. Vickery's point only suggests, it seems to me, that Hun Sen was not as pacifistic as some socialist writers may believe. Vickery, however, does not clearly specify whether Hun Sen's enemies like Ranariddh and Sam Rainsy were more murderous than the Second Prime Minister, but implies that they were at least equally murderous. This point demands concrete evidence!
23. U.N. Secretary-General's Implementation Report, U.N. Document S/23613, 19 February, pp. 20–21.
24. Michael Doyle, *UN Peacekeeping in Cambodia: UNTAC's Civil Mandate* (Boulder, Colorado: Lynne Rienner Publishers, 1995), pp. 35 and 68.
25. Report of the Secretary-General on the Situation of Human Rights in Cambodia, U.N. Document, A/52/26 September 1997, pp. 11–12.
26. *Far Eastern Economic Review*, 21 August 1997, pp. 14–17.
27. Ibid., p. 17.
28. Joint Statement of U.N. Special Representatives to Cambodia on the Occasion of the Second Consultative Group Meeting, 1–2 July 1997, p. 1.
29. The German Statement on Macroeconomic Issues, Consultative Group Meeting, 1–2 July 1997, p. 2.
30. Statement by the representative of the Australian Agency for International Development, Dr Peter McCawley, 1–2 July 1997, p. 5.
31. Japanese Statement on "Aid Co-ordination Issues", Second Consultative Group Meeting, 1–2 July 1997, p. 4.
32. U.S. Statement, Consultative Group Meeting, 1–2 July 1997, p. 3. Other state representatives like those of the European Union, Great Britain, Denmark, Norway expressed the same concern.

33. See ibid., p. 3; statement by Hubert Neiss, IMF Representative, 1–2 July 1997; and Asian Development Bank, Statement on Macroeconomic Management, 1–2 July 1997.
34. Keat Chhon's Opening Remarks at the Consultative Group Meeting, 1–2 July 1997.
35. A paper written by the minister, 16 July 1997.
36. "We didn't understand that the world would react to the coup the way it did." (Interview, 3 December 1997). In my early works, I discussed the international community's anti-Khmer Rouge stand, which worried me because I viewed this policy attitude as having the potential to encourage the government to use violence against anyone seen as being pro-Khmer Rouge. Sorpong Peou, *Conflict Neutralization in the Cambodia War: From Battlefield to Ballot-Box* (Kuala Lumpur, Singapore, and New York: Oxford University Press, 1997) and "Cambodia's Post-Cold War Dilemma: Democratization, Armed Conflict, and Authoritarianism", *Southeast Asian Affairs 1996*: 113–29.
37. Interview, 3 December 1997.
38. *Udom Katte Khmer*, 23 September 1997.
39. Interview, 6 December 1997.
40. *Reaksmey Kampuchea*, 22 November 1997.
41. Ann Masson, "Component III: Civil Service Renewal Programme, National Programme to Reform the Administration", 18 October 1996, p. 2.
42. See Augustine J. Kposowa and J. Craig Jenkins, "The Structural Sources of Military Coups in Postcolonial Africa, 1957–1984," *American Journal of Sociology* 9, no. 1 (July 1993): 126–63.

CAMBODIA 2017
Plus ça change...

Khatharya Um

While election years in Cambodia are always eventful, 2017 proved to be even more so than expected. While the months leading to the June commune elections brought the customary machinations and jitters, it was the post-election developments that dashed whatever hope for political change may have been engendered by the results of the last two elections. As the ruling Cambodian People's Party (CPP) moved to consolidate its power in anticipation of the forthcoming elections in 2018, the country spiralled away from whatever measure of political openness may have been achieved in recent years. While election-related violence is not unprecedented, as forecast in the frequent references to "colour revolution" and imminent eruption of "social chaos", the crackdown against regime opponents in the months following the June elections was wholesale and decisive. The consequences affect not only the upcoming 2018 elections but potentially the next electoral cycle as well. The hoped-for democratic transition into which the international community had poured massive financial and political investment over the last quarter of a century appears more elusive than ever.

Still smarting from its precarious win in the 2013 elections, the CPP was confronted with yet another disconcerting outcome in the 2017 commune elections. Despite the ruling party's efforts to turn the political tide, the Cambodian National Rescue Party (CNRP) successfully secured 5,007 council seats (to the CPP's 6,503) and 489 out of the 1,646 commune chief seats, a tenfold increase from their win in the 2012 elections. Though short of the

---

Reprinted from Malcolm Cook and Daljit Singh, eds., *Southeast Asian Affairs 2018* (Singapore: ISEAS – Yusof Ishak Institute, 2018), pp. 97–111. At the time of original publication, Khatharya Um was a political scientist, Associate Professor and Chair of Asian American and Asian Diaspora Studies at the University of California, Berkeley.

60 per cent that the party had projected, the CNRP did secure 44 per cent of the vote, compared to the CPP's 51 per cent. This narrowing margin is significant because it reveals not only a wide base of support for the opposition in urban centres but, even more significantly, an erosion of the CPP's political control in rural areas that have been the party's traditional base, where the majority of Cambodians live and where the ruling party has long-established political infrastructure. At 85 per cent of registered voters, voter turnout was impressively high, an indicator of popular optimism about the prospect of change, bolstered in no small part by the earlier performance of the opposition party, despite the preponderant power and repressive grip of the CPP.

These shifting terrains are not lost on the CPP. While transgressions against civil society and fundamental freedoms, particularly of expression and assembly,[1] have been unrelenting, the violent measures taken by the ruling party against its political opponents reached a new height in the months surrounding the June elections. Arrests and imprisonment of activists and members of the CNRP, many charged with participating in the 2014 popular demonstration that the government has labelled an "insurrection", preceded the commune elections in June. The systematic attack escalated after the elections, spurred no doubt by the CNRP's notable performance at the polls, culminating in the late-night arrest and imprisonment of Kem Sokha, head of the CNRP, on 3 September 2017, in disregard of his parliamentary immunity. Citing as evidence a 2013 speech he made to the Cambodian community in Australia in which he mentioned receiving advice from American experts, Kem Sokha was charged with treason, accused of plotting and conspiring with "foreign elements" to overthrow the government, and, through the CNRP, of inciting a "lotus revolution" in Cambodia.[2] Earlier, the government had introduced a law stipulating that parties cannot be headed by someone with a criminal record, which had already forced CNRP president Sam Rainsy, who is facing multiple charges and a $1 million fine for libel against Hun Sen, to resign in an effort to save the party.

With Sam Rainsy in exile, Kem Sokha's imprisonment essentially decapitated the party. Fearing their own arrest, a number of CNRP officials and party supporters have fled the country, many to Thailand. Others defected to the CPP. The final move to destroy the opposition came on 16 November when the Supreme Court issued a decree to dissolve the CNRP under the charge of attempting, with American support, to destabilize the government through a "colour revolution". The government also imposed a five-year ban on political activities of the 118 senior CNRP members, which essentially undercut the possibility of any party-led mobilization for the upcoming 2018 elections and beyond. Amidst rumours of his leaning towards the CNRP, Nhek Bun Chhay, head of the Khmer National United Party (KNUP) and a former royalist commander who fought against Hun Sen's forces in 1997 but who broke away from FUNCINPEC last year to form KNUP, was stripped of his bodyguards and his position as adviser to the government (a rank equal to that of deputy prime minister) for not being "loyal to the government". Besides the CPP and CNRP, KNUP was the only other party to secure a commune chief position in the June elections.

In what the regime termed "a slight correction on democracy for the common public good",³ the dissolution of the CNRP was followed by amendments to the election laws to allow for the redistribution of the party's electoral seats in the National Assembly, Senate, communes, and district councils to other parties. Once a rival, but now aligned with the CPP, the royalist party, FUNCINPEC, which had advocated the redistribution of CNRP seats, was catapulted from its politically insipid status by an exponential gain of over a third of the National Assembly seats through the reallocation.⁴ In 2013 the party had won less than 4 per cent of the vote and was unable to secure a single assembly seat. In the Senate, remnants of the Sam Rainsy party who regrouped under the newly minted Candlelight Party were allowed to retain their seats. With the lion's share of the commune seats going to the CPP, the ruling party now controls over 95 per cent of seats at the commune level,⁵ along with the majority control of over 55 per cent of the National Assembly.

The redistribution of CNRP seats — which Phil Robertson, deputy director of Human Rights Watch–Asia, describes as "a looting of democracy" — essentially nullified the will of 44 per cent of registered voters who cast their ballots in June. Calling the amended laws "unconstitutional", legal analyst Yoeurng Sotheara noted: "the constitution says the National Assembly should represent the people.... It's no longer representative if the seats of the opposition party which supporters voted for ... are distributed to parties they don't support.... the government doesn't have the authority to redistribute the will of the people."⁶ Evoking the need to defend national interests, a twelve-man working group has been tasked with looking into constitutional amendments, alluding to the likelihood of additional changes, which does not bode well for the rapidly shrinking democratic space. Concern about the fairness of the upcoming elections in 2018 was reinforced by the resignation of the three CNRP representatives from the National Election Committee (NEC), including the vice chair of the committee, and their replacement with members from minor parties.

Combined, the imprisonment, flight, exile and ban on political activities of the CNRP leadership and the defection of party members has effectively neutralized the only viable oppositional force for the upcoming 2018 elections. FUNCIPEC's renewed rapprochement with the CPP and resulting political resurgence are suggestive of a familiar replay of the 1990s political theatre in which an uneasy alliance was expediently forged between the CPP and its weaker non-communist ally to give a veneer of multiparty democracy in Cambodia that was necessary and sufficient for regime legitimation in the eyes of the international community. This newly found symbiosis notwithstanding, the CPP has already admonished FUNCINPEC for its attempt to solicit Chinese aid for the 2018 elections in contravention of a recently passed law that prohibits parties from accepting foreign funds. With the party dismantled and banned from political activities and with most of the leadership in exile, a faction of the former CNRP led by Sam Rainsy has announced the launch of the Cambodian National Rescue Movement (CNRM) to continue mobilizing for regime change, a move that has been rejected by Kem Sokha, who insists on the legitimacy of the CNRP and its three million voter–supporters.

In the concerted campaign to undercut the political strength of the opposition and ensure an uncontested win at the national polls in 2018, the regime also tightened control over the media, rights organizations and activists, further silencing dissent. While the independence of the media has always been compromised by state surveillance and censorship, the forced closure of the English-language newspaper *The Cambodia Daily*, curtailment of the in-country operations of the U.S.-funded Voice of America (VOA) and Radio Free Asia (RFA), and the cessation of operations of fifteen local stations that aired their programmes and those of the CNRP were unprecedented developments. As it was with the $6.3 million tax bill levied against *The Cambodia Daily*, VOA and RFA also faced potential tax liabilities and licensing issues, and were compelled to close their Cambodia offices. Two former RFA reporters, Oun Chhin and Yeang Sothearin, were arrested in November and detained at Prey Sar prison for engaging in espionage, charged with providing "a foreign state with information which undermines national defence",[7] for which each could face up to fifteen years in prison. According to RFA, the men had not been in the station's employment since the termination of its Phnom Penh–based operations in September. Similarly, the government ordered the closure of the U.S.-funded National Democratic Institute and the prompt departure of its foreign staff for allegedly failing to register the organization in accordance with Cambodia's NGO Law. Rights organizations such as the Cambodian Human Rights and Development Association (ADHOC), the Cambodian League for the Promotion and Defense of Human Rights (LICADHO), the Committee for Free and Fair Elections (COMFREL), and the Cambodian Center for Human Rights (CCHR) founded by Kem Sokha in 2002 also came under scrutiny. Rights activists, particularly those working on labour and land disputes, continue to be in the crosshairs of the state that seeks to emphasize stability and growth amidst political turmoil.

International Relations

The attack on the CNRP not only neutralizes oppositional forces, thus calling into question the possibility of a free and fair election in 2018, but also destabilizes U.S.–Cambodia relations that were already on unsteady ground, particularly given the accusation of U.S. complicity in the supposed CNRP "colour revolution". Denouncing the "meritless and politicized allegations" used to justify the dissolution of the CNRP, and noting the "unnecessary damages" to U.S.–Cambodia relations, the Trump administration stated "it is becoming increasingly evident to the world that the Cambodian government's restrictions on civil society, suppression of the press, and banning of more than 100 opposition leaders from political activities have significantly set back Cambodia's democratic development and placed its economic growth and international standing at risk".[8] Citing concern that "next year's election will not be legitimate, free or fair",[9] the United States withdrew the two-year $1.8 million grant to Cambodia's National Election Committee that it had pledged in April. The U.S. Senate also passed a unanimous motion urging the listing of key Cambodian officials on the Specially Designated Nationals list, a move that could mean the freezing of assets and curtailment of business relationships with American companies. On 6 December the United States announced that it would be imposing visa restrictions on individuals involved in "undermining democracy in Cambodia", and made the lifting of the ban contingent on the reinstatement of the opposition and reversal of the regime's political course. U.S.–Cambodia relations were also rocked by the temporary stall of the deportation programme, affecting some 1,900 Cambodians in the United States with felony convictions or undocumented status, though Cambodia's Ministry of Foreign Affairs and International Cooperation attributed this moratorium to protests from the Cambodian diaspora and some congressional members. The programme has since resumed.

The European Union (EU) was equally condemning of the deteriorating political situation in Cambodia and what Commissioner Karmenu Vella described in his address to the European Parliament as "a significant step away from the path of pluralism and democracy enshrined in Cambodia's constitution and supported over more than two decades by Cambodia's international partners including the European Union".[10] In her meeting with the Cambodian Foreign Minister Prak Sokhonn on 20 November, High Representative Mogherini insisted that EU development cooperation and assistance to Cambodia, including trade preferences under the EU's Everything But Arms (EBA) scheme, are predicated on the country's respect for human and labour rights. In December, the EU suspended its funding support for the 2018 elections, noting that "an electoral process from which the main opposition party has been arbitrarily excluded cannot be seen as legitimate".[11] The European Parliament has also passed a resolution calling for visa restrictions and the freezing of assets of Cambodian officials, as well as a temporary suspension of preferential trade access under article 19 of the EBA. In November, Sweden announced that it would not provide new aid to Cambodia except to support education and research. Concerns were also registered by the Inter-Parliamentary Union, which called for a fact-finding mission to Cambodia, and by ASEAN Parliamentarians for Human Rights (APHR), which insists that "anyone who thinks genuine, participatory, and inclusive elections are still possible in 2018 under these circumstances is gravely mistaken. The international community's engagement with Cambodia, including monitoring of the elections, should be conditional upon the restoration of democracy...".[12] The Geneva-based International Commission of Jurists, in turn, expressed concern over the "weaponization" of the country's judicial system in the CPP's campaign against its political opponents and critics. Rhona Smith, UN Special Rapporteur on Human Rights in Cambodia, underscored that what distinguishes "rule of law" from "rule by law" is respect for human rights, fairness, justice and public participation. At a UN forum, Kem Monovithya, a spokeswoman for the banned Cambodia National Rescue Party and daughter of jailed CNRP leader Kem Sokha, urged member states and signatories of the Paris Peace Accord to request a fact-finding and monitoring mission to Cambodia and to "review Cambodian membership at the UN".[13] The latter issue drew harsh admonishment from the Phnom Penh regime, citing the importance of protecting "national interests".[14] In the face of international pronouncements that under these circumstances the 2018 elections will not be free and fair, and the consequent withdrawal of aid, Prime Minister Hun Sen has defiantly declared that the elections will proceed as scheduled — 25 February for Senate seats and 29 July 2018 for the national election — pointing out that "the Cambodian constitution or around the world doesn't state one country needs another country's president or the U.N. Secretary General to acknowledge its election is legitimate".[15]

Limits of Sanctions

Despite its dismissive attitude, the Hun Sen regime is not oblivious to international opinion, particularly with an economy that is reliant on external, essentially Western, markets. With the EU the destination of an estimated 50 per cent of Cambodia's total exports, mostly in sugar and garments, preferential trade access is important, accounting for some $5 billion. Combined, the United States and the EU absorb some 60 per cent of Cambodia's exports, markets that cannot easily be replaced by China, which only imported $609 million of goods from Cambodia in 2016,[16] or by regional partners with much smaller markets and whose economies are more competitive than complementary. Additionally, the EU also provides development assistance to Cambodia — totalling nearly $170 million in 2016 — for projects in agriculture, education, governance, administration and electoral reform and in support of the Extraordinary Chambers of the Courts of Cambodia (ECCC).

Sanctions, however, have their limitations, not the least of which is the frequent subordination of international principles to the imperatives of realpolitik. Demand for accountability has been less than consistently applied by Western countries and by the donor community at large. In fact, Cambodia was granted and allowed to retain its EBA preferential trade status over the last decade, effectively spurring the exponential development of the sugar industry, despite widespread land disputes and forced evictions linked to economic land concessions that the European Parliament had found to have displaced over 400,000 Cambodians.[17] In 2016, members of the EU Parliament and civil society groups had also called for the withdrawal of tariff preferences for Cambodia because of negative social and environmental impacts and violations of labour and other rights. The same concerns about the unravelling of democratic processes and regime repression of political opposition have also been raised in the past, all with little enduring impact. At present, the EU is also engaging countries such as Myanmar and Vietnam that have yet to embark on democratic reforms. Finally, while the EU may be willing to issue public rebuke of state repression, they are more challenged in their ability to arrive at a consensus on what constitutes viable concrete action, given some states' concern that removal of preferential trade access would only adversely impact the 700,000 low-wage garment workers and not the leadership, and without any assurance of meaningful change.

The paramount nature of realpolitik is evident in the varied responses to developments in Cambodia. Despite American condemnation of the violent crackdown, President Trump did not raise human rights concerns during the ASEAN Summit in Manila in November. International outcry in general, including from the West, was relatively tempered. The circumspection of Asian governments, including ASEAN with its member states' spotty records and policy of non-interference, was notable though not unexpected. Tokyo's expressed concern about the dissolution of the CNRP was offset by Japanese Minister of Foreign Affairs Kazuyuki Nakane's assertion that Japan will continue its assistance to the NEC while "keep[ing] dialogue" with the Cambodian government.[18] Besides the EU, Japan is the biggest funder of the upcoming elections. On 7 August the Japan International Cooperation Agency (JICA) signed an agreement with Cambodia to provide a Japanese official development assistance loan (ODA) of up to 23.502 billion yen (approximately US$208 million) for the Sihanoukville Port New Container Terminal Development Project.

Tokyo's policy stance is likely informed by China's expanding influence in the region. While the West is an important market, China is not only Cambodia's largest source of international aid but also of foreign investment, amounting to ten times the size of U.S. investment, which accounts for only 3 per cent of the country's total foreign investment capital. It is also Cambodia's largest trade partner and a major source of foreign tourists, on whom the country remains highly dependent. Significantly, Chinese aid is also directed to critical sectors. With high economic growth and an annual increase of 20 per cent in electricity demand, the Cambodian government has given priority to the development of hydropower. The six operational hydroelectric plants account for 47 per cent of available electricity in Cambodia.[19] The seventh and biggest hydropower dam, the Lower Sesan II in northeastern Cambodia, is scheduled to be fully operational in 2018. With the exception of the Lower Sesan II project — which is a joint venture between Chinese, Cambodian and Vietnamese companies, with China holding 51 per cent control — all hydropower projects in Cambodia have been fully financed by Chinese companies.[20] In addition to almost US$2 billion in concessional loans, Chinese firms had also committed to investing an additional $7 billion in Cambodia for infrastructural projects, including a highway connecting Phnom Penh with Cambodia's main port, Sihanoukville. In recent years, Chinese investment has also extended beyond largely infrastructural projects to real estate, as investors seek additional safety nets in the event of an economic bust.

Even more than the size and sectoral importance, Chinese aid is not tied to human rights or other aspects of social accountability. As Cambodian government spokesman Phay Siphan puts it, "the Chinese always support us in economic growth and they never interfere in our decisions".[21] Undoubtedly seizing the opening provided by the retraction of Western aid as an opportunity to also lure Cambodia away from Vietnam's sphere of influence, China was quick to affirm its commitment to "support Cambodia's efforts in maintaining political stability"[22] and to extend aid to the NEC in the form of some 60,000 polling booths and 15,000 ballot boxes for the 2018 elections, which sent a clear and bolstering signal to the Hun Sen regime that it can proceed on its political course with relative impunity.

Chinese support is, by no means, uncalculating or unconditional, nor is its economic presence without adverse consequences. As part of the One Belt, One Road initiative backed by the Asian Infrastructure Investment Bank (AIIB) and the Silk Road Fund, these development projects are critical aspects of China's strategic calculus to enhance its influence among regional states in Asia. This deployment of soft power is important given China's economic and strategic interests in Southeast Asia, which is projected by the World Economic Forum to have the world's fifth-largest economy by 2020, and through which the planned maritime Silk Road will pass. With growing economies and populations, the infrastructural needs of ASEAN member states are vast, making China's economic backing indispensable to the Southeast Asian countries, and the latter an economically and geopolitically important site for Chinese investment. With China's territorial claims and undeterred expansion in the South China Sea (despite the unfavourable ruling of the Arbitral Tribunal in 2016) a source of contention and concern in the region, the support of some ASEAN member states is critical for China. With Cambodia's support, for which it was rewarded with a generous aid package, China was able to block any mention of the South China Sea in the joint communiqué of the 45th ASEAN Foreign Ministers Meeting in Phnom Penh. Despite the disconcertion of some regional states over Cambodia and Laos' pro-China position, the importance of Chinese goodwill is not lost on an ASEAN that is feeling the uncertainty of America's Asia policy, as evidenced by the conciliatory tone of the statement issued at the conclusion of the November summit in Manila.

Though Chinese aid has been indispensable, Chinese projects have also been controversial. While they may have brought electrification to some 79 per cent of the villages, as reported by the Ministry of Mines and Energy, and enabled the reduction of the country's dependency on costly imported electricity, the Chinese-financed hydropower plants in Cambodia have also engendered mass displacement. The Lower Sesan II project alone affects 860 mostly indigenous minority families who were forced to abandon their ancestral villages. Despite the government offer of compensation of $6,000 or five hectares of land per family, many are reluctant to relocate because of their cultural and spiritual rootedness and because some of the resettlement sites are yet to be cleared for cultivation or are prone to inundation. Some 60 families have refused the government compensation and were given until the end of December to accept the deal, after which time the government will no longer compensate them for their losses.[23] Experts have also warned against the adverse impact of the dams on the ecosystem and fish migration routes that, in turn, affect fish supplies. In response to widespread concern about the social and environmental impacts of these projects, Prime Minister Hun Sen commented that "there is no development in the world that does not affect environment; it's just small or big impact only", arguing that "this project will provide great benefit to socio-economic development and poverty reduction, especially in the northeastern region".[24]

Growth, Development and Social Justice

With economic growth of 7 per cent, the Hun Sen regime has stood on the platform of peace and development. With signs of slowing down in the construction and textile export sectors, continued growth is contingent on an expected rise in other manufacturing exports and robust tourism. This rests on Cambodia being able to maintain or even increase its competitive edge and to diversify its export manufacturing sector, and on a stable social and political environment. Uncertainties in the past had adversely impacted business confidence. In the agricultural sector, growth remains hindered by poor infrastructure and difficult access to markets, rural indebtedness and landlessness.

As Transparency International country director Preap Kol noted, however, "for a growth of a country like Cambodia to be sustainable, development of economy should ideally go hand in hand with development of social justice and democracy". Though growth has been impressive, the challenges to sustainable and inclusive development — improved land administration, natural resource management, good and equitable public service delivery, transparency, and overall good governance — remain to be effectively addressed. Disparity between the rich and poor and between urban and rural areas persists. While the poverty rate continues to fall and the country has reached lower-middle-income status with a per capita gross national income of $1,079 in 2015, over 28 per cent of the population continues to live in economic precarity. With the living wage a major catalyst in the mass labour protests of 2013 that resulted in violent clashes and deaths of protesters, the government has been particularly attentive to this issue, especially as it pertains to the garment and footwear industries that employ over 700,000 workers and generate a revenue of $7 billion annually. Though wages for workers in the footwear and textile industries had jumped 150 per cent over the past five years — from $61 per month in 2012 — they are struggling to keep up with the cost of living. Currently at $153, the government has recently promised another 11 per cent increase by next year. Though it will improve workers' living conditions, there is also concern, shared by the unions, that this minimum wage increase would reduce the country's competitiveness in the global labour market.

In the rural areas, where 80–90 per cent of the population resides, the inequities and dislocations of development continue to register. Land disputes and forced displacement continue to plague many communities. Among many peasant protests, nearly a hundred villagers from Banan and Bavel districts of Battambang demonstrated in front of Prime Minister Hun Sen's home and the Ministry of Land Management to protest against the illegal occupation of their social land concessions by government soldiers. In many forested regions, such as the northeastern province of Rattanakiri, the creation of largely foreign-owned export plantations and illegal logging continue to destroy the country's rapidly shrinking forestland, upon which many communities, including a large number of indigenous minorities, rely for their livelihoods. A recent international survey revealing a 30 per cent increase in forest cover loss between 2015 and 2016[25] has been heatedly contested by the government. Protests by villagers and activists — such as the one mobilized to stop illegal logging in the Preah Roka Wildlife Sanctuary, a 223,287-acre national park that has been designated as a protected refuge for endangered wildlife — are numerous, despite the violent consequences that they engender. Forest defenders have underscored the importance not only of stepped-up efforts to stop illegal logging in Cambodia but also of the EU and the United States to terminate their timber export agreements with countries such as Vietnam where illegally felled timber has reportedly been exported.

In Phnom Penh, development has also seen to the demolition of one of the capital's historic landmarks, popularly known as the "White Building". The land was purchased by Arakawa, a Japanese developer, with plans to build an $80-million twenty-one-storey complex. Constructed in the 1960s as an affordable housing project, it was home, in its derelict state, to 493 families, some 25 of which had refused to be relocated.

Meanwhile, six years after the early morning demolition of their homes, 11 evicted families of the yet-to-be-resolved Borei Keila development controversy are still awaiting fair compensation for their losses. While the government has moved to address the problems of illegal logging and corruption, the initiatives, though important, have not amounted to systemic reform. Pointing to regime failings as the basis for popular dissatisfaction[26] reflected in the June electoral outcomes, PM Hun Sen has called for officials to "bathe and clean themselves".

Migration

For many of Cambodia's land poor and landless, migration is the only viable option. According to government records, 116,000 have migrated to Thailand through official channels over the last decade. Other estimates place migrants currently working across the border at closer to one million, of which an estimated 500,000 are undocumented. Labour exploitation and abuses persist. The passing of a new law in Thailand that penalized both undocumented workers and their employers saw to the mass return exodus of over 8,000 Cambodian migrant workers in June, 10–15 per cent of whom were reported to be minors.[27] Though the official cost of a passport is $100 ($200 for expedited processing), migrants often have to pay much more to an agency — as high as over $800 — a sum that few can afford, given the menial work and earnings they stand to secure in Thailand. Despite the Ministry of Labour's plan to legalize more migrant workers through the issuance of travel documents in Thailand, the cost and lack of personal documents remain major obstacles to the registration effort, which is scheduled to continue until the end of 2017. At home, the Cambodian government has tightened its own immigration policies with a more stringent review of identity cards and residency papers. As of October, these measures stand to affect some 70,000 migrants, the majority of whom are ethnic Vietnamese, prompting Vietnam to urge the Cambodian government to guarantee the legal rights of those "waiting for their legal documents to be completed". With the 7 January anniversary in view, this immigration policy and general pivoting towards China are testing Cambodia–Vietnam relations in unprecedented ways.

Conclusion

As this chapter goes to print, the anniversary of the Veng Sreng demonstrations in which some fifty thousand protesters took to the streets calling for regime change came and went unceremoniously, as fear effectively silenced critique. The outcry of earlier months against the dismantling of a meaningful multiparty democratic system enshrined in the Paris Accords had fizzled. Back-door diplomacy and economic pressure may continue but are unlikely to reverse the course of a regime moving unapologetically towards shedding any pretence at political liberalization and democratic reform in a "descent into outright dictatorship", as the ASEAN Parliamentarians for Human Rights chairman put it.

That the hope for a democratic transition for Cambodia is more elusive now than ever should not come as a surprise. Arguably, the stage was set twenty-four years ago when the international community endorsed a fait accompli presented not by the will of the Cambodian people but the right of force, when the CPP stared down the international community and walked away with the election they did not win and proceeded to rule for the next two decades: "Their dreams of democracy wilted. They blinked."[28] Thus began a performance politics in which all participated, with Cambodia presenting a façade of political openness with elections and their predictable outcomes that are sufficient to nurse the justification of continued aid. Democracy was exchanged for purported stability, with liberalization success measured against the infernal days of the Khmer Rouge. Indeed, the ability of the Hun Sen regime to consolidate power — political, military, economic — in a single party and its willingness to exercise force unflinchingly have effectively prevented the possibility of war. It has not, however, been able to foster peace, just governance or equitable access to basic rights — to freedom from fear; to education, jobs and life opportunities; or to equal protection under the law — for the majority of the Cambodian people. Whatever liberalization we may have witnessed over the last two and half decades have largely been economic. While it did move the country out of the cloister of the socialist economy, it has also engendered a widening of socio-economic gaps and the unrelenting disenfranchisement of millions of Cambodians in the process.

With the Western gaze fixed on the geopolitical balancing game in East Asia — pivoting around China and North Korea — Cambodian leadership is once again astutely playing the China wildcard. It is unlikely that the country's autocracy and violent crackdown on opponents and dissent are going to provoke more than symbolic condemnation by the international community. This much is evident and is not lost on the ruling regime, or on the Cambodian people. If anything, recent developments affirm that rule of and by force is effective, made even more so by its seeming impunity. With the CNRP refraining, to prevent bloodshed, from calling for mass protest, the only resolution is a political one, which is not unimaginable. In previous impasses the Hun Sen regime had eased its grip, with entry bans lifted and detainees released at the eleventh hour. Whether this will happen in time to make any difference to the electoral outcomes in 2018 remains to be seen. With the gains and losses of the recent elections a looming reminder of possibilities and challenges, the stakes are indeed very high.

Notes

1. See Amnesty International, "Cambodia 2016/2017" <https://www.amnesty.org/en/countries/asia-and-the-pacific/cambodia/report-cambodia/>.
2. Ben Sokhean and Leonie Kijewski, "PM Accuses Kem Sokha–founded NGO of Serving Foreign Interests, Says It 'Must Close'", *Phnom Penh Post*, 27 November 2017.
3. Andrew Nachemson, "Cambodia: From Pet Project to Problem Child", *Phnom Penh Post*, 27 November 2017.
4. Prak Chan Thul, "Cambodia's Hun Sen Warns His Party It Could Still Lose Election", Reuters, 22 November 2017.
5. Leonie Kijewski and Khouth Sophak Chakrya, "CPP Big Winner in Local Seat Reallocation", *Phnom Penh Post*, 4 December 2017.
6. Mech Dara and Andrew Nachemson, "Breaking: National Assembly Passes Election Law Amendments to Allow CNRP Seat Distribution", *Phnom Penh Post*, 16 October 2017.
7. Mech Dara and Yesenia Amaro, "Ex-RFA

Reporters Provisionally Charged with 'Espionage' Sent to Prey Sar", *Phnom Penh Post*, 20 November 2017.
8. Mech Dara and James Reddick, "US Withdraws Election Funding Following CNRP Dissolution", *Phnom Penh Post*, 17 November 2017.
9. Amy Sawitta Lefevre and Prak Chan Thul, "Cambodia Faces U.S., EU Action after Banning Opposition", Reuters, 16 November 2017.
10. <https://eeas.europa.eu/delegations/cambodia/37658/speech-commissioner-karmenu-vella-european-parliament-urgency-debate-banning-opposition_en>.
11. Reuters, "EU Suspends Funding for Cambodian Election", 12 December 2017.
12. See APHR statement, 13 October 2017 <https://aseanmp.org/2017/10/13/asean-parliamentarians-condemn-moves-to-eliminate-opposition-in-cambodia/>.
13. Voice of America, "UN General Assembly Urged to Review Cambodia Membership", 22 December 2017.
14. Mech Dara and Andrew Nachenson, "Kheng Seeks Constitutional Ban on Individuals Harming Cambodia's 'Interests' ", *Phnom Penh Post*, 29 December 2017.
15. Neou Vannarin, "Hun Sen: CNRP Dissolution, NEC Resignations, and Aid Cuts Will Not Affect 2018 Election", Voice of America, 23 November 2017.
16. David Hutt, "Why the EU is Dallying over Possible Cambodian Sanctions", *Forbes*, 3 November 2017.
17. See European Parliament resolution on Cambodia, 26 October 2012 <http://www.europarl.europa.eu/meetdocs/2009_2014>.
18. Daphne Chen, "Japan 'Expresses Concern' over CNRP", *Phnom Penh Post*, 22 November 2017.
19. Terence Chong, "The Politics behind Cambodia's Embrace of China", *ISEAS Perspective* 2017, no. 59 (2 August 2017).
20. *China Daily*, "Chinese Investment in Energy Creates New History for Cambodia: Cambodian Minister", 10 October 2016.
21. Reuters, "China's Big Money Trumps US Influence in Cambodia", 11 September 2017.
22. Neou Vannarin, "Hun Sen: CNRP Dissolution, NEC Resignations, and Aid Cuts Will Not Affect 2018 Election", Voice of America, 23 November 2017.
23. Phak Seangly, "Relocation Site for Sesan Villagers Flooded", *Phnom Penh Post*, 2 November 2017.
24. Xinhua, "Chinese-Built Biggest Dam in Cambodia to Start Operation in November", 25 September 2017.
25. See <https://earthobservatory.nasa.gov>.
26. Van Roeun and Ben Paviour, "Wary of Losing Votes, Hun Sen Makes Rare Call for Reform", *Cambodia Daily*, 27 June 2017.
27. Leonie Kijewski and Yon Sineat, "Voices from the Border", *Phnom Penh Post*, 14 July 2017.
28. Paul Millar, "Why the West was Doomed to Fail in Cambodia", *Southeast Asia Globe*, 1 January 2018.

Indonesia

INDONESIA'S ARMED FORCES
Rejuvenation and Regeneration

Donald E. Weatherbee

On 5 October 1981, Indonesia's Armed Forces, ABRI (*Angkatan Bersenjata Republik Indonesia*), celebrated its thirty-sixth anniversary with a massive display of military pomp and muscle. At the Cilegon naval centre, on the shores of West Java, in front of an audience of thousands, 20,000 members of ABRI took part in a war-like exercise that featured a fly-past of fifty planes including American built F-5E "Tigers", A-4 "Skyhawks", and OV-10 "Broncoes", and a naval parade of thirty-seven vessels showcasing Indonesia's two NATO class submarines and the French Exocet surface-to-surface missile systems of the Navy's new corvettes and fast-attack craft. Combat troops stormed ashore in a mock amphibious landing, putting their newly acquired Western-made armour on the beach. Similar, albeit more modest, demonstrations of Indonesia's military hardware took place at Medan, North Sumatra, and Ujung Pandang in South Sulawesi.

Although at one level of analysis obviously a show of force in a troubled regional international environment, this year's ABRI display again illuminates the central position that the Armed Forces occupy in Indonesia's national life. In the words of Defence Minister and ABRI's Commander, General Mohammad Jusuf, Armed Forces Day was meant to underline ABRI's role in "strengthening national resilience and enhancing the unity of the country and people" (*Straits Times*, 5 October 1981). From the point of view of ABRI's leadership, this is a critical task

---

Reprinted in abridged format from Huynh Kim Khanh, ed., *Southeast Asian Affairs 1982* (Singapore: Institute of Southeast Asian Studies, 1982), pp. 149–63. At the time of original publication, Donald E. Weatherbee was the Donald S. Russell Professor of Contemporary Foreign Policy at the University of South Carolina and, for the academic year 1981/82, was a Fulbright Research Fellow at the Institute of Southeast Asian Studies.

in an atmosphere in which the traditional cleavages of race, ethnicity, and religion are exacerbated by the social and political antagonisms engendered by uneven patterns of economic change, perceived inequalities in income distribution, and corruption — in 1981 heated up by the run-up to the 1982 general elections to be followed by the presidential selection process in 1983.

The military portion of "national resilience" is conceptualized in the formulations of the People's Defence System, HANKAMRATA (*Pertahanan Keamanan Rakyat Semesta*), which seeks to unite functionally the wider society with the Armed Forces in the territorial defence of the *wawasan nusantara* — the indivisible unity of the land and sea elements of the archipelago. The doctrine explicitly relates the economic, political, social, and psychological factors of national development to the tasks of defence. Implicit is a defence-specific justification for the military penetration of non-military social sectors, thus further legitimizing the military's "dual function". On the other hand, the People's Defence System realistically focuses on the problem of internal security and domestic warfare. At its core is the notion of the Armed Forces operating with the active assistance of the wider population organized into local resistance groups. In many respects the current articulation of the HANKAMRATA is a restatement of the long controlling military doctrine of territorial warfare and management which has its experiential origins in the lessons of Indonesia's revolutionary struggle. Although ABRI continues to move towards professionalization, modernization, and bureaucratization, in HANKAMRATA its guerrilla warfare genesis is still valued.

Theoretically the People's Defence System provides the framework for the vertical and horizontal integration of ascending levels of territorial military commands, governmental units, and social groups — from village to nation — for the purpose of defence against any enemy that might threaten the territorial or political integrity of the *wawasan nusantara*.[1] The central assumption, common to doctrines of people's warfare anywhere, postulates the unity and ideological solidarity of the people and the Armed Forces in their determination to resist by conventional and unconventional warfare the enemies of the Republic and Constitution. Great stress, therefore, is laid on qualities and attributes such as motivation, self-confidence, tenacity, heroism, and morale.

The command structure of ABRI gives organizational effect to the People's Defence System, creating a kind of military "spider web" enclosing the *wawasan nusantara*. Given Indonesia's limited economic and technological capabilities, in conjunction with the definition of the principal security threat being internal, it is theoretically logical (as well as politically realistic) that the territorial defence concept emphasizes the role of the Army, both in its combat and quasi-administrative functions. The doctrinal assertion is the requirement that all defence and security efforts should be unified in one organization which can be centrally managed and controlled. This principle rationalizes the fact of army dominance in the joint staff structure installed in 1969, which ended the operational autonomy of the services and signalled Suharto's consolidation of power.[2]

At the national level, integration is accomplished in the Department of Defence and Security (HANKAM) headed by the Minister of Defence and Security, concurrently Commander-in-Chief of the Armed Forces. There are four Area Defence Commands (KOWILHAN):

I — Sumatra and West Kalimantan;
II — Java, Madura, and Nusatenggara;
III — Sulawesi and the rest of Kalimantan;
IV — Malaku and Irian Jaya. From the Area Commands, the organization proceeds downward into smaller and smaller units providing intensive territorial control and administration. The basic operational unit is the Army Regional Command (KODAM) covering one or more provinces. Currently there are sixteen KODAMs. The regional commanders are one or two-star army officers who are responsible for the defence of their territory, having operational control over the forces assigned, as well as responsibility for the People's Defence Forces (HANSIP). Co-ordination of military civic-action is carried out at this level. The combat striking or mobile force is one or more brigades. This is the basic tactical unit. Below the KODAM is the Army Sub-Regional Command (KOREM) supervising parts of provinces or regencies; District Command (KODIM); Sub-District Commands (KORAMIL); down to the village which is considered to be the basic territorial unit.

Through this territorial hierarchy, paralleling the governmental structure, the military have input at all levels of political, economic, and social decision-making from the village upwards, replicating as it were the formal and informal national model in the sub-national scene. The military's wider social and political role thus is further sanctioned by the fact that in addition to fulfilling the principles of People's Defence and providing the framework for civic action, the territorial organization of the Army has created a *de facto* shadow government giving continuity to the political substance of a martial law regime without the legal structure of martial law. This is emphasized by the pervasive influence of the internal security activities of KOPKAMTIB (Command for the Restoration of Security and Order) and BAKIN (Intelligence Co-ordinating Board).

The militarization of administration in Indonesia is a crucial area of civilian-military tension. The concept of "dual function" is, after all, defined by the military not the whole society. It is particularly resented by civilian intellectuals. Certainly it is easy enough to cite examples of irritation on the part of civilians with what is viewed as the expensive and expansive lifestyles of some segments of the officer corps. Nearly every Indonesian has had some contact with corruption and arbitrariness on the part of military personnel, enlisted or officer. This type of criticism, however, tends to be particularized and difficult to aggregate in terms of potential for ABRI-civilian estrangement. ABRI as the bulwark against the dangers threatening Indonesia, internal or external, whatever might be the shortcomings of some of its personnel, is challenged by only an élite minority. To debate on their terms, however, is not to debate doctrine, but the more fundamental question of the role of ABRI in Indonesia.

The Rejuvenation Process

The imperfections of civil-military integration does raise questions about the assumptions of the solidarity of the population with the military, the very basis of the People's Defence System. This was the first task to which General Jusuf addressed himself on taking command. In order to restore pride and morale among the enlisted ranks, welfare measures have been taken to increase pay and benefits, improve housing, and provide expanded dependent care. At the same time there has been an upgrading of skills, more training time, and re-indoctrination. The long-range pay-off is expected to be a better disciplined, more professional military whose conduct will be more correct at the civilian interface. This is particularly important for the territorial forces at the KODIM level and below who have daily face-to-face contact with the greatest part of the Indonesian population; they are ABRI's exemplars for the people.

To improve this image a programme was begun in 1980 to "bring ABRI to the villages" (ABRI *masuk desa*). Company-sized units would spend weeks at a time in the rural areas engaged in what can be called civic action programmes to demonstrate the unity of ABRI and the people. Although some critics have seen an ulterior motive in "ABRI *masuk desa*", having to do with the 1982 elections, it does seem founded at least in the desire to revivify the "organic" link between soldier and citizen demanded by both ideology and doctrine. Finally, at various times in the past few years, schemes to broaden the civilian population's acquaintance with ABRI through expanded military training have been bruited. Given the huge population bulge at the military age — some forty million between fifteen and thirty years of age — it would seem doubtful that much impact could be made, even if funds were available.

A less political, more immediately military issue over the appropriateness of HANKAMRATA has to do with the question of what kind of war should Indonesia prepare to fight. The lessons on which the People's Defence System is founded are drawn from the independence struggle sharpened in the later combat experiences of ABRI down to Timor. The policy question today is whether a military capability based on internal security considerations meets the requirements of the new international environment. Since 1976, a number of ABRI officers, army as well as air force and navy, argue that greater emphasis should now be given to the conventional warfare capabilities of the Armed Forces.

ABRI's "World View"

Although the ABRI élite is by no means monolithic in its outlook, there is a pattern of commonly shared values, attitudes, and perceptions which serve to define the world view of the "Generation of '45".[3] These provide conceptual continuity to policy choices at a different level of ends-means judgements than the developmentally oriented civilian technocrats. For the "Generation of '45", security and stability are the pre-conditions for the achievement of those developmental ends that in terms of resource allocation are more attractive interests to the civilian spokesmen for rational development.[4] The principal themes of the ideology of the "Generation of '45" can be briefly (but not inclusively) listed.

(1) ABRI has both a military and a "social/political" role to play in Indonesia's development. This is the theory of the "dual function" (*dwifungsi*) that postulates not only the propriety but the necessity of military intervention into all aspects of public life. The practice of "dual function" goes well beyond the idea of a civic action role for the military. It legitimates ABRI's political role, participation in economic activities, bureaucratic penetration, and so forth. The "dual function" concept derives from a claim to a special mission of the military to guarantee the fruits of its revolutionary struggle. President Suharto, implicitly answering domestic critics of the "dual function" in his 1978 report to the Consultative Assembly (MPR),

denied that the military's social role was militarism because in carrying out its "role as a dynamic force to create stability and unity for the nation and the state", ABRI relied on reason and consultation, not coercion, to achieve consensus (Jakarta Domestic Service, reported in *FBIS: AP*, 17 March 1978). To oppose ABRI's concept of "dual function" is to challenge the basis of authority in the State itself. The contemporary issue stirring élite politics is how extensive should that "dual function" be. Simply put, opponents (including some influential retired officers) of the way in which ABRI has penetrated all important governmental organs and state-owned enterprises, argue that *dwifungsi* should not mean ABRI monopoly. Will the next generation of ABRI leaders be *dwifungsi* "maximalists" or "minimalists"?

(2) The ABRI élite's perception of the problem of internal security is coloured by a perfervid anti-communism. Although this anti-communism is sometimes criticized as a cynical justification for continued military dominance in national life, its reality as a background for policy-making cannot be ignored. The leading decision-making elements in Indonesia do not accept the proposition that communism as an imminent internal threat to Indonesia's basic security interests has abated. All challenges to "stability" (which in politically realistic terms can be defined as no overt opposition to ABRI's authority) open the door to communist subversion. However, after more than fifteen years since Gestapu, there is beginning to be a willingness to frame the problem of communism in terms of governmental performance at the crucial level of responding to the basic aspirations of the population. There is evidence that the siege mentality view of communism is eroding as some key officers adopt a broader definition of security threat to include the relationship between society and authority.

In the urban centres the disparities between the "haves" and the "have-nots" is most drastically displayed in the vivid contrast between the life-styles of the economic and political élites and the masses of the dispossessed. Although General Jusuf has made an effort to limit ostentatious displays and conspicuous consumption by senior officers, this is only an outward manifestation of a more deeply rooted problem. The obvious symbol of the gap between the élite and the wider population is the widespread corruption that has become the object of popular scorn and bitterness. Here, the "Generation of '45" itself is divided between those who would "stonewall" the issue and those (a much smaller group) who would attempt to purge the system. What will be the new generation's attitudes towards economic inequality and internal security?

(3) The international environment in which Indonesia must find security is basically hostile. A key is that the outside world is fundamentally exploitative (Weinstein, *Indonesian Foreign Policy*). This is paralleled by the belief that Indonesia is vulnerable. Indonesia's élite approaches its friends as well as its potential enemies with suspicion about ultimate motives. This orientation to the international system is one more conceptual foundation giving continuity to Indonesian policy. A psychological support to these assumptions is the sometimes poorly concealed anti-foreignism which has a degree of racial antipathy lurking in the background. It would seem that the new generation's acquaintance with the world — particularly given to the erosion of foreign language skills — is narrower, less "cosmopolitan".

Does a touch of xenophobia lurk in the future background?

(4) ABRI, and especially the Army, through its homogeneity and internal cohesiveness is the only bureaucratic institution that can provide the cement to ensure unity of territory and unity of politics. Part of that cement has been the Javanization of key commands and informal patterns of decision making. Against a historical background of internal revolt and separatist tendencies in the archipelago, compounded by political division and factionalism in the political system, the Army sees itself as the vehicle for national integration, stressing military virtues of solidarity and loyalty in a civilian setting. Although the cohesiveness of the Army may be strained in the future as the new generation of officers replaces the "Generation of '45", it is difficult to imagine an alternate ideological framework developing in ABRI that would significantly change the way that ABRI views its role in the society. On the other hand, despite the ideological recycling of Pancasila and ABRI's secularizing institutional environment the tantalizing question remains as to what degree of influence Islamic political forces may have within the new generation of officers as well as their responsiveness to the kinds of issues raised by the dissident retired officers.

(5) The "Generation of '45" is deeply suspicious of the workings of an undisciplined political party system. As guarantors of the revolution and the 1945 Constitution, ABRI's emphasis is on consensus and unity as opposed to the divisive and disruptive activities of civilian politicians. Although the ABRI sanctioned political system is legitimized in the electoral process and through the parliamentary institutions, this takes place in a carefully constructed and ABRI controlled environment. Real interest conflict in the form of free political competition is not allowed to legitimately enter the system. Those intellectuals who would insist on challenging the consensus risk arrest and imprisonment, or worse, being branded communist. Social grievances and frustrations must not be aggregated in a way that would tarnish the ideal of unity or threaten ABRI's commanding position. In the electoral process ABRI's overt intervention on the side of GOLKAR, the government's non-party political party, continues. Suggestions that ABRI should be aloof from political competition or play a neutral role are rejected. When General Jusuf, with his eye on the professionalization of ABRI, suggested that ABRI should stand above the political fray, he was quickly contradicted. In uncharacteristically tough language, President Suharto made it clear that, if necessary, force would be used to ensure that ABRI as a "socio-political" force would "work closely with other socio-political forces that are truly faithful to Pancasila in defending it and the Constitution". (*Far Eastern Economic Review* [hereafter cited as *FEER*], 2 May 1980, p. 23.) For the other "socio-political" force, read GOLKAR. Will the new generation be any less distrustful of open political competition?

(6) The commitment of the "Generation of '45" to a secular, modernizing nationalism is ideologically grounded in the Pancasila and the 1945 Constitution. The former denies the exclusivity of Islam while the latter is the legal foundation for the ABRI-dominated political system. The developmental component is contained in the notion of "national resilience" (*ketahanan nasional*) which calls for the marshalling of all state capabilities and resources,

material and moral, that give substance to national existence. It is a concept that is explicitly developmental, recognizing the interdependent linkages between security, political stability, economic development, and social welfare. The emphasis is on self-reliance and the maximization of indigenous resources. Although the permeability of the state is recognized as a fact, the doctrine is one that rejects dependence — economic, political, or military. The Indonesian interpretation of "national resilience" minimizes the objective fact of a relatively low base of economic capability by emphasizing less easy-to-measure and offsetting elements of strength such as "the people's determination" and good leadership qualified by adjectives like "tough", "tenacious", "inspirational", "efficient", and "skilled".

It is difficult to generalize about the quality of leadership in Indonesia. The civilian technocratic-bureaucratic élite approaches the problems of Indonesian economy and society in a rational way. On the other hand, they must function within a political framework dominated by patterns of loyalty that can serve to frustrate problem solving. Extensive corruption and the attendant social waste of scarce assets continue to eat away at the regime's legitimacy. But even as one details the internal weaknesses of incumbent leadership, this is done with the realization that in fact there is no readily apparent prospect of an alternative form of authority. One element of "stability", if that is the appropriate word, is the entrenchment of the New Order's system. When Suharto leaves the scene, there are few who do not expect but that he will be succeeded by someone whose basic constituency is in the Army. The question is, what changes are taking place in that constituency?

Notes

1. An extended statement of the HANKAMRATA is in Lt. Gen. Sayidiman Suryohadiprojo, *Beberapa Fikiran Tentang Sistim Pertahanan Keamanan Rakyat Semesta* (Jakarta: HANKAM, Lembaga Pertahanan Nasional, 1976).

2. For the evolution of the Indonesian Army's command structure, see Ruth McVey, "The Post Revolutionary Transformation of the Indonesian Army", Part I, *Indonesia* 11 (April 1971), pp. 131–75; Part II, *Indonesia* 12 (October 1971), pp. 147–81; Nina Vreeland, et al., *Area Handbook for Indonesia*, 3rd edition, (U.S. Department of Army Handbook, DA Pam 550–39), pp. 41ff; Ulf Sundhaussen, "The Military Structure, Procedures, and Effects on Indonesian Society", in *Political Power and Communications in Indonesia*, eds. Karl Jackson and Lucien Pye (Berkeley and Los Angeles: University of California Press, 1978), pp. 57–67.

3. What follows is based on the author's interviews over the period 1967–81 and is confirmed by the works of others, *inter alia*, Franklin B. Weinstein, *Indonesian Foreign Policy and the Dilemma of Dependence* (Ithaca: Cornell University Press, 1976), hereafter cited as *Indonesian Foreign Policy*; Harold Crouch, *The Army and Politics in Indonesia* (Ithaca: Cornell University Press, 1977); Harold W. Maynard, "A Comparison of Military Elite Role Perceptions in Indonesia and the Philippines" (Ph.D. dissertation, American University, 1976), hereafter cited as "A Comparison of Military Elite Role Perceptions"; Donald G. McCloud, "Indonesian Foreign Policy in Southeast Asia: A Study of Patterns of Behavior" (Ph.D. dissertation, University of South Carolina, 1974).

4. John James MacDougall has concluded that the Indonesian technocrats "seem impressively agreed upon a coherent and materially-based modernizing strategy that is a highly functional ideology in that it allows them to enjoy and to order a whole view of a complex economic-political system in crisis". But it is one that rests on considerable coercion. "The Technocratic Model of Modernization: The Case of Indonesia's New Order", *Asian Survey*, XVI, no. 12 (December 1976): 1183.

INDONESIA
The Pancasila State

Donald E. Weatherbee

Ever since Indonesia's "New Order" regime under President Soeharto seized authority from Sukarno's "Old Order" in 1966, political scientists have attempted with varying degrees of objectivity and involvement to characterize the elements of policy and control that have allowed an outwardly authoritarian military oligarchy to maintain and consolidate power for nearly two decades. Thousands of academic and journalistic words have been written seeking to explain the political dynamics of Soeharto's rule. For example, it is tempting to fix it squarely in its indigenous cultural setting: Soeharto as a Javanese king and Indonesia as his kingdom.[1] Ben Anderson saw the major tendencies of the modern state replicating the colonial state.[2] Some western analysts have applied the bureaucratic polity paradigm as explanatory.[3] Donald Emmerson has identified growing "bureaucratic pluralism" as the key feature of the polity.[4] Indonesian social scientists themselves are not averse to playing the model game. In a trenchant structural criticism of the New Order, Gajah Mada University's Dr Mohtar Mas'oed reacted to 1984's contentious draft legislation (discussed below) that would further consolidate the New Order as the regime moves towards a possible 1988 leadership watershed. Dr Mohtar described Indonesia as a "hegemonic-bureaucratic-corporatist" state: that is, it is institutionally led by the military which co-operates with civilian technocrats who are supported by national entrepreneurs who in turn join forces with the international business community.

Reprinted in abridged format from Lim Joo-Jock, ed., *Southeast Asian Affairs 1985* (Singapore: Institute of Southeast Asian Studies, 1985), pp. 133–51. At the time of original publication, Donald E. Weatherbee was the Donald S. Russell Professor of Contemporary Foreign Policy at the University of South Carolina.

Policy making is done in a bureaucratic-technocratic framework avoiding prolonged bargaining.[5]

To the degree that Indonesian leaders are even cognizant of the esoteric analyses of their political system, often they must seem in a "real world" sense irrelevant to the task of unity in a plural society in the context of rapid economic development with its attendant social dislocations. In a *realpolitik* sense this requires in the last analysis coercive controls to back up authoritative decision making. Indonesian leaders insist, however, on the uniqueness of their experience in that they are giving expression to an identity defined by the *Pancasila* — the Five Principles of the Indonesian State: belief in one God, humanitarianism, national unity, consensual democracy, and social justice. First enunciated in 1945 as the basis for unity in the prospective independent state, the vague and general universal values embodied in the Pancasila became the constitutional basis for unity in a society characterized by plural ethnic and religious groups. Today, as state ideology, the Pancasila has become the criterion against which the citizens' activities in the state are measured. The Indonesian model is held up as a Pancasila model. The issue that dominated Indonesian politics in 1984 was how to give practical policy effect to the concept of Pancasila.

Pancasila Democracy

Since 1967 the Soeharto government has explicitly sought to operationalize the Pancasila in terms of policies and practices. The 1973 rationalization of the political party system, for example, was a step towards Pancasila democracy. Beginning in 1978 a major indoctrination programme through P-4 courses was undertaken to eventually implant Pancasila values in the hearts and minds of all Indonesian citizens.[6] Beginning in 1985 P-4 courses will be required in all junior and senior high schools in addition to a new subject "History of the Indonesian People's Struggle". Students are already formally introduced to Pancasila indoctrination in the Pancasila Moral Education courses (PMP) in the lower schools. Even those Indonesians who have not yet been through a P-4 course are oriented to a heightened Pancasila consciousness through the general information activities of the state. The government's ambitious effort to make the Pancasila instrumental guidelines to actual behaviour has required value specification that has not been without controversy. Two issues in particular continued to plague the building of Pancasila democracy as the drive in 1984 was to make it the sole principle for all political and social organizations: the role of opposition and the position of religion.

Pancasila democracy is presented as an idealization of the pattern of political behaviour that supposedly characterized indigenous society.[7] It is stated to grow out of particular Indonesian characteristics. Harmony, cohesion, and consensus are to be strived for. Individualism must give way to the common interest. The role of the government is to express the unity of purpose of the Indonesian people in their aspirations and developmental endeavours. In Pancasila democracy the struggle is to consolidate independence through continuous development. The Indonesian Armed Forces (ABRI) have a special role in Pancasila democracy. Their dual function (security/development) is part of their historic duties as a stabilizing and dynamic force — "including a force which preserves and continuously refreshes Pancasila democracy" (Soeharto, 16 August 1984).

To reject this interpretation is to reject the basis of legitimacy of the New Order society. To oppose the regime is to oppose Pancasila. To oppose Pancasila is to oppose the constitutional foundation of the state. Therefore, opposition is by definition "extremism". For years opposition in Indonesia has been dichotomized as "left" (PKI/communism) and "right" (Darul Islam/Tentera Islam Indonesia/radical Islam). One of the practical political functions of the implementation of Pancasila democracy has been further curtailment of opposition such as advocates of liberal democracy and frustrated ex-generals (the "Petition of 50" group).

The New Order's answer to the problem of opposition and political conflict is to force all social/political forces in the state to conform legally to the Pancasila as their sole ideological and organizing principle. By doing so, according to President Soeharto, they, "will liberate us from the remnants of mutual suspicion resulting from the concrete expressions of the past". The drive for the imposition of the Pancasila as sole principle was particularly felt in 1984 by Muslim groups that see the issue in terms of the subordination of Islam to a secular state ideology manipulated by a regime that is inherently biased against Islam.

Political Parties

The focus of political party activity during the year was continued efforts to put into practice the 1983 mandate contained in People's Consultative Assembly's (MPR) "Broad Outlines of State Policy" that all political parties and functional groups adopt Pancasila as their sole ideological principle. Political party competition in Pancasila democracy is conceived of only in terms of advancing the best programmes and leaders to achieve the consensual goals of development. Opposition based on ideological competition or appeal to partisan interests growing out of social, ethnic, or economic cleavages has no place. In President Soeharto's words, the adoption of Pancasila by the parties, "will facilitate the prevention of conflict among various political groups, which in their efforts to attain their respective goals may cause clashes detrimental to national unity and integrity".

GOLKAR, the non-party government grouping of various functional groups, vigorously promotes Pancasila. It celebrated its twentieth anniversary on 20 October. From a party based on functional groups and association, GOLKAR is being transformed into an organization based on individual membership. The 1984 Congress launched an ambitious cadre training programme. According to GOLKAR chairman, State Secretary Sudharmono, by the 1987 elections eight million cadres will be prepared by 500,000 qualified trainers to campaign to win at least 67 per cent of the votes. The fact that the cadres will include officials down to the village level means that GOLKAR has no plan to let the masses "float". Overt organizational activities by the other parties below the district level apparently still continues to be prohibited.

The United Development Party (PPP) held its first national congress since its 1973 formation on 20–22 August. The PPP is the umbrella party in which the four Muslim parties were forced to merge for electoral purposes while maintaining their separate organizational identities.[8] The rivalry between the two largest factions, MI and NU, was suppressed through government intervention so that the congress could be held to adopt Pancasila as the sole ideological principle. PPP general chairman H.J. Naro, who was named PPP "formateur", orchestrated the proceedings in such a way that his supporters from MI dominated the new executive board, getting 20 of the 38 seats. NU, the largest of the four component parties only received 13 seats. The decline of NU's influence in the PPP strengthened the position of the Situbondo faction led by the traditionalist *ulama* (religious teachers) who would withdraw from the political process and concentrate on Islamic social and religious activity. Certainly the so-called Cipete faction headed by Idham Chalid, who was alleged to have bent with the government wind, could not demonstrate any rewards from staying in the PPP camp. Idham Chalid was deprived of his PPP presidency and not one of his supporters was selected by Naro for the executive board.

The acceptance by the PPP of the Pancasila as the sole ideological principle meant that the three "pillars of Pancasila democracy" were in place with both GOLKAR and the Indonesian Democratic Party (PDI) — the umbrella party for the secular nationalist and non-Muslim religious parties — having already endorsed the concept. The PPP pillar was still wobbly, however. The "ideological" question was raised — that if the PPP's sole principle was the Pancasila, was it any longer a Muslim party? Although expressed in personal attacks on Naro's leadership from leading Sarekat Islam figures, the issue is real both in terms of suitable projection of the party's image, for example, the appropriateness of the Kaabah party symbol (which apparently will not be used in the next general election), and in organizational terms. With the Pancasila as the sole principle, the PPP, as well as of the other parties, is open to membership by any Indonesian. GOLKAR, for example has always claimed to be a "Muslim" grouping given the general population of Indonesia and has its own *dakwah* organization. More importantly, one can ask what is the *raison d'être* of the PPP if its Islamic character is denied.

Fresh from NU's organizational humiliation at Naro's hands at the PPP Congress, a chastened Idham Chalid and his Cipete group formally reconciled with the Situbondo *ulama* at a meeting in Surabaya on 10 September, opening the door for the 27th NU Congress held at Kiai As'ad Syamsul Arifin's Salafiyah Syafiiyah religious school (*pesantran*) in Situbondo 7–12 December. This was after some initial hesitation as to whether the government would allow it take place before the ratification of the bill on mass organizations. Once the *ulama* agreed to constitutionally accept the Pancasila as NU's sole principle, making concrete thereby its rather ambiguous position of a year earlier, the government moved rapidly to expedite the congress. President Soeharto expressed his appreciation for that in his address officially opening the congress. In addition to the President, ten other senior officials spoke giving the 3,500 delegates "guidance". The armed forces provided the logistical support. The congress's slogan was "Back to the NU's Original Programme of Action of 1926", which demonstrated the dominance of the *ulama* and service to the religious sphere as opposed to secular matters. The burning issue was whether NU would leave the PPP. While such a move would reinforce the already perceptible tacit withdrawal of the *ulama* from the formal organized political sphere as Islam was supplanted by the Pancasila as the ideological principle of the PPP, such a decision would have been seen by the government as destabilizing. The problem was finessed by a formulation that held that political party membership was a personal decision, and thus the individual NU member was not obligated to the PPP.

Meanwhile, the PDI limped through the year not fully recovered from the internal dispute spurred by its First Chairman Sunawar Sukowati's statement on the "secular state" in 1983. It was not until November that the party's full 15-member executive committee could meet and then only after the intervention of Interior Minister Supardjo Rustam to invite the PDI to maintain internal harmony.

In his 16 August 1983 Independence Day address to parliament, President Soeharto denied any intention of forcing a single party system on Indonesia. "That fear is without grounds," he said. Yet, with the ideological homogenizing processes of Pancasila democracy, GOLKAR's now "non-opposition" opposition has an identity crisis. What in fact do the religious parties represent — not just those in PPP but the Christian parties under the PDI umbrella — now that religion is excluded as a legitimate basis for political activity? What can they offer that will attract and hold followers in terms of legally approved alternative platforms distinct from GOLKAR that relates to any electoral function? The traditional role of political parties of aggregating and articulating competitive interests has been both conceptually and legally constrained. From a political sociology vantage point, given the military's dominance in the New Order, one can, in fact, begin to question whether the PPP and PDI will continue to have what Duverger[9] calls a political party's deepest significance in the creation of new élites, providing the framework for the masses to recruit their leaders from amongst themselves. Like the other structures of society the parties now must be viewed as essentially GOLKAR's adjuncts in the mobilization of the population to the tasks of national development.

Mass Social Organizations

Not just political parties, but all voluntary organizations are to be geared to national development on the ideological foundation of the Pancasila. If the social organizations of Indonesia, in particular those based on religious profession, could not be persuaded to the Pancasila as their sole principle, the new 1984 legislation would require the adoption of the Pancasila on pain of dissolution.

In June 1984 five draft bills were introduced in Indonesia's parliament (DPR). The five draft laws include a bill on the revision of the general election law; a bill on the revision of the law on the composition and position of the constitutional representative bodies (MPR, DPR, and the DPRD); a bill on the revision of the law on political parties and functional groups (GOLKAR); a bill on constitutional referendum; and a bill on social/mass organizations. The legislation was billed as a perfection of Pancasila democracy, providing a framework within which all citizens could cultivate their contribution to national development. Once adopted, the legislation would be another step in the consolidation of the army-based New Order regime as it prepared for generational change at its most senior official levels, guaranteeing continuity of authority.

The draft law on mass organizations was the most divisive as it requires all voluntary social groups to adopt the Pancasila as their sole ideology. It also gives the government the right to direct their activities in the interests of national development and dissolve them if necessary. According to Home Minister, Suparjo Rustam, under whose jurisdiction the implementation of the measure will fall, all kinds of organizations, no matter how small, will be subject. The only exception will be non-voluntary governmental organizations or organizations set up by non-Indonesians.

In a carefully worded commentary, the leader writers of *Kompas* (19 September 1984) picked up on Juwono Sudarsono's testimony before the DPR's GOLKAR faction reflecting a view that the intellectual source of the proposed legislation — and particularly the mass organization bill — was to be found in the politically and economically privileged establishment. The fundamental concern, in *Kompas*' words, is that Pancasila not become the "guarantor of the social status quo", a conservative ideology for social control unconnected to the interests of the politically and economically weaker majority of the Indonesian population. According to the Jakarta Legal Aid Institute (LBH) the most disturbing articles in the political bills were those on "cultivation, suspension and dissolution of social/mass organizations". Cultivation, it was felt may turn into control, supervision into restriction, and the reasons for suspension and dissolution have not been specified, and thus the government is free to make its own interpretations.

Liberal, intellectual criticism of the legislation was mild compared to the response propagated through the teaching and missionary activity (*dakwah*) of traditional Islamic spokesmen. From mosque and meeting hall, in pamphlets and wall posters, the mass organization bill was denounced as putting the secular ideology of Pancasila before Islam. Although government spokesmen from President Soeharto downwards constantly reiterated that the law on mass organizations was not anti-religious or anti-Islam, their explanations tended to fall on the deaf ears of the "true believers" who saw the Pancasila guarantee of freedom of religion in the sense of tolerance an unacceptable equation of Islam with the other religious streams in Indonesia despite the fact that more than 90 per cent of the population is, statistically at least, Muslim.

Indonesia's committed Muslims (*santri*), perhaps 40 per cent of the Islamic population, have long felt that the New Order regime is hostile, encompassing as it does the cultural values of heterodox Javanism (*abangan*), political secularism, corrupt alliance with much disliked Chinese entrepreneurs (*cukong*), and Christian penetration (it is not unremarked that General Murdani is a Catholic). The *santri* community is deeply offended, for instance, by the fact that in Pancasila education Javanese mysticism (*kebatinan*) is given the status of religious belief (*kepercayaan*) in a way deemed fundamentally subversive to Islam.

The government has sought to be sensitive to Islamic concerns in some non-strategic areas of national life. In 1973 when confronted by vigorous Islamic protest it backed away from a controversial marriage bill. The government periodically campaigns against gambling, prostitution, pornography, and the other manifestations of what Muslim critics call the moral decay of a society contaminated by secular values. The latest crackdown on vice was initiated by President Soeharto himself on 24 October. Religious and legal officers of the government are quick to act to control efforts to convert the Muslim faithful by other religious communities. A scandal in April 1984 surrounded the activities of a Christian cult called the "Children of God" whose foreign members in the guise of language teachers allegedly enticed young Muslims by communal sex. The government is not prepared, however, to give way to demands that somehow the state should express an Islamic quality. It is not prepared to sacrifice hard won unity to particularistic demands.

The mass organization bill was a kind of last straw for many Muslims. They had been forced to acquiesce to religious pluralism as the basis of the state. The Islamic political parties had been first emasculated in the legal framework of electoral competition, then made redundant in terms of opposition by the Pancasila as a single principle. Now any organization that had an Islamic base must become a Pancasila organization. The government's assurance that Muslims were not threatened and that they could freely practice their religion seemed in fact to restrict the profession of Islam to family, mosque and prayer, whereas devout Muslims believe that their religion expresses a total way of life and the fullness of human activity and organization is supposed to reflect this expression.

While Pancasila democracy may have disciplined the political structures of Islam, religious teachers were less compliant. Muslim grievances and calls to action are transmitted through the *dakwah* ("Call to the Truth"), the Islamic proselytizing mission. Fiery orators, practitioners of the "hard" *dakwah*, preached a polarizing anti-government, anti-Pancasila as sole principle social and political message. An environment was created in which the more radical and uncompromising Muslims were prepared for more direct opposition including political violence.

ABRI

The Indonesian Armed Forces special role in society continues to be acknowledged as the core institution in Pancasila democracy. ABRI's own appreciation of the internal threat from extremism — left or right — has been enhanced. For the institution, 1984 was essentially the completion of the process of generational change in ABRI's active duty officer corps as the last of the '45 generation reached the age of retirement. However, President Soeharto made rhetorically clear what was already practically understood: that is that the '45 generation will continue to lead the Indonesian people "as long as they are needed".

General L.B. Murdani is the ABRI chief. With his multiple commands, which in June 1984 saw direct responsibility for presidential security added, General Murdani has become the most powerful ABRI chief since 1967. The 1983 reorganization of the defence establishment which split the formerly unified position of ABRI commander and Minister of Defence does not seem to have diminished Murdani's influence. Certainly his profile has been high, not only in narrow security matters but in the diplomacy of the Kampuchean crisis as well. The question remains, of course, as to how much of that influence is attributed to his institutional role as opposed to his personal relationship with President Soeharto. There was some speculation that he might have gone too far. This was fuelled when in March, President Soeharto raised the navy, airforce, and police commanders to four-star rank, an active duty status that only Murdani had enjoyed.

In 1984 ABRI began the most thoroughgoing reorganization since Soeharto's centralization of authority in the 1969 reorganization. When it is completed in April 1985, ABRI will theoretically have shorter and tighter lines of command and a greater concentration of forces for strategic purposes. In the army the four three-star military theatre commands (*Kowilhan*) will be abolished. The number of two-star regional commands (*Kodam*) is being halved, from 17 to eight plus the Jakarta command. These changes will be phased in as the present incumbent generals retire. The vertical hierarchy from *Kodam* to *Korem* (sub-regional command), *Kodim* (district) and *Babinsa* (non-commissioned village presence) will be maintained, but the *Korem* will have greater operational authority. One result of the reorganization will be fewer general officer command billets which means that selection will be tighter.

The navy will also be drastically restructured. The current eight naval regional headquarters will be reduced to the two fleet bases at Surabaya and Teluk Rantai on Sumatra's West Coast. Rationalization of the airforce command structure is meant to return it to the 1950–1966 RAF model. Only the army will maintain a general staff. The general staffs of the navy and airforce will be replaced by directorates with direct access to lower executive units.

Alleged ABRI involvement in the so-called "mysterious killings" or elimination by "death squads" of criminal elements continued to capture attention in 1984, although the issue was less burning as the actual number of "death squad" hits declined. Jakarta's Legal Aid Institute estimates that since 1982, at least 4,000 suspects have been eliminated. By the end of 1984, in the words of GOLKAR's Secretary General Sarwono Kusumaatmadja, "There is a general feeling all over the place that it [the killing] has practically disappeared" (*Straits Times*, 9 October 1984). The decrease in incidents (bodies discovered) was probably more a function of the fact that the purpose of "exemplary justice" as a criminal deterrent, which apparently had wide popular support, had largely been accomplished, rather than any Indonesian deference to external human rights groups. The question of the killings was embarrassingly raised, for example, by Dutch Foreign Minister Hans van den Broek during his January 1984 visit to Jakarta. General Murdani made it clear that a discussion of the issue was interference in Indonesia's domestic affairs. As for Amnesty International, Sarwono caustically challenged, "Let them live in a remote village in Indonesia".

The Economy

According to President Soeharto the essence of the implementation of a Pancasila society is national development. Indonesia's development ambitions are framed in its five-year plan, the fourth of which began in 1984, a year that saw the favourable macro-economic trends discerned in late 1983 continue.

The World Bank's annual report on Indonesia showed that the economy had made a remarkable recovery from the lows of the early 1980s. A realistic strategy of prudence and austerity in coping with lower oil prices had worked with exports climbing, current account deficits narrowing, and foreign exchange reserves increasing. Gross Domestic Product

(GDP) grew 4.5 per cent in fiscal year 1983/1984 with a predicted 5.1 per cent growth rate in 1984/85. Inflation rose to 12 per cent as a result of devaluation and increases in domestic fuel costs. Indonesia is the world's seventh largest borrower with a gross external debt at the end of 1982 of US$24.4 billion. Its debt of US$8.1 billion to the World Bank and the International Development Agency (IDA) make Indonesia those organizations' third largest borrower. Indonesia's foreign exchange reserves closed in 1983 at more than US$8.6 billion, and although its debt service ratio is high, nearly 23 per cent, there is little concern about repayment capability. The ability of Indonesia's economic managers with political backing to make tough decisions in 1983 with the 28 per cent devaluation of the rupiah and the cancelling or rephasing of 47 industrial projects certainly contributed to the turnaround. International approval of Indonesia's economic course was given by the 1984 aid pledge of US$2.46 billion by the International Governmental Group on Indonesia (IGGI) made up by the World Bank and 12 major creditors. This was underlined by the subscription of the US$750 million jumbo loan covering the largest part of 1984's commercial borrowing needs. The World Bank signalled two major priorities: reduction in dependency on oil exports and job creation. These are addressed in Indonesia's fourth five-year plan (Repelita IV).

Foreign Relations

After years of carefully projecting a non-threatening, co-operative low profile in its region and beyond, Jakarta now is beginning to claim an international role more consonant with its deeply felt need for leadership. The reasons for Indonesia's current policy stance include self-confidence born from successful internal political and economic consolidation and the weathering of the recession; the leadership's new-found desire to obtain greater recognition on the international stage as a middle-range power; growing disenchantment with the political lead being given to ASEAN by the front-line state; and concerns about the regional impact of policies of external powers. To these intangibles the factors of population, size, geostrategic location, resources, and national pride can be added to define a foreign policy identity that is more forceful and assertive in promoting national interest.

Although in a manner analogous to the domestic scene it might seem tempting to project the Javanese palace model of politics to the international stage, viewing Indonesia as a kind of latter day Majapahit, we would argue that a stronger case could be made for viewing Indonesian foreign policy in terms of rational adjustments to a changing foreign policy environment in a period of incrementally increasing capabilities. In other words, myths of the past are not necessary to interpret the contingent responses to the interests of the present. In 1984, Indonesia's new assertiveness was particularly evident in its Indochina policy, towards its western and southern neighbours, and in its great power relations.

East Timor

Total security in East Timor continues to elude Indonesian authority nearly a decade after the forcible integration of the former Portuguese colony into the republic. After clashes in August 1983, terminating a period of several months in which policies of peaceful reconciliation were pursued, Indonesian troops in the province were reinforced to perhaps 12,000 men for a final drive against several hundred remnant Fretilin guerillas. By July 1984, Armed Forces chief Murdani could announce that unrest had been quelled with Fretilin confined to remote mountains and reduced to small bands of men foraging for food. With the passage of time, the international aspects of Indonesia's East Timor problem have gradually receded to the background. For the second year in a row debate on the East Timor item on the U.N. General Assembly's agenda was postponed to the next session. Continuing bilateral contracts between Indonesia and Portugal furthered by Secretary-General Perez de Cuellar's quiet diplomacy created an atmosphere in which it was felt that renewed open debate would be counterproductive.

The question remains as to what substantial alterations in Indonesia's vigorous assertion of sovereignty in the territory might be produced by quiet diplomacy. "Our principle," says Foreign Minister Mochtar, "has already been clear, namely, that there is no longer any problem as regards East Timor which has been an inseparable part of Indonesia" (*Antara*, 29 July 1984). This is no reason to expect, in the absence of compelling sanctions, Indonesia to retreat from its position. Obviously, then, negotiations will be limited to facilitating international activity (UNICEF, ICRC, UNHCR) in meeting the humanitarian needs of the Timorese and the programmes of repatriation and family reunion. On the human rights issues, Indonesia firmly rejects the continued interventions of outside forces whether Amnesty International, the Australian Labor Party, American congressmen, or, as in 1984, even the Pope.

Indochina Diplomacy

In 1984 Indonesia began what came to be called its "dual track" diplomacy towards Vietnam; that is, while continuing to operate within the consensual framework of ASEAN, it would nevertheless explore bilaterally possible avenues for compromise. The pursuit of a more "realistic basis" for settlement than that officially endorsed by ASEAN in the ICK (International Conference on Kampuchea) formulations, is based on Indonesia's perception that the long term threat to Southeast Asia is China, not Vietnam and that the stalemate that has been created by frontline-led ASEAN diplomacy has made the region more vulnerable to that threat.[10]

The most dramatic event which to some observers suggested a potential Indonesian break with the ASEAN position was the 13–18 February visit to Vietnam of General Murdani. The ABRI chief had twice before visited Hanoi as President Soeharto's trouble shooter. The 1984 visit was different, however, because of his institutional role. He was the first senior government official of an ASEAN country to visit Hanoi since 1980. There was speculation that the visit and agenda was without, it seems, prior ASEAN consultation. General Murdani, probably reflecting the general attitude in the Indonesian military, indicated that Indonesia does not think that Vietnam is a threat to Southeast Asia and, in fact, expressed understanding of Vietnam's own threat perceptions from China. Murdani's trip was followed in the same month by a Hanoi seminar co-sponsored by Jakarta's influential Centre for Strategic and International Studies on problems of peace and stability in Southeast Asia.

Indonesian expectations about possible diplomatic breakthroughs were disappointed when Vietnamese Foreign Minister Nguyen Co Thach visited Jakarta in March. Thach, perhaps missing an opportunity, embarrassed his hosts by insisting on the common problem of China as opposed to a "realistic", that is, mutually satisfactory to Vietnam and ASEAN formula to settle the Kampuchean crisis. Foreign Minister Mochtar, who had a special charge as the 1984 Chairman of the ASEAN standing committee, carried the search for a "realistic" settlement to Moscow in April. Although Indonesian-Soviet bilateral relations were warmed, no progress on Kampuchea was evident.

Indonesia's "dual track" diplomacy was consensually sanctioned by ASEAN when it was designated the ASEAN "conduit" or "interlocutor" with Vietnam at the special ASEAN Ministerial Meeting in May. The 9 July Indochinese Foreign Ministers Meeting welcomed the prospects of the continuation of the Vietnamese-Indonesian dialogue. This was promised in the scheduled January 1985 official visit by Foreign Minister Mochtar to Hanoi. The question is what is meant by the Indonesians when they speak of a "realistic" approach. Increasingly it appears that the answer may lie in misgivings about the role of the Khmer Rouge in Kampuchea. Jakarta does not yet seem to have worked out the modalities for this in the face of probable Thai, and behind Thailand, the People's Republic of China's resistance to such a move.

The People's Republic of China (PRC)

Indonesia, together with Malaysia, still views the PRC as the long term strategic threat in the Southeast Asian region. Vague and ambiguous as it might be, there is a generalized concern about some form of Chinese political expansionism as China acquires new capabilities, including military, as a result of the process of the "four modernizations". China's potential as a future commercial rival in world markets has Indonesia's attention as well. Although the China "threat" is not manifest yet in any concrete fashion, it is the looming background against which short and intermediate range Indonesian China policy is fashioned. In part, for example, Indonesia's initiatives in the Indochina question stem from its deep misgivings about the ultimate goals of China both with respect to Vietnam and, more pertinently, the PRC's strategic penetration of Thailand.

The desultory debate over the quality of bilateral Indonesian-PRC relations brought no changes to their frozen status in 1984. Although Beijing continues to woo Jakarta, the Indonesian military élite in particular rejects the dualism implicit in China's policies towards the ASEAN governments and the ASEAN communist parties. Although influential civilian, political and business voices argue for normalization, the official position remains that so long as there is no explicit guarantee from the PRC that it will not support communist subversive activities in Southeast Asia there can be no normalization. Beneath the surface of the issue, of course, are the long standing suspicions about PRC links to Indonesia's Chinese minority. This is covered by the code words "political stability". To the criticism that this somehow impedes Indonesia's ability to interact diplomatically with the PRC, Foreign Minister Mochtar replies that there is ample opportunity for the necessary bilateral exchanges through the multiple multilateral fora in which both countries participate. As for the mounting pressure for formal Indonesian-PRC trade relations, Mochtar, in a 6 November speech before the American Chamber of Commerce in Indonesia, implied that some form of direct contact might be possible and, in fact, serve to pave the way for normalization of relations. It should be recalled, however, that Dr Mochtar, backed by elements in the Foreign Ministry, has often been out in front on the normalization question. This time, however, ABRI Commander General Murdani agreed that Indonesian political stability would not be disturbed by direct trade relations with China. Mochtar later pointed out that the decision to resume direct trade was not necessarily a prelude to renewed diplomatic ties.

The bilateral issue of normalized Indonesian-PRC relations intersected Indonesia's Indochina diplomacy during the year. Foreign Minister Mochtar was the ASEAN Standing Committee Chairman and thus the co-ordinator of ASEAN's position. Unlike his immediate predecessors, Dr Mochtar did not make any visits to Beijing in this capacity despite his initial statement at the June 1983 Bangkok ASEAN Ministerial Meeting that he might go. In March 1984, former Vice President Adam Malik, since 1972 a vocal advocate of normalized relations with China, urged Mochtar as the ASEAN Chairman to go to Beijing in the cause of peace. Although Mochtar agreed that such a trip would be useful, he cautioned that a visit might "give the wrong signals" noting that because of other considerations, "the time has not yet come" (*Straits Times*, 10 March 1984). This position was reiterated in May when Mochtar revealed that President Soeharto had ruled out any such trip.

Conclusion

Indonesia had, some years before, insisted that its foreign policy voice be heard. Its tone was threatening, the rhetoric revolutionary, the policy confrontation. Some of the variables that led to the external projection of the ultra or radical nationalism of Sukarno's Old Order persist in the New Order. History, geography, self-esteem, etc., are not discontinuous. That which has changed is leadership and its relation to domestic political and economic forces. But this is also not constant. Leadership may be in the process of transition in Indonesia. The events of the past year show too, that the leadership's relation to domestic forces is dynamic, not static. Soeharto's New Order is, after 20 years, itself becoming an establishment order. It is, therefore, too early to say what the ultimate dimensions of Indonesia's foreign policy claims will be.

Notes

1. Susumu Awanohara, "Suharto's kingdom", *Far Eastern Economic Review*, 9 August 1984, pp. 32–36.
2. Benedict R.O'G Anderson, "Old State, New Society: Indonesia's New Order in Comparative Perspective", *Journal of Asian Studies*, XLII, 3 (May 1983): 477–96.
3. Karl D. Jackson, "Bureaucratic Polity: A Theoretical Framework for the Analysis of Power and Communications in Indonesia", in Karl D. Jackson and Lucien Pye, eds., *Political Power and Communications in Indonesia* (Berkeley: University of California Press, 1978), pp. 3–23; J.L.S. Girling, *The Bureaucratic Polity in Modernizing Societies*, Occasional Paper No. 64, (Singapore: Institute of Southeast Asian Studies, 1981).
4. Donald K. Emerson, "Understanding the New Order: Bureaucratic Pluralism

in Indonesia", *Asian Survey*, XXIII, 11 (November 1983): 1220–41.
5. This analysis was contained in a paper delivered to a panel discussion in Yogjakarta and reported in *Panji Masyarakat*, 21 October 1984.
6. P–4, *Pedoman Penghayatan dan Pengalaman Pancasila* (literally, "Guide to Pancasila Living and Practice").
7. Textual bases for the description of Pancasila democracy abound. In 1984, for example, President Soeharto's 16 August Independence Day Address before parliament. In general, for Pancasila democracy see Geoffrey C. Gunn, "Ideology and the Concept of Government in the Indonesian New Order," *Asian Survey*, XIX, 8 (August 1979): 751–69 and Michael Morfit, "Pancasila: The Indonesian State Ideology According to the New Order Government," *Asian Survey*, XXI, 8 (August 1981): 838–51.
8. Nahdatul Ulama (NU), Parti Muslimin Indonesia (PMI), Syarikat Islam (SI), and Perti.
9. Maurice Duverger, *Political Parties: Their Organization and Activity in the Modern State*, 2nd revised English edition (New York: John Wiley & Sons, 1959).
10. ASEAN and Indonesian diplomacy in the Kampuchean crisis is the subject of Donald E. Weatherbee, "The Diplomacy of Stalemate," in Weatherbee, ed, *Southeast Asia Divided: The ASEAN-Indochina Crisis* (Boulder: Westview Press, 1985).

THE INDONESIAN ECONOMY FACING THE 1990s
Structural Transformation and Economic Deregulation

Sjahrir

The decline in oil prices that started in the early 1980s adversely affected the Indonesian economy, partly contributing to the recession in 1982 and part of 1983. However, the decline in oil prices also forced the country to restructure its economy to one that is more diversified and balanced, and thereby more resilient to face the 1990s.

The new series of gross domestic product (GDP) figures announced in the presidential speech in Parliament on 16 August 1989 shows that the non-oil and gas sector grew at a rate faster than the oil and gas sector in the economy during 1983–88. The Indonesian economy grew at an annual average rate of 5.1 per cent during the Fourth Five-Year Plan period (1984–88). The GDP growth rates were 6.74 per cent in 1984, 2.47 per cent in 1985, 5.88 per cent in 1986, 4.98 per cent in 1987, and 5.65 per cent in 1988. The non-oil and gas sector grew by 4.91 per cent in 1984, 5.45 per cent in 1985, 6.24 per cent in 1986, 5.62 per cent in 1987, and 7.36 per cent in 1988.

The structure of production, pattern of export, and structure of government revenue all changed with the decline in oil prices. The importance of the non-oil and gas sector increased in the production structure while the reliance on oil and gas exports declined. Within the non-oil and gas sector the export of manufacturing products increased compared with that of primary products. Sources of government revenue shifted more from oil and gas taxes to income and value-added taxes.

Another major factor which contributed to the shift in the structure of production

---

Reprinted from Ng Chee Yuen and Chandran Jeshurun, eds., *Southeast Asian Affairs 1990* (Singapore: Institute of Southeast Asian Studies, 1990), pp. 117–31. At the time of original publication, Sjahrir was Managing Director of the Institute for Economic and Financial Research, Jakarta, and a Lecturer in the Faculty of Economics, University of Indonesia.

that resulted in an increase in the export of manufactured goods was the government's commitment to the liberalization of the economy. In this connection, financial market liberalization was one of the major programmes of the liberalization policy.

As a result of the above factors, the year 1989 also observed spectacular growth in its capital market. Within a short period of twelve months, market capitalization soared to 5 trillion rupiah from 1 trillion rupiah at the end of 1988. Several new banks comprising both national private banks and foreign joint-venture banks were opened in the country. With increasing optimism and confidence, the Indonesian Government calculated that these developments through liberalization would help mobilize the resources required for the Fifth Five-Year Plan (1 April 1989 to 31 March 1994). The estimated resource required for the plan is 239.1 trillion rupiah, out of which 55 per cent is expected to come from the private sector and the rest from the government.

This article examines the structural transformation of the Indonesian economy in the context of the government's liberalization policy, addressing the issues and problems involved.

Structural Transformation, 1983-88

The average annual GDP growth rate, according to revised figures of the Central Bureau of Statistics was 5.1 per cent for 1984-88. However, it was achieved with varying growth rates in different sectors, and each sector's growth rate, with the exception of the agricultural sector, surpassed the annual population growth of 2.1 per cent.

Table 1 presents the structure of the Indonesian economy in percentages of GDP by industry and by main economic sectors in 1983-88. It is clear from the table that the contribution of agriculture to GDP declined while that of manufacturing rose significantly during the period.

Table 2 shows Indonesia's growth rate by industry and by main sectors. From the table it is apparent that the secondary sector had been growing at a much faster rate than the primary sector. Between 1984 and 1988, the average growth rate in the secondary sector was more than 10 per cent compared with less than 2 per cent in the agricultural sector.

When the New Order of President Soeharto came into effect in 1966/67 the agricultural sector's share in GDP was more than 55 per cent, with 75 per cent of the labour force working in this sector. Despite a rate of growth that was low in the agricultural sector and high in the secondary sector, 55 per cent of the total labour force in 1987 continued to be employed in the agricultural sector whilst the manufacturing sector absorbed only 8.3 per cent of the labour force. The remainder of the labour force was in trade (14.9 per cent), services (15.9 per cent), and others (5.9 per cent). Such a situation shows that the structure of employment had not shifted in accordance with the structure of production. More specifically, this development indicates that despite the heavy investment which gave rise to healthy growth in the industrial sector, this sector was not able to absorb the excess labour at the rate at which the country's labour force was increasing. Given that 2.3 million new workers are expected to join the labour force annually in the current Five-Year Plan period, it is unclear how the unemployed and new entrants will be absorbed into the national economy. This is a serious problem for Indonesia and calls for greater attention to

TABLE 1
Indonesia's Structural Transformations, 1983–88
(As a percentage of GDP)

Sector	1983	1984	1985	1986	1987	1988
Primary	43.52	42.88	40.83	40.00	38.71	37.05
Agriculture	22.78	22.23	22.61	21.88	21.35	21.07
Farm food crops	14.24	13.99	14.00	13.54	13.05	12.84
Farm non-food crops	2.95	2.83	3.03	2.87	2.86	2.84
Estate crops	0.48	0.54	0.60	0.62	0.60	0.58
Livestock and products	2.26	2.28	2.40	2.29	2.24	2.22
Forestry	1.28	1.08	1.00	0.99	1.03	1.02
Fishery	1.57	1.51	1.58	1.58	1.58	1.58
Mining and quarrying	20.74	20.65	18.22	18.12	17.36	15.98
Crude petroleum and natural gas	19.44	19.52	17.08	16.93	16.14	14.74
Others	1.29	1.13	1.14	1.19	1.22	1.25
Secondary	18.66	19.87	21.12	21.43	22.31	23.53
Manufacturing industry	12.74	14.57	15.81	16.31	17.22	18.40
Non-oil and gas manufacturing	9.87	10.45	11.47	12.03	12.79	13.80
Petroleum refinery	0.46	0.75	0.90	1.03	0.99	0.98
LNG	2.41	3.37	3.44	3.25	3.43	3.61
Construction	5.92	5.30	5.31	5.12	5.09	5.13
Tertiary	37.82	37.25	38.05	38.57	38.98	39.42
Electricity, gas, and water supply	0.40	0.39	0.42	0.48	0.52	0.55
Trade, hotel, and restaurant	14.86	14.22	14.58	14.94	15.23	15.71
Transport and communications	5.28	5.36	5.28	5.19	5.24	5.24
Banking and other financial intermediaries	3.04	3.38	3.53	3.85	3.74	3.61
Ownership of dwelling	3.03	2.91	2.90	2.83	2.81	2.77
Public administration and defence	7.35	7.23	7.60	7.62	7.81	7.96
Services	3.86	3.76	3.74	3.66	3.63	3.58
Gross domestic product (GDP)	100.00	100.00	100.00	100.00	100.00	100.00
GDP without oil and gas	77.69	76.36	78.58	78.80	79.44	80.67
GDP without oil	80.86	80.64	82.95	82.95	83.79	85.21

Source: Central Bureau of Statistics, *National Income of Indonesia, Main Tables 1983–1988*, November 1988.

TABLE 2
Annual Growth Rates of Sectors and Industry in the Economy, 1984–88
(At constant 1983 prices)

Industries in Each Sector	1984	1985	1986	1987	1988
Primary	5.17	−2.42	3.8	1.37	1.2
Agriculture, animal husbandry, forestry, and fishery	4.15	4.22	2.55	2.22	4.33
Mining and quarrying	6.29	−9.58	5.35	0.35	−2.64
Secondary	13.65	8.9	7.52	9.08	11.51
Manufacturing industry	22.05	11.19	9.29	10.61	12.96
Construction	−4.42	2.60	2.24	4.21	6.58
Tertiary	5.13	4.67	7.39	5.88	6.89
Electricity, gas, and drinking water	3.22	11.39	19.09	15.08	10.70
Trade, hotel, and restaurant	2.19	5.05	8.57	6.75	9.09
Transportation and communications	8.42	0.99	4.04	5.76	5.83
Banks and other financial institutions	18.79	7.02	15.55	1.89	1.89
House-rent	2.38	2.05	3.42	4.27	4.05
Government and defence	4.99	7.64	6.31	7.34	7.68
Other services	3.87	2.03	3.72	3.74	4.32
GDP	6.74	2.47	5.95	4.76	5.72

Source: Central Bureau of Statistics, *The Economics Census of 1986* (August 1989). The figures are taken from table 6 of a new series of GDP produced using an improved survey method.

the agricultural sector in the form of greater investments in supporting infrastructures to improve productivity.

It is estimated that even with greater investments in the agricultural sector which should alleviate the problem of unemployment, Indonesia would still continue its course towards an industrial state. If we assume a higher growth rate in agriculture, say 4 per cent per annum, and a lower growth rate in industry, say 10 per cent, it can be shown through projection that by 1992 at least, the manufacturing sector will surpass the agricultural sector in its share of GDP. With the above assumptions, the share of agriculture as a percentage of GDP would be 20.46 per cent in 1989, 20.67 per cent in 1990, 20.28 per cent in 1991, and 19.90 per cent in 1992. During the same period the share of the manufacturing industry as a percentage of GDP would be 18.72 per cent in 1989, 19.09 per cent in 1990, 19.81 per cent in 1991, and 20.56 per cent in 1992.

If this is the case, then the Indonesian economy is well on its way to being at a "semi-industrialized" stage of development, according to the classification of Unido (United Nations Industrial Development Organization), in which the share in GDP of the manufacturing sector excluding oil and gas ranges between 20 and 30 per cent.

Distributional Aspect in Structural Transformation

Structural transformation in any economy is generally observed to occur concomitantly with changes in income distribution and at times may even exacerbate the problem of poverty in certain sections of the society. In this regard it is interesting to note that President Soeharto, in his presidential speech on 16 August 1989, provided figures regarding the social well-being of the Indonesian society from 1969 (the start of the First Five-Year Plan) to 1988. President Soeharto[1] underlined the marked improvement which had occurred in nearly all aspects of basic needs and the provision of public utilities in the country.

Per capita food consumption rose impressively. Between 1969 and 1988 the per capita annual availability of rice increased from 107 to 161 kg.; eggs from 0.5 to 2.7 kg.; milk from 0.3 to 1.5 litres, fish from 10.7 to 16.4 kg. Approximately over the same period, the availability of cloth per capita had quintupled, the number of medical doctors per head of population had more than trebled, and other services for public utilities such as the provision of clean drinking water, community health clinics, electricity, roads, and transport facilities all saw marked improvement and expansion.

The poverty line, which measures the level of poverty, also dropped significantly. Indonesia's poverty line is derived from the National Census Survey (SUSENAS), which is essentially a survey on the consumption expenditure of the Indonesian population. The poverty line is set at the rupiah cost of 2,100 calories per day for each person based on a basket of foods, plus a mark-up for basic necessities such as housing, clothing, education, health, and transportation. For the urban area an important part of cost is electricity bills whereas in the rural area the use of electricity is substituted by kerosene oil consumption.

Table 3 shows that the poverty level in urban areas had declined less significantly compared with rural areas. The total number of people classified as poor declined from 54 million in 1976 to around 30 million in 1987. Although the figures themselves are impressive, one has to question the validity of using a "static" approach in measuring the poverty line. This "static" approach is different from that being used in relatively more industrialized economies. In the West, the poverty line is measured by calculating income per capita minus a certain percentage (say, 40 per cent). If the income per capita of Indonesia is US$500, then the poverty line is US$500 minus 40 per cent of US$500, that is, US$300. If the measurement had been done in this more "dynamic" fashion, then the poverty line of Indonesia would be different, and the number of people living below the poverty line would have been higher than 30 million in 1987. But whether one uses 30 million or 50 million (the number obtained using the "dynamic" approach), the important question is "What is the policy agenda for those living below the poverty line?" Food subsidy is definitely out of the question for a country with a per capita income of less than US$500, a foreign debt of more than US$50 billion (with a debt-service ratio of 35–37 per cent), and an under-employment

TABLE 3
Number and percentage of Population Living below Poverty Line, 1976–87

Year	Number of Poor People (millions)			Percentage Living below Poverty Line		
	Urban	Rural	Total	Urban	Rural	Total
1976	10.0	44.2	54.2	38.8	40.4	40.1
1978	8.3	38.9	47.2	30.8	33.4	33.3
1980	9.5	32.8	42.3	29.0	28.4	28.6
1981	9.3	31.3	40.6	28.1	26.5	26.9
1984	9.3	25.7	35.0	23.1	21.2	21.6
1987	9.7	20.3	30.0	20.1	16.4	17.4

Source: Central Bureau of Statistics, *Poverty, Income Distribution and Basic Needs* (Jakarta, August 1989).

level which is high, with four out of every ten persons underemployed in the labour force.

In the past, probably the only "policy agenda" available was the "Inpres Program", which provided funding for different regions through topical subsidies (such as for education, health, and environmental concerns) and direct subsidies to regions (from villages to subdistricts, regencies, and provinces) to be used in developing infrastructure such as roads and tertiary channels for irrigation. However, this method of addressing problems in Indonesia in the past had not been very satisfactory given that the availability of funds fluctuated in tandem with the price of oil. For example, during the oil boom years of the 1970s, funds were readily available for these programmes as government revenue increased rapidly from oil exports and loans were easily obtained internationally. Concomitantly, debts also increased significantly. With the decline in oil prices in the 1980s, funds for such programmes dried up very quickly though the momentum for such investments continued, giving rise to serious political and economic repercussions. This state of affairs prompted the Indonesian Government to focus more attention on economic stabilization policies, commonly known as the concept of "constant format" in Indonesia. Future funding for such programmes would thus be considered within a macroeconomic framework that accords greater priority to stabilization and job creation.

Macroeconomic Policies and Deregulation

The macroeconomic policies in recent years and possibly in the 1990s, which are based on the concept of "constant format", have the following objectives: a balanced budget, a freer foreign exchange regime, a more stable flow of foreign aid through the IGGI (Inter-Governmental Group on Indonesia), and a relatively low rate of inflation.

These policies have already brought about some positive results. To maintain a more balanced budget, a number of large capital-intensive projects were rephased, with billions of dollars of foreign exchange saved; austere budgets were implemented in 1986–88; and central government capital spending was cut by more than 25 per cent. This was supplemented by a sweeping tax reform implemented over 1984–86, which increased non-oil tax revenue and improved the efficiency of the tax system. Domestic inflation was brought under control as the inflation rate was reduced from double- to single-digit for the greater part of the 1980s. There were two currency devaluations, in 1983 and 1986, which resulted in the maintenance of competitive exchange rates that provided strong incentives for non-oil exports.

In addition to these macroeconomic policy reforms, the government also initiated the following deregulation programmes to reduce regulatory impediments and to hasten up economic recovery:[2]

1. Deregulation of banks first started in June 1983. This reform introduced flexibility in allowing state banks to determine the level of interest rates, which were previously set by the Central Bank's "guidelines". Likewise, credit ceilings have also become more flexible for state banks.
2. The New Tax Law, which became effective beginning with budget year 1984/85, is relatively less complicated to administer. Income taxes are fixed at three rates: 55, 25, and 15 per cent. A value-added tax was also implemented, starting from 1 April 1985. Among other things, the government also initiated the "self assessment" system in which official "interferences" in the system are significantly reduced. These measures help increase revenue and efficiency in the Indonesian budget.
3. Under Presidential Instruction No. 5/1984, licensing and regulation powers of government departments are reduced.
4. Responsibility in the area of customs of the Director-General of Customs and Excise was transferred to a Swiss-based private company under Presidential Instruction No. 4/1985.
5. The 6 May 1986 package allows exporters who require imported inputs for their exports to import such goods directly.
6. Another reform which started on 25 October 1986 allows domestic firms which produce goods for the domestic market to import direct raw materials that previously were channelled through only a few state-owned enterprises (SOEs).
7. Reforms on non-tariff barriers were implemented on 15 January and 24 December 1987; non-tariff barriers have been simplified; in some cases, complicated quota systems are brought under the simplified tariff system; and licensing obstacles for investment in some sectors are reduced. The capital market enjoys more laxity with the removal of regulations that prohibited a fluctuation of more than 4 per cent in the price of a stock market share.
8. Deregulation in the financial sector is particularly significant after the 27 October 1988 package. For the first time the opening up of new banks is allowed. The opening up of new branches is made much easier and joint ventures between foreign banks and private national banks are also permitted. This package is responsible for the spectacular activities and expansion in the banking sector in 1989.
9. The 21 November 1988 package covers

trade, shipping, and the industrial and agricultural sectors. In general, non-tariff barriers are further reduced. For example, regulations on shipping lanes are abolished, and regulations on the import of plastics, which is a politically sensitive issue, are relaxed.

10. Capital markets are opened for greater foreign participation in investment under the 20 December 1988 package. Under this scheme, other financial activities such as those involving venture capital and insurance have also been opened up.

11. The March 1989 package is an extension of the October and December 1988 packages. This package, among other things, strengthens the foreign-exchange holding position of domestic banks.

12. Finally, the June 1989 package provides criteria to measure the efficiency of SOEs (called BUMN, Badan-badan Usaha Milik Negara). In a way this move forces SOEs to be more efficient. However, the problem with the criteria is that it is heavily accounting-oriented in its measurement and does not take institutional factors into consideration in its assessment. It uses solvency, liquidity, and profitability as the criteria for evaluation regardless of the nature of the market within which SOEs operate. But a high rate of profitability may not necessarily have any bearing on efficiency level, as in the case of SOEs with monopoly power.

It should be noted, however, that the Cabinet is divided as to how deregulation should proceed in the future. While most of the technocrats from the Ministry of Finance, the Central Bank, and the Ministry of Planning are strong advocates of deregulation, the minister who co-ordinates the committee of ten state-owned "strategic industries", B.J. Habibie, Minister of Research and Technology, is not known to be keen or supportive of deregulation policies.[3]

The financial sector, in particular the capital market, seems to have been most affected by the deregulation. Deregulation in the capital market, together with that in trade, plays an important role in the spectacular growth of Indonesia's non-oil and gas exports.

Banking and the Capital Market

The 28 October 1988 policy decree altered the banking environment substantially. The old bank law of 1967, which effectively prohibited the establishment of new banks, has been superseded by the deregulation package of 1988, which allows private national banks as well as foreign joint-venture banks to be established. Established local banks meanwhile expand rapidly, opening up new branches and sub-branches all over the country.

In addition to the above reforms, the scope of banking activities has also been widened. For instance, national banks are now permitted to deal in transactions related to foreign exchange. Similarly, reserve requirements have been reduced from 15 to 2 per cent. With deregulation, banks began to provide competitive interest rates. To raise additional funds, some banks have not only increased their interest rates but also started a new savings package called TAHAPAN (Tabungan Hari Depan or Saving for the Future) and KESRA (Kesejahteraan Rakyat or the People's Welfare). It is therefore not surprising that Indonesia is awash with liquidity.

Table 4 shows the structure of bank funding. Until 1988, liquidity credit (that is, credit extended by the Central Bank) played an important role in the banking funds of Indonesia. This liquidity credit, which ranged from 25.8 to 34.0 per cent must have been an important inflationary factor in the economy. The data for 1989 on liquidity credit is not available but it is not expected to change significantly from that of previous years.

On the other hand, the mobilization of funds appears to be successful after the deregulation measures of 1988. The Central Bank Governor in his speech at the annual bankers' dinner in January 1990 gave details on the performance of the banking sector in 1989. From the end of 1988 to the end of 1989, M1 increased by 32 per cent and M2 by 35 per cent. Specifically, savings deposits increased from 2.2 trillion to 4.7 trillion rupiah and time deposits also increased by 34 per cent to 8.6 trillion rupiah. Given that the inflation rate for 1989 was less than 7 per cent, the deregulation measures seem to have been successful in mobilizing funding resources, at least in 1989.

To further activate the stock market, the following additional measures have been undertaken: share prices which were previously not allowed to fluctuate by more than 4 per cent are now relaxed; and foreigners are allowed to invest in the capital market, but their participation is limited to 49 per cent of the shares listed. These measures, together with those discussed earlier, resulted in the most spectacular performance in the Jakarta Stock Market. Market capitalization jumped from 1 trillion rupiah at the end of 1988 to 5 trillion rupiah at the end of December 1989. Over this period we observed not only the opening of the Surabaya Stock Exchange but also the marked increase in the number of companies listed: from twenty-four to fifty-seven. In Jakarta, an over-the-counter market for shares has also been started. Table 5 shows the growth in transactions of the Jakarta Stock Market

TABLE 4
Structure of Banking Funds in Indonesia, 1981–88
(As a percentage of total)

Year	Demand Deposit	Time Deposit	Savings Deposit	Liquidity Credit
1981	47.7	21.3	5.1	25.8
1982	41.5	21.8	4.9	31.9
1983	32.5	34.0	4.5	29.0
1984	27.6	34.1	4.3	34.0
1985	25.5	40.1	4.6	29.8
1986	24.4	40.4	5.3	29.9
1987	20.8	46.3	4.9	28.0
1988	19.2	46.4	5.1	29.3

Note: Liquidity credit came from Bank Indonesia, Indonesia's Central Bank.
Source: Bank Indonesia, various weekly and monthly reports.

TABLE 5
Shares Transactions in the Jakarta Stock Market, 1977–89

Year	Total Shares Sold ('000)	Value of Sales (Rp billion)	Average Daily Sales (Rp million)
1977	14.6	0.2	1.6
1978	19.5	0.2	0.9
1979	119.3	1.3	5.4
1980	1,656.3	5.7	22.8
1981	2,891.3	7.7	30.1
1982	5,018.5	12.6	50.7
1983	3,505.7	10.1	40.4
1984	1,218.8	2.1	8.7
1985	1,610.9	3.2	13.1
1986	1,428.2	1.8	7.3
1987	2,532.7	5.2	21.4
1988	6,944.6	30.6	121.9
1989	92,038.2	948.7	3,794.6

Note: The OTC (over-the-counter) market for 1989 produced 16,158,500 shares at Rp41.5 billion.
Source: Badan Pelaksana Pasar Modal.

(excluding the over-the-counter market and the Surabaya Stock Market).

Balance of External Payments

Other measures which affected the external position of Indonesia, such as trade deregulations and the two devaluations of the 1980s, helped to cushion the adverse impact of the decline in oil prices. Manufacturing exports performed creditably from 1986 to 1989. In 1989 manufacturing exports not only dominated the export structure but also accounted for nearly half of Indonesia's total exports. Table 6 gives a breakdown of Indonesia's exports in 1981 and from 1986 to August 1989.

Specifically, the value of non-oil and gas exports in 1989 was estimated to be over US$13 billion, or a monthly rate of more than US$1.1 billion. Until the month of August 1989, the value of exports was US$8,615 million, of which US$6,930 million, or 80.5 per cent, was made up of manufactured goods.

Besides the issue of competitiveness, the Indonesian Government is taking steps to encourage higher "value-added" manufacturing exports using various trade policies, although this move may contradict GATT (General Agreement on Tariffs and Trade) rules. This is specifically reflected in the ban on rattan and higher taxes for semi-processed exports in order to increase the export of higher value-added rattan products

TABLE 6
Exports, 1981 and 1986–89
(In US$ billion)

Year	Oil and Gas	Non-Oil and Gas	Manufactures	Total	Manufactures as % of Total
1981	20.7	4.5	2.6	25.2	10.3
1986	8.3	6.5	4.4	14.8	29.7
1987	8.6	8.6	6.7	17.1	39.2
1988	7.7	11.5	9.3	19.2	48.4
1989*	5.6	8.6	6.9	14.2	48.6

*January–August.
Source: *Indikator Ekonomi*, August 1989; *Buletin Ringkas*, October 1989; Central Bureau of Statistics.

such as furniture. However, this policy to enhance higher value-added products may not necessarily lead to an increase in the total value of exports. For instance, the ban imposed on the export of rattan in August 1988 did not induce a surge in furniture exports. Meanwhile, the value of rattan exports declined from US$162.1 million in fiscal year 1987/88 to only US$36.8 million in fiscal year 1988/89.

Likewise, the prohibitive taxes imposed on sawmill exports did not induce a proportional change in furniture exports. The tax on sawmill exports increased tenfold from US$100 to US$1,000 per cubic metre. In total, around US$600–700 million of exports will be affected and export losses would almost certainly approximate that amount.

Historically, the high volume of rattan and sawmill exports implies that these Indonesian products are highly competitive in the world market. However, this may not necessarily be the case with furniture exports, which require higher skills and marketing techniques. Given the circumstances, if there is no inverse relationship between the increase in furniture exports and the decline in raw material exports, the impact of this trade policy may adversely affect exports and result in higher unemployment. Therefore, before extending this policy to other sectors of the economy, due attention must be given to these considerations. In an environment of increasing globalization of capital and technology, such protectionist measures are unlikely to improve the trade environment and export performance of Indonesia.

In any case, the deregulation measures improved the non-oil and gas balance significantly. As a consequence, despite the lower oil prices, the overall trade balance improved, which prevented the current account deficit from worsening during fiscal years 1984/85 to 1988/89, except for 1986/87 (Table 7). The sharp decline in oil prices in 1986 resulted in lower oil-export revenue in 1986/87 and this adversely affected the current account deficit. Oil exports declined from US$8,816 million in 1985/86 to US$4,798 million in 1986/87.

Fairly stable current account deficits during the period enabled the Indonesian

TABLE 7
Summary of Balance of Payments, 1984/85 to 1988/89
(1 April to 31 March yearly)
(In million US$)

Description	1984/85	1985/86	1986/87	1987/88	1988/89
A Goods and services					
1 Export (f.o.b.)	19,901	18,612	13,697	18,343	19,824
Non-oil and natural gas	5,907	6,175	6,731	9,502	12,184
Oil	10,625	8,816	4,798	6,159	5,007
Liquid natural gas	3,369	3,621	2,168	2,682	2,633
2 Import (f.o.b.)	−14,427	−12,552	−11,451	−12,952	−14,311
Non-oil and natural gas	−11,630	−10,078	−9,356	−10,597	−12,239
Oil	−2,605	−2,282	−1,908	−2,190	−1,912
Liquid natural gas	−192	−192	−187	−165	−160
3 Services (netto)	−7,442	−7,892	−6,297	−7,098	−7,372
Non-oil and natural gas	−4,061	−4,052	−4,010	−4,372	−4,864
Oil	−2,175	−2,530	−1,464	−1,635	−1,560
Liquid natural gas	−1,206	−3,310	−823	−1,091	−948
4 Current account (netto)	−1,968	−1,832	−4,051	−1,707	−1,859
Non-oil and natural gas	−9,784	−7,955	−6,635	−5,467	−4,919
Oil	5,845	4,004	1,426	2,334	1,535
Liquid natural gas	1,971	2,119	1,158	1,426	1,525
B Government borrowing	3,519	3,432	5,472	4,575	6,588
1 Program and	52	38	585	1,296	2,192
2 Project and	1,471	1,379	1,973	1,894	2,406
3 Other project and	1,795	1,473	1,495	1,185	1,005
4 Direct and other borrowing	201	542	1,419	200	985
C Government debt repayment	−1,292	−1,644	−2,129	−3,049	−3,763
1 Debt before July 1966	−31	−36	−123	−84	−95
2 Debt after July 1966	−1,261	−1,608	−2,006	−2,965	−3,668
D Other capital inflows (netto)	499	572	1,232	1,709	−211
1 Direct investment	496	561	514	814	878
2 Repayment of investment loan	−251	−262	−262	−270	−293
3 Other loans	34	166	321	543	707
4 Repayment of other loans	−442	−476	−478	−488	−470
5 Other capital	662	583	1,137	1,110	−1,033
E Special drawing rights (SDRs)	—	—	—	—	—
F Monetary movement	−667	−30	738	−1,585	677
1 IMF credit position (netto)	6	−15	−9	−8	5
2 Short-term loan (netto)	—	—	—	—	—
3 Short-term money owned but not yet received	−672	−15	747	−1,577	672
G Unaccounted difference	−91	−498	−1,262	57	−1,432

Source: Presidential speech in Parliament on 16 August 1989, on the implementation of the Fourth Five-Year Plan (1 April 1984 to 31 March 1989), table V-1, page V/18/.

Government to better manage its debt situation, although debt repayment increased from US$1,292 million in 1984/85 to US$3,763 million in 1988/89 — an increase of almost 200 per cent. The debt crisis was also eased with a new debt management policy, under which greater preference have been given to loans which can be obtained under concessionary conditions and with low interest rates rather than commercial loans that carry higher interest rates.

If Indonesia continues its prudent debt management policy, if it is able to control its current account deficits by raising non-oil and gas exports, and if oil prices do not decline sharply, then it is possible that in the 1990s Indonesia's external balance situation could be further improved. Despite the increasing role played by the non-oil and gas sector, the importance of oil and gas remains significant to the Indonesian economy. As a manifestation of this fact, the current account deficit of more than US$4 billion in budget year 1986/87 was directly related with the drastic decline in oil price to US$9 per barrel in 1986. Thus, if the current trend continues, the Fifth Five-Year Plan target of a debt-service ratio of 25 per cent is achievable.

Economic Institution: State-Owned Enterprises and the Indonesian "Conglomerates"

One of the important policies initiated in 1989 under the Ministerial Declaration by the Ministry of Finance attempts to increase the efficiency and productivity of SOEs. This policy, using the "profitability", "liquidity", and "solvency" criteria (known as BUMN, or Badan-badan Usaha Milik Negara), evaluates the enterprises and categorizes them as "very healthy", "healthy", "less healthy", and "unhealthy". The categorization is then used to promote efficiency and profitability through "merger" and even divestment of these enterprises. Out of 213 SOEs, 188 were evaluated and classified thus: thirty-five very healthy, twenty-five healthy, thirty-seven less healthy, and the rest unhealthy. After the evaluation, the Minister of Finance announced that fifty-two SOEs are ready to "go public" as early as 1990. Since the total assets of all SOEs amounted to 123.478 trillion rupiah, an amount that is larger than Indonesia's GDP (at 114.520 trillion rupiah) in 1987,[4] it is very important to understand policies related to the operation of SOEs.

The criteria developed to evaluate the SOEs have some problems. To begin with, the institutional aspects of the market within which these enterprises operate are not taken into consideration. There are many SOEs which get concessions and monopoly power to import inputs and some of them even get protected market access to their products. For example, before the removal of non-tariff barriers on the import of plastics, PT Mega Eltra, an SOE, in co-operation with a private company monopolized the import of plastics. Companies needing plastics for their inputs were forced to pay the price set by this SOE since direct importation was forbidden. In these circumstances the profitability of PT Mega Eltra would be inflated while companies that buy plastics from this company as inputs in their production would register lower profitability. Under such distorted market conditions the relevance of the profitability criteria is thus questionable.

Similarly, PLN (Perusahaan Listrik Negara), the state electricity company, has been classified as "unhealthy". The problem with PLN is that the company has to pay the price set by another SOE, PERTAMINA, for its energy inputs, and its output price is also fixed by the government. In such a situation it is difficult to evaluate PLN on the basis of profitability.

The above problems are compounded by the establishment of a new board called BPIS (Badan Pengelola Industri Strategis), which controls ten SOEs classified as "strategic". Since the definition of strategic industries is ambiguous, enterprises which may not be strategically important may likewise want to be so classified to escape evaluation under the Finance Minister's criteria of deregulation, and eventual divestment.

With regard to private companies, the main concern has been the growth of operation and market share of a few companies. According to one source,[5] the total sales of the largest 300 Indonesian conglomerates approximate 70 trillion rupiah, which is nearly twice the budget of fiscal year 1988/89. Given the growing size of these conglomerates and their domination by Indonesian Chinese, the current debate in the media may have ethnic and political repercussions in Indonesia.

Concluding Remarks

If present trends continues, it is expected that the role of market forces will play an increasingly important role in the 1990s. With further trade deregulation, financial liberalization, and the privatization of SOEs, it is hoped that the economy will move towards a higher level of development. However, certain problems that require special attention remain. The politicization of the issues of conglomerates and SOEs needs to be better managed and the question of redistribution warrants greater focus.

The economic development experienced in the past two decades shows that the economy has not been able to adequately absorb the rising labour force in the secondary and tertiary sectors alone. This fact has to be taken into consideration in formulating future development policies.

With the decline in oil and gas revenue, the bulk of the budget should come from income tax, value-added tax, and duties. This is only possible with the growth of the private sector, which is dependent on a conducive business climate that is competitive. In the end, the key to the success of the policy, which aims to increase the role of the market in the economy, lies in the capability of the government to change its role from taking an omnipotent and omnipresent position to one that facilitates a competitive economic environment.

Notes

1. Jamie Mackie and Sjahrir, "Survey of Recent Development", *Bulletin of Indonesian Economic Studies* 25, no. 3 (December 1989); figures taken from the presidential speech on 16 August 1989.
2. Mostly from Sjahrir, "Indonesian Financial and Trade Deregulation: Government Policies and Society Responds" (Paper delivered at the Workshop on the Dynamics of Economic Policy Reform in Southeast Asia and Australia, Griffith University, Queensland, 7–8 October 1989).
3. Mackie and Sjahrir, op. cit., pp. 31–33.
4. *Profit & Anatomi BUMN*, vol. 1, 2nd ed. (Pusat Data Business Indonesia, 1989). The English translation is *Profile & Anatomy of the State-Owned Enterprises* (Indonesian Business Data Center, 1989).
5. *TEMPO* (weekly news magazine), 6 January 1990, pp. 102–3.

A YEAR OF UPHEAVAL AND UNCERTAINTY
The Fall of Soeharto and Rise of Habibie

Leo Suryadinata

On 21 May 1998 Soeharto announced that he was unable to continue leading the nation and had decided to step down. His deputy, B.J. Habibie, was immediately sworn in as the new President. This dramatic three-minute event ended the Soeharto era. It was the culmination of several dramatic months of rising political violence and protest, but failed to usher in a much hoped-for era of political stability.

Economic Crisis

The Indonesian economy deteriorated rapidly following the onset of the regional economic crisis that began in the middle of 1997 in Thailand. Indonesia, forced to accept a US$43 billion bail-out under the International Monetary Fund (IMF) in September, was the hardest hit by the crisis. The value of the rupiah dropped from Rp 2,350 per U.S. dollar in June 1997 to Rp 16,500 in January 1998. By early April, it was back to Rp 9,000 per U.S. dollar. However, the low value of the rupiah made it impossible for Indonesian companies to import goods and to pay debts. Prices of imported and domestic products rose drastically and many companies faced bankruptcy. Unemployment rates also jumped. These developments affected Indonesian politics. The presidential election in March was conducted under the shadow of economic turmoil and increasing discontent.

There were two interpretations of the economic crisis in Indonesia. The government view was that the causes were mainly economic. The problems could be solved by undertaking economic reforms. The situation would then improve, and political reforms would not be required.

Reprinted from Daljit Singh and John Funston, eds., *Southeast Asian Affairs 1999* (Singapore: Institute of Southeast Asian Studies, 1999), pp. 111–27. At the time of original publication, Leo Suryadinata was Associate Professor in the Department of Political Science, National University of Singapore.

The other view was that the crisis was both economic and political in nature. Economic problems included over-expansion of the Indonesian economy without sound infrastructure, overuse of foreign investments in non-productive sectors (for example, real estate), and rampant corruption and cronyism, which resulted in large debts being incurred by both private (US$74 billion) and state (US$63.4 billion) sectors. Indebted private companies were mostly owned by the New Order élite and Chinese conglomerates. Many argued that this was the root of the problem.

Rampant Corruption

Under authoritarian rule, the power of the Indonesian state was strong, and it was concentrated in the hands of Soeharto. The spoils distribution system was used to co-opt the élite. When there was enough money to distribute, and the economy was healthy, the situation appeared to be stable. However, when the economic crisis set in the weakness of the system began to reveal itself.

Some Indonesian observers had predicted that the Soeharto government would end in the late 1970s, as corruption was already rampant then. Yet the government remained for another twenty years. Apart from authoritarian rule, what were the other reasons that contributed to the duration of the New Order?

In fact, the legitimacy of the New Order was based on growth and development. For almost three decades, Indonesia experienced healthy economic performance measured by any conventional economic indicator: there was gross national product (GNP) growth, large foreign investments, and low inflation rates. Massive foreign capital and short-term loans poured into Indonesia.

Once there was a crisis of confidence, however, investors withdrew their short-term loans, and the banking system collapsed as banks were unable to pay debts. The country was thrown into turmoil. In the view of Harvard Professor Jeffrey Sachs, Indonesia "was paying the price for increased reliance on foreign capital to finance domestic investments, and for the erosion of export competitiveness by rapid capital inflows. Alongside, the financial system had grown fragile with excessive short term debt."[1]

Sachs suggested that as long as the banking system was rescued, the economic situation would become stable again. But many disagreed, arguing that the economic crisis would not be solved as long as the existing system continued. In the last twenty years corruption and cronyism had become rampant. The first family had businesses in almost every field, and according to *Forbes* magazine, accumulated wealth amounting to US$4 billion.[2] They and their cronies monopolized the Indonesian economy from the 1980s. Corrupt practices thus placed a heavy burden on the public.

The Indonesian middle class, although small in number, began to be critical of government practices. The labour force had grown, and the gap between the rich and the poor had widened. The economic crisis caused many factories to be shut down and the number of unemployed increased dramatically. Worse still, the prices of food began to rise and went beyond the reach of many poor people. The situation became serious.

IMF and the Political Crisis

As mentioned earlier, the government regarded the turmoil as an economic problem. Once reforms were made in the economic field, the government could go on as usual. Nevertheless, to solve the economic crisis, IMF aid was needed. However, the IMF was either not very sensitive to the Indonesian problem or did not really understand the situation. IMF conditions for its massive bail-out required Indonesia to undertake financial reforms, dismantle monopolies, and withdraw subsidies on basic commodities.

Nonetheless, IMF assistance did not produce any immediate economic improvement. The IMF blamed the Indonesian Government for not implementing the reform programme. Its requirements for the dismantling of the monopolies and lifting of subsidies for basic food and commodities were resisted by the Soeharto government, as it felt that these measures would only cause further price hikes and in turn worsen the socio-political conditions. Although the government estimated that the inflation rate in 1998 would be about 45 per cent, the cost of many food items and other commodities had been raised by 100 per cent early in the year.

A Gathering Storm

From the onset of the monetary crisis, social unrest intensified. Riots against the Chinese minority became frequent, targeted mainly at Chinese shopkeepers who dominated the retail trade. The riots started in small towns in central and east Java before spreading to Sulawesi, West Java and Sumatra in early 1998. Protests against the hike in food prices and basic commodities were the major cause of the disturbances. University students in Java and the outer islands staged demonstrations calling on the government to introduce both economic and political reforms. They even demanded that Soeharto should step down. Initially, the demonstrations were confined to the campus, and were peaceful.

Attempting one last try, Soeharto planned to establish a Currency Board to boost the value of the rupiah, pegging it at around Rp 5,000 to the U.S. dollar. Many economists argued that this was unrealistic as the Indonesian monetary system was ailing, its foreign reserves were low (US$14–17 billion), and foreign debt amounted to US$137.4 billion. Both the United States and the IMF opposed the proposal, urging Indonesia to concentrate on IMF mandated reforms. However, fearing that an Indonesian collapse could have a drastic impact on the region, they eventually allowed some subsidies for basic food, commodities and medicine.

Soeharto still appeared to be unaware of the seriousness of the Indonesian political problem triggered by the economic crisis. In March 1998, he announced a new "crony" Cabinet, with his daughter as Social Minister, and his golf partner, Mohamad "Bob" Hasan, as the Trade and Industry Minister. Earlier, he had also appointed Habibie, a controversial figure, as Vice-President. When the students and critics demanded reform, Soeharto replied that it would be done only in the year 2003!

Soeharto was so confident that in early May he allowed the removal of the fuel and electricity subsidies, which ranged between 20 per cent and 70 per cent. The price of gasoline increased from Rp 600 to Rp 1,200 per litre. Food prices rose immediately after the removal of the fuel subsidies. Students in the Sumatran city of Medan rioted. On 11 May Soeharto flew to Cairo to attend the G-15 Summit of non-aligned leaders. During his absence, large demonstrations developed, particularly after the killing of four students from Trisakti, a private university in Jakarta, by the army Special Force. The following day, the unemployed, workers, urban poor and even gangsters joined the students. Intellectuals also supported the students, demanding immediate economic and political reforms, and asking Soeharto to step down. The peaceful demonstrations developed into major riots. Soeharto shortened his stay in Cairo and flew home in the morning of 15 May, promising reforms but still refusing to step down.

The situation in Jakarta deteriorated, as burning, looting and killing became common. Over one thousand people were killed. Ethnic Chinese were again the main target of the mob, causing many to flee the country. Foreign countries began to evacuate their citizens, deepening the sense of crisis. Demonstrations and riots occurred nation-wide. Rumours spread that students and the opposition would lead a nation-wide demonstration on 20 May, the National Awakening Day. On 17 May, Amien Rais, a critic of Soeharto and leader of Muhammadiyah, the second largest Muslim association in Indonesia, announced that he would organize the National Awakening Day demonstration.

On 18 May, Harmoko, the Speaker of Indonesia's House of Representatives (Dewan Perwakilan Rakyat or DPR) as well as the Assembly (Majelis Permusyawaratan Rakyat or MPR) shocked the country by calling on Soeharto to step down. General Wiranto, chief of the armed forces (ABRI or Angkatan Bersenjata Republik Indonesia) and Minister of Defence and Security, rejected this call as unconstitutional. Soeharto sought to fight back. On 19 May he invited nine moderate/conservative Islamic leaders to his residence and asked for their support — non-Muslims were not invited.[3] Soon after the meeting, Soeharto promised reform and a new general election within one and a half years. Some Muslim leaders asked the people to support Soeharto's plans. However, the effort was too little, and too late.

The Fall of Soeharto

On 20 May, Parliament threatened to impeach Soeharto if he did not step down by 23 May. Fourteen of his ministers, including Ginanjar Kartasasmitra and General Wiranto asked him to resign. On 21 May, Soeharto suddenly agreed to do so. He made a brief speech telling the Indonesian people that under the present situation, it was "very difficult to perform the government task and [to promote] development of the country anymore." He had therefore decided to resign (*berhenti*) from the presidency.[4]

Since 1997, Soeharto had talked of *lengser ke prabon*, a Javanese wayang term referring to a Javanese king withdrawing himself from worldly matters to enter a rich spiritual world. But there was no indication that he really wanted to give up power. What caused his sudden change of mind?

Three factors were important. First, Soeharto realized that the military, especially General Wiranto, was no longer solidly behind him. This could be seen from the military's soft attitude towards the students, especially when the students marched to occupy the Parliament building. The military displayed no willingness to crush the students. Wiranto eventually lent his support to those asking Soeharto to resign. Secondly, when close associates such as Harmoko and Cabinet ministers asked him to resign, Soeharto realized he had been abandoned. Perhaps he felt a deep sense of betrayal. He was suddenly standing alone. Thirdly, on 20 May, Madelene Albright, American Secretary of State, openly stated that the Clinton administration wanted Soeharto to resign.

Thirty-two years earlier, it was the student movement that had brought down Soekarno and given rise to Soeharto. This time it appeared that "student power" was also behind the downfall of Soeharto. Nevertheless, there are differences. In 1966, the student movement was largely confined to Jakarta and Bandung and no support came from their teachers. In 1998, the movement was nationwide and it had the support of their teachers, many of whom had been student leaders in 1966. In 1966 the students were supported by the military. In 1998 the army initially sided with Soeharto; only towards the end, did the army side with the students. The neutrality, and eventual support, of the military were crucial factors to the victory of "student power".

Habibie's Accession

Habibie was appointed President by Soeharto. Some have questioned whether this was legal without the approval of the MPR, as Soeharto was answerable to the MPR. The pro-Habibie group argued that under extraordinary circumstances, this was acceptable. According to Soeharto's announcement, Habibie was to rule Indonesia for the rest of Soeharto's term (1998–2003). Many, however, saw him as a transitional President. Opposition groups considered Habibie to be Soeharto's man, and hence not able to meet the aspirations of the Indonesian people. They wanted an immediate general election, and the election of a new President. Knowing his precarious position, Habibie responded by planning to hold an early extraordinary session of the MPR, and a general election in the following year. The opposition felt that this was too long, but the military, led by Wiranto, appeared to support this schedule.

Habibie's government was an extension of the New Order. His Cabinet included sixteen ministers who had served under Soeharto. The positions of Minister of Defence and Chief of the Armed Forces continued to be held by General Wiranto. Most MPR and DPR members also remained unchanged, although Habibie replaced some government critics with his own men.

Nevertheless, it would be wrong to say that the system of government remained unchanged. The upheaval which led to the fall of Soeharto unleashed new social forces. Students and the Indonesian Muslim groups became very militant and outspoken. The indigenous middle class, although small in number, had joined the movement demanding *reformasi* (reform). These groups called for both a more democratic political system and the immediate reduction of food prices. Many radicals even asked Habibie to step down at once. Habibie faced a situation which required him to be more responsive towards the opposition groups.

The Role of the Military

The fall of Soeharto also witnessed a decline in the role of the military. This decline can be attributed to the Indonesian military's conduct before and after Habibie became President, and the publicity given to this in 1998. Indonesians became aware that the ABRI was involved in the kidnapping and killing of civilians who were suspected to be against the so-called New Order regime on the eve of Soeharto's fall. Some of the military members were involved in the killing of students who staged demonstrations. The military was also held responsible for the riots and subsequent looting in May, as they were conspicuously absent during those crucial days. The media and human rights groups also focused on the military's brutal suppression of ethnic minorities in Irian Jaya, East Timor and Aceh in the last ten years. These incidents tarnished the image of the military and strengthened popular distrust of it. ABRI could no longer claim its traditional moral authority.

The decline in military power was also due to continuing splits within ABRI. These divisions were fully exploited by Soeharto so that the generals could not unite against him. The main split was between the "Islamic" and "nationalist" generals. In 1993 Benny Moerdani — known as the leader of the "nationalist" group — was purged. After this, the military leadership remained divided. By early 1998 the main group — identified as "Islamic" — was led by Major General Prabowo (head of KOSTRAD, the Army Strategic Reserve Command, and Soeharto's son-in-law) and Feisal Tanjung (Armed Forces chief from 1993 to March 1998). The rival "nationalist" faction was led by General Wiranto (who in March succeeded Feisal Tanjung as head of the Armed Forces, and was also appointed Minister of Defence). Soeharto had overall control over these groups. After Soeharto's resignation, a third pro-reform group emerged, led by Lieutenant-General Susilo Bambang Yudhoyono (Chief of the Socio-Political Section of the Armed Forces). In the contest for influence that followed, Wiranto used his positions to remove Prabowo from his KOSTRAD post.

The fall of General Prabowo was surrounded by controversy. The rise of the student movement and growing opposition to the Soeharto regime had angered many generals. The Special Forces (Kopassus), which was led by Prabowo, abducted student activists. Many disappeared and never returned. It is possible that Soeharto wanted to use the military — probably the Prabowo group — to create some minor incidents so that he would be able to prolong his control. By this interpretation, the May riots in Jakarta were believed to have been masterminded by the Prabowo group.

Another interpretation of the May riots focuses on a conflict between the Prabowo and Wiranto groups. The Jakarta Commander Safrie Syamsuddin, a close friend of Prabowo, and the Jakarta Police, refused to act on 13 and 14 May, thus allowing looting, raping, killing and arson to take place. Wiranto eventually brought in troops from outside Jakarta and the marines. It was these marines who allowed the students to occupy the Parliament building, thus ending Soeharto's thirty-two-year rule.

Whether Prabowo was acting on behalf of Soeharto or in opposition to Wiranto, the fact is that he had committed an offence. He was put on trial in August 1998 and found guilty of being involved in illegal activities, and eventually dismissed from the military service. Nevertheless, the culprits of the shootings remained at large.

The military was placed on the defensive after the fall of Soeharto. Many civilian politicians wanted to abolish the socio-political role of the Armed Forces. The ABRI itself also wanted to "redefine" its role. In late September 1998, a military seminar was held in Bandung to discuss ABRI's role. Lieutenant-General Susilo Bambang Yudhoyono suggested that the term *dwifungsi* (dual function) be changed to *Peran ABRI* (Role of the ABRI), a more neutral term.[5] The military, however, refused to abandon the concept of *dwifungsi*.

In fact, Habibie continued to be in coalition with the military. While co-operating with Wiranto, Habibie also had his own military supporters. General Feisal Tanjung and Major-General Maulani, head of Bakin (military intelligence) were identified as his men. By year's end, the struggle between various groups was still evident.

Riots, the Students and Opposition

Although some Muslim groups and the mainstream in ABRI supported Habibie, the students and most party leaders were critical, seeing his government as a continuation of the Soeharto regime. When the MPR held a Special Session in November, the opposition, especially the students, sought to pressure the meeting to incorporate their demands into the resolutions. Some students might also have intended to disrupt the session. However, the Habibie government was determined to ensure that the session would not be disrupted. During the session, the regular troops were mobilized, but most controversial was the creation of the "self-made security forces" (*pengamanan swakarsa*) to "safeguard" the session by the government. These "civilian security forces" consisted of pro-government youths, including hooligans who were hired to do the dirty jobs.

As Habibie moved to legitimize his regime by calling for the Special Session of the MPR, anti-Habibie and anti-military students began nation-wide demonstrations. In Jakarta, the students wanted to march to the MPR/DPR building but were stopped by troops. Clashes took place between the students and the civilian supporters of the government. The military also moved to suppress the students.

The student strategy was to join forces with other opposition groups to pressure the Habibie government to step down. In fact, soon after the fall of Soeharto, Indonesian students in West Java, including Jakarta, formed the Communication Forum of the Students Senate Jakarta, which aimed at inviting eminent reformists to form a presidium to take over from Habibie. This transition government would be assigned to organize the general election.

The reformists, however, were far from united, and failed to co-ordinate their activities. Only on 10 November (the day the Special Session started) was the Communication Forum able to organize four major reform leaders — Abdurrahman Wahid (Chairman of the Nahdlatul Ulama [NU], the largest Muslim organization in Indonesia), Megawati (Chairperson of the Partai Demokrasi Indonesia-Perjuangan [PDI — Perjuangan] and daughter of former President Soekarno), Amien Rais (Chairman of the Partai Amanat National [PAN], and former chairman of Muhammadiyah, the second largest Muslim organization) and Sultan Hamengkubuwono X (Governor of Yogyakarta) — to discuss the nation's future at Wahid's residence in Ciganjur. These four eminent leaders issued an eight-point declaration — later known as the Ciganjur Declaration — demanding a clean and democratic government based on the 1945 constitution, in order to preserve unity and to realize a prosperous society.[6] Four points were crucial:

- Implement honest and fair general elections by May 1999, as a democratic way to end the transitional government led by Habibie. Three months after the general election, the new government must be formed through a General Session of Parliament;
- Removal of ABRI's dual function by stages, to be completed in six years;
- Sincere efforts to end *korupsi, kolusi,*

nepotisme (KKN), preceded by an investigation of Soeharto's wealth;
- Immediate dissolution of all "self-made security forces" of the MPR's Special Session.

However, this reformist group refused to form a presidium to take over the government, as there was no strong legal basis for this. Radical students decided to continue their demonstration, which put strong pressure on the MPR session. They demanded the immediate trial of Soeharto and the end of the ABRI's dual function. The students gathered in the universities near the MPR/DPR building and eventually came into conflict with civilian security guards and troops. In the two-day conflict, there were twelve casualties, six of whom were students from the Atma Jaya Catholic University. The mob joined the students. Looting, arson, and chaos occurred again, reminiscent of the May riots. The situation in Jakarta became very tense and the MPR session ended under the shadow of these riots.

After the 13 November riots, Indonesian politics became more unstable. Student demonstrations continued and the authorities appeared unable to curtail them. Muslim leaders linked to the NU were assassinated in Banyuwangi, East Java. Religious conflicts escalated. The Ketapang Incident (22 November) in Jakarta, originating from a territorial conflict between gangster groups, developed into religious conflicts.[7] Churches were burned down and this was followed by the burning of mosques in Kupang, West Timor, then the burning of more churches in Sulawesi. Responsible religious leaders came together and appealed to the masses to be calm and not to destroy religious buildings, in order to preserve the unity of the country. NU leader Abdurrahman Wahid even argued that if this was not controlled, a social revolution might result.

According to a widespread rumour, the ethnic and religious conflict was engineered by the pro-Soeharto group to divert attention away from the call to investigate Soeharto's wealth. On 25 September, under constant pressure from students and others Habibie eventually instructed Andi Ghalib, the Attorney General, to conduct the investigation, but no significant results emerged. Students in Jakarta demonstrated again in December, but Habibie's government still appeared reluctant to conduct a proper investigation. Many observers believed that as long as Soeharto and his family were free to move around there would be no solution to the Indonesian problem.

The MPR resolutions took into account the student demands in three of twelve resolutions, although they were still far from what the students had asked for.[8] The investigation of Soeharto and his cronies was included as a clause in one of the resolutions but it was not an independent resolution on its own. The political role of ABRI would be reduced in stages. Pancasila would no longer be recognized as the sole ideological foundation of the state. Does this mean the end of the Pancasila ideology, or the implementation and interpretation of Pancasila ideology as practised during the Soeharto era? What will be the impact on Indonesian unity? These points will be discussed later.

Religion and the State

To place the religious conflicts in context, it is worth noting that they were on the increase in the last decade of Soeharto's rule. A survey in *Tempo* is indicative.[9]

Churches destroyed or burned down (1945–97)

Period	1945–54	1955–64	1965–74	1975–84	1985–94	1995–97
No. of Churches	0	2	46	89	132	131

Mosques destroyed or burned down (1970–98)

Period	1970–79	1980–89	1990–Nov 1998
No. of Mosques	2	11	17

In the first fourteen years of Indonesian independence, only two churches were destroyed. But during the Soeharto era, the number increased remarkably. Between 1985 and 1994, 132 churches were destroyed and in the last three years alone, 131. Although the reasons for this religious conflict are complex, the perceived threat posed by the non-Muslim community, and Muslim dissatisfaction towards Soeharto's political policy, were significant. Also important was weakening government control. The number of mosques destroyed has always been small as the non-Muslims form a relatively weak minority. However, the non-Muslim minority (mostly Christians) also responded under stress, hence the destruction of some mosques.

Islam as the majority religion in Indonesia was cultivated by the Soeharto regime from the late 1980s to counter-balance the *abangan* (nominal Muslim) military group. With the resurgence of Islam world-wide from the 1970s, the Muslims in Indonesia also became more confident. They felt they had been relegated to a minority position, and it was time to reassert their role. Islamic identity was increasingly highlighted. In every public function, for example, Muslims tried to show their Islamic identity by saying grace in Arabic. Muslim attire was also encouraged. The establishment of the Islamic Intellectual Association (Ikatan Cendekiawan Muslim Se-Indonesia, or ICMI) in December 1990 — endorsed by Soeharto and led by Habibie — was a symbolic triumph for Islam in politics.

Not all Muslims supported ICMI however. Abdurrahman Wahid of NU, for example, was a leading critic. In fact, Muslims remained split between the moderates and the radicals, the former continuing to accept Pancasila (read: religious pluralism) as the state ideology, while the latter favoured a Muslim state (Islam as a state religion), if not an Islamic state (a state based on Islamic law). Nevertheless, in 1985 NU, Muhammadiyah and the Soeharto-created and -approved Partai Persatuan Pembangunan (PPP), were forced to accept Pancasila. After Soeharto changed his policy towards Islam in 1989, Islam as a religious and political force grew rapidly. When Soeharto resigned, many began to question Pancasila and disagreed with the use of Pancasila as the sole ideology for mass and political organizations. Following this, at the Special Session of the MPR in November, the law on Pancasila as the sole ideology was abolished.

This does not mean that Pancasila as a state philosophy has been abandoned, but Pancasila is no longer imposed on mass organizations and political parties. The PPP, for instance, in its recent congress held in November/December, decided to revert to Islam as the ideology of the party, and re-adopt the Ka'bah as the symbol of the party.[10] Islam as a socio-political force has been used again, this time not by the opposition, but by the new authority. An article in the influential Jakarta magazine, *Tajuk*, on 12 November, stated that the first two presidents (Soekarno and Soeharto) did not use Islam as their foundation; Habibie was the first president to use Islam as his political base. This view is extreme but it is true that Islam has been used by Habibie to support his regime. The number of Islam-based parties suddenly increased in the last seven months.[11]

As a result of the resurgence of Islam, and its use by Indonesian politicians, religious conflict has dramatically increased. Abdurrahman Wahid of the NU was outspoken in urging Indonesians of various religious persuasions to get together to maintain Indonesian unity. He also warned that Pancasila should not be made into a political issue, and urged the Habibie government to pursue national reconciliation through dialogue, to stop a social revolution. His appeal was initially ignored by the government. In December, General Feisal Tanjung even said that no such dialogue was needed because it was difficult to identify who would really represent the people. He suggested that this should be done only after the general election of 1999 — implying that Abdurrahman Wahid's actions were merely to gain votes for the forthcoming elections.

Habibie continued to play the religious game in order to survive. While paying lip service to Pancasila, he also projected himself as a Muslim leader. He selected many ministers who had strong Muslim backgrounds — some were even known to be anti-minority religions. Dr A.M. Syaefuddin, his Agriculture Minister, said in October that people from a minority religion could not become President of Indonesia,[12] and claimed that Megawati was a Hindu, and therefore unsuitable to be President. His statements angered the Balinese who demanded his public apology and resignation. Syaefuddin reluctantly apologized, but refused to step down, and continued to receive Habibie's support. However, he was defeated by Hamzah Haz of the NU, the Minister of Investment in Habibie's Cabinet, in the contest for the new PPP chairmanship.[13] Perhaps the PPP felt that it could not afford to have a controversial figure if it wanted to do well in the June 1999 elections.

Syaefuddin's comments were part of a broader, concerted attack on Megawati. The government continued to support the Soerjadi faction of the PDI and refused to acknowledge Megawati as the legitimate leader of the PDI, so that Megawati's influence could be undermined. Pro-Habibie Muslim groups even met and declared that the Indonesian President and Vice-President could not be women as this was against Islamic law.

East Timor and Other Regional Rebellions

Ethnic as well as religious conflicts escalated in the post-Soeharto period. Separatist movements in three provinces — East Timor, Irian Jaya and Aceh — made international headlines. East Timor, which was annexed by Indonesia in 1976, has never been recognized by the United Nations as part of Indonesian territory. In June 1998, East Timorese students and youths began to stage demonstrations demanding a referendum on the independence of their province. Habibie rejected the demand but offered limited autonomy to the twenty-seventh province of Indonesia. He also declared his willingness to release Xanana Gusmao, the leader of the Timorese opposition group Fretilin, in exchange for international recognition of East Timor. Affected by continuing conflict in the province after the fall of Soeharto, Indonesia eventually agreed to resume talks with Portugal, the former master of East Timor. The two countries agreed to hold in-depth discussions on Indonesia's proposals for a "special status, based on a wide-ranging autonomy" for East Timor.[14]

In Irian Jaya, students and youths also made use of the *reformasi* era to stage their demands. In early July, Irianese protesters hoisted the separatist West Papuan flag. One person was killed by the police. In the next few days, more flag-hoisting events took place, resulting in further clashes with the police. Up to seven Irianese were killed. Wiranto described the hoisting of a non-Indonesian flag as an act of treachery that could not be tolerated. In fact, the Irianese have suffered injustice under Indonesian rule. The head of the Association of the Irian community in Jakarta stated that 200,000 Irianese had been "eliminated" over the past thirty-five years.[15] Government resources were unevenly distributed, and most Irianese continue to live below the poverty line.

Irian Jaya has suffered from Indonesian rule in similar ways to Timor. However, many Irianese leaders have demanded autonomy rather than complete independence. They want "one nation, two systems". Since Irian Jaya has long been recognized by the United Nations as part of Indonesian territory, obstacles to obtaining independence are considerably greater.

The Aceh independence movement also re-emerged as the power of the central government declined. Compared to the East Timorese and Irianese, the Acehnese have been better integrated, though resentment against the central government has never been far from the surface. On 25 August 1998 there was a shocking revelation that between 1989 and 1998, when Aceh was treated as a Special Military Operation, 781 people had been killed, 163 people had disappeared, and 368 people had been tortured.[16] Public outcry forced the military to apologize to the Acehnese people and reduce its presence in Aceh. However, conflict between the Acehnese and the military continued, resulting in many casualties. At year end military–civilian relations in Aceh, and Jakarta–provincial relations, remained tense.

Because of these tensions in the unitary government system, some scholars and politicians have suggested the introduction of a federal system to halt the process of disintegration. The Habibie government appeared uninterested.

The Chinese Minority

The ethnic Chinese experienced a trauma on 13–14 May when they were targeted for lootings, arson and gang rape. Many Chinese who could afford it fled the country. About 150,000 people reportedly left Indonesia during the May riots, of which 70,000 were ethnic Chinese.[17] (If the figure is accurate, this means that 1.2 per cent of the Chinese population left the country). Many indigenous Indonesians condemned the barbaric acts. There was also an international outcry pressuring the Indonesian Government to investigate and punish those who committed the crimes. Under international and domestic pressure, on 22 July Habibie eventually announced his decision to form a committee to investigate the violation of human rights in Indonesia, not only for the Chinese community but for Indonesians as a whole. Since the composition of the committee was mixed — including government officials and others — understandably there were differences of opinion. The report, scheduled for submission in three months, was delayed a week and released on 3 November.[18] This acknowledged that 52 women had been raped, a figure considerably lower than most estimates. It found no proof that the riots and rapes had been planned, or that ethnic Chinese, who formed the majority of the victims, were specially targeted. The government firmly denied that there was any organized terrorism against the Chinese, although independent reports pointed in that direction.

There have been many theories seeking to explain the terrorism against the ethnic Chinese. One argues that its purpose was to drive all the Chinese out of Indonesia. The Chinese role would then be taken over by *pribumi*. Of course, this theory is very naive. But the terror indeed frightened a large number of Indonesian Chinese and many fled the country, taking their capital with them. Many migrated to neighbouring countries. Singapore, Australia and the United States were favourite destinations, followed by Malaysia where the cost of living was lower. Some even sent their children to Hong Kong, Taiwan and mainland China just to escape the turmoil. Nevertheless, the majority of the Chinese Indonesians — more than 95 per cent — had nowhere to go, and had to stay and fight for their rights.

Following the fall of Soeharto, three ethnic Chinese parties were formed: Partai Reformasi Tionghoa Indonesia (Parti), Partai Pembauran Indonesia (Parpindo) and Partai Bhinneka Tunggal Ika Indonesia (PBI). Parpindo, however, was dissolved not long after its establishment, partly because of a lack of response. Many Chinese leaders felt that their safety and prosperity could only be guaranteed if they formed an alliance with indigenous Indonesians. Not surprisingly, many ethnic Chinese leaders joined indigenous-dominated political parties, despite the uncertainty in the future. For instance, Kwik Kian Gie (a leading economist and a Soeharto critic) continued to stay with the PDI, while Junus Jahja (an economist) and K. Sindhunata (a Chinese Catholic and a leader of the assimilationist movement) joined PAN.

The Chinese exodus made Indonesia's economic recovery more difficult. The Indonesian authorities urged Chinese Indonesians to return — both in person and with their capital. Although the majority have returned, only a small part of their capital has been brought back as business opportunities remain bleak. Businessmen are taking a wait-and-see approach, and will not reinvest their money before making sure that there will be good returns.

Habibie's ambiguous attitude towards the ethnic Chinese also contributed to the uncertainty. Soon after the May riots, Habibie visited Chinatown and urged the Chinese to continue to help stabilize the situation. But in July 1998 he told the *Washington Post* that he did not care whether the Chinese returned — if they did not return, their role would be taken over by others. He also noted that Indonesia "will not die" without the Chinese.

Economic Conditions and the Poverty Line

Under Habibie, the Indonesian economy showed some improvement, particularly in the slowing of inflation and the stabilization of the rupiah *vis-à-vis* the U.S. dollar. When Habibie became Vice-President in March 1998, the rupiah plunged to Rp 17,000 per dollar. However, after Habibie was made President, he extended full co-operation to the IMF, resulting in the resumption of IMF assistance. The rupiah stabilized, then improved to Rp 8,000 per U.S. dollar by December 1998. Inflation also slowed. There was no shortage of basic food, at least in the short term.

The general performance of the Indonesian economy, however, was poor, contracting between 13 per cent and 15 per cent, the largest since Indonesia's independence. The banking system was not improved as a new bankruptcy law was not passed. Although Indonesia closed 16 banks considered insolvent and 54 banks were placed under the supervision of a restructuring agency, Indonesia still had to restructure private debts. The reform in the monetary system was slow. Without drastic reform in the political field, and a marked reduction in corruption, economic recovery is unlikely.

Most serious is the problem of poverty. In the last two years of Soeharto's rule, the number of people who lived below the poverty line began to increase, reducing gains made in earlier years. After Soeharto's fall, the number of poor accelerated rapidly. According to one Indonesian economist, at the end of 1996, about 28 million people lived below the poverty line. By the end of 1997 this had increased to 72 million, and in the first three months of 1998 the number reached 128 million, or 65 per cent of the population.[19] Central Bureau of Statistics data released in July 1998 stated that 79.4 million (40 per cent of the total population) lived below the poverty line, and this would increase to 95.8 million (or 48 per cent of the Indonesian population) by the end of 1998, as no economic improvement was in sight.[20]

General Election Outlook

Although the pro-Habibie group insisted that the Habibie regime was legitimate, opposition groups saw him as a transitional figure who would soon give up power. In their view, Habibie's job was to oversee the smooth conduct of the general and presidential elections. The MRP Special Session in September agreed that a general election would be held on 7 June 1999, and the presidential election on 28 October 1999. Generally, opposition groups accepted the schedule and prepared to contest the elections.

The ruling party, Golkar, made its own electoral preparations. Simmering rivalries between one group wanting to make it a party for retired generals, and another wanting a civilian party, came to a head at an extraordinary national congress on 9 to 11 July. General (retired) Sudradjat, former Chief of Armed Forces and Akbar Tanjung, State Secretary, competed for the top position. Akbar Tanjung, supported by Habibie, won the election and became the new head. General Wiranto was also reportedly in favour of Akbar Tanjung, as he did not want his former boss to become the leader. Some retired generals were disappointed with Golkar, and left the organization. Sudradjat later established a new party called Partai Keadilan dan Persatuan (Justice and Unity Party). The extraordinary congress also saw the decline of Soeharto's influence in Golkar. The Supervisors' Council, headed by Soeharto, was abolished. Sons and daughters of Soeharto were purged from the organization. In October, the new Golkar held a regular national congress and declared officially that Golkar was a political party, the Partai Golkar. Habibie and Akbar Tanjung sought to project a "new image" to help Golkar win the forthcoming elections.

By year's end, about 110 new parties had been established. But as the Election Commission must approve the parties before they can contest, at election time in June 1999 the number of parties is likely to be much smaller.

If the election is free and fair, four or five major parties are likely to gain support, but none will be dominant. These major parties, apart from the government party Partai Golkar, include the Islamic PPP, opposition parties PAN, the Partai Kebangkitan Bangsa (PKB, an NU party), and the PDI-Perjuangan. The results are likely to be similar to those in 1955 — the most democratic election in Indonesian political history — and demonstrate a continuing division of Indonesia's political culture into secular nationalists and Islamic nationalists.

In the 1955 elections, the nationalist and Islamic parties were able to divide the votes, with secularist/nationalists having a slight majority. In the June 1999 elections, the votes will be distributed among these secular and Islamic parties, perhaps with the Islamic-based parties having a slight majority, owing to the rise of Islam in the last few decades in Indonesia. In November 1998, a survey was made on the strength of the "Islamic" parties in the forthcoming general elections. Of eight "Islamic" parties, the PAN received 47 per cent, the PKB 23 per cent, the Partai Bulan Bintang 4.4 per cent, and the PPP only 4.2 per cent. The rest received less than 2.3 per cent.[21] If the survey is correct, the PAN and PKB are far ahead of other Islamic political organizations.

The PDI-Perjuangan appears to be quite popular, especially in Central Java and Bali. It may emerge as a major party. However, many Islamic voters may not give their votes to the secular PDI-Perjuangan.

Partai Golkar is also likely to get some votes as its structure remains intact; it benefits from being the government party, and has a strong financial base. The role of (pro-Golkar) bureaucrats and the military will still be significant in influencing the outcome of the votes, especially in the rural areas where the largest number of Indonesians live.

None of the parties will have a landslide victory. There will be a new coalition government, indicating that the political situation in the future might not be as stable. But a general election is the only means to establish a legitimate government, and hence the possibility of political stability.

Foreign Relations

Towards the end of Soeharto's rule, Indonesia focused on domestic economic problems and was unable to take a leadership role in ASEAN. When Soeharto appointed Habibie as his Vice-President, he assigned Habibie to look after foreign affairs, but when the G-15 Summit was held in Cairo in May 1998, it was Soeharto, not Habibie, who attended the meeting. When Habibie was sworn in as the President, he was preoccupied with domestic problems.

Habibie's relations with Indonesia's immediate neighbours were not cordial from the beginning of his administration. Negative comments by Senior Minister Lee Kuan Yew on Habibie's possible nomination as Vice-President in February 1998 influenced early relations with Singapore. His State Enterprise Minister, Tanri Abeng, visited the city state and complained that it was not sincere in helping Indonesia. In an interview with the *Asian Wall Street Journal* in early August, Habibie described Singapore as a little red dot on the map. This was the lowest point in Indonesia–Singapore relations for more than two decades.

Jakarta's relations with Kuala Lumpur also encountered difficulties. Habibie was critical of Mahathir's dismissal of Anwar Ibrahim, showing solidarity with the sacked Malaysian Deputy Prime Minister. Anwar's letter and criticism against Mahathir were published in *Republika*, an ICMI paper that Habibie has close links with. Habibie also cancelled a bilateral visit to Malaysia, and for a time mooted not attending the Kuala Lumpur APEC (Asia-Pacific Economic Cooperation) summit in November. He did, however, eventually attend APEC, and the December ASEAN Summit in Hanoi, showing Indonesian support for both organizations.

Indonesia–China relations remained quite cordial. When there was ethnic conflict in Indonesia in early 1998, China refrained from making any comments. On 17 February, when asked about Beijing's attitude towards the ethnic Chinese who were victims of the riots, a Chinese spokesman only noted that he believed the Indonesian Government was able to handle the situation and racial harmony would prevail.[22] On 12–13 April, Tang Jiaxuan, the new Foreign Minister of China, had visited Soeharto's Indonesia, and reiterated Beijing's readiness to provide a grant of US$4 billion (one source says US$3 billion) through the IMF package.[23] Soeharto expressed his gratitude to China.

When the ethnic Chinese — the majority of whom were Indonesian citizens — were targeted for looting, arson and rape during the riots in May, China remained quiet. Only on 7 July, did Chen Shigu, Beijing's ambassador to Jakarta, appeal to the Indonesian Government to investigate the rape cases thoroughly. He also noted that it was the responsibility of the Indonesian Government to protect the safety of its citizens, including those of Chinese descent.[24] A month later, Foreign Minister Tang repeated the appeal, urging the Indonesian Government to treat its citizens equally.[25] However, Beijing continued to affirm that it would honour its pledge to the IMF bail-out package for Indonesia.[26] Apparently, China was concerned to avoid making other Southeast Asian countries anxious that China would intervene in ethnic Chinese affairs.

When the United States and the United Kingdom jointly bombed Iraq in December, the Islamic-oriented Habibie government refrained from any criticisms. Perhaps because Indonesia needed foreign economic aid, it could not afford to antagonize Washington.

Conclusion

Reformasi was the most frequently used slogan in 1998, but the year is best described as one of upheaval and uncertainty. The fall of Soeharto produced both change and continuity. Freedom of speech, freedom of the press, and freedom of organization have been very obvious. This has come as a fresh breeze, after thirty-two years of authoritarian rule under Soeharto. The role of the ABRI also appears to have declined. However, the old leadership still remained at the apex, with Habibie and Wiranto representing an extension of the Soeharto regime. Nevertheless, central authority was weak, and riots and demonstrations never ceased throughout 1998.

Arguably, Habibie's most notable achievement in 1998 was to survive. At the beginning of his rule, many predicted that he would not last the year. He faces even greater difficulties in 1999, in particular the challenge of presiding over credible elections, and inaugurating a new presidency.

Notes

1. *Ascent* 7, no. 2 (April 1998), p. 1.
2. "Suharto family, net worth: At least $4 billion, maybe much more", *Forbes*, 6 July 1998, p. 54.
3. The Muslim leaders were Abdurrahman Wahid (NU), Ahmad Bagja (NU), Ma'aruf Amin (NU), Emha Ainun Najib (intellectual/writer), Dr Nurcholish Madjid (intellectual), Ali Yafie (Head of Majelis Ulama Indonesia), Prof Malik Fadjar (Muhammadiyah), Prof Yusril Ihza Mahendra (Law Professor at the University of Indonesia), Cholil Baidawi (Muslimin Indonesia), Umarsono (Muhammadiyah), and Sutrisno Muhdam (Muhammadiyah). S. Sinansari Ecip, *Kronologi Situasi Penggulingan Soeharto: Reportase Jurnalistik* (Bandung: Penerbit Mizan, July 1998), p. 99.
4. For the text of the speech, see ibid., pp. 136–39.
5. "Dwifungsi ABRI dihapus, Diganti 'Peran ABRI'", *Republika*, 21 September 1998. See also "ABRI Lakukan Redefinisi atas Doktrin Dwifungsi", *Media Indonesia*, 23 September 1998.
6. "Empat Tokoh Reformasi Akhirnya Bertemu", *Kompas*, 11 November 1998.
7. "Peristiwa Ketapang", *Suara Pembaruan*, 23 November 1998. Ketapang is the name of a street in Jakarta.
8. "SI MPR 1998 Hasilkan 12 Ketetapan", *Suara Pembaruan*, 14 November 1998.
9. "Ketika Ika Menindas Bhinneka", *Tempo*, 14 December 1998, pp. 24–25.
10. "PPP Kembali Ke Lambang Ka'bah dan Asas Islam," *Suara Pembaruan*, 1 December 1998.
11. *Tajuk*, 12 November 1998, p. 21.
12. "Menyoal Ucapan AM Saefuddin", *Media Indonesia*, 1 November 1998.
13. *Kompas*, 1 December 1998.
14. *Tempo Interaktif*, 6 August 1998.
15. *Tempo Interaktif*, 29 July 1998.
16. *Suara Merdeka*, 25 August 1998.
17. *Waspada*, 6 June 1998.
18. "Assessing the May Riots", *Asiaweek*, 13 November 1998.
19. Sjahrir, "Dampak Negatif Kontraksi: Sampai Hancurkan Kita?" *Warta Ekonomi*, 6 July 1998, p. 8.
20. *Tempo Interaktif*, 3 July 1998.
21. *Tajuk* 1, no. 19 (12 November 1998): 28.
22. Leo Suryadinata, "China's Hand-off on Indonesia", *Far Eastern Economic Review*, 16 April 1998.
23. *Lianhe Zaobao*, 14 April 1998.
24. "Dubes RRC Sesalkan Terjadinya Perkosaan Saat Kerusuhan," *Suara Pembaruan*, 7 July 1998.
25. *Xinhua*, 3 August 1998, transcribed in FBIS-CHI-98-218, 6 August 1998.
26. "Tang: $3 billion Aid Package to Jakarta Will Go Ahead," *Hong Kong Standard*, 4 August 1998.

INDONESIA
The New Regional Autonomy Laws, Two Years Later

Gary F. Bell

I. Introduction

Indonesia is a fascinating amalgam of ethnicities, languages, cultures, and religions, united by history, by a common national language, by political will and sometimes by sheer force, and spread over thousands of separate, distinct, and often distant islands. That such a country would have a high degree of regional autonomy would seem to make sense but surprisingly the regions in Indonesia until recently did not have much autonomy and were administered mainly by the central government. This led to a lot of resentment towards the centre and particularly towards Java and the Javanese who dominate in politics and in the central government.

Addressing a call for more regional autonomy, the Habibie government passed new laws that promised the broadest autonomy to the regions and the Wahid government adopted regulations under the new laws. The laws and regulations came into force on 1 January 2001. This decentralization has been referred to by some as the "Big Bang" — Indonesia moved from a government structure that was highly centralized to one of the most decentralized in the world (at least on paper) and did so in about 27 months from the People's Consultative Assembly (MPR) decree opening up the regional governance reform in October 1998[1] until the coming into force of the laws on 1 January 2001. Many believe that no country has ever decentralized so much so suddenly.

This article will look at the provisions of the new regional autonomy laws. It will, in particular, examine the political context that led to their adoption, their contents including their shortcomings, the many difficult tasks faced during the

---

Reprinted from Daljit Singh and Chin Kin Wah, eds., *Southeast Asian Affairs 2003* (Singapore: Institute of Southeast Asian Studies, 2003), pp. 117–31. At the time of original publication, Gary F. Bell was Associate Professor at the Faculty of Law of the National University of Singapore.

implementation of the laws over the past two years, and the possibility of amending the laws. It will then look very briefly at the separate autonomy laws adopted for special regions.

I have elsewhere made a detailed legal analysis of the laws and regulations just before their coming into force[2] and also written on the legal consequences of the regional autonomy laws on regional minorities in Indonesia.[3] Jurists should refer to these other articles for a more detailed legal analysis. The purpose of this article will be to explain some of the legal difficulties generated by the law to non-lawyers and to give a more general overview of the law and its early implementation over the last two years — though still from a jurist's point of view. Admittedly, a jurist's point of view is not the only way of looking at the regional autonomy laws and other points of view might shed a better, or at least a more complete light on the topic. Nonetheless the legal point of view must be taken into account in analysing many consequences of the regional autonomy laws.

II. The New Regional Autonomy Laws

A. The Political Context that Led to their Adoption

Regional governments are not a new phenomenon in Indonesia. There were regional governments in the provinces (*propinsi*), regencies (*kabupaten*), and villages (*desa*) (to name the main levels of government) and there were laws setting up and regulating these governments.[4] In reality, however, these local governments were not democratic and were politically controlled by the central government. They behaved more like implementers of central orders than as autonomous governments. This led to recriminations in the regions and demands for autonomous and democratic regional governments. In particular, there was a sense that the regions, particularly resource-rich regions, were not making sufficient profits from their own resources and that the central government was unjustly exploiting them.

Following the fall of Soeharto in 1998, Vice-President Habibie, of the same Golkar Party, took over the presidency. He wanted to be seen as a reformist and did put in place many new laws. One of the reforms he promised was regional autonomy. At the time of this promise, Indonesia was in turmoil, and East Timor, Aceh, and Irian Jaya were fighting for independence. Promising more autonomy was seen by some as the only way to keep Indonesia together. A promise of more regional autonomy was not surprising since Habibie himself was not originally from Java and the promise could boost support for Golkar outside Java in the then coming elections.

B. The New Law and the Constitutional Amendments

The two main laws relating to regional autonomy were adopted in 1999 and came into force on 1 January 2001. The first is the Law on Regional Governance commonly referred to as the Regional Autonomy Law.[5] The second is the Law on Fiscal Balance between Central and Regional Governments ("Fiscal Balance Law").[6] In this essay, the focus will be mainly on the Regional Autonomy Law and its implementation.

Before going into the details of the new laws, it should be pointed out that although the powers of regional governments have increased drastically and their role has changed, the different levels of government remain essentially the same. At the top is the central government, which the law simply refers to as the government (*pemerintah*). Every other level of government is referred to as a regional government (*pemerintah daerah*). There are many levels, but the only important ones for our purposes are the provinces (*propinsi* or *provinsi*), headed by a governor (*gubernur*); and one level below them, either the regency (*kabupaten*), in rural areas, headed by the regent (*bupati*) or the city (*kota*), in urban areas, headed by a mayor (*walikota*). Then, at the very local level in rural areas are the villages (*desa*). For our purposes, we need not describe the other levels of government between the regency and the village. It should be pointed out that the term *kabupaten* is sometimes translated in English as "district" rather than "regency". Both English terms refer to the *kabupaten*, and there is therefore no difference between a regency and a district. As we will see, if the different levels of regional governments have not changed, the relationship between them is now drastically changed. The governments at the regency or city level are now autonomous and are therefore in principle independent from the provincial and central governments.

1. Constitutional Status of the Regional Autonomy Laws

Notwithstanding the incredibly broad devolution of powers to the regions, the Regional Autonomy Law does not adopt the concept of federalism. It adheres to the principle of the "Unitary State of Indonesia" enshrined in article 1 of the Constitution[7] and restated in the newly amended article 18 of the Constitution relating to regional autonomy.[8] Federalism would involve the recognition of a central state and of regional states with constitutionally protected powers which the central government cannot reduce without amending the Constitution. Such is not the case under the Regional Autonomy Law even though the Constitution now mentions regional autonomy as a constitutional principle.

The new article 18 of the Constitution adopted as part of the second amendment in August 2000 states that: "regional administrations can put in effect the broadest autonomy, except in governmental matters that by virtue of legislation are defined as matters for the Central Government."[9] The Constitution therefore leaves the definition of the powers of the regions to legislation (*undang-undang*) adopted by the Central Parliament. Unlike in a federation, the powers of the regional governments can be modified by simple legislation from the central government — there is no need for a constitutional amendment.

What is clear, however, from article 18 of the Constitution is that unless a law specifically assigns a power to the central government, then that power belongs to the regions. In legal terms we would say that the residual powers belong to the regions.

2. The Autonomy Laws, their Objectives, and their Shortcomings

The Confusing Division of Powers

In a manner consistent with the second amendment, the Regional Autonomy Law gives the residual powers to the regions. Interestingly it states in article 11(1) that "the powers of Regencies and Cities shall include all government powers other than the powers that are the object of an exception in Article 7 [powers of the Central Government] and those regulated by Article 9 [powers of the province]".[10] It is therefore not the provinces that inherit the residual powers and most of the powers devolved but the regencies and cities. It is indeed surprising that such wide powers are transferred not to the 30 provinces but to the 350 regencies and cities.[11] For example in Bali, the broadest government powers were granted to the eight regencies and one city of Bali rather than to the provincial government of Bali. The fear seems to have been that provinces could be politically more difficult to control and may use their new powers to foster dreams of independence.

The powers transferred are indeed very broad. Basically the regencies and cities have powers over everything that is not by law assigned to the central government or the provinces, and frankly, very little is left to the central government or the provinces. The problem, however, is that the provisions dividing the powers between the different levels are very unclear and confusing.

The central government powers are limited by article 7(1) of the Regional Autonomy Law to "responsibilities for foreign affairs, defence and security, the administration of justice, monetary and fiscal matters, religion and responsibilities in other sectors". This is an incredibly short list. It should be added however that the central government remains entitled to make policies in "other sectors" which article 7(2) further defines as including

> policies on national planning and control of national development at a macro level, funds for fiscal balance, the state administrative system and state economic institutions, the development and the empowerment of human resources, the efficient use of natural resources along with strategic high technology, conservation and national standardisation.

It remains nonetheless a very short list. The main problem however, especially on the list in article 9(2), is that it will be very difficult to apply this division of powers in practice. How can the central government make "policies on national planning" without encroaching on many powers now devolved to the regions (education, health, the environment, natural resources, etc.)?

The provincial powers are even fewer. Article 9(1) states that the powers of the provinces include "the powers in government sectors that cross the borders of regencies and cities along with the powers in other specific government sectors". There is no other definition in the law of what constitutes a cross-border government sector. In fact this is very confusing since many responsibilities clearly assigned to regencies and cities (public works and the environment for example) could arguably be cross-border sectors (intercity roads, environmental impact beyond a regency). The division of powers is therefore not clear.

Even less clear is what is included in "other specific government sectors" over which provinces have jurisdictions. There is no list of such sectors except in the elucidation to the law. The wisdom of legislating a list of sectors through a commentary or elucidation rather than in the law itself is questionable — the elucidation is not a binding source of law. However, and even though elucidations are given a lot of weight in interpreting statutes in Indonesia, the elucidations cannot contradict the clear text of the law. For example the elucidation gives "environmental control" as an example of a sector that is provincial, contradicting article 11(2) of the law which clearly states that the environment is a matter for the regencies and cities. The law should prevail.

To add to the confusion, article 9(2) mentions that the provinces have jurisdiction over "the powers which have not, or have not yet, been implemented by regencies and cities". This is a *de facto* jurisdiction — to know whether a certain power belongs to the regency or the province one would have to check whether the regency has exercised that power. If not, then that power belongs to the province, at least with respect to that regency — if other regencies in the same province have exercised that power, then they would have jurisdiction. This is bound to be a very time-consuming and error-prone process even if one were to check only the "recognition of powers" which the ministry of home affairs has issued for each specific regency (see below).

The Confusing Regulations and the Lack of Co-ordination with Existing Laws

Given that the law is not entirely clear as to the division of powers, one would have hoped that the government regulations authorized by the law and adopted before its coming into force would have been more illuminating. Unfortunately, the main regulation on the division of powers only added to the confusion.[12] Drafted by sectors that seem to correspond to existing ministries (or vested interests), it reads as if the different ministries had decided to make a last ditch effort to keep their powers and prevent their transfer to the provinces.

The law was adopted so quickly that there was insufficient time to review most of the national laws. Since so many powers were to be transferred to the regions, many of the national laws should have been amended to reflect the more limited powers of the central government. For example, the mining law that provides for mining licences should have been amended before the coming into force of the regional autonomy law so that those applying for a licence know that they now had to deal with the provinces. Due to lack of time the many amendments required were not adopted and therefore many national laws still read as if the central government has most powers, thus adding to an already confusing situation.

C. The Implementation of the New Laws

Many observers had predicted the worst on the coming into force of the Regional Autonomy Law. As we will see, many of the dire predictions did come through. The situation is far from perfect and much work will need to be done to improve the laws and their implementation. Yet, one must admit that in some respects the transfer of powers went much more smoothly than had been expected.

1. Administrative Success

The most successful aspect of the implementation has been the transfer of more than two million civil servants as well as about 16,000 facilities (schools, hospitals, etc.) to the regions.[13] There were some difficulties here and there, but overall it has gone rather smoothly considering the magnitude of the task.

The transfer of funds has also to a large extent been successful. There has of course been a decentralization of corruption, and a series of abusive regional taxes have been imposed to raise local revenues. The regions do complain that they do not have enough funds to cope with their new responsibilities, which might be true, but is not convincing coming from the often corrupt local officials. Nevertheless the transfer of funds from the central to the regional governments did occur and most government facilities (schools, hospitals, etc.) are open and functioning. With very few exceptions, there has been no serious disruption of service. It is amazing that the transfer went relatively smoothly, and the authorities must be congratulated for proving wrong the critics, including myself, who expected a rougher fiscal and administrative transition. The civil servants who were transferred to the authority of the regions must also be congratulated for their resilience — at times some continued working even though they were not exactly sure who would pay them and when.

2. The Continuing Legal Uncertainties

Unfortunately, however, not everything went well and there are quite a few other problems that have arisen in the implementation of the law. First and foremost, the legal uncertainties have led to many difficulties and have had a negative impact on trade and commerce as well as on investments. The nature of the legal uncertainties in the law and regulations has been described above. Now let us see what these uncertainties led to in the implementation stage.

Adding to the Confusion: New Regulations that might be Ultra Vires and therefore Invalid

The Ministry of Home Affairs and Regional Autonomy must be commended for drafting and adopting many regulations, decrees, and instructions (or having them adopted by the government). As mentioned above, there is a great need for clarification of the laws and regulations on regional autonomy and the fact that the ministry is trying to clarify the laws is appreciated. A lot of work has been put into this.[14]

There are, however, a few difficulties with the means chosen to clarify the law. At the risk of being too legally technical, it needs to be pointed out that many of the regulations that attempt to bring clarity are themselves based on doubtful legal grounds. Under the principle of the hierarchy of sources of laws, a law or regulation of a lower level that contradicts a higher law or regulation is invalid. For example a statute that contradicts the Constitution is unconstitutional and therefore, in principle, invalid. The same principle applies to a law and regulation (a regulation that contradict a law is invalid).

The recently adopted decree of the People's Consultative Assembly (MPR) on sources of law[15] gives a hierarchical order to most sources of law. Interestingly however, it does not list ministerial decrees as a source of law and therefore it is unclear how the many decrees of the Minister for Home Affairs and Regional Autonomy can prevail over regional regulations — the latter are listed as sources of law in the MPR decree but ministerial decrees are not. Therefore, one could think that ministerial decrees could not prevail over regional regulations.

The very basis of both article 18 of the Constitution and article 11 of the Regional Autonomy Law is that regional governments (the *kabupaten* and *kota* says the law) have all powers except those granted to the central government by a statute (*undang-undang*). The grant of powers to the central government cannot be done by regulation, and even less by a presidential or ministerial decree. At least one presidential decree protecting some central powers seems to go directly against the Regional Autonomy Law[16] thus again bringing legal uncertainty.

In particular it is unclear why the regions should first have to seek the authorization of the Minister for Home Affairs and Regional Autonomy before exercising the powers clearly conferred onto them by the law. Of course for greater certainty, a system which records at the ministry the powers the regions decide to exercise seems like a good idea. However as it stands now the system seems to allow the Minister not to recognize or acknowledge the powers granted to a region by the Regional Autonomy Law. It is difficult to see how this can be done under the authority of a government regulation or presidential decree. This kind of supervision by the Minister was first authorized by a simple presidential decree[17] and then a ministerial decree.[18] It is, therefore, based on doubtful authority since the Constitution and the law state that regions can only be denied their powers by a statute.

After the Minister for Home Affairs and Regional Autonomy acknowledges regional powers, the supervision of the regions continues to be exercised through another government regulation[19] which grants the Minister, and in some instances the governors, the power to effectively cancel regional regulations that contradict "the public interest, a higher law or/and other law". The regulation states that regions which do not accept this cancellation can appeal to the government through the Ministry of Home Affairs (article 10). There is a ministerial decree to the same effect.[20] This regulation and this decree directly contradict article 114 of the Regional Autonomy Law which states that the government, not the Minister, can cancel a regulation and that the appeal is to the Supreme Court, not to the government. Again, a regulation or decree that contradicts a law should be invalid. The Riau province has threatened to take the central government to the Supreme Court after it revoked one of its regulations.[21] This would be the first time the Supreme Court (Mahkamah Agung) would have to apply the Regional Autonomy Law.

The above discussion may seem rather technical to non-jurists but it points to the fact that the regulations adopted since the coming into force of the regional autonomy law have often added to the legal uncertainty rather than resolved it.

It is important to have efficient supervision of the regions to make sure that they do not in any way exceed their jurisdiction or usurp powers that rightly belong to the central government. This, we will see, is essential for increasing foreign and domestic investments in the regions, for insuring that all citizens are treated equally and that Indonesia remains a common market for all Indonesian workers and businesspersons. Such efficient and strong supervision would have been better based on clear authority in a statute, rather than on a regulation or decree that seems to contradict a statute.

Regional Taxation and other Doubtful Exercises of Powers

There are many examples of regional regulations that are clearly *ultra vires* and that should be challenged by the central government. Many regions have purported to exercise powers that they clearly do not have. For example, some regions have purported to enforce religious dress in schools[22] or regulate some other religious matters.[23] This is clearly beyond their powers (*ultra vires*) as religion is one of the matters reserved exclusively to the central government. It does not seem however that the Ministry of Home Affairs has been particularly quick to cancel these regulations.

The main area in which the regions have exceeded their powers seems to be the imposition of taxes and levies. Many regions have raised many kinds of taxes and levies that exceeded the taxation powers they were granted and the ministry did intervene to cancel some of these regulations.[24] These illegal taxes and levies affect not only investments, but also internal trade. Taxes on the value of goods passing through a region hinder trade within Indonesia and threaten the concept of a common market within Indonesia.

Continuing Need for a Review of Legislation to Curb Contradictions and Uncertainties

Much of the political debate has been about whether there should be a revision of the Regional Autonomy Law but what is not debated much but nonetheless important is the need for a systematic revision of other national laws to take into account the devolution of powers to the regions. Unfortunately not much progress has been made in this respect and it is hoped that the numerous national laws in need of a revision will be looked at in a systematic fashion. For example, the country needs a new Investment Law that would clearly state which level of government is responsible for the approval of investments in different sectors. A bill is only now being prepared.[25]

3. The Regionalization of Corruption and the Emergence of Local Democracy

All too often in Indonesia, with power comes corruption. The decentralization of powers has led to a decentralization of corruption. There is ample evidence of such corruption and evidence also of money politics in securing elections and political appointments in the regions. Is the situation worse than under Soeharto and is that why foreign investors are no longer investing?

It is hard to compare levels of corruption between the New Order and the present situation. While the long-term goal to fight corruption should of course remain, it must be recognized that corruption does not necessarily hinder investments as long as the corruption is reliable and predictable — after all there was a high level of foreign investments during the Soeharto regime. Unfortunately the decentralization of powers has made corruption unpredictable and unreliable. It has become unpredictable because now you never know how many regional governments will want a take your profits either through official (though perhaps illegal) licence fees or taxes, or through unofficial bribes. The new powers have emboldened local authorities, and the amounts they want are unpredictable as they vary from region to region and from time to time. The corruption has also become unreliable: because of the legal uncertainties in the delegation of powers, even if you pay a certain regional government, you can never be sure that it can deliver since another level of government might claim to have the power to grant you what you want.

Fortunately however, there is a counterpart to the decentralization of corruption: local democracy. There seems to be in many regions an increased popular awareness of the newly devolved powers and a desire to make local politicians accountable.[26] One way to encourage this emerging local democracy would be to amend the Regional Autonomy Law to provide for the direct election of Governors and Regents as opposed to the present indirect mode of election that encourages money politics and other forms of corruption. This has been promised recently by the Minister for Home Affairs and Regional Autonomy.[27]

4. The Effect on Foreign Investment and the Economy

The effects of legal uncertainties regarding regional autonomy and in particular the cost and uncertainties created by illegal taxes, levies, and regional bribes have hurt foreign and domestic investment. Direct foreign investment approvals have diminished by 42 per cent in the first semester of 2002.[28] It is of course impossible to isolate regional autonomy from other factors discouraging investments such as the increasing labour costs and labour unrest, security concerns, more general legal and political risks as well as better conditions in competing countries like China and Vietnam. However, the uncertainties relating to regional autonomy are definitely an important factor in discouraging investments. Even investments by the mining industry which is used to roughing it out in tough and unpredictable regions have been affected by the difficulties relating to the new regional autonomy laws.[29] Many existing investors are moving their investments to competing countries.

5. The Lack of Protection for Minorities under the Regional Autonomy Law

Even before the implementation of regional autonomy laws, fishermen from some regions were preventing fishermen from other regions from fishing in "their" waters. Unfortunately there have been an increasing number of instances of discrimination against Indonesian citizens who do not belong to the main ethnic group of the region where they reside. This is now referred to as the *Putra Daerah* issue (son of the region issue). As I have pointed out elsewhere,[30] regional regulations that discriminate between citizens based on ethnicity, religion, or origin are unconstitutional and therefore invalid.

Luckily some regional authorities have recently taken a stand against discrimination based on ethnicity and origins in regional administration,[31] but much more should be done.

D. Can the Regional Autonomy Law be Amended?

Will the Regional Autonomy Law be amended in the near future, perhaps before the elections in 2004? This is hard to tell but the issue is certainly hotly debated. As mentioned above, the law was adopted under President Habibie and offered very broad regional autonomy. Already under President Wahid, the regulations adopted to implement the regional autonomy laws clearly signalled that the central government wanted to keep responsibilities that many thought would go to the regions judging from the broad wording of the laws and the repeated statements of President Habibie. In a way, though not in an obvious or very public one, President Wahid did slow down the move to devolve almost every power to the regions.

The fear of many in the regencies and cities is that President Megawati is not fully committed to regional autonomy and wants to recentralize powers either to Jakarta or to the provinces. Given the President's nationalistic and pan-Indonesian political views, this fear might be in part justified. By now, however, the Regional Autonomy Law has become something of a sacred cow and anyone suggesting amendments to it is accused of wanting to recentralize everything. President Megawati often feels the need to deny that she wants to recentralize, which shows that she realizes that there might be a political price to pay if she is perceived as opposing regional autonomy. This political reality makes it difficult for the government to make the necessary amendments to the laws. When government officials want to mention the possibility of amending the law, they do so by talking of improvements (*penyempurnaan*) rather than revisions (*revisi*). Even the MPR decree that suggested evaluating and considering amending the Regional Autonomy Law carefully talks of "improvements".[32]

After the 2004 elections it might become even more difficult to amend the law. The third amendment to the Constitution introduces a new assembly for the representation of the regions, the House of Representatives of the Regions (Dewan Perwakilan Daerah, or DPD). Each province is equally represented at the DPD. It seems that the agreement of the DPD will be required for matters that relate to regional autonomy ("it shall participate in the discussion" [*ikut membahas*] of these matters says the Constitution).[33] Given the nature of this assembly, it is unlikely that the DPD will agree to any perceived recentralization of powers. It therefore seems that it will be politically much more difficult to amend the law to clarify the division of powers after the elections in 2004. There is however very little time, and very little political enthusiasm, to amend the law before 2004.

III. Special Autonomy Laws

In addition to the Regional Autonomy Law applicable to most provinces, regencies, and cities, some special statutes apply to some regions. These special statutes are very different from the Regional Autonomy Law and from one another. The comments here are limited to introducing briefly each of them.

The province of the special region of the national capital Jakarta is constituted by a separate statute and most of the powers normally granted to regencies are granted to the province itself. The heads of the main subdivisions (regents and *walikotamadya*) play an administrative role and are not elected but appointed by the Governor.[34] Given this undemocratic structure and the indirect election of the governor himself, it is not surprising that the recent re-election of a former general as Governor of Jakarta has been marred by accusations of a complete disregard for democratic principles, of corruption and of money politics. Governor Sutiyoso was originally put in place by Soeharto in 1997 for a five-year term and is the very general who, in 1996, had a role in commanding the troops that crushed peaceful demonstrators of Megawati's own party and killed some of them. Hardly a man with democratic credentials, yet he was re-elected with Megawati's personal support amid accusations of corruption and money politics. Jakarta might now have the unenviable record of being perceived as one of the least democratic regions in all of Indonesia.[35]

A special law was also adopted for Aceh.[36] It was not however negotiated with the Free Aceh Movement (GAM) and thus far has not been accepted by them as the basis for peace in that conflict-torn region. The most noted feature of this new law is the fact that the province of Aceh is given the power to implement *sharia* law although it remains unclear what exactly that means given that it must do so within the secular unitary state of Indonesia.

The Province of Papua, formerly known as Irian Jaya, also now has its own statute constituting it as a special region.[37] The statute seems to clearly endorse affirmative action in favour of the Papuans (or, as some would say, it institutes discriminations against non-Papuans). The governor must be an ethnic Papuan (*orang asli Papua*, article 12) and priority in employment and opportunity must be given to ethnic Papuans (article 62). In addition to the Regional Legislative Assembly, Papua has a special "Papua People's Assembly" (*Majelis Rakyat Papua*) made up of native Papuans. The consent of this ethnic-based assembly is required for the passing of certain types of regulations and for choosing the Governor.

Unlike the general Regional Autonomy Law, all three special laws concentrate most powers at the provincial level rather than at the level of regencies and cities.

Finally it should be mentioned that the special region of Yogyakarta feels a bit less special these days since it does not have its own statute. A draft special statute for the region, that would secure a special position for the sultan, is under study in the province.[38]

IV. Conclusion

Regional autonomy is very much a work in progress in Indonesia. It is however remarkable that such a radical decentralization done over such a short period of time has not led to more disastrous results, and in fact has led to some positive outcomes (more democracy and empowerment in the regions). The good work of all involved in the process and the significant efforts of the Ministry of Home Affairs must be commended.

There are however many shortcomings, as one would expect given the unrealistic time frame in which the transition took place. These shortcomings are unfortunately affecting the Indonesian economy by bringing more legal uncertainty and increasing the local political risks for businesses. These problems should be addressed urgently.

It seems to me that the way to go is to "improve" (i.e., amend) the laws so as to make clearer the division of powers between the different levels of government and to put in place efficient and quick ways to curb any excessive power of local governments.

Notes

1. MPR Decree number XV/MPR/1998(ii).
2. See Gary F. Bell, "The New Indonesian Laws Relating to Regional Autonomy: Good Intentions, Confusing Laws", *Asian Pacific Law and Policy Journal* 2 (2001): 1–44. Available at <http://www.hawaii.edu/aplpj/2/1.html>.
3. See Gary F. Bell, "Minority Rights and Regionalism in Indonesia: Will Constitutional Recognition Lead to Disintegration and Discrimination?", *Singapore Journal of International and Comparative Law* 5 (2001): 784–806.
4. See, for example, Undang-undang No. 5, Th. 1974 Tentang Pokok-pokok Pemerintahan di Daerah [Law Number 5 of 1974 on the Fundamentals of Governance in the Regions] and Undang-undang No. 5, Th. 1979 Tentang Pemerintahan Desa [Law Number 5 of 1979 on the Governance of Villages].
5. Undang-Undang No. 22, Th. 1999 Tentang Pemerintahan Daerah [Law Number 22, Year 1999 on Regional Governance] (7 May 1999) [hereinafter referred to as Regional Autonomy Law].
6. Undang-Undang No. 25, Th. 1999 tentang

Perimbangan Keuangan Antara Pemerintah Pusat dan Daerah [Law Number 25, Year 1999 on Fiscal Balance between the Central Government and the Regions] (19 May 1999) [hereinafter referred to as Fiscal Balance Law].
7. Article 1, paragraph 1 of the 1945 Indonesian Constitution states: "The state of Indonesia is a unitary state in the form of a Republic." ("*Negara Indonesia ialah negara kesatuan yang berbentuk Republik*"). Undang-Undang Dasar Negara Republik Indonesia Tahun 1945.
8. "The unitary State of Indonesia is divided into provinces and these provinces into regencies and cities and each and every of these provinces, regencies and cities form a regional government in accordance with the law." "*Negara Kesatuan Republik Indonesia dibagi atas daerah-daerah provinsi dan daerah provinsi itu dibagi atas kabupaten dan kota, yang tiap-tiap provinsi, kabupaten dan kota itu mempunyai pemerintahan daerah, yang diatur dengan undang-undang.*"
9. "*Pemerintahan daerah menjalankan otonomi seluas-luasnya, kecuali urusan pemerintahan yang oleh undang-undang ditentukan sebagai urusan Pemerintah Pusat.*" Perubahan Kedua Undang-Undang Dasar Negara Republik Indonesia Tahun 1945 [Second Amendment to the Basic Law of Republic of the State of Indonesia 1945] article 18(5), in Putusan Majelis Permusyawaratan Rakyat Republik Indonesia, Sidang Tahunan [Decisions of the People's Representative Assembly of the Republic of Indonesia, Annual Session], 17–18 August 2000 [hereinafter Second Amendment to the Basic Law].
10. "*Kewenangan Daerah Kabupaten dan Daerah Kota mencakup semua kewenangan pemerintahan selain kewenangan yang dikecualikan dalam Pasal 7 dan yang diatur dalam Pasal 9.*" The text in square brackets in the English version is added by the author.
11. The number of provinces and regencies is increasing. These numbers are our best estimate at the time of going to press.
12. See Peraturan Pemerintah R.I. No. 25, Th. 2000 Tentang Kewenangan Pemerintah dan Kewenangan Propinsi Sebagai Daerah Otonom [Regulation of the Government of the Republic of Indonesia, Number 25, Year 2000 on the Responsibilities of the (Central) Government and the Responsibilities of the Provinces as Autonomous Regions].
13. Bert Hofman and Kai Kaiser (of the World Bank), "The Making of the Big Bang and its Aftermath — A Political Economy Perspective", available at <http://www.gtzsfdm.or.id/documents/dec_ind/o_pa_doc/hofmankaiserAtlanta_3.pdf>.
14. To see the large number of regulations, decrees, and instructions that has been prepared and the amount of work that went into this, see the excellent website maintained by the German Technical Assistance Project for Policy Support for Decentralisation (Gtz Poyek P4D) at <http://www.gtzsfdm.or.id/>.
15. Ketetapan Majelis Permusyawaratan Rakyat Nomor III/MPR/2000 Tentang Sumber Hukum Dan Tata Urutan Peraturan Perundang-Undangan [Decision of the MPR Number III/MPR/2000 on Sources of Law and the Hierarchical Order of Legislative Rules], 18 August 2000.
16. See Presidential Decree (Keppres) no. 62/2001 which purports to allow the National Land Bureau (Badan Pertanahan Nasional) to remain part of the central government for two years when the law clearly states at article 11(2) that land is a matter that the regency or city must regulate.
17. Presidential Decree (Keppres) no. 5/2001.
18. Ministerial Decree 130–67/2002.
19. Peraturan Pemerintah Nomor 20 Tahun 2001 Tentang Pembinaan dan Pengawasan atas Penyelenggaraan Pemerintahan Daerah [Government Regulation Number 20 of 2001 on Fostering and Supervision of Local Governance].

20. Keputusan Menteri Dalam Negeri Nomor 41 Tahun 2001 Tentang Pengawasan Represif Kebijakan Daerah [Decision of the Ministry of Home Affairs no. 41/2001 on the repressive supervision of regional policies]. The decision conveniently adds the decisions of the Minister as a source of law higher than regional regulations, something the MPR decree on sources of laws had failed to do.
21. See Decentralisation News No. 31, 19 July 2002 available at <http://www.gtzsfdm.or.id/documents/dec_ind/newsletter/Newsletter31.pdf>.
22. See for example "Governor to quiz mayor on Muslim attire directive", *Jakarta Post*, 5 June 2002.
23. "Besides in Aceh, *sharia* also has been introduced in Pamekasan regency in East Java; Maros, Sinjai and Gowa regencies in South Sulawesi; and the regencies of Cianjur, Indramayu and Garut in West Java. In Indramayu, *sharia* has been implemented in the form of requiring civil servants to wear Muslim clothes on Fridays, to recite from the Koran for 30 minutes before beginning work and to fast every Monday and Thursday. In Gowa regency, South Sulawesi, it has been ruled that thieves will have their hands amputated, as required by *sharia*. However, no one in the regency has yet been punished in this manner." As reported in "*Sharia* has 'little chance in the country'", *Jakarta Post*, 13 December 2002. I should point out that only Aceh is authorized to implement Islamic law.
24. Decentralization News No. 27, 3 May 2002, available at <http://www.gtzsfdm.or.id/documents/dec_ind/newsletter/Newsletter27.pdf> reports, for example, that the Ministry of Finance has identified 123 regional regulations that contradict the law on regional taxations, thus proving that the ministry of finance is monitoring the situation. See also, for example, "Government revokes, reviews regional rulings", *Jakarta Post*, 19 February 2002.
25. "House urges govt to complete crucial investment bill", *Jakarta Post*, 6 September 2002.
26. "Decentralization encourages democracy, researchers say", *Jakarta Post*, 1 March 2002.
27. See Decentralization News, no. 37, 29 November 2002, available at <http://www.gtzsfdm.or.id/documents/dec_ind/newsletter/Newsletter37.pdf>.
28. "FDI approvals fall 42% in first semester — BKPM", *Jakarta Post*, 24 July 2002.
29. "According to the Indonesian Mining Association (IMA) there had been relatively few new investments in the mining sector since 1998, partly due to the legal uncertainties created by poor implementation of the regional autonomy policy". "Govt revokes 68 bylaws in energy and mineral sector", *Jakarta Post*, 3 October 2002.
30. See note 3 above.
31. "Everyone should enjoy equal opportunities — Jambi governor", *Jakarta Post*, 10 September 2002, p. 5.
32. See point 1(f) of the annex of the Ketetapan VI/MPR/2002 Tentang Rekomendasi atas Laporan Pelaksanaan Putusan Majelis Permusyawaratan Rakyat Republik Indonesia Oleh Presiden, DPA, DPR, BPK, MA Pada Sidang Tahunan Majelis Permusyawaratan Rakyat Republik Indonesia Tahun 2002. [Decision VI/MPR/2002 on the recommendations on the report on the implementation of decision of the MPR of the Republic of Indonesia by the president the DPA, DPR, BPK, Supreme Court at the annual session of the MPR of the Republic of Indonesia in year 2002.]
33. See articles 22C and 22D of the Constitution introduced by the Third Amendment to the Constitution.
34. See articles 9 and 20 of the Undang-

Undang 34/1999 Tentang Pemerintahan Propinsi Daerah Khusus Ibukota Negara Republik Indonesia Jakarta (Law 34/1999 on the Governance if the Province of the Special Region of the National Capital Jakarta).
35. "Sutiyoso reelected Jakarta governor despite suspect status", *Jakarta Post*, 26 December 2002.
36. Undang-Undang 18/2001 Tentang Otonomi Khusus Bagi Provinsi Daerah Istimewa Aceh Sebagai Provinsi Nanggroe Aceh Darussalam [Law 18/2001 on the Special Autonomy for the Special Provincial Region of Aceh as the Province of "Nanggroe Aceh Darussalam"] [in the Acehnese language].
37. Undang-Undang 21/2001 Tentang Otonomi Khusus Bagi Provinsi Papua [Law 21/2001 on Special Autonomy for The Papua Province].
38. "Public, elite divided over Yogyakarta's special status", *Jakarta Post*, 5 September 2002.

THE IMPACT OF DOMESTIC AND ASIAN REGIONAL CHANGES ON INDONESIAN FOREIGN POLICY

Dewi Fortuna Anwar

The past decade has seen fundamental and dramatic changes in Indonesian national politics which have affected all aspects of public life. The forced resignation of President Suharto amid the Asian financial crisis in May 1998 ended the stranglehold of the authoritarian New Order regime which had ruled Indonesia for thirty-two years, and ushered in a new *reformasi* era characterized by rejection of many key features of the New Order. In a zeal to outlaw authoritarianism and build a more pluralistic democracy, Indonesia carried out four successive amendments to the 1945 constitution which, among others, abolished the social-political role of the armed forces, ensure a clear separation of power between the executive, the legislative, and the judiciary, enshrine the principles of human rights in the constitution, and allow the development of a truly multiparty system. To prevent the rise of another long-term leader like Suharto who was able to manipulate the Consultative Assembly to elect him for seven consecutive five-year terms, the presidential term has been limited to two non-renewable five-year terms while the president and vice-president are to be directly elected by the people. As a reaction to the overt centralization under the New Order which gave little room for regional initiatives, the post-Suharto governments have also introduced sweeping regional autonomy.

After difficult early years of transition, marked by various internal conflicts and political instability, relative normalcy and political stability seemed to have been restored by 2004 as Indonesia succeeded in holding its first direct presidential election, affirming its status as the world's third-largest democracy. The newly democratic

---

Reprinted from Daljit Singh, ed., *Southeast Asian Affairs 2010* (Singapore: Institute of Southeast Asian Studies, 2010), pp. 126–41. At the time of original publication, Dewi Fortuna Anwar was Deputy Chairman for Social Studies and Humanities at the Indonesian Institute of Sciences (IPSK-LIPI), Jakarta.

Indonesia recognizes freedoms of expression and association as key principles, giving rise to a vibrant and increasingly critical civil society, free-wheeling media, and numerous political parties. These fundamental changes in Indonesia's political landscape have led to a re-structuring of relations between the state and society, between the central government and the regional governments, and between the various institutions of the state, which in turn has transformed the ways that decisions are made. One of the key areas affected by these political changes is in the making and implementation of Indonesian foreign policy, which during the previous era had been the prerogative solely of the predominant executive.

Besides the political transformation which has changed some of the ways that Indonesia looked at itself and the world, including new foreign policy priorities and strategies, Indonesia's economic development in the aftermath of the Asian financial crisis has also affected its regional and global standing. After several years of turning inward to deal with its myriad domestic problems, Indonesia's recent economic recovery — though its growth has been well below the pre-crisis level — and its relative ability to weather the latest global financial meltdown which started in the United States in early 2008, has helped to improve Indonesia's international image and also injected a new sense of self-confidence in the articulation and implementation of its foreign policy.

While domestic political changes have influenced the way decisions are made, introduced new national priorities, and influenced how these priorities are expressed, the changing regional dynamics have also led to some re-alignments in Indonesia's external relations. The rise of major regional powers, China and India, has re-focused Indonesia's attention on these two countries, particularly on the former, reviving memories of the particularly close relations between Jakarta and Beijing throughout the 1950s till the mid 1960s under President Sukarno. At the same time relations with other key regional and global powers have also reached new heights, including with Australia and the United States, indicating that Indonesia's "Free and Active" foreign policy principle could in fact only really be implemented in the post–Cold War international political climate. While reaching beyond the region, ASEAN has also continued to be a major factor in Indonesia's foreign policy, through which Indonesia tries to promote its core national values as well as enhance the ability of the regional members to shape policies in the wider East Asian region.

This chapter will examine how Indonesia's transition to democracy has had an impact on the way that decisions related to foreign policy are made, how democratization has introduced new priorities and attitudes, especially in Indonesia's relations with its ASEAN (Association of Southeast Asian Nations) neighbours, and how Indonesia has adapted to the rise of China.

Making Foreign Policy under Multiple Centres of Power

Throughout the New Order period most strategic decisions were made by the executive dominated by President Suharto at the top supported by the military-bureaucratic elites. No other power centres existed, and while the House of Representatives (DPR) had the sole power to ratify treaties and was supposed to be consulted on major policies, the DPR for the most part acted as a rubber stamp for the government. It is true that except during special circumstances, such as when a country is involved in external conflicts, foreign policy does not usually engage the interests of the general public even in well-established democracies. In Indonesia under Suharto the crafting and implementation of foreign policy remained largely in the hands of the Department of Foreign Affairs, which received a large infusion of senior military figures who often occupied ambassadorial positions in key foreign capitals. With a tame DPR, repressed countervailing forces, and media that practiced self-censorship to avoid closure, Indonesia's foreign policy throughout the New Order period was quite insulated from forces outside of the bureaucracy. Except on issues related to the Israeli-Palestinian conflict, which usually attracted the interest of Islamic groups who supported the Palestinians and opposed any moves by Indonesia to have relations with Israel, public interest on foreign policy as a whole was low. The fall of Suharto brought this government monopoly over the decision-making process, including in foreign policy, to an end.

One of the most significant outcomes of the *reformasi* has been the amendment of the 1945 Constitution — four times since 1999. With the constitutional amendments, the power of the DPR has increased exponentially, fully matching that of the executive. Although Indonesia has a presidential system with a powerful presidency, new checks and balances have been put in place, with a fully independent judiciary and an equally powerful DPR which is quite eager to flex its muscle.

The first constitutional amendment stipulates in Chapter 13, Article 1 that the DPR must be consulted on ambassadorial appointments, which in practice has in fact given the DPR the right to approve or reject the government's ambassadorial candidates. This provision was introduced to prevent the recurrence of old practices such as when Suharto used ambassadorial postings either as rewards for senior military figures for services rendered or as a means of getting rid of rivals,[1] and to ensure that the ambassadors sent overseas are of sufficiently high quality. The DPR has exercised this power over ambassadorial appointment with great enthusiasm, often rejecting the candidates who have been carefully selected by the Department of Foreign Affairs for trivial reasons, such as being unable to sing the national anthem properly, or being unable to fluently translate *Pancasila*, the state ideology, into English. The DPR has also switched the placements of candidates from those originally put forward by the Foreign Ministry, such as when the nominee for ambassador to Moscow was considered by the DPR to be better suited to serve in the more difficult post in Canberra. The upshot was that the ambassadorial candidate originally intended to head the Indonesian Embassy in Moscow was given the post in Canberra, and vice versa.[2]

Carried away by the zeal for reform and the desire to curtail the prerogatives of the president, the reformers have also included a provision in the first constitutional amendment which gives the DPR the right to approve the ambassadors being sent to Jakarta by other countries. This is in fact quite unique and contrary to common diplomatic practices, as the names of ambassadors are usually kept secret until official agreement by the host country has been received. The important roles played by the DPR in both the appointment of Indonesian ambassadors overseas and the approval of incoming ambassadors have sometimes resulted in long delays in filling these posts.

According to the 1945 constitution the DPR has always had the authority to ratify international treaties, but throughout the New Order period every international agreement signed by the government had been ratified by the DPR without exceptions. Under the current democratic setting, however, the process of treaty ratification is no longer just a formality since the DPR can as easily refuse to ratify a treaty if it believes that the treaty is not in the best national interest. Such a refusal became a reality in 2007 when the Defence Cooperation Agreement (DCA) signed by the Indonesian and Singaporean governments was met by public resistance in Indonesia who lobbied the DPR to reject the agreement. The failure of the DCA to get through the DPR was illustrative of the challenges of making foreign policy in a political setting where the views and aspirations of the general public can no longer be ignored with impunity. At the same time the DCA debacle also demonstrated the growing power of the regions, although under Indonesia's far reaching decentralization policy introduced in 1999 defence and foreign policy remain in the domain of the central government.

In February 2007 the governments of Indonesia and Singapore signed the Defence Cooperation Agreement (DCA) in Bali, in tandem with another agreement, a bilateral extradition treaty. Indonesia has long sought to secure a bilateral extradition agreement with Singapore, which became more urgent since the Asian financial crisis when it was alleged that several economic criminals from Indonesia had taken refuge in Singapore. For its part Singapore wished to renew its defence cooperation with Indonesia, particularly to gain access to Indonesian territory for its military to conduct exercises. In Indonesia the two negotiations were conducted separately, the extradition treaty led by the Ministry of Foreign Affairs, and the DCA by the Ministry of Defence, and given the sensitivities and complexities of both issues the public had mostly been kept in the dark about the details contained in the agreements. It was generally perceived in Indonesia that the Indonesian Government agreed to the signing of the DCA as a quid pro quo for Singapore agreeing to the extradition treaty. The two agreements were tied up and sent to the DPR for ratification in tandem, clearly in the hope that support for the extradition treaty would help to smooth the ratification of the defence cooperation agreement.

When details of the DCA became public however there were howls of protest from various quarters, particularly from the three provinces directly affected by the DCA. The terms of the DCA allowed Singapore to conduct military exercises in three separate areas; in Siabu (Kampar, Riau Province), Natuna waters (Riau Islands Province), and Baturaja (South Sumatra Province). All three regions protested that the Singaporean military exercises would have an adverse impact on the people's livelihood and called on the DPR to reject the DCA.[3] A number of political parties, such as the Islamic United Development party (PPP) and the National Mandate Party (PAN), also openly opposed ratification of the DCA. In the end both the DCA and the extradition treaty failed to pass through the DPR.

The making of foreign policy in Indonesia, therefore, just as in other democracies, must increasingly involve wider public consultations and participation and become more sensitive to popular sentiments. Failure to do so can lead to embarrassment to the government as in the case of the DCA or, even more serious, the president may be openly called to account by the DPR if Indonesia adopted an international stance that is contrary to the prevailing opinions in the DPR. For instance, in March 2007, as a non-permanent member of the United Nations Security Council, Indonesia supported UNSC Resolution No. 1747 imposing sanctions on Iran for its nuclear programme, which had been suspected of violating the nuclear non-proliferation treaty (NPT). Public perception in Indonesia, however, shared by a significant number of the DPR members, was strongly opposed to this as the resolution was regarded as being driven by the United States, which was seen to be unfairly targeting Iran, a fellow Muslim country. At the time the United States under President George W. Bush was still highly unpopular due to the American invasion and occupation of Iraq and Washington's war on terror, which was mostly perceived by Muslims as a war against the Islamic world.

The DPR, therefore, employed its right of interpellation by calling President Susilo Bambang Yudhoyono to come to the DPR to be questioned over Indonesia's support for the resolution. A stand-off occurred when the President did not come in person to the DPR but only sent a delegation of ministers, comprising the Coordinating Minister for Political and Security Affairs, the Foreign Minister, and the State Secretary Minister in July 2007, whom the DPR refused to meet. It was only after intensive lobbying of the DPR leadership by the President that the DPR softened its position and was willing to hear the government's explanation from another delegation of ministers.[4] It is to be expected that after this incident in which the President was put through a difficult political position over a relatively minor vote at the UN Security Council, Indonesian diplomats and the Indonesian foreign ministry as a whole must become much more circumspect in adopting an international position, especially on issues that attract public attention. On the Iranian nuclear issue henceforth Indonesia abstained every time the UN Security Council voted on another sanction against Iran.

Besides having to defer more closely to the wishes of the DPR, notably to Commission I in charge of defence and foreign policy, the Foreign Ministry has also recognized the importance of involving other stakeholders so as to ensure a wider sense of ownership towards Indonesian foreign policy. There was a conscious effort by Foreign Minister Nur Hasan Wirajuda (2001–9) to democratize the process of foreign policy making by actively consulting and engaging with think tanks, academics, religious groups, the media, and civil society organizations as well as with members of Parliament. The Foreign Ministry frequently commissioned papers from leading academics which would be openly discussed in workshops to provide policy inputs to the ministry. It also held regular closed briefings with these opinion makers through forums such as the "foreign policy breakfasts".[5] In one of his speeches soon after being appointed as Foreign Minister, Wirajuda's successor, Marty Natalegawa, reiterated that he will continue the democratization of Indonesia's foreign policy making, both in terms of substance as well as in terms of process.[6] Even then the Foreign Ministry has to accept more public scrutiny and criticism for every perceived shortcoming than ever before.

Democracy as the New Foreign Policy Agenda

In his first foreign-policy speech in 2005 President Susilo Bambang Yudhoyono outlined what he considered to be Indonesia's "international identity", comprising three key elements. These are the fact that Indonesia is the world's fourth most populous nation, that it is the home to the world's largest Muslim population, and that it is the world's third largest democracy. Yudhoyono took pride in the fact that Indonesia is "also a country where democracy, Islam and modernity go hand-in-hand".[7] The themes of Indonesia being the world's largest Muslim nation and the third largest democracy with a modern outward looking society have been emphasized over and over again as Indonesia projects itself onto the international stage, including in the newly formed forum of the major world economies, the G-20, in which Indonesia is the only member from Southeast Asia. In his first annual press briefing Indonesia's new Foreign Minister Marty Natalegawa stated that "As G-20 confirms its status as the premier forum on economic issues, Indonesia is challenged to carve a niche within the Group that is unique to itself as the world's third largest democracy, the country with the world's largest Muslim population and a voice of moderation."[8]

Indonesia has always been the home to the largest Muslim population, who are predominantly moderate, yet this fact was not considered as of any special value to the country's external relations before. It was the emerging problems of international terrorism linked to extremist Islamic movements, and the perceived clash of civilizations between Islam and the West, which drew international interest to the new phenomenon of Indonesia, where democracy is taking root in the world's largest Muslim nation. Indonesia has, therefore, been quick to seize the opportunity to project this new international identity and to capitalize on its unique position to try to act as a bridge between the Islamic world and the West. Promoting dialogue between civilizations and interfaith dialogues have become an important part of Indonesia's foreign policy agenda, which is also regarded as important in overcoming religious extremism at home.

The most important impact of Indonesia's political transformation on the substance of its foreign policy in the past decade, however, has been the mainstreaming of democracy and human rights issues in its foreign policy agenda, particularly in its policy towards ASEAN. Since its establishment ASEAN has been regarded as the cornerstone of Indonesia's foreign policy, and Jakarta had been a staunch supporter of the "ASEAN Way", which includes non-interference in each other's internal affairs, decision making by consensus, and a minimalist approach towards regional integration. With the dramatic political transformation at home, however, the foreign-policy establishment came under increasing pressure to align Indonesia's external stance with its core values at home, which now include respect for democracy and human rights. Indonesian pro-democracy activists have become increasingly critical of ASEAN's traditional non-interference policy which has prevented the association or its members from taking a critical stance when a fellow member committed gross violations of human rights. ASEAN is popularly perceived as an elitist regional organization with little relevance to the lives of the common people and the issues that matter to them most. The political situation in Myanmar, particularly the long imprisonment of the democratic leader Aung San Suu Kyi who had won the general elections in 1990, has long been a focus of pro-democracy activists around the world, and lately also in Indonesia. The result is that the Indonesian Government has been under considerable domestic pressure to push for the promotion of democracy and human rights as one of the key political agendas for ASEAN.

When Indonesia took over the chairmanship of ASEAN in 2003 it proposed the establishment of an ASEAN Security Community (ASC) — later renamed as ASEAN Political-Security Community (APSC) — to complement the ASEAN Economic Community which had been put forward by Singapore earlier as one of the three pillars of the ASEAN Community. Besides re-emphasizing the key treaties and agreements of ASEAN which have governed interstate relations since the establishment of ASEAN in 1967, the APSC for the first time also talks about democracy and human rights as being part of the core values of ASEAN as well as goals to which all members aspire. The third pillar, the Social-Cultural Community has been put forward by the Philippines. The Declaration of ASEAN Concord II (Bali Concord II) of 2003 formally agreed to the establishment of an ASEAN Community comprising the three pillars by 2020, later brought forward to 2015. The ASEAN Community initiative is envisioned to transform the primarily intergovernmental regional organization into a more people-oriented one.

The correlation between Indonesia's democratic transition and ASEAN's move towards a more people-oriented organization has recently been highlighted by the new Foreign Minister, which is worth quoting at length: "Almost mirroring Indonesia's democratic transformation over the past decade, the period since 2003 when Indonesia last held the Chairmanship of ASEAN has witnessed ASEAN's own evolution towards an ASEAN Community. This development has not been an accident. For Indonesia, the evolution of an ASEAN that is more alert to democratic principles and good governance is critical to ensure that there would not be a disconnect or divide between the transformation that has taken place in Indonesia and the regional milieu."[9]

Given the existing political differences within ASEAN it is to be expected that not all of the suggestions put forward by Indonesia, with many of the initiatives coming from civil society, will be accepted by the other ASEAN members. While the Indonesian Government has in fact been accommodative to the domestic demands that democracy and human rights take centre stage in Indonesia's policy towards ASEAN, and ASEAN has adopted some of the key proposals put forward by Indonesia, Indonesian public discontent towards ASEAN has continued to grow in the past years. Important elements of Indonesian civil society were deeply dissatisfied that the ASEAN Charter, which was finally adopted by the ASEAN governments in December 2007, was a watered down version from the original draft, with a much weaker provision for the protection of human rights and no provision for sanctions in the case of non-compliance.

A number of influential opinion-makers who in the past had been most active in promoting ASEAN regional co-operation, such as Rizal Sukma who was commissioned by the Foreign Ministry to help draft the ASEAN Security Community proposal in 2003, had in fact called on the Indonesian Parliament not to ratify the ASEAN Charter.[10] After intensive lobbying by the Foreign Ministry the DPR finally ratified the ASEAN Charter in late 2008, with Indonesia among the last ASEAN members to do so.

The establishment of the ASEAN Intergovernmental Commission on Human Rights (AICHR) in July 2009, which is a much weaker body than that initially envisioned by its champions, with no real power to monitor and protect human rights in the region, has also caused general disappointment. The former Minister of Foreign Affairs, Hasan Wirajuda, admitted that it was a case of one against nine between Indonesia and the rest of the ASEAN members as Indonesia's proposal to give real teeth to the ASEAN human rights commission was overwhelmingly outvoted, resulting in a fairly weak commission.[11] The Foreign Ministry has, however, appointed Rafendi Djamin, a well known human rights activist to represent Indonesia in the AICHR, so far the only commissioner in the AICHR who is from an NGO. This appointment clearly reflects Indonesia's seriousness in trying to develop the AICHR into a credible human rights body in ASEAN.

Members of the Indonesian Government, particularly the President and the Foreign Minister, have in recent year repeatedly reiterated the importance of ASEAN to Indonesia, that it remains the cornerstone of Indonesia's foreign policy. Marty Natalegawa in his speech at the Seventh CSAP General Conference quoted earlier said that "Indonesia's engagement in ASEAN is not optional in its nature. ASEAN is a fact of life."[12] The frequency of government pronouncements that ASEAN remains central to Indonesian foreign policy interests in part may be seen as a response to the growing call that Indonesia should not be investing so much of its time and energy in ASEAN. For instance, Rizal Sukma and Jusuf Wanandi from the Center for International and Strategic Studies (CSIS) — CSIS is a member of the long-established ASEAN-ISIS network which had actively promoted regional integration — have in the past year been agitating for Indonesia not to allow itself to become a hostage of ASEAN. In one of his many articles on the subject, Sukma wrote, "Indonesia has always been forced into compromise or into a corner by other members for the sake of ASEAN". Among his litany of complaints against ASEAN, Sukma listed Indonesia's bilateral dispute with Malaysia over Ambalat, Indonesia's failure to convince fellow ASEAN members to have a credible human rights body, and the fact that Indonesia's views on the ASEAN Charter were largely ignored. Sukma wrote that "there is nothing more irritating than being ignored" and then went on to say "that enough is enough. It is enough for Indonesia to imprison itself in the 'golden cage' of ASEAN for more than 40 years." Sukma concluded that "Indonesia, therefore, needs to begin formulating a post-ASEAN foreign policy. ASEAN should no longer be treated as the only cornerstone of Indonesia's foreign policy."[13]

The frustrations expressed towards ASEAN and the nationalist calls for Indonesia not to be held hostage by ASEAN within certain quarters reflect a combination of factors. The first is clearly the growing divide in core values between Indonesia, which is now in the midst of trying to consolidate its undoubtedly still messy democracy, and some of the other ASEAN members which still limit political freedom and have resisted Indonesia's efforts to give ASEAN the authority to enforce democratic and human rights principles through a more binding ASEAN Charter and a stronger human rights body. The second is that after recovering from several years of crisis, Indonesia's confidence has been restored and with it a certain assertiveness, which had been deliberately suppressed throughout the

New Order period when Indonesia adopted a low profile foreign policy in ASEAN. With the existence of multiple actors seeking to influence foreign policy it is no longer possible for Indonesia to adopt a low profile in ASEAN if this conflicts with public opinion at home. The third is the reality of ASEAN, that it is after all an association of sovereign states in which decision making is made through consensus; and while Indonesia is by far the largest member, it is not able to force its will on the association without fatally damaging ASEAN, which has been the lynchpin of peace and stability in Southeast Asia over the past four decades.

While continuing to emphasize the importance of ASEAN to Indonesia and accepting compromises on its proposals on democracy and human rights, which have disappointed so many activists at home, the Indonesian Government has in fact not limited its promotion of the democratic agenda to ASEAN. In December 2008 Indonesia launched the Bali Democracy Forum as the first governmental or first track forum for dialogues on democracy in Asia. The Bali Democracy Forum (BDF) is part of Indonesia's public diplomacy which tries to showcase Indonesia's attainments in democracy as well as promote an inclusive dialogue about democracy by inviting not only countries that are already democracies but also those "aspiring to be democracies". While the BDF was the initiative of the Foreign Ministry, the President has taken a direct interest in the matter and presided over the two BDFs held in 2008 and 2009.

The Bali Democracy Forum has four stated goals and objectives.[14] First, to establish a regional cooperation forum that promotes political development, through dialogue and sharing of experience, aiming at strengthening democratic institutions. Two, to initiate a learning and sharing process among countries in Asia as a strategy towards the maintenance of peace, stability, and prosperity in the region and beyond. Three, to initiate and build a platform for mutual support and cooperation in the field of democracy and political development. Four, to establish a working institution which would function as a resource base and information centre for research and study as well as a pool of expertise in the various sectors relevant to democracy. To prepare and support the BDF the foreign ministry, in collaboration with the Udayana University in Denpasar, Bali, has established the Institute for Peace and Democracy (IPD), which acts as the secretariat of the BDF.[15]

When it was first launched on 10–11 December 2008 the BDF received mixed reviews. On the one hand it was warmly received, as could be seen by the numbers of countries that sent high-level delegations. Australia, Brunei, and Timor Leste were represented by their respective heads of government while many countries sent delegations led by cabinet ministers. In 2008, thirty-one countries from Asia and observers from outside of the region attended. There was, however, also scepticism, especially from well-established democracies, at the inclusive nature of the dialogue, which also included countries that cannot be categorized as democratic, like China and Myanmar. However, interest in the BDF has grown since to date it is the only forum in Asia where government officials can talk openly about issues related to democracy and the political development in their respective countries and the region as a whole. As part of its programme, Indonesia invited the BDF participants to observe Indonesia's 2009 presidential election, with the expectation that inviting outside observers to watch elections, which can help ensure electoral fairness and transparency, would become generally acceptable in Asia. In the second Bali Democracy Forum in 2009, thirty-six countries sent delegations, including the Sultan of Brunei, the Prime Minister of Japan, and the Prime Minister of Timor Leste. The number and rank of observers from outside the region also increased, with the United States sending the Under Secretary for Political Affairs, Williams J. Burns, to attend.

Adapting to the Rise of China

Like other countries in the region, Indonesia has had to adapt its foreign policy to the changing regional dynamics, in particular the rise of China and India. As far as Indonesia is concerned the biggest transformation in its external relations in the past decade has been in its relations with China. It is worth remembering that after very close relations between Jakarta and Beijing throughout the 1950s and early 1960s under President Sukarno, from 1966 to 1990 Indonesia froze diplomatic relations with China. The strongly anti-communist New Order government under President Suharto not only banned any direct contact with mainland China, it also prohibited Chinese cultural influences, including Chinese language and writings. China was seen as the primary external threat to Indonesian security. After the end of the Cold War Indonesia normalized diplomatic relations with China, but interactions between the two countries were still strictly regulated. Yet by 2005 Indonesia and China had signed a strategic partnership agreement and the top leaderships of the two countries had exchanged state visits. The strict visa control for visiting Chinese nationals has been lifted and Chinese visitors can now obtain visas on arrival. Past suspicions of China's intent have clearly diminished as Indonesia also granted concessions and permits to Chinese companies to be involved in Indonesia's strategic industries, such as oil and gas and the construction of power plants.

Indonesia has clearly come to realize that it cannot afford to ignore China's huge economic potential, which other countries are also eager to tap. China's "charm offensive" towards Southeast Asia, including coming to Indonesia's assistance during the 1997–98 economic crisis and the December 2004 tsunami in Aceh, has also helped to remove some of Indonesia's earlier suspicions of China. China's technological prowess has also attracted Indonesia's attention, with moves to develop closer science and technology cooperation between the two countries, including in the area of defence. The last few years have, therefore, witnessed increasing interaction between Indonesia and China in almost all fields.

At the same time that Jakarta's relations with Beijing have blossomed, Indonesia has also intensified its relations with other regional powers, such as with Australia, Japan, South Korea, and with India. Indonesia's sometimes volatile relations with Australia, mostly due to political and security differences, have been anchored with the signing in 2006 of the Agreement on the Framework for Security Cooperation (Lombok Treaty), which came into force in February 2008, a wide-ranging security cooperation agreement replacing an earlier framework security agreement (which Indonesia unilaterally revoked in 1999 in the wake of Australia's role in East

Timor after the ballot). Indonesia has also signed a strategic partnership with India and South Korea and an economic partnership agreement with Japan. With the improvement of the United States' international standing after the election of President Barack Obama, Jakarta is also seeking to finalize a comprehensive partnership agreement with Washington.

In his annual press briefing quoted earlier, the Foreign Minister stated that Indonesia's foreign policy is multi-directional with the aim of having a thousand friends and zero enemies. The proclivity of Indonesia's strategic or comprehensive partnership agreements clearly point in that direction. Taking a more realist perspective and using the rise of China as the backdrop, however, it can also be argued that Indonesia, like many of its ASEAN neighbours, is pursuing a multi-hedging policy of both engaging China and counterbalancing it by engaging several other regional and extra-regional powers at the same time. Indonesia's support for an enlarged East Asia Summit to include Australia, India, and New Zealand, rather than simply accepting the transformation of the ASEAN Plus Three (China, Japan, and South Korea) into a new East Asian regional architecture, is clearly indicative of Jakarta's policy of "the more the merrier", hence preventing any one regional power from becoming overly dominant. Indonesia's support for ASEAN continuing to be in the driver's seat of wider regional initiatives also reflects Indonesia's unchanging attitude regarding the importance of regional resilience and ASEAN as a regional actor. Lately the Indonesian Foreign Minister has voiced support for the inclusion of Russia and the United States in the East Asia Summit, a forum still primarily driven by ASEAN, while rebuffing the initiatives from Australia and others to form a wider supra-regional architecture such as the Asia-Pacific Community which will not be anchored in ASEAN.

It should be noted, however, that voices critical of ASEAN in Indonesia have also cast doubts about the ability of ASEAN to continue to aspire to be in the driving seat of various regional fora or to provide the necessary support to Indonesia in the face of various challenges. Thus, contrary to the official stance of the Foreign Ministry, there has also been some support in Jakarta for the establishment of a wider East Asian forum to include the United States. Jusuf Wanandi for instance wrote, "It may be necessary for the East Asian region to establish an overarching summit to deliberate on strategic issues, including traditional security issues, with the participation of the United States."[16] Even here, however, there is clearly no support for an East Asian regional architecture that is exclusively Asian in nature.

Conclusion

Indonesia's foreign policy since the fall of President Suharto has shown both continuity and change. The basic doctrine of an independent and active foreign policy, of commitment to ASEAN, supporting multi-lateralism, and the central role of the United Nations in maintaining international security has not changed. The role of foreign policy in serving Indonesia's national interests, particularly its economic development, has also remained the same. At the same time there have also been major changes, as consequences of domestic political transformations, both in the process and substance of Indonesian foreign policy. In terms of process, the making of foreign policy has been democratized, with the existence of multiple power centres and a diversity of stakeholders, which present both constraints and opportunities to the traditional foreign policy establishment. On the one hand, the government has to defer increasingly to the DPR and listen to the aspirations of the various opinion-makers. On the other hand, the foreign ministry is greatly assisted by the inputs provided by independent scholars and think tanks in formulating foreign policy, who together with the media and other civil society actors also help in disseminating foreign policy issues to the wider public.

In terms of substance Indonesia's transition to democracy has also influenced its foreign policy agenda. Issues related to democracy and human rights now occupy an important position in Indonesia's foreign policy agenda, particularly towards ASEAN as support for the development of an ASEAN Community grows. Indonesia is also actively projecting its image as the world's largest Muslim democracy as a national asset in the wider international fora.

With the end of the Cold War and the concurrent rise of China as a global economic power, Jakarta's formerly aloof attitude towards China has also changed. In the past five years in particular, relations between Jakarta and Beijing have intensified in almost all fields. Nevertheless, Indonesia remains wary of China or any other regional power becoming too dominant within an overarching East Asian regional architecture. Indonesia's position that ASEAN should be in the driving seat of any wider regional initiatives has remained unchanged, though there are already voices in Indonesia which, dissatisfied with ASEAN, support the establishment of a new East Asian or Asia Pacific architecture.

Notes

1. During much of the New Order period key diplomatic posts, such as ambassadors in the major ASEAN capitals, Washington, Tokyo, and Canberra, were held by senior military figures, mostly from the army. Powerful members of the elite whom Suharto could not simply dismiss were often sent overseas as ambassadors, popularly known by the term, *di Dubeskan*, or to be made an ambassador as a punishment rather than an achievement.

2. In July 2003 the DPR rejected the nomination of Susanto Pudjomartono, a former chief editor of the English daily, the *Jakarta Post*, as the new Indonesian Ambassador to Australia. The soft spoken Javanese was considered to be unsuited to be Indonesia's chief envoy in Australia, where the media were often highly critical of Indonesia. The outgoing Ambassador, Sabam Siagian, who was also a former chief editor of the *Jakarta Post* and regarded to have been a fairly successful Ambassador, is a blunt outspoken Batak from North Sumatra. The DPR instead preferred Imron Cotan, a career diplomat who had served as the Deputy Chief of Mission in Canberra and was nominated to be the new Ambassador to Russia, to return to Canberra as the new Ambassador. Imron Cotan is also a straight-talking Batak. In the end the DPR's views prevailed and the ambassadorial appointments for Canberra and Moscow were switched.

3. Since the onset of *reformasi* it has become increasingly common for delegations from the regions to put their aspirations or demands directly to the relevant commissions in the DPR, something that did not really happen in the earlier New Order period when the DPR had little control over legislation. In the case of the DCA, for instance, members of the legislative assembly of the affected districts came to Jakarta to lobby DPR Commission I in charge of foreign affairs and defence.

4. The president invited the top leaders of the DPR to the palace for consultations and a briefing on Indonesia's vote at the UN

Security Council on UNSC No. 1747. The DPR then agreed that another delegation of ministers comprising the Coordinating Minister for Political and Security Affairs, the Minister of Foreign Affairs, and the State Secretary Minister will be allowed to explain the government's policy to the DPR Commission I <http:www.tempointeraktif.com/hg/timeline/2007/03/20070330-01.id.html>.

5. The writer has participated in these workshops and foreign policy breakfasts several times.

6. Remarks by H.E. Dr Marty Natalegawa, Foreign Minister of the Republic of Indonesia on the occasion of the 7th General Conference of the Council for Security Cooperation in the Asia Pacific, 16 October 2009, Grand Hyatt Hotel, Jakarta <http://www.cscap.org/uploads/GeneralConfReport/7GenConfMinistersRemarks.pdf>.

7. Speech by President of the Republic of Indonesia before the Indonesian Council on World Affairs (ICWA), Jakarta, 19 May 2005 <http://www.presidensby.info/index.php/pidato/2005/05/19/332.html>.

8. Annual Press Briefing, Minister for Foreign Affairs of the Republic of Indonesia, H.E. Dr R.M. Marty M. Natalegawa, "Indonesia and the World 2010". Indonesian Ministry of Foreign Affairs, Jakarta, 8 January 2010.

9. Ibid.

10. Rizal Sukma, "To Be Responsible, Indonesia Should Not Ratify ASEAN Charter", *Jakarta Post*, 22 July 2008.

11. Rakaryan Sukarjaputra, "Badan HAM ASEAN Jauh di Bawah Standar", 9 August 2009, Kompas.com <http://m.kompas.com/xl/read/data/2009.08.09.06163052>.

12. Remarks by H.E. Dr Marty Natalegawa, 7th General Conference of the Council for Security Coopearation.

13. Rizal Sukma, "Indonesia Needs a Post-ASEAN Foreign Policy", *Jakarta Post*, 30 June 2009.

14. See The Bali Democracy Forum website <http://balidemocracyforum.org>.

15. The writer is a member of the Board of Governors, later named Board of Advisors, of the Institute of Peace and Democracy.

16. Jusuf Wanandi, "The ASEAN Summit and Indonesia's National Interests", *Jakarta Post*, 19 March 2009.

ISIS IN INDONESIA

Sidney Jones and Solahudin

A steep decline in terrorist acts in Indonesia in 2014 should have been good news, especially because it underscored that police vigilance was high and extremist capacity was weak. But a third factor was also involved that was not such good news: more extremists were focused on getting to Syria and joining what they believed was a more important jihad than any they could wage at home. By late 2014, about 100 Indonesians, possibly more, were believed to have left to fight in Syria, some with their wives and children, and most to join the Islamic State.

Violent Extremists in Indonesia in 2014

By early 2014, Indonesia's jihadist community was divided between those who supported violence inside Indonesia, with the police as the primary target, and those who believed that at least for the moment, violence at home was counter-productive. The former generally supported the Islamic State and its predecessor, the Islamic State in Greater Syria and Iraq (ISIS). The latter were more likely to support IS's main rival in Syria, the al-Nusra Front, and its allies.

Prominent in the first group was Mujahidin Indonesia Timur (MIT), a group of some thirty armed men led by Santoso alias Abu Wardah in the hills outside Poso, Central Sulawesi. Santoso had run a series of military-style training camps in Poso beginning in 2011, and graduates and supporters are now scattered across Java, Sumatra, Sulawesi and Nusa Tenggara Barat (NTB). Despite being effectively under police siege during the year in his jungle

---

Reprinted from Daljit Singh, ed., *Southeast Asian Affairs 2015* (Singapore: Institute of Southeast Asian Studies, 2015), pp. 154–63. At the time of original publication, Sidney Jones was Director and Solahudin was Co-Director at the Institute for Policy Analysis of Conflict (IPAC), Jakarta, Indonesia.

camp, Santoso managed to smuggle out videos periodically to YouTube and radical websites. While neither he nor any other group managed any bombings in 2014, the few attacks on police during the year were all linked to MIT.[1] Santoso was the first Indonesian to publicly pledge loyalty to the Islamic State after its leader, Abubakar al-Baghdadi, announced the establishment of the new caliphate on 29 June 2014 (1 Ramadan).

The pro-violence group also included remnants of Mujahidin Indonesia Barat (MIB), many members of which had previous ties to an old Darul Islam network led by the now-imprisoned Abdullah Umar. It included some but not all members of Abu Bakar Ba'asyir's organization, Jamaah Anshorul Tauhid (JAT), and many followers of the imprisoned cleric Aman Abdurrahman who had no specific organizational affiliation.

The group that argued most strenuously that the costs of jihad in Indonesia outweighed the benefits was Jemaah Islamiyah (JI), best known for its involvement in the 2002 Bali bombing. Since 2007, it had forbidden its members to engage in attacks on the grounds that there was no community support, and there was no justification for collateral Muslim deaths since Indonesia was under neither occupation nor attack. It was vilified as a result by other jihadists for having abandoned jihad but its early and strong support for anti-Assad Islamists in Syria reburnished its jihadi credentials and strengthened its recruitment potential. Through 2014 JI remained strongly anti-ISIS but it also remained the only jihadi group with the capacity for long-term strategic thinking and the question was what its ultimate goals were.

The Attraction of Syria

From the beginning, the conflict in Syria had exerted a strong pull for Indonesians, stronger than other conflicts such as in Afghanistan, Somalia, Yemen and elsewhere that were seen as part of the global jihad. The reasons were several. First, according to several prophetic traditions (*hadith*), the final battle at the end of time, called *Malhamah al-Kubra*, would take place in Sham (Greater Syria), when the Imam Mahdi would lead the forces of Islam to victory.[2] The appeal of taking part in that victory was high, especially as radical Indonesians were avid readers of books on Islamic eschatology, with one Jemaah Islamiyah-affiliated publisher in Solo, Central Java, issuing a whole series on events that would mark the end of the world. Many of the discussions on the Syrian conflict that took place around Indonesia from 2012 onwards were explicitly linked to these apocalyptic predictions.

Second, many Indonesians were moved by the humanitarian suffering of Sunni Muslims in Syria and wanted to help. These included many in the radical community. Two groups close to JI became active in 2012. One was Syam Organizer <www.syamorganizer.com>, which sponsored lectures and fund-raising events across Indonesia. Another was the Red Crescent Society of Indonesia (Hilal Ahmar Society Indonesia, HASI). In late 2012, HASI began sending delegations to Syria to provide medical assistance, initially to Ahrar al-Sham, a group that was initially independent but some factions of which eventually allied with al-Nusra.

Some, particularly in the Salafi community, were attracted to the idea of fighting Shi'ism and saw Assad, a member of the Alawite sect, as a murderous Shi'a massacring Sunnis.

Finally, some of Indonesia's most militant extremists saw in the struggle of ISIS in particular a chance for the re-establishment of a caliphate that would unite all Muslims in a single political entity. Many Muslims who see a caliphate as the most perfect form of governance reject violence as a means of achieving it. But in Indonesia, some have long believed that it would be achieved only through jihad and the creation of individual Islamic states. They closely followed the creation of the "Islamic State of Iraq" in 2006 — an entity that existed in name only — and admired its leader, the late Abu Musab al-Zarqawi. (Santoso of MIT, for example, calls himself the Zarqawi of Indonesia.) Thus when ISIS, the successor to ISI, began to control territory and apply a draconian form of Islamic law, the hopes of these militants rose. When al-Baghdadi declared a caliphate, they immediately pledged support.

The Syrian conflict thus stirred interest among many different Islamist groups in Indonesia, but the common concern masked different motivations and deep differences about which faction in Syria to support.

How Support for ISIS Spread in Indonesia

Early support for ISIS in Indonesia spread through two related channels: the website www.al-mustaqbal.net, run by a man named M. Fachry, and the teachings of detained cleric Aman Abdurrahman. Fachry had been initially inspired in 2005 by the teachings of a then U.K.-based cleric named Omar Bakri Muhammad, founder of an organization called al-Muhajiroun. Bakri taught that a caliphate could be built through the establishment, by force if necessary, of territorial zones called *imarah Islam*, in which Islamic law would be applied.[3] Fachry and a few friends were determined to set up such a zone in Indonesia, and they became increasingly hostile toward other Islamists whose views differed from theirs. They also became increasingly interested in developments in the Middle East.

When Arab Spring activism led to the fall of authoritarian leaders in Tunisia, Egypt and Libya, Fachry and several friends were convinced that the caliphate was at hand, because they saw these developments as fulfilment of a prophecy about the political cycle of Islam. In the prophecy, the Prophet's own rule would be followed by a government of his successors (caliphate), then by inherited kingdoms, then by dictators and finally, at the end of time, by a return to the caliphate (*khilafah minhajul nubuwah*). Fachry's friends included a few followers of Aman Abdurrahman.

Aman Abdurrahman himself, a superb Arabic linguist, became the main translator of ISIS propaganda, and though serving a nine-year sentence in a maximum-security prison, those translations appeared regularly on radical websites, including Fachry's. His support for ISIS was ironic. He had long been a critic of al-Zarqawi, faulting him for lacking a long-term strategy and only concerned with striking at the enemy. He called this approach *qital nikayah* which he contrasted with what he clearly believed to be the superior strategy, *qital tamkin*, which used jihad as a way of removing barriers to the establishment of an Islamic state. But as Zarqawi's successors began to hold territory and apply Islamic law, he strongly supported them and suggested that any Muslim who did not was tantamount to being an unbeliever (*kafir*). He also used his authority in prison to bring other prisoners around to his point of view. Outside prison, his many followers distributed his analyses as leaflets and kept his blog, millahibrahim.wordpress.com, updated.

Fachry and friends had initially taken a wait-and-see attitude after the rift between the al-Nusra Front and ISIS exploded into the open in April 2013, unsure of which to support. But Fachry's mentor, Omar Bakri Muhammad, came out in support of ISIS in October 2013 and from that point on, he and other ISIS supporters began organizing discussions designed to build local support for the pro-ISIS position. One of the activists who appeared frequently as a discussant or moderator in these events was a young preacher named Bahrum Syah, one of Aman Abdurrahman's disciples. On 16 March, Fachry and Bahrum Syah together organized a big pro-ISIS demonstration around central Jakarta's main traffic circle; two months later, Bahrum Syah left for Syria. Two months after that, he appeared in an ISIS recruiting video, posted on YouTube, urging other Indonesians to join.

By the time Bahrum Syah left, a critical mass of Indonesians was already there. Some had left from study abroad. One group of four had left from the International Islamic University in Islamabad; they were all from the school founded by former JI head Abu Bakar Ba'asyir in Ngruki, Solo. Another left from a university Yemen, two others from a technical institute in Turkey. Another contingent had left from West Java. Several had left with families, attracted by the prospect not just of taking part in an exciting political and religious enterprise but by the stipends offered for housing and schooling. The Facebook and Twitter posts sent back to friends in Indonesia almost certainly attracted others, but most of those who left from Java already had ties to radical groups.

After victories in Mosul and other Iraqi cities and al-Baghdadi's declaration of the caliphate just as the fasting month was starting, Fachry and al-Mustaqbal started organizing induction ceremonies across Indonesia, where anywhere from a dozen to several hundred participants would take an oath of allegiance to the new leader. These ceremonies took place from Jakarta to Poso, from Malang to Bima. To the shock of many Indonesians, one such ceremony took place in mid-July in one of Indonesia's supposedly most tightly controlled prison complexes, where both Aman Abdurrahman and Abu Bakar Ba'asyir were detained. A photo of the inductees, together with an ISIS flag, was posted on the Internet.

It remains unclear whether anyone who attended the pledging ceremonies left for Syria on the strength of the oath alone, but the number of people believed to have taken part in the ceremonies across Indonesia in July and August alone was estimated to be about 2,000.[4]

In Syria

Information on how to get to Syria was available from several different sources. One was from social media sources. One of the teenagers who left his studies in Turkey to join the fighting was particularly active, sending photos and information back to his friends in Indonesia. Another husband-wife team, known on Facebook as Abu Qaqa and Siti Khadijah, wrote detailed accounts of how they left, where they crossed, how much money they spent, how they made contact and what their lives were like when they finally reached Aleppo.

Another source was prison networks. It became clear in early 2014 that some of the extremist prisoners were a key node in the sending networks. One such individual was Iwan Dharmawan alias Rois, the field coordinator for the 2004 Australian embassy bombing. Rois remains an important leader of the old West Java Darul Islam network known as Ring Banten that split off from the main DI body in 1999. He was sentenced to death for his role in the bombing and remains on death row in the same prison as Aman Abdurrahman, where he has become a strong pro-ISIS ally. Sometime in January, a former prisoner from Ring Banten, who had been by all accounts fully rehabilitated and not interested in conducting attacks in Indonesia, visited Rois as an old friend. He spoke to Rois about wanting to go to Myanmar to help defend Muslims under attack from Buddhists. Rois convinced him to go to Syria instead and gave him a contact number in Bogor. He followed up the lead, left for Turkey via Doha and by February was in Syria, on his way to battle in Iraq. He died in Ramadi in May 2014.

In Porong prison, Surabaya, another prisoner named Sibghotullah played a similar role, advising would-be mujahidin in the East Java area who came to visit whom to contact. After he was released in mid-2014, he wasted little time in leaving himself, except that he was caught en route and returned to Indonesia. Another prisoner was reportedly playing a similar role in Malang prison.

The prison network was only one of several operating in Indonesia for assisting those who wanted to leave to join ISIS. Unlike the generation that left for the Pakistan-Afghan border twenty-five years earlier, the fighters going to Syria have to pay their own way. Neither the Saudi funding, nor an equivalent of the "services bureau" set up in Peshawar to guide foreign fighters to the training camps, exists for the thousands making their way to the ISIS armed forces. A rudimentary system of vetting takes place, however, so that Indonesians leaving have to have a recommendation from someone already there before they are given the contact number on the Turkish-Syrian border and helped to cross over.

ISIS has made appeals for women to join, as teachers, nurses, cooks and wives for the fighters. All of Indonesian women known to be with ISIS in late 2014, however, were wives of men who went to fight.

These men seemed to have mostly joined a unit for Indonesian and Malaysian fighters initially called Kabila Nusantara and as of 26 September 2014, called Majmu'ah Persiapan Al Arkhabily, or the "Archipelago Group-in-Preparation".[5] The goal of the new unit was to facilitate the incorporation of Malay- and Indonesian-speaking fighters into the ISIS forces because language had proved to be a serious problem, with few Indonesians fluent in either Arabic or English. It would also help widows and women left behind when their husbands went to fight; offer religious instruction; and provide the basis for a future Indonesian-Malaysia army of the Islamic state.

An announcement posted on Indonesian websites noted that "the new group is recruiting members so that it can meet the qualifications that IS requires for all its elite units: each *majmu'ah* must include fighters with combat experience and skills in sniper shooting, heavy weaponry, field engineering, military strategy and war tactics, and military management."[6]

The exact size of the unit was not known but one estimate was that it had or was aiming to have the strength of a military company, about 100 men.

Impact on Terrorism at Home

The fact that those most committed to violence in Indonesia have been those most excited about going to join ISIS in Syria has advantages and disadvantages for the Indonesian Government. On the one hand, it has meant that the groups most focused on committing terrorist attacks in Indonesia now have another goal that may be at least temporarily diverting them from planning operations at home, especially as very few of those operations have worked. As of late 2014, there had not been a successful bombing in five years, and the three attempts at suicide bombing had killed only the would-be bombers.

If the Indonesian Government turned a blind eye to departures of men who wanted to fight, some of them might well be killed. At least eight Indonesians and probably more had died either in battle or as suicide bombers between November 2013 and October 2014, three of them killed by Kurdish forces in the battle for Ras al-Ayn near the Turkish border in October. If they did not return, one view held, that meant fewer terrorists to worry about.

But the bigger worry was what would happen if even a small percentage returned with the leadership credentials, ideological commitment, combat experience and weapons skills to turn the largely incompetent Indonesian extremists into a more serious risk. The danger was high enough to warrant trying to prevent anyone from leaving; the problem was that Indonesia had no tools to do so. It is not against the law in Indonesia to go overseas to fight or even to join an organization that has been put on a terrorist list by the United Nations. There is no precedent for cancelling passports, as some other countries have done.

Even though the government's concern was high enough to declare ISIS a banned organization on 4 August 2014, the declaration had no force of law. It was more a policy directive and was followed by instructions to step up security at prisons, be more selective in the issuance of passports and improve monitoring of those known to be in Syria and those who had returned. One challenge for the new government of President Jokowi installed in October 2014 was whether additional legal tools could be developed.

The Corrections Directorate of the Indonesian Ministry of Law and Human Rights, responsible for overseeing prisons, was well aware of the problems it faced, with terrorists detained or serving sentences in twenty-seven different institutions, and most having access to handphones. By mid-2014 it had begun a concerted effort to improve security and training for prison officials, with some indication by the end of the year that it was paying off, as support for ISIS seemed to be declining.

Jemaah Islamiyah

Another challenge for the Indonesian Government is how to respond to the many extremist groups in Indonesia who rejected the caliphate announced by al-Baghdadi but supported the al-Nusra Front, the official al-Qaeda affiliate in Syria. These groups included JI, Majelis Mujahidin Indonesia (MMI) and a significant part of JAT. Indeed, when Abu Bakar Ba'asyir as the founder of JAT declared his support for ISIS, many in the organization, led by its chair, Mochammad Achwan, broke away to found a new group, Jamaah Anshorul Syariah (JAS).

If the groups who support al-Nusra in Syria do not support violence in Indonesia, what is the problem if they go there to fight? The problem is that al-Nusra, while focused more on bringing down Assad than on establishing a global caliphate, also employs brutality and a harsh system of Islamic law, and has also engaged in terrorism. Anyone fighting with al-Nusra is also likely to return to Indonesia with increased skills and ideological commitment and could well move away from the positions now espoused by the JI leadership. Moreover, there have been many reports of defections from al-Nusra to IS since the caliphate was announced; at least one Indonesian from IS has defected the other way. The point is that al-Nusra is not a moderate organization, and Southeast Asian governments, including Indonesia, should also be monitoring their nationals allied with it.

The alliance of JI with al-Nusra raises a particularly difficult set of issues. JI since 2007 has focused on *dakwah* (religious outreach) and education. Its imprisoned leaders have been models of cooperation with prison authorities and have preached that if jihadists do a cost-benefit analysis of attacks, they will see that at the moment, without community support, the costs far outweigh the benefits. The problem is that no one is quite sure when the calculus will shift. Of all extremist organizations in Indonesia, JI has the longest history, the most resilient membership and the best capacity for thinking long term. Its leadership remains committed to the establishment of an Islamic state in Indonesia. What impact will Syria have on that goal?

A partial answer was provided in March 2014 when police discovered a military camp in Klaten, Central Java where new JI recruits were training. In September they arrested a man who had been taking part in monthly JI fitness trainings in the hills outside Bandung and Semarang in Java. The man in question had been inducted into JI at the height of its strength in 2000 but became inactive after 2007. In early 2011, he was approached by a JI leader and asked to resume his activities in the organization, suggesting that a systematic rebuilding was underway. In late 2013, police discovered an end-of-year report that showed the extent that JI was concentrating on attracting professional recruits from universities — engineers, doctors, linguists, chemical technicians and IT specialists.

If the recruitment has been successful, JI's link to Syria and its early involvement in providing humanitarian aid through HASI may have contributed to its appeal. As of late 2014, police and prison authorities saw the senior JI leadership as partners in combating IS and generally had no problem with their going back and forth. Senior JI figures were indeed very critical of IS. They argued that IS was an organization, not a state, and that al-Baghdadi had not been selected as caliph by a religious council (*majelis syuro*), as Islamic law mandates. They also strongly objected to IS's practice of declaring anyone who did not swear a loyalty oath as an enemy and a legitimate target for killing.

But JI's rejection of IS does not make them moderate. Especially given its past, it is important that the organization not be seen as having abandoned violence or jihad. They decided in 2007 it was counterproductive, not illegitimate, and conditions could change.

Looking Forward

The Syrian conflict will reverberate in Indonesia for years to come. There are several ways it could have an impact. As noted, fighters could return with skills. Indonesians and Malaysians who fought together could retain those bonds at home and attempt to found a cross-border alliance for jihad — something that has not existed since JI had a presence in five countries just before the 2002 Bali bombing (Indonesia, Malaysia, Singapore, Philippines and Australia). IS could try to set up a structure in Southeast Asia through returning fighters or sympathizers. In the near term, would-be fighters who have not had the chance to leave for Syria could decide to undertake an action in Indonesia to attract the attention of IS leaders and demonstrate their own commitment.

All of this suggests that the current lull in terrorist activities could be temporary. Just as there were no major attacks in Indonesia between 2005 and 2009, the lull could be shattered as it was then by the attack on two luxury hotels in Jakarta.

The government of Jokowi may have been given some breathing room to decide on a strategy but this is a problem that is not going to go away.

Notes

1. These included three killings of police in Bima; the fatal shooting of an informer allegedly linked to the military; and an armed clash with the police in Poso that led to the death of a paramilitary police officer.
2. Institute for Policy Analysis of Conflict, "Indonesians and the Syrian Conflict", IPAC Report No. 6, 30 January 2014.
3. Institute for Policy Analysis of Conflict, "The Evolution of ISIS in Indonesia", IPAC Report No. 13, 24 September 2014.
4. Some of the pledging ceremonies, announced on radical websites and through text messaging, were as follows: Poso, 1 July 2014; Kembang Kuning prison, Nusakambangan (Aman Abdurrahman), 2 July 2014; Ciputat, Jakarta, 6 July 2014; Solo, Central Java, 15 July 2014; Ambon, 16 July 2014; Pasir Putih prison, Nusakambangan (Abu Bakar Ba'asyir), 18 July 2014; Bima, Sumbawa, 20 July 2014; Malang, East Java, 20 July 2014; Bekasi Selatan, outside Jakarta, 3 August 2014. Ceremonies also reportedly took place in Lampung and East Kalimantan.
5. "Update on Indonesia-Malaysia Military Unit in Syria", IPAC Update, 6 October 2014. The update is based on an Indonesian website source, available at <http://panjimas.com/citizens/2014/09/29/allahu-akbar-majmuah-al-arkhabiliy-cabang-daulah-islamiyyah-terbentuk/>.
6. Ibid.
7. These were the attempted bombings of the police mosque in Cirebon in April 2011, a church in Solo in September 2011, and the police command in Poso in June 2013.

Laos

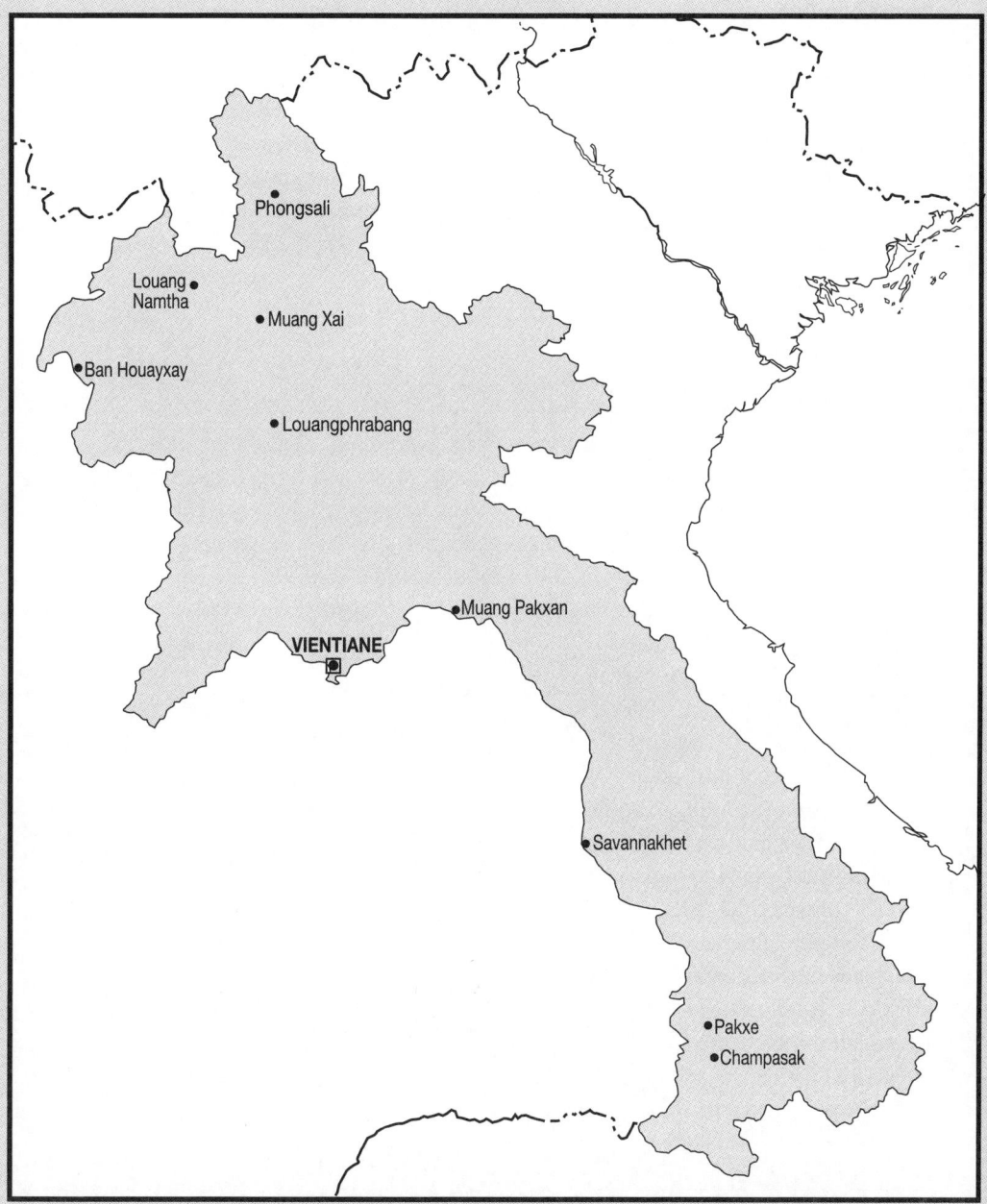

LAOS
Coping with Confinement*

Joseph J. Zasloff and MacAlister Brown

Leadership

In 1981, the Lao People's Democratic Republic (LPDR) was led by the same small, cohesive band of revolutionaries who had directed the Pathet Lao since 1949, the year that the latter had split from the Lao Issarak (Lao Freedom Movement). A contingent of leaders, including Souphanouvong, Phoumi Vongvichit, and Phoune Sipraseut, had emerged in 1973 from their mountain redoubt in Sam Neua Province to accept ministries in the coalition government established by the Vientiane Agreement (an outgrowth of the Paris Agreement concluding the war in Indochina). In 1975, a second contingent of leaders — which included the number one and two men in the Lao People's Revolutionary Party (LPRP), Kaysone Phomvihane and Nouhak Phomsivan — descended to Vientiane. It was at this point that, following the collapse of the non-communist regimes in Saigon and Phnom Penh, the LPRP moved to consolidate its power, without violence.

A Politburo of seven members (Khamthay Siphandone and Sisomphon Lovansay, in addition to the five leaders mentioned above) and a 33-member Central Committee constitute the core of the party leadership. One striking characteristic of this leadership is that it is overwhelmingly Lao Loum (Lowland Lao). Only one alternate member of the Central Committee, Nhiavu Lobaliayo, is a Hmong (or Lao Soung) and perhaps one or two are Lao Theung. The paucity of minority representation in the LPRP leadership is significant in a country whose estimated 3.2 million population is divided between about 50% lowland Lao and 50% highland tribes. For two decades of their revolutionary struggle, the LPRP had its base in the mountain regions of

---

Reprinted from Huynh Kim Khanh, ed., *Southeast Asian Affairs 1982* (Singapore: Institute of Southeast Asian Studies, 1982), pp. 211–28. At the time of original publication, Joseph J. Zasloff was Professor of Political Science at the University of Pittsburgh. MacAlister Brown was Professor of Political Science and Chairman of the Political Economy Program at Williams College.

Laos, and after 1964 it controlled most of the mountain area, which constitutes almost two-thirds of the country's land. Many analysts assumed from this that the Lao Communist movement had tribal representatives among its top leadership, an assumption clearly put in question when the Party revealed its leadership lists.

The contradiction between LPRP claims of ethnic egalitarianism and the limited representation of tribal minorities in the policy-making levels of the Party has several possible explanations. The communist leaders, like their Royal Lao Government (RLG) predecessors, have been nurtured in an environment in which the lowland Lao feel a sense of superiority toward the highlanders and they are little inclined to take them into the highest circles of command. Like most of the dominant peoples of Southeast Asia, the lowland Lao have regarded their mountain people as backward and "uncivilized". (The Lao word which is still commonly used in Vientiane to refer to the highland peoples is *Kha,* meaning slave.) Further, in Laos as elsewhere, the leadership of communist revolutionary movements in colonized countries has been recruited largely from middle-class nationalists with some education. The mountain communities of Laos have had few members with education, and fewer with a well-developed sense of Laotian nationalism. A number of the tribal chiefs with promise were co-opted by the French or the Americans, including Hmong leaders Touby Lyfong and General Vang Pao.

The most prominent minority leader associated with the Lao communist movement was Sithon Kommadam, a Lao Theung (Alak/Loven) tribal chief from southern Laos. Sithon held honorific posts in the Lao Patriotic Front, was a Vice-President of the Supreme People's Council, and upon his death in May 1977, five days of mourning were declared to celebrate this "great patriot of the Lao nation and representative of the Lao Theung nationality". Despite this public recognition, Sithon never achieved membership on the Party Central Committee, where real political power resides. Another prominent minority personality associated with the Lao communist movement is Faydang, a Hmong chief (and a relative of Nhiavu), who along with Sithon, Kaysone, and Souphanouvong, was named one of the "four heroes of the revolution". But Faydang did not achieve membership in the Party Central Committee. In view of the highly plural nature of its society, the LPDR is unlikely to avoid the ethnic tensions common among its neighbours in Southeast Asia or to escape the demands for power that excluded ethnic groups have been making throughout the Third World. The LPDR has been sending some highland minority youths for education in Vietnam, Eastern Europe, and the Soviet Union, and it is possible that there will be greater diversity in the decision-making echelons as they return, and as attrition reduces the incumbent leadership.

Cohesion or Factionalism in the LPRP Leadership?

A favourite subject among the diplomatic community in Vientiane for more than a decade now has been the possible existence of factions in the Lao communist leadership. In view of the history of factionalism in the Soviet and Chinese parties, and in ruling communist parties elsewhere, it is not unreasonable to expect that factions may have developed in the LPRP.

In the early period of the Lao revolutionary movement, some observers divided the leaders into an "Indochinese communist-oriented" group, with members closely linked to the Vietnamese, versus a "Lao nationalist" group, with members thought to be guided by Lao national interests, who co-operated with the Vietnamese out of expediency (like Souphanouvong and Phoumi Vongvichit). These two groups were said to have been reinforced by social class characteristics — those who sprang from modest social origins and had strong Vietnamese links versus those of Lao upper-class origins who had close family and social ties to the Lao Issarak and RLG élite.

During the brief coalition government following the Vientiane Agreement, from 1973 to 1975, speculation continued that the leadership was still divided, this time into a "Sam Neua" group (including Kaysone and Nouhak) who remained in the caves of Sam Neua to direct LPRP policy versus a "Vientiane" group (including Souphanouvong and Phoumi) who had been dispatched to take posts in the Provisional Government of National Union (PGNU). Those remaining in Sam Neua seemed tougher, more pro-Vietnamese, harder-line communists, less prone to accommodate with the feudal and bourgeois RLG élite, while those in Vientiane appeared more ready for compromise with their RLG cousins, more interested in putting distance between Laos and Vietnam, and less antagonistic toward non-communist foreigners.

After the creation of the LPDR in 1975, these divisions were thought to merge into two categories: (1) "ideologues", the more zealous Marxist-Leninists, eager to impose a rapid, thorough socialist transformation on feudalist Laotian society, closely patterned on the Vietnamese communist model; and (2) "pragmatists", believed to be more indulgent toward traditional Lao Buddhist practices and to favour a slower, more comfortable transition to socialism.

By early 1978, as the tensions between Vietnam and China increased, the Lao leadership was faced with a problem of orientation toward these two powers and chose to align with Vietnam. There was speculation that this issue continued the leadership cleavage between the "pro-Vietnamese" group and the "nationalists" who judged it a disservice to the Lao national interest to provoke China and favoured a neutralist posture in the dispute. Some evidence for this division can be drawn from the reaction to Hong Kong press reports in the summer of 1978 of a secret (and improbable) visit to Beijing by General Vang Pao, the former CIA-supported Hmong leader, who was said to be working on the creation of a "Meo Kingdom" in Northern Laos and Vietnam. These reports were featured in the Soviet and Vietnamese press, while the Chinese denounced them as "Soviet black propaganda". In his 12 October Independence Day speech, Souphanouvong deplored the "vicious, insidious and dangerous rumours alleging that China is a new patron of Lao elements in exile, that China will attack Vietnam and proceed to attack Laos, etc."[1] In contrast with Souphanouvong's denunciation of those who would "sow division" between Laos and China, Kaysone, in his National Day address on 1 December, denounced the "despicable, ferocious schemes" of the "international reactionary forces" (the Vietnamese code word for China) to divide and sabotage the revolutionary movement.[2] In early 1979, after Vietnam's invasion of Kampuchea followed by China's invasion of Vietnam, spokesmen supported Vietnam unequivocally, and *all* Politburo members uniformly used the Vietnamese slogans to denounce "Chinese aggression".

Since the rise of tensions with China, there have been stories of purges of pro-Chinese elements within the middle ranks of the government bureaucracy and, to a lesser extent, within the same ranks of the Party. In April 1979, a Central Committee member, Sanan Soutthichak, who was also Minister of Communications, Public Works and Transportation, was placed under house arrest, reportedly for pro-Chinese activity. About the same time, Khampheng Boupha, Minister of Posts and Telecommunications was arrested, some say under charges of corruption, others because of pro-Chinese activity.

Although the speculation about divisions within the Lao communist leadership seems plausible, a more impressive case can be made for their record of continuity. The Lao leaders have served in a closely-bound group since the late 1940s, a record of cohesiveness in the communist world that may be surpassed only by their Vietnamese mentors. They have remained united during periods of relative peace, when there were strong material enticements to abandon their cause, as well as during arduous periods of their struggle from the caves. This long revolutionary experience together — particularly the periods of privation — has forged powerful links among the leaders. While they may have differing tendencies on certain important issues — and our information about their decision-making processes is severely limited — for almost thirty years they have shown and continue to show, a remarkable capacity to present a united front.

The Semi-Secret Ruling Party

The LPRP continues to maintain a secrecy — more accurately, a semi-secrecy — about its mode of operation and the identity of its rank and file members. An offshoot of the Indochinese Communist Party (ICP), the LPRP was, according to its official history, founded in 1955 by "twenty-five members of the ICP". The Party's existence was kept secret from the Lao public until 1973, when its name and the fact that it had directed the revolution were revealed. Previously, the Neo Lao Issarak (Lao Freedom Front) and subsequently the Neo Lao Hak Sat (NLHS or Lao Patriotic Front) — both Front organizations headed by Prince Souphanouvong — had been publicly presented as leading the revolution. In 1975, after it was in full control, the LPRP released the names of its seven-member Politburo and, during the following five years, the names of its thirty-three-member Central Committee and the party committees in each of the fourteen provinces. As to the size of the Party, a long-time party official, during an interview in Vientiane in December 1980, was willing to disclose that the Party has "several ten thousand members". The LPRP follows the standard communist practice of planting party members within all principal institutions of the society — in government, the Army, the mass organizations, the collectives — as leaders and as a transmission belt for party policy. Party members act as the eyes and ears of the central party organization.

Although party members are admonished not to reveal themselves, and any public discussion of the clandestine membership is forbidden, it would not be difficult for knowledgeable observers to pick out the party members in their work organization. In each Ministry, for example, the key power-wielders are party members. Former RLG civil servants who have been retained by the new regime are inevitably guided by a party member, generally a cadre who has come from the "liberated zone". All party members do not, of course, hold positions of authority; they also are drawn from the lower ranks such as messengers, drivers, and maintenance personnel. (During the past few years, the LPRP has emphasized the recruitment of workers and peasants, according to a party official.) Some former civil servants, now in refugee camps, noted that they could guess who the party members were in their organization by their periodic joint absences, presumably during party meetings. Many asserted, too, that party members — especially those from inferior rank and social position — could be identified by their haughty or presumptuous behaviour.

A number of factors explain this persistent semi-secrecy of the Party. Clandestine behaviour is an old habit which members do not shed easily. It was useful in the twenty-five-year struggle against their adversaries in the Royal Lao Government (RLG), who were fooled by it. Secrecy gives the Party its mystery, inspires anxiety and fear, and thus simplifies the function of control. Party "difficulties", acknowledged by a party official in an interview, probably include fear of infiltration and subversion. During the first three years of the LPDR, the Lao People's Revolutionary Party (LPRP) focused its fear of subversion upon "CIA and Thai-reactionary-inspired agents", working upon the vulnerable segments of Laotian society. After mid-1978, when China became the principal threat to Vietnam, and by extension Laos, LPRP cautionary statements contain frequent allusions to "big power hegemonism", a code-word for China.

Party leaders seem to think that the Party is still not sufficiently strong, and its security will be better assured by continued secrecy. The LPRP is relatively small, compared to other incumbent communist parties. Assuming 30,000 LPRP members (based on the party official's figure of "several tens of thousands"), the proportion of party members to population (estimating 3.2 million inhabitants), would be slightly less than 1%. Vietnam in 1979 had 1.5 million members in a population of 53 million, or approximately 3%. One LPDR official who was willing to discuss the Party, noted that Kaysone had spoken publicly about "bad elements" within the Party — those who had succumbed to corruption, abuse of power, deterioration of sexual comportment, and to loss of political zeal. Perhaps these must first be purged, he ventured, before the Party can open up. During the fall of 1980, there were arrests of civil servants in all ranks, apparently guilty of some of these offences, although the charges were not made public. There have also been rumours of arrests for pro-Chinese activity, an issue on which the party leadership may now feel particularly sensitive.

LPRP "Special Relations" with Vietnam

Lao relations with Vietnam, often characterized officially as "close as lips to teeth", are based on the concept of a "special relationship". All the leaders of the Lao People's Revolutionary Party (LPRP) have had long and intimate ties with the Vietnamese communist movement. Many are linked to the Vietnamese by family, education, and work experience. Almost all of the chief LPRP leaders speak Vietnamese. They fought against the French from 1946 to 1954, during the First Indochina War, under Vietnamese guidance. In the brief period of relative peace in Indochina from 1954 to 1960, they synchronized their strategy and relied upon advice and assistance from Hanoi. Vietnamese communist troops remained stationed in LPRP-dominated areas during this period. It was direct Vietnamese military assistance which made possible the substantial military advances achieved by the Pathet Lao from 1960 to 1962, culminating in the Geneva Accords of 1962 which provided for Pathet Lao participation in a tripartite government in Vientiane as an equal partner. After 1964, when the tripartite government collapsed and the Indochina War escalated, the LPRP leaders remained heavily dependent upon their Vietnamese senior partners for strategic guidance, logistic support and troop assistance. Thus, LPRP leaders have seen their military and political fortunes inextricably linked to the Vietnamese communists for more than a quarter of a century.

The predominant Vietnamese influence in Laos is transmitted through a number of channels. First, and probably foremost, are the Party-to-Party channels, both formal and informal. Formal Party-to-Party relations are conducted through the LPRP's Office of the Secretariat, headed by Secretary-General Kaysone, according to a party official in Vientiane. Within the Vietnamese delegation posted in Laos, presumably there is a Vietnamese Communist Party (VCP) bureau responsible for liaison with the LPRP Secretariat. Informally, there are frequent contacts between LPRP Politburo and Central Committee members, and VCP officials. Since Kaysone and other LPRP leaders were members of the Indochinese Communist Party, this party channel is a familiar and natural one. LPRP leaders travel frequently to Hanoi, and VCP delegations regularly visit Laos.

Another important channel through which the Vietnamese exercise influence upon the LPDR is their sizeable advisory staff. The Prime Minister's Office and each of the LPDR ministries, according to refugees, have a staff of Vietnamese advisers who provide both political and technical counsel. Party and government training schools have a complement of Vietnamese advisers who guide curricula for political instruction, provide documents which are translated from Vietnamese to Lao, and sometimes directly conduct training sessions.

The Vietnamese military presence in Laos is another important channel of Vietnamese influence. In 1979 and early 1980, Western diplomatic sources estimated Vietnamese troops in Laos to be 40,000, while the Lao People's Liberation Army (LPLA) was estimated at 20,000. By the end of 1980, following the Thai closure of the Laotian border, a presumed increase of Chinese support to insurgents in Laos, and an augmented Vietnamese road-building programme, Vietnamese military presence was thought to have risen to from 50,000 to 60,000 troops.

Monarchy, Religion, and Political Change

Prior to their seizure of power, the Lao communist leaders consistently proclaimed their support for the monarchy and for Buddhism. This support of the 600-year-old monarchy was clearly a political tactic, based upon the fact that the King commanded widespread devotion within traditional Laos, particularly from the Lao peasantry. The LPRP calculated that the Lao population was not "mature" enough to understand the need to depose the King and establish a socialist republic. Party leaders waited until they were firmly in control before abolishing the monarchy, in December 1975, with the proclamation of the Lao People's Democratic Republic.

In deposing the King, LPDR officials accepted his "voluntary" abdication and renunciation of royal wealth. They appointed him as "Supreme Adviser" to the President of the LPDR, and the Crown Prince was named a member of the Supreme People's Council (SPC). These appointments were typical of the incremental Lao-style of revolution — relatively gentle when compared with Cambodia and Vietnam — in which the Party gradually adjusted the population to the new political realities.

The Royal Family continued to live in their modest palace in Luang Prabang, restricted in their movements. The Crown Prince had attended only the first meeting of the SPC, and although the King was invited as a guest — apparently to lend legitimacy to this fledgling institution — neither attended subsequent sessions. Their refusal to attend may have angered party leaders. There was increasing anti-government guerrilla activity in the vicinity of Luang Prabang in early 1977, accompanied by rumours that dissidents were aiming to involve the King and Crown Prince in their activities, perhaps by "liberating them" and making them a popular rallying point. In March 1977, LPDR authorities arrested the King and Crown Prince and sent them to a remote location in Sam Neua Province to "ensure their safety". Although refugees report intermittent rumours about the death of members of the Royal Family, government officials state that they are still confined in Sam Neua Province, and are permitted to engage in gardening at the residence.

Prince Souvanna Phouma, former RLG Prime Minister, has fared better than the Royal Family. He holds the honorific title of "Adviser" to the government, moves freely about Vientiane and Luang Prabang, and has visited France since the communist take-over. Souvanna celebrated his 80th birthday in 1981 in apparent good health, having made a remarkable recovery from a massive coronary in 1974 when, as head of the PGNU coalition government, he was treated by no less than seven physicians, at least one from each of the major powers interested in the political outcome in Laos. Souvanna has abandoned his constant cigar, on doctors' orders, but he is still a regular bridge player at the weekly public international bridge evening in Vientiane.

Souvanna consented to an interview with the authors in December 1980, graciously receiving his visitors in the comfortable villa on the Mekong River where he lives alone, attended by a small personal staff. He has been legally separated from his wife for some years and his children live abroad. He is lucid and thoughtful, speaks impeccable French, and is responsive to questions, with good recall of events and dates. Souvanna is selective in his recollections of history, synthesizing the past in a manner that justifies his present, lonely position. He contends that the Vientiane Accords of 1972 might have been preserved if the RLG ministers and generals had been more courageous, instead of fleeing in May 1975. When asked what they could have accomplished, he responded, "We could have talked. Laos is not the same as other countries. It has been very special — different from other communist systems."

Souvanna's reproach of his RLG colleagues is incongruent with the position he took in November 1974, when, in a speech he said that those RLG leaders "who do not want peace should leave". Former right-wing leaders whom the authors interviewed in Paris and elsewhere recall these words with particular bitterness, asserting that this was Souvanna's capitulation. Souvanna contended that his primary mission, at all times, was to serve as a peacemaker, and to protect the territorial integrity of Laos. He was proud that there had never been an official partition of Laos, as there had been of Vietnam.

Souvanna obviously felt that his half-brother shared his conviction about serving the fundamental interests of Laos. Though they had long periods of political antagonism, Souvanna said that he had remained in correspondence with Souphanouvong and always looked on him as a brother and a patriot. Souphanouvong is now a regular visitor at Souvanna's house.

Reorganization of Buddhism

Buddhism has been substantially reorganized under the new regime. Not long after deposing the King, the LPDR authorities, in 1976, abolished the office of Supreme Patriarch (Sangha-raj), the spiritual leader of Lao Buddhism. The Supreme Patriarch, Thammayano, born in 1892, had served in that office for forty-five years prior to his divestiture. LPDR spokesmen maintain that the former Supreme Patriarch had been designated "Supreme Consultant" on Buddhist affairs to the President, and that adequate support for medical care and other needs had been provided to him. The Patriarch's aides and supporters in Thailand point out that he was restricted to his temple in Luang Prabang, could receive few visitors, and could not preach. Following medical treatment in Vientiane, the ailing Supreme Patriarch, with the help of his aides, fled to Thailand in March 1979.

Deposition of the Supreme Patriarch has a significance similar to the deposition of the King. No longer does a single religious leader, endowed with charisma that flows from an esteemed office, rule over a religious institution that has links in every Lao village. His office has been replaced by a committee which directs a series of newly-formed committees. All Buddhist sects in the country have been brought under the umbrella of a single organization, the Lao Buddhist Fellowship Association.

At the apex of the new Buddhist organization are the President, three Vice-Presidents, a Secretary-General and his Deputy, who make up an executive committee with headquarters in Vientiane. There are administrative departments directed by committees at the national level, with subordinate committees at the provincial level, which are charged with economics and finance, religious affairs, education, health, and maintenance of the wats (pagodas). An executive committee directs Sangha affairs at the province (*khoueng*), district (*muong*), and canton (*tasseng*) level. Thus, committees have replaced individual leaders at each level and the Sangha is under close party supervision. There are regular political indoctrination sessions for village monks, and a variety of conferences and training courses organized by the Party for higher-ranking monks.

The LPFP recognizes the significant role that monks could take in spreading the party gospel, and in legitimizing the regime. Buddhist monks in Laos, as in other Theravada Buddhist societies, are highly respected. The monk's life is seen to be clean, pure, self-denying and intellectual, and is admired for its austerity and discipline. In a graduation address at the conclusion of a political training course for monks in Vientiane, in October 1976, Phoumi Vongvichit, Minister of Education, Sports and Religious Affairs, indicated the political function the LPRP envisages for the monks:

> The success of your study will benefit the nation because, as Buddhist monk teachers,

you are now a resource for the country. You will be able to correct some past mistakes in our society. You will become a group of political cadres who will closely co-operate with revolutionary political cadres in teaching and guiding our people to walk along the same path to the same destination, thereby making our nation more prosperous in the future.[3]

The first President of the Lao Buddhist Fellowship Association was (Maha) Khamtanh Thepboualy, a native of Champassak Province, born in the early 1920s. In 1978, he disrobed to become Head of the Department of Religious Affairs of the Ministry of Education, Sports and Religious Affairs. Although this would seem to be a promotion up the political ladder, some refugee monks maintain that he has been reduced in influence. His replacement as President is (Maha) Thongkhoun Anantasountone, born about 1923, who was a monk at Wat That Luong in Vientiane during the RLG regime.

The Buddhist organization is responsible for the maintenance of the 2,469 wats which Buddhist spokesmen claimed, in December 1980, were still operating throughout the country. The wat has traditionally been the centre not only of religious affairs for the village, but also of social and civic matters. An important part of merit-making in Theravada Buddhist countries is providing alms to the monks and offering cloth and money for the repair and upkeep of the wat. Reports by refugees differ significantly with those of official Buddhist spokesmen within Laos regarding maintenance of the wats, and the monks who inhabit them.

Khamtanh Thepboualy claimed, in an interview in October 1980, that in the past two years, the government made a generous allocation of 8 million old kip (approximately US$2,500 at the 1979 exchange rate) for maintenance of wats, and that popular contributions continued to be generous in support of local wats. By contrast, refugee monks claim that government contributions have declined drastically, and that many wats are in bad shape. They say that people now give far less to the village wat, first, because their resources are so meagre, and secondly, because they are discouraged by political cadres. Many refugees report they were told that monks should practice "self-sufficiency", as everyone else must, and should not be parasites, "eating the rice of the people". *Bouns* (temple festivals), which once provided a source of income for the wats and merriment for villagers, are now frowned upon, refugees report angrily.

(Maha) Thongknoun Anantasountone, in an interview in December 1980, acknowledged that *bouns*, gambling, and garish celebrations at the wats have been discouraged by the new leaders. "We prohibit spectacles, and those things that violate the principles of Buddhism. We wish to purify the practice of Buddhism and return to our genuine tradition.... During the old regime, there was too much waste, gambling and alcohol. People came to amuse themselves at bouns, which had nothing to do with religion." This theme of "purification" may have an appeal to some in Laos. There had been criticism before 1975, as there is today in Thailand, that the actual practice of Buddhism had degenerated, and was too suffused with materialism. The *bouns* and feasts, *lamvong* dancing, and gambling on temple grounds had often played a larger role than worship, some felt.

Reports differ substantially about the extent to which the regime requires monks to support themselves by farming, and about the religious significance of such a requirement. A student of Buddhism in Thailand, where traditions are similar to those in Laos, writes that monks should not dig earth or cause it to be dug, a rule that is derived from the prohibition against taking life, which has a strict interpretation for monks. This would exclude, in effect, a monk from doing agricultural work.[4] The President of the Lao Buddhist Fellowship Association stated, however, that the Lao Buddhist tradition is for monks to plant and care for their own gardens, but not rice-fields. He was emphatic in stating that the LPDR, contrary to the contentions of some refugees, does not oblige monks to work in the rice-fields.

There is also a wide divergence between the official figures for the size of the Sangha and the claims of Lao refugee monks in Thailand. (Maha) Thongkhoune stated that there were 13,400 monks in Laos in 1980, and 12,059 in 1979. Noting the constant flow of monks in and out of the Sangha, he stated that 2,440 novices and monks had entered during 1980, and 2,020 had entered in 1979. The Sangha, he claimed, remained approximately the same size after 1975 as before.

In sharp contrast, the secretary to the former Supreme Patriarch told an American journalist that since 1976, the number of monks had shrunk from 20,000 to 1,700. Many had escaped to Thailand, he said, and 1,000 were believed to be confined in detention camps.[5] Other refugee monks give higher estimates for the number of monks still active in Laos. The abbot of the Nong Khai refugee camp estimated, in an interview in December 1980, that there were not more than 5,000 active monks and novices. A refugee monk from Vientiane reported that by the end of 1976 the number of monks in wats in the capital had fallen to about one-third, and another monk from the south reported that by mid-1978 the numbers had declined to one-twentieth or less.[6] These refugee monks contend that wats without monks become schools, barracks, or storage barns and Buddha images and other ritual objects are consigned to museums.

The fundamental thrust of these widely divergent claims is clear: official spokesmen wish to demonstrate that Buddhism continues to flourish under the LPDR, while refugee monks wish to show that Buddhism is withering away under government pressure.

ECONOMIC, POLITICAL, AND SOCIAL PROBLEMS

The New Economic Policy

By the latter half of 1979, LPDR leaders, faced with deteriorating economic conditions in the towns and popular discontent with collectivist measures in the countryside, were convinced of the need to launch a series of policies aimed at "liberalizing" the economy. The Vietnamese Communist Party, confronting comparable economic disintegration, had announced a similar package of "liberal" policies in September 1979, with the promulgation of "Resolution 6".[7] Thus, the LPRP, following the lead of its Vietnamese mentor, adopted a resolution in December 1979 which embodied policies designed to slow down collectivization, ease restraints upon the sale of farm produce in the free market and introduce incentives for controlled private enterprise in the towns. LPRP Secretary-General Kaysone counselled that Laos needed to proceed toward socialism "step by step", and that capitalism should not be eliminated too rapidly.[8] At the urging of international experts, a new pricing policy was put into effect, attempting to co-ordinate official prices more closely with the forces of market supply and demand. Subsidies on food and other items were to be limited to between 5 and 15% of the free market prices, in an attempt to bring a balance between the official and free market prices and, perhaps more important, to stimulate agricultural production and delivery to market.

The new pricing policy caused official producer prices to rise fourfold and official retail prices to rise fivefold. Wages and salaries were also increased. The government hoped these measures would increase producer incentives, expand food supplies, improve the financial viability of state enterprises, and generally ameliorate the budgetary situation.

It is not yet evident how substantially this new economic policy will affect the economy. Collectivization was proceeding at a slower pace in 1980 and 1981, and more goods were coming from the farm to the free markets. Although foodstuffs are more abundant in the markets, manufactures were cut down both by the Thai blockade in the summer of 1980 and the subsequent reopening of only two border points and prices are painfully high in relation to income. Some shops have reopened in Vientiane, a few small enterprises have been undertaken with private participation, and there have been modest signs of social relaxation under the new policies.

Political and Social Obstacles

The Lao People's Democratic Republic faces serious obstacles to the achievement of its announced economic goals. It seems likely that Laos will be dependent for many years in the future, as it has been in the past, upon external assistance. Now that the Soviet Union and its socialist allies have replaced the richer United States and its allies as the principal donors, the level of external funding may be a problem. External assistance declined in the first six years of the LPDR, with the termination of most Western assistance.

Probably a more basic problem than finding adequate foreign assistance funds is the ability of Laos to absorb this aid and achieve self-generating economic growth, as the Five-Year Plan (1981–85) envisions. Perhaps the country's most serious deficiency is the paucity of skilled managerial, administrative, and technical manpower. The distressing dearth of competent personnel is, in part, a self-inflicted wound. Although many of the country's limited number of well-trained administrators and professionals who served the RLG fled in the early months of the communist accession to power, the new regime has poorly used those who stayed. Some who hoped to contribute their talents to post-war reconstruction under a new leadership were sent to re-education camps, where many are still held. Others were given posts in the new government, but rarely has their responsibility been commensurate with their training and experience. Clearly, political reliability is a more important factor than technical competence in assignment to jobs, and the trusted revolutionary cadres who accompanied the LPRP leadership as they descended from the caves in the liberated zone to Vientiane in 1975 have been placed throughout the government in supervisory positions. Few of these cadres have much formal education or experience in operating a modern economy. The strength of the Pathet Lao movement was in political mobilization and fighting a revolution, not in directing a developing economy.

The principal long-term hope for improving the deficiency in trained personnel lies in the students returning from the Soviet Union and Eastern European countries. If they return endowed with effective skills and dedication, the fragile administrative capacity of the LPDR would be strengthened.

Another problem seriously affecting the LPDR's economic potential — perhaps more fundamental than its weak administrative capacity — is its lack of popular support. At the outset of the regime many Lao, tired of war and the corruption of the old regime, were favourably disposed toward the new rulers. But with six years of their economic and political policies, the LPDR leaders have squandered much of the goodwill that greeted them. Collectivization, controls, and taxes have caused widespread discontent in the countryside, and inflation and economic deterioration contribute to the deep malaise in the towns. Throughout the country there are negative attitudes toward the severe regulation of travel, the monitoring of personal behaviour, the heavy socialist propaganda, and boring seminars required for all groups. The heavy dependence upon Vietnam, an historic enemy, further erodes the legitimacy of the regime. It is difficult to discern a base of support in any significant segment of society. Perhaps the students returning from education in the socialist countries might feel gratitude, although the experience of many underdeveloped countries does not suggest that former students retain an abiding affection for the regime that sponsors their education.

Detention Camps

The LPDR authorities have followed the Vietnamese example in establishing detention camps for persons charged with political crimes, past or present. Testimony from former inmates makes clear that there are at least three categories of detention camps: 1) prisons; 2) centres for "remoulding and reconstruction"; 3) "re-education" camps. Prisons are primarily for common criminal offences but political prisoners are also detained in them for short terms, typically six to twelve months. Centres for "remoulding and reconstruction" are expressly for political prisoners who serve three- to five-year terms, or even longer. As with the prisons, there is a severe regimen of hard work and short rations and, despite the camps' label, there is almost no political indoctrination. The "re-education" camps, also designed for political prisoners, are less severe than the "remoulding and reconstruction" centres. Inmates work hard, conditions are rugged, and food is limited, but importance is placed upon political indoctrination. Inmates receive a very small stipend and an issue of clothes and supplies, and since 1979 some have been able to invite their families to join them.

Detention camp prisoners are not given a trial but are incarcerated simply by administrative fiat of the authorities. Former prisoners say that they were arrested, told by the security officials that they had been charged with crimes, and were sent off to a camp. Their terms of detention are, in all cases, indeterminate. Typically, prisoners are told one day prior to their release to prepare for departure.

Although figures have appeared in the Western press estimating numbers in the detention camps between 15,000 and 30,000 during recent years, there is no firm basis for these calculations. Government authorities discuss publicly only the "re-education" centres in Sam Neua Province, which held from 1,450 to 1,700 "students" at the end of 1980. But the accounts of former inmates, now refugees, make it abundantly clear that there are centres for "remoulding and reconstruction" as well as prisons in each region of the country where political prisoners are held, probably in each of the fourteen provinces.

In November and December 1980, government authorities released approximately 100 "re-education" camp inmates who had been high-level civil servants in the former government, and in 1981 another group was released. In releasing them the regime was taking a calculated risk that most would remain in the country — it assumes that some would leave. The authorities must have justified the release and promise to liberate others soon with several reasons. After five years in the camps, it could be argued that those "students" had learned their lessons. Further, the release was bound to meet with public support, particularly welcome in this period of economic deterioration and rising political tensions, as relations with China are aggravated. The families who have waited five years for the return of their relatives attract the sympathy of large numbers in Vientiane, where social relations are closely intertwined. Perhaps the most compelling reason is the utility of putting into service the trained personnel now incarcerated in camps. As former RLG civil servants continue to flee, there is further need for the skills of those in the camps. Although it is unlikely that the LPDR leaders will dismantle the detention camps as long as the Vietnamese maintain theirs, it is possible that a certain segment of former RLG officials who have been held since 1975 will continue to be liberated.

Refugees

Since 1975, more than 350,000 refugees have fled Laos — at least 10% of the population. In 1980, some 70,000 fled to Thailand, the largest number in any year since the outflow that accompanied the communist seizure of power.

The reasons for this continuing flow more than five years after the establishment of the new regime can he summarized under the rubriques of "push" and "pull" factors. The "push" factors combine economic and political elements. The dismal economic conditions provide a discouraging atmosphere in which political demands and stresses grow more onerous. The high cost of living, shortages of food and essential goods, and inadequate pay are universal complaints of refugees. Those associated with the former regime who have somehow escaped incarceration in detention camps claim they have little chance for advancement, and they feel under constant tension. Many claim that they see few opportunities for their children. They say that their hope for a better life for themselves, or their families, has been exhausted. Families who have a member in a detention camp, a father or son, often wait for his release, and take flight at the first opportunity. Young men flee the military draft, and both young and older men object to service in the village guard. Peasants who flee express serious discontent with the cooperative programme. A large percentage of the Hmong population, as well as other highlanders, who were associated with the CIA-sponsored military effort, feel a special sense of vulnerability. Some of these continued insurgent activity against the new regime.

Among the important "pull" factors is the promise, at least for some, of resettlement in third countries. The hope for a better life, especially for one's children, free from economic hardship and political oppression is an important theme. Reunion with family in third countries, or in refugee camps is a strong pull for some, and it sustains a continued refugee flow as family networks outside Laos grow.

The Thai Government, concerned by the continuing arrival of refugees, launched a programme in early 1981 aimed at discouraging the refugee flow. Refugee holding centres were made "austere", with a minimum provision of food, shelter, and medical care; international personnel are not admitted and third country representatives are not given access. This policy has been labelled "humane deterrence" of the refugee flow. Thai officials appear to believe that these policies have already had a desirable effect, and published figures on the refugee flow since the beginning of this policy show a decline. It is too early to conclude that such a policy will actually deter the flow. If the refugees continue to come, even in reduced numbers, it seems likely that the Thai Government will wish to facilitate resettlement of the refugees in third countries. (Thailand opposes their permanent settlement in Thailand, and would face international obloquy if it forced the refugees back into Laos.) Thus, the deterrent effect of making resettlement impossible would be nullified.

The LPDR has deplored the departure of its ordinary Lao citizens for the economic promise of resettlement in the United States or Europe. They contend that this outflow has been encouraged by outside governments, treated as a measure of political persecution in Laos, and used as a recruitment base for resistance commandos. Laos has not used strenuous measures to block communication with refugees or prevent the flow, though shootings take place from time to time along the river. Yet the disaffection with the economic and political condition of the nation which the exodus implies is a nagging reproach to the leadership. The Lao Government's desire to keep productive citizens at home and the Thai Government's desire to keep the refugee population within manageable dimensions that can be readily resettled have harmonized at least one aspect of Lao relations with Thailand. It is not certain that the Thai policy of spartan reception camps will be continued, nor that the outflow of Lao people will decline, but both countries seem to have an interest in maintaining the trend.

The United States remains a major factor in the refugee equation because it provides the largest portion of resettlement opportunities for Indochina refugees and it provides much of the financial support for the holding camps. Some elements in the U.S. Congress have begun to question whether the country should continue to admit a maximum of 14,000 Indochina refugees a month, during a period of unemployment and recession, and the Immigration and Naturalization Service (INS), in 1980, began seriously to question whether persons from Laos should be classified as refugees who would suffer persecution if they returned home, rather than as economic migrants seeking better economic opportunity. Although the Secretary of State insisted successfully that the INS question must be answered in favour of "refugee" status for persons leaving a communist country, a subsequent study by a State Department–appointed committee acknowledged that the economic "pull" factor might be drawing lowland Lao out of impoverished Laos. Members of Congress also seemed to be growing more sensitive to that aspect of the refugee flow and moderately lower resettlement quotas have been set for 1982.

External Relations of Laos

Since 1979, Laos has been locked in the vice of Sino-Vietnamese antagonism, which produced the Vietnamese invasion of Kampuchea in December 1978 and the Chinese counter-blow along the Sino-Vietnamese border. However friendly and mutually supportive the relations of the Pathet Lao and the People's Republic of China (PRC) had been during thirty years of revolutionary struggle, the leadership in Laos had little choice but to line up squarely with Vietnam in support of the overthrow of the Pol Pot government at the end of 1978 and in condemnation of China's punitive invasion of Vietnam in February 1979. Such loyal adherence to the policy line of the Socialist Republic of Vietnam (SRV) can be seen as a natural extension of the LPRP's revolutionary history as a junior partner in the two Indochina "Resistance Wars" from which the Pathet Lao reaped the harvest in 1975 with the seizure of full national power.

The LPDR's alignment with Vietnam has placed them in diplomatic isolation at the United Nations on the Kampuchea issue, which the General Assembly took up in 1980. It has also resulted in greater economic dependence on the Soviet Union, greater reliance on Vietnamese military forces in relation to China, more volatile relations with Thailand (the "front-line state" vis-à-vis Vietnamese-occupied Kampuchea) and unwillingness of the United States to consider bilateral relations outside the context of Vietnam relations.

Relations with China

Recent Lao relations with China have been antagonistic but usually not vituperative or aggressive. The LPDR officially called for the Chinese to terminate their road-building projects and withdraw their personnel in March 1979, and three months later the Chinese Embassy was obliged to cut down to twelve persons. But at the same time the LPDR has publicly called for the Sino-Vietnamese negotiations (undertaken after China's punitive blow in 1979) to continue. The Lao Foreign Ministry utters frequent charges against the "dark design" of the reactionary ruling circle in Beijing, such as trying to divide and sow discord among the peoples of Indochina and incite Thailand against Indochina. Yet, in public statements or in private exchanges, the most strident level of accusation is seldom reached by Lao officials.[9] Although China is accused of sending spies and commandos into northern provinces of Laos to create dissension and subversion (among the ethnic minorities of this area), Lao spokesmen usually make clear that no direct military action has been launched by China. Alleged Chinese training and equipping of refugees from Laos are seen as serious threats, as are the formation of anti-government resistance fronts by Lao refugees. Vietnamese troops may have moved into northern Laos in areas that they previously did not frequent, to heighten the vigilance against subversion or attack. So far, however, the threat from China is a potential that neither side is interested seeing unleashed.[10]

China's alleged formation of a Lao Socialist Party (LSP) in exile, which the radio of Democratic Kampuchea reported in May 1979, the support of a unified front of Lao resistance groups (the Lao Peoples' National Liberation United Front — LPNLUF), which was reported in Bangkok on 30 September 1980, and the alleged creation and training of a "Lanna division" of six to seven thousand Lao exile soldiers in China, create psychological pressure on Vientiane. However, the unsubstantiated nature of the LSP and the "Lanna division", and the factional incoherence to be expected within the variegated LPNLUF, make these assets less threatening to the Lao Government than they might appear. China could easily cut off their support to these groups, should it see fit, in return for Vientiane's agreement to stop abetting Vietnam in Kampuchea, to exclude Vietnamese forces from at least the northern provinces of Laos, and to respect Chinese primacy as the leading power in the region.[11]

Relations with Thailand

During Prime Minister Kriangsak's control of Thai foreign policy, from October 1979 to March 1980, a thaw developed between Thailand and Laos. Notwithstanding the Vietnamese invasion of Kampuchea, and a provocative gunboat shooting incident on the Mekong River border at about the same time, Kriangsak visited Vientiane on 4–6 January 1979 and entertained Premier Kaysone in return in Bangkok in April. The two leaders boldly pronounced their agreement to make the Mekong a "river of peace". This diplomatic thaw steadied the commerce in household goods and personal consumer items from Thailand into Laos which slightly brightens the drab scarcities of Lao markets. During the first five years of the LPDR this flow was interrupted periodically by Thai blockades following border incidents. With the ouster of Kriangsak by General Prem Tinsulanond in March 1980, however, the Thai Government was more affected by feelings of suspicion and anxiety, as well as traditional feelings of superiority toward their Lao cousins, than by conviction that a *détente* could be sustained along the river. The presence of Vietnamese troops in Laos as well as Kampuchea, made it difficult for Bangkok to follow a policy of adamant opposition to the puppet regime in Phnom Penh on the one hand but friendly relations with the special partners of the Vietnamese in Laos on the other.

As the desperate exodus of Kampuchean people moved into internationally-supported camps on the Thai border, to escape starvation caused by warfare and disruption, Thai anxieties mounted concerning the ultimate "disposal" of these unwanted populations that the Indochina revolutions had cast into Thailand. The effort of the United Nations High Commissioner for Refugees (UNHCR) to sponsor some voluntary repatriation of Khmer refugees from camps in Thailand raised warnings from Vietnam that Pol Pot guerrillas (the armed force of Democratic Kampuchea) should not be infiltrated back into Kampuchea to fight the Heng Samrin government. Shortly thereafter, on 22–23 June, a localized Vietnamese military thrust on a refugee village inside Thailand took place, which was sharply repulsed by Thai Armed Forces resulting in casualties and considerable shock and indignation among the Thai. A week earlier, two Thai gunboats on the Mekong River had been fired upon by a Lao shore battery, allegedly without provocation, killing a Thai officer. Bangkok subsequently perceived the Lao action as part of a pattern of intimidation orchestrated by Vietnam. Once again the river crossings and commerce to Laos were closed and an apology and compensation were righteously demanded of Laos.

It appears equally credible that the river incident was not co-ordinated with the Vietnamese incursion into Thailand, but it is perception that counts. Laos explained the shooting as a case of Thailand trying to retrieve the body of a Thai smuggler who had been killed in an internal dispute on Lao territory. Lao forces responded appropriately. Whatever the true circumstances, the Lao economy had to pay the price for Vietnam's policy of signalling Thailand, by means of military attack, its rules of the game regarding the Democratic Kampuchean forces in Thai sanctuaries. During the blockade, Thai imports dried up in the Lao markets and Thai military collusion with Laotian resistance elements probably proceeded with less self-restraint, in view of the hostile, bilateral relations.

Laos had little to gain from the controversy except a heightened recognition of the economic importance of a secure, reliable truck route and pipelines to the ports of Vietnam to avoid the Thai Government's stranglehold over vital imports from abroad and daily commerce. The Vietnamese road construction project to improve the route from Savannakhet to Danang port was apparently accelerated during the summer of 1980, even at the expense of shifting engineering equipment from other projects. The general policy of reliance on the SRV to escape economic dependence on Thailand doubtless received another boost within the councils of the LPDR. The proportion of Lao external trade entering through the port of Danang at the time was estimated at about one fifth.[12]

The side effects of Thailand's indignant policy were recognized by Thai policymakers and a formula was devised under which Lao expressions of regret that the incident occurred were treated as equivalent to an apology. Two river crossings were reopened, to the satisfaction of many Thai merchants in the legal trading sector. Subsequently, Laos and Thailand held their traditional boat races opposite Vientiane, in October, but in February 1981 the old pattern recurred as Thailand closed two river crossings near Vientiane in retaliation for reported shooting by Lao troops into a Thai village. Thai forces also responded with artillery and mortar fire.[13]

Relations with the Soviet Union

The Soviet Union plays an important role in Laos. It is the LPDR's principal donor, now providing approximately 60% of the country's external assistance, with some help from its European allies. The Soviet Union is the principal guide to the fledgling Laotian Air Force, to which it has delivered eighteen MIG aircraft.

The number of aid technicians and administrators seems to be growing, with estimates ranging from 1,200 to several thousand. Unlike Vietnam, Laos has not been invited to join the Council for Mutual Economic Aid (COMECON), but it sits as observer at the meetings. Given the rather abrupt manner in which the SRV was invited into the organization in August 1978, apparently without much consultation among the non-Soviet members, and in view of the weakness of the Lao economy, the LPDR is not likely to be accorded full membership. The East European states would probably regard the imposition of still another poor Indochina state upon COMECON as a Soviet-imposed burden, notwithstanding their friendly Party-to-Party relations. As many as two thousand Lao students are studying in the socialist bloc states (primarily the USSR and East Germany) with perhaps thousands more studying in Vietnam.[14] This training lasts as long as six years, and some students who were sent after the cease-fire in 1973 have begun to return to jobs in the ministries.

Press reports have intermittently suggested that Vietnam, jealous to preserve its dominant role in Laos, might be disturbed by substantial quantities of direct Soviet aid to Laos (and to Kampuchea), preferring to have assistance channelled only through Vietnam. Although the possibility of Vietnamese suspicion of Soviet motives in Laos cannot be excluded, it seems more likely that the Vietnamese, at least for the present, see their interests served by the flow of Soviet resources into Laos. The Vietnamese geographical proximity to Laos, their long-standing guidance of the Lao communist movement, their substantial military presence, and their military advisory role insure their dominant influence in Laotian affairs.

The Soviet involvement in Indochina affairs was revealed by the discreet summit meeting of Indochina leaders and President Leonid Brezhnev in August 1981. Prime Minister Kaysone Phomvihan, although reported to be on a vacation in the USSR, apparently joined Vietnam's communist party leader Le Duan and the new Cambodian Prime Minister Pen Sovan (also on vacation) in a meeting with Brezhnev on the Black Sea. Later, bilateral discussions of each Indochinese leader with the Kremlin leaders were acknowledged in early September and Le Duan indicated that "identity of views and co-ordination of actions among the communist parties and states in the socialist community have become more necessary than ever".[15] The Soviet leader in turn urged that discussions seeking a regional solution to questions of security in the area not be broken off. In his view Beijing and Washington were responsible for the trouble between Indochina and ASEAN and careful diplomacy toward Southeast Asian states, and India and Japan — not military pressure — should be pursued to overcome this problem.

Relations with ASEAN

The crux of the problem between ASEAN and the Indochina states has been the Vietnamese military presence in Cambodia and ASEAN's more or less concerted support of Thailand, the frontline state, in countering this situation. This effort has ranged from blocking any seating of the Heng Samrin government at the United Nations General Assembly to complicity with China in the sustenance of Democratic Kampuchean guerrillas which harass the Vietnamese troops in Cambodia. ASEAN also secured a U.N. General Assembly resolution in 1980 calling for an international conference on the Cambodia question, and in anticipation of that gathering (which the Indochina states refused to attend) the rival Cambodian refugee groups (under Khieu Samphan, Prince Sihanouk, and Son Sann) were encouraged to compose a united front. The unlikely nature of this marriage revealed itself at the eighty-three-nation conference on Cambodia which eventually took place in New York in July 1981, and betrayed the mutual distrust with which the three Cambodians regarded one another. Nonetheless, they officially agreed to work together at a meeting in Singapore on 4 September 1981. The Lao Government has stood beside Vietnam and even helped take diplomatic soundings, through all of the manoeuvring between ASEAN and Vietnam, in preparing for the crucial U.N. votes in 1980 and 1981 on rejecting the credentials of the People's Republic of Kampuchea to sit in the General Assembly, and on the Secretary-General's task of convening a conference on Cambodia. In July 1980 an Indochina Foreign Ministers' meeting was held in Vientiane to review the situation. A previous meeting of the group took place in Phnom Penh six months earlier. The Vientiane meeting's statement endorsed a four-point proposal made by the People's Republic of Kampuchea for the establishment of a demilitarized zone in the border areas between Thailand and Cambodia and a joint commission to implement measures guaranteeing peace and stability and international control in the border areas. This suggestion was rejected by Thailand as a wrong definition of the problem — which is the presence of foreign troops in Cambodia — and an unwarranted demand for Thailand to relinquish sovereignty in its own territory.

Later, as the U.N.-organized conference approached in 1981 (with no communist states agreeing to participate), Lao Foreign Minister Phoun Sipraseut visited ASEAN Foreign Ministries, no doubt to take stock of their solidarity and inclinations. The major tension at the one-sided conference was between the Democratic Kampuchean (DK) delegation, supported by China, and the other parties, over whether the various groups that would contest in a free election envisioned for Cambodia would have to give up their arms. The Chinese support for not disarming the DK group creates suspicion and distrust among the Cambodian refugee opposition groups, which the Indochina bloc will no doubt do their best to exploit. Allowing the Lao Foreign Minister to carry the ball occasionally may provide some variation in the personalities involved, but the message and strategy will remain constricted by Vietnam's sense of its own best interests.

Relations with the United States

Whatever hopes the Lao People's Revolutionary Party might have nourished in 1975 of continuing to receive American aid without political conditions and USAID infrastructure — hopes were dashed by the manner in which party-inspired Lao students took possession of U.S. facilities and ousted the administrators. Under existing American laws, Laos may receive no economic assistance except "humanitarian" aid which was provided during the severe food shortage of 1978. With economic aid relationships cut off, the American Embassy in Vientiane has been ordered to operate with no more than twelve non-local employees.

A lingering issue between the United States and Laos is the accounting for Americans missing-in-action (MIAs) which the U.S. Government believes the LPDR, like the Vietnamese, are withholding. A U.S. State Department briefing paper, released in July 1981, categorized the Americans missing in Laos during the Vietnam War as: missing-9; POW-1; presumed dead-360; killed in action/body not recovered-189. Between 1962 and 1975, 20 Americans who had been missing in Laos were returned (9 in Hanoi in 1973 after the signing of the Paris Peace Accords). In August 1978, the LPDR returned four sets of skeletal remains (two of which were later determined to be non-American) to a U.S. congressional delegation led by Representative Montgomery.

Vietnam inexplicably released the skeletal remains of three Americans on 7 July 1981, just prior to the U.N.-sponsored conference on Cambodia. Perhaps the Vietnamese were tantalizing the United States with MIA information to stimulate an American appetite for normalized relations. Laos, which doubtless has less MIA information to deal with and, unlike Vietnam, has no problem of establishing diplomatic relations with the United States, will probably not act independently of the Socialist Republic of Vietnam in this matter. The U.S. fixation on this issue was demonstrated to Laos again in May 1980 when a raid was made from Thailand by infiltrators, perhaps trained by the CIA, to investigate reports of a prison camp in central Laos which seemed to be signalling the presence of American pilots. The site was found to be completely devoid of Westerners, and the Lao Government made rather pro-forma protests. The raid may have been launched with CIA backing to pre-empt more amateurish attempts by interested but unofficial parties.

Another issue raised by the U.S. Government to the LPDR concerned the alleged use of a chemical agent in fighting Hmong insurgents in the mountainous regions of central Laos. Hmong refugees, who had fled from pockets of resistance within Laos, reported that villages had been sprayed with what they called "yellow rain", which caused choking, acute vomiting, serious stomach illness, and death to some who breathed its fumes. A U.S. Congressional Committee in 1979 had taken testimony from Hmong refugees and from U.S. Army medical and chemical warfare officers. The latter asserted that the substance which had been sprayed was not related to chemical agents left behind in Indochina by the United States.

On 13 September 1981, in Berlin, Secretary of State Alexander Haig announced that U.S. chemists had solved the riddle of identifying the substance, a mycotoxin, from a leaf and stem sample procured within Cambodia. A sample from Laos was under investigation and the Department of State's report seemed to portend a similar identification of the lethal substance, which does not grow naturally in Southeast Asia. The United States was pointing an accusing finger, without directly saying so, at the Soviet Union, which made indignant denials. The United Nations General Assembly resolved in 1980 to investigate charges of chemical warfare, which had also been raised for Afghanistan and South Yemen, but a field investigation by a panel of experts has yet to be organized by the U.N. Secretariat, and the willingness of Laos to admit such a group is unlikely. With strong congressional support the Department of State will probably maintain a campaign to substantiate its charges and keep Vietnam and the USSR on the defensive.

In Conclusion

Much as it might serve the economic interest of Laos to maintain uninterrupted friendly relations with Thailand and to receive assistance again from the United States and France, and to end the threatening subversive actions of China, it does not appear possible for the LPDR to break away from the Indochina bloc which Vietnam has fashioned and the Soviet Union supports as a counterweight to Chinese influence in the region. Thus the Vietnamese force of around fifty thousand soldiers will remain in Laos not only with China on their mind, but also to deal with internal security problems and growing resistance intrusions. Vietnamese technicians and advisers will remain important in the countryside where a wider range of foreign development assistance might otherwise have been available. This degree of dependence on a few close friends is not likely to stimulate Lao national tranquillity nor productivity any more than it did during the period of American dominance, when resources were more plentiful. So Lao foreign policy, largely dictated by its revolutionary history, will largely determine its rate of economic development and political consolidation — which will remain slow and uncertain.

Notes

* This report draws upon the authors' joint visit to Vientiane, Laos, in December 1980, and upon an earlier visit to Vientiane by Professor Brown in October 1980. While in Vientiane, the authors interviewed Lao government officials, international organization experts, and members of the foreign diplomatic community. In addition, this article draws upon Professor Zasloff's interviews with Lao refugees in camps in Thailand during January and December 1980.
1. *Foreign Broadcast Information Service: People's Republic of China, Daily Report* (hereafter cited as *FBIS:PRC*), 19 October 1978; see also 11 September and 12 November 1978, for signs of tension in the Party over this issue.
2. *FBIS: Laos*, 4 December 1978.
3. *Summary of World Broadcasts*, 1 November 1976, FE/5352/13/6-8. Quoted in Trevor Ling, *Buddhism, Imperialism and War* (London: George Allen and Unwin, 1975), pp. 148–51.
4. Somboon Suksamran, *Political Buddhism in Southeast Asia* (London: C. Hurst and Company, 1977), p. 3.
5. Henry Kamm, "Laotian Buddhist Ex-Chief, 87, is Given Refuge in a Temple", *New York Times*, 15 March 1979.
6. Interviews with Mahabunkong, Bangkok, 13 November 1978 and Vanna, Nong Khai, 18 November 1978, cited by Martin Stuart-Fox and R.S. Bucknell, "Communism and Therevada Buddhism: The Lao Experience", in manuscript.
7. "Resolution 6" was promulgated at the 6th Plenum of the Central Committee of the Vietnamese Communist Party.
8. "Kaysone Speech to Supreme People's Council", Vientiane Domestic Service in Lao, 27 December 1979; *FBIS*, 18 January 1980.
9. Cf. Speech of Mr Phoune Sipraseut, Minister of Foreign Affairs of the LPDR, at the 35th Assembly of the United Nations, 1 October 1980. Other impressions have been obtained from interviews in the Lao Ministry of Foreign Affairs, October and December 1980.
10. M. Stuart-Fox develops this theme in detail in "Laos in China's Anti-Vietnam Strategy", *Asia and Pacific Community*, Winter 1981.
11. See the analysis of M. Stuart-Fox, ibid., for a fuller development of this relationship. During the April 1979 Sino-Vietnamese negotiations on normalizing relations, the Chinese proposal called for the withdrawal of Vietnamese troops stationed in other countries (not simply Cambodia). Cf. G. Porter "Vietnamese Policy and the Indochina Crisis", *The Third Indochina Conflict*, ed. D.W.P. Elliott (Boulder Colorado: Westview Press, 1981), p. 112.
12. *Bangkok Post*, 26 November 1980, p. 9.
13. *New York Times*, 9 February 1981.
14. Premier Kaysone alluded at the fifth anniversary of the LPDR to "tens of thousands of students studying abroad", but this would seem to be an inflated figure.
15. *Far Eastern Economic Review*, 18 September 1981, pp. 11–12.

LAOS
The Chinese Connection

Martin Stuart-Fox

The title of my first contribution to Southeast Asian Affairs in 1980 was "Laos: The Vietnamese Connection". A great deal has happened in the Lao People's Democratic Republic (LPDR) over the past three decades, both internally, and in its relations with its neighbours. The Lao People's Revolutionary Party (LPRP) is still in power, but it is a party riven by ambition and greed. The country is wealthier than it was thirty years ago; but the urban-rural divide is more marked than ever. Wealth is concentrated in the cities, most of it in the hands of Party members and their families. The resources of the country, which the French had glimpsed a century before, most of which are located in rural areas, are now being rapidly exploited, but not for the benefit of the rural majority. Neighbouring states have hungrily eyed these resources, and seized their opportunities to obtain a share — none more so than China. So just as what was interesting about Laos in 1980 was the Vietnamese connection, so in 2009 what is interesting is the developing Chinese connection, and what this means for Lao politics and policies.

To focus on the Chinese connection is not to suggest that the Vietnamese connection no longer matters. It certainly does. Rather it is to focus on economic and political changes that are now taking place. What I want to do in this article is to examine the changes that were becoming apparent in 2008 in three areas: in politics; in economic development; and in international relations. But I shall deal with these in the reverse order, for Lao politics are all but opaque in the absence of any media reporting or discussion, and it is only by examining the shifting influence of neighbouring states, and popular responses

---

Reprinted in abridged format from Daljit Singh, ed., *Southeast Asian Affairs 2009* (Singapore: Institute of Southeast Asian Studies, 2009), pp. 143–69. At the time of original publication, Martin Stuart-Fox was Professor Emeritus, University of Queensland, Brisbane, Australia.

International Pressures

(a) The Rise of China

In early 2008, for the first time the growing Chinese presence became a matter of popular concern and debate in the LPDR. The trigger was an announcement in September 2007 that a consortium of three Chinese companies would build a new 20,000-seat stadium in Viang Chan (Vientiane) in time for Laos to host the Southeast Asian games in December 2009. In return, the consortium, coordinated by the Suzhou Industrial Park Overseas Investment Company, would be given a 50-year concession to develop 1,640 hectares of swampy land known as the That Luang marshes, not far from the hallowed That Luang stupa.[1]

The agreement had been secretly negotiated through the China Development Bank, which had agreed to provide credit of US$100 million to build the stadium, on the surety of the land concession. A Lao company, whose political associations are unclear, was given a five per cent stake in the project, which would include not just up-market housing, but also an industrial zone, a shopping complex and hotels. Buildings would be sold or leased for the duration of the concession, which according to the agreement could be extended for a further 25 years. Thereafter ownership would revert to the Lao government.

On the face of it, the "New City Development Project" looked like a good deal: Laos would obtain a stadium free, plus a modern housing estate in the heart of Viang Chan. But then concern grew and the rumour mills began to grind. People were unsure how much land would be resumed and what compensation would be paid. Promised compensation is often not paid in Laos, but rather ends up in the pockets of officials. Rural victims have no recourse, but reportedly some of the land covered by the That Luang development belonged to Party members, who began to ask questions.

Of greater popular concern, however, was Chinese ownership of the project, and what the consortium intended to do with it.[2] The Lao are well aware that the Chinese business presence is expanding in Laos, and they know how Chinese businesses operate. Already there is a large shopping complex in Viang Chan, known simply as the Chinese Market, where mainly Chinese shopkeepers sell consumer products imported from China through business networks that effectively exclude Lao from competing. Moreover Chinese businesses usually employ only Chinese workers. The Chinese company contracted to build the stadium has brought in as many as 3,000 Chinese construction workers rather than employ Lao labourers.

It was not entirely surprising therefore that a rumour was soon circulating that the "new city" was being built exclusively to house 50,000 Chinese residents. So persistent was the rumour that the Party felt it necessary to hold a rare press conference specifically to deny it. Deputy prime minister (and former foreign minister) Somsavat Lengsavat, who reportedly facilitated the deal, revealed to reporters many of the details given above, and assured them that anyone with the necessary means would be able to buy a house in the new estate, for there would be "no discrimination among buyers and no special concessions for Chinese citizens".[3]

More details were released about the development itself, which an artist's impression depicts as modern and multi-purpose, overlooking open water. But rumours about the project persisted — particularly that it would become a luxury "Chinatown" for wealthy Chinese who would come to control the Lao economy. By August, Voice of America was quoting unnamed "Lao authorities" as saying that many landowners were refusing to relocate because of inadequate compensation, and that as a result the government was looking for land elsewhere.[4] Another rumour was that the That Luang development would be cut to one third of the original plan.

What feeds such rumours is the lack of transparency that characterises most government and Party business in Laos, where decisions backed by powerful political figures can overrule any existing regulations. But the furore over the That Luang marshes development project reflects growing unease over the Chinese presence in Laos. That presence is evident for all to see, as is the influence of Chinese business, which is willing to pay for useful political connections.

A small Chinese presence in Laos goes back centuries, but the Chinese population grew steadily during the French and Royal Lao periods (1893 to 1975) to reach more than 40,000.[5] Most of this Sino-Lao community left after the LPRP seized power in 1975 and relations between Laos and China deteriorated in 1979. But with the restoration of normal relations in 1987 and transition to a market economy, a few began to return. By 1997, the Chinese population in Laos was estimated to be around 10,000,[6] divided between Sino-Lao families who had returned to reclaim property and restart businesses in the Mekong towns of central and southern Laos, and an influx into northern Laos of new entrepreneurs and small traders from Yunnan, who can enter Laos with no more than Chinese identity papers and a border pass.

Today the Lao government puts the number of Chinese living in Laos at 30,000. This is widely believed to be a gross under-estimate, but even the government's figures still represents a tripling of the Chinese population over the last decade. In the northern Lao provinces down to Udomxai, the Chinese presence is very evident. Many shop signs are in Chinese, and in some towns most commerce is now in Chinese hands. Over the last five years, Chinese from Kunming and further away still, many of them young single men, have begun trading in Luang Phrabang and Viang Chan. Some have moved even further south.

These newcomers have little in common with the older Sino-Lao community. Many hardly speak Lao and most have little sensitivity towards Lao culture. They are more brashly nationalistic and tend to stick together.[7] But the Chinese are nothing if not adaptable. Already intermarriage is occurring (partly due to the gender imbalance in China), and once young men acquire Lao wives they are more likely to stay in Laos, learn Lao, and adapt to Lao ways.

Another recent trend has been a rapid increase in large-scale Chinese investment in Laos, principally in mining and agriculture, but also in energy production, telecommunications, and construction materials. Chinese companies are involved in mineral exploration, and are exploiting deposits of limestone (for cement) and potash. A consortium in which the Aluminium Corporation of China holds a 51 per cent stake and another Chinese company holds 19.5 per cent has been awarded the right to mine half of a vast bauxite deposit in southern Laos,[8] while a second Chinese-led consortium has applied to develop the other half. The investment needed, including power stations, will run into billions of dollars.

China's rapidly growing demand for agricultural and forestry products, particularly rubber and food, has driven investment in plantations in northern Laos. Rubber was first planted in northern Laos (400 ha in Luang Namtha province) in 1994. By 2006 the area under cultivation had increased to 7,341 ha, with planned expansion that will take the total to 119,000 ha by 2010. This is almost double the planned cultivation area for central and southern Laos over the same period.[9]

Much of this massive expansion is in the form of plantations run by Chinese companies. Some, however, is being driven by smallholders who are planting rubber on their own land, usually with inputs provided by Chinese buyers. Rubber trees take seven years to come into production, but thereafter the return for the farmer per hectare (US$880) is almost as much as for opium (US$903). Agarwood and teak are also being grown on plantations for the China market.

Food crops include corn, cassava, bananas, sesame, and soy beans. These too are either produced on land leased to Chinese companies, or grown by smallholders who sell to Chinese buyers on contract (usually for a period of fifteen years). If land concessions are less than 100 ha, deals can be concluded with provincial authorities. For larger plantations central government approval is required. Abuses occur when land to which peasant farmers claim traditional rights is expropriated on the grounds that they do not have legal title.[10]

The areas of land involved are substantial. Over a ten-year period from 1996 to 2006, the area contracted to grow corn for China in Udomxai province alone increased from 3,000 ha to 13,000 ha, producing around 100,000 tonnes. Meanwhile in Luang Namtha province, closer to China, 40,000 ha were devoted to growing sugarcane and 60,000 to cassava. Production of each crop was expected to reach 1 million tonnes in 2008.[11]

Chinese construction companies have also been active in Laos. Most of the construction work has been on Chinese aid projects, but a Chinese construction company was contracted to build the Malaysian-owned Don Chan Palace Hotel, the tallest building in Viang Chan, in time for Laos to host the ASEAN Summit of 2004. Chinese construction companies have also been successful in bidding for road construction projects funded by the Asian Development Bank. A Chinese airline has bought a stake in Air Lao.

The figures for Chinese direct investment in Laos tell the story. From 2001 to August 2007, according to the Lao Committee for Planning and Investment, US$1.1 billion of Chinese investments was approved, second only to Thailand's US$1.3 billion.[12] But for the fiscal year 2006–07, Chinese investment accounted for over 40 per cent of the total US$1.1 billion approved; and 45 out of the 117 projects were Chinese.[13]

In view of the increase in Chinese investment project designed to produce goods that China needs, from food to minerals, it is not surprising that trade is growing. China has unilaterally reduced tariffs on a wide range of imports from Laos, and the target is for two-way trade to reach US$1 billion. That goal is some way off, however. In 2006, China imported US$45.1 million from Laos and exported US$185.6 million; so trade runs strongly in China's favour. What is surprising is that these figures are still but a fraction of the trade in both directions between Laos and Thailand (see below).[14]

Chinese aid has focused on improving communications between China and Laos. Chinese engineers have been building roads in northern Laos since the early 1960s. Until they were withdrawn in 1979, the work was done by military construction units. With the resumption of normal relations, a selective Chinese aid programme also resumed. For example, a ground satellite reception centre was built in 1990–91, and the capacity of the Vang Viang cement factory was expanded in 1992–94. (A second factory has subsequently been built.)

The expansion of China's aid programme to Laos dates from 1999, when China provided a substantial loan to enable Laos to weather the Asian economic crisis. The Lao were grateful for the assistance, and relations warmed between the two countries. China undertook two showy projects in Viang Chan: construction of the Lao National Cultural Hall, and reconstruction of the Avenue Lan Xang, and the gardens around the Patouxai monument at the head of the avenue, leaving Japan (by far the largest aid donor to Laos) to deal with the other major thoroughfares with their more demanding associated sewage and drainage problems.

Over the last several years Chinese financial assistance has mainly been in the form of cash grants and no-interest loans for projects agreed upon with the Lao government, plus credits for commercial ventures by Chinese companies in Laos. Roads and bridges continue to be a priority. In 2008, National Route 3 from the China-Laos border at Boten to the Mekong River port of Huayxai opposite Chiang Saen in Thailand was completed.[15] China will build a connecting bridge to be jointly financed with Thailand and completed by 2011, after which it will be possible to drive from Singapore to Beijing. Other road construction is underway or planned, notably in Udomxai province. Commercial credits have gone towards building hydropower stations on three rivers in northern Laos, to the Hongsa lignite-fired power station in Xainyaburi province, and to power transmission lines and telecommunications. China has also built part of the GMS Information Super highway in Laos, which went into operation on 31 March 2008.[16] Total Chinese development aid granted to Laos to mid-2007 has been estimated at US$280 million, but China has reportedly also cancelled loans to the value of US$1.7 billion.[17]

Since 1991, China has provided scholarships (currently 55 per annum) for Lao students to study in China; Chinese advisers are assigned to work with Lao counterparts on specific programmes; and Chinese youth volunteers spend six-month terms teaching IT and languages (Chinese and English), coaching in various sports, or performing medical service. Groups of Lao government and Party officials attend management and training courses in China, including military training for young officers.

Laos and China exchange official government, Party and military delegations on a regular basis. In November 2000, President Jiang Zemin became the first Chinese head of state to visit Laos, following an official visit to China by Lao president Khamtay Siphandone. Premier Wen Jibao attended the 2004 ASEAN Summit in Viang Chan, and arrived again for the 2008 Greater Mekong Subregion (GMS) Summit, an indication of the importance China attaches to the regional grouping. While in Laos, the Chinese premier signed seven agreements covering aid, trade, investment, infrastructure, communications and power generation, including provision of a US$100 million export credit facility for the purchase, among other items, of a Z9 military helicopter.[18] The Chinese have said they are happy with the state of military relations, which "have developed very well";[19] and China is believed to provide military equipment to the cash-strapped Lao army, though no details have ever been published.

China and Laos have no outstanding problems to resolve. The border has been demarcated. They do, however, share concern over such transnational problems as smuggling (especially of drugs, but also of people) across their porous common border, and the spread of infectious diseases (from HIV/Aids to bird flu). There is reportedly some Chinese concern about the operation of the Boten casino, just across the Chinese border in the Lao province of Luang Namtha. The turn-off to the casino is actually north of the Lao immigration and customs post, which means that Chinese visitors do not have to pass through any Lao checkpoint. The casino operates solely for a Chinese clientele, catering for gambling, prostitution and money laundering. For this cosy arrangement, the Hong Kong Chinese operators pay Lao provincial authorities.

There has been much debate over the evolving Chinese relationship with the states of mainland Southeast Asia, and speculation over Chinese intentions towards the region.[20] As the smallest and most under-populated state, Laos is the most vulnerable in the face of China's growing might. There is little doubt that both the Chinese presence and Chinese influence will increase. But Laos has little to fear as long as Chinese interests are kept in mind in Viang Chan. And there is every indication that they are. When Wen Jiabao visited Laos in March 2008, the Chinese media quoted Lao prime minister Bouasone Bouphavanh as assuring him that Laos highly valued its ties with China and would make "concerted efforts ... to step up the friendly and cooperative relations".[21]

What the Chinese want for their grant aid and loans are three things: backing for Chinese policy on everything from Taiwan to Tibet; access for Chinese companies to exploit Lao resources; and lines of communication through Laos to Thailand. The Lao provide all three. What the Lao regime seeks in addition to aid and investment is political support in the face of Western pressure for reforms, both economic and political, that the Lao are reluctant to accept. It receives this support in the guise of China's policy of non-interference in the internal affairs of sovereign states. Not only will China exert no such pressure itself, but as in the case of Burma/Myanmar, China looms as a potential alternative source for any aid or investment the West can provide, thus vitiating Western influence.

As China's own influence is undoubtedly on the rise, the obvious question is: what implications does this have, both for Laos' relations with other neighbouring states, particularly Vietnam and Thailand, and for Lao politics? Let us take Vietnam first.

(b) Party-to-Party: The Continuing Influence of Vietnam

Just as there has been debate over China's intentions towards Laos, and mainland Southeast Asia more broadly, so there has been discussion over whether China and Vietnam are actively competing for influence in Laos.[22] And if so, whether this has resulted in, or reflects, divisions within the Central Committee of the LPRP.

For several years there has been speculation over whether there exist defined pro-Vietnamese and pro-Chinese factions in the LPRP. Some observers have suggested that the basis for such a division is generational: the old revolutionaries have close ties to Vietnam, while younger Party members have no such historical baggage and look rather to China. Others point to geographical factors: northerners, led by former foreign minister Somsavat Lengsavad (who is ethnic Chinese and speaks fluent Mandarin) favour China,[23] southerners less so. But neither argument is very convincing.

The only time when there may have been pro-Vietnamese and pro-Chinese factions was in 1979, when some in the Party were purged following the Vietnamese invasion of Cambodia to overthrow the Khmer Rouge, and during the subsequent Sino-Vietnamese conflict when Laos fell into line with Vietnam. But those purged were not so much pro-Chinese as anti-alignment: though they may have had some sympathy for China, they argued that Laos should remain neutral in the conflict between China and Vietnam. Their expulsion from the LPRP was engineered by the Vietnamese.

Historically the Lao have been adept at balancing one external power off against another, and it is part of their international relations culture to do so. This is true whether they are of the revolutionary or the younger generation. As for Somsavat, he is Sino-Lao, but formed by his immersion in the Lao revolutionary movement. He has benefited from Chinese contacts, but there is no evidence that he ever took the risk of being labelled pro-Chinese. Besides, he had little influence in a party dominated by military men with close ties to Vietnam.

Lao policy is to be as even-handed as possible between China and Vietnam. When the new leadership team of Lieutenant General Choummaly Sayasone as Party and state president and Bouasone Bouphavanh as prime minister were appointed in 2006, both men first visited Hanoi, then immediately went on to Beijing. This would suggest that Vietnam still retains an edge over China in the closeness of its relations with Laos.

But if there are no pro-Vietnamese versus pro-Chinese factions, are the two countries nevertheless competing for influence in Laos? Some indication may be provided by figures for aid, trade and investment. Like China, Vietnam releases few figures or details of its aid to Laos, though over the years this has been substantial. Occasionally announcements are made of emergency aid or aid for specific projects. Thus in 2008, Vietnam gave US$100,000 of aid for flood victims in Laos, and said it would assist Laos in preparing to host the 2009 Southeast Asia games by building a training centre and sending instructors (with no dollar value attached). Assistance is also provided from one organization to another, such as medical supplies donated by a hospital in Vietnam to a hospital in Laos, or by one province to another with which a "sister" relationship exists.

Vietnam avoids giving large sums for prestige projects of the kind China favours; nor can it provide anything like the assistance China gave Laos during the Asian economic crisis (though Vietnam did do what it could). Vietnam has funded major road and bridge construction, and built airstrips. Overall, however, Vietnamese aid is more comprehensive than Chinese aid, and many more Vietnamese experts are sent to work with their Lao counterparts in fields as diverse as the media, education and agriculture. Vietnamese experts also advise in such sensitive areas as Party organization, security, and in the military.

As for trade, Vietnam is ahead of China as a destination for Lao exports (at US$107.2 million as against US$45.1 million for China for 2006, the last year for which figures are available), but provides half the value of imports that China does (with US$90.8 compared with US$185.6 for China in 2006).[24] Two-way trade, though more evenly balanced, thus lags behind China, and the gap is likely to have widened in the last two years. As with China, however, the goal is to increase two-way trade between Laos and Vietnam to US$1 billion per annum by 2010, and to double that again by 2015.[25] This is overly ambitious, but by then Vietnam will be purchasing substantial amounts of Lao electricity, and a number of Vietnamese investment projects will be in production. Vietnam has facilitated trade by building roads and making the port of Danang available for Lao exports. A railway to connect Savannakhet with the Vietnamese rail network is also planned.

Vietnamese investment in Laos comes in third after Thailand and China, but is not far behind and on the rise. Total investment in 117 projects underway or planned was put at US$1.28 billion, with US$600 million committed in 2007 alone and another US$240 million in the first seven months of 2008.[26] A large proportion of this sudden increase is in hydropower. Dams under construction or planned on the Xekaman River in Attapeu province will be producing 4 billion kWt of electricity for sale to Vietnam by 2013.[27]

A more controversial hydropower dam is planned on the Mekong River in northern Laos.[28] Other projects include mining and mineral exploration, rubber and agricultural plantations, wood processing, garment factories, and other light manufacturing. Vietnamese commercial banks also operate in Laos. Just as most Chinese investment is located in northern Laos (but for bauxite), so most Vietnamese investment is concentrated in the south and east.

Vietnam certainly does not rely on historical ties between aging revolutionaries as the sole basis for its continuing influence in Laos. Up-and-coming Lao Party members regularly attend ideological training courses at the Ho Chi Minh National Politics Institute in Hanoi,[29] which enables Vietnam to build contacts with successive generations of Lao Party leaders. Far more Vietnamese than Chinese possess good Lao language skills, and many Lao speak Vietnamese (including ten out of the eleven Lao Politburo members, the exception ironically being prime minister Bouasone who was educated in Moscow). This allows the Vietnamese embassy (the largest in Viang Chan) to maintain contacts across the LPRP. As a result, the Vietnamese have a better understanding of Lao politics than any other foreign embassy.

Even though the 25-year Treaty of Friendship and Cooperation that comprises the core of the "special relationship" between Vietnam and Laos expired in 2002, Vietnam does all in its power to keep the memory alive. A joint history of the relationship is being written, and Vietnam has funded a US$1.6 million Laos-Vietnam History Museum near Savannakhet. The military debt has been acknowledged in the form of memorials, and small, but well publicized, ceremonies take place as the remains of Vietnamese soldiers killed in Laos are repatriated. The phrase "special relationship" may no longer be used in official communiqués, but it has simply been replaced by reference to the two countries' "traditional friendship, special solidarity and comprehensive cooperation".[30]

Like China, Vietnam has no outstanding issues with Laos. The border is delineated, including the crucial tri-border marker between Vietnam, Cambodia and Laos (placed in August 2008). Development of the tri-border area is a priority for all three countries. Smuggling from Laos to Vietnam remains a problem, including notably timber and illegally caught wildlife. Despite a ban on the export of whole logs dating from 1999, timber smuggling continues on a large scale, abetted by the military of both countries, to feed the voracious Vietnamese furniture trade.[31]

So in view of the evidence, are Vietnam and China competing for influence in Laos? On the face of it, it would appear so. The recent upsurge in Vietnamese investment in Laos suggests that Hanoi is determined to match China in obtaining a share in Lao resources. And both countries foresee a similar increase in trade. Their aid programmes are very different, however, and so may be their unstated political goals.

For China, political influence appears to be directed mostly towards obtaining economic opportunities,[32] though a strong Chinese presence in Laos also offers some strategic benefit to Beijing. For Vietnam, the strategic importance of Laos for the defence of its long and vulnerable western border has always been of primary concern. The price Hanoi was prepared to pay to maintain control of eastern Laos was demonstrated during the Second Indochina War. For Vietnam, a politically friendly regime in Laos is essential. Thus for Vietnam the first priority is to preserve the closest possible political relationship, which for Hanoi has always taken precedence over the economic relationship. And the political relationship rests squarely on party-to-party relations between the Vietnamese Communist Party and the Lao People's Revolutionary Party. This is why Hanoi's political goal in Laos is to promote a strong and cohesive LPRP.

Of course China also supports Laos politically, and will continue to do so for as long as its economic interests are served; but China could obtain concessions from, and dominate, any Lao regime of any political persuasion simply by virtue of size. Because China does not need to have particularly close party-to-party relations, Beijing sees no need to overtly challenge Hanoi's political influence. The continuing cohesion and effectiveness of the LPRP is thus a Vietnamese responsibility, and Vietnam takes it very seriously.

Vietnam takes a close interest not only in Lao politics, but also in how the Lao government is performing. Marxist-Leninist instruction of Lao Party members in Vietnam emphasises their moral responsibility to improve the lot of the "masses". Vietnamese advisory teams visit important ministries (including finance and defence) to suggest improvements in administrative efficiency. Reforms are designed to make the Party more responsive to popular demands, in particular to limit corruption, which is the principal criticism many Lao voice in private. There is no suggestion of regime change, which the Lao always suspect lies behind Western advice: just the opposite for the Vietnamese.

Apart from corruption, another concern the Vietnamese reportedly have is over the cohesion of the LPRP, not in relation to ideological differences, but rather with regard to the ambitions and activities of powerful individuals and their patronage networks. Where these are in conflict, rivalries and jealousies may cause divisions that have the potential of weakening Party cohesion, and so need to be managed. Already the wealth accumulated by certain families is a cause of envy on the part of others. For these reasons, according to some sources, the Vietnamese have lent cautious support to moderate reforms that prime minister Bouasone has indicated he would like to introduce.[33]

(c) ASEAN and the West

Lao membership of ASEAN has significantly altered the perception the country has of its place in the region and the world. Lao leaders repeatedly stress their commitment to regional integration, through which landlocked Laos will become landlinked, as the mantra goes. Certainly Laos is strategically situated, for it shares common borders with the other four mainland states.[34] But of these two loom much larger than the others. Vietnam is one, of course: the other is Thailand.

Relations between Laos and Thailand have been bumpy at times, as several outstanding issues create difficulties for both sides. These include border demarcation, refugees and security, trafficking, and smuggling. The border problem has been dragging on for years. While the land frontier (with Xainyaburi province in the north and Champasak province in the south) is determined but for a small stretch over which the two countries fought a brief border war from December 1987 to January 1988, there has been no agreement even on the principles of demarcation of the longer river frontier.

Over the past decade, security concerns have mainly focused on the Hmong minority. A small remnant group of Hmong in the mountains to the south of the Plain of Jars have refused Lao government offers of amnesty and continued their armed insurgency, though few insurgents now remain. Others have escaped to Thailand as refugees. The Thai want to send them back to Laos, but Lao authorities have been reluctant to accept them. The Hmong themselves do not want to return; nor are they keen to take up offers of resettlement in the U.S. or elsewhere.[35]

The Lao have also accused the Thai of harbouring Lao dissidents responsible for making armed incursions into Laos, attacking a border post, and probably exploding a number of small bombs between 2000 and 2004. On the other hand, several such dissidents have been mysteriously assassinated in Thailand, in which, if rumour is to be believed, the Lao secret service has been implicated. These murky events have done nothing to improve Lao-Thai relations.

Trafficking and smuggling are other perennial problems that bedevil Lao-Thai relations. Young Lao women are trafficked for prostitution and young Lao men for employment in conditions of virtual slavery. Drugs are also trafficked through Laos, from Burma and China into Thailand. Smuggling is two-way, of timber and livestock into Thailand and of manufactured and consumer goods into Laos. If one route is closed off, others open along the long and porous border.

Concerted efforts have been made on both sides to deal with these problems. Thai and Lao representatives meet regularly, from the local to the national level. There is close cooperation on health matters in particular (HIV/aids, bird flu). Moreover there is political goodwill on both sides — with good reason, for despite the rise of China and the political influence of Vietnam, in trade terms Thailand is more important than both combined. Over half of all Lao exports go to Thailand, while Thailand accounts for almost 70 per cent of Lao imports.[36]

Amounting to US$1.3588 billion in 2007, Thai investment in Laos still remains greater than that of China, although it slowed in 2007, and in 2008 will again be less than for China, due to the political turmoil in Thailand and the world financial crisis. Large projects include power generation (mainly in the form of hydroelectricity), mining and agriculture. And there are also many smaller Thai investment projects (more than for any other country) in areas such as tourism, transport and manufacturing.

Thailand exercises influence by other means, however. Many Lao have extended family members in northeast Thailand. Most Lao can understand, and many can read Thai, and as relatively little is published in Lao, Thai publications provide much of the information educated Lao have about the world. Lao students study in Thailand, and a large, but unknown, number work there, legally or illegally. For many Lao, therefore, Thailand provides their model for development.

Of the other ASEAN countries, only Malaysia (with US$138.6 million) and Singapore (with US$100.6 million) have significant investments in Laos (in tourism and timber, industry and services).[37] Trade is on the increase, and will be boosted by full Lao accession to the ASEAN Free Trade Area (AFTA), but it will continue to be overwhelmingly with Thailand and Vietnam. Only Malaysia (for exports) and Singapore (for imports) currently figure in Lao trade statistics.

Japan (with US$420.3 million) and Korea (with US$296.9 million) also have significant investments in Laos,[38] Japan mainly for a hydropower project and plantations for woodchips in southern Laos and Korea in a wide variety of smaller enterprises, including garment manufacturing and plantations of cassava and jastropha (for biodiesel production). Ten Korean companies have teamed up with Lao partners to build an entire satellite city close to Luang Phrabang. The 3,000 ha development will include hotels, a shopping mall and a golf course in addition to residential housing, all at an estimated cost of US$2 billion.[39] An Indian multinational is investing US$350 million in eucalypt plantations and a paper pulp mill.

Japan has consistently been the most generous donor of bilateral aid to Laos, contributing more than the next four donors combined (France, Germany, Sweden and Australia), and more than the multilateral aid provided by either the World Bank or the Asian Development Bank. Major projects have included hospitals, bridges and roads, notably in Viang Chan, and the Viang Chan water supply.

Western aid donors have been less generous, though Laos still manages to attract one of the highest per capita aid provisions in Asia. After more than two decades of assistance, especially to the forestry sector, Sweden has announced it will terminate its aid to Laos as current projects are completed, but France as the former colonial power and Australia are committed to continuing their aid programmes. Germany is a late comer, and the United States has only had a very small programme focusing mainly on opium reduction along with some clearance of unexploded ordnance left over from the Second Indochina War.

The point of this brief overview is to note that no ASEAN or Western state is in a position to exert the sort of influence over the Lao government that Vietnam or China do. The Lao-Thai relationship has been too fraught for too long, and carries too much historical baggage for Bangkok to have a decisive influence in Viang Chan. Japan has a much more consistent relationship as the Lao PDR's principal aid donor, but has invested relatively little and would be reluctant to urge reform, for fear that the Lao regime might interpret it as covertly working towards regime change.

This leaves the multilateral donors. Both the World Bank and the Asian Development Bank provide substantial loans to Laos for infrastructure development and poverty reduction. Both are thus in a position to include provisions in contracts to improve governance and financial transparency. As both banks are avowedly non-political, however, there is a limit to how much pressure for reform they can exert.[40]

Notes

1. The stupa is the symbol of Lao culture and identity, in the same way Angkor Wat is for Cambodia. When the LPDR introduced a market economy, the That Luang replaced the red star at the apex of the Lao national crest. A three-day national holiday marks the That Luang festival in November, the most important in the Lao Buddhist year.
2. Brian McCartan, "New-age Chinatown has Laotians on edge", *Asia Times Online*, 26 July 2008.
3. Editorial statement, "Govt [sic] explains That Luang Marsh Development", *Vientiane Times*, 12 February 2008.
4. Dara Baccam, "Laos: Chinese firms will not develop That Luang marshland", *Voice of America News*, 12 August 2008.
5. Prior to the French period, Lao contacts with China were via Yunnan, in the form of tribute (via Kunming) and trade (conducted by Yunnanese Muslims or Hui). Very few Chinese lived in northern Laos. The Chinese who arrived during the French period came via Saigon or Bangkok to southern and central Laos. Most were Chaozhou, Hakka, Hainanese and Cantonese, roughly in this order. See "Chinese in Laos" in Martin Stuart-Fox, *Historical Dictionary of Laos*, 3rd ed. (Lanham, MD: Scarecrow Press, 2008), pp. 54–55.
6. Florence Rossetti, "The Chinese in Laos: Rebirth of the Laotian Chinese community as peace returns to Indochina", *Chinese Perspectives* no. 13 (1997): 26.
7. See Bertil Lintner, "China Ascendent — Part 1: Checkbook diplomacy raises China's standing with Laos and Cambodia", *YaleGlobal*, 25 April 2008 at <http://yaleglobal.yale.edu/display.article?id=10702> (accessed 30 April 2008).
8. The other partners are Italian-Thai 19.5 per cent (Bangkok-based and owned by a Sino-Thai family) and Saha Bolisat Lao 10 per cent (a Lao company controlled by the family of former Lao state and Party president Khamtay Siphandone).
9. Sounthone Ketphanh, Khamphone Mounlamai, and Phoui Siksidao, "Rubber Planting Status in Lao PDR", paper presented to a workshop on Rubber Development in Laos held at the National Agriculture and Forestry Research Institute of Laos, Viang Chan, 9–11 May 2006 at <http://nafri.org.la/05_news/workshops/rubber/papers/Sess1_p2_rubber%20status.pdf> (accessed 12 November 2008).

10. Brian McCartan, "China Farms Abroad", *Asia Sentinel*, 1 August 2008 at <www.asiasentinel.com/index.php?option=com_content&task=view&id=1361&Itemid=32> (accessed 11 November 2008).
11. David Fullbrook, "Beijing pulls Laos into its orbit", *Asia Times Online*, 25 October 2006.
12. The figure for 2002–07, according to the IMF, was US$1.188 billion. *IMF Country Report* no. 08/340, Lao People's Democratic Republic, Statistical Appendix.
13. "Chinese investors invade Laos", *The Nation* (Bangkok), 8 October 2007.
14. Thailand accounts for 51.3 per cent of Lao exports and 70.6 per cent of imports, as against figures for China of 8.9 and 8.6 per cent. *EIU ViewsWire*, New York, 5 June 2008 and 23 September 2008.
15. The cost of US$97 million was shared between China, Thailand and the Asian Development Bank (US$30 million each), with the Lao government making up the remainder. "New overland route links Singapore to Beijing", *The Nation* (Bangkok), 1 April 2008.
16. Laos has announced suspension of further foreign investment in telecommunications because the sector is "saturated". *KPL Lao New Agency*, 28 October 2008. Mining concessions are also on hold until 2010.
17. "Chinese investors invade Laos", *The Nation* (Bangkok), 8 October 2007; *Radio Free Asia*, 12 May 2007.
18. Qin Jize, "China, Laos to enhance ties", *China Daily*, 31 March 2008.
19. "Sino-Laotian bilateral ties", *People's Daily Online*, as updated 16 November 2006 <http://english.peopledaily.com.cn/200611/16/eng20061116_322139.html> (accessed 13 November 2008).
20. Bertil Lintner calls the movement of Chinese into mainland Southeast Asian states "a creeping invasion", which Beijing is doing nothing to prevent (in "China's Third Wave, Part 1: A new breed of migrants fans out", *Asia Times Online*, 17 April 2007). Grant Evans prefers the term "drift' (in his paper "The Southward Drift of the Chinese" presented at the 17th Biennial Conference of the Asian Studies Association of Australia, Melbourne, 1–3 July 2008). With respect to Laos, Evans rejects C.P. Fitzgerald's alternative models of sinicization: the Vietnam model of wholesale adoption of Chinese culture; and the Yunnan model of Chinese settlement followed by political administration. Instead he favours a third model in which limited Chinese migration will bring some sinicization of Lao culture, but not political control. I have argued that the pattern of power relations between China and Southeast Asia that is emerging, while it is by no means a modern replay of the tributary relationship that existed until the nineteenth century, does preserve cultural and historical elements of it that both sides implicitly recognize. See Martin Stuart-Fox, *A Short History of China and Southeast Asia: Tribute, Trade and Influence* (Crows Nest, Australia: Allen & Unwin, 2003). Milton Osborne argues similarly that China seeks recognition from Southeast Asian countries as the paramount power: Chinese interests will come first, but China also wants Southeast Asia to be a prosperous partner. Milton Osborne, *The Paramount Power: China and the Countries of Southeast Asia* (Sydney: The Lowy Institute for International Policy, 2006).
21. "Special Report: Premier Wen visits Laos, attends GMS Summit", *Xinhua*, 30 March 2008.
22. See, for example, Ian Storey, "China and Vietnam's tug of war in Laos", *China Brief from the Jamestown Foundation*, vol. 5, issue 13 (7 June 2005).
23. Bertil Lintner, "Laos: Signs of Unrest", in *Southeast Asian Affairs 2001*, edited by Daljit Singh and Anthony Smith

(Singapore: Institute of Southeast Asian Studies, 2001), pp. 177–86.
24. *EIU ViewsWire*, New York, 5 June 2008. IMF Country Report no. 08/340 (Laos), October 2008.
25. "Laos sets to boost trade with Vietnam", *Vietnam News Agency*, 27 October 2008.
26. "Vietnam pours 1.28 billion USD investment in Laos", *Vietnam News Agency*, 12 August 2008. According to the IMF, however, the total for 2002–07 was US$539.2 million. *IMF Country Report* no. 08/340, Lao People's Democratic Republic, Statistical Appendix. See also Andrew Symon, "Regional race for Laos' riches", *Asia Times Online*, 30 August 2007.
27. "Vietnam, Laos ink supplements to major hydro-power project", *Vietnam News Agency*, 16 June 2008.
28. To be constructed over 2010–16 at a cost of US$2 billion. *Voice of America News*, 30 October 2008.
29. According to the *Vietnam News Agency* (27 August 2008), since 2005, 947 Lao officials have graduated from the Institute.
30. Used twice in the joint statement issued on the occasion of Lao president Choummaly to Vietnam in 2006 at <http://www.vnanet.vn/pPrint.aspx?itemid=151083> (assessed 16 August 2006).
31. Supalak Ganjanakhundee, "Illegal logging hits Lao forests", *The Nation* (Bangkok), 1 April 2008.
32. Tina Qian argues in "Communist capital flows downstream: China's aid to Laos" (China Development Brief at <http://www.chinadevelopmentbrief.com/node/454/> accessed 11 November 2008) that China wants an economic quid pro quo for its aid, rather than greater political influence. Others argue that China is waiting for the revolutionary generation to pass on (Brian McCartan, "China and Vietnam square off in Laos", *Asia Times Online*, 30 August 2008), and that this is a deliberate long-term strategy (Storey, "China and Vietnam's tug of war over Laos"; Pavin Chachavalpongpun, "With a little help from Laos' friends" at <http://www.nationmultimedia.com/2006/12/04/opinion/opinion_30020631.php> (accessed 6 December 2006).
33. See, for example, his speech to the National Assembly in June 2007. "PM announces improvements to Govt [sic]", *Vientiane Times*, 25 June 2007.
34. Burma/Myanmar, Thailand, Cambodia and Vietnam; Malaysia being commonly grouped with the maritime states of Indonesia, the Philippines, Brunei and Singapore.
35. Of close to 8,000 Hmong refugees in Thailand, almost a thousand returned to Laos in May and June 2008 and have been resettled. Others refuse to go. The Lao have complicated things by preventing independent monitors from verifying that returnees have been properly treated.
36. Lao exports to Thailand have declined from 50 per cent in 2005–06 to 30 per cent in 2007–08, while imports remained at 68 per cent. Department of International Cooperation, Ministry of Planning and Investment, Lao PDR, *Background Document: Achievements, Challenges and Future Directions within the Implementation of the National Strategies and Policies* (Roundtable Implementation Meeting, Vientiane, 24 November 2008), p. 8. Major import items include petroleum products, vehicles and machinery; while exports include minerals, timber, and electricity. Two-way trade stood at almost US$1.5 billion in 2006, a figure both sides intend to double by 2010. *Mekong News*, 28 December 2006 at <http://209.85.173.132/u/sumernet?q=cache:FRYSamSaVAEJ:www.sumernet.org/news/mekongnews_detail.asp%3Fid%3D28+investment+laos&hl=en&ct=clnk&cd=2&ie=UTF-8> (accessed 24 November 2008).

37. *IMF Country Report* no. 08/340, Lao People's Democratic Republic, Statistical Appendix.
38. *IMF Country Report* no. 08/340, Lao People's Democratic Republic, Statistical Appendix.
39. *Voice of America News*, 30 October 2008.
40. For an assessment of progress in such matters as public expenditure, financial sector reform and the reform of state-owned enterprises, all of which the World Bank has been pressing for, see The World Bank Office, Vientiane, *Lao PDR Economic Monitor*, November 2008.

Malaysia

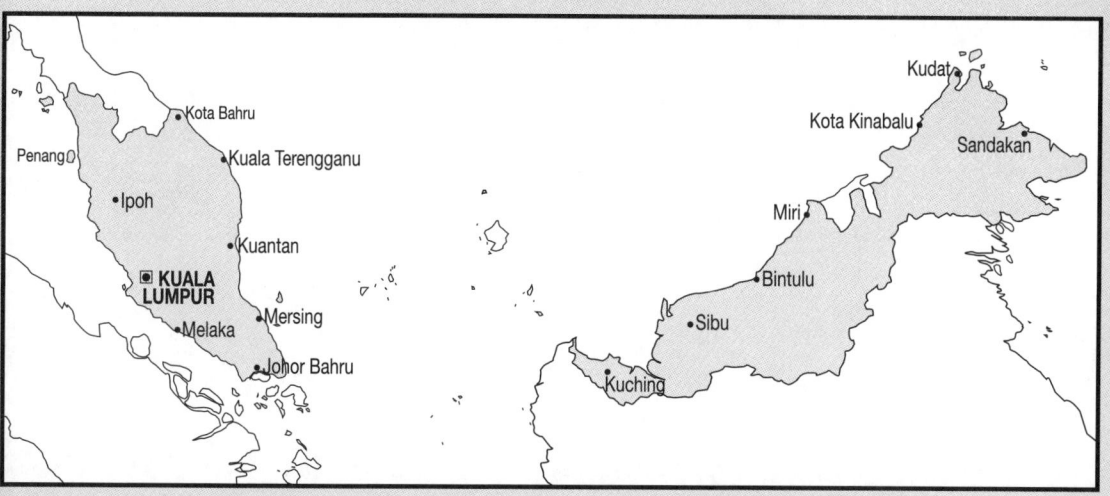

Malagasy

THE SECURITY "GAP" IN PENINSULAR MALAYSIA

Chandran Jeshurun

Events during the last twelve months since November 1974 have, if anything, convinced even most sceptics of the undeniable seriousness of the security situation in Peninsular Malaysia. Burgeoning, as it has, in the wake of the historic victories of the communist forces of Vietnam and Cambodia, the terrorist activities of the Communist Party of Malaya (CPM) and the rising toll of security forces personnel have indeed created a sense of concerned anticipation among outside observers. It is, of course, only too tempting to become somewhat alarmed about the developments in Malaysia in view of the disappointingly phlegmatic reaction of the other Southeast Asian states to the communist takeover of Vietnam, Cambodia and Laos and, for the prophets of doom, the equally disheartening way in which the much acclaimed domino theory appears to be fizzling out. Moreover, the grim forebodings of some Malaysia-watchers ever since the tragic days of May 1969 might understandably find a new lease of life with the revival of the undisguised racial connotations of the CPM's terrorist and propaganda campaign against the ruling Barisan Nasional (National Front) Government of Tun Abdul Razak.

New Trends in Communist Strategy

In the heat of the moment, especially after several sensational attacks such as the blowing up of the National Monument in August, the grenade-throwing incident at the Police Field Force Brigade Headquarters in Kuala Lumpur in October, and the daylight assassination of the Perak Chief Police Officer in Ipoh in November, it is easily forgotten that the authorities had, in fact, warned almost a year ago of the imminence of an escalation in communist

---

Reprinted from Lim Joo-Jock and S.B.D. de Silva, eds., *Southeast Asian Affairs 1976* (Singapore: Institute of Southeast Asian Studies, 1976), pp. 234–41. At the time of original publication, Chandran Jeshurun was a Research Fellow at the Institute of Southeast Asian Studies, Singapore.

terrorist activities following the disclosure of the three-way split within the CPM. The rationale for this anticipated course of events, as pointed out in the background paper, was that each of the rival factions would try and outdo the others in its revolutionary fervour by stepping up its terrorist tactics. The evidence, so far, certainly indicates the exceptionally virulent policy of the CPM (Marxist-Leninist) faction. Official reports of the Perak Chief Police Officer's assassination specially mentioned that pamphlets of the CPM (M-L) were found at the scene of the incident, while at least two clashes between the security forces and the communists in August in the border areas of Kroh in Kedah and Betong in Thailand were reported to have involved the CPM (M-L) elements. The first anniversary of the proclamation of the CPM (M-L) faction on 1 August, 1975, was also celebrated with the usual flurry of banners and flags in Kuala Lumpur and surrounding areas, and even as far south as Tampoi in the state of Johore.

While it might possibly be said that there has been little, if any, change in the guerrilla warfare on the Malaysia-Thailand border front, it does appear that there has been an upsurge in the number of contacts between the security forces and the communists compared with the twelve-month period before November 1974. One of the most significant developments in this respect has been the apparent infiltration of communist guerrillas into the Jerantut district of Pahang where there was a clash with the security forces in early October. The elimination of several guerrillas close to the border of the state of Kedah and Penang on the mainland also demonstrates how far away from their border sanctuary the communists have managed to extend their activities. Another disturbing feature of the jungle operations against the communists has been the vulnerability of the security forces patrols to being blown up by skilfully laid booby-traps and, judging by the numerous cases of death and severe maiming, this particular aspect of communist tactics might effectively undermine morale among the government's troops. On the other hand, there has been no comparable instance of the use of high explosives as in the East-West Highway incident of last year although there was the occasional attack against railway trains and road and river convoys close to the border.

The seemingly systematic assassination of Special Branch officers in various parts of Peninsular Malaysia which had been noted for its daring and frequency during the year ending November 1974 has proceeded unhindered during the past twelve months. It reached a climax on 13 November, 1975, with the brazen killing of the Perak Chief Police Officer and his driver, a police constable, in the heart of Ipoh at midday, and the apparent escape of the killers. As it was pointed out in last year's review of the communist campaign in Peninsular Malaysia, the victims of the killer squads have all been, without exception, members of the Special Branch and of Chinese descent. The Perak Chief Police Officer had, in fact, been brought over in February from Sarawak, where he had been serving for about two decades, as an obvious choice of officer to hold the most senior position in the police force in his own home state where the CPM had been particularly successful in penetrating the local Malaysian Chinese populace. The satisfaction of the Chinese community at his appointment was, in a sense, expressed by the spontaneity of the indignant condemnation of his murder by some leaders of the community. The question must therefore surely be asked as to the practicability of putting certain senior Malaysians who are for some reason — ethnic or otherwise — vulnerable to the assassin's bullets in the forefront of the war against the communists.

Perhaps most effective, in terms of publicity and its effect on public confidence, has been the series of bold attacks in urban areas, especially in the Federal capital, Kuala Lumpur. A warning of what was to come had actually been given in early July by the Malayan People's Liberation Army (MPLA), the fighting arm of the breakaway factions of the CPM, when it announced in a pamphlet that they would soon wage war in the urban areas. Accusing the government of racial and class discrimination, it declared that it would not only make its presence felt in the jungle but also in the towns. Hitherto, practically every incident in an urban situation had involved the assassination of Special Branch Officers but it was apparent from the tone of the MPLA's language that it was switching its strategy to a more obvious political line.

On 26 August, five days before the country was to celebrate National Day, a mobile sabotage squad of the CPM set off explosive devices at the National Monument in the parkland of Kuala Lumpur, hardly a few hundred yards from Parliament House, which blew off various parts of the imposing edifice which had been erected in memory of those who gave their lives in the 1948–60 Emergency. The plan had allegedly misfired for the bombs had been set to go off when the morning reveille was held at the foot of the monument but the incident nevertheless served to create a general sense of alarm in the public mind and to that extent the attempt can be considered to be a major success for the CPM's urban guerrilla warfare tactics.

Hardly had the excitement and fears of Kuala Lumpur's public died down before the communists struck again on 3 September when grenades were lobbed into the compound of the Central Brigade of the Police Field Force in the heart of the city, killing two men on the spot and injuring fifty-one others. Apart from the fact that the attack once more demonstrated the seeming impunity with which the guerrillas were able to carry out their operations, it was beyond question in the minds of the average laymen that they had established themselves firmly among the local squatter population. These two events in the Federal capital seen in conjunction with the assassination of Special Branch officers, earlier rocket and bomb attacks against the Royal Malaysian Air Force base on the outskirts of Kuala Lumpur, the camp of the 5th Battalion, Malaysian Rangers, at Port Dickson, and the 8th Battalion, Police Field Force camp at Sungei Renggam in Johore, have led some observers to conclude that "the current strategy of the communist terrorists in Malaysia is to undermine public confidence in the security forces and to damage the morale of the police and servicemen." On the other hand, it has been suggested that, as the majority of the casualties in the government's forces has been Malay and the attempted blowing up of the National Monument was an affront that touched on Malay nationalist susceptibilities, the communists have, in fact, embarked upon a more politically-oriented campaign.

It is, however, difficult to assess in any meaningful way the current trend in the CPM's strategy given the restrictions on available evidence as well as the yet unknown nature of the effects of the three-way split within the party. Official disclosures in several cases as quoted above appear to suggest that the CPM (M-L) has indeed gone on the offensive and that it was the CPM (M-L)'s MPLA — the CPM (Revolutionary Faction) is also supposed to have named its fighting arm the MPLA — which issued the proclamation of urban guerrilla warfare in July. The evidence is also strongly suggestive that the urban terrorism in Kuala Lumpur was the work of the CPM (M-L) for the Central Committee of the CPM itself has alleged that one of its underground organizations in Selangor, the Selangor Liberation League, went over to the CPM (M-L) almost to a man, calling itself the Malayan People's Liberation League (MPLL), which is the political wing of the CPM (M-L). As late as 22 March, the CMP Central Committee and the CPM (M-L) were still at each other's throats judging by the vitriolic "pamphlet war" that was raging between the two groups but there has been, oddly enough, hardly any news about the progress of the CPM (RF). A somewhat cryptic overseas report in mid-1975 has raised the possibility of "major new developments" since March but, so far, there has been no sign of any readjustment in the relations between the warring factions.

On 27 November 1975, the "Voice of the Malayan Revolution" broadcast a bitter castigation of the "so-called Marxist-Leninist faction" and made an undisguised appeal to those who had broken away from the Central Committee of the CPM, especially in the 2nd District of the 12th Regiment, to return to the fold. The commentary, in repeatedly referring to the "principal chieftains of the so-called Marxist-Leninist faction," quite clearly hoped to win back some support and, while conceding that the CPM (M-L) elements had carried out "a few military operations" recently, it accused the government of having deliberately given them "wide publicity ... to create the impression that the so-called Marxist-Leninist faction was also intent on waging armed struggle." However, it was pointed out that the CPM (M-L)'s guerrillas had adopted the "unusual practice" of camping in the "guerrilla zone", were moving about fully armed in the towns and along the main roads, and were also fraternizing openly with "enemy personnel" — indications of the "active co-operation" between the government and the CPM (M-L). The breakaway faction was also accused of having "flagrantly refused" to move south and, instead, of having created trouble in the border areas as well as sabotaging the southward operations of the CPM Central Committee's "shock brigades". All this rhetoric, in the context of the CPM's statement, "The CPM is the Force at the Core of Leading the Malayan Revolution," issued on its forty-fifth anniversary on 26 April 1975, does induce the impression that the split within the party is still a fundamental problem and remains unsolved. To that extent, at least, the Malaysian Government is unlikely to overreact to the recent upsurge in communist terrorism.

The Government's Response

The Malaysian Government, in the light of these developments, has naturally been put on the defensive both in facing the domestic population as well as in maintaining its image externally. Not unlike other governments faced with similar situations, it has undoubtedly boosted its military effort and deployed a greater number of troops against the communists than at any time since the end of the 1948–60 Emergency. Indeed, the reports of the frequent contacts with the guerrillas are a clear indication of the expanded scale of operations especially in the border region. The emergence of the urban guerrilla threat, on the other hand, is bound to test the nation's military resources severely and the government has, in fact, announced further increases in the strength of the armed forces and plans to acquire more sophisticated weapons. Nothing, of course, can be said about the counter-intelligence activities of the Special Branch but there can be little doubt that the entire machinery of the government in this respect will come under close scrutiny and, probably, result in a degree of resuscitation. Rather strangely, the Minister of Home Affairs himself revealed in late October that government agents had been penetrating the CPM for the past thirteen years, the implication being that the situation was well under control. Notwithstanding such self-confidence on the part of the authorities, it would be indeed difficult to believe that active steps are not, in fact, being taken to bolster the varied traditional instruments of combat in the fight against the CPM, the more so because of the country's unique experience in the past.

Despite the paucity of information regarding the government's reaction to the increased tempo of CPM terrorist and subversive operations on the military and intelligence levels, one of the recent symptoms of an official awareness of the need to involve the ordinary public more closely with internal security measures has been the launching of the Rukun Tetangga scheme, which might be loosely translated as a Community Self-Reliance project. After having gazetted the Emergency Essential (Community Self-Reliance) Regulations 1975, the government announced that all able-bodied men between the ages of eighteen and fifty-five would be compulsorily liable to register and serve in unarmed patrols of their own neighbourhoods within areas that are designated Rukun Tetangga sectors. It was apparent from the start that the scheme was primarily directed towards the densely populated urban centres of Peninsular Malaysia and the first sector to be designated for the Rukun Tetangga scheme was in Kuala Lumpur.

Public response to the Rukun Tetangga scheme, especially among the English-educated middle-class residents of Kuala Lumpur and other major towns, has naturally been rather encouraging and subsequent events such as the grenade attack on the Police Field Force Brigade Headquarters in Kuala Lumpur have no doubt brought added justification to the idea. Far more significant in the long run will be the great impetus that the scheme can give to the growth of communal goodwill and understanding, an objective that is particularly vital in the haphazardly created urban residential areas along the west coast of the Peninsula. As it is common knowledge that there has been a visible desire on the part of Malaysian Chinese leaders for some time for greater opportunities for their community in the armed services and the police, the government has attempted to partly diffuse the pressure in this respect by proclaiming that the Rukun Tetangga scheme is in fact a form of national service. However, a certain amount of doubt has, admittedly, been created owing to the fact that neither the Ministry of Defence nor the Ministry of Home Affairs has anything to do with the scheme directly, the chief political co-ordinator being in the Prime Minister's Department. However, there seems to be some provision for the security authorities to have a say in the management of the Rukun Tetangga scheme through the National Security Council whose Secretary is the Deputy Director General of the organization.

At another level of legislative counter measures against the rampant terrorism in the country, the government came out with the rather more ominous Essential (Security Cases) Regulations 1975. Without going into the legal details of the new legislation, the government's objectives might be summarized in the words of the Attorney General himself as: (*a*) the protection of witnesses who are at present unable through fear of reprisal to give evidence in cases involving national security; (*b*) to obtain more convictions in a court of law of persons engaging in the subversion of national security who are getting away scot-free under existing laws; and, generally, (*c*) "to gain the people's confidence" in the government and the rule of law. One of the provisions of the new regulations which permits the evidence of a witness to be given in camera in the absence of the accused and his counsel and, if given in his presence, allows the witness to wear a mask or hood to hide his identity appears to have caused quite a lot of uneasiness both among the legal profession and the ordinary public.

Initially, there was some consternation as to the lack of any definition of what constitutes a "security case" and questions were raised as to whether the new laws were "intended to be used selectively ... as a deterrent ... or to be used widely, on every possible occasion." The government's announcement having been made only a few days before the Third Malaysian Law Conference in mid-October, it was inevitable that the Regulations came under sustained fire from the assembled delegates while other bodies such as the Associated Chinese Chambers of Commerce expressed alarm at the possibility of the new system of prosecution degenerating into some of the terrifying practices of the Japanese Occupation. The Opposition parties not unexpectedly rejected the legal measures on the grounds that the government "cannot legislate against communism" and that "no amount of laws can bring peace and security if the government does not solve the basic grievances and needs of the people." Probably as a result of all these criticisms, the government relented somewhat from its original tough line and a number of important amendments, which are discussed in the previous paper, have been made to the new regulations. Meanwhile, the Prime Minister himself has given the assurance that the regulations would be enforced with great care and that they would be withdrawn when the security situation returned to normal.

One of the most unhealthy and worrying features in the general security situation that came to light in the latter half of the year is the widespread circulation of rumours, all of which are ostensibly designed to discredit the government and national leaders as well as to fan racial tensions. The Prime Minister, Tun Razak, drew attention to them in September saying that the stories of ministers packing their bags getting ready to flee the country in the event of trouble, presumably in the footsteps of Thieu and Lon Nol, were the work of antinational elements. Since then there have been numerous warnings of the threat to security that is posed by these rumours, notably by the Deputy Prime Minister, Datuk Hussein Onn, the Minister of Home Affairs, Tan Sri Ghazali Shafie, and the Deputy Minister in the Prime Minister's Department, Datuk Abdullah Ahmad. The president of the Malaysian Chinese Association (MCA), Datuk Lee San Choon, has also pointed to the possibility of the

CPM outrages, such as the attack on the National Monument and the Police Field Force Brigade Headquarters, being directly intended to heighten racial tensions in the country. One of the specific targets of these rumours has been the security forces and the campaign in the Ipoh area appears to have been sufficiently virulent to merit a public denial by the late Chief Police Officer of Perak that armed men in camouflage uniform were going around arresting anyone who possessed red cloth. Nevertheless, it would seem that there had been some misunderstanding over the house-to-house searches conducted by the Police in the course of their antisubversive investigations, for a delegation from the MCA Youth body called on the Inspector General of Police in September reportedly to obtain clarification. It is also interesting that the Inspector General of Police is supposed to have said that if any of the captured or surrendered communists and their agents were to give the names of any Malay comrades he would personally direct every Malay house to be searched as well. But all said and done, it is difficult to believe that the government will treat the "smear" campaign lightly in view of the dangerous potential for violence that unfettered rumour-mongering has had in the country since the troubled days of 1969.

Some Gaps in Security

In reviewing the CPM's strategy, one foreign journal recently noted: "Obviously, the guerrillas hope to exploit the 'sensitive issue' of the communal balance within Malaysia, cultivating the seeds of discontent among the non-Malays while meting out 'punishment' to those non-Malays who publicly identify themselves with the forces of law and order." It then bemoaned the fact that, although Malaysia "once boasted a propaganda machine which, during the years of the 1948–60 Emergency, played almost as important a role as the security forces," in the face of the new threat to security "this once superb 'agitprop' machine is almost idle." It must be admitted that the government has not, either by its actions or by its statements of policy, so far shown any particular awareness of the tremendous use that can be made of its vast mass media resources. Both through Radio and Television Malaysia and the Information Services, not to mention a host of other ancillary units, the government should be able, under efficient and pragmatic management, to effectively counter much of the erosion of confidence that is taking place in the public mind through the invidious process of the local "grapevine". It is no secret in Kuala Lumpur and the major towns that, quite apart from the prevalence of subversive rumours, there has been an epidemic of anonymous letters and pamphlets or *surat melayang* mostly to do with political power struggles and the alleged corrupt practices of people in high places within the ruling party which are hardly a credit to the government. But the government's mass media services seem curiously oblivious to this aspect of public opinion-making and instead plod on wearily along the old nation-building trail of slogans and rosy pictures.

Although there is no reliable measure of public reaction to official broadcasting policy, not many will quarrel with the former Prime Minister, Tunku Abdul Rahman's laconic comment about television programmes: "Too much of a good thing can have the effect of stultifying the efforts of government. They start off with the news of what each Minister is trying to do and end up with what the Assistant Ministers are trying to do. In the meantime, the public is interested to know what is happening in the country and what is happening in the world." In the context of the boringly obvious assertion that "the engagement of the people in the struggle" against the CPM is imperative, it might justifiably be asked if the government is not committing the grave blunder of neglecting one of its major channels of communication with the society at large in allowing the broadcasting and information services at its disposal to be squandered away. Among other things, the invaluable lessons learned during the 1948–60 Emergency in wearing down the revolutionary fibre of the CPM cadres and guerrillas through the sustained use of the mass media — in the place of the "voice aircraft" and the air-dropping of pamphlets, there is now the transistor and the television set — can surely be brought up to date under intelligent planning. At the same time, unlike in the previous case, there is more than ample justification for making the building of a new Malaysian nation the crux of the whole exercise in terms of the New Economic Policy and the restructuring of society instead of being merely limited to the winning of the war. That is possibly one important scenario in which the reappraisal of current radio and television programmes as well as broadcasting policy as a whole might be meaningfully conducted.

Another urgent area for government's action is that of the New Villages, the nomenclature of which, having been set up almost a quarter of a century ago, was aptly described by the first Cabinet Minister appointed to look into their affairs, Dr. Lim Keng Yaik, as "a misnomer". While the statistics regarding New Villages are not always in agreement, they, nevertheless, offer an intriguing insight into the problem that exists today. In 1954, it was estimated that there were 480 New Villages throughout Peninsular Malaysia with a population of some 573,000 of whom 86% were of Chinese descent. Dr. Lim Keng Yaik in 1973 quoted a figure of 420 New Villages with a population of 840,000. His successor to the ministerial post, Michael Chen, recently stated that there were 1.5 million people living in 465 New Villages of which 150 were in the state of Perak where the CPM's underground network has been particularly well entrenched. There is no escaping the reality of the security threat in the New Villages which is beginning to closely resemble the pattern of subversion and infiltration that prevailed during the 1948–60 Emergency. The Prime Minister himself has said as much in referring to the cultivation of food for the guerrillas by their sympathizers in the Jerantut district of Pahang and the Perak Government has been repeatedly harping on the subversive activities of the inhabitants of its New Villages.

Dr. Lim Keng Yaik, perhaps the most sympathetic voice for the New Villages in the government so far, listed their chief problems in 1973 as: (*a*) the lack of land for cultivation and housing and the difficulty in converting Temporary Occupation Licenses (TOLs) to leases; (*b*) the breakdown of administration in the New Villages which has left them in something of a limbo as far as development was concerned, not to speak of the day-to-day running of their affairs; (*c*) the lack of employment opportunities especially for the young; and (*d*) the poor provision of social amenities and other facilities. Despite the government's acceptance of the need for positive action in hauling the New Villages out of the economic and social rut that they had been allowed to fall into, it had only spent the meagre sum of M$60,496 on Dr. Lim's portfolio in the first six months of 1972. Nevertheless, major advances were made in 1973 in solving the problem of landlessness through negotiations with individual state governments and plans were drawn up for the long-term economic development of the New Villages. Under these plans, New Villages which had economic potentialities were to be developed into integrated townships while those which were not viable were to be gradually disbanded and their inhabitants given the opportunity to migrate to more viable ones.

Despite these hopeful initiatives, Michael Chen in September 1975 was still stressing the problem of finding new land for agricultural and housing purposes. More significantly, he revealed that under the tender system in the past only about one-third of the funds allocated for the building of roads, drains and other social amenities was actually used for those purposes. Almost M$3 million were to be distributed among the New Villages in grants during 1975 and the Minister also hoped to use a M$10 million revolving fund to solve the acute housing problem. But it is clear, however, from the mention of the "sites and services scheme" and of the need for the *gotong royong* (self-help) spirit among the New Villagers, that for the time being, at least, the government does not intend to embark upon any massive scheme of redevelopment of the New Villages comparable to other government land development schemes.

There is no gainsaying that the New Villages constitute one of the major security "gaps" in the country and that the task of improving their welfare and transforming them from, as one scholar once put it, "reservoirs of resentment into bastions of loyal Malayan citizenry" is a challenge that the government will have to face squarely, sooner than later. Moreover, as Johore, Pahang and Selangor have the largest number of New Villages next to Perak and would naturally be the focuses of the CPM's attempts to expand its underground network, the urgency of the matter can hardly be exaggerated. If there is a justification for punitive action against some of the New Villages in Perak and Pahang where the security situation is especially grave, it should not be blandly assumed that such action will necessarily act as a deterrent on those in Selangor and Johore who are disaffected for one reason or other. The MCA's remarkable lack of enterprise in pursuing the cause of the New Villages objectively should also not be regarded as an excuse for the government to drag its feet.

The facts, meagre as they are, simply militate against any further indifference to the plight of the New Villages. In a little less than twenty years their population has almost trebled while living conditions and economic opportunities have worsened rather than improved. Half a million tradition-minded people of Chinese descent have been left to multiply in the same mental isolation that they had been in as squatters twenty years ago. Neither education, nor the mass media, nor indeed the political process has served to assimilate them into the mainstream of national life. In the interval, it may indeed be true, as Michael Chen and Tun Razak have asserted, that some of the original New Villagers have embarked upon business ventures and also undoubtedly engaged in secret society activities which have enriched them to the point where they are now able to afford "cars which are usually referred to as status symbols". It would surely be a strange logic, however, to use this as the *raison d'etre* for demanding the undivided loyalty of the majority to a concept which it is least able to comprehend. The remarkable preference of the major New Villages around Kuala Lumpur for the Opposition when the rest of the country was giving Tun Razak's National Front such a thumping victory in last year's General Elections is an ominous pointer of the real state of things. In fact, given the essential good sense of the present political leadership and the new nationalism of the concerned Malaysian, it would not be too much to expect an enlightened policy of gradually winning over the youth of the New Villages to the common ideals of the New Economic Policy. Certainly, for a start, there is an excellent case for refurbishing the services of the Information Department and gearing them for a determined "hearts and minds" offensive not unlike what was so successfully conducted on at least two occasions in the recent past. In this respect, it is of interest to note that the Sultan of Perak has urged Radio and Television Malaysia to give priority to special programmes for the inhabitants of New Villages and the Orang Asli (aboriginal people) settlements. It is a telling testimony on the need to fill this particular security "gap" that such advice from a high personage has to be proffered in public.

THE "BATTLE ROYAL"
The UMNO Elections of 1987*

Shamsul A.B.

UMNO (United Malays National Organisation) has occupied a unique position and has played a crucial role in the growth of the post-war Malaysian social system, particularly in the political sphere. Since its formation in 1946, it has been the single most influential institution to have shaped not only the political contours but also the overall social terrain in Malaysia. Since independence in 1957, it has remained the backbone of the Malaysian Government until today.

Central to any discussion of UMNO is its leadership. This is unavoidable because whatever happens within the leadership, particularly at the top among its national leaders — whether there is consensus or conflict amongst them — determines to a large extent UMNO's internal stability and hence to a great extent that of the country too. This was amply demonstrated, for example, when a leadership crisis which occurred in UMNO in the mid-1970s led to a series of other crises within the National Front coalition with the political situation in Malaysia becoming very tense during that period. At that time, UMNO was experiencing a "changing of guards" at the top initiated by the late Tun Abdul Razak in the early 1970s after he took over the premiership and the UMNO presidency from Tunku Abdul Rahman. It was under him that the now famous New Economic Policy (NEP), aimed mainly at "eradicating poverty" and "restructuring society" within Malaysia, was introduced. This policy clearly favours the Malays and other indigenous groups collectively known as *bumiputera* (literally, "son of the soil"), especially in the economic and educational spheres. As Razak saw it then, the successful implementation of this pro-

---

Reprinted in abridged format from Mohammed Ayoob and Ng Chee Yuen, eds., *Southeast Asian Affairs 1988* (Singapore: Institute of Southeast Asian Studies, 1988), pp. 170–88. At the time of original publication, Shamsul A.B. was an Associate Professor in the Department of Anthropology and Sociology, National University of Malaysia, Bangi, Selangor.

Malay affirmative action strategy could only be carried out by the better-educated and technocratically oriented leaders. Therefore, the 1974 general election witnessed the rise of an élite group of Tun Razak's protégés, mostly hand-picked by him, some of whom became politicians and Cabinet ministers overnight. Amongst them were Dr Mahathir Mohamad and Musa Hitam, both expelled from UMNO by Tunku Abdul Rahman for "insubordination" after the 1969 general election, and Tengku Razaleigh, considered by many then as a "Malay economic genius".

This move by Tun Razak was resisted by the *pimpinan lama*, or "old leadership", within UMNO and subsequently a crisis erupted within UMNO's national leadership which affected the grass-roots leadership as well. The latter crisis has received less attention from most analysts than the former although it was as serious as, or perhaps more serious than, the national crisis. The "old leadership", both at the national and grass-roots level, resisted Tun Razak's move because they were slowly losing their influence which had traditionally been based on patronage-distribution activities. The *pimpinan baru*, or "new leadership", began to gain political clout through the effective implementation of their centralized and technocratic administration which was strongly and positively felt by grass-roots supporters as well as the emerging Malay entrepreneurial group. The "new leadership" owed its political success to the excellent overall economic conditions that existed in Malaysia then. Unfortunately, before Tun Razak and his group of protégés could establish and consolidate their positions, especially within UMNO, Tun Razak died in January 1976. Down but not out, the "old leadership" within UMNO fought back to restore their power and influence. Hence an intense and complex leadership struggle within UMNO took place in 1976–77, one which set the tone for successive ones.[1] However, the "new leadership", now under the business-like and no-nonsense leadership of Datuk (later Tun) Hussein Onn, eventually emerged victorious. But this victory was not without its toll, with three of Tun Razak's protégés ending up as political detainees for alleged involvement in "communist activities".[2] One of the more influential personalities from the "old leadership" group, Harun Idris, ended up in Pudu Jail, Kuala Lumpur, after being convicted of corruption. By the time of the July 1978 general election, the "new leadership" had consolidated its position as the central leadership both within UMNO and in the National Front coalition. They achieved a resounding victory in the election.

However, it was in that same month (July 1978) that for the first time ever in UMNO's history its incumbent president was challenged. Datuk Hussein Onn, who was actually the acting UMNO President at that time having taken over Tun Razak's position after the latter's death, was challenged by Sulaiman Palastin, a candidate put up by the "old leadership" during the 31st UMNO General Assembly in order to register their disapproval over the way Hussein Onn treated Harun Idris who by then had been expelled from UMNO and convicted of corruption. Although Hussein Onn won hands down, a "sacred" UMNO tradition was "demystified". By 1978 all the top UMNO leadership posts had been contested, except that of the deputy president, an extremely important one in UMNO's and Malaysia's context because virtually everyone who had held that position, with the exception of Tun Dr Ismail, became deputy prime minister, subsequently UMNO president and later prime minister.

Therefore, the claim made by some observers in 1976, after Datuk Harun's expulsion from UMNO, that UMNO is still "peasant in outlook with traditional values that regard any form of open defiance of the leadership as impolite"[3] was proven inaccurate and insensitive to the social reality prevailing in Malaysia. This reality was that the Malays, mainly as a result of the implementation of the NEP, were experiencing tremendous socio-economic change, necessarily uneven in nature. This in turn had sharpened their social consciousness, particularly their critical and political consciousness. Furthermore, those who voted at the UMNO General Assemblies of the 1970s and early 1980s were mainly rural intelligentsia, educated urban upper- and middle-class professionals and bureaucrats, old and new Malay entrepreneurs but not peasants anymore as in the 1950s and 1960s. They were not only highly democratically conscious but also critical and vocal as many of them were pre-1974 local university graduates who received their education both in lecture theatres or at speakers' corners listening to fiery anti-government speeches and on the streets breathing tear gas and fighting baton-wielding police. Though very much mellowed by the comfortable life they led soon after graduation they were anything but dumb yes-men and often became the "backroom boys" or "think tanks" for various top UMNO leaders, who were constantly conducting silent guerrilla war–like activities against one another to preserve their dominant positions within the party. The combination of these external and internal factors have transformed the ground rules of UMNO internal politics from one that had been guided by the so-called traditional values in the 1950s and 1960s, to one which has come to be dictated by crude materialistic values (or "money politics" as Dr Mahathir himself called it) and characterized by open but controlled hostility and opposition in the 1970s and 1980s.[4]

It is against this background that one must situate and understand the origins of the intense and bitter personal rivalry that developed and continued for about half a decade (1980–85) between Musa Hitam and Tengku Razaleigh in their battles for the post of UMNO's deputy president, first in 1981 (when the post was contested for the first time ever in UMNO's electoral history) and then in 1984. Therefore, by 1981 all of UMNO's top posts (president, deputy president, vice-president and those in UMNO Youth and UMNO Women wings) had been contested. This is significant in UMNO's context because after 1981 any challenge to its top leadership was seen by its members, at all levels, as a sign of their "political maturity" and not as being "un-Malay", because before this any form of open defiance of the leadership had been considered not only impolite but heretical in terms of Malay traditional values.

It was during the protracted battles between Musa and Razaleigh that this "political maturity" developed and was realized. Two identifiable factions developed within UMNO, led by Musa and Razaleigh respectively. Before this any such division was only felt at the top but this time it went down to the grass roots — to the *warung* ("stall") and Malay-dominated trade union meetings in the urban areas and to the *kedai kopi* ("coffee shop") and *surau* ("small prayer house") in the rural areas. *Orang Musa* ("Musa's man") and *orang Razaleigh* ("Razaleigh's man") were not only labels but often became the "key phrases" which opened or terminated a business or any other discussion, guaranteed or denied an individual getting a contract or a scholarship, and expedited or delayed an application for a job, a licence, or even the transfer of a school teacher from an *ulu* ("remote") to an urban school and vice versa. In short, the idiom of political interactions, especially at the grass roots, whether amongst UMNO members or its sympathizers, became highly divisive in content and nature, articulating the leadership conflict at the top in the dialect of local issues, in a manner never seen before within UMNO.[5]

Although Musa won in both the contests, both he and Razaleigh were embittered and bruised. Their supporters suffered greatly too, despite the fact that Musa and Razaleigh patched up again, at least in public, after the event. The "Musa faction" and the "Razaleigh faction" remained at the grass roots long after these battles and they were in fact preparing for the next round of contests when Musa suddenly resigned from his ministerial posts, although not his UMNO deputy presidency in February 1986. This was a decision which shocked Mahathir and his men. This sudden turn of political events certainly complicated matters at the top level within UMNO but things became even more complicated and confused at the grass-roots level especially within the "Musa faction", where there were many supporters of Mahathir as well, because Musa was the Mahathir-endorsed candidate in the contest for the post of UMNO deputy president both in 1981 and 1984. Some supporters of the "Razaleigh faction" were overjoyed to see the Musa-Mahathir split and saw it as clearing the path for Razaleigh's comeback to the top. However, as later events demonstrated, this was not the general feeling of the "Razaleigh faction". They might have disliked Musa but they hated Mahathir for his alleged double-dealing now made obvious by Musa's resignation and Mahathir's exposé of Musa's letter to him in July 1984 asking that the defeated Razaleigh be kept out of the Cabinet, a request to which Mahathir did not accede. So the stage was set for what was dubbed, by a local daily, as *peperangan antara gergasi*, or the "war of the giants", in UMNO's 1987 elections.

The "War of the Giants": Its Origins

The implementation of the NEP has resulted in a rapid, almost phenomenal, expansion of the Malay middle class. A large proportion of the new Malay middle class, comprising civil servants, professionals, and entrepreneurs, belongs to UMNO. Like middle classes elsewhere, its expansion in Malaysia has engendered its own internal contradictions as different factions within this class struggle for the control of economic resources and access to political positions, in turn heightening competing interests and aspirations and, therefore, increasing the potential for open conflicts. In the Malaysian state where there exists a concentration of political power and, of late, a sizeable portion of economic wealth in the hands of the Malay middle and upper classes, it is inevitable that when the state cannot accommodate all the competing interests and aspirations, its negative expressions are mediated through UMNO politics. This is not at all surprising for UMNO as a political party, since its inception has embodied and articulated all that the Malay middle and upper classes want to protect, preserve, and achieve. This increasingly intense struggle for power within UMNO, which began in the mid-1970s, continued through the early 1980s, reaching its height at the 34th UMNO General Assembly when the incumbent UMNO President was seriously challenged. It was not simply a personal challenge to Mahathir, the President, but to his whole team by an alternative team led by Razaleigh and Musa. UMNO was offered an unprecedented alternative involving not only an alternative president and deputy president but also vice-presidents and Supreme Council members. The stakes were high — the highest in the country — for they involved the prime ministership and other important Cabinet posts. In short, Malaysians for the first time in their country's post-war history were offered a team of alternative leaders.

The struggle for power within UMNO would not have escalated to such a height if Malaysia's economy had not been suffering from a prolonged economic recession. As long as the economy was booming, the competing interests and aspirations of the Malay upper and middle classes were relatively easily met and fulfilled by those in power. However, when the economy suffered from serious set-backs, those who were adversely affected, especially the group of Malays mentioned above, became bitter and frustrated and ultimately turned against those in power because they were desperate, disenchanted, and disillusioned. It is, therefore, not surprising when those who were looking for scapegoats transformed their dissatisfactions into political action, first, by publicly denouncing the government and its leaders and, subsequently, by challenging them openly in the political arena. However, it was not only the upper and middle classes who were feeling the negative effects of the economic downturn. Petty-traders, civil servants, even rural dwellers, were affected adversely. Therefore, the question of the recession and the need to revive the economy immediately became the rallying point for the Razaleigh-Musa team. On its own, the economic issue was not sufficient to attract enough supporters to the Razaleigh-Musa team. But a combination of this issue and a host of other issues which came into public attention from 1980, namely, the financial scandals within UMNO and its National Front partners, the mismanagement of the economy, the "kitchen Cabinet" issue, and Mahathir's allegedly "dictatorial approach" in running UMNO and the country, enabled the Razaleigh-Musa team to command and mobilize the support of UMNO dissidents and to openly challenge Mahathir's leadership.

From 1980 onwards various financial scandals, many of them associated with Mahathir's close associates within and outside his Cabinet, became public. The Pan-Electric scandal, which resulted in the arrest and conviction of Tan Koon Swan, the MCA (Malaysian Chinese Association) President and a Cabinet minister, by the authorities in Singapore, was one of the bigger scandals. There were other scandals too, such as those involving the government-controlled Sports Toto and Employment Provident Fund, and the UMNO-owned United Engineering Malaysia and Fleet Group. These scandals were used by Mahathir's opponents within UMNO as proof of his alleged tolerance of corruption and nepotism amongst individuals closest to him. When a company called Zenecon Bumi Sdn. Bhd., controlled by Mahathir's sister-in-law, was awarded a huge subcontracting job to build the Dayabumi forty-storey office block owned by the government-controlled Urban Development Authority (UDA), the host of accusations made by Mahathir's opponents became more credible in the eyes of UMNO members and of the general public. This scandal-ridden image certainly did not help the Mahathir leadership to fight off the accusation that his government was facing a "crisis of confidence". It was made more difficult by another accusation, that is, the alleged mismanagement of the already deteriorating economy.

The Razaleigh-Musa camp repeatedly mentioned that the economic crisis experienced by Malaysia could not be attributed solely to adverse international economic conditions. The opposition claimed that Mahathir's wrong priorities implemented at the wrong time and resulting in the mismanagement of the economy were equally responsible for the country's economic crisis. The most popular example cited as a "proof" of Mahathir's mismanagement was the Proton Saga car project and related heavy industries schemes which the country could ill-afford during bad times. A number of other projects, such as the Penang Bridge and Dayabumi, were cited by Mahathir's critics within UMNO to emphasize the "truth" of their claims although a few of the projects were necessary in view of the expanding industrial activities in the whole country despite unfavourable economic conditions. Objectively it was unfair to hold Mahathir solely responsible for all the economic woes suffered by Malaysia but in an increasingly hostile political situation fuelled by the economic recession every single thing he did, particularly his "mistakes", came under close scrutiny by all parties concerned, especially his opponents in UMNO, and were often exaggerated. In the popular mind Mahathir became "the man who caused all the problems".

It is not difficult to understand why such a perception prevailed if we take into consideration the fact that Mahathir was seen as being very "cliquish" and "dictatorial" in the way he ran the government and conducted business, political or economic, both as UMNO President and as Prime Minister. He was accused of having a small business clique which he favoured and a smaller "kitchen Cabinet" within his Cabinet, thus giving the general impression that the economy and the politics of the country were in the hands of the "élite of the élites". As a consequence, those outside this very close circle of Mahathir's allies claimed that they had only limited access to him. Besides, he was also accused of paying little attention to views different from his, from within his Cabinet, from UMNO national officials, and from those outside the government; hence the accusation that he was "dictatorial".[6]

Rightly or wrongly, these serious accusations and allegations were made not only by his opponents within UMNO but also by those outside, mainly non-governmental organizations (NGOs) such as Aliran and the Consumer Association of Penang, and UMNO's traditional political opponents, Parti Islam (PAS) and the Democratic Action Party (DAP). In short, Mahathir was fighting a many-sided battle, within and outside his political party. Although he was unable to deal effectively with the opponents within UMNO, despite declassifying documents pertaining to three major controversial projects (the Penang Bridge, Dayabumi, and the Proton Saga) which had previously been classified official secrets thus demonstrating that Razaleigh and Musa were partly responsible in endorsing the projects which they now criticized, Mahathir to a certain extent was able to dent the image of his opponents outside UMNO. Through his ministers and his own statements Mahathir announced to the public that the government knew that some NGOs received aid from abroad and suspected that at least two of them, which were never identified, had Zionist backing — a severe charge indeed to be made in a Muslim country. PAS, DAP, and NGOs were portrayed by UMNO stalwarts as thorns in the flesh of the country, attempting to tear the country's political and social fabric apart by perennially conducting smear campaigns against the government and constantly working to create unrest and destroy the government.[7] As far as Mahathir's opponents inside UMNO were concerned, any washing of dirty linen in public by those outside UMNO, at that point in time, was a great help to their cause of bringing about change in UMNO. This objective was clearly indicated in their slogan for the campaign "*Kami Mahu Perubahan, Razaleigh-Musa, Azam Baru 1987*" [We Want Change, Razaleigh-Musa, New Resolution 1987] which was inscribed even on cheap throw-away cigarette lighters distributed to those who attended their rallies.

It was very clear that the "war of the giants" that broke out within UMNO in 1987 had been the result of a simultaneous interplay of the larger social forces and UMNO's specific internal circumstances. The very same factors had also heightened the critical consciousness of UMNO members and forced them to boldly evaluate their leadership and seriously consider alternatives, something which had never entered their minds before. In a sense, UMNO and the Malay community, as a result of the "war", became more democratic and increasingly uninhibited in expressing dissenting views. This, of course, has not been without its costs as recent events in Malaysia in October and November 1987, including detentions under ISA and the banning of newspapers, have painfully shown. The consequences of all this were felt not only by UMNO members, from top to bottom, but also by the rest of the Malaysians.

The "Battle Royal": Clutching at Straws

Even in late February 1987 it was not very clear what the challenge to Mahathir would be at the 24 April contest, and who exactly his opposite number was going to be — Musa or Razaleigh. However, anticipating a no-holds-barred fight, the UMNO Supreme Council decided in December 1986 to set up an Ethics Committee, consisting of party veterans, to deal with unfair election practices at the grass-roots and national UMNO elections. But it was quite clear that the committee was ineffective, as pointed out by its Chairperson, Khir Johari, because reports on vote-buying practices, which the committee had been set up to stop, were not forthcoming despite allegations by both opposing camps in UMNO that vote-buying was rife.[8]

Although Razaleigh and Musa did not declare officially that they were contesting for the posts of president and deputy president, respectively, until the eleventh hour, from the weeks when divisional party elections began on 6 February to the end of February, both Mahathir and Razaleigh received nominations for the post of president while Musa and Ghafar were nominated for the post of deputy president. As the weeks went by, the rumour that Razaleigh had sealed a pact with his former archrival, Musa, to oppose the expected Mahathir and Ghafar combination no longer remained a rumour. Things came out into the open at a symbolic divisional party meeting on Musa's homeground, Segamat, Johor, on 27 February, when Razaleigh, invited to officiate at the meeting, fired his first salvo (of course, aimed at Mahathir) by asking his supporters not to wait till after midnight to see him because of fear of being blacklisted and harassed by the cronies of the incumbent UMNO leader. At the same time, he reminded them not to fear the one they vote in every three years even more than they fear God. Before making this statement, Razaleigh invited Musa, and the latter accepted, to officiate at the former's divisional meeting in Gua Musang, Kelantan, on 20 March. With that, as far as UMNO members were concerned, the Razaleigh-Musa pact was confirmed but it was ignored by the party's Ethics Committee which would have had to take action against Razaleigh and Musa had it recognized that such a pact existed.[9]

What took place during the next seven weeks, throughout March and up to 24 April, was the fiercest electoral battle and campaign ever conducted in UMNO's forty-year history with nothing spared by both sides. Almost every day, there were official functions throughout the peninsula attended by leaders from both camps; seminars, conferences, and book launchings also proliferated. In short, both camps were desperate for public attention and for their side of the story to be heard. But it was obvious that the local newspapers, especially the English and Malay dailies owned by UMNO interests, were giving more space in their front pages to the Mahathir-Ghafar camp and in the inside pages to the Razaleigh-Musa team. The television stations gave even less coverage to the latter. However, one had to attend the various UMNO division meetings to get the real picture and to feel the intense campaigning that was carried on by both camps, particularly for the election of the all-important team of delegates to attend and vote at the UMNO General Assembly. Eleven delegates were to be elected from each division with each parliamentary constituency forming one division.[10]

More often than not the incumbent divisional chiefs were either Members of Parliament (MPs) or state assemblymen who formed the core supporters of the Mahathir-Ghafar camp, since their appointments were the result of patronage by the incumbent UMNO leaders. But other members of the divisional committees were not automatically loyal to Mahathir. In fact some of them were UMNO businessmen, public servants, and members of the local intelligentsia who were disgruntled over the recession or for other reasons. Therefore, it was at the divisional level where the conflict between Mahathir-Ghafar and Razaleigh-Musa was expressed most clearly and often crudely. Issues such as economic recession, Mahathir's "kitchen Cabinet", and financial scandals within UMNO, which were important at the national level, were taken for granted and often relegated to peripheral status at the local level. Instead, juicy personal stories about Musa's sex life, Razaleigh's favourite whisky, Mahathir's preference for Daimler over Proton Saga and the imported Italian marble in his toilet at Sri Perdana, his official residence, Ghafar's impending bankruptcy case, Anwar's divorce from his first wife and his attempt to ABIMize UMNO (ABIM is the Malay acronym for the Malaysian Islamic Youth Movement founded by Anwar), Daim's three-tier swimming pool (though he does not swim), and the colour scheme of the built-in cupboards in Rafidah's newly constructed mansion at Bangsar hill, became hot topics for discussions and in speeches made by local supporters of both camps. The personal smear campaign style adopted was directed at local divisional chiefs and politicians irrespective of which side they belonged. Undoubtedly the battle at the grass roots was not only bitter but savage!

Therefore, it was not surprising at all when division heads, like Mohamed Rahmat of UMNO Pulai Division in Johor, who urged members to nominate Mahathir and Ghafar for the top posts, were ignored or opposed by the delegates at the divisional meetings who, instead, voted to nominate Razaleigh and Musa. However, overt displays of loyalty, such as the one quoted above, were meaningless if Mahathir supporters were being voted in as delegates to the UMNO General Assembly which was to elect the leadership. To complicate matters further at the local level, the Razaleigh faction and the Musa faction still remained, especially in Johor and Kelantan and in some other UMNO divisions throughout the peninsula. This was the result of the bitter battles between the two figures for the deputy president's post, in 1981 and 1984, the wounds of which were not healed even though the Razaleigh-Musa pact was now on. As a consequence, although there was an understanding that Razaleigh was to contest for the presidency and Musa for the post of deputy in the April 1987 elections, nominations for Musa to be president and Razaleigh to be his deputy were quite substantial in number. Therefore, in effect, at the local level, there were three main factions operating, those of Mahathir, Musa, and Razaleigh. Of the three, Musa's seemed to be the weakest for many of his supporters had been Mahathir's men earlier and who returned to Mahathir's camp after the elections. Many UMNO divisional leaders and committee members believed that it was for this reason that Musa agreed to become Razaleigh's running mate, although many armchair analysts argued that Musa felt safer to enter the race as an incumbent despite the fact that he was seen more as the challenger because his anticipated opponent was Ghafar, the Deputy Prime Minister. In other words, none of the camps could be sure as to who amongst the elected divisional delegates were their supporters or opponents, or were merely fence-sitters.

By the end of March when the full list of delegates to the UMNO General Assembly was finalized, comprising official delegates who could vote (a total of 1,479, of which 1,434 were from the 133 UMNO divisions, thirty-five were Supreme Council members, and five each were from the Women and Youth wings) and observers from UMNO branches and divisions (about 13,500), the contenders were already on the road visiting as many divisions, and meeting as many elected delegates as possible. During that period the campaigns were conducted openly and covered extensively by the mass media. Although the media favoured the Mahathir-Ghafar team, the rallies of Razaleigh-Musa were often well attended, giving a sense of popular ground swell against Mahathir-Ghafar, which was not necessarily reflected among the official delegates. Owing to the unfavourable mass media coverage, the Razaleigh-Musa camp had to resort to the use of video and cassette tapes to bring their message beyond the UMNO circle, to a wider audience, a strategy used by PAS in its campaign during the 1986 general election. Despite the favourable media coverage given to Mahathir-Ghafar, it was mainly their allies who took the stage and conducted the battle, with the central figure in the gripping party drama, Mahathir, keeping silent, as if waiting for the Razaleigh-Musa camp to exhaust their "political capital".

It was not until about mid-March that Mahathir decided to break his silence in the title defence for the "UMNO heavyweight championship", as *Watan*, a local Malay magazine, called the contest. He did this in deep "enemy" territory, when he opened the new UMNO headquarters in Kelantan, as a guest of Razaleigh and in front of thousands of the latter's noisy supporters. His message was loud and clear though couched in the familiar subtle metaphor of Malay proverbs, *ayer dicincang tidak putus* ("slashed water is never severed"), expressing the brother-like relationship that he has had with Razaleigh. However, he warned that if he was pushed too far, *air boleh jadi ais dan ais boleh retak, macam hati manusia* ("water could become ice and ice could break, like the human heart"). And as he stepped up his campaign he became more and more direct in his attacks on Razaleigh, to which Razaleigh replied in equally harsh terms. So the *silat*-like[11] verbal exchanges continued unabatingly for about three weeks, covered extensively by the media, especially the *Star*, an MCA-owned English daily, and *Watan*, both of which had been consistently giving a more balanced coverage of the campaigns of the two opposing camps since the "war of the giants" began.

By 11 April, after all the nominations for the various posts to be contested in the Assembly had been received, the public encounters subsided as the "research and intelligence headquarters" of both camps began juggling with figures to gauge the number of voters they had "captured". However, it was a difficult exercise because some delegates appeared to be counted by both camps and the number of uncommitted voters was still high, about 20–25 per cent of the total 1,479 votes. The open, noisy, and road show–like phase of the campaign had by then passed and was replaced by the closed-door and silent meetings attended by those who mattered most. This phase was punctuated once or twice by Mahathir's public speeches at official opening functions during which he rebutted his rivals' charges of his alleged cliquish and dictatorial style. It was inevitable that the closed-door sessions turned into skeleton-digging exercises of rivals' cupboards because both camps, in essence, did not really differ in their overall philosophy, policy, and approach to many important national issues. Since both belonged to UMNO, which is committed to preserving and promoting Malay interests, it was said that the difference between them was akin to that between Pepsi-Cola and Coca-Cola. Be that as it may, the rest of the UMNO chips, the vice-presidencies, the Supreme Council posts, had by then fallen rapidly along both sides of the cleavage. Confounding the theorists yet again, the factions ruled out any sort of compromise, despite the many behind-the-scene attempts made mostly by the Mahathir-Ghafar camp.

The six contenders vying for the three vice-presidential posts were split into two camps. The three from the Mahathir-Ghafar camp were Anwar Ibrahim (a Cabinet minister), Wan Mokhtar, and Ramli Ngah Talib (both state chief ministers), and from the Razaleigh-Musa camp were Abdullah Badawi, Rais Yatim (both Cabinet ministers), and Harun Idris (ex-state chief minister). The two incumbents were Abdullah Badawi and Wan Mokhtar while Harun Idris had occupied the post once, Rais Yatim had tried and failed twice, and Ramli Ngah Talib was reputed to be a strong newcomer for he was the leader of

UMNO Perak, which had the largest single block of 256 delegates in the Assembly. In order to avoid being branded "greedy" and to enhance his chances of winning, Anwar Ibrahim resigned as UMNO Youth wing chief, thus automatically relinquishing his ex-officio vice-presidency

There were sixty-nine candidates for the 25-man Supreme Council, the largest number of candidates in UMNO's electoral history. The number was originally seventy-two but three withdrew from the contest. Like the contenders for the vice-presidential posts they could be grouped into the two major camps, which indicated an obvious desire by both camps to control the powerful inner circle. For the first time ever, none of these candidates stood for any higher post, particularly for the vice-presidency, which was a common practice before. In short, everyone contesting all the top posts and the Supreme Council positions was going for broke.

What was more significant was the fact that even the thirteen UMNO Cabinet ministers were split into two camps, with six each behind Mahathir and Razaleigh and one, Najib Tun Razak, sitting on the fence. At least four deputy ministers and four parliamentary secretaries had openly declared their support for Razaleigh and Musa. However, Mahathir received the support of all the state chief ministers who, as early as 26 February, had pledged their loyalty to him, yet another move unprecedented in UMNO's history. This move was not surprising for all of them owed their offices to Mahathir. But at least two of them owed to Ghafar directly, namely, the Chief Ministers of Negri Sembilan and Selangor, who were not appointed after the general election of 1986 until Ghafar had successfully pleaded on their behalf with the Yang Di-Pertuan Besar of Negri Sembilan and the Sultan of Selangor, respectively.

About a week before D-day the race for the party leadership looked a very close one. The number of fence-sitters narrowed to as few as 10–15 per cent of the total 1,479 delegates, with the 85–90 per cent committed votes being shared equally by Mahathir and Razaleigh. Musa was still considered to have the edge over his opposite number Ghafar. Mokhtar, Abdullah Badawi, and Anwar were surging forward ahead of the other three contenders for the vice-presidencies. According to detailed surveys by the "research and intelligence headquarters" of both camps, sited at "secret locations" in Kuala Lumpur, the profile of the delegates to the 24 April UMNO General Assembly had undergone a drastic change over the years and this could indirectly influence the voting pattern. For example, teachers, who made up 40 per cent of the delegates in 1981 and 32 per cent in 1984, were now down to 19 per cent, a figure on which both camps concurred. Their role as leaders had been taken over by a new breed of middle-class Malays comprising businessmen and entrepreneurs who totalled 25 per cent of the delegates in 1987. Civil servants made up 23 per cent, MPs and state assemblymen 19 per cent, community development officers 5 per cent, and professionals and others 1 per cent. The total number of delegates to the Assembly had also increased over the years: from 1,158 in 1981 to 1,244 in 1984, and to 1,479 in 1987. The increase was a result of the creation of additional parliamentary constituencies in 1982 and 1986, each of which had a corresponding new UMNO division.

When the big day came, which was Friday, 24 April, the numbers-game was still confused, but both sides appeared supremely confident as they waited for the "judgement hour". Delegates had arrived in Kuala Lumpur since 20 April together with the 13,500 official observers from all UMNO branches and divisions and a large number of local and foreign mass media representatives. Altogether they occupied no less than 5,000 hotel rooms, from the five-star hotels to the starless ones, costing UMNO millions of ringgit, excluding the 150,000 ringgit bill to feed all those present for the four-day historic occasion at the UMNO-owned Putra World Trade Centre. The venue of the meeting was sealed off from the public by no less than 500 uniformed and plain-clothes security personnel, mainly from the police.

During the voting period which began early on Friday, 24 April, delegates voted by secret ballot and individually instead of by divisions, thus reducing the influence of divisional heads who traditionally were believed to be able to sway delegates' choices. Voting started immediately after the President's speech thus leaving no time for last-minute campaigning. Though the original plan by the Supreme Council was for the voting to end before the Friday prayers of Muslims, that did not happen. There was a lot of confusion amongst the delegates over whom to vote for because there were no candidates' names on the ballot papers but only numbers that had been assigned to each candidate; voting thus did not finish at the scheduled time. It was, therefore, suspended for about three hours to allow delegates to attend Friday prayers and then continued until late afternoon. It was during this break that further canvassing was undertaken by both camps. Some believed that this break was crucial to Mahathir's success. However, the counting of votes for the five top posts — president, deputy president, and the three vice-presidents — took about eight hours to complete and the results were not announced until after midnight because the votes were recounted a number of times. The results for the Supreme Council posts were declared early the next morning. Without doubt, the day was truly a record-setting and record-breaking one for UMNO and the outcome and its repercussions were to have major repercussions for the organization. It also signalled the birth and the quick consolidation of what is now known within UMNO as Team A and Team B, the former referring to Mahathir and his supporters and the latter to Razaleigh and his sympathizers.

"Ashes If You Lose, Charcoal If You Win": The Marginal Victory and Its Aftermath

Mahathir won the battle but with a very narrow margin of merely forty-three votes, that is, only 51.45 per cent of the 1,479 votes cast. So did Ghafar, who made it by just forty votes, or 49.96 per cent of the total votes cast. It was indeed a photo-finish victory for the Mahathir-Ghafar combination. They were both happy and shocked. Happy because they had won: "I simply wanted to win," said Ghafar in his victory speech; and shocked because a photo-finish victory was hardly the kind of victory they had wanted or even envisaged. The results clearly indicated that Mahathir's popularity had been drastically reduced, his image dented, his authority eroded, his "cleanliness" questioned, his "efficiency" doubted, and his "trustworthiness" under suspicion.[12] In short, the Mahathir-Ghafar combine had won the battle but not necessarily the war.

Razaleigh and Musa knew from the beginning that they had entered what was going to be a "winner-takes-all" contest. This was confirmed by Mahathir in his closing address at the Assembly on 26 April when he said, "If we win we get something, if we lose we get nothing." In fact Razaleigh had cleared his office at the Ministry of Trade and Industry knowing that whichever way it went he would be vacating it. All his supporters knew that they had burnt their bridges the day they decided to openly throw their support behind him, and the prospect of losing their jobs stared in their faces. However, while they lost the election and their jobs, they had not lost the "moral battle". Razaleigh received 48.55 per cent of the total votes cast, a more-than-respectable figure considering their limited ability to mobilize any form of government machinery during the campaign.

Kalah jadi abu, menang jadi arang ("ashes if you lose, charcoal if you win"), says a Malay proverb. In some sense the proverb summarized quite accurately the fate of both camps. The narrow margin of victory or defeat meant that they both suffered, burnt and black like ashes and charcoal. The degree of the suffering, of course, differed. Mahathir received only a half mandate to run UMNO and the country, hardly a confidence-boosting prospect. More importantly, he will have to take stock of the criticisms levelled against him if he is to avoid a repeated open confrontation in the 1990 UMNO General Assembly. Indeed a trend had been set in 1987 and any future UMNO leader could ignore it only at his peril. This is the burden that Mahathir will have to carry for the years to come.

On the other hand, in the immediate- and short-term future, Razaleigh and Musa would suffer in silence because of the diminution in their status as public figures. They would be hounded by frustrations for some time because they came so close to tasting the fruits of victory. Their supporters, especially at the grass roots, would suffer equally, perhaps more, because their losses would be concrete and real: no more party perks, business licences, scholarships for their children, no hope for their loan payments to be rescheduled, with prospects of bankruptcy imminent for some. But Razaleigh and Musa left no doubt that they would return in 1990, although whether this would be on a joint ticket or separate ones remains unpredictable.

Viewed from any angle, the real winner to emerge from both the "war of the giants" and the "battle royal" was Anwar Ibrahim. It was Razaleigh who conducted all the negotiations with Anwar and successfully brought him into UMNO in 1982, of course with the full endorsement of Mahathir, although the latter was given the full credit publicly by the mass media for Anwar's political "conversion". By March 1982 Anwar was accepted as an UMNO member. In the April 1982 general election he contested for the Permatang Pauh parliamentary seat and won handsomely. Soon after he was made a deputy minister, and later in the year elected as UMNO Youth president toppling the incumbent, Suhaimi Kamaruddin, by only ten votes. Thus, he automatically became an ex-officio vice-president of UMNO. Not too long after that he joined the Cabinet as a full minister at the Ministry of Youth, Sports, and Culture, and after the 1986 general election was elevated to the position of Minister of Education. And now, after April 1987, he emerged as an elected UMNO vice-president in his own right and no longer in an ex-officio capacity. Indeed his rise to power has been truly meteoric for it was accomplished within five years of his entering UMNO, a political achievement unparalleled in UMNO's, or for that matter Malaysia's, history. What is more significant is the fact that he achieved all this during a period when UMNO was facing its biggest and most intense leadership crisis ever. With Musa and Razaleigh fighting bitterly for political supremacy, Musa and Mahathir, to everyone's surprise, went their separate ways, and then Razaleigh and Musa, the two former archrivals, teamed up to challenge the Mahathir-Ghafar team. Somehow Anwar survived all this unscathed, always on the winning side and a winner too. Perhaps the short but very intense initiation and baptism of fire that he went through has now more than prepared him for the next "promotion", the much sought-after UMNO deputy presidency and the post of deputy prime minister. This possibility is not at all far-fetched. One has only to consider the fact that despite the bitter struggle between Team A and Team B in the buildup to the 1987 UMNO elections, many delegates when interviewed after the event openly admitted that they voted for Anwar although they were Razaleigh supporters. The cross-tickets voting at first seems puzzling. But if one considers Razaleigh's role in bringing Anwar into UMNO and in providing Anwar the vital ten votes to win the post of UMNO Youth chief in late 1982, this incident of cross-voting is not very puzzling. Thus one should not rule out a Razaleigh-Anwar team in future UMNO elections — the former for president (read prime minister) and the latter for deputy president (read deputy prime minister)!

Besides Anwar, the other two successful candidates for the post of vice-president were Wan Mokhtar Ahmad and Abdullah Ahmad Badawi. The success of Anwar and Wan Mokhtar gave the Mahathir-Ghafar combination a clear edge over the Razaleigh-Musa team at the top level. However, it was in the Supreme Council that the Mahathir-Ghafar team won decisively. At least fifteen of the twenty-five elected Supreme Council members were considered Mahathir allies. To these Mahathir added ten more for he had the prerogative as the president to appoint the secretary-general, the treasurer, the information chief and seven additional councillors, in addition to the twenty-five elected ones, thus ensuring that his authority remained unchallenged in the powerful inner circle of the party's policy-making body. Taken as a whole, the victories of Anwar, Wan Mokhtar, and Abdullah Badawi for the vice-presidencies, and especially of Yusof Noor for the Supreme Council — he received the highest vote of 1,030 — cannot but lead one to conclude that the Islamic factor did play an important role in the 1987 UMNO elections since all of them are Islamicists in their own right. Wan Mokhtar, Abdullah Badawi, and Yusof Noor were educated in Islamic studies while Anwar, who was a graduate of Malay studies, has been championing the Islamic cause since the early 1970s, first, as the leader of the Islamic Youth Movement (ABIM) and, later, in his capacity as an UMNO leader. However, one could also argue that all these personalities had enjoyed personal followings in their respective states and to a certain extent outside their states as well. This might have been sufficient to carry them through and to win their respective positions. None the less, their victories engendered a sense of unease among many political observers outside UMNO who feared the Islamic shift within UMNO and believed this trend to be "bad" for the nation, as a whole.

In the light of the overwhelming victories of the members of the Mahathir-Ghafar team, both in the vice-presidential and Supreme Council contests, it is even more difficult to explain why their own victory margins were so small. Several theories were offered in local dailies, foreign and local magazines, and in post-UMNO election seminars held mostly in Kuala Lumpur. Even after all the "rebels" were purged from the Cabinet on 30 April, no convincing explanation for the narrow margin by which Mahathir and Ghafar had won was forthcoming. Only after the announcement of the much-awaited Cabinet reshuffle on 19 May did there emerge an indication, stronger than any of the theories propounded by political pundits, as to where the forty-three votes, which made the difference between Mahathir's victory and defeat, had come from.

The inclusion of Mohamed Rahmat and Mustaffa Mohammad in the Cabinet, and of Abdul Ghani Othman as a deputy minister, all of them from Musa's stronghold of Johor, and the retention of Najib Tun Razak clearly indicated their decisive roles in obtaining the crucial votes for Mahathir. Najib had been neutral during the intense months of campaigning by the opposing camps, until after he was handed the UMNO Youth chief post, though in an acting capacity, by Anwar, a staunch Mahathir supporter. This put Najib firmly in Mahathir's camp. Anwar (read Mahathir) would not have given the post to him if there had not been an agreement that Najib, as the division chief, would deliver the votes. Mohamed Rahmat and Mustaffa Mohammad (both of whom lost in the Supreme Council contests) openly supported Mahathir and Ghafar despite early opposition from within their respective UMNO divisions. However, they would not have been appointed Cabinet ministers solely on the basis of their vocal attempts to counter the overwhelming support for Musa in Johor. In a life and death contest (metaphorically speaking) that Mahathir faced, votes certainly mattered most, and both Mohamed Rahmat and Mustaffa Mohammad must have been able to sway their divisions' delegates to deliver them to Mahathir, hence the handsome rewards. The ex-academic Abdul Ghani Othman, the MP and division head for Ledang, Johor, was once Musa's protégé but, at the same time, was also known to be Sanusi Junid's man in the board of directors of Bank Rakyat. He was only a member of the UMNO Youth Executive Committee, in charge of its Economics bureau, when appointed by Mahathir as a deputy minister in the Ministry of Energy, Telecoms and Posts. In many ways he was a not-so-important figure in UMNO Youth and of lesser consequence within UMNO as a whole. There were many other well-known and experienced figures amongst the losers in the Supreme Council contests belonging to Mahathir's camp who were not appointed as deputy ministers or even parliamentary secretaries in the new government formed by Mahathir. Ghani must have delivered the priceless eleven votes from his division to Mahathir. If we total the number of votes these four personalities could muster, they could have been just enough to allow Mahathir to retain the presidency. This might explain their induction into the government.

The narrow victory margin had also put Mahathir in a position where he was not able to make any compromise, for the sake of UMNO's future unity, with the opposite camp, either in the form of retaining some of the "rebel" ministers or appointing those "rebels" who lost in the vice-president and Supreme Council contests. He had to reward those who were immediately responsible for his victory and had shown unwavering loyalty to the leader. He had repeatedly said during the campaign that he could only run the government with loyal Cabinet ministers. If these remarks were to be taken as a reflection of Mahathir's true stand then it could be assumed that he had no intention to compromise at all with the opposition, irrespective of the negative repercussions UMNO would suffer in future by his ignoring the wishes of the 48.55 per cent of the delegates who had voted against him. However, this is very much in line with Mahathir's "Malaysia Incorporated" concept, whereby the majority shareholders rule, even if the majority is only a wafer-thin 2.9 per cent. As a result, this has led to the consolidation, in fact entrenchment, of the Team A "shareholders" (Mahathir's team) at all levels and in all areas of Malaysian political and economic life. This has also meant that UMNO, and to a certain extent Malaysia, has suffered the loss of several good, experienced leaders, mostly technocrats brought in by the late Tun Razak to administer the NEP. It also signalled the end of the "new leaders" group groomed by Tun Razak in the mid-1970s, which has now been fragmented into three major factions: those of the re-elected Mahathir, his defeated challenger Razaleigh, and his former deputy-turned-detractor Musa Hitam.

It was not a coincidence, therefore, that after the elections a weakened UMNO, like a human body low in terms of internal resistance, suffered many "attacks" from within the National Front coalition and also from outside it. Dissension within UMNO during the same period continued despite Mahathir's tireless attempts through a country-wide "unity campaign" in September and October, to bring back Team A and Team B together before his departure for Vancouver, Canada, to attend the Commonwealth Prime Ministers' Meeting. The biggest threat from within UMNO was the court suit filed by Razaleigh-Musa supporters, against UMNO party management, including the Secretary-General Sanusi Junid, on the grounds that the management had deliberately and negligently allowed delegates from fifty-three unregistered branches to attend divisions' meetings which then elected the all-important delegates to the April 1987 UMNO General Assembly. They, therefore, sought a declaration from the court that the party's General Assembly was unconstitutional and illegal and its decisions null and void. Considering Mahathir's narrow margin of victory, the suit was crucial. However, neither side had fully anticipated the decision that was handed down in February 1988.

UMNO was busy at the same time fending off non-stop attacks from within the National Front components — the MCA, MIC, Gerakan, and so forth, on various issues relating to language, education, and culture. The biggest and the latest of these attacks came after the Education Ministry's appointment of non-Chinese-educated teachers to senior administrative positions in Chinese primary schools. Led by Chinese and Chinese-based government parties and joined by the opposition DAP and fifteen other Chinese associations in a rare public display of Chinese unity, almost the entire spectrum of Chinese political opinion opposed the government's action on this issue. Before this the non-UMNO government parties had also voiced their unhappiness over a range of issues, including a decision by the University of Malaya's Malay-dominated Senate to teach elective courses in the English, Chinese, and Indian studies departments in Malay; a requirement introduced by the Malacca state government that non-Muslim school students take an Islamic-style pledge; the suggestion by UMNO Youth asking the government to withdraw aid to a Chinese-dominated tertiary institution; and the opposition by some Malay-dominated voluntary groups and UMNO Youth to a decision by the government to help to pay back the millions of ringgits lost by hundreds of thousands of depositors, mostly Chinese, as a result of the deposit-taking co-operative (DTC) scandals involving many MCA leaders.

As if all this was not enough, the Mahathir government had to face numerous attacks from outside the National Front as well, both from opposition parties and from the NGOs. There were two that really rattled the government. The first, involving the opposition DAP, was related to the signing of a proposed contract between the Malaysian Government and United Engineers Malaysia (UEM), technically an UMNO-owned and controlled company, for the privatization of the 900-km. North–South Highway in Peninsular Malaysia. The leader of DAP, Lim Kit Siang, successfully obtained a court injunction preventing the signing of the contract and filed an underlying suit alleging corruption in the award of the letter of intent. Both the government and UEM attempted, but failed in court, to remove the injunction and to strike out the underlying suit. The suit will now be brought to trial in January 1988. It will involve the following Cabinet members: Mahathir, Ghafar, Daim, and Sanusi Junid, all from UMNO, and Samy Vellu, the MIC leader.

In the past, charges of corruption have been successfully brought against three state Chief Ministers — Ahmad Said of Perak, Ibrahim Fikri of Trengganu, and Harun Idris of Selangor — all of whom were convicted.

This, however, is the first-ever charge of corruption brought against federal Cabinet ministers, including the Prime Minister himself. In a weak response to the DAP attack and in an attempt to get UMNO members on side, Mahathir explained that the building of the North–South Highway, the award of the contract to UEM and the charging of the tolls, were all related to his general plan which would facilitate the payment of debts incurred by UMNO in the construction of the massive and impressive new UMNO building. Many suspected that the success of Lim Kit Siang in assembling a case against the government and UEM was possible because of the detailed information he was said to have received from Hasbudin, a Malay-owned and pro-Razaleigh-Musa company, which had successfully constructed the Penang Bridge but failed to win the contract for the privatization of the North–South Highway despite its lower tender offer compared with Hatibudi,[13] an UMNO-owned company. If this was true, the battle between Team A and Team B had gone outside UMNO and seems to be hardly over. In fact it appears to have intensified and expanded.

The second major attack on the government was related to the suggestion that the Constitution be amended to suit the changing situation after thirty years of independence. The suggestion was made by Aliran, a social reform movement, at its tenth anniversary celebrations held on 15–16 August at which Tunku Abdul Rahman Putra, Malaysia's first Prime Minister, officiated. The Tunku also supported this move. The suggestion drew wide public comment from various quarters of Malaysian society, including high-ranking ex-judicial officers as well as the royalty. Mahathir and his allies replied to the suggestion by stating that it was unnecessary to amend the Constitution because it already contained all the necessary provisions to cover every aspect of change that Malaysian society had experienced and could possibly experience. In the course of the heated exchanges that took place over a period of weeks, Mahathir and his allies even argued that the judiciary should refrain from making political statements that could jeopardize its neutrality and hence reduce the public's confidence in judicial institutions. However, it was not very long ago, in what was dubbed as the 1983 constitutional crisis, that Mahathir had gone to the people through massive public rallies in an effort to amend the Constitution so as to curb the powers of the royalty. He had then succeeded, though not totally, in achieving his objective. In fact, it was his success in 1983 and what was thought to have been a demonstration of his liberal attitude on a very important matter that perhaps spurred Aliran and others to make suggestions regarding constitutional amendments which had a similar thrust.

It was the volatile combination of these events — within UMNO, within the National Front and outside both of them — which brought the racial situation almost to the boil in the capital city, Kuala Lumpur. Mahathir came home from Vancouver in the last week of October, after a successful bid to bring the next meeting of Commonwealth Prime Ministers to Kuala Lumpur, only to face the grim prospect of an outbreak of racial violence in the country. That would have become a distinct possibility if the planned UMNO rally and public procession to celebrate the forty-first anniversary of the party, scheduled for 1 November in Kuala Lumpur and to be attended by about 500,000 members, had gone out of organizers' control. Mahathir responded swiftly to this perceived threat. He ordered the arrest of all those considered "threats to national security". From 27 October to 20 November a total of 106 people were arrested and detained without trial under the draconian Internal Security Act (ISA). However, by 29 December, fifty-five had been released and at least five were sent for a further two-year detention, including Lim Kit Siang, the DAP chief. Those arrested were a mixed bunch: opposition party members, National Front party members including MCA's Chinese educationists, members of public interest reform groups, environmentalists, unionists, academics, church workers, Muslim religious teachers, and private individuals. Publishing licences of three newspapers, *Star*, *Sin Chew Jit Poh*, and *Watan*[14] were suspended and, as of the end of the year, none of them has been allowed to operate again. All public rallies of a political nature, in the open or behind closed doors, have been banned, including the planned mammoth anniversary rally by UMNO.

In conclusion, the challenge that had begun within UMNO has spread outside. The overall economic slow-down has definitely played an important underlying role, by exaggerating the tensions both within and outside UMNO. The latter took the form of racial tensions, not a new phenomenon in Malaysia. What went on outside UMNO seems to have been brought under control by the exercise of powers invested in the government under ISA, but the tensions within UMNO are expected to continue for a long time. The 1987 UMNO elections are not really over yet because the court cases asking that they be declared null and void are scheduled to be heard some time in January 1988. Attempts to have the court cases withdrawn have failed.[15] Will the plaintiffs fail, or, will there be a sequel, "The 1987 UMNO Elections II"? This remains the sixty-four million dollar question.

Notes

* This essay is based upon data collected in a series of field research begun in October 1986 for a larger project, "Socio-Economic Change and Cultural Transformation in Rural Malaysia", under the joint patronage of the JSPS (Japan Society for the Promotion of Science, Ministry of Education, Japan) and the VCC (Vice-Chancellors' Council of the National Universities of Malaysia), and funded by the Hitachi Scholarship Foundation, Japan.

1. For an excellent account of the crisis, see Harold Crouch, "The UMNO Crisis: 1975–77", in *Malaysian Politics and the 1978 Election*, edited by Harold Crouch, Lee Kam Hing, and Michael Ong (Kuala Lumpur: Oxford University Press, 1980), pp. 11–36.
2. The names and detailed background of the detainees are found in Kassim Ahmad, *The Second University: An Account of Detention under the ISA* (Petaling Jaya: Media Intelek, 1983).
3. See the editorial of the *New Strait Times*, 28 March 1976; also cited by Crouch, ibid., pp. 34, 35.
4. For some empirical examples regarding "money politics", see Shamsul A.B., "The Politics of Bumiputera Policy", in *From British to Bumiputera Rule: Local Politics and Rural Development in Peninsular Malaysia* (Singapore: Institute of Southeast Asian Studies, 1986), chap 5.
5. Details of the Musa-Razaleigh conflict and its effects on UMNO internal politics are found in A. Ghani Ismail, *Razaleigh Lawan Musa Pusingan Kedua 1984 (Latar Belakang)* (Taiping: IJS Communications, 1983).
6. Statements to this effect have been made by many of Mahathir's former Cabinet ministers, such as Abdullah Badawi, and UMNO Supreme Council members, such as Marina Yusof; see *Malaysian Business*, 16 April 1987, pp. 9, 12–13.
7. See *Utusan Malaysia*, 15 December 1986, for a full press statement by Abu Hassan Omar, the then Federal Territory Minister, detailing government views on the public activities of the NGOs and the opposition parties.
8. An important article on the success and failure of the UMNO Ethics Committee has been written by Rustam A. Sani, "Mengapa UMNO Perlukan Etika Pemilihan Pemimpin", *Utusan Malaysia*, 18 December 1986.
9. Forming "shadow Cabinets", "package groups", or "teams" within the party is outlawed by the UMNO Ethics Committee because such practices are defined as "unfair election practices". Those found to be involved in such practices could be suspended from UMNO membership thus denying them further participation in the UMNO elections. For details, see Rustam A. Sani, ibid.
10. From early February to the end of March 1987, the 133 UMNO divisions had to meet and select their eleven delegates for the April 1987 UMNO General Assembly. The author attended twenty-one of such meetings spread over five states — Johor, Kelantan, Kedah, Selangor, and Negri Sembilan — covering both the Mahathir-Ghafar and Razaleigh-Musa strongholds. He also conducted interviews with divisional leaders and ordinary members of the UMNO areas he visited, obtaining first-hand information on the "war of the giants" as seen by the "dwarfs".
11. *Silat* is a form of Malay martial art.
12. "*Bersih, Cekap and Amanah*" [Clean, Efficient, and Trustworthy] was a Mahathir-introduced slogan for the 1982 general election, the first election after he became the Prime Minister.
13. Hatibudi controls and owns UEM. The former is a small private Malaysian company of which Prime Minister Mahathir Mohamad, Deputy Prime Minister Ghafar Baba, Minister of Agriculture Sanusi Junid, and Minister of Finance Daim Zainuddin, in their capacity as leaders of UMNO, are trustees.

14. *Watan* has been a much-neglected and misunderstood source of Malay *realpolitik* especially by foreign correspondents mainly because of its dramatic if sensationalized style of journalism. Its predecessors *Suara Rakyat* and *Suara Merdeka* have been banned, too. But it remained the most informative and balanced in its coverage of the 1987 UMNO elections, in fact of Malay politics in general. For example, it was the only newspaper in Malaysia which gave the full list of all the 1,479 delegates and their backgrounds, a crucial information indeed.

15. On 4 February 1988, the judge who was presiding over the suit brought against the UMNO party management by the eleven UMNO members from the grass roots declared UMNO an unlawful society.

MALAYSIA
A Fateful September

John Funston

In December 1974 thousands of demonstrators in Kuala Lumpur were dispersed by baton-wielding police, aided by tear gas. Hundreds were arrested. Among those detained under the Internal Security Act (ISA) was youth leader Anwar Ibrahim, probably at the behest of Education Minister Dr Mahathir Mohamad.[1] In September 1998 the two key actors held different positions, but the scenes played out were much the same.

September began with the unexpected imposition of currency controls on day one. More dramatically, on day two Prime Minister Mahathir sacked Anwar from the Deputy Prime Minister and Finance portfolios. In the early hours of day four Anwar was stripped of both the deputy leadership and even membership in the United Malays National Organisation (UMNO), the dominant party in the ruling coalition. On 20 September balaclava-clad, M16-wielding police Special Forces broke down an open door and arrested Anwar, who was then held under the ISA for allegedly endangering public security. At the end of the month he was arraigned before the court, charged with five counts of corruption (abuse of power) and five of sodomy.

The drama of September brought Malaysia unsought international prominence, and opened up many questions. What went wrong between the Prime Minister and his designated heir? Did the fall-out from these events threaten Dr Mahathir's long rule? How strong was the movement for *reformasi*? Could Anwar make a comeback? Was this yet another power struggle between UMNO factions, or did it represent something more profound?

Reprinted in abridged format from Daljit Singh and John Funston, eds., *Southeast Asian Affairs 1999* (Singapore: Institute of Southeast Asian Studies, 1999), pp. 165–84. At the time of original publication, John Funston was a Senior Fellow at the Institute of Southeast Asian Studies, Singapore.

What Went Wrong?

Relations between Mahathir and Anwar have long been complicated. They first came in contact in 1969, when both were in opposition to Prime Minister Tunku Abdul Rahman. Mahathir spoke at student meetings organized by Anwar, and a student journal under Anwar published a chapter from Mahathir's *Malay Dilemma*, after the book had been banned. Their paths diverged in the 1970s as Mahathir returned to the UMNO fold and Anwar strengthened his position as a youth leader, particularly with the Malaysian Islamic Youth Movement (known by its Malay acronym, ABIM). In 1982 Mahathir persuaded Anwar to join UMNO, and the two of them worked closely together until Anwar became deputy party and government leader in 1993. From that time the relationship was strained, and both local pundits and the international media frequently predicted a split.

Nonetheless, at the beginning of 1998 Anwar's position as apparent heir seemed secure. The economic downturn was extremely serious, but affected the corporate sector more than the population as a whole. Both Mahathir and Anwar stressed the importance of maintaining party and national unity in addressing economic problems. Political stability was one of the advantages Malaysia trumpeted over less fortunate neighbours.

Economic Differences

Most analyses in the Western media have focused on economic differences to explain the falling out. According to this view, Anwar sought to solve economic problems by focusing on internal problems, and worked closely with the International Monetary Fund (IMF), promoting reforms based on the free market and greater transparency, and adhering to tight monetary and fiscal policies. Mahathir, in contrast, was seen as placing all the blame for Malaysia's economic problems on external factors, being implacably opposed to the IMF, favouring loose monetary and fiscal policies, and wanting to continue with "crony capitalism".

Such an assessment sits oddly with history. A fair assessment of Mahathir's economic policies would have to acknowledge that the seventeen years of his rule have seen a major transformation in the direction of liberalization, while fiscal and monetary policies have remained prudent. Anwar made a contribution towards these policies, but only since becoming Finance Minister in 1991.

Until around the middle of 1998, economic policies were worked out in close consultation with the IMF. While many observers saw these as reflecting the views of Anwar in opposition to the wishes of Mahathir, such an assessment reflects a naïve understanding of political power in Malaysia. The Prime Minister is much more powerful than his deputy, or any other minister, and all policies require his acquiescence at least. After the National Economic Action Council (NEAC) was announced in November 1997 Mahathir, Anwar and the NEAC executive director, Tun Daim Zainuddin, met daily to discuss economic issues. Daim, a former Finance Minister and long-time confidant of Mahathir, and Anwar both had a forum to argue their case, but the final decision rested with Mahathir. The outcome of consideration by these three, and the broader NEAC, was brought together in the 200-page National Economic Recovery Plan (NERP), released to the media on 23 July 1998. This represented a move towards looser monetary and fiscal policies, but within a framework that economic commentators acknowledged as prudent.

Mahathir's and Anwar's views on the international and domestic aspects of the crisis were not as far apart as has generally been argued. Mahathir accepted the logic of domestic reforms and continuing liberalization until the second quarter of 1998. In response to questions over his differences with Anwar around late April, he commented:

> People keep on wanting to publish when he says about liberalisation. I say the same thing but nobody mentions it. He admits and I admit we have done things that may be considered wrong in the eyes of foreign investors.
>
> Question: What are you referring to?
>
> About crony capitalism, about corruption. We don't have a monopoly on that. In other countries, they have this. We are willing to do away with that.[2]

Anwar, on the other hand, began by denying that internal factors contributed to the financial crisis. At the UMNO general assembly in September 1997, he spoke of an "economic war carefully organised by a Western syndicate on our shares and currency".[3] Later that month, he described currency traders as "buccaneering speculators" and "gun-slingers".[4] While he subsequently gave more attention to internal factors, he remained critical of international financial arrangements. And his willingness to work with the IMF to address economic problems never inclined him to support an IMF programme for Malaysia. In May 1998 he called on Malaysian youth to be patriotic and "help the government save the state from foreigners like the IMF... We do not want our politics, social life and economy organised by the IMF".[5]

It would, of course, be an overstatement to argue that there were no differences between the two leaders. As economic recession began to bite in early 1998 there were evident disagreements over how much monetary and fiscal policies should be loosened, and in particular over the maintenance of high interest rates. But these were essentially issues of fine-tuning, and reflected a wider international debate which, around mid-year, saw even the IMF move to a more flexible policy. (A similar debate took place in Thailand between the Finance and Commerce ministers, but received less critical international attention.) As the economy slowed dramatically, Anwar made no attempt to stick with an austerity policy that even the IMF had abandoned. By the end of June his views on maintaining high interest rates had been modified to the extent that he described Malaysia's rates as "prohibitively high".[6]

Even the issue of "crony capitalism" is not clear-cut. While Anwar and his circle echoed the Indonesian slogan of opposing *korupsi*, *kronyisma* and *nepotisma* (KKN) — and also highlighted *ketelusan* (transparency) — they did, on a smaller scale, have cronies of their own. Mahathir, on the other hand, did not oppose this message until around June 1998. The reasons for his opposition after this time may be more closely linked to political than economic differences (see below). Even after June Mahathir supported reforms in the direction of greater transparency on the Kuala Lumpur Stock Exchange. It should also not be forgotten that as recently as the 1996 UMNO General Assembly, Mahathir was so upset by burgeoning corruption in Malaysia that he shed tears, and initiated tougher legislation to oppose this.

But economic factors did poison the relationship between Mahathir and Anwar in three important ways. The first flowed from the difference in style between the two of them. Mahathir's attacks on currency traders, and occasional interventions in the management of the stock market, unnerved markets and antagonized everyone. Anwar calmed international and domestic markets and charmed the rest, particularly the international media — thereby violating what a current best-selling book has identified as the first of 48 laws of power, "Never Outshine the Master".[7] Mahathir deeply resented this. Nothing was more likely to strengthen his desire to reassert control than calls by the international media for him to step down in favour of Anwar.

A second destabilizing factor was the effect of the economic crisis on economic management. For many years the Malaysian Government has played a major direct role in economic affairs, both with a view to hastening the creation of a modern industrial society, and fostering a Malay entrepreneurial class that could compete with non-Malay citizens and foreigners. It offered numerous incentives to selected entrepreneurs to achieve these ends, set up government corporations to invest in the private sector, and distributed government contracts and privatization deals to favoured corporate players. Many of the larger Malay corporations also had close links with factions in the ruling UMNO. When the economy boomed, this worked well. But when the economy went into recession Malay corporations were the worst hit. Difficult decisions had to be made about which corporations would receive support, how much support would be given, and the form this would take. As Prime Minister, Mahathir had the biggest say on such issues, but as Finance Minister Anwar also had some authority.

Since his sacking Anwar has spoken and written at some length about conflicts with Mahathir over several government-linked corporations — including Perwaja Steel, Renong, and Malaysian Airlines System. Perhaps the most difficult case, in March 1998, was the buy-out by Petronas (the national oil company) of the shipping company, Konsortium Perkapalan, owned by Mahathir's son, Mirzan. Petronas comes under the Prime Minister's Department, and so Mahathir did not intervene in the transaction. Anwar as Finance Minister acceded to it, on the basis of an independent assessment by an international shipping valuer, but Mahathir was reportedly displeased that the price paid was below market expectations.

Thirdly, Anwar did not share Dr Mahathir's fondness for mega and prestige projects. Anwar did not oppose all mega projects — contrary to several reports, he did not criticize the new administrative capital, Putrajaya — but after his sacking, he did complain bitterly about extravagances, such as houses for the Prime Minister and his deputy in Putrajaya, and a top-of-the-range corporate jet ordered for the Prime Minister.

Political Power Conflict

In Malaysia, the relationship between a Prime Minister and his deputy has often been a difficult one. To a much greater extent than in most countries, the deputy is the heir apparent, and is treated as someone almost as powerful. Mahathir has always chaffed under this system. With his first deputy, Musa Hitam, Mahathir was infuriated when the media dubbed his administration the "2 Ms" — implying in his mind that Musa was accorded a position of near equality. Conflict between a Prime

Minister and his deputy is, to a degree, institutionalized.

However, it is simplistic to argue, as some have, that Mahathir always changes his deputy every five to six years. It is a moot point whether Musa would have been sacked, as he resigned without testing this. His successor, Ghafar Baba, retained Mahathir's support until just about everyone else in the party had deserted him.

In retrospect, the immediate origins of the Mahathir-Anwar fall-out can be dated to mid-1997. In May that year, Mahathir went on two month's leave, putting Anwar fully in charge. This and Anwar's forceful intervention on corruption issues alarmed his opponents within UMNO. They redoubled efforts to discredit him. Just before the UMNO General Assembly in September, copies of a poison-pen letter, accusing Anwar of sodomy, infidelity and fathering an illegitimate child, circulated widely. Mahathir dismissed the allegations, but took no action against those responsible. At the Assembly, Mahathir alienated a significant section of the party with a blistering attack on Islamic fundamentalists.

Mahathir's actions at the 1997 UMNO Assembly, and his controversial response to the financial crisis, alienated both Islamic groups and the middle class. In the second half of 1997 and the first half of 1998 numerous articles appeared in the local media asking fundamental questions about political and economic policies, with some even criticizing Mahathir directly. Popular resentment was manifested in UMNO's shock defeat at the hands of Parti Islam (PAS) in a July 1998 parliamentary by-election for Arau, in Perlis state. PAS won focusing on the issue of KKN.

Around May/early June a chasm opened up between Mahathir and Anwar over KKN. Mahathir began to deny that this existed in Malaysia, and placed all blame for economic problems on external factors. He saw the focus on this issue by Anwar and others as designed to achieve the same result as that in Indonesia, namely, the ouster of the government.

As the June UMNO general assembly loomed, Anwar increased pressure on Mahathir, in what was intended as a "message" — in 1995 Mahathir had said that he would not stay on if UMNO members sent a message that they were not happy with him. On 7 June, Anwar warned of the need for reform if Malaysia were to avoid the fate of Indonesia. On 18 June, the day before the party assembly, UMNO Youth head, Datuk Ahmad Zahid, criticized the existence of KKN at the Youth general assembly. However, the precise nature of Anwar's "message" was unclear. Anwar said later that he did not plan to oust Mahathir at the meeting, but wanted a commitment to reform. Mahathir may not have interpreted his actions in such a benign way.

Mahathir's political skills have often been most apparent when under pressure. These were much to the fore in the lead-up to and at the UMNO assembly. In March, he rebuffed moves for change by getting UMNO's endorsement to limit contests for divisional heads — people who play a key role in the assembly. By outlawing contests where a Supreme Council member was a divisional executive, only 36 of 165 divisions changed hands. At the assembly, Mahathir won endorsement for his view that external threats were the cause of Malaysia's problems, then cut the ground from under Anwar's feet by releasing a list of all Malay beneficiaries to government contracts and privatizations. Among the named beneficiaries were Zahid and members of Anwar's family. While these listings said little about the wealth of Anwar's supporters, the ploy worked. Mahathir even managed to turn *kronyisma* into a positive by linking it to the constitutionally defined *bumiputera* "special position" — all Malays were cronies because all had benefited from this.

Another unusual development just prior to the assembly was the publication of a book entitled *50 Dalil Mengapa Anwar Tidak Boleh Jadi PM [50 Reasons Why Anwar Cannot Be Prime Minister]*, a work reviving charges made at the previous assembly, and adding further embellishments. Anwar obtained a court injunction preventing its distribution prior to the determination of a libel action against the author and publisher. Nonetheless, the book appeared among the hand-outs given to assembly delegates by the party secretariat.

Events thereafter can, in retrospect, be seen as a well-planned series of moves — using both the state and party — to weaken Anwar's position before the ultimate *coup de grâce*. The main steps included:

- Anwar quickly became the main target for investigations into the *50 Dalil*, not the author and publisher.
- On 24 June, Daim was reappointed to the Cabinet, with imprecise responsibilities for co-ordinating all efforts to overcome the economic crisis.
- In July, the editors of the two major Malay dailies — *Utusan Malaysia* and *Berita Harian* — and a director of TV3 were forced to resign. All held strategic positions in the media, and were known to be close to Anwar.
- On 20 July, ninety UMNO MPs (minus Anwar, who was then overseas) declared their loyalty to Mahathir.
- On 31 July, Datuk Nallakaruppan, a businessman and tennis partner of Anwar, was taken into custody for questioning in relation to the *50 Dalil*. On 13 August he was charged under the ISA for possession of live ammunition, an offence carrying a mandatory death penalty.
- Throughout August Dr Mahathir toured all states, allegedly to explain Malaysia's economic problems to the people, but in the process shoring up his popular support and warning of "drastic" measures to come.
- Mahathir foreshadowed further use of the ISA by praising its usefulness in his National Day speech on 30 August.
- On 1 September, currency controls were introduced.

Even external events favoured Mahathir at this time. A bitter dispute with Singapore provided an opportunity for him to rally support as the country's leader. The Malaysian media were able to represent Anwar's position as similar to that of U.S. President Clinton — a political leader who had denied sexual wrongdoing, but had subsequently been found out. And an internationally prominent economist, Paul Krugman, published a sophisticated argument for currency controls just a few days before Malaysia imposed its own.

On 2 September, Anwar was sacked at 5.30 p.m., and the following evening the UMNO Supreme Council decided "unanimously" to expel him from the party. On 3 September, an affidavit lodged by the police in relation to legal actions by Datuk Nallakaruppan contained lurid claims of sexual misdemeanours, corruption, intimidation of witnesses, and possible sedition. This was dramatically reported in the local media — an unprecedented use of an affidavit — and foreshadowed much of the case later made against Anwar.

Until the sacking, both sides manoeuvred with the subtlety often associated with characters in the Malay *wayang* (shadow puppets). Mahathir and Anwar declared their mutual loyalty at the UMNO assembly, and continued to deny rumours and media reports of rifts. On 11 August, Anwar said he would not challenge Mahathir for the leadership in 1999, declaring that it would be like challenging his "father". One day before the sacking Mahathir described relations with Anwar as "good".

Did this amount to a "conspiracy" as Anwar has claimed? Anwar had over the years developed strained relations with several senior UMNO figures, and differences between the two leaders were often incited by their followers. Opposition to Anwar had intensified from mid-1997, as already noted. Whether or not there was something more sinister may become apparent as the court case unravels. By year's end that possibility could not be ruled out.

A Morality Issue

Mahathir publicly rejected claims that economics or politics were behind Anwar's sacking, and attributed it solely to Anwar's sexual misdemeanours. It was, he declared, all because of Anwar's moral shortcomings — "In the West, homosexual ministers are accepted. In Malaysia we cannot accept leaders involved in strange activities. I sacked him because of this."[8]

In view of the issues discussed above, such an explanation may seem unlikely, but it cannot be dismissed entirely. Mahathir does have strong puritanical views and, as frequently revealed in his criticisms of immorality in the West, a particular disgust with homosexuality. Mahathir made his own investigations into the *50 Dalil*, interviewing six of Anwar's accusers. He subsequently declared that he had "incontrovertible proof" that allegations of Anwar's sexual misdemeanours were soundly based.

That said, it is also clear that Mahathir did not seek to check the claims in the *50 Dalil* until after the heated UMNO assembly. Evidence in Anwar's trial has revealed that Mahathir's interview of one of the key witnesses was conducted only on 26 August, just a week before Anwar's sacking. By this time, dismissal preparations were well in hand.

Anwar's Challenge

Anwar's sacking led to an outpouring of public protest. After the UMNO meeting that expelled Anwar, Dr Mahathir was pelted with used paper drinking cups, an unprecedented act of public defiance towards a prime minister. In the days that followed, tens of thousands flocked to Anwar's house nightly, to hear his talks (*ceramah*) and lend moral support. Between 12 and 20 September he addressed meetings around the countryside — including at his home district of Permatang Pauh, and at Alor Setar, Malacca, Kuantan, Kuala Terengganu, Kota Bahru, Batu Pahat, and Kuala Lumpur. Precise numbers at these meetings are difficult to obtain, but all probably exceeded 20,000, with meetings in excess of 50,000 in Alor Setar and Kota Bahru. The 20 September rally in Kuala Lumpur, at the National Mosque and Dataran Merdeka (Independence Square), was the biggest in the city since 1969, with estimates ranging from 35,000–100,000 people.

After being sacked Anwar categorically denied all accusations against him, and criticized the government for its failure to observe basic principles of justice. After his expulsion from UMNO he became progressively more critical and militant, accusing Dr Mahathir of dictatorship, corruption and protection of cronies, and calling on him to resign. A formal statement of principle, (Permatang Pauh Declaration) issued on 12 September, emphasized justice through the rule of law, democracy, economic justice, eradication of corruption, and commitment to peaceful protest. These themes, which had enjoyed great popularity in the media before the July dismissal of senior media figures, were taken up enthusiastically by his supporters. Reformists also resurrected past controversies during Mahathir's rule, and gave these extensive airing on the Internet.[9]

Rallies continued throughout September. On 21 September some 10,000 people gathered outside the court where Anwar was expected to appear. A complete ban on protests was announced on 23 September, but 5,000–10,000 supporters still gathered at the National Mosque two days later. Further rallies of 3,000–5,000 occurred at Dataran Merdeka on 26 September, 30,000–100,000 at Parti Islam headquarters on the outskirts of Kuala Lumpur on 27 September, and another 3,000 at Dataran Merdeka on the following day.

By the end of September, a large number of Malaysians had taken part in anti-government protests, and had gained a sense of empowerment from doing so. Government leaders reluctantly admitted that many people did not believe their case against Anwar.

The momentum of demonstrations in Kuala Lumpur was maintained during the first half of October, with some 10,000 people participating in Saturday afternoon "shopping". Tougher police action on 17 October led to 134 arrests, 30 of whom had to be hospitalized. A week later, a few demonstrators fought back against the police, resulting in what was described as "riots", and 178 arrests. The massive police presence, the formal laying of charges against those arrested on 17 October, and constant warnings against demonstrating, finally reduced the numbers to around 1,000 in subsequent outings, and the venue shifted from the centre of town to the vicinity of the mosque in the nearby Malay area of Kampong Baru. There, on 14 November, TV crews recorded a confrontation in which two police motorcycles were set alight, and a policeman fired a pistol into the air before making good his escape. Once the Asia-Pacific Economic Co-operation (APEC) summit ended in Kuala Lumpur (18 November) a powerful incentive for demonstrations was removed, and the momentum declined further. However, some 1,000 university students demonstrated on 27 November, and 300 lawyers on 4 December, to protest against legal proceedings in relation to the Anwar case.

Anwar's cause was helped by the establishment of two loosely structured coalitions — the Majlis Gerakan Keadilan Rakyat Malaysia (Gerak), and Gagasan Demokrasi Rakyat (Gagasan) — organized around PAS and the Democratic Action Party (DAP) respectively, on 27 September. Membership overlapped, but included two smaller political parties and more than a dozen non-governmental organizations (NGOs) representing professional, human rights and Islamic groups.[10] Some NGOs, including the Bar Council and the International Movement for a Just World, continued to issue public statements critical of the government, and had some of these reported in the mass media.

On 10 December, the Pergerakan Keadilan Sosial (Social Justice Movement), or ADIL (Justice), was launched as the specific vehicle of the reform movement. It was headed by Anwar's wife, Dr Wan Azizah bte Dr Wan Ismail, and its 27 committee members, and 24 "supporters" read like a "who's who" of Malaysian NGO movements and academia. ADIL's registration as an NGO was still under official consideration at year's end.

In addition, Anwar supporters made their views widely known through the Internet — particularly the news discussion group *soc.culture.Malaysia*, and dozens of pro-Anwar sites — and through a pre-recorded Anwar interview aired on CNBC (available by satellite to some 250,000 Malaysians) on 24 September. The PAS bi-weekly *Harakah* increased its sales from 65,000 to 300,000. After Anwar was released from the ISA on 14 October he was also able to maintain a constant flow of letters, press releases, and press articles, despite continuing detention under remand at Sungai Buloh prison. The foreign media provided an outlet for pro-Anwar views. Sales of Anwar's speeches on video and cassette, together with *reformasi* T-shirts and stickers, also did a brisk trade. Members of the public donned white ribbons, as a symbol of justice.

Government Response

The government sought to manage Anwar's sacking with a multi-pronged strategy. First, it launched a massive campaign to try and discredit Anwar, using the resources of state, party and the media. Allegations of sodomy and other sexual misdemeanours were at the centre of this. But he was also accused, *inter alia*, of being out to topple Dr Mahathir, willing to lead Indonesian-style riots, a "puppet" of foreign powers, and the architect of the country's economic problems.

Secondly, it attempted to create fear in those who might be inclined to support Anwar, particularly through the use of the police and ISA. Rallies organized by Anwar and his supporters were all proclaimed "illegal", and subject to various forms of harassment, ranging from close surveillance to violent dispersal. The regular police had the support of the Special Branch, the anti-riot Federal Reserve Unit, and the anti-insurgency Police Field Force. Some twenty-seven Anwar supporters were held under the ISA, and nine hundred were arrested during rallies. Police closely monitored Anwar's wife. University lecturers, students and public servants were threatened with strong disciplinary action, including expulsion, if they gave any support to the opposition.

Government leaders encouraged fear in a different way by painting grim scenes of the potential for bloodshed, and claiming that public protests were both dangerous and incompatible with Malaysian democracy. Warnings that public demonstrations could lead to Indonesian-style racial clashes were repeated frequently.

Thirdly, government leaders sought to shore up unity in UMNO and the Barisan Nasional, behind Mahathir's leadership. Teams of veterans, led by former deputy Tun Ghafar Baba, were sent around the countryside on information tours. Party leaders made strong public statements of support for Mahathir. Dissidents, or suspected dissidents, were expelled from UMNO, or asked to "show cause". And an extraordinary UMNO General Assembly in December passed constitutional changes designed to give more power to the leadership, and thwart any possible return by Anwar in the near future. One of the changes — allowing triennial party elections to be deferred for eighteen months — was invoked the following month.

Finally, the government sought to rally the population around an alleged international threat to "re-colonize" Malaysia. Currency controls were justified on these grounds. U.S. Vice President Al Gore's open support for "the brave" supporters of *reformasi* at the APEC summit in November led both UMNO and the Information Ministry to organize signature campaigns protesting against foreign intervention in Malaysia's affairs; corporations also expressed their support for Mahathir in large newspaper advertisements. This campaign was sustained into December when Mahathir's *bête noire*, George Soros, called for his overthrow, and the United States and British air forces launched attacks on Iraq.

The government did have some success in these efforts. The patriotic campaigns sustained a degree of popular support for the government. Police actions eventually ended regular demonstrations. And UMNO avoided any major split in the party, as had happened in 1987. However, even on these counts success was not unqualified. Patriotic fervour had begun to wane by year's end. Public attendance at Anwar's trial increased dramatically every time proceedings moved in his favour, suggesting the possibility of demonstrations resuming should circumstances change. And UMNO's apparent unity could not prevent strong opposition to Mahathir's attempts to avoid appointing a deputy (eventually resulting in Abdullah Badawi's instatement in early January 1999). At the grass-roots, feelings ran more deeply. Media reports cited government surveys showing that some 70 per cent of UMNO members did not believe the case against Anwar. Thousands left UMNO and joined PAS.

The government also faced other, deeper problems. It was unable to convince the public that Anwar was guilty as charged, or that he was fairly treated. The court case made slow progress throughout 1998, but the unambiguous evidence of Anwar's guilt that the political leaders had promised did not emerge. Government statements repeatedly acknowledged that their case against Anwar was not going well. In late December, UMNO Secretary-General Sabarrudin Chik claimed that Anwar had deliberately courted arrest, and the government had fallen for this.[11] In early January 1999, Mahathir announced plans for a nation-wide tour because the people were "confused" over the Anwar issue.[12]

Several aspects of the case raised questions about the possibility of Anwar receiving a fair trial. Two stand out. The first was Mahathir's declaration from the outset that he was convinced of Anwar's guilt, his claim on 22 September that he had "incontrovertible proof" of this, and regular reaffirmations of Anwar's guilt, notwithstanding a court ruling against such statements. The second was Anwar's appearance in court with his famous black eye. It did not help the government's case that the police chief had just given public assurances that Anwar was "safe", that Mahathir initially speculated that it might have been self-imposed or provoked, and that no results of a police enquiry had been announced by the end of the year (three months later).[13]

The harsh measures against protestors were also not without cost. Widespread use of the ISA (which enables indefinite detention without trial) had not occurred since the late 1980s. It provoked a strong outcry, particularly on the Internet, from a public that felt Malaysia had matured beyond such measures. The same was true of forceful police tactics, including the use of tear gas (not seen since 1974), and the use of chemically-laced water sprays for the first time ever.

The government and government-controlled media suffered an unprecedented loss of credibility. Many boycotted UMNO-controlled newspapers, such as the *New Straits Times*, *Berita Harian* and *Utusan Malaysia* — circulation reportedly dropped by over 20 per cent — and stopped watching television. A spate of instant books appeared, most supporting Anwar's cause. And unlike previous crises, the public had ready access to alternatives. Satellite TV made foreign news channels available for Malaysia's middle class. The international media, including locally produced editions of the *International Herald Tribune* and *Asia Wall Street Journal*, and *Harakah*, provided extensive reporting on Malaysian developments. And the Internet was a new source of information, with dozens of pro-Anwar sites appearing. The quality of Internet sites was mixed, but some had well-researched pieces, and many carried literary pieces that made powerful use of satire. And even information that was wrong could cause unease — such as a September report that UMNO leaders Datuk Najib and Datuk Abdullah had resigned from the government.

The government's handling of Anwar's dismissal, and the trial, also gave rise to what many described as "collateral damage". Sordid, explicit descriptions of Anwar's alleged sexual misdemeanours in the local press, on television, in court, and even in Mahathir's news conferences, generated considerable public unease and contravened Malay traditions that abhor shaming a rival in public. "Every new development in the Anwar Ibrahim trial deepens the disgust of it all", wrote a leading Malay literary figure. "The headlines local newspapers now run would curl the whiskers of a sewer rat. Does anyone up there care what this is doing to the Malays? This is shaming the Malays".[14] The trial has also revealed unflattering details about links between the government and private business, and the administration of justice. The reputation of the police in particular has been tarnished by the revelation of Special Branch "turning over" and "neutralization" procedures, and the acknowledgement of a former Special Branch head that he might lie in court if the Prime Minister asked him to.

In retrospect, it is apparent that problems faced by the government were to a large extent created by its determination to move quickly against Anwar and, once he had declined a trouble-free exit, to declare his guilt before this had been confirmed by the courts. Had Anwar remained as deputy until after the Commonwealth Games and the APEC summit he would not have been the focus of so much international media attention, and the police would not have been diverted from other tasks. Had UMNO followed its traditional practice of suspending officials until legal processes had taken their course, and UMNO leaders refrained from public declarations of Anwar's guilt, Anwar would not have had such strong grounds for claiming injustice.

At year's end, the government was facing perhaps its most severe test in Mahathir's eighteen-year rule. Previous conflicts had been confined within UMNO. This time the government faced opposition within the party, as well as broader opposition from the public at large. An additional difference was that communications had changed — ready access to the international media and the Internet made this conflict far more difficult to manage than those in the past.

Conclusion

Malaysia at the beginning of 1998 did not seem a likely candidate for major unrest. Like many neighbouring countries, the economic crisis prompted a broad reassessment of development strategies, and an opening up of politics as the local media offered a forum for discussion of alternative ideas. Both inside and outside Malaysia, analysts were critical of Dr Mahathir's response to the crisis, and many expected that he would either step down, or be forced to step down by his deputy, Anwar.

Mahathir confounded his critics, as he has done so many times in the past. Alone in the region, Malaysia reversed cautious moves towards democratic opening, and departed from traditional liberal economic policies.

This is unlikely to be the end of the story. Sustained opposition to these moves demonstrated the emergence of a new political culture, unwilling to accept instructions from above as in the past. The Internet has made it possible to disseminate information widely — to a much greater extent than the "flying letters" (*surat layang*) of the past. With elections due by August 2000, the government, in particular UMNO's leadership, will have to respond to this.

Notes

1. As Education Minister, Dr Mahathir had no direct authority to invoke the ISA, but he has said he believes his intervention was responsible. *Straits Times*, 24 May 1997.
2. *Straits Times*, 4 May 1998, quoting from *Business Week*.
3. *Utusan Malaysia*, 5 September 1998.
4. *Utusan Express* (an English language paper published on the Internet by *Utusan Malaysia*), 17 September 1997; and *New Straits Times*, 20 September 1997.
5. *Utusan Malaysia*, 16 May 1998.
6. *Straits Times*, 30 June 1998.
7. R. Greene and J. Eifters, *The 48 Laws of Power* (Viking Penguin, 1998).
8. *Business Times* (Singapore), 26 September 1998.
9. These past controversies have included: multi-billion dollar losses sustained by government-owned Bank Bumiputra, and from efforts to corner the international tin market in the early 1980s (Maminco); even greater losses in the 1990s from Central Bank currency speculation (in rivalry with George Soros) and mistakes by the government-owned Perwaja Steel; mass arrests under the ISA in 1987 (Operation Lalang); the sacking of three top judges in 1988; reducing the powers of the sultans in 1984 and 1991; an armed clash with an Islamic group in 1985 (Memali); and the crushing of the Islamic group Darul Arqam, and arrest of its leaders under the ISA in 1994.
10. Objectives and membership of Gerak can be found on its website, http://www.members.tripod.com/gerak_org/index.html, and that of Gagasan at http:// www.malaysia.n et/dap/ggs-m.htm.
11. *Financial Times* (London), 22 December 1998.
12. *Straits Times*, 11 January 1999.
13. The Attorney General's acknowledgement on 5 January 1999 that police had been responsible for *some* of Anwar's injuries, the announcement of an independent enquiry on 27 January, and the former police chief's admission on 28 February that he had struck Anwar did a little to clear the air, but there are still many issues to resolve. More detailed comments on the legal aspects of the case can be

found on Internet sites for the Bar Council of Malaysia, http://www.jaring.my/barmal/; the International Movement for a Just World, http://www.jaring.my/just/, particularly their section on the Anwar Ibrahim Crisis, http://www2.jaring.my/just/Anwarpage.htm; and an independent legal site, http://www.geo cities.com/CapitolHill/Congress/5544/.

14. Rehman Rashid, "The Politics of Contempt", posted on soc.culture.Malaysia, Thursday, 17 December 1998, 10:23 am.

TEARS AND FEARS
Tun Mahathir's Last Hurrah

Bridget Welsh

Amidst tears and apprehension about a future without a man who became synonymous with Malaysia for over a generation, Malaysia's fourth and longest-serving prime minister stepped down after a sixteen-month transition on 31 October 2003, making way for the tenure of his appointed deputy, Abdullah Ahmad Badawi. Malaysia's new prime minister faces an extraordinary set of challenges, many of which were the direct result of his predecessor's twenty-two-year premiership that ended on a high note of international stature and strong domestic support, especially among non-Malays. Mahathir's last year in office was indeed a tribute to his service to Malaysia, yet it was riddled with controversy at home and abroad as his style of rule and views provoked strong criticism. Abdullah's first few months in office sent a signal that his leadership differed both in style and substance. However, he needs to obtain a strong political mandate in the general election and party elections in 2004, before he can effectively implement reforms and initiate policies that address some of the problems Tun Mahathir left behind.

Grand and Controversial International Exit

Over the course of his twenty-two years in office, Mahathir propelled Malaysia on to the international stage, citing its success in managing ethnic tensions, promoting economic development and projecting an anti-Western stance as a calling card for the developing world and Muslim nations. While the merits of Mahathir's record in

---

Reprinted from Daljit Singh and Chin Kin Wah, eds., *Southeast Asian Affairs 2004* (Singapore: Institute of Southeast Asian Studies, 2004), pp. 139–55. At the time of original publication, Bridget Welsh was Assistant Professor of Southeast Asian Studies at the Paul H. Nitze School of Advanced International Studies (SAIS) of Johns Hopkins University in Washington, D.C.

these areas remain contentious, 2003 was used to solidify his role as an international spokesman on issues of co-operation and social justice in the international community. The year saw the culmination of a gradual progression of a foreign policy over the last third of his years in office involving extensive overseas travel and the systematic expansion of his exposure in Africa, the Middle East, and Latin America.[1] At its core Mahathir projected himself as one of the leading critics of the United States, whose policy in Iraq isolated itself from the international community.

The grand exit unfolded in three acts, involving three different gatherings that drew international attention. In February, Malaysia hosted the Non-Aligned Movement (NAM) conference in Kuala Lumpur. The event served to galvanize opposition to perceived unilateralism on the part of the Bush administration. Tensions were building within the United Nations over a military response to the Saddam regime. The Bush administration, supported by a neo-conservative approach to foreign policy built on the doctrine of pre-emption, was seeking U.N. approval to oust Saddam Hussein from power. Underscored by deep reservations about the justification for war in Iraq and suspicion of U.S. involvement in the Middle East, Mahathir avidly opposed the effort and appealed to his electorate for support. With government backing, a broad-based social movement numbering in the thousands, known as Malaysians for Peace, reinforced Malaysian opposition to the U.S. attack "on Iraq". Mahathir argued that war should be "outlawed", that "no single nation should be allowed to police the world", and that a broad multilateral mandate was needed to effectively curb terrorism.[2] Attention centred, however, on the references in his speech in which he called the victims of the September 11 attacks "collateral" damage for long-standing mistakes in U.S. foreign policy, notably the Palestine-Israeli conflict. The comments split the Malaysia-America Friendly Caucus that had formed on Capitol Hill in the wake of a thawing of relations between the Mahathir administration and the United States in 2001, and set in place a waiting mode in many circles in the United States that counted the days until Mahathir's departure. Behind the scenes, Mahathir used the NAM meeting to organize opposition to Bush's policy towards Iraq in the United Nations. This soured U.S.-Malaysia relations over Iraq even further. Mahathir's calls for greater responsibility on the part of the West for development in the developing world were drowned over the U.S. Iraq policy, even though the NAM conference itself was held to be a partial success in rejuvenating (albeit temporarily) the movement that had lapsed in influence since the heyday of the 1955 Bandung conference.

In June Mahathir used highly racial anti-Western discourse at the United Malays National Organisation (UMNO) General Assembly. In what has become typical of Mahathir's combative style, his main address to UMNO delegates focused on the moral degeneration of the "West" as a root cause of domestic problems in the West, ranging from theft to incest.[3] As he highlighted "European" moral decay, he continued his pattern of using a Western enemy to minimize domestic conflict. Yet, unlike the rhetorical anti-globalization attacks at the height of the *reformasi* years (1998–2001), the speech primarily served to reinforce perceptions of Mahathir's racial view of the world. The circulation of Henry Ford's treatise against Jews at the assembly enhanced this interpretation.[4] The party infighting within UMNO that the speech hoped to minimize continued to simmer as the leadership transition was unfolding. Throughout the assembly Mahathir did not explicitly acknowledge his retirement, fueling speculation that he might stay on as he continued to hold on to power and promote his views internationally. Those expecting a passing of the baton were sorely disappointed.

It was not until the Organization of Islamic Conference (OIC) meeting in mid-October that Mahathir was to deliver his final decisive international speech while in office. When Mahathir launched an Islamization drive in 1982 with the co-optation of Anwar Ibrahim he began to articulate a stronger Islamic dimension in his foreign policy.[5] From Bosnia to Iraq, Mahathir projected the image of Malaysia as a developed and comparatively open political system in the Muslim world that was closely connected to issues in the *ummah*. In October, he focused on two issues: concern for a fairer settlement for Palestinians and misperceptions of a connection between Islam and terrorism. In a speech that openly called on Muslims to rethink their beliefs and actions, his voice of moderation was drowned out by twenty-eight controversial words about Jews in which he claimed they ruled the world.[6] The anti-Semitic comments provoked outrage in the West leading to a rebuke by President Bush at the APEC meeting in Bangkok and overshadowed the overall intent of his speech to address problems within the Muslim world.[7] His speech and the response illustrated the significant role that Mahathir had acquired as an international anti-West spokesman, one whose combative rhetoric included important messages for greater moderation and social justice. His retirement shortly after the OIC speech, however, reinforced the controversy associated with his racial worldview and marred his international image. Mahathir's international profile served to project Malaysia far beyond its borders, yet ultimately with mixed results.

Neighbourhood Squabbles, a Weaker ASEAN and an EAEC Reality

Behind the grand international curtain, regional relations between Malaysia and its neighbours changed significantly in 2003, particularly with Singapore, Brunei, and Myanmar (Burma).

The year began with "strained" Singapore-Malaysia relations that continued to sour until Mahathir's departure, with full-page advertisements and booklet publications as part of campaigns launched by both governments in an all-out effort to defend their respective positions on issues such as the ongoing water talks, sovereignty over Pedra Branca/Pulau Batu Putih, gas prices, and immigration processing. While relations had waxed and waned during the Mahathir years, Malaysia was angered by the 2002 publication of a booklet *Water Talks? If Only It Could* in Singapore that discredited Malaysia's case in the water negotiations. The publication stated that an agreement on the price of water had been reached and Malaysia was violating the agreement.[8] This spiralled into a series of responses, rhetorical and substantive, by both countries, which included petty actions to open condemnation on both sides. The main problems involved a breakdown of the water talks and sovereignty of a small island neighbouring both countries, which was eventually transferred to the International Court of Justice in the Hague for arbitration. Trust between leaders, Mahathir and Goh

Chok Tong, had apparently evaporated. Mahathir was not willing to retire without staking out Malaysia's position, irrespective of the bad blood spilled. The official strain, however, did not extend into the robust economic links, labour flows and tourism, as most Singaporeans and Malaysians ignored the diplomatic spat.

Ties between Malaysia and Brunei also took a turn for the worse. At stake was control over the rich Kikeh oil reserves estimated to comprise over 700 million barrels, 21 per cent of Malaysia's current reserves.[9] Unlike the longstanding tensions between Malaysia and Singapore, the Kikeh oil find in the Baram Delta off the coast of both countries opened wounds that were healing between Malaysia and Brunei as border disputes had eased, even over the Limbang River. From the year 2000, however, each country claimed the Kikeh area as part of its "exclusive economic zone", 200 nautical miles off its coastline. They launched deals with international oil companies to explore the area. Unlike the prospecting in the Gulf of Thailand, parties in Kikeh were unable to form a joint-venture for exploration. The potential gains were just too high, and the underlying dependence of the countries on oil obscured efforts to reach a compromise. In March, Brunei sent a gunboat to the area and Malaysia responded by sending several gunboats in April to prevent a Total ship in partnership with Brunei from entering the contentious waters. As the year drew to a close, both countries appeared willing to resolve the dispute, yet the problem remained. Mahathir as the longest-serving prime minister in office again flexed his muscles as a regional leader, staking out Malaysia's claim with the armed warships.

Further afield, Mahathir reversed a cordial relationship with the Burmese military junta, the SPDC (State Peace and Development Council), after Nobel Laureate and the National League for Democracy leader, Aung San Suu Kyi's convoy was attacked on 30 May. The clash led to the arrest of "The Lady" and members of her party and an outpouring of international criticism. Mahathir, close to Special U.N. Envoy Razali Ismail who visited the country in his tenth visit in June, joined the condemnation of the attacks, suggesting that Myanmar (Burma) could be expelled from the Association of Southeast Asian Nations (ASEAN).[10] This claim reversed a long-standing position advocated by Malaysia for a broader and more inclusive regional grouping and alienated the Burmese junta. With the appointment of Khin Nyint as prime minister in August and the announcement of the road-map, ASEAN's pressure on the regime has eased, but the relationship between Malaysia and the SPDC was scarred. Malaysia was excluded from the Bangkok discussions of the road-map in December, and Abdullah will have to work hard to rebuild the relationship.

Regional tensions in 2003 illustrated Mahathir's inability to become the dominant leader in ASEAN, even on the eve of his retirement. Tensions with Singapore and the rising ambition of Thaksin Shinawatra curbed Mahathir's impact and the regional organization was weakened by the vexing question of how to address the Myanmar (Burma) "problem" and by divisions over the invasion of Iraq. Mahathir's retirement, however, reduced Malaysia's influence in ASEAN, as Abdullah joined the queue in leadership tenure. As the eldest statesman, Mahathir was respected, as the tribute of regional leaders at the APEC meeting in October showed. Yet he failed to fully resolve the problems of regional expansion of which he had been the leading advocate, despite his threat to expel Myanmar, and fuelled conflict within ASEAN by fostering bilateral tensions, leaving the organization comparatively weaker.

In contrast, his dream of a greater East Asian community materialized further in 2003. Under the rubric of ASEAN+3, Mahathir, along with Goh Chok Tong, had pushed for stronger links with China, Japan, and Korea, and the region has followed suit. At the First East Asia Congress in August Mahathir acknowledged that his goal had been obtained and reaffirmed a twenty-year commitment to Japan in the Look East Policy.[11] While Malaysia's relationships with countries in Greater East Asia still contain suspicion, China's "charm offensive" has made headway.[12] Abdullah's prominent visits to China and Japan as deputy prime minister were widely publicized. Japan's star, however, has dimmed, making way for China. In 2003, trade between Malaysia and China reached RM77 billion.[13] Even after the impact of severe acute respiratory syndrome (SARS), 557,647 Chinese tourists visited Malaysia in the year 2003. The government has also opted to open a China Studies Centre at the University of Malaya. While China poses an economic challenge to Malaysia, 2003 fostered greater co-operation and deepened economic and cultural ties.

Institutionalizing Malaysia's "War on Terror"[14]

In 2003, Malaysia continued with its firm approach to regional terrorism, even though this issue resonated more abroad than domestically. Up till 2001, Malaysia had been serving as a critical transshipment point and organization centre for terrorism in the region, notably the leading regional organization Jemaah Islamiyah (JI). From 2001, Malaysia began to exercise a more vigorous enforcement role in addressing terrorist issues, which mirrored stronger regional enforcement, particularly in Singapore. The August 2003 capture of Hambali, the leader of JI married to a Malaysian, was a critical success in a year where the August JW Marriott bombing in Jakarta reminded the region of the persistent terrorist threat. Two of the current leaders of the JI, for example, Noordin Mohammed Mop Top and Asahari Husin (also known as Amran Mansour) are thought to be Malaysians.

While Malaysia's response to terrorism was firm, it couched its initiatives within the rubic of regional co-operation or domestic initiatives rather than a close connection with the United States' "war on terror". In September the government publicly listed the twelve groups that have been deemed as national threats and acknowledged that it was actively looking for 273 JI members. The government estimated that there were 465 JI members in Malaysia, 69 of whom were held in Kamunting prison.[15] It introduced four terrorist-related laws, including changes to the penal code and money-laundering-related measures. Malaysia also established a special naval police force for anti-terrorism patrols. The patrols have been concentrated in waters off Sabah, near a known route of terrorist movements between Malaysia, Indonesia, and the Philippines. Building on close security co-operation with Singapore and Thailand and to a lesser extent the Philippines, Indonesia, and the United States, Malaysia deepened intelligence-sharing. The Special Branch arrested Zulkifli Abdul Hir in December, another of the JI's leaders. Malaysia built on its regional ties by offering in September to broker talks between the

Philippine government and the Moro Islamic Liberation Front (MILF) based in Mindanao. Before 2001, Malaysia had provided sanctuary for many of the MILF leaders, and, as such, is in a unique position to mediate between the separatist group and Philippine government. The offer to broker negotiations indicates an increasing decisiveness on the part of the Malaysian government to address transnational terrorism.

Still, problems over co-operation remain. In July the Malaysian government set up a regional terrorism centre in Kuala Lumpur, which has been less than effective. The centre was strongly supported by the United States, but Malaysia carefully distanced itself in the funding and selection of personnel, illustrating persistent reservations about a U.S.-led "war on terror" and the difficulty of balancing international pressure with a suspicious domestic constituency. The activities of the centre have been extremely limited — a prescheduled course on financing. The centre still lacked a curriculum at the end of the year, even though it had been open for about six months. More serious is the lack of regional ownership in the centre, as the Malaysians have yet to galvanize regional involvement. Rather, a pattern of separate country-specific centres has evolved in the region, dampening a regional response to terrorism. Serious questions also persist over the use of Malaysian-based companies as fronts for terrorist financing.[16]

In spite of its initiatives, Malaysia's "war on terror" remains shrouded in secrecy and lacks broad domestic credibility. The government primarily relies on the draconian Internal Security Act (ISA), which has been highly politicized after the arrest of Anwar Ibrahim and members of the opposition party keADILan during the *reformasi* era. By year's end there were seventy-nine people held for terrorism, including Abu Jibril, believed to be among the most extreme religious preachers in the region. Yet, many observers question the incarcerations under the ISA because of inadequate transparency and a failure to justify the detentions, even in a White Paper. The 2003 anti-terrorist laws are questioned on human rights grounds, especially the money-laundering bill which places a higher burden of responsibility on lawyers and accountants to report clients and subjects them to a RM1 million fine.[17] To some, Malaysia is seen to be responding to demands of the United States in their "war on terror", whose own record on human rights since 9/11 in places such as Guatanamo Bay has raised serious concerns world-wide.

This places the Malaysian government in a difficult position; on the one hand, it co-operates with the United States, and on the other, the government faces pressure from the human rights community to justify the co-operation. When thirteen Malaysian students in Pakistan were arrested in July on U.S. advice, for example, the Malaysian government had them extradited and held them under the ISA. Yet, in November the government released them, responding to public pressure for leniency during the Hari Raya holidays.[18] It remains unclear whether the government released potential JI organizers or innocent students who were marked by an association with a Pakistani *madrasah*. Rather than opt for greater disclosure, the Malaysian government has chosen to hide behind the U.S. umbrella and the ISA, which in the climate of broad anti-Americanism within Malaysia, especially among the Malay community, undermines its own credibility and ultimately efforts to tackle terrorism within Malaysia. Ultimately, Mahathir's tenure has created a context in which the politicization of the ISA and overall weakening of professionalism within the state has led to greater dependence on measures that curb human rights in security matters and, ironically, a closer affinity with the United States in the post 9/11 world.

Settling Scores and Cleaning House

On the domestic scene Mahathir continued to shape events until his retirement. While talk of a deal over the release of former Deputy Prime Minister Anwar Ibrahim circulated, especially in April, Mahathir left office with Anwar behind bars, one appeal exhausted, another delayed, and facing debilitating back problems without surgery. Even though Mahathir openly acknowledged in October that he regretted the treatment of Anwar, the pivotal events of 1998 darkened assessments of his premiership. In June he freed five activists in keADILan, after two years in prison under the ISA. While it remains unclear whether supporters of Anwar will hold the same degree of antagonism towards Abdullah, Mahathir failed to reach any compromise on the Anwar issue and reach out to the Malay community more broadly, especially many among the *reformasi* youth that he alienated.

Overall, Mahathir appeared inclined to settle scores in 2003 rather than let issues slide. In October the trial of activist Irene Fernandez was moved forward before his retirement and she was convicted to one year in jail, currently on appeal, for the publication of a report on deplorable conditions for illegal immigrants. Malaysia's longest trial — eight years — came to an abrupt end under Malaysia's longest-serving prime minister.

Mahathir also appeared inclined to sort out affairs within the Barisan Nasional (BN). The most openly contentious conflict was in the Malaysian Chinese Association (MCA), which had divided into different factions supporting the president, Ling Liong Sik, and challengers to his rule led by Lim Ah Lek. According to Ling's opponents, his son's debts and his long tenure were not rejuvenating the party. Ling openly offered an open undated resignation letter in 2002 in an effort to reduce party infighting and repeated his offer in January 2003. Tensions within the MCA continued to simmer between Ling's "Team A" and Lim's "Team B" factions. By July, with pressure mounting and the nod and encouragement from Mahathir, Ling resigned, opening the way for new leadership, the young grassroots-oriented compromise leader Ong Ka Ting.

One of the first measures Ong introduced was a nine-year term limit to the party presidency at the MCA Congress in August. This move went a long way to reducing tensions within the party, which continued to surface through the fall. Ong experienced some teething problems, as charges of ties between him and triads circulated widely in the first few months of his presidency. These eased somewhat after a known triad leader, "Jackie Chan" (Ong King Ee) of the Sio Sam Ong (Three Little Emperors), resigned from the party in August.[19] Ong has strong support within the MCA. He has to work, however, to build ties and establish credibility with the Chinese business community, especially the tycoons, who remained close to Ling even as they directly lobbied UMNO for contracts and state access. With the leadership issue resolved and the potential for infighting dampened, the MCA was in a stronger position for the 2004 general election. The party, however, continued to face a generation gap among its membership due to the MCA's inability to attract the Chinese youth. More importantly, the MCA faces a changing demographic trend that reduces the number of Chinese Malaysians, their main supporters.

Mahathir's resolution of the MCA crisis stood in stark contrast to his efforts to address factionalism within UMNO. His repeated calls on UMNO members to refrain from jockeying among each other fell on deaf ears. On the surface, the infighting was a product of the extended transition, which was riddled with insecurity. Members shifted alliances and personal loyalties for positions within UMNO, in some cases, advancement. Mahathir muddied the situation by not definitively handing the reins to Abdullah. Through September rumours continued to circulate that Mahathir might not step down. He called on Abdullah to appoint Defence Minister Najib Tun Razak as his deputy to curb infighting, but Abdullah refused, opting to make the choice of his number two at his own pace. This fuelled further speculation among the UMNO rank and file about the transition itself and portfolios after October.

Party infighting within UMNO had deeper roots, however. Since 1987, Mahathir had systematically weakened UMNO as an institution, personalizing ties and prioritizing personal loyalty, especially to himself.[20] His removal of Anwar had sent a strong signal to members who had opted for independent positions or had challenged the status quo, and reinforced the importance of personal relationships in a feudal party leadership hierarchy. Members rely heavily on "social capital" — patronage and personal networks, school ties, family ties, marriage, and membership in party cliques to solidify loyalties — rather than on routinized rules and procedures to organize party positions.[21] Mahathir changed and defined the rules of the game so comprehensively during his tenure that status within the party became more uncertain, subject to whims and rumours. This pattern developed as the stakes of leadership within the party increased. Mahathir fostered a climate of unchecked state patronage, which was dependent on position and state access. Even private domestic capital within Malaysia became increasingly subservient to political favour. Structurally, the combination of a more personalized and powerful UMNO has instilled a factionalized and unstable climate within the party.

Even if infighting within UMNO is not a new phenomenon, the transition only served to exacerbate the uncertainties. Through October, the question overshadowing the transition was whether Mahathir would step down. After that, members wondered whether Abdullah, lacking his own mandate within the party, would have enough power to win over the support of the rank and file and stave off challenges to his leadership. The central issue was the choice of Abdullah's deputy, which was announced in early January 2004, and major cabinet portfolios. Najib was appointed as deputy prime minister (DPM) over UMNO vice-president Muhyiddin Yassin after months of speculation. The decision points to the persistence of infighting under Abdullah, geared towards two contests — the upcoming general election expected by April 2004 and the UMNO party elections to be held by June 2004.

The infighting suggests that UMNO is searching for a new political identity.

With Mahathir's departure, a process of soul-searching has begun. Many are turning to their rural roots. This rejuvenation of traditional Malay identity underlies some of the shifting of support to Chief Minister of Selangor Khir Toyo, closely tied to rural *kampung* life, away from Youth Chief Hishamuddin Onn in what is expected to be a contest for the Youth Chief position next year. While Hishammuddin maintains strong support, many in the rank and file are rethinking what and who the party represents. In the same vein, of late some members have consciously rejected foreign "public school" ties for local education. The élite-trained "Melayu Baru" with handphones and snazzy cars are nostalgic for their *kampung*, not co-incidentally the areas where the party lost most support in the 1999 contest. It remains to be seen whether this move is an electoral ploy, political jockeying, or serious reconfiguration of party identity.

An integral component of the changing identity within UMNO involves rising religious conservatism, a greening of the party, as some members are drawn to leaders who are seen as conforming to the increasing Islamization in Malay society. The wearing of the *tudong* (head scarf) by party wives, for example, solicits greater member support, as does the introduction of measures deemed more "Islamic", such as Perlis Chief Minister Shahidan Kassim's attempts in January to change the polygamy law and impose a state curfew.[22] While these measures were rejected by the more liberal majority in the UMNO Supreme Council — which maintains a strong moderate position — they point to a conservative stream within the party, which may become more prominent as members search for support in their constituencies. To date, Abdullah has not fostered conservatism within UMNO; his Islamic scholar credentials have given him the space to avoid deepening the competition with PAS for religious legitimacy that Mahathir began in 1982.

Mahathir left UMNO in a stronger electoral position, despite the internal conflicts. The passage of the new electoral districts in July 2003 strengthened the position of UMNO and the BN as a whole. The delineation exercise created twenty-six seats, most of which involved greater multi-ethnic pluralities. At least ten of these seats are expected to increase UMNO's electoral fortunes.[23] The creation of new multi-ethnic constituencies works in favour of the governing coalition; many non-Malays fear the influence of Parti Islam Se Malaysia (PAS), especially after the implementation of *hudud* law in Terengganu in 2002. The BN's growing electoral confidence has helped to ease tensions within the coalition. Disagreements over construction of the Penang Outer Ring Road in 2002 had ebbed as the two MCA-suspended members that voted against the initiative were quietly brought back into the fold. Mahathir left behind a more confident and comparatively less divided governing coalition.

Opposition Divisions and Tactics

The BN's confidence stemmed in part from the weaknesses within the opposition. The Barisan Alternatif (BA, or Alternative Front) had split over differences regarding PAS's articulation of the Islamic state in 2002. Uncomfortable with a position that was perceived to violate the secular foundations in the constitution and potentially undermined the rights of non-Muslims, the Democratic Action Party (DAP) opted to go it alone, although promised not to compete directly against other opposition parties. The opposition no longer offers a broad multi-ethnic alternative to voters. Throughout 2003, the differences among and within parties continued to simmer. KeADILan, dependent on PAS for electoral machinery and supported primarily by a Malay Muslim constituency, was caught in the middle between PAS and the DAP. These differences became less critical as the party became enveloped in its own internal battles over its merger with Malaysian Peoples' Party, or Parti Rakyat Malaysia (PRM). It was less clear what keADILan represented, as the issue of Anwar Ibrahim served less to unite members and mobilize voters. The conflicts manifested themselves in public squabbles. Youth members in keADILan, for example, resigned over the merger with the PRM in September.[24]

PAS remains the strongest opposition party, largely because it challenges the legitimacy of UMNO among the Malays. In 2003 the party deepened its religious conservatism, as the dominance of the *ulama* or *kepimpinan ulama* was reinforced at its 49th General Assembly in September. Ulama Hassan Shukri was elected as deputy-president defeating Mustafa Ali, the University of Malaya economics graduate. Hassan's victory and the overall new leadership composition highlight the decreasing influence of professionals who joined the party in the 1990s and, not surprisingly, corresponds to measures that are less receptive to the non-Malay community.[25] While the party stated that it would field women candidates, for example, it continued to claim that women were "neither half of nor equal to men", evoking a narrow interpretation of women's rights. The party's conservatism has been increasing steadily, since the early 1980s, corresponding to changes taking place within Malaysia, but it was the death of former president Fadzil Noor in 2002 that strengthened the position of Hadi Awang and fellow *ulama*, who have parochial roots and less exposure to multi-ethnic communities.[26]

On 12 November, PAS launched its Islamic Blueprint, setting out guidelines on Islamic governance at the state level.[27] The document lacked clarity and raised wide concerns over rights and public accountability, particularly among non-Malays. Yet, for some Malays, the blueprint reinforced the perception that PAS has greater religious legitimacy. PAS has gradually introduced Islamic law in the two states it governs, with the most comprehensive measures in Terengganu from July 2002. The party has capitalized on its religious credentials in an effort to win state governments in Malay-dominant areas, with its sight set on Kedah in particular. The focus on religion, however, obscures the party's organizational strength.[28] PAS rivals UMNO in its ability to mobilize voters. The organizational capacity of the party will be tested in the 2004 election with the leadership transition to Abdullah; PAS no longer holds the same moral high ground on issues such as corruption as it did under Mahathir. Personalities, local party networks, and religious postitions will be contested in rural constituencies.

With PAS focusing on winning states, the other opposition parties will try to maintain their national positions. KeADILan, holding a handful of seats, faces fierce competition from the BN, especially in rural Malay areas. The DAP equally will be challenged to hold on to its seats, as its "929 campaign" (named after the day Mahathir declared Malaysia an Islamic state in 2001) opposing Islamic governance has not won widespread support. The DAP has focused on promoting the issue of secular government. The message has not yielded substantially greater support for the party, although the message has touched a chord among many Malaysians. The problems of the 929 campaign illustrate the party's frayed connection with its base of Chinese voters. Both keADILan and the DAP do not have clearly defined electoral issues, beyond Anwar and 929 respectively. The ISA has faded for voters in the post 9/11 climate. The opposition does not appear to have a comprehensive winning electoral strategy.

Railways and Economic Engines

The opposition has a long hill to climb, in part due to strengths in the economy. Mahathir's crowning glory was economic legitimacy (albeit tarnished by corruption), which sustained support for his tenure as he became increasingly authoritarian. He left office with the economy growing steadily: in 2003 Malaysia's GDP (gross domestic product) growth registered 4.8 per cent, up from 4.1 per cent the previous year. Inflation declined to an impressive 1.1 per cent. The current account showed a record surplus of RM48.2 billion or 13 per cent of GDP while reserves soared to US$44.9 billion. Growth in 2003 was driven primarily by exports of petroleum and palm oil. With sharp price increases in these commodities, 19 per cent and 16.4 per cent respectively, and steady rise in electronic manufacturing profits, Malaysia underscored the largest trade surplus with its largest trading partner, the United States (RM74.7 billion from RM51.5 billion the year before). By the end of the year Malaysia became the United States' tenth largest trading partner.

These impressive figures hide deep uncertainties. Malaysia's economy has been driven by foreign investment and, since 1997, public expenditure. Substantial new foreign investment remains elusive, although it did increase in 2003 from 0.3 per cent of GDP to 1.9 per cent. This new investment was concentrated in the oil and gas sector, and not located in cutting-edge industries like pharmaceuticals and biotechnology, despite the efforts on the part of the Malaysian government to promote these sectors. With limited capital flowing into the country, the government has relied on public expenditure to stimulate the economy, particularly domestic consumption. The outpouring of funds has sustained five years of deficit spending which has reached 5.5 per cent of GDP, the second highest in the region after the Philippines. The level of public funding was illustrated in the tabling of the mid-review of the Eighth Malaysia Plan in October. In his last task in Parliament, Mahathir added RM50.8 million to the initially projected RM100 million allocation for public contracts, which had exceeded the initial five-year projection by RM9.2 million half-way through the five-year plan. The majority of these contracts — 60 per cent — are allocated to Malays in a patronage effort on the part of UMNO to appeal to voters.[29] Deficit spending relies on incoming revenue. Currently, Malaysia's external debt stands at RM194.5 billion, 49.9 per cent of GDP. Abdullah inherited serious structural financial vulnerabilities.

In response to these vulnerabilities, Abdullah has opted to curb spending on "big projects". In December, a high-speed rail project linking the Asian railway from Singapore to China was postponed under the guise of cutting spending. Closer inspection showed that Abdullah opted not to grant the Malaysia Mining Corporation Berhad and Gamuda Berhad the RM14.5

billion ringgit (US$3.8 billion) contract as a signal that closed bidding on projects would not be tolerated. The postponement sent a signal that Abdullah was willing to reform economic policy.

Yet Mahathir's economic policy-making legacy extends beyond public finance to a strong connection with specific policies and the policy-making process. The pegging of the Malaysian ringgit tied to a bundle of capital control measures has been viewed as Malaysia's saving grace during the 1997 crisis. It remains unclear whether the peg currently strengthens the economy. With the depreciation of the U.S. dollar, Malaysia faced increasing pressure on the peg throughout the year. Exports are no longer as profitable as they were when the peg was introduced, and the pressure is reducing Malaysia's competitiveness in an increasingly competitive regional economic environment. Abdullah will have to decide whether to change the policy and choose the form that this policy will take. In making any changes, he will be distancing himself from the stability and recovery associated with the currency peg, and possibly open himself to criticism in economic management. Similar problems are associated with the Proton Saga, which has relied heavily on protectionism for profits. Abdullah's reduction of tariffs at the end of the year suggests that he is cautiously willing to introduce reforms.

Policy reforms are only part of the terrain Abdullah must navigate. During the later years of Mahathir's tenure he increasingly depended on a small group of advisers to formulate economic decisions, reducing the role of the technocrats in the bureaucracy in economic policy-making. This relationship allowed for personalization of decision-making and reduced transparency. While the decisions overall were sound, including significant reforms in the banking sector, they rested on the skills of key individuals, including Mahathir himself and were open to criticism over corruption. Abdullah needs to build on the existing system in the short term and broaden the economic policy-making process in the longer term. Unlike Mahathir, he lacks the same familiarity with economic issues. With competition from China, the country needs a new engine of growth, beyond petroleum, electronics, and palm oil.

Abdullah Badawi's Populist Honeymoon

Abdullah has managed to divert attention from the country's economic vulnerabilities in a widespread populist campaign for his own political mandate. When he took office, there was an air of uneasiness, as the volume from the Prime Minister's Office immediately quietened. Abdullah's first speech set a different tone, one of compromise and consultation. Building on his "likeability", Pak Lah as he is affectionately called, initiated a series of measures that distanced him from his predecessor. Foremost is an open and public anti-corruption campaign, clearly illustrated in the railway project postponement. Open bidding as well as a back-handed rebuke against Syed Mokhtar, who owns Malaysia Mining Corporation Berhad, a close ally of Mahathir, has sent a strong signal that a new style of governance has emerged. He strengthened the Anti-Corruption Agency which immediately investigated Mohd Nazri Abdul Aziz, an UMNO cabinet minister.

At the same time, Abdullah launched significant initiatives to clean up the police force with the creation of the

Police Commission in January 2004.[30] This reflects greater appreciation of the increasing prevalence of crime, especially rape and murder, and concerns about the professionalism of the police force to address crime. Crime has dominated the press throughout 2003, with headlines featuring items such as the gruesome murders of Canny Ong in June (she had returned from America to visit her sick father) and trial of the murder of the second wife of the Raja Jaafar Raja Muda Musa, a Perak prince. She was chopped on the neck and thrown over a five-story bridge in October 2002.

Badawi has also championed the "ordinary" person. In December he stemmed an effort to stop people withdrawing savings from the Employees Provident Fund (EPF) at fifty-five, even though the initiative made financial sense.[31] He also began restructing the public funds away from "big" projects to "smaller" projects, focused on the rural areas.

Abdullah's populist initiatives reflect political realities, and to a certain degree his own grassroots orientation. He lacks strong links within Mahathir's UMNO. His participation in "Team B" in 1987 split the party. Upon assuming office in October his power has come from the institution of the executive rather than through strong party support. He needs his own mandate. Ironically, some of the initiatives weaken his base within UMNO, particularly his anti-corruption campaign. His aim is to get enough popular support in the election to offset a party leadership challenge. Whether these initiatives are viable and sustainable remains to be seen, in particular after the election. They require structural changes. Mahathir essentially neutered the bureaucracy, emphasizing loyalty over performance. Abdullah will need greater professionalism for his initiatives to be effective.

Emerging New Social Contract

The populist measures point to changing political dynamics within Malaysia, a reshaping of the relationship between the state and citizens. Mahathir left behind a different society than he inherited in 1981, one with greater religiosity among Muslims, a shrinking non-Malay population, and a growing younger generation. Each of these dynamics will present a challenge for Abdullah. Islamization in Malaysia has become deeply entrenched. In April the Ministry of Information banned thirty-five books, including the Iban Bible, on grounds that it was detrimental to public peace.[32] They rescinded the ban on the Bible in May. Yet, the incident points to potential vulnerability of non-Muslims. The upholding of the 2002 apostasy decision involving four deviant Muslims in Kelantan illustrates the growing role of religious courts in everyday life.[33] In this case the individuals involved were denied the right to leave Islam. Beyond the rights of the individuals, the case points to the increasing importance of religious law over secular statutes. With the implementation of Islamic law in Terengganu in 2002, there are growing concerns that the state is redefining the rights of Malaysians according to the interpretations of *ulama*. This is transforming the nature of legitimacy of the state, politicizing moral issues and behaviour, and potentially limiting the rights of those who do not follow the "correct" practices, especially Muslims who are subjected to these laws.

This dynamic also seriously impacts the non-Malays who comprise a decreasing share of the population. In 2003 the two Chinese-majority parties within the BN — the MCA (Malaysian Chinese Association) and Gerakan — tabled a possible merger.³⁴ At issue was the role of the Chinese within the polity and the protection of the rights of this community. Mahathir's departure has increased uncertainty among non-Malays. By the end of Tun's tenure he had gained the trust and loyalty of the majority of the non-Malay community. Abdullah has yet to receive this support, and the transition has fostered reflection on the position of the communities within the polity. The merger discussions suggest further reflection on the status of the Chinese within Malaysia and intense discussion of traditional issues associated with political identity, particularly cultural rights and the scope of the New Economic Policy (NEP) affirmative action policy. It is unlikely that the Indian community will face the same degree of reform until the retirement of the MIC (Malaysian Indian Congress) leader Sammy Vellu.

The demographic pressure for change has increased, and the state has responded in kind. Younger Malaysians comprise a larger share of the population and the political parties recognize that they lack strong connections with the youth. The 2003 public campaign to register younger voters failed; only 40,365 out of 2.1 million have bothered to register by September.³⁵ The government went further with the introduction of a National Service programme in June. The programme will recruit 90,000 youths in three-month separate intakes in 2004, with the aim of eventually enlisting 480,000 people.³⁶

The six-month programme, which includes military training and social service, aims to foster loyalty to the state and promote inter-ethnic integration. Mahathir left behind a disengaged, and in some cases in the post-*reformasi* period, disenchanted youth, which Abdullah will have to harness.

New Leadership and New Promises

Until his retirement, Mahathir continued to dominate politically. In 2003 he left his imprint on a swath of issues, from Singapore-Malaysia relations to the MCA leadership struggle. As his OIC remarks show, he did not end his tenure quietly. He maintained a combative style and positions, even on issues such as the treatment of Anwar Ibrahim that have marred his legacy. When he handed over the key to his office in October to Abdullah, many Malaysians shed tears in gratitude for years of service and in some cases over anxiety (and hope) about the future. Surprisingly, Mahathir, at least in the short term, has given Abdullah space to set his own path.

Abdullah has quickly stepped out of Mahathir's shadow. Using populist initiatives, he has taken on the mantle of anti-corruption and "ordinary" people, in a less controversial style. The focus has been on consolidating his domestic position. The 2004 national and party elections will test his success. The changes, however, will have to go beyond populism and mandates to address the weakening of institutions in the Mahathir era, vulnerabilities in the economy, and regional security.

Notes

Special thanks to Edmund Terence Gomez, who reviewed the draft. All errors in the article are mine.

1. Joseph Liow, "Personality, Exigencies and Contingencies: Determinants of Malaysia's Foreign Policy in the Mahathir Administration", in *Mahathir's Administration: Performance and Crisis in Governance*, by Ho Khai Leong and James Chin (Singapore: Times Books, 2001), pp. 120–60.
2. Speech by Mahathir Mohamad at the Opening Session of the XIII Summit Meeting of the Non-Aligned Movement at Putra World Trade Centre, Kuala Lumpur, 24 February 2003.
3. Speech by Mahathir Mohamad at the UMNO General Assembly at Putra World Trade Centre, 19 June 2003.
4. Simon Cameron-Moore, "Mahathir's Party Hands Out Anti-Semitic Book", Reuters, 21 June 2003.
5. Patricia Martinez, "Mahathir, Islam and the New Malay Dilemma", in *Mahathir's Administration: Performance and Crisis in Governance*, by Ho Khai Leong and James Chin (Singapore: Times Books, 2001), pp. 120–60.
6. Speech by Mahathir Mohamad at the Tenth Session of the Islamic Summit Conference in Putra Jaya, 16 October 2003 <http://www.oicsummit2003.org.my/speech_03.php>.
7. The Malaysian government adamantly denied the rebuke in the national newspaper, *New Straits Times*, 22 October 2003.
8. Government of Singapore, *Water Talks? If Only It Could* (2003) <http://www.mita.gov.sg/SgMy.htm>.
9. S. Jayasankaran and John McBeth, "Oil and Water", *Far Eastern Economic Review*, 3 July 2003, p. 17.
10. "ASEAN May Expel Myanmar", *New Straits Times*, 21 July 2003.
11. "Building the East Asian Community: The Way Forward", Speech by Prime Minister Mahathir Mohamad at the First East Asia Congress, Putra World Trade Centre, 4 August 2003.
12. "China Challenge and Opportunity", Speech by Deputy Prime Minister Abdullah Ahmad Badawi, at the Great Hall of the People, Beijing, China, 16 September 2003. Reprinted in *New Straits Times*, 17 September 2003.
13. "China Challenge and Opportunity", Speech by Deputy Prime Minister Abdullah Ahmad Badawi, at the Great Hall of the People, Beijing, China, 16 September 2003. Reprinted in *New Straits Times*, 17 September 2003.
14. Special thanks to Zachary Abuza for his assistance in this section of the paper. For a broader discussion, see his *Militant Islam in Southeast Asia* (Boulder, Co.: Lynne Rienner Publishers, 2003).
15. These groups include Tentera Sabillulah (1967), Golongan Rohaniah (1971), Koperasi Ankatan Revolusi Islam Malaysia (1972), Kumpulan CRYPTO (1977), Kumpulan Mohd Nasir Ismail (1980), Kumpulan Revolusi Islam Ibrhaim Mahmood@Ibrahim Libya (1985), Kumpulan Jundullah (1987), Kumpulan Mujahiddin Kedah (KMK) (1988), Kumpulan Perjuangan Islam Perak (KPIP) (1988), Kumpulan Al-Ma'unah (2000), Kumpulan Militan Malaysia (KMM), and Jemaah Islamiyah (2001). "Takeover attempts by 12 Groups", *New Straits Times*, 26 September 2003 and "Cops Still Looking for 273 JI Members", *Star*, 26 September 2003.
16. Zachary Abuza, "Funding Terrorism in Southeast Asia: The Financial Network of Al Qaeda and Jemaah Islamiyah", *NBR Analysis* (Washington: National Bureau of Asian Research) 14, no. 5 (December 2003).
17. Beh Lin Yi, "Major Overhaul of Legislation to Tackle Terrorism Offences" <www.malaysiakini.com>, 22 October 2003.
18. Suaram, "13 Students Detained Without

Trial under the ISA" <http://www.suaram.org/update/urgent_appeal_20031117.htm>.
19. See Lim Kit Siang, Speech at the 37th DAP anniversary dinner organized by the DAP Klang Parliamentary Liaison Committee <http://www.malaysia.net/dap/lks2459.htm>.
20. Hwang In-Won, *Personalized Politics: The Malaysian State under Mahathir* (Singapore: Institute of Southeast Asian Studies, 2003).
21. Bridget Welsh, "Malaysia's Transition: Elite Contestation, Political Dilemmas and Incremental Change", in *Woodrow Wilson Center: Special Report* (Washington, D.C.: Woodrow Wilson Center, September 2003).
22. "CM Perlis Curfews Kids", *Star*, 10 January 2003.
23. Ong Kian Ming, "The Process of the Delimitation Exercise — A Critical Examination", IKMAS Election Project (Forthcoming, 2004).
24. Yoon Szu-Mae, "Ezam: Four Want Out of Keadilan Youth Exco", 17 September 2003 <www.malaysiakini.com>.
25. Jocelyn Tan, "I am Not a Radical, Says Hadi", *Star*, 13 September 2003.
26. Farish Noor, "Blood, Sweat and Jihad: The Radicalization of the Political Discourse of the Pan-Malaysian Islamic Party (PAS) from 1982 Onwards", *Contemporary Southeast Asia* 25, no. 2 (August 2003): 200–32.
27. http://www.harakahdaily.net/islamicstate.pdf.
28. Bridget Welsh, "Real Change? Electoral Behavior in the *Reformasi* Era", in *The State of Malaysia: Ethnicity, Equity and Reform*, edited by Edmund Terence Gomez (London: RoutledgeCurzon, 2004), pp. 162–93.
29. Deborah Loh, "8th Plan Gets Fresh Engine for Growth", *New Straits Times*, 31 October 2003.
30. "Royal Commission set up to Modernise Force, Improve Image" <http://www.malaysiakini.com/news/2004010200113497.php>, 2 January 2004.
31. Foong Pek Yee, "Government 'No' to EPF", *Star*, 18 December 2003.
32. U.S. Government, *International Religious Freedom Report: Malaysia* (Bureau of Democracy, Human Rights and Labor, December 2003).
33. Ibid.
34. Alina Simon, "MCA and Gerakan May Merger to Strengthen BN", *Star*, 19 December 2003.
35. "Lackluster Registration Campaign", *New Straits Times*, 16 October 2003.
36. "Malaysia's National Service Not Like Singapore's: Najib", *Straits Times*, 29 June 2003.

MALAYSIA
Political Transformation and Intrigue in an Election Year

Johan Saravanamuttu

The year 2008 will be remembered as a watershed for the Malaysian political system and for the forward trajectory of Malaysian democracy. This election year saw a refurbished coalition of oppositional political forces, the People's Pact (Pakatan Rakyat), deprive the ruling National Front (Barisan Nasional) coalition of its two-thirds majority of seats in Parliament. Even more significantly, four state governments fell, making it a total of five governments in Opposition hands. I suggest here that this development has created a de facto two-party system for a maturing Malaysian democracy. Economically, Malaysians will be facing a severe downturn though not a technical recession. The year also saw the denouement of a leadership crisis within the United Malays National Organisation (UMNO) leading ultimately to the anticipated departure from the political stage in March 2009 of the fifth Malaysian Prime Minister Abdullah Ahmad Badawi. The political terrain remains fraught with pitfalls for premier-in-waiting Najib Abdul Razak and for Opposition Leader, Anwar Ibrahim, who awaits his sodomy trial.

The Malaysian Prime Minister Abdullah Badawi already had more than his fair share of a baggage of problems to deal with even before his tenure headed into 2008. Let me briefly recollect. After 25 November 2007, five HINDRAF lawyers remained in detention under the draconian ISA, while one was at large. The V.K. Lingam video exposé in September 2007 and the Royal

---

Reprinted in abridged format from Daljit Singh, ed., *Southeast Asian Affairs 2009* (Singapore: Institute of Southeast Asian Studies, 2009), pp. 173–92. At the time of original publication, Johan Saravanamuttu was Visiting Senior Research Fellow at the Institute of Southeast Asian Studies, Singapore.

Commission inquiry into it in January 2008 remained much in the public consciousness,[1] so too the Altantuya murder trial which had dragged on from 2007. Inter-faith fractures which had surfaced since 2005 remained largely unresolved and so too internal squabbles within the ruling coalition parties. Most sensationally, the MCA Minister for Health had to resign because of the circulation of a sex video by his detractors. Finally, the economy was not in great shape with petrol prices and inflation spiking and Mahathir still sniping from the sidelines. Yet speculation was rife by early 2008 that an early election would be called presumably to salvage the premier's beleaguered situation, more than one year in advance of the mandatory five years. In a CNN interview Abdullah did admit that a fresh mandate was necessary for him to address a host of new issues and to make good his unfulfilled anti-corruption agenda.

In the event, parliament and state assemblies, with the exception of Sarawak, were dissolved on 13 February 2008. The Election Commission called for nominations on 24 February for the 12th General Election of Malaysia to be held on 8 March 2008. An unusually long 13 days were given for campaigning and some 222 parliamentary seats were in contention along with 505 state seats. Malaysians were in for an exciting 2008, whatever the prospective outcome of the election. Hardly anyone got it right. Two days before election day, Malaysian analysts (including this one) speaking at a seminar at the Institute of Southeast Asian Studies (ISEAS) in Singapore were not prepared to concede that the Barisan Nasional (BN) would lose its two-thirds majority in parliament, let alone four more state governments.[2]

The Election Outcome

It could well be that the 8 March General Election (GE) has surpassed some of the outcomes of the 1969 watershed general election which led to the outbreak of riots in Kuala Lumpur on 13 May.[3] In 2008, the outburst of election rallies throughout the campaign period by Opposition parties was also reminiscent of May 1969, but perhaps eclipsing 1969 by the sheer numbers that attended such rallies throughout the country. One large rally in Penang saw some 50,000 in attendance, clearly unprecedented.[4] Despite the ruling coalition of Barisan Nasional (BN) losing its two-thirds majority of seats held, no untoward events occurred after 8 March, speaking well for the fact that Malaysian society had arrived at a political threshold where violence as an instrument of change was now no longer tolerated. Equally significant, I would argue, is that Malaysia edged closer to a formal parliamentary two-party system but as an outcome of 8 March already has a de facto two-party system at the state-level of governance. Let us now turn briefly to the election results (for a summary of the results, see Table 1).

Some of the salient outcomes of 8 March could be said to be the following:

- The BN barely got half (50.1 per cent) of the 7.9 million ballots cast nationwide and lost the popular vote on the Peninsula, garnering only 49 per cent of the ballots.
- The BN lost its two-thirds majority in parliament, winning 140 federal seats and 307 state seats, the Opposition taking 82 and 198 respectively.
- The BN lost the state governments of Selangor, Penang, Perak and Kedah, while Kelantan remained in Opposition hands. (In its worst performances of

TABLE 1
Results of Parliamentary Election, 2008

Party	Votes	%	Seats	%
Barisan Nasional	4,090,670	50.14	140	63.1
UMNO	2,381,725	29.19	79	35.6
MCA	849,108	10.41	15	6.8
MIC	179,422	2.20	3	1.4
Gerakan	184,548	2.26	2	0.9
Others	495,867	6.08	41	18.5
Pakatan Rakyat	3,786,399	46.41	82	36.9
DAP	1,107,960	13.58	28	12.6
PAS	1,140,676	13.98	23	10.4
PKR	1,509,080	18.50	31	14.0
Others	28,683	0.35	0	0
Independents	63,960	0.78	0	0
Spoilt Votes	175,011	2.14	—	—
Unreturned votes	41,564	0.51	—	—
Total	8,159,043	100	222	100

Source: Computed from Election Commission data.

the past, BN had failed to capture only two state governments, Kelantan and Terengganu in 1959 and 1999.)
- BN casualties included the Women, Family and Community Development Minister, Sharizat Abdul Jalil; Information Minister Zainuddin Maidin; presidents of the Malaysian Indian Congress, S. Samy Vellu; People's Progressive Party (PPP), M. Kayveas; and Gerakan, Koh Tsu Koon.
- Parti Islam Se-Malaysia (PAS)'s women's wing chief Lo' Lo' Mohd Ghazali became the second woman from the party to win a parliamentary seat (the first was Khadijah Sidek in 1959).

One of the more significant aspects of the 2008 GE in contrast to previous elections, was the comprehensive vote swing of all major ethnic communities away from the BN parties. Political scientist Ong Kian Ming has estimated that some 30–35 per cent of non-Malay voters swung to the Opposition parties, compared with the popular vote in the previous election of 2004. Although the overall corresponding swing for Malays was only about 5 per cent, Ong has argued the following:

> It is important to highlight that these vote swings are not uniformly distributed. For example, the Malay vote swing in the West Coast states, especially in Penang, Selangor and Kuala Lumpur was higher than the estimated 5 per cent and was closer to 10 per cent or even higher in certain constituencies like Balik Pulau, Gombak and Lembah Pantai. It would not have been possible for the opposition, PKR in these cases, to win without a sizeable swing in the Malay vote (Ong 2008).

Nationwide, in mixed seats where the electorate formed 40–60 per cent of Malay voters, the BN won 28 seats and the Opposition 26 seats, showing that the alternative People's Pact (Pakatan Rakyat, PR), had become a veritable contender to the BN and in some sense was emulating BN's model of electoral success.[5] It could well be argued that cross-ethnic voting accounted for a significant number of victories of the People's Pact and, had the pattern of cross-ethnic voting which occurred in Kelang Valley been replicated in states like Pahang, Malacca, Negeri Sembilan and Johor, the BN government would have been toppled on 8 March.[6]

A De Facto Two-Party System

The fact that Malaysia may have become a de facto two-party system at the state-level can be attributed to the stunning victories of the People's Pact coalition of forces led by Anwar Ibrahim as shown in Figure 1. In fact, some analysts have pointed out that the sixth state to fall was the federal territory of Kuala Lumpur, where all but one parliamentary seat out of 12 seats went to the People's Pact.[7]

Anwar further demonstrated about six months later that the 8 March outcome was no fluke by sweeping the Permatang Pauh by-election with a majority of well over 15,000 votes on 26 August and was subsequently officially anointed as Leader of the Opposition in Parliament.

First, it must be stressed that the major change in the political landscape is still the nascent, two-party (or two-coalition) system at the state level, where PR governments run five governments, namely, Selangor, Penang, Perak, Kedah and Kelantan. In

FIGURE 1
Malaysian Election 2008: Distribution of Seats Won in Each State Legislature

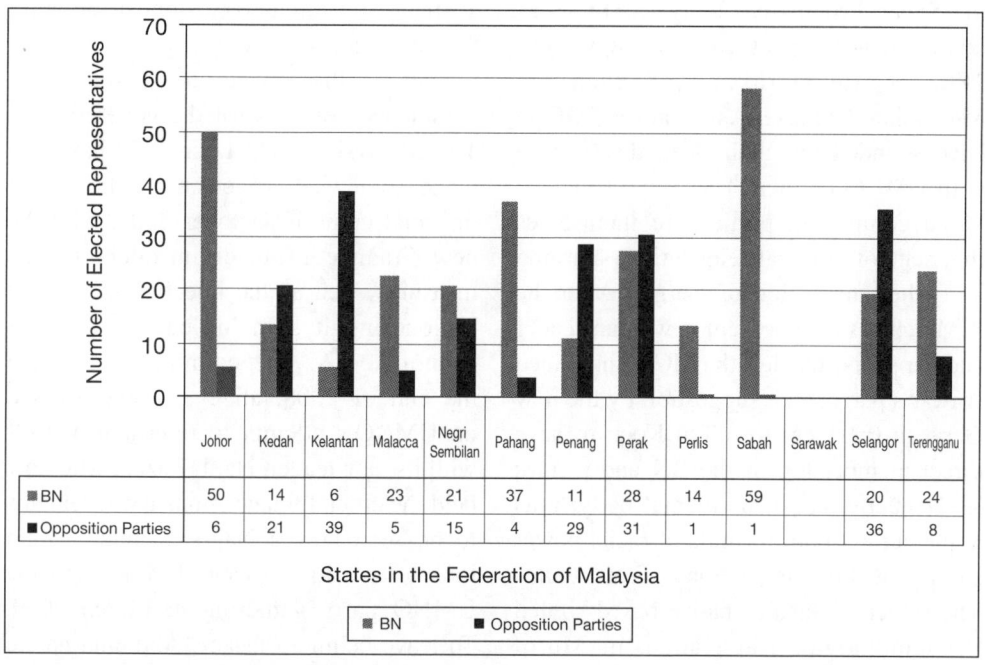

	Johor	Kedah	Kelantan	Malacca	Negri Sembilan	Pahang	Penang	Perak	Perlis	Sabah	Sarawak	Selangor	Terengganu
■ BN	50	14	6	23	21	37	11	28	14	59		20	24
■ Opposition Parties	6	21	39	5	15	4	29	31	1	1		36	8

States in the Federation of Malaysia

Source: Computed from Election Commission data.

these states, the BN now finds itself in the unfamiliar role of opposition, except in Kelantan where this has been the case for about two decades. One could well argue that Malaysian democracy has perhaps arrived at a new threshold and that citizens can now have the opportunity to judge four alternative state governments and choose to re-elect or reject them the next time around. As such, the formalization of the People's Front as an alternative coalition to the National Front appears to be *fait accompli*. Unlike its predecessor, the Alternative Front (Barisan Alternatif) of 1998–99, the People's Pact governmental presence seems guaranteed for some time to come by virtue of power at the state level. The next move would be to have a common logo, like the BN.

Second, the obverse may be true for the BN coalition. This long-standing coalition is clearly in a state of transformation if not turmoil. Already one component party, the Sabah Progressive Party (SAPP), has abandoned the pact (on 17 September 2008) while Gerakan and even the Malaysian Chinese Association (MCA) have sounded out their deep disaffection with UMNO politics. These two Chinese-based component parties are themselves in a state of political reinvention, spurning an earlier suggestion of merger. After the 8 March result, one senior woman leader and her supporters left the MCA and joined Anwar's party.[8] The suggestion by the new Gerakan President Koh Tsu Koon to have direct membership in the BN and to turn it eventually into a multiracial party hints at the current poor formula of racial power sharing within the National Front today. The leader of Sabah's native-based United Pasokmomogun Kadazandusun Murut Organization (UPKO), Bernard Dompok, has also expressed grave concern about the failure of the National Front government to deal with three urgent matters, namely, the unequal exchange of economic benefits to Sabah and its concomitant status as Malaysia's poorest state, the issue of religious freedom and the unresolved problem of the influx of more than one million illegal immigrants into Sabah.[9]

However, not all is rosy for the PR. Taking the example of Penang, the DAP-led People's Pact government may have weathered a number of UMNO-generated political storms and self-inflicted *faux pas* but the going has been tough, admitted as much by Chief Minister Lim Guan Eng.[10] Similarly, the PKR-led Selangor government has also had its fair share of challenges but it seems to be holding firm. The PAS-led governments of Perak and Kedah also have their own sets of political hiccups.

At the federal level, the formation of a strong parliamentary opposition with 82 seats seems to be having a noticeable impact on the BN, even without a no-confidence vote against the government.[11] The Malaysian budget for 2009 has been made somewhat irrelevant by the global financial crisis in October 2008, with the new Finance Minister introducing new measures such as the injection of a RM7 billion ringgit stimulus package for the economy.[12] As the country approached the end of 2008, all eyes were focused on UMNO's attempt to re-establish itself with its new leader, Najib Razak, who now held the crucial finance ministry. It remains to be seen how a Najib's cabinet would look after a likely reshuffle following the UMNO party gathering in March 2009. To leave behind a legacy, Abdullah has in the month of December 2008 introduced three reform bills affecting the Judiciary, the Anti-Corruption Agency and the Police, which will be discussed further below.

Anwar's New Sodomy Trial[13]

Not long after successes of the People's Pact in 8 March came another accusation of the perpetration of sodomy by Anwar Ibrahim. Dubbed "Sodomy II", this sensational development surfaced in late June when a 23-year-old political aide of Anwar, one Mohd Saiful Bukhari Azlan, lodged a police report claiming that he had been sodomised by Anwar. Anwar's wife Wan Azizah immediately countered the allegation by revealing photographs that Mohd Saiful had been seen to be associated with political aides of Deputy Prime Minister Najib Razak. The suggestion was that the young man may have been a 'plant' who had offered to work for the PKR during the general election. It was also later revealed by Najib himself that Saiful had come to his residence to inform him of the alleged act and to seek advice before he lodged the police report. Almost immediately after the accusation, there was a dramatic incident of Anwar seeking asylum or refuge in the Turkish Embassy on 30 June alleging that his life was under threat.[14] In the event, charges were then proffered against Anwar for sodomy. A series of dramatic developments then occurred as follows:

- On 2 July, the police confirmed the charge of sodomy based on a Kuala Lumpur Hospital medical report by the alleged victim, Mohd Saiful Bukhari Azlan.
- On 9 July, Anwar asked an Islamic court to investigate his former aide. Under *syariah* law, accusations of a sexual crime, such as sodomy, needed four witnesses to support the claim.
- On 16 July, Anwar was arrested by a contingent of 10 police cars with 20 balaclava-clad officers, under Section 377A of the Penal Code, outside his home, one hour before he was due to make a statement at the police HQ.
- Anwar was released without charges filed on police bail after overnight detention, and after recording a statement.
- On 29 July, Anwar Ibrahim demanded that the police drop the sodomy investigation against him, producing a medical report he said showed no assault had taken place.
- In a statutory declaration on 1 August, Mohamed Osman Abdul Hamid of Pusrawi Hospital reiterated his findings that after examining Mohd Saiful, he found no evidence of sodomy. The doctor made his first public appearance after having been missing for more than a month since his medical report was leaked to the media.
- On 15 August, Mohd Saiful swore on the Qur'an at the Federal Territory Mosque that he was sodomized by Anwar Ibrahim. Imam Ramlang Porigi subsequently said that Mohd Saiful's Quranic oath or "sumpah muhabalah" was technically wrong. "I was only there as a witness, to listen in", he elaborated, noting that Saiful made two errors while reciting the oath: the first when he mispronounced the word for God and had Ramlang correct him; and the second when he confused the date of the alleged sodomy incident and corrected himself.
- Anwar Ibrahim, on 7 August, pleaded not guilty to sodomy or "unnatural sex" (defined as "carnal intercourse against

the order of nature") and was released by Sessions Court Judge Komathy Suppiah on a personal bail bond of RM20,000 (US$6,090).
- On 7 November 2008, the judge in the Sessions Court struck down the request by Malaysia's Attorney-General Abdul Gani Patail to transfer the case to the High Court. The reason given was that the certificate signed by the AG was invalid.

Despite Anwar's minor court victory, his political trajectory remains stymied as long as the sodomy trial is ongoing. It is difficult to see how he would function effectively even as the leader of the parliamentary Opposition when the trial gets into full-swing presumably in 2009. The worse-case scenario would be that he was found guilty and would have to serve another jail term, in which case he would be disqualified to be a parliamentarian.

An Aborted Numbers Game

The year 2008 was noted for the turbulent politics of a possible or impending takeover of the government by the People's Pact through the parliamentary move of attracting crossovers of government MPs to the Opposition bench. With the PR holding 81 seats,[15] it needed exactly 31 crossovers to give it a majority of one in a parliament of 222 MPs. This stratagem was the brainchild of Anwar Ibrahim, the newly crowned Opposition leader. With his resounding victory in his former constituency, vacated by wife and PKR leader Wan Azizah, Anwar's moment to topple the government seemed palpable as he cleverly kept alive a strategy of baiting crossovers of BN parties and politicians, especially from Sarawak and Sabah. However, the deadline of 16 September 2008 passed with a Parliament out of session and Anwar not making good his claim of toppling the BN. The Malaysian government has always designated 31 August as national day somewhat ignoring the sentiments of the two East Malaysian states which only joined Malaysia (indeed made it possible) on 16 September 1963.

Anwar's stratagem of choosing 16 September for a takeover seemed clever enough. He also called for 16 September to be a public holiday in the five PR-governed states, with the standing offer of a 20 per cent state royalty on oil and gas. Many have suggested that sequestering some 50 MPs in Taiwan from 7–19 September on a supposedly study trip was specifically aimed at blocking Anwar's 16 September plan and discrediting him when it did not materialize. It seemed to many that the Abdullah government was genuinely worried that Anwar had the numbers and the Taiwan tour was a desperate attempt to foil Anwar's plan. Anwar on his part dispatched some five of his political lieutenants to Taiwan to pursue the BN MPs. Tian Chua, the PKR MP for Batu, who led the group was quoted as saying that: "We have the numbers already. We are just going there to have coffee and spend time with them and also learn about agriculture from Taiwan so that we do not get left behind when Pakatan Rakyat takes over."[16]

Anwar's sodomy trial could certainly be seen as another stratagem by his opponents not just as an attempt to block his takeover plans, but in the worst-case scenario take out the Opposition Leader with a 20-year prison sentence. The Session Court's decision to not transfer the case to the High Court is perhaps a minor victory for Anwar although the fact remains that as long as the trial is still on, this would mean that Anwar's overall political situation remains in limbo. 16 September arrived without the much anticipated crossovers which Anwar claimed he had. One hypothesis was that Anwar may have got enough crossovers (or pledges) to form the government but PAS was uncomfortable with an imbalance in favour of non-Muslims. There was also the prevalent suggestion that Anwar was either playing a psychological game or merely bluffing with the hope that his stratagem would bring about a bandwagon effect of a swing in his favour.[17] In the event, by October 2008, as the crossovers were not forthcoming, Anwar was forced to put his takeover plan on the backburner and probably even abandon it altogether.

Political Turbulence of a New Politics

The year 2008 will also definitely be remembered for the political turbulence it generated in Malaysian race relations, although one hastens to add, without any hint of a racial riot. Indeed, the idiom of a "new politics" in which a political society resists the worst attempts by extremist elements to tilt the political balance in the direction of violence has been greatly and assiduously practised. The racist outburst by one Ahmad Ismail of UMNO in September could have easily stirred a hornet's nest and led to undesired incidents but it did not. Indeed good sense seemed to have prevailed although the general public appeared to be somewhat dissatisfied with the Prime Minister's less then stern sanction against the offending individual. After his provocative act of smashing and ripping apart the framed portrait of the former Chief Minster of Penang, the UMNO Bukit Bendera chief was suspended by UMNO for three years.[18] Even so, the UMNO recalcitrant still refused to apologise for a serious alleged remark in which he alluded to all non-Malays as being "temporary visitors" to the country.

Politics took an ugly turn with the ISA arrests of *Sin Chew* reporter Tan Hoon Cheng and Seputeh MP Theresa Kok, and then the ISA detention of blogger Raja Petra Kamarudin, all occurring in the month of September. The *Sin Chew* journalist detained was the same person who had reported on the Ahmad Ismail statement, allegedly made during the Permatang Pauh election campaign. Although she was held for only a day, many thought it incredulous that the reason given for her detention was to protect her from harm, as stated by the Home Minister Syed Hamid Jaafar Albar.

However, Theresa Kok's detention was a much more convoluted affair. The DAP parliamentarian, winner of the largest parliamentary majority on 8 March,[19] was arrested under the ISA on 13 September and detained for seven days in an undisclosed location. Just before her arrest, the Malay daily *Utusan Malaysia* in an article had claimed that Teresa Kok "advised" a mosque in Puchong not to use loudspeakers while making the *azan,* the Islamic call to prayer, which she denied doing. It turned out later that a faulty loudspeaker system was the reason why the mosque did not broadcast the *azan* although it was true there was a petition to the mosque by a neighbourhood group requesting a mosque to lower the volume during ceramahs or sermons but not during *azan*. The administrator of the mosque as well as the petitioners also confirmed that Kok was not involved in the petition. PAS MP for Kota Raja, Siti Mariah Mahmood, lodged a police report against a blog website called Pembela Melayu and Selangor Opposition

Leader Mohd Khir Toyo for defaming Kok by alleging that Kok had supported a petition by the Chinese in Kinrara against the *azan* in their area. After her release, Kok filed a RM30 million legal suit against *Utusan Malaysia*. On 27 September, two Molotov cocktails were thrown into the Kok family home in Taman Rainbow, Jalan Ipoh, together with a warning letter containing threatening words but Teresa's parents and her siblings were not in the house and nobody was hurt.

What was rather unexpected was the release of Raja Petra on 7 November by the Shah Alam High Court after he had spent just over a month in Kamunting. The High Court ruled that the detention of Raja Petra under the ISA was illegal and ordered his immediate release. Judge Syed Ahmad Helmy Syed Ahmad said that Raja Petra's detention was unconstitutional and that the home minister had erred procedurally under Section 8 of the ISA to issue the detention order against Raja Petra.[20] Raja Petra, 58, had named the Home Minister as the defendant in the habeas corpus application which sought among others for his immediate release and an order that his detention under the ISA was unlawful.

The minister had given three reasons for Raja Petra's detention, namely, that he owns and operates the *Malaysia Today* website and published articles and readers' comments intentionally and recklessly which were critical of and insulting to Muslims, affecting the purity of their religion and the personality of Prophet Muhammad; published articles deemed defamatory or false concerning Malaysia's leaders, with the intention of undermining public confidence and inciting hatred against the government; and that these articles are alleged to be a threat to national security. The articles in question were "Malays, the Enemy of Islam", "Let's send the Altantuya murderers to hell", "I promise to be a good, non-hypocritical Muslim" and "Not all Arabs are descendants of the Prophet".[21]

It seems evident from the ISA detentions of Tan, Kok and Raja Petra that the UMNO-led government remained insensitive or impenetrable to the idiom of new politics ushered in by the 8 March General Election. The use of the draconian ISA against political opponents, for that matter, politicised trials such as the sodomy charge against Anwar Ibrahim, increases the government's credibility gap and tends to reinforce a public's declining confidence in government institutions such as the police or the judiciary. The Home Minister's own reasoning that the ISA detention of the *Sin Chew* journalist was to "protect" her was the butt of considerable public ridicule. Civil society groups have reacted to the draconian moves of the Home Minister by organizing such events as candlelight vigils, peaceful protests and signature campaigns. Spokespersons of Gerakan have also called for the reform of the ISA.[22] Undoubtedly, political parties within the government coalition, such as Gerakan, MIC and MCA, are uncomfortable with the use of the ISA on these recent occasions.

A Minister's Resignation

As a matter of fact, the Abdullah government's use of the ISA in September directly led to the resignation of de facto Law Minister Zaid Ibrahim proving that the new idiom of politics had made inroads into UMNO itself. In a thoughtful open letter to the Prime Minister, on 30 September, Zaid wrote that events of the last three weeks compelled him to review his position within the government and that the way in which the ISA had been used led him to the conclusion that "the government had time and time again failed the people of this country in repeatedly reneging on that solemn promise made by Tunku Abdul Rahman", which he cited as follows:

> My cabinet colleagues and I gave a solemn promise to Parliament and the nation that the immense powers given to the government under the ISA would never be used to stifle legitimate opposition and silent lawful dissent.[23]

In his letter, Zaid listed the many times Malaysian governments (including that of the Tunku) reneged on this promise, mentioning in particular its recent use by Abdullah on the HINDRAF 5 and on Tan, Kok and Raja Petra. He opined:

> Malaysians today want to see a government that is committed to the court process to determine guilt or innocence even for alleged acts of incitement of racial or religious sentiment. They are less willing to believe, as they once did, that a single individual, namely the minister of home affairs, knows best about matters of national security.[24]

Zaid goes on to write about his failure to bring about the sort of judicial reform he was trying to advocate in the Abdullah government. High on his list of priorities was the reinstatement of "judicial review" as a concept and practice which was virtually removed by the 1988 constitutional amendment during the Mahathir era after Operation Lalang. He writes that he sought to introduce the means by which steps could be taken to assist the judiciary to regain its reputation for independence and competence but "unfortunately, this was viewed as undesirable by some since an independent judiciary would mean that the executive would be less 'influential'."[25] Not long after writing this letter, Zaid Ibrahim was sacked from UMNO.[26]

Before his resignation, Zaid did try to salvage or repair the reputation of former Lord President Tun Salleh Abas and five other former supreme court judges of the Mahathir period. But even this attempt at resuscitation of the judiciary turned awry. In a dinner in April attended by the Bar Council and politicians, on the urging of Zaid, the Prime Minister made ex-gratia payments to these judges for the injustice meted out to them by the Mahathir government. Abdullah said that their pain and loss could not really be compensated by monetary payments although the Prime Minister would not apologise for the events of 1988. Apart from Salleh Abas, a second judge, Azmi Kamaruddin, and families of the other four judges were at hand. At the same event, the Prime Minister announced that he would set up a Judicial Appointments Commission. However, later developments soured Zaid's efforts when the amount of the ex-gratia payments was announced even though Zaid had promised not to do so in deference to the ex-judges and their families.[27]

Any form of judicial repair was further damaged by the controversial appointment of a new Chief Justice in Tan Sri Zaki Tun Azmi on 21 October who succeeded Datuk Abdul Hamid Mohamad. Zaki's appointment has been criticized by the DAP citing his swift promotion and the fact that he had been a legal adviser to UMNO. Opposition Member of Parliament Karpal Singh said he was in possession of an audio recording of what Zaki allegedly said to the media: "It took me six months to be nice, to bribe each and every individual to get back into their good books before our files were being attended to." Zaki later issued a clarification, published in the *New Straits Times* on 9 November, saying that the reporter misinterpreted what he said. He said "I have never in my life bribed or received any bribe."[28] Karpal has persisted in calling for Zaki to step down from his Chief Justice post and has upbraided the Bar Council for not objecting to Zaki's appointment.[29]

UMNO Transition

Ever since the Barisan Nasional's disastrous showing on 8 March, the likes of Mahathir and Tengku Razaleigh had been calling for Abdullah Badawi to step down as President of UMNO. The Kelantan politician-prince immediately offered himself as candidate for the UMNO presidency in the UMNO polls originally due for December. Abdullah managed to resist these calls until his own minister Muhyiddin Yassin also threw down the gauntlet in early May, stating that he was willing to contest one of the two top positions in the December UMNO polls.[30] The Minister for International Trade and Industry subsequently decided only to contest the Number Two spot. This left Najib Razak with only Tengku Razaleigh to take on but the latter's bid fizzled out in November when Najib's massive accumulation of nominations shut out any challenger. Meanwhile, UMNO provided a face-saving device for Abdullah when it postponed the polls till March 2009. Abdullah has indicated that he will not contest the presidency in March.[31] The UMNO contestants to key posts, with the requisite number of nominations, at the point of writing are as follows:

President:	Najib Tun Razak
Deputy President:	Muhyiddin Yassin, Ali Rustam, Muhammad Muhd Taib
Vice Presidents (3):	Hishammuddin Hussein, Ahmad Zahid Hamidi, Khaled Nordin, Shafie Apdal, Syed Hamid Albar, Mohd Isa Samad, Jamaluddin Jarjis, Rais Yatim, Rahim Tambi Cik
UMNO Youth Chief:	Mukhriz Mahathir, Khairy Jammaluddin, Mohd Khir Toyo
Wanita Chief:	Rafidah Aziz, Shahrizat Abdul Jalil

Abdullah Badawi has turned out to be the biggest casualty of the 8 March political tsunami and will step down in March 2009 in favour of the incoming UMNO president Najib Razak. Another casualty in the future may be the political fortunes of Abdullah's son-in-law, Khairy Jamaluddin, who at the time of writing trails far behind Mukhriz in nominations.[32] With such major changes to the Malay political landscape, one could expect some political ramifications for Malaysian politics in 2009 such as a cabinet reshuffle with Najib loyalists. However, whatever happens at the March 2009 party gathering, UMNO's position of primacy within the ruling coalition is unlikely to change. The new leadership is likely to see the continued influence (if not interference) of former Prime Minister Mahathir Mohamad. Moreover, if his son, Mukhriz, assumes the leadership of the UMNO Youth Movement, he would act as a natural conduit for his father's continued presence and influence in UMNO. Najib, as UMNO's new leader with his likely deputy Muhyiddin Yassin are bound to be more accommodating to Mahathir and his ideas as compared to Abdullah Badawi before.

The Closing of the Abdullah Era

It is fitting that one ends with a section on the denouement of the Abdullah Badawi tenure. Abdullah's final curtain closes with the tabling of three bills to recoup a severely dented reputation and to presumably bestow some kind of belated legacy to his tenure as the fifth prime minister of Malaysia. The bills, presented in quick session during the December sitting of Parliament, were: the Malaysian Commission on Anti-Corruption (MCAC) Bill, Judicial Appointments Commission (JAC) Bill and the Special Complaints Commission (SCC) Bill. Had such bills been tabled during his earlier term, he may have been spared the criticism of doing too little too late. The SCC is now lambasted by critics as the watered-down version of the Independent Police Complaints and Misconduct Commission (IPCMC) submitted three years ago after a veritable study by a Royal Commission. Abdullah's failure to implement this was one of his egregious failures which cost the BN many votes on 8 March. The JAC is Abdullah's supposed answer to judicial reform which we have discussed at some length above but the legislation has now been critiqued for its various flaws, in particular the stipulation that judicial appointments still have to be ultimately screened by the Prime Minister.[33] Finally, the MCAC has been criticized for the requirement that corruption charges have to be made via the Attorney General's office and that the new commission, replacing the ACA, still has no power of prosecution.

It may be Abdullah's unfortunate fate that history may judge him harshly as the leader who showed more promise than he had the capacity to fulfil. Even on the question of foreign policy, Abdullah who began self-assuredly by debunking some Mahathirist stances and policies, unfortunately ended with even scandals[34] and with the personally damaging loss of a piece of territory, Pulau Batu Puteh/Pedra Branca, to Singapore.[35] Worse, Abdullah's administration is now held responsible for the massive landslide on 6 December which saw five people killed and thousands evacuated at Bukit Antarabangsa, an up-market residential spot near Kuala Lumpur.[36]

Furthermore, two major unresolved issues will continue to exercise Malaysian political actors whether in government, opposition or civil society. First would be detention under the Internal Security Act (ISA) of five Hindu Rights Action Force (HINDRAF) leaders. Civil society groups and the opposition will continue to press for their release and the debunking of the ISA, while the credibility and legitimacy of the Malaysian Indian Congress (MIC) and its leader, Samy Vellu will remain in limbo until the HINDRAF issue is resolved. Malaysia has the dubious distinction of two persons "missing in action" abroad, *personae non grata* Waytha Moorthy of HINDRAF and P. Balasubramaniam, the private detective who made a statutory declaration about Najib Razak and his association with the murdered Mongolian model, Altantuya Shaariibuu.

The second serious issue in the immediate post-Abdullah period could be the progression of the Altantuya murder trial and the Anwar sodomy trial. Despite the unexpected acquittal on 31 October of political analyst Razak Baginda for abetment, a long trial may ensue for the two other accused whose defence has been called. This could still have grave implications for the new Prime Minister Najib Razak as the two who will be in the dock were special police officers assigned to Najib as Deputy Prime Minister. Similarly, the course and outcome of Anwar's sodomy trial will not only affect his own political fortunes but also his leadership of the People's Pact. Abdullah has left Malaysia with an uncertain political future. Both the leaders of the government and the opposition will have unpredictable political trajectories in 2009 and beyond. Who will navigate through the political minefields and emerge as the victor? As Malaysians edge gingerly into 2009, a still fluid and uncertain political scenario awaits them. What is certain is that the political terrain has palpably shifted after 8 March and politics of the old mould would have become ineffectual.

Notes

1. The video clip showed lawyer V.K. Lingam allegedly speaking to former Chief Justice Fairuz Abdul Halim about his appointment as Chief Justice of the Federal Court. A commission of inquiry found the video to be authentic but till date, no action has been taken on the matter.
2. Most pundits could not see the Opposition winning more than 40 seats. At a pre-election seminar in ISEAS, two days before polling day, main speaker Dato' Dr Michael Yeoh of the Malaysian think-tank ASLI and other speakers were confident that the BN would retain its two-thirds majority.
3. Cf. Ooi, Saravanamuttu and Lee, *March 8: Eclipsing May 13* (Singapore: Institute of Southeast Asian Studies, 2008).
4. See Ooi's "the Opposition's Year of Living Demonstratively", in Ibid., pp. 17–20.
5. See Maznah Mohamad, "Malaysia: Democracy and the End of Ethnic Politics? *Australian Journal of International Affairs*, vol. 62, no. 4 (December 2008): 446.
6. This is the thesis proffered by Lee (Ooi et al. 2008, pp. 113–14).
7. See Lee's analysis of the Kuala Lumpur voting (Ooi et al. 2008, pp. 92–103).
8. On 17 July 2008, MCA former women's wing deputy chief and former cabinet minister, Tan Yee Kew, quit her party and in August joined the PKR with 1,700 supporters <http://anilnetto.com/malaysian-elections/tan-yee-kew-and-1700-mca-members-cross- over-to-pkr/>.
9. Dompok raised these issues in a 21-page keynote policy address at his party's 12th triennial meeting in October 2008 ("Dompok: Tide against BN in Sabah", *Malaysiakini*, 12 October 2008).
10. See Lim's statement in Malaysiakini. com, 21 December 2008 <http://www.malaysiakini. com/news/95227> (accessed 29 December 2008).
11. The threat of crossovers remains possible although Opposition leader Anwar Ibrahim appears to have dropped the idea, as will be suggested in the section below.
12. Najib made this announcement on 4 November. The government had earlier also announced that there would be an injection of RM5 billion into the Malaysian Bourse, the money being sourced from the Employees Provident Fund (EPF). *Malaysian Insider*, 4 November 2008. <http://www.themalaysianinsider.com/index.php/malaysia/11792-najib-epf-loan-to-valuecap-is-guaranteed-by-government> (accessed 29 December 2008).
13. I have sourced most of this set of events from Wikipedia and corroborated them with other news reports, especially in Malaysiankini.com.

14. The Turkish Embassy denied that they were granting Anwar asylum.
15. Although there are 82 seats on the Opposition bench, one is held by an independent, Ibrahim Ali, MP for Pasir Mas, Kelantan.
16. Tian Chua said this when he was met by reporters at the KL International Airport before boarding, with five others, a 2.20 p.m. China Airlines flight to Taiwan on 12 September. See *The Star*, 13 September 2008.
17. I have made such an argument elsewhere. See "Are Malaysian Parliamentarians caught in a Prisoner's Dilemma?", *Opinion Asia*, 11 September 2008.
18. Compare this to Zaid Ibrahim's sacking. See below.
19. Kok retained the Seputeh constituency with a majority of 36,492 votes.
20. See *Malaysiakini*, 7 November 2008 <http://www.malaysiakini.com/news/92620> (accessed 29 December 2008).
21. See Ibid.
22. Newly elected Gerakan president Koh Tsu Koon in October called for the government to expedite reforms to avoid a repeat of 8 March. Among others, he called for a judicial commission and reforms to the Internal Security Act (ISA), Printing Presses and Publications Act (PPPA) and the University and University Colleges Act (UUCA). See *Malaysiakini*, 11 October 2008 <http://www.malaysiakini.com/news/91078> (accessed 29 December 2008).
23. Zaid's open letter was carried in full by *Malaysiakini* <http://www.malaysiakini.com/news/90602> (accessed 30 December 2008).
24. Ibid.
25. Ibid.
26. On 2 December, the UMNO Supreme Council rescinded Zaid's membership in UMNO. Zaid has complained that he was not given a chance to defend himself and that UMNO practised a double standard <http://www.malaysiakini.com/news/94294> (accessed 30 December 2008).
27. Minister Mohd Nazri Aziz revealed that RM10.5 million was paid out and also insisted that the judges were not sacked and were paid government pensions. Salleh Abas received the largest amount of RM5 million <http://www.malaysiakini.com/news/92589> (accessed 30 December 2008).
28. As reported in *The Sun* <http://www.thesundaily.com/article.cfm?id=27751> (accessed 30 December 2008).
29. See report in *The Sun*, Ibid.
30. See *The Star* <http://thestar.com.my/news/story.asp?file=/2008/5/11/nation/21218890&sec=nation> (accessed 30 December 2008).
31. Najib Tun Razak had practically won the presidency with 134 nominations out of a possible 191 and would make him prime-minister-in-waiting. He will assume the UMNO presidency at the general assembly scheduled for 24–28 March 2009.
32. Mukhriz has obtained 63 nominations while Khairy has secured 36.
33. See the studied analysis of its various provisions, including those problems related to the central idea of a nine-member commission, by constitutional expert Shad Saleem Faruqi in his column, *Reflecting on the law*, "Many unanswered questions", *The Star*, 31 December 2008. Faruqi says that "the law is adroitly silent" on whether the PM is bound by the JAC's nominations.
34. The oil-for-food issue involving relatives and the transporting of centrifuges by a company headed by his son are two examples.
35. However, one should note that the agreement to have the Pulau Batu Puteh/Pedra Branca dispute adjudicated by the ICJ was already decided during the Mahathir period.
36. Derived from various news reports.

Myanmar

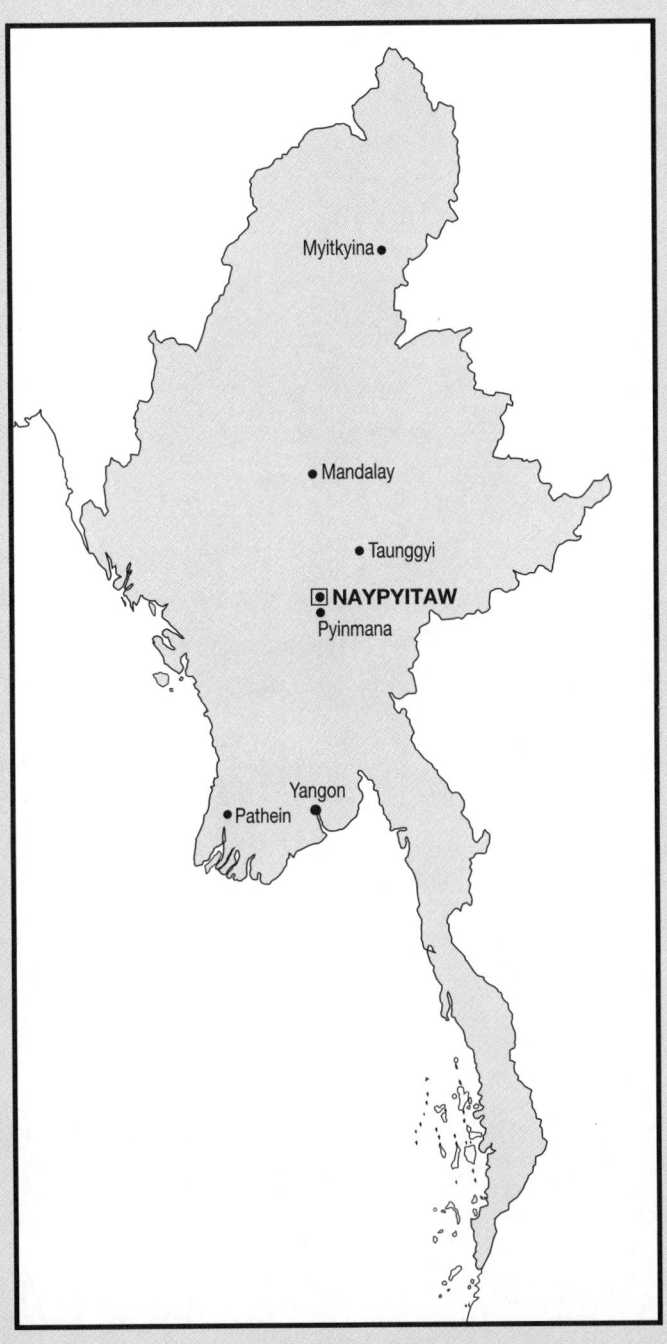

BURMA IN 1988
Perestroika with a Military Face

James F. Guyot

CONTEXTS FOR CHANGE

Nineteen eighty-eight marks a system break in Burma's modern history. To understand the significance of the events of the year we should set them in two different contexts. One is the context of states with command economies and Leninist parties which have undertaken *perestroika* with or without *glasnost*. The polar reform cases include the Chinese model, with economic liberalization starting in agriculture and politics being restrained after an initial opening, and the Soviet model, with economic liberalization attempted across the board and political openness encouraged as a spur to the *perestroika* process. These models offer only a partial context for our understanding of Burma since in both instances the movement can be characterized as reform rather than revolution: while there are significant redistributions of power and authority among state institutions and between state and society, and there are changes in external relations as well, still the basic legitimacy of the system remains in place, élite replacement is moderate, and the level of violence and coercion is low.

The other context is Burma's own cycles of reform and revolution during the last half century as shown below. (The numerologically inclined will note a periodicity of about a dozen years — actually 13.67 plus or minus 0.83 years.)

THE POLITY IN 1988

While the operative effects of any changes in direction for the economy during 1988 were obscure, political changes verged on

---

Reprinted in abridged format from Ng Chee Yuen, ed., *Southeast Asian Affairs 1989* (Singapore: Institute of Southeast Asian Studies, 1989), pp. 107–33. At the time of original publication, James F. Guyot was Professor of Political Science and Public Administration at Baruch College, The City University of New York.

Burma's Reform and Revolution Cycles

		Politics	Economics
Revolution	1948	Independence	Buddhist Socialism (economic nationalism)
Revolution	1962	Military coup Revolutionary Government	Burmese Way to Socialism (command economy)
Reform	1974	Socialist Republic Expansion of the Burma Socialist Program Party (BSPP)	Internal rice price raised Loans from World Bank, Asian Development Bank, and foreign countries.
Reform or Revolution?	1988	Ne Win's abdication Popular revolt Military coup	Free trade in grains Opening of economy to private domestic and foreign firms

revolution. The level of violence was high, the legitimacy of the regime collapsed, and the ruling élite, while maintaining its core institution, the army, went through a complete change of personnel at the top. Before analysing these fundamental changes, the chronological line of action will first be set out.

Chronology of the Crisis[1]

The system break of 1988 began in March with a tempest in a teashop which grew into a full-scale student riot and brought on full-scale police repression. In contrast to the previous fall's student protests over demonetization, this series of riots spread to downtown Rangoon. The stage for public protest had been set by spiralling inflation and a shortage of fuel for transport, which left some areas of the country, and particularly the cities, short of rice. The overture and subsequent accompaniment for the drama were played by Brigadier Aung Gyi in a series of semi-public letters to his old comrade in arms, Bogyoke Ne Win, documenting the decline of the Burmese economy, reopening old wounds of past conflicts among the entourage of the Revolutionary Government, and pointedly criticizing police violence against student protesters.

In April, after the universities had been closed and the students sent home, many of them to the countryside, a government commission investigated the riots. Late that month the Minister of Planning and Finance was warned by his Japanese counterpart that substantial economic reforms must be undertaken if Japan were to continue its economic support. There is some evidence that the Japanese also recommended political reforms.

In mid-May, the Commission of Enquiry released its report, saying that two students had been killed and three wounded by police weapons in the March riots. In late July, the government admitted that an additional forty-one had been suffocated in police vans, for which the Director General of Police and the Home Minister would be sacked.

On 21 June, massive student demonstrations, joined by the general public, wrought widespread destruction and brought on severe repression with heavy loss of life, including six policemen. The universities were closed again, public assemblies banned, and a dawn to dusk curfew imposed on Rangoon.

Early in July, the government announced an extraordinary congress of the BSPP to be held at the end of the month. Rioting and curfews flickered throughout various district towns. On 23 July, at the extraordinary party congress, Chairman U Ne Win announced his retirement from politics, "[b]ecause I believe I am indirectly responsible for the tragic events of March and June, and because of my old age." He took with him five other leading members of the party, including Joint General Secretary U Sein Lwin, and recommended a referendum on the people's "lack of trust in the government and the party that guides it" to decide whether the country should have a multi-party or a single party system.[2] Events moved swiftly and in unpredictable fashion. Sein Lwin, a noted *apparatchik* and astrologer, accepted his party's call to remain and become both Chairman of the Party and President of the Republic. The party also rejected Ne Win's suggestion of a September meeting to consider a multi-party system. Students assembled at the Shwedagon to protest the appointment of Sein Lwin, whom they held responsible for directing the riot police not only during the spring uprisings but as far back as the U Tham riots of 1974. At the end of the month Brigadier Aung Gyi and ten associates were arrested.

During the early days of August, the cycle of resistance and repression spiralled upwards with martial law declared on 3 August and a Rangoon-wide protest beginning on 8 August. The army, which had been standing by, replaced the police and on the following day medical personnel at Rangoon General Hospital appealing for an end to the bloodshed were shot. While a new Prime Minister appealed for calm in Rangoon, the U.S. Senate passed the Moynihan Resolution condemning the killing and calling for the end of one-party government. On 12 August, Sein Lwin resigned, after only seventeen days at the helm. He was replaced by Dr Maung Maung, formerly Chief Judge and recently appointed Attorney General, as one of two civilians in leading positions in the military-dominated government. As massive street demonstrations in Rangoon and Mandalay encompassed lawyers, doctors, dock-workers, and many others cutting across the sectors of urban life, Dr Maung Maung's government released Brigadier Aung Gyi and the other opposition leaders and lifted martial law. In the waning days of August, pressure for a more open political system mounted as an All-Burma Students Union was formed and an Alliance for Democracy and Peace brought together such disparate political elements as former Prime Minister U Nu, former Generals Tin Oo and Aung Gyi, and Daw Aung San Suu Kyi, the daughter of Bogyoke Aung San, the founder of both independent Burma and the Burmese army. The government newspapers were taken over by staff members who published news of the demonstrations and pressed opposition demands. At the end of the month, a riot at Insein Jail led to considerable loss of life and the escape of thousands of prisoners. At this time several foreign embassies began evacuating their personnel.

The first half of September found the Maung Maung government making a succession of concessions in the midst of a crescendo of opposition demands and expanding disorder. The Executive Committee of the Burma Socialist Program Party hurriedly endorsed a system of multi-party democratic elections without waiting for the referendum it had earlier foresworn, but the opposition groups called for an interim government to supervise the elections. Government employees had been resigning from the BSPP and then went on strike demanding an interim government. Next, the government itself severed its ties with the BSPP and required civil and military officials to resign from the party. The tipping point came when uniformed members of the civil, police, and even military services joined the protesters, and when demonstrators before the Ministry of National Defence had to be restrained by Brigadier Aung Gyi one day, and on the next day crowds surrounding the Foreign Trade Ministry captured soldiers who had shot at them and who had to be rescued by monks. The following afternoon, Sunday 18 September, the Defence Minister, General Saw Maung, staged a consensual coup, relieving the Maung Maung government of the burdens of office, reimposing a curfew and restrictions on daytime activities, and calling on all government employees to return to work within eight days or face suspension.

The four-point rationale offered for this *sui coup* (in which a government run by the army is replaced by the army) was to restore law and order, to ensure transportation and communication, to ease the food and shelter needs of the population, and after those goals were accomplished, to stage democratic multi-party elections. The public response was quick and bloody. The shooting of demonstrators and looters lasted several days in Rangoon, started later and lasted longer in Mandalay, and resulted, according to an official statement a month afterwards, in 451 dead. Ambassadors from the United States and the West European countries, together with those of Australia and India, condemned the killings. While Japanese aid had already been suspended *de facto* (it was to be officially suspended in January 1989), U.S. economic aid was formally suspended, as German aid had been the previous month. The opposition National League for Democracy (led by Aung Gyi, Tin Oo, and Aung San Suu Kyi) urged non-violence and the continuation of the civil service strike to press for an interim government. During the next week and a half, the State Law and Order Restoration Council (SLORC), the body through which the army ran the country, issued back-to-work statistics ranging from 65 to 95 per cent for most areas of the country and government agencies, and extended the deadline for compliance to 3 October. Meanwhile, many student and other protesters (subsequently estimated by the government to number 3,000) left Rangoon for the insurgent areas on the Thai border or went underground.

The process of pacification continued in more orderly fashion during October and November. The State Law and Order Restoration Council appealed to students who were following the wrong path to return to the care of their parents, and set up centres for their reception, claiming 1,139 returnees by 24 November. Porters were conscripted and public donations were accepted to support the army in its fight with the insurgents, particularly in Methawaw, where the Karen National Union had recaptured a stronghold in mid-October with the help of newly insurgent students. Many civil servants who had participated in the protests were transferred or forced into early retirement. Political parties were encouraged to register, which they did in profusion, and their office-bearers and programmes were publicized in the sole legal newspaper. The parties were warned not to criticize the army or each other, or to organize rallies, but the leaders of the main opposition, Brigadier Aung Gyi and Daw Aung San Suu Kyi, were permitted to make tours upcountry, where they were greeted by large crowds.

In mid-December, the Saw Maung government's international isolation was broken by a "brotherly" visit by General Chaovalit at the head of a Thai goodwill delegation. From this followed such concrete results as the repatriation of Burmese students by air from the Thai border and agreements on Thai private ventures to exploit Burma's teak and fishery resources. At year's end the tally of students who had returned to the fold, both internally and by air, stood at 1,835. On 20 December the curfew was relaxed by one hour to 10 p.m. Methawaw was recaptured from the Karen National Union on 24 December. By 30 December, one hundred and seventy-four political parties had been registered for the as yet unscheduled multi-party elections. Although Brigadier Aung Gyi had left the National League for Democracy at the beginning of the month, the League continued to be strong, confirming its legitimacy by assuring a peaceful, massive funeral for Daw Khin Kyi, the mother of Daw Aung San Suu Kyi. This was the first large public assembly since the coup and was attended by numerous foreign and government officials on 2 January, two days before a quite muted Independence Day.

Violence and Coercion in a Suspended Revolution

A traditional Burmese lament asks, "may we be spared the misfortune arising from a change of kings". Some ninety degrees to the west, Thomas Hobbes generalized this complaint as "that miserable condition of war ... when there is no visible power to keep [men] in awe, and tie them by fear of punishments to the performance of their covenants". Although much that happened in the politics of the "change of kings" in Burma in 1988 was neither violent nor coercive, the disappearance of the power to keep men in awe and the resort to visible punishments direct us to pay special attention to these two dimensions of political action. The sheer volume of violence engendered by the rebellion requires some accounting. Moreover, an examination of the shifting shape of the coercion that suppressed the rebellion may provide some insight into the prospects for stability and democracy in coming years.

A chart of the events of the year would show five peaks of protest with varying degrees of both violence and coercion. The data for marking out a comparative analysis of these events are uneven and often contradictory since the extent of under-reporting by the government apparently varied over time as did the openness to foreign reporting.[3] Nevertheless, the general shape of events seems clear. In the riots of 12–17 March the violence on the part of protesters was directed against property. The riot police (Lon Htein) killed 43 students (unofficial estimates were around 200) and arrested 625 persons at the Rangoon Institute of Technology, Rangoon University, and downtown Rangoon, releasing 484 of them within a month-and-a-half. No life was lost on the government side and the affair was limited to the Rangoon area.[4]

The protests that began at the Institute of Medicine on 21 June resulted in the death of six policemen together with three protesters (outside sources suggest a "great loss of life"). Seventy-seven persons were arrested, the universities were again closed, and Section 144 restraints on public activities were imposed (prohibiting gathering, speeches, marching, agitation, exhortation, and demonstrations) along with a dawn to dusk curfew in Rangoon. This time around, disturbances spread quickly to Mandalay, Pegu, Taunggyi, Magwe, Moulmein, and Akyab, where curfews were imposed. A long week of disturbances in Prome, Bogyoke Ne Win's home-town, resulted in an appeal for calm by the State Sayadaws and the proclamation of martial law under Section 144 by President San Yu. Subsequent events in Pegu, the second city of the Rangoon Division, were said to have left thirteen civilians and two policemen dead.[5]

The next major set of protests began in Rangoon on 8 August as an organized response to the ascent of the leader of the Long Htein, General Sein Lwin, to supreme power as both President and Party Chairman. The official toll after five days of public protest, looting, and police response in Rangoon was between 112 and 182 killed, including six on the government side. In addition, some 1,626 persons were arrested.[6] Martial law had been declared for the greater Rangoon area five days before and the army, which had evidently been standing by during previous protests, joined the riot police in suppression duties. Similar events, with losses among civilians, police, and the military, were reported in district towns throughout the country, notably 31 killed at a police station at Sagaing, the religious centre across the river from Mandalay. Outside estimates of deaths made at the time were 500–1,000 in Rangoon and 3,000 countrywide.[7]

The fourth surge of protest came after the advent of Dr Maung Maung's ostensibly civilian government. Troops had been withdrawn from the streets and the large, nonviolent demonstrations on 22 August and subsequent days were organized by nascent political organizations and directed towards demands for an interim government and multi-party elections. In the midst of the protests, martial law was officially lifted and major opposition leaders were freed. Although extensive looting was reported, the only significant loss of life during the month of the Maung Maung government seems to have followed from the rioting and release of prisoners at Insein Jail, the Mandalay Prison, and lesser jails around the country.[8]

The final spasm of public protest in the 1988 rebellion provoked the largest official death toll. A month after the Saw Maung *sui coup*, the government put the number killed in the post-coup crackdown at 451. Four months later, in a large-scale briefing tour for foreign correspondents, the official statement was that only fifteen demonstrators had died in the first two days and subsequently "560 were killed when law-enforcing authorities had to shoot and disperse looters".[9] In its Human Rights Practices report, the U.S. Department of State estimated that a thousand protesters may have been killed in September.[10] During the immediate post-coup period, reports of violence and confrontation centred on Rangoon and Mandalay. As the army closed down strike centres around the country and scattered reports of looting came in, the locus of violent opposition shifted to the insurgent areas.

Subsequently, the SLORC pacification programme advanced, using forms of control that were more organizational. All schools remained closed until the end of the year. Many civil servants who had been active in the protests were transferred or retired, notably those in the Foreign Ministry (a number of whose overseas members sought asylum), Posts and Telecoms, the Irrigation Department, and the Road Transport Corporation. Nurses were cautioned by the Minister of Health to be polite when being interrogated. And "persistent troublemakers who have no steady jobs" were drafted as porters for the army.[11] Perhaps the most pervasive form of coercion was the government's control over rations of oil and rice, the items most often sought by looters.

Contrary to the crescendo of governmental violence from the March riots to the September *sui coup* that official figures portray, unofficial sources give a larger size and a different shape to the summer rebellion. Brigadier Aung Gyi said a month later in an *Asiaweek* interview.[12]

> Well, I think in this military coup the casualties won't be more than 500 in Rangoon. But the previous August, all those killed in the Rangoon area [may total] about four or five thousand. That is my estimate. In August in the whole country I think it may be around 8,000 people.

To be sure, this view may have been shaped in part by Aung Gyi's experience of imprisonment during Sein Lwin's brief rule. To the extent that his observation of a downward trend is accurate, that the Saw Maung government was less brutal than the Sein Lwin government, it encourages a more positive expectation for the development of civil politics under the aegis of the SLORC.

Another perspective on the volume of the violence of the 1988 rebellion would put it in the broader context of Burmese history by comparing this rebellion to the Oilfield Strike of an even half century before, one of the hallowed events in the advance of the Burma independence movement. From January 1938 the oilfield workers in Yenangaung and Chauk had struck and, with the encouragement of the Thakins of the Dobama Asiayone, had staged a 400-mile-long march to Rangoon. The durable Section 144 was imposed and marchers were confronted by police and soldiers along the way, with the main Thakin leaders arrested in Magwe. But from its beginning until the triumphal march around the Shwedagon in January 1939 there had been no killing except for one student who had been fatally clubbed in a baton charge during a protest surrounding the Secretariat and who became known as "the first student to shed blood for the sake of his country".[13] Or again, in the 1946 turmoils, which included a police and civil service strike that forced the pace of independence, the only casualties inflicted by the police were four persons killed in the Tantabin Incident.[14] Apart from World War II itself and the endemic political and ethnic insurgencies that plagued independent Burma from 1948 onwards, the only human losses matching the summer of 1988 would be those of the Saya San rebellion of 1930–32, when some 40–50 civil and military officials and an estimated 1,300 rebels were killed.[15] Perhaps a more parallel and contemporary standard for comparing violence can be found in neighbouring Thailand, where estimates are that more than 100 students and others died in the student-led revolt that toppled forty years of military rule in October 1973, and 46 were killed in the coup that temporarily restored military rule in October 1976.[16]

Having put the size of the violence into context, let us now consider its shape, that is, the geography and the groups involved, in order to clarify our understanding of both its causes and some of its likely consequences.

Beginning with the students in Rangoon in March, the turmoil had spread by June to Mandalay and other major district towns, and by August it had encompassed towns throughout the whole country. Little is known, however, about what was happening at the village level. The March and June protests included non-student elements and were rather unorganized. The massive demonstrations against the Sein Lwin government beginning on 8 August brought Buddhist monks, young and old, into the protest, and monks were shot, as were some medical personnel. The more organized and violence-free demonstrations of late August included identifiable middle-class elements among the marchers, first lawyers and medical personnel and then more segments of the civil service, as well as a sprinkling from the security services. The components of the post-coup protesters, to the extent that they can be characterized, appear to have been the hard-core youth — high school and university students along with amorphous urban workers. The one significant social group which seems not to have been involved in the rebellion is the peasantry. While absence of evidence is not evidence of absence, there are other reasons for assuming that the rebellion may not have penetrated significantly to the village level. For instance, the social chaos that almost wrecked the urban economy was at its peak during the period when rice was being transplanted. If there had been considerable disruption in the agricultural sector at that time, Burma would have been less likely to increase paddy production during the 1988–89 crop year, as it now seems to have done.

A motivational argument could also be advanced to support the proposition that the protest was a purely urban phenomenon. This would follow the line that, as several knowledgeable observers have suggested, the confrontation of the masses with the military regime should be explained largely in economic rather than in political terms.[17] Apart from the military élite, the major segment of Burmese society that suffered the least from the recent economic reverses was those who could provide food for themselves or could market it at the rising prices that plagued the urban workers during 1988. At least until the government reverted to extractive methods for obtaining the share it felt it needed of the 1988–89 paddy crop, the farmers could consider themselves relatively well off. Specialists studying political development and praetorianism during the 1970s used to argue that seizing and maintaining power required a coalition of two out of three elements: guns, brains, and numbers — in other words, the army, the urban middle class, and the peasantry. Those observing Burma during the rebellion of 1988 noted that the army could afford to shoot many students as long as it kept one of the three elements, the farmers, happy.

Élite Succession

A snapshot of Burma's top governmental leaders on 4 January 1988, the celebration of the 40th anniversary of independence, would show mostly military and ex-military men who had been guided by the Burma Socialist Program under the direction of Bogyoke Ne Win. A second picture, a year later on the 41st anniversary would show all the faces but one (the doctor who was Minister of Health) to be military and Bogyoke Ne Win would be leading from the shadows. The Burma Socialist Program Party would not be in the scene, having been officially severed from its governmental connection in the meantime. General Saw

Maung, the Chief of Staff of the Armed Services, Chairman of the State Law and Order Restoration Committee, Minister of Defence, and Minister of Foreign Affairs in the second, would have appeared in the first snapshot only if Deputy Ministers were included; all ministerships in the second shot were held by new personages. But a change in person does not mean a change in character, since the new incumbents of office come from the same social formation as their predecessors, merely migrating from allied élite statuses

What is significantly different is the appearance of a legitimated counter-élite outside the government. Within the government itself there have been no significant counter tendencies, no cracks in the military monolith nor between the military and the civil services. The *sui coup* showed none of the characteristics of the stillborn coup of 1977 which pitted the younger trained officers of the Defense Services Academy who had been serving in the jungle against those whose careers had been enhanced by party and economic enterprises. Early September rumours of the incipient defections of Brigadier General Nyan Lin of the Southeast Command in Moulmein and Brigadier General Tun Kyi of the Northwest Command in Mandalay were effectively stilled by their appearance as chairmen of their respective regional Law and Order Restoration Councils later that month.[18] This does not mean that there were no tensions within the higher command structure or potential for warlordism. Indeed, the month that Dr Maung Maung tried to govern may have been used by General Saw Maung as Defence Minister for checking on the reliability of various units. Though the protesters appealed for the servicemen to join them, the only documented defections were by lower level personnel, primarily in the peripheral services, the police, the air force, and the navy.[19]

Neither did the civil bureaucracy pose a counterbalance to military hegemony. Unlike the situation in neighbouring Thailand, there has been no patrimonial or technocratic tradition in independent Burma; during the parliamentary period, the politicians dominated the civil servants and after 1962 the military both directed and penetrated with their own men the once proud steel frame of administration. During the summer rebellion, various organizations of government workers had sprouted up to condemn one-party dictatorship, the falsification of data, and the ignoring of expert advice (Institute of Economics Teachers Union). They also condemned the firing of demonstrators (All Burma Construction Corporation) and demanded the formation of an interim government (Timber Corporation). After the September coup, members of the state administration or of government boards and corporations were forbidden to join other than purely religious or economic organizations, and individuals prominent in the protests were disciplined.[20]

What of party-government relations? The constitutional protections and the leadership role of the BSPP as a Leninist party had been extinguished before the coup. Afterwards the government was re-constituted in a number of Law and Order Restoration Councils (LORC) at divisional, township, township sector, and ward or village levels. Down to the township level, the LORCs are composed of the respective heads of the military, police, and general affairs departments, together with a secretary, and are chaired by the military man. This replicates the Security and Administration Committee system through which the army had governed during its first dozen years in power. At the ward or village level, "respected citizens" who do not belong to any political party comprise a LORC chaired by a member of the township LORC.[21] This compromise with the BSPP system which was set up after the 1974 constitution presumably abolishes the principle of democratic centralism under which that system operated. As noted by Brigadier General Myo Nyunt, the Rangoon Division Commander: "Unlike before, when the state selected the local councillors, ward and village level councils today are formed after consultations with the Sangha Nayaka Committees and the local elders".[22] So the government is now officially not under the control of the party — that is, the party is currently out of the business of governing. Still, if one could get a look at the local level élites the same faces as before would probably appear.

During the heady days of the Maung Maung government, a variety of natural counter-élites had arisen, principally the students who had mobilized mass demonstrations and re-established the tradition of student political organizations. Underground organizations had begun after the March riots and the All-Burma University Students' Democratic League came to light in late July with an announcement on the BBC that they would lead national demonstrations against the Sein Lwin government. After the lifting of martial law, the All-Burma Students' Union became official, with Min Ko Naing as chairman. After the Saw Maung coup he announced a dual-track strategy of both registered political party activity and underground links with the insurgents.[23]

The more conventional counter-élites were a combination of political figures from the independence movement who had been active during the parliamentary democracy period and break-aways from the post-1962 military regime. Once the SLORC had extinguished the option of an interim government, the major opposition group legitimated itself within the new rules of the game by registering as the National League for Democracy, with Brigadier Aung Gyi as Chairman, General Tin Oo as Vice-Chairman, and Daw Aung San Suu Kyi as Secretary when a party registration procedure was in place at the end of September. That same week witnessed the birth of the Democracy Party under the patronage of Bohmu Aung, who was one of the Thirty Comrades present at the creation of the Burma Independence Army, and who later became a minister in U Nu's government during the parliamentary period. In the following week seven more parties signed on and a week after that the old Burma Socialist Program Party appeared under the new name of National Unity Party. Party registration, thus, took off on a growth spurt that can be described by the sigmoid curve characteristic of such biological events as a "virgin field epidemic" or the appearance of new species on earth during the "Cambrian explosion".[24] The rate of growth decelerated after 4 November, when the Election Commission announced that parties should obtain the consent of patrons and executive committee members before registering, and the total reached 174 by the end of the year (see Figure 1). It is difficult to define the political significance of this efflorescence of organizations. Most party names included the words "democratic" or "people" and espoused a variety of goals (the first aim of the National Fitness and Peace Party was "to obtain genuine national fitness and peace") which were dutifully published in the *Working People's Daily* and announced on the radio.[25] What they could do to advance their causes was quite limited, however. Although allocated a petrol ration and a number of phone lines, they were forbidden to criticize the army or each other, or to organize rallies. The mass of them were, in effect, signboard organizations, and even that characteristic was curbed as no sign could be erected for units below the township level.

The National League for Democracy was permitted to play a distinctive role, perhaps in recognition of the particular legitimacy of its core leaders. Brigadier Aung Gyi and Daw Aung San Suu Kyi each travelled about upcountry during the early pacification period, speaking to large and enthusiastic crowds, and granted interviews with foreign news sources. Military restraints on these activities and on their local level organizations varied among regional commands.

The SLORC is officially a transition government, quite unlike the Revolutionary Council that seized power in March 1962, but perhaps a little like the caretaker government of 1958–60 that gave General Ne Win and his young colonels their first taste of running a government, during which they ran a fair election and afterwards turned power over to U Nu although they had backed his opponents. The preconditions the SLORC has set for holding multi-party elections are eminently elastic — even if law and order were reasonably restored and the trains ran on time, the third condition, meeting the food and shelter needs of the population, could, if *perestroika* does not deliver the goods, become a convenient excuse for

FIGURE 1
Cumulative Party Registrations, 1988

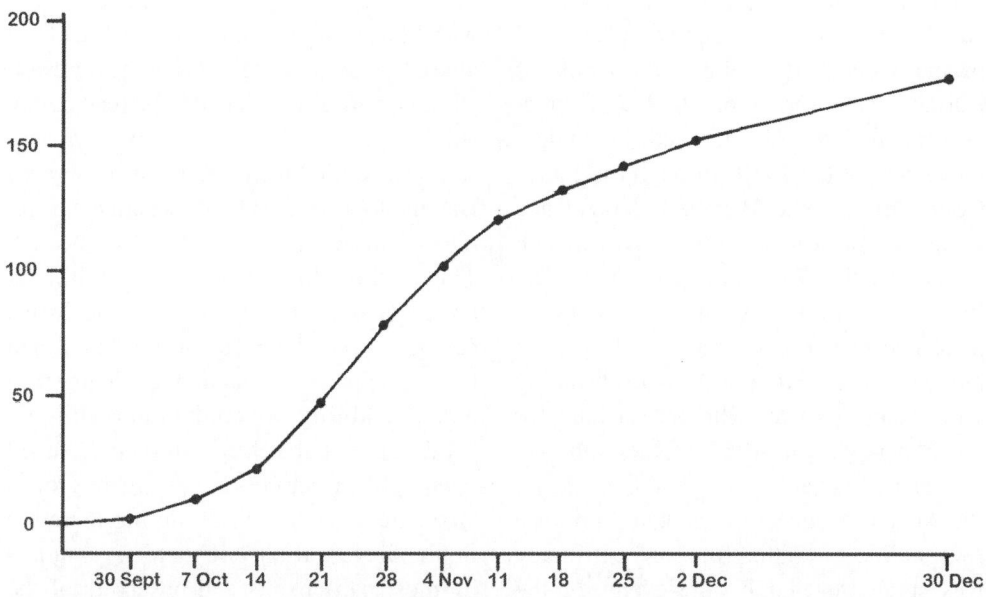

Source: Compiled by Hugh C. MacDougall in *Burma Press Summary*. Weekly data points from 30 September to 2 December 1988.

endless delay. So far, several cautious steps towards elections have been taken, under prodding from local and external opinion. If a fair and open process of élite succession does eventually evolve, it might contribute a new base for the legitimacy of the Burmese state.

The Question of Legitimacy

States may derive their legitimacy from several sources. Fundamental, of course, is the Hobbesian justification that they are maintaining order and the rule of law. This justification the Sein Lwin government lost by definition when it unleashed the violence of early August. The Maung Maung government had tried in vain to retain it by insisting on existing constitutional procedures for the transition to a system of multi-party elections. The major claim that Saw Maung's SLORC could make by year's end was that it had met the minimum requirements of governmental stability and public order for almost four months.

The main line of legitimacy claimed by the Socialist Republic of the Union of Burma in the spring of 1988 was direct descent from the Thakins and the student movement of the 1930s through the Thirty Comrades and the Burma Independence Army of the 1940s, down along a path defined by the *Tatmadaw* (the army). The importance of this connection may be measured by the devotion of fully half of Ne Win's resignation address to disputing with Aung Gyi over who was at fault for the blowing up in 1962 of the Rangoon University Student's Union building, and by the Maung Maung government's promise to rebuild it.[26] This line of legitimacy was surely severed by the events of the summer and by the alternative claims on the independence struggle tradition by the rekindled student's union, Brigadier Aung Gyi, an assortment of the remaining Thirty Comrades, and Daw Aung San Suu Kyi. The SLORC struggled to refurbish the military image through martial slogans and the celebration of persons who donate money for the welfare of soldiers fighting the insurgents, but they were slow to reweave connections to the military tradition, waiting several months before even mentioning Bogyoke Ne Win in the press. Perhaps the most significant event emblematic of national solidarity was the funeral of Daw Khin Kyi, the widow of Aung San, who was buried between the graves of Queen Supayalat, wife of the last reigning Burmese king, and Thakin Kodaw Hmaing, a revered independence fighter, in a massive ceremony which the government had to share with the opposition National League for Democracy.[27]

For over a quarter of a century Bogyoke Ne Win had ruled Burma with an iron hand. As a result he developed considerable inertial legitimacy, identifying the state with himself in the minds of friend and foe alike.[28] After his regime-shaking farewell address, part of which had to be read out by another person, Bogyoke Ne Win was not seen at a public function until Armed Forces Day the following March.[29] Charisma is not only evanescent; it is also quite specific. Thus, while his hold on the public at large has slipped, in the eyes of successive cohorts of post-independence military men he has apparently maintained legitimacy and the ability to compel institutional loyalty, a feat that has historically eluded open political parties and insurgent groups alike. Beyond that, his enduring direction of the larger affairs of state is assumed by most participants and observers of the Burma scene, an assumption documented by rumour and the counting of the traffic flow in and out of his residence prior to important scene changes in the play of politics.

Another source of legitimacy cultivated by the army's Burmese Way to Socialism, as by U Nu's Buddhist Socialism before it, was the creation of prosperity through socialist economic development. This, too, failed for major segments of Burmese society, especially in 1988, as has been documented above. This failure was symbolized in the dropping of "socialism" with the name change from the Socialist Republic of the Union of Burma to simply the Union of Burma. Yet another of U Nu's consensus-building, legitimacy-enhancing ventures (which actually led to dissension, and helped precipitate his fall from power) was the return to the traditional role of the state as the protector of Buddhism. This role the Revolutionary Council abjured in keeping with Aung San's ideal of a secular republic and as a way to reduce the political weight of the activist monks. With the further institutionalization of state power following the 1974 constitution, the government moved into the conferring of titles for members of the Sangha, and then went forward in the 1980s with two "Congregation[s] of the Sangha of All Orders for Purification, Perpetuation and Propagation of the Sasana". The resulting registration of monks and the creation of a structure of governance for the Sangha paralleling that of the secular government not only helped legitimate the state but also provided one of the instruments of control to which the SLORC has turned in its attempts to bring about order.[30]

The BSPP is probably the one legitimacy-building institution that suffered the most. It lost its name, its government funds, its government membership, its monopoly on political leadership, and it was excoriated by its last chairman, Dr Maung Maung, quoting Lord Acton on the corruption of power. The party had been constructed along Leninist lines and in accord with the state ideology, The System of Correlation of Man and His Environment, in order to take the place of the king in giving balance to the Burmese state. This the single party system clearly failed to do. What kind of legitimacy a multi-party system (with or without dominance by the military-favoured BSPP successor) will be able to establish in Burma remains an open question.[31]

Outward-Looking?

External recognition and support is one form of legitimation that Burma has not sought under Ne Win as his stance was politically and economically inward-looking. Under Aung San, the Union of Burma had cut the colonial connection more decisively than the other Asian nations emerging from the British Empire. U Nu's non-aligned involvement in the international scene, revered by Ne Win's Revolutionary Government as a carefully correct doctrine of non-involvement in regional and international affairs, was honed so sharply as to require leaving the Conference of Non-Aligned Nations when it became too obviously aligned with the Eastern bloc. The economic reforms of the 1970s necessitated participation in multinational institutions such as the Asian Development Bank and an increasing reliance on bilateral economic aid, particularly from Japan and West Germany. The economic reform programme, set in train in the fall of 1987 and trundled with formal zeal and much uncertainty throughout the rebellious months of 1988, requires even greater interpenetration of the Burmese economy with the global economy.

What were the political implications of the announced outward-looking economic policy? A strongly held belief during the days of autarky was that foreign businessmen would rob Burma of its unspoiled riches if given half a chance, just as they had done during the British times.[32] A similar suspicion covered those citizens of non-indigenous background, as Chairman Ne Win had warned when announcing the internal liberalization of the economy. The fear of political intervention runs even deeper, harking back, among other things, to the U.S.-supported Kuomintang (KMT) incursions thirty-five years ago, and was doubtless heightened by the extraordinary attention that Burma found the rest of the world paying to the daily events of the 1988 rebellion. Let us consider the political economy of Burma's interactions with three distinct sets of nations: the Western democracies; Burma's immediate neighbours, India, China, and Thailand; and Japan.

The first set of countries has little security interest in, and few economic ties with, Burma. Consequently, they could be rather principled in their response to the rebellion, celebrating the spontaneous surge towards democracy and actively deploring the repression of human rights, in several cases by cutting off economic aid. In response, the Burma Government frequently criticized both the Voice of America and the British Broadcasting Corporation for exaggerating incidents and encouraging lawlessness. Particular outrage was expressed at the U.S. statement that students returning under the amnesty were being punished.

Within the region itself, India chided its former province and accepted its refugees, China revived negotiations to expand trade once the dust had settled, while Thailand's stance reflected political sensitivity, energetic economic interests, and the tripartite division of foreign policy-making between an established foreign minister, a newly elected civilian prime minister, and an ambitious army commander. The Burmese students hiding out on the border presented a problem, particularly since they aroused support among Bangkok university students and recalled Thailand's successful student-led revolution of fifteen years before. Burma's relatively unexhausted teak forests presented a timely opportunity since the Thai King's new year's gift to the nation was to be the abolition of commercial logging that had denuded the countryside. Disagreement between the foreign minister, whose party in the government coalition included bankers, and the prime minister, whose party was heavy with industrialists, left the field to the army commander, whose military associates had quickly opened up logging operations in Laos once he smoothed over border conflicts with Thailand's eastern neighbour. General Chavalit became, as General Saw Maung happily noted, "the first dignitary to visit us after the new situation has developed in Burma".[33] Thus, Burma's old belief, that there are many out there who covet its natural riches, may be validated in the competition to participate in the economic opening of the Golden Peninsula.

Japan has certainly been the leader among nations in its influence on Burma, a responsibility that it has carried with considerable self-effacement. In part, this reflects the personal ties that the ruling generation of today's Liberal Democratic Party feels to a country where many of them had served and where many of their classmates had died in the last war. During several of the cycles of Burma's post-war history a web of relationships had formed — trade connections blossoming from reparations payments and loans, personal ties with Brigadier Aung Gyi and the modernizers of the caretaker government, and technical and financial support of the reforms of the late 1970s. By the late 1980s Japan was providing four-fifths of the development aid upon which Burma had become increasingly dependent. Brigadier Aung Gyi's open letters in the spring of 1988 carried the Japanese message of the need for economic reform along with the opportunity for enhanced assistance.[34] Coverage of the summer and fall events in the Japanese press and on TV was extensive. Japanese economic assistance was quietly suspended in 1988 and the government refrained from recognizing the Saw Maung regime. But they did maintain contacts, with the Burmese noting the visit of the Counsellor of the Japanese Embassy to the Office of the Commission for Holding Multi-party Democratic General Elections.[35] Early in 1989 the Japanese announced recognition of the government and the resumption of aid while the Burmese announced the coming of an election law, with elections to follow in 1990.[36] The contingency of one event upon the other is suggested by more than their coincidence in time.

THE PROSPECTS FOR *PERESTROIKA*

Burma went through four governments and one name change during 1988. Throughout, two constants have been: the central role of the army in affairs of state; and a dogged, at times desperate, promotion of economic and political reform. How has *perestroika* fared? The liberalization of the rice trade may well have accomplished its efficiency goal of increased production, but the loss of control reduced the supply available for government distribution and export, so that there was a partial reversion to command deliveries. The reality of massive cross-border trade with China and Thailand was legitimized in the hope of gaining greater control. The opening to foreign enterprise appears to be advancing, though the mutuality of the benefits cannot yet be calculated. Political reform made at least pro forma progress in the extinction of Leninist party control, but the reality of this development remains to be seen.

Glasnost, which may be taken to mean "open debate", "the legitimacy of public criticism", and the "availability of information", burst upon Burma beginning with the Aung Gyi letters in the spring of 1988.[37] At high tide, the newspapers were taken over by their staffs and even a branch of Amnesty International was formed in Rangoon. Following the Saw Maung coup, however, only highly constrained forms of information flow and public discussion were permitted. The political year ended mixed, with the large and peaceful funeral for Bogyoke Aung San's widow, a unique joint-venture of the State Law and Order Restoration Council and its main opposition, the National League for Democracy. A Burmese social scientist, observing the revolutionary summer with scholarly detachment from abroad, commented that, "in Burma you can't have *perestroika* without *glasnost*". Whether *perestroika* in Burma follows the Chinese or the Russian model will be an intriguing question for 1989.

Notes

1. The sources for this chronology include various issues of FBIS, East Asian Service; the "Burma Press Summary" from *Working People's Daily*, by Hugh C. MacDougall; *FEER*; *Asiaweek*; and the *New York Times*. Also useful were occasional issues of the English language press in Tokyo; a summary of the crisis up to September, by David I. Steinberg; and a talk by U.S. Ambassador Burton Levin at The Asia Society, New York, 29 November 1988.
2. FBIS, Rangoon Domestic Service, 23 July 1988.
3. The most evident under-reporting of deaths was the official statement that only two students were killed in the 18 March disturbances, a figure which was contradicted at the time by informal reports from the hospital, morgue, and cemetery. Four months later, the government admitted an additional forty-one deaths, with the explanation that "[t]he delay in the release of news concerning these incidents is due to the fact that all proper care had to be taken in the interest of law and order and so as to prevent exacerbation of the situation and proliferation of such disturbances." *Working People's Daily*, 20 July 1988. From late August until the coup, government newspapers were less "official" than Rangoon radio.
4. *Working People's Daily*, 13 May and 19 July 1988; and *Christian Science Monitor*, 28 June 1988, p. 9.
5. *Working People's Daily*, 19, 22, 23 June 1988; *Asiaweek*, 8 July 1988, p. 9; and 29 July 1988, p. 14.
6. The *Working People's Daily* reported that as of 20 August 112 of the 379 persons hospitalized had died. Previous reports gave individual daily totals, which would presumably include some persons who were never hospitalized. The arrest figure is a compilation of daily totals. *Working People's Daily* 9, 11, 12, 21 August 1988.
7. *Asiaweek*, 19 August 1988, p. 11; and *Far Eastern Economic Review*, 25 August 1988, p. 10.
8. Official reports gave the figure of 57 killed at Insein (unofficial estimates were 1,000) and 20 at various other jail breaks. *Asiaweek*, 9 September 1988, p. 31; and *Working People's Daily* 28, 29, 30 August 1988.
9. FBIS, 12 October 1988, p. 42; and *New York Times*, 22 Jaunary 1989.
10. Country Reports on Human Rights Practices for 1988, quoted in the *New York Times*, 8 February 1989.
11. *Asiaweek*, November 1988; *FEER*, 24 November 1988, p. 40; *New York Times*, 22 January 1989; FBIS, 29 September 1988; and *Working People's Daily*, 10 October 1988.
12. "Interview/Aug Gyi: Ne Win Wants an Election", *Asiaweek*, 21 October 1988, p. 31.
13. Subsequent protests against the coercive actions of the Ba Maw government led in February to a demonstration in Mandalay in which seven monks and ten others were killed by police. Khin Yi, *The Dobama Movement in Burma (1930–1938)* (Ithaca: Southeast Asia Program, Cornell University, 1988), pp. 112; 83–131.
14. John F. Cady, *A History of Modern Burma* (Ithaca: Cornell University Press, 1958), pp. 534–35.
15. Taylor, op. cit., p. 198; E. Sarkisyanz, *Buddhist Backgrounds of the Burmese Revolution* (The Hague: Martinus Nijhoff, 1965), p. 163.
16. David Morrel and Chai-anan Samudavanija, *Political Conflict in Thailand: Reform, Reaction, Revolution* (Cambridge: Oelgeschlager, Gunn & Hain, 1981), pp. 147, 275.
17. The Australian Ambassador, Chris Lamb, noted on the Melbourne Overseas Service: "A lot of the problems that we have had in the last 6 months in Burma have been caused by high prices of food ... for the people of Burma ordinarily won't make a

tremendous noise about political difficulty; they will do so if there are food shortages. This is ... interpreted outside Burma as being a political scream, but it's not really; it is a food, clothing, and shelter scream". FBIS, 13 December 1988.
18. FBIS, 16 September 1988.
19. A broadly reproduced still from a Japanese TV newsreel shows student protesters with their palms on the pavement shikoeing a line of soldiers with fixed bayonets. From the sound track it is clear that they are not begging for mercy but asking the soldiers to join them. *FEER*, 25 August 1988, p. 13; *New York Times*, 11, 15 September 1988; and *Washington Post*, 13 September 1988. The case of several paratrooper privates and a corporal joining a strike centre was reported in *Working People's Daily*, 7 September 1988.
20. *Guardian*, 5 September 1988; *Working People's Daily*, 9, 17 September 1988; and FBIS, Rangoon Domestic Service, 30 September 1988.
21. *Working People's Daily*, 28 September 1988.
22. FBIS, Rangoon Domestic Service, 11 January 1989; and 3 October 1988.
23. FBIS, 29 July 1988; *Asiaweek*, 9 September 1988, p. 32; and 28 October 1988, pp. 28–30.
24. Stephen Jay Gould, "Is the Cambrian Explosion a Sigmoid Fraud?" in *Ever Since Darwin: Reflections in Natural History* (New York: W.W. Norton & Company, 1977), pp. 126–33.
25. FBIS, Rangoon Domestic Service, 15 December 1988.
26. Jon Wiant, "Tradition in the Service of a Revolution: The Political Symbolism of Taw-hyan-ye-khit", in *Military Rule in Burma since 1962: A Kaleidoscope of Views*, edited by F.K. Lehman (Singapore: Maruzen Asia, 1981), pp. 59–72.
27. FBIS, 3 January 1989, pp. 40–43.
28. John Badgley, "Kammic Socialism", in Josef Silverstein, op. cit.; and Robert H. Taylor, op. cit., pp. 366–71.
29. *FEER*, 13 April 1989.
30. Tin Maung Maung Than, "The *Sangha* and *Sasana* in Socialist Burma", *Sojourn* 3, no. 1 (February 1988); pp. 26–61.
31. Two specialists who approach Burma from quite diverse perspectives both argue that multi-party democracy faces severe incompatibilities with Burmese social and cultural conditions. See Taylor, op. cit., pp. 360–64; and Lucian W. Pye, *Asia Power and Politics: The Cultural Dimensions of Authority* (Cambridge: Harvard University Press, 1985), pp. 41–46, 95–107.
32. Ne Win's suspicion of businessmen, especially foreigners, was often relayed in the form of pithy anecdotes, in a manner similar to that of his age-mate, Ronald Reagan. *Working People's Daily*, 9 October 1987.
33. FBIS, Rangoon Domestic Service, 14 December 1988.
34. John Badgley, op. cit.
35. FBIS, Rangoon Domestic Service, 13 January 1989.
36. *New York Times*, 18 February 1989.
37. They are available in the Echols Collection, Cornell University.

MYANMAR 1990
New Era or Old?

R.H Taylor

The political impasse between an entrenched military regime and a restive civilian opposition that followed the massive demonstrations and protests throughout Myanmar in 1988 remained unresolved at the end of 1990. Despite the holding in May of the first multi-party general election for thirty years, with victory by its most outspoken critics, the National League for Democracy (NLD), the State Law and Order Restoration Council (SLORC) government remained in an apparently unassailable position. But faced with sporadic protests and other expressions of discontent and alienation, the military's ability to develop a new and publicly acceptable political order appeared uncertain. In the meantime, however, the economic reforms begun in 1988 continued to gather pace, though without the clear policy guidelines which might have restored confidence more rapidly. In the midst of this domestic political and economic uncertainty, foreign economic and political pressures on the government were unrelenting from major Western governments including Japan, the United States, and the countries of the European Community, though relations with most neighbouring countries continued to be strengthened. The events of the year which have led to such a mixed and contradictory summary of the condition of Myanmar are easier to identify than the causes, which remain a subject of passionate disputation.

Domestic Politics and the Election

That the election would be the central political event of the year, holding the promise of the amelioration of the

---

Reprinted in abridged format from Sharon Siddique and Ng Chee Yuen, eds., *Southeast Asian Affairs 1991* (Singapore: Institute of Southeast Asian Studies, 1991), pp. 199–219. At the time of original publication, R.H. Taylor was Professor of Politics at the School of Oriental and African Studies, University of London.

nation's major political problems, was the expectation of all. As the head of the government, General Saw Maung, said in a speech to an SLORC co-ordinating meeting on 10 January,[1]

> The reason why the rule of law and order and the prevalence of peace and tranquillity is being given so much emphasis is because the Pyithu Hluttaw [People's Assembly] election to be held this year is not an ordinary one. It is an election of historic significance, a veritable milestone in the annals of history marking the change from one era to another, from one system to another and a turning point in our history itself.

Despite widespread scepticism expressed inside and outside the country that elections held by the military could be "free and fair", and that only an interim civilian government, as demanded in 1988, could be entrusted with election management, there was general agreement that the elections themselves were conducted honestly. However, there were significant restrictions on freedom of speech and assembly and some party leaders were detained throughout the campaigning period and beyond. The fact that the NLD coalition of civilian and ex-military leaders formed after the 1988 demonstrations overwhelmingly won the election, provided proof to sceptics that the final results were honest. The fact that the military remains in government provides evidence of the deep and unresolved political tensions which the election was unable to release.

Indicative of the new political expectations engendered by the elections, 2,310 candidates from 100 political parties plus 82 independents were nominated for the 491 seats established in the new Pyithu Hluttaw. Subsequently, voting was postponed indefinitely in five remote constituencies in the Shan State and one in the Kachin State because of alleged transport and communications difficulties. These are areas where insurgency remains a major threat to security and population is relatively sparse. The constituencies established were based on the system used in forming the national legislature under the 1974 Constitution, providing a seat for every township regardless of population but creating multiple seats for populous townships. This resulted in constituencies of widely disparate electorates, with two having less than 700 voters while four had over 100,000 persons on the electoral rolls. The system did, however, provide additional representation for areas populated by ethnic minorities in the border regions.

Controversy surrounded the election campaign throughout. The nomination of Daw Aung San Suu Kyi, the General-Secretary of the NLD who had been under house arrest since 19 July 1989, to stand in a central Yangon constituency was opposed by the National Unity Party (NUP) candidate for the same seat. The NUP, the name taken by the re-formulated Burma Socialist Programme Party (BSPP) after its fall from power in 1988, was widely perceived as the party closest to the army and was expected to rely on strong government support in the election. In the event, the party made a poor showing at the polls. The success of the challenge against Daw Aung San Suu Kyi's nomination in the Yangon Election Commission was interpreted by many as bias by the authorities against the NLD. The ban on her candidature was justified by the government because of her alleged connections with Britain and contacts with insurgent groups, especially the Kachin Independence Organization (KIO). The other key figure in the NLD leadership, former General Tin U, remained in prison throughout the year, thus also barred from standing in the election.

Claims of arrests and harassment of NLD and other candidates were denied by the authorities, though they did concede that some were taken in for questioning from time to time. The actual conditions of the campaign were set forth in SLORC Order 3/90 which required that rallies and speeches be approved in advance by local Law and Order Restoration Councils. Any publications or speeches which could be interpreted as undermining the sovereignty, independence or territorial integrity of the state, impairing the unity of the country and its various ethnic minorities, undermining the dignity or unity of the armed forces, impairing education, or inciting religious or ethnic conflict, were banned. The political parties were each given two opportunities of presenting their policies in 15-minute radio and 10-minute television speeches. Most other forms of campaigning seemed to be confined to party offices in the constituencies, though party documents and tapes of Daw Aung San Suu Kyi's speeches were available for sale in some markets. The formal campaigning commenced with the first television speeches on 12 March.

Government actions during the campaigning provided mixed signals as to what the army leadership's post-election plans might be. The gradual lifting of martial law in various townships throughout the campaign period seemed to augur a lessening of political repression. The promotion in rank of most of the key SLORC leaders, including SLORC Chairman, General Saw Maung, to the new and unprecedented rank of Senior General in early March, suggested that the army was preparing to solidify itself internally, before handing over power to a new government. By the beginning of April the government was making it clear that it did not care which party or coalition of parties might win the elections. Plans became clearer on 12 April when Secretary 1 of the SLORC, Major-General Khin Nyunt, widely perceived as the second most prominent member of the leadership, stated that the military would remain in office after the elections until a new constitution was drafted and a "strong government" was formed.

Though troops had been apparent on the streets of the cities in the months leading up to the election, and the 10 p.m. to 4 a.m. curfew imposed in 1988 remained in effect, on election day the military presence was less obvious and polling took place without incident. Election results began to be announced the day after voting and it was soon clear that the NLD would be successful. In the end, 72.59 per cent of the 20,818,313 eligible voters turned out, the highest participation rate of any election in Myanmar's history. Voter turn-out varied from a high of over 75 per cent in the six largest divisions and Rahkine State to around 66 per cent in the Kachin and Mon States, and the mid-50 per cent range in all other states and divisions, except for the lowest, the Shan State, which recorded an approximately 48 per cent participation rate. Slightly over 12 per cent of the votes cast were declared invalid. A number of the parties led by major political figures of different political allegiances in the 1950s, such as former Prime Minister U Nu, Thakin Chit Maung, and former Brigadier Aung Gyi, as well as parties claiming derivation from the old Anti-Fascist People's Freedom League (AFPFL) coalition, failed to gain any significant support. Indeed, only 1,049 of the 2,296 candidates managed to gain one-eighth or more of the votes cast in their constituencies.

The NLD won a total of 392 seats in the Pyithu Hluttaw. Its next nearest party was the allied Shan Nationalities League for Democracy (SNLD) which gained 23 seats. The NUP won only 10 seats, while the regionally based Rahkine Democracy League (RDL) managed to take 11. In all, of the 93 parties which ultimately fielded candidates, 27 were successful in winning one or more seats. Twelve parties elected one member, while five elected two, four elected three, and one elected four or five members, along with six independents. The overwhelming success of the NLD was based on its winning just under 60 per cent of the valid votes cast. As all the other successful parties were regionally or ethnically based, the only other party able to gain a more than two per cent of the national vote was the NUP, which garnered slightly over 21 per cent of the total valid votes in winning its ten seats, while the NUP's subsidiary Peasants, Workers, and Youth Unity Organizations together managed to gain an additional 3.5 per cent of the national total. (See Tables 1 and 2.) Non-regional or non-ethnically designated party candidates who were able to win a seat, such as the Democracy Party's U Tun Hlaing, who won Bahann 1 where Daw Aung San Suu Kyi was to have stood, usually ran in constituencies where there was no NLD candidate.

As the success of the NLD became apparent, expectations of a handover of power were constrained and it was not until 21 June that the publicly recognized leader of the party, 72-year-old former Colonel Kyi Maung, an officer who left the army with Brigadier Aung Gyi in the 1960s, stated that he would send a message to the SLORC for talks without conditions on a speedy transfer of power on the basis of the 1947 Constitution which, slightly amended, was already prepared for use. The army leadership had made it clear previously that they viewed this Constitution as fatally flawed because of its grant of the right of secession to the Shan and Kayah states as well as the fact that it had been written before independence and was therefore tainted with a colonial heritage.

The SLORC refused to respond to overtures from the NLD leadership for talks leading to a transfer of power on the obscure grounds that it was not a political but a military government. The absence of any capacity to force the army to hand over power apparently led to disputes on strategy and tactics within the NLD. Rumours emerged that the party was facing serious internal rifts between its more militant backers, many of whom came from amongst the students and youths who led the 1988 upheaval and would not tolerate compromise with the army government, and older figures, many of whom had previously served in the army.[2] While it was suggested that the League's divisions could be personified in terms of a split between a Daw Aung San Suu Kyi identified group and a U Tin U faction, such labelling merely served to simplify a complex set of political pressures within the League, made more intense by the frustration the party's supporters felt in the face of military intransigence.

The conflict between the SLORC and NLD leadership was more than merely a struggle for power, but went to the heart of the relationship between the military and any future civilian government. As in similar situations in other countries where the army has faced the prospect of leaving office, personal security as well as issues of state policy were at issue.

TABLE 1
27 May 1990 Myanmar Election Results by State or Division and Party

State/Division	NLD[a]	NUP[b]	Independent	National	Regional	Total
Kachin	14	2			3[c]	19
Kayah	4	2			2[d]	8
Kayin	10			1[e]	3[f]	14
Chin	4	1	2		6[g]	13
Sagaing	52	1	2		3[h]	58
Tanintharyi	13					13
Bago	47	1		3[i]		51
Magway	39					39
Mandalay	55		1			56
Mon	16				4[j]	20
Rahkine	9				17[k]	26
Yangon	59			2[l]		61
Shan	22	1		1[m]	32[n]	56
Ayeyarwady	48	2	1			51
TOTAL	392	10	6	7	70	485

a National League for Democracy
b National Unity Party
c KSNCD – Kachin State National Congress for Democracy
d KSNLD – Kayah State Nationalities League for Democracy
e POCL – Patriotic Old Comrades League
f KSNO – Karen State National Organization, 1
   MNDF – Mon National Democratic Front, 1
   DOKNU – Democratic Organization for Kayan National Unity, 1
g CNLD – Chin National League for Democracy, 3
   MPP – Mara Peoples Party, 1
   ZMC – Zomi National Congress, 2
h NHRPP – Naga Hills Regional Progressive Party, 2
   UNLD – United Nationalities League for Democracy, 1
i PND – Party for National Democracy
j MNDF – Mon National Democratic Front
k NDPHR – National Democratic Party for Human Rights, 4
   RDL – Rahkine Democracy League, 11
   M/KNSO – Mro (or) Khami National Solidarity Organization, 1
   KNLD – Kamans National League for Democracy, 1
l DP – Democracy Party, 1
   GOSDA – Graduates and Old Students Democratic Association, 1
m UNDP – Union Nationals Democracy Party
n SNLP – Shan Nationalities League for Democracy, 23
   UPNO – Union Paoh National Organization, 3
   UDLDP – Union Danu League for Democracy Party, 1
   SSKDP – Shan State Kokang Democratic Party, 1
   T(P)NLD – Tayang (Palaung) National League for Democracy, 2
   LNDP – Lahu National Development Party, 1
   DOKNU – Democratic Organization for Kayan National Unity, 1
Source: Working People's Daily, 28 May to 3 July 1990.

TABLE 2
27 May 1990 Myanmar National Election: Numbers of Pyithu Hluttaw Seats and Percentage of Valid Votes Won by Successful Political Parties

Parties	Seats Won	Seats Contested	Percentage Total Votes
National Parties			
National League for Democracy	392	447	59.87
National Unity Party[a]	10	482	25.12
Patriotic Old Comrades League	1	3	0.02
Party for National Democracy	3	3	0.48
Democracy Party	1	105	0.48
Graduates and Old Students Democratic Association	1	10	0.08
Union Nationals Democracy Party	1	247	1.48
Regional Parties			
Kachin State National Congress for Democracy	3	9	0.11
Kayah State Nationalities League for Democracy	2	8	0.08
Karen State National Organization	1	3	0.05
Mon National Democratic Front	5	19	1.05
Democratic Organization for Kayan National Unity	2	3	0.11
Chin National League for Democracy	3	13	0.38
Mara Peoples Party	1	4	0.04
Zomi National Congress	2	4	0.14
Naga Hills Regional Progressive Party	2	6	0.08
United Nationalities League for Democracy	1	4	0.07
National Democratic Party for Human Rights	4	8	0.97
Rahkine Democracy League	11	25	1.21
Mro (or) Khami National Solidarity Organization	1	4	0.17
Kamans National League for Democracy	1	3	0.08
Shan Nationalities League for Democracy	23	58	1.68
Union Paoh National Organization	3	15	0.27
Union Danu League for Democracy Party	1	4	0.17
Shan State Kokang Democratic Party	1	2	0.05
Ta-ang (Palaung) National League for Democracy	2	9	0.18
Lahu National Delopment Party	1	7	0.12

a Including Peasants Unity Organization, Youth Unity Organization, and Workers Unity Organization.
Source: *Working People's Daily*, 1, 2, 3 July 1990.

This was highlighted in a post-election interview of U Kyi Maung with a foreign journalist in which he made reference to the holding of a Nuremberg type trial in Yangon after the NLD came to power. Denying the threat was a major problem, he did suggest that some individuals such as Major General "Khin Nyunt might reasonably feel themselves pretty insecure".[3] Subsequently, Major General Myo Nyunt, the commander of the Yangon Division, drew together U Kyi Maung's Nuremberg reference with earlier claims by Daw Aung San Suu Kyi that the Myanmar army was composed of fascists. Later in the year Senior General Saw Maung drew attention to an alleged demand of young Buddhist monks and others opposed to the regime that the army be broken into smaller, regionally based units and that all currently serving officers from the rank of colonel up would be removed from office.[4] Such perceptions of intended revenge heightened the leadership's fears about the ultimate consequences of passing power to a civilian government while maintaining the corporate solidarity of the officer corps.

The centrality of the army in Myanmar's politics is apparent in the conflict which has developed between the SLORC and the NLD. Both the SLORC and the older leadership of the NLD were all once subordinates of former General Ne Win, who, while apparently playing little or no role in current affairs, has left a conflicting legacy of loyalty and distrust which has been impossible so far to overcome. U Kyi Maung and his cohort were among the former Brigadier Aung Gyi faction of officers placed under arrest by General Ne Win in the 1960s; former General Tin U was the popular Minister for Defence who was jailed along with other officers for being implicated in a plot to assassinate U Ne Win in the mid-1970s. Army factionalism and the legacies of successive military generations have provided one of the distinctive features of the élite level conflict of the post-1988 political struggle.

After the final election results were released at the beginning of July, sporadic demonstrations led by students began to develop in Yangon and elsewhere. Though quickly curbed by the military, they were evidence of growing tension among the public. In the meantime, the government claimed it could not call into session the new Pyithu Hluttaw because the final election formalities, such as appeals on election misconduct and reports of election expenses, had not been submitted to the Election Commission and the latter could not issue its final report.

In order to regain the political initiative as it had done when it established the date of the 1990 election in February 1989, the SLORC issued its Declaration No. 1/90 on 27 July. This subsequently became the basis of the government's post-election plan to which the party leaders would have to accede if they were eventually to gain any semblance of governing power. The steps set out in Declaration No. 1/90 followed from the refusal of the army since 1988 to concede power to civilians under an interim constitution. Rather, eventually the government would hold a national conference to draft guidelines from which the Pyithu Hluttaw would draft a new, permanent constitution. To facilitate this activity, the SLORC had earlier commissioned the writing of a political history of Myanmar from 1945 to 1962 in order to reveal the alleged deficiencies of the immediate post-independence civilian order. The SLORC leadership also made it clear that in drawing up the new constitution the views of the alleged 135 "national races" of the country would have to be consulted and that perhaps a referendum would have to be held on the new document. In the eyes of the opposition, such a programme seemed no more than a set of ruses established to forestall any meaningful transfer of power.

The timing of SLORC Declaration No. 1/90 was apparently intended to pre-empt the results of a meeting of NLD Pyithu Hluttaw members held in Yangon on 28 and 29 July. The meeting ended with the issuing of what came to be known as the Gandhi Hall Statement, after the venue. Noting that the SLORC had not responded to the NLD's requests for talks, it stated that the new legislature had not been elected to be a constituent assembly but to form a national government. As the party had already prepared an interim constitution, it insisted that the Pyithu Hluttaw meet in September and, after forming a government, draft a final constitution.

The SLORC's rejection of the Gandhi Hall Statement was made clear in a speech at Pa-an on 4 August by Brigadier-General Khin Nyunt. Restating the points made in Declaration No. 1/90, he reiterated that the SLORC was a military government acting under martial law. It therefore held de facto powers of government and would not allow the disintegration of the union. Denying that the military was stalling to remain in power, he said the SLORC was "performing its activities according to its planned programmes step by step" and that the politicians should be completing their arrangements with the Election Commission and doing "necessary preparatory work". He noted finally that, "Some parties are making demands and confrontations. Since the work [of the military] has already been planned, the SLORC will not accept any demands or confrontations."

This uncompromising statement, following on the Gandhi Hall Statement, came just four days before the second anniversary of the general strike called by the anti-government demonstrators in 1988. This date, 8-8-88, has become a powerful symbol of opposition to the military throughout the country. In the event, demonstrations did take place in several towns and cities, and it was alleged by opposition leaders and foreign diplomats that two laymen and two Buddhist monks were killed by troops suppressing a demonstration in Mandalay. This allegation was stoutly denied by the government but to little avail, and opposition to the regime mounted as September and the planned meeting of the Pyithu Hluttaw approached.

The political solidity of the opposition to the military was underscored on 30 August when a coalition of 21 ethnically and regionally designated parties, known as the United Nationals League for Democracy (UNLD), issued its declaration, named after Bo Aung Kyaw Street where they met in Yangon. Their Declaration 1 endorsed the Gandhi Hall Statement and insisted, as had the NLD, on the release of Daw Aung San Suu Kyi and U Tin U from detention, as well as the lifting of restrictions on democratic rights and freedoms. The views of SLORC Chairman Saw Maung in the face of this pressure were set forth in discussions he held at the end of August with a visiting Japanese Diet member, Mr Michio Watanabe, who had come to Yangon in the hope of speeding a political transition. According to published reports, Senior General Saw Maung said that Daw Aung San Suu Kyi would be released if she left the country or promised to refrain from any political activities, conditions she would doubtless refuse to accept. As to discussions with the NLD leadership, the Senior General claimed this was impossible because the party was split into several factions but that he would at some point in the future open a dialogue with party leaders. An apparent sense of isolation among the military leadership was underscored by his alleged statement that the country's universities could not be reopened because the student body might return armed.[5]

The arrest of party leaders, students, and monks for refusing to comply with the military's programme dominated the politics of the final third of the year. NLD spokesman U Kyi Maung, along with another senior figure, U Chit Khaing, were taken into custody together with four Mandalay NLD leaders on 6 September for allegedly passing "state secrets" to diplomats and foreign journalists, presumably about the 8 August demonstrations in Mandalay. Further arrests followed, including those of members of the NLD and the Democratic Party for New Society in Kayan for distributing pamphlets. Protests continued, however, and became more pointed as some monks, initially in Mandalay, but subsequently elsewhere, stepped up a campaign to deny religious ceremonies to military officers and their families. This form of tacit excommunication from the institutions of Buddhism was designed to show a strong moral disapprobation of the army and to press military families to oppose government policies. The action prompted the arrest and disrobing in October and November of many monks after the army had consulted with the elderly leadership of the national *sangha* (community of monks) organization. Subsequently legislation was reinforced, making illegal any monastic sects or organizations other than the nine officially recognized by the state.

As the year ended, the army remained in control of the government and had forced the few remaining party leaders to sign SLORC Declaration No. 1/90 accepting its programme for political change. According to Chairman Saw Maung, NLD leader U Aung Shwe, also a former officer, signed along with representatives of the National Democratic Party (NDP), the NUP, and other groups. The importance of this remained obscure, however, as the general was unable to provide a timetable for constitutional development in the new year and the government announced the arrest of a further group of NLD Pyithu Hluttaw members and organizers at the beginning of December for plotting to establish a parallel government during September and October. Several other NLD Pyithu Hluttaw members were said to have "absconded" and it was reported that they had gone to the Thai border area in order to join with student and minority opposition groups. Eight persons elected to the Pyithu Hluttaw, led by a cousin of Daw Aung San Suu Kyi, subsequently declared the formation of a "parallel government" at the headquarters camp of insurgent organizations on 18 December but two later returned to Yangon and announced that they had been misled. The "parallel government" received no encouragement from other states and its identification with armed ethnic insurgents probably undermined its appeal for legitimacy in the eyes of most of the Myanmar population.

Insurgencies Suffer from Policy Initiatives

Parallel with the events taking place in Yangon, Mandalay, and other central areas of the country during the year, the insurgencies which have provided a background to national politics since independence continued. Though conflicting reports of success of the army against the insurgents were issued by the government and its armed opponents during the year, it seems likely that the strengthened armed forces were able to keep pressure on their various foes. Since 1988 the size of the armed forces has been increased to approximately 230,000 men and women, and new and better arms were reportedly purchased from China and Yugoslavia. Improved relations with countries bordering on Myanmar's north and east seem to have facilitated military action in these zones.

By the end of January, for example, the government claimed to have taken eight camps from the Karen National Liberation Army (KNLA), the armed force of the Karen National Union (KNU), leaving only two major camps in their hands. Unsubstantiated reports from sources who had recently been to the Thai border area in early April suggested that the KNU was left in secure control of only one major camp, but just how permanent is control of these areas by the government was not revealed. Fighting in the Kachin State also continued during the year, with the government claiming it had captured two KIA brigade headquarters in the first two months of the year. Whatever the success of the various government and insurgent forces, the annual recitation of battle causalities issued in March made for grim reading.

In the Shan State the government continued to develop its links with the Wa people who had until 1989 provided the bulk of the armed forces of the now largely defunct Burma Communist Party (BCP). The government media gave prominence to a programme to resettle the population and wean them away from the cultivation of opium poppies. Other reports suggested that Wa troops, operating under the name of the United Wa State Army (UWSA) were receiving assistance from government forces in attacks on troops of Khun Sa's opium smuggling Mong Tai Army. The truth of these claims, and counter-claims, remained to be demonstrated and the negative press coverage which the government's treatment of its civilian opponents received made it harder for foreign reporters to accept reports on its programmes in the remoter parts of the country at face value. The international concern in recent years over the significant place of Myanmar in the Golden Triangle drug-producing zone of northern Southeast Asia has been one more complicating factor in the country's foreign relations, as well as a drain on its military, economic, and financial resources. Whatever else, however, the government vowed that it would not negotiate with the insurgents and would continue its armed struggle until all of its armed opponents surrendered or were destroyed. In the meantime, the fiscal base of the insurgents appears to have been significantly shaken as a consequence of the opening up of legal border trade, undermining part of the black market.

Relations with Western Governments Strained but Economic Ties with Asia Growing

As far as most Western governments were concerned, Myanmar had reached the status of a near pariah state. Throughout the year a variety of protests were presented to the government from the countries of the European Community and Scandinavia, the United States, Japan, Australia, Canada, and New Zealand over the detention of Daw Aung San Suu Kyi and U Tin U, the failure to transfer power to the NLD after the election, the detention (some reportedly on embassy grounds) of locally employed embassy staff, and general denials of human rights, including the relocation of thousands of persons from the centre of Yangon, Pathein, Taunggyi, and other cities.

The latter is a prime example of the often distorted claims and counter-claims exchanged between the government and resident diplomats and their governments during the year. The government's version of the relocation of 150,000 persons from Yangon was that many were squatters and homeless who were happy to be relocated. Others were government employees who were being provided inexpensive land on which to develop for the first time their own homes. The programme was provided further justification, in the eyes of the authorities, because it was a scheme drawn up four years earlier on the basis of a plan developed by the United Nations Commission on Human Settlement. Critics of the government, whose views were widely distributed outside the country, claimed that the relocation was a politically inspired scheme to break up centres of opposition to the military and thus undermine the voting strength of the NLD. While the latter was a nonsense, the government did not strengthen its case by denying that there were major problems of water, sanitation, employment, housing, and family disruption surrounding the compulsory relocation of so many people in such a short time. Similar to the resettlement of many squatters from the centre of the city to the now established suburbs of North and South Okkalapa under the military "Caretaker Government" in the late 1950s, this programme which, if properly planned and financed, was probably essential for the healthy and structured development of the city, became instead another example of government callousness in the eyes of its foreign and domestic critics.

The human rights issue which was at the centre of so much of the criticism of the government was aired in February at the 46th meeting of the United Nations Commission on Human Rights in Geneva. The meeting accepted a French proposal to send "an independent expert to establish direct contacts with the Government of Myanmar on developments relating to the human rights situation in Myanmar and to report thereon to the Commission at its next session". In November, Professor Sadako Ogata from Japan spent several days in Yangon attempting to carry out her mission. While the official press reported her meetings with government officials, little else was revealed about her investigation other than that she had been unable to travel to Mandalay and other areas as she had planned.

Relations with the United States were especially strained during the year. In March the U.S. Government announced that it had indicted Khun Sa, the head of the Mong Tai (Shan United) Army, reportedly the largest opium smuggler in the region. While the Myanmar Government reported that it would be happy to co-operate with the American authorities in suppressing the drug trade, and put on three significant exhibitions of its efforts in this regard during the year, it would not allow an American Panama-type raid in order to bring Khun Sa out for trial in an American court. Relations became additionally strained later in the year when the original agreement of the Myanmar Government to accept the nomination of a former Central Intelligence Agency official as the Bush Administration's ambassador designate was reversed.

The deterioration of relations with Western governments that had set in after the 1988 coup has not yet led to the breaking of diplomatic relations with any regime. This point was noted in the 27 July SLORC Declaration No. 1/90 and reiterated in a Foreign Ministry press release on 5 October detailing a meeting with the dean of the diplomatic corps at which the government protested at the application of pressure on it by some other governments. Comments on domestic Myanmar politics made by diplomats to journalists in Bangkok and elsewhere, and then broadcast back into the country via British, American, and Indian radio stations, were also viewed as privileged and unwarranted interference in the internal affairs of the state. Condemnation of the Burmese language services of the British Broadcasting Commission (BBC), Voice of America (VOA), and All India Radio (AIR) continued throughout the year, including Senior General Saw Maung's Resistance Day speech on 27 March. The fact that claims in foreign publications that these external broadcast media have been significant shapers of the activities of opponents to the military since 1988 has contributed to the launching of these attacks. The reporting of events in Western countries, and the unsubtle cartoons published about foreigners in the official *Working People's Daily*, served as a constant reminder of the government's strained relations with Western states.

Given the training and experience of the leaders of the Myanmar army, it is not surprising that they have responded to the critical comments advanced by foreign governments and news media, including two more condemnatory reports by Amnesty International, in a highly nationalistic manner. The result has become a dialogue of the deaf, as calls for the release of political leaders such as Daw Aung San Suu Kyi and the immediate handover of power to the NLD has been interpreted as an attempt not only to facilitate the removal and trial of the officer corps, but also as an attempt to suborn the nation's population. The view of the army is represented in the following excerpt from General Saw Maung's Independence Day statement on 4 January 1990. After recalling how Myanmar had lost its independence to Britain in the 19th century because of a combination of domestic feudalism, ethnic disunity, military unpreparedness and imperialist avarice, he went on to say,[6]

> In this 20th Century although the colonialists do not blatantly commit aggression on small nations and occupy them as in the olden days, they employ the method of breeding minions using social, economic, and cultural means as well as ideological means so that the small nations may fall under their influence, think highly of them and become subservient to them. We must defend and protect our nation with greater caution and vigilance so that our nation never becomes a colony under any form.

In the logic of this reasoning, foreign pressure to establish an NLD government, release political opponents from detention, improve human rights, and govern in a different manner are part of a plan to weaken the army's capacity to continue to carry out its goal of maintaining national independence. As the military's opponents view this argument, it is no more than a sham to justify remaining in power, and thus no attempt at a genuine dialogue has been made.

Future Remains Uncertain

Despite the expectation, underlined by Senior General Saw Maung in his speech in January quoted above, that the year promised to be one seeing the end of one era and the beginning of another, no resolution of current political problems was found. The transition to a civilian government held out by the elections did not eventuate and the impasse of 1988 remains. Economic recovery has been patchy, with severe problems of inflation and trade imbalance which have not been addressed because resources are scarce.

The criticisms of foreign governments cannot dislodge the military regime; but the Myanmar Government cannot in the short term effectively reform the economy with the limited resources at its disposal. Political uncertainty makes long-term foreign investment in agriculture and manufacturing difficult except for the most speculative of industries. Few believed after the 1988 coup that the military could remain in office and transform the polity to a democracy with a market economy. The doubters were not forced to change that judgement in 1990. Will the military government be able to confound its critics in 1991 without resort to methods which in the end will be self-defeating?

Notes

1. According to Major General Khin Nyunt, SLORC Secretary 1 and head of the Directorate of Defence Services Intelligence (DDSI), of the 485 Pyithu Hluttaw representatives election, "there are 42 persons who were given retirement by the Defence Services.... There are 145 retired public service personnel; 54 lawyers; 50 doctors; and 194 civilians." Of the latter group, none, Major General Khin Nyunt said, could be described as a student. Ibid., 5 August 1990.
2. *Asiaweek*, 13 July 1990.
3. *Working People's Daily*, 13 November 1990.
4. Kyodo News Agency, 30 August 1990.
5. *Working People's Daily*, 4 January 1990.

MYANMAR
No Turning Back

Moe Thuzar

The year 2011 was one of change for Myanmar. It was the year of the country's administration becoming "civil" in the eyes of many in the country and the world at large. A civilian government, albeit with a military past, was sworn in on 30 March 2011. President Thein Sein's inaugural speech to the parliament, outlining priorities for economic renewal, sustainable development, poverty alleviation, human rights and good governance, and recognizing the plight of ethnic minorities involved in armed conflict, was initially dismissed by many as "just words".

Six months later, however, observers within and outside the country were recognizing the steps outlined in this inaugural speech when changes started showing in Myanmar's political and economic scene. These changes include the freedom of movement (and speech) of Nobel laureate Aung San Suu Kyi, the loosened restrictions on the media, a law allowing workers the right to strike, amnesties for prisoners (including political prisoners), and steps taken towards economic reform. The pace set by the government on this road to reform seemed almost exhilarating to citizens and observers used to setbacks and stonewalling from the authorities in the past. The pace continued to surprise as 2011 progressed, peaking with the National League for Democracy (NLD) rejoining the political process, the agreement by the Association of Southeast Asian Nations (ASEAN) to Myanmar's bid to be the ASEAN Chair in 2014, and the landmark visit of U.S. Secretary of State Hillary Clinton to the country.

Indonesian Foreign Minister Marty Natalegawa has described the reform process in Myanmar as irreversible. Op-

Reprinted from Daljit Singh and Pushpa Thambipillai, eds., *Southeast Asian Affairs 2012* (Singapore: Institute of Southeast Asian Studies, 2012), pp. 203–19. At the time of original publication, Moe Thuzar was Visiting Research Fellow at the Institute of Southeast Asian Studies, Singapore.

timists and critics share concerns on whether the "flickers of progress" described by U.S. President Obama will develop into a steady flame. Having cited the reforms as a key reason for its decision to give Myanmar the ASEAN chair for 2014, ASEAN, too, has much at stake.[1]

Reviewing developments in Myanmar in 2011, the picture that emerges shows the beginning of a convergence of interests, the first in decades, between the military-backed government, the polity in Myanmar, the forces for democracy symbolized by Aung San Suu Kyi, and the international community.

The Year in Review

The year 2011 saw a newly elected "civilianized" government in Myanmar. It had come to power in what many around the world had largely decried as sham elections in November 2010. The Hluttaw, or parliament, convened on 31 January. The government — comprising a large number of officials from the previous military regime — took office in March,[2] headed by Thein Sein as President. The appointment of Thein Sein as President surprised many. As a retired general and immediate past Prime Minister under the State Peace and Development Council (SPDC) government, his appointment was met with scepticism that the new administration would take on the necessary reforms. The appointment of several technocrats as deputy ministers (with implementation responsibilities) did not alleviate the scepticism either. There was further scepticism when Myanmar proposed to chair the ASEAN Summit in 2014, to resume the turn she gave up in 2006.

That scepticism is now giving way to cautious optimism. The series of measures oriented towards reform undertaken by a country which, as recent as twelve months ago, was the problem child of ASEAN, has given rise to new hope for Myanmar.[3] Viewed in the context of the half-century of political and economic stagnation, the reform agenda and delivered promises appear particularly impressive. In the same context, expectations are high for the government to continue delivering.

The starting point for the first flickers of change can be counted from the release of Aung San Suu Kyi on 13 November 2010 and the subsequent laissez-faire attitude of the government with regard to her movements and the activities of the NLD, which then was technically an illegal association after its de-registration from the 2010 election process. The steps taken towards more media freedom, reinvigorating the economy, recognition of poverty as a priority, efforts to improve human rights, and the national political scene have all added to the aspirations for change.

The Press Finds its Voice

Thein Sein took up the necessity of media freedom in an address to his Cabinet. Referring to the media as the "fourth estate", he recognized the role of the media and the need to respect that role. The first visible instance of the tight controls over the local media being relaxed started with the ominously titled Press Scrutiny and Registration Division (PSRD) allowing stories on five genres — entertainment, health, children, information technology, and sports — to be published without prior submission of drafts. This benefited a total of 178 journals in the country, a majority of them in the local language. On 9 December, stories covering business and crime were allowed to be published freely, benefiting

54 publications. This left only stories on political news and religion subject to scrutiny. Still, there is now more leeway in the reporting of political news. Journalists can now report on interviews with political parties and political news, including the activities of Aung San Suu Kyi.[4] This is a clear contrast to the prohibitions in the past. The relaxation of press censorship regarding stories on Aung San Suu Kyi became more evident after her first meeting with Thein Sein on 19 August and especially after the publication of her article in a local journal in September.

In an interview with Radio Free Asia in October, the PSRD head stated that press censorship should be abolished in the near future, as it is "not in harmony with democratic practices".[5] Many will remember this remark as 2012 progresses, with expectations now heightened for greater freedom of expression.

Media freedom certainly had a vital role in covering public opposition, online and in print, to the construction of a multi-billion dollar hydroelectric dam on the Ayeyarwady River with Chinese funding. The President's decision to suspend the dam construction is partly due to the media's active role. The *Weekly Eleven News Journal* — conferred "Best Media Award of the Year" for 2011 from Reporters Without Borders (RSF) — was particularly effective.

Starting September, previously blocked websites are now accessible, with the exception of pornographic websites. The problem now is bandwidth. Many netizens in Myanmar complain of the slow speed of connection.

On 18 September, many noticed that the government newspaper, the *New Light of Myanmar*, no longer carried slogans denouncing the influence of foreign media. In October, foreign and local media were allowed to cover the Hluttaw sessions in Naypyitaw for the first time. Foreign journalists were also allowed into the country on official visas, the most prominent example being the BBC (previously banned) accompanying the visit of Andrew Mitchell, the United Kingdom's Secretary for International Development, in November.

Changing the Economic Scene

On 9 April, the Minister of Commerce briefed officials of the Union of Myanmar Federation of Chambers of Commerce and Industry (UMFCCI) that in future the Ministry alone would be responsible for granting import/export permits. Up to then, the issuing of licences was a monopoly of the Trade Council, which had been in existence since 1964,[6] and which was notorious for corruption and cronyism. The April briefing by the Minister of Commerce effectively abolished the Trade Council.

On 27 April, nine presidential advisors were appointed: three each for economics, politics, and legal affairs.[7] This attracted attention, not least because it was unprecedented, but also because the chief economic advisor, Dr U Myint — a former economist with UNESCAP — is close to Aung San Suu Kyi and has a reputation for not mincing words. Dr U Myint also heads a new think tank, called the Myanmar Development Resource Institute, which was established in May with the aim of providing necessary academic and technical inputs to poverty alleviation programmes.[8]

Another step towards economic-related reform was the exemption from export tax of rice and six other items — corn, beans and pulses, sesame seeds, rubber, and seafood — for six months effective 15 August. This was to improve competitiveness, according to the announcement in the government newspaper, the *New Light of Myanmar*. The exemption followed a reduction in the rice export tax on 1 July, from eight to five per cent.

In October, a delegation of the International Monetary Fund (IMF) paid its annual visit to Myanmar to assess the financial situation. In their discussions with officials from the Central Bank, private banks and the UMFCCI, and other key business figures, one of the main topics was unifying the exchange rate in the country. This is significant as the Myanmar kyat is officially as strong as the French franc, i.e., approximately 6 kyats to US$1, while the black market rate is about 800–850 kyats to US$1. There continues to be scepticism that the IMF can assist in Myanmar's currency rate unification. Many small and medium enterprises, which comprise the bulk of the country's economy, would be affected if a unified rate were to be stabilized below the current black market rate.[9]

Scepticism notwithstanding, starting 1 October, U.S. dollars can now be openly exchanged for Myanmar kyat at designated counters at six private banks at the going black-market rate. There were some teething issues: some counters quoted higher buying and selling rates in USD than the going black-market rate.

A widely popular measure in the country was the unification of pension rates on 30 June, of those who had retired prior to 1 January 2010 and their counterparts who had retired since then. As pension calculations were previously based on salary at the time of retirement, any civil servant who had retired prior to pay rises implemented in April 2006 and January 2010, had been drawing substantially less than those who had retired subsequently. The pension hike on 30 June cost the government the equivalent of several hundred million U.S. dollars, as the unification of rates translated into a hundred-fold increase in the allowance of many pensioners.[10]

In 2012, legislators will deliberate on a bill to amend the foreign investment law of November 1988. The amendment of this law is aimed at raising more foreign investment in the country. Current top investors in Myanmar are China, Thailand, South Korea, Britain, and Singapore.[11]

Political Reforms: Listening to the People

On 16 May, an amnesty reduced the sentences of 14,578 prisoners, 55 of whom were political prisoners. Another amnesty on 11 October pardoned 6,359 prisoners, some 200 of whom were political detainees. Another release was expected in November, coinciding with the timing of the 19th ASEAN Summit in Bali, Indonesia where Myanmar's bid for ASEAN chairmanship would be decided. ASEAN's decision was made but the release did not take place. What did happen was the transfer on 16 November of several prominent political detainees to prison facilities closer to their families. Among them were the influential leader of the 1988 student demonstrations Min Ko Naing and the activist Reverend Ashin Gambira. A Home Ministry official was quoted saying that those due to be freed would be released "gradually" and that "things are in the process".[12]

The government started meetings with Aung San Suu Kyi on 25 July. Minister Aung Kyi, who had been appointed by the SPDC government in 2007 as the liaison minister for Aung San Suu Kyi, continued this role. Aung San Suu Kyi and Aung Kyi had a second meeting on 12 August before "the Lady and the President" met on 19 August in Naypyitaw. Many watchers parsed the symbolic nature of the meeting where the President was seated under a portrait of General Aung San, Aung San Suu Kyi's father and the country's independence hero. While in Naypyitaw, Aung San Suu Kyi also attended a national workshop on economic reform convened by the President, and was accorded ministerial treatment.[13]

Also in August, the President publicly invited exiles who have not committed "serious crimes" to return and help in rebuilding the country. In the absence of any formal policy or procedure safeguarding their return, very few exiles have done so. The *Irrawaddy* reports that those who return are expected to sign a five-point document essentially binding them not to engage in actions and words that can harm national stability.[14]

On 5 September, the Myanmar National Human Rights Commission was formed. The commission came into prominence with its first open letter to the President on 10 October, appealing for the release of political prisoners, just a day before the 11 October amnesty of over 6,000 prisoners. The commission followed up with a second open letter on 12 November, clarifying the numbers of political prisoners (some 500 out of which 200 had been released on 11 October) and requesting the release of the remaining prisoners. The letter's last point stated that if "for reasons of maintaining peace and stability, certain prisoners cannot as yet be included in the amnesty, the Commission would like to respectfully submit that consideration be made for transferring them to prisons with easy access for their family members".[15] A more recent statement by the commission on 14 December warned of conflict trauma for children and adults in Kachin State, after commission members had visited the area to observe the condition of refugees.[16]

The world sat up and took notice on 30 September, when the government acceded to popular demands by suspending work on the controversial US$3.6 billion Myitsone hydroelectric dam project financed by China at the confluence of the two rivers forming the Ayeyarwady. In announcing his decision, the President stated that he was listening to the people's will. He had received recommendations not only from Dr Myint but also petitions from many citizens from all walks of life.[17] There is no precedent for such reversals in the face of public opposition. It also shows that the President — the top decision-maker — is willing to listen and act on recommendations. China was apparently taken by surprise at the decision and urged the Myanmar Government to protect the rights of Chinese investors. The government-owned Chinese company backing the dam threatened to start legal proceedings, but has taken no steps so far. The Myitsone story has a symbolic stature as an instance of Myanmar clearly stating a preference to pursue her "independent and active" foreign policy.

Also at the end of September the government passed a law allowing the formation of trade unions while granting the workers the right to strike. The *Economist*[18] reported that Myanmar's labour ministry consulted the International Labour Organization (ILO) on the legislation to ensure that it was up to international standards. Steve Marshall, the ILO's representative in Myanmar said that the move was a momentous policy decision.

November saw the NLD rejoining the political process. The decision on 18 November by the NLD that it would register to run in the parliamentary by-elections was seen by many as the leading opposition party's recognition of the government's reform process. However, the assurance given by the President to Aung San Suu Kyi that all political prisoners would be released soon still needs to be realized. The Hluttaw approved the NLD's request for registration on 12 December and scheduled the by-elections for 1 April 2012. Aung San Suu Kyi is sure of a parliamentary seat, and perhaps even a Cabinet position. If the latter happens, it would be the result of consultation between the NLD and the government.

The Hluttaw passed the "Peaceful Assembly and Procession Bill" on 22 November. Although still restrictive in the freedom to assemble, the bill is significant, given Myanmar's recent past.[19] Under the present bill, demonstrators are required to inform authorities about their planned protest at least five days in advance, and are also required to avoid government buildings, schools, hospitals, and embassies.

A Year of Prominent Visitors

The year 2011 ended on a high note for Myanmar. In early December, U.S. Secretary of State Hillary Clinton made a landmark visit to the country, the first official visit by a U.S. Secretary of State since John Foster Dulles in 1955. Although high-level visits by U.S. officials — including Senator John McCain, U.S. Special Envoy Derek Mitchell, and State Department Assistant Secretary Joseph Yun — had taken place throughout the year, Mrs Clinton's visit signalled U.S. recognition of Thein Sein's reform moves. The visit took place just after Myanmar was given the 2014 chairmanship of ASEAN and just before Myanmar was due to take on the role of country coordinator of the ASEAN-U.S. Dialogue for 2012–15. ASEAN — and Myanmar's role in ASEAN — will be an important reference point as the United States and Myanmar continue to communicate over the country's reform agenda.

Mrs Clinton's visit was preceded and followed by many other visits of foreign dignitaries, all of whom were keen to meet with the key players in Myanmar's reform process, and make their individual cases for engagement. UN Special Envoy Vijay Nambiar visited twice: in May and October. UN Special Rapporteur for Human Rights Thomas Quintana visited in August and probably catalysed the formation of Myanmar's National Human Rights Commission. Australian Foreign Minister Kevin Rudd visited in June. The European Union sent two delegations. From ASEAN, Indonesian Foreign Minister Marty Natalegawa and newly elected Thai Prime Minister Yingluck Shinawatra also visited twice. Former Malaysian Prime Minister Mahathir Mohamad visited in October and gave a rousing business talk in Yangon. Singapore Foreign Minister K. Shanmugam followed on the heels of Mrs Clinton. Japanese Foreign Minister Koichiro Gemba paid a Christmas visit. Billionaire philanthropist George Soros — whose Open Society Foundation donates some US$2 million to projects in Myanmar — became the next big name to visit Aung San Suu Kyi, scheduling a visit in early January 2012. Doubtless, many high-profile visitors will follow. The norm is now to meet both Thein Sein and Aung San Suu Kyi.

What Next for Reforms?

The reforms and their continued implementation in 2012 are dependent on several influences, including personalities, processes, and relationships.

The Lady and the President

President Thein Sein shot into prominence with his reform agenda for a "modern and developed democratic nation" and his commitment to implement it. Prior to his presidency, he was a nondescript personality as Prime Minister for the SPDC regime. His credibility as President does not seem to have suffered from the initial favouring of Thura Shwe Mann (now Speaker of the Lower House) as heir apparent to succeed Senior General Than Shwe. While he may not have the charisma of Aung San Suu Kyi, his strengths as an administrator are now coming to the fore in his role as a cautious reformer. He is aware of what needs to be done and of the implementation gaps which became evident in the post-Nargis follow-up. While he has the expertise of advisors and technocrats to tap on in implementing his reform agenda, he walks a delicate line between pushing reforms and managing the concerns of the hardliners.

Daw Aung San Suu Kyi has expressed satisfaction with her talks with the Thein Sein administration, including her meeting with the President. At the same time, she continues to be the voice of conscience publicly as well as during her meetings with the government. One recent example is her call for the rule of law as "essential in every sector for the development of the country" in a speech made on the anniversary of her release from house arrest. Emphasizing that the rule of law was vital for Myanmar's transition to democracy, particularly with regard to economic development and foreign investment, she also expressed her aspirations for the emergence of a free and fair judiciary.[20] Aung San Suu Kyi has also expressed her concern over the use of force in clashes between the military and some ethnic armed groups, calling for immediate ceasefires and peaceful resolution of the conflicts and offering her support to further this, in an open letter to the President in July. The mild reaction by the government to this letter is a departure from the SPDC regime's attitude of jealously separating democracy and ethnic issues.[21]

Two common strands link the interests of Thein Sein and Aung San Suu Kyi. They are both inextricably and inseparably linked to the reform movement. The excitement surrounding reforms is due to the real possibilities for change that supporters see resulting from the sincerity of Thein Sein and the charisma of Aung San Suu Kyi. But both also lack obvious successors. Morbidity aside, they need a contingency plan in the event that a disgruntled military decides "enough is enough" and steps in. Their combined knowledge and experience of the military will be assets in planning a role for a peacetime army as reforms progress. This depends substantially on how the decades-long conflict with ethnic groups will be resolved.

The Ethnic Factor[22]

The ethnic issue remains serious and poses a challenge to the country's democratization. Recent steps taken by the government have been positive although marred by the continuation of fighting with some armed groups.

President Thein Sein's prioritization of the ethnic minority issue in his inaugural speech met with scepticism as there was an upsurge in fighting around the same time he took office. The olive branch proffered for dialogue and reconciliation was not taken up. In June, a seventeen-year ceasefire with Kachin rebels collapsed, threatening to derail reform efforts. The government has reached out to all armed groups, in secret and publicized meetings, offering more flexible terms and dropping the demand (made by the SPDC regime) for the groups to become border guard forces. Incentives that were offered include economic development and freedom of travel for unarmed ethnic leaders, among others. A planned national conference to seek political solutions to ethnic differences has not yet taken place, although the government's offers did persuade some of the major ethnic groups to sign peace agreements. Others agreed initially to verbal ceasefires, followed by written agreements signed in the last months of 2011. One of the most significant breakthroughs is the preliminary ceasefire agreement with the Shan State Army, one of the biggest rebel groups. However, clashes with the Kachin rebels[23] broke out again in December, which does not bode well for the government's reform efforts.

As Myanmar prepares for ASEAN chairmanship, and as business and tourist visits increase, a peaceful resolution of the situation with the ethnic armed groups is a definite priority.

Opening up through ASEAN

ASEAN had faced much criticism in standing by its decision to admit Myanmar as a member. ASEAN's brokering of space for humanitarian aid workers in the aftermath of Cyclone Nargis in 2008 created opportunities for non-governmental organizations to operate in Myanmar. The tripartite mechanism among the United Nations, ASEAN, and the Myanmar Government to coordinate cyclone relief and recovery became a reference point for options on how capacities for change could be built in the country.

ASEAN has responded to the steps taken towards reform by agreeing to Myanmar's request to chair and host the ASEAN Summits in 2014. The NLD — which will soon have a greater role in Myanmar's parliamentary process — sees ASEAN's move as paving the way for stepping up political reform. ASEAN's decision is thus a blend of incentive and monitoring. The Indonesian Foreign Minister has described the reform process as irreversible. With ASEAN chairmanship and credibility at stake, there can be no back-tracking on reforms. There is also no turning back for ASEAN. Having justified its decision, ASEAN has to ensure that the reforms result in democracy and development beyond 2014. To address concerns by rights groups and parliamentarians, ASEAN must now step up its strategy of enhanced interaction with Myanmar.[24]

This will be most needed in the next few years leading up to Myanmar's ASEAN chairmanship. By agreeing that Myanmar take up ASEAN Chair responsibilities for 2014, ASEAN has also agreed that Myanmar will chair important high-level meetings with ASEAN Dialogue Partners, including the East Asia Summit, the ASEAN Regional Forum and Post-Ministerial Conferences, and the individual summits with Dialogue Partners, including China and the United States. The summits are preceded by meetings of senior officials and ministers. ASEAN's internal coordination meetings also involve ministerial-level coordinating councils for each of ASEAN's three community pillars.

All this requires skilful organization and coordination and, more importantly, an understanding of ASEAN institutions and cooperation mechanisms and the role of the association in regional and international dynamics. Myanmar will need to pay more attention to the latter two requirements if she is to lead regional priority-setting as ASEAN Chair. There are several learning gaps to address in the years before Myanmar takes up ASEAN chairmanship. These are partly because Myanmar's integration in ASEAN has largely been driven at the senior levels of government, and messaging to working-level officials and the general public has been limited in scope and depth.

The year 2012 will see Myanmar engaging more closely with fellow ASEAN members, more closely with some than others. There is a marked regard for countries such as Indonesia which had supported Myanmar's re-entry into the Non-Aligned Movement in 1992 and under whose chairmanship Myanmar obtained agreement for chairing the 2014 ASEAN Summits. Indonesia was also the first ASEAN country to follow the ASEAN Summit decision with a bilateral visit in December, to assess collaboration potential under the Myanmar-Indonesia Joint Commission. Indonesia and Vietnam will be among the first that Myanmar turns to in preparing for the ASEAN Chair responsibilities.

Parliament's Check-and-Balance Role

Despite the inexperience of its members, the Hluttaw seems to be stepping up to the role that is expected of it. The national legislature is more active than the provincial legislatures and has shown that it is not a rubber-stamping authority. The role of the military-appointed Members of Parliament is another interesting factor. Contrary to expectations that they would vote in a bloc against opposition-proposed motions, military legislators supported a motion in the lower house that the President grant a general amnesty for political prisoners. MPs have shared that after some initial mistrust, relations are improving between elected and military representatives.[25] At local government levels, the regional commanders have not intervened in legislation and administration, despite their past positions of power and authority in the various regions.

Debate and discussion continue in the eight permanent parliamentary committees (four each for both the upper and lower houses) formed in early March. About one-third of the representatives elected to sit on each of the committees are not from the dominant Union Solidarity and Development Party (USDP). This provides a window for the opposition to have a voice through the parliamentary system.[26]

As 2011 drew to a close, a media bill was still under consideration. With the new, more relaxed atmosphere in reporting and press movement now taking stronger hold, legislators and journalists share concerns that any legislation on the media should ensure freedom of speech and the security of reporters.[27]

A Balancing Act

Myanmar's reform moves in 2011, especially the decision to halt construction of the Myitsone dam project with China, gave rise to speculation that the country was seeking to emerge from its long-standing and at times stifling embrace of friendship with China. The thaw in U.S.-Myanmar relations was also ascribed to the U.S. desire to balance China's strides in the region. The United States, Myanmar, and China all deny this is so. One of Thein Sein's political advisors has stated that Myanmar aims for a "win-win-win" situation for change in the country by leveraging relations with both the United States and China. Derek Mitchell, the U.S. special envoy for Myanmar said on 13 December — at the end of a visit to Beijing — that improved U.S.-Myanmar relations were not aimed to have any negative influence on China's ties with Myanmar. The Chinese Foreign Ministry has stated that Beijing welcomed the enhanced relations between Myanmar and the West. The latter statement was noted by Aung San Suu Kyi, who referred to China as a "very close neighbour".[28]

Myanmar will continue to balance this "win-win-win" act in 2012. Hillary Clinton's visit opened up opportunities for more collaborative projects in health care, poverty alleviation, and education. More "enhanced interactions" may follow as part of Myanmar holding the role of country coordinator of ASEAN-U.S. Dialogue. There may be many interpretations of the halting of the Myitsone dam project, but the reality is that China has several other investments in Myanmar, including the building of oil and gas pipelines across the country that would allow an alternative access route to Middle Eastern crude. On the other hand, Chevron Corp. is one of the few U.S. companies operating in Myanmar in the oil and gas area. U.S. investment in Myanmar is less than 1 per cent, while China accounts for about 35 per cent, with US$13.947 billion.[29]

Continuing the Pace

The pace set for reform in 2011 and the expectations it has raised highlight the importance for the reform measures to continue with a steady momentum. Success lies with the ability of the government to formulate and implement a development policy appropriate for Myanmar's specific situation, including progressing reforms at a pace that the Myanmar people can adapt to and absorb. The year 2012 will continue to see Myanmar slowly emerge from decades of relative isolation.[30] The aspiration at many levels and walks of life seems to be to catch up with the rest of the world (or at least ASEAN).

Starting from a low base, one can argue that the only direction for Myanmar to go is upwards. Notwithstanding its stance of maintaining independence in foreign policy matters (thus not putting all eggs into one basket), Myanmar will draw on ASEAN and its dialogue system to facilitate her upward mobility through closer connectivity with the region and immediate neighbours. The short-term adjustment challenges are quite formidable. The effects of these adjustments will be most felt by the public in policies regarding exchange rate unification and getting the economy on an even keel. Managing and coordinating the inflow of donors and investors is another challenge. It is important to engage the polity in the transition processes, transparency, and communication. This is a lesson that the present government is learning fast.

Will 2012 bring the easing of sanctions? The United States and European Union — and the opposition in Myanmar — have been consistent in maintaining the conditions necessary for this to happen. These include the release of all political prisoners, peaceful resolution of the armed conflicts with ethnic groups, the holding of free and fair elections, and effectively addressing human rights abuses.

Thant Myint-U, the well-known historian on Myanmar, in his latest book *Where China Meets India*, presents a potential best-case scenario where Myanmar will emerge from her former isolation, with balanced development, cognizant of the need for environmental protection, and social mobility, all of which will assist Myanmar on the road to democratic governance. This optimum scenario will require foremost a resolution of the armed conflict with ethnic groups. Several other issues also need to be addressed. These include social protection (and more equitable distribution of wealth) through poverty alleviation programmes, and balancing economic growth with environmental protection and resource conservation. Myanmar will eventually need to consider her role in ASEAN and the world at large, with a foreign policy that integrates economic, environmental, and social priorities.[31]

Meanwhile, there continues to be a sense of euphoria surrounding the reforms. This will become more pronounced in the run-up to the by-elections in April 2012. It is unlikely that the government will tighten controls on rallies as in the past. There is optimism that the by-elections will be free and fair, resulting in Aung San Suu Kyi taking a formalized role in the reform process. The sense of expectancy and the force of expectations surrounding Myanmar's reforms brings to mind the mood of the country's pre-independence days, when General Aung San and the British Government were negotiating the transition to independence. General Aung San had cautioned the Myanmar people that independence did not mean the freedom to do as one pleased, that there were obligations accompanying freedom. In the same vein, people caught up in the move towards democracy in Myanmar today will need to be aware of the role and participation of the citizenry in the process, particularly how the citizens understand the public issues at stake and the power of their informed decisions. The civil society — the independent, non-governmental organizations as well as the government-approved entities — have a crucial role in representing and advocating the interests of the people, be they farmers, workers, students, activists, teachers, professionals, business owners, housewives, the unemployed, or the elderly, and in educating these people on the power they hold to make democracy work.

While credit must be given to the Thein Sein administration for setting reforms in motion, there are still many uncertainties going forward. One fact, however, is certain: there is no turning back.

Notes

1. Some ASEAN members had voiced their concern over Myanmar's chairmanship bid for 2014, citing that it (2014) was a "crucial" year, falling just before 2015, the date set for achieving a single integrated ASEAN community.
2. The State Peace and Development Council was dissolved on 30 March 2011. The *Myanmar Times* noted the date as a "historic" day.
3. Moe Thuzar, "ASEAN and Myanmar: No Turning Back", ISEAS Viewpoints, 18 November 2011 <http://web1.iseas.edu.sg/?p=6015>.
4. "A Year in Review 2011", A *Myanmar Times* Special Feature, December 2011.
5. "Press Censorship Should Cease as Part of Reforms: PSRD Head", *Myanmar Times*, 10–16 October 2011 <http://www.mmtimes.com/2011/news/596/news59603.html>.
6. The application for an import/export permit previously required submission to the Trade Council. The process, a five-step procedure, took at least eight days

but could easily take a month or longer. Many businesspeople hired agents for speed and convenience, further feeding the corrupt cycle. See Juliet Shwe Gaung's news article, "New Govt Changes Import/Export Licence System", *Myanmar Times*, 2–8 May <http://www.mmtimes.com/2011/business/573/biz57303.html>.
7. The economic advisors are Dr Myint, Winston Sett Aung, and Dr Sein Hla Bo. The political advisors are led by Ko Ko Hlaing, a former military officer and consultant for the Ministry of Information's News and Periodicals Enterprise. The other two political advisors are Dr Nay Zin Latt and U Ye Tint. The three legal advisors are former police colonel U Sit Aye, Daw Khin Myo Myint, and U Than Kyaw. Khin Myo Myint is the sole female of the nine advisors. See also "Thein Sein Appoints Presidential Advisors" by Ba Kaung. *Irrawaddy* online, 27 April 2011 <http://www.irrawaddy.org/article.php?art_id=21193>.
8. U Myint, "New Economic Perspectives for Myanmar", paper presented at ASEAN 2030: Report Finalisation Workshop, EDSA Shangri-La Hotel, Manila, 14 December 2011. According to U Myint, the proposal was made by him in May 2011 and approved by Thein Sein in June 2011.
9. Aye Thidar Kyaw and Stuart Deed, "IMF Visits Myanmar on Article VIII Mission", *Myanmar Times*, 31 October–6 November 2011 <http://www.mmtimes.com/2011/business/599/biz59904.html>.
10. Nyunt Win, "Pensioners All Smiles as Government Unifies Monthly Payments", *Myanmar Times*, 11–17 July 2011 <http://www.mmtimes.com/2011/news/583/news58305.html> (accessed 5 December 2011).
11. "Foreign Investment in Myanmar Hits over 40 Bln USD in 23 Years", Myanmar Business Network, 23 December 2011 <http://www.myanmar-business.org/2011/12/foreign-investment-in-myanmar-hits-over.html> (accessed 30 December 2011).
12. At the time of writing, two more amnesties have taken place, the first on 4 January 2012 releasing 32 prisoners and the second on 13 January 2012 releasing over 200, including Min Ko Naing, comedian Zarganar (in the earlier release), and former Prime Minister and notorious intelligence chief Khin Nyunt. Khin Nyunt's release sparked controversial comments at home and abroad.
13. "Myanmar: Major Reform Underway", International Crisis Group Asia Briefing No. 127, 22 September 2011.
14. Sai Zom Hseng, "Invitation to Return Falls Flat among Exiles", *The Irrawaddy*, 28 October 2011 <http://irrawaddy.org/article.php?art_id=22346>.
15. "Myanmar National Human Rights Commissioner Sends Open Letter to President", *New Light of Myanmar*, 12 November 2011 <http://www.myanmar.com/newspaper/nlm/Nov13_04.html>.
16. Saw Yan Naing, "Kachin Children in War Trauma: Burma Rights Commission", *The Irrawaddy*, 14 December 2011 <http://irrawaddy.org/article.php?art_id=22652>.
17. Thein Sein's comment that he was listening to the will of the people finds an echo in a remark made by Aung San Suu Kyi on the topic. The BBC quoted her as saying, "We understand the president in his memo to the national parliament has asked to suspend the Myitsone dam because of public concerns. Since every government should listen carefully to people's voices and tackle the concerned problems, I welcome this move."
18. *The Economist*, London, 8 October 2011.
19. Compare the bill on peaceful assembly to the situation of only four years ago. In September 2007 Myanmar was criticized internationally for the brutal repression of peaceful protests by monks — later joined by civilians — over fuel price hikes.
20. Yadana Htun and Shwe Yinn Mar Oo, "Daw Aung San Suu Kyi Calls on Govt to Ensure Rule of Law", *Myanmar Times*, 21–27 November 2011 <http://www.

21. Minister Aung Kyi acknowledged that the ethnic issue was "one of the issues under discussion" with Aung San Suu Kyi. Aung San Suu Kyi had sent open letters to both the President and the leaders of four armed groups (Kachin, Shan, Karen, and Mon) urging "immediate ceasefire and peaceful resolution of the conflicts". For more details on the content of the open letter, see Tun Tun's article, "Suu Kyi's Open Letter Calls for Immediate Ceasefire in Ethnic Areas", Mizzima online <http://www.mizzima.com/news/inside-burma/5691-suu-kyis-open-letter-calls-for-immediate-cease-fire-in-ethnic-areas.html>.
22. "Myanmar: A New Peace Initiative", International Crisis Group Asia Briefing No. 214, 30 November 2011. It warns that the resumption of fighting in Kachin areas is the "most serious threat to peace in Myanmar".
23. The Kachin rebels had led strong opposition to the Myitsone dam project halted in September. The suspension of work on the dam was a contributing factor to restart talks with the Kachin armed groups before fighting broke out again in December 2011.
24. Moe Thuzar, "ASEAN and Myanmar".
25. The *Myanmar Times* actually termed this the most surprising development of all in a year of surprises. Apparently, the military and elected MPs now engage in discussions on "issues of shared interest" in Hluttaw corridors. See Sandar Lwin, "In the Hluttaws, More Green Shoots", *Myanmar Times*, 2–8 January 2012 <http://www.mmtimes.com/2012/news/608/news60802.html>.
26. The four committees are the Bill Committee; Public Account Committee; Hluttaw Rights Committee; and Government's Guarantees, Pledges and Undertakings Vetting Committee. See Shwe Yin Mar Oo and Soe Than Lynn, "MPs encouraged by committees", *Myanmar Times* <http://www.mmtimes.com/2011/news/566/news55605.html>.
27. "Media Law Bill", Voice of America Myanmar language broadcast on 30 December 2011 <http://www.youtube.com/watch/?v=6mwXk_i6jus>.
28. On 8 December 2011, Aung San Suu Kyi met with the Chinese Ambassador to Myanmar in Yangon. The Chinese Foreign Ministry stated that the meeting took place in response to her (Aung San Suu Kyi's) request. There are different interpretations of Myanmar's position regarding relations with the United States and China. It is more of a balancing act rather than "crawling out of China's umbrella". See Daniel Ten Kate, "Myanmar Seeks 'Win-Win-Win' in Balancing US-China Competition" <http://www.bloomberg.com/news/2011-12-04/myanmar-seeks-win-win-win-in-balancing-u-s-china-competition.html> and Brigadier S.K. Chatterji (retd), "Myanmar, the US, China: Shifting Sands", rediff.com, 2 January 2012.
29. Thailand follows China with US$9.5 billion, followed by Hong Kong (US$6.3 billion), South Korea (US$2.9 billion), Britain (US$2.65 billion), and Singapore (US$1.8). "Foreign Investment in Myanmar".
30. Moe Thuzar, "Myanmar: Facing the Future", in *Regional Outlook: Southeast Asia 2012–2013*, edited by Michael J. Montesano and Lee Poh Onn (Institute of Southeast Asian Studies, Singapore, 2012).
31. Ibid.

MYANMAR'S GENERAL ELECTION 2015
Change Was the Name of the Game

Tin Maung Maung Than

"Time for Change"; "For Real Change Let's Vote for NLD"[1]

On 8 November 2015, in Myanmar's sixth multiparty general election (hereafter GE2015) since independence in 1948,[2] voters' desire for "change" swept away the conservative forces associated with more than five decades of military dominance in the politics of Myanmar. That simple catchy C-word, reminiscent of Barak Obama's U.S. presidential campaign battle cry in 2008,[3] proved more effective than the "goodies" delivered during the five years of USDP (Union Solidarity and Development Party) rule under President U Thein Sein,[4] as well as the last-minute deluge of amenities, goods and services brought in by powerful USDP candidates to their designated constituencies to garner votes from the weary public. The National League for Democracy (NLD), led by Daw Aung San Suu Kyi, the charismatic daughter of Myanmar's martyred independence hero, "Bogyoke" (general) Aung San, clinched supermajorities in both houses of parliament, stunning pundits, competitors, detractors, supporters and the NLD itself, not only in Myanmar but also in the international community.[5] Thus, GE2015 appeared to herald the dawn of a new era in Myanmar politics, whose troubled experiment in parliamentary democracy was truncated by the military coup of 2 March 1962. However, both powerful agencies and rigid structures stand in the way of "real change" as envisaged by the NLD leadership and aspired to by those who voted in the popular party led by their beloved hero's daughter.

Reprinted from Malcolm Cook and Daljit Singh, eds., *Southeast Asian Affairs 2016* (Singapore: ISEAS – Yusof Ishak Institute, 2016), pp. 241–64. At the time of original publication, Tin Maung Maung Than was Visiting Senior Fellow at the ISEAS – Yusof Ishak Institute, Singapore.

The Bumpy Road to GE2015

One could say that the re-entry of the NLD, especially its chairperson Aung San Suu Kyi, into the mainstream political playground through the by-elections in April 2012 set the stage for the race to win GE2015. People took notice of the NLD's comeback when it won forty-three of the forty-fives seats it then contested. It allowed the party and its leader to play a high-profile role in and out of the parliamentary system and capture the imagination of a public apathetic to electoral politics since the huge setback when the junta ignored the results of the 1990 general election.

Meanwhile, the government of President U Thein Sein, formed in March 2011, carried out significant political and economic reforms as well as administrative restructuring and attempted to achieve performance legitimacy and overcome its image as a quasi-civilian government comprising many retired military officers and serving generals.[6] The failure of the electorate to recognize the reforms contributed to the outcome of GE2015.

The Union Election Committee: Best Is Not Good Enough?

The Union Election Commission (UEC) established by the military junta in March 2010 to oversee the 2010 general election and supervise the political parties was reconstituted in February 2011 with U Tin Aye (a former three-star general belonging to the same cohort in the Defence Services Academy as President-elect U Thein Sein) as chair. It established (provincial) election commissions in all fourteen states and regions, which in turn formed respective district and township branches. The UEC then started preparations for GE2015 after successfully conducting the by-election in April 2012. Towards the end of 2014 there was much speculation about the election date for GE2015, with the UEC indicating that it would be held towards the end of 2015. Registration of new political parties with the UEC gathered pace in the months preceding the deadline of 30 April 2015. Meanwhile, the UEC announced that it would accept foreign observers to monitor GE2015, and issued relevant regulations on 26 June.

The electoral process gained further impetus when the UEC announced on 8 July that the election date would be 8 November. Thereafter, the UEC went into high gear to roll out its programme for the successful conduct of "free and fair" elections come November. As such, a series of dates and deadlines were announced together with a slew of instructions and rules covering all aspects of the electoral process.[7] Some of the significant dates and deadlines were as follows:

- Candidate lists accepted from 20 July to 8 August; later extended to 14 August due to severe flooding in upper and central Myanmar.
- Withdrawal deadline for candidates set at 11 August; later extended to 17 August.
- Scrutiny of candidate lists from 12 to 21 August; later extended to 31 August.
- Voter list announcement beginning 7 September; subject to revision on feedback from voters.
- Campaign period from 8 September till 6 November.
- 7 November designated as "cooling" period in which no campaign-related material would be allowed to remain in public view.
- Polls on 8 November: 6 a.m. to 4 p.m. local time.

The UEC expected to spend four billion kyat (about US$4 million) for the elections, including allowances for schoolteachers assigned to man the more than 47,000 polling stations throughout the country.[8]

In August, the UEC also established strict campaigning rules, which, inter alia, included the following restrictions:[9]

- Permission to publicly display campaign material had to be obtained from the relevant township municipal authorities.
- Permission to hold campaign rallies had to be sought from the relevant election commission, with applications needing to provide the details of the venue, date, time and expected number of attendees.
- Party members needed to seek approval from or register with the local election commission branch before speaking in public or to the media.
- Anyone wishing to campaign on behalf of the official candidate needed to register with and get permission from the local election commission branch.
- Parties that wanted to broadcast on television or radio would be permitted fifteen minutes each, subject to the approval of the content by the Ministry of Information.

The vetting of candidates by the UEC resulted in a number of disqualifications, mainly due to a breach of the citizenship criteria. Initially, 124 candidates were disqualified, of which more than a third were reportedly Muslims, mainly from Rakhine State. However, 11 Muslim candidates were reinstated on appeal.[10] By 2 November the UEC-approved list contained 6,039 candidates[11] vying for 1,149 seats[12] in the three parliamentary categories (upper house, or Amyotha Hluttaw; lower house, or Pyithu Hluttaw; and provincial legislature, Region/State Hluttaw). Meanwhile, the number of parties registered to contest the elections had swelled to 91, with 60 of them claiming to represent non-Bamar ethnic groups or religious minority communities.[13]

Compiling and correcting electoral rolls turned out to be a Herculean task for the UEC, and a nightmarish exercise for potential voters. Computerized for the first time in Myanmar, the voter lists were plagued by a huge number of errors and omissions, given the enormity of the data pertaining to some 33 million people, most of whom had only given names. This was attributed to software shortcomings, staff inexperience and the apathy of the potential voters who balked at giving feedback to rectify mistakes. The process went through two cycles of revisions and concluded with much reservation on the part of the public. This was probably the single-most confidence-sapping episode in the UEC's bumpy ride to GE2015.[14]

In October there appeared an apparent twist in the plot when the UEC mooted the idea of postponing GE2015 due to severe flooding that could hamper the electoral process. Ten parties, including three ethnic parties, were reportedly invited by the UEC on 13 October to discuss the option of postponing but then decided, on the same day, to stick to the original schedule. This incident caused some confusion and elicited adverse comments that reinforced the mistrust and suspicion generated since early September by the furore over error-prone voting lists.[15] Meanwhile, some 40,000 unarmed "special police" formed from civilian volunteers were assigned duties as additional security personnel on polling day. They underwent a short training stint (20 to 31 October) at their respective regional centres to be deployed at polling stations.[16]

Although it had been announced over a year in advance that voting would require stamping (with a pre-inked stamp) instead of ticking the box on the ballot paper, and repeated assurances by UEC officials that a vote would still be valid even if the stamp did not fall squarely on the desired box, apprehension and suspicion remained throughout the months leading up to election day. It reflected, in one way, the public distrust of the electoral process managed by the UEC as an independent and non-partisan body.[17] The issuing of voter identity slips, which must be presented at the polling station in order to vote, on 1 November (first announced in mid-September) was also seen as confusing for voters.[18]

However, the UEC's decision to allow local and international observers (non-governmental observers were allowed for the very first time) on a large scale as election watchers was seen as a right step towards greater transparency and indicative of its attempt to conduct a free and fair election. The UEC stated that 1,118 foreigners, 9,406 locals and 291 media personnel from 45 agencies were issued identity cards as official election observers. International observers included 470 people from 32 diplomatic missions, 465 people from 6 international election monitoring INGOs (international non-governmental organizations) and 183 people from 9 international organizations assisting Myanmar's democratic transition and electoral process. Local observers were from 13 domestic election-monitoring organizations.[19] The international organizations that sent observers included the U.S.-based Carter Center (which has had long-term observers in Myanmar since December 2014), the EU Election Observation Mission (European Union) with some 150 personnel and the Asian Network for Free Elections (ANFREL, a Bangkok-based INGO consortium) which sent 47 long- and short-term observers. The domestic contingent included PACE (People's Alliance for Credible Elections), which fielded some 2,000 volunteers as observers.[20]

Disenfranchisements

There were three kinds of disenfranchisement in GE2015. Those deemed ineligible due to their residency status, eligible voters living in officially cancelled constituencies, and potential voters excluded from the voting list.

In the first category were the so-called "white card" holders who were allowed to vote during the constitutional referendum of 2008 and the 2010 general election but denied voting privileges after the government changed its mind in early 2015 under pressure from Buddhist extremists.[21] They were mainly Muslims of Bangladeshi origin and mostly living in Rakhine State. Identifying themselves as Rohingya, their claim as a distinct ethnic group has been rejected by the authorities, who do not accept the name *Rohingya*, but call them "Bengalis" instead. Their population could number anywhere between 600,000 to a million.[22] Most of the mainly Buddhist Bamars and other ethnic nationalities, as well as the political parties (both mainstream and ethnic-based), either remained silent or applauded this disenfranchisement, while the foreign media, human rights organizations and Western politicians deplored the action, but to no avail.[23]

The second group comprised voters who could not vote due to the cancellation of five entire constituencies, as well as those who could not vote in their respective constituencies because they were residing in insecure village tracts where there was fighting between Ethnic Armed Organizations and the Myanmar armed forces. Altogether nearly 600 village tracts in Kachin, Kayin, Mon and Shan states, as well as Bago Region, were affected, compared to 498 in the 2010 general election. There was no official announcement on the number of voters who lost their opportunity to vote, but it could be up to several hundred thousand.[24]

The last group comprised potential voters who were abroad and failed to register with the respective Myanmar diplomatic missions, despite attempts by the UEC to extend its reach through advanced overseas voting scheduled from 13 to 23 October. The most conspicuous omission was the huge migrant population in Thailand, that could encompass some two million documented and undocumented workers, of which fewer than 20,000 were reported to have registered by early September.[25] There could also be hundreds of thousands of overseas Myanmars staying in Southeast Asia, Australia, Europe and the Americas who missed the opportunity to register due to ignorance, logistical difficulties, documentation issues and inadequacy of registration arrangements.[26] The top UEC official was reported to have indicated that it was a "struggle" for the UEC as well as the Ministry of Foreign Affairs "to manage the process". There were reportedly nearly 35,000 overseas applications, of which some 30,000 were successful. The official, citing lack of experience, said "sorry" to all migrants who did not get to vote.[27]

Influential Players: Fumbling, Dodging, Scrambling and Prevailing

Apart from the political parties, there were several other influential players involved in the electoral process, viz., the government, the military, Buddhist nationalists, media and civil society organizations (CSOs).

Political Parties

Myanmar's political parties contesting for GE2015 lacked clear ideologies, and tended to depend on personalities rather than concrete policies; especially the scores of small national parties and the five dozen ethnically designated parties.[28] The ethnic parties, however, aspired to play a swing role in national politics and a major role in state (provincial) politics, provided either of the two major national parties (USDP and NLD) failed to secure a super majority in the two houses of parliament.[29] The two major contenders for power, the NLD and the incumbent USDP, both had their share of contentious or controversial episodes in their quest for victory in the polls.

The NLD had, all along, been betting on its chairperson Daw Aung San Suu Kyi's charisma and popularity to deliver victory at the polls. She was a one-woman election machine, relentlessly leading the charge, exploiting the polity's frustrations over the incumbent regime's apparent failure to deliver reform dividends to the grass roots and falling short on its ambitious objectives of rooting out corruption and drastically reducing poverty. Emphasizing that there was no "real" change despite the multitude of reform measures instituted by the government, she travelled extensively in Myanmar in what could be described as quasi-campaigning well before the official campaign period began. She made it a point to tour flooded areas as well as Kachin, Rakhine and Shan states, where public support for the NLD was presumably weak under the twin shadows of ethnic nationalism and strong local identity. Nonetheless, the NLD refused to yield to ethnic parties and contested the ethnic constituencies.[30] It also did not field Muslim candidates in the elections; its sole

Muslim nominee was not accepted by the UEC.³¹ That, together with the decision not to endorse some veteran party stalwarts, popular activist leaders and prominent personalities — like U Ko Ko Gyi of the 88 Generation Peace and Open Society and outspoken independent MP Daw Nyo Nyo Thin — as NLD candidates disappointed many NLD supporters. These omissions in the candidate list announced on 3 August drew criticism from many quarters. It also resulted in some demonstrations and resignations among supporters of the NLD grass roots.³² Thereafter, the party leader emphasized the need to vote for the party, instead of considering the merits of individual candidates (1,151 in all).³³ While campaigning, the NLD leaders voiced the party's concerns over and dissatisfaction with the UEC's handling of its complaints, its rulings on candidate eligibility, and its inability to rectify errors in the voter list, but stopped short of questioning the UEC's integrity.³⁴

As the NLD campaign gained momentum, its chairperson's rallies drew large crowds in a sea of red (NLD's colour). Her promise to bring "change" caught on, and the question in the minds of its leader and supporters became not whether the NLD would win but by how big a margin.³⁵ During the home stretch, on 5 November Daw Aung San Suu Kyi held a press conference at her residence and dropped a bombshell in answering a question on leading a possible NLD government by pronouncing, "I said I am going to be above the president", causing consternation and confusion all around.³⁶ This provocative remark overshadowed her conciliatory reply to a question on forming a government: "We do want to go for a government of national reconciliation.... even if we win 100 percent, we would like to make a government of national reconciliation in order to set a good precedent for our country." She then added, "It shouldn't be a zero-sum game where winner takes all and loser loses everything. This is not what democracy should be."³⁷

While the NLD was rooting for change, the USDP, identified with the incumbent administration, was emphasizing development, stability and continuity,³⁸ drawing strength from its immense financial and organizational resources and capitalizing on its chairman President U Thein Sein's popular wholesome image. Its candidate selection process, overseen by acting chairman Thuya U Shwe Mann (Speaker of the lower house and chairman of the combined houses of parliament), became controversial when out of around 150 senior officers proposed by the military, only 57 were accepted as candidates, and 2 ministers known as President U Thein Sein's close aides were denied "safe" constituencies. On the other hand, some 57 per cent of the incumbent USDP MPs from the two houses of parliament were among the 1,147 selected as candidates. The strategy appeared to be banking on incumbents, government ministers and freshly retired senior military men to carry the ball.³⁹ However, the projected image of stability and continuity suffered a setback on 12 August when the conservative party leaders took a desperate measure to remove the party's wayward acting chair Thuya U Shwe Mann. In a late night operation at the party headquarters in Nay Pyi Taw, involving government security personnel, Thuya U Shwe Mann and his supporters (including the General Secretary U Maung Maung Thein) in the Central Executive Committee (CEC) were stripped of their CEC membership and a new CEC was installed (adding recently retired generals and government ministers who resigned to take up party positions) immediately. General Secretary U Htay Oo was appointed as co-chair, in lieu of chairman President Thein Sein, who was barred by the Constitution from engaging in party activities while in office. Apparently, Thuya U Shwe Mann was seen as increasingly forsaking party, government and military interests and moving too close to Daw Aung San Suu Kyi, the USDP's nemesis, in pursuing his personal ambition to be the next president.[40] Despite putting on a brave face, the party seemed unable to get its act together in the aftermath of its unprecedented shakeup, with its leadership scrambling to gain traction with less than three months left to face the ultimate test. However, in an upbeat mood on the last day of campaigning on 6 November, party leader U Htay Oo told the Radio Free Asia Myanmar language service that the USDP could win up to 80 per cent of the seats.[41]

Government

The government itself was not directly involved in the electoral process, but, as individuals, ministers (16), and deputy ministers (22) as well as region and state chief ministers (14) joined the USDP party slate to contest the elections.[42] The two vice-presidents also stood for election as USDP candidates.[43]

Ever since he took office in 2011, there had been much speculation on whether President Thein Sein would seek a second term and contest in GE2015. Rumours abounded of his reluctance to run again, but he had never publicly renounced the option, and would often say that he would consider continuing if called to serve, to the consternation of Thuya U Shwe Mann's camp in the USDP leadership who were working towards having their leader installed as the USDP presidential candidate in due course. Finally, a senior USDP official revealed that U Thein Sein would not run in GE2015.[44] However, since Myanmar's 2008 Constitution (Article 60-c) allows a non-MP to be nominated for the presidential election, he could still be in the running if the USDP managed to garner enough support among the elected MPs and military representatives (25 per cent of the total allocated). In fact, it was reported that USDP General Secretary U Tin Naing Thein told the BBC on 16 October that the party would nominate U Thein Sein as a presidential candidate if it could secure a majority in the elections.[45] Moreover, some detractors questioned whether President U Thein Sein's touring of flooded areas and his regional tours since August, extensively covered by the state media, amounted to canvassing for the USDP.[46] It did not help when President U Thein Sein, during his visit to Ngapudaw town in Ayeyarwady Region on 29 October, reportedly said, "What more change do you want? If you want more, go for communism. Nobody wants communism, do they?", presumably as a counterpoint to the NLD's appeal to vote it in for change. This drew a rebuke from Daw Aung San Suu Kyi, who capitalized on it as indicating a preference for stasis.[47]

Military

By constitutional mandate, the military known as the Tatmadaw (royal force) is entitled to 25 per cent of the seats in all the parliaments: the Pyithu Hluttaw (people's assembly or lower house) and Amyotha Hluttaw (national assembly or upper house) at the national level as well as all the fourteen Hluttaws (assemblies) at the Region or State level. The military representatives in the parliament are nominees of the Tatmadaw Commander-in-Chief (C-in-C), who has the authority to replace individual military representatives at any time. This military cohort in the parliament is meant to serve as a check against elected representatives from political parties as a deciding factor in changing important articles in the Constitution, which requires a majority of 75 per cent plus one vote to be successful before it can be endorsed by a national referendum requiring affirmation by more than 50 per cent of the eligible voting population. In fact, the Tatmadaw faction in the parliament played a significant role in defeating the motions to change articles in the Constitution pertaining to the relaxation of requirements for presidential candidates (that would bar Daw Aung San Suu Kyi from the presidency) and to reduce the voting threshold for changing important articles in the Constitution.[48] The military's autonomy in its own internal affairs is also assured by the Constitution.

Moreover, the military faction in the Pyidaungsu Hluttaw (Union Assembly; a combined sitting of both house of parliament) is entitled to nominate a presidential candidate, who is assured of the vice-presidency even if that person had lost in the vote by the Presidential Electoral College (a troika assembly comprising the two houses of parliament and the Tatmadaw faction from those two houses) to one of the two other candidates (one nominee each from the two houses of parliament), as the runner-up and the second runner-up would automatically become vice-presidents. The C-in-C also nominates serving officers (usually lt. generals) as ministers for the important portfolios of defence, home affairs and border affairs. As such, the military personnel under the C-in-C's authority outnumber the elected representatives in the powerful National Defence and Security Council (NDSC, which has eleven members).[49] Since the Constitution stipulates that cabinet ministers and deputy ministers appointed by the President need not be elected MPs, the number of retired military personnel in the executive branch could be quite substantial. Furthermore, the six-decade old practice of accepting retired military officers into the civil service ensures that the military continues as a significant force to be reckoned with in the governance of Myanmar.

Notwithstanding the aforementioned structural and situational conditions that allow the Tatmadaw to be a major player in Myanmar's politics and government, the military also plays a significant part in the electoral process through a quasi-symbiotic relationship with the USDP, whose founders had strong military roots. The soldiers' extended families, numbering millions, could be captive voters for military-backed candidates.[50] Moreover, in GE2015 around 140 senior officers resigned to apply for USDP nomination as candidates, and among those accepted were the Tri-service chief of staff (a full general and number three in the Tatmadaw command hierarchy), the Defence Minister, several theatre commanding generals, defence agency heads, regional commanders and senior command and staff officers (colonels and brigadier generals).[51] Finally, one cannot rule out the current C-in-C (Senior General Min Aung Hlaing) being nominated as a presidential candidate by the Tatmadaw faction in the parliament.[52]

Buddhist Nationalists

Following anti-Muslim riots in Rakhine (2012) and later in central and southern Myanmar in 2013, a constellation of Buddhist nationalists, including monks and lay followers, became active lobbyists for "protection of race and religion" in Myanmar. The movement culminated in the formal establishment, in January 2014 at Mandalay, of the "Association for Protection of Race, Religion and [Buddha's] Dispensation", commonly known by its Myanmar language acronym, "Ma Ba Tha", with an apparent agenda to rally Buddhists against all perceived threats to the perpetuation of Myanmar nationality and Buddhism. It has grown into a powerful organization with extensive reach throughout the country through local chapters and branches under a central body, all headed by monks. Its leaders include not only learned, conservative and respectable senior monks but also firebrands like U Wirathu who was featured on the cover of *Time Magazine* in June 2013 as "the face of Buddhist terror", and is well known for his highly controversial anti-Muslim rhetoric. Its critics see Ma Ba Tha as an extremist organization mainly directed against the Muslim minority, while its sympathizers regard it as a necessary defender of the Buddhist faith.

Ma Ba Tha rose to prominence in the election year when it successfully lobbied for the passing of four laws popularly known as "race and religion laws" in July and August. Its members and supporters took umbrage when NLD MPs voted against the laws, seen as discriminatory and repressive by human rights lobbies. Some of Ma Ba Tha's leading monks and luminaries then became involved in espousing rhetoric that could be construed as anti-NLD and pro-government and USDP.[53] During the campaign period there were allegations of anti-NLD rhetoric and actions by either Ma Ba Tha members or their associates as well as of their lending support to the USDP campaign. Nevertheless, the top Ma Ba Tha leadership denied that the organization was supporting any political party or instructing people to vote or not to vote for anyone or any party. However, it is quite obvious what they were alluding to when they made accusatory statements that NLD senior official U Tin Oo's earlier comments were "aimed at destroying the protection of race and religion" and adding that "we don't want people to vote for the person who destroys our race and religion".[54] Moreover, it was reported that on the sidelines of a Ma Ba Tha rally in Yangon on 4 October, U Wirathu remarked that, "The current government is the best choice for the elections."[55]

Media

GE2015 attracted much attention at home and abroad in both the print and electronic media, as well as in the popular social media that has expanded tremendously within Myanmar in recent years with the advent of cheap SIM cards and affordable smart phones, allowing voter education and campaigning through Facebook and message applications.[56] The private print media, consisting of weekly journals and daily newspapers, were awash with election-related stories, op-eds and news accompanied by cartoons and photo-spreads, with rumours and innuendos abounding. The majority of the information in the private print media was critical of the government and the ruling party and supportive of the so-called opposition exemplified by Daw Aung San Suu Kyi and the NLD. The local media's bias was tantamount to campaigning for the "opposition", stretching the limits of "press freedom". Though the impact of this unprecedented media coverage on actual voting is difficult to ascertain, it certainly added colour, vibrancy and flair to the election landscape, especially for the urban polity.⁵⁷

On the other hand, state-owned media concentrated on factual reporting, voter education and official statements on the electoral process. During the campaign period, both print and broadcast media gave extensive coverage to the tours and interviews of the President and C-in-C, while highlighting the developmental accomplishments of the government. This looked like attempts to raise the profile and enhance the performance legitimacy of the incumbent regime.

Civil Society

Civil society played a greater role in GE2015 than in the previous two elections (1990 and 2010) under military rule. Taking advantage of the greater freedom enjoyed under President Thein Sein's government, CSOs were engaged in many areas related to the electoral process months and even years ahead of polling day. They were very active in areas such as voter education, checking electoral rolls and election monitoring. They also collaborated with the authorities and international organizations in performing those tasks.⁵⁸ On the other hand, the popular former student activists who belong to the quasi-political CSO named 88 Generation Peace and Open Society did not form a party to contest in GE2015. Instead they campaigned for "change" in an alliance with the NLD, as well as undertaking voter education drives.

The Polls

There were neither major disturbances nor serious untoward incidents on 8 November, the polling day, throughout the country. Despite long queues, voters were orderly and well behaved in a "positive and calm environment" as observed by the ASEAN delegation comprising electoral management bodies from Indonesia, Laos, Malaysia, Thailand and Timor-Leste.⁵⁹ Other international observers agreed that it was a smooth and peaceful election.⁶⁰

It was reported that the actual turnout was 69 per cent, lower than that recorded in 2010 (77 per cent) and 1990 (73 per cent). Around 6 per cent of the votes were disqualified, amounting to 1.5 million for the lower house and some 1.2 million for the upper house. The advanced votes accounted for about 5 to 6 per cent, which was half of that for the 2010 election.⁶¹

Even before the day was out the NLD supporters sensed victory and gathered outside the NLD headquarters in Yangon, blocking the roads leading to it and spilling over into side streets in the vicinity, cheering as the results rolled slowly in on the large LCD screen set up in front of the NLD office. They eventually dispersed late in the night at the request of the NLD leadership.⁶² The next day, U Htay Oo, the USDP co-chair (who also lost his seat), conceded defeat in an interview with Reuters by simply saying "We lost";⁶³ perhaps the biggest understatement of the year in Myanmar politics. However, there were no victory parades or organized celebrations, as Daw Aung San Suu Kyi refused to endorse such actions.⁶⁴ The President and C-in-C congratulated the NLD leader and acknowledged the letter she sent to them on 10 November requesting to meet in order to discuss power transfer and "national reconciliation". They initially indicated that the meeting should wait until after the settlement of election disputes, but later agreed to meet separately on 2 December. Thuya U Shwe Mann (who lost his seat) also received the request, and he promptly accepted the meeting proposal.[65]

There was some grumbling and allegations of irregularities in advanced voting, but actual formal complaints contesting the result numbered only thirty-three on the day before the closing date set by the UEC. There were also a number of police cases for criminal breach of election law.[66]

Results and Implications

The NLD virtually swept the polls, despite fielding many rookie candidates, given that it had only forty-three incumbent legislators in the two houses of parliament, of whom 73 per cent were re-nominated.[67]

It took about two weeks for the UEC to complete the announcement of the outcome in all constituencies, mainly due to logistical difficulties. The extent of the NLD's overwhelming dominance in the new legislature can be seen in Table 1, which shows the collated results for the two major contenders. While the number of elected MPs falls short of full strength due to cancellations of seats (see above), the military nominees are of full strength.

From Table 1 it is evident that the NLD now has a supermajority (more than two-thirds) of elected representatives, but only a simple majority if the military MPs, who could vote as a block, are included. In practice, even if the NLD is able to convince all other MPs to support its motions, it cannot achieve the threshold of 75 per cent plus one (in the combined sitting of the two houses) to change significant articles in the Constitution, even without taking into account another bar in the form of a national referendum where more than 50 per cent of all eligible voters (not just those who vote) must agree to

TABLE 1
NLD and USDP Election Results

Political Party	Amyotha Hluttaw (upper house) 168 balloted 56 military nominees	Pyithu Hluttaw (lower house) 323 balloted 110 military nominees	Taing/Pyinai Hluttaw (region/state assembly) 629 balloted 220 military nominees
National League for Democracy (NLD)	135 (80.4% of balloted seats, 60.3% of total seats)	255 (78.9% of balloted seats, 58.9% of total filled seats)	476 (75.7% of balloted seats, 56.1% of total filled seats)
Union Solidarity and Development Party (USDP)	11 (6.5% of balloted seats, 4.9% of total seats)	30 (9.3% of balloted seats, 6.9% of total filled seats)	73 (11.6% of balloted seats, 8.6% of total filled seats)

Source: *Burma Bulletin*, November 2015, p. 2.

endorse the proposed changes agreed to by the parliament. Thus, the winning margin is not sufficient to change the Constitution.

All the eighteen other political parties scored poorly in the two national-level parliaments and the respective provincial (seven ethnic states; seven Bamar-majority regions) parliaments. The results are shown in Table 2.

As Table 2 shows, only the Arakan National Party (ANP) and Shan Nationalities League for Democracy (SNLD), among the eighteen successful ethnic-based parties, secured a noticeable number of seats. The ANP, led by the outspoken leader Dr Aye Maung, an incumbent MP, drew its strength from the highly nationalistic Rakhine (Arakan) nationals who subscribed to the party's strong anti-migrant policy directed against the so-called Bengali (stateless) residents and their self-identifying Rohingya identity. Ironically, the veteran politician lost his bid for re-election. Similarly, the SNLD (tiger head symbol) that also won big in the 1990 election, led by the charismatic Khun Htun Oo, also seemed to have taken

TABLE 2
Results for Parties Other Than NLD and USDP

Political Party	Amyotha Hluttaw (upper house)	Pyithu Hluttaw (lower house)	Taing/Pyinai Hluttaw (region/state assembly)
1. All Mon Regions Democracy Party	0	0	1
2. Arakan National Party*	10	12	22
3. **Democratic Party (Myanmar)**	0	0	1
4. *Independents*	2	1	1
5. Kachin State Democracy Party	0	1	3
6. Kayin People's Party	0	0	1
7. Kokang Democracy and Unity Party	0	1	1
8. La Hu National Development Party	0	0	1
9. Lisu National Development Party	0	2	2
10. Mon National Party	1	0	2
11. National Unity Party	1	0	0
12. PaO National Organization	1	3	6
13. Shan Nationalities League for Democracy*	3	12	25
14. Ta'ang (Palaung) National Party	2	3	7
15. Tai-Leng Nationalities Development Party	0	0	1
16. Unity and Democracy Party of Kachin State	0	0	1
17. Wa Democratic Party	0	1	2
18. Wa National Unity Party	0	0	1
19. Zomi Congress for Democracy	2	2	2

Note: * denotes ethnic-based parties which fared relatively well. The non-ethnic based party is in bold.
Source: *Burma Bulletin*, November 2015, p. 3.

advantage of resurgent Shan nationalism and the tarnished image of its main rival, the 2010 election winner, Shan Nationalities Democratic Party (white tiger symbol), which was perceived as collaborating with the government.

Ethnic-based parties generally suffered substantial setbacks, even in their own ethnic constituencies for provincial seats. Of the seven ethnic states, only in Rakhine and Shan did the ANP and SNLD respectively secure a larger share of seats than the NLD. Nevertheless, once the military seats are included, their respective shares dipped to 48.9 per cent and 17.6 per cent. In the remaining five states (Chin, Kachin, Kayah, Kayin and Mon), the NLD's share (inclusive of military seats) ranged from 49.1 per cent in Kachin to 61.3 per cent in Mon State. Among the six Self-Administered Areas (one level below the state or region in the administrative hierarchy), no ethnic-based party won in three of them (Danu, Kokang and Naga), while the local parties won the rest (Pa O, Ta'ang [or Palaung] and Wa). Moreover, in the thirteen states and regions where twenty-nine (separately polled) "ethnic affairs" seats were contested, representing ethnic minority populations in the territories concerned, ethnic-based parties won seats in only three (Sagaing Region, Shan State and Yangon Region).[68]

Contrary to a common belief that the ethnic-based parties suffered because of disunity leading to vote splitting, the likely explanation for their poor showing could be a conjunction of two factors: tactical voting to "block a disfavoured party" (read USDP) and turning to the NLD with its message of change; and insecurity in ethnic areas that favoured the powerful incumbent or the NLD, the largest "national" party offering hope.[69]

The non-ethnic based or "national" parties were even bigger losers than the ethnic-based parties. The only national party that gained representation in the (provincial) parliament is the Democratic Party (Myanmar), chaired by veteran politician U Thu Wai who was closely associated with the late former premier U Nu of the parliamentary democracy era.

Among the dozens of national parties which did not win any seats are four large parties that fielded hundreds of candidates, but to no avail. The National Unity Party is the reincarnation of the defunct Burma Socialist Programme Party that imploded in 1988. It had 61 seats in the current legislature and fielded 763 candidates. The National Development Party founded by former presidential political advisor U Nay Zin Latt, which put up 354 candidates, was registered in July 2015. Some regarded it as a proxy party for the USDP or U Thein Sein.[70] The third largest was the National Democratic Force formed in July 2010 by NLD veterans who broke away to contest the 2010 election when the NLD refused to participate. It had 274 candidates, with a current parliamentary representation of just 7. The Myanmar Farmers Development Party was also a newcomer, with 268 hopefuls. It was registered in November 2012 and claimed to have 2 million members. Yet they were all unable to overcome the tsunami that was the NLD.[71]

Then there were the independents. Out of the 310 independents running (as against 82 in 2010) only 4 (6 in 2010) succeeded. Some high profile people contested as independents; most were unsuccessful. U Aung Min, U Thein Sein's chief peace negotiator and President Office Minister (POM), lost, while U Soe Thane, another POM, ran successfully in a small constituency. Both of them were denied "safe" constituencies by Thuya U Shwe Mann and ran in Kayah State as upper house candidates. Another unsuccessful competitor was Daw Nyo Nyo Thin, who, apparently rejected by the NLD, ran for the lower house in Yangon. President U Thein Sein's personal aide, U Ko Ko Kyaw, ran against Thuya U Shwe Mann (USDP) for the lower house in the latter's hometown, Phyu, where the NLD won. U Phone Zaw Han, former mayor of Mandalay and ex-military officer, contested in Mandalay and lost too. Independents had virtually no chance against the NLD onslaught, which the USDP discovered the hard way.

The USDP lost most of their veterans and big guns in their battles against seemingly undistinguished NLD opponents. Beginning with the party leader, most of the CEC members, cabinet ministers and deputy ministers lost their bids under the USDP ticket. The few exceptions were the two vice-presidents, the speaker of the upper house, and three chief ministers. The senior military officers who joined the USDP slate in August did not fare much better. Only ex-General Hla Htay Win (Tri-service chief of staff), a retired naval C-in-C, and one theatre commander won from among the many general officers who opted for politics. The most notable casualties from the military were the two former defence ministers of the current regime and the military appointments general.[72]

The "Why?" in election results can never be satisfactorily answered. The aggregate of revealed preferences of individual voters on that day of reckoning are reflected in the overall results. Pundits and laymen alike, not to mention the winners and losers, have tried to explain the results from their own perspectives. Nevertheless, to hazard a guess, the major reasons for the USDP's humiliating loss could be attributed to the following: the incumbent's disadvantage of people forgetting the good things they had done but remembering bad experiences, like the forced eviction of squatters, the violent suppression of demonstrators, the pardon of Chinese illegal loggers from life sentences and the rude behaviour of some high officials; perceived unfulfilled promises in terms of resolving land-grab complaints, reducing poverty, eradicating corruption and ensuring clean government; unresolved labour disputes; fears of rising inflation; complacency; losing touch with the polity; and the fiasco of the palace coup against Thuya Shwe Mann. All these had translated into a desire for change that resonated with the NLD's simple promise of bringing change. It was hope and dissatisfaction, pulling and pushing; the strongest pull came from Daw Aung San Suu Kyi, whose stamina and determination to tour the countryside seemed to have generated a big payoff.

To NLD supporters, the long wait for popular representation seemed to be over with the NLD's overwhelming victory in GE2015. As such, enormous expectations await the NLD's rule, and at this stage the future of Myanmar seems to rest squarely on the shoulders of "the lady"; not so encouraging for those who believe in strong institutions, collective leadership and shared responsibilities. On the other hand, one may find out that democratic authoritarianism is not an oxymoron and not incompatible with freedom and liberty. The NLD's "tactics" of promising "change" prevailed over the seemingly ossified USDP's elusive performance legitimacy, but it remains to be seen whether the NLD can come up with a strategy to govern Myanmar effectively and bring peace, justice and prosperity to its people. Meanwhile, the transition period lasting through January 2016, when the new parliament convenes, to the election of the new president and the formation of the government before the end of March, is crucial for all stakeholders in Myanmar.

Will a "dream team" emerge? Perhaps not, but muddling through is probably the norm in this era of uncertain democracies and rising authoritarian tendencies. After all, hopes and dreams are the stuff that inspires those who perspire to achieve their goals.

Notes

1. The NLD's election slogan during its campaign.
2. There were elections every four years under the one-party socialist constitution, from 1974 to 1988, where only a "yes" or "no" vote for the ruling BSPP (Burma Socialist Programme Party) candidate was allowed. The NLD won by a landslide in the 1990 (fourth) general election conducted by the military junta that seized power in September 1988. However, the junta refused to transfer power to the winning party and decreed that a new constitution must be formulated first. The military-supervised constitution was endorsed by a referendum in May 2008, thereby paving the way for a multiparty general election. The NLD boycotted the 2010 (fifth) general election where the military-backed USDP swept the polls.
3. One of the many catchy slogans was "Change We Need" and another was "Change We Can Believe In". A list is available at <https://en.wikipedia.org/wiki/List_of_U.S._presidential_campaign_slogans>.
4. Despite the constitutional provisions requiring suspension of party activities by government members, the USDP chaired by President U Thein Sein has been seen as the ruling party.
5. See, for example, Nirmal Ghosh, "Aung San Suu Kyi" in "Looking Back: People Who Shaped the Year" under the headline "The Year of the Unlikelies", *Straits Times*, 21 December 2015, p. A14.
6. As stipulated in the Constitution, three important ministries, viz. Defence, Home Affairs and Border Affairs, are reserved for serving general officers nominated by the military Commander-in-Chief (C-in-C). Cabinet ministers need not be elected representatives, and their appointment is the prerogative of the President, except for the three aforementioned portfolios, though theoretically the President can reject the C-in-C's nominees; which is extremely unlikely.
7. For details, see the UEC website at <http://uecmyanmar.org/>.
8. "Kyat Four Thousand Million to be Used in the 2015 Election" (in Myanmar language), 21 July 2015 <https://www.facebook.com/TheNewEducationDigestJournal>; reproduced in *Thit Htoo Lwin* online news website at <http://www.thithtoolwin.com/>.
9. *Burma Bulletin*, August 2015, p. 2.
10. No USDP candidate was disqualified. See *Burma Bulletin*, September 2015, p. 2.
11. There were 1,733 for the lower house, 886 for the upper house and 3,420 for the Region/State legislature, competing for 323, 168 and 658 seats, respectively. See the UEC website at <http://uecmyanmar.org/>; and Richard Horsey, "The Myanmar Election Results", SSRC Report, 23 November 2015. For another source, which stated an overall figure of 1,150 with 659 available in the Region/State constituencies, see Guy Dinmore and Wade Guyitt, "Final Results Confirm Scale of NLD Election Victory", *Myanmar Times*, 23 November 2015 <http://www.mmtimes.com/index.php/national-news/17747-final-results-confirm-scale-of-nld-election-victory.html>.
12. The number of seats for polling was

reduced from the 1,171 in the initial UEC list due to cancellations for security reasons.

13. "Election Parties", *Myanmar Times*, 2 September 2015 <http://www.mmtimes.com/index.php/election-2015/parties.html>. Three of them were identified as Muslim-based parties. See Burma Bulletin, September 2015, p. 2.

14. See, for example, ibid., pp. 3–4; Catherine Trautwein, "The Election's Digital Challenge", *Myanmar Times*, 7 October 2015 <http://www.mmtimes.com/index.php/business/technology/16874-the-election-s-digital-challenge.html>; Win Ko Ko Lat et al., "Myanmar Election Body Cancels Vote in Two More Shan State Townships", RFA, 27 October 2015 <http://www.rfa.org/english/news/myanmar/election-10272015172919.html>; and "Naut Sone Mei Sayin Hset Let Hma Ywin" [Latest voters list still incorrect], BBC Burmese, 4 November 2015 <http://www.bbc.com/Burmese>.

15. The ethnic parties did not turn up, and only the NLD objected to the postponement. The USDP and two other parties agreed, while the remaining three were ambivalent. For details, see *Burma Bulletin*, October 2015, p. 2; and Ye Mon and Ei Ei Toe Lwin, "Vote to Go Ahead after Day of Confusion", *Myanmar Times*, 14 October 2015 <http://www.mmtimes.com/index.php/national-news/16971-vote-to-go-ahead-after-day-of-confusion.html>.

16. *Burma Bulletin*, October 2015, pp. 8–9.

17. See, for example, Ye Mon and Lun Min Mang, "Voters to Stamp Ballots Once Again", *Myanmar Times*, 24 October 2014 <http://www.mmtimes.com/index.php/national-news/12066-voters-to-stamp-ballots-once-again.html>; and Maung Zaw, "No Second-chance Ballots, Voters Warned", *Myanmar Times*, 26 October 2015.

18. *Burma Bulletin*, September 2015, pp. 4–5.

19. "Union Election Commission News Release" (in Myanmar language), Nay Pyi Taw, 2 November 2015.

20. *Burma Bulletin*, October 2015, p. 8; "Carter Center Election Observation Delegation Arrives in Yangon Wednesday", Carter Center, 2 November 2015 <http://www.cartercenter.org/news/pr/myanmar-110215.html>; "EU Election Observation Mission Deploys 62 Short-term Observers — Over 150 EU Observers in Total to Observe on Election Day", EOM Press Release, 5 November 2015; "ANFREL Deploys Short-Term Observers in Myanmar Hoping to See a Transparent and Fair Final Week before Polling", ANFREL, 3 November 2015 <http://anfrel.org/anfrel-deploys-short-term-observers-in-myanmar-hoping-to-see-a-transparent-and-fair-final-week-before-polling/>; and "2000 PACE Observers Watch Election Process around the Country", PACE Press Summary, 8 November 2015.

21. Paul Vrieze, "Revoking White Card Holder Voting Rights 'Counter Reconciliation': US Official", *The Irrawaddy*, 13 February 2015 <http://www.irrawaddy.org/burma/revoking-white-card-holder-voting-rights-counter-reconciliation-us-official.html>.

22. See, for example, Lun Min Mang, "Former White-Card Holders Cut from Rakhine V Lists", *Myanmar Times*, 24 June 2015 <http://www.mmtimes.com/index.php/national-news/15191-former-white-card-holders-cut-from-rakhine-voter-lists.html>; and Kayleigh Long, "When Myanmar Votes, Rohingya Must Stay Home", IRIN News, 1 September 2015 <http://www.irinnews.org/report/101936/when-myanmar-votes-rohingya-must-stay-home>.

23. Thomas Fuller, "Myanmar Striking Rohingya from Voter Rolls, Activists Say", *New York Times*, 23 August 2015.

24. Lun Min Mang and Ei Ei Toe Lwin, "Vote Cancellations in Conflict Areas Higher Than in 2010", *Myanmar Times*, 14 October 2015 <http://www.mmtimes.

com/index.php/national-news/16991-vote-cancellations-in-conflict-areas-higher-than-in-2010.html>; and *Burma Bulletin*, October 2015, p. 3.
25. See *Burma Bulletin*, September 2015, p. 4.
26. *Burma Bulletin*, October 2015, p. 7; and Amy Sawitta Lefevre and Antoni Slodkowski, "Around 4 Million Voters Shut Out of Historic Myanmar Election", Reuters, 20 October 2015 <http://www.reuters.com/article/us-myanmar-election-voters-insight-idUSKCN0SE2GN20151020>.
27. In the 2010 general election there were only 6,567 overseas votes. See Khin Su Wai, Wa Lone, and Swan Ye Htut, "Rush Begins as Myanmar Expats Return Home to Vote", *Myanmar Times*, 3 November 2015 <http://www.mmtimes.com/index.php/national-news/17345-rush-begins-as-myanmar-expats-return-home-to-vote.html>.
28. For a survey-based finding on Myanmar political parties, see Suzanne Kempel, Chan Myawe Aung San, and Aung Tun, "Myanmar Political Parties at a Time of Transition: Political Party Dynamics at the National and Local Level", Pyoe Pin Programme Report, April 2015 <https://www.umb.edu/editor_uploads/images/mobilize/mgs/mgs_conflictres/Political_Parties_at_a_Time_of_Transition_Report_FINAL_April_2015_Aung.Tun.pdf>.
29. Ibid., p. 17; and Aubrey Belford, "In Myanmar, Ethnic Loyalties Could Crimp Suu Kyi's Party", Reuters, 7 July 2015 <http://www.reuters.com/article/us-myanmar-politics-parties-idUSKCN0PH2DQ20150707>.
30. Htet Khaung Linn, "Interview: 'We Need Genuine Competition and Respect the Public's Choice'", Myanmar Now, 4 September 2015 <http://www.myanmar-now.org/news/i/?id=5f9d3706-ba79-4ddb-8423-9e9e4a5ea24a>.
31. *Burma Bulletin*, September 2015, p. 2.
32. *Burma Bulletin*, August 2015, pp. 4–6.
33. Kyaw Zaw Win et al., "Aung San Suu Kyi Urges Support for NLD amid Myanmar Candidate Row", RFA, 10 August 2015 <http://www.rfa.org/english/news/myanmar/support-08102015151253.html>; and Kyaw Phone Kyaw, "Behind the Numbers and Names, an Election Picture Emerges", *Myanmar Times*, 2 September 2015 <http://www.mmtimes.com/index.php/national-news/16277-behind-the-numbers-and-names-an-election-picture-emerges.html>.
34. Lun Min Mang, "NLD Details Laundry List of Complaints against UEC", *Myanmar Times*, 22 September 2015 <http://www.mmtimes.com/index.php/national-news/16585-nld-details-laundry-list-of-complaints-against-uec.html>.
35. Esther Htsuan and Jocelyn Gecker, "Despite Critics, Support for Suu Kyi Strong before Election", Associated Press, 30 October 2015 <http://bigstory.ap.org/article/8bdf84c1290a490d8de825446e07dd69/despite-critics-support-suu-kyi-strong-election>.
36. Andrew R.C. Marshall and Timothy Mclaughlin, "Myanmar's Suu Kyi Says Will be above President in New Government", Reuters, 5 November 2015 <http://www.reuters.com/article/us-myanmar-election-idUSKCN0SU0AR20151105>; For excerpts from her hour-long session with over a hundred media personnel, see Kyaw Phyo Tha, "Takeaways from Suu Kyi's Marathon Pre-Poll Presser", *The Irrawaddy*, 5 November 2015 <http://www.irrawaddy.com/election/news/takeaways-from-suu-kyis-marathon-pre-poll-presser>.
37. Ibid.
38. Swan Ye Htut and Pyae Thet Phyo, "USDP Campaigns in Strongholds, Promises Development", *Myanmar Times*, 14 September 2015 <http://www.mmtimes.com/index.php/national-news/16455-usdp-campaigns-in-strongholds-promises-development.html>.
39. Ei Ei Toe Lwin, "USDP Rejects Requests for Safe Seats", *Myanmar Times*, 17 July

2015 <http://www.mmtimes.com/index.php/national-news/15545-usdp-rejects-requests-for-safe-seats.html>; and Chit Win , "Myanmar's Ruling Party Gambles on Incumbent Lawmakers", *Nikkei Asian Review*, 20 October 2015 <http://asia.nikkei.com/Viewpoints/Perspectives/Myanmar-s-ruling-party-gambles-on-incumbent-lawmakers>.

40. Sithu Aung Myint, "Why Was Thura U Shwe Mann Fired?" *Myanmar Times*, 26 August 2015 <http://www.mmtimes.com/index.php/opinion/16150-why-was-thura-u-shwe-mann-fired.html>.

41. Khin Maung Soe, "Myanmar's Ruling Party Predicts Victory ahead of General Elections", RFA, 6 November 2015 <http://www.rfa.org/english/news/myanmar/victory-11062015153007.html>.

42. Democratic Voice of Burma, "2015 Election: USDP Unveils Candidate List", DVB online, 24 August 2015 <http://www.dvb.no/news/2015-election-usdp-unveils-candidate-list/55895>.

43. Members of the government need not resign to contest the elections so long as they do not take up party positions. But they must give up their seats in the legislature once they are appointed as members of the new government.

44. Ko Ko Lat, "Thein Sein Will Not Seek Second Term as Myanmar's President", RFA Myanmar Service, 12 August 2015 <http://www.rfa.org/english/news/myanmar/thein-sein-will-not-seek-second-term-as-myanmars-president-08122015165802.html>.

45. "USDP Backs President Thein Sein for Second Term: Party Official", *The Irrawaddy* online, 19 October 2015 <http://www.irrawaddy.com/election/news/usdp-backs-president-thein-sein-for-second-term-party-official>.

46. "Is the President Personally Campaigning?", *Eleven Myanmar* online, n.d. <http://www.elevenmyanmar.com/opinion/president-personally-campaigning>.

47. Ei Ei Toe Lwin, Wa Lone, and Simon Widmer, "NLD Leader Challenges President over Mantle of Change", *Myanmar Times*, 2 November 2015 <http://www.mmtimes.com/index.php/national-news/yangon/17316-nld-leader-challenges-president-over-mantle-of-change.html>.

48. Hnin Yadana Zaw, "Myanmar Military Retains Veto after Constitution Change Vote Fails", Reuters, 25 June 2015 <http://www.reuters.com/article/us-myanmar-politics-idUSKBN0P50Q820150625>.

49. The members are the President, two Vice-Presidents, the Speakers of the lower house and upper house, Ministers of Defence, Home Affairs, Border Affairs and Foreign Affairs. The C-in-C and Deputy C-in-C are also included.

50. The C-in-C Senior General Min Aung Hlaing was reported to have said on 20 October in Nay Pyi Taw that the military's families should vote for candidates "who have an empathy for the army, are able to correctly guard the race and religion and who have no influence from foreign organizations and foreigners". See Swe Win, "Can Soldiers Vote in Myanmar Elections without Fear?", Myanmar Now, 1 November 2015 <http://mizzima.com/news-election-2015-election-features/can-soldiers-vote-myanmar-elections-without-fear>.

51. See, for example, *Burma Bulletin*, August 2015, pp. 8–9; and Renaud Egretaau, "A Generals' Election in Myanmar", *The Diplomat*, 4 November 2015 <http://thediplomat.com/2015/11/a-generals-election-in-myanmar/>.

52. Maung Aung Myoe, "Presidential Hopefuls in Myanmar's 2015 Elections", *ISEAS Perspective*, no. 62, 3 November 2015.

53. See *Burma Bulletin*, September 2015, p. 3; *Burma Bulletin*, October 2015, p. 5; and Aung Kyaw Min, "Divisions as Ma Ba Tha Begins 'Campaigning'", *Myanmar Times*, 15 October 2015 <http://www.mmtimes.com/index.php/national-

news/17010-divisions-as-ma-ba-tha-begins-campaigning.html>.
54. Ei Ei Toe Lwin, "Ma Ba Tha Takes Aim at Defamation Accusations", *Myanmar Times*, 25 September 2015 <http://www.mmtimes.com/index.php/national-news/16691-ma-ba-tha-takes-aim-at-defamation-accusations.html>.
55. Aung Kyaw Min, "Divisions as Ma Ba Tha Begins".
56. Connor Macdonald, "Smartphone Freedom Fuels Rise of Social Media in Myanmar Politics", *Myanmar Now*, 21 December 2015 <http://www.myanmar-now.org/news/i/?id=e50cf392-1a2e-4341-b199-e27ed6d89b0d>.
57. Sui-Lee Wee, "Myanmar Media Stack the Deck for 'Mother' Suu Kyi ahead of Polls", Reuters, 29 October 2015 <http://www.reuters.com/article/us-myanmar-election-media-idUSKCN0SN0QG20151029>.
58. "Partnering with Myanmar's Civil Society to Build Democracy", IFES, 15 December 2015 <http://www.ifes.org/news/partnering-myanmars-civil-society-build-democracy>.
59. Sophia Fernandes, "Myanmar Election Observers Witness Large Voter Turnout", International IDEA, 11 November 2015 <http://www.idea.int/asia_pacific/myanmar/myanmar-election-observers-witness-large-voter-turnout.cfm>.
60. *Burma Bulletin*, November 2015, p. 3.
61. R.J. Vogt, "UEC Puts Election Turnout at 69 per cent", *Myanmar Times*, 3 December 2015 <http://www.mmtimes.com/index.php/national-news/nay-pyi-taw/17948-uec-puts-election-turnout-at-69-percent.html>.
62. Personal observation in Yangon, 8 November 2015.
63. Timothy McLaughlin, "Myanmar Ruling Party Chief Concedes Defeat, Will Accept Result", Reuters, 9 November 2015 <http://www.reuters.com/article/us-myanmar-election-usdp-idUSKCN0SY0W920151109>.
64. James Coe, "Where's the Victory Rally? Suu Kyi Waits!", *Mizzima*, 13 November 2015 <http://mizzima.com/news-election-2015-election-news/where%E2%80%99s-victory-rally-suu-kyi-waits>.
65. *Burma Bulletin*, November 2015, pp. 6–7.
66. "Ywe Kauk Pwe Kant Kwet Hmu 33 Hmu Shi" [Thirty-three cases of election objections], RFA Myanmar, 29 December 2015 <http://www.rfa.org/burmese>, reproduced in *Thit Htoo Lwin* online news website at <http://www.thithtoolwin.com/>; and Htet Khaung Lin, "Litany of Election Complaints Submitted to Myanmar Police", *Mizzima*, 5 December 2015 <http://mizzima.com/news-election-2015-election-news/litany-election-complaints-submitted-myanmar-police>.
67. See Chit Win, "Myanmar's Ruling Party Gambles". The NLD has only two incumbent MPs in the provincial legislature.
68. All the figures are from boxes numbers 3 to 5 in, "The 2015 General Election in Myanmar: What Now for Ethnic Politics?", Myanmar Policy Briefing No. 17, Transnational Institute, December 2015 <https://www.tni.org/files/publication-downloads/bpb17_web_def.pdf>. There are special seats allotted to represent each ethnic group constituting a substantive minority in the population of the state or region concerned. For a state named after the non-Bamar majority ethnic group, these seats represent other ethnic minorities in that state as well as the Bamar ethnic group, provided they qualify population-wise. For a region where the majority population is Bamar, the seats represent non-Bamar ethnic groups who qualify in terms of population threshold defined as either equal to or greater than 0.1 per cent of Myanmar's total population (51.4 million). Moreover, the ethnic group that has its own designated self-administered area within a state or region does not qualify for such a representative seat for the said state or region. Once elected, the MP becomes Minister for Ethnic Affairs

in the government of the respective state or region. See, "Myanmar 2015 General Elections Fact Sheet", IFES, 15 September 2015 <ihttp://www.ifes.org/sites/default/files/ifes_2015_myanmar_election_fact_sheet_final.pdf>.
69. Ibid., pp. 9–10.
70. Larry Jagan, "National Development Party: Phoenix or Third Force?", *Frontier Myanmar*, 10 September 2015 <http://www.frontiermyanmar.net/en/national-development-party-phoenix-or-third-force>.
71. The figures are from Kyaw Phone Kyaw, "Behind the Numbers and Names, an Election Picture Emerges", *Myanmar Times*, 2 September 2015 <http://www.mmtimes.com/index.php/national-news/16277-behind-the-numbers-and-names-an-election-picture-emerges.html>.
72. Renaud Egreteau, "The (Few) Generals That Don't Exit in Myanmar", *The Diplomat*, 20 November 2015 <http://thediplomat.com/2015/11/the-few-generals-that-dont-exit-in-myanmar/>.

Philippines

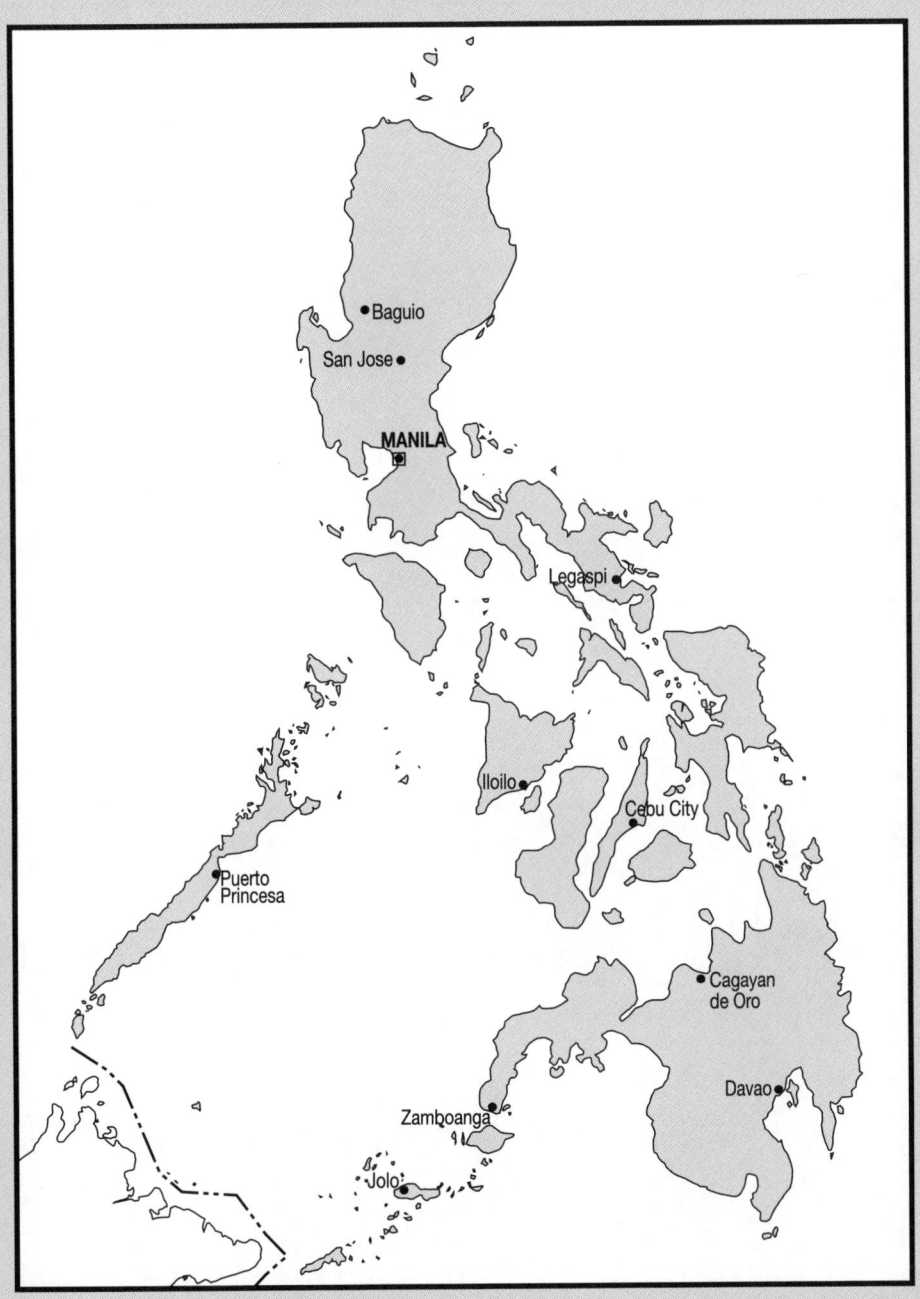

AN OVERVIEW OF THE PHILIPPINES

Lim Yoon Lin

On 23 September 1972 President Marcos invoked martial law under the country's Constitution to meet what he termed "the threat of a violent overthrow of our Republic" and "to reform the social, economic and political institutions in our country." Simultaneously there was an almost total clampdown on the press, television and radio stations, and the mass arrest of prominent citizens, among them opposition politicians and publishers. The declaration of martial law was quickly followed by a number of vigorous measures aimed at controlling the possession of weapons and weeding out the corrupt and incompetent within the government service, and bringing certain basic industries and communications under state control. It is noteworthy that although the communist threat was the justification for martial law the initial measures of martial law rule could also be seen as having been aimed at breaking the power of the oligarchy such as the arms' ban, detention of political opponents, appropriation of private property, seizure of newspapers and the initial ban on foreign travel.

The immediate reaction of political observers to the imposition of martial law was that it was a move on the part of President Marcos to perpetuate his power indefinitely and suppress all criticisms against his rule which had been mounting since his re-election in 1969. The ordinary Filipino however, tired of the increasing violence and anarchy in Manila during the months preceding September, and burdened by serious food shortages and spiralling prices following devastating floods in June 1972 was more anxious to see the

---

Reprinted in abridged format from *Southeast Asian Affairs 1974* (Singapore: Institute of Southeast Asian Studies 1974), pp. 175–201. At the time of original publication, Lim Yoon Lin was a Research Officer at the Institute of Southeast Asian Studies, Singapore.

implementation of much needed reforms in the country and the reconstruction of what President Marcos has proudly proclaimed as the New Society.

One of the first to benefit from martial law was the armed forces. On 30 September 1972 President Marcos announced increased rates of monthly pay for the enlisted personnel of the Philippine Armed Forces, increased monthly pay for commissioned officers and promotions for a number of officers. While reforms and improvements in the armed forces had for long been recommended, the Presidential Order coming almost immediately after martial law had the appearance that it was made with the aim of ensuring military backing for the President. Since the imposition of martial law the armed forces have been brought increasingly to the fore with increased political and administrative responsibilities. However, great pains have also been taken by the government to stress that martial law in the Philippines, unlike in other countries, is not a military take-over but is based on the constitutional powers of the President and that civilian authority will remain supreme at all times.

Two months after martial law there appeared to have been some signs of relaxation when President Marcos announced that he was going "to allow free and open debate on the draft Constitution," then before the Constitutional Convention, and a nation-wide plebiscite was set for 15 January 1973. He even hinted that he might lift martial law after the referendum. Earlier on 25 October 1972, the Constitutional Convention under the influence of forces loyal to President Marcos had adopted a new Constitution which provides for the President to head the interim government (during the transition period from the old to the new Constitution), combining in his person the powers of president and prime minister, until he calls upon the interim Parliament to choose the executive and parliamentary head of a new government. No time limit was set for the interim parliament, leaving the President the sole judge of deciding when the transitional period should end.

By the end of December, however, unwilling to risk a national debate on the draft Constitution and perhaps influenced by an unsuccessful assassination attempt on Mrs. Marcos on 7 December, President Marcos postponed the referendum on the draft Constitution. Instead he decided to submit the matter to the 35,000 *barangays* or citizens' assemblies throughout the nation, using the threats posed by rightist conspirators and Maoist elements against his New Society reforms as justification for revoking his earlier ruling to allow free discussion on the draft Constitution. Thus between 10–15 January 1973 a nation-wide "consultation" was held wherein some fifteen million Filipinos participated and voted overwhelmingly in favour of the continuation of martial law. Ninety-seven per cent of the *barangays* were recorded as having approved the new Constitution, 93% voted against the need for a constitutional plebiscite and 89% against the holding of national elections in November 1972. The result was the ratification of the new Constitution on 17 January 1973 by President Marcos under which he became President and Prime Minister concurrently, with a mandate to rule for the next seven years. Dubbing his regime "constitutional authoritarianism", he also announced the suspension of the interim National Assembly provided under the new Constitution and warned that he would "no longer tolerate any attempt to undermine the Republic." In April the Supreme Court by a majority vote upheld the validity of the new Constitution, dismissing five petitions which had sought to challenge the process adopted to ratify the new Constitution. While it may appear that the right to appeal to a civil court still remains under martial law, the Supreme Court proceedings in April however received scant attention in the controlled media.

Perhaps of more significance to the martial law regime was the 27 July 1973 referendum. Constantly held up by the martial law administration as the most effective base for citizen participation in the government process as opposed to political parties, the citizens' assemblies were convened for the second time in 1973 in a further effort on the part of President Marcos to demonstrate the popularity of his New Society as well as the constitutionality of his regime. This time only one question was put before the voters: whether they wanted President Marcos to continue in office after 30 December 1973 and complete the reforms he has initiated under martial law. The official message stressed throughout was that the issue in the 27 July 1973 referendum was not President Marcos himself so much as the reforms he had set in motion. A novel feature in the July referendum was the provision of "remarks sheets" on which voters could write their comments on the present administration and explain their votes. The Commission on Elections (Comelec) promised that these would be analyzed by a group of experts and their findings serve as a "persuasive" guide to the President in the formulation of future policies.

A slight relaxation on the eve of the referendum was allowed with the lifting of the midnight to 4.00 a.m. curfew from 23 July to 28 July and the armed forces and other government agencies enjoined "to encourage and not to interfere in public and free discussions on the question" to be resolved on 27 July. But despite the official promise of freedom of debate there was no discussion in the media of the merits and demerits of the continuation of martial law rule nor was much publicity given to a petition by some Filipino citizens requesting a month-long postponement of the referendum, the reappearance of free speech and press and the setting up of an independent committee of citizens to oversee the referendum.

Repeating their motion in January 1973, the voters voted overwhelmingly for President Marcos' continuance in office beyond 1973 and thus also endorsed the reforms he had initiated since martial law was imposed. The official count was 18,052,016 "yes" votes (90.67%) and 1,856,744 "no" votes (9.33%). The Comelec was quick to point out the predominance of "yes" votes in the affluent communities in Greater Manila such as Forbes Park and in the traditional bailiwicks of opposition leaders. Official reports disclosed that from the remarks sheets, a great majority were in favour of the indefinite deferment of the convening of the interim National Assembly and a more extensive reorganization of the government than was being undertaken then. From the voting results it would appear that the majority of ordinary Filipinos were convinced that the answer to their poverty and the country's lack of progress lies in the promised New Society.

There is as yet no indication as to when martial law would end although Filipinos are constantly assured that martial law was only "a transitory period." President Marcos recently indicated his intention to hold another plebiscite in 1974 for the *barangays* to decide on the lifting of martial law. No time period was specified but it would have to depend he said on the "quality of permanence the government is able to give the reforms in the New Society."

It is undeniable that martial law rule has brought benefits to many sectors of Philippine society. They are manifested in the general tonedown in lawlessness and violence so endemic of Filipino politics prior to September 1972, the streamlining of the government service making possible speedy and effective actions than was the case in pre-martial law days, the implementation of a nation-wide land reform programme, the stepping up in infrastructure and increase in economic activities and the entry of foreign investments. Before we look at the major programmes and developments under the New Society, it should be mentioned that the achievements of the New Society are also marred by certain flaws. Chief among these is the "transitory" provisions of the new Constitution which repose all powers in the hands of one man and make him the sole judge of what is good for the country. While rule by decree has enabled quick action to be taken on many pressing problems, it also means that there is no recourse to an independent body from arbitrary or mistaken presidential decisions.

Another discouraging aspect of martial law rule is the strict censorship of the local media and the general paucity of information in the country except when they are doled out through the official media. The Secretary of Information, Francisco Tatad, head of the newly created Department of Information, has said that the government would be able to provide all the "necessary, accurate, straight news of positive, national value." It would appear that Filipinos have not been able to learn more than what their government wants them to on certain "sensitive" issues as a result of the tightly controlled press. After the initial clampdown, a number of newspapers and magazines were allowed to resume publication but they did not include the "big three": *The Manila Times, The Herald* and *The Manila Chronicle* which the President had branded as "adjuncts and tools of vested economic interests." Today, all newspapers and radio and television stations are subject to a six-month licensing which is renewable by applying to the watchdog Mass Media Council. It is ironic that what was once "the freest press in the world" is now in the words of the Foreign Secretary, General Romulo, "rigid with conformity." Even the Information Secretary, Mr. Tatad, complained that the "press today is too timid."

As with the muzzled press, the indefinite detention of an unspecified number of political opponents and the tough measures taken against some members of the clergy, is symptomatic of the intolerance of the martial law administration. One of the first to be arrested under martial law, Liberal Party Senator, Benigno Aquino, Jr., one of Marcos' fiercest critics, remains in jail while many of those detained with him have been released. In a show to demonstrate that "everything is being done to ensure utmost fairness, impartiality and objectivity in the prosecution of the charges against the accused," President Marcos in August 1973 ordered the creation of a five-man panel with only two government representatives for the purpose of re-investigating subversion charges against Senator Aquino. But the latter has indicated he intends to boycott any court set up by Marcos to try him just as he had earlier refused to be tried by a military tribunal.

Of late according to the Catholic Bishops' Conference of the Philippines

(CBCP), certain church institutions had been subjected to raids by government troops and a number of priests and nuns detained for interrogation. Among the latest to be taken into custody on charges of subversion against the government is Father Edward Gerhock of Maryknoll, the first American to stand trial since martial law. While it is true that certain disaffected individuals of the clerical order have gone underground, this is hardly indicative of any link between the underground communist movement, the New People's Army, and the "Christian Left." What has happened is that among the younger members of the clergy, especially those active in social work among poor plantation workers and subsistence farmers, there is growing disillusionment with government development. Many are beginning to question certain aspects of martial law rule and insist on "critical cooperation" with the government. The harsh measures taken by the government to cope with what has been officially alleged as subversion acts are seen by many Catholics as attempts at intimidation. They have elicited pastoral letters of protest complaining of "harassment" and the suppression of human rights. But these have found no place in the controlled press.

One and a half years after martial law, the mood of the government remains much the same as the day martial law was imposed. It is a mood that will brook no criticism from whatever quarter least of all when the legality of the regime is called into question. At the same time despite being firmly in control the government remains wary of any move that it suspects might bring resistant groups together be they communists, Muslim insurgents, rightist oligarchs or the Christian Left. While many thinking Filipinos are concerned with when the "transitory period" of martial law rule will end, what is of more import to the great majority of ordinary Filipinos is whether the martial law regime can fulfil its many promises or whether they can expect to see its performance steadily being outstripped by its promises.

UNFINISHED REVOLUTION
The Philippines in 1986

David G. Timberman

Introduction

The unfolding of the affairs of nations rarely corresponds neatly with the beginning and end of the calendar year, and the experience of the Philippines in 1986 was no exception. The dramatic events of 1986, the high point of which was the toppling of the Marcos regime by a non-violent revolution in February, were inextricably rooted in the political and economic crises that had wracked the country since the assassination of Benigno "Ninoy" Aquino, Jr. in August 1983. Likewise, many of the daunting problems and challenges facing the Philippines in the post-Marcos era will not begin to be resolved until well into 1987, if at all.

Despite this seamless flow of events, the changes that occurred in the relatively short span of twelve months created a dramatically new political environment in the Philippines by the end of 1986. At the beginning of the year, for example, Ferdinand Marcos, weakening but still powerful, was marshalling the intimidating powers of his presidential office and political machine to assure his re-election in the face of the strongest political challenge ever to his twenty-year rule. At year end, Marcos was in exile in Hawaii and President Corazon ("Cory") Aquino sought to fend off challenges from both the left and the right as she struggled to consolidate her still shaky political position and define and pursue the policy agenda of her coalition government.

In January, the leadership of the Philippine Armed Forces appeared to be loyal to President Marcos, despite the growing prominence of the Reform the Armed Forces

---

Reprinted from Mohammed Ayood, ed., *Southeast Asian Affairs 1987* (Singapore: Institute of Southeast Asian Studies, 1987), pp. 239–63. At the time of original publication, David G. Timberman was a Manila-based writer and consultant specializing in political and economic affairs.

Movement (RAM). By December, however, Defence Minister Juan Ponce Enrile and his RAM followers had gone from being heroes of the February revolution to being outcasts as a result of their challenge to the Aquino government. Meanwhile, General Fidel Ramos, the other "Hero of EDSA (Epifania de los Santos Avenue)", opted to support the Aquino government, and by doing so, strengthened his position as a key figure in the Aquino administration.

At the start of the year the communist insurgency continued to grow, and perversely, the insurgency issue was used effectively by Marcos to criticize the Aquino candidacy and justify his continued rule. By December the communists had recovered from their politically damaging boycott of the February election and were using a fragile sixty-day cease-fire to mount an effective public relations campaign.

In January, the country's economic crisis, brought about by corruption, mismanagement, and unfavourable international economic conditions, showed few signs of ending as the economy had just suffered its second consecutive year of negative growth. By December, the dramatic recovery hoped for by many had not materialized, but a boom in the stock market suggested increased optimism about the country's economic prospects — optimism that was only partially justified by key economic indicators at the end of the year.

As 1986 began, the majority of Filipinos, though divided into two opposing camps, participated in a passionately contested presidential campaign. The campaign and its aftermath raised the average Filipino's political awareness, commitment to democratic ideals, and sense of nationalism to levels that were perhaps unique in Philippine history. At year end, Filipinos were experiencing both the pleasures and the pains of their newly gained freedom, as exemplified by a proliferating and often rumour-driven press and the regular appearances of pro-Marcos "loyalists" and communist revolutionaries alike on television talk-shows.[1]

The Snap Election

The chain of events that led to the downfall of Ferdinand Marcos began with the assassination of Benigno Aquino in August 1983, but the final stage of the process began in the autumn of 1985.[2] On 16 and 17 October, conservative U.S Senator Paul Laxalt visited Manila to convey to President Marcos the Reagan Administration's growing concern over the deteriorating political and economic situation in the Philippines. The visit was intended to emphasize to Marcos that these concerns — and the belief that significant political and economic reforms were needed — were not only felt by the State Department but were also shared by President Reagan. President Marcos was unreceptive to Laxalt's call for reforms and was reported to have dismissed the senator's suggestion that he hold an election prior to the mandated 1987 election in order to re-establish his credibility.

In late October 1985 the Reagan Administration further underscored its concern during Senate Foreign Relations Committee hearings on the Philippines at which Assistant Secretary of State, Paul Wolfowitz, and Assistant Secretary of Defense, Richard Armitage, both painted a grim picture of the economic crisis and growing communist insurgency. Following these hearings, Senator Dave Durenberger's Intelligence Committee released an alarming report on the situation in the Philippines, prompting Durenberger to call for Marcos to step down.[3]

It was against the backdrop of mounting U.S. pressure that President Marcos announced, on 3 November 1985, his decision to hold snap presidential and vice-presidential elections on 17 January 1986. Several weeks later, in a compromise to gain opposition endorsement for the contest, he agreed to postpone the elections until 7 February.

The fact that Marcos made his announcement on the American television programme, "This Week With David Brinkley", suggests that the election was called for American government consumption as much as for domestic political reasons. However, in addition to seeking to silence his American critics, there were a number of other, perhaps equally important, factors that were part of the calculus of his pivotal decision. One certainly was the likelihood that the ruling party, the Kilusang Bagong Lipunan (KBL), would suffer significant losses in the local elections scheduled for May 1986, thus seriously eroding the ability of his political machine to deliver the vote in the 1987 presidential contest. A second probable factor was Marcos' supreme confidence that the opposition would be unable to field a unified ticket against him; and if they did, that none of the likely opposition candidates was a match for his political skill and power. And finally, if Marcos foresaw his health deteriorating further by 1987, it would have made sense to hold the presidential election sooner, while his health was relatively better, rather than later. But whatever the combination of reasons, Marcos' decision gave new purpose and focus to the widespread but fragmented opposition to his regime.

On 2 December 1985 the Sandiganbayan, the three-member court appointed to try Chief of Staff Fabian Ver and twenty-five others for conspiracy in the August 1983 murder of Benigno Aquino and Rolando Galman, exonerated all the defendants on all accounts. Following the announcement of the decision, largely a foregone conclusion to most Filipinos, Mrs Corazon Aquino observed that "justice is not possible so long as Mr Marcos continues to be head of our government". And on the next day, 3 December, Aquino announced her long-awaited decision to run for president. For the next week it appeared that the opposition would field two major candidates, "Cory" Aquino and Salvador "Doy" Laurel, head of the United Nationalist Democratic Organization (UNIDO), thus assuring a Marcos victory before the campaign had begun. But on 11 December, the last day of registration, after the intervention of Jaime Cardinal Sin, a "shotgun wedding" between the two was arranged. Laurel abandoned his decision to run for president and instead accepted the vice-presidential slot. Aquino, on her part, agreed to run for president under the UNIDO banner rather than under the Pilipino Democratic Party-Lakas ng Bayan (PDP-LABAN) coalition.

On the same day, Marcos selected as his vice-presidential running mate 75-year-old Arturo Tolentino, a KBL Member of Parliament (MP) and Marcos' former Foreign Minister. The campaign slates were set, despite recurring rumours that Imelda Marcos would replace Tolentino at the last moment, or that Laurel would switch parties and become Marcos' vice-presidential candidate (either of which would have been legal under the Philippines' byzantine election code).[4] One last major uncertainty was removed on 19 December when the

Marcos-appointed Supreme Court voted 7 to 5 to throw out eleven petitions questioning the constitutionality of the snap election (including one filed by Tolentino before he joined the Marcos ticket). The battle lines were drawn and the battle was set to begin.

The Election Campaign

The 1986 presidential campaign was not unlike past campaigns in that it was primarily a contest between personalities and less of a public debate over issues. But the contest in 1986 was made unique by the magnitude of the contrast between the two presidential candidates and by the great difference in the power of their political organizations.

The campaign was above all a contest between two dramatically different people. Ferdinand E. Marcos, with his shrewd legalistic mind and his great ability to manipulate the Philippines polity and people, was the unrivalled master of Philippine politics. But all the bravado of the 69-year-old strongman could not overcome the deepening sense shared by many Filipinos that his failing health reflected his failed policies and that he was a captive of his own corrupt regime, unable to reform it even if he had wanted to. In stark contrast to this stood fifty-three-old Corazon C. Aquino, the wife of the martyred opposition leader Benigno Aquino, who inherited with great reluctance her husband's role as leader of the anti-Marcos opposition. Although generally admired for her integrity and common sense, she was a self-proclaimed political neophyte.

Equally contrasting were the resources at the command of the two camps. Marcos had at his disposal the almost unlimited powers of the government as well as the KBL's well-entrenched, if somewhat rusty, nation-wide political machine. He controlled directly or indirectly all of Manila's television stations and most of the radio stations and newspapers as well. He also controlled the Commission on Elections (COMELEC) responsible for seeing that his tailor-made election code was followed. The KBL had the necessary majority in the Batasang Pambansa (National Assembly) to ensure that the Assembly would proclaim Marcos president after it "canvassed" (that is, certified) the validity of the election returns. And finally, he could count on his hand-picked judiciary to be unreceptive to any legal challenges filed by the opposition.

At the critically important local level the KBL, though not monolithic, still controlled 69 of 73 provincial governments, 53 of 59 city governments, 1,218 of 1,469 municipal governments, and virtually all of the more than 41,000 *barangay* (village) captainships throughout the country. Most places Marcos visited during the campaign had crowds bussed to the site where they were usually given T-shirts, food, or money. A star-studded variety show and, often, a singing performance by the First Lady herself preceded Marcos' appearance. In his speeches he invoked the spectres of a communist take-over, Muslim secession, and civil war if Aquino were elected. And as a further enticement for votes — as well as a reminder of the totality of his power — he issued presidential decrees raising salaries, lowering prices, giving land, granting new loans or writing off old ones. Marcos' campaign stops and speeches received extensive coverage in the government-controlled media while Aquino's activities received brief, if any, mention.

Against this intimidating array of campaign weapons Aquino and Laurel mounted a tireless campaign. Deprived of equal access to the media, they took to the road. By the first week in January they had visited 24 of 73 provinces while Marcos had left Manila only occasionally. By late January they had visited 50 provinces and by election day they had visited 68.

Aquino's campaign emphasized her continuation of the cause begun by her husband's martyrdom, her sincerity and integrity, and her courage to stand up to Marcos whatever the cost. Her positions on major issues were moderate but lacking in detail. She pledged to restore democracy and human rights, pursue a peaceful solution to the insurgency, encourage a free, but equitable economy, and honour the agreement on military bases with the United States until its expiration in 1991. But it was her sincerity, commitment and courage, probably more than any of her policies, that held such strong appeal to the average Filipino. As the crowds grew, she became less "Ninoy's widow" and more a political figure in her own right; and as this happened, she began to exude more self-confidence and exert more control over her candidacy.

Mrs Aquino was not totally alone in her campaign against the Marcos machine. Assisting her in different ways and varying degrees were the Roman Catholic church, the international media and, to a lesser degree, the National Movement for Free Elections (NAMFREL) as well as the U.S. Government.

In mid-January Jaime Cardinal Sin, the influential Archbishop of Manila, issued a pastoral letter titled "A Call to Conscience" in which he warned that the Church would not forgive election fraud and urged voters to accept bribes if necessary, but to vote as their conscience dictated. In late January the Catholic Bishops' Conference of the Philippines issued a pastoral letter urging voters to combat a "conspiracy of evil" that threatened to thwart the people's will during the election. And on 5 February, just two days before the election, Cardinal Sin virtually endorsed Aquino, saying that if she were elected she would make a good president.

The international media played a major role in providing Aquino's candidacy with the recognition and legitimacy that the Marcos media machine was intent on denying.[5] Filipinos could learn more about the Aquino campaign by reading the international editions of *Time* or *Newsweek* available at any news-stand than they could by reading most Manila newspapers. *Washington Post* and *New York Times* stories in late January questioning Marcos' war record were seized upon by the opposition and effectively used to challenge his honesty and bravery. And as election day approached Marcos and Aquino regularly traded barbs in interviews on U.S. news and talk-shows that were watched live or video-taped by the many Filipinos who had access to the U.S. military's Far East Network.

NAMFREL, a non-governmental election "watch-dog" organization with close ties to the Catholic Church, played a particularly critical role during and after election day. But the presence of some 400,000 NAMFREL volunteers throughout about 90 per cent of the country created outposts of accountability during the campaign that served to counter-balance the local dominance of the KBL.

Finally, the U.S. Government, already associated with the election because of the pressure it had put on Marcos, found itself riding the tiger down a path filled with uncertainty and risk. A week after Marcos called the snap election, Assistant Secretary of State Paul Wolfowitz stressed in Congressional testimony that overall U.S. policy towards the Philippines was not "hostage to the bases". Washington repeatedly emphasized the importance of free, fair, and honest elections and listed four pre-conditions necessary to make a fair election possible: the authorization of NAMFREL as a legal election monitor; the accreditation of UNIDO as the dominant opposition party; equal media access; and the appointment of independent commissioners to two vacant COMELEC positions.

Throughout the campaign, U.S. Ambassador Stephen Bosworth emphasized that while the U.S. Government was not taking sides, it was deeply concerned that the electoral process should reflect a renewed commitment to democratic processes and institutions.[6] On 27 January, Bosworth said that the United States would work with whichever side won the election, but that the "quality" of the relationship would depend on the credibility of the election. And on 30 January, one week before the election, President Reagan pledged to increase U.S. aid if the election was fair and if the new government committed itself to reforms. Predictably, the American position was criticized by both the pro-Marcos press, whose charges of U.S. meddling masked a growing fear that the United States was deserting Marcos, and the opposition press, whose criticisms of continued U.S. neutrality were fuelled by a desire for the United States to intervene more directly in support of Aquino.

During the last two weeks of January the intensity of the campaign reached typhoon force, as reflected by the increase in campaign-related violence (the death toll reached 40 by the end of the month and would total at least 90 by 7 February), the movement of huge amounts of money into and out of government coffers (estimated at over US$400 million) and the heightened pitch of campaign rhetoric on both sides.

Marcos, perhaps finally realizing the magnitude of the challenge presented by Aquino, ordered his cabinet ministers to get out of Manila and on to the campaign trail. In his speeches and campaign advertisements on television, he repeatedly accused Aquino of not having the experience or strength to lead the country in the face of the numerous threats it faced. According to one observer, "the overriding theme of Marcos TV ad campaigns was fear.... If the country didn't want to end up like Vietnam, like Iran, like Iraq, it had better give the job to a counter-insurgency expert."[7]

Aquino countered just as forcefully, blaming all of the country's problems on Marcos and his twenty years of "experience". During a visit to the southern island of Mindanao she called Marcos a coward for not visiting the island in ten years. Several days later she labelled him an inveterate liar and described his government as "a dictatorship cleverly crafted by an evil genius".

At the same time NAMFREL and COMELEC were engaged in on-again-off-again negotiations to arrive at a mutually acceptable procedure for a joint "quick count" of the election returns. The opposition considered a prompt count as essential to ensure that the returns would not be manipulated by the Marcos camp. But with COMELEC unwilling to let NAMFREL play an equal role in the counting and announcing of the results the talks ultimately broke down. On 30 January NAMFREL said that there was only a 50–50 chance of a reasonably clean election and estimated that there were up to a million "flying voters" (voters illegally registered in more than one precinct) still on COMELEC's registration lists. The stage was set for the bitter controversy generated by the two different election tallies.

On the evening of 4 February, the opposition staged what was then considered to be the largest political rally ever, drawing between 500 thousand and one million supporters to Manila's Luneta Park. Marcos, in his final rally the following day, accused the opposition of fomenting "hatred, anger and revolution". The following night, election eve, the military was placed on red alert, as Vice-Chief of Staff Lt. Gen. Fidel Ramos called for calm. U.S. Senator Richard Lugar, who headed a twenty-member official U.S. mission to observe the election, emphasized the importance of a quick count of votes beginning the following day.

To be contested for, on election day, were 21 to 23 million votes (80 to 90 per cent of the 26.2 million registered voters) likely to be cast in some 90 thousand precincts around the country. Marcos was expected to win the lion's share of votes in the "solid North" (Ilocos, Cagayan, and Central Luzon) and to carry the Eastern Visayas (the home of his wife) and much of Mindanao (where he had entered into alliances with local warlords). If the elections were free, Aquino was expected to post strong showings in Metro Manila, Cebu, and Southern Mindanao and to win a majority in the Southern Tagalog and Western Visayas regions.

Blas Opie, Marcos' Labour Minister, confidently predicted that Marcos would win by two million votes. The opposition camp claimed that Aquino would win 65 per cent of the vote if the election was fair. In contrast to these confident projections many other observers predicted a close contest in which Aquino would have to win by a big majority in Metro Manila (where 4.3 million votes were at stake) and in the other major cities in order to overcome the KBL's control of the rural areas. But none came close to anticipating the scale of the fraud that actually occurred on 7 February and during the week of vote counting and canvassing that followed.

"An Appearance of Fraud"

Describing election day, Francis Clines of the *New York Times* wrote:

> The day dawned at crescendo, the complaints of fraud and ballot thievery pouring in as a single tide from the scores of thousands of island precincts: ballot boxes allegedly stuffed with Marcos votes even before the polls opened; voting precincts suddenly moved overnight; "goon" intimidators loitering in the path of voters; tally sheets reportedly missing; mercenary voters allegedly commuting across a swatch of precincts to vote early and often.[8]

The vote-buying, violence, and fraud of election day were followed by a more subtle form of cheating that occurred as the votes were counted. Employing its own "quick count" NAMFREL showed Aquino leading by nearly one million votes on 8 February. The COMELEC count at the same time, however, showed Marcos with a slight lead. From that point on, the difference between the two counts continued to grow, prompting thirty COMELEC computer operators to walk out on 9 February to protest discrepancies between the figures on their computer printouts and the results publicly posted by COMELEC.

By 10 February the gap was its most glaring: the COMELEC count, which had stopped following the walkout, showed Marcos winning 51 per cent of the vote, but with only 28 per cent of the total vote counted. NAMFREL, however, had Aquino getting 53 per cent with 48 per cent of the total vote in. According to NAMFREL the national average for voter-turnout was about 80 per cent, but in Metro Manila, a heavily pro-Aquino area, it was only 73 per cent because voter registration lists had been tampered with, making it impossible for many to vote.

At this critical juncture President Reagan, in off-the-cuff comments on 10 February, dismissed the mounting evidence of widespread fraud by Marcos and suggested instead that the fiercely contested election was evidence of a "strong two-party system" in the Philippines. Apparently unaware of the polarization of Philippine society that was occurring as he spoke, he urged the two sides to "work together to form a viable government". A day later, after meeting with members of the U.S. observer team, he further damaged American credibility by conceding that there was "an appearance of fraud", but that it "was occurring on both sides". U.S. Ambassador Bosworth visited Aquino to try to explain away Reagan's statements; but he was unable to erase the public's perception that the United States was going to support Marcos until the bitter end. In an effort to buy time, the White House dispatched diplomatic troubleshooter Philip Habib to Manila to consult with government and opposition leaders.

Over the next two days the percentage of the total vote counted by COMELEC edged up to about 50 per cent. But the differences in the two counts remained more or less constant: COMELEC had Marcos winning with over 52 per cent, while NAMFREL had Aquino ahead by about the same margin. Stalemated, COMELEC washed its hands of the mess and on 12 February the KBL-dominated Batasang Pambansa (National Assembly) began to canvass the election certificates.

On 15 February, amid growing domestic and international criticism of the election, the Batasan declared Marcos the winner, with 53.8 per cent of the votes as against Aquino's 46.2 per cent, representing a margin of about 1.5 million votes. The final Batasan tally was based on a total turnout of only 20.1 million votes or only 77 per cent of registered voters. (In the May 1984 elections for the Batasan the turnout was 89 per cent.) But even more damaging to the Aquino cause — and damning to the Batasan's count — was the fact that only 71 per cent of the Metro Manila vote was counted.

NAMFREL, in its final tabulation based on slightly less than 15 million votes, showed Aquino with 7.84 million and Marcos with 7.05 million. It estimated that some 3.3 million people, mostly in opposition inclined areas, were unable to vote and that about 660 thousand of these were in Metro Manila alone.

In the eyes of many Filipinos and most foreign observers the numerous reports of fraud and intimidation on election day, the glaring discrepancy between the two tallies, and the Batasan's heavy-handed canvassing of the certificates combined to form a powerful indictment of the government's handling of the election. On 14 February, the Catholic Bishops' Conference of the Philippines supported this view, calling the fraud "unparalleled" and condemning the KBL's tactics as "a criminal use of power to thwart the sovereign will of the people". On 15 February, Reagan finally echoed the findings of the U.S. and international observer missions when he said that the abuse was "so extensive that the election's credibility has been called into question". But most important of all, Aquino refused to accept the Marcos "victory", and on 16 February called for a nation-wide general strike and boycott of government and "crony" firms. Marcos, it appeared, had "won" the election, but at the considerable cost of losing the last vestiges of his credibility and legitimacy.[9]

From Snap Election to "Snap Revolution"

The details of the three-day "people power" revolution in February are too complex and still too uncertain to be fully described here.[10] Furthermore, the drama and imagery of the event — the sea of people surrounding Marcos' tanks and troops and the feelings of fear and uncertainty amidst the fiesta-like atmosphere — were broadcast live around the world by the international media. This account will, therefore, touch on only the most critical aspects of the revolution.

By Aquino's own admission, if it were not for the military revolt started by Defence Minister Juan Ponce Enrile and Lt. Gen. Fidel Ramos on 22 February she might have spent the following weeks and months leading a national campaign of civil disobedience against the Marcos regime.[11] It took the civilian-backed military revolt (or the "Miracle of EDSA", as it is reverently referred to by many Filipinos) to remove the discredited regime. In addition to closing one chapter in Philippine history, the non-violent, centrist, and urban nature of the revolution has important implications for Philippine politics in the wake of Marcos' departure. Among these are the prominent role it guaranteed the military in the new government, the relatively minor role it accorded the left, and the glorification of non-violent mass action, or "people power".

The revolt was triggered, as Juan Ponce Enrile himself said during his initial press conference at the Ministry of National Defence in Camp Aguinaldo, by the imminent arrest — by Chief of Staff Fabian Ver — of Enrile's supporters in the RAM movement, and perhaps of Enrile as well. But what Enrile neglected to say at that time was that Ver's action was prompted, in turn, by the general's discovery of Enrile's intention to break with the government on 24 February and of a RAM plot to attack Malacañang Palace to force President Marcos to resign.

Upon learning of Ver's intentions, Enrile hastily changed his plans and headed for the protection of his Ministry on Saturday afternoon, 22 February. As Robert Shaplen observed:

> Emile panicked by jumping the gun on his resignation, but he managed to preempt the plans of Marcos and Ver, who had a pretty good idea of what the Reformists were up to.... But they also knew that if they overreacted they would split the military, make more trouble for themselves and for the country, and create a serious problem with the United States.[12]

Once at Camp Aguinaldo, Emile called Lt. Gen. Ramos to ask for his support. (The previous week Marcos had announced his intention to replace Ver with Ramos, but without specifying when. In preparation for this Ver began appointing his followers to key posts, prompting Ramos to protest about the "midnight appointments" to Marcos.) Ramos agreed to join him and at 6.30 p.m., protected by no more than 300 soldiers, Enrile and Ramos held a news conference broadcast over Radio Veritas, the radio station of the Catholic

Church. They announced their resignations from the Marcos government in protest of the fraudulent election results and called for Marcos to step down.[13] Ramos then went to his headquarters in Camp Crame, across Epifanio de los Santos Avenue or EDSA, leaving Enrile with "more correspondents than troops". As it turned out, the correspondents provided the most effective protection.

At 9.00 that evening, Cardinal Sin broadcast a message on Radio Veritas urging people to go to Camps Crame and Aguinaldo to protect the rebels and give them food. By late Saturday night an estimated 10 to 15 thousand people had gathered at EDSA. At 11 p.m. Marcos countered with a televised press conference in which he claimed, with unusual veracity, that he was the target of a coup by the reformists in the military. At about the same time the White House issued a statement calling for the peaceful resolution of the conflict, adding that the resignations of Emile and Ramos "strongly reinforce our concerns that the recent elections were marred by fraud, perpetuated overwhelmingly by the ruling party".

The twenty-four hour period from early Sunday morning, 23 February, to Monday morning, 24 February, proved to be decisive. On early Sunday morning, before the crowds began to mass, Marcos' forces could have overwhelmed the rebels in a conventional armed attack. But by delaying, either because of his uncertainty about the situation or his confidence in his ability to cut a deal with Emile, Marcos' military option quickly evaporated. By mid-Sunday morning about 20 thousand civilians had gathered at the gates of Camps Aquinaldo and Crame, making a "surgical strike" against the rebel forces impossible.

The crowd grew all day, but then dissipated Sunday night, leaving the rebels vulnerable again and fearing the worst. But once again, except for a half-hearted and ineffective attempt to disperse the remaining civilians with tear-gas before dawn on Monday, Marcos and Ver were unable or unwilling to seize the opportunity. Later in the morning, faced with the defection of eight Air Force helicopters, growing "people power", and a stern warning from the United States that military aid would be immediately cut off if the rebels were attacked, Marcos could only hope to somehow co-opt Emile. This he tried the following day, by offering to make Emile the head of a new government — an honour Emile declined.

The military stand-off coincided with an actively contested war of words that was finally decided by a battle for control of Manila's (and therefore the nation's) airwaves. One of Marcos' first acts, early on that Sunday morning, was to order his troops to destroy the transmitting tower of Radio Veritas, which had become the rebel's main vehicle for mass communication. Following the temporary shut down of Radio Veritas (it began broadcasting again on Sunday evening from a commercial station), Marcos went on Channel 4, the government-owned television station, to demand that the rebels stop "this stupidity" and surrender peacefully. Later in the morning Emile countered with his own press conference in which he reiterated his call for Marcos to resign, saying he had "lost the support of the people". Shortly afterwards, Aquino, who was in Cebu when the revolt began, issued a public statement calling for people to go to EDSA to lend their support to the rebels.

On Monday morning the media battle intensified as rebel troops captured

Channel 4 after a skirmish that resulted in the death of two loyalist troops. The television station was captured and its signal cut off in the middle of a press conference called by Marcos to dispel rumours that he had fled the country. Within six hours the station was on the air again, in time to announce Enrile's declaration of a provisional government headed by Aquino. With the loss of Channel 4, loyalist troops then secured another station, Channel 9, and that evening Marcos again went on television to announce the immediate imposition of a curfew and to urge his civilian followers to bring their guns to the capital to defend the republic "to the last breath". At about the same time the U.S. government, in a belated but still dramatic statement, called for Marcos to step down. The White House said, "Attempts to prolong the life of the present regime are futile … a solution to this crisis can only be achieved through a peaceful transition to a new government."

Marcos, unconvinced that the U.S. statement reflected the view of President Reagan, called Senator Paul Laxalt at 3.00 on Tuesday morning (Manila time). In addition to seeking confirmation of Reagan's position, Marcos indicated his lack of interest in resigning and in going to the United States, where he feared congressional harassment. In increasing desperation he also proposed a variety of possible power-sharing arrangements. Laxalt said he would consult President Reagan (who apparently would not talk to Marcos directly) and promised to call Marcos back. Two hours later, after meeting with the White House crisis team, Laxalt called Marcos and, in response to Marcos' request for advice, told him to "cut and cut cleanly. The time has come."[14]

Marcos, however, proceeded with plans for his inauguration at noon on 25 February, the same day that Aquino planned to take her oath of office. At about 10.00 a.m. Aquino held her inaugural and "in the name and will of the Filipino people" was sworn in as the 7th president of the Philippines. Afterwards Laurel was sworn in as Vice-President, Enrile as Minister of National Defence, and Ramos as Chief of Staff of the Armed Forces. After the triumph of "people power" it was ironic, as Robert Shaplen has noted, that the Aquino ceremony was held at Club Filipino, an exclusive club in Makati that has long been a gathering place for the country's élite.

At noon Marcos took his oath as president in a melancholy ceremony at Malacañang attended by about 1,000 people comprising family members, staff, and supporters. Conspicuously absent, however, were "Vice-President" Arturo Tolentino and Cesar Virata, Marcos' long-time Finance Minister and Prime Minister. But even as the ceremony was under way, preparations were being made to leave the palace. Finally, at 7.15 p.m. Marcos informed the American Ambassador that he would relinquish office and leave the palace but that he wanted to stay in the country. At 9.00 p.m. four U.S. helicopters picked up Marcos and his family, Ver, and about thirty others and flew them to Clark Air Base, about 100 km. north of Manila, where they spent the night. The following morning, Marcos' request to stay having been denied by Aquino, the deposed president and his party of about fifty-five were flown to Guam and then to Hawaii. Accompanying them were US$1.1 million in pesos and other assets reported to be worth US$30 million.

The Marcos government had ended after more than twenty years of increasingly authoritarian, corrupt, and damaging rule. It was up to Corazon Aquino and her shaky coalition to pick up the pieces. As *Time* magazine succinctly predicted in its cover story following the departure of Marcos, "Now for the hard part."

The First Hundred Days of Aquino

Upon taking her oath, Mrs Aquino became head of a bankrupt government that faced an intimidating number of potential threats to its survival.[15] Most immediate was the continued existence of the Marcos political apparatus that, though leaderless, still remained intact and possessed the ability, it was feared, to thwart the new government's initiatives. Still in place at the national level were the KBL-controlled Batasan, and the Marcos-appointed military leadership and judiciary. Related to this was the issue of the constitutional basis for the Aquino government, for if Aquino came to power under Marcos' 1973 Constitution and if the 1973 Constitution was still considered to be in effect, then the government was dependent upon the Batasan to confer it with legitimacy. Equally vexing was the near total control of provincial and local governments by KBL officials — officials whose terms, under the existing election code, did not expire until June.

Another immediate challenge facing President Aquino was to form a cabinet which was both satisfactory to the disparate groups that shared a role in overthrowing Marcos and which could agree upon a set of policies to solve the long list of pressing problems.[16] Salvador Laurel, the head of UNIDO, wore several hats as Vice-President, Minister of Foreign Affairs, and Acting Prime Minister (until the Batasang Pambansa was abolished on 25 March). But the bulk of the cabinet positions went to Aquino's campaign advisers and to the leaders of PDP-LABAN. These included human-rights lawyer Joker Arroyo in the traditionally powerful position of Executive Secretary; former Mindanao MP Aquilino Pimentel as Minister of Local Government, lawyer Neptali Gonzales as Minister of Justice, Ernesto Maceda who was a close friend of the Aquino family as Minister of Natural Resources; businessman Jaime Ongpin as Finance Minister; economist Solita Monsod as Minister for Economic Planning; NAMFREL head and businessman Jose Concepcion as Minister of Trade and Industry; former Senator Jovito Salonga as head of the Presidential Commission on Good Government (PCGG); and former Senator and human-rights lawyer Jose Diokno as head of the Presidential Commission on Human Rights (PCHR). And finally, held over from the Marcos Cabinet, were Juan Ponce Enrile as Minister of National Defence and banker Jose Fernandez as Governor of the Central Bank.

The Cabinet included prominent leaders of the moderate left as well as more traditional and conservative politicians such as Enrile and Laurel. The economic ministers, however, shared a general orientation in favour of a market-driven, international economy. The Cabinet's diversity made disagreements and disunity inevitable. At the top of the new government's agenda were rebuilding a democratic political system, stimulating economic recovery and finding solutions to the communist and Muslim insurgencies. The Cabinet moved decisively to address several of these issues, but was divided and seemingly paralysed in its handling of others.

The Aquino government moved rapidly to dismantle the Marcos legacy. In the first week, over the objection of Enrile and the military, the government released about 500 political prisoners including Jose Maria Sison, the founder of the Communist Party of the Philippines (CPP), and Bernabe Buscayno, alias Commander Dante, the alleged head of its military arm, the New People's Army (NPA). On 2 March, at a "thanksgiving" rally in Manila that drew an estimated one million people, Aquino reinstated the writ of habeas corpus and officially retired Fabian Ver and 22 of Marcos' overstaying generals.

The following day, 3 March, Local Government Minister Pimentel announced that some fourteen thousand locally elected officials would be subject to replacement by new "Officers in Charge" or OICs, at the discretion of the government. The announcement began one of the most controversial policies of the new government. The KBL challenged the legality of replacing the elected local officials. But what really was at issue was the sweeping transfer of the power of local office — traditionally used by the national party leadership to cultivate party loyalty at the local level and by the local office holders to benefit their families and followers — from the KBL to the opposition. The KBL's hyperbolic description of the replacements as "revolutionary terror" underscored the importance of local patronage to national politics. For the same reason Laurel and other UNIDO stalwarts criticized Pimentel for appointing members of his party, PDP-LABAN, to the majority of OIC positions. The military leadership, which was much more restrained in reshuffling its local commands, expressed concern about the destabilizing effect of the massive and sometimes arbitrary changes.

On 12 March Aquino froze the funds, assets, and properties of Marcos, his family, and business associates. This was the first step in the PCGG's arduous task of discovering and reclaiming the "hidden" and "ill-gotten" wealth of Marcos and his "cronies". By mid-year the PCGG, under the direction of Jovito Salonga, had identified over US$860 million in Marcos assets abroad (out of an estimated US$5–10 billion) and had "sequestered" or temporarily taken over some 200 firms including giants such as San Miguel Breweries and the United Coconut Planters Bank. At year end 268 firms with assets worth $1.1 billion were sequestered.

The new government was also faced with the critical question of what to do about the 200-seat Batasang Pambansa. The options under consideration included establishing a legislative coalition with enough "reformist" KBL MPs to give the pro-Aquino bloc a majority, dissolving the body and electing new members in May, or doing away with the body completely. Despite some promising preliminary discussions between the government and various factions within the rapidly disintegrating KBL, the government eventually decided it was necessary to begin with a completely clean state. On 25 March, after one month in office, Aquino issued Presidential Proclamation Number 3 establishing an interim "freedom constitution" that gave the president virtually unlimited powers and abolished the Batasan. The Aquino government, according to Justice Minister Neptali Gonzalez, was "revolutionary in origin, democratic in essence and transitory in nature". In response to their sudden unemployment, a group of KBL MPs and several previously "opposition" MPs announced their intention to convene a "rebel parliament" in April. Former Labour Minister Blas Ople exclaimed, "This is an act of revolt and we are ready to be arrested and jailed." But his bravado, and the self-righteous cries of injustice by the other leaders of the discredited Batasan, rang hollow in the ears of most Filipinos and the rump parliament movement eventually fizzled out.

In mid-April, Aquino moved to cleanse another Marcos tainted institution by swearing in ten new Supreme Court justices and setting into motion a review of all judicial appointments. Justice Claudio Teehankee, a Marcos appointee who became known for his independent opinions (and for this reason was passed over twice by Marcos to head the court), was appointed Chief Justice. Later in the year, the court reviewed the December 1985 Sandiganbayan acquittal of Ver and his other co-defendants in the Aquino-Galman murder trial, and declared a mis-trial, setting in motion new legal proceedings against the original defendants.

On 25 May, three months after coming to power, Aquino took perhaps her most important step in shaping the country's political future when she announced the appointment of forty-four people to a commission to draft a new constitution. Although lawyers were preponderant, the commission included representatives of almost every major group in the Philippines, from the Catholic Church to farmers and labour unions. Five appointments were left to be filled by the KBL and one by the Iglesia Ni Kristo, an independent religion that had consistently supported Marcos.

When the Constitutional Commission (CONCOM) convened on 2 June, only four former-KBL members, lead by Blas Ople, agreed to join, while the Iglesia Ni Kristo declined to be represented, making for a total membership of 48 commissioners. Justice Cecilia Munoz-Palma, President-elect of the Commission, described the group's task as "to pick up and sort out the broken pieces of our shattered democracy". The task would prove to be an exhausting one, with the group deliberating on a wide range of issues from the appropriate form of legislature to the constitutionality of abortion and the presence of U.S. bases. Although blocs formed and changed depending on the issues under consideration, the commission's output bore the mark of its moderate reformist majority.

By 5 June, the 100th day of the Aquino administration, the broad thrusts of the new government had begun to emerge. So too had many of its problems and contradictions. To its credit the Aquino government had faithfully restored individual, political, and press freedoms, and through the initiation of the Constitutional Commission, had begun the process of building new democratic institutions. It had also reached an agreement with the communist National Democratic Front (NDF) to begin ceasefire talks, but only after it belatedly realized that the majority of the 22,000 armed members of the New People's Army (NPA) were not going to "come down from the hills" simply because of the change in government.

The Aquino government, however, often seemed paralysed by indecision and internal disagreements — even though the "Freedom Constitution" gave it powers equal to or greater than those possessed by Marcos. Tensions had grown between Enrile and the left of centre Ministers such as Executive Secretary Joker Arroyo over the government's policy of seeking reconciliation with the communists. Additionally, the rift continued to grow between Laurel and Pimentel over the appointment of OICs. Finally, a heated debate over the scope and speed of import liberalization erupted between Solita Monsod and Jose Concepcion.

Progress on key socio-economic issues was frustratingly slow. Although the government's economic programme called for a reduced role for the government in the economy, it became clear that the government would have to take an active and leading role in stimulating demand if an economic recovery was to begin. And although Aquino had called for major reforms during the election, it became apparent that her government was not prepared to take quick action on controversial issues such as land reform.

As the Aquino coalition grappled with its own inherent disunity other centrifugal forces were at work in the Philippine political universe. Perhaps most dramatic was the rapid disintegration of the ruling KBL party following the departure of Marcos. Even though Marcos "loyalists" continued to stage noisy and sometimes violent weekly rallies in Manila, the thin veneer of KBL unity quickly disappeared. With the change of government the more pragmatic KBL leaders saw the necessity of breaking with Marcos and began to form their own political organizations. On 15 March, forty-four KBL officials led by Blas Ople formed the Partido Nacionalista ng Philipinas (PNP). With the creation of PNP they openly broke with Marcos and offered "critical co-operation" to the Aquino government. By late March the number of KBL leaders joining PNP had grown to about seventy and at least two other emergent factions threatened to fragment the party further. The moribund Nacionalista Party (NP) was also revitalized by Renato Cayetano, a former MP and close associate of Enrile, increasing speculation that it would become Enrile's new party.

At the same time that the right was regrouping, so was the left. On the far left, the CPP went through a Chinese-style self-criticism to assess why it had misjudged the revolutionary potential of the election and to plan steps to improve its tarnished image as leader of revolutionary forces in the Philippines. Significantly, it concluded that it had not been flexible enough in its willingness to enter into temporary coalitions or united fronts with non-communist but nationalist groups. Following their release in March former political prisoners such as Jose Ma. Sison and Ed de la Torre became instant celebrities and began to form their own socialist and democratic socialist parties. BAYAN (Bagong Alyansang Makabayan), the umbrella organization representing 1,000 left-leaning "cause-oriented" groups that claim membership of two million, also sought to recoup its losses caused by the boycott of the election. Taking advantage of the unprecedented "democratic space" available under Aquino, BAYAN recast itself into a political party, the Partido ng Bayan, and set its sights on mobilizing grass-roots support in preparation for the 1987 constitutional plebiscite and local elections.

Living with the Military ...

If the first half of the year was marked by the steps taken by the new government to consolidate its power in the face of the threats posed by the remnants of the Marcos regime, then much of the second half of the year was dominated by a search for a *modus vivendi* between the civilian and the military leadership. The tensions between the new civilian leadership and the military were rooted in the politicization of much of the military under Marcos. Furthermore, the unexpected joining of the opposition with elements of the military in February had thrust the two groups together without the benefit of time or preparation. The new civilian leaders, many of whom had suffered at the hands of the military during martial law, or had defended Filipinos whose human rights had been violated by the military, had a deep distrust of the military. Conversely, a number of the leaders of the New Armed Forces of the Philippines or NAFP (as it had been renamed) had little respect for some members of the new government whom they viewed as anti-military, left-leaning, or simply naïve. The military's concerns were reinforced by the new government's release of captured communist leaders and by the establishment of a commission headed by former senator and human rights activist Jose Diokno to investigate alleged human rights violations by the military, particularly since no similar action had been taken to investigate alleged human rights violations by the communists themselves.

Further complicating matters was the lack of cohesion within the NAFP caused by the realignment of factions following the revolution and the retirement and reshuffling of much of the senior command. At mid-year, divisions existed between units that had participated in the February revolt and units that had resisted it, between groups that accepted the legitimacy of the new government and those that did not, and between factions of the now influential RAM movement that were loyal to Enrile and factions that were loyal to Ramos.

All of these tensions surged to the surface during the "Manila Hotel Incident" of 6–8 July. On Sunday, 6 July, following the weekly loyalist rally at Luneta Park in Manila, Arturo Tolentino and a group of loyalists moved to the nearby Manila Hotel. There Tolentino proceeded to publicly take an oath as Acting President of the Philippines and offered the posts of Prime Minister and Defence Minister to Enrile. Tolentino's quixotic bid for power was backed, in an apparently premeditated fashion, by 200–300 heavily armed troops from bases outside of Manila under the command of fifteen serving or recently retired senior officers. On Sunday evening a tense stand-off developed as the loyalists occupied the luxurious hotel and government troops created a cordon sanitaire around it.

Enrile negotiated on behalf of the government in the absence of Aquino and other senior officials who were visiting the southern city of Davao. He announced that he was not interested in joining Tolentino but that he was prepared to forgive and forget the incident in the interest of the unity of the NAFP. On Monday, once it became clear that Emile did not support Tolentino's escapade and that there was little popular support for the loyalists, the rebel troops began to surrender. Early Tuesday morning Tolentino and his cohorts were allowed to slip out of the hotel and by noon the hotel was vacated.

Upon returning to their barracks the rebel troops were meted a "punishment" of thirty push-ups. In order to avoid being charged with sedition, they were also required to pledge allegiance to the "freedom constitution" and so on 28 July the entire NAFP participated in a mass pledge of allegiance led by Emile and Ramos. With that the government closed the book on the incident, preferring not to press the case against Tolentino and several of the other loyalist leaders who refused to pledge allegiance to a constitution they did not consider legitimate.

The incident at the Manila Hotel ended peacefully and consequently had a comic cast to it. The absurdity of occupying (and also plundering) the venerable hotel discredited — perhaps irrevocably — Tolentino and his loyalist followers. But it also had an ominous side to it. Many of the soldiers involved claimed afterwards that they had joined the hapless coup because they had heard reports that Emile was one of the leaders. Many also said that they had joined in response to what they viewed as the Aquino government's leniency towards the communists. These comments indicated the military's growing disenchantment with the civilian government and the key role Emile played as broker between the military and the government. Although the public, in Filipino fashion, tried its best to laugh away the incident, the spectre of a military coup had been released and would continue to haunt the national psyche for the rest of the year.

... And Talking to the Communists

In the midst of this growing unease and in the face of continuing NPA-NAFP hostilities, government and National Democratic Front (NDF) representatives began formal cease-fire negotiations on 5 August. Agriculture Minister Ramon Mitra and former Senator Jose Diokno were the government's negotiators. Representing the NDF, the Communist Party dominated umbrella organization for twelve "peoples organizations", were Satur Ocampo, NDF Chairman, and Antonio Zumel, from the CPP Central Committee. Later, Commission on Audit Chairman Teofisto Guingona joined the government panel when Diokno went to the United States for cancer treatment.

At issue was the future of the seventeen-year-old armed insurgency being waged by the communist New People's Army. The NPA, by mid-1986 had grown to between 22,000 and 23,000 armed regulars with a base of supporters estimated to be anywhere from one to two million in size. Philippine and U.S. military specialists estimated that the NPA "influenced" about 20 per cent of the country's 40,000 villages, meaning that at least occasional "revolutionary" indoctrination, taxation, and justice were administered by the NPA or CPP. The CPP claimed that it "controlled" about 25 per cent of all villages and had nominal control over parts of several large cities such as the Agdao section of Davao City. Whatever the differences in estimates, there was no doubt that the insurgency was growing and threatened the government's control of large portions of the country from Mindanao to central Luzon.[17]

The Aquino government, perhaps blinded by its own commitment to non-violence, tended to view the insurgents of 1986 as similar to the Hukbalahap communists of the late 1940s and early 1950s. It assumed that the large majority of insurgents had "gone to the hills" in response to the poverty and injustice of the Marcos era and that the reforms promised by the new government, combined with a programme of amnesty and rehabilitation, would bring all but the most hard core of the insurgents back into the fold. However, the continuation, and in some areas intensification, of NPA attacks on the military soon underscored the fact that the insurgency would not be quickly or easily ended. In late September, General Ramos reported 1,489 violent incidents from 1 March to 15 September, of which 70 per cent were said to have been initiated by the NPA. By October only 250 NPA regulars were reported to have surrendered.

The cease-fire talks between the government and the communists became politically desirable to both sides. Aquino was committed philosophically and politically to exhausting all peaceful means for ending the insurgency. Although her willingness to negotiate was criticized by the right, her role as peacemaker was generally well received by the conflict-weary public. Negotiations also demonstrated the civilian government's primacy over the military (which was not represented in the negotiations) and its independence from what was perceived to be Washington's hardline stance.

In the face of Aquino's sincerity and popularity the communists did not want to be perceived as spurning her olive branch. But equally important, the peace talks provided them with new legitimacy, respectability, and publicity. Although their efforts to acquire belligerent status were not successful, the fact that the government was prepared to negotiate with them was recognition of their importance if not of their equal stature. The safe conduct passes provided to Ocampo and Zumel enabled them to participate in interviews with the generally sympathetic Manila media. Soft-spoken and smiling as they explained the CPP's ideology and objectives, they were able to counteract the rightists' shrill warnings that the communists were ruthless, godless murderers intent on seizing power by force.

Just as there were compelling reasons for both sides to enter into negotiations, so too were there reasons for both sides to desire a cease-fire. Aquino had staked her reputation on finding a peaceful solution to the problem. Failure to reach an agreement would have intensified criticism from both the right (for the government's *naïveté* in expecting solutions from negotiations with the communists), and the left (for proving that Aquino was a captive of the hardliners in the military and in Washington). The Aquino government saw a cease-fire as, at best, the beginning of the demilitarization of the conflict or, at worst, as a needed respite that would give the government and the military time to prepare for the resumption of the hostilities.

The communists also felt a cease-fire would be to their advantage, judging from their willingness to give up or moderate a number of their original demands such as for belligerent status and "comprehensive negotiations" as a pre-condition for a cease-fire. Another indication of this was their willingness to return to the negotiating table after the capture of CPP leader Rudolfo Salas on 29 September and the brutal murder of labour leader Rolando Olalia on 12 November. The potential benefits of a cease-fire to the communists seemed to be primarily in the areas of political organization and propaganda, as was later revealed by their campaign of highly visible and sometimes provocative armed parades and rallies.

The Cory Constitution

At the same time that the government was talking with the NDF, the Constitutional Commission (CONCOM) was slowly piecing together a document that was likely to shape the country's political affairs for years to come.[18] After taking more than a week to agree upon the seventy-one word preamble, the Commission's pace picked up and by early August the outline of the proposed future government had emerged. So too had a major split between the Commission's "nationalist" minority and the centrist majority.

Perhaps the most important decision made by the commission was the selection by just one vote of an American-style presidential system with a bicameral legislature instead of a parliamentary system. The president, vice-president, and twenty-four senators are to be selected in national elections every six years. Local elections to fill the 250-seat lower house will be held every three years. In reaction to Marcos' twenty-year rule, future presidents beginning with Aquino are limited to one term in office. As one of its last acts, the commission fixed the terms of Aquino and Laurel until 30 June 1992 and set 11 May 1987 as the date for national legislative elections.

Other key provisions place numerous restrictions on the president's use of martial law powers, establish an independent judiciary, make all types of croplands subject to land reform but leave implementation to Congress, allow regional autonomy for the Muslim and Cordillera peoples, guarantee universal secondary school education, prohibit capital punishment and abortion, require that any future agreements permitting foreign bases be ratified by the Senate and subjected to a plebiscite, and ban nuclear weapons in the Philippines but with the key and open-ended proviso that it be done "consistent with national defense".

Almost as revealing as what is contained in the new Constitution is what is not. Deleted was language in the preamble of the 1973 Constitution that had been interpreted as a Philippine claim to the Malaysian state of Sabah. Reflecting the strong influence of Catholicism on the Commission, a provision in the 1973 Constitution that gave the state responsibility for setting and achieving population growth targets also was eliminated. Also rejected by the majority of commissioners were "nationalist" efforts to forbid or significantly reduce foreign ownership in certain industries, to guarantee "direct and indirect protectionism" for local industry and agriculture, to implement sweeping land reform, and to ban foreign military bases.

On 12 October, a month and a half late, the Commission approved the 109-page final draft by a vote of 44 to 2. Political scientist and columnist Alex Magno, a self-styled "critical ratificationist", offered this description of the document:

> ... it is a conscious repudiation of the preceding dictatorship.... There are flashes of surprising progressivity in the draft charter. But these are reined in by the phraseology of conservative restraint.... All potentially explosive provisions were left to the congress to sort out.... It is as if the conservatives and progressives intentionally left things hanging so that they could clash another day.[19]

When the draft charter was presented to her on 15 October Aquino said, "Democracy is safe with this constitution." She might have added that the tenure and authority of her government would be protected, too. To ensure the passage of the Constitution prominent Aquino supporters led by Justice Minister Neptali Gonzales on 8 November formally launched Lakas ng Bansa (LAKAS), an "umbrella organization" that seemed destined to evolve into Aquino's political party. After characteristic vacillation, Laurel and UNIDO also gave their qualified support to the charter. Later Cardinal Sin gave his blessing to the document, calling it "unique, perfect and beautiful".

However, other quarters were not as enthusiastic and the charter quickly became a political football. Leftist groups such as Partido ng Bayan and the KMU (Kilusang Mayo Uno or First May Movement) labour union had lobbied hard to have "democratic nationalist" provisions written into the

Constitution so that they could not be blocked by the new legislature, which they assumed would be as conservative as its predecessors. Their hopes frustrated, they criticized the charter's provisions on land reform, foreign ownership, and military bases. The KBL and Nacionalista parties, recognizing that the document would firmly establish the Aquino government for the next five years, vowed to campaign against it, condemning it as partisan, socialist, and pacifist. The Filipino people would have less than four months to consider the strengths and weaknesses of the charter — and the implications of its rejection for the Aquino government's stability — before voting on it in a nation-wide plebiscite scheduled for 2 February.

Rambo, RAM Boys, and Ramos

The beginning of negotiations with the communists, the slow but significant progress of the Constitutional Commission and the success of Aquino's mid-September visit to the United States set the stage for the next and final drama of the already melodramatic year: Emile's confrontation with Aquino. During the months after the revolution the 62-year-old minister continued to enjoy considerable public popularity because of his role in unseating Marcos and because he was perceived to be a smart and tough leader. But he also had been one of the chief architects of martial law and the official Cory Aquino had to appeal to in order to visit her imprisoned husband. As such, Enrile's personal and political relations with Aquino and the majority of her cabinet were destined to be strained.

Enrile disclaimed any desire to replace Aquino as president, but was reported to envision himself as the key power-broker in the Cabinet because of his considerable following among the right and the military. However, as the months passed, there were reports that Aquino's inner circle of advisors increasingly had excluded Enrile from the decision-making process. Whether it was in response to this ostracism, or because he wanted to force a dramatic change in the Aquino Cabinet's composition and policies, or as the first step in a calculated plan to seize power, by early September it became clear that Enrile had decided to challenge Aquino. In a much publicized speech he threatened that he might soon lose his patience, and said that when he did he was "like Rambo", the trigger-happy, grenade-throwing renegade soldier of the American movies. Throughout most of September and into October, Enrile became more and more vocal in his criticisms of the government's shortcomings and in particular its willingness to negotiate with the communists while the NPA continued to attack the Armed Forces.

In October Enrile's campaign intensified as he charged, among other things, that Aquino "threw away" her mandate when she dissolved the 1973 Constitution. His continued outspokenness led to rumours of a "show-down" at the cabinet meeting scheduled for 22 October, prompting Vice-President and Foreign Minister Laurel to cancel a trip to an ASEAN-EEC meeting in Jakarta in order to make himself available as a mediator. However, on the night of the 21st, while the Manila press waited breathlessly for the following day's bloodbath, Aquino and Enrile met with a handful of close advisers to discuss their differences. Enrile reportedly asked Aquino to replace eight cabinet members, reconvene the Batasan, reinstate most local officials, and set a deadline for the cease-fire negotiations. Aquino agreed to impose a cease-fire deadline and to sack incompetent, absentee, or pro-communist OICs. At the cabinet meeting the following day it was business as usual. The crisis was temporarily defused.

After a brief "cease-talk" however, Enrile was soon on the offensive again, criticizing the government in front of a predominantly loyalist rally on 26 October. Enrile's campaign was viewed with sufficient concern by the U.S. Government to prompt Washington to publicly declare on 29 October its "complete and unequivocable" support for the Aquino government and to privately communicate its displeasure to Enrile.

The buffeting of the Aquino government intensified in November, a month that began to resemble the chaotic period before the imposition of martial law in 1972. The month started with a spate of bomb explosions in Manila. This was later followed by three political assassinations and the kidnapping of a senior expatriate Japanese businessman. All the while, rumours of a possible coup by members of the RAM movement loyal to Enrile added to the atmosphere of crisis and loss of control.

Ironically, the month had begun on a hopeful note when, on 1 November, the NDF made a major concession to the government by expressing its willingness to agree to a temporary cease-fire in advance of "comprehensive negotiations" and tabled a proposal for a 100-day cease-fire beginning on 10 December. But as the prospects for a truce brightened, disgruntled elements in the military and other extremist opponents of the Aquino government intensified their efforts to destabilize the government. On 5 November reports surfaced in the Manila press of an imminent military plot, entitled "God Save the Queen", that involved a "surgical strike" against the government to force a major revamping of the Cabinet. The ultimate objectives apparently were the elimination of leftist influences in the government and a significant diminution in the power of Aquino. In response, Ramos, in a significant show of support for the Aquino government, warned "adventurers" in the military against carrying out the plan. On 9 November, on the eve of a three-day trip to Japan, Aquino declared, "This queen doesn't want to be saved," and warned that she would call for her supporters to take to the streets if a coup were attempted.

Aquino's trip to Tokyo provided no respite from the crisis. On 12 November the horribly mutilated bodies of KMU President and Partido ng Bayan Vice-Chairman, Rolando Olalia, and his driver were found outside Manila. A general strike called by the KMU to protest the murders was not widely followed, but some 300,000 workers and students joined the Olalia funeral procession as it wound its way through Manila. In a further blow to the government, the day after Aquino returned from Tokyo the Japanese head of Mitsui in the Philippines was kidnapped and was still missing at year end.

Events came to a head over the weekend of 22–23 November. Malacañang received reports that at least 100 members of RAM were preparing to take over the Batasang Pambansa building and key communications centres, reinstate the legislature, and call for new presidential elections. General Ramos went on radio and television to notify all military personnel to disregard any orders that did not come from the normal chain of command, and particularly any orders from Col. Gregorio "Gringo" Honasan, one of the founders of RAM and Emile's chief security officer. On Sunday morning Aquino called an emergency cabinet meeting at which the crisis was discussed and it was agreed that the entire Cabinet would offer to resign. Later that afternoon Enrile, who had not attended the cabinet session, offered his resignation to Aquino during a short meeting. She promptly accepted it and appointed General Rafael "Rocky" Ileto, Enrile's deputy and a respected former ambassador, the new Minister of National Defence.

Four days later, on 27 November, the country's sense of relief was further bolstered by the signing of an agreement with the NDF for a sixty-day preliminary cease-fire to run from 10 December to 8 February 1987. The next day, in an anti-climatic response to her pledge to "start anew", Aquino announced her acceptance of the resignations of just two of her cabinet members: Ernesto Maceda, Minister of Natural Resources, and Rogaciano Mercado, Minister of Public Works. Neither resignation generated much political controversy as both men were widely thought to have indulged in the corruption endemic to the ministries they headed. However, in another reshuffle on 3 December, Pimentel was removed as head of local governments and named Minister of National Affairs. And on 10 December, in a move that provoked the ire of the left, Aquino announced that her controversial Labour Minister, Augusto Sanchez, would also resign by the end of the year.

The Philippines' two-week Christmas holiday began in mid-December and with it the year effectively came to a close. The end of the year brought the start of a fragile and controversial cease-fire, a new role for Enrile as head of the Nacionalista Party, and a temporary respite for the Aquino government. And from Honolulu Imelda Marcos tearfully proclaimed, "We will return to serve again the small, the needy, and the poor." Amid the year-end revelry Filipinos looked back on 1986 with an equal mixture of exhaustion and exhilaration and tried to catch their breath before the new year brought a round of new challenges.

Conclusion

Nineteen eighty-six was a year of great, but incomplete and uneven, change in the Philippines. It is clear that it was a year of political transition away from the authoritarianism of Ferdinand Marcos' regime. But it is not clear in what direction the process of change ultimately will lead. Will the Aquino government be able to formulate and successfully implement moderate reforms that satisfy the majority of Filipinos who are impoverished, without seriously alienating the small but powerful élite? Will the new Philippine leadership have the political will and the resources to address head-on fundamental problems afflicting the country such as the unequal distribution of land and income, rapid population growth, and an inefficient economy? And failing this, is it possible that Philippine society will abandon its traditional conservatism and opt for the radical change advocated by the left?

Also unclear is what other elements of Philippine society, if any, have had their values and behaviour permanently transformed by the February election and subsequent non-violent revolution. Preliminary indications suggest that the changes of 1986 may not be as widespread or as lasting as some might hope. But a more definitive judgement must await two tests in 1987: the constitutional plebiscite on 2 February and the national legislative elections scheduled for 11 May. These contests will reveal the level of President

Aquino's popularity after one year in office and will test the Aquino camp's ability to build a political organization to rival the parties of the left and right. But equally important, the manner in which these two political exercises are conducted will give the first concrete indications of whether the unseating of Marcos has begun a new, more genuinely democratic, era in Philippine politics or, instead, has left intact the country's traditional politics based on patronage and narrow self-interest.

Notes

1. By year end more than twenty-five daily newspapers and weekly magazines were vying for readers in Metro Manila, with only a minority of the publications profitable.
2. For a review of Philippine affairs in 1985, see Robert Youngblood, "The Philippines in 1985: A Continuing Crisis of Confidence", in *Southeast Asian Affairs 1986* (Singapore: Institute of Southeast Asian Studies, 1986) or Eduardo Lachica, "The Philippines: A Critical Transition", in *Asian Issues 1985* (Lanham, MD: University Press of America, 1986). For a review and assessment of the entire Marcos era, see John Bresnan, ed., *Crisis in the Philippines: The Marcos Era and Beyond* (Princeton: Princeton University Press, 1986).
3. U.S. Senate Select Committee on Intelligence, *The Philippines: A Situation Report* (Washington, DC: US Government Printing Office, 1985).
4. Also contesting the election were former Senator Eva Kalaw, who ran for vice-president under her wing of the Liberal Party, and Reuben Canoy, who ran for president under the banner of the Social Democratic Party.
5. See Jonathan Kolatch, "Could There Have Been a Revolution Without Television?", *Manila Sunday Times Magazine* (reprinted from TV Guide), 29 June 1986, p. 22 and 6 July 1986, p. 24.
6. US Congressman Stephen Solarz was less concerned about maintaining an air of impartiality. During the final week of the campaign his Sub-Committee on East Asian and Pacific Affairs held widely publicized hearings to investigate charges that Marcos and his wife had purchased US$350 million in New York real estate.
7. Kolatch, op. cit., 6 July 1986, p. 24.
8. *New York Times*, 8 February 1986, p. 10. See also Robert Shaplen, "From Marcos to Aquino", *New Yorker*, 25 August 1986, p. 33 and 1 September 1986, p. 36.
9. For a detailed analysis of the conduct of the election see the U.S. observer delegation's final report: U.S. Senate Committee on Foreign Relations, *Report on the February 7, 1986 Presidential Election in the Philippines* (Washington, D.C.: U.S. Government Printing Office, 1986).
10. Colourful accounts of the election and revolution are given in James Fenton, "Snap Revolution", *Granta*, no. 18 (Spring 1986): 33–109; Cecilio Arillo, *Break Away* (Manila: CTA & Associates, 1986); *Bayan Ko!* (Hong Kong: Asia 2000, Ltd., 1986); Al McCoy, Gwen Robinson, and Marian Wilkinson, "How the February Revolt was Planned", *Philippine Sunday Inquirer*, 5 October 1986, p. 1 and 12 October 1986, p. 1; and Shaplen, op. cit.
11. A paper prepared anonymously, reportedly for the Catholic Bishops' Conference, and widely circulated at the time of the election listed five "post-election scenarios", none of which foresaw a military-civilian revolt against Marcos. Instead the scenarios were: the re-imposition of martial law or the staging of a pro-Marcos military coup; Marcos victory, either through massively fraudulent or relatively clean elections;

12. Shaplen, op. cit., 1 September 1986, p. 46.
13. The *New York Times* reported on 25 February 1986 (p. 141) that Enrile's admission of government-sponsored election fraud was a "turning point" in the White House's decision to call for Marcos to step down.
14. See Paul Laxalt, "My Conversations With Ferdinand Marcos: A Lesson in Personal Diplomacy", *Policy Review*, Summer 1986, pp. 2–5.
15. For thoughtful assessments of the challenges facing the Aquino government see the report of an Asia Society study mission entitled *The Philippines: Facing the Future* (New York: The Asia Society, 1986); and Carl Lande and Richard Hooley, "Aquino Takes Charge", *Foreign Affairs*, Summer 1986, pp. 1087–107.
16. In addition to UNIDO and PDP-LABAN, the Aquino coalition included the Liberal Party (Salonga wing), the Mindanao Alliance headed by Homobono Adaza, and the Muslim Federal Party.
17. For differing views on the nature of the communist insurgency see William Branigan, "The Rebels May Be Communists, but They're Not the VC", *Washington Post* (National Weekly Edition), 25 November 1985, p. 16; Ross Monro, "The Kew Khmer Rouge", *Commentary*, December 1985, pp. 19–38; Steve Lohr, "Inside the Philippine Insurgency", *New York Times Magazine*, 3 November 1985, pp. 40–60; and the U.S. Senate Committee on Foreign Relations, *Situation in the Philippines* (Washington, D.C.: U.S. Government Printing Office, 1984).
18. For a helpful comparison of the 1986 draft constitution with previous constitutions, see *The Constitution of the Republic of the Philippines* (Manila: National Bookstore. Inc., 1986).
19. Alex Magno, "Reconciling with a Yellow Charter", *Newday Magazine*, 10 November 1986, p. 4.

Aquino wins but Marcos refuses to step down; and Aquino wins and Marcos concedes.

TERRORISM
Evolving Regional Alliances and State Failure in Mindanao

Kit Collier

The death of Azahari bin Husin in a shoot-out with Indonesian police near the East Java town of Malang on 9 November 2005 was widely acclaimed as the most important victory against the regional terror group Jemaah Islamiyah (JI) since the capture of Hambali.[1] But it became increasingly clear during the year that Malaysian-born Dr Azahari — known as the "Demolition Man" for his skills in assembling the first Bali bombs that killed 202 three years earlier — did not answer to the JI hierarchy and was operating as his own man. Indeed, in 2005 it became obvious that old ways of thinking about JI and regional terrorism were no longer adequate — if they ever were in the first place.

The dominant model, perpetuated in the media by prominent commentators Rohan Gunaratna and Zachary Abuza, views JI as an al-Qaeda franchise, with a clearly demarcated command structure and organizational boundaries, dedicated to the establishment of an Islamic caliphate embracing much of Southeast Asia. To the extent this image was ever valid, as Sidney Jones points out, it represents a five-year-old "snapshot" of JI with little relevance today.[2] A fluid pattern of alignment and realignment between autonomous jihadi factions characterized the terrorist threat in 2005, and this trend is likely to strengthen in the future.

What knits these factions loosely together is not "a very horizontal and exceptionally compartmentalized organization" with a "very rigid cell structure", as Abuza insisted after Bali's second series of suicide bombings on 1 October 2005,[3] but a shared world-view based on personal

---

Reprinted from Daljit Singh and Lorraine C. Salazar, eds., *Southeast Asian Affairs 2006* (Singapore: Institute of Southeast Asian Studies, 2006), pp. 26–38. At the time of original publication, Kit Collier was Consultant to the International Crisis Group and Visiting Fellow at the Research School of Pacific and Asian Studies, Australian National University.

allegiances forged in exile, training camps on the Afghan border, or the conflict zones of Sulawesi, Maluku, and — looking forward — Mindanao. Gunaratna has even declared Mindanao the "new strategic base of Jemaah Islamiyah", but like Abuza, misperceives the nature of this threat.[4]

This overview examines Mindanao's growing role as *the* regional terrorist crossroads in 2005, but from the perspective of local realities, not externally imposed organigrams. It demonstrates a kaleidoscopic interplay of foreign and domestic jihadi groups only possible in Mindanao's lawless enclaves, where for all practical purposes the Philippine state has failed.

Perspectives on Southeast Asian Terrorism

Carlyle Thayer identifies three basic ways of looking at terrorism in Southeast Asia: from a global, a regional, or a national perspective.[5] The global view rests on an "al-Qaeda-centric paradigm" that places Osama bin Laden at the centre of analysis and evaluates local political violence largely in terms of its purported "links" back to the terrorist mainspring. Gunaratna is the most widely cited exponent of this view, portraying JI as "al-Qaeda's instrument" and "al-Qaeda's Asian arm".[6]

Regional specialists like Abuza take this perspective a step further. While showing more interest in local context and specifics than globalists, Abuza agrees that al-Qaeda "established" JI as "a regional arm of its own", then extends the argument to apply a JI-centric paradigm to developments in Southeast Asia.[7] Like al-Qaeda, JI is seen as an organizational monolith, to be analysed like a wiring diagram. Regionalists are often inattentive to contingency and factionalism, and, for country specialists, their interest in local history and culture seems shallow, unsupported by the necessary learning.[8]

The dominance of global and regional perspectives is partly due to the reluctance of many country specialists to take terrorism seriously as a legitimate field of inquiry. Until the first Bali bombings, prominent Indonesianists downplayed globalists' and regionalists' assertions of an emerging terrorist threat.[9] The latter's often cavalier approach to evidence, sources, and referencing, their lack of area knowledge and languages, and suspicions of intelligence laundering by persons too close to security services for comfort, all help explain the initial scepticism of most country specialists.

But some of them question the value of the entire enterprise. "When it comes to clandestine terrorist activity," asserts Natasha Hamilton-Hart, "scholars and journalists are rarely in a position to contest or add to official information." For Hamilton-Hart, this renders fine-grained examination of terrorist networks "quite pointless".[10] As if in parody of the gross causal attributions favoured by the globalists and regionalists she critiques, Hamilton-Hart regards terrorism as just another form of resistance, best understood in terms of the grievances that — it is assumed — motivate it. Like Abuza's al-Qaeda-centric organigrams, this approach circumvents the active agency of Southeast Asian terrorists themselves, substituting US foreign policy for "militant Islam" as a crude, undifferentiated "root cause".

The worth of cataloguing individual terrorists' movements, contacts, and orders would be dubious indeed if its purpose were merely to demonstrate an author's privileged access to classified information. All the more so if the author lacked the area knowledge to interpret these connections in ways that add meaningful value to a list of names and dates — or even to render such minutiae accurately. But in the hands of appropriately qualified, open-minded country specialists, such details — derived from a variety of government, public, and private sources, and scrupulously cross-checked — become vital clues in understanding the real world, face-to-face relationships that make specific terrorist attacks possible.

JI and the Second Bali Bombings

As CNN viewers have come to expect, the triple suicide bombing of Raja's Café in Kuta and the Nyoman and Menega Cafés in Jimbaran beach, Bali, on the evening of 1 October 2005, which killed 20 innocent bystanders, was soon followed by "expert" pronouncements that JI was "the only group with the intention and the capability" to mount such attacks.[11] This phrase, which is Gunaratna's and Abuza's typical response to major bombings in Indonesia, misses the significance of both the new attack, and of others stretching back more than five years to the attempted car-bomb assassination of the Philippine ambassador in Jakarta — that JI is deeply divided over such operations, which are the initiative of a few ultra-militants drawing on diverse personal networks, not a cohesive corporate entity.

Media consumers may prefer digestible sound bites and familiar faces (bin Laden, Abu Bakar Ba'asyir) symbolizing well-defined organizations with clear international links. But appreciating the true complexity of these networks demands a longer attention span.[12] From the time Ba'asyir took over as *amir* (commander) of JI following the death of co-founder Abdullah Sungkar in 1999, ultras associated with Hambali and the Malaysia-based Mantiqi 1 group rankled at Ba'asyir's vacillating leadership and flirtations with open mass politics. The majority around JI's Java-based Mantiqi 2, on the other hand, became increasingly uneasy with the consequences of the ultras' bombing campaign, in which Ba'asyir acquiesced. These internal tensions mounted with successive attacks on Bali (12 October 2002), the Jakarta Marriott Hotel (5 August 2003), and Australian Embassy (9 September 2004), all causing Muslim casualties and prompting a police crackdown that has crippled JI's formal structures.[13]

Like the Marriott and embassy attacks, the second Bali bombings were masterminded by the Malaysians, Azahari and Noordin Mohammed Top, who relied on personal networks to recruit operatives, not the JI command structure. The embassy suicide bomber, Heri Golun, was drawn into the plot through a West Java splinter group of Darul Islam (DI), known as the Banten Ring — as was the operation's field commander, Irwan Dharmawan, alias Rois, sentenced to death by a Jakarta court in September 2005. The three Bali II suicide bombers, identified as Salik Firdaus, Aip Hidayat, and Misno, appear to have belonged to yet another DI faction that kept its distance from more renowned leaders. The three are said to be quite unknown to JI prisoners shown their photographs.[14]

Like Rois, the suspected leaders of this faction, Muhammad Akram and his deputy, Enceng Kurnia, owe their web of contacts to shared experiences in Poso (Central Sulawesi), and Ambon (Maluku), where autonomous DI groups, notably Mujahidin KOMPAK, were quicker to exploit communal conflict after 1998 than JI's ponderous bureaucracy.[15] These continue to foment discord in alliance with

JI — but not under its command. A raid on a paramilitary police post on Ceram island, Maluku, in May 2005, and marketplace bombings in Tentena (near Poso) in May and Palu, Central Sulawesi, in December, were all likely ad hoc attacks drawing on men with a variety of organizational affiliations.[16] Here, too, a rigid hierarchical model provides little insight into dynamics on the ground.

The distinction between Azahari and Top's bombers and the mainstream JI leadership crystallized in January 2006, when Indonesian national police chief General Sutanto announced that Top had formed an organization of his own — Tanzim Qaedat al-Jihad.[17] This is probably a formalization of the pair's existing network hitherto known as *Thoifah Muqatilah*, composed of younger militants inspired by direct action against Western targets.[18] Mainstream opinion in JI questions the legitimacy of such attacks outside Indonesia's conflict areas, focusing instead on the need to build up the organization's ideological and military strength for a decisive confrontation with the Indonesian state in 25 to 30 years' time.

What the bombers and the mainstream group do share is a commitment to passing on the lethal skills of a generation of Afghan veterans decimated by the regional wave of arrests since late 2001, when JI was first unveiled in Singapore. Communal conflicts in eastern Indonesia were intended to create a secure base area (*qoidah aminah*) where sharia law could be applied in an embryonic Islamic state, and more fighters could be trained. During the short post-Soeharto transition to democracy, some armed forces elements had enough interest in destabilization to allow jihadis a free hand. As Susilo Bambang Yudhoyono continues to consolidate Indonesia's traditionally strong bureaucratic state, however, space to train is increasingly constricted. Militants must look beyond Indonesia for safe haven, to the lawless enclaves of the southern Philippines.

Finding New Partners in Mindanao

Conventional globalist and regionalist accounts of Mindanao's role in Southeast Asian terrorism provide as outdated a snapshot as their image of JI, again assuming a world of clearly bounded organizations. In fact, numerous arrests — mostly by Indonesian and Malaysian authorities — have smashed the Mantiqi 3 structure that managed JI activity in Sulawesi, Kalimantan, Sabah, and the southern Philippines, contributing to the collapse of JI's administrative apparatus in Mindanao, Wakalah Hudaibiyah (WakHud). Its surviving members were forced into closer cooperation with local insurgents in 2005, as well as with "freelance" Indonesian and Malaysian jihadis operating outside what remains of the JI command structure. The resulting pattern of blurred organizational distinctions and new alliances was further complicated by factional rivalries within Southeast Asia's strongest secessionist group, the Moro Islamic Liberation Front (MILF).

Chronic insurgency is the most visible symptom of state failure in Mindanao, a condition described by America's top diplomat in Manila in April 2005 as "the next Afghanistan".[19] As the International Crisis Group observes, the MILF rebellion is "powerful enough to limit state capacity in much of the South, yet so decentralised that what ensues is not a shadow government, but pockets of anarchy".[20] Some of these enclaves are presided over by rebel commanders who continued to shelter foreign jihadis during the year, threatening a delicately poised peace process that holds the only real hope for long-term stability in this increasingly important regional terrorist sanctuary.

While Gunaratna ignores the MILF's indigenous dynamics, portraying the movement as a corporate subsidiary of al-Qaeda, Abuza insists that it is "a more unitary organization than it is given credit for", and that internal factionalism is not significant enough to "hamper decision-making".[21] Events in 2005 take on an even more worrying cast from this perspective than in the light of Crisis Group's assessment, for it implies that the MILF's central leadership with whom Manila is negotiating actively approves of commanders' ongoing terror ties — notwithstanding those leaders' official disavowals.

JI's formal links with the MILF date back to 1994, when late MILF chairman Salamat Hashim approved a proposal to relocate JI's training facilities from Afghanistan to Camp Abu Bakar, the MILF's headquarters in Mindanao.[22] This arrangement began to disintegrate after Philippine armed forces overran Camp Abu Bakar in July 2000, but what replaced it was a more dispersed pattern of mobile facilities, more difficult for the government to pinpoint and for MILF leaders to control.[23] At the same time, WakHud head Ahmad Faisal, alias Zulkifli, sanctioned an increasingly intimate relationship with Kadaffy Janjalani's Abu Sayyaf Group (ASG), diversifying JI's refuge and operational options.[24]

In 2004–2005, these included joint training between JI, ASG, and freelance jihadis, under MILF protection, together with members of a volatile new group — the Rajah Solaiman Movement (RSM), militant Filipino converts to Islam who have carried out two successful bombings in Manila and plotted several more.[25] On Valentine's Day 2005, a bus bomb in the capital's business district was coordinated with two near-simultaneous blasts in Davao City and General Santos City, killing eight. The attacks demonstrated that "structural" elements of JI identified with WakHud could still reach out to strike urban centres even in the Philippines' northern heartland — but only with the aid of an expanding roster of local partners, exposing JI to new security risks.[26]

Dulmatin, Freelance Jihad, and Creeping US Intervention

The US announcement within a week of Bali II of a US$10 million reward for the capture of Dulmatin, a prime suspect in the first Bali bombings, drew renewed attention to Mindanao and, in particular, the growing role of freelance jihadis there. Dulmatin had fled Central Sulawesi, moving through Tawau, Sabah, to the southern Philippines in April 2003, two months after his Bali co-conspirator Umar Patek made use of the same DI contact to escape increasingly effective law enforcement in the would-be *qoidah aminah*. Once in Mindanao, the duo established an independent relationship with Kadaffy Janjalani, who had also sought refuge on the mainland from joint US-Philippine military activity in the ASG's traditional Sulu archipelago stronghold. They began instructing recruits in MILF territory in Palimbang, Sultan Kudarat province, as part of a joint DI-KOMPAK training programme.[27]

This programme was run by a former head of KOMPAK in Ambon, Abdullah Sonata, captured in Jakarta in July 2005. Sonata is indicative of the independent mindedness of the new generation of freelancers, for he is said to have declared a formal "split" with Dr Azahari over the issue of suicide attacks in non-conflict areas (thus siding with the Mantiqi 2 mainstream, though Sonata is not himself JI). Yet he also worked closely with Umar Patek to bring suicide recruits for training in the Philippines.[28] These included members of Muhammad Akram's DI faction that furnished the Bali II suicide bombers.[29]

Dulmatin's US$10 million bounty is second only to those offered for Osama bin Laden and Abu Musab al-Zarqawi, reflecting heightened US strategic concern over Mindanao in the wake of Bali II. But American intervention acquired a new assertiveness a full year before the 1 October atrocities, when a series of air strikes on jihadi targets began. Although executed by Philippine air assets, the strikes were planned jointly on the basis of shared intelligence and observed by US military advisers in the field. In November 2004, January 2005, and again in April 2005, strikes were mounted on a cluster of municipalities in southern Maguindanao province, where a maverick MILF commander, Ameril Umbra, harboured Dulmatin, Patek and Kadaffy Janjalani, as well as "structural" JI elements. Multibattalion ground sweeps followed from July to September, with US advisers again taking part.

This escalation in the Mindanao conflict, regulated by a formal ceasefire since 2003, elicited a surprisingly restrained response from the central MILF leadership. Umbra, also known as Commander Kato, had had a strained relationship with the leadership for at least six years, and in October 2005, just two days after Dulmatin's bounty was announced, his command was publicly "deactivated". This was an unprecedented show of open dissension within the MILF, and the leadership's first indication that it took its obligations to isolate terrorists within its ranks seriously. It remains unclear what substance there is to reports that Kato and his key sub-commanders have actually been disciplined, and whether such action flowed from their known collaboration with Janjalani and Dulmatin, or from pursuing a series of violent private feuds in 2005 that also threatened the ceasefire.[30]

The diplomatic framework for separating the Mindanao conflict from the regional jihad took a leap forward in December 2004, with the long overdue creation of an Ad Hoc Joint Action Group (AHJAG) composed of government and MILF representatives who would share information on terrorist activity in Mindanao. Manila provided the MILF with a list of 32 foreign terrorists it believed were finding sanctuary in the south in April 2005: it consisted of 31 Indonesians and one Malaysian, Zulkifli bin Hir, head of the Kumpulan Mujahidin Malaysia. It is not known what, if any, reciprocal intelligence the MILF has supplied, but in a significant goodwill gesture, several hundred MILF guerrillas were temporarily cantoned in July 2005 to allow counter-terrorist pursuit operations to proceed unhampered. A number of minor skirmishes with MILF forces still occurred, however, and Dulmatin and Janjalani, now working closely together, made good their escape.

American military pressure on the ASG and its foreign jihadi allies, and by extension the MILF, continued to mount into early 2006. "Balikatan" and "Balance Piston" exercises and "Bayanihan" training, civic action and psychological operations were extended from their initial theatres on Basilan island and Zamboanga City (beginning in 2002), to include North Cotabato and the Zamboanga peninsula, and, after a false start in 2003, the island of Jolo. Jolo, cradle of the Philippines' Muslim separatist rebellion and the ASG's principal redoubt, presents an enormous challenge to counter-terrorist strategy in the region, and a crucial opportunity. Among the most volatile of Mindanao's terrorist sanctuaries, its Tausug inhabitants are fiercely independent, and resent Manila's failing 1996 peace agreement with the MNLF. Many also nurture collective memories of US colonial repression a century ago.

Tentative US civic action deployments on Jolo began in September 2005, with full-scale Balikatan manoeuvres scheduled there in February and March 2006. If the exercises follow the pattern of Balikatan '02 on Basilan — dubbed at the time the "second front" in the global war on terror — the American presence may puncture the ASG's psychological grip over the population and begin to fill the vacuum of extra-local authority at the root of state failure. If, on the other hand, the ASG and its foreign jihadi allies decide to confront the Americans, and the US response appears indiscriminate, the former colonial power risks catalysing a new coalition that embraces MNLF and MILF forces, as well as its regional terrorist foes.

Conclusion

Far from being pointless, a detailed, accurate understanding of interpersonal terrorist relationships is fundamental to avoiding the distortions that often arise from both global/regional and country specialist perspectives. These distortions persisted in much of the commentary on Southeast Asian terrorism during 2005. Among the insights generated by more careful research, particularly by Sidney Jones, the following bear consideration by scholars, journalists, and practitioners:

- JI is not "an integral part of al-Qaeda".[31] Its roots are thoroughly Indonesian, and its ultimate objective is an Islamic state in Indonesia. Its ties to al-Qaeda, like those to related offshoots of the DI movement and Moro insurgents, are incarnate in individual associations, not bureaucratic flow charts.

- The history of these individual associations — names and dates, understood in context — is an indispensable guide to the shifting, often ad hoc, alliances between autonomous jihadi factions. After kinship, the most resilient ties cutting across organizational boundaries are built during shared, formative experiences in exile, training camps, and combat.

- Terrorist and insurgent organizations in Southeast Asia resemble bundles of personal associations more than integral corporate bodies. They are riven by internal rivalries, and members of one group may be closer to like-minded members of another than to their nominal comrades. This makes for constant flux as individuals break away and recombine in new associations. Practitioners need a keen awareness of these tendencies if they hope to defeat organized terror, not inadvertently strengthen it.

- "It's not just JI".[32] Although it has become a convenient shorthand for the terrorist threat in Indonesia, JI in its strict organizational sense may be less of a danger here and now than at any other time since 2002. As more Mantiqi 2 mainstreamers fill the shoes of detained ultras, the immediate threat, to Western targets in particular, comes

from freelancers who may not answer to JI at all.
- Despite its Indonesian roots, JI's extended family is much more than an Indonesian phenomenon. Media coverage often remained trapped in a parochial national framework in 2005, as the familiar litany of past outrages — Bali I, Marriott, Australian Embassy — was reinvoked as background to Bali II. Almost universally overlooked were the Filipino victims of JI-related bombings — General Santos, Davao, Superferry, Manila — who now rival in number those killed in Indonesia.[33]
- Equally artificial is a notion of state failure defined by national boundaries. Unlike Afghanistan, the Philippines is not a failed state, but it encompasses impenetrable enclaves within which transnational terrorists continue to find sanctuary, weaving their cause into those of local insurgents with widespread support.
- These sanctuaries in the southern Philippines remain the weakest link in the entire regional counter-terrorist effort. Effective law enforcement in the stronger states of the region — Indonesia, Malaysia, and Singapore — has driven their jihadis out of preferred safe havens and would-be base areas, and into the arms of Moro militants. A new generation of Indonesian terrorists bred on the battlefields of Mindanao probably already outnumbers Indonesia's Afghan veterans, and will pose a continuing danger for years to come.

Finally, fine-grained analysis of actual processes of terrorist mobilization helps to temper popular myths on both the left and right. Suicide bombings are conscious acts of human agency. They require painstaking planning, logistics, and coordination. Tracing these acts in all their deliberate murderousness should put paid to outlandish and destabilizing conspiracy theories, as well as gross causal attributions not susceptible to proof or disproof.[34] Understanding need not imply empathy, and regional governments — especially the Philippines and Malaysia — can contribute to public understanding by putting more terrorist suspects on open and transparent trial.

Notes

1. Hambali, also known as Riduan Isamuddin and born Encep Nurjaman, was arrested in Ayuthaya, north of Bangkok, by Thai police and CIA operatives in mid-August 2003, and remains in US custody. Although his testimony would aid regional police forces enormously, US officials refuse to share access to him.
2. Sidney Jones, "The Changing Nature of Jemaah Islamiyah", *Australian Journal of International Affairs* 59, no. 2 (June 2005): 169–78.
3. Zachary Abuza, "To Bali via Mindanao: What the Bali Investigations Tell Us So Far", http://counterterror.stypepad.com/the_counterterrorism_blog/2005/10/to_bali_via_min.html#more.
4. This phrase was earlier used by Maria Ressa. See "The New Strategic Base of Jemaah Islamiyah", *Newsbreak* (Manila), 25 April 2005, pp. 16–17.
5. Carlyle A. Thayer, "New Terrorism in Southeast Asia", in *Violence in Between: Conflict and Security in Archipelagic Southeast Asia*, edited by Damien Kingsbury, pp. 53–74 (Clayton and Singapore: Monash Asia Institute and Institute of Southeast Asian Studies, 2005).
6. Rohan Gunaratna, *Inside Al-Qaeda: Global*

Network of Terror (London: C. Hurst, 2002), pp. 192–93.
7. Zachary Abuza, *Militant Islam in Southeast Asia: Crucible of Terror* (Boulder: Lynne Rienner, 2003), p. 122.
8. It is tedious to recount the numerous errors of fact, spelling, and interpretation that plague Abuza's work. This may explain why there has been so little published criticism of it. For country specialists, these errors expose a weak grounding in the history, geography, and culture of the peoples described. Unfortunately, the errors are reproduced by other regionalists drawing on Abuza. Note, as just one example, David Wright-Neville's reference to "Taussig" speakers who "make up the bulk of the MNLF [Moro National Liberation Front]" and the "majority of the more violent Abu Sayyaf Group". Like many regionalists, Wright-Neville does not indicate the source of his information, but Abuza's earlier work consistently makes the same mistake. Surely such a significant population — actually the *Tausug* — should be familiar to a serious analyst of Southeast Asian terrorism. See David Wright-Neville, "Dangerous Dynamics: Activists, Militants and Terrorists in Southeast Asia", *Pacific Review* 17, no. 1 (March 2004): 36.
9. Thayer, op. cit., claims Indonesianists such as Greg Fealy "went into denial". A review of Fealy's articles in the months before Bali I reveals a more nuanced position. Fealy's main complaint was the authorities' failure to back up allegations with credible evidence. See Greg Fealy, "Is Indonesia a Terrorist Base? The Gulf between Rhetoric and Evidence Is Wide", *Inside Indonesia* (July–September 2002).
10. Natasha Hamilton-Hart, "Terrorism in Southeast Asia: Expert Analysis, Myopia and Fantasy", *Pacific Review* 18, no. 3 (September 2005): 303–25.
11. "Indonesia Must Ban JI, Says Expert", 3 October 2005, http://edition.cnn.com/2005/WORLD/asiapcf/10/02/bali.terror/.
12. Critics of the war on terror are quick to recognize such simplifications, but usually display a similar impatience for the detail of terrorist activity themselves.
13. Sidney Jones, "The Changing Face of Terrorism in Southeast Asia: Weaker, More Diffuse, and Still a Threat", speech delivered at the Australian Strategic Policy Institute, 15 September 2005, http://www.crisisgroup.org/home/index.cfm?id=3717&I=1.
14. Darul Islam, from which Ba'asyir and Sungkar broke away in 1992–93 to form JI, was established in 1948 by S.M. Kartosoewiryo. Strongest in West Java but with offshoots in Central Java, Sumatra, Sulawesi, and Kalimantan, the movement rebelled for an Islamic state but was crushed by the mid-1960s. Revival since the late 1960s has spawned an extended family of squabbling sects with often overlapping memberships. The most important factions today are Panji Gumilang's KW9, Kang Jaja's Banten Ring, and groups led by Kartosoewiryo's son Tahmid, Ajengan Masduki, and Gaos Taufik. Related splinter groups include AMIN, RPII, and KOMPAK, the last ostensibly operating as a charity. See Greg Fealy and Aldo Borgu, *Local Jihad: Radical Islam and Terrorism in Indonesia*. Australian Strategic Policy Institute, September 2005.
15. International Crisis Group, *Indonesia Backgrounder: Jihad in Central Sulawesi*, Asia Report No. 74 (Jakarta/Brussels, 3 February 2004).
16. International Crisis Group, *Weakening Indonesia's Mujahidin Networks: Lessons from Maluku and Poso*, Asia Report No. 103 (Jakarta/Brussels, 13 October 2005).
17. Sian Powell, "Bomber in Shift from JI to al-Qa'ida", *The Australian*, 31 January 2006.

18. *Tanzim Qaedat al-Jihad* means "jihad-base organisation", and *Thoifah Muqatilah*, "combat unit". Mainstream Mantiqi 2 leaders include Ustadz Muhaimin Yahya (alias Ustadz Ziad), Ustadz Abdullah Anshori (alias Abu Fatih), Ahmad Roihan (alias Saad), and Ustadz Abdul Manan. See Fealy and Borgu, op. cit., p. 34.
19. US Charge d'Affaires Joseph Mussomeli told Australian television that "certain portions of Mindanao are so lawless, so porous ... that you run the risk of it becoming like an Afghanistan situation", referring to al-Qaeda's exploitation of the failed state to export global terror. See *Philippine Star*, 11 April 2005, p. 4.
20. International Crisis Group, *Southern Philippines Backgrounder: Terrorism and the Peace Process*, Asia Report No. 80 (Singapore/Brussels, 13 July 2004).
21. Zachary Abuza, *Balik-Terrorism: The Return of the Abu Sayyaf* (Carlisle, PA.: US Army War College, September 2005), p. 38.
22. International Crisis Group, *Southern Philippines Backgrounder: Terrorism and the Peace Process*, p. 14.
23. Abuza mistakenly dates this major government offensive to 1999. See "Al Qaeda in Southeast Asia: Exploring the Linkages", in *After Bali: The Threat of Terrorism in Southeast Asia*, edited by Kumar Ramakrishna and See Seng Tan (Singapore: Institute of Defence and Strategic Studies, 2003), pp. 133–57.
24. Faisal was captured off Sabah in September 2003, along with his deputy, Ahmad Saifullah Ibrahim. Next in command of WakHud was Qomarudin bin Zaimun, arrested in Java in 2004; his successor is Usman, but it is not clear whether survivors in Mindanao still follow directives from the centre. See International Crisis Group, *Philippines Terrorism: The Role of Militant Islamic Converts*, Asia Report No. 110 (Jakarta/Brussels, 19 December 2005).
25. The February 2004 Superferry bombing was the worst maritime terrorist attack in recent memory, killing at least 116, while a plan to car-bomb Manila's L.A. Café was foiled in March 2005.
26. The principal JI co-conspirator was Rahmat Abdulrahim, a Mindanao training batchmate of Faisal's. Rahmat was convicted in the Philippines' first successful murder prosecution of a foreign terrorist in October 2005.
27. *Philippines Terrorism: The Role of Militant Islamic Converts*, pp. 9–10.
28. "Mengenal Jejak Noordin-Azahari", *Tempo* (Jakarta), 16 October 2005. Three of Sonata's recruits were captured arriving in Zamboanga from Sabah in December 2004, and three more in Tawau in June 2005. These arrests were instrumental in tracking down Sonata and other key bombing suspects in Jakarta in July. They also demonstrated ongoing Arab, possibly al-Qaeda, financial support. See Simon Elegant, "On the Trail of the Bali Bombers", *Time*, 17 October 2005, p. 17.
29. Akram is also a Mindanao (and Afghan) veteran, having run DI's Camp Ash Syabab under MILF protection until the 2000 offensive. Sonata's programme picked up from Akram's. See *Philippines Terrorism: The Role of Militant Islamic Converts*, p. 9.
30. For background, see Kit Collier, "Precarious Peace in Mindanao", *Asia-Pacific Defence Reporter*, December 2004–January 2005, pp. 16–17.
31. Abuza, "Al Qaeda in Southeast Asia", p. 144.
32. Jones, "The Changing Face of Terrorism in Indonesia".
33. Even the International Crisis Group remained trapped in this paradigm, flagging a "Terrorism in Indonesia" link on its website, despite its closely related research on the Philippines. The Group maintained during 2005 that there was as yet no firm evidence of foreign terrorist involvement in southern Thailand's deteriorating situation.

See International Crisis Group, *Southern Thailand: Insurgency, Not Jihad*, Asia Report No. 98 (Jakarta/Brussels, 18 May 2005).

34. Former Indonesian President Abdurrahman Wahid, for example, continued to court the limelight by maintaining that Indonesian police or intelligence staged the 2002 Bali bombings — despite a solid body of evidence to the contrary now ventilated in court. With regard to the common argument that bombings in Indonesia are a direct response to Western policy in Iraq — a form of globalism that needs no concrete knowledge of Indonesia, or any other Islamist conflict zone — Sidney Jones notes that "anger at the West is so widespread that it becomes less of an explanatory factor as to why some groups turn to violence and others don't". The same might be argued of another "root cause" explanation of terrorism, poverty. See Sally Neighbour, "Weird Wahid Claim May Inflame", *The Australian*, 13 October 2005, pp. 1, 6; and Sidney Jones, "Terrorism in Southeast Asia, More Than Just JI", *Asian Wall Street Journal*, 29 July 2004.

Singapore

SINGAPORE'S FOREIGN POLICY IN THE SEVENTIES
The Reconciliation of Global and Regional Interests

Kawin Wilairat

Although it is false to assume that a new decade ushers in a new era, in the study of international politics it is in many ways convenient to think in terms of decades, because it allows for a point in time to assess the past, to analyse the present and to point to the future. With this proviso made, it can nevertheless be asserted that the first three years of the 1970's have marked a watershed in the international affairs of Asia and particularly Southeast Asia. The events which have changed the pattern of international relations in Southeast Asia and will clearly distinguish the present decade from the past include:

First, the *rapprochement* between China and the West and the rest of Asia, heralded by President Nixon's visit to Peking in February 1972 and the seating of China in the United Nations in 1971.

Second, the reshaping of American policy in the region along the lines of the Nixon Doctrine of self-help and put into effect through the winding down of the Vietnam War, the signing of the Vietnam Ceasefire Agreement in January 1973, and the phased withdrawal of American troops from Vietnam and Southeast Asia.

Third, the withdrawal of British military bases from Malaysia and Singapore initiated in 1968 and completed in 1971 and succeeded by the more fluid and ambiguous Five Power Defence Arrangements between Australia, New Zealand and the United Kingdom (ANZUK) and Malaysia and Singapore.

Fourth, the increasing Sino-Soviet rivalry, and the growing Soviet involvement in South and Southeast Asia marked by the Soviet-Indian Treaty of 1971 and the expanding Russian naval presence in the Pacific and Indian Oceans.

Fifth, the growing Japanese domination of the economies and markets of Southeast

---

Reprinted from *Southeast Asian Affairs 1974* (Institute of Southeast Asian Affairs 1974), pp. 278–301. At the time of original publication, Kawin Wilairat was Research Fellow at the Institute of Southeast Asian Studies, Singapore.

Asia, and the shaping of a new political role for Japan in Asian affairs commensurate with her economic power.

Finally, the shifting of the foreign policies of Australia and New Zealand to a more Asian orientation and to a greater involvement in Asian affairs following the Labour Party victories in both countries.

Despite a reduction in tension, however, Southeast Asia still remains in a state of flux and transition. None of the powers or potential powers in the area have yet established clear and well-defined long-term policies towards the region which could form the basis for a new political order. Though the Soviet Union has revived the Brezhnev concept of an Asian collective security system, though a neutralization proposal has been endorsed by ASEAN, and numerous other regional proposals advanced by other states, ambiguity and instability still seem to be characteristic of the international system in Southeast Asia. As the Soviet Union raises its profile, the United States military presence has been made even more problematical with the restructuring of the Southeast Asia Treaty Organization (SEATO), the overthrow of the military regime in Thailand, and the move by Thailand and the Philippines towards an accommodation with China.

It is against this background — one that Prime Minister Lee Kuan Yew has described as "fluid, nebulous ... marked by confusion and anxiety" — that the major international problems confronting Singapore, as she enters her second decade as an independent republic, must be considered. But it must also be recalled that though these changes in the international scene have been swift and sudden, rapidity and abruptness in shifts of policy are not new to Singapore. The 1960s, in fact, had been the most revolutionary decade for her; no other country has undergone so many significant changes in so short a period. The sixties, indeed, saw the transition of Singapore from a colony to an internally self-governing state (1959–63), to becoming a part of the Federation of Malaysia (1963–65), and thence to an independent republic. Furthermore, challenges which threatened her economy and viability as a state, were sprung upon her in rapid succession in the 1960s. These included: (1) the separation from Malaysia with its political and economic repercussions; (2) Sukarno's Confrontation which disrupted her important Indonesian trade and threatened her security and (3) Britain's decision in 1968 to withdraw her military bases by 1971, which left Singapore with the task of absorbing 40,000 employees who contributed to 20% of the GNP, and creating a credible defence force all within three years.

That Singapore, which found herself in August 1965 an independent republic without "administrative machinery for defence or diplomacy," has fashioned and implemented successful domestic and foreign policies, must be apparent to the most casual observer. The city-state is today the most prosperous nation in Southeast Asia, enjoying a standard of living considered second only to Japan's in Asia. She is also the third busiest port in the world, the home of a thriving Asian Dollar Market whose operations have exceeded the US$1,000 million mark, a booming tourist centre visited by over a million tourists in 1973, and is projected to become by 1975 the world's second largest oil refining centre. Other economic and social indicators add to the same picture, one often described as an "economic miracle."

Because Singapore was suddenly thrust into world politics in a very vulnerable position, it is not surprising that the theme which dominated her foreign policy was, and to an extent still is, "survival." The case against her was not negligible. It seemed that, in the words of Foreign Minister Rajaratnam, "a small city state without a natural hinterland, without a large domestic market and no raw materials to speak of [had] a near-zero chance of survival politically, economically or militarily."

Singapore's formula for success has since been put by Mr. Rajaratnam into a theoretical "global policy" framework, the content of which is basically "a judicious mixture of well-trained and well-equipped defence forces, friendly alliances ... and giving as many countries as possible a tangible stake in the security, prosperity and integrity of Singapore." The twin objectives of this policy are, not unnaturally, security and prosperity.

Singapore's foreign policy, reflecting the government's painful awareness of the city-state's physical constraints and economic dependence on trade, was from the beginning grounded in the belief that survival meant making as many friends and as few enemies as possible. Upon separation from Malaysia, Singapore announced a policy of non-alignment and declared herself uncommitted to any bloc and open to trade and commercial relations with all nations. She also insisted that her non-alignment, sometimes called "qualified non-alignment" or "positive neutralism," was not incompatible with her defence ties with Britain.

As her spokesmen have explained, Singapore's policy of non-alignment does not mean non-commitment and "does not preclude us from expressing our own conviction on specific issues based on our own experience and circumstances, and our own judgement on the effect it would have on our international relations."

Thus, though itself severely anti-communist in its internal affairs, the Singapore Government has sought friends and trading partners among all countries regardless of ideology or politics. It has, for example, concluded trade agreements with communist countries such as Bulgaria, Hungary, North Korea, Poland, Rumania, the USSR, and Yugoslavia.

At the same time as Singapore has been endeavouring to gain friends, she has just as earnestly been trying to avoid arousing enmity. Through a cautious and carefully balanced diplomacy she has been able to maintain good relations with both sides in most international disputes, ranging from the cold war antagonists, communist China and Taiwan, the Arab states and Israel, to divided countries such as the two Koreas and the two Vietnams. In 1973, forty-two states were represented by their diplomatic missions in Singapore (and eight other states had already established consulates or trade representatives), an unusually large number for a small state but as one ambassador remarked:

> Where else can you find a city-state which provides port facilities to some 500 Russian merchant ships a year, one which has absorbed massive investment from the United States and other countries of the western world, trades with China and is an active member of regional organizations like ECAFE and ASEAN?

This political-security aspect of Singapore's foreign policy has been aptly described as "a conscious search for a political personality to be built around the traditional trading personality." It also involves the pursuit of what has been called "multiple involvement" or "multilateral underpinning." Basic to it all has been an unceasing and tenacious effort (notably by Mr. Lee Kuan Yew who has made almost annual trips to the United States and Europe and visited Russia in 1970 and East Europe in 1971) to convince great and major powers, east and west, that they have a stake — strategic and economic — in the existence of a viable and independent Singapore.

While the majority of Southeast Asian observers at most hope for a multipolar balance of power in Asia in the form of a quadrilateral arrangement between the U.S., the USSR, China and Japan, Singapore leaders have characteristically looked further ahead to a more distant (and less likely) five-polar relationship involving the participation of a "more independent, outward-looking, and responsible" Europe. This view has been particularly reiterated in the most recent speeches of the Prime Minister. Typical is the following plea made in Brussels in December 1972:

> For Southeast Asians, European multilateral sharing of responsibilities could be critical.... If we are to move towards a more peaceful and stable world, the major countries must move now towards a more multi-lateral sharing of world responsibilities. If the Europeans take an interest beyond just the Mediterranean Basin and Africa, they will help make this a more prosperous and stable world.

Singapore from the beginning also identified herself with the Afro-Asian movement and shortly after separation, a trade and goodwill mission led by the Foreign Minister toured Africa for two months. It was Nigeria who sponsored Singapore's admission to both the United Nations and the Commonwealth, and in 1967 Singapore became a member of the Afro-Asian Solidarity Conference.

Although Singapore has participated in Afro-Asian cooperative efforts (she sponsored an Afro-Asian Housing Conference in 1967; had hosted the Afro-Asian Trade Union Bureau; and maintains a National Afro-Asian Peoples' Solidarity Committee) she has mainly pursued a policy of non-involvement. Singapore has also, over the years, it seems, realized that given the different rates and forms of economic development between Africa and Southeast Asia and the different political issues that occupy them (this was made very apparent by the threatened disruption of the 1971 Commonwealth Prime Ministers Meeting in Singapore by some African leaders), the most that can be expected from Afro-Asian relations is the occasional airing of views and support for similar ideological concerns.

Singapore, similarly, has shown increasing disenchantment with the non-aligned nations group. Although Singapore has sent delegates to all the non-aligned nations conferences since 1965, she has called for a rethinking of the concepts of non-alignment in the light of shifting Great Power relations, and has bluntly suggested that the conferences should be less given to political rhetoric but be more concerned with the real issues of economic development.

Thus, after the latest non-aligned nations summit conference in Algiers in September 1973, Foreign Minister Rajaratnam again expressed disappointment and said that more could have been achieved "if members talked less politics and more economics.... The concept of non-alignment is still valid, but to give it substance demands great exertion and discipline which, I think, the Third World countries are not ready to undertake." Indicative, perhaps, of the diminishing importance of these conferences to Singapore was the fact that she was represented at this Fourth Non-Aligned Summit only by the Foreign Minister, whereas Prime Minister Lee himself attended the Third Summit at Lusaka in 1970.

Underlying the economic aspect of Singapore's foreign policy was the realization that Singapore could no longer remain dependent on her entrepôt trade, but had to restructure her economy, expand her economic activities and build a sound industrial base. For almost a decade, Singapore has been developing export-oriented manufacturing industries based on foreign capital and imported raw material. At first Singapore welcomed and encouraged practically every industrial proposition — the object was to attract capital and provide employment (a chronic problem then aggravated by the liquidation of the British military base). Today she is in a position to be selective and the emphasis is now on capital-intensive high-technology industries which, according to Prime Minister Lee, "have very little pollution, very little noise, high added skills to pay high wages, and world-wide markets so [Singapore is] not a pawn to any single regional market."

In theoretical terms, this "economic pragmatism" meant turning Singapore, in addition to being a regional centre, into a "Global City" whose "world hinterland" would more than make up for the lack of natural resources, raw materials, and a large domestic market. This global city which Singapore is to become, is based on modern technology — "electronic communication, supersonic planes, giant tankers, and modern economic and industrial organization."

The Foreign Minister has suggested that a measure of the extent to which Singapore has already become a global city can be gauged by looking at "the daily movements of aircraft and ships, the contacts made by telephone and cable and external trade and money transactions." However, the strongest evidence would be, according to Mr. Rajaratnam, Singapore's "absorption into the emerging system of global cities ... [and] its link-up, more and more, with international and multi-national corporations." By "plugging-in" into the framework of the world economy, via these corporations, Singapore, he believes, has found "a short-cut to catch up or at least keep pace with the most advanced industrial and technological societies ... [and] can achieve in twenty to thirty years what otherwise would have taken ... a century or more to achieve." This can come about because,

> The international and multinational corporations introduce us to high technology, complex managerial and marketing skills in addition to bringing in investments ... [and] established markets. For these firms the world is their hinterland; the world is their market and through them we are automatically linked to the world hinterland and world markets that would on our own be unavailable to us.

Attesting to the success of Singapore's global policy are recent statements of American officials. The then Secretary of State, William Rogers, said in 1973 "Growing U.S. trade and investment in Singapore and its strategic location make friendly relations with Singapore an important factor in our overall Asian policies." In June 1973, the visiting U.S. Deputy Assistant Secretary of the Commerce Department declared that his country's position as Singapore's leading investor and second largest trading partner, and the recent shift of the U.S. Regional Development Centre to Singapore, constituted a "vote of confidence in the future of Singapore by the Government of the United States." Total trade between Singapore and the United States in 1972 reached S$2,289 million.

Similarly, the Russian Ambassador in Singapore in an article marking the fifth anniversary (June 1973) of the establishment of diplomatic relations, stressed "the development of equal and mutually beneficial ties" over the past five years. The Soviet Union has maintained a bank in Singapore since 1971, brought in its national airline in 1969, and began a joint venture, the Singapore-Soviet Shipping Company, in 1967. Singapore-Soviet trade totalled S$130 million in 1972.

Additional evidence of the success of Singapore's global policy lies in the diversity of her substantial trading partners and in the amount and origin of foreign investment. In 1972 Singapore's top ten trading partners were Malaysia, the United States, Japan, Indonesia, the United Kingdom, Australia, Hong Kong, West Germany, Thailand, and China; and her total trade of S$15,687 million exceeded that of the two giants of Asia: India and China. Foreign investment in Singapore's manufacturing industries totalled almost S$2,000 million at the end of 1972, the leading investors being the United States, the United Kingdom, Holland, Japan, Hong Kong, Malaysia and West Germany. Other countries that have invested in Singapore include Australia, Canada, Denmark, France, Italy, India, Indonesia, New Zealand, Norway, Sweden, Switzerland and Taiwan.

Singapore's economic success, it must be pointed out, has also been due to two "lucky accidents" that came about — the Vietnam War and the oil exploration boom in Southeast Asia. By the beginning of the 1970's Singapore has become the third largest exporter (mainly of petroleum products) to South Vietnam, had become a ship-repair base for the United States, and was, till 1970, used as a Rest and Recreation Centre for American troops. As for the oil boom, a 1971 report stated that the investment in the Singapore oil industry had already meant at least S$250 per capita and no less than a S$25 increase in the annual per capita income.

In contrast to the success of her global policy, Singapore's regional policy has not been as well received. Though a founding member of ASEAN, Singapore's relations with her ASEAN partners were considered until last year (when the situation underwent a noticeable improvement) at best "cool and correct." It was particularly embarrassing that until 1972 and this past year, though Prime Minister Lee had made frequent trips to Europe and the United States, he had never visited the ASEAN countries.

A reason for this, perhaps, was that until the past two years or so, Singapore's regional relations were not considered as significant as her global ones. Never expecting more than it could gain from any relationship, Singapore had never really put too much by way of regional cooperation except as a long-run ideal goal. In the meantime she viewed her association with regional organizations as forums to express and exchange views, to develop habits of cooperation, and to promote limited cooperative projects in areas such as tourism, education and communication.

The criticisms aimed at Singapore's regional policy thus centred on what was variously called, her "diffident" or "wait-and-see" attitude to regional cooperation. Ironically the most extreme and provocative criticism (that of Prime Minister Gough Whitlam, in August 1973, who accused Singapore of pursuing "a thoroughly selfish attitude" in Southeast Asia and being "the richest country in Southeast Asia which did nothing to help its neighbours") came from outside the region and after new regional efforts had been initiated by Singapore.

In 1970, however, it was still possible for a study of regional cooperation to see Singapore's involvement in ASEAN as appearing "so far to have been more of a diplomatic manoeuvre than an expression of deep commitment to regional cooperation." Some observers had also remarked that Singapore joined ASEAN as a move to improve regional relations that would involve little risk and in the hope that the new organization would bring early economic benefits. This was, perhaps, due to the heavy emphasis put by Singapore on the need for ASEAN to remain economically oriented. Thus, Singapore's Prime Minister and Foreign Minister have constantly stressed the need for ASEAN to concentrate on solving economic and social problems and not become involved in other matters such as regional security.

To Singapore, the urgent and vital problems of Southeast Asia are economic — even with the recent international developments and their repercussions on the region. Because, as Mr. Rajaratnam pointed out, if the nations of the region are not able to solve their economic problems reasonably and expeditiously, their chances of contending with the new problems that the new alignments of power will bring about will be that much diminished.

There have also been criticisms to the effect that Singapore is the "weakest link in the show of ASEAN unity." If this is so, it is due to the tendency of Singapore to deal strictly in realities — what Mr. Rajaratnam calls putting everything "through the sieve of what is possible and not possible; what is practical and not practical" — and to present to her ASEAN partners the "harsh facts of life" and "unwelcome truths." Representative of this realism is the penchant Singapore delegates have for meticulously counting the actual achievements and activities of ASEAN, and presenting the facts to their ASEAN colleagues. Thus, at the official opening of the Fifth ASEAN Ministerial Meeting in April 1972, Mr. Lee Kuan Yew noted:

> Measured by the implementation of recommendations made by ASEAN committees, ASEAN has made progress in regional cooperation. In the first year, August 1967 to August 1968, there were 102 recommendations. None were implemented. In the second year, August 1968 to December 1969, of 161 recommendations, 10 were implemented, i.e. 6.2%. In the third year, December 1969 to March 1971, of 207 recommendations, 22 were implemented — 10.6%. In the fourth year, March 1971 to April 1972, of 215 recommendations, 48 were implemented — 22.3%.

In her stand against "grandiose schemes" and "illusions about regionalism" Singapore has stressed two points. First, the acceptance that regional cooperation at this stage, and for some time to come, will be evaluated in terms of its actual contribution to national interests and national development. The slow progress of regionalism is due to the need to reconcile the theory of regionalism with the practice of nationalism. Singapore, therefore, is not, in the words of the Foreign Minister:

... unduly dismayed by this approach. On the contrary, given present-day realities in the area this approach to regionalism may be the sounder one.... There is a real contradiction in striving towards regional cooperation through promoting and strengthening national economic interests.... If the concept of regionalism can assist national consolidation and the transformation of ASEAN states into stable modernized societies, then prospects for regionalism will be better.

Second, that cooperation between weak and developing economies despite the best of intentions and mutual goodwill cannot ensure rapid growth and development. Southeast Asian countries therefore have to cooperate with the more industrialized countries outside the region; regionalism must go hand in hand with internationalism. This oft-stated view was bluntly put by Mr. Lee Kuan Yew just after the founding of ASEAN:

> Cooperation between educationally not advanced and industrially underdeveloped countries can only produce miniscule economic gains to be divided between large numbers of poor and hungry people.... The underdeveloped countries of Southeast Asia must be associated with the more industrially advanced and prosperous....

Singapore regards the desirability of regional cooperation to be a truism but has taken pains to point out that a number of factors in the Southeast Asian context actually "delimits the scope for regionalism." These include:

1. The need to give priority to solving more urgent domestic problems — social, economic and political.
2. The reluctance to compromise newly gained sovereignty over economic matters by newly independent states.
3. Heterogeneity of the region in socio-cultural terms and also the great disparities in levels of development, technology and economic infrastructure.
4. The incompatibility in economic policies — as far as Singapore is concerned — between those favouring an "inward looking policy" (industrialization through import-substitution and tariff protection) and those favouring an "outward looking policy" (industrialization by encouraging foreign investment and export promotion with minimum tariff protection).

Singapore, therefore, does not see a Southeast Asian common market as a practical proposition in the foreseeable future. What should be encouraged is economic cooperation in "projects that have a regional basis" (e.g., buffer stock arrangements in the tin mining industry). Different projects, she points out, may require different regional groupings, so rigid regional groupings should be avoided; objectives such as the establishment of an ASEAN common market can best be achieved gradually through small steps rather than by drawing up grandiose schemes and rigid time-tables.

Singapore's maverick image has been heightened by the fact that at a time when multinational enterprises are being condemned in Southeast Asia and other developing countries for "exploitation" and "interference," the Singapore Government has worked out a mutually beneficial relationship with them (American, European and Japanese) that has made a substantial contribution to the country's progress in terms of real income and rising employment.

Although Singapore until recently (1972) followed a rather self-effacing role in regional affairs and might have displayed a "wait-and-see" attitude towards regional cooperation, she has nonetheless fully participated in ASEAN and other regional activities. Thus, after the headline-making charges by the Australian Prime Minister, Mr. Gough Whitlam, that Singapore had done nothing to help her neighbours, Dr. Goh Keng Swee, the Singapore Deputy Prime Minister, produced figures to refute the charges which showed that: (1) Singapore was in 1972 only second to India among Asian countries contributing awards under the Colombo Plan; (2) special scholarships are reserved in Singapore schools and universities for students from ASEAN countries, the value of these amounting to over five times that of the Colombo Plan scholarships; and (3) Singapore at the end of 1972 had invested a total amount of S$360.5 million in Malaysia and Indonesia — making her the fourth largest investor in Indonesia and one of the largest in Malaysia.

Though her contributions may be modest overall, Singapore feels that she can make a significant contribution in the areas of science, technology and education. The Singapore Meteorological Department has collected data for aircraft and shipping in the region, and has used its telecommunications facilities as a link in the exchange of meteorological data between centres in the northern and southern hemispheres. Under the Colombo Plan and the ASEAN technical cooperation scheme, Singapore has provided scholarships for trainees from the rest of the region in a wide-ranging number of fields including engineering, construction, nursing, radiography, and public health; in 1972, 186 such scholarships were awarded by Singapore. Singapore also hosts research and training institutions, such as the Regional English Language Centre and the Regional Institute of Higher Education and Development, which serve the whole region. In addition a non-profit "think-tank, "the Applied Research Corporation, has recently been set up by the Singapore Government to offer professional consultancy and technical services (in the broad areas of economics, management science, applied sciences, and engineering) to the whole region.

Furthermore, if a country's contributions to regionalism (its participation and perceptions) are measured according to indicators suggested by theorists of regional integration, there is additional evidence to back Singapore's claim that she is as interested and as much a participant in "regional affairs" as her ASEAN partners. A study of four indices — voting record in the United Nations, diplomatic exchanges, shared membership in the inter-governmental organizations and trade — shows that Singapore's orientation is no more extra-regional, if not less, than her ASEAN partners.

Turning to trade as an index of cohesiveness or orientation, it is clear that the extra-regional trade links of ASEAN countries are much stronger than intra-regional ones. Intra-ASEAN trade increased from 1966 to 1970 at 5.2% per year, whereas total ASEAN trade grew by 9.1% per year over the same period. Trade within ASEAN as a percentage of total ASEAN trade shrunk from 18.3% in 1966 to 15.7% in 1970. What is interesting in these trade figures is the fact that at the beginning of the 1970s, only Singapore among the ASEAN countries had consistently more than 25% of its total imports and exports with its ASEAN partners.

A comparative study of Singapore's voting pattern in the United Nations General Assembly, from 1965 to 1970, showed that her votes were more in line with ASEAN countries than with any other group of countries. The degree of similarity of her voting position was measured against those of her ASEAN partners, Commonwealth nations, West European countries, and the major powers, for three sets of issues — East : West, North : South, and Colonial.

A study of Singapore's diplomatic missions (extra-regional compared with intra-regional) and membership in intergovernmental organizations reinforces the findings of the trade and voting analyses.

Since 1969 the Singapore Government has also actively encouraged, through tax-exemption incentives, its entrepreneurs to invest in Malaysia and Indonesia. In addition, among the guidelines set up for foreign investment in Singapore was the consideration that Singapore be used as an "investment base or launching site for branching out manufacturing operations to other Asian countries," and as a "centre for the development of software systems and professional services adapted to regional requirements and practices."

Though regional cooperation has not become any more economically attractive in the six years of ASEAN's existence, Singapore has in the past two years or so become more attentive to regional matters. There is now evidence that a more active and leading role in regional affairs is in the making, and that Singapore is paying more attention to projecting an image of herself as an integral part and not a "pariah" in the region, as her critics claim. She now wishes, it seems, to make sure that her usefulness as a regional partner is fully recognized, not only in her traditional role as an entrepôt centre, but as a new economic force promoting development in and channelling investment to her neighbours and providing educational, technological, and professional services.

Singapore's three leading foreign policy spokesmen have, in their speeches and statements, constantly touched upon this theme. Speaking at the University of Singapore in November 1970, Dr. Goh Keng Swee warned that "if we are not careful" Singapore's relations with her neighbours would get worse as "the gap between our standard of living and theirs widens in the 1970s." In a major policy speech in February 1972, Mr. Rajaratnam noted:

> It is said that Singapore's prosperity is the consequence of the failure of our neighbours to realize their full potentialities. When they do ... it will be curtains for Singapore.... The opposite is true. The more prosperous our neighbours become, the more dynamic their economies become ... the better our economic prospects.

And one of the points stressed in a recent speech by Mr. Lee Kuan Yew was the need for Singapore to foster better relations with her neighbours — "the fusing of national imperatives with regional and neighbourly interest."

In addition to the growing awareness of her unsatisfactory regional image, there are several other factors which have probably contributed to this shift in policy. First, is the changing power alignments in the region discussed above. Second, is the felt need in Singapore for a more unified stand of ASEAN on such matters as the oil crisis and trade negotiations with the industrial powers (especially after Britain's entry into the EEC and the ending of Commonwealth privileges). Finally, is the need to match or counteract the increasing aspirations of Indonesia to attain a position of leadership in the region and to direct and shape the region's future.

There is also, of course, the ever present awareness among Singapore's leaders that she is willy-nilly a part of Southeast Asia, dependent on her neighbours for such vital things as her water supply, food, and raw materials and that, because of her size and location and economic structure, it is difficult for her to be insulated from the repercussions of her neighbours' foreign policies and internal politics.

Besides the innumerable policy statements the most important evidence of Singapore's new assertive policy are the recent visits made by Prime Minister Lee to all the ASEAN countries. Since March 1972 when Mr. Lee visited Malaysia, the Prime Minister has visited Thailand (January 1973), Indonesia (May 1973) and the Philippines (January 1974). In each case the visit was the first made by the Prime Minister since Singapore became an independent republic in 1965. The visits were widely acclaimed both in Singapore and in the other ASEAN countries and have done much to improve the relations between Singapore and her neighbours. Although there were some critical comments (particularly in Indonesia) the region's press and political commentators in general welcomed Singapore's "new regional role," the "raising of her profile" in regional affairs, and the end of the pattern of "marked mutual indifference" between Prime Minister Lee and the other Southeast Asian leaders.

However, despite the seven years of separate existence and the exchange of visits by the two Prime Ministers, relations between Malaysia and Singapore are only slowly heading towards the "brisk and businesslike" nature both governments desire. There is still a fair amount of contention between the two countries over a series of issues symptomatic of the separation trauma. The friction stems from the fact that in order for the two countries to reach an acceptable *modus vivendi* separation has to be total. Thus, each country finds itself having to assert its own identity and sovereignty over matters in which, prior to separation, both had had a say. Malaysia, furthermore, seems committed to a policy of reducing those hitherto close economic links with Singapore which are viewed as a sign of Malaysian dependency on Singapore and inhibiting Malaysian economic growth.

In the past year, for example, differences and bad feelings occurred over such matters as the Malaysian termination of the currency interchangeability pact; the separation of the joint stock exchange and rubber market; the Singapore decision to float her currency; the Malaysian ban on log exports to Singapore; the extension of port regulations to Singapore vessels hitherto exempted from them; and Singapore's imposition of new restrictions on Malaysian cars entering the Republic and the subsequent Malaysian retaliatory requirements for visiting Singapore cars.

There are also differences over the structure and future of the Five Power Defence Arrangements. A lack of co-operation in defence matters is clearly shown by Malaysia's steady refusal to allow Singapore access to her jungle warfare training facilities in nearby Johore, and the use of an uninhabited islet suitable for bombing practice.

In spite of these problems, there is still a great deal of empathy between the two countries based on their long historical association, and the family and business ties that remain between the peoples north and south of the causeway. Malaysia-Singapore trade totalled S$2,785 million in 1972, and Malaysia remains Singapore's leading trade partner while Singapore is one of the largest investors in Malaysia.

Relations between Indonesia and Singapore have clearly improved over the past two years, especially after Prime Minister Lee's visit to Jakarta last May. The "psychological barriers" are said to be coming down and the image each country has of the other is steadily being improved through an increase in the number of official and unofficial exchanges ranging from trade missions, parliamentarians, and defence staff, to youth delegations, student groups, goodwill and study tours, and other forms of "people-to-people" programmes.

Relations between the two countries are, however, far from perfect; mutual suspicion and questioning of intentions still exist. One source of contention is Singapore's refusal to release statistics of her trade with Indonesia. This is due (but denied by Singapore) to the discrepancy that will appear because of the substantial smuggling or "unregistered trade" that takes place from Indonesia to Singapore. Indonesians are also resentful of the spillover to Singapore of profitable economic activities (servicing and refining) accompanying the oil exploration boom and feel that such activities should remain in Indonesia. Regulations have been passed to ensure this but so far have not been very successful. Singapore, on the other hand, is quite wary of Indonesia's aspirations for leadership in the region and of her moves to divert shipping and entrepôt activities from Singapore.

Nevertheless, there is now a definite trend towards closer economic cooperation between the two countries. Indonesia with a total trade of over S$1,500 million with Singapore in 1972 is the latter's fourth largest trading partner, and Singapore now ranks as the fourth largest investor in Indonesia. There have recently been proposals for Singapore to participate in the development of Sumatra's Lake Toba as a major tourist resort and in the development of a major industrial complex on Batam Island twelve miles from Singapore.

Singapore's relations with her two other ASEAN partners, Thailand and the Philippines, have not, for historical, political and economic reasons, been as important. In 1972 Singapore's trade with Thailand and the Philippines totalled S$483 million and S$69 million respectively. Of the two countries, Thailand is perhaps more important to Singapore in that she is the largest supplier of rice and is considered in Singapore strategic thinking the most crucial buffer state against the spread of Indochinese inspired insurgency. After Mr. Lee Kuan Yew's visit to Thailand in January 1973, two agreements were reached whereby a detachment of Singapore commandos will be trained annually in Thailand, and Singapore will build patrol crafts and carry out maintenance and repairs for the Thai Navy. Consultations and visits between defence officials of the two countries are becoming more frequent.

Despite her real contributions to regional cooperation and her recently more active regional policy, Singapore will have to live with the fact that for the time being she will be regarded somewhat with a mixture of suspicion and envy by her neighbours. The roles of regional centre and global city have emerged and merged and become for Singapore at one and the same time complementary and incompatible. The more Singapore is to succeed in attracting investment and trade, the more she has to portray her "local personality" and project her uniqueness in relation to her neighbours, and "nobody likes anyone who makes a profession of being different from them."

Three regional issues in particular face Singapore in which divergent pulls of her international and regional interests will have to be carefully balanced: the neutralization of Southeast Asia, the "nationalization" of the Malacca Straits, and the recognition of China.

Though the Malaysian proposal for a neutralized Southeast Asia is now considered a main feature of diplomacy and international politics in Southeast Asia, it is still at the "drawing board" stage and is seen, at least in Singapore, as only a framework for discussion. Singapore, in fact, is far from enthusiastic about the proposal, the success of which would achieve a Southeast Asian region free from external interference. She has pointed out that, so far, none of the Great Powers upon whose cooperation the success of neutralization depends, has even expressed an interest in it let alone endorsed it.

Singapore sees the move to make Southeast Asia a zone of peace and neutrality as desirable but urges her ASEAN partners not to bank on idealized statements and unilateral declarations. The countries of the region have to accept the fact that the Great Powers will contend for their interests in the region because of its strategic location and resources, and trying to exclude one or all is unrealistic. The best course is for Southeast Asian countries to show the Great Powers that it is in their best interests to promote peace and stability in the region, and to withstand externally instigated turmoil by putting their houses in order and maintaining domestic stability.

Furthermore, following her concept of "multilateral underpinning" for her security, Singapore's interpretation of what neutralization should entail and how it should be achieved is somewhat different from that of her neighbours, especially Malaysia and Indonesia. The thinking in Singapore is that a balance, not only of power but of interests, must exist among the Great Powers in the region. Without this balance, the vacuum created would make for instability and encourage nations in the area to fend for themselves leading to tension and disputes and great power involvement, even though none of the parties might actually seek to exploit the situation. It is believed that, as in the case of Europe, the relaxation of tension can only come about by the establishment of a situation whereby the security of the region is guaranteed by the mutual interests of and tacit understanding among the Great Powers to maintain the status quo.

The Singapore Government's persistence in stressing the dangers of a power vacuum and in calling for a continued United States' presence, and indeed the presence of all Great Powers in a balanced situation, is also to be explained partly in terms of her economic stake in having their continued economic interests in the region, partly in her fear of instability and insurgency, and partly in her apprehension of being open to pressures from her immediate neighbours (the so-called "nutcracker theory") without a countervailing Great Power presence.

One Singapore proposal, in particular, to achieve a *de facto* neutralization of Southeast Asia, came in for a heavy round of criticism from her neighbours. During his 1973 visit to Japan, the Singapore Prime Minister had suggested that a joint naval task force consisting of American, West European, Australian, and Japanese units would be desirable for maintaining security and stability in Southeast Asia in the light of increasing Russian naval build-up in the region and in the Indian Ocean.

Singapore is understandably wary of any move which would disrupt the flow of shipping through the Straits — a flow which is Singapore's life-line to the export markets of the world. The development of the controversy over the move to "nationalize" the Straits of Malacca by Indonesia and Malaysia, in November 1971, has put Singapore in an uncomfortable position.

Firmly adhering to the position that the Straits should remain "freely accessible to all nations without discrimination" with "unimpeded passage of all ships of nations," Singapore has felt it necessary to cooperate with her neighbours to the extent of formally "taking note" of their positions in their tripartite statement of November 1971. What Singapore does hold to be a legitimate matter of littoral state responsibility are the problems of navigational safety and pollution control; the fact that the Tripartite Declaration of 1971 separated the two issues — de-internationalization and safety of navigation — is perhaps what made it possible for Singapore to participate in the Declaration.

The Singapore position of reservation (i.e. holding open options) was explained by Foreign Minister Rajaratnam in a parliamentary statement:

> Singapore ... could not go any further than to take note of the views of our two neighbours. The reason is that, in Singapore's view, the status of the Straits of Malacca and of Singapore should not be considered in isolation but in conjunction with the status of some 114 straits scattered throughout the world and which are considered vital links in international sea communication.

Singapore, according to Mr. Rajaratnam, feels that there must be a uniformity of agreement in regard to the status of all straits of international importance, otherwise there would be "a dangerous scramble for the carve-up of not only straits, but of oceans as well." The forum for the settling of the controversy "by mutual accord and agreement and in a rational way" should be the United Nations Law of the Sea Conference to be held in 1974.

Singapore in fact, views the "nationalization" issue as a setback for the movement to end Southeast Asia as an arena for Great Power rivalry. While the United States, the Soviet Union and Japan have all made strong statements defending the international character of the Straits and the right of free passage, China has condemned the "collusion" of the "Soviet revisionist social-imperialism" and the "Japanese reactionaries" and their "attempt aimed at interfering in the affairs of the Straits [and] encroaching upon the sovereignty of the states on both sides of the Straits." The apparent impossibility of the littoral states enforcing their claims was amply illustrated by the recent flurry of Soviet and American warships through the Straits during the latest Middle East War without any notice being given, let alone permission requested, as insisted upon by Malaysia and Indonesia.

What also adds to Singapore's anxiety is the suspicion that the move was initiated by Indonesia to strengthen her "archipelago principle" (sovereignty over all inland waters) and to bolster her position within the region and her conception of regional order. Other motivations for the Indonesian move could be the prospect of diverting shipping from Singapore and an economic leverage to be used on Japan.

The question of establishing formal ties with China is one which requires the most careful and sensitive handling by Singapore. The potential repercussions, internal and external, of such a move cannot be down-played for a country who has in the past been called a Third China and whose Southeast Asian identity has been questioned by her neighbours.

Singapore's official position is that such ties are only a matter of time, but that she would prefer her ASEAN partners to take the initiative and make the first moves. Throughout the latter part of 1973, Malaysian-Chinese ties seemed imminent and the apparent delay is said to be due to the problem of the status of Chinese non-citizens in Malaysia. This would also appear to be a problem Singapore will face, but her main concerns lie, (1) in the need to reassure her neighbours that diplomatic recognition will not make her an "outpost of Chinese influence", and (2) in the danger of a revival of Chinese chauvinism accompanied by communal tension. Hence, a "no hurry" policy and a meticulous avoidance of displaying any enthusiasm for recognition.

In the meantime, Singapore maintains her long-standing and unbroken trade links with both China and Taiwan. Singapore, furthermore, is host to the only communist Bank of China in Southeast Asia. (Established in 1936 it was taken over by the People's Republic of China in 1949). She has also in the past few years allowed the setting up of eleven Chinese emporiums as retail outlets for Chinese goods.

Although their trade is not very large at present (total trade in 1972 was S$456.5 million) Singapore sees good prospects for her future trade and shipping relations with China. In 1971, in fact, China assisted the Singapore shipping community in its efforts to break the monopolistic "contract system" of the Far East Freight Conference by providing cargo space on her ships. In October 1973, China also agreed to send more ships to carry Singapore cargo at lower rates and to consider sending her commercial vessels to Singapore for dry-docking and repairs.

As for the strategic-security considerations of the emergence of China and Chinese influence in the region, Singapore sees no immediate threat. Though she does not down-play the potential and constant danger of Chinese support for internal subversion, she does not see the possibility of this in Singapore at present. The Singapore Government was, in fact, confident enough of its control over internal security and political stability to release, during the past year, several political detainees who were known to have been involved in communist activities. Prime Minister Lee has also dismissed any immediate strategic threat from the "emergence" of China:

> I do not see a Chinese Navy, a Chinese 7th Fleet complete with missile cruiser in the South Pacific or the Indian Ocean in the 1970s. More trade — particularly in the simpler manufactures — cheap garments, footwear, processed foods, lathes and simple machinery, yes.

To Singapore the more important question as far as China is concerned is the larger problem of long-term overall regional security and stability. In this context the problem posed by China will not be direct military aggression or invasion. Instead, as Dr. Goh Keng Swee argues:

> The great problem ... to which in Asia we have yet to find a solution is this. If by the 1990s or in the early decades of the twenty-first century, the communist system in China were to produce a modern industrial state equipped with all the technological advances, what will happen to the rest of Asia if it fails to achieve similar progress? The disarray in Asian countries ... hardly inspires confidence in the ability of non-

communist Asian countries to bring about the modernization of their societies and economies.... It is this development which, if unmatched by performance in other Asian countries, will be the real long-term challenge of communism in Asia.

There are other important issues which Singapore faces in her international relations than those discussed above, such as the oil crisis and the signs of what could be a Great Power naval build-up in the Indian Ocean. But these are problems which at least do not add to Singapore's fundamental "international dilemma" — the conflict between her regional and global interests. Whether or not Singapore can continue to "enjoy the best of both worlds," whether or not her foreign policy will be ultimately successful, depends on a careful balancing of these two divergent pulls — the regional (centripetal) and the global (centrifugal).

Singapore's leaders are apparently undaunted by this and other problems. Energetic, confident, and standing on a unparalleled record of success, they convey the impression of thriving on overcoming such challenges. Furthermore, over the relatively few years of Singapore's history as an independent republic, what could be called an intellectual-philosophical framework has evolved within which foreign policies and objectives are generated and pursued. This framework is one which stresses pragmatism and self-reliance, open-mindedness and flexibility, and the constant interpretation and reinterpretation of external developments and constant adjustment of policy to ensure the realization of the objectives of national security and prosperity. Thus, though foreign policy positions may change and policies may shift, the style will continue to be the same — a blunt hard-nose pragmatic approach that is pre-emptive rather than reactive.

In the meantime, the fragmented condition of domestic political opposition together with a style of leadership that is at once convincing, authoritative and successful (and requires at most a tacit consensus within the ruling People's Action Party) creates an environment that is suited for the kind of foreign policy-making that is required for the current fluid and shifting international situation of the 1970s.

THE DOWNTURN IN THE SINGAPORE ECONOMY
Problems, Prospects and Possibilities for Recovery

Cheah Hock Beng

Our economy is in the process of transforming itself from a low-wage, low productivity regime to a high-wage, high-productivity regime. The process is well under way....

We are like a man on a flying trapeze, who has let go of one swing and is now sailing through mid-air. He cannot stop now. He must make it to the next swing if he is to recover safely. In the same way, we too have no choice but to press on with our economic restructuring (*Straits Times*, 27 July 1985, p. 1).

The above remarks were made by the then Minister of State for Trade and Industry, and head of the government-appointed Economic Committee, in connection with a sharp downturn in the Singapore economy. They reflected the government's perception of the acute precariousness of the city-state's economic position. The rate of economic growth declined from 8.2 per cent in 1984 to −1.7 per cent in 1985. Domestic demand declined by 3 per cent and trade also contracted by 4 per cent during the year. A total of 90,000 jobs were lost and the unemployment rate had risen to 6 per cent at the end of the year. Observers also expect that the depressed economic conditions would continue over the next two to three years.

In the course of 1985, the government introduced several measures in an attempt to steer the economy back on to its original course. That course had been set earlier when the government announced its strategy for economic re-structuring in 1979. That strategy was intended to promote a general upgrading of the economy, so as to move out of low-wage, labour-intensive activities

---

Reprinted from Lim Joo-Jock, ed., *Southeast Asian Affairs 1986* (Singapore: Institute of Southeast Asian Studies, 1986), pp. 296–312. At the time of original publication, Cheah Hock Beng was Lecturer in the Department of Economics and Management, University of New South Wales, Canberra.

and into skill- and higher technology-intensive activities in manufacturing and services. It was believed that the latter activities would be capable of sustaining higher wages for the work-force, and would also be less vulnerable to trade competition and protectionist restrictions. Consequently, it was believed that Singapore would be less likely to encounter economic difficulties.

Why then did the strategy "fail" to avoid the present economic difficulties? Was it due to some unforeseen and unavoidable circumstances, or could the cause be attributed to some inherent aspects of the strategy itself? What are the prospects for a viable and sustained economic recovery?

External Developments Contributing to the Downturn

Singapore's economy has been and will continue to be strongly affected by external developments because it has been closely integrated with the international economy. In this respect, the downturn in Singapore's economy is, in part, a direct consequence of the more adverse conditions in the international economy. The reasons for this include the following.

Firstly, a slow-down in the economies of the mature industrialized countries in Europe and North America, combined with the catching-up by Japan, and a host of newly Industrializing countries, has led to a relative convergence of economic structures and massive duplication of productive capabilities. This has resulted in intense competitive pressures for numerous products and many industries. Even in the 1970s, it had become clear to some observers that,

> Ships, steel, textiles — these are a few of the sectors of the world economy in which there has recently developed a marked surplus in productive capacity and in which there has been consequent earnest and often heated discussion among the governments and producers over the share-out of markets and the rules, not of free trade, but of "fair" trade. Shoes, color television sets, ball bearings, furniture — the list of manufacturing sectors in which similar international negotiations have been conducted grows each year. Ahead lie new and possibly even greater problems of surplus capacity.[1]

While the existence of surplus production capacity, combined with constraints on the growth of demand, leads to a need for structural adjustments in the economy, in many countries these adjustments are often difficult to undertake because of the massive scale of the problems and the keenness of the competition.

Secondly, rapid technical change, involving the revolutionary transformation of methods of production, has promoted a substantial improvement in the efficiency potential of manufacturing processes in the world.[2] While these improved processes have the potential for very positive benefits over the long term, for a period of time, they intensify recessionary and deflationary pressures because of their immediate impact in displacing labour and increasing competition. Consequently, for a period of time, there is the prospect of a contradiction between a massive expansion of the productive potential with the introduction of new technology, and constraints upon (if not actual reductions in) the growth of demand, resulting from the general recession and from the rise in unemployment.

Thirdly, deflationary tendencies arise from widespread price-cutting among a host of products and industries. These have ranged from agricultural commodities to petroleum products, integrated circuits and computers, all of which have experienced a substantial fall in prices. It has been argued in this connection, that:

> We are entering a long period of deflation ... Deflation will mean that prices will be falling across an extremely broad front, from raw materials to services ... Deflation will also aggravate the debt burdens of many companies ... The overall lay-offs will mean that the depression must deepen. This in turn will mean that the pace of deflation will quicken, eroding corporate cash flows so that more firms in more industries will be forced to cut prices drastically, even though they will not be able to offset [price] cuts by cost cuts. Decreasing demand will mean that companies will be unable to absorb price cuts through increased sales. Many companies will be forced to make further cuts in investment, and slash payrolls as the economy keeps sliding. The deflationary spiral will ultimately resemble the inflationary spiral to which we have become accustomed, but up-side down.[3]

For a period of time, a revival of economic growth in the United States and the large increase in U.S. imports helped to sustain growth in other countries, including Singapore, and to postpone the economic downturn. However, the United States has almost reached the limits of its willingness to sustain a continued rapid growth of imports. Consequently, recessionary and deflationary tendencies are likely to be further intensified in the years ahead.

Fourthly, the intensification of demand constraints leads to a resurgence of protectionist restrictions, particularly among countries which have large foreign debts and substantial trade deficits. These trade restrictions break up existing markets and reduce the scope for many previously successful producers and exporters. These will have to compete more keenly with each other for the remaining markets.

Moreover, countries which have foreign debts and substantial trade deficits, if they are not to default on their repayments, will also be under great pressure to increase their exports. That is, foreign debts and trade deficit problems lead countries to impose more restrictions on imports while simultaneously trying to promote their own exports. However, the adoption of similar policies by others leads to greater difficulties for all (would be) exporters. And because keener competition makes the search for a solution through increased exports more difficult, it increases the tendency to seek a solution through a (further) reduction in imports. Consequently, there is again a real possibility of a more widespread outbreak of trade wars and a downward spin of the international economy. This compounds the other recessionary and deflationary tendencies in the international economy.

In particular, this creates serious difficulties for countries like Singapore which seek to maintain open economies, and rely upon access to foreign markets. In Singapore's case, the small size and openness of its economy, plus its strong dependence on trade (which amounts to more than three times the value of its gross national product), means that it would inevitably be more seriously affected by the adverse effects of recession in the international economy than many other countries.[4]

As a result of the slow-down in the international economy and the politicization of international economic relations, Singapore will find it increasingly difficult to export to developed-country markets, including the export of manufactures for which investments were previously undertaken with that aim by foreign investors.

Thus, the city-state should expect a continuation of recession in the international economy, the possibility of further losses of privileges under the Generalised Scheme of Preferences, increased protectionism in Western markets, a fall in the capacity of other developing countries to finance imports, and increasing unwillingness among private investors, domestically and abroad, to take risks.

Moreover, while the process of economic restructuring has been promoted in various ways, several complications have been encountered which lay open to question a number of key assumptions of the general development strategy.

Difficulties in Economic Restructuring

Firstly, the economic downturn has affected virtually all sectors and all firms. This has served to undermine a major assumption of Singapore's development strategy, that is, that economic diversification would provide balance and greater stability. This perception had provided the rationale for the initial industrialization programme and, more recently, for the promotion of new service activities. In the 1960s and 1970s, a more diversified economy had indeed helped the city-state to become less vulnerable to the vagaries of any one industry or sector. However, when the recession is generalized throughout the economy, as it has been on this occasion, affecting not just the manufacturing sector but also construction, the tourist industry and retail activities, as well as banking and finance (see Table 1), then the strategy of diversification loses its efficacy.

In particular, the generalized recession means that greater reliance on the service sector is not an alternative which would, in itself, be free of difficulties. For many activities in the service sector too have been severely affected by the economic downturn. It is also likely that in the future, competition will continue to intensify in the service sector. This development would encourage further the introduction and spread of new technology in that sector. To the extent that the new technology is labour-saving, this means that not as many jobs would be created in that sector as could otherwise be expected. This means that the potential capacity of the service sector to absorb labour displaced from other sectors in the economy would also be reduced.

Secondly, another assumption of the economic restructuring strategy is that substantial improvements in productivity would help to improve the city-state's competitiveness, and to sustain economic growth. However, it will become increasingly difficult to raise productivity in a situation of substantial over-capacity and constrained demand. Indeed, declining sales and output lead to loss of scale economies and other positive dynamic effects, with the possibility that productivity levels will fall. Investments in new equipment and plant will also be constrained by poor business expectations. This too will further constrain productivity growth.

Thirdly, Singapore has for long relied heavily on foreign multinational corporations (MNCs) to provide better skills, technology and access to foreign markets. Recent experiences with Rollei, General Electric[5] and other companies, have shown that the MNCs are not immune to economic setbacks. MNCs in the electronics industry, for example, have been hit seriously by the slump in that industry. As a result of this and other developments, some MNCs are shifting production to final markets, and the inflow of foreign investment

TABLE 1
Percentage Change in Real Gross Domestic Product by Industry

	1980	1981	1982	1983	1984	1985 1st qtr	1985 2nd qtr	1985 3rd qtr
TOTAL	10.2	9.9	6.3	7.9	8.2	2.7	-1.2	-3.5
Goods sector	11.1	10.7	2.0	8.7	10.2	-1.7	-9.8	-11.7
Agriculture & fishing	1.9	-2.3	-7.0	1.9	4.3	5.3	-11.2	-11.6
Quarrying	7.4	29.7	26.5	20.5	-1.6	2.5	-3.3	-7.1
Manufacturing	11.8	9.7	-5.7	2.1	8.8	-2.9	-7.4	-10.1
Construction	10.9	17.5	36.3	29.3	15.3	0.0	-15.6	-15.6
Services sector	11.9	10.9	9.1	8.2	8.0	4.7	2.6	0.3
Utilities	7.7	7.3	4.8	9.0	7.9	9.4	6.0	2.1
Commerce	7.2	5.7	5.9	4.4	5.7	4.1	2.2	-4.2
Transport & communications	13.9	13.8	12.0	7.9	10.2	5.0	1.3	0.9
Financial & business services	22.4	19.0	10.8	12.8	10.5	3.7	3.5	3.0
Other services	5.7	6.0	9.4	8.8	4.1	6.3	3.1	3.0

Notes: Real gross domestic product refers to GDP at 1968 factor cost. Percentage change refers to the change of the current period over the corresponding period of the previous year.
Source: Department of Statistics, Singapore.

has slowed down. This slowing down of foreign investments impinges adversely on the speed and the scope of the industrial restructuring process.

Fourthly, the most capital-intensive activities and the ones with the highest value-added per worker, such as petroleum refining, shipbuilding and repairing, oil-rig construction activities, and other industries which are high on the government's list of priorities, such as electronics, were among the industries most severely affected by the economic downturn. This is because even the more capital-intensive, high value-added and priority industries have encountered intense international competition, arising from the emergence of new competitors and coinciding with a decline in demand in export markets.

Fifthly, Singapore's policies of promoting the upgrading of manufacturing industry towards higher value-added, more skilled and more capital-intensive activities, are also in competition with similar efforts in other countries. Indeed, to the extent that its industrialization efforts move increasingly into higher-technology products and industries, they become subject to the intense international competitive pressures that exist in this arena. It is likely that the competitive pressures in these industries will be as intense as, and perhaps even more so than, in the older, mature industries. For the former is an arena which is dominated by the principal international economic competitors. In this respect, Singapore's development efforts to move into higher technology products and industries are drawing it closer to "big league" competition. And in this competition, the stakes and the risks are substantially greater.

Moreover, because of the difficult international economic situation, many governments are more inclined to adopt interventionist measures. In many cases, this means targeting the same "sunrise" industries that other countries have chosen. This too implies that intense economic competition can be expected even among the city-state's targeted priority industries.

As there is no international institution or forum where the different national strategies and policies are co-ordinated before they are implemented, the validation of strategic choices has to occur through direct competition in the international economy. On this basis, co-ordination is achieved *ex post*, with potentially disastrous consequences for those defeated on the international battleground. In short, the economic restructuring strategy is not unambiguously leading Singapore towards a safer haven.

Higher Domestic Costs and Declining International Competitiveness

Another constraint on the economic restructuring process arose directly from various measures which contributed to rising domestic costs. These had the unintended consequence of lowering Singapore's international competitiveness. Reduced competitiveness contributed to the economic downturn, and that outcome in turn undermined the capacity of many firms to continue with the process of upgrading their operations. The origins of this sequence of events may be analysed as follows.

In the late 1970s, the city-state was at or nearing the end of the "easy phase" of its export-promotion drive. Furthermore, its economic planners and their advisors believed that they had learnt a lesson from the failure to allow wages to rise to higher levels earlier during the 1970s. They believed that economic restructuring and more substantial improvements in productivity would have been promoted if wage increases had not been restrained during that period. It was noted that higher wage increases in other newly industrializing countries were accompanied by more substantial improvements in productivity in those countries. In comparison, a lower level of wage increase in Singapore was accompanied by a lower growth rate of productivity. The "lesson" that was drawn was that if Singapore wanted to spur the process of economic restructuring in general, and productivity growth in particular, it should encourage significant wage increases to "correct" the deficiencies of the previous wage-restraint policy.

Consequently, in the late 1970s, the government, through the National Wages Council (NWC) launched a policy which boosted the level of wage increase. This was accompanied by increased contributions to the Central Provident Fund (CPF) and the introduction of the Skills Development Fund (SDF) levy, which contributed to a rise in labour costs, together with other measures which led to higher costs of housing, transportation and public utilities. These, and other financial impositions, raised the costs of undertaking economic activity and the general cost of living in the city-state.

This effect was, in part, intended. For the policy-makers believed that if firms were confronted by higher costs and lower profitability, it would spur them towards more extensive mechanization, computerization, and automation. In particular, those firms engaged in labour-intensive, low-wage and low value-added activities would be "encouraged" to upgrade their activities, or move those activities abroad, or cease their operations and release their resources to be redeployed and better utilized elsewhere in the economy. It was further reasoned that firms engaged in high value-added, more skilled and high technology-intensive activities, which are highly mechanized, computerized and automated, would not be adversely affected. In this way, it was expected that the economic restructuring process would be speeded up, with substantial benefits perceived to accrue in the long run.

However, the adverse developments had not been fully anticipated. The Economic Committee, a high-level advisory committee set up to review the country's economic restructuring strategy, revealed in its interim report that unit labour costs in Singapore, taking productivity changes into account, had risen 39 per cent between 1980 and 1984.[6] This increase was significantly higher than that in Taiwan, Hong Kong and South Korea. It even exceeded similar growth rates in Japan, the United States and the United Kingdom.

Moreover, the Economic Committee recognized that the substantial rise in wage costs was only one part of an escalation of cost increases over a broad front. It reported:

> In addition to the increase in wage costs, increases in indirect taxes and other costs have also hurt businesses in Singapore. These other costs include: rental payments which, after steep increases in 1980–84, have only recently begun to come down; interest costs which rose sharply since 1980 with the rise in interest rates; statutory board rates and fees, which have generally risen each year; indirect taxes, notably property taxes which have increased with the rise in property values; and taxes on transportation, where deliberate increases to meet specific policy objectives have added to business

costs. These increases have made the process of adjustment even more difficult for employers.[7]

One adverse consequence of the increased costs of undertaking economic activity was that the benefits of the economic restructuring strategy were offset to a significant degree by the increased financial burden. While some of these measures had been adopted to promote other national objectives, such as to reduce traffic congestion through greater reliance on public transport, conservation in the use of scarce water, land and other resources, and so forth, one unintended consequence was that they acted at cross-purposes with the objective of improving Singapore's international competitiveness — by cutting into the gains to be expected from greater automation, higher productivity and better management.

Difficulties also arose because, in many cases, the cost increases could not be passed on through price increases, as in the past, because increasing competition, domestically and from abroad, was generating strong deflationary pressures in the economy. In this situation, the previous inflationary trend could not be sustained.

Table 2 shows the change in the pattern of inflation in Singapore, with imported inflation becoming progressively less important between 1980 and 1984, while domestic sources of inflation rose in significance. Indeed, in 1983 and 1984, domestic inflation was wholly responsible for price increases in Singapore, even offsetting the fall in the general price level of imports.

This change in the pattern of inflation is again reflected in Table 3, where the Wholesale Price Index reveals the deflationary pressures most clearly. That index also shows that the price level of imported products has declined. More importantly, it shows that the price levels of Singapore manufactured products, and of exported products, have also fallen significantly since 1981. It is this fall in the prices of domestic output and of exports, combined with the substantial rise in the domestic costs of undertaking economic activity in Singapore (which also offset the benefits from the lower cost of imports), that has contributed to a serious profit squeeze on producers in the city-state.

Despite Singapore's heavy reliance on imports for consumption and intermediate goods, and the deflationary trend of import prices, the Consumer Price Index (CPI) and the gross domestic product (GDP) deflator both show only a disinflationary trend. In the case of the CPI, it is again

TABLE 2
Sources of Inflation (in per cent)

	1980	1981	1982	1983	1984p
Imported	55	40	28	−37	−4
Domestic	45	60	72	137	104
Total	100	100	100	100	100

Source: Ministry of Trade and Industry, *Economic Survey of Singapore 1984* (Singapore: Ministry of Trade and Industry, 1985).

TABLE 3
Percentage Change in Price Indicators

	1980	1981	1982	1983	1984	1985 1st qtr	1985 2nd qtr	1985 3rd qtr
Wholesale Price Index								
General	19.6	3.9	-4.2	-3.7	-0.6	-1.6	-1.4	-2.5
Imported products	16.8	1.6	-4.4	-2.6	-0.7	-3.3	-2.1	-2.5
Exported products	23.3	3.7	-3.1	-4.7	-3.9	-2.3	-1.4	-1.6
Singapore manufactured products	23.4	2.9	-5.2	-3.8	-2.1	-2.7	-2.6	-4.4
Local farm products	10.7	13.6	4.3	-1.0	-10.6	-24.1	-2.6	11.5
Building materials	14.9	6.5	-4.1	-4.0	-6.9	-8.8	-7.4	-6.1
Consumer Price Index								
General	8.5	8.2	3.9	1.2	2.6	0.2	0.6	0.5
Food	7.7	9.6	5.0	0.3	1.5	-2.2	-1.7	-0.7
Housing	11.2	4.3	2.2	0.3	2.1	4.2	4.2	1.4
Clothing	1.9	1.8	0.4	0.1	-0.4	-2.5	-2.8	-2.5
Transport & communications	12.9	9.5	2.4	0.8	3.8	0.8	4.8	4.8
Miscellaneous	7.0	8.6	4.4	4.8	5.6	2.6	0.7	0.2
Gross Domestic Product Deflator	8	7	4	3	1	n.a.	n.a.	n.a.

Notes: Percentage change refers to the change of the current period over the corresponding period of the previous year.
Source: Department of Statistics, Singapore.

important to note that the fall in the price levels of food and clothing (both of which have a large import component) was offset by a significant rise in the price levels of housing, and transport and communications (caused to a large degree by government-induced price increases).

Thus, up to the second quarter of 1985, the government did not fully appreciate the intensity of the tendencies towards recession and deflation, arising from a more competitive international economy, and the implications of these developments (see *Straits Times*, 2 February 1985, p. 1; 5 March 1985, p. 1; and 20 March 1985, p. 1). Various well-intended measures which it introduced had the unintended consequence of raising the costs of undertaking economic activity in the country, offsetting the benefits from imported deflation and from the economic restructuring process itself, and working at cross-purposes with the general objective of increasing the city-state's international competitiveness.

The Implications for Future Strategy

The recent problems have highlighted the limitations of and the growing constraints upon the earlier strategy of economic restructuring. In many ways, the difficulties also suggest that the "developmental state" in Singapore has increasingly been confronting the limits on its capacity to intervene in the economy, and to direct successfully the pattern of change. In the 1985 Budget Speech, one indication of the limits was revealed when it was announced that the government would restrict the range of activities of statutory boards, facilitate the privatization of state enterprises, encourage the private sector to take the lead in the economy, and permit greater scope for the operation of market forces.

Other reasons for the recent inclination for privatization stem from criticisms about the "unfair" advantages enjoyed by state enterprises, and from the recent difficulties encountered by a number of state joint-ventures in Singapore. The most prominent cases are to be found in the shipbuilding and repairing, and the petroleum-refining and petrochemical industries, where a number of major investments have met with serious difficulties in the midst of a world-wide deterioration of prospects in these industries.

However, the move towards privatization is also likely to meet with serious constraints. For the question here revolves around the willingness of the private sector to take up the challenge. There is a distinct possibility that, in a recessionary situation, the private sector itself would be hesitant in initiating major new investments, or becoming involved in major new projects, because of the greater risks and the prospects of lower profits. If this were the case, it is likely that privatization would proceed at a relatively slow pace. Indeed, when the private sector perceives that a previously active government has rather suddenly become reticent in undertaking new investments, or sustaining earlier ventures, it may choose to follow that lead in withdrawing from commitments, rather than take over the lead by increasing investments. If so, recessionary pressures would be intensified, rather than moderated — an unintended consequence of the change in government policy.[8] For this and other reasons, it is likely that the government will continue to play an important role in the economy, despite the fact that a greater degree of liberalization in various areas would be very helpful for the economy.

The Economic Role of the Government

The government's earlier and continuing efforts to promote greater mechanization, automation and computerization, and its campaigns to raise productivity, are all helpful and important measures to promote positive changes in the economy. However, these may not be sufficient to meet the challenges. It would be necessary to reduce substantially the costs of undertaking business activity in the country, if international competitiveness and economic growth are to be enhanced.

Two broad areas in which the government could make a useful contribution are in relation to the lowering of production and operating costs, and the general cost of living. Both of these are not mutually exclusive. Indeed, improvements in each area could have significant beneficial effects for the other. The government could help to lower production and operating costs by continuing to reduce rentals for Jurong Town Corporation (JTC) factories, the price of public utilities, the costs of commercial transportation, and other economic services relied upon by industry. It could help to lower the costs of living through greater efforts to reduce the costs of housing, food, and personal transportation, among other things.

Indeed, if substantial reductions in the cost of living can be achieved, it would even be possible for workers to accept a reduction in (nominal) wages, where necessary, without suffering a fall in their standard of living. On the contrary, if the cost of living could fall at a more rapid rate than the fall in nominal wages, workers would still be able to enjoy a higher standard of living based upon an appreciating real wage. In areas where such wage reductions are feasible, companies could further reduce their production and operating costs and, thus, further enhance their competitiveness.

For the above reasons, the recent cost-reduction measures introduced by the government in July, in August and in October 1985, are significant steps in the right direction. These actions, undertaken after the severity of the economic downturn in the second quarter was realized, included fiscal concessions to firms on property tax, rental of JTC and Housing and Development Board (HDB) premises, fuel, transportation, storage, public utilities, and communications services. These concessions have been estimated to amount to more than S$1 billion in revenue foregone, equivalent to 6.2 per cent of the gross national product in 1984 (*Straits Times*, 26 October 1985, p. 1). Together with the suspension of the payroll tax and the reduction of the Skills Development Fund levy, announced in March 1985, they constitute a significant start in the drive to make Singapore more cost competitive.

Given the scale and severity of the problems that exist, the extent and speed of the government's recent response is entirely appropriate. However, that response must also be sustained in the future, and become a part of a comprehensive and integrated strategy for cost reduction at the national level. This should be the important new element in the general economic restructuring strategy in the years ahead.

It must be anticipated that the government's efforts to reduce costs, would ease the pressures on some producers to rationalize their operations. As the cost reductions offered by the government would benefit all industries, some producers of low-wage and labour-intensive manufactures and services would acquire a renewed lease of life. On the one hand, this would not be bad in the present difficult economic situation, as it would help to sustain output and employment levels. But, over the longer term, it could slow down the economic restructuring process and produce an effect opposed to what was intended in the long-term development strategy, which was to hasten the phasing-out of labour-intensive, low-wage, low value-added economic activities.

The solution for this problem would be to encourage competition to prevail. If the government enabled new enterprises to be set up more easily, and to compete with earlier-established firms, this would itself generate pressures in the market for resources to be put to the best possible use. In this way, it would also limit the ability of firms to capture unduly high profits, and to slacken in the economic restructuring process. In particular, this reliance on market forces to sustain the incentives for firms to continue to improve the efficiency and sophistication of their operations, relieves the government of the need to devise other intervening measures to sustain those objectives.

There is, however, a possibility that cost-reduction measures by the government, involving a foregoing of a substantial amount of public revenue, could result in budget deficits in the years ahead, despite the government's well-known aversion to such a situation. This possibility and its associated difficulties would be minimized to the extent that the cost reductions offered by the government and its statutory bodies spring, firstly, from genuine reductions in the costs of providing public services, because of significant improvements in the efficiency of public administration, and in the production and delivery costs of public goods and services; and, secondly, from a recovery of public revenue when a viable and sustained economic recovery gets under way. Nevertheless, if for a period of time a deficit is incurred, this should not immediately lead to the reversal of the fiscal and other concessions, which can be expected to bring substantial benefits over the longer term.

In short, the greatest positive impact for private industry and for the economy as a whole could be achieved if the government itself were to continue to promote a comprehensive and integrated strategy for cost reduction at the national level, including reductions in a host of direct and indirect taxes. This would be a powerful adjunct to the earlier efforts to promote economic upgrading and restructuring, because it would enhance the capacity of the private sector and of the country as a whole to be internationally competitive.

The Controversy over Wage Policy and CPF Contributions

With the economic downturn, there have been numerous complaints from various quarters that wages in Singapore are "too high". Business circles have pressured the government to take measures to lower labour costs. The calls include suggestions for a general wage freeze and a reduction in CPF contributions. The latter would, in effect, result in a diminution of total wages for all employees. However, in this area, government initiatives may be problematic or even counter-productive.

At present, a "temporary" general wage restraint appears to be an expedient answer to the problem of the country's declining international competitiveness. It has been argued that Singapore should practice wage restraint for two or three years, allowing wage increases among its competitors to close the gap and enable it to regain international competitiveness.

However, would wage restraint prove counter-productive for the future, just as the 1979–81 "wage correction" policy has now been held responsible for the city-state's reduced international competitiveness, and just as the wage restraint policy of the late 1960s to mid-1970s was previously held responsible for the slow productivity growth during that period? In short, would a general wage restraint (or reduction) be a backward step in relation to Singapore's own earlier experiences of wage policy?

While the general wage level is higher in Singapore than in other newly industrializing countries such as Hong Kong, Taiwan and South Korea, this partly reflects the greater relative scarcity of labour in Singapore compared to those countries. Given the declining trend in Singapore's birth rate, and the difficulties that would be associated with any attempt to resort to a large-scale influx of foreign workers, the situation of relative labour scarcity is unlikely to change significantly (unless business activity in Singapore declines dramatically. In that case, market pressures would themselves force wages downwards.)

Consequently, efforts to reduce artificially any component of total wages (salary plus employer's CPF contributions) by a significant amount in Singapore could miss this important factor and seriously distort market signals. The potential problems associated with any attempt to implement an economy-wide wage freeze (or cut) would include the following.

Firstly, a contraction of domestic demand. Domestic demand contracted by 3 per cent in 1985. A wage freeze or wage cut would not help to improve the situation. Indeed, increased anxieties over "rainy days" ahead, plus the likelihood of a reduced rate of savings resulting from a large cut in employers' CPF contributions, may lead employees to reduce personal and household expenditures further, and also to increase voluntary savings to compensate for the lower rate of compulsory savings. The net effect could be a larger contraction of domestic demand. This would compound the difficulties.

Secondly, the need to improve productivity and spur the upgrading and restructuring of the economy provided the rationale for earlier efforts to boost wage increases. Based on that reasoning, a general wage freeze/cut could halt or reverse the effects of the earlier measures and reduce incentives among firms to continue with the upgrading of their operations. If so, a wage freeze/cut could in fact turn out to be the "soft option", not the stiff, but necessary, medicine that it has been portrayed to be.

Thirdly, a general wage freeze/cut policy is too inflexible. It does not differentiate between the different conditions of different firms and industries. Furthermore, there are serious uncertainties about the best level at which to restrain or lower wages. Even if that level could be established, based on a host of assumptions, as an average for the whole economy, how should that be translated in relation to the particular conditions of specific sectors, industries and firms? This has been a long-standing imponderable of the earlier wage policy, and it will continue to bedevil any general attempt to restrain or cut wages.

At the same time, wage restraint, based conveniently on the present general wage level until the general wage levels in competing countries "catch up", ignores the fact that since independence, Singapore's wage level has always been higher than those of Hong Kong, Taiwan and South Korea. It could be a mistake to wait for wages in those countries to catch up, just as it could be folly to wait for wages in Indonesia, Bangladesh and China to catch up. Based on the inherently greater relative scarcity of labour and, thus, inherently higher wage level, Singapore must learn to do different things, or perform them better, relative to its competitors. Waiting for their wages to catch up could be a poor solution to the problems, for those problems could be compounded in the interim, rather than resolved.

It cannot be denied that in certain cases, at the present time, a wage freeze/cut is needed to restore the viability of particular business activities, and that this fact is appreciated by and agreeable to the employees of the enterprises concerned. In those cases, the employers and workers concerned should be encouraged to take the appropriate measures to improve the prospects of their firms. But this should not be translated into a blanket imposition of a uniform level of restraint or rate of wage reduction on the whole Singapore work-force, which may not be necessary or appropriate in other situations.

Fourthly, such a policy would affect the lower-income group more seriously than those in the higher income group who, with better skills and greater demand for their services, would possess greater leverage in avoiding the wage restraints or reductions. Consequently, the policy could have regressive effects. Moreover, it could lead to a bigger "brain drain" of domestic talent abroad, and also make it more difficult to recruit the foreign expertise that may be needed.

Fifthly, a general wage freeze or cut would constitute a "stop-go-stop" experience which would be unsettling and incompatible with a consistent long-term development strategy. Indeed, "temporary" policy reversals may have unforeseen and unintended but, nevertheless, serious adverse long-term consequences. In view of previous unforeseen problems encountered with wage policy, such as the "wage correction" policy, the second-tier wage increase, and other measures, it may be best to allow wage levels to be determined through the market mechanism. In this respect, a general wage freeze/cut would constitute intervention by the state in the workings of the labour market, in a manner inconsistent with the present policy preference for the freer operation of market forces.

If the continuation of the higher wage policy is perceived to be no longer feasible, and if a policy of wage restraint/cut may, from past experience, lead to difficulties, what is the alternative? The alternative could be an attempt to work towards freeing the wage-determination mechanism, so as to permit each enterprise to determine the wages of its workers, while focusing government attention largely on other efforts to reduce the general cost of production and the general cost of living in the economy. Individual enterprises can then be left with the task of determining how best to exploit the benefits of the general lowering of costs in the economy, and how much to reward their workers, in relation to the specific labour requirements of their operations, the competitive pressures they face domestically and abroad, and the effectiveness of their management. Such an alternative would, in effect, be a flexible wage policy, which facilitates differentiated responses at all levels, related to the specific requirements of the diverse sectors, industries and firms in the economy.

Furthermore, if there is a clear need to lower the rate of CPF contributions, it may be best to credit the difference to the employees. This would, in the first instance, boost the take-home pay of employees and help to sustain or to raise domestic demand, thus countering other contractionary forces in the economy. Secondly, the release of a portion of existing CPF contributions to the work-force would assist them to reduce the burden of any wage reduction that may be necessary for particular enterprises. This could also help to encourage the workers concerned to accept wage reductions in cases where this is important for the continued viability of their enterprises. In this way, the lowering of the rate of CPF contributions could accompany and facilitate, to a greater extent than at present, the determination of wages at the enterprise level. This could help to resolve a number of difficulties related to wage policy which have plagued the city-state for many years.

Export Promotion and Negotiating Strategy

In the present circumstances, even if Singapore's continued pursuit of export-oriented industrialization continues to be the "correct" strategy, that approach is likely to meet with diminishing returns.[9] Thus, while there is undoubtedly a need for more trade promotion efforts to minimize the decline in exports, it is also important for the city-state to intensify its efforts in international economic diplomacy, to create more favourable conditions for trade and investment.

In this respect, a campaign on the basis of the general benefits of free trade could achieve paltry results, at a time when many countries, and the special interest groups within them, are inclining towards an increasingly narrow definition of their national (sectional) interests. It may thus be important to formulate new negotiating strategies which take this development into account, and which challenge it on different grounds. Specifically, Stewart has argued that developing countries will gain little from the pursuit of general demands for improvements in the international system. They should instead concentrate on influencing specific interests which are important to or influential in the developed countries. In her view,

> Detailed information on bilateral and multilateral relationships and interests are needed to establish the full potential [for LDC negotiating strategy] ... the mechanism is to use and make operational particular interests, rather than appeal hopefully to general interests. The area of potential action does not only concern interests already in being, but from a longer term perspective, includes the ways in which interests develop ... Policies can then be selected which are likely to produce a favourable constellation of interests.[10]

In a similar vein, Ballance and Sinclair have recommended a sectoral approach to industrial and trade negotiations, to take into account the unique features of different industries.[11]

There is also a need for a better appreciation of the possibilities for latecomers in development to gain special advantages when the new competes with the old in a process of dynamic change. This and other Schumpeterian insights suggest that while the proliferation of trade restrictions could create serious difficulties, it does not necessarily spell doom for a small exporting country. There may, in fact, be opportunities for turning adversity into advantage, a knack which has been characteristic of the Japanese. Thus, it has been argued by Yoffie that a newly industrializing country could improve its trade earnings in the face of restrictions if it were politically adept and had an industrial structure that could adapt to changing market trends.[12]

According to Yoffie, both Taiwan and South Korea found the restrictions on their export of footwear so helpful to the upgrading of their industrial capabilities and less to their trade earnings that they implemented their own unilateral voluntary export restraints (VERs) after the United States formally discontinued the bilateral orderly marketing agreements (OMAs) with these countries.[13] He also made the observation that:

> ... there are political and economic weaknesses in the structure of modern protectionism. The industrial nations, particularly the United States, have not employed orderly marketing arrangements and voluntary export restraints as well conceived tools of industrial intervention. On the contrary, OMAs and VERs have been used as ad hoc, short-run political policies that may not be as dangerous as UNCTAD and others believe. By emphasizing adjustment in their trade relations rather than intransigence, bargaining rather than coercion, and the substance of international agreements rather than their form, those less powerful exporting countries have found a way to turn an adverse situation into advantage ... the politics of trade have paradoxically created opportunities for the "weak" to beat the "strong" at their own game.[14]

Greater awareness of such possibilities could be very useful for efforts to find new avenues out of difficult and contentious situations.

Exchange Rates and Competitiveness

In the past few years, the Singapore dollar has strengthened relative to a number of other major currencies. This has led to complaints from business circles of greater difficulties in promoting exports. However, the converse effect of the currency appreciation is that imports are cheaper, and this helps to lower production costs. It may be contended that a large part of the negative impact on exports stemmed not from the rise in the exchange rate but from the rise in the domestic costs of undertaking economic activity in the country.

Consequently, if domestic costs can be held down, or progressively lowered, the higher exchange rate need not constitute a formidable problem. Indeed, given Singapore's need to import most of its final consumption goods, capital equipment and intermediate inputs, the appreciation of the Singapore dollar could make a significant contribution to the lowering of the cost of living and domestic production costs. This positive effect would help to enhance the city-state's international competitiveness.[15]

However, for this to be the case, it is important that active steps be taken to exploit the benefits of this development, by establishing appropriate mechanisms to feed a greater part of those benefits back into the processes of production and consumption, so as to achieve increasing competitiveness over time. In this connection, problems will arise, as they did earlier, not from the appreciation of the currency in itself, but from the failure to exploit fully its positive effects, and from other adverse developments which offset those benefits.

Undoubtedly, there are limits to the adjustment process in the short term, particularly if the changes in exchange rates are very large and/or very volatile. Consequently, it is necessary to be aware of the possibility of very serious adverse consequences stemming from such changes in relation to other major currencies, in particular, the U.S. dollar. Thurow has argued in effect that if the exchange rate of the U.S. dollar falls, the United States would become a relatively lower-cost producer, while other countries would become relatively higher-cost locations.[16] If this shift is substantial enough, production that had previously been moved offshore from the United States would be likely to be moved back there.

Given Singapore's heavy reliance on U.S. investments and on the operations of U.S. MNCs, the danger is a very serious one. Thurow had suggested that a collapse of 60 per cent in the value of the U.S. dollar could be possible. That gives some indication of the magnitude of the adjustment which may have to be confronted. As the time span available to make such an accommodation cannot be known in advance, the earlier the process of adjustment to such a possibility begins, the better. Once again, that process of adjustment implies strenuous efforts to achieve substantial and genuine cost reductions in Singapore.

Corporate Responses to Competition and Change

Finally, as competition continues to intensify in the years ahead, firms operating in Singapore will also have to bear a great responsibility for meeting the challenges ahead. One key element in corporate strategy in response to competitive pressures will be the need to achieve substantial improvements in the production process so as to attain lower unit costs ahead of the competition. This must constitute the core of the competitive strategy, the organizing principle, on the basis of which other elements of competitive strategy are integrated.

This strategy may be related to the experiences in the electronics industry, where deflationary pressures have been very strongly felt. In that industry, many of the companies which were able to achieve substantial product-performance improvements, together with significant cost savings, had adopted the strategy of "pricing down the experience curve".[17] For these companies, increases in the accumulated volume of production were associated with positive learning effects which, together with economies of scale, reduced significantly the unit costs of production. This enabled companies to lower prices while maintaining profit levels over time. The falling price encouraged the expansion of demand for the product, and the continuation of the positive dynamic effects. The company which achieved cost savings ahead of its competitors was also able to capture a growing market share.

However, earlier versions of this strategy need to be improved because market size for any product is not infinite, because many products are subject to technical obsolescence as a result of rapid technological advances, because of the proliferation of competitors, and because of the spread of protectionism and other constraints on demand. These considerations are reflected in the non-linear shape of the product life-cycle, which manifests phases of growth, maturity and decline.

In view of these factors, attempts to capture economies of scale and of learning must be supplemented by other efforts to acquire economies of scope,[18] and the strategy of pricing down the experience curve must be pursued not just over the life-cycle of a single product, but over that of a series of products, each of which is superior to the previous one.

Thus, at the level of the firm, an integrated strategy for multi-dimensional competitive advantage must combine attention to cost reduction with product improvement, and improvements in the production process, so as to achieve significant economies of scale, scope and learning. Within this integrated strategy, companies must also take advantage of competitive pressures on their suppliers of primary and intermediate inputs. The ability to achieve and to capitalize upon lower costs for those inputs would help to enhance overall competitive advantage; that is, to be able to offer better products at lower prices.[19]

Local manufacturing enterprises in Singapore should also give greater consideration to the possibilities of investing abroad. This could be an important means for them to obtain cheaper production inputs, and to acquire better access to foreign markets. To the extent that the higher value-added activities of local firms need raw materials, components and other inputs from the less-sophisticated manufacturing activities which can no longer be competitively located in Singapore, and to the extent that the sourcing of these inputs from non-affiliated firms abroad may not be the most satisfactory way of acquiring these inputs, it could be profitable for these enterprises to establish subsidiaries abroad where the simpler manufacturing processes can be located, and links with the more sophisticated production activities retained in Singapore can be maintained.[20]

This would enable local firms to utilize their acquired managerial and technical expertise in the simpler manufacturing activities in setting up and managing those foreign operations. They would also be able to obtain returns from those operations in the form of profits, royalties, benefits from vertical or horizontal integration between the Singapore plant and its foreign subsidiary, as well as better knowledge of operational and marketing conditions abroad.[21] This outcome could be much more desirable than the total abandonment of the simpler manufacturing operations by local firms, with the consequence in some cases of the complete cessation of operations and the demise of the local enterprise.

Conclusions

A combination of domestic and external factors have contributed to the downturn in the Singapore economy in 1985. The economic restructuring strategy has itself come up against a number of constraints. Some of those constraints could have been anticipated but, even then, their effects could not have been fully and precisely determined *ex ante*. What needs to be done now is to direct greater attention to those constraints, and to test various possibilities for a breakthrough at diverse points. As the situation is significantly different from that in the past, this will require modifications in the general development strategy as well as in corporate strategies.

Among other things, the government should endeavour to lower further the present burden of direct and indirect taxes, and also strive harder to achieve greater economies in the costs of transportation, public utilities, and other public goods and services, and pass on these savings to domestic producers and consumers. This would assist producers to be more cost competitive, and enable consumers to gain real wage increases through the falling cost of living. Firms, too, should improve organizational and operational efficiency by persisting with their efforts to upgrade their products and production processes, exploiting the benefits of lower cost inputs and equipment, and adopting more aggressive pricing and marketing strategies.

Even if these efforts are successful, and economic recovery is achieved, it is unlikely in the near future to reach the growth levels attained in previous years. But in view of the severe bottlenecks which the very rapid growth rates caused during the earlier periods, this may have some positive aspects. Economic recovery at a slower pace reduces the likelihood and the severity of potential bottlenecks in the future, because the economy would have more time and greater scope to respond to the shortages which might occur. Thus, slower growth has its advantages. Another of these benefits is that the economic downturn, combined with labour-saving technical change, will alleviate the previous labour-supply constraints in the economy. Furthermore, continuing deflationary pressures on the prices of a host of goods and services could produce significant reductions in the cost of living and in the costs of undertaking business activity in Singapore.

While cost reduction is crucial for Singapore at present, such efforts must be undertaken with great caution in relation to wages. It should be realized in this connection that artificially restraining or depressing the general wage level could have one or more of the following adverse consequences: an unduly low and, in time, unsustainable wage level; a further contraction of domestic demand immediately or in the future; a reversal of the incentives for firms to press for productivity improvements and to continue with the upgrading of their operations, and the undermining of the long-term strategy for economic upgrading and restructuring.

Despite the uncertainties, there are grounds for cautious optimism that small and responsive countries like Singapore will continue to discover sufficient profitable niches in the international economy to survive the present difficulties. For, despite the more difficult economic situation, Singapore, as a follower of the more advanced industrial countries, could continue to gain special advantages from discoveries and innovations made in those countries. Singapore entrepreneurs and policy-makers should thus be alert to the unique opportunities which will be created by new products, new technologies, new skills, new organizational systems and new markets, and be prepared, through greater ingenuity, flexibility and speed, to capitalize upon those opportunities ahead of other competitors.

This Schumpeterian outlook may prove to be particularly useful in coping with the complex and deeply entrenched economic difficulties in the world today.[22] For those difficulties portend major transformations within the economic system which, in Schumpeter's view, constitutes the process of "creative destruction".[23] That process will weed out those activities, organizations and institutions which fail to respond to the new conditions, with severe consequences for those who continue to rely upon them.

In the years ahead, therefore, we are likely to observe, in a more forceful fashion, the collapse of many established companies, and the disintegration of some previously viable economies. For Singapore too, if the various efforts to turn the economy around do not take effect, the principal concern of the "man on the flying trapeze" would be whether any "safety net" is in place, and whether it would hold up against the impact of the crash.[24]

Given the scale and the severity of the current problems in Singapore and abroad, the concerns in the years ahead could revert to a struggle for economic survival, rather than be focused on economic recovery and visions of a better life. However, despite the current difficulties, from our perspective, the intense competitive pressures are transforming the international economy into a comparatively new and more efficient system. When the foundations of that new system have been laid, a revival of the international economy will again become a real possibility. A viable economic recovery in Singapore will be bound up with and dependent upon that possibility.

In the interim, there are measures that can be undertaken to orient the Singapore economy in a direction congruent with the developments which larger forces are producing in the international economy. Fundamentally, these measures are all related to making Singapore's economy more flexible, more innovative and more cost competitive. If, in the midst of the present difficulties, the city-state can perceive the means and the opportunities for achieving these aims, then it shall not only have reason to hope but, more importantly, it can begin to put together the elements of a viable strategy for economic recovery.

Notes

1. Susan Strange, "The Management of Surplus Productive Capacity", in *Economic Issues of the Eighties*, edited by N.M. Kamrany and R.H. Day (Baltimore: Johns Hopkins University Press, 1979), p. 226.
2. See Gary Anderson, "Planning for Restructured Competition", *Long Range Planning* 18, no 1 (1985): 21–29; and Paul Sillitoe, "Get Smart — That's the Message for Future Factories", *Far Eastern Economic Review*, 31 October 1985, pp. 82–84.
3. Robert Beckman, *The Downwave: Surviving the Second Great Depression* (London: Pan, 1983), pp. 164–65.
4. See R.S. Sayers, *The Vicissitudes of an Export Economy* (Sydney: Sydney University Press, 1965).
5. Rollei, a German camera manufacturer, suffered serious set-backs from Japanese competition and liquidated its large Singapore subsidiary in 1981. More recently, General Electric, a major American multinational company, faced with rising costs and strong competition, has transferred a large part of its Singapore operations to neighbouring countries, and scaled down its manufacturing activities in the city-state.
6. Ministry of Trade and Industry, *Economic Survey of Singapore, Second Quarter 1985* (Singapore: Ministry of Trade and Industry, 1985).
7. Ibid., p. 21.
8. In many cases, simply allowing market forces greater rein in the midst of an economic downturn is itself likely to lead to a deepening of the recession, at least for a period of time. The net results of that experience will have to be assessed in the future.
9. See the criticisms of Bela Balassa made by Albert Fishlow in *World Development* 12, no. 9 (1984): 979–82.
10. Frances Steward, "Brandt II — The Mirage of Collective Action in a Self-serving World", *Third World Quarterly* 5, no. 3 (1983): 646–47.
11. Robert Ballance and Stuart Sinclair, "Reindustrializing America: Policy Makers and Interest Groups", *World Economy* 7, no. 2 (1984): 197–214.
12. David Yoffie, *Power and Protectionism* (New York: Columbia University Press, 1983).
13. Ibid., p. 207.
14. Ibid., p. 9.
15. This perception has led the government to resist appeals for the exchange rate to be lowered. See *Straits Times*, 17 September

1985, p. 1; and V.G. Kulkarni, "Strongman's Dollar", *Far Eastern Economic Review*, 3 October 1985, pp. 50–51.
16. Lester Thurow, "America, Europe and Japan: A Time to Dismantle the World Economy", The *Economist*, 9 November 1985, pp. 17–26.
17. See Edmond Sciberras, *Multinational Electronics Companies and National Economic Policies* (Greenwich, Conn: JAI Press, 1977).
18. See Joel Goldhar and Mariann Jelinek, "Plan for Economies of Scope", *Harvard Business Review* 61, no. 6 (1983): 141–48.
19. See William Hall, "Survival Strategies in a Hostile Environment", *Harvard Business Review* 58, no. 5 (1980): 75–85; Arthur Thompson, "Strategies for Staying Cost Competitive", *Harvard Business Review* 62, no. 1 (1984): 110–17; and Gary Anderson, loc. cit.
20. See Raj Aggarwal, "Emerging Third World Multinationals: A Case Study of the Foreign Operations of Singapore Firms", *Contemporary Southeast Asia* 7, no. 3 (1985): 193–208.
21. See William Rapp, "Strategy Formulation and International Competition", *Columbia Journal of World Business* 8, no. 2 (1973): 98–112; Bruce Kogut, "Designing Global Strategies: Comparative and Competitive Value-added Chains", *Sloan Management Review* 26, no, 4 (1985): 15–28; and Bruce Kogut, "Designing Global Strategies: Profiting from Operational Flexibility", *Sloan Management Review* 27, no. 1 (1985): 27–38.
22. See Herbert Giersch, "Schumpeter and the Current and Future Development of the World Economy", in *Schumpeterian Economics*, edited by Helmut Frisch (New York: Praeger, 1981).
23. "Joseph Schumpeter, *Capitalism, Socialism and Democracy*, fifth edition (London: Allen and Unwin, 1976), pp. 82–83.
24. One aspect of the potential "safety net" is constituted by the substantial foreign reserves of the country, accumulated during the earlier period of rapid growth. These amounted to S$24.7 billion in July 1985. Monetary Authority of Singapore, *Monthly Statistical Bulletin* 6, no. 10 (1985): 32.

A RETURN TO NORMAL POLITICS
Singapore General Elections 2011[1]

Terence Chong

Introduction: Change from New to Old

Change is not always about the new. Occasionally, it is about the reappearance of the old. This is easily missed in a country that takes deep pride in perpetual self-transformation, and nowhere was this more evident than in the 7 May 2011 Singapore General Election (GE2011). In the wake of the most thoroughly contested general elections in generations, the mainstream media and pundits alike sought to capture this sense of change with a variety of phrases such as the "new normal"[2] and "watershed",[3] suggesting that the 61 per cent of the popular vote won by the People's Action Party (PAP) — its lowest since independence — has resulted in a different Singapore, one that has broken away from the norm. Such hyperbole is understandable and not entirely inaccurate, but greater contextualization will show that sometimes the old reappears as the new.

GE2011 was historically important for a couple of reasons. It saw the largest number of voters ever — 2.3 million, increasing from 2.1 million in 2006 and 2 million in 2001. It also gave us a quick glimpse into the future of Singapore politics because it saw the largest ever participation of first-time voters — 200,000 — as well as the largest number of younger voters with an estimated 600,000 out of 2.3 million between the ages of 21 and 35. The candidates from the various political parties reflect this youthful demographic too.[4] However, the fact that the ruling PAP was not returned to government on Nomination Day is not new. While 2011 saw 82 out of 87 seats contested, it must be remembered

---

Reprinted from Daljit Singh and Pushpa Thambipillai, eds., *Southeast Asian Affairs 2012* (Singapore: Institute of Southeast Asian Studies, 2012), pp. 284–98. At the time of original publication, Terence Chong was Senior Fellow at the Institute of Southeast Asian Studies, Singapore.

that 2006 saw 56 per cent of the seats contested (47 out of 84). And if we cast our minds back further to 1980, we will remember that 38 out of 68 Parliamentary seats were contested; in 1976 53 out of 69 seats were contested; and in 1972 57 seats out of 65 were contested. The lesson: the PAP could only take its incumbency for granted from the 1980s onwards. GE2006 and GE2011 mark a return to the old.

GE2011 was also keenly contested because of the credible slate of Opposition candidates. Running under the Opposition banner were individuals who bore the widely recognized credentials of education and academic success, from PhD holders, successful lawyers, to government scholars, as well as a former Principal Private Secretary to a Prime Minister. Nevertheless, such high credential Opposition candidates are not unprecedented either. JB Jeyaratnam, a former District Judge, broke the PAP's stranglehold over Parliament by winning over Anson constituency in the 1981 by-election. Former Solicitor-General Francis Seow contested in the Eunos Group Representative Constituency (GRC) in 1988, losing narrowly with 49.1 per cent of the vote. High profile lawyer Tang Liang Hong, who contested in Cheng San GRC with J.B. Jeyaratnam in 1997, won 45.2 per cent of the vote. The lesson: while the Opposition has attracted its fair share of unqualified candidates, it has also put up individuals with strong credentials. The performance of local Opposition parties in 2011 will only heighten its attractiveness to younger, more educated Singaporeans.

Beyond the demographics, GE2011 was, to all intents and purpose, poised between two camps — the PAP and the Workers' Party (WP). On one hand, the PAP campaigned on party leadership renewal, the induction of a fourth generation of national leaders from which the future Prime Minister would emerge, as well as a steady and trustworthy government. On the other, mounting the most coherent campaign of all the Opposition parties, the WP brought out the message for a more democratic Parliament with greater representation and accountability, greater government transparency, crystallized by its "Towards a First World Parliament" slogan. In essence, Singaporeans were asked to choose between a trusted brand and greater government accountability.

The Run-up to GE2011: A New Public Discontent

Less than a month before Polling Day, former Prime Minister Goh Chok Tong observed that "the ground may not be sweet" for the PAP.[5] It was a strange admission given the stellar economic growth of 14.5 per cent in 2011.[6] Goh's pessimism sprung from the fact that this growth had not trickled down fast enough to the ordinary Singaporean. The high cost of living — top of most concerns — saw the consumer price index rise to 4.5 per cent in April 2011. The age increase from 62 to 65 for Central Provident Fund (CFP) withdrawal had also caused considerable angst amongst older Singaporeans who wondered if they would ever get to enjoy their savings. The widening wage gap was another reason for the bitter ground. With a per capita GDP of $29,000, second only to Japan in Asia, Singapore's Gini coefficient, however, had risen from 42.5 in 1998 to 47.2 in 2006.[7] High-income earners were benefiting more from economic growth than low-income earners were, thus making the widening wage gap a clear political concern, especially in an election year.[8]

A new form of public discontent, however, was discernable in the run-up to the elections. In the past, public discontent was generally over so-called "bread and butter" issues that exposed the side effects of an open economy. Such perennial bread-and-butter issues included the high cost of living, employment, liberal immigration policies, and the widening wage gap. These issues have long been, and rightfully, framed by the PAP as the unavoidable consequences of globalization, beyond the ambit of any government. The government's response has always been the emphasizing of skills-upgrading programmes in order to move local labour further up the value chain and employment-based welfare assistance such as Workfare.

In the run-up to GE2011, however, the object of public discontent had shifted to something new, something previously unquestionable — the government's judgement. This time around, augmenting these perennial issues, were concerns such as not building enough public housing or expanding public transportation infrastructure to accommodate the surge in foreigners, the high profile escape of terrorist suspect Mas Selamat, the expenditure of public funds on the Youth Olympic Games in 2010, and the flooding in downtown Singapore. These new concerns, unlike globalization's side effects, were seen primarily as policy missteps which have, rightly or wrongly, put into question the government's ability to meet the high demand for public transport and housing infrastructure, its capability to incarcerate terrorist suspects, as well as misreading the international impact of megaprojects, resulting in negligible benefit to the nation. This discontent, no doubt genuine and heartfelt, was amplified in cyberspace where specific mistakes or policy missteps were constantly revived on news sites like the Online Citizen or Temasek Review, and repeated on Facebook, creating an echo-chamber effect. The ire of this discontent was aimed at the government's perceived easy dismissal of its critics and its repeating of stock answers to public questions. In the end, it was the PAP's inability to adequately counter this new public discontent and the Opposition's ability to exploit it to the hilt that contributed to the incumbent's poor electoral showing.

(De)Personalizing Personalities: The Double-edge Sword of Social Media

If there was something new about GE2011, it was the degree of familiarity that the electorate perceived it had with Opposition candidates. Unlike past elections, where the mainstream media had a monopoly over information distribution, this time every new face, party defection, rumour and half-truth was covered extensively by social media and other news websites. It was the Internet, more than any other agency, that truly levelled the playing field in the area of information distribution, making the elections so much more personal to ordinary Singaporeans. With many citizens able to complement their diet of state-controlled media like the *Straits Times*, *Today* or Channel NewsAsia with online sources like the Online Citizen and Yawning Bread for information on the Opposition, many of these candidates were able to avoid being rigidly portrayed by the mainstream media as angry irrational belligerent people far removed from the everyday concerns of Singaporeans and who had an axe to grind with the PAP. Social media wrestled this image prerogative from the mainstream media to offer a more sympathetic and human face of Opposition parties at the introduction of their candidates, face-to-face interviews, and rally speeches.

The availability of rally speeches on the Internet also multiplied the viewership many times over, allowing people to watch more than one party's rally each night, thus drastically altering the political consumption process. Candidates like Singapore Democratic Party's (SDP) Vincent Wijeysingha and National Solidarity Party's Nicole Seah were elevated to celebrities by the online buzz. Youtube and Razor TV effectively eradicated the physical discomforts of attending live rallies, and offered personalities on demand with each click of the mouse. Staring into the camera, candidates morphed from distant (both literally and figuratively) figures in the crowd into real Singaporeans with a direct line to other Singaporeans. Not only did the snowball effect of social media turn friends, relatives, and colleagues into a ready audience, but it also allowed opinions and biases to enjoy an echo-chamber effect, thus doing what the mainstream media could not (or would not) do — personalize the Opposition.

If so, then conversely, the ruling party quickly found that social media could also depersonalize candidates. New PAP candidates like Tin Pei Ling and Janil Puthucheary, for different reasons, were turned into embodiments of public dissatisfaction with the ruling party.[9] These personalities ceased to be individuals as they underwent countless instances of satire and censure in cyberspace and, consequently, came to signify a host of criticisms of the PAP such as elitism and arrogance. Again, the PAP's limited ability to counter these perceptions in cyberspace only served to reinforce the view that it was ill-prepared for social media.

One reason for its limited ability was that these criticisms were not made by Opposition candidates who could be isolated and attacked by the ruling party but, instead, by members of the public. Without the benefit of new ideas or novel approaches to occupy the public's imagination, the PAP had reverted to campaigning on the strength of its track record, thus leaving online journalists, bloggers, and active netizens free to fill the vacuum. Such a move was further aggravated by a host of political missteps which put the ruling party constantly on the back foot. One such example was the inherent unfairness of the GRC system, with the PAP's fielding of Chia Shi-Lu, a surgeon, as a last minute replacement of Steve Tan who dropped out for unknown reasons. Chia, unknown to the electorate the day before, became a Member of Parliament on Nomination Day when he was uncontested at Tanjong Pagar GRC. This episode was put through the mill in cyberspace and drove home for many Singaporeans the unfairness, even farcical ramifications, of the GRC system without Opposition candidates even having to utter a single word of complaint. Left without an obvious target, the ruling party chose to ignore such online criticisms in the hope that they would die away or at least be confined to cyberspace.

Old Instincts and the New Apology: Political Responsiveness

The PAP's campaign strategy was, like the rest of GE2011, an uneasy mix of the old and the new. Contingent on unfolding events, the campaign was fluid and dynamic, and it is uncertain whether the ruling party had a coherent or fixed strategy. Instead, the campaign saw an initial indulgence of old campaign instincts, before it changed tact towards the end.

One such old instinct was to identify an individual within the Opposition to train its sights on. It was a tactic that highlighted an individual's perceived flaws, magnified them in the mainstream media, and presented them as symptomatic of the broader defects of the Opposition as a whole. In past GEs these included Francis Seow, Chee Soon Juan, and James Gomez, where such personalities were made to epitomize all that was wrong with the Opposition. This time round, WP's celebrity candidate Chen Show Mao, a high-achieving corporate lawyer, came under fire. The PAP's organizing secretary, Ng Eng Hen, publicly questioned Chen's ability to sympathise with the aspirations of Singaporeans, after spending most of his adult working life in the United States and China.[10] The implication was that Chen was out of touch with ordinary Singaporeans and that his WP candidacy was not a serious one. This line of questioning was quickly abandoned when it threatened to backfire.[11]

Soon after Chen, SDP's Vincent Wijeysingha was put under the spotlight. Wijeysingha and his team were contesting against Minister Vivian Balakrishnan and his team in Holland–Bukit Timah GRC. On 24 April, the Minister furtively told the media that "It has been brought to my attention — in fact it is the SDP which is suppressing a certain YouTube video, which raises some very awkward questions about the agenda and motivations of the SDP and its candidates."[12] After prompting much public speculation, the PAP team issued a press statement that suggested that Wijeysingha had a gay agenda which he wanted to promote if elected into Parliament. Throwing in some moral panic for good measure, the statement even noted that the video contained discussions that "touched on sex with boys and whether the age of consent for boys should be 14 years of age"[13] — a discussion that Wijeysingha had no part in. The suggestive tone of the press statement was of no small significance given the highly divisive public furore over the AWARE saga in 2009 when a group of Christian women took control of a high profile women's rights group in the belief that the latter was promoting homosexuality in schools.

Meanwhile, then Senior Minister Goh Chok Tong began the campaign by calling for a "clean fight" in his Marine Parade GRC Facebook account. There he emphasized that there should be "no personal attacks, no rude language", and that Singapore is "a gracious, generous community".[14] A few days later, however, deep into the hustings, Goh looked to be questioning the abilities of his former Principal Private Secretary, Tan Jee Say, who was running on an SDP ticket. Goh was quoted as saying, "He was an able, hardworking PPS, but I did not think he would make it as a Permanent Secretary",[15] thus seeming to go back on the gentlemen's agreement to eschew personal attacks.

Perhaps most reminiscent of old-style tactics was then Minister Mentor Lee Kuan Yew's comments about the closely contested fight in Aljunied GRC. As it became increasingly clear that the biggest fight of GE2011 was shaping up in Aljunied GRC, and that then Foreign Minister George Yeo stood a real chance of losing his seat, Lee remarked rather curiously that it would not be the "end of the world" if the PAP lost Aljunied and warned that "if Aljunied decides to go that way [vote WP], well Aljunied has five years to live and repent".[16]

These individual-based attacks and stark warnings did not go down well with much of the electorate. In addition to the generally coordinated campaign of the Opposition parties, these old instincts of the ruling party began to cause it to lose ground. In an unprecedented move, the Prime Minister, at his lunch time rally on 3 May at Boat Quay, apologized for the government's mistakes, including Mas Selamat's escape and the downtown floods.[17] During his forty-minute speech in the heart of the financial district, PM Lee promised that the government would learn from these mistakes and urged the country to come together as one after the elections. This public apology, for a brief moment, equalized the asymmetrical relationship between the ruling elite and Singaporeans.

Nevertheless, that the PM felt the need for a public apology is less indicative of his government's incompetence but more of the way the campaign had spun beyond the ruling party's control. After all, there was no public clamour for a government apology of any sort. The timing of the apology was tactically astute. Instead of addressing and countering every public criticism, which ran the risk of aggravating public discontent, the apology from the erstwhile infallible PAP was rare enough to steal media attention from Opposition parties in the last days of the campaign, yet vague enough to avoid being pinned down on specifics. In conclusion, the way in which the ruling party eschewed old campaign instincts for a game-changing public apology suggests that the PAP continues to demonstrate some political responsiveness in the face of challenges. The key question is: if the ruling party has realized the political cost of its old instincts, what new instincts will it develop to be more palatable to an electorate that is increasingly concerned with fair play?

Aljunied GRC: National Interests vs. Municipal Concerns

Although it was clear by Nomination Day that the PAP had a real fight on its hands when Low Thia Khiang, leader of the WP, joined Sylvia Lim to contest in Aljunied GRC, the sheer size of its task was realized during the campaign walkabouts. When the PAP team comprising former Foreign Minister George Yeo and Minister Lim Hwee Hua made their rounds, it was met with relative detachment from residents, prompting Yeo to concede that there "was a lot of resentment towards the ruling party because it was too arrogant and high-handed".[18] This was in contrast to the WP team's warm reception as it made its way through food markets and hawker centres in the area.[19] The warm reception should not have come as a surprise as the WP had history with the area, having contested there when it was known as Eunos in 1988 and 1991, and in 1997 for Cheng San GRC, and most recently in 2006.

In the end, the WP won with 54.7 per cent of the votes. This win may be down to several factors. Most crucially, the WP fielded a strong and credible team. It had a mixture of familiarity in the form of Sylvia Lim who had been Non-Constituency MP and Low, MP for Hougang for twenty years. It also received a boost in credentials with star lawyer Chen Show Mao, a graduate of Harvard, Oxford, and Stanford. This line-up drove home the point that the WP was a serious party capable of running a GRC. The WP's campaign message of "First World Parliament" also resonated with the residents. Because of the country's first-past-the-post system, the 30–35 per cent of Opposition votes in every General Elections are not represented proportionately in seat numbers, leaving residents of smaller constituencies like Potong Pasir and Hougang to shoulder the burden of Opposition presence in Parliament. The WP team forced the issue of a more democratic Parliament on to Aljunied residents, challenging them to make their political decision based on national and democratic interests, instead of narrowly defined municipal self-interest like estate upgrading or property value. The PAP team lost not because of its incompetence but because the WP forced the constituency to choose between nurturing a viable Opposition for the long-term survival of the country and putting all their eggs in the PAP basket. For good measure, the spectre of a Parliament with all 87 seats occupied by the PAP was raised by the Opposition at every opportunity. Indeed, the significance of the PAP's loss of Aljunied does not end at the historicity of the event, but extends also to the way the WP team succeeded in convincing Aljunied voters to think beyond their bus stops, street lamps, or lifts.

Other external factors also went in favour of the WP. Serangoon Gardens, a middle-class area in Aljunied GRC, was generally dissatisfied with the decision a couple of years ago to build dormitories for foreign construction workers in its vicinity. Media reports note that Lim Hwee Hua, in charge of Serangoon Gardens, was the lowest scoring of the PAP team, with 40 per cent of the vote.[20] Lee Kuan Yew's remarks that Aljunied voters would have to "repent" for voting unwisely also did not go down well with more-educated and younger voters in the constituency. According to George Yeo, Lee's remarks had "created greater anger, greater resentment in many people".[21] Perhaps more pertinently, Lee's earlier observations in his book — *Lee Kuan Yew: Hard Truths to Keep Singapore Going*[22] — that all religions and races except Islam could be integrated and that Malays were distinct and separate from other citizens, also served to upset Malay voters. Malay MP Zainul Abidin Rasheed, who helmed the Eunos division where Malay voters made up 20 per cent of the voters, a higher proportion than the 15 per cent demographic, later admitted that Malays "were hurt by those remarks and remain so".[23]

The Aftermath: Cabinet Reshuffle

Just a week after the results on 7 May, came the announcement that Lee Kuan Yew and Goh Chok Tong would step down from the Cabinet. The two senior politicians, having "studied the new political situation and thought how it can affect the future", decided that it was time for "a fresh clean slate".[24] The resignation of the nation's founding father as well as his immediate successor heralded the first possibility of concrete change in post-GE2011 Singapore, even if they remained as MPs. However, the initial shock of their resignation has since given way to tacit acceptance that the two personalities are not likely to retire from public life in light of Lee's continued high profile appearances at public forums and dialogues, together with Goh's new designation as "Emeritus Senior Minister". Months later, both Lee and Goh, together with Lim Boon Heng, Wong Kan Seng, George Yeo, and Lim Hwee Hua resigned from the PAP's executive committee.[25]

The subsequent Cabinet reshuffle saw Wong Kan Seng, Raymond Lim, and Mah Bow Tan left out, although they remain MPs. All three performed poorly in their respective GRCs, garnering below average scores. Wong and Mah won 57 per cent of the vote, while Lim fared the worst with 54 per cent. Both Mah and Wong are older than the PM at 63 and 65 respectively, thus making their exit reasonable on grounds of renewal. However, one question lingers over why voters were not informed of their impending exit prior to the elections? If indeed these three Ministers had expressed their desire to the PM to quit politics prior to GE2011,[26] then the hard choice was between letting familiar (if unpopular) faces go or giving the voters the impression that their would-be MPs would still be full-fledged ministers after the elections. The politically expedient choice had to be made.

Meanwhile, the rest of the Cabinet reshuffle saw Tharman Shanmugaratnam promoted to Deputy Prime Minister, while helming the Finance and Manpower Ministries. S. Iswaran was appointed Minister (without portfolio) in the Prime Minister's Office, with former Army chief Chan Chun Sing made Acting Minister at the Ministry of Community Development, Youth and Sports. Yaacob Ibrahim left the Ministry of Environment and Water Resources in the hands of Vivian Balakrishan, and took over the Ministry of Information, Communications and the Arts. Gan Kim Yong replaced Khaw Boon Wan as Health Minster, while the latter took over the National Development Ministry.

Renewal and Transformation

At the end of GE2011, the electorate was left with the promise of political renewal and party transformation. Political renewal was always on the cards. After all, PM Lee had made GE2011 primarily about nurturing fourth-generation leaders to form a new team, and with the resignation of five Cabinet Ministers as well as the introduction of two new faces, he has delivered on the promise of renewal. The promise to transform the ruling party in light of its perceived arrogance and emotional disconnect from the ground was first made by George Yeo on the eve of Polling Day.[27] The promise was reiterated by the Prime Minister in his post-elections press conference in which he admitted that the PAP needed to do some "soul searching" and that Yeo's call for a "transformed PAP" would not go unheeded.[28]

PM Lee began post-GE2011 life with a bang. At his government's swearing-in ceremony, he announced that a committee would be set up to review ministerial salaries, the source of so much public discontent. Through the years the government had steadfastly argued that high ministerial salaries were needed to attract talented individuals into politics and to keep the government honest. More than any other issue, the issue of ministerial salaries has come to symbolize the emotional disconnect between citizens and their leaders. This is not the first time unpopular policies have been reversed; the Graduate Mothers' scheme and the female quota on applications to study medicine at university being two such examples. As such, it would be erroneous to interpret the review as evidence of the government's new-found post-GE2011 responsiveness in light of the fact that it has never shied away from dismantling unpopular policies. Instead, the announcement of the ministerial salary review may be argued to have been calculated to produce a "feel good" factor after such a divisive election. If the resignation of five ministers was a gesture of renewal, then a big gesture was also needed to signal the PAP's will to transform. After all, though promises of transformation were made, no one was clear as to exactly what the ruling party had in mind or what this transformation entailed. In this light, the ministerial salary review would be momentous enough to suggest that real transformation was under way.

Meanwhile, a major opportunity for genuine institutional reform was missed with the People's Association (PA) issue. At the heart of the saga was the electorate's desire for political fairness and respect for the choice made by Aljunied voters. Soon after the elections, the new WP MPs in Aljunied GRC highlighted the perceived unfairness of appointing ousted PAP MPs as "grassroots advisors". The PA's response was that the PA was established to carry out government policies and programmes, and that because WP MPs were not part of the government, they could not be expected to champion such policies and programmes.[29] Such a rationale was puzzling. After all, the government is made up of three branches — the executive, the judiciary (courts), and the legislative (Parliament) — and the WP MPs were part of government by virtue of being part of the legislative. Conversely, ousted PAP MPs are no longer part of government, only members of the ruling party. PM Lee's affirmation of the PA's position may, unfortunately, give rise to cynicism over the PAP's ability (or willingness) to enact institutional reform.[30] The lesson here is that institutional reform is not on the cards. The PA issue is probably a sign that the PAP is laying down the political battle-lines, to which the WP and other Opposition parties would, no doubt, respond. More divisive politics is on the way.

The Presidential Elections: Three Lessons

Close on the heels of GE2011 was the Presidential Elections (PE2011) on 27 August. A relatively young institution, the elected presidency had only witnessed one election since its inception in 1991, when Ong Teng Cheong, in 1993, defeated Chua Kim Yeow, a former Accountant General, who was persuaded by the government to offer a contest. This time four candidates emerged, namely Tony Tan, former Deputy Prime Minister; former PAP MP Tan Cheng Bock; Tan Jee Say, former senior civil servant; and former head of the National Trade Union Congress' insurance arm, Tan Kin Lian. Coming so close after the May GE2011, public anger and ground resentment no doubt spilled over into the PE2011, affecting different candidates accordingly.

Tony Tan, the government's favoured candidate, became the nation's seventh President by the slimmest of margins — 0.34 per cent; less than a quarter of the spoilt votes. However, unlike GE2011, which forced Singaporeans to ask difficult questions such as whether they were willing to trade slower immigration influx for slower economic growth, the limited powers of the Presidency made it a relatively straightforward referendum on the PAP. In the end, Tony Tan won with 35.2 per cent; Tan Cheng Bock garnered 34.8 per cent; Tan Jee Say came in with 25 per cent; while Tan Kin Lian lost his deposit with only 4.9 per cent of the votes. Taken collectively, these figures offer three lessons.

Firstly, the PAP brand is still credible but it is no longer all persuasive. It is tempting to conclude, as some have, that the PAP brand is still attractive in light of the 70 per cent of combined votes won by Tony Tan and Tan Cheng Bock, the two candidates with the strongest ties to the ruling party.[31] However, this conclusion misses out several points. Some of Tan Cheng Bock's voters were not PAP voters but those who voted tactically with a "best man to defeat Tony" attitude. Also, Tan Cheng Bock's siphoning of votes from

Tony Tan does not suggest that voters were equally happy with either ex-PAP man, but that reform and ideological distance from the PAP elite were prized. Both Tony and Cheng Bock took great pains to disassociate themselves from the PAP throughout the campaign. Unlike the new PAP candidates in GE2011 who harped incessantly on the party's "track record", the two front runners campaigned on their disagreements with the PAP and on their personal achievements.

Secondly, court politics have been unveiled in Singapore. An array of trade unions, business groups, civic and clan associations lined up to endorse Tony Tan throughout the campaign. Nevertheless, the razor-thin margin of his victory also makes crystal clear that the leaders of these unions and associations do not speak for their members. There is a discernable gulf between the interests of these leaders and those they represent. If so, this PE2011 has demonstrated with clarity what endorsement exercises really are — the jostling of individuals to find favour with the elite. Endorsements do not make a difference to voters who have already made up their minds but, instead, serve to affirm or legitimize someone's choice. Furthermore, a more educated and sophisticated electorate would not be compelled to vote a particular way because union or clan leaders publicly laud someone, especially since today's unions do not have the same sway those in the 1950s and 1960s did. Instead, these endorsements can be seen as public displays of favour. Individuals were building their social capital with the candidate they thought would be President in the hopes that they may later draw on this social capital if their favourite takes office. This is court politics unveiled; and it is by no means a new phenomenon in Singapore. For years, this type of "endorsement" has been (mis)interpreted as public recognition of the PAP's monopoly on talent and credibility, as well as the dearth of credible opposition candidates. But this time around, the 0.34 statistic has single-handedly exposed the sheer theatricality of the endorsement exercise.

To be sure, such political endorsements are not particular to Singapore. Special interests groups in the United States and media institutions in the United Kingdom often publicly align themselves with a candidate or party. However, in Singapore, it does strain the assertion that NTUC unions and local institutions are non-partisan. Will this lead to a divide between institutional leaders and those they represent? Will court politics become more overt and public in the future as the political stakes are raised? If so, how will it impact on the credibility of such supposedly non-partisan organizations?

Finally, there is little doubt that ideological profiles in Singapore have grown sharper. The traditionally understood values of the "right", "centre", and "progressive left" or "liberal" have always echoed in Singapore. Whether it was the PAP's gradual shift from the left to the centre right of politics, or the "English-educated liberal" and "Chinese leftists" labels, Singapore has long been a cauldron of such ideological politics. The absence of politics and political consciousness in the last two decades has meant that this cauldron has been simmering with the lid on. PE2011 has blown it off again. Broadly speaking, Dr Tony Tan, with his emphasis on business interests and the political status quo, came to epitomize the right in the public's mind. The votes against Tony Tan were probably votes against the way market liberalism is seen to have informed public policies. Tan Cheng Bock was centrist in that he was acceptable to

PAP and opposition voters, while Tan Jee Say's position on 377A, the death penalty, and ISA put him squarely centre left. The 35 per cent, 34 per cent, and 25 per cent roughly represent the ideological profiles running through our nation today. Many Tan Jee Say voters cast their ballot based on his position on the above issues despite the rational appeal of tactical voting. These were conscience voters who placed values above pragmatism. Such ideological divides have always existed in the country, even if they have not been exposed given the lack of competitive politics in the last couple of decades. The reinvigoration of the Opposition, together with an increasingly educated and cosmopolitan electorate, will only bring such divides to the fore.

Conclusion

The absence of competitive politics in Singapore has made GE2011 and PE2011 seem like watershed events. Nevertheless, as this chapter has sought to show, such competition has only been stamped out in the last few decades during a period which coincided with sustained economic growth and an efficient yet authoritarian government. This state of affairs has fuelled the myth of Singapore's exceptionalism in a region often embroiled in political turmoil. A variety of factors like the socioeconomic side effects of market liberalism, policy missteps, and the emergence of a younger, more educated, and liberally minded electorate, has emerged to challenge this myth.

The question now is whether the Opposition parties will use GE2011 as a springboard to greater gains, or if the ruling party will mobilize and apply its considerable resources to halt the attrition of its votes or, indeed, claw back some ground. The ability of the PAP to tweak unpopular policies such as the withdrawal age for CPF, HDB waiting times, or immigrant flows should not be underestimated. In fact, only two fears prevent the government from addressing such policies in a speedy and unambiguous manner — the fear of being perceived as populist, often interpreted by the government as weakness and a lack of strong leadership; and the fear of shaking investor confidence. For the moment, government leaders seek platforms to assuage the concerns of voters, and that their voices would not be ignored, while assuring investors that the country will not change economic direction and will remain a business-friendly environment.

Finally, more than any other party, the WP, has the most to lose. No longer will it be viewed indulgently by Singaporeans as just another Opposition party finding its feet. The presence of credible candidates and favourable publicity have moved the WP from the periphery of national discourse to its centre, where its every move, decision, and utterance will be scrutinized by both the mainstream and online media. And it is certainly no exaggeration to say that the performance of the WP's eight representatives in Parliament in the next five years will influence the way Singaporeans judge the merits of a more robust democracy.

Notes

1. This chapter was presented at the Conference on Elections and Democracy in Malaysia 2011, Universiti Malaysia Sarawak, 9–10 November 2011.
2. Leong Wee Kiat, "WP Gearing Up to Form Govt", Channel NewsAsia, 9 July 2011.
3. Shamim Adam and Weiyi Lim, "Singapore's Election 'Watershed' May Loosen Political Hold of Lee's Party", Bloomberg, 9 May 2011.
4. There was a high number of candidates aged 39 years and under across the political parties: 15 of 87 candidates were 39 years old and under in the PAP; 11 of 23 candidates were 39 years old and under in the Worker's Party; 7 of 24 candidates were 39 years old and under in the National Solidarity Party; 2 of 7 candidates were 39 years old and under in the Singapore Progressive Party; 3 of 7 candidates were 39 years old and under in the Singapore Democratic Alliance; and 6 of 11 candidates were 39 years old and under in the Reform Party. There was also the highest number of first time candidates too: PAP – 24; WP – 16; NSP – 12; SPP – 3; SDP – 9; SDA – 5; RP – 9.
5. Maria Seow, "Ground May Not Be Sweet for GE: SM Goh", *Today*, 19 April 2011.
6. Ministry of Trade and Information, "MTI Forecasts GDP Growth of 4.0 to 6.0 per cent for 2011 Following Strong Rebound in 2010", Press Release, 17 February 2011.
7. Melanie Lee, "Singapore's Economic Boom Widens Wage Gap", Reuters, 9 November 2007.
8. S. Ramesh, "Widening Income Gap a Concern", Channel NewsAsia, 4 January 2011.
9. Tin Pei Ling, wife of the Prime Minister's then Principal Private Secretary, was lampooned for being childish and materialistic, while Janil Puthucheary, a new citizen, was perceived as playing down the sacrifices of National Servicemen.
10. Teo Cheng Wee and Robin Chan, "PAP Salvo Targets Workers' Party 'Star' Chen", *Straits Times*, 19 April 2011.
11. "Personal Attacks on WP's Chen Will 'Backfire': Analysts", *Straits Times*, 20 April 2011.
12. Judith Tan and Amresh Gunasingham, "'Strange Bedfellows' in SDP Team", *Straits Times*, 24 April 2011.
13. "Dr Balakrishnan Fires Another Salvo at SDP", Asiaone, 25 April 2011 <http://www.asiaone.com/News/AsiaOne+News/Singapore/Story/A1Story20110425-275604.html> (accessed 23 August 2011).
14. S. Ramesh, "GE: SM Goh Urges "Clean Fight" in GRC Contest", Channel NewsAsia, 21 April 2011.
15. Chang Ai-Lien and Mavis Toh, "Tan Jee Say Did Not Make the Cut: SM Goh", *Straits Times*, 1 May 2011.
16. "'Not End of the World if PAP Loses Aljunied GRC': MM Lee", *Straits Times*, 30 April 2011.
17. Raju Gopalakrishnan and Kevin Lim, "Singapore PM Makes Rare Apology as Election Campaign Heats Up", Reuters, 4 May 2011.
18. Eugene Wee, "George Yeo: PAP Must Change", *New Paper*, 6 May 2011.
19. Chong Zi Liang, "Workers' Party 'A' Team Gets Warm Reception at Markets", *Straits Times*, 30 April 2011.
20. "Reasons Behind Aljunied Swing", Asiaone, 9 May 2011 <http://www.asiaone.com/News/AsiaOne%2BNews/Singapore/Story/A1Story20110509-277921.html> (accessed 23 August 2011).
21. Alicia Wong, "George Yeo: We Need a 'Transformed' PAP", 5 May 2011 <http://sg.news.yahoo.com/blogs/singaporescene/minister-george-yeo-transformed-pap-155058643.html> (accessed 25 August).
22. Lee Kuan Yew, *Lee Kuan Yew: Hard Truths to Keep Singapore Going* (Singapore: Straits Times Press, 2010).
23. Alicia Wong, "MM Lee's Remarks Hurt

Malays: Zainul Abidin Rasheed", 12 May 2011 <http://sg.news.yahoo.com/blogs/singaporescene/pap-decide-ll-contest-next-ge-zainul-abidin-111049437.html> (accessed 23 August 2011).
24. Prime Minister's Office, "Joint Statement by SM Goh Chok Tong and MM Lee Kuan Yew", 14 May 2011.
25. Li Xueying, "Lee Kuan Yew Steps Down from PAP Central Executive Committee", *Straits Times*, 6 Oct 2011.
26. Ion Danker, "They Wanted to Quit, I Asked Them to Stay On", 18 May 2011 <http://sg.news.yahoo.com/blogs/singaporescene/3-key-ministers-retire-cabinet-115352420.html> (accessed 25 August 2011).
27. Wong, "George Yeo".
28. Rachel Chang, "PAP to Adapt to New Electorate: PM", *Straits Times*, 9 May 2011.
29. Hui Mei Ooi, "Why Opposition MPs Can't Be Advisers to Grassroots Bodies", *Straits Times* Forum Page, 31 August 2011.
30. "'PA Grassroots Adviser Works with the Govt': PM Lee", *Straits Times*, 11 September 2011.
31. Monica Kotwani, "PE Showed Strong Support for PAP", *Today*, 31 August 2011.

Thailand

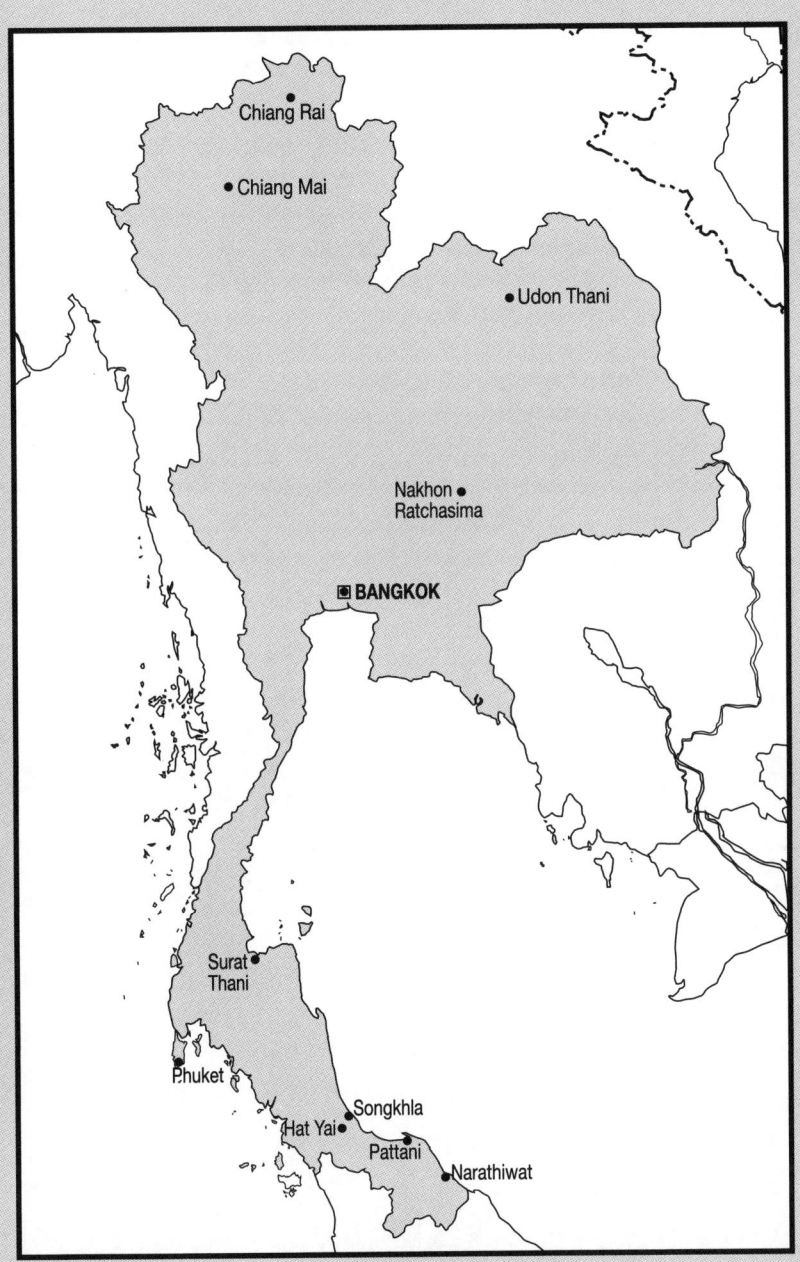

THE REVOLUTIONARY SITUATION IN THAILAND

Boonsanong Punyodyana

Downfall of the Military Régime

In September 1973 one hundred Thai people from many walks of life — university students, farmers, labourers, ex-members of the dissolved elected Parliament, artists, writers, government officials, medical doctors, and professors — signed their names to endorse a statement petitioning the military government for a democratic constitution. On 6 October, some members of this group went about distributing leaflets and copies of their demand for a democratic constitution at a few public spots. Thirteen of them were immediately arrested and charged with illegally holding a political assembly of more than five persons, committing communist acts, and insurrection. On Tuesday 9 October, the second day of the final examinations at Thammasat University, thousands of Thammasat University students walked out of their examinations and forced the university to be closed. They began a vigorous campaign against the military régime and demanded an immediate and unconditional release of all the arrested members of the constitutionalist group, which included students and one professor from Thammasat University. They staged a sit-in on the Thammasat University campus for five consecutive days and nights, taking turns to make continuous anti-government speeches. During the rally, they were joined by nearly 100,000 high school, vocational school, and university students from Bangkok and many provinces. Arriving by bus or on foot, they came equipped with national flags, loudspeakers, placards, and leaflets, some of which they had distributed along the way.

Reprinted in abridged format from *Southeast Asian Affairs 1975* (Singapore: Institute of Southeast Asian Studies, 1975), pp. 187–95. At the time of original publication, Boonsanong Punyodyana was Chairman, Department of Sociology and Anthropology, Thammasat University, Bangkok.

At Thammasat, students were organized into teams of tactical planners, donation collectors, food distributors, speech makers, negotiators, militiamen, as well as bottle-bomb makers. At noon on the fourth day of the rally, the National Student Center of Thailand (NSCT), acting on behalf of all students, served an ultimatum to the military government to release the prisoners unconditionally and proclaim a democratic constitution within six months. The ultimatum required that the military government act within twenty-four hours; otherwise, the students would take ultimate action. At 7.00 p.m. the same evening, the government announced that it would release the prisoners on bail and agreed to have a new constitution ready within one year, but the students refused to accept the government's move and continued demonstrating at Thammasat University through the fourth night. At the same time the prisoners, confined at a police centre on the outskirts of Bangkok, also refused to be released on bail, arguing that they had not committed any crime. They informed the military government that they would leave their prison cells only if told by the NSCT. But the NSCT reiterated that the government must free all the prisoners without any condition. (At one point the government indicated that it could never release one of the thirteen prisoners, who was kept in solitary confinement, because he was an ex-member of Parliament, and not just a student or professor.)

From 8.00 p.m. the government began announcing that a "third-hand" element was supplying deadly weapons to the demonstrators; parents should, therefore, advise their children not to continue demonstrating. Later it also announced that communist infiltrators were operating among the demonstrators. The students promptly denounced the government's announcement as a lie, and declared, in speech and in writing, that they accepted the government's allegation that they were all rebels.

At the end of the twenty-four hour period, that is, at noon on the fifth day of the rally (Saturday, 13 October 1973), the students marched out of Thammasat University and were joined, according to most estimates, by about half a million people from Bangkok and the provinces. Together, they established command posts at several places along the five-kilometre route from Thammasat University to Chitralada Palace where the King and Queen of Thailand reside. At each post they maintained vigil by making continuous speeches castigating the military government and leaders.

At 8.00 p.m. that evening the military government and some student leaders announced that the government had released all prisoners without any condition, and would grant a new constitution within one year. Government radio and television stations, as well as some student leaders, then urged the demonstrators to disperse. The majority of the participants did leave, but tens of thousands lingered on all night and marched to the Palace, apparently in disbelief.

At 6.00 a.m. on Sunday, 14 October, the police started firing at the students and people who tried to force their way through the police cordon outside the Palace, claiming that they wanted to return to their homes along the adjacent road. The shooting triggered the "Bloody Sunday", which quickly escalated to the deployment of army troops, tanks, and helicopters. Fighting broke out all over the city between the people and uniformed men. Students and others threw rocks and molotov cocktails at the soldiers. Snipers fired from roof-tops. Several students and one trash collector were killed crashing trucks against army tanks. Government buildings, including two police-stations, were set on fire. Most of the traffic lights and police booths all over the city were smashed. One group of vocational school students hijacked a water tanker, refilled it with gasoline obtained from a willing gas-station owner, and sprayed the gasoline on a big building to set it ablaze. Thammasat University was attacked by tanks and helicopters. When frightened students tried to escape by crossing the river on the west side of the campus, they were shot at from helicopters. The "war" lasted until the night of Monday, 15 October, leaving hundreds of students and other people wounded and, according to an official body-count, seventy-one dead. (Even now many people suspect that the number of casualties was higher than what the official figure shows.) At the reported request of King Bhumibol on the night of the "Bloody Sunday", the military government resigned, and three military leaders — Prime Minister Field Marshal Thanom Kittikachon, Deputy Prime Minister Field Marshal Prapas Charusathira, and Colonel Narong Kittikachon (the former's son and the latter's son-in-law) — and their families flew secretly out of Thailand. The King appointed Professor Sanya Dhammasakti, Rector of Thammasat University and a member of the Privy Council, the new Prime Minister, thus initiating the post-October political process in Thai society.

Formation of Political Groupings and their Anti-Government Actions

During the past four decades of limited monarchy, Thai people have been held, for the most part, under strict military control. While the military junta, civil service bureaucrats, and certain Chinese merchants have accumulated excess wealth, the masses of farmers and workers have been left in poverty, landless and indebted. The longer the tripartite (the military, the civil bureaucracy, and the privileged business strata) maintain their power, the greater the gap between the rich and the poor. On the face of it, rural Thai people might seem politically apathetic and subordinated, but under economic hardship they have migrated in large numbers to Bangkok and raised their voices in protest. They have by-passed the "legitimate" channels to protest illegally by committing crimes or joining the communist movement whose specific goal is to turn the existing society upside down.

On 2 March 1957, student leaders at Chulalongkorn University led nearly 100,000 students and other people in demonstrating against the rigged elections held in Bangkok on 26 February 1957. The protesters demanded new elections and the resignation of Premier Field Marshal Pibul Songgram.

The student-led demonstrations on 2 March 1957 were the first massive ones in Thai political history, but not the first student protest against the military oligarchy. In the late 1940's there was a rally at Thammasat University in which a number of students shed their blood as a gesture of protest against the National Guard Unit which had used the campus as its headquarters during the Second World War and had refused to leave after the war was over.

The National Student Center of Thailand was established on 20 December 1969. It comprised the elected presidents of all student bodies. The stated objective of the NSCT was to "eliminate immature conflict among students of different institutions". At the beginning, the NSCT was engaged in humanitarian causes, such as projects to aid the rural poor and provide relief to flood victims. In 1972/73, under the leadership of Thirayudh Boonmee, the NSCT rapidly became active in politically significant campaigns. It first attacked Japanese economic imperialism by promoting Thai goods and organizing the "Anti-Japanese Goods Week". When the Thanom Government issued Decree No. 299 to transfer the judicial authority from the Judicial Board to the politically appointed Minister of Justice, the NSCT supported the law students in their protest so effectively that the military government had to revoke it.

In the first half of 1973, two events took place which prompted the NSCT to take strong measures. The first event was connected with the illegal use of army helicopters and guns by high ranking military and police officers to hunt in a forest reserve. Their misconduct was reported to the press and the NSCT by some forestry students. The NSCT successfully forced the government to bring all persons concerned (including a movie actress and a businessman) to justice. In prosecuting these offenders, the military government of Marshal Thanom suffered a big loss of credibility. The second event was the dismissal by the Rector of Ramkhamhaeng University of nine students who had written critically and satirically about the hunting incident and had severely condemned the military government. The two-day student rally on 21 and 22 June 1973, led by the NSCT, resulted in the reinstatement of the nine students and the removal of the Rector himself. The political role of the NSCT was most manifest when it took the leadership in the October 1973 protest against the arrest and imprisonment of the thirteen constitutionalists. The NSCT itself did not initiate the move for a constitution, but one of the leaders of the constitutionalist group was Thirayudh Boonmee who had just finished his term as Secretary-General of the NSCT.

The changeover from military government to civilian government in October 1973 must be primarily credited to the student movement. Nonetheless, the massive force underlying the Thai people's victory over the military oligarchy was made up, in the main, of people from many walks of life. Among the heroes and heroines who sacrificed their lives or suffered physical or mental injuries (in some cases crippling) during the fighting on 14 and 15 October 1973, more were non-students than students. Among the students who were killed or injured by government personnel, more were from the lower levels of schooling, that is, high schools, technical schools, and teachers' training colleges, than from institutions of higher learning. This datum would seem to suggest that the less privileged elements in Thai society had fought more aggressively against the *status quo* under the military régime than the more privileged ones.

Since the Bloody October of 1973, a number of politically oriented groups and voluntary associations have been formed in Bangkok and other communities and have exerted themselves as pressure groups. Their emergence is clearly in response to the following conditions: (1) the long suppression of freedom of expression; (2) the lack of means by which various occupational groups of people and the common people at large could express their grievances and induce change; (3) the overall oppressive situation in Thai economy and society; and (4) the lack of confidence in the post-October government to solve the people's problems.

Among the groups and associations that have emerged are: the People for Democracy Group (PDG), the Federation of Independent Students of Thailand (FIST), the National Education Students' Center of Thailand (NESCT), the National Vocational Students' Center of Thailand (NVSCT), the Graduate Group, the National Center for the Protection of Teachers' Rights, the Civil Liberty Union (CLU), the Environmental Protection Club, the Consumers' Association, etc. In addition, hitherto non-political workers' associations and the National High School Students' Center of Thailand have elevated their stands and become politically active. The rice farmers in many provinces have also successfully organized themselves into collective bargaining and politically relevant entities.

All of these groups have engaged themselves in protests against one matter or another. Issues of protest range from the government's plan to construct a second airport in Bangkok and water pollution to the undemocratic draft of the new constitution, Japanese and American imperialism, and the burning of village houses and the killing of innocent people by anti-communist troops. Foremost among these groups are the PDG, NSCT, and FIST, which have rallied extensive support not only of students, but also of the people at large. The PDG evolved from the one hundred constitutionalists who originated the October 1973 event. Its membership is now nation-wide. This group has maintained close links with radical student groups. On 7 February 1974, when the PDG protested against the burning and killings at Ban Na Sai village by government personnel and held a rally in Bangkok, over 50,000 people turned out to join them. The PDG, NSCT, and FIST have also been active in supporting the workers' and farmers' fights against capitalists.

In the process of social conflict and change, people naturally divide themselves into opposing sides. While some activist groups, notably, PDG, NSCT, and FIST, have fought bravely on the side of the oppressed workers, farmers, and poor citizens (including those brutalized on charges of communism), some students and others have tried unceasingly to preserve the position of the oppressive ruling class whose vested interests are shared by exploitative capitalists and imperialists. The process of struggle inevitably becomes focused on class conflict. As class consciousness grows, the people's movement shifts more and more toward the revolutionary end.

Revolutionary and Counter-Revolutionary Trends

The Sanya Government which was appointed by the King on 15 October 1973 declared its mission as being to proclaim the permanent democratic constitution in accordance with the people's wishes within six months. That deadline was not met. In late May 1974 the Prime Minister led his Cabinet in resignation, but the King reinaugurated Professor Sanya on the advice of the National Legislative Assembly. Professor Sanya formed a new Cabinet which, like his first, was composed of civil service bureaucrats and some generals, including some members of the first Sanya Cabinet itself. The difference was only in personalities. Those who had served in the military government and those openly accused by the public as corrupt were dropped.

In December 1973 King Bhumibol appointed the "National Convention", comprising 2,346 members from many occupational backgrounds, both urban and rural, except students. The National Convention was assigned to elect among its members 299 persons to serve as members of the National Legislative Assembly. The outcome of the election saw most members of the new assembly coming from the top strata of the civil service bureaucracy and the wealthy echelon of the business community. The National Legislative Assembly then elected a member of the royal family, a wealthy businessman and conservative writer, as the Assembly's Speaker.

The Sanya Government and the National Legislative Assembly were expected to carry out the important duty of producing a democratic constitution and laying the ground rules for a progressive democratic system in Thailand. They were assumed to serve as caretaker bodies pending national elections. But because both these groups of men are members of the Establishment or *bourgeoisie*, they have not brought about any real change in the political system and have even opposed the people's demand for change. For example, they have introduced a two-house system of Parliament in the constitution. As the upper house will be an appointed one, the new constitution is anti-democratic. They have refused to change the policy concerning the U.S. military presence in Thailand, Thailand's relations with the People's Republic of China and the Democratic Republic of Vietnam, and communist insurgency. They have retained the Anti-Communist Act of 1952, and continue to conduct counter-insurgency activities and receive the secret budget from the U.S. and Thai governments for this purpose, without any hint of change.

Thai people continue to be in danger of "McCarthyism", and the great gap between the privileged and unprivileged classes has not begun to narrow. Most of the many hundreds of political dissidents who were imprisoned by the military government have not been released. Under these circumstances, it is no wonder that Thailand, since the overthrow of the military oligarchy in October 1973, has witnessed widespread and continuous unrest throughout the country. The aftermath of Bloody October is clearly characterized by the struggle between the forces of *status quo* and the growing forces of change. Within one year, about six hundred protest rallies have been staged in sixty-seven out of the seventy-one provinces.

As the ruling élite continue trying to convince the masses of the importance of peace and order, political stability, elections, and parliamentary democracy, more and more Thai people realize their real problems and claim that they are inherent in the very structure of their quasi-capitalist, quasi-patrimonial (*sakdina*) society which is dominated by external imperialist powers. While progressive left-wing students, intellectuals, workers, and farmers have grown increasingly conscious of the reality of *bourgeois* and capitalist oppression, reactionary elements from all of these groups have also become sensitized to the threatening signs and pace of change. They have turned to serve the power élite by organizing counter-revolutionary groups. They have used the government-controlled radio and television facilities and capitalist-controlled newspapers as means of character assassination and distortion of facts about students' and workers' movements. They have supported a reactionary constitution promulgated by a *bourgeois* government and Assembly.

The groups previously mentioned can easily be classified as leftist, rightist, and middle-of-the-road groups. The PDG, FIST, as well as larger elements in the NSCT, workers' and farmers' leadership, which are uncompromising in their stand regarding people's democracy and socialism and have displayed their ideological commitments in the Ban Na Sai incident and in anti-capitalist and anti-imperialist campaigns, can be termed leftist. The Graduate Group and the Civil Liberty Union are liberal or liberal-progressive (termed middle-of-the-roaders), inasmuch as they concern themselves primarily with seeking justice within the system, concentrating their efforts on corruption of public officials, government misappropriation of funds, and the like.

The notoriously rightist and reactionary group is the so-called Students' and People's Front (SPF). This group has its headquarters in the office of the Thai People's Freedom League which is an anti-communist group established over ten years ago by Marshal Sarit with financial support from the U.S. Government. On the evening of 3 July 1974, just a day before the American Independence Day, when many activist groups throughout Thailand were preparing to hold rallies opposing the presence of American air-bases, SPF leaders were active in the centre of the Chinese section of Bangkok, instigating and rousing the emotions of innocent citizens to confront the police. The outcome of the riot, which still leaves many people in doubt as to its real cause, was twenty-seven persons dead and nearly one hundred others injured, all victims of police gunfire. This incident effectively redirected the attention of the Thai people from the anti-American campaigns.

The revolutionary and counter-revolutionary struggle is an on-going process not limited to the urban scene. As already pointed out, the rice farmers, who constitute the bulk of the population of Thailand, have shown increased class consciousness and greater ability to mobilize and organize among themselves. Discounting the communist movement, it would seem that the future of Thai society depends to a large measure on the alliance between unprivileged urban workers and farmers. In the long run, the force of progressive students and intellectuals would only be recast into a supportive role. When the farmers and workers are united (they probably would be), it would seem unrealistic to predict that any amount of traditional and reactionary forces would suffice in preventing real change to happen to the structure of Thai economy and society.

AMERICAN MILITARY WITHDRAWAL FROM THAILAND

Thanat Khoman

American troops came into Thailand twice, in 1961 and 1963. They were contingents of Marines sent to this country when communist Pathet Lao forces advanced towards the Mekong River which serves as a border between Thailand and Laos. The objective was to deter the aggressive communist side from seeking excessive military and political gains in Laos. When the communist forces retreated, the Marines as well as other SEATO forces from the United Kingdom, Australia and New Zealand which joined the U.S. troops in 1963 were repatriated. The U.S. left only a contingent of Army Engineers to help build the strategic road from the naval base of Sattahip to Northeast Thailand.

Why did the U.S. want to send its armed forces into Thailand?

Since I am not an American and privy to the deliberations which led to such a decision, I can only guess at the reasons which a foreigner like myself can detect. As I see it, the reason is not of a selfish nature. The U.S. did not hope to derive any particular benefit from such a move. To my mind, the U.S., in those days, must have felt a sense of mission, a certain responsibility for safeguarding peace and preventing war, particularly aggressive wars. In other words, the U.S. was conscious of its role as "world policeman", since it has been blamed for allowing wars to break out because it failed to take the necessary actions or to take part in the activities of international organizations like the League of Nations. As a result of those accusations, some of them unfounded, the U.S., since World War II, took it upon itself to bar the road to aggressors and to extinguish the flames of international conflicts. The despatch of

---

Reprinted in abridged format from *Southeast Asian Affairs 1976* (Singapore: Institute of Southeast Asian Studies, 1976), pp. 394–97. At the time of original publication, Thanat Khoman was a Senator in the Vudhisapha. He was formerly the Foreign Minister and Adviser to the Prime Minister of Thailand on Foreign Affairs.

U.S. Marines came within the purview of that mission.

Later on, perhaps around 1965 (the exact date is unknown to me as the talks or negotiations were conducted in secret between the then Prime Minister, Field Marshal Thanom Kittikachorn, and the American authorities), the U.S. sent its military personnel, drawn mostly from the Air Force, and war equipment into Thailand. As it was learnt later, this action was necessary because of greater U.S. involvement in the Vietnam War. The military aircraft and the use of air-bases in this country were needed to support U.S. operations in Vietnam. It was regrettable, however, that the move was made in secret and the public in both Thailand and the U.S. were completely left in the dark, which was not quite in keeping with democratic processes. It was only after the press in the U.S. discovered the American presence in Thailand that the people in both countries were informed of the important military build up in various places in Thailand. The climax was reached when the U Tapao base was ready and the famous B-52s began to move in and start operations from there. The use of that air-base and others located in various places in North and Northeast Thailand for war purposes continued relentlessly until the cease-fire agreement was signed in Paris in February 1973, and ground to a complete halt after the U.S. Congress adopted a resolution banning all military activities on the part of American forces in Thailand.

This is a brief genesis of the U.S. military presence in Thailand.

As to the problem of its withdrawal, no difficulty should have arisen if it were tackled in an objective and straightforward manner. Regarding the introduction of the U.S. Marine contingents, as soon as the situation in neighbouring Laos improved, I conducted negotiations with the competent American authorities on the withdrawal, and never experienced any difficulties on that score. When I pointed out that the development in the situation was such that foreign military presence was no longer required, the U.S. as well as other government members of the South East Asia Treaty Organization willingly acceded to the Thai Government's request and withdrew their forces. Even concerning the current build up which came to as many as 42,000 men in 1970, I obtained government authorization to discuss withdrawal with the American side which made no difficulties and redeployed some 12,000 men after President Johnson ordered the cessation of air attacks on North Vietnam in late 1968, shortly before he retired from politics. That decision rendered the strong military presence unnecessary, even superfluous. However, after I left office in 1971, the number of American forces in Thailand shot up to some 50,000 men, which was much higher than at any time I was in the government. That increase had no valid justification and could be explained only by the fact that after the 1971 self-inflicted *coup d'etat*, the entire government, including the Foreign Office, was under the direction and control of military officers who wanted to see Thailand more and more committed to military ventures in place of the U.S. which was seeking to ease off from Vietnam and elsewhere in Indochina.

The reason I advanced in discussions with American officials was that since the stationing of the American forces in Thailand was predicated on the requirement of the Vietnam War and not for the defence of this country, the reduction of air activities decreed by the U.S. Government should make it possible for a corresponding reduction of American military personnel. That argument was accepted and resulted in the redeployment of American forces which caused no difficulty either to the Thai or American side.

Why did I advocate the withdrawal of American forces, as indeed I did, from as far back as 1961 until the last day of my tenure of office in November 1971?

These are the reasons.

To begin with, the introduction of foreign forces is not something that should be desired. It can only be tolerated so long as it serves the national interests of the host country or at least if such interests coincide with those of the sending party. If and when the military presence serves only the interests of the latter and ceases to be advantageous to the host, then it loses its *raison d'etre* and justification.

This is so because the presence of military forces, even the friendliest ones, in a foreign country always creates problems. It affects to a major or minor degree the sovereignty and independence of action of the host. It may also interfere directly or indirectly with the latter's domestic affairs and politics and, therefore, cause friction. Above all, it creates adverse social, moral, psychological and even human problems and undesirable effects on the local society, not to speak of economic disruptions caused by the influx of substantial funds as well as by the subsequent reduction or termination thereof. This is what Thailand has been experiencing and we have not reached the end of it yet.

Such problems are not peculiar to us. They exist elsewhere, even in Europe. They are more pronounced here because, as in France, the differences of cultures and civilizations are sharper.

The question is whether these drawbacks are counterbalanced by whatever gains the host country is supposed to have derived, and some propaganda statements have attributed great advantages to Thailand for playing host to American forces. The truth is that the U.S. spent millions of dollars building air-bases and other military installations, but who used them, Thailand or the U.S.? Furthermore, when the U.S. Government decided to construct, at considerable cost, the U Tapao air-base for the use of its B-52 bombers, did not the U.S. realize enormous savings on fuel, wear and tear of materials and, above all, in human lives, because those planes did not have to come from Guam and were readily available to support ground troops fighting in Vietnam? The real gain for the Thai side was in the employment of a few hundred low-wage workers as the U.S. could not bring in its own labour for expenses would have been infinitely higher, and it was doubtful whether American workers would be able to adjust themselves to local conditions. In reality, the advantages accruing to Thailand are considerably fewer than those realized by countries like Japan and Taiwan through offshore procurement contracts, or even by the U.S. itself, as mentioned above.

Be that as it may, the criteria for allowing foreign forces to remain should rest on the national interests of the host country, or at least on the concord between the former and those of the foreign party. Otherwise, foreign military presence cannot be justified.

In the case of the U.S. forces, from the moment that their government, for a variety of reasons, decided to relinquish its role and responsibility in the Vietnam venture and, later on, were manacled by their legislative authorities who prohibited them from engaging in combat activities, their presence in a foreign land could no longer be explained or justified. Politically, they may cause inconvenience to their hosts.

All this does not mean that they should be summarily and arbitrarily shown the door. All along, my advocacy for the withdrawal of foreign forces has been predicated on mutual discussions and negotiations, and I have never failed to put this principle into practice on the numerous occasions when I requested the U.S. and other SEATO governments to pull out their military personnel. Between the Thais and Americans, in particular, whose countries have entertained cordial relations for more than a century, the way to deal with this matter should be to sit down and talk it over a cup of coffee or tea or better still, a highball. The Thai Government should not unilaterally fix a date for their departure without even a semblance of consultation. For this reason, I find the Kukrit Government's haste to have American troops out by March 1976 an amateurish and naïve decision not in keeping with our national interests.

Why is this so? Firstly, because a matter like this involves two parties, even though Thailand is playing host. Secondly, at least in the past, before the U.S. Government signed the Paris cease-fire agreement and before the U.S. Congress passed the resolution forbidding American forces to perform combat duties, American military presence concurrently served the interests of both the U.S. and Thailand. Although the situation has now changed, there is no reason not to discuss the withdrawal on a practical and friendly basis. Moreover, there is a tradition in diplomacy to transact official business on the basis of mutual discussions, particularly with a friendly country of such long standing.

I would go even further and contend that discussions should also be held with our antagonistic neighbour, North Vietnam, which has been clamouring for the departure of those foreign forces and has set the withdrawal of American forces as a condition for normal relations with this country. In this connection, over a year ago when I served as Adviser to Prime Minister Sanya and anticipating the final outcome in South Vietnam, I obtained the Prime Minister's agreement to contact North Vietnamese officials in Europe to pave the way for the future normalization of relations between Thailand and the emerging new régimes in Indochina. The conversations were courteous and free from disagreeable and acrimonious charges and countercharges. They suggested a distinct possibility of reaching an agreement on joining the question of the use of the bases by foreign forces to that of the support of insurgency. However, because of regrettable weakness and short-sightedness on the part of the government and those who pulled the strings behind it, the right course was not pursued and a favourable opportunity thrown down the drain with unfortunate loss for the nation.

Now it is more than obvious that while a unilateral declaration is sterile, offensive to friends and counter-productive for the country, mutual discussions with the U.S. on the one hand and with North Vietnam on the other, could have yielded more beneficial results.

More importantly, the events of last April and May culminating in the downfall of the Lon Nol and Thieu régimes have brought about a radical change in the situation as well as in the attitude of the victorious North Vietnamese leaders and the new masters in South Vietnam and Laos. The latter, in particular, has been behaving in an intentionally provocative and abrasive manner with little doubt as to whom they were acting for and why.

Under these circumstances, the unilateral declaration on the withdrawal of U.S. forces does not fit any longer into the present context of international contingencies. It should be scrapped and voided as long as relations between Thailand and North Vietnam are not normalized. Only after normalization should the question of the withdrawal of foreign forces be taken up again not unilaterally, but on the basis of mutual consultation and discussion, on new terms and conditions to regulate the matter, exactly in the same manner as in the cases of the Turkish and Spanish bases.

In my opinion, this is the course which will serve the interests of Thailand and free Southeast Asia whose interests in this matter are in no way different from those of this country. Therefore, in dealing with this matter, we should think not only of ourselves but also of our friends and neighbours whose destiny, in terms of security, is so closely linked with ours.

•

THE THAI ECONOMY
From Boom to Gloom?

Peter G. Warr

Following elections in November 1996 a new coalition government took office in Thailand, led by incoming Prime Minister and New Aspiration Party leader General Chawalit Yongchaiyut. The new administration began its work in an atmosphere of great concern about the state of the Thai economy. Throughout 1996 Thai economic commentary was dominated by signs that the export-led boom that began in the late 1980s may be coming to an end. Most important of these signs were an apparently dramatic slow-down in the annual rate of growth of total exports and revelations that some investment and securities institutions may be unable to meet interest obligations. Confidence in Thailand's capacity to sustain high levels of economic performance was seriously damaged. The economic situation had clearly contributed to the downfall of the previous government of Banharn Silpa-Archa and posed immediate dangers for the new government. Identifying the causes of these and other economic problems is the central theme of this article.

Economic Boom, 1988-95

The background to the economic gloom of 1996 was the unprecedented boom which began in 1988. Over the eight years ending in 1995 the Thai economy was the fastest growing in the world (Table 1). The average rate of real GDP growth was unprecedented, at 10.4%, and inflation was low, averaging 5.3%. Two factors produced the dramatic growth: growth of exports,

---

Reprinted from Daljit Singh, ed., *Southeast Asian Affairs 1997* (Singapore: Institute of Southeast Asian Studies, 1997), pp. 317–33. At the time of original publication, Peter G. Warr was the John Crawford Professor of Agricultural Economics in the Department of Economics, Research School of Pacific and Asian Studies, Australian National University.

TABLE 1
Thailand: Main Economic Indicators

	1985	1990	1991	1992	1993	1994	1995	1996
GDP (US$ bn)[a]	38.9	85.6	98.7	111.3	125.0	143.0	167.1	185.0
Population (millions)[a]	51.6	56.1	56.9	57.8	58.6	59.4	60.2	61.1
Growth (% p.a.)	1.9	1.6	1.5	1.5	1.4	1.4	1.5	1.4
GNP per capita (US$)[a]	742	1,508	1,709	1,889	2,087	2,356	2,714	3,028
Share in GDP (%)[b]								
Agriculture	15.8	12.7	12.7	12.0	10.0	10.4	10.3	10.0
Industry	31.8	37.0	38.8	38.5	39.2	39.4	40.3	40.4
(Manufacturing)	21.9	27.2	28.4	28.0	28.5	28.6	30.2	30.0
Services	52.3	50.2	48.5	49.5	50.5	50.2	49.4	49.6

Source: [a]International Monetary Fund, International Financial Statistics (IFS) series.
[b]World Bank, World Development Tables.

especially exports of labour-intensive manufactured goods; and very high inflows of foreign capital, including direct foreign investment. The two went together, in that much of the foreign investment was in the labour-intensive manufacturing sector. Export growth over this period averaged an extraordinary 28% per annum and as a share of GDP exports surged from 23% in 1988 to 34% in 1995. Economic inequality increased during this period but this should not be taken to mean that the benefits of growth were confined to the rich. The boom coincided with dramatically reduced incidence of absolute poverty, which fell from 22% in 1988 to under 10% in 1994, using the most common definition of poverty incidence.[1]

Economic Gloom, 1996

In 1996 GDP growth in real terms fell to "only" 6.8%, the first year since 1993 of annual growth below 8%. Inflation was moderate at just under 6%. The government's budget ended the calendar year in deficit and the new government promised to cut public spending, in particular that involving military purchases. The current account deficit was a focus of public concern, at 8.3% of GDP, compared with 8.1% in 1995. Export growth slowed from 20% or more in the immediately preceding years to less than 2% in 1996. During 1996 the baht remained under speculative pressure and rumours of impending devaluation were common. The Thai property and stock markets also ended 1996 in a slump which damaged confidence in the country's immediate economic prospects.

The export slow-down and the problems of the financial sector have different origins but they are linked in the present economic crisis through speculation on the exchange rate. The export slow-down was primarily the result of a slow-down in international demand for Thailand's exports, a real appreciation of the baht caused by the fact that it has remained pegged to the U.S. dollar while the Japanese yen has depreciated, and — most importantly — increases in real wages within Thailand. The last of these causes means that Thailand is facing a structural adjustment problem requiring that resources be reallocated away from labour-intensive export industries and towards more skill-intensive exporters.

The financial crisis was a consequence of the boom combined with inadequate public sector supervision. Several large investment institutions have become over-extended by excessive and unhedged borrowing abroad and domestically, leaving these firms highly vulnerable to exchange rate and interest rate risk. They were also suffering the effects of bad loans within Thailand. During late 1996 speculation about devaluation resulted from the county's poor trade performance and this speculation induced a capital outflow, raising domestic interest rates. Bankruptcies in the property and financial sector seemed inevitable unless the government agreed to large "bail-outs".

The Export Slow-down

Table 2 shows the levels of Thailand's exports by destination for the years 1994 to 1996. The slow-down was widespread among Thailand's export destinations but was greatest in exports to Japan, NAFTA and the Chinese economies. By looking at the composition of exports by commodity (Table 3) it can be seen that the slow-down was concentrated in manufactured exports from labour-intensive industries.[2] The reasons for the export slow-down are discussed in depth below.

The Budget Deficit

Thailand's financial year runs from 1 October to 30 September. In the current 1996/97 financial year, the first quarter ending 31 December 1996 revealed a government cash deficit of 54 billion baht (US$2.1 billion). This compares with a surplus of 16.2 billion baht a year earlier. The first quarter fiscal result produced concern that the current full financial year may produce a budget deficit for Thailand for the first time in nine years. Thailand's revenue base is highly responsive to the overall growth rate and even small slow-downs in growth produce significant reductions in revenue.[3]

In the past, the policy response in similar budgetary circumstances has been a contraction of public investment spending. Responses of this kind have already been announced for 1997 and 1998. Thailand's financial planners are known for their conservatism and the policy issue is not whether expenditure cuts will occur but where the cuts will be concentrated. In

TABLE 2
Thailand's Export Trade Flows

Destination Share (%)	1994	1995	1996
ASEAN	18.2	19.9	19.3
Chinese economies	9.5	10.5	8.7
Japan	17.1	16.8	16.7
European Union	14.9	14.5	15.8
NAFTA	22.6	19.1	18.5
Rest of World	17.7	19.2	21.0

Note: Chinese economies means China (PRC), Hong Kong and Taiwan.
Source: *Bangkok Post Year-End Economic Review*, December 1996.

TABLE 3
Commodity Structure of Thailand's Export Slow-down

	1994	1995	1996
Total exports (million baht)	1,137,602	1,406,310	1,401,392
Growth rate (%)	20.9	23.6	–0.35
Growth rate by major commodity:			
1 Computers and parts	44.9	38.7	31.3
2 Garments	12.4	1.3	–21.9
3 Rubber	43.3	46.5	1.4
4 Integrated circuits	27.5	28.4	3.4
5 Gems & jewellery	8.3	11.5	8.4
6 Rice	18.9	24.1	8.4
7 Sugar	41.2	67.2	11.7
8 Frozen shrimps	29.9	2.3	–17.8
9 Television & parts	26.2	12.7	14.1
10 Shoes & parts	40.5	37.0	–40.9
11 Canned seafood	24.7	4.1	–0.3
12 Airconditioner, & parts	62.1	49.6	33.6
13 Plastic products	–29.1	102.2	51.4
14 Tapioca products	–13.6	–2.8	16.7
15 Textiles	4.5	22.1	–4.4

Note: Growth rates by major commodity for 1996 based on nine months data, January to September.
Source: *Bangkok Post Year-End Economic Review*, December 1996.

Thailand's current economic circumstances it is clearly important that cuts in expenditure not exacerbate the export slow-down already experienced in 1996. Because Thailand's infrastructure is already heavily congested, reductions in infrastructure spending would threaten just that.

The government has announced that the 50 billion baht expenditure cuts planned for each of 1997 and 1998 were to be concentrated on military expenditure. There was also to be a 40 billion baht cut in the budget of the state enterprises. But the bulk of government savings will come from a slow-down in military expenditures. It remains to be seen whether the military will accept that outcome. The paradox may be that as Prime Minister a former general is capable of implementing military spending cuts that would not be accepted from politicians with purely civilian backgrounds.

The Current Account Deficit

The Thai baht is loosely pegged to the U.S. dollar. As in all (approximately) fixed exchange rate countries, Thailand's economic commentary focuses perhaps excessively on the current account balance. The 1996 slump in export growth obviously contributed to the current account deficit experienced in 1996 but the deficit was almost as high in 1995 and then recorded export growth was at 20%. The export slowdown is not the sole cause of the current account deficit. The continued high rate of capital inflow into Thailand is a more significant explanation for the high current account deficits of recent years and the economic debate in Thailand has largely missed the relevance of this point.

As Thailand continues to industrialize, its high rate of capital inflow generates a corresponding current account deficit. The high level of foreign investment into Thailand contributes to the current account deficit because of the imported inputs of capital equipment and intermediate goods required during the production process. More significantly, as foreign investment enters the country and foreign exchange is converted to baht at the (approximately) fixed exchange rate, the domestic money supply is increased as these baht are spent within Thailand. The demand for all goods increases, including both imports and goods which might otherwise have been exported. The current account deficit thereby increases but this is not a "problem", to the extent that autonomous capital inflow is the originator of this process. The problem potentially arises when a capital inflow, in the form of borrowing from abroad, is not autonomous but is undertaken in order to finance a payments problem due, say, to loss of international competitiveness of the country's exports.

How can we tell which of these factors is the more important cause of Thailand's current account deficit? An indicator of the health or otherwise of the country's trade position is the state of its foreign reserves. When autonomous capital inflow is the cause of the current account deficit the level of reserves increases. When a loss of competitiveness is the cause, and capital inflows are accommodating, the level of reserves declines. Table 4 indicates that Thailand's foreign exchange reserves continued to increase in 1996, measured both in millions of US$ and in months of imports, in spite of the supposed current account crisis. The level of Thailand's international reserves is more than adequate by international standards and by Thailand's own very conservative historical standards.[4] It is appropriate that these issues should continue to be monitored closely, but the evidence does not indicate that a significant payments problem currently exists. What exists is a crisis of confidence.

Exchange Rate Management

Thailand has a long and proud history of stable monetary policy, a stable exchange rate and low inflation. The independence of the central bank, the Bank of Thailand (BOT), has been seen as an important contributor to that record. During the government of Prime Minister Banharn Silpa-Archa the autonomy of the BOT was threatened by what was seen in the press as political interference from the government. Negative public reaction to this perceived interference contributed to the Banharn government's growing unpopularity. But a more serious threat to the Bank's independence in setting monetary policy derived indirectly from the economic reforms of the early 1990s.

For several decades, Thailand has maintained a virtually fixed exchange rate relative to the U.S. dollar.[5] If international movements of capital were entirely free, then the fixed exchange rate would mean that the BOT did not have effective control of Thailand's domestic money supply. The reason is that if the Bank tried to reduce the money supply by raising domestic interest rates, speculative capital would flood in

TABLE 4
Thailand: External Indicators, 1985–96

	1985	1990	1991	1992	1993	1994	1995	1996
Merchandise exports, fob. (US$bn)[a]	7.1	22.8	28.2	32.1	36.4	44.5	55.4	56.2
% change	-3.8	15	23.8	13.7	13.4	21.3	24.5	1.0
% GDP	18.1	26.6	28.8	29.1	29.4	31	34	29.5
Merchandise imports, fob. (US$bn)[a]	8.4	29.6	34.2	36.3	40.4	47.9	63.0	68.1
% change	-9.1	29.9	15.8	6	11.8	18.5	31.6	8.1
Merchandise trade balance (US$bn)[a]	-1.3	-6.8	-6	-4.2	-4.3	-3.7	-8	-11.9
Net invisibles (US$bn)[a]	-0.2	-0.5	-1.6	-2.6	-2.5	-4.3	-5.6	-4.1
Current account (US$bn)[a]	-1.5	-7.3	-7.6	-6.3	-6.3	-8	-13.6	-16.0
% GDP	-4	-8.5	-7.7	-5.8	-5.6	-6	-7.2	-8.6
Foreign exchange reserves (US$bn)[b]	2.2	13.3	17.5	20.4	24.5	29.3	36	39.5
Months imports	3.1	5.4	6.1	6.7	7.2	6.8	6.3	6.9
Exchange rate (baht/US$)[b]	27.16	25.59	25.52	25.4	25.32	25.15	24.92	25.5
Real exchange rate (1990 = 100)[c]	94	100	100	102	103	104	105	100
External long-term debt (US$bn)[d]	13.2	19.9	23.5	24.9	26.1	31.8	33.5	35.5
% GDP	34	23.2	23.9	22.5	21.1	10.8	20.4	18.7
External long-term debt-service ratio[d] (% exports)	25.2	13.9	10.7	12.1	16.5	17.9	11.7	14

Sources:
a IMF, Balance of Payments data series.
b IMF, International Financial Statistics data series.
c Real exchange rates are calculated with Thailand's export shares as weights, using price indices and exchange rates data from source b.
d World Bank, World Development Tables and Asian Development Bank, *Asian Development Outlook, 1996 and 1997* for 1995 and 1996 debt service data.

from abroad to take advantage of the high interest rates. This inflow would raise the domestic money supply as the funds were converted to baht at the fixed exchange rate, thus defeating the monetary objective. Likewise, if the Bank wished to raise the domestic money supply by lowering interest rates this objective would be defeated by a capital outflow.

Historically, what prevented the above mechanism from destroying the BOT's monetary independence was that the Bank imposed several forms of controls on capital movements into and out of Thailand. These measures preserved for the Bank a considerable degree of monetary autonomy.[6] But in the early 1990s most of these capital market controls were dismantled in a liberalization programme intended partly to facilitate Thailand's challenge to Singapore and Hong Kong as a regional financial centre. The Bangkok International Banking Facility (BIBF) was established in 1993 to promote this objective. The unintended effect was that it left the BOT with very little control of the domestic money supply so long as the fixed exchange rate policy remained in place.

One policy recommendation was to move to a truly floating exchange rate. Another was to reinstate some controls on international capital movements. The latter proposals seem to have won, at least temporarily. In June the Bank set a 7% cash reserve requirement on short-term lending through the BIBF. In October the fear of capital flight induced the Bank to withdraw policy changes which would have liberalized the raising of loans offshore. The Bank also reduced the maximum ratio of non-baht borrowing to total liabilities. Further measures designed to limit speculative capital movements remain possible.

During 1996 there were suggestions that the Bank of Thailand may move to a flexible exchange rate system. It was announced that the band within which the baht is pegged had been widened, and this was interpreted by some as an indication that a switch to a flexible exchange rate policy was imminent. Such a prospect was apparently under discussion, but for the time being it seems the debate was resolved by reinstating some controls on capital movements removed during the capital market liberalizations of the early 1990s.

During 1996 rumours of an impending devaluation of the baht were frequent and these rumours had powerful financial effects. The expectation of a devaluation induces an outflow of speculative capital and deters the holding of money. It is well known that such expectations can actually force a devaluation that might not otherwise have been required. The speculative capital outflow may explain in part the property market and stock market slump experienced in 1996. The export slow-down presumably contributed to the lack of confidence in Thai financial markets as well, but the expectation of a devaluation was probably its most powerful financial effect.

Explaining the Export Slow-down

The apparent export slow-down has attracted many attempted explanations from observers of the Thai economy. They are reviewed here, arranged in what would seem to be increasing order of importance — that is, with the least important explanations first, followed by the more important.

Politics

The government of Prime Minister Banharn

Silpa-Archa had taken office after the election of July 1995 but was disrupted by repeated scandals and by allegations of corruption and other misdemeanours. The public perception was also one of incompetence in economic management and other areas. In November 1996 the government was forced by the threat of a parliamentary censure motion to call a general election. Economic management was a major issue in the campaign and the Banharn government was blamed for a range of economic problems including the export slow-down, the deterioration in the current account and slumps in both the property market and the stock exchange.

Corruption and incompetence of the levels attributed to the Banharn administration are nothing new for Thailand. In the past, corruption at the top of government did not lead to serious economic failure because policy continued to be controlled primarily by technocrats, rather than the politicians. Consequences of the kind experienced in 1996 did not occur. For this reason it seems unlikely that the Banharn government was truly responsible for more than a little of the export slow-down. The government's apparent incompetence seems to have been more a source of public embarrassment than of extensive policy failure.

There were worrying instances in which the Banharn government had attempted to interfere with the bureaucracy's economic management, including an apparent challenge to the independence of the central bank, the Bank of Thailand, but it would seem that, to some extent, the Banharn government was merely "unlucky" to have been in office when more powerful economic forces induced the economic problems of 1996. The prospects for economic management are better under the new government, but the reported deficiencies of the Banharn government were insufficient to explain the 1996 export slowdown.

Monetary Policy

The Bank of Thailand responded to above normal inflation in 1995 by tightening monetary policy. Inflation eased, but the apparent effect on real output was greater than expected. By early 1996 an export slow-down was already evident and slower growth for 1996 was being forecast. The Bank of Thailand eased its monetary policy and interest rates declined. Monetary tightness in late 1995 and early 1996 may have contributed to the export slow-down but was presumably responsible for only a small part of the large decline in export growth that was reported. There is no obvious reason why exporters should be more negatively affected by a tight monetary policy than producers for the domestic market, and also no reason why labour-intensive exporters should be affected the most.

As discussed above, liberalization of the movement of capital into and out of Thailand has reduced the Bank of Thailand's capacity to control the domestic money supply but exchange rate expectations have powerful effects on financial markets. Expectations of exchange rate adjustments have major effects on capital movements, and rumours of impending devaluation of the baht have circulated in Bangkok financial circles since at least May 1996. By inducing capital outflow these expectations have a contractionary effect on the domestic money supply. These financial movements could not reasonably be cited as a cause of the export slow-down but they do provide a credible explanation for the property and stock market slumps of 1996.

Trade Liberalization

During the late 1980s and early 1990s, Thailand liberalized its import protection regime significantly. The expected effect of this liberalization is a gain in overall economic efficiency, reflected partly in a surge of exports. The efficiency gains raise overall productivity and the *level* of exports permanently, but they will not necessarily raise growth *rates* permanently. That is, the gains are expected to be primarily static rather than dynamic. The surge in export growth rates experienced in the late 1980s and early 1990s thus reflected, in part, the efficiency gains from the earlier liberalizations. By the mid-1990s the efficiency gains from these liberalizations had been fully realized. The level of exports had been permanently raised by these liberalizations, but the growth *rate* of exports had been raised only temporarily. The growth rate of exports would have been expected to slow down on this account some time around the mid-1990s. This effect may therefore explain some but not all of the slow-down that actually occurred at that time.

Congested Infrastructure

The unprecedented rate of Thailand's industrial expansion since the late 1980s, concentrated on export oriented production, has placed enormous strain on the country's already congested infrastructure facilities. Despite very high levels of public investment in infrastructure facilities during the period of the Seventh Five-Year Plan (1992 to 1996), it has not been possible to keep up with the demand. Average levels of infrastructure investment over this period exceeded baht 250 billion per year (US$10 billion). Of this, transportation accounted for 40%, energy 35%, telecommunications 18% and other utilities 7%. Roads, ports and telecommunications are increasingly overcommitted. The congestion of infrastructure has clearly contributed to the export slow-down but could not in itself explain the apparent severity and suddenness of the 1996 export problems.

Falsified Export Data

A new value-added tax (VAT) system was introduced in the early 1990s at the rate of 7%. Under this scheme exporters may receive rebates of value-added taxes at the rate of 7% of the value of goods exported. The rebates are paid on production of documentary evidence that the exports actually occurred. By 1995 a market had developed in falsified export documents, so that VAT rebates were being claimed for exports which did not actually take place. Empty containers were reportedly being shipped abroad as part of this form of tax fraud. It has been estimated that of the 1,406 billion baht of exports officially declared for 1995 at least 100 billion baht were fictitious.[7]

If this estimate was correct and the official export data for both 1994 and 1996 were both correct, the true growth rate for 1995 would have been lower than the reported rates. Similarly, the true export growth rate for 1996 would then have been higher than the reported rate because the true 1995 base on which it is calculated would have been below the reported level. If the 100 billion baht estimate for export overstatement in 1995 was correct, export growth for the years ending 1995 and 1996 would be 14.8 and 7.2%, respectively, rather than the 23.6 and 1.6% actually reported. If the true overstatement of 1995 exports was 150 billion baht the true growth rates for 1995 and 1996 would have been 10.4 and 11.4%, respectively.

The overstatement of exports for the purpose of claiming VAT rebates presumably began a year or two earlier than 1995, when it was officially uncovered. This means that the true growth rates for 1994 and 1995 were also presumably lower than the reported rates and the 1996 export slow-down was correspondingly smaller than the official data indicate. In short, the overstatement of exports probably disguised a moderate slow-down in exports which actually began a year or two earlier. A slow-down really does seem to have occurred, though not as sudden or as large as the 1996 slow-down indicated by the official export data.

Real Appreciation

Over the year 1995 to 1996 the Thai baht/ US$ exchange rate depreciated somewhat, from an average of 24.9 to 25.5 — a depreciation of 2.4%. Much more significant, however, was that the Japanese yen depreciated relative to the dollar, from an average of 93.5 to 107.5 yen/US$ — a depreciation of 15%. This means that the baht appreciated relative to the Japanese yen by more than 12%.

When these calculations are conducted in real terms, to take account of differences in rates of inflation, the story is even more dramatic. The 2.4% nominal depreciation of the baht relative to the U.S. dollar was offset by the difference in rates of inflation between the two countries, as measured by CPI movements — 5.8% for Thailand and 2.8% for the United States. Thailand's real exchange rate relative to the U.S. dollar barely changed; there was in fact a small real appreciation of 0.6%. But Japan's rate of inflation was only 0.2%, so the yen depreciated in real terms relative to the U.S. dollar by a striking 17.6%. The baht appreciated in real terms relative to the yen by more than 18%! In 1996 Thailand's overall real exchange rate with respect to all trading partners appreciated by about 5% compared with 1995.[8]

Along with the goods of other countries which peg their exchange rates more or less to the U.S. dollar, Thai goods became less competitive in Japanese markets as a result of this large real appreciation. For the same reason, Thai goods also became slightly less competitive in U.S. export markets relative to U.S. goods and markedly less competitive in U.S. markets relative to Japanese goods. The large real appreciation of the baht relative to the yen explains part of Thailand's export slow-down in 1996, but it does not explain why labour-intensive industries suffered the most.

Demand Slow-down in Importing Countries

In 1996 export growth declined relative to the previous year in almost all Asian countries. Thailand was not alone, although Thailand's reported export slow-down was one of the largest (Table 5). As the table also shows, the principal reason was a slow-down of demand from major importing countries. Japan is a major market for all of the East Asian exporting countries and slow growth of the Japanese economy over several years has produced a slow-down in Japanese import growth.

To the extent that international demand side factors were responsible, the 1996 slow-down in the growth of exports from Thailand and similar exporting countries does not indicate a decline in their export competitiveness. There is little these countries can do about a decline in international demand. To some extent, they must wait for demand to recover and maintain their

TABLE 5
Asian Economies Export and Import Slow-down (Percentage change)

Country/Territory	Exports		Imports	
	1995	1996	1995	1996
China	21.0	−11.8	15.3	−2.2
Hong Kong	13.3	0.0	4.0	1.0
Taiwan	20	3.9	21.3	−2.2
Indonesia	18.5	7.5	26.8	10.3
Japan	4.5	−8.2	17.5	3.4
Korea	25.5	4.3	28.2	7.3
Malaysia	20.4	8.7	25.3	−0.4
Philippines	20.6	24.8	18.9	38.7
Singapore	19.3	11.5	16.6	11.7
Thailand	19.4	1.5	22.8	12.8

Note: Indonesian export data relate to non-oil exports only.
Source: Except for Taiwan, growth rates computed from International Monetary Fund, Direction of Trade data series in US$, current prices. Taiwan data from Ministry of Finance, Republic of China, Taipei.

efficiency in the meantime. Desperate schemes intended to "promote" exports have the potential to introduce inefficiencies that will only impede their capacity to respond efficiently to increased international demand when recovery occurs.

The slow growth in international demand for electronic products is well known and was also significant for Thailand, but it should be recalled (from Table 3) that electronic products were not the slowest growing of Thailand's exports. Exports of labour-intensive products such as garments, textiles and footwear actually fell the most. Once again, slow growth of international demand does not account for that difference. Internal factors, operating within the Thai economy, must be responsible (see below).

Real Wages

Recently available data on real wages provide the single most significant explanation for Thailand's export slow-down and its concentration in labour-intensive industries. Research at the Thailand Development Research Institute has recently produced a reliable series of real wage data for Thailand. These data are reproduced in Figure 1 for the years 1982 to 1994. The data describe an index of nominal wages for the manufacturing sector deflated by the consumer price index and are indexed in the chart below so that the level for 1982 is 100. Over the 13 years from 1982 to 1994, real wages increased by 70%, but this increase was heavily concentrated in the years since 1990. Over the years 1982 to 1990 the increase was from an index of 100 to 117, an average compound rate of increase of 2%. But over the following four years to 1994 the real wage increased to an index of 170, an average annual rate of increase in real wages of almost 10%!

Why the sudden increase in real wages? During the early stages of Thai economic growth the rising industrial and services sector demand for labour could be

FIGURE 1
Thailand: Index of Real Wages, 1982–94

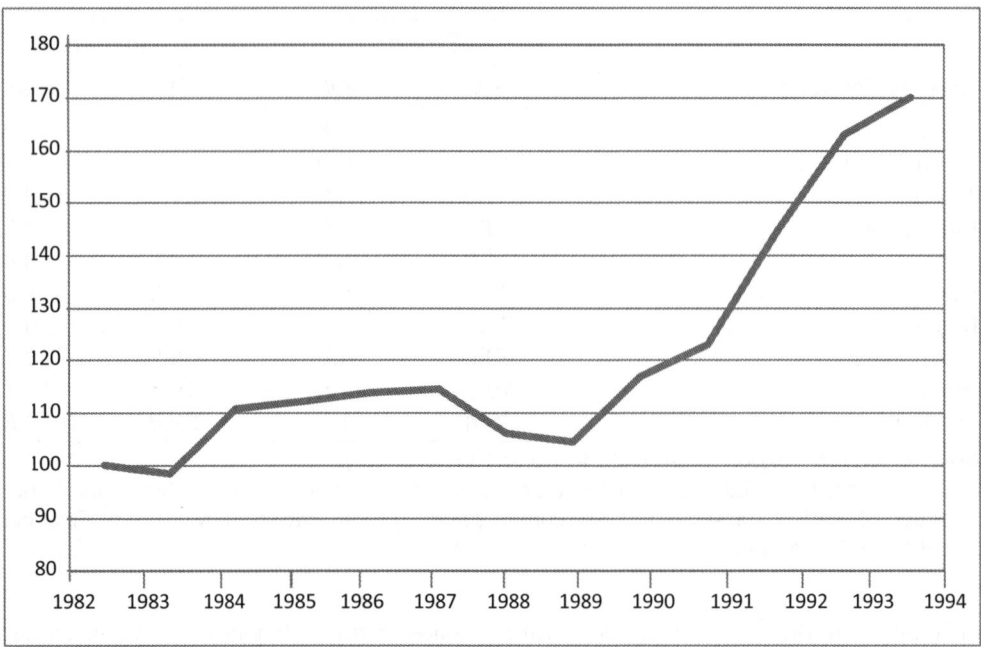

Source: Thailand Development Research Institute, Bangkok.

TABLE FOR FIGURE 1
Thailand: Real Wages, 1982–94
(1982 = 100)

Year	Index
1982	100.0
1983	98.5
1984	110.8
1985	112.3
1986	113.8
1987	114.5
1988	106.2
1989	104.6
1990	116.9
1991	123.1
1992	144.6
1993	163.1
1994	170.1

Source: Thailand Development Research Institute, Bangkok.

satisfied from a very large pool of rural labour with relatively low productivity. The potential supply of unskilled rural labour was so large that as workers moved from agriculture to more productive jobs in the manufacturing and services sectors, it was possible for these sectors to expand their levels of employment without significantly bidding up real wages. But as this process continued that pool of "cheap" rural labour was largely used up, so that by the early 1990s labour shortages were becoming evident. Agricultural industries were themselves experiencing serious problems of seasonal labour shortages. Further increases in the demand for labour outside agriculture then led to rising wages.

Thailand's export industries are especially vulnerable to increases in real wages for two basic reasons. First, many of Thailand's most successful export industries are highly labour intensive, implying that a given increase in real wages has large effects on their costs. Second, these export industries face highly competitive international markets for their products, where they must act as price-takers. This means that cost increases cannot be passed on in the form of increases in product prices. Producers for the domestic market may have greater scope for doing so.

The implication of rising real wages is a loss of competitiveness in the labour-intensive export-oriented industries that have been the basis of much of Thailand's growth over the past decade. This information helps explain the export slow-down of the mid 1990s. With the end of the era of "cheap labour", Thailand's labour-intensive exports face the prospect of declining competitiveness. The importance of this point is confirmed by the fact that the export slow-down was concentrated in labour-intensive industries such as garments, footwear and textiles.[9]

For the export-oriented labour-intensive industries, large real wage increases raise serious problems. Unlike most of the potential causes of the export slow-down reviewed above, the increase in real wages is presumably (and hopefully) permanent. This means that the export competitiveness of these labour-intensive industries has declined permanently, given their present technology. They must adjust or face steadily declining market share. To adjust, these industries must find less labour-intensive and more capital- and skill-intensive ways of producing their goods. Thailand as a whole must move out of these industries as wages continue to rise and move into more skill-intensive industries. Here, the performance of Thailand's education sector in supplying the skilled labour force required becomes crucial.

Past indications raise serious concern about the capacity of the Thai education sector to deliver the skilled work-force that will be required. Thailand's primary school participation rates are high but retention rates at the secondary level are low by Southeast Asian standards. The reasons for this include the concentration of upper secondary schools in urban areas and the resulting high cost for rural people to participate, since students must stay away from home to attend school. In addition the secondary curriculum has been described as unsuitable for vocational type students.[10] These features of the education system combined with Thailand's high rate of industrialization have produced severe shortages of skilled labour. The long-term prospects for the Thai economy depend on its capacity to upgrade its manufacturing base. But the country's capacity to move from forms of manufacturing dependent on abundant unskilled labour and towards more skill-intensive forms of production will depend crucially upon the capacity of the education system to produce the skilled work-force required.

The increase in real wages may be bad news for some manufacturers, but it is obviously good news for Thailand's poor, who derive most of their incomes from their own labour. Observers of Thailand's economic development have for some years expressed concern at the rising inequality evident from consumer expenditure surveys. The income share of the richest quintile group (richest one fifth of the population) increased continuously at least from 1975/76, the earliest year for which reliable data are available, until 1992. The income share of each of the other four quintile groups continuously declined. Nevertheless, the same household survey data sources also reveal that the proportion of the population whose incomes fell below a designated poverty line — held constant in purchasing power terms — declined significantly over the same period. The poor became better off in absolute terms over this period, which is why absolute poverty incidence declined, but the rich became better off at an even faster rate, which is why relative inequality simultaneously rose (Table 6).

There is roughly a two-year lag between conduct of the household surveys and publication of the survey results. The data for 1994 recently became available and Table 6 includes these results. Poverty incidence continued to decline, but the increase in relative inequality evident until 1992 was reversed over the interval to 1994. The experience of Thailand illustrates an empirical phenomenon first noticed in 1955 by Simon Kuznets: economic growth often produces rising inequality in the early stages of development followed by reduced inequality as the process matures.

In the Thai case, the fundamental reason for the transition from rising to declining inequality as growth proceeds is clear. It is the increases in real wages that began in the early 1990s. As the process of industrialization continues, "surplus" rural labour is eventually absorbed and real wages then begin to rise. As real wages

TABLE 6
Thailand: Income Distribution and Poverty, 1981–94

1981		1986	1988	1990	1992	1994
Income Share by Quintile Groups (%)						
Quintile (poorest)	5.41	4.55	4.60	4.20	3.94	3.99
Quintile 2	9.10	7.87	8.13	7.38	7.02	7.29
Quintile 2	13.38	12.09	12.46	11.50	11.06	11.60
Quintile 2	20.64	19.86	20.66	19.26	18.95	19.60
Quintile 5 (richest)	51.47	55.63	54.16	57.67	59.04	57.52
Ratio of Income Share of Quintile 1 to Quintile 5		9.5	12.2	11.8	13.7	15.0	14.4
Gini coefficient		0.453	0.500	0.485	0.522	0.536	0.525
Poverty incident (head count ratio %)		23.0	29.5	22.2	16.6	13.1	9.6

Source: Bangkok Post Year-End Economic Review, December 1996, p. 22.

rise, the real incomes of all labour-income earners rise accordingly and inequality declines, but this may occur only after a prolonged period when, as in the case of Thailand, real wages remain relatively constant for many years and inequality increases.

Prospects for 1997 and Beyond

The new government is expected to boost investors' optimism in the future of the Thai economy by restoring confidence in the government's capacity for competent economic management. Public investment is expected to decline in real terms in an effort to restore a more sustainable level of the budgetary deficit.

The International Monetary Fund predicts that global economic growth will recover from 3.8% in 1996 to 4.2% in 1997. The growth of world trade is expected to increase slightly, from 6.8% in 1996 to just over 7%. The United States and Japanese economies are expected to slow down slightly, however. Because of these two countries' importance as sources of demand for Thailand's exports, the prospects for demand for Thailand's exports are probably only slightly, if at all, more favourable in 1997 than the experience of 1996.

Some further real appreciation of the baht relative to the yen may occur in 1997. Slow recovery of Thailand's exports in 1997 relative to 1996 is probably the best that can reasonably be expected. Gradual recovery may be expected in subsequent years provided Thai producers can adjust their product mix appropriately in response to rising real wages. The very high rates of export growth experienced in the late 1980s and early 1990s will probably not be repeated.

The Thai economy may be expected to continue to grow at 6% per annum or better in real terms — high by international standards but below the unprecedented rates of over 10% achieved during the boom of 1988 to 1995. This growth slow-down need not be a source of gloom. The boom period growth rates were recognized to be environmentally unsustainable; in so far as they were based on unlimited supplies of cheap labour, they were economically unsustainable as well. In adjusting to lower growth rates Thailand may find ways to manage the social and policy conflicts produced by economic growth better than was possible during the hectic days of the boom.

Notes

1. This is the headcount measure of poverty incidence, discussed later in this article.
2. The fifteen commodities represented in Table 3 comprised between 52 and 54% of total exports in each of the three years shown.
3. See Peter G. Warr and Bhanupong Nidhiprabha, *Thailand's Macroeconomic Miracle: Stable Adjustment and Sustained Growth* (Washington, D.C.: World Bank and Kuala Lumpur: Oxford University Press, 1996).
4. Measured in months of imports, Thailand's reserves were the highest in Southeast Asia, with the possible exception of Brunei, for which data were not available. At the end of 1996 Thailand's reserves were US$42.7 billion, equivalent to 7.3 months of imports. Note that Table 4 describes annual average levels of reserves, rather than year-end levels. Corresponding end-of-year data for other Southeast Asian countries (with months of import coverage in parentheses) were: Malaysia US$21.4 billion (3.3 months), Indonesia US$17.2

billion (4.6 months), Singapore US$78.2 billion (7.1 months), and the Philippines US$ 7.8 billion (2.8 months). [*Source*: HG Asia, *Economic Snapshot*, February 1997.]
5. The main exceptions were devaluations in mid-1981 (roughly 10%) and late 1984 (roughly 15%). For further detail, see Peter G. Warr and Bhanupong Nidhiprabha, *Thailand's Macroeconomic Miracle: Stable Adjustment and Sustained Growth* (Washington, D.C.: World Bank, and Kuala Lumpur: Oxford University Press, 1996).
6. For further detail, see Peter G. Warr and Bhanupong Nidhiprabha, *Thailand's Macroeconomic Miracle: Stable Adjustment and Sustained Growth* (Washington, D.C.: World Bank, and Kuala Lumpur: Oxford University Press, 1996).
7. *Bangkok Post Year-end Economic Review*, December 1996, p. 26.
8. Since we are interested in the implications for Thailand's export industries, this calculation uses Thailand's export shares to weight the bilateral real exchange rates with respect to individual trading partners.
9. The frozen shrimp industry is a special case, where U.S. import restrictions were important, effectively banning non-farm shrimp imports from Thailand. Fortunately, these bans are due to be lifted in 1997.
10. For further detail, see Sirilaksana Khoman, "Education Policy" in *The Thai Economy in Transition*, ed. Peter G. Warr (Cambridge: Cambridge University Press, 1993), pp. 325–54.

THAILAND
A Year of Diminishing Expectations

Naruemon Thabchumpon

At the end of 1997, many Thai people hoped that 1998 would be the starting point for reforming the country. Even though the Thai economy was severely hit by the economic crisis, the new government of Chuan Leekpai promised economic recovery and better governance. As time went by, however, and the economy went into a sharp decline, expectations slowly diminished. The Chuan government rode out these difficulties, and had some success in projecting itself as the only option, but encountered increasing pressures from a critical civil society.

Thailand under the IMF

When the International Monetary Fund (IMF) was asked by Thailand to help in the crisis after the devaluation of the baht in July 1997, many sectors of Thai society welcomed it as a force that could discipline what was perceived as an irresponsible gang of politicians and businessmen whose ineptitude had brought the country to its knees. Many technocrats even hoped that the structural adjustment programme might help dismantle crony capitalism in Thailand.

Initially, the IMF imposed a largely traditional formula on Thailand, involving cuts in government funding, increased taxation, high interest rates, greater disclosure, and financial sector reforms. It did, however, require much greater reforms of the financial sector than was normal for such programmes, together with other structural reforms to open the country up to foreign investment, and accelerate the spluttering pace of privatization. Thailand had experienced IMF tutelage before — in

---

Reprinted from Daljit Singh and John Funston, eds., *Southeast Asian Affairs 1999* (Singapore: Institute of Southeast Asian Studies, 1999), pp. 311–24. At the time of original publication, Naruemon Thabchumpon was a lecturer at the Faculty of Political Science, Chulalongkorn University, Bangkok.

the mid-1980s when a period of global recession had a particularly debilitating effect on the financial sector. It was prepared to accept new IMF controls because officials felt that the key to recovery was to win back the confidence of foreign capital, and to do this it had to adhere to the IMF programme.

The Chuan government was more willing than its predecessor to take tough decisions, and to implement them. However, there was no initial easing of the economic problems. The baht declined to an all-time low against the U.S. dollar in January (US$1 = 55.5 baht) before it began to strengthen as part of a broader regional trend in February. Even as the currency stabilized, the economy plunged deeper into recession, contrary to the expectations of the IMF and others. As a result, the government's second Letter of Intent (LOI) with the IMF projected a deficit of 2 per cent of gross domestic product (GDP) (rather than earlier plans for a 1 per cent surplus), more focus on social safety nets, and more flexible use of interest rates. Subsequent LOIs continued such policies. The deficit was pushed to 3 per cent of GDP in May, and 5 per cent in December, and the May agreement focused on reforms in the financial sector. In the second half of 1998, the IMF also allowed the Bank of Thailand to pressure commercial banks to lower interest rates, bringing the cost down from more than 20 per cent to single digits.

Under IMF tutelage, the Chuan government moved purposefully to reform the financial sector, widen opportunities for foreign investment, and improve transparency and bankruptcy procedures. In many areas, however, government intentions were not backed up by legislative action — for instance, eleven key economic reform bills were still before Parliament at the end of the year. However, progress was gradually made across the board, and in August the government announced a major reorganization of the banking sector. Central to this was the promised injection of some US$7 billion into the larger banks (in return for a write-down of capital held by existing shareholders, and a reduction in their management role), the merging of others, and foreign take-over of the rest. Coming on top of the closure of 56 finance companies in late 1997, and increased capitalization of US$1 billion each for the two largest banks from share placements on the international market, many analysts saw Thailand as having gone further than other crisis-hit countries in clearing up this troubled sector. In practice, implementation proved slow and difficult, but by year's end one medium-sized bank (Siam Commercial) had agreed to the proposed restructure. The difficulty of reform in this sector was again illustrated when the much vaunted "world's largest ever one-day asset sale" resulted in only about 10 per cent of the 371 billion baht of core assets of the closed finance companies being disposed of — and even these at highly discounted prices. Subsequent negotiations led to about one-third of the offer being accepted, still well below the expected take-up.

Some clear economic gains were made. Perhaps the most notable was the stabilization of the exchange rate. From March, the rate stayed at around 38–42 baht to US$1 (an increase of about 35 per cent from January), despite a volatile external environment and stock market. Its value was sustained by monthly balance of payment surpluses of around US$1 billion, positive capital inflows, more foreign investment, and an increase in net foreign reserves (minus forward commitments) from only US$800 million in August

1997, to US$11.4 billion in May 1998, and US$22 billion by the end of the year. Exports fell nearly 7 per cent in U.S. dollar terms, but increased 6 per cent in volume, and 24 per cent in baht terms. Tourism boomed, increasing by 7 per cent. Inflation remained under double digits, and the stock market rose some 60 per cent in the first quarter, then fell by the same amount by August, then gained a further 30 per cent by December.

Further complicating this somewhat mixed picture was plummeting growth, forcing the IMF progressively to revise its estimates from positive growth of 1 per cent to a negative 8 per cent. As the real economy ground down, the corporate sector sank even deeper into debt, and banks' non-performing loans ballooned to over 40 per cent. Many Thai economists, economic journalists, and politicians declared that the IMF policies were not working.

Social Impact of the Crisis

Throughout 1998, many Thai people experienced a twilight zone, even those who retained their jobs. Although they still occupied their houses and went to work, they had a feeling that all could be gone any day soon. They had to hold on to whatever job they had very tightly. The World Bank estimated that unemployment would rise from 1.3 million to 1.8 million at the end of 1998. The 1.8 million jobless represented 5.6 per cent of the work-force, and many observers feared this could trigger social unrest. Other negative effects resulting from the economic crisis included an increase in problems such as child labour, child abuse, prostitution, drugs, homelessness, and HIV/Aids.

Despite economic growth in the last decade, about eight million Thais — some 12 per cent of the population — were living on less than US$2 a day before the crisis. These people benefited little from the boom, and were among the first to suffer from the bust. The poor were affected particularly by higher inflation, with some basic foodstuffs costing more than the overall inflation of 9 per cent, and the staple, rice, almost doubling. But a buoyant agricultural sector in the first three quarters of the year — boosted by high prices for its exports and a generally favourable season — provided some respite for those losing jobs in the construction and industrial sectors.

Almost all sectors of the economy were affected by the rapid slowdown, the rising cost of imports, the high price of credit, failing businesses and cuts in government expenditure. The crisis also had a deep impact on the middle and lower-middle classes. Tens of thousands in the financial sector lost their jobs. Those with money in failed finance companies saw their assets tied up until the affairs of these companies were sorted out. Stock market investments evaporated. Interest on home mortgages climbed for properties that were declining rapidly in value. Private education became much more expensive, particularly for those with children overseas. Some 40 per cent of the year's university graduates were unable to find ready employment. And the middle class unemployed found it difficult either to seek jobs in the unofficial urban sector, or return to the villages.

Political Fall-out

The economic crisis had several political consequences. It intensified a debate among academics and competing civil society groups over the most appropriate development paradigm for Thailand. And it had a direct impact on the political fortunes of the ruling coalition — causing conflict within Chuan's Democrat Party, and strengthening criticisms from civil society, the parliamentary opposition, and the Senate.

Debating Development

In Thai civil society, there is a contrasting picture between the urban groups (élite-urban) and the countryside (rural-popular).[1] As a result of thirty years of rapid economic development, the élite-urban civil society — including progressive civil servants, some in the business community, and the middle class — is growing and gaining more political power. Since the crisis in 1997, this group has demanded political reform in order to achieve a better standard of efficiency and "rational" administration, rather than the corrupt and paternalistic ways of old. By comparison, economic development has not fostered the same political participation among the peasants. This has contributed to the concentration of economic and political power in the hands of a few, and caused marginalization and disempowerment among the villagers.[2] However, rural grassroots organizations, often led by urbanites, have begun to emerge as an essential part of the social democratic movement in Thailand. In 1998, these two groups proposed different ways to solve the economic crisis, and push forward social reform.

Rural-Popular Nationalism: By mid-1998, many Thai intellectuals associated with the rural-popular side of civil society were arguing that the crash of the Thai economy was not only the result of several years of resources mismanagement, but of at least four inherent weaknesses in the country's economic condition. First, the economic structure had been centralized under the control of a small élite group who were proponents of the idea of turning the country into a "capitalist satellite" state. Under élitist guidance, people were not encouraged to boost their capabilities and discipline themselves to build a stronger economy. Secondly, the majority of the leaders both in government and finance lacked the honesty, professionalism and longer-term vision to cope with rapid changes on a global scale. Thirdly, development policy had been focused largely on foreign investment without proper attention being given to building up a domestic capital base for sustained business development. Finally, the educational system had failed to produce innovative thinkers and professionals.

After the economic crisis, two radical "nationalist" movements emerged. Both shared the same idea on the essential causes of the crisis. "Globalization", understood as the expansion and penetration of Western multinational companies into the economy of Southeast Asia, was seen as the major factor.[3] Another was the "imperialist design" of the Group of Seven (G7) powers in attempting to put the "Asian tigers" under the yoke of economic colonialism.[4] For these groups, solutions such as a self-sufficient, low-technology agricultural economy were the answer for economic recovery. Instead of foreign capital and technology, Thailand should use traditional "Thai intellectual resources", and not rely totally on the IMF. The crisis should be transformed into an opportunity for people to become more self-reliant, and to abandon the old thinking of entrusting the government and the IMF with the responsibility of steering the country out of economic trouble.

One of the most important of these groups was the People's Liberation Alliance (Neaw Rom Prachachon Ku Chat). The Alliance was launched on 5 May 1998, made up of thirty non-governmental organizations (NGOs) and people's organizations, including the farmer-based organization known as the Assembly of the Poor, the NGO Co-ordinating Committee on Development (NGO-COD), the State Enterprise Worker Confederation, the Campaign for Popular Democracy, and the Student Federation of Thailand. These groups had played a key role during the campaign for constitutional reform in 1997, which culminated in a new, more democratic, constitution. They decided to form an alliance after exchanging ideas and opinions about the impact of the IMF bailout package on government attitudes, and attempts to address long-lasting problems of the poor.

The Alliance's initial demands were for the government to suspend its drafting of the fourth LOI to the IMF (due in September) to enable public hearings on this; disclose all terms with the IMF; identify clearly public debt and debt that belonged to the private sector, and impose a foreign debt moratorium; and set up a Popular Economic Restoration Fund (PERF). It also urged the government to review its support to the Financial Institution Development Fund (FIDF) — an institution set up to inject liquidity into banks and finance companies — since it benefited only a small number of people in the financial sector. "The FIDF", it argued, "should be considered a 'black hole' that sucked most of the money out of the market without solving any problems facing the people at large. Instead, the government should pay attention to the PERF which would be able to minimise the impact of the economic crisis".[5] In June 1998, the group organized a seminar on the Social Investment Fund — funded by a World Bank loan, and administered through civil society groups — and its impact on the poor. The leaders argued that the World Bank should have *given* the social investment money to Thailand instead of in the form of a loan, to acknowledge its responsibility for the social problems facing Thailand at the time. They also suggested a moratorium on foreign debt, and a debt moratorium for poor farmers.

Established at about the same time as the Alliance was the National Restoration Civic Group (Prachakom Kob Ban Ku Muang). This organization comprised people from three main sectors: academics and thinkers led by prominent physician and social activist Dr Prawese Wasi; affected business leaders from both the public and private sectors; and those involved in rural civil society activities, especially the network of rural doctors. The group aimed to establish social communication with the public, without pressuring or accusing any particular groups or individuals. It was keen on promoting social awareness about frugal and beneficial consumption, and encouraging people to work towards a self-sufficient economy and peaceful coexistence.

In May 1998, the Group organized several meetings in Bangkok. These centred on informing the public of the seriousness of the country's debt burden, and urging them to maintain their morale and to look for solutions to their predicament wisely. The Group also made plans to travel to different provinces to hold academic forums in co-operation with local civic groups, down to sub-district and village levels.

Subsequently, the Group organized a series of forums directed at forming an alliance to rescue Thai society from the crisis. It questioned the government's direction in solving the economic problem by passing the debt burden to the general public, as required by the IMF. Dr Prawase used the medical practitioners' network to inform the public in Bangkok of the real economic danger facing the country. The Group also proposed setting up a "Thai Peoples Share-owning Democracy" to encourage the public to buy the shares of the Bangchak Petroleum Company. The government-owned company was popular because of its support for the rural Thais, and a strong public campaign was launched to prevent its privatization, as mandated by the IMF, leading to foreign control. The leader of the group also urged the people and the government to strengthen Thailand's bargaining power with the IMF, and to provide a full disclosure of all government agreements with this organization.

Élite Urban Nationalism: In 1988, there was increasing talk in Thai academic and media circles, particularly among the élite-urban elements in civil society, about "good governance".[6] The Thai word *thammarath* — from *thamma* (Buddhist teachings), and *rath* (state) — was coined to convey this concept. The term was publicly used by sociologist Thirayuth Boonmee, a former leader of the 1973 revolution, who wrote a best-selling book on it. Good governance, involving "transparency, accountability and citizen's participation", was supposed to help Thailand survive the economic crisis and ensure that another crisis would not occur. The main supporters of this concept were the middle class, businessmen and capitalist leaders, such as former Prime Minister Anand Panyarachun and former Commerce Minister Amaret Sila-on. They received strong support from journalists and academics. During 1998, at least ten forums were held on "good governance", analysing its relevance for economic recovery, national security, bureaucratic reform, politics, the poor, corporate management, and social reform. The group saw the economic crisis as the result of several years of resources mismanagement, or in other words, as a crisis of political governance. The problems would go away if competent ministers or administrators were guiding government policy.

To its critics, this campaign displayed little awareness of the root causes of the crisis — that they were linked to broader problems in the global economy. This approach was also criticized by some people's organizations, such as the Assembly of the Poor, for ignoring marginalized groups. The Assembly argued that the "good governance" model was focused on industrial and financial reform, rather than broader social reform. It emphasized participation from all sectors of the society, including the state, business and civil society sectors, rather than equality between different sectors. The key issue relating to "good governance", in the eyes of the critics, was the question of "whose governance it is"?[7]

Self-Sufficiency and Good Governance: While it rejected extreme criticisms of its association with the IMF, the government generally sought to identify with proposals for a greater focus on self-sufficiency and assisting the poor, and promotion of good governance. Besides the broad public support for such objectives, the government had also to bear in mind the King's speech on 4 December 1997, in which he had urged the development of a self-sustained, agriculture-based economy, and the use of more domestically-produced goods. As a direct response, the Interior and Agriculture ministries, using loans provided by the World Bank and the Asian Development Bank, built small reservoirs upcountry in order to support self-sustaining farms and to create more jobs.

More generally, the government used World Bank loans to provide direct assistance at the village level. Some 16 billion baht was administered by government departments, and 4.8 billion by civil society groups. A Social Investment Fund (SIF) set up for the latter represented the first time that a development budget had not been administered by state agencies. Its objective, as SIF executive chairman, Ammar Siamwalla explained, was "to revive the intermediary web of relations, which the organisers believe was a basis for stronger communities, and thus it will not only ensure the well-being of the poor or those affected by the economic downturn, but also reduce their dependence on government money".[8] The SIF subsequently ran into problems of disbursement, since civil society groups were not well-equipped to meet the standards of accountability demanded by the World Bank. But a start was made in channelling funds directly to the grass-roots.

Government leaders also sought to demonstrate sympathy when confronted by mass action from civil society in making strategic concessions, in particular by setting up a high-level committee to advise on problems of the poor. Established in June, this comprised prominent social activists, business leaders, and the head of the army. Prawese Wasi, who proposed the setting up of the committee, was appointed an adviser.[9]

Despite these efforts the government, at times, still found it difficult to avoid the charge that it was pro-rich and unsympathetic to the poor — for reasons that are discussed below.

One Year of the Chuan Government

When Prime Minister Chuan Leekpai was nominated as Thailand's twenty-third premier on 8 November 1997, many people welcomed this and dubbed him "the hero on the white horse". The media analogy for Chuan's government at the end of 1998 was "the hero on the wooden horse".

In spite of formidable economic and social problems, Chuan's government initially gained strong support from a public tired of the indecisiveness and internal bickering of its predecessor, headed by Chavalit Yongchaiyut. Chuan gave an interview saying that he expected a turnaround in the economy within six months. He was confident that "faithful" implementation of the bail-out packages provided by the IMF would ease the government's task as "Thailand's economic fundamentals are still sound because Thailand is still one of the world's largest net exporters of food".[10] His government gained from keeping all major portfolios in Democrat hands — Finance, Commerce, Interior, Defence and Foreign Affairs. Chuan's own reputation for probity helped, and he appeared to have learnt from mistakes in the past. In particular, he began by demonstrating decisiveness, where previously he was seen as prevaricating. In addition, the government benefited from working in close association with respected former Prime Minister Anand Panyarachun, and from quiet signals of royal endorsement.

Chuan enjoyed remarkable support during his first six months in office. He was, however, tested by a conjunction of events from late April. A split became evident between the Deputy Prime Minister and Commerce Minister, Supachai Panitchpakdi, and Finance Minister Tarrin Nimmanaheaminda, with the former favouring an easing of fiscal and monetary policy to inject more liquidity into the system, and the latter adherence to IMF austerity requirements. Their views were eventually reconciled by concessions on both sides, and an easing of IMF austerity requirements (though differences between the two were resurrected in early 1999). At about the same time, Thirayuth Boonmee struck a popular chord when he accused the government of being unsympathetic to the poor, particularly for its use of public funds to pay off debts accumulated by government institutions that had loaned money to the private sector. And a government report on the Bank of Thailand — leaked to the media — reopened old wounds and reminded the public that no-one had yet faced legal proceedings over billion dollar bank and finance company losses. Riots in neighbouring Indonesia in the lead-up to Soeharto's overthrow also created fears that Thailand might follow the same path.

At mid-year, civil society also appeared to be mobilizing, with plans announced for a 50,000 strong demonstration by farmers in Bangkok on 24 June. As with a similar threat of mass opposition in January, government leaders rushed to meet the organizers and promised to look into their concerns. The government leaders also promised to roll-over loans from the Agriculture Bank for one year, to form a high-level committee (mentioned above), and to address farmers' concerns through legislation. While Chuan was never considered to be as sympathetic to farmers' as Chavalit had been — unlike Chavalit, he never personally met with them — these tactics worked. Only 2,000 farmers eventually turned up for the demonstration, and dispersed quickly, with only vague threats of returning if the government continued to ignore their concerns.

There was, however, no return to Chuan's early popularity after these events. From around June the Cabinet was plagued with a succession of corruption scandals, leading to several resignations. Most did not involve Democrat ministers — some were even centred in the bureaucracy — but all caused the government to lose some of its lustre. Public opinion surveys showed a government on the slide. Chuan, however, defied this trend, maintaining a high popularity rating throughout the year.

In early October, an Election Commission ruling allowing an opposition party to expel parliamentarians who had crossed to the government forced a major Cabinet reshuffle. This saw the Chart Pattana party rejoining the government, giving Chuan a healthy parliamentary majority, but potentially making cooperation between the coalition members more difficult. Democrat members also were divided over this change — one of several issues that caused growing intra-party tensions in the second half of the year.

The parliamentary opposition sought to take advantage of these events, and demonstrated their growing hostility towards the IMF. Former Prime Minister Chavalit charged that the government had allowed itself to come under the domination of the IMF and the United States. Other ministers under Chavalit, particularly former Deputy Prime Minister Dr Virabongse Ramangkul, a key negotiator of the first LOI with the IMF, presented a more measured critique. In their view, Thailand's IMF-directed economic stimulus measures had been based on its forecast that the Thai economy would recover in 1998. However, the IMF's predictions were based on wrong assumptions, and it adopted the wrong formula of raising revenue through tax increases, more borrowings to replenish reserves, and selling local assets. These policies had failed and would lead the nation to a dead end. Three factors would determine the timing and strength of any recovery: favourable external factors, healthy exports, and the complete restructuring of finance institutions. These factors were not improving even though the Finance Minister had tried to set up many mechanisms, including the 14 August banking policy.[11]

The Senate Speaker Mechai Ruchupan also strongly attacked the government for trying to please the IMF at the cost of misery to the people. According to Mechai, the IMF required laws to protect the interest of foreign creditors, and the government had been complying without considering the interests of the local people. The Senate, he argued, would have to keep the country's interests in mind. The ultimate goal was to make laws which would benefit Thais and the country, rather than foreigners.[12]

These criticisms evoked a broad popular response, and were often supported in the media. Chuan, however, placed his trust in Finance Minister Tarrin and refused any major change of course. To a degree, the Democrat leaders were able to deflect such criticisms by pointing to vested interests involved, particularly among some of the Senators. Their strongest card, however, was that Chavalit remained discredited by his own record in office, and as he was the only potential alternative the public felt it safer to stay with Chuan. The formation of the Thai Rak Thai Party (Thai Patriotic Party) by telecommunications billionaire Thaksin Shinawatra in July provided momentary hope for a third way, but the party failed to build on initial favourable media coverage.

Political Reform

The constitution promulgated in October 1997 sought to transform Thai politics, in particular to make it more democratic and to reduce corrupt practices common in public life. The economic crisis had strengthened the need to make the decision-making process more legitimate, efficient and involve people's participation. Hence, the constitution sought to establish a broader political system than one which had long been monopolized by traditional politicians and bureaucrats. Among the provisions addressing these issues were requirements that elected officials and their families had to declare their assets before and after taking office, citizens with 50,000 signatures could petition a new anti-graft commission to investigate officials suspected of corruption, and an independent election commission would look after the electoral process to ensure that it would be free and fair. In 1998, some progress towards these goals was made, although putting the constitution into practice, and changing the political culture, proved extremely difficult.

Parliament passed three "organic" laws — legislation deemed essential to implement the constitution. These were for the creation of a constitutional court, and conduct of elections (a political and party bill, and a national election commission bill). Some progress was made towards setting up an independent and powerful National Human Rights Commission (NHRC). The proposed law was drafted by the office of the Attorney General, and adopted by the Cabinet in October 1998, after a public hearing that facilitated public participation in the process. (Early in 1999, however, this work appeared threatened by a revised draft prepared by the Council of the State, and accepted by the Cabinet, that watered down the powers and independence of the NHRC.)

Other provisions of the new constitution also made an impact. The public was, for the first time, advised of the income and assets of all Cabinet members, including those of the preceding administration. (Most were millionaires — in baht terms — though almost invariably their wives were much richer. Chuan was the second poorest.) The right of 50,000 electors to impeach officials perceived to be corrupt was invoked in September, in relation to a scandal over public medical purchases involving ministers and senior health ministry officials. While this could not be taken further as envisaged under the constitution, because of the absence of a National Counter Corruption Commission (NCCC), the action placed great pressure on the officials involved and led to the resignation of the Public Health Minister and his deputy. Threats of a similar petition in relation to other scandals — over illegal logging early in the year, and government purchase and distribution of vegetable seeds later in the year — put pressure on the government, and in the latter case led to the resignation of the Agriculture deputy minister. The government was also forced to account for its actions in the first annual report to Parliament, in November.

Civil society institutions continued to play an influential role. While the efforts of rural groups were inconclusive, urban groups maintained pressure on the government to focus on issues of sustainable economic policy, governance, and opposition to corruption. The media played an important role, highlighting and investigating the major scandals throughout the year. The newly-formed Press Council, established to exercise a degree of self-regulation over the media industry, helped to further strengthen the fourth estate.

Complementing the new constitution, the State Information Act, passed in September 1997, was a major step towards making government actions more accountable. The initial response to it was poor, attributed to obstacles such as lack of knowledge about the information obtaining process, reluctance to bother state officials in charge of providing information, and distrust of the system. Eventually, the media took the lead. *Prachachat Thurakij*, a business newspaper, petitioned the State Information Committee to reveal the details of the army's television operation contract (and later asked for details of the side letters of the LOIs, in 1999). *The Nation* newspaper asked the Foreign Affairs Ministry to look into the 200 files on Thai foreign policy towards Cambodia between 1970 and 1980. Both requests were under consideration at year's end.

The military kept a low profile throughout the year, notwithstanding a sharp reduction in its budget, and controversial plans for restructuring and reducing its numbers. As Defence Minister (only the second civilian to occupy this post), Chuan reinforced the concept of civilian dominance in Thai politics. Rumours that an officer implicated in the harsh suppression of civilian protesters in 1992 might become the new army chief heightened anxiety for a time, but the eventual appointment of General Surayud Chulanont won wide support. He reaffirmed the army's willingness to remain outside the political arena, and became the first general to resign from the Senate in support of this principle. However, behind the scenes, the outgoing army head, General Chettha Thanajaro, did leave a problem for Chuan when he insisted that former Prime Minister Thanom Kittikatchorn should receive an honorary military award. Chuan questioned this, but felt unable to resist what was presented as an internal military arrangement. He came under strong attack in early 1999 when the award became public knowledge.

In a related field, the police force was transferred from the Ministry of Interior to an "independent" status in the Prime Minister's Office, following Cabinet agreement in August. This was widely welcomed as a positive move towards breaking down excessive powers in the hands of the Interior Ministry, and a step towards making the powerful police force more accountable.

Against these generally positive developments, progress was extremely slow on a number of fronts. None of the remaining eight "organic" laws — which must be completed by October 1999 — had been considered by Parliament. And some proposed laws also violated the spirit of the constitution. For example, Article 46 of the constitution stated that local communities have the right to protect and manage their natural resources, but a community forestry bill proposed by the Royal Forestry Department (RFD) sought to recruit local farmers to grow tree plantations in forests under the supervision of the RFD. The purpose of these RFD proposals was to relocate hill-tribe people and other poor farmers living in the conservation forest, and to ensure that the Department had power to control forestry management policy. NGOs and grass-roots members argued that forestry problems would never be solved if the Department ignored the participation of local people in managing the forest, and proposed an alternative draft putting the public firmly in control. The issue remained unresolved at year's end.

Foreign Policy

The economic crisis left its imprint on most areas, and foreign policy was no exception. Funding for the Ministry of Foreign Affairs (MFA) was drastically cut. Although no overseas posts were closed, seventy-three officers who had returned from overseas postings were not replaced. Other departments also cut down on overseas positions, and the MFA Permanent Secretary headed a high-level committee that looked at ways of rationalizing all such posts.

A great deal of effort was focused on strengthening relations with the United States and other great powers, in an attempt to gain their support for economic reform efforts. For this purpose, Prime Minister Chuan was given an unusual amount of international exposure. After attending the APEC summit in November 1997, he went to the World Economic Forum at Davos in January 1998 (the only Southeast Asian leader to do so), then visited Washington two months later. Chuan has generally shunned international politics — his English is halting, and he is not at ease — but at these meetings he successfully represented himself as the personification of democracy and economic rationalism. In March, he graced the covers of both *Time* and *Business Week*. Thailand's economic reform efforts were undoubtedly boosted by this favourable exposure.

Another economic issue that preoccupied the MFA for much of the year was supporting the candidature of Deputy Prime Minister Supachai Panitchpakdi for the leadership of the World Trade Organization. A great deal of prestige — if not direct economic benefit — rested on this campaign, and by the end of the year he was the front runner but not assured of victory. The United States, helpful on many other issues, was not supportive on this one.

Thailand's most controversial international initiative was its proposal, at the ASEAN Annual Ministerial Meeting in July, for the organization to adopt a form of "constructive intervention". Viewed by many observers as a challenge to ASEAN's traditional policy of non-intervention in the affairs of regional neighbours, it attracted the support of only the Philippines, and was quickly rejected. While the specifics of the proposal were not absolutely clear — spokesmen issued conflicting statements on whether it did or did not challenge ASEAN traditions — its primary purpose seems to have been to address concerns raised both at home and abroad that ASEAN's non-intervention principle was being used to cover up human rights abuses. There was economic concern here also, as ASEAN's stand on issues such as Myanmar was making it difficult for the ASEAN countries to have cordial relations with the great powers across the board. That Thailand was not proposing a radical shift in ASEAN policy became clear later in the year when the leaders adopted a relatively low-key stance on human rights issues associated with the sacking of Malaysian Deputy Prime Minister Anwar Ibrahim.

Thailand experienced no great dramas in bilateral relations for the year. Ties with Myanmar remained difficult because of continuing border clashes, notwithstanding Thai attempts (unsuccessful) to act as an intermediary for Myanmar with the European Union. Continuing political unrest in Cambodia after the general election there also complicated relations with this immediate neighbour.

Thailand's hosting of the Asian Games in December finished the year with an undoubted public relations triumph. For many months, it looked like a disaster in the making, as the construction of facilities fell behind schedule because of the economic crisis. In the end, all went relatively smoothly, and Thailand won plaudits for its warm hospitality, and impressively choreographed opening and closing ceremonies.

Conclusion

The economic crisis led to intensified conflict over resource management, with a strong articulation of the view that the Chuan government favoured the well-to-do at the expense of the poor. In the view of critics, the coalition government would like to return to a model where villagers stayed "out there" and were looked after by paternal staff officials; and it was reluctant to consult regularly and seriously with farmers in the way it dealt with bankers and businessmen. Government leaders sought to dispel this image, but made only limited headway.

At the same time, people's organizations and NGOs, backed by the King, sought a return to a focus on self-sufficient agriculture. To some degree, this was romanticizing a countryside that had already vanished, but a start was made towards preparing a programme that was both visionary and pragmatic. The challenge is to unite all groups affected by the economic crisis, and bring about democracy in a deeper sense.

Notes

1. Vitit Muntarbhorn and Charles Taylor, *Road to Democracy: Human Rights and Democratic Development in Thailand* (Montreal: International Centre for Human Rights and Democratic Development, 1994), p. 47.
2. Suthy Prasartset, "The Rise of NGOs as Critical Social Movement in Thailand", in *Thai NGOs: The Continuing Struggle for Democracy*, edited by Boonyaratanasoontorn (Bangkok: Thai NGO Support Group, 1994), p. 97.
3. Pittaya Wongkul, *People's Liberation Alliance* (Bangkok: Vithithat Project, 1998), p. 6 (in Thai).
4. Yook Sriareeya, *The Asian Crisis* (Bangkok: Vithithat Project, 1998), p. 55 (in Thai).
5. *The Nation*, 5 May 1998.
6. Thirayut Boonmee, *Good Governance and Social Reform* (Bangkok: Amarin Printing, 1998), p. 55 (in Thai).
7. Nitirat Sapsoomboon, *People's Voice* (Bangkok: Assembly of the Poor, June 1998), p. 57 (in Thai).
8. *Bangkok Post*, 9 September 1998.
9. *The Nation*, 26 June 1998.
10. Speech of Prime Minister Chuan Leekpai on the occasion of the fifth APEC forum of economic leaders in Canada, *The Nation*, 26 November 1997.
11. "Thai Economic Outlook, 1999: Will Thailand's Economy Recover?", annual seminar organized by the Thammasat Economic Association on 26 November 1998. See the *Bangkok Post*, 27 November 1998.
12. *The Nation*, 21 November 1998.

THAILAND
A Reckoning with History Begins

Michael J. Montesano

Introduction: Wat Thepsirin, 12 November 2006

On the clear, sunny afternoon of 12 November 2006, a sliver of Bangkok's great, good, and merely loyal gathered at Wat Thepsirintharawat Ratchaworawihan to participate in the royally sponsored cremation rites for General Kriangsak Chomanan. Thailand's prime minister during 1977–80, Kriangsak had passed away in late 2003. Three years on, his cremation offered a rare, even reassuring moment of calm and order during a year of disorientating and discouraging developments for Thailand.

Thais present at Wat Thepsirin included a number of those who had shaped recent history. Former Foreign Minister Air Chief Marshal (Retired) Siddhi Savetsila attended the cremation. So did former Prime Minister Chuan Leekpai and several of the leading technocrats of the late 1970s and early 1980s. Dhanin Chearavanont of the Charoen Pokphand (CP) Group was also present — perhaps in recognition of Kriangsak's engagement with the People's Republic of China, where CP was an important early foreign investor, during his tenure as premier.

For all their reminders of yesteryear, the rites had a particularly timely aspect, too. Not least, they came less than two months after a military coup in Bangkok, executed on 19 September 2006. In his time, Kriangsak had been no stranger to coups. He was a leading participant in the October 1976 coup that ended Thailand's three-year experiment with open democratic politics. A year later, the extreme rightist orientation of judge Thanin Kraivixien's government led Kriangsak to lead a further

---

Reprinted from Daljit Singh and Lorraine C. Salazar, eds., *Southeast Asian Affairs 2007* (Singapore: Institute of Southeast Asian Studies, 2007), pp. 311–39. At the time of original publication, Michael J. Montesano was Assistant Professor, Southeast Asian Studies Programme, Faculty of Arts and Social Sciences, National University of Singapore.

coup, this time without prior royal approval, and to assume the premiership himself. During his years in office, Kriangsak moved to limit the political influence of the right-wing, pro-monarchist mass movement, the Village Scouts. Determined to place the Thai monarchy truly above politics and convinced of the need for a systematic approach to the challenges facing the country, he consulted with the King only minimally.[1] This determination is said to have earned him the lasting dislike of the palace.

With no member of the royal family present, and in the King's stead, Privy Council president General (Retired) Prem Tinsulanonda presided over the 12 November cremation rites. His role was not without irony. Prem had served in Kriangsak's cabinet until, in February 1980, a meeting between the two officers and the King resulted in Kriangsak's resignation, Prem's replacing him as prime minister, and the inauguration of the latter officer's eight-year tenure as Thailand's chief of government. Despite Kriangsak's status as a distinguished career army officer, a former armed forces supreme commander, and a former prime minister, none of the active-duty officers in the 19 September junta attended his cremation rites. The privy councillor and retired general whom that junta had installed as prime minister in early October, Surayud Chulanont, spent the day in Khao Yai National Park on an outing with young people from Thailand's troubled, Muslim-majority far south.[2] One of his deputy prime ministers (and concurrent finance minister), Pridiyathorn Devakula, did attend the cremation, as did the defence minister.

The lack of security measures at General Kriangsak's cremation rites, a publicly announced outdoor event drawing a number of the more prominent political figures in a country fighting a violent war within its own borders, was conspicuous. So were the unmistakable enthusiasm and interest generated by the arrival at Wat Thepsirin that afternoon of Chaturon Chaisang, acting leader of exiled former Prime Minister Thaksin Shinawatra's Thai Rak Thai (TRT) party.

Thaksin Defiant: 1 January to 19 September 2006[3]

The campaign to oust an elected premier

Thaksin's premiership was from the start a high-wire act.[4] His brashness and outspoken determination to reshape the Thai political order, his unabashed plutocracy and utter insouciance about glaring conflicts of interest, and his persistent unwillingness to make the adjustments necessary to veil his disreputability always involved real risks. Of course, a measure of disreputability has characterized many of the leading Thai political figures of the last three decades. Unlike most such figures, too, Thaksin had a number of characteristics that appealed to an urban, relatively affluent, public. That public tolerated least the *chao pho* or "god-father" style of the provincial politicians whose ascendancy had defined national politics during those three decades. Thaksin was himself a rich urbanite who talked the talk of globalization straight out of light-weight business best-sellers. While his business success depended entirely on concessions from the Thai state, at the very least pagers, cable television, cell-phones, and satellites were high-tech. And Thaksin did have a Ph.D., in "criminal justice".[5]

Nevertheless, the Bangkok voters whom such "positives" most impress have long proved a notoriously fickle lot. That trait had manifested itself in the second half of 2005. During a period of just a couple of weeks some eight months after his and his TRT Party's overwhelming general election victory of February 2005, their second in four years, that group had begun unmistakably to sour on Thaksin. Casual conversation with professionals, office workers, and others in the Thai capital left little doubt about their astonishingly swift change of heart. By the start of 2006, a four-month old protest movement led by the maverick media entrepreneur and former business associate of Thaksin, Sonthi Limthongkul, drew crowds numbering in the thousands to its regular rallies. If his movement was not going to tail off gradually into irrelevance rather than do any serious damage to the prime minister, however, Sonthi needed either heavyweight allies or a lucky break. In the mean time, and with long-reported frictions between Prime Minister Thaksin and King Bhumibol clearly in mind, Sonthi somewhat outlandishly labelled his campaign a fight for the King. To honour the monarch, he began to appear in a yellow shirt and to urge his followers to do the same.

Powerful allies for Sonthi and his followers took some time to enter the scene, at least publicly. But late January saw Thaksin himself give the movement against him its lucky break. This break took the form of agreement that Singapore's diversified state holding company, Temasek, would purchase Shin Corporation (Shin Corp), the telecommunications conglomerate that Thaksin had founded and built into what was arguably Thailand's leading corporate concern. But in agreeing to sell it, Thaksin had finally stumbled and fallen from his high wire.

The Shin-Temasek deal proved controversial on numerous grounds.[6] One was the prime minister's apparently direct involvement in the deal, in violation of provisions in Thailand's 1997 Constitution prohibiting cabinet ministers from substantial executive roles in the private sector. Another was that, having effected the transaction on the Securities of Exchange of Thailand, neither Thaksin nor those of his relatives who legally held the family's Shin shares owed taxes on the proceeds of a US$1.85 billion sale. Further, that sale came just days after Thaksin's government had succeeded in raising the ceiling on foreign ownership of telecoms firms, and it effectively transferred to foreign interests a number of lucrative concessions granted by the Thai government.

The resultant furore re-energized Sonthi's movement. It drew crowds of first tens and then hundreds of thousands to anti-Thaksin rallies on the streets of Bangkok. It led to the conversion of what had been a one-man campaign into a broader People's Alliance for Democracy (PAD). It emboldened first Sonthi and later the PAD to petition King Bhumibol to intervene and appoint a new prime minister, perhaps with the legal cover of Article VII of Thailand's 1997 Constitution. Taking Thaksin up on his suggestion that Thais wear yellow during 2006 to honour the sixtieth anniversary of the monarch's ascent to the throne,[7] a significant number of protestors wore head-bands or sport-shirts of that colour. Striking order and good humour marked the rallies that they joined.

Similarly striking was the unmistakable effect on the movement to oust Thaksin of Major General (Retired) Chamlong Srimuang's decision to join the PAD. A former secretary-general to General Prem during the latter's tenure as premier, Chamlong's history of demonstrating against elected prime ministers went back three decades, to his involvement in rallies against Seni Pramoj in 1976. He had taken a hand in orchestrating Kriangsak's replacement by Prem in 1980 and led the protests against Suchinda Kraprayoon in 1992.[8] Chamlong had first brought Thaksin into politics in the early 1990s as a member of the political party that he led at the time. Now, crucially, he led members of his ascetic "Dharma Army" into the movement to oust his former protégé.[9]

On 23 February, Prime Minister Thaksin met with Privy Council president Prem. He announced the next day that he would dissolve parliament and call new elections. The run-up to the resultant polls, held on 2 April, proved surreal. PAD rallies continued, hopes that the palace would arrange appointment of a new — if unelected — premier persisted, and opposition parties refused to participate in the election. Not the Democrat Party leader and prospective prime minister Abhisit Vejjajiva but rather that party's shrewd former secretary-general Major General (Retired) Sanan Kachornprasart apparently orchestrated this decision. The Democrats, Mahachon, and Chat Thai thus sat out an election in which TRT would certainly have crushed them. Its electoral base among Bangkok's less affluent voters and in the rural north and northeast would have assured that victory.

Thailand's 1997 constitution required a complete lower house before a government could be chosen, and it mandated that unopposed candidates receive the support of at least 20 per cent of eligible voters. The 2 April polls saw TRT facing only a grab-bag of previously unknown parties of poorly explained origins. But up to 10 million Thai voters declined to indicate a party preference in polls for the 20 per cent of parliamentary seats filled by proportional representation; these so called "no votes" were generally understood as votes against Thaksin. Their total compared with a party-list vote total of 16 million for TRT, somewhat lower than its tally of 19 million votes in the 2005 polls. In Bangkok and the south, TRT effectively lost the election. Voters in all but nine of the capital's 36 constituencies cast more "no votes" than votes for TRT.[10] And, in 36 of the southern region's 54 constituencies, TRT candidates running unopposed failed to receive the 20 per cent of total possible votes needed to win election to parliament.

Thaksin greeted these results as an electoral endorsement of his government. But another closed-door meeting, this time not with the Privy Council president but with King Bhumibol himself, led him abruptly to disavow plans to reassume the premiership when the newly elected parliament convened. Then, three days after his victory at the polls, Thaksin granted himself a leave of absence from government; a deputy prime minister would fulfil his duties during the leave, due to last until the formation of a new government. The legality or constitutionality of this arrangement was left unaddressed, but royal intervention had had some effect.

The PAD persisted in its protests against the "Thaksin regime". The need for supplementary polls to fill all seats in the parliament notwithstanding, the country faced the prospect of a single-party lower house. Calls for royal intervention to appoint a prime minister resumed. As throughout the entire first half of 2006, the example of 1992 continued to condition expectations and some hopes at this time. That year had seen the King stage two forceful and effective interventions in Thai politics. First, he had dressed down Suchinda and Chamlong on television, thus ending the violence on Bangkok's streets and forcing the former's resignation as premier. Second, less openly but more significantly, he had arranged for the re-appointment of Anand Panyarachun to that position, despite the manifest intention of the recently elected parliament to install someone else.[11]

On 25 April 2006, the King intervened again, though again not to appoint a prime minister. Declaring elections contested by a single party undemocratic and declining to name a new premier on his own authority, the monarch charged the judges of the Administrative and Supreme Courts and the justices of the Constitutional Court with resolving the country's "mess".[12] His words produced action. In short order, the Constitutional Court found pretexts to annul the 2 April election. The three courts together requested the resignations of the entire Election Commission. Charges were filed against TRT for engaging dummy parties to compete in that election and against the Democrat Party for boycotting it and for asking the King to appoint a prime minister.

While Thaksin ended his leave after seven weeks, in time for the celebrations to mark the King's sixtieth jubilee, pressure on him only mounted. Two respected legal advisers resigned from his administration. Leading members of the Prem-centred Network through which the palace has exercised its considerable influence over Thai government and politics for the past three decades[13] also abandoned all pretense of neutrality. As Privy Council president, Prem served a royal institution purportedly above politics. Not only, however, did he give a series of widely reported anti-Thaksin speeches, but he also used those speeches to advocate military loyalty to King and country rather than to the government of the day.[14] Anand Panyarachun and Dr Prawes Wasi, two of the most prominent servants of Thailand's "network monarchy", also chimed in to damn the care-taker prime minister. In retrospect, it is evident that the baton was being passed, from PAD to Network. In the race to oust Thaksin, the former had done what it could. What remained to be done required the latter.

By the end of July, that race had clearly turned the final bend. The King had decreed April's elections useless. The courts had moved to dissolve the Election Commission that had organized those elections. Ideally, with a new commission in place, TRT could be denied the sort of overwhelming victory that it had scored in three successive general elections. But three members of the former commission stubbornly refused to step down. In a deft move to break this impasse, King Bhumibol on 20 July signed a royal decree scheduling elections for mid-October.[15] Understanding the signal thus sent, the Criminal Court promptly convicted the three hold-out commissioners on charges relating to the conduct of the 2 April polls; they were, briefly, denied bail and jailed.[16]

Further, army commander General Sonthi Boonyaratkalin ordered the abrupt reassignment of more than 100 mid-ranking officers, many in command of troops in the Bangkok area and thought to have ties to senior officers close to care-taker prime minister Thaksin.[17] A former business partner of the latter, the American cable-television operator William Monson, revived an old perjury suit against him. And on 24 August police reported thwarting an attempt to assassinate the premier by means of a car bomb meant to have exploded as he drove from his Thonburi home to Government House. Was this a genuine assassination attempt? A TRT or Thaksin publicity stunt? An effort to alert Thaksin to the lengths to which his antagonists were prepared to go in their campaign against him? A clear answer has proved unforthcoming. In the event, within a month, those antagonists opted for a putsch to have their way.

Thaksin toughs it out

In response to the phased onslaught mounted against him during the first nine months of 2006, Prime Minister Thaksin assumed a posture of flexible and, by Thai historical standards, brave defiance. The need for his opponents to resort to a *coup d'état* against him — and this in the first decade of the twenty-first century! — testified to the success of this response.

At the heart of Thaksin's defiance lay his continued insistence that, both in February 2005 and in April 2006, a majority of Thailand's voters had turned out to cast their ballots for TRT and for him. He repeatedly stressed the democratic basis of his premiership and the anti-democratic nature of the forces determined to drive him from power. Those forces had two wings, one led by Sonthi Limthongkul and the other by Privy Council president Prem. Thaksin thus had to aim his verbal attacks at two rather different targets.

In announcing his decision to dissolve parliament and call the April elections, for example, Thaksin accused his enemies of attempting "mob rule". He contrasted his own electoral mandate with the desires of "one group of people". And he referred to "attempts to overthrow the government by people who stand to lose their benefits".[18] During the first half of the year, the contest between Thaksin and the PAD seemed to define Thailand's political crisis; these comments seemed to reflect that understanding of the crisis. It remained possible to read Thaksin's reference to "one group of people" as criticism of affluent Bangkokians disdainful of the TRT's rural power base and effectively to ignore his allusion to people who stood to lose benefits. Competing visions of democracy appeared to be what was at issue. If the PAD and its supporters attached importance to the procedural norms, press freedom, and the oversight bodies that Thaksin's premiership had so thoroughly undermined, Thaksin's own emphasis on the will of the electoral majority exposed the awkwardness of his enemies' claims to the mantle of Thai democracy.

In early February, Thaksin said that a mere whisper from the King Bhumibol would be sufficient to bring his resignation.[19] Pundits would make much of this remark in the following months. In fact, it really reflected rather formulaic public acknowledgement of the stature of the ninth Chakri monarch. Half a century after Field Marshal Sarit Thanarat put his military regime actively behind the revival of Thai royalism,[20] easy deference to the King's will had long since come to be equated with loyalty to the Thai nation-state. But expressing loyalty thus understood and acting in compliance with the royal will were not the same thing. The substance of Thaksin's conversations with Privy Council president Prem in late February and with the King himself in early April remains unknown. In one form or another, however, each of these meetings almost surely brought the whisper that Thaksin had promised to heed. Indeed, as noted above, the latter encounter resulted in Thaksin's taking leave from the care-taker premiership and promising not to return to that office during the new parliament.

In fact, however, these announcements proved stalling tactics. Seven weeks after making them, Thaksin reassumed the care-taker premiership. By the time of the 19 September putsch, he was leading TRT towards another probable electoral victory and the formation of a new government, maybe or maybe not under his leadership. He had succeeded in thwarting the royal-judicial gambit to install a less TRT-friendly Election Commission.[21] He was preparing to reshuffle senior commanders in Thailand's armed forces in a way that might give him a lock on military power for a number of years to come.[22] He continued to base his defiance on the repeated support of electoral majorities, voting in a democratic system. But, most importantly, he had all-but-explicitly refocused that defiance on the second wing of the forces against him.

This change of focus became clear in early July, when Thaksin used a meeting with senior civil servants to denounce the efforts of a "charismatic, extra-constitutional figure" — *phu mi barami nok ratthathamanun* — to overthrow him. If the reference was to the King, then this comment amounted to a stunning charge, in a country where *lèse-majesté* remains a serious crime and no serious public discussion of the advantages and disadvantages of monarchical rule has occurred for many decades. No commentator on or participant in the crisis, whether for or against Thaksin, dared openly acknowledge the import of Thaksin's charge, and its possible reference to the King. And it would take the Network nearly three more months before, other means of ousting Thaksin exhausted, it finally found the confidence to act decisively and send tanks on to the streets of Bangkok.

Currents and undercurrents

In the aftermath of the Thai military's seizure of state power on 19 September, the junta's leadership alluded often to political "undercurrents", in apparent reference to pro-Thaksin forces bent on effecting the ousted premier's return to power. In the event, concrete evidence of an organized, clandestine movement to undermine the military regime and restore Thaksin never materialized. It was during the nine months preceding the putsch rather than in its aftermath that a wide range of currents and undercurrents most significantly shaped Thai affairs. Each of these currents merits an article in its own right, but a brief treatment must suffice here. If 2006 proved a year of deep crisis and even deeper uncertainty about what the future might hold for Thailand, the range of visions for and understandings of the country's social and political orders espoused in 2006 offered grounds both for despair and for hope. It revealed both troubling divisions and promising alternatives.

One current was royalism. The year began with the expectation that its highlight would be celebrations of the sixtieth jubilee of King Bhumibol's astonishing reign. Those celebrations did indeed come off very successfully in early June, with the representatives of tens of reigning monarchies in attendance and up to a million of the King's subjects gathering in Bangkok's Royal Plaza to catch a glimpse of their sovereign. Throughout the year, and above all on Mondays, Thais rich and poor alike wore their yellow sport-shirts in the King's honour.

Chakri royalism, vintage 2006, was thus a complex phenomenon. At its moment of greatest apparent triumph, it also faced its deepest crisis in living memory. A reign of 60 years could only be approaching its end, for example. The question of whether King Bhumibol's resuscitation of the monarchy as a central force in Thai life would outlive him remained open. At least one of the institutions on which the continued influence of the palace will depend, the Privy Council, received unaccustomed public attention during the year.²³ Its president, General Prem, emerged early on as a central figure in the country's political crisis. When the PAD ceded the leading role in the effort to oust Thaksin to the Network, Prem led the assault from the front. Less openly, as early as February sources in Bangkok reported that the Privy Council was deliberating the merits of direct royal action to dismiss Thaksin and appoint a new premier; Privy Councillor General (Retired) Surayud Chulanont was said to be their favoured candidate.

But the King never intervened to name a prime minister. In his 25 April audience with the judges, he ascribed his inaction to a respect for parliamentary forms. Some observers attributed such inaction to concern that direct intervention could fail, with serious consequences for royal prestige. In the eyes of many arch-royalists, avoidance of dramatic intervention protected the royal institution from exposure to a dangerously divisive political situation. Ironically, then, some of those most committed to royal power favoured restraint in its exercise. Another irony justified such arch-royalist fears. Sonthi Limthongkul, who had done as much as anyone else to draw the Thai monarchy into the popular movement against Thaksin, was widely regarded not as a sincere royalist but rather as a convinced republican. Too close an alliance between the palace and such a figure could hardly be deemed advisable.

The caution, at least during the first half of the year, of the palace, its Network, and arch-royalists, did not in the end prove viable. But the PAD's conviction, shared by opposition parties and much of the public, that the rescue of Thai democracy from Thaksin Shinawatra required the active assistance of a hereditary sovereign nevertheless sat poorly with many Thais. This unease gave rise to an undercurrent of apprehension which is fundamental to any appreciation of the year's developments.

Above all in the country's energetic, influential, intellectual circles, the call for royal intervention sparked violent debate.²⁴ Well-developed censorship of critical public discussion about the role of the monarchy in Thai life kept this debate out of the press. But online webboards offered a new forum for frank, intense exchanges. Thailand's failure to come to grips with the 6 October 1976 atrocities committed by security forces, Village Scouts, and rightist vigilantes at Thammasat University sharpened these exchanges.²⁵ The realization that, but for the bumbling of military dictators Thanom Kittikachorn and Prapas Charusathien in 1973, royal intervention to resolve political crises might never have been established as a Thai political norm became increasingly clear. The "democracy" ostensibly at issue during 2006 might, but for this contingency, have developed in a far more robust, self-sustaining form. Such counter-factual speculation aside, even before the royalist putsch of 19 September what was said, written, read, and debated about the Thai monarchy during 2006 took the country well into unfamiliar territory.

The relative stealth with which some Thais debated their monarchy during the year contrasted dramatically with the flamboyant, unashamed social bigotry displayed by many in the anti-Thaksin movement.²⁶ Coupled to a belief that Thaksin had undermined the ethical, procedural, and institutional norms crucial to democratic governance was open disdain for the judgment of his rural electoral base. That base lived, above all, in the north and northeast of the country. In the period following the coup, the military-backed government would try to direct this current of concern over support for Thaksin in the northern and northeastern regions to its own ends.

A further regional current took the form of continued separatist violence in Thailand's far south.[27] By year's end, that violence had taken nearly 2,000 lives over three years. Insurgents staged a number of dramatic attacks: numerous bombings and other acts of destruction in a single day, nearly simultaneous explosions in some 20 Yala bank branches, shooting a former Narathiwat senator, and planting bombs in central Hat Yai. In many ways, however, the slow grind of increasingly routine violence and the failure of Thai security forces to protect ordinary citizens — Muslim and Buddhist alike — or school-teachers and other civil servants defined the year's ongoing tragedy. If the Thai army took care to avoid repetition of its bloody blunders of early 2004, it also failed to demonstrate success in mastering appropriate counter-insurgent tactics.

The June–August period did bring a number of important milestones in Bangkok's attempts to grapple with the rebellion in the south. June saw the release of the report of the National Reconciliation Commission (NRC) on the conflict.[28] It advocated the use of Patani Malay as a "working language" in the far south. It called for the establishment of unarmed peace-building units. It stressed the need for improved governance and more effective communication between the Thai state and southern Muslim society.[29] Privy Council president Prem mounted quick, strong criticism of the suggestion about using Malay.[30]

The complexity of dialogue with southern Muslims became all too clear as southern Muslim elites began more readily to voice their own concerns with the danger posed by their co-religionists' campaign of violence. A milestone in its own right, this altered posture underlined the role of new currents within southern Muslim society in the ongoing insurrection. It suggested the tenacity of the *political* threat facing the Thai state in its three southernmost provinces. Increasingly, too, the state's forces found themselves facing a formidable *military* threat. Late August brought another noteworthy development. In the aftermath of the Yala bombings, army commander General Sonthi Bunyaratkalin spoke of entering into talks with southern rebels.[31] In the first instance, however, reaction to this idea within official Thai circles was generally negative.

The ongoing pattern of violence in Thailand's far south during the year stood in marked contrast with almost total lack of violence resulting from the national political crisis. Peaceful demonstrations of hundreds of thousands of people on the streets of Bangkok reflected well on Thai political culture. But to take the absence of violence for granted would be a mistake. As early as February, one could encounter pro-PAD elements hoping to see rallies turn so confrontational and bloody as to force direct royal intervention to replace Thaksin. It is to the credit of the PAD's leadership that it succeeded in keeping such elements in check. Similarly, ideological homogeneity does not characterize the Thai army's office corps; some soldiers' apparently proto-republican inclinations also numbered among the undercurrents of the January–September period.

Restoration Miscarries: 9 September to 31 December 2006

Concern that an imminent reshuffling of senior commands would give Thaksin control of the Thai military for years to come may have precipitated the 19 September putsch. But plans for a military seizure of state power much like the one that actually took place appear to have been ready for up to seven or eight months before the coup.³² By the second half of September, alternative means of ridding the kingdom of Thaksin seemed to have come to naught. With Thaksin in New York to attend the annual session of the United Nations General Assembly, Thai army commander General Sonthi Boonyaratkalin and his fellow plotters made their move.

Prominent among those plotters appear to have been the commanders of two of Thailand's four army regions: Lieutenant-General Anupong Paochinda of the Bangkok-based First Army and Lieutenant-General Saprang Kalayanamitr of the northern Third Army, headquartered in Phitsanulok. The extent of Privy Council president Prem's active involvement in plotting the putsch is impossible to know. The latter's incorporation of General Sonthi, like General Surayud, into the Network is a clearer matter.³³

Calling itself the Council for Democratic Reform under Constitutional Monarchy (CDRM) or *khana patirup kanpokhrong nai rabop prachathippatai an mi phramahakasat songpenpramuk*, the junta that informed the people of Thailand that it had taken over their government on the evening of 19 September included, in addition to General Sonthi, the commanders of the navy, air force, and national police, and the supreme commander of the armed forces. Despite this show of inter-service solidarity, apparently not effected without some tense exchanges, the putsch was an army affair. To explain its decision to seize state power, the new junta cited deep social divisions, corruption and the undue politicization of state insitutions, and the Thaksin regime's disrespect for the monarchy.³⁴

The coup succeeded without bloodshed or loss of life. The 1997 constitution was abrogated, political activity proscribed, martial law declared, and elections promised in a year or so. A photograph of General Sonthi, several fellow officers, and Privy Council president Prem seated on the floor before the king and queen during a middle-of-the-night meeting at Chitralada Palace was released.³⁵ The substance of that meeting remains necessarily unclear, as in fact does the state of the king's health at the time of the putsch. He had undergone a reported spinal procedure several weeks after the sixtieth jubilee celebrations.

The 19 September coup by no means enjoyed universal approval in Thailand. But martial law and retro-active royal appointment of Sonthi as head of the junta³⁶ attached some risk to vocal expressions of disapproval. At the same time, the putschists' devotion to the royal cause and the widespread hatred of Thaksin that his months of success in defying his enemies had only intensified won the coup widespread support. The world learned that Thais regarded this one as a "good coup".³⁷ Foreigners had to come to grips with the willingness of a range of Thailand's civilian politicians and putatively progressive intellectuals to endorse a military seizure of power, one of whose central goals was to rescue hereditary monarchy from an elected politician. Still, among Thais, many erstwhile admirers of these politicians and intellectuals struggled to keep their disillusionment to themselves.

Soon rechristening itself the Council for National Security (CNS), the junta named Privy Councillor and former army commander General (Retired) Surayud

Chulanont as prime minister on 1 October. This appointment came after Supachai Panitchpakdi turned the job down. Currently heading the United Nations Conference on Trade and Development, Supachai previously served as director-general of the World Trade Organization and as deputy prime minister and commerce minister in Chuan Leekpai's Democrat-led governments. While respected both domestically and internationally for his economic expertise, Supachai proved unacceptable to the junta when he asked for the right to name his own cabinet. CNS interest in stewardship of the Thai economy came second to its determination to use its spell in power to restore the Thai political order to what it and its backers regarded as acceptable condition.

Within ten days of royal endorsement of his premiership and with the reported "final nod" of Privy Council president Prem Tinsulanonda, Privy Councillor Surayud named his cabinet. Among major portfolios, Finance went to Bank of Thailand governor Pridiyathorn Devakula, Foreign Affairs to Nitya Pibulsonggram, and Interior to Ari Wongaraya. Pridiyathorn also became one of Surayud's deputy prime ministers. Both Nitya and Ari had previously served as permanent secretary of the ministries for which they now took responsibility; they had been career civil servants. A Central Thai Muslim and long-time protégé of former prime minister Banharn Silpa-archa (of whose native province and political bailiwick Ari had served as governor), Ari had for a time held the post of deputy minister of education under Thaksin. Son of Mahidon family nemesis Field Marshal Plaek Pibulsonggram, Nitya's rapprochement with and acceptability to the Network seems to have grown out of his American wife's service as Prem's English-language tutor when the latter was prime minister during the 1980s.[38]

A number of other cabinet choices offered indications of the political bases and orientation of the Surayud government. Kosit Panpiemras, an expert on agricultural and rural-development policy who served as finance minister in General Suchinda Kraprayoon's short-lived 1992 government, became deputy prime minister and industry minister. He returned to government from the Bangkok Bank, where Prem had arranged a sinecure for him. The defence portfolio went to General (Retired) Boonrod Somthat, Surayud's military-academy classmate, long-time aide, and golf partner. Like the prime mininister and CNS leader Sonthi, Boonrod's military background lay in special warfare. In Kroekrai Chiraphaet, the government enlisted an able, articulate commerce minister.

The stated rationale for the 19 September coup bore only general resemblance to the mission to which the Surayud government and its CNS sponsors committed themselves. Like that rationale, however, this mission was threefold: slay the political monster that was the Thaksin phenomenon, make the country's politics safe for the monarchy, and fix the south.

Through the end of the year, prosecution of that first goal proved rather farcical. Unaccountably, the junta did not at the time of its putsch immediately confiscate those of Thaksin's assets that remained in the country. Instead, it focused on finding legal means of ridding Thai politics of his malignant presence for good. Such means proved elusive. The former prime minister, in the meantime, repeatedly rattled both the CNS and the government by appearing here and there in Asia, as he toured and shopped at leisure. The success of these stunts underlined two realities. One was that the masterful political touch that Thaksin displayed so often in the early part of his premiership had not deserted him. The other was that he had the Network that had overthrown him very much on the defensive. Surayud's government began to look hapless.

That government also appeared extraordinarily poor at public relations at a time when effective communication of its goals and plans took on immense importance. Investigation of Thaksin necessarily involved re-opening the murky matter of the Temasek-Shin deal. In structuring that deal, Temasek had apparently used nominees to duck Thai restrictions on foreign ownership. Scrutiny of the deal and determination to use that scrutiny to damage Thaksin proved risky, however. For such scrutiny called attention to the fact that nominee and other arrangements for the evasion of foreign-ownership restrictions had long been standard practice in Thailand.[39] That attention confronted many foreign firms with the prospect of having dramatically to re-think the way that they did business there. Extreme pessimists even envisioned the forced sale, at fire-sale prices, of foreign holdings to Thai interests eager to restore the pre-1997 national economic order. The intensification of the "sufficiency economy" vogue during the post-coup period[40] only deepened some observers' fears of Thai economic nationalism and its consequences.

In truth, that vogue related above all to the second important goal of the CNS and the government that it had installed. In his first major public address as prime minister, to a large dinner hosted by the Foreign Correspondents' Club of Thailand on 7 November, Privy Councillor Surayud stated baldly, "successful political reform is our top priority".[41] Less publicly, holders of major economic portfolios in his cabinet made clear to interlocutors that their mandates were more political than economic. That reform, and those mandates, had two dimensions.

Nothing spooked the Network so much as Thaksin's emergence as its — in fact, the palace's — political rival among the large rural populations of the north and northeast. That development must be checked. For it challenged one of the king's proudest accomplishments: putting his time, his expertise in irrigation and interest in agriculture, and his *barami* or charisma at the service of rural Thais. Of course, the rural Thailand of earlier decades of the ninth reign was no more. In proclaiming its concern with income inequality,[42] the Network acknowledged the rationality of rural support for Thaksin and his TRT. It would, then, need to reconnect villager and palace, both ideologically and organizationally. No mere political party must be allowed to come between them.

Surayud was the son of an army officer who went over to the banned Communist Party of Thailand (CPT) and underground. Both Surayud and his fellow royalist officers on the CNS were also products of a Thai army proud of its own counterinsurgency record and influenced by Cold War doctrines of civic action, special warfare, and psychological operations. In recent years, as both a member of the Privy Council and the son of a respected comrade, Surayud had cultivated relationships with CPT veterans. As prime minister, he devoted parts of his first trips to the north and northeast to meeting former CPT grass-roots organizers.[43] In their top-down corporatism and resistance to liberal capitalism, royalist and both erstwhile communist *and* anti-communist counterinsurgency-era visions of rural mobilization had much in common.

Realization of such a vision, somehow, counted as one of the Network's most significant post-coup priorities. Reports of an ongoing revival of the Village Scouts[44] are clearly to be understood in this context.

Odds hardly favoured this approach to integrating rural Thailand into the political order that Surayud, his government, and the CNS sought to build. It had never really worked before, for either the right or the left, and today's far more intensive interaction between capital and countryside only made it more difficult still. Success in the second dimension of the post-coup effort at political reform seemed equally unlikely.

That dimension related to the restoration of civilian parliamentary rule to its condition during the 1980s and 1990s. Under the general management of Prem Tinsulanonda, the Network operated during that period to oversee fractious multi-party coalition governments.[45] The inherent instability of these coalitions made the Network's periodic intervention necessary; it served to empower the network monarchy in an age of apparently more and more democratic civilian parliamentary government. These operations often brought considerable success, but the rise of a figure like Thaksin and the dominance of TRT made them impossible (and, of course, also unnecessary).

From his exile in London, Thaksin resigned from TRT in early October. Chaturon Chaisang, a bright former student activist who hailed from a dominant political family in Chachoengsao province and had served as Thaksin's education minister, became the party's acting head. TRT still faced the possibility of forced dissolution. But it appeared at least equally likely to emerge as one among several middle-sized parties in a new Network-managed parliamentary order. Crucial to the restoration of that order would be the promulgation of a new constitution, and the terms of that document. The CNS arranged for the drafting process to begin. It made the reckless promise of submitting its proposed charter to a popular referendum. *Barami* would, then, face an early test at the polls.

Not least for its dependence on the unique figure of General Prem, himself older than King Bhumibol, the parliamentary order to which Surayud and the CNS seemed determined to return Thailand would not be easy to restore. Thailand had changed. Thaksin Shinawatra had helped see to that. In its determination to effect a restoration, then, the Network was taking a gamble. Yet on this gamble, and on its approach to the Thai countryside, appeared to rest its hopes to build sound foundations for the tenth Chakri reign.[46]

The third part of the mission that Surayud and the CNS undertook related to the crisis of the Thai south. On one level this mission was one of reconciliation. The new Prime Minister's earliest initiatives included a trip to the region to offer his apologies to southern Muslims for their treatment at the hands of the Thai state. Dramatic as this departure proved, that apology was intended as much as anything to distinguish the Network's approach to the south from Thaksin's.[47] The re-establishment of the Southern Border Provinces Administrative Center (SBPAC), which Thaksin had dissolved in 2001, sent a similar message. As chairman of the revived SBPAC, the CNS named a career official of the Ministry of the Interior, whose brother had held the same post before joining the Privy Council.[48] The ongoing war in southern Thailand is markedly more serious than the conflict that an earlier incarnation of the SBPAC helped bring to an end. But in opting to relaunch the Center, the CNS acted on more than mere unimaginative faith in old solutions. For the old SBPAC had represented perceived royal success in serving the King's southern Muslim subjects and their receptiveness to his goodness. Some in the post-coup regime, perhaps including Surayud himself, genuinely believe that the key to resolution of the southern crisis lay above all in showing more goodness than Thaksin.

Surayud's first visit to Kuala Lumpur as prime minister and revived talk about negotiations further signalled a change in Bangkok's approach to its war in the south.[49] However, whether it viewed negotiations as tactical, a means to divide those insurgents with whom compromise was possible from those who must be defeated in battle, remained unclear. The inability of Thai security forces to inflict such a defeat without unacceptable totals of civilian deaths was rather less open to doubt. That southern insurgents responded to the new government's gestures of conciliation with escalated violence only underlined the military challenge facing Bangkok.[50] So too, as the southern crisis grew deeper and deeper, concerns mounted in Bangkok that Surayud focused on it at the expense of attention to numerous other problems facing his government. Of course, that focus doubtless also reflected a privy councillor's appreciation of the concerns of the man whom he ultimately served.

As every year, the King addressed his country on 4 December, the eve of his birthday. Televised coverage of his speech showed him riding in a golf cart across the grounds of Bangkok's Chitralada Palace, his children walking alongside, to the throne hall in which Surayud, his cabinet, senior military officers and civil servants, and others waited to hear him. He rode past thousands of his assembled subjects; seated on the palace lawns, every last one of them appeared to wear the scarf of the Village Scouts around his or her neck.[51] King Bhumibol's 2006 birthday address stressed the advantage of a government of the aged and experienced, like Surayud's. Its import was publicly to signal the sovereign's support for that government.[52]

As December progressed, that same government continued to stumble. Steep rises in the value of the Thai baht and resultant pressure on exports led to dramatic intervention on the part of the Bank of Thailand on 18 December. It announced a 30 per cent reserve requirement, for a term of one year, on capital brought into Thailand by foreigners. Announcement of this measure triggered an immediate drop of 15 per cent in the Securities Exchange of Thailand (SET) index; it wiped out more than 800 billion baht in share value. Quickly back-pedalling, the government exempted capital inflows for certain purposes from the policy. But Finance Minister Pridiyathorn's denial of involvement in formulating the policy served only further to tarnish the image of the government.[53]

The day-to-day working relationship between Surayud's government and Sonthi's CNS also remained unclear. Among factors accounting for these officers' lack-luster performance in power, the relative importance of indecision, gentlemanliness, commitment to process, and simple lack of understanding of the country that Thailand had become was difficult to gauge. That performance notwithstanding, even sympathetic observers agreed, and some worried, that the interests, positions, and perhaps the fortunes of the palace and its soldiers — Prem, Surayud, Sonthi, and the rest — had become indistinguishable and inseparable.

Legacies of History

In the mercilessness of the crisis to which 2006 subjected Thailand, the year highlighted a number of related legacies of the country's recent history. Many, though not all, of them mirrored the currents and undercurrents so important in the pre-putsch period.

Dismal in its own right, the Thai military's recourse to a coup in the first decade of the twenty-first century also reflected a long-term failure to confine soldiers to matters of national defence.[54] Having taken a hand in the 1932 coup that ended absolute monarchy, military officers soon succeeded in sidelining their civilian partners in that coup. In the late 1940s, the Thai army restored itself to power; it remained in power through the 1970s. Soldiers also emerged as the palace's favoured political partners[55] (and so, in time, the servants of the network monarchy). Thailand's latest coup made clear that, endless reports of increasing military professionalism in the post-1992 period notwithstanding, the upper echelons of the Thai army continued to view themselves as guardians of the nation's well-being. The basis of that vision in chauvinistic conceptions of that well-being and in unrivalled coercive power undermines efforts to institutionalize accountable representative government in Thailand.

A complementary legacy of the past half-century of Thai history that assumed great significance was the success of King Bhumibol's reign. The King returned from Switzerland in 1951 as a young, untried, and even isolated figure. The support first of a small circle of senior princes and later of the unlikely figure of Field Marshal Sarit Thanarat gave him the opening to put his own considerable native talents to work.[56] But in its achievements and in the restoration of monarchy to the centre of Thai affairs by the early 1970s, the ninth Chakri reign was in itself another high-wire act for Thailand. It exposed the country not so much to the risk of stumbling and falling but rather to the inevitability of the act's end.

The Thailand that King Bhumibol will pass on to his successor is a far more complex country than the Thailand that he inherited upon the demise of his older brother in 1946. Its population is larger, generally more affluent, better educated, and infinitely more thoroughly exposed to the wider world. Education, affluence, and exposure have led Thais to form expectations for their social and political orders. Yet fears of straying into *lèse-majesté* and natural reluctance to speak openly about the inevitable passing of the current King have served to choke off all serious debate about the institutional, practical, and political future of monarchy in Thailand. The result, after months of unending crisis for Thailand during 2006, is deep-seated national anxiety. Widespread approval of the 19 September coup stemmed in some part from this late-in-the-reign dread. The sentiment is also apparent in the ugly reactions that have greeted some critics, Thai and foreign alike, of the post-putsch political dispensation.

Thaksin Shinawatra's ability to dominate Thailand as he did during 2001–2006, and the possibility that he should do so again, highlights a further legacy of the ninth reign. A period of prosperity for the royal institution proved one of poverty for the range of other institutions basic to a competitive, open, democratic order.[57] In combination, the after-effects of the 1997 financial crisis, the fickleness of Thailand's urban electorate, and the political genius of Thaksin and some close to him put paid with hardly a hiccup to what had appeared a hardy civilian parliamentary order during the late 1980s and through the 1990s.

The quick collapse of that order raises a series of awkward questions, to which 2006 offered rather disconcerting answers. To what degree did the fundamentally undemocratic machinations of the network monarchy, deftly managed by Prem Tinsulanonda, underpin Thai democracy's apparent success in the pre-Thaksin period?[58] What forces account for the long-term underdevelopment of robust structures of governance, regulation, and justice in Thailand? Clearly, utopian constitution-drafting, such as that culminating in the country's 1997 charter, cannot conjure such structures out of thin air. But to what degree does the absence of such structures underlie, at least in part, a wide variety of pressing problems?

In the months following the 19 September putsch, for example, some in Thailand were suddenly struck with pity for the more than 2,000 victims of extra-judicial killings during Thaksin's savage 2003 "war on drugs" and their families.[59] This sentiment brought small consolation, indeed; it offered no check on the Thai state's ability to launch comparable campaigns in future, with or without the legal fig-leaf of martial law employed by the CNS junta.

Likewise, it became clear during the year that an emphasis on "justice" for the Muslims of the Thai south, such as the NRC report expressed, actually served in some respects as a cover for parties determined to resist meaningful administrative decentralization. "Apologize, but do not devolve power", seemed to be the approach. It reflected a commitment to the structures of internal colonization developed by King Chulalongkorn and his brother Prince Damrong Rajanuphap.[60] History had long proved these structures antithetical to the institutional correlates of democratic governance to which Thaksin's enemies claimed such attachment during 2006. Some observers of the Thai scene fret that, in the next reign, the maintenance of these structures will give rise to frictions not just between Bangkok and the Muslim south but between the capital and other regions, too.

The divide between Bangkok and much of provincial Thailand — above all the north and northeast — that characterized the battle over Thaksin during 2006 represented an even more tangled legacy of recent history. This divide owed in part to Thailand's chronically poor investment in human capital development, a problem to which economists had called attention for nearly two decades and a factor in excluding what is perhaps a majority of the Thai population from decent opportunities in the dynamic sectors of today's economy. The structure of opportunity in that economy in turn owes much both to long-term declines in Thailand's international competitiveness and to the restructuring that followed the financial crisis of 1997.[61]

In a number of ways, then, the Thaksin-TRT phenomenon was a creature of that 1997 crisis. Not so much the financial collapse of that year but rather the ensuing processes of adjustment accelerated the deprivation of those voters to whom TRT's "populist" policies appealed most. One element of that appeal was, nevertheless, unrelated to the financial crisis. For all the alleged development of "civil society" and non-governmental organizations (NGOs) in recent decades, the political spectrum from which the Thai electorate chooses parties to support remains surprisingly truncated. Voters lack a left-wing option. The structure of the Thai party system appears fossilized, as if Cold War–era fears of being branded communist remain alive.[62] Their vast number and flamboyant hyper-activity notwithstanding, NGOs and their supporters have left Thailand's economically and socially disadvantaged voters without even a vaguely socialist or social-democratic option. Rationally, then, those voters have turned out for TRT.

Those post-1997 processes also did considerable damage to many of the erstwhile pillars of Thailand's business-dominated political economy. For those tycoons that emerged from the crisis either relatively undamaged or even better off than before, like Thaksin and a number of his political associates, the path to power lay virtually wide open.[63] It is in no way to minimize Thaksin's own rather sinister political talent to say that, if he had not charged aggressively down that path, another similar figure would probably have done so.

In another respect, too, Thailand's crisis of 2006 was a legacy of its crisis of 1997. The diminished Thai economy that has emerged since that latter year sees international capital have its way in domestic markets more than at any previous moment in the country's history. The domestic banking sector has long served as the linchpin of that national economy and the incubator of successive Thai governments' economic-policy talent. It has now become the object of criticism among foreigners with no comprehension of its previous role and success. The range of assets and the span of control now in foreign hands leave Thailand unrecognizable to serious students of its economic and business history. Just as Thaksin represented, then, a product of the financial crisis of a decade ago, so in many respects was Temasek's ability to purchase Shin a result of the same crisis. The vulnerability of the Thai telecoms sector to foreign control had, however, far less to do with the still opaque circumstances of the Shin-Temasek deal than to the more general vulnerability of post-1997 Thailand.

Finally, economic disorientation can call forth political extremes. The political struggle that engulfed Thailand during 2006 ultimately pitted two inherently undemocratic forces against each other: plutocracy and hereditary monarchy.[64] The country seemed to face the prospect of addressing the legacy of its recent history — military rule, revived monarchy, a widening socio-economic divide, weak institutions, and the 1997 crisis in its multiple dimensions — with a very narrow range of options.

Conclusion: Saphan Khwai and Victory Monument, New Year's Eve 2006

The utter lack of provisions for security notwithstanding, the cremation rites for General Kriangsak proceeded with dignity and in peace. Just over six weeks later, bombs exploded hours before public gatherings, both far larger and of a very different sort, were due to begin in central Bangkok. Starting soon after six in the evening of New Year's Eve, a series of six small blasts struck the capital — the first several at Saphan Khwai and near the Victory Monument and the last, six hours later, near the site of a planned outdoor celebration to welcome 2007. By the time of that last blast, authorities had called the event off. The night's explosions killed at least three persons and left more than 35 injured. Three years after the intensification of armed insurgency in the Thai south and nearly a year after the sale of Shin Corp re-energized the campaign to oust Thaksin, violence had come to Bangkok.

In the immediate aftermath of these attacks, it remained impossible to determine who was responsible. Thaksin loyalists? Elements in the armed forces dissatisfied with the post-putsch division of spoils and posts? Southern insurgents? Parties close to the CNS junta itself? One of countless other actors who might be determined either to take advantage of the collapse of the Thai political order during 2006 or to dominate what was left of that order through particularly sinister means? Any answer would be irresponsible speculation. But the Bangkok explosions of 31 December 2006 made utterly clear that the end of the year found Thailand far from the end of its deep crisis. The future roles in the nation's life of Thaksin Shinawatra, of the royal institution, of the country's armed forces, of the discredited intellectual class, of parliament, and even of the Thai electorate were impossible to guess. Late in the ninth Chakri reign, Thailand was beginning an awkward, difficult reckoning with its history.

Notes

The author acknowledges the many in Thailand and outside the country whose thoughts and observations shaped his understanding of the developments treated herein.

1. Kriangsak's involvement in the politics of the 1976–80 period and his relations with other major figures of the era are treated in Paul Handley, *The King Never Smiles: A Biography of Thailand's Bhumibol Adulyadej* (New Haven: Yale University Press, 2006), chaps. XIV and XV (pp. 257–98), on which the discussion here and below draws extensively. The general's life and career are documented in *Chiwit lae phon ngan phanathan phon ek Kriangsak Chommanan* [The life and achievements of the Honourable General Kriangsak Chomanan] (Bangkok, 2006), one of two cremation volumes distributed on the occasion of the 12 November rites.
2. "PM Quashes Thaksin Return", *Nation* (Bangkok), 13 November 2006; see photo caption.
3. For perhaps as the most valuable analysis of the first phase of the year's anti-Thaksin movement, see Suphalak Kanchanakhundi, "Khabuankan prachachon kuengsamretrup" [A semi-realized people's movement], *Fa Diaokan* IV, no. 2 (April–June 2006): 166–87. A detailed treatment of the long run-up to the coup also appears in Michael J. Montesano, "Political Contests in the Advent of Bangkok's 19 September Putsch" in a forthcoming collection of papers presented at the 2006 Thailand Update Conference, edited by John Funston (Canberra: National Thai Studies Centre, 2007). But both that piece and the present article offer necessarily summary coverage of a year of daunting complexity for Thailand. So many forces converged in Thailand's crisis of 2006 that it has proved necessary to omit much material of direct, if specialist, interest and relevance. At the same time, this article represents an attempt to capture and synthesize perspectives and analyses perhaps slighted in the extensive extant body of writing on the year's events, in newspapers, magazines, academic articles, and — of course — on the Internet, in Thai, English, and other languages.
4. Two fine studies of the Thaksin phenomenon are Pasuk Phongpaichit and Chris Baker, *Thaksin: The Business of Politics in Thailand* (Chiang Mai: Silkworm Books, 2004), and Duncan McCargo and Ukrist

Pathamanand, *The Thaksinization of Thailand* (Copenhagen: Nordic Institute of Asian Studies, 2005).
5. "Thaksin Shinawatra to Receive Sam Houston Humanitarian Award", http://www.shsu.edu/~pin_www/T@S/2002/ShinAwardRel.htm (Sam Houston State University news site, 20 October 2002), downloaded 11 February 2007. On Thaksin's earlier appeal to upwardly mobile urban Thais, despite his actual resemblance to many of the politicians that members of this class most loathed, see James Ockey, "On the Expressway, and Under It: Representations of the Middle Class, the Poor, and Democracy in Thailand", in *House of Glass: Culture, Modernity, and the State in Southeast Asia*, edited by Yao Souchou, pp. 313–37 [esp. pp. 321ff.] (Singapore: Institute of Southeast Asian Studies, 2001).
6. To date, far too little about the entire transaction is clear. One very early attempt to make up for its lack of transparency is Phinyo Traisuriyathamma et al., *25 Khamtham Bueanglang Thekowoe Chinkhop* [25 questions: the inside story of the Shin Corp. take-over] (Bangkok: Openbooks, February 2006).
7. Duncan McCargo, "A Hollow Crown", *New Left Review* 43 (January–February 2007): 135–44 [esp. 135–36].
8. The author is indebted to Dr Michael Nelson for sharing his observations on Chamlong's career as premier-slayer.
9. "Thailand's Tiny Buddhist 'Army' ", *Christian Science Monitor*, 9 March 2006.
10. "Poll: 70% in Bangkok Query Election Winners' Legitimacy", *Bangkok Post*, 4 April 2006.
11. Handley, *The King Never Smiles*, pp. 356–57, very usefully discusses the circumstances surrounding Anand Panyarachun's re-appointment as prime minister in June 1992. The palace also had the "May events" of that year and the royal role in resolving them on its mind in early 2006. On the evening of 12 March and at the command of the Bureau of the Royal Household, television stations rebroadcast — without explanation — the King's 20 May 1992 meeting with Suchinda and Chamlong; see "King Whispers Out", *Nation*, 13 March 2006.
12. He used the term *mua*. For the text of the King's comments to the judges, see "Phraratchadamrat Nai Luang Naew Thang Kae 'Wikrit Chat' " [Royal addresses: the way to solve the "national crisis"], *Matichon* (daily), 27 April 2005.
13. On Thailand's "network monarchy" and its functioning, see Duncan McCargo, "Network Monarchy and Legitimacy Crises in Thailand", *Pacific Review* XVIII, no. 5 (December 2005): 499–519, and "Thaksin and the Resurgence of Violence in the Thai South: Network Monarchy Strikes Back?" *Critical Asian Studies* (Thematic issue on "Patani Merdeka — Thailand's Southern Fire") XXXVIII, no. 1 (March 2006): 39–71. This essay and others from the special issue of *Critical Asian Studies* on the Thai south are available in Duncan McCargo, ed., *Rethinking Thailand's Southern Violence* (Singapore: NUS Press, 2007). On Prem Tinsulanonda's emergence as the leading servant of the royal institution in the second half of the ninth Chakri reign, see Handley, *The King Never Smiles*, above all, chap. XV (pp. 276–98), "In the King's Image: The Perfect General Prem".
14. "Troops 'Belong to King' ", *Bangkok Post*, 15 July 2006; "Prem Slams 'Unethical Leaders' ", *Bangkok Post*, 29 July 2006; and "Prem Pours Scorn on Money Politics", *Bangkok Post*, 19 August 2006.
15. "King Endorses Election Decree", *Nation*, 21 July 2006.
16. "Ex-EC Trio Released on Bail", *Nation*, 28 July 2006.
17. "Sonthi Stuns by Shifting PM's Allies", *Nation*, 21 July 2006.
18. "Thaksin Tackles Critics: 'Me or Them' ", *Nation*, 25 February 2006.

19. "PM Would Go Only If King Tells Him", *Bangkok Post*, 5 February 2006.
20. Kobkua Suwannathat-Pian, *Kings, Country, and Constitutions: Thailand's Political Development, 1932–2000* (London: RoutledgeCurzon, 2003), pp. 155–63; Handley, *The King Never Smiles*, chapter VII (pp. 139–55), "Field Marshal Sarit: The Palace Finds Its Strongman".
21. "New Election Commission: 'Anti-Thaksin' 3 Lose Out", *Nation*, 9 September 2006.
22. "Thai Coup Pre-empted Shake-up of the Military", *Asian Wall Street Journal*, 22–24 September 2006.
23. James Ockey, "Monarch, Monarchy, Succession and Stability in Thailand", *Asia Pacific Viewpoint* XLVI, no. 2 (August 2005): 115–27 [esp. 120–23], offers a brief history of the Privy Council, a body with whose role and composition many in Thailand are unfamiliar in the extreme.
24. Patrick Jory, "The Silence of the Intellectual Lambs", *Bangkok Post*, 23 February 2007.
25. Thongchai Winichakul, "Remembering/Silencing the Traumatic Past: The Ambivalent Memories of the October 1976 Massacre in Bangkok", in *Cultural Crisis and Social Memory: Modernity and Identity in Thailand and Laos*, edited by Shigeharu Tanabe and Charles F. Keyes, pp. 243–83 (London: RoutledgeCurzon, 2002).
26. "Chang Noi: Giving Up on Democracy for Thailand", *Nation*, 27 November 2006, analyses this current of bigotry with great clarity. (The pseudonymous Chang Noi's columns, going back to 1996, are available online at http://www.geocities.com/changnoi2/.)
27. Events in the Thai south since early 2004 have generated a voluminous literature, of very uneven quality. Among useful works are Nithi Iaosiwong, "Mong sathannakan phak tai phan waen kabot chao na", *Sinlapa Watthanatham* XXV, no. 8 (June 2004): 110–24 (available in English as "Understanding the Situation in the South as a 'Millenarian Revolt'", *Kyoto Review of Southeast Asian Studies* 6, March 2005, http://kyotoreview.cseas.kyoto-u.ac.jp); and Duncan McCargo, ed. *Rethinking Thailand's Southern Violence*. McCargo's forthcoming Cornell University Press monograph on the southern crisis will likewise prove valuable. For a broad historical treatment of southern Thailand, see Patrick Jory and Michael J. Montesano, eds., *The Plural Peninsula: Studies in the History of Ethnic Interactions in Southern Thailand and Northern Malaysia* (Singapore: NUS Press, forthcoming).
28. National Reconciliation Commission (NRC), *Raingan khanakammakan itsara phuea khwamsamanachan haengchat ao chana khwamrunraeng duai phalang samanachan* [Report of the National Reconciliation Commission: besting violence through the power of reconciliation] (Bangkok: NRC, Office of the Cabinet Secretary, 2006), available at http://www.nrc.or.th. *Fa Diaokan* (http://www.sameskybooks.org), Thailand's most important journal of current affairs, devoted much of its April–June 2006 (*Fa Diaokan* IV, no. 2) to enlightening critiques of the NRC report and its proposals, offered from a variety of perspectives.
29. Michael Connors, "Addressing the Southern Conflagration", *Bangkok Post*, 13 June 2006.
30. "Prem Not Happy with NRC's Idea", *Nation*, 27 June 2006.
31. "Thai General Urges Talks with Muslim Insurgents", *Financial Times*, 1 September 2006.
32. "Chang Noi: The Persistent Myth of the Good Coup", *Nation*, 2 October 2006.
33. "Profile: Gen Sonthi Boonyaratglin — Meteoric Rise to Power", *Nation*, 21 September 2006. This incorporation cannot have been difficult. While both after Thaksin's decision to name General Sonthi army commander in October 2005 and after the 19 September coup, much was made in both the foreign and domestic press of his Islamic faith, more ought to

have been made of other details of his biography. Sonthi is a second-generation military officer. Each of his paternal grandparents' last names — Ahamatchula and Bunyaratkalin — had been personally bestowed on members of their respective extended families by King Wachirawut (r. 1910–25). Apparently to further his military career, Sonthi's father chose to use his own mother's less Muslim-sounding maiden surname, Bunyaratkalin, which the King had originally granted to an officer of the Siamese Navy in 1915 (some three years *before* he would grant "Chunhawan" to an army second lieutenant named Phin, who went on to found twentieth-century Thailand's most important politico-military dynasty). See Charin Chaesakhon, *Phon ek Sonthi Bunyaratkalin: khunsuek ku phaendin* [General Sonthi Bunyaratkalin: the warrior who redeemed the land] (Bangkok: Green Libra Publisher, 2007), pp. 17–33, and *Akkharanukrom namsakun praratchathan nai phrabatsomdetphramongkutklaochaoyuhua* [Directory of royally bestowed last names from the reign of Rama VI] (Bangkok: Rama VI Memorial Foundation, 1991), pp. 72, 135, 358. These sources do raise the possibility that, at some point, a member of the family made a minor adjustment to the Thai spelling of "Bunyaratkalin". Whatever the case, the coup leader was hardly an outsider to Thailand's ninth-reign royalist-military caste, his religion notwithstanding.

34. "Statement from the Administrative Reform Council", *Nation*, 20 September 2006, http://www.nationmultimedia.com/2006/09/20/headlines/headlines_30014072.php. Also see "Must Read: CNS Coup White Paper", *Nation*, 12 December 2006 (available in unofficial translation, at http://www.nationmultimedia.com/2006/11/27/headlines/headlines_30020056.php).

35. Available in "Thais Put Their Trust in the Military", *Age* (Melbourne), 23 September 2006, http://www.theage.com.au/news/world/thais-put-their-trust-in-the-military/2006/09/22/1158431902364.html, accessed 23 February 2007.

36. "Chronology: Coup as It Unfolds", *Nation*, 2 October 2006.

37. The popularity of the 19 September putsch and the resultant crisis of Thai liberal democracy merit detailed study in their own right. But see "Chang Noi: The Persistent Myth of the Good Coup". Also see Jory, "The Silence of the Intellectual Lambs", which offers preliminary consideration of the weak commitment to liberalism of Thailand's intellectual class.

38. "The Surayud Cabinet", *Nation*, 23 October 2006; "Analysis: Retired Diplomat Nitya to Retain Foreign Policies", *Nation*, 10 October 2006.

39. "Thais to Clarify Foreign Ownership Laws", *Financial Times*, 4/5 November 2006; Thanong Khanthong, "Old Money Strikes Back Like a Blast from the Past", *Nation*, 15 December 2006; and "Thais May Redraw Law on Foreign Ownership", *Financial Times*, 28 December 2006.

40. See, for example, Korn Chatikavanij, "On 'Sufficiency Economy': A List of Achievable Aspirations", *Bangkok Post*, 9 December 2006; Korn is a leading member of the Democrat Party. In tandem with yellow shirts, 2006 saw great promotion of the King's "new theory" of *setthakit phophiang* or "sufficiency economy". On the history of this concept, see Paul Handley, *The King Never Smiles*, esp. chap. XXI (pp. 407–26), "The Economic Crash and Bhumibol's New Theory", and also pp. 389–90 and 432–34.

41. The text of this speech, as originally delivered in English, is available in "PM's Speech at FCCT", *Nation*, 8 November 2006, http://www.nationmultimedia.com/2006/11/07/regional/regional_30018323.php.

42. Ibid.

43. "Surayud Calls for Equality in Society", *Nation*, 12 December 2005; "Comrades-in-Arms: Their War Gone By", *Nation*,

12 January 2006; "Interim Government: Renewing Old Connections", *Nation*, 15 October 2006; "Surayud Calls on Former Communists to Help Govt", *Nation*, 21 October 2006. A very important biography, Watsana Nanuam, *Senthang lek phon ek Surayut Chulanon chak luk khommiwnit su pho. bo. tho bo* [The iron path of General Surayud Chulanont: from communist's son to army commander] (Bangkok: Matichon, 2003), devotes considerable attention to Surayud's relationship to his father.

44. Handley, *The King Never Smiles*, pp. 222–36, discusses the Village Scouts, their ties to the palace, and their involvement in right-wing agitation and violence during the 1970s. See also Katherine A. Bowie, *Rituals of National Loyalty: An Anthropology of the State and the Village Scout Movement in Thailand* (New York: Columbia University Press, 1997). Repeated efforts to build connections and solidarity between King Bhumibol and his rural subjects are an important theme of the Handley book; see, for example, the fascinating discussion of those efforts as they unfolded during the Prem years on pp. 289–97.

45. McCargo, "Network Monarchy and Legitimacy Crises in Thailand", explains the origins and operations of this order.

46. A more extreme statement of this same point is found in Paul Handley, "What the Thai Coup Was Really About", *Asia Sentinel*, 6 November 2006, http://www.asiasentinel.com/index.php?option=com_content&task=view&id=249&Itemid=31.

47. "Surayud Issues Tak Bai Apology", *Nation*, 2 November 2006; "Time for Peace, Reconciliation", *Nation*, 3 November 2006.

48. "Sonthi Backs Ending Emergency in South", *Nation*, 31 October 2006; "Peace Initiative: Pranai to Head Up Revived Southern Border Committee", *Nation*, 2 November 2006. On the SBPAC and its approach as creatures of network monarchy, see McCargo, "Thaksin and the Resurgence of Violence in the Thai South: Network Monarchy Strikes Back?"

49. The stimulating, well-informed commentator on far-southern affairs who calls himself "Barun" used his regular column to assess the realities of the proposed negotiations; "'Kaptak Cheracha' khong Nakkha Fai Tai" [The southern fire mer-chants' 'negotiations trap'], *Nechan Sutsapda*, 13 October 2006, p. 86. A collection of Barun's earlier columns — indispensable reading on the war in the south — is Barun, *Yihat Si Thao* [Gray jihad] (Bangkok: Sarika Press, 2005).

50. "Fear Is Now the Rule in Thailand's South", *International Herald Tribune*, 26 February 2007.

51. See note 44 above.

52. "HM Backs Surayud Govt", *Nation*, 5 December 2006. An unofficial English-language translation of the speech is available at "His Majesty's Full Birthday Speech", *Nation*, 5 December 2006, http://www.nationmultimedia.com/2006/12/05/headlines/headlines_30020787.php.

53. "Baht Crisis: BOT Bid to Limit Currency Dealings", *Nation*, 19 December 2006; "Bt 820-billion Blunder", *Nation*, 20 December 2006; "Credibility Damaged by Fast U-turn", *Nation*, 21 December 2006; and "Capital-Control Fiasco: Pridiyathon Denies Any Intervention", *Nation*, 22 December 2006.

54. Fewer than 24 hours after the Army putsch, a bitterly anti-Thaksin and thus ebullient Kraisak Chunhawan put an astonishingly positive spin on precisely this point from the rostrum of the Foreign Correspondents' Club of Thailand on the evening of 20 September 2006. Until recently chairman of the Foreign Affairs Committee of Thailand's first-ever elected senate, Kraisak is of course the grandson of Field Marshal Phin Chunhawan, a leading participant in the coup of 1947 that initiated a quarter-century of military dictatorship in Thailand. He is the son of

General (Retired) Chatichai Choonhavan, who as an elected member of parliament (MP) replaced General Prem as prime minister in 1988 after his Chat Thai won the most seats of any party in the general elections of July of that year. In his assumption of the premiership as an elected MP and also in his style of government Chatichai thus played a leading role in the entrenchment of civilian parliamentary rule in Thailand. Kraisak served as an influential adviser to Chatichai, until a military junta ousted his government in February 1991. He stated on 20 September 2006 at the FCCT that, in Thailand, military involvement in politics was a fact of life and that — as in 1973, so in 2006 — military backing for popular uprisings against bad regimes could be necessary. One wondered if he felt the same way about 1976. The ability of a figure such as Kraisak to speak in such terms and such tones spoke volumes about the crisis of liberal democratic ideals in Thailand during 2006.

55. See Handley, *The King Never Smiles*, pp. 139ff., 187ff., and 283–84, on some of the important moments in the evolution of this partnership, with it various strands.

56. See ibid., chaps. V–VII (pp. 80–155). Its critical — even controversial — posture notwithstanding, Handley's book is an unmatched resource for understanding the revival of the Thai monarchy during the second half of the twentieth century. The assertion of continuities between King Phumiphon and his grandfather King Chulalongkorn has distracted not only most Thais but also most foreign observers from the near insignificance of the royal institution in the quarter-century from the mid-1930s. But even so Chakri-friendly a scholar as the late David Wyatt pointed this reality out more than two decades ago; see David K. Wyatt, *Thailand: A Short History* (New Haven: Yale University Press, 1984), p. 245. In its treatment of the past two decades, Duncan McCargo, "Network Monarchy and Legitimacy Crises in Thailand" is an indispensable complement to Handley.

57. In fact, no single argument figures so importantly as that one in Handley, *The King Never Smiles*.

58. On this point, see McCargo, "Network Monarch and Legitimacy Crises in Thailand".

59. "DSI to Probe Four Murders from 'War on Drugs'", *Nation*, 14 December 2006.

60. See Tej Bunnag, *The Provincial Administration of Siam, 1892–1915: The Ministry of the Interior under Prince Damrong Rajanubhab* (Kuala Lumpur: Oxford University Press, 1977), and, for an attempt at fresh interpretation of the extension of Bangkok's power into the former Patani sultanate, Tamara Loos, *Subject Siam: Family, Law, and Colonial Modernity in Thailand* (Ithaca, NY: Cornell University Press, 2006), esp. chap. 3 (pp. 72–99).

61. These comments draw on the remarks of Chris Baker — one of contemporary Thailand's savviest and shrewdest interpreters — to a panel discussion on "Does Thailand Need a New Government?", Foreign Correspondents' Club of Thailand, 17 August 2006. He stressed the concentration of industrial production in the post-1997 Thai economy in multinational concerns, and anticipated points later made in "Chang Noi: Giving Up on Democracy for Thailand", cited above.

62. A fascinating discussion of this matter appears in Satya Sagar, "Thai Coup in Hot Soup", *Znet*, 17 October 2006, http://www.zmag.org/content/showarticle.cfm?SectionID=44&ItemID=11205. Also see Michael J. Montesano, "Rational Debate on FTA Nearly Impossible", *Nation*, 29 June 2006, and "Letters to the Editor: By Avoiding Electoral Politics ...", *Nation*, 13 July 2006. Since 2005, the People's Coalition Party (*phak naewruam phak prachachon*, http://www.pcpthai.org/

web01/) has tried to fill the void on the left of Thailand's party-political spectrum. One of its organizers, Giles Ji Ungpakorn, put its creation into context in "There Was a Democratic Alternative to the Coup", *New Mandala*, 25 September 2006, http://rspas.anu.edu.au/rmap/newmandala/2006/09/25/there-was-a-democratic-alternative-to-the-coup/.

63. See Thanong, "Old Money Strikes Back Like a Blast from the Past"; and Pasuk and Baker, *Thaksin: The Business of Politics Thailand*, esp. pp. 57–59 and 69–74.

64. But for an important reminder of the ability of certain segments of Thai society to imagine their King as a patron of democracy, see the final passages of Chris Baker, "Revival, Renewal, and Reinvention: The Complex Life of Thailand's Monarch", *Asia Sentinel*, 8 September 2006, http://www.asiasentinel.com/index.php?option=com_content&task=view&id=154&Itemid=34.

WHAT WENT WRONG WITH THE THAI DEMOCRACY?

Suchit Bunbongkarn

The coup on 22 May 2014 in Thailand has, for the present, caused a break in the political divide and impasse, a problem that the previous elected government was unable to solve. Many were worried that the deeply entrenched political polarization which had existed for almost a decade would lead to bloodshed if it was allowed to continue. So many questions were asked on what went wrong with the presumed Thai democracy. Why did the coup happen? What would be the future of democracy in Thailand? How can it be consolidated? These questions reflect that Thailand is facing a serious problem of democratic consolidation.

Many scholars on democratization agree that the road to a stable democracy is not always smooth. They agree that democratic consolidation in many countries is not an easy task, and Thailand is no exception.

Democratic consolidation depends on a variety of factors which vary from one country to another. Nonetheless, one of the major causes for the instability of a democratic regime is related to political legitimacy. Any political regime which does not secure legitimacy will find it hard to survive since its legitimacy depends on its acceptance by its citizens as expressed through major political forces. There is no need at this stage to debate in detail here how to develop and fortify a democratic regime's legitimacy. However, it is accepted that the essential requirement for strengthening such legitimacy is the regime's effectiveness in meeting the needs of its people and the implementation of democratic values, practices and procedures.

Reprinted from Daljit Singh, ed., *Southeast Asian Affairs 2015* (Singapore: Institute of Southeast Asian Studies, 2015), pp. 359–68. At the time of original publication, Suchit Bunbongkarn was Professor Emeritus in the Faculty of Political Science, Chulalongkorn University and Senior Fellow at the Institute for Security and International Studies (ISIS), Thailand.

Political Polarization and the Crisis of Political Legitimacy

In the case of Thailand during the past decade, we have witnessed a deeply entrenched political polarization which had never reached such extreme levels in the past. This divisiveness, initially caused by a conflict between the pro- and anti-Thaksin groups, later developed into a crisis of political legitimacy. The anti-Thaksin group was formed around 2001 by a mass media tycoon, Sonthi Limthongkul, and later joined by some prominent political elites, notably Chamlong Srimuang, former Governor of Bangkok. In the beginning, the group was composed of thousands from the urban middle class and some upper-middle class who believed that Thaksin was leading the country towards one party rule. He was accused of trying to amass his family's fortunes through "policy corruption". For example, when he was the Prime Minister, the Parliament, presumably under his influence, passed a law enabling him to sell his family's telecom company, Shin Corp, to Temasek of Singapore and be tax exempt for the profits made. In addition, some of his populist policies, especially the provision of village funds (one million baht (US$31,000) per village) and medical care (thirty baht per one hospital visit), were criticized by a number of scholars. They argued that such policies would, in the long run, affect the national economy detrimentally. However, what the anti-Thaksin groups were most concerned about was the fact that Thaksin seemed to allow the left-wing elements in his party to freely criticize the monarchy even though most of the criticisms were unfounded. The anti-government protest rapidly received more popular support both in urban and rural areas. This gradually led to an erosion of the political legitimacy of Thaksin's government.

On the Thaksin side, the then Prime Minister and his political colleagues established a political movement, commonly known as the "Red Shirts" movement to counter the "Yellow Shirts" (People's Alliance for Democracy, PAD) and to strengthen Thaksin's legitimacy. The movement mobilized rural villagers mostly from the north and the northeast to rally in Bangkok to demonstrate the strength of their support. The movement also wanted to show how popular the government's populist policies were especially in rural provinces and towns in the north and the northeast. The political figures playing an important role in establishing the power bases of Thaksin in these two parts of the country were left-leaning party members, some of them being former student activists who fled into the jungle after the coup in 1976 to join the Communist Party of Thailand (CPT). In addition, Thaksin, through the use of his wealth, was able to bring in a large number of politically ambitious local leaders in these areas of the country to his side by enabling them to run for the seats in the Parliament under Thaksin's party. At the top echelons of the party, apart from Thaksin, there were a number of wealthy businessmen whose financial contributions helped to oil Thaksin's political machine. However, it was known that Thaksin was the one who contributed the most financially.

The coup in September 2006 neither put an end to political divisiveness in the country nor did it eliminate Thaksin's influence. He was forced out of power, but his political clout remained. The coup-appointed government did not make serious efforts to uproot Thaksin's influence. It also did not attempt to educate the people on "what is right, what is wrong" in politics. Hence, the rural people in the north and the northeast continued to believe that Thaksin had done much good for them, and that he was the only political leader who had really helped them. To no one's surprise, therefore, when the new Constitution was put into effect and General Elections were held in 2007, the Thaksin-backed People's Power Party won.

From 2007 to the coup in May 2014, the political polarization remained a chronic problem in Thai politics, and there was no sign of reconciliation. Almost immediately after the People's Power Party won the elections and formed the government with Samak Sudaravej as Prime Minister, the Yellow Shirts (PAD) started campaigning against the government on the grounds that the government was only a "puppet of Thaksin". Thus, it was deemed no longer legitimate to govern. It was not long before the Constitutional Court ruled that Samak was disqualified to be prime minister because he had received money from a television show producer for performing as a cook on a cooking show. He was then succeeded by Somchai Wongsawat, Thaksin's brother-in-law in September 2008. The PAD stepped up its campaign against the government demanding that Somchai step down. Protesters argued that Somchai was Thaksin's puppet and that the government was not legitimate. The economy was almost crippled when the protest leaders, including Chamlong Srimuang, led a large crowd to seize Don Muang and Suvanaphumi international airports in Bangkok, causing all the international and domestic flights coming to Bangkok to divert their course to other airports and stop flying to Thailand. However, the government kept on insisting on its legitimacy, arguing that it came to power through elections. Nevertheless, it made no effort to regain its control of the airports.

Somchai's government did not last long. In early December 2008, the Constitutional Court ordered the People's Power Party, the major party in Somchai's coalition government, to be dissolved as one of its executive members was found guilty of breaking the election law during the General Elections in 2007. The dissolution immediately led to the downfall of Somchai's government, and the PAD which had then occupied Bangkok's two airports in protest.

Nonetheless, the situation did not return to normal. When the Parliament voted Abhisit Vejjajiva, the leader of the Democrat Party, the main opposition, to be the next prime minister, the pro-Thaksin group rejected Abhisit's government outright. It argued that Abhisit was not a legitimate prime minister because he was not the leader of the largest party in the Parliament, although the majority of the members of the Parliament voted for him. The Red Shirts of the United Front of Democracy Against Dictatorship (UDD) attacked the vote as being unfair and illegitimate because, they believed, the vote was undertaken under the pressure of the military.

The Democrat-led government under the premiership of Abhisit was the first anti-Thaksin government since the elections in 2007. It was not unexpected, therefore, that the UDD would launch a large-scale protest against the government. The main objective of the UDD was to bring Thaksin back home without serving a jail sentence. It intended to destroy the image of the Prime Minister and his ability to run the country. A rally organized by the UDD disrupted the ASEAN Summit meeting in

Pattaya in 2009, and in 2010 around some 10,000 UDD protesters, mostly from the north and northeast, occupied Ratprasong, the main shopping area of Bangkok for several months. They exerted pressure hoping to force the government to resign. Eventually, the government decided to use army troops to disperse the protesters. The army took utmost precautions to avoid violent clashes with the protesters. However, during several months of pressure and suppression, sporadic clashes occurred causing a number of deaths and injuries on both sides. Finally, the army was able to put an end to the protest but not without casualties. Some buildings were set on fire, including some department stores in Bangkok and city halls in some provinces.

The UDD's agreement to end the protest did not mean that the political polarization was about to end. On the contrary, the divisiveness was getting worse, soon resulting in profound hatred on both sides. The UDD condemned Abhisit for the loss of life on the UDD side during the army suppression. The community radio stations in the north and northeast and the red shirt television channel accused Abhisit's government of ordering the government troops to use live ammunition and lethal weapons with the intention to kill the protesters. Hate speech was often used in their broadcasts attacking the government. Freedom of speech, guaranteed in the previous Constitution, had provided opportunity for such mass media to play an effective role in instilling a belief among rural villagers in the north and northeast that Abhisit's government was illegitimate while strengthening popularity of Thaksin and his Pheu Thai Party in these two parts of the country.

The General Election in 2010 demonstrated an increasing divisiveness among the Thai electorate. Thaksin's Pheu Thai Party won a majority of seats in the Parliament while the Democrat Party came in second. As expected, Pheu Thai captured most of the seats in the north and northeast whereas all the seats in the south went to the Democrat Party except in one or two Muslim-dominated provinces. The result of the elections confirmed that the political influence of Thaksin remained very strong. Yingluck Shinawatra, Thaksin's sister, ran in his place as the Pheu Thai Party leader, although she had no political experience. She was elected by the Parliament to be the prime minister. Most people believed that she won due to her family ties with Thaksin.

Soon after Yingluck's government had assumed power, several anti-Thaksin groups became active again. However, they were not capable of organizing mass protests until 2013 when the government tried to amend the Constitution and introduce an amnesty bill. These actions were believed to be part of the government's effort to bring Thaksin back to Thailand without serving a two-year imprisonment.

On the issue of enacting an amnesty law, Yingluck's government was accused of abusing power. The fact that the government was trying to use the majority it enjoyed in the House of Representatives to pass this law despite strong protests from both inside and outside the House added fuel to the fire. In addition to a fierce debate against the bill in the House, the Democrat Party, the main opposition, took to the streets with some 10,000 people in Bangkok in protest against the bill. However, the government continued without heeding the protest, believing that the protest was just a tactical move of the opposition, and that it was supported only by a small group of people. However, a serious political crisis was triggered by the fact that the House of Representatives decided to vote on this bill at 4:00 a.m. without allowing full discussion. This was not only highly unusual, but also very arbitrary and presumptuous of the government, thus leading to a large-scale mass protest.

It was not only the amnesty bill that had eroded the government's legitimacy. There was also the rice pledging scheme[1] in which Yingluck's government failed to pay back farmers on time. Most critics and experts on rice trading believed that it was a wrong policy and that there was large-scale corruption at almost every level from the policymakers downward. The country's economy and the reputation of Thai rice were damaged. It was reported that the government had lost several hundred thousand million baht due to corruption and mismanagement of this policy. The most serious consequence was the suffering of the farmers due to the lack of government payment.

The Strengths, Base of Support and Weaknesses of the Anti-Yingluck Government Movement

The government's insistence on enacting the amnesty bill had resulted in widespread demonstrations, indicating a rapid increase in the strength of the government opponents and an expansion of the base of support for them. A huge number of people had decided to join the anti-government, anti-Thaksin movement, especially the one called the People's Democratic Reform Committee (PDRC) led by Suthep Teuksuban, former deputy leader of the Democrat Party. The government's abuse of power and large-scale corruption in the government were the issues picked up by the protesters to attack and condemn Yingluck and her brother, Thaksin. They hoped to obtain as large a number of people as possible, not only in Bangkok but in other urban towns and in the south which was the stronghold of the Democrat Party, to join in the protest against the government and thus force Yingluck, the Prime Minister, to resign. Hundreds of thousands of people in Bangkok from all walks of life joined the demonstration. They were government officials, professional and business people, private entrepreneurs, state enterprise workers, university teachers, medical doctors, nurses and public health workers. There were demonstrations in other provinces as well, including major provinces in the north and the northeast. However, the strongest and most solid support came from the south.

The strength of the PDRC did not rely only on the number of the protesters, but also on the financial contributions from the protesters and others who shared a similar belief with the protesters in rejecting the legitimacy of Yingluck's government. The way the people contributed money to Suthep and his organization was a phenomenon to behold. Wherever he held an anti-government rally, people would surround him, handing him thousands of banknotes. It was estimated that throughout the several months of protest the PDRC received contributions of millions of baht.

In addition to those contributions, the PDRC received support from the mass media. The most important one was the Blue Sky TV channel which was known to be pro-Democrat. Throughout the whole period of the protest, it switched to broadcast programmes supporting the PDRC. The Thai television medium was a very effective means to mobilize people to join the PDRC movement. It was a great success in expanding the base of support for the PDRC to bring in various groups of people to participate in political rallies and to donate money and other necessities for a prolonged protest, for example, food, drinking water, camping tents and blankets.

Another important factor contributing to the success of the PDRC in expanding and strengthening mass support was Suthep's leadership. Throughout the period of demonstration, Suthep had shown his perseverance, strong determination, and devotion to his cause. He campaigned tirelessly to overthrow PM Yingluck and the so-called "Thaksin system". Apart from such strength of character, his oratorical skill enabled him to capture the hearts and minds of millions of people.

Despite the strengths mentioned above, the PDRC still had some weaknesses. One of them was the lack of strong and effective coordination with other anti-government groups. Since the introduction of the amnesty bill to Parliament, there had been a number of anti-government groups formed in addition to the PDRC. One led by one of the most respected Buddhist monks, Buddha-issara, was very influential and gained the support of the masses. In fact, the group was part of the PDRC, but Buddha-issara wanted to be independent from Suthep. Other smaller groups led by some political activists, including the one which called itself the "People's Army to Dethrone Thaksin's System" and another called the 'Network of Students and People for National Reform', were actively campaigning for the same cause as the PDRC. However, effective coordination between them was absent.

Another weakness was the lack of a clear-cut reform plan. The PDRC had launched a campaign for a national reform before elections. They were successful in mobilizing voters to boycott the General Election on 2 February 2014, but what they failed to do was to present to the public the specific national reform programmes, both for the short term and long term. Another important issue the PDRC faced was how to overhaul the so-called "Thaksin system". They had announced that if the government failed to agree to the PDRC's demand, then they would launch a people's revolution. However, it was obvious that they did not know how.

The Yingluck Government's Legitimacy Crisis

Amidst the mass protests, Yingluck's government insisted on its legitimacy to rule, arguing that it was elected by the people. A legitimacy crisis occurred when the government failed to maintain law and order. Arrest warrants were issued by the Criminal Court at the government's request to arrest Suthep and a number of his colleagues on sedition charges, but the government failed to arrest them. The government was unable to disperse the protesters and prosecute them. These failures indicated that Yingluck's government was facing a very serious problem of eroding legitimacy. When the government sought loans from the government-owned banks to pay the farmers who joined the rice pledging scheme, quite a number of bank customers threatened to withdraw their deposits from these banks, thus forcing them to turn down the government's request. What was even worse was that the government could not provide a political environment favourable for organizing general elections within the time frame stipulated in the Constitution. Due to the protests and the Democrat Party's threat to boycott the elections, the government and the Election

Commission had to organize the elections beyond the constitutional deadline, making the elections unconstitutional as ruled by the Constitutional Court. The government and the Red Shirts (the UDD) mobilized rural villagers, mostly from the north and northeast, to come to Bangkok to support the government and to counter the PDRC. However, the UDD's demonstration was politically ineffective. It could not compare with the PDRC in terms of the number of people involved, and the UDD could not afford to pay those villagers to stay in Bangkok for more than two or three days.

On the eve of the coup on 22 May 2014, Thailand was, therefore, plagued with an insurmountable conundrum over political legitimacy with no solution in sight, as there was no resolution acceptable to both the government and the opponents. It this situation it was impossible to find a way out though constitutional means.

The Military and National Reform

At present, the country is in the hands of the military or the National Council for Peace and Order (NCPO). They have agreed that extensive political, as well as other reforms, are urgently needed. It is hoped that the reforms would lead to political reconciliation as well as a stable democratic political system. The NCPO set up the Cabinet, the National Legislative Assembly, the National Reform Council (NRC) and the Constitutional Drafting Committee. These institutions have been assigned to launch national reform programmes and draft a new permanent Constitution.

The political reform, under consideration of the NRC and the CDC, is focusing on the development of political institutions and processes, including the election system and the political party system to ensure that elected governments in the future would be honest, responsible and serve public needs. It has been agreed that such a government must be able to accommodate the needs of various political and social groups. The people's liberty should be respected. Equality in all aspects should be encouraged, and law and order must be observed and maintained. The gap between the urban rich and the rural poor must be narrowed, and the wealth and economic power should not be in the hands of the very few.

Another reform issue which is of public concern is the relationship between politicians and government bureaucrats. The people want the reforms to ensure that the government bureaucracy, including the police and the armed forces do not become the political tools of politicians.

The devolution of the government administration is also a reform issue of importance. The NRC and CDC have agreed that the political and administrative authority must not be concentrated in the capital. More authority should be transferred from the national government to the local ones. There has been a proposal for direct elections of provincial governors and some local government officers. This is a very sensitive issue. How can we make sure that such devolution of authority will not end up providing opportunities for greedy local politicians who have an insatiable hunger for power and wealth as their personal interests prevail over national interests?

The next reform issue is the development of an effective system of checks-and-balances. This involves the strengthening of the authority and independence of public prosecutors, the national counter-corruption and human rights commissions and the judiciary.

It has also been agreed that the reforms should focus not only on the political institutions but also on the cultural and psychological aspects. The political ethics and morality of politicians and government officers must lead to a conviction that politics and government administration are public service. Joining politics must be to serve the people not to seek personal wealth, power and influence. A sense of citizenship needs to be instilled in the people. This sense of citizenship will encourage the people to participate more actively in their local affairs. They will learn how to stand on their own feet and rely less on the patronage offered by local leaders or politicians.

One of the most important reforms is the strengthening of the people's sector and civil society. The development of a sense of citizenship will empower the people's sector. The people are the foundation of democracy. If the people's sector is weak, the democracy will also be weak and unstable. In the past, Thailand did not pay enough attention to the development of the people's sector, hence the democratic system had been exploited by politicians for their personal benefit. To strengthen the Thai democracy, the people's sector must be strengthened.

Those reforms mentioned previously are only a few of the important ones facing the Thai body politic. There are many more reforms that need attention. All the reforms would lead to the development of a more effective system of checks-and-balances, the rule of law, and a greater opportunity for the citizenry to participate in the formulation and implementation of decisions affecting their lives. It is hoped that the reforms undertaken would ensure that a more stable, effective and responsible democratic government emerges in the not too distant future. This seems to be a very formidable task which cannot be completed easily within a few years as there are a number of obstacles to be tackled. Also, how these reforms can be achieved remains to be seen.

Note

1. The "rice pledging policy" was implemented by Yingluck Shinawatra's Pheu Thai government after it won the July 2011 Thai General Election. The Thai government purchased rice from farmers for 15,000 baht per tonne, around 50 per cent above market prices, which it then stockpiled. The rationale was that with Thailand as the world's leading rice exporter, this sudden price hike and potential market shortage would force global rice prices higher. This would then allow the government to sell its rice for a premium, causing minimal impact on the budget, and generating a bigger pay-off for Thai farmers in the government's electoral stronghold.

Vietnam

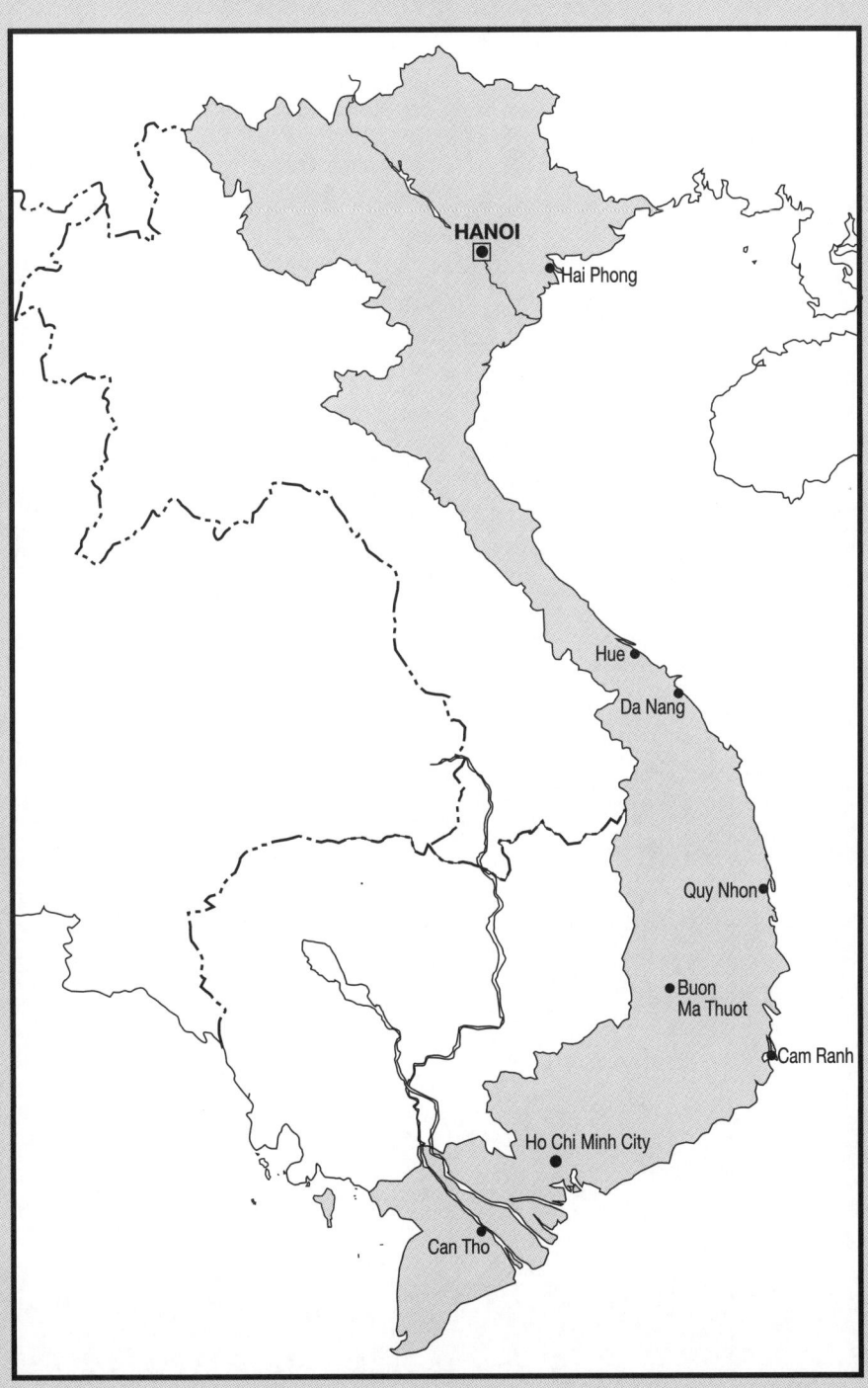

VIETNAM IN PERSPECTIVE

Ng Shui Meng

The wheel of fortune turns for most people but for the Vietnamese, it seems to have long remained immobile. Nearly two years ago, when the Paris Peace Agreement was signed, war-weary Vietnamese took heart that somehow the wheel would finally turn to their advantage. Although few were naïve enough to expect miracles, or that the next couple of years would be an easy time, many began to talk of post-war reconstruction. Most people had hoped that the framework established in the Paris Agreement, agreed to by signatory parties, would somehow transform the bloody struggle of the battlefields to a less violent competition in the political arena. Unfortunately their hopes did not materialize. Indeed, all that the Paris Agreement has achieved thus far has been to put an end to the direct U.S. involvement in the Indochina conflict and allow President Nixon to fulfil his promise of bringing the "boys" home. As far as Vietnam is concerned, the fighting has continued unabated; casualties are still high; and the prospects for a rapid political settlement is just as illusory today as when the Agreement was signed. With the South Vietnamese economy rapidly deteriorating, ordinary Vietnamese discover that living in "post-war" Vietnam is not much of an improvement from the days of the war itself.

This paper attempts to review and assess the significant political, economic, and social events that took place in South Vietnam in 1974. In so doing, the major trends of the country will be brought into sharper focus.

Major Political Trends

The year 1974 was one in which the government of the Republic of South Vietnam (GVN) has had to face some of the most

---

Reprinted in abridged format from *Southeast Asian Affairs 1975* (Singapore: Institute of Southeast Asian Studies, 1975), pp. 201–11. At the time of original publication, Ng Shui Meng was a Research Officer at the Institute of Southeast Asian Studies, Singapore.

serious challenges since it came into power. Jostled along by political currents, both external and internal, the political base of the government has been seriously eroded.

Adversary Challenges

On the military front, GVN's competition with the Provisional Revolutionary Government (PRG) and the Democratic Republic of Vietnam (DRV) has not diminished as a result of the cease-fire agreement. In fact, there has been little doubt as to the PRG's and DRV's capability of launching a full-scale military offensive. It is variously estimated that, at present, there are at least 300,000 North Vietnamese troops and an unknown quantity of armament and ammunition supplies in South Vietnam, ample for sustaining a high level of warfare for a few years. Although there is still no evidence of an imminent major DRV offensive, the current "nibbling" operations of the PRG forces have already taken a very heavy toll of the 1·1 million-strong South Vietnamese Army.

Since the Paris Agreement, PRG's efforts to expand its control over the country have continued to undermine the government's territorial base. The PRG has direct control over no more than 10% to 15% of the total area of South Vietnam and less than 10% of the total population. However, if the areas under "contested" control are included, then the PRG network probably extends over more than 30% of the country. ("Contested" areas are under nominal GVN control, but for all purposes are completely accessible to the PRG propaganda teams and military units.) Much of South Vietnam's most valuable timber lands and rice lands are within the PRG controlled zones and, hence, of strategic importance to its economic warfare against the GVN. Aided by the economic adversities which South Vietnam now faces, the PRG may continue to score successes at the expense of the GVN by merely exploiting simple "bread and butter" issues and the existing internal political contradictions within the country.

Diminishing Aid

Most of the serious problems that beset the South Vietnamese Government in 1974 have been, in one way or another, linked to the substantial reduction in U.S. military and economic aid. The South Vietnamese economy has since the escalation of the Vietnam war depended on large amounts of U.S. aid for its solvency. Indeed, it is not an exaggeration to say that the fate of South Vietnam herself would have been in doubt years earlier had it not been for U.S. assistance in the form of money, men, and munitions. At the height of the U.S. involvement, the United States expedited half a million of her best trained men and spent as much as US$30 billion a year to assist South Vietnam. However, the policy of *détente* initiated during the presidency of Richard Nixon has led to the ultimate withdrawal of U.S. troops and the gradual abandonment of American interest in the country.

The abandonment of U.S. interest in South Vietnam became most apparent during 1974. Despite pressures from the White House, the U.S. Congress was determined to trim economic and military aid to Vietnam. Thus the U.S. House of Representatives voted, on 8 August, to reduce military aid to Vietnam from the requested sum of US$1.4 billion to US$700 million for fiscal year 1975 (July 1974–June 1975), which is US$500 million short of that for fiscal year 1974. Economic aid would also be slashed from the requested US$750 million to US$450 million, about US$150 million less than the previous year's amount. The ceiling for both military and economic aid for fiscal year 1975 as passed by the House of Representatives would be a maximum of US$1.2 billion.

Such a drastic reduction in U.S. assistance has had important consequences for South Vietnam. Coming as it did so soon after the withdrawal of American troops, diminishing aid has merely aggravated the serious economic ills (inflation, unemployment, and others) which have in recent years plagued the South Vietnamese economy. With the rising costs of fuel and the depletion in the stock of ammunitions, it has become increasingly difficult for the South Vietnamese Army to sustain its military drive. Thanks to some juggling of its complicated accounting system, the Pentagon was able to come up with another US$266 million to help tide the South Vietnamese Army over the last three months of fiscal year 1974, before funds for fiscal year 1975 became available. It is not expected that the Pentagon would continue to work such wonders for Vietnam in future years, given the hostile climate of the U.S. Congress and the depressed state of the U.S. economy. The only way that the South Vietnamese Government can continue with current military activities is to raise its own funds for defence or to reduce the level of fighting. Already approximately one-quarter of the more remote outposts in Military Region IV in the Mekong Delta had to be abandoned in August to reduce expenditure.

Internal Political Competition — The Third Force

The Paris Agreement, which raised false hopes for peace within Vietnam, created a special problem for the government. Article 12 of the Agreement stipulates the establishment of a tripartite National Council of National Reconciliation and Concord to be made up of the two conflicting parties in South Vietnam (the GVN and the PRG) and a "third political segment". This Council, theoretically, would provide a framework within which the two competing governments and the other existing political groups could somehow work out a mode for peaceful coexistence. Unfortunately, no one, including those who signed the Agreement, was certain as to what or who should constitute this third political segment, the so-called "Third Force". The numerous and disparate political groupings which are opposed to the Saigon Government but profess no support for the PRG, consider themselves the Third Force. The GVN, however, chooses to interpret the third segment in the Council as one to be appointed by both the conflicting parties. The PRG, although offering no specific definition of its own for the third segment, has, for its own reasons, given tacit support to South Vietnam's opposition groups.

The Saigon Government in staunchly refusing to accept a third political force in the country has alienated most non-PRG political groups. In denouncing the Third Force as communist initiated and in persecuting its more articulate proponents, the Saigon Government has further pushed the Third Force members to align themselves, if not ideologically, at least tactically, with the PRG. However, having neither a single identifiable leader nor an efficient organization to champion its cause, the Third Force has been slow in developing into an influential political movement. Nevertheless, it has gained some momentum in mounting pressure against the government.

Ironically enough, the catalyst for the Third Force movement was supplied by the Vietnamese Catholics — one of the pillars of the Saigon Government's political base. Spearheaded by an energetic priest, Father Tran Huu Thanh, the People's Movement against Corruption for National Salvation was formed. What had begun as a series of small proclamations against corruption in high places, culminated in the publication of the explosive "Indictment No. 1" in Hue on 8 September. This Indictment contains a six-point accusation of corruption against President Thieu and members of his family. (In the Indictment, President Thieu is accused of seizing government houses and prime government land for his personal use; halting an investigation of a fertilizer company in which his brother-in-law was charged with having illegally made a fortune in fertilizer speculation; allowing his wife to profit from a supposedly charitable hospital which she founded; collaborating with Prime Minister Tran Thien Khiem in the running of a narcotic smuggling organization; and condoning the profiteering activities of his aunt and other relatives in government-subsidized rice shipments to Central Vietnam.)

Like a magnet, the movement quickly attracted the support of the opposition groups, especially those which professed to belong to the Third Force. On 14 September, a group backed by some militant Buddhists of An Quang Pagoda, once the hotbed of political dissent, proclaimed the formation of the Forces for National Reconciliation (NRF) under the leadership of Opposition Senator Vu van Mau. Picking up the cue, a number of journalists, Opposition Senators, and Deputies of the Lower House who had earlier organized themselves into the South Vietnam Committee for Freedom of the Press and Publication (SCFPP) called upon the fifteen or so Vietnamese language newspapers to defy the censorship code by publishing Indictment No. 1. Only three newspapers responded. Threatened with confiscation, the publishers publicly burned their papers and, with the support of some Buddhists and Catholic priests, turned the occasion into a demonstration. Together with some other organizations, like the Association of Disabled Veterans, and a couple of well-known individuals, like Duong van Minh (Big Minh) and the leading Buddhist figure, Thich Tri Quang, a loose political front was formed. Thus, thanks to the anti-corruption efforts, the Third Force has finally gained the status of a political movement. Believing that the country's serious military, economic, and social problems can only be solved when there is peace, the expressed objective of the movement is reconciliation and peaceful coexistence with the PRG.

Corruption

One of the major issues that surfaced constantly during the year to undermine the government's position was that of corruption. In Vietnamese society where relationships are still to a large extent determined by one's position in the social hierarchy, the use of power, influence, or money to extract benefits or to smooth one's way through an often inefficient bureaucracy is not only tacitly accepted, but also, if somewhat illegal, institutionalized. Under the best of conditions, there are kickbacks for everyone, commensurate with each person's position within the system. Corruption becomes unacceptable and an issue for protest only when there is a breakdown in the system. This occurs when there are not enough kick-backs for all, benefiting only those at the very top of the social strata, or when, as a result of the "squeeze", the masses of the population become so impoverished that their very existence and livelihood are threatened. In the case of South Vietnam, given the present difficult economic conditions, official corruption allowing a few people to rake in huge profits becomes more than just an irritation to most; it proves to be an unbearable burden, especially for those at the lowest levels of society.

Three major scandals involving sugar, rice, and fertilizers — each touching some of the most sensitive nerves of the still essentially agricultural Vietnamese society — fuelled public discontent. In the sugar scandal, the Director-General of the state-owned Viet Nam Sugar Company, Nguyen van Hai, and other top members of the management were charged with the hoarding of and speculation in sugar worth more than a billion piastres. This was done just before the announcement of the doubling of the retail price of sugar. Also implicated, but not charged, was the former Minister of Economy, Pham Kim Ngoc, whose involvement in providing the official cloak for such illegal activities was hinted at. The outcome of the charges was much delayed and inconclusive. The case dragged on for more than a year without the accused being convicted.

The rice scandal was another *cause célèbre* in South Vietnam in 1974. Rice has always been the staple food of the Vietnamese and South Vietnam was once able to export her rice surpluses. However, years of war have resulted in her becoming a substantial rice importer. In 1973, her rice imports amounted to about 304,000 metric tons. As a war strategy to deny rice to the PRG areas, rice distribution throughout the country is tightly controlled and vested in only a few authorized agents. Herein lies the greatest opportunity for unscrupulous dealers to profit at the expense of the public, especially when the commodity is in extremely short supply, as in the months just preceding a harvest. In densely populated Central Vietnam, where a lack of suitable rice lands has traditionally caused rice shortages, the people have to face this vexing problem every year. For the poor, any malfunction in the distribution, deliberate or otherwise, can mean starvation. In the scandal, two persons responsible for transporting rice into Central Vietnam and distributing it in the area were charged with purposely withholding the commodity for personal gain. The accused were Pham Sanh, the President of Nam Viet Bank and Ngo Thi Huyet, an aunt of President Thieu and mother of Hoang Due Nha, the influential former Minister of Information. Though they denied all charges, the public remained sceptical.

Speculation in and hoarding of fertilizers also plagued the Vietnamese farmers from the beginning of 1974. In her pursuit of the "green revolution", South Vietnam has in recent years expanded the acreage under miracle rice cultivation. Miracle rice, while it has the advantage of a higher yield potential, requires much more chemical fertilizer than ordinary rice. Unfortunately, following the oil crisis of October 1973, the price of this oil-based commodity increased significantly, thereby forcing a reduction in its import into Vietnam. The shortage in supply was further aggravated by illegal hoarding which caused the price of the product to rise beyond the means of ordinary farmers. Such manipulation of the market system imposed tremendous strain on the farming community and exerted great pressure on the government to probe into the causes of fertilizer shortage. Fanning the flames of discontent were rumours that President Thieu himself had blocked investigations because his own brother-in-law was involved.

The inability or unwillingness of the authorities to penalize the involved officials effectively and quickly enough was the major cause of public discontent. The foot-dragging and half-hearted investigations made by the government merely added to the cynicism of the public who viewed this as evidence of the lack of sincerity on the part of the government to seriously eradicate corruption. Thus, when the movement against corruption gained momentum, it very rapidly took on a much more serious political overtone. In failing to curb the canker of corruption, the government's efficiency was called into question. In condoning the corrupt practices of appointed public officials, the President's personal integrity was tainted. Confidence in his leadership was shaken and, hence, during the anti-corruption movement, demands for his resignation became increasingly strident.

Cabinet Reshuffle

The ills that threaten the stability of the Vietnamese society and the impact such defects have on the political structure of the government have not gone unnoticed by the President. Time and again pledges were made by the government to revamp the system. The oft-repeated pledge to "clean" the system and prevent corruption as a means of consolidating national security and increasing economic production was, however, not acted upon with any concerted effort on the part of the authorities. The normal response was to remove a number of the most inept officials from their positions, or to go through the motions of a Cabinet reshuffle which brought about neither a change in policy nor any significant improvement. Two Cabinet reshuffles took place in 1974, the first was effected in February, only four months after the October 1973 reshuffle, and the second took place in October.

The February reshuffle was carried out with the declared intention of improving the efficiency of the government by co-ordinating the work of the various ministries in order to tackle the serious economic problems of the country. Twenty-two ministers resigned from a twenty-four member Cabinet on 16 February. However, with the formation of the new Cabinet, announced on 18 February, fifteen of the ministers who had resigned were reinstated. Of the new appointments, two attracted most attention — that of ex-General Tran van Don as one of the three Deputy Prime Ministers and the other of Hoang Due Nha as Minister of Information. Don, one of the generals in the junta which ousted President Diem in 1963, is among President Thieu's most trusted friends. As a former general, Don still has a very large following within the military ranks, and his appointment was seen as an attempt to further Thieu's hold over the army. The reason for the appointment of Hoang Due Nha was less obvious. Nha is the President's cousin and adopted nephew and has a very strong influence in the President's Office. However, his appointment as a minister in the new Cabinet might not have been a promotion. Had he remained in his former post as Commissioner General of Information, Nha would have had direct access to the President and would have wielded greater influence on presidential decisions than he could as a member of the Cabinet under the direct control of Prime Minister Tran

Thien Khiem. It was rumoured that there had been a power struggle between Khiem and Nha to gain Thieu's confidence. The appointment of Nha to the Cabinet was thus conjectured to be a victory of Khiem over Nha. This interpretation seems to have been borne out by the fact that in the October reshuffle, Nha was one of the first ministers to be dropped.

The October reshuffle was an attempt to defuse the rising tension following the wave of anti-corruption and anti-government demonstrations. In this reshuffle ten ministers, including Nha, resigned. This time, unlike in February, when the reshuffle was accomplished within thirty-six hours of the mass resignation, Prime Minister Tran Thien Khiem found it extremely difficult to find replacements for his new Cabinet. Individuals were known to have turned down offers of ministerial positions. More than six weeks passed before Premier Khiem could form a new Cabinet. Not unexpectedly the new nominees, with the exception of Dr Nguyen van Hao, a well-known economist and former head of the National Economic Development Fund, excited little interest. Dr Hao, in his new position as Deputy Prime Minister in charge of Economic Development, is expected to be able to introduce some innovative measures to right the ills of the depressed economy. And unless this can be done shortly, Vietnam, at least economically, would find the year ahead more unbearable.

Foreign Relations

In the last few years, as the superpowers progressively moved towards *détente*, their respective allies have been anxious not to be left too far behind. Countries which have formerly aligned themselves with either of the two power blocs are currently sending out feelers for the establishment of some kind of rapprochement with heretofore "less friendly" nations. In the case of South Vietnam, who is still in the midst of fighting an alleged communist threat, there are certain constraints against the pursuit of a more flexible foreign policy. Having associated herself closely with the Western "Free World" bloc since 1954, South Vietnam maintains no relations with the communist countries. With regard to the non-aligned Third World countries, she has had only a lukewarm relationship. In the post-Paris era, however, the country has felt a greater need to establish relations with the Third World countries to gain international standing. As an indication of this new attitude, South Vietnam has abandoned the policy of terminating relations with any country which recognizes North Vietnam (although she still protests strenuously against the recognition of the PRG). Her efforts to broaden ties with Third World countries have met with some success within the last two years. In spite of the tensions between the Arab countries and Israel, South Vietnam has scored a major diplomatic breakthrough by establishing diplomatic ties with Saudi Arabia while still maintaining her long-standing friendship with Israel. As a result of this new connection, the Saudi Arabian Government has promised to supply oil to South Vietnam. Friendly visits have also been made by the Foreign Minister, Vuong van Bae, to various countries in Central and South America in search of new diplomatic links. In another surprise move, President Thieu announced in his 9 November speech at the National Public Prosecutors' Convention in Saigon, South Vietnam's willingness to recognize the major communist powers on condition that they refrain from interfering in the internal affairs of the country. While this may be interpreted as an approach consistent with the new foreign policy of South Vietnam, the statement, coming at the end of the nearly two months of fierce anti-government protests, has been regarded as designed more for internal consumption than as a serious overture to the communist bloc.

Relations with the West

It seems that South Vietnam, after having served the West in its attempt to stall the "communist threat" to the "Free World", has suddenly found herself left out in the cold in the post-*détente* era. While North Vietnam is increasingly gaining recognition among Western countries, South Vietnam is beginning to feel a chilling effect in her relations with the West.

South Vietnam-U.S. relations have been dampened over the question of aid. President Thieu has repeatedly lashed out at the drastic reduction in aid as evidence of failure on the part of the United States to fulfil her commitment to the country. Unfortunately, such tirades have had less and less impact since Richard Nixon's resignation from the U.S. Presidency. President Ford does not have the same degree of personal commitment to the Thieu Government as his predecessor and has proven himself less eager to offend the U.S. Congress on behalf of South Vietnam over the question of aid. As far as most Americans are concerned, the Vietnam War has ended and their commitment to the country terminated at the signing of the Paris Agreement. It would therefore be increasingly difficult for the U.S. Government to justify continued military aid to South Vietnam. When the full impact of the economic recession in the United States makes itself felt, there will be even greater pressure to lobby against any more aid to that country.

With the U.S. influence declining in South Vietnam, it appears that France would like to step in and play a greater role in her former colony. As of April 1973, France has restored diplomatic relations with South Vietnam and has promised to assist her in her post-war reconstruction programme. But as it turned out French economic aid to South Vietnam in 1974 amounted to only US$25 million, a mere drop in the bucket.

Relations with the People's Republic of China

South Vietnam-PRC relations have never been more hostile than in the past twelve months. Relations between these two countries have been further soured by their conflict over the Paracels and the Spratlys. These islands forming mere specks of sand in the South China Sea had never been of much interest to anyone, except fishermen and sulphur collectors. But the increased interest in oil within the region has changed the picture significantly. Geological surveys seem to indicate substantial quantities of oil under the sea-bed of the South China Sea. As a result, the countries within the region have been reassessing the value of every piece of real estate on shore and off shore. South Vietnam has, as of 1973, begun granting oil concessions for exploration and exploitation to international oil companies.

In mid-January 1974, Chinese ships were spotted around the Paracel Islands and Chinese fishermen were seen landing on the island group. South Vietnam, who also claims the islands, responded with a show of power. On 19 January the South Vietnamese Navy sank a Chinese gunboat, but in the subsequent two-day battle, the South Vietnamese, overpowered by superior

Chinese air, sea, and land forces, lost the islands to Chinese control. South Vietnam's diplomatic attempt to gain U.N. support on the Paracel issue was unsuccessful. Even the U.S. 7th Fleet stationed within the Pacific steered clear of the conflict.

Another near clash with the Chinese occurred immediately after the Paracel defeat. On 1 February, for fear of losing the Spratlys also, about 200 South Vietnamese troops landed on two of the islands of the Spratly chain. A tense atmosphere prevailed for more than a month, with Peking issuing repeated warnings against infringement of its territorial claims. The storm blew over by itself, with the issue of disputed claims over the Spratlys still left unsettled.

The issue of disputed off-shore claims will continue to be an open sore irritating both South Vietnam and China. As oil exploration activities intensify, the opportunities for future conflicts will be abundant until there is some mutual agreement on each other's legitimate claim. Another incident in November 1974 illustrates the seriousness of the problem. On 10 November three Chinese trawlers were sighted slowly circling an oil rig operated by Shell Pecten, located about 240 kilometres southeast of Saigon. Saigon immediately alerted its new F5E Tiger jet-fighters to be ready for any outbreak of warfare and also sent in a large fleet of warships to protect the rig. Though no clash occurred, the potential for armed confrontation nevertheless remains.

Relations with other Southeast Asian Countries

Relations between South Vietnam and the other countries in Southeast Asia, especially ASEAN, can only be described as correct. Still showing a degree of suspicion over the region's call for neutrality, South Vietnam has, in a way, purposely kept a posture of coolness. Some events which took place in 1974 have certainly not been conducive to bringing about any closer ties. The dispute with the PRC over the Paracels and the Spratlys also involved the Philippines and Taiwan. Also claimants to the islands, these two countries had already stationed small units of troops there. Using utmost diplomatic tact, South Vietnam managed to avoid serious dispute with these two allies. And in face of what might turn out to be a greater threat if a show-down with the PRC really materialized, the Philippines and Taiwan went along without making things more difficult for South Vietnam. The two countries merely issued diplomatic notes urging all the claimants to settle the issue through negotiations.

Another oil-related incident sparked off yet another near conflict, this time with the Khmer Republic. Cambodians who have, for historical reasons, shown a distrust and dislike for Vietnamese became agitated when, on 4 September, South Vietnam issued a warning to the Khmer Republic to remove an oil rig operated by Elf du Cambodge in the Gulf of Thailand near Wai Island. The rig was operating in a concession which although granted by the Khmer Republic, was within a disputed area. To back up the threat, the South Vietnamese sent in a small fleet of naval vessels and gave the oil company ten days' notice to tow away the rig or suffer the consequences of its being forcibly removed. A clash was avoided when the oil company agreed to remove the rig, but a more unpleasant repercussion of the incident occurred when an anti-Vietnamese outburst in Phnom Penh caused the temporary evacuation of some South Vietnamese Embassy officials and their families.

A surprising development in South Vietnam's foreign relations occurred on 21 November when President Thieu announced at the twentieth General Conference of the Asian People's Anti-Communist League what he considered to be a plan to bring lasting peace and economic prosperity to the region. He called for a conference of the ten Southeast Asian countries with also the possible participation of Australia, Japan, India, Taiwan, and Iran to "seek a way to establish a lasting peace and lay the foundations for constructive economic and cultural relations among the countries in this area". Significantly enough, North Vietnam was included in his invitation but not the PRC. The inclusion of the DRV and the exclusion of China were interpreted as an attempt by South Vietnam to isolate China by forming a united front with the other countries in the region against this Red giant. It was also thought to be an attempt to drive a wedge between North Vietnam and China. There has been no direct response from the invited countries to the suggestion, but considering the fact that most Southeast Asian countries are all much more anxious to build bridges with the PRC, President Thieu's suggestion may turn out to be a seed cast in the wind.

Conclusion

Looking back, 1974 was not a politically favourable year for South Vietnam. The government was plagued by problems from within and without the country. Watergate and the subsequent fall of President Nixon terminated the golden era of American aid. The policy of *détente*, a hostile U.S. Congress, and a general psychological abandonment of South Vietnam by the U.S. public were among factors which led to a substantial reduction in U.S. military and economic aid. Within the country, the regime was continually jostled by events which tended to destabilize the already precarious political situation. The notorious scandals, the campaign against official corruption, and the Cabinet reshuffles were among events which further eroded the regime's popular support. Worse still, even the Vietnamese Catholic Church, which had, from the beginning of the Republic, been the most important organizational pillar of the regime, began to show signs of possible desertion. In denouncing official corruption and appealing for national reconciliation, the Church seemed to indicate a new stand *vis-à-vis* the administration.

The task of crystal-ball gazing is a hazardous one. However, there is little indication that 1975 is going to be a good year for South Vietnam. The very same problems which afflicted the country during the past year — the persistent and debilitating war, widespread corruption, and administrative inefficiency — are still present. If anything, the deepening economic crisis would preclude the government's ability to deal effectively with these social, political, and military issues. It would appear then that the incipient opposition movement which had emerged by the end of 1974 would continue to grow and push the government to work towards reconciliation and peaceful coexistence with the PRG.

YEAR ONE OF POSTCOLONIAL VIETNAM

Huynh Kim Khanh

The year 1976 for Vietnam was the first since 1858 — a total of 117 years — that the country was entirely free of Western colonial intervention. During this first year of independence, the country had to face a multifaceted challenge: that of bringing back national unity (disrupted since 1862), repairing the massive physical destruction, and overcoming the economic, cultural and social dislocations that had occurred during the Thirty-Year War (1945–75). Beyond these immediate problems, the first year of peace was also one when the foundations were laid for the country's future ideological, economic and institutional structure and for its self-assertion in international affairs. In more specific terms, 1976 was a year of hectic transitional activities which included the administrative restructuring of the country, nationwide elections for a National Assembly of the reintegrated country, a new formal name for the country ("The Socialist Republic of Vietnam"), and planned industrial and agricultural transformations designed to give the country a foundation for rapid economic and social development.

This article attempts to review the principal aspects of Vietnam's public life during 1976. This is done while recognizing the hazards of such an undertaking. Aside from the risks inherent in "instant history" — in effecting from afar a year-end review of the development process of any society — there are special problems awaiting those who study contemporary Vietnam. Most of these problems are associated with the fact that Vietnam, unlike other societies, is a divided country in the process of becoming one. While it is true that formally and

---

Reprinted from Huynh Kim Khanh, ed., *Southeast Asian Affairs 1977* (Singapore: Institute of Southeast Asian Studies, 1977), pp. 287–305. At the time of original publication, Huynh Kim Khanh was Senior Research Officer at the Institute of Southeast Asian Studies, Singapore.

juridically the country was reintegrated on the State plane during 1976, due to long years of partition and especially the difference in the socio-political regimes that governed the two regions, the reality of the existence of the two zones remains vivid. This could be observed in the post-war reconstruction efforts and in the transformations of the social, economic and institutional aspects of each zone. The North, as we shall see momentarily, greatly suffered from the war in material terms (far more than the South in many ways, due to the massive terroristic bombings); yet, it has the advantage of a stable political, social and economic structure and an experienced leadership. Thus, except for the accelerated pace of activities, for the northern zone, 1976 was a year of *economic* reconstruction on the basis of a firm social and political structure. It is in what was formerly "Free Vietnam" (south of the 17th Parallel) that a true "revolutionary process" was taking place, not only affecting the socio-politico-economic institutions but also upturning the daily life of the people. Twenty years of American occupation, misleadership by Vietnamese *collaborateurs* and wartime activities leave a legacy of corruption, mismanagement and a general social and economic *malaise*. The problem in South Vietnam in 1976 involved more than just "healing the wounds of war" or economic reconstruction; it entailed no less than a radical reconversion of the socio-economic structure and political values of the people, making it possible for the southern zone to be fully integrated in the planned development of the entire country. All considered, to review at this stage the developments in Vietnam as one country is to expose oneself to the hazards of probable misrepresentations; these, however, are risks that are not avoidable.

War Damages

In addition to whatever long-term aspirations, the "healing of the wounds of war" was among the principal concerns of the new Vietnam throughout the second half of 1975 and the whole of 1976. Most of these "wounds" — material damage and socio-economic dislocations, let alone political and value distortions — with which today's Vietnamese concern themselves are the products of the U.S. phase (1954–75) of the Thirty-Year War (1945–75). In fact the most extensive damages to Vietnam occurred during the period between the massive introduction of American armed forces and the concomitant massive aerial bombardment from 1965 until the signing of the Paris Peace Agreements in January 1973. During this period, several types of war were conducted in Vietnam, often simultaneously. The types of damages which occurred followed the types of war conducted. For instance, the war in *North Vietnam* was for the most part an *air war of destruction*. The damages, in this case, largely involved the material infrastructure of North Vietnam: railroads, industrial yards, bridges, factories, power stations, dams, schools, and in the latter months of the war, dykes and hospitals. During the same period, however, three types of war were being conducted more or less simultaneously in *South Vietnam*: a *guerilla war* in the populated rural area; a *conventional war* (air, sea, ground-pitched combats) largely away from populated areas; and a *chemical war*, designed to deny food supplies and cover to the "enemy", conducted in the areas beyond the effective control of the U.S.-Thieu régime. The damages, in this case, involved not so much the man-made material infrastructure as the ecological balance of South Vietnam. Also an untold amount of social and economic dislocations in Vietnamese society must be attributed to the "forced urbanization" programme, which, designed to drain the support base of the guerilla, forced the peasants to move into urban areas.

Most of the material damages could be attributed to an unusually large amount of munitions expended by both sides, especially by the U.S. and its "allies". Although no information is available on the amount of munitions used by the Vietnamese side, we do have official figures for the American side of the war. According to U.S. Department of Defence (DoD) figures, between 1965 and 1972 the U.S. expended 7,403,610 tons of bombs in Indochina. This figure is the approximate equivalent of *three times* the amount of bombs dropped in *all war theatres* throughout World War II. If we add to this figure the tonnage of munitions expended in ground and sea actions, the total comes to 15,056,403 tons.[1] It is worth noting that these figures were recorded almost three years before the end of the fighting. In addition to the munitions expended, the U.S. armed forces sprayed between 1962 and 1970 approximately 19,000,000 gallons of chemical agents (herbicides and defoliants) on 5.7 million acres or one-seventh of the South Vietnamese land mass. This chemical warfare was designed to strip away foliage in areas believed to be occupied by North Vietnamese or Viet Cong troops. Noxious chemicals were also used for the destruction of crops, particularly in the Central Highlands, in the "food denial" campaigns.

Putting aside the extent of war casualties,[2] the wounds of war which most likely affect Vietnam's rehabilitation programmes involved almost every aspect of Vietnamese economic and social life. According to the Report of the United Nations Mission to Vietnam (March 1976), the U.S. bombing strikes and artillery barrages virtually wiped out the North Vietnamese infrastructure of transport, agriculture, industry, communications and fisheries. All railway systems were damaged, with many completely destroyed, including stations and warehouses. "Practically all the *bridges*, in particular the large and medium-sized ones on the Hanoi–Lang Son and Hanoi–Vinh lines, were destroyed, often five to seven times in succession (after being provisionally repaired)" (p. 32).[3] Except for the large Red River dyke near Hanoi, a substantial number of water control and dyke systems were destroyed: "183 dams and canal areas and 884 water installations were hit" (p. 16). "Thousands of villages [were] damaged, about 1,000 devastated and several dozens completely destroyed. Practically all the provincial capitals of North Vietnam (29 out of 30) were damaged and nine of them were completely destroyed." (p. 6) The situation in the South, according to this Report, appears to be less unfavourable. The marks of destruction on bridges, roads, railways and houses appear to be those of sabotage rather than bombings. Herbicide damage, however, created a large number of "blank zones", where all vegetation was ruined by defoliants (p. 6). In this connection, a report of a similar character indicated that one-fifth of South Vietnam's forests, including the most valuable timber land, had been sprayed with defoliants.

> As a result, some 62 billion board feet of valuable timber are estimated to have been destroyed. This represents South Vietnam's entire domestic needs, based on current demands, for the next 31 years. The trees must be replanted, and if nothing drastic has happened to the soil, then it may take

anywhere from five years for the fruit trees to a century or so for the rare timber trees to become productive again. (Le Anh Tu, "Vietnam: The Legacy of the War" (Philadelphia, 1976); reprinted in *Indochina Chronicle*, May–June 1976).

Urgent measures to rehabilitate the country were undertaken by the Vietnamese authorities as soon as the war ended in April 1975. Here again a distinction should be made between the postwar reconstruction efforts in the North and those in the southern zone.

Reconstruction in the North

In actual wartime activities affecting the country, the war ended in North Vietnam more than two years earlier than in the South. The last major wartime event in North Vietnam took place in late December 1972, when, in a futile attempt to force a change in the terms of the tentative Paris Peace Agreement, the Nixon-Kissinger Administration unleashed a twelve-day-long saturation bombing of Hanoi, Haiphong and other northern cities by its fearsome B-52 armada. While the war continued in the South, at a slower pace, there had been no warfare in North Vietnam as of the signing of the Paris Peace Agreement in January 1973. Thus, by the time peace came to South Vietnam in April 1975, North Vietnam had almost completed its three-year postwar reconstruction plan (1973–75).

Healing War Wounds in the South

Postwar rehabilitation and reconstruction in South Vietnam during the last twenty months was far more complicated than that in the North in fundamental ways. It involved resolving a wide range of problems — practical, institutional and ideological — of an almost unbelievable magnitude. While in the North, Herculean efforts were required to replace damaged or destroyed material installations and then to develop them according to accepted principles, procedures and institutions, it is not possible to talk of rehabilitation or reconstruction in the South in similar terms. What was required in the South was the founding, if not to say creation, of a totally new polity on the basis of the ruins of an old socio-political régime built upon concepts and standards diametrically opposed to revolutionary change. This was considered and expected officially as a necessity, if Vietnam were to advance as an integrated society. This was also the greatest challenge that faced the Vietnamese authorities during the last twenty months.

The legacy of the U.S.-Thieu régime was an economic and social *malaise* of unknown proportion: an economy that was on the verge of bankruptcy; a threatening famine in the northern provinces of Central Vietnam; more than three million unemployed people, excluding an army of a half-million prostitutes about to be out of work; six to seven million refugees who had been forced by wartime activities to flee their native villages into the cities; etc. The lightning collapse of the Saigon politico-administrative house of cards, which had been propped up for twenty years with American money, weapons and 500,000 U.S. troops, made possible a rapid takeover but also meant the necessity to create an administrative apparatus to govern the country. To have to provide administration quite suddenly to an additional two-thirds of the territory and over twenty million people (before April 1975 the PRG controlled over less than 30% of the land and about 10% of the population of the South) was a difficult task, especially when an overwhelming majority of *the best* PRG administrative and political cadres had been eliminated in the aftermath of the Winter-Spring (*Tet*) Offensive of 1968 and as a consequence of the CIA-sponsored Phoenix Programme.

Beyond these practical and institutional problems are psycho-ideological problems that must be overcome. In the wake of liberation, the "winning over of the hearts and minds" of the people and their ideological remoulding have been and continue to be the most difficult challenge to the Vietnamese authorities. Contrary to what Hanoi wanted themselves and the world to believe in the early days after liberation, in general the South Vietnamese population did *not* welcome the revolutionary forces with outstretched arms. Everyone was relieved that the war was over and few, if anyone, with the possible exception of some corrupted generals, regretted the passing of the old régime. This, however, was not translated into an enthusiastic reception for the revolutionary régime (a French report at the time indicated that roughly one-third of the people of Saigon appeared to have welcomed the arrival of the revolutionary forces, while the rest were either apathetic, fearful or hostile). Had it been so, the difficulties for the new régime would have been greatly reduced — and so would the extent of its accomplishments to date, In fact, if anything, the Provisional Revolutionary Government (PRG) forces did not enter into an empty ideological house either. Except for a very small minority of the South Vietnamese population (possibly 15% to 20%) who had had previous contact with "the other side" and possibly thought they could live with them, for most people the "Viêt Công" was an unknown quantity and most therefore were apprehensive of, and some hostile to, the new régime. There were in South Vietnam at the time of liberation about 2,000,000 Catholics (among the most retrogressive Catholics in the world), 1,500,000 supposedly anticommunist members of the Hoa Hao religious sect, 1,100,000 South Vietnamese troops, and approximately 2,000,000 members of the police, civil guards, militia, administrative officials, etc. That is to say, in April 1975, virtually every South Vietnamese family had some members who were involved with the former régime in some capacity and otherwise had some good reasons to be suspicious of the "Viêt Côngs".

As the PRG assumed power in May 1975, it had immediately to tackle a wide range of problems. It had first to assure the population that the revolution meant to bring about national reconciliation and not further division, and the myth of the "bloodbath" disseminated by American propaganda was just that — a myth. [Everywhere they went during the first weeks of May 1975, Saigonese were treated with well-trained and more or less mechanical smiles from the youthful *bo-doi giai phong* (liberation soldiers).] But aside from the winning over of men's hearts and minds, the work which was considered as of highest priority included, first, the provision of sufficient food for the population and the finding of gainful work for the unemployed. Food shortage had been a serious problem. During the last ten years or so of the U.S. occupation, South Vietnam had every year to import 300,000 to 700,000 tons of foodstuffs. The immediate task, especially given the confusion in the South during the last two moments of the War, was that of averting a probable famine. Unemployment was another serious problem which could have social and political ramifications and had to be dealt with urgently. Peasants displaced in the U.S.-Thieu "forced urbanization" schemes, refugees, former soldiers of the *collaborateur* armed forces, office workers and labourers temporarily out of jobs made up about 3 million people, not counting approximately 5 million family members dependent on them. A third immediate priority was the reestablishment of communications facilities (roads, railroads, bridges, etc.) for transporting the people to their home villages or to be resettled, the family members to be reunited, the means of production to rural areas, and the agricultural products to be brought into cities. These spheres were considered by the Vietnamese authorities as of overriding urgency in their attempts to heal the wounds of war.

In order to cope with the difficulties just mentioned, the Vietnamese authorities decided to give absolute priority to the rehabilitation of agriculture and the improvement of crop production in the *immediate future*. The authorities decided upon a two-pronged programme: the encouraging of displaced peasants to return to their native villages and the creation of "new economic zones" (*vùng Kinh-tê mới*) for the systematic resettlement in specified rural areas of unemployed people, military and civilian personnel of the former régime and those who prefer to be resettled. By this operation, the authorities hoped to resettle in the rural areas in the short-term approximately 2.5 million people who would reclaim for agricultural production 500,000 hectares of land abandoned because of warfare.

In addition to the specifically economic tasks just reviewed, there was a plethora of war-related social problems that must be attended to. Among the legacy of the former régime is a population of 60% illiterates (as compared to 3% in North Vietnam), about three million cases of venereal disease, 450,000 to 500,000 prostitutes, half-a-million drug addicts, and corruption in every sphere of life. These wounds of war had to be healed during the first months after liberation. A literacy campaign which was begun in June 1975 continued throughout 1976. In addition to the official objective of eradicating the "bandit of ignorance" (*giác dôt*), the campaign was also part of the political mobilization of the people. For the treatment of V.D. (suspected to be "made in U.S.A."), there was established a Center for Treatment of Venereal Disease and Skin Diseases in Saigon. Drug addiction is another serious problem. Estimates of the number of drug addicts range anywhere between 100,000 (Indochina Resource Center) and 500,000 (U.N. Report). Instead of penalizing drug addicts, as did the former régime, the new authorities opened an experimental rehabilitation centre. There is no available figure on the number of cured addicts, but it has been accepted generally that a great deal of progress has been made in this area.

How did South Vietnam fare in its efforts in "healing the wounds of war"? Although the picture is far from entirely clear in all its details, in general, and given the multitude and magnitude of the problems that it faced on 30 April 1975, the country did very well indeed. This appears to be the consensus of foreign observers and this is also the picture that emerges from a careful reading of Saigon's two daily newspapers— *Saigon Giai Phong* (Liberated Saigon) and *Tin Sang* (Morning News), the latter is a nongovernmental newspaper published by Ngo Cong Duc, formerly a Third Force leader and a member of the National Assembly in the former régime. This is not to say that all the postwar problems have been solved, or that everything has gone well, or that life has been easy. While it is true that nowhere in South Vietnam has famine occurred, life, especially urban life, has been much more difficult since liberation. Salaries are much lower than before liberation, but the costs of living have become much higher. [On 16 August 1976 the Prime Minister's Office published a decree determining the salary régime for a more equitable distribution of income — that would make the basic salary of a highest paid person (for example, a Government Minister) approximately four times the lowest (for example, an unskilled worker. An unskilled worker earns about 42 dong monthly.)] There are still approximately one million unemployed people in Saigon alone as of September. While it is true that in general revolutionary cadres have maintained a high standard of discipline, not a small number have fallen victim to the temptations of the "decadent bourgeois way of life" that was Saigon. There are well-known incidents of cadres accepting bribes or even joining in schemes of extortion. Other cadres gave work to unemployed prostitutes (perhaps out of humanity?). (*Le Monde* reported that northern cadres who stayed at Hotel Miramar in Saigon were entertained by prostitutes who lived in the Hotel.) Let us now review the results of postwar rehabilitation in the South.

Probably the greatest accomplishment of the new authorities, aside from averting a famine, was its ability to provide security. This was no easy task as it may appear. While it is true that at the time of the liberation, the *collaborateur* armed forces were in disarray, it is worth recalling that there were at the time 1,100,000 South Vietnamese (ARVN) troops who were much more numerous and better armed than their adversaries (the ratio for men was 3:1 and the weapons ratio was 10:1 in favour of ARVN). How to control and reeducate these people, making them accept the authority of their former enemies, was a difficult task. About 1,000,000 ARVN troops, including 40,000 officers were registered and controlled. While common soldiers were allowed to go home to their families and to attend sessions of *hoc tap cai tao* (reform education) for three days like civilian adults, officers were sent to reeducation camps where they are kept under the watchful eyes of revolutionary cadres while they internalize revolutionary concepts and learn a profession for future employment. At the time of this writing, it is reported that with a few exceptions, all former military officers with the rank of captain and above are still under detention. While an occasional act of sabotage and a few sniping incidents still take place, there is no question as to the internal security in South Vietnam.

No less outstanding an accomplishment was the new régime's ability to get along with South Vietnamese Catholics. This is a community of over 2,000,000 Christians, well-known for their anticommunism and religious conservatism. More than half of the Church's membership derived from the 800,000 Catholics who left North Vietnam in 1954, having sided with the French in the Franco-Vietnamese War (1946–54). Around 1964 and 1965 when it appeared as if the communists could take over South Vietnam, several Catholic leaders openly talked of developing a resistance base, or else evacuating the entire Catholic community abroad. So conservative is the Church that its hierarchy refuses to distribute to

Christians important encyclicals, such as *Pacem in Terris, Mater et Magistra and Populorum Progressio*, all of which represent the modern, "progressive" trend in the Holy See since Vatican II. Yet, the Vietnamese Church appears to have acquiesced in, although not to say supported, the rule of the new régime. This has taken place despite the government's decision to nationalize all private schools and hospitals (before April 1975, the Church owned 435 health and charitable institutions, 1,060 elementary schools, 145 secondary schools and 2 universities) and to dissolve the 500,000-member Catholic Workers' Union. When on 13 February 1976 an armed rebellion, the only outbreak of organized resistance known thus far, was led by Father Nguyen Quang Minh and based at the Vinh Son Church in Saigon, the Church under the leadership of Archbishop Nguyen van Binh, rallied to the régime.

The trend toward reconciliation between the Church and the communist régime improved when it became known that, contrary to popular opinion, freedom of worship is respected in the North, where the number of Catholics had doubled since 1954. This was vividly testified to when in August Archbishop Trinh Nhu Khue of Hanoi travelled to the Vatican to be consecrated as Cardinal, the only Cardinal in all of Vietnam. Late in the summer Archbishop Nguyen van Binh of Saigon journeyed to Hanoi and had friendly discussions with the communist authorities. Although widespread mutual suspicion continued to exist, the government hopes that a "silent church" will not be developed in Vietnam.

Next to these accomplishments in neutralizing possible opposition, the government has made important progress in preparing for social and economic development. The development of the "new economic zones" (*vùng Kinh-tê mới*) was more than just a temporary measure designed to relieve the urban areas of population pressure; rather, it is part of a long-term programme to rationally redistribute the population throughout the country. In its serial study on the new economic areas, from 18 to 24 September, the daily *Saigon Giai Phong* claimed that by the end of August 1976, 600,000 people *from Saigon alone* had gone to the new economic areas. Radio Hanoi reported on 6 December 1976 that 60% of the population of the city of Danang had on Liberation Day been resettled. Other cities such as Hue, Nha Trang, Can Tho, etc. had also resettled "tens of thousands" of persons. In the prospectus of the Second Five-Year Plan (1976–80), read by Prime Minister Pham van Dong at the Fourth Congress of the Vietnam Workers' Party (now the Communist Party of Vietnam), the government called for a further resettlement of four million people during the next four years in order to reclaim 1,000,000 hectares of virgin land which will be used in specific crops and plantations. (This would entail mainly the resettlement of crowded communities of the Red River Delta in North Vietnam in the higher, mountainous regions of the North West and those in the Central Highlands in Central Vietnam.)

Life has not been easy for the settlers, to say the least, during the first year in the new economic zones. Despite the government's promise of land and a house with a well in the new land, settlers in the early days often found their land consisted of scrubby soil which had been left unused for several years, and their "house", two flimsy thatched roofs perched precariously on a few poles. The "well" was often a shallow hole in the ground. Worse, mines left behind by the war resulted in casualties sometimes. (In this connection, Viêt Công mines designed for non-discovery often proved to be more deadly than "Allied" mines.) The government claimed that those were instances of the past, when due to the confusion of the situation contractors had taken advantage of the government's liberal policies and when preparations were less than adequate. Settlers who came to the new economic areas in the last six months apparently fared better, since the organization of the administration in the South had improved, and the régime wanted to do away with the bad image of the new settlements. Also, thanks to the rich soil and favourable climate of the South, those who had settled earlier already reaped the benefit of their cash crops (potatoes, beans, cauliflowers, etc.).

Postwar rehabilitation and transformation in the educational field have also registered great progress. To ensure that the socialization process is a monopoly of the State, all private schools were nationalized immediately following liberation. All former schools have been reopened, and new schools have been created, particularly in the new economic zones and rural areas, which were formerly neglected. For the 1976–77 school year, over four million students have registered in nearly 10,000 general schools throughout South Vietnam. They are given free education and provided with free textbooks by the State. Saigon, which hopes to eradicate illiteracy by the end of 1977, for the first time ever opened "hundreds of" nurseries and kindergartens for children of the poorer districts. Higher education is also reorganized. In the past, more than half the university students registered in the Faculties of Law and Letters. The new régime closed down the Faculty of Law for a time (it was reopened in September 1976, though not for teaching law, but economic development) and drastically reduced the number of students in literature and the arts. According to *Saigon Giai Phong* (26 September 1976), over 40,000 sat for college entrance examinations to enter Saigon's 11 colleges this school year. Seven other universities and colleges also reopened their doors: four in the Hue-Danang region, one in Nha Trang (oceanography), one in Can Tho and one in Dalat.

The régime has also tried to deal with an unexpected, yet apparently proved to be most serious, problem that had occurred since liberation, that is, corruption and bureaucratism among revolutionary cadres. In the few months following liberation, the population of Saigon was astonished beyond belief to discover that there were among the supposedly puritanical and morally upright communist cadres those who willingly accepted bribes or demanded them. Others appeared to enjoy vices normally thought to be a monopoly of capitalists. Still others appeared to be arrogant, bureaucratic, causing a great deal of inconvenience to the population. Throughout the first half of the year, the Party and government leadership made a determined effort to eliminate the "bad elements" from the official ranks. It was discovered that in addition to cadres and officials who had "changed their nature" (*biên chât*) and became corrupted (*hu hoá*), the officials' ranks had been infiltrated by what was popularly called "the 304th Division". This is a reference to those who styled themselves "revolutionaries" and joined the loosely-structured "people's committees" in the early days after liberation. To the chagrin of the communist authorities, some were discovered later to be former "cowboys" (hoodlums) or even former CIA agents. [304 stands for 30 April. The 308th Division is the best known infantry ("steel") division in the Vietnam People's Army. It played an important role in the Dien Bien Phu and also Ho Chi Minh campaigns.]

Using methods which had been proved effective in the North, the government decided to unleash the population against corrupted officials. The people were encouraged to report to the government cases of official corruption, extortion, etc. Arrests, trials, and jail sentences of officials and cadres (including the Head of the Provincial Office of the Foreign Trade Department in Danang) were widely publicized. Finally the government decided to reorganize the "people's committees", following an intensive investigation and elimination of corrupted cadres. In Saigon, for instance, the government organized a kind of "group therapy" (the cathartic type) sessions — a five-day (14–18 August 1976) "Conference to Evaluate the Régime" (*Hoi nghi Kiem diem Chinh quyen*) throughout the various districts of the City, at which the public openly denounced corrupted and otherwise inefficient officials. As a consequence of this Conference, the entire People's Administrative Committee for the Fifth District, governing Cholon (Saigon's Chinatown), were incarcerated. Also new "people's administrative committees" were set up throughout the City (*Saigon Giai Phong*, 19 August 1976). The confidence that the new authorities had in the people, as expressed in its appeal to the people to help clean its own ranks, should be taken as an indication of strength and self-confidence. It is, in any case, a far cry from the days, twenty months earlier, when barbed wired barricades, tear gas and riot police symbolized the relationship between the government and the people.

In this brief review an attempt has been made to present the different dimensions of the rehabilitation of a devastated country. For reasons of lack of space I have refrained from describing in detail some of the "spectaculars", for example, the completion on 4 December of the Thong Nhat Railway (Hanoi–Ho Chi Minh City), the basic completion of the hydraulic works in the South, irrigating an additional 500,000 hectares, the resumption of foreign trade, etc. I have chosen to emphasize the political and administrative aspects, and some of the "human" dimensions, of rehabilitation; for ultimately the success or failure of a revolution depends on these dimensions. Only the future can tell whether and to what extent the Vietnamese communist authorities have succeeded in eliminating deficiencies and attaining their ambitious projected goals.

National Unity and Socialism

No less important an event than postwar rehabilitation was the decision by the VWP Political Bureau, made at its Plenum held in September 1975, to effect national reunification at the level of state institutions as soon as practicable and for the South to embark immediately on "socialist construction", bypassing a transitional stage generally thought to be necessary. This was a bold step and no doubt the most important decision made for Vietnam in several decades. While healing war wounds was the immediate and concrete task, the two issues of when and how to reunify the country and to bring about socialism for the entire country are of long-term significance. Yet, at the threshold of the attainment of such ideals, the Vietnamese leadership discovered pitfalls ahead on the road to completion of unity and socialism.

Given the particular situation of Vietnam at the time of liberation, and the ideological constraints of the Party, the decision on these twin issues was thus fraught with risks and uncertainties.

During the months immediately following total liberation, the VWP leadership was confronted with several practical and ideologically-derived considerations on Vietnam's future. In practical terms, although there was no longer any question about the fact of one Vietnam, yet a decision had to be made on the *timing* and *modalities* to effect the forms of national reunification. The entire country was now governed by the decisions of one centralized revolutionary party, the Vietnam Workers' Party, and under the effective military control of one armed forces, the People's Army of Vietnam, also under the command of the Party. Yet, in juridical and symbolic terms, even after liberation, the country was still divided into two states and ruled by two separate governments.

While it was desirable for such an anomaly to be resolved as rapidly as practicable, the advantages and disadvantages of a rapid reunification had to be carefully balanced against one another. There appeared to be no unanimity within the Vietnamese leadership on this issue. Despite the ultimate decision for a rapid reunification, there existed cogent arguments based on practical considerations for a more gradual process and for a temporary preservation of two separate states for some years. In fact there had been an official policy for a gradual reunification of the country following liberation. The South Vietnam National Front for Liberation and, later on the PRG, had advocated the establishment of a democratic and nonaligned state in South Vietnam which would retain a separate political identity from the North until such time when reunification could be effected by peaceful means. In this formulation, national reunification could take place gradually over a period of twelve to fourteen years. During this interim period there would be one country but two states, governed separately until reunification. It was thought that such an arrangement would be beneficial to Vietnam in many ways. In terms of internal Vietnamese politics, it was thought that a gradual reunification might serve to minimize the risks of offending southern sensitivities and allow an orderly phasing out of potential organized opposition among the southern population. It would also permit the South a period to prepare the people's mental mould and to overhaul its socio-economic institutions and political apparatus for an eventual reunification.

The VWP was also confronted with awkward ideological considerations in its desire to effect a rapid reunification of the country. Although in terms of Vietnamese history, the total liberation of the country represented a clearcut beginning of a new historical period, this is not the case in the ideologically inspired explanation for the process of the Vietnamese revolution. The liberation of the South did not automatically signify the completion of the "revolutionary tasks" of a certain designated historical phase.

Should the Party and Government leadership try to integrate in the immediate future an essentially "semifeudalist" and "compradore bourgeois" economy of the South with the socialist, largely state-owned, state-controlled, and state-managed economic system of the North? Chairman Truong Chinh raised this question in his Political Report to the Consultative Conference,

At present, when it [South Vietnam] has been completely liberated, should South Vietnam limit itself within the people's national democratic revolution for a period of time before embarking on the socialist revolution and socialist construction?

And, reflecting the collective opinion of the VWP leadership, he answered his own question

> I think that is not necessary. The great victory of the general offensive and uprising in Spring this year has put a victorious end to that phase of the people's national democratic revolution in South Vietnam and opened up for the South Vietnamese people a new phase of revolution with a new strategic task, that of socialist revolution.

Chairman Truong Chinh also offered the official explanation as to why re-unification should be effected sooner and not later. Immediate reunification should be effected because the two zones had "essential and decisive similarities, whereas differences are conditional and temporary." Among the essential similarities cited by Chairman Truong Chinh are the following elements: one "single and genuine Marxist Leninist party" which had "always led the revolutionary cause of our people in both zones" in the last forty-five years; a national united front in each zone which is based on the worker-peasant alliance; a people's armed forces in each zone, comprising three different categories: the regular army, the regional army and the militia and homeguards; and a revolutionary administration in its zone with its own security forces. This explanation, while having its merits, fails to satisfy queries as to the felt need for *immediate* reunification.

It appeared that the decision to reunify the country so soon following liberation was made out of expediency and was partly necessitated by the situation in the South. Also it was a difficult decision made by an experienced leadership, which, after carefully weighing various alternatives, saw both opportunities and risks and little choice but to make such a decision. The absence of an organized opposition in the South to a communist take-over appeared to be one reason. The coalition government envisioned in the earlier official communist policy had been predicated upon possible vigorous opposition by noncommunist or anticommunist groups (the Catholic Church, the Hoa Hao, the Cao Dai religious sects, the anticommunist parties, etc.) to a rapid reintegration of South Vietnam with the North. Such an opposition never materialized. The communist authorities also wanted to take advantage of the momentum of events and the psychological preparedness of the southern population to accept radical changes in the aftermath of the precipitous collapse of the U.S.-Thieu régime. In this connection, a separate southern régime may after a few years develop its own jealously guarded independence and may cause future difficulties for national reintegration.

A third factor had to do with the insufficiency of southern cadres to handle political-administrative and socio-economic chores. A great number of southern cadres had been eliminated in the aftermath of the *Tet* Offensive of 1968 (Radio "*Giai Phong*" [Liberation], Saigon on 15 January 1976 reported on this problem: "where we had 30 comrades, there were 2 or 3 left; in places where we had 100 cells, there were left 5 or 6.") Several of the survivors were killed in the CIA-operated Phoenix Programme (which the former Saigon régime officially claimed was responsible for the death of 27,000 Viet Cong cadres).

The problem of southern sensitivities would have proved to be much worse, had there been a separate southern state which were staffed principally by northern cadres. In this connection, it is difficult to believe that the Vietnamese authorities would have sufficient staff members to man two separate diplomatic staffs, trade missions, etc. in over ninety countries which would have recognized both regimes, short as they are of trained personnel.

Finally, one should not discount the "human" factor. The age of the VWP leaders may have something to do with the decision. It is not totally unimaginable that the ageing revolutionary leaders of Vietnam (average age: 68) would like to witness the realization of the political dreams and completion of the ideals for which they have devoted their entire adulthood (virtually all the top-level leaders of the VWP joined the revolutionary movement around the years 1926 to 1929 when several were about 17 to 19 years old).

Vietnam Is One

On 2 July 1976 the newly reunified Vietnamese state was officially founded. The National Assembly unanimously adopted resolutions of symbolic importance to the country:

1. "Vietnam is an independent, unified and socialist country, bearing the name of The Socialist Republic of Vietnam.
2. The National flag ... has a red background with a five-point gold star in the middle.
3. The national emblem ... is round-shaped with a red background, a gold star in the middle, two sheaves of rice on either side, half a cogwheel and the inscription 'Socialist Republic of Vietnam'.
4. The capital city ... is Hanoi.
5. The national anthem ... is the song *Tien Quan Ca* [March to the Front]."

The National Assembly also elected the national leaders of Vietnam. Ton Duc Thang, formerly President of the Democratic Republic of Vietnam, was elected President of the newly founded Socialist Republic. Nguyen Luong Bang, formerly Vice-President of the DRV, was elected Vice-President. Nguyen Huu Tho, formerly President of the Advisory Council of the PRG, was also elected Vice-President. Truong Chinh, formerly Chairman of the Standing Committee of the DRV National Assembly was elected Chairman of the new Standing Committee of the National Assembly. Pham van Dong formerly Prime Minister of the DRV, was elected Prime Minister of the Government of the new Socialist Republic. As its plenary session on the following day, 3 July 1975, the National Assembly approved the list of the members of the Government Council (Cabinet) presented by Premier Dong. This list includes seven Deputy Prime Ministers: Pham Hung (South), Huynh Tan Phat (South), Vo Nguyen Giap (Centre), Nguyen Duy Trinh (?) Le Thanh Nghi (North), Vo Chi Cong (South), Do Muoi (North). Five of these Deputy Premiers also cumulate ministerial posts. The list includes thirty-six members of the Government Council who hold ministerial or equivalent posts. The process of national reunification in Vietnam was thus officially concluded. Also, the process of building Vietnam as a socialist state was thus begun.

Conclusion

1976 was a difficult but purposeful year for Vietnam. By deliberate choice, the leaders and people of Vietnam doubled their efforts in rebuilding a wartorn country and in building a foundation for a rapid socio-economic development which, they hoped, would permit them to escape from the conditions of underdevelopment in a relatively brief period of time. It was also a year in which the Vietnamese had to create a new political structure for the reunified country. In retrospect, it is possible to say that the Vietnamese could justifiably be satisfied with the accomplishments in postwar rehabilitation to date. (And this had been repeatedly expressed in year-end messages by leaders such as Ton Duc Thang, Pham van Dong, Le Duan, etc.) Yet the road ahead for them appears full of pitfalls — most of these are not related to either the ambitious plans of development, or the apparatus for the attainment of the objectives of such plans, but have to do with the character of those who man them. It appears, judging by the accelerated pace of activities during the past year, that the Vietnamese have succeeded in part to build a firm foundation for future economic expansion and social progress. Yet, the goals of the triple revolutions that they have set out for themselves appear to be still beyond their grasp. Only in the future can anyone fairly say whether the self-confidence and optimism of the Vietnamese in their future prospects are justified.

Notes

1. We have the following figures from DoD for the period 1965–72 (as of 30 November 1972:

Year	Air	Ground	Sea	Total
1965	315,000	—	—	315,000
1966	512,000	590,177	5,000	1,107,177
1967	932,763	1,203,530	30,000	2,166,293
1968	1,431,645	1,484,403	50,500	2,966,548
1969	1,387,237	1,405,823	30,000	2,823,060
1970	977,446	1,181,534	13,000	2,171,980
1971	763,160	832,968	5,293	1,601,421
1972	1,084,359	805,565	15,500	1,905,424**
1965–72	7,403,610	7,504,000	149,293	15,056,403*

* through November 30
** through June 30

Source: Department of Defence; reprinted in "A Statistical Fact Sheet on the Indochina War," February 1973, by the Indochina Resource Centre, Washington, D.C.

2. In February 1973, the Indochina Resource Center, using statistics provided by DoD and the Saigon Army (ARVN), arrived at the following table of "Estimated Casualties in South Vietnam":

	U.S. (hostile and non-hostile)	South Vietnam	Third Country	Enemy	Civilian	Total
Killed	56,244	195,137	5,221	927,124	415,000	1,598,726
Wounded	303,635	495,931	11,880	1,390,686	935,000	2,202,132
Total						3,800,858

It is worth noting that war ended two years after the estimates above were made. Also, the figures do not include casualties in North Vietnam.

3. In this connection, Harold Brown, formerly U.S. Secretary of the Air Force and currently Secretary of Defence, is reported to have claimed that in the first half of 1966 alone, the U.S. Air Force destroyed 7,000 trucks, 3,000 railway cars, 5,000 bridges and 5,000 barges and boats in North Vietnam. In September 1966 alone, roads were cut at 600 points. "This," Secretary Brown added in his report, at that time, "is a serious degradation of the North Vietnamese logistical net." (William Greider, "Carter Chooses the Painful Past," *Washington Post*, 16 January 1977).

VIETNAM, ASEAN AND THE INDOCHINA REFUGEE CRISIS*

Frank Frost

The problems posed by the exodus of people from Indochina were of critical concern to all the Association of Southeast Asian Nations (ASEAN) members in 1979. Thailand, the first ASEAN state to be seriously affected by the post-1975 outflow, had had to receive tens of thousands of overland refugees, primarily from Laos. By comparison with the influx from Laos into Thailand, the scale of the outflow from Vietnam in the first three years after 1975 was relatively small; about 35,000 "boat people" had arrived in ASEAN states by mid-1978. After mid-1978, however, the serious refugee situation in Southeast Asia was aggravated further by a mass departure of people from Vietnam, in a process that became the focus of worldwide attention and concern.

The exodus of Indochinese refugees after 1975 was, of course, only one instance of a series of movements of people in Southeast Asia in recent decades. Since World War II, there have been many such mass movements of people in the wake of political change and internal conflicts — movements which have occurred both within countries (most notably, the mass creation of refugees inside the Indochina states during the Second Indochina War), and between different states (the exodus of people, predominantly Catholics, from the northern to the southern zone in Vietnam in 1954, and the movement of Muslims from Southern Philippines to Sabah from the late 1960s and from Burma to Bangladesh in the late 1970s). All these population movements involved extensive social and economic disruption and human suffering. The Indochina refugee movements after 1975, however, became the focus of regional concern, and international attention

---

Reprinted from Leo Suryadinata, ed., *Southeast Asian Affairs 1980* (Singapore: Institute of Southeast Asian Studies, 1980), pp. 347–67. At the time of original publication, Frank Frost was a Legislative Research Specialist in the Commonwealth Parliamentary Library, Canberra.

and diplomatic activity of a kind not directed towards other refugee situations in Southeast Asia in recent years.

Partly a result of the legacy of thirty years of conflict and partly stemming from internal policies pursued by the Indochina states and from the tensions generated by the Sino-Vietnamese conflict, the Indochina refugee exodus has been a source of enormous human and political problems. For the refugees themselves, it has involved intense suffering and often death, particularly during the voyages in overcrowded boats across the often dangerous waters of the South China Sea. For the states receiving them, the refugees have been a source of political and often racial tension, a potential security threat, and an administrative and economic burden while they await resettlement. For the Indochina states, especially Vietnam, the refugee exodus may have alleviated some social and political tensions posed by unassimilable minority socio-economic and ethnic groups, but at the cost of international denunciation and widespread alienation and antipathy among neighbouring states. For the international community (especially the U.S., Western Europe, Canada and Australia), the refugees have challenged the capacities of "developed" states both to respond to the immediate humanitarian and political problems involved, and to try to contribute to developing policies that might produce long term solutions.

To assess the problems raised by the refugees for Southeast Asia, this article will focus on the stages and origins of the refugee outflows, the response of the ASEAN states in 1979 to both the boat and land refugees, and the impact of the crisis on ASEAN and on the prospects for regional security and détente.

Vietnam and the Refugee Exodus

The departure of people from Vietnam since 1975 can be seen as having taken place in five phases. The initial phase of the departures involved the evacuation by U.S. forces of 130,000 people just before the fall of Saigon (Ho Chi Minh City). A second phase from mid-1975 to early 1978 saw the arrival of a further 30,000 people in neighbouring states, in small boats after privately organized clandestine escapes (see Table 1). From early 1978 to the end of that year, a third phase saw the departure of over 200,000 ethnic Chinese from Vietnam to China and the arrival of over 60,000 Chinese and Vietnamese in the ASEAN states and Hong Kong by boat. After a falling-off in arrivals in January and February 1979, which coincided with the monsoon season, a fourth phase occurred after the Chinese invasion of Vietnam in February and March. By July 1979, a further 175,000 people had arrived in neighbouring states. A fifth phase was ushered in from mid-1979 as Vietnam agreed to a "moratorium" on the outflow and the numbers of boat people fell sharply to a level more like that experienced between 1975 and early 1978. Whether the most recent phase continues or is replaced by another resumption of mass departures is highly uncertain, as will be pointed out. It must also be noted that while the arrivals of boat people in neighbouring states can be accurately accounted for, the numbers leaving Vietnam were clearly greater, and there were many tragic cases of overloaded and ill-equipped boats sinking or landing in deserted areas where no supplies or help were available. While the estimates of a 50% casualty rate among boat refugees were probably exaggerated, there can be

TABLE 1
Numbers of People arriving by Boat in Southeast Asia and Hong Kong

1975	—		377
1976	—		5,248
1977	—		15,657
1978	—		85,544
1979	—	January —	8,954
		February —	5,737
		March —	11,157
		April —	26,600
		May —	51,550
		June —	56,941

Source: United Nations High Commissioner for Refugees (UNHCR).

no doubt that thousands of people lost their lives during the exodus: after examining the evidence, one estimate in late 1979 put the number of deaths at over 28,000 (see *Far Eastern Economic Review* or *FEER*, 26 October 1979).

The departures of such large numbers of people from Vietnam resulted from a variety of factors which it is useful to distinguish, even if in practice the factors often combined together to produce the pressure for individual people to leave. The factors included the socioeconomic and political problems of postwar Vietnam, the attempts of the government to reorganize southern society and to gain control of the economy, the conflict between Vietnam and Kampuchea, the tensions arising from the deterioration in Sino-Vietnamese relations and the impact of China's "punitive" invasion in February–March 1979, and the involvement, unofficially and officially, of elements of the Vietnamese Government.

Vietnam faced a host of problems after 1975. During the Second Indochina War, Vietnam's economic development in both the North and South was severely circumscribed and neither sector approached self-sufficiency. To its inherent problems of poverty and resource scarcity, however, were added dislocation and devastation on a staggering scale. In Southern Vietnam alone, about 16% of the population were killed or wounded during the war and 57% were made homeless between 1965 and 1974. Many roads and bridges were destroyed and agriculture was severely disrupted. Cities and towns had been swollen by internal refugees who gained employment primarily through the military machines and their service industries, or who lived unproductively from various types of foreign (primarily U.S.) economic assistance.

In such a war-torn and artificially developed society, the impact of the sudden end of the Thirty Years' War was inevitably dislocating and destabilizing. In the South, several million people found themselves unemployed, with the collapse of the noncommunist military machine and the service industry sector that had supported the U.S. involvement. In the North, the end of the war saw a perhaps inevitable slackening of tension and motivation and the releasing of pent-up demands for more basic necessities and consumer goods. Economic problems were accompanied by acute political problems, especially in the South. While some sectors of Southern society had a history of long term support for the communist cause, other sectors such as several minority religious groups (the Catholics, Hoa Hao and Cao Dai) and many urban dwellers had little sympathy for, and much suspicion of, the new communist authorities. These problems produced pressures which made some refugee departures likely. It is probably true to say that, even if the cadres of the Vietnam Communist Party (VCP) in the South had been willing and able to govern the divided Southern society in an entirely equitable and efficient manner, there would still have been great dissatisfaction among some sectors in the South (such as the Catholics and the Hoa Hao) who, by virtue of the collapse of the old regime, faced a decline in their degree of community autonomy and economic and political influence. In reality, as David Elliott eloquently pointed out in *Southeast Asian Affairs 1979*, the VCP had been gravely weakened in the South during the war and after 1975 had the greatest difficulty in trying to maintain an effective government in the North and develop one in the South: mismanagement and corruption were common problems. The immediate implications of the end of the war, then, provided one pressure for the development of a refugee outflow.

As the VCP attempted to organize the reunification and economic reconstruction of Vietnam after 1975, further pressures arose. The Fourth Party Congress in 1976 adopted an ambitious five year development plan emphasizing agriculture and light industry over heavy industry and involving a massive programme of population relocation to alleviate overcrowding and unemployment in urban areas and open up abandoned lands (in "new economic zones"). The total cost of the plan was estimated at US$7.5 billion, much of which was expected to come from foreign sources, including Vietnam's traditional allies, and Western countries and financial institutions with whom Vietnam's leaders were eagerly expanding relations. This ambitious economic plan began to founder almost immediately, undermined by a variety of problems including low morale, lack of raw materials, mismanagement, corruption and (especially after 1977) natural disasters and serious shortfalls in foreign assistance. The net result of these conditions was that, at the end of 1978, living conditions throughout Vietnam were about the same as they had been in the early 1960s, annual per capita income was US$140, the average daily calorie intake was 1,500, and unemployment remained at over 3,000,000.

Further problems arose as the VCP attempted to establish political authority and economic control in the South. Up until early 1978, the socialist Northern economy and the capitalist Southern economy coexisted uneasily. Although the VCP suffered from grave political and administrative weaknesses, it was decided to assert control over the Southern economy, particularly by abolishing the role of private traders and by collectivizing land ownership and cultivation. The abolition of the private trade in rice and other commodities was effected in March 1978 and 30,000 businesses, mostly Chinese-owned, were closed in Ho Chi Minh City alone. A subsequent sudden currency change had the effect of wiping out much of the profits and savings of these traders (although much wealth was held in gold). This policy left tens of thousands of people with a choice of either remaining in Vietnam with a greatly reduced social and economic status, possibly as farmers in "new economic zones", or leaving by boat. Many chose the latter course, and their departure ushered in the third and fourth stages of the Vietnam refugee crisis: the mass exodus from mid 1978 to mid 1979.

A third, closely related, source of pressure for refugee departures was the developing conflict between Vietnam and Democratic Kampuchea and the serious deterioration of Vietnam's relations with China. After 1975, Vietnam faced an increasingly tense situation in relations with the radical regime in Kampuchea. The scale of border clashes grew, particularly after the major Vietnamese incursions in October 1977. Diplomatic relations between the states were broken off at the end of 1977. The conflict with Kampuchea and its government's policies produced several major problems for Vietnam: farming settlements and new economic zones in border regions were disrupted, Vietnam had to accommodate over 150,000 Kampuchean and Vietnamese refugees, and the renewal of military mobilization and the expansion of conscription had an adverse effect on morale in a war-weary country. In the same post-1975 period, long-term tensions in relations between China and Vietnam came increasingly to the fore, with Kampuchea a major focus of hostility. In both Northern and Southern Vietnam, the Hoa minority became an important factor in the Sino-Vietnamese dispute. In the South, the Hoa bore most of the brunt of the restrictions on private traders, although there were clearly a number of motives behind the Vietnamese policy decisions and the socialization measures were not simply "anti-Chinese" in intent. In the North, the Hoa had been comparatively far more integrated into society and they played important roles in the professions and in industries, including mining and fishing. In mid 1978 as Sino-Vietnamese political tensions heightened, over 150,000 Hoa departed for China. Each government blamed the other for the outflow and the balance of factors involved is difficult to establish precisely, but the exodus from the North seems to have been encouraged by fears of discriminatory Vietnamese policy and of the possibility of armed conflict. In the first extensive published account of the refugee crisis (Bruce Grant, Michael Richardson, et al., *The Boat People*, Melbourne, 1979), it is argued that

The movement out of Vietnam and into China ... was fueled by a potent mixture of rumour, panic and the increasingly virulent propaganda war between China and Vietnam. Once started, it became self-generating. The shock waves from the northern exodus to China almost certainly spread to the Chinese community in southern Vietnam, just as nationalisation measures and currency reform in mid 1978 which hit the Chinese-dominated business community in southern Vietnam the hardest, also had an unsettling effect on Chinese in the north (p. 87).

China closed its border in July 1978, but Hoa continued to depart for China and Hong Kong by boat. After the Chinese "punitive" invasion (from 17 February to mid March 1979) the situation of the Hoa further deteriorated, as they were subjected to intensified suspicion of disloyalty and discriminatory measures in employment and education. The Sino-Vietnamese conflict did place the ultimate loyalties of the Hoa under intense pressure, and some were prepared to acknowledge to journalists after their arrival in Hong Kong that they had in fact primarily sympathized and identified with China in the conflict (*The Boat People*, p. 94). At the end of 1979, the future of the remaining Hoa in Vietnam was one of the major outstanding and unresolved issues of the refugee crisis. While few Hoa remained in the North, almost a million were still in Southern Vietnam and their future in the wake of the bitterness generated by the Chinese invasion was highly uncertain.

To these pressures on residents of Vietnam to leave the country was added, in 1978 and 1979, the apparently active encouragement and involvement of elements of the Vietnamese Government. The refugees who left Vietnam in the second phase of the outflow (mid-1975 to early 1978) did so in small boats through privately organized escape groups. In early 1978, however, the Vietnamese Government became involved in the outflow when the Hoa began leaving in substantial numbers. A number of accounts of this official involvement in the traffic appeared in 1979, based on interviews with refugees and the trials of a number of seamen and businessmen involved in the transport of refugees by large freighters, which were employed in the traffic for a period of several months in late 1978. According to one such account,

> In southern Vietnam the PSB (Public Security Bureau) staffed or supervised several offices in Ho Chi Minh City, as well as in Cholon, the "China town" where an estimated one million Sino-Vietnamese lived. Subordinate offices were set up in coastal provinces of the Mekong delta and central Vietnam. They were usually run by centrally appointed officials under a provincial chief of public security. The role of the PSB was usually limited to initial registration and approval of applicants wanting to go abroad, and to final checks before those leaving joined their boats. The actual organisation of passengers was left to middlemen. Offices handling the organised exodus were seldom located in government buildings, the police and security officials were in plain clothes, and the program was not publicized in the media, merely by word of mouth (*The Boat People*, p. 109).

The system seems to have been geared primarily to the outflow of Hoa; ethnic Vietnamese could participate with false identity papers identifying them as Chinese, and an extensive fake document business developed. The cost of departure for adult Chinese was commonly US$2–3,000, although there were considerable variations and the cost of leaving the North was much less than that for leaving the South. There were a variety of estimates of how much the government had earned from the payments by refugees by mid-1979; ranging from US$115 million, for the year up to June (*FEER*, 15 June 1979) to over US$2 billion (Hong Kong Government official, quoted by Reuter's news agency report, 7 June 1979). The levying of payments on the refugees may have seemed a legitimate policy of taxation of wealth to the elements in the Vietnamese Government sponsoring it, but the practice attracted almost universal condemnation, both in Southeast Asia and internationally.

In 1978 and the first half of 1979 (up to the Geneva Conference), statements by Vietnamese leaders acknowledged the problems caused by the outflow of boat people and emphasized, on a number of occasions, that the Vietnamese Government disapproved of illegal departures and would do what it could to co-operate with the United Nations High Commissioner for Refugees (UNHCR) and with neighbouring states to alleviate the problem. There was, however, no acknowledgement of government involvement, and it was suggested that the outflow was, to a considerable extent, beyond the control of the government. Nguyen Duy Trinh, Vietnam's Deputy Premier, stated during a visit to Bangkok in December 1978 that Vietnam realized "that the escape from Vietnam had created problems for neighbouring countries" and that Vietnam was co-operating with the UNHCR to alleviate the problem (*Nation Review*, Bangkok, 12 December 1978). Prime Minister Pham Van Dong, in a strongly worded birthday message to Malaysia's Prime Minister Hussein Onn in March 1979 expressed Vietnam's understanding of the difficulties faced by Malaysia in relation to illegal immigrants and emphasized Vietnam's "determination" to "unswervingly and scrupulously" carry out what had been agreed upon between the two countries during Pham Van Dong's visit to Malaysia in October 1978 (British Broadcasting Corporation [BBC], *Summary of World Broadcasts* [SWB], FE 6058/A3/14, 5 March 1979). During an interview with the Indonesian news agency Antara in April, Prime Minister Dong reiterated in relation to the refugee issue that,

> We have on many occasions expressed our regret about this. We are doing our utmost to avoid whatever can create difficulties to other countries in the region (*SWB*, FE 6097/A3/8, 21 April 1979).

It was also argued that the refugee exodus was not sanctioned by the Vietnamese Government and that it was beyond government control. Nguyen Duy Trinh, for example, speaking in Bangkok in December 1978, stated that,

> Some groups of people who do not want to live with us have escaped from the country. What we can do is merely ask them to abide by the law.... We have not adopted a policy of permitting Vietnamese people (to) leave the country. We have tried to stop them but they however managed to escape. You should sympathise with us (*Nation Review*, ibid.).

Pham Van Dong, in a similar vein, when asked by a visiting Indian official why Vietnam was not controlling the outflow, was reported to have "pointed out the long coastline and the impossible task of policing it" (*SWB*, FE 6127/A3/6, 28 May 1979). Vietnamese leaders also placed stress on the arrangement for "orderly", legal departures which was negotiated with the UNHCR. This programme was designed to authorize the exit from Vietnam of people who were allowed to leave by the Vietnamese Government and who were granted an entry visa by a receiving country. Although the programme was finally agreed on in May 1979, it was very slow to begin and had accounted for only a tiny proportion of those leaving Vietnam by September (see next section).

While the Vietnamese Government did not acknowledge that the mass outflow of people could be effectively restricted, or indeed was resulting partly from direct official sponsorship, the effects of the outflow on regional opinion were clearly being closely monitored. As the reaction from the ASEAN states mounted, Vietnam sent several officials to countries in the region to consult on the issue. As the Geneva Conference on refugees approached in July, it was apparently decided to place limitations on the outflow of people and halt, at least for a time, the government-sponsored refugee programmes. This new policy was duly announced at the Geneva Conference (discussed in detail below), and by August Vietnam was claiming to have made mass arrests of 4,000 people involved in planning and conducting passage of refugees. A "temporary" moratorium was now in force.

In response to the criticism directed towards the refugee outflow by the ASEAN states and states outside the region including the U.S., Britain and Australia, Vietnam issued a document in mid-1979 which gave an interesting indication of Vietnam's interpretation and defence of the outflow and of the Vietnamese Government's attitude towards it. The document, entitled "Those Who Leave" (published by *Vietnam Courier*, Hanoi, 1979), emphasized the social and economic problems of postwar Vietnam, the impact of natural calamities "of unprecedented scope", and the impact of China's "aggressive" policies towards Vietnam. The enormous problems of postwar reconstruction of a society distorted by war were stressed. The government's actions in restricting private trade in the South were justified on the grounds that the Hoa traders were distorting and manipulating trade in commodities for their own benefit, but to the detriment of the economy generally, China, it was argued, began a campaign of manipulation of the Hoa in 1977, inducing them to leave and then utilizing groups of them as guides in its invasion in 1979. The document stressed that the primary motivation of the refugees in leaving were economic difficulties, particularly for those whose jobs and professions were redundant and those (especially professionals) who faced unacceptable losses of wealth and status. It denied that Vietnam forced anyone to leave, arguing that the refugee departures (especially of professionals) "disorganises the economy and disturbs social order". It was also firmly asserted that the outflow involved corruption but not official government involvement, and that the problem of corruption was a particularly difficult one in the South.

> There may be cadres who have availed themselves of the situation to get their palms greased, but this is not government policy. What government can claim that none of its employees has ever been tempted in certain circumstances to fill his pockets?... In a country that has been ravaged by war and where Phoenix operations conducted over long years by the American command had literally decimated the ranks of revolutionary militants — in some sectors 85% of the cadres were murdered — it has been particularly difficult after liberation to set up a State apparatus without opportunist or degenerate elements worming their way into it (*Those Who Leave*, p. 32).

The document highlighted the problems and limitations in Vietnam's official position on the refugee outflow. While it offered some credible evidence and arguments on the economic and political problems of postwar Vietnam, it did not successfully rebut allegations of official involvement in the outflow. The assertion, made in mid-1979, by Secretary of State for Foreign Affairs, Nguyen Co Thach, that it was not official policy to make people pay to leave, "But there are cases of Lockheed and Watergate scandals not at the top but at lower levels", did little to clarify the real situation, especially since the Watergate scandal in the U.S. had indeed involved corrupt practices instigated by high government officials (*FEER*, 27 July 1979; see also *Asiaweek*, 15 June 1979). Vietnam's declaration that the refugee departures were a result merely of corrupt officials was undermined to a considerable extent by the announcement of a moratorium on departures in July and the subsequent sharp decline in the numbers of refugee arrivals in Southeast Asia. Vietnam's difficulty in providing a credible explanation for the scale of the exodus in 1978 and 1979 was an important element in the increasing concern and antipathy which greeted the refugee arrivals in the ASEAN states.

ASEAN and the Boat People

The refugee exodus was at the centre of ASEAN's attention and concern in 1979. As Table 2 indicates, the scale of the influx reached massive and frightening proportions by mid-year. Coming as it did after Vietnam's invasion of Kampuchea in late December 1978, the refugee influx

TABLE 2
Refugee Arrivals in Countries of First Asylum – 1979[1]

	January	February	March	April	May	June	July	August	September	October
Malaysia	4,202	3,166	6,033	13,250	17,508	3,529	–	164	3,499[2]	960
Indonesia	1,831	406	3,101	4,610	10,035	22,743	3,876	813	434	329
Philippines	200	802	254	476	814	2,191	1,149	473	1,053	410
Singapore	–	–	–	266	317	51	1,262	1,552	1,307	574
Hong Kong	3,151	2,901	3,114	5,702	18,718	22,835	8,768	2,975[3a]	2,673[3b]	686
Thailand (boat)	467	996	620	1,471	2,780	2,432	709	163	208	193
Australia	–	44	–	248	–	–	–	–	–	–
Other countries	80	341	1,301	1,106	967	669	446	630	492	108
Total boat refugees	9,931	8,568	13,423	26,602	51,139	54,500	13,210	6,770	9,666	3,260
Thailand – land refugees	7,223	3,608	6,024	5,741	4,976	14,943	9,540	3,076	4,616	3,482
Total refugee arrivals	17,154	12,176	19,447	32,343	56,115	69,443	25,750	9,846	14,282	6,742

Source: UNHCR Monthly Statistics.

Notes: (1) These figures do not take into account those refugees still not registered at UNHCR or Hong Kong Government camps. Refugees rescued at sea are included under countries of first asylum.
(2) 577 arrivals and 2,922 persons who had arrived in previous months on Malaysian beaches and who were transferred to UNHCR camps in September.
(3) Of whom (a) 2,499 arrivals and (b) 1,723 arrivals purporting to come from North Vietnam under investigation as having been previously resettled in China.

raised disturbing questions about Vietnam's attitudes and intentions towards the ASEAN members. The refugees also posed a variety of challenges to the ASEAN states. The influx imposed severe economic and political burdens upon several states and challenged their capacity to respond in an effective and humanitarian way. The influx challenged the ASEAN states' capacity to co-operate to alleviate the immediate impact of the crisis and to minimize dissension within the group. The crisis also challenged ASEAN's ability to exert pressure on Vietnam to restrict the outflow and pressure on the international community to accept and resettle refugees.

While the Vietnamese refugee influx was of concern to all the ASEAN members, some members felt the impact far more than others. The Philippines had received about 5,000 refugees by June 1979, but the difficulty of the voyage and the unfavourable currents meant that only a small proportion of the refugee boats attempted to gain asylum there. While the Philippine Government was concerned at the influx, and took a firm stance on a large freighter, the *Tung An*, which brought 2,000 people to Manila in January, the refugee problem did not become a major domestic issue. Thailand was a more likely destination for refugee boats and since 1975 had received a large number. From November 1977, however, the government had authorized local officials to re-supply arriving boats and push them on to other destinations. A further deterrent to boat arrivals were the activities of Thai pirates who made a large number of savage attacks on refugee boats, which made generally defenceless and lucrative targets. As a result, by 1979 refugee boats tended to avoid Thailand as a destination and the numbers of boat refugees it received were comparatively low. Singapore was also a likely destination for boats, but its government pursued the toughest policy on refugee arrivals of any ASEAN member and its small size and short coastline enabled the policy to be effectively carried out. After 1975, Singaporean forces regularly refused to accept refugee boats, although repairs and supplies were provided. Refugees arriving by merchant ship were subject to stringent provisions which required their resettlement within ninety days. In November 1978, a ceiling of 1,000 was imposed as the maximum number of people whom Singapore would temporarily accommodate at any one time. The policy was justified on the grounds of the republic's small size and limited capacity to receive refugees in large numbers (*FEER*, 10 November 1978). The policy resulted in Singapore having the lowest number of arrivals of refugees of any ASEAN member in 1979.

Malaysia and Indonesia were far more severely affected (see Table 3). Malaysia was in the most direct path of the boats leaving Vietnam, and the lights of offshore oil rigs provided a helpful navigation guide for the often poorly equipped vessels. While Malaysia received only 77 boats in 1975, 1,080 in 1976, and 5,812 in 1977, the numbers began to rise rapidly in 1978: between January and March, 3,800 arrived; 13,219 had been received by June; and the monthly arrivals for October, November and December were 9,934, 19,227 and 10,721. In a prophetic statement in May, Prime Minister Hussein Onn foresaw the problems that were to arise:

> We are very concerned because more and more are coming. They are creating social, political, economic and security problems. We don't know exactly who is coming in,

TABLE 3
Refugee Population Trends

		June		July		August		September[1]		October
Malaysia		74,817		65,045		55,975		49,748		42,681
Indonesia		42,939		46,810		45,708		43,978		40,715
Thailand		172,145		175,227		172,805		168,897[2]		64,347[3]
	(Lao	146,039	(Lao	147,857	(Lao	148,333	(Lao	144,882	(Lao	n/avail.
	Viet.	9,502	Viet.	9,180	Viet.	8,860	Viet.	8,540	Viet.	
	Kam.	16,604)	Kam.	18,195)	Kam.	15,612)	Kam.	15,475)	Kam.	
Philippines		5,131		5,526		5,651		6,311		6,259
Singapore		445		1,098		1,260		2,025		1,580
Hong Kong		59,003		66,651		66,106		65,206		62,591

Source: UNHCR Statistics.

Notes: (1) Small concentrations of refugees in other countries, for example, Macao and Brunei, bring the total in September to around 300,000.
(2) In addition, on 30 September, there were 5,294 displaced persons in Transit Centres in Bangkok, awaiting movement to countries of resettlement. An estimated 200,000 Kampucheans also arrived in Thailand in October.

and local people are starting to complain. I can see a situation ... when we will have to turn them away (*FEER*, 26 May 1978).

By the end of 1978, the inflow of refugees into the east coast areas of Peninsular Malaysia was causing considerable tension and unrest. The predominantly Chinese refugees were highly unpopular among the residents of the staunchly Muslim, Malay-dominated east coast states. Concern was heightened by price rises which were blamed on the local purchasing of food and supplies by the UNHCR, allegations of bribery by refugees of Malaysian officials, and the dangers of imported diseases to the local population and to livestock (*FEER*, 24 November, 1 December, 15 December 1978). The Malaysian federal government came under increasing political pressure from state leaders, local United Malays National Organisation (UMNO) branches and from the opposition Parti Islam to take a firmer stand against the refugees.

From late 1978, the Malaysian Government took several major steps to alleviate the tensions caused by the refugees. As far as possible, the refugees were located in camps isolated from the Malaysian populace, such as the island of Pulau Bidong, which became a community of over 40,000. Conditions were harsh for the refugees in the camps, but they were at least able to stay and await resettlement. The government also moved to improve its coastal patrols and began to "shoo off" boats which attempted to land. In late June, a government spokesman claimed that 275 boats carrying more than 41,000 Vietnamese had been stopped and towed out to sea since the beginning of the year (*SWB*, FE 6152/A3/12, 27 June 1979). Some of the rejected boats attempted to make further efforts to land in Malaysia. However, people making such attempts risked being held in temporary holding centres rather than in the UNHCR sponsored camps. While the people held in UNHCR sponsored camps were secure from expulsion, those held in temporary centres existed in great insecurity; there were some 10,000 so-called "beach people" in this situation in mid-June (*Asian Wall Street journal* or *AWSJ*, 19 June 1979.) The "shoo off" policy did not prevent the arrival of large numbers of refugees in Malaysia up to June as the figures indicate, but the influx would clearly have been much larger if the policy had not been pursued.

Indonesia was also subject to a major influx of boat people. While only 2,932 people arrived in 1978, in 1979 Indonesia began to receive large numbers in April (4,610), May (10,035) and June (22,743). The refugees generally landed on a number of islands in the Riau and Natuna archipelagos to the southeast of Malaysia and their impact created tensions similar to those experienced in Malaysia. The rapid influx of people created shortages of food and other commodities and drove up prices. The conditions of the refugee camps themselves were usually very poor. The Indonesian Government was also concerned at the security problems which could arise from the uncontrolled arrival of thousands of Indochinese. The Chief of Staff of the Army, General Widodo, warned on 28 June that many of the arriving refugees were ex-servicemen and said that "...it was feared that they were sent here deliberately for certain purposes disguised as refugees" (*SWB*, FE 6157/A3/17, 3 July 1979).

In the first six months of 1979, the problems posed by the arriving boat people grew steadily worse. Although the UNHCR was actively involved in registering refugees and arranging for their resettlement, the rate of intake by the Western countries prepared to take large numbers of refugees (primarily, the U.S., Canada, France and Australia — see Table 4) fell far behind the arrival rates. In Malaysia, for example, Home Secretary Ghazali Shafie told an UMNO meeting in early July that, of the 170,000 Indochina refugees who had arrived in Malaysia since 1975, 56,000 had been expelled and only 44,000 so far resettled (*Straits Times*, 8 July 1979). In the case of Indonesia, government figures provided by an Indonesian official, speaking at a conference on refugees in Canberra in July, indicated that while there were 45,000 refugees in the country on 14 July, the UNHCR had been able to resettle only 2,017 people in the period from 1975 up to June 1979: at that rate, the acceptance of refugees from Indonesia would take over 10 years. The ASEAN countries burdened by the boat arrivals were particularly frustrated by what they saw as the inconsistent and hypocritical attitudes of the Western states who insisted on screening and processing refugees to be accepted, while they simultaneously encouraged the ASEAN states to accept as temporary residents all who approached their shores without question (*Straits Times*, 15 May 1979). An exasperated Ghazali Shafie told a press conference on 18 June that if the arriving Indochinese were, in fact, refugees

> there should not be any restriction, any selection ... We cannot find the logic of those countries who claim these people to be refugees and yet will categorise. When a person cannot speak English he falls into a different category. When a person has tuberculosis he is not accepted anywhere ... There is no point in calling them refugees and treating them as normal immigrants (*FEER*, 29 June 1979).

As well as the internal pressures caused by the refugee arrivals, the ASEAN states by mid 1979 also faced the problem of interstate tensions arising from individual members' attempts to cope with the crisis. Relations between Malaysia and Indonesia were of particular concern. The policy pursued by Malaysia of rejecting arriving boats placed an increasing refugee burden on Indonesia, since many of the boats headed for the nearby Indonesian islands. While Indonesia was aware of the internal pressures faced by Malaysia, there was evidence of Indonesian irritation at Malaysia's policy by mid-1979. Foreign Minister Mochtar Kusumaatmadja was reported to have said, after a tour of ASEAN members just before the Geneva Conference, that Indonesia

> could not agree with the attitude of any recipient country to tow the refugees out to the high seas without taking into consideration the interests of neighbouring countries (*SWB*, FE 6169/A3/4, 17 July 1979).

The Foreign Minister told the Rosenthal Congressional Delegation on 6 August that his government

> planned to meet with the Malaysians and state to them clearly that the Malaysians must not push their refugees out to sea since their subsequent arrival in Indonesia is causing grave problems.[1]

By the time of Dr. Mochtar's latter statement, the refugee flow from Vietnam was already abating, but the problem of transfers of refugees clearly had created some tension between Malaysia and Indonesia, which could have seriously worsened, had not the regional refugee situation improved after July.

TABLE 4
Refugee Resettlements and Resettlements' Commitments

Country	Numbers Resettled April 1975–30 September 1979	Programme 1979/80
U.S.A.	259,054	168,000
France	57,057	15,000
Australia	25,693	14,000
Canada	22,348	36,000 (50,000 by December 1980)
West Germany	7,934	(20,000 – no time period)
China, People's Republic	270,000	10,000
Hong Kong	14,000	(total of 10,000 to be resettled)
New Zealand	1,262	900 in 1979; 1,800 by June 1981)
Argentina	94	4,500
Austria	431	580
Belgium	1,683	2,060
Brazil	65	63
Denmark	1,106	800
Finland	100	100
Greece	52	150
Iceland	34	30
Israel	168	200
Ireland	109	200
Italy	1,650	1,000
Japan	62	500
Luxembourg	51	100
Malaysia	2,137	600
Monaco	–	25
Netherlands	1,062	1,360
Norway	1,105	2,400
Paraguay	31	(total of 3,000 to be resettled)
Spain	1	–
Surinam	–	1,000
Sweden	689	750
Switzerland	2,822	2,000
United Kingdom	3,531	3,000
Other resettlement countries	840	10,000
Total	675,171	360,118

Source: UNHCR statistics except for U.S., Australia, China and Hong Kong.

Both the internal problems and the interstate tensions raised by the refugee inflows for the ASEAN members underlined the pressing need for a regional response by the ASEAN group to a situation which could clearly not be effectively approached on an individual basis. In 1979 the ASEAN members did devote a considerable amount of attention to the crisis and they pursued several major goals — ultimately, with considerable success. The major aims pursued were the alleviation of the immediate impact of the crisis by joint action (particularly to establish "refugee processing centres"), the exertion of pressure to increase international involvement and particularly to raise resettlement rates, and the exertion of regional and international pressure on Vietnam to stem the flow of boat people. These aims were pursued concurrently in a series of consultations, meetings and policy changes from May to July, the period leading up to the crucial Geneva Conference on 20–21 July.

The idea of establishing centres where refugees might be temporarily accommodated while awaiting resettlement was first suggested by Malaysia and presented at the conference on Indochina refugees held in Geneva in December 1978. It was envisaged that island "refugee processing centres" could be established which could alleviate the socio-economic and political pressures on countries of first asylum and also improve conditions for the refugees themselves: proponents of the concept, including Home Affairs Minister Ghazali, initially hoped that the centres could be located outside the ASEAN region. The proposal was adopted as an ASEAN initiative by the ASEAN Standing Committee on 21 February 1979. Indonesia and the Philippines indicated that they would be prepared to offer islands for the purpose provided that the host country would retain full control over the centres, resettlement of the refugees in them would be guaranteed and the costs would be met by extraregional countries and/or by the UNHCR (*AWSJ*, 22 February 1979). Indonesia subsequently offered the island of Pulau Galang, part of the Riau group southeast of Singapore, and the proposal was discussed at an international conference in Jakarta on 15–16 May attended by twenty-four countries, including the ASEAN members and Vietnam. The planned capacity of the centre was 10,000, a relatively low figure in the context of the numbers of refugees present in ASEAN states at the time. The proposal was none the less adopted, and centres subsequently established on Galang, and on Tara Island, northeast of Palawan in the Philippines (*FEER*, 31 August, 29 September 1979).

While the refugee processing centres were a useful ASEAN initiative, they could not hope to make a serious impression on the inflow that the members experienced from April to June. As has already been noted, the rate of inflow dramatically outstripped the rate of resettlement and threatened Malaysia and Indonesia with unsustainably high numbers of refugees. In mid-June, Malaysia, Indonesia and Thailand made a series of dramatic announcements on refugee policy to heighten awareness of the extent of their problems in both the international community and in Vietnam. Malaysia announced on 12 June that it would no longer accept any further Vietnamese refugees and the Foreign Minister, Tengku Rithaudeen, warned the Vietnamese Ambassador that the influx of boat people had reached "a critical phase" and could affect bilateral relations (*SWB*, FE 6141/A3/3, 14 June 1979). Deputy

Prime Minister Dr. Mahathir Mohamed was quoted as saying that Malaysia would shoot incoming refugees, and although he denied the alleged statement several days later (*SWB*, FE 6145/A3/2, 19 June 1979), it had already gained wide international publicity. Prime Minister Hussein Onn conveyed Malaysia's new policy of nonacceptance of refugees to the U.N. Secretary General in a strongly-worded message (*SWB*, FE 6146/A3/l, 20 June 1979). At the same time, President Suharto announced on 12 June that Indonesia would no longer accept any Indochina refugees and a fleet of ships was deployed to attempt to drive incoming boats away (*SWB*, FE 6142/A3/9, 15 June 1979). Thailand's Prime Minister, General Kriangsak Chomanand, also announced that his country could accept no more refugees: he told a special envoy of the U.N. Secretary General on 18 June that further refugees would be refused, no matter what other countries might say. He stated that, as of 12 June, the Thai authorities had already repatriated 42,986 Kampuchean refugees back to their country (*SWB*, FE 6146/A3/5, 20 June 1979).

These statements and policy changes had a major international impact. The International Committee of the Red Cross and the League of Red Cross Societies criticized the prohibitions on refugee entry, but their criticism was rejected by the ASEAN Standing Committee, which "strongly deplored" the comments and pointed to Vietnam as the responsible party in the exodus (*SWB*, FE 6161/A3/11, 7 July 1979). More importantly, the ASEAN statements were followed by a number of proposals for action and offers of aid from the U.S., Western Europe and Japan. It was reported that, in response to Prime Minister Hussein Onn's message to the U.N. Secretary General and in response to other calls for action, particularly from the British Government which was gravely concerned at the refugee burden being imposed on Hong Kong (see Tables 2 and 3), another international conference was to be held to consider the refugee crisis. At the Tokyo "summit" meeting of seven industrialized states (the U.S., Japan, the U.K., France, West Germany, Italy and Canada) in late June, the refugee issue was extensively discussed. The U.S. made the important announcement that it would double its refugee intake to 168,000 for the forthcoming year, and the states attending the "summit" called for an immediate halt to the refugee outflow, stated that "the plight of refugees ... poses a humanitarian problem of strategic proportions and constitutes a threat to the stability of South East Asia", called on the U.N. Secretary General to convene a conference on the problem as soon as possible and said that as part of an international effort they would "significantly increase their contributions to Indochina refugee relief and resettlement".

Having gained increased international recognition of their problems in June, the ASEAN members used their annual Foreign Ministers' meeting at the end of the month as a forum to continue their efforts to exert international pressure. In their "special meeting" in Bangkok on 12–13 January, just after the invasion of Kampuchea, the Foreign Ministers had expressed their "grave concern" at the increasing influx of refugees, stated that a continuation of the flow of refugees would seriously affect the stability of the region, and

> stressed that the Government of Vietnam, which has pledged to promote regional peace and stability, and other countries from which such people come, should take appropriate measures to tackle the problem at the source (*SWB*, FE 6018/ A3/7–8, 17 January 1979).

The conviction that the refugee problem must be tackled at the source and that the source was Vietnam, was reiterated as a theme by the Foreign Ministers at Bali, but the stronger language of some Ministers reflected the more serious regional situation. Dr. Mochtar stated in his opening address that "Vietnam must be made to accept its responsibility with regard to the problem". The Philippine Foreign Minister, General Carlos Romulo, likened the Vietnamese treatment of the boat people to Nazi atrocities during World War II. The most outspoken comments came from Singapore's Foreign Minister, S. Rajaratnam, who said that

> ... once you go into causes [of the exodus] you enter into the secret world of wild Vietnamese ambitions and their even wilder dreams. [The refugee problem] ... is linked with a number of other things — with the Vietnamese invasion and occupation of Kampuchea, the military alliance with the Soviet Union, its confrontational relations with China, the forging of the Indochinese states into a military bloc, the abandonment of the policy of peaceful reconstruction in favour of feverish militarisation through foreign aid and less than four years after the ending of the war, the presence of nearly 150,000 Vietnamese troops along the Thai border. Seen in this context the refugee problem is not an exercise in humanitarianism. It is a military exercise to further the ambitions which the Vietnamese have concealed from us but not from their own people or their allies.... Their ambitions are hegemony in Southeast Asia.... In other words each junkload of men, women and children sent to our shores is a bomb to destabilise, disrupt, and cause turmoil and dissension in ASEAN states. This is a preliminary invasion to pave the way for the final invasion ... (Vietnam and the Refugees [Singapore: Ministry of Foreign Affairs, July 1979], p. 23).

The language of the Ministers' joint communiqué was more reserved, but it contained a firm declaration of ASEAN policy on the crisis. The Ministers expressed their

> grave concern over the deluge of illegal immigrants, [and] displaced persons ... from Indochina which has reached crisis proportions and has caused severe political, socio-economic and security problems in ASEAN countries and will have a destabilising effect on the region.

The Ministers gave notice that refugees not resettled or not reaccepted by the Indochina countries "within a reasonable time frame" would be sent out. They stated that Vietnam, as the country responsible for the exodus, had a decisive role to play in the resolution of the problem and they "appealed to the international community to prevail upon Vietnam to stop the exodus". The Ministers urged that a higher resettlement rate be adopted and welcomed the increased intakes announced at the Tokyo summit of industrialized countries. Although Rajaratnam expressed some disappointment at the Bali meeting and said that ASEAN could have gone further on the refugee issue, the other Ministers appeared to be satisfied with the meeting overall (*FEER*, 13 July 1979; *SWB*, FE 6156/A3/5–6, 2 July 1979).

The Ministers followed up their joint statement with discussions with the Foreign Ministers of the U.S., Japan, Australia and New Zealand. These discussions saw considerable agreement on the seriousness of the problem, but Secretary of State Cyrus Vance was reported to have emphasized that strong U.S. support for increased resettlement rates was contingent on the maintenance by ASEAN states of the "principle of first asylum" whereby Indochina refugees would in fact be accepted. While Secretary Vance's request ran counter to the views expressed in the joint communiqué, the joint meetings at Bali had provided a valuable opportunity for ASEAN to gain further publicity for, and awareness of, their policy on refugees.

While they were dramatizing the impact of the refugee influx and firmly criticizing Vietnam's role in the problem, the ASEAN members also had some direct contact and discussions with Vietnamese representatives in May and June. Vietnam attended the Jakarta conference in mid May and its representative, Ambassador Tran My, stated that Vietnam would do what it could to lessen the difficulties caused by the refugee problem to other countries, (*SWB*, FE 6118/A3/8, 17 May 1979). In late June, a Vietnamese envoy, Mai Van Bo, held discussions with Indonesian and Malaysian officials: he was reported to have acknowledged in Jakarta that the refugee situation had reached a "critical stage" (*SWB*, FE 6151/A3/9, 26 June 1979). It is possible that these discussions with ASEAN officials, combined with contacts with Vietnamese Ambassadors and a visit to Hanoi in June by U.N. Secretary General Kurt Waldheim during which he was reported to have warned Vietnam of the serious nature of the impact of the refugee outflow in the region, may have influenced Vietnamese policy-making in the period before the Geneva Conference. There appeared to be a significant change in tone in Vietnamese comments on the situation when the Vietnam News Agency (VNA) on 13 July said that illegal departures from Vietnam constituted "an intolerable burden for the ASEAN countries" (*SWB*, FE 6168/A3/4, 16 July 1979), a statement which was welcomed by Indonesia's Foreign Minister (*Straits Times*, 16 July 1979).

The Geneva Conference in July 1979 was different in character from the meeting which had preceded it in December 1978: more countries attended (66 compared to 38), the level of delegation leadership was higher and it was chaired by the U.N. Secretary General, not the High Commissioner for Refugees. There was a considerable amount of political comment during the meeting, with Vietnam receiving strong criticism from a number of representatives from countries including China, the U.S. and Australia. On the eve of the Geneva Conference, there was considerable doubt in ASEAN official circles about the meeting's chances for success: Ghazali Shafie was quoted as saying that, "I do not think that Vietnam will give a tinker's cuss about what we say in Geneva, but the rest of the world should" (*Straits Times*, 19 July 1979). In his speech to the conference, Vietnam's delegate, Phan Hien, declared that Vietnam was aware of the difficulties caused by the "emigration" from Vietnam. The cause of the outflow was essentially the difficulties experienced in Vietnam after the war. Vietnam's agreement with the UNHCR for an orderly, legal process of emigration was stressed and Phan Hien called on the Western states to increase their economic assistance and resettlement programmes. He claimed that illegal emigration from Vietnam was severely dealt with under Vietnamese law, but did not state whether the massive outflow in the past year had been subject to control by the government (*SWB*, FE 6174/A3/1–3, 23 July 1979). However, after extensive discussions between the Vietnamese representatives and U.N. officials, the U.N. Secretary General stated in his closing address that,

... as a result of my consultations, the Government of the Socialist Republic of Vietnam has authorised me to inform you that for a reasonable period of time it will make every effort to stop illegal departures. In the meantime the Government of Vietnam will co-operate with the UNHCR in expanding the present seven point program designed to bring departures into orderly and safe channels.

He added, "I may also recall that a proposal was made here, supported by a number of countries, for a moratorium on unorganised departures from Vietnam". In addition to this breakthrough, the conference also produced other positive results: the numbers of places offered for resettlement rose from 125,000 to 260,000; commitments of financial assistance for refugees rose to US$190 million; Japan reaffirmed its commitment to provide substantial funds for refugee assistance; support for the existing refugee process centre on Galang Island was confirmed and a site for 50,000 refugees was offered by the Philippines; and sea rescue measures for boat people were announced (*FEER*, 3 August 1979; *AWSJ*, 24 July 1979).

The outcome of the Geneva Conference represented a turning point in the international effort to develop an effective response to the plight of the boat people, and ASEAN had played a leading role in publicizing and defining the terms of the debate. The announcement of a "moratorium" on departures by the U.N. Secretary General represented a tacit admission by Vietnam that it was necessary to control the outflow and that it did have the capacity to do this. The dramatic fall off in the rate of arrivals of boat people in the three months after the conference (see Table 2) demonstrated the Vietnamese Government's capacity in the area of controlling emigration. The Geneva Conference, however, left important questions unanswered. In particular, it was far from certain that the Vietnam-UNHCR "orderly departure" procedures could be effectively implemented, and that resettlement countries would be as eager to accept Vietnamese legal emigrants as they had been Vietnamese boat people. By 11 September, only 879 people had left Vietnam legally under UNHCR auspices and in November it was reported that numerous problems still confronted implementation of the policy (*Guardian Weekly*, 18 November 1979). With Vietnam at war in Kampuchea, subject to continuing tensions in its relations with China and experiencing extensive and possibly worsening economic problems, the pressures for further departures of both ethnic Chinese and Vietnamese seemed likely to continue. While the ASEAN states were seeing the real possibility of a major reduction in their populations of boat refugees in late 1979, the prospects overall continued to be highly uncertain.

Thailand and the Refugee Crisis

Thailand was the first ASEAN country to be seriously affected by refugee outflows from Indochina after 1975. While it had received over 130,000 Indochinese people by mid-1977 — well before the mass exodus of Vietnamese boat people — Thailand's problems tended to attract less regional and international attention. This was possibly because the departure of the "land people" from Laos (who consistently constituted the great majority of Thailand's Indochina refugees) involved a less obviously dramatic passage and because the ethnic similarities between the lowland Laotians and the people of Northeastern Thailand meant that many of the incoming refugees aroused less antipathy than, for example, Sino-Vietnamese boat people in Peninsular Malaysia's east coast. While Thailand had a consistently large number of refugees after 1975, its problems became significantly more serious in 1979 after Vietnam's invasion of Kampuchea. By late 1979, Thailand's refugee problems were gaining the recognition they deserved as the most serious in the region.

Thailand received refugees from three sources after 1975. From Laos, thousands of ethnic Lao and hill tribespeople crossed the Mekong as the Second Indochina War ended and the communist Pathet Lao assumed full control of the government at the end of 1975. As with Vietnam, part of the outflow represented a legacy of the preceding war; in this case, the involvement of Meo (also called Hmong) tribespeople in U.S.-sponsored operations against Pathet Lao and Vietnamese forces. The Hmong have come under considerable pressure from Pathet Lao and Vietnamese forces since 1975, and reports of the conflict have included allegations of poison gas attacks against the tribespeople. Refugees from Laos have also included former residents of Vientiane and lowland Lao farmers, who have fled from economic hardships and austerity and the introduction of compulsory military service. By May 1979, according to UNHCR figures, there were in Thailand 73,665 Lao (46%), 50,645 Hmong (32%) and 13,495 other refugees from Laos. Departures continued from Laos in 1979 at a rate of about 5,000 per month. Thailand also received Kampuchean refugees and boat people from Vietnam. The number of Kampucheans who sought refuge in Thailand up to the end of 1978 was comparatively low, which seems to have resulted from the tight controls maintained by the Democratic Kampuchean regime: 13,281 Kampucheans were registered with the UNHCR at the time of the invasion. While Thailand received a relatively high proportion of the initial flow of boat people from Vietnam after 1975, official action and the activities of Thai pirates meant that in 1978 and 1979 Thailand received only a small proportion of the outflow from Vietnam.

The refugee influx into Thailand, particularly from Laos, created extensive social, economic and political problems. The refugees themselves lived under harsh conditions in camps and what assistance they did receive was liable to cause resentment from local Thais, especially in the Northeast — the poorest region in the country. Laotian refugees in Thailand had difficulty in gaining resettlement and, as a result, Thailand's population of refugees continued to rise: from 75,866 in 1976, to 97,595 in 1977 and 138,727 in 1978. In July 1977, General Kriangsak (then Deputy Supreme Commander) protested against what he saw as the selective policies of resettlement being pursued by the U.S. and other Western countries which selected the "cream" and left Thailand with the overwhelming majority "who cannot help themselves or have no skills to contribute to our progress" (*FEER*, 22 July 1977).

Thailand's situation was greatly worsened in 1979 by internal developments in Kampuchea. While the forces of the government of Democratic Kampuchea had been responsible for a series of disturbing border incidents, the Pol Pot regime from the Thai point of view acted as a buffer between Thailand and Vietnam and had not been the source of a massive flow of refugees. The Vietnamese invasion from 25 December 1978 and the ensuing disruption which exacerbated the problems of food shortages, created a new source of displaced persons, many of whom sought refuge in Thailand. From early 1979, Thailand was faced with the entry of tens of thousands of Kampuchean civilians, many ill and on the edge of starvation, and large groups of the remnant forces of the Pol Pot regime, who sought to use the Thai border areas as a zone for regroupment and resupply. The civilians who entered Thailand were primarily ethnic Kampucheans but also included thousands of ethnic Chinese forced from the country at the instigation of Vietnamese forces (*SWB*, FE 6122/A3/9, 22 May 1979). While the civilians imposed an economic and administrative burden on the Thai authorities, the presence of Pol Pot forces posed a most serious security threat since there was a very real danger of the conflict in Kampuchea spilling over into Thailand as Vietnamese and Pol Pot forces clashed near the border.

Thai policy towards Indochina in 1979 concentrated on attempting to maintain workable relations with Laos and Vietnam, while acting to minimize the dangers posed by the conflict in Kampuchea. With Vietnam, there were a number of consultations between senior leaders and the Thai Government received assurances that Vietnam would respect its territorial integrity and would not allow the Kampuchean conflict to spill over into Thailand. Although the refugee inflow from Laos continued, the Thai Government was able to maintain extensive contacts: an agreement on co-operation was reached during Prime Minister Kriangsak's visit in January and a number of delegations were subsequently exchanged.[2] Kampuchea posed the gravest problems. Thailand supported the ASEAN joint stand on opposition to the presence of foreign forces (and therefore to Vietnam's presence) in Kampuchea, but there was no sign of a Vietnamese reappraisal of its involvement. As the year progressed, the refugee problems posed by the Kampuchean situation worsened. Thailand refused to accept Kampucheans entering its territory after 8 January 1979 (the date of the inauguration of the People's Republic of Kampuchea [PRK] as "refugees" eligible for UNHCR assistance: it classed them as "displaced persons". Thousands of people entered Thailand after January, but efforts were also made to limit the numbers arriving: some thousands of people were apparently induced to return (*SWB*, FE 6127IA3/8, 28 May 1979). In mid June, as was earlier noted, when regional concern about the refugee crisis was at its height, over 40,000 Kampucheans were forced back inside their country: the move brought some expressions of international concern, but Prime Minister Kriangsak, in letters to President Carter and Britain's Prime Minister, Mrs. Margaret Thatcher, was reported to have stated that

> Cambodian refugees had been repatriated because they were not genuine refugees but had been "exported" by force from their own countries. Repatriation was therefore the only solution for Thailand since it could not count on third countries taking them for resettlement (*SWB*, FE 6141/A3/2, 14 June 1979).

As the dry season approached, Thailand faced a further influx of Kampucheans fleeing from the intensifying fighting near border areas. It was reported that over 70,000 people crossed into Thailand in a ten day period in mid October (*Sydney Morning Herald*, 10 November 1979). At this point, the Thai Government announced a policy change. It was now stated that people from Kampuchea would be allowed to enter Thailand, but that they would be transferred from areas immediately adjacent to the border to inland camps established with UNHCR aid. This move seemed to be aimed at reducing the dangers posed by the tens of thousands of people on the border whose presence threatened to draw Thailand into the fighting between the Vietnamese and Pol Pot forces. By 2 November, the Deputy Secretary General of the National Security Council said that there were now 170,000 Kampucheans in Thailand and more than 130,000 were ready to cross over into Thailand if the fighting escalated: camps were being constructed to hold a total of 300,000 Kampucheans (*SWB*, FE 6265/A3/9, 7 November 1979).

By late 1979, Thailand's refugee crisis continued to look forbidding. The influx from Laos was continuing and the rate of intake from Kampuchea had greatly increased and showed no sign of abating. The regional diplomacy and international attention directed towards the refugee crisis in 1979 had been of relatively limited benefit to Thailand, since so much of it had been directed towards the boat people. Thai leaders were acutely aware and highly critical of the orientation of both regional and international attention towards the boat people for most of 1979 and there were a number of expressions of dissatisfaction at this emphasis: just after the Geneva Conference, for example, it was reported that the returning Thai delegation had called for another conference on the refugee crisis since the Geneva meeting had mainly focused on the boat people (*SWB*, FE 6176/A3/6, 25 July 1979), and Prime Minister Kriangsak told the Rosenthal Delegation that he was "particularly concerned that the Geneva Conference on Refugees focused only on the problem of the boat people, which ignores Thailand's problems" (*The Indochina Refugee Situation*, op. cit., p. 14). While it had been possible to reach a compromise at Geneva in July which did result in a significant alteration of Vietnamese policy towards boat refugees, there was no agreed basis for a political solution in Kampuchea which might alleviate the conditions encouraging a mass flow of refugees. The ASEAN members repeated their call for a withdrawal of Vietnamese forces from Kampuchea in a motion put to the U.N. General Assembly in mid-November and carried by a large majority (91 to 21, with 29 abstentions), but this resolution was predictably bitterly denounced by Vietnam and the Heng Samrin regime. It seemed unlikely that Vietnam would modify its policies of firmly supporting the Heng Samrin regime and seeking the destruction of the residual Pol Pot forces, even if this meant continued large scale creation of refugees and continued tension and instability for Thailand.

Vietnam, ASEAN and the Indochina Refugee Crisis

The Indochina refugee crisis had important ramifications for ASEAN, Vietnam and the prospects for regional détente and security. For ASEAN, the refugee crisis had the effect of further expanding its role and scope as a regional organization and of enhancing its international standing. Despite differences in individual emphasis and approach, the ASEAN members demonstrated a capacity to consult and co-operate in developing policies for alleviating the impact of the refugee arrivals, to minimize the discord between members arising from conflicting national interests and policies (as in the case of Malaysia and Indonesia) and to gain international action on issues that were of vital concern to all. The collective declarations by the ASEAN Foreign Ministers on the issue of the boat refugees and on the Kampuchean crisis, and the joint ASEAN diplomatic effort at Bali, Geneva and in the U.N. brought ASEAN its most extensive and significant international recognition so far. The prestige of ASEAN and its members was also effectively advanced by international criticism of Vietnam's role in the refugee exodus, and the resultant contrast with the relatively much more humanitarian image maintained by the ASEAN states.

However, while the ASEAN response to the refugee crisis in 1979 clearly marked an important stage in its development, the success of its response should not be exaggerated. ASEAN devoted most of its attention to the issue of the boat refugees and the members were able to develop an approach which did achieve a considerable success at Geneva; resettlement and financial assistance for refugees were greatly expanded, and Vietnam restricted the outflow. In relation to the land refugee crisis in Thailand, however, ASEAN had not achieved a comparable impact by late 1979. In spite of widespread international support for ASEAN's position on Kampuchea, there were no signs that Vietnam was prepared to respond in a manner that might slow down the exodus of Khmer refugees into Thailand. It appeared that while Vietnam was prepared to discuss the impact of the boat refugees in the region and make concessions on this issue, it was not prepared to consider the possibility of negotiations or compromise on support for the pro-Vietnamese Heng Samrin regime, no doubt because its leaders felt that Vietnam's national interests were much more crucially at stake in Kampuchea. The net effect of the differential ASEAN success was that Malaysia and Indonesia derived more obvious benefit from ASEAN's diplomacy on refugees than did Thailand, but Thailand still benefited from the solidarity and international support of ASEAN in bolstering its position in relation to the Kampuchean crisis.

The refugee crisis also had important ramifications for Vietnam's relations with the ASEAN members and for the prospects for regional détente. Vietnam's role in the refugee outflow clearly resulted in increased suspicion of its intentions among the ASEAN members. Whatever the exact course and rationale of official policy-making in Vietnam, it was hard to avoid the conclusion that the Vietnamese Government did have a considerable role in the outflow, that its leaders made a number of expressions of concern for the problems of neighbouring states while the mass outflow was in progress, and only acted to restrict the outflow when regional and international pressures became too great. How significant a barrier the refugee exodus issue would be for the long term prospects for Vietnam-ASEAN détente was uncertain. While Singaporean leaders expressed very strong condemnation of Vietnam, leaders of other ASEAN countries while criticizing Vietnam's policies were ready to acknowledge its immense economic and political problems and also the role of continuing Sino-Vietnamese tension and Chinese "threats" to Vietnam in exacerbating the problem.[3] While Vietnam's credibility undoubtedly suffered as a result of the refugee crisis, an extensive series of discussions and communications between Vietnam and ASEAN representatives took place in 1979 (especially between May and July) and the scale of communications was certainly higher than in the tense period in 1975 and 1976 immediately after the end of the Second Indochina War. The continuation of discussions and contacts provided grounds for some optimism, but the doubts raised by Vietnam's role in the exodus and its approach to the issue seemed likely to remain an important factor in ASEAN members' attitudes for a considerable period of time.

A further vitally important aspect of the refugee crisis in late 1979 was that whatever the progress made during the year in alleviating its impact and restricting the outflows, at least from Vietnam, the fundamental causes of the outflows remained unresolved. The continuation of severe economic and political problems in Vietnam and Laos, the continuing tension in Sino-Vietnamese relations and the possibility of a further Chinese "punitive" attack, and the uncertainty of the situation in Kampuchea left the region with ongoing sources of tension and instability. The ending of the human suffering and the political dangers created by the Indochina refugee outflows ultimately depends on the resolution of these intractable problems.

Notes

* The author wishes to thank John Funston and Dr. Carlyle Thayer for their most helpful comments on a draft of this article.
1. *The Indochinese Refugee Situation August 1979; Report of a study mission of the U.S. House of Representatives, August 2–11 1979*, 16 September 1979 (Washington: U.S. Government Printing Office, 1979), p. 18.
2. John Funston, "Thailand and the Indochina Conflicts," *Dyason House Papers*, 6, 1, September 1979, pp. 1–7.
3. See the comments by Malaysia's Deputy Prime Minister and Indonesia's Foreign Minister in the Rosenthal delegation report, op. cit., pp. 18–19, 23–24; and the statement by Ghazali Shafie that every time China "rattles its sword or swings its cane" the Chinese in Vietnam panic and leave the country (*Straits Times*, 12 July 1979).

VIETNAM AND ASEAN
A First Anniversary Assessment

Carlyle A. Thayer

Paradigm Lost — Changing Foreign Policy Models

During the mid- to late-1980s, a major transformation took place in how Vietnam's policy élite conceptualized foreign policy. The roots of this transformation are twofold. They lie in domestic circumstances arising from the socio-economic crisis which confronted Vietnam at that time. And secondly, they lie in external influences arising from the "new political thinking" fashionable in Gorbachev's Soviet Union. Vietnam turned from a foreign policy model heavily structured by ideological considerations to a foreign policy model which placed greater emphasis on national interest, balance of power and *realpolitik*. Vietnamese analysts now tend to emphasize global economic forces and the impact of the revolution in science and technology over military aspects of power when weighing the global balance. The old and new foreign policy models are not mutually exclusive. Ideology and national interest are not dichotomous terms; they can and do overlap and co-exist.

The influence of ideology on Vietnam's foreign policy prior to the mid- to late-1980s may be illustrated as follows. From the inception of the Democratic Republic of Vietnam as an established state in Southeast Asia in 1954, its élite accepted the "two camp" thesis that the world was divided between the forces of socialism and imperialism. In the late 1960s Vietnam adopted a framework known as the "three revolutionary currents". According to this model, global order was determined by three trends (or revolutionary currents): the strength of the socialist camp headed

---

Reprinted from Daljit Singh, ed., *Southeast Asian Affairs 1997* (Singapore: Institute of Southeast Asian Studies, 1997), pp. 364–74. At the time of original publication, Carlyle A. Thayer was Associate Professor and Head of the School of Politics at the Australian Defence Force Academy.

by the Soviet Union; the strength of the workers' movement in advanced industrial countries; and by the strength of the forces of national liberation in the Third World. In practical terms, Vietnam allied itself with the Soviet Union as the "cornerstone" of its foreign policy. Hanoi's leaders also viewed Indochina as a strategic entity and sought to develop an integrated alliance system with Laos and Cambodia. Vietnam's 1978 invasion of Cambodia and 25-year treaty of friendship and co-operation with the Soviet Union were logical end products of this orientation. They resulted in a decade-long polarization of regional relations. Vietnam was left isolated and dependent on the Soviet Union and Eastern Europe for economic support.

ASEAN was in the forefront of diplomatic efforts to secure the withdrawal of Vietnamese military forces from Cambodia. This partly took the form of an embargo on trade, aid and investment. These pressures eventually played a part in convincing Hanoi's leaders to seek a negotiated end to the conflict. In December 1986, at the Sixth National Party Congress, as is well known, Vietnam adopted the policy of *doi moi* or renovation. This policy was mainly concerned with overcoming a domestic economic crisis by the adoption of socio-economic reforms whose centrepiece was the dismantling of the central planning apparatus in favour of a market-orientated economy. Vietnam also sought to open its economy to foreign investment.

It was clear to Hanoi's leaders that *doi moi* could not be accomplished without a comprehensive settlement of the Cambodian conflict. In 1987, the Politburo of the Vietnam Communist Party secretly adopted Resolution No. 2 which set in motion a strategic readjustment in Vietnam's national security policy. Vietnam made the decision to withdraw from Cambodia and Laos and to downsize its large standing army.

Vietnam's ideologically-derived worldview began to change in tandem with a rethinking of Soviet foreign policy. It was not until May 1988, however, that Vietnam's new foreign policy orientation was codified. This took the form of Politburo Resolution No. 13 which stressed a "multi-directional foreign policy" orientation.[1] This resolution is now recognized as a major landmark. It is important to note that this followed, and was not contemporary with, the adoption of renovation in economic policy. The emphasis was "to maintain peace, take advantage of favourable world conditions" in order to stabilize the domestic situation and set the base for economic development over the next ten to fifteen years. Politburo Resolutions nos. 2 and 13 set in motion changes in Vietnamese national and foreign policies which contributed to a diplomatic settlement of the Cambodian conflict in October 1991.

An important modification of Vietnam's "multi-directional foreign policy" was adopted by the Seventh National Party Congress in June 1991. Vietnam now sought "to be friends with all countries". This meant intensifying the process of diversification of foreign relations. The major accomplishments of this new orientation were fivefold: normalization of relations with China (November 1991), the restoration of official assistance from Japan (November 1992) and in 1995 normalization of relations with the United States, membership in ASEAN and the signing of a framework agreement with the European Union. For the first time, socialist Vietnam had established relations with all five permanent members of the UN Security Council and equally importantly, with the world's three major economic centres: Europe, North America and East Asia. Vietnam's overall diplomatic relations have expanded to include diplomatic ties with 163 countries by the end of 1996. In 1989 Vietnam had diplomatic relations with only 23 non-communist states.

During 1995 Vietnam exchanged thirty-five major delegations with ASEAN states including the visit of President Le Duc Anh to the Philippines and the visit of the King of Malaysia to Vietnam. Figures released at the end of that year revealed that ASEAN states had invested in 234 projects with total investment capital reaching US$3.2 billion. Singapore ranked first in both the number of projects (108) and capital invested, US$1.4 billion. A year later these figures had risen to 273 projects with a total capitalization of US$4.6 billion. On 15 December 1995 Vietnam signed the protocol acceding to the agreement on the Common Effective Preferential Tariff (CEPT) scheme as a first step in joining the ASEAN Free Trade Area. Vietnam is now obligated to extend most-favoured nation and national treatment to ASEAN member countries. Under the terms of this protocol Vietnam is also required to provide information on its trade regime and move to meet a series of tariff reduction deadlines starting 1 January 1996. Vietnam uses 2,218 tariff lines. It nominated 857 lines in its immediate inclusion list (nearly 39% of the total). Of these, 548 have a zero tariff while the remaining 309 items attract a tariff in the 1–5% range. Vietnam has already met the deadline of January 2006 by which tariffs on all items in the immediate inclusion list must be lowered to between 0–5%.

Vietnam has retained 1,189 tariff lines (54% of the total) on its temporary exclusion list and 26 tariff lines on its sensitive list (1% of the total). It must phase in tariff reductions on the temporary exclusion lines in five equal instalments beginning in January 1999 and ending by January 2003. Thus, by 2003, ninety-two percent of all tariff lines used by Vietnam would fall under the CEPT scheme. Most of Vietnam's sensitive list includes unprocessed agricultural products; these must be phased in starting January 2001 and ending by January 2010.

In sum, in both political and economic relations Vietnam has achieved very favourable circumstances for its integration with the region and the global economy. This chapter will offer an assessment of how Vietnam views the advantages and disadvantages of membership in ASEAN.

First Anniversary Assessments — Advantages

Vietnamese officials state that three main factors accounted for Vietnam's decision to join ASEAN: the desire to have amicable relations with regional states, to attract foreign investment and as a catalyst to its domestic reform process.[2] After joining ASEAN, Vietnam reorganized its bureaucracy by creating a National ASEAN Committee headed by a Deputy Prime Minister with responsibility of co-ordinating all institutions which interact with ASEAN or ASEAN-affiliated bodies. An ASEAN Department was created within the Foreign Ministry. Vietnam participated in the first Asia-Europe Summit Meeting and Fifth ASEAN Summit. Vietnam has agreed to host the Sixth ASEAN Summit meeting in 1998.

Vietnam also received support from ASEAN members, other states and international organizations, such as the United Nations Development Program, to assist in overcoming domestic impediments to full participation in ASEAN's myriad programmes. Priority attention has focused on the reform of the underdeveloped legal system, and overcoming red tape, bureaucracy, and the lack of accountability and transparency in decision-making and policy. Specifically, Vietnam has come under pressure to speed up tax reform, liberalize the financial sector, develop the private sector, reform state enterprises and liberalize trade.

In July 1996 when Vietnam celebrated the first anniversary of its membership in ASEAN it was more committed to the regional association than previously. Among the foreign policy élite there was a general consensus that the decision to join ASEAN was correct and had been a success despite the difficulties it was facing in trying to liberalize its economy and catch up with the other members. This assessment must be viewed within the context of the multiple economic and political objectives Vietnam sought to achieve when it first joined.

In 1994 when Vietnam made the decision to apply for membership in ASEAN it did so with the prime strategic objective of securing of a more peaceful international environment in which to guarantee Vietnam's national security against external threat. According to one Vietnamese writer, "Politically, due to ASEAN's high international prestige, ASEAN membership would enhance Vietnam's diplomatic standing and integrate Vietnam's security with the security of the whole of Southeast Asia, thus creating an external environment favourable for economic development."[3]

A secondary objective was to secure the most favourable external conditions for carrying out economic renovation. Within these broad strategic objectives Vietnam specifically sought to transform its relations with ASEAN states from suspicion to trust and from competition to partnership by moving to resolve such problems areas as the repatriation of Vietnamese refugees, demarcation of continental shelves, overlapping territorial claims (involving Malaysia, the Philippines and Thailand) and fishing disputes. These legacies of history were seen as irritants which could impede the development of closer ASEAN-Vietnam relations. An improvement in Vietnam's relations with ASEAN would also serve to change Vietnam's image (see below) and increase its prestige in global affairs.

Vietnam also sought membership in ASEAN to enhance its bargaining position with other states, specifically China and the United States. Vietnam is now more strategically important to Beijing and Washington as a member of ASEAN. Despite the normalization of relations with China in late 1991, there had been no resolution of overlapping territorial claims in the South China Sea. Indeed, Chinese assertiveness in the Spratly Islands in 1992 served as a catalyst for ASEAN membership. Joining ASEAN, in Hanoi's view, transformed this particular problem from a bilateral one between Beijing and Hanoi to a multilateral one involving China and ASEAN as a group. At the same time as Vietnam conducts bilateral talks with China on territorial disputes, as it does with other ASEAN members such as the Philippines, it also stands behind ASEAN declaratory policy on the settlement of territorial conflicts. However, as Vietnamese analysts point out, "Vietnamese history shows that one-sided relations have led to political isolation and economic difficulties.... Therefore, Vietnam's ASEAN membership should be achieved in a way that would strengthen instead of harm Vietnam's relations with China."[4]

Likewise, Vietnam sought membership in ASEAN as a means of improving its relations with the United States. In 1994 when Vietnam applied for membership in ASEAN it was still subject to a U.S.-imposed trade and aid embargo. By securing membership in ASEAN Vietnam hoped it would transform its image from a "communist trouble maker" to that of a socialist developing country striving to develop a "market-orientated economy". In Hanoi's view, its conversion into a potential "partner for peace" would be attractive to decision-makers in Washington. ASEAN membership would also provide some measure of protection for Hanoi from Washington on such issues as human rights and democratisation. According to one Vietnamese political analyst Vietnam would be "quite happy to hide behind" Malaysia and Singapore on those issues.[5]

Vietnam also set the broad objective of achieving external support for its economic development which it saw as a concomitant of an improvement in the strategic environment. In other words, a transformation in Vietnam's political relations would also lead to a transformation in Vietnam's economic relations which in turn would reinforce its domestic policy of renovation. As a first priority, Vietnam sought to integrate its economy with that of the Asia-Pacific region and global economy. Joining ASEAN meant participation in the ASEAN Free Trade Area (AFTA) and gaining familiarity with the norms and practices of international trade. This in turn will facilitate membership in the Asia-Pacific Economic Co-operation forum (APEC) and eventual membership in the World Trade Organization.[6] As a member of ASEAN, Vietnam could also expect to learn from the developmental experience of its individual members. This would accelerate the development of a competitive market-orientated economy.

As a member of ASEAN and a participant in AFTA, Vietnam expects to benefit from increased trade and investment from ASEAN states. Intra-ASEAN trade is expanding and Vietnam has already reorientated its exports to take advantage of this large market. This trend was evident even before Vietnam formally joined the Association. Imports from ASEAN account for nearly one-half of Vietnam's total imports. About 30% of Vietnam's total trade goes to ASEAN states. The volume of trade with ASEAN countries has risen markedly in dollar value terms and is expected to expand further with Vietnam's participation in ASEAN's CEPT scheme. Admitting Vietnam into AFTA will not greatly affect the other ASEAN economies as trade with Vietnam comprises about 2.5% of the existing intra-ASEAN total. But participation in AFTA may result in trade creation and trade diversion benefits for Vietnam. Vietnam is expected to increase its imports from ASEAN, particularly from Singapore. These imports will replace more costly domestically manufactured goods and may even have the indirect affect of dampening the smuggling of Chinese goods. ASEAN, Thailand in particular, will divert its trade by importing more from Vietnam under AFTA arrangements. Vietnam may also import quality materials from ASEAN not only for domestic production but for export. As an ASEAN member Vietnam enjoys the Generalized System of Preferences status in selling to Europe and North America. Vietnam's textile, garment, leather and electronic assembly industries are expected to benefit most.

Vietnam expects that membership of AFTA will result in increased foreign direct investment to the extent that the ASEAN region as a whole is seen as a stable and profitable market. Vietnam also expects to receive from member states transfers of high technology which was created by foreign investment initially. Four ASEAN countries — Singapore, Malaysia, Thailand and Indonesia — rank among the largest fifteen foreign investors in Vietnam, particularly in tourism and real estate. ASEAN investment in Vietnam is expected to rise as investors seek to exploit Vietnam's lower labour costs in resource and labour intensive industries.

Eighth Party Congress

Vietnam's paradigm shift in foreign policy from a model stressing ideology to one with an emphasis on national interest has provoked internal party debate. Vietnam's diversification of foreign relations, including developing ties with the United States, has not been without its critics as well. This became particularly evident immediately following the normalization of U.S.-Vietnam relations and Vietnam's admission into ASEAN. These events took place during the process of preparing the first draft of the party's Political Report to the Eighth National Party Congress.

In August 1995, Politburo member (and Prime Minister) Vo Van Kiet prepared a twenty-one page classified memorandum for consideration by the Politburo.[7] Kiet touched on a number of internal party issues and warned that if Vietnam did not step up the process of renovation the leadership risked being removed from power. In his discussion of foreign relations Kiet argued that confrontation between socialism and imperialism had given way to multipolarity as the dominant feature of the global system. According to Kiet, "Unlike the past, national interests, regional interests, and other global interests (peace, environment, development, globalization of manufacturing) play an ever more important role in creating conflicts and forming new alliances..." In his view the four remaining socialist countries (China, Vietnam, North Korea and Cuba) "cannot act and have no international value as a united economic force" as each was still searching for a suitable path of development. Kiet also mentioned "hot spots" which could flare up, a pointed reference to Chinese actions in the South China Sea.

According to Kiet, changes in the international system resulted in greater acceptance of Vietnam's one-party state by the international community. He listed normalization of diplomatic relations with the United States and membership in ASEAN as two major achievements of his government. In so doing he downplayed the threat posed by the United States to Vietnam. Indeed, he argued for a strengthening of relations with Washington: "Vietnam will benefit more if we go down that path". In sum, according to Kiet, Vietnam now faced the most favourable international environment since 1945 and it should take determined steps to take advantage of this situation.

Vietnam's ideological conservatives, in contrast, still stressed the importance of conflict and competition between socialism and imperialism. In their view socialism was temporarily on the decline and capitalism inevitably would be replaced. Party conservatives are particularly concerned by the threat to one-party rule posed by the process of "opening up" and "integration into the world economy". These critics argue that Vietnam's "socialist orientation" will be undermined by the development of a market economy at home and by political and cultural influences from abroad. In its starkest form, Vietnam is seen as the victim of a campaign of "peaceful evolution" orchestrated by "foreign reactionaries and imperialists" (overseas Vietnamese and the United States). Conservative Le Xuan Luu has argued that ideology — Marxism-Leninism and the Thoughts of Ho Chi Minh — must be defended equally along with the country's air space and land and sea territory (writing in *Tap Chi Cong San*, May 1996).

At least two major drafts of the Political Report were drawn up before the final version was presented to the Eighth Congress.[8] When all three versions are compared it is notable that the foreign policy section was the most heavily edited and amended. Most remarkably, the foreign policy sections of the first two drafts failed to mention ASEAN (Vietnam's membership in ASEAN was noted in passing in the first section which dealt with successes achieved after ten years of renovation). A reference was finally inserted as the fourth point in a nine point list of Vietnam's foreign policy objectives. Vietnam's fourth foreign policy objective was: "To strengthen our relations with neighbouring countries and ASEAN member countries, to constantly consolidate our ties with traditional friendly states, and attach importance to our relations with developed countries and political-economic centres in the world while at the same time upholding the spirit of solidarity and brotherliness with developing countries in Asia, Africa and Latin America, and with the Non-Aligned Movement." The inclusion of a reference to ASEAN was made as a result of the strenuous objections by ASEAN Ambassadors stationed in Hanoi after they saw the public draft released in April. They were reportedly furious that such as important event as Vietnam's membership in ASEAN had been given such scant attention.

A Political Report to a national party congress is, by its nature, a concensus document. Each section of the Political Report is drafted by a specialist committee and is circulated internally before being released for wider discussion. Draft copies of the Political Report are routinely discussed at provincial party congresses held prior to the national congress. It is not surprising then to find that the section of the 1996 Political Report which dealt with "the characteristics of the international system", reflected the views of ideological conservatives as well as the more pragmatic orientation of policy practitioners. The Political Report, for example, noted that "with the collapse of socialism in the former Soviet Union and Eastern European countries, socialism has suffered a temporary set-back. This does not change the characteristics of our times, however; humanity is still living in the transitional period from capitalism to socialism..." The Report goes on to note that the "scientific and technological revolution is developing at an increasingly rapid pace, thereby accelerating various production forces and the process of globalisation of the world economy and social life". The Political Report also juxtaposes the potential for conflict arising from competition in the areas of economics, science and technology with the potential for co-operation arising from global peace and stability. Or, to round out this point, the Political Report notes the role of "socialist countries, communist and workers parties and revolutionary and progressive forces" alongside peaceful coexistence and cooperation by "nations under different political regimes".

National defence, internal security and foreign relations are seen as mutually reinforcing. According to the 1996 Political Report, Vietnam's first foreign policy priority is "to consolidate a peaceful environment and create more favourable international conditions in order to accelerate socio-economic development, implement national industrialisation and modernisation, and support the cause of national defence and construction". Vietnam's once highly secretive military establishment is now seeking to expand international relations with its ASEAN counterparts as well as other countries. During 1996, for example, defence contracts were made with at least fourteen non-ASEAN countries. The list includes: Australia, Bulgaria, Burma, Cambodia, Canada, China, Cuba, India, Japan, Laos, Russia, South Korea, United Kingdom and the United States. Beginning in 1994 Vietnam's Defence Minister visited all ASEAN states except Brunei. Since joining ASEAN Vietnam has hosted visits by Thailand's Defence Minister, Chief of Staff, Army Commander-in-Chief and a delegation from the National Defence Institute; the Chiefs of Staff from Indonesia's Armed Forces and Air Force; the Philippine's National Defence Secretary and Commander of the Infantry Force; a delegation from Malaysia's Armed Forces Staff College; and Singapore's Defence Minister and a military delegation led by a Brigadier-General. Going in the opposite direction were the Vietnamese Defence Minister and the head of the Army's General Department of Technology who both visited Singapore.

The Vietnamese military are also making their first appearances at region-wide security meetings. At the same time as Vietnam joined ASEAN it became a member of the ASEAN Regional Forum (ARF). Vietnamese representatives have attended the ARF inter-sessional meetings on confidence-building held in Tokyo in January and Jakarta in April, and the Asia-Pacific Security Dialogue hosted by Thailand in March. Vietnam also sent representatives to the Forum for Defence Authorities in the Asia-Pacific Region, the first regional meeting of defence planners, held in Japan in October.

Vietnam's military is one of the most ideologically conservative groups in the Vietnam Communist Party. While the sudden burst in developing new military relations appears impressive, on closer examination little has been accomplished. Vietnamese military officials restrict bilateral discussions to generalities. They are mainly concerned to work out the details of how they might acquire needed spare parts and other equipment. They are extremely wary of developing any relationship in depth. Foreign observers who have sought to engage the Vietnamese in discussions on regional security issues and draw them further into the process of regional security dialogue have become frustrated by Vietnam's stonewalling tactics.

Conclusions

Vietnam joined ASEAN primarily for the political and strategic benefits it calculated it would gain *vis-à-vis* China and the United States. Perhaps the major political disadvantage for Vietnam, long accustomed to asserting its sovereignty and independence, has been the need to meld Vietnam's position to fit in with the ASEAN consensus. As noted by one Vietnamese writer, "despite announcing its commitment to the Treaty of Amity and Co-operation signed in Bali in 1976, Hanoi is not so certain whether it accepts the rules of the game, that is, accepts all the written and unwritten norms of the relationship among ASEAN countries without any exceptions".[9]

Vietnam faces several possible economic disadvantages as a result of ASEAN membership. Vietnam and the other ASEAN economies are essentially competitive not complementary, particularly in the areas of foreign investment and development assistance. Vietnam's developing industry faces potentially stiff challenges from its ASEAN counterparts. In August ASEAN Secretary-General Ajit Singh told Vietnam it would need to end its quota system (which favours state enterprises), eliminate other non-tariff barriers, and enhance the transparency of its trade regime. These steps may aggravate Vietnam's trade imbalance with ASEAN and increase an already growing trade deficit. More than half of Vietnam's trade deficit of US$3.5 billion (1996 figures) is with other ASEAN countries. There is also the possibility that Vietnam's tax base could be undermined by the in-flow of goods from ASEAN states as part of the AFTA regime. At present Vietnam earns a portion of its domestic revenue from tariffs on imported goods. When these tariffs are lowered or eliminated the flow of revenue from this source to the central government will decline. Vietnamese policy-makers are now considering off-setting taxes, such as consumption and turnover taxes, to offset these expected losses. This is a highly complex issue with the finer technical points being debated by Vietnamese economists and party officials.

The major disadvantage of ASEAN membership in the eyes of some ideological conservatives lies in the potential for economic success to contribute to political instability if not speed up the erosion of one-party rule in Vietnam. Ideological conservatives are presently fighting a rearguard action trying to bolster the state-owned sector of the economy while placing constraints on the private sector. Reformers and foreign policy pragmatists argue that sometime between the Seventh and Eighth National Party Congresses Vietnam has "lost direction" or suffered from a "loss of orientation". In sum, not only has a "paradigm been lost" but Vietnam is still suffering from a crisis of faith in its foreign relations.

Vietnam's Foreign Minister Nguyen Manh Cam has called for a "deepening of relations" with foreign countries. What does this mean in practical terms? On the surface it means going beyond the simple framework of "diversifying relations" and "making friends with all countries" to develop multifaceted relations. But Vietnam has hardly succeeded in going beyond the economic dimension. After foreign direct investment, aid, and trade, where does the relationship go? Vietnam emphasizes its own independence, stability, socialist orientation and integration with the world. This had led to a shallowness or flatness in relations, especially on the political and security and defence planes. Ties are advancing at glacial pace in these areas. Note the anodyne flavour of the following report:

> The party leader [Do Muoi] said that the visit of the Singapore defence minister would make an important contribution to the promotion of mutual understanding and to the consolidation of bilateral friendship and co-operation between the two countries.
>
> He expressed his pleasure at the fruitful development of relations between Vietnam and Singapore as well as between Vietnam and other members of the Association of Southeast Asian Nations (ASEAN), thus creating favourable conditions for Vietnam's socio-economic development. He further said that Vietnam wished, together with other ASEAN countries, to build Southeast Asia into a region of peace, stability, co-operation, development and prosperity.
>
> Prime Minister Vo Van Kiet highly appreciated the friendship and cooperation

between the two countries. He briefed his guest on the socio-economic situation of Vietnam.[10]

Vietnam's "loss of orientation" has led to a certain formalism in the conduct of its foreign policy. Relations are established but not consummated. It would appear that deep-seated insecurities within the party structure account for this. There is a fear about developing close political ties with non-socialist states and the impact this might have on domestic affairs. This results in superficial professions of friendship and co-operation across a spectrum of activities, but substantial relations fail to develop further. The initiative in bilateral relations is left to the foreign partner.

All in all, the development of Vietnam's international relations and defence ties with its fellow ASEAN members are vitally dependent on a deepening and quickening of the process of socio-economic reform. Vietnam must increasingly work harder to preserve the gains it has already won.

Notes

1. Nguyen Dy Nien, "Tiep tuc doi moi va mo cua vi su nghiep cong nghiep hoa, hien dai hoa dat nuoc", *Tap Chi Cong San*, no. 12, June 1996.
2. Doan Manh Giao, "Why Vietnam Joins ASEAN", Paper presented to international seminar on "Vietnam in ASEAN: Business Prospects and Policy Directions", Kuala Lumpur, 19 December 1995.
3. Hoang Anh Tuan, "Why Hasn't Vietnam Gained ASEAN Membership?" *Contemporary Southeast Asia*, 15, no. 3 (December 1993): 283.
4. Ibid., pp. 288–89.
5. Quoted by Adam Schwarz, "Joining The Fold", *Far Eastern Economic Review*, 16 March 1995.
6. Vietnam has applied for membership in both APEC and the WTO. The 1996 APEC Summit in Subic Bay decided to admit Vietnam by 1998 most probably at the summit scheduled for Kuala Lumpur.
7. "Thu Vo Van Kiet goi Bo Chinh Tri", *Viet Luan* [Paris], no. 1053, 5 January 1996, pp. 30–31 and 58–60. I am grateful to Thaveeporn Vasavakul for providing a copy of this source.
8. Dang Cong San Viet Nam, *Du Thao Cac Van Kien Trinh Dai Hoi VIII cua Dang (Tai Lieu Dung Tai Dai Hoi Dang Cap Co So)*, Mat (Secret), Luu Hanh Noi Bo (Internal Circulation), December 1995; "Du Thao Bao Cao Chinh Tri cua Ban Chap Hanh Trung Uong Dang Khoa VII Trinh Dai Hoi Lan Thu VIII cua Dang", *Nhân Dân*, 10 April 1996 supplement; and "Bao Cao Chinh Tri", Quan Doî Nhân Dân, 30 June 1996. For a general overview of the Eighth Congress and foreign policy, see: Vu Khoan, "Dai hoi VIII va cong tac doi ngoai", *Tuan bao Quoc Te*, no. 26, 26 June–2 July 1996, pp. 1 and 10.
9. Pham Cao Phong, "How Asean's newest member is coping", *Trends, in Business Times Weekend Edition*, 29–30 June 1996.
10. Vietnam News Agency, 2–6 November 1996.

VIETNAM
In Search of a New Growth Model

Jonathan Pincus

Vietnam suffered two major domestic financial crises on either side of the global economic crisis of 2008. This extended period of turbulence destabilized the economic model that had been in place for most of the *doi moi* or "renovation" period since the late 1980s. The model had consisted of export-oriented and labour intensive "vent for surplus" sectors welded to a state-dominated economy producing goods and services for the domestic market. The former generated employment and export earnings, while the latter distributed economic rents throughout Vietnam's highly commercialized and fragmented state apparatus.

By the early 2000s, rapid credit growth was fuelling speculative investments in equities, property and other risky ventures by domestic businesses and households, both in the state and non-state sectors. This process gradually undermined bank, corporate and household balance sheets. By 2011 the decay could no longer be concealed, and major scandals broke in the state economic groups, notably in the shipbuilder Vinashin and the state shipping company Vinalines. The export sector continued to grow, led by surging exports of mobile phones and other electronic goods as global producers sought to diversify production bases away from China, where wages and other costs were rising quickly. However, domestic investment and consumption stagnated as businesses and households struggled under the weight of a heavy debt burden, frozen asset markets and tight credit conditions. Moderate rates of growth have been sustained but they remain heavily dependent on foreign

---

Reprinted from Malcolm Cook and Daljit Singh, eds., *Southeast Asian Affairs 2016* (Singapore: ISEAS – Yusof Ishak Institute, 2016), pp. 379–97. At the time of original publication, Jonathan Pincus was affiliated with the Open Society Foundations and the Centre for Development Studies, University of Cambridge.

direct investment and external demand. The challenge facing the government is to devise a new growth model that builds on the country's export success and stimulates investment in domestic supplier and downstream industries, while at the same time opening domestic markets to greater competition.

This chapter sets out to do three things. First, it briefly describes the growth model that evolved during the *doi moi* period and remained intact until the crises of 2008–11 played themselves out. One of the most interesting features of the model is the concentration of domestic commercial activity within the state, and the resulting absence of large-scale private firms in the dynamic export sectors or the import-substituting sectors. Second, we revisit the crises of 2008 and 2010 to emphasize the central importance of these events to the breakdown of the old model. Finally, we consider some of the constraints that policymakers face in fashioning a new model that would build on the achievements of *doi moi* while avoiding the pitfalls of state commercialization and the resulting obstacles to autonomous private sector development.

The Old Growth Model

The *doi moi* model evolved over the two decades beginning in the late 1980s and marked a gradual turning away from central planning and towards a mixed or "socialist market economy", to use the government's preferred terminology. As many scholars have pointed out, economic reform was less a conscious reorientation of policy than an unintended outcome of defensive actions to relieve conditions of extreme shortage while maintaining the Communist Party's monopoly on political power.[1] Agriculture was decollectivized in stages, domestic prices were liberalized and the state's domination of foreign trade relaxed. Greater space was allowed for foreign investment and private sector activity.

These changes made it possible for millions of Vietnamese households and small businesses, and foreign invested enterprises, to mobilize underutilized land and labour in the production of goods for export. The noted Burmese economist Hla Myint borrowed Adam Smith's term "vent for surplus" to describe this process, which he viewed as a common pattern in Southeast Asia.[2] Vietnam's vent-for-surplus growth started in the agricultural sector and gradually expanded into labour-intensive manufacturing. A net food importer in the 1980s, Vietnam was by 2000 the second-largest rice exporter in the world, the second-largest exporter of coffee, the top exporter of pepper and cashews, and an important producer of fish, shellfish, fruit, vegetables and cut flowers. Most of these commodities were produced on small farms and marketed through state trading companies. Garment exports expanded by 20 per cent per annum, and footwear by 13 per cent in the decade following implementation of the Bilateral Trade Agreement with the United States. The wages earned by these workers — like the profits going to small farmers — drove increases in domestic demand, which accounted for more than half of Vietnam's output growth over the period 1990 to 2010.

Agriculture and labour-intensive manufacturing were the growth engines of the *doi moi* period. As shown in Figure 1, exports as a share of GDP rose from about one-third to nearly 90 per cent after 1990, making Vietnam one of the most open economies in the region. In the aid donor literature, the explosion of production on

FIGURE 1
Exports as a Percentage of GDP, Vietnam and Comparator Countries

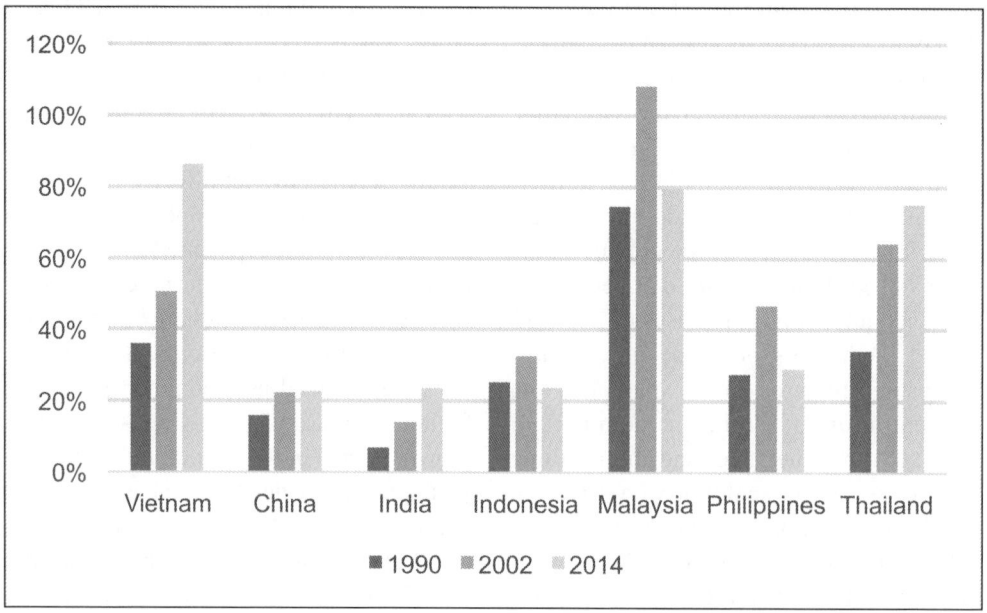

Source: World Development Indicators.

family farms, in small workshops and foreign enterprises is usually interpreted as the retreat of the state and its replacement by a thriving private sector. There is certainly an element of truth to this reading of events, as the shift from rationing under central planning to market allocation, and the relaxation of restrictions on inward investment and private business removed important segments of trade, agriculture and manufacturing from state entities and placed them in private hands. However, what is often missed in these accounts is that the state did not so much withdraw from these sectors as strategically reposition itself in the most lucrative segments and activities, such as control over natural resource exploitation, domestic and international commodity trading, distribution and retail, manufacturing for the domestic market, transport, finance, construction, property development and telecommunications.

In effect, the state retained control over the commanding heights of the economy — in other words, large scale and strategic domestic industries — while leaving small-scale, less profitable activities to household enterprises and small firms. Part of the explanation for the continuing dominance of state-owned enterprises and state agencies despite the growing acceptance of private activity lies in the absence of influential groups outside of the state that had the power and self-awareness to demand limits on the ability of government to manipulate domestic markets. Private activity had been strictly controlled under the war economy and largely prohibited during the brief attempt at central planning after reunification. But even before then, Vietnam had never produced a significant domestic commercial class. The exodus of much of the ethnic Chinese community in the 1970s was a significant loss of commercial experience and entrepreneurialism. The resulting vacuum was filled by state-owned enterprises, central and provincial agencies and government personnel working on their own account or linked to nominally non-state businesses and individuals. These state and state-related entities were well positioned to mobilize state power to achieve commercial ends. They had the experience, connections and control over land and capital that was required. No genuinely independent commercial interests existed that could put pressure on government to rein in the state enterprises and open opportunities for non-state actors. As Jonathan London notes, against expectations that liberalization would give rise to independent capitalists, "what occurred was the development of a business class within the state".[3]

Thus the *doi moi* growth model comprised small-scale domestic producers, foreign firms and medium-to-large-scale domestic enterprises under state control or closely linked to the state. Large private domestic firms are rare, and virtually non-existent in the manufacturing sector. The largest domestic manufacturing firm in Vietnam by market capitalization is the Thai Nguyen Iron and Steel Company, a partially equitized state-owned enterprise with a registered capital of just US$135 million. The ten largest Vietnamese companies consist of three banks, the state-owned insurer Baoviet, three mobile network operators, Electricity of Vietnam, joint-venture oil producer Vietsovpro, and the state railway company. There are no genuinely private companies among the largest thirty enterprises in Vietnam.

Equitization, or the process of converting state-owned enterprises into joint-stock companies, was seen by many as a vehicle through which a genuine private sector could be created from the reallocation of state assets. But in the event, equitization never represented a real challenge to state domination of the commanding heights of the economy. Martin Gainsborough has shown that managers of state-owned enterprises and provincial officials were well placed to control the process and to channel public assets, particularly land, into joint-stock companies under their control.[4] The government retained a controlling share in 36 per cent of equitized state-owned enterprises over the period 2001–11, and ownership of 57 per cent of all shares sold over the same period.[5] In Gainsborough's formulation, equitization did not represent a retreat of the government from the economic sphere but rather "state advance".[6] The fact was that no other group of people existed that had access to the capital, knowledge and connections to take control over the new joint-stock companies formed by equitization.

State domination of the commanding heights of the economy left little room for private firms to expand without the support of government agencies or people connected to state decision-making in some way. Private companies find it difficult to get the permits or access to land and bank credit that they need to mount a serious challenge to incumbents from the state sector.[7] Constraints on private activity are closely associated with the presence of state companies in the same sector or location. For example, Nguyen and Freeman report that provinces with a high density of state-owned enterprises provide less credit to private firms and require more time to issue Land Use Rights Certificates (LURC) than other provinces. Malesky and Taussig find that the allocation of bank credit is related to the presence or absence of political connections, and that the most profitable private firms do not even attempt to get bank loans.[8] Nguyen and Le show how state enterprises' easier access to land, credit and export quotas in the textile and garment sector reduces the profitability and viability of private firms.[9] Nguyen and Van Dijk find that corruption disproportionately harms private firms.[10]

State companies themselves are fragmented geographically, oriented to local markets and technologically unsophisticated. The government has made several attempts to construct national champions from these firms, combining local and regional entities into General Corporations and later Economic Groups in mining, energy, transportation, telecommunications, manufacturing and utilities. Inspired by Korea's chaebol and large Chinese state business groups, the government sought to concentrate its resources and scarce managerial capacity on a limited number of firms that it hoped would develop technological capabilities and realize economies of scale. However, the state proved unable or unwilling to impose discipline on these companies, which set about capitalizing on their easy access to state credit and land to speculate in Vietnam's booming property and financial markets.[11] For the most part, these business groups did not consolidate or rationalize their operations, but instead added new subsidiaries in a wide range of activities, often unrelated to the core business of the group. Vinashin, the state shipbuilder, controlled 445 subsidiaries and twenty joint venture companies and had taken on $4.5 billion in debt by the time of its collapse in 2010. But much the same could be said for other groups, including Vinatex (textiles and garments), PetroVietnam (energy), Vinacomin (mining) and Vietnam Airlines (aviation).

Diversification of state economic groups was financed by rapid growth of the banking system and in particular the rise of the joint-stock banks. Domestic credit rose from 5 per cent of GDP in 1995 to a peak of 115 per cent in 2010. Investment as a share of GDP rose from less than one-quarter in 1994 to a high of 35 per cent in 2007 (Figure 2). High rates of investment without a corresponding acceleration in growth resulted in falling levels of capital efficiency. Vu Minh Khuong points out that total factor productivity growth, which was high in the 1990s, came to a virtual standstill after 2000 as state companies borrowed heavily to invest in speculative activities.[12]

Thus, on the eve of the first domestic crisis, the *doi moi* model was still intact, although fault lines had begun to emerge. Rapid growth of exports from the vent-for-surplus production created millions of jobs and generated billions of dollars in foreign exchange, and in doing so had supported the growth of domestic demand. These activities were largely carried out by small farms and workshops and by foreign-invested enterprises. The commanding heights of the economy remained in the state sector, but failure to impose discipline on these groups opened the way for them to invest heavily in speculative, non-core activities. Financial liberalization, including the rapid growth of joint-stock banks, provided the finance for these ventures. The absence of large-scale, genuinely private firms, and a politically important domestic commercial class, meant that there was little pressure on government to curtail the power of state groups and companies.

FIGURE 2
Gross Fixed Capital Formation and Domestic Credit as Percentage of GDP

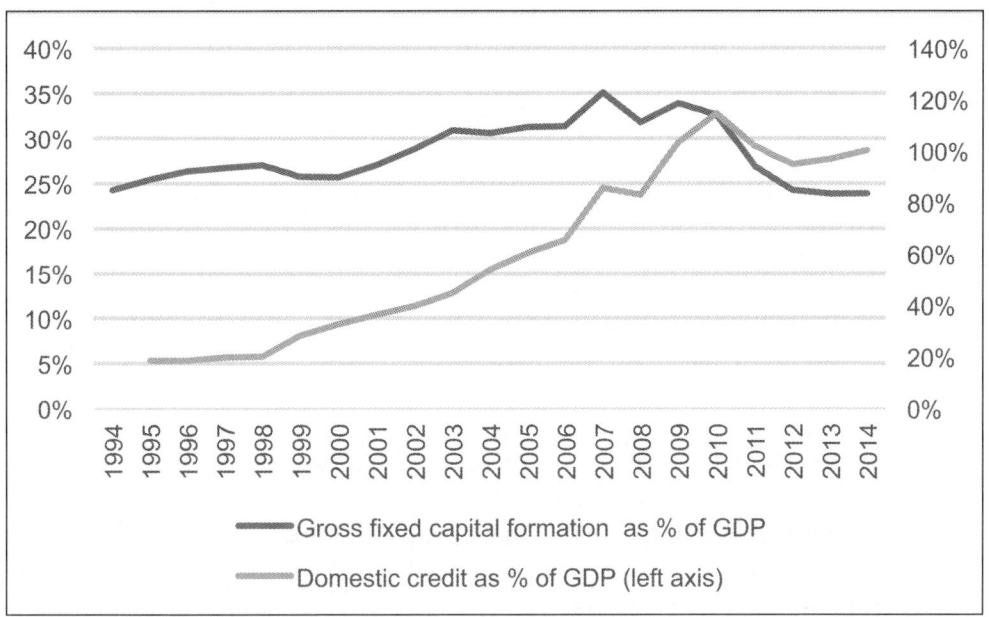

Source: World Development Indicators.

Although vulnerabilities were increasingly apparent, the model did succeed in delivering relatively high rates of growth with modest price inflation, until the first crisis hit in 2008 (Figure 3).

Three Crises

The reaction of global and domestic financial markets to Vietnam's accession to the World Trade Organization in 2007 was nothing short of euphoric. Inward portfolio investment in bonds, equities and other financial instruments, which amounted to about 2 per cent of GDP in 2006, spiked to 8 per cent the following year. Foreign direct investment also rose sharply (Figure 4). The result was a classic emerging-market crisis driven by a sudden flood of foreign capital. The State Bank of Vietnam (SBV) lacked the policy instruments to sterilize an inflow of dollars on this scale, or in other words to avoid a situation in which the flood of dollars fed directly into the domestic money supply. Short of capital controls, it is difficult to see what SBV could have done given the instruments available to it. The resulting monetary shock drove up asset and consumer prices and the real value of the Vietnamese dong, which encouraged imports and threatened to choke off export growth.

The government's response was to slam on the brakes, raising interest rates and reserve requirements, and tightening control over the foreign exchange market. The tight money policy worked, with inflation subsiding by the third quarter. But just as

FIGURE 3
GDP Growth and Consumer Price Inflation

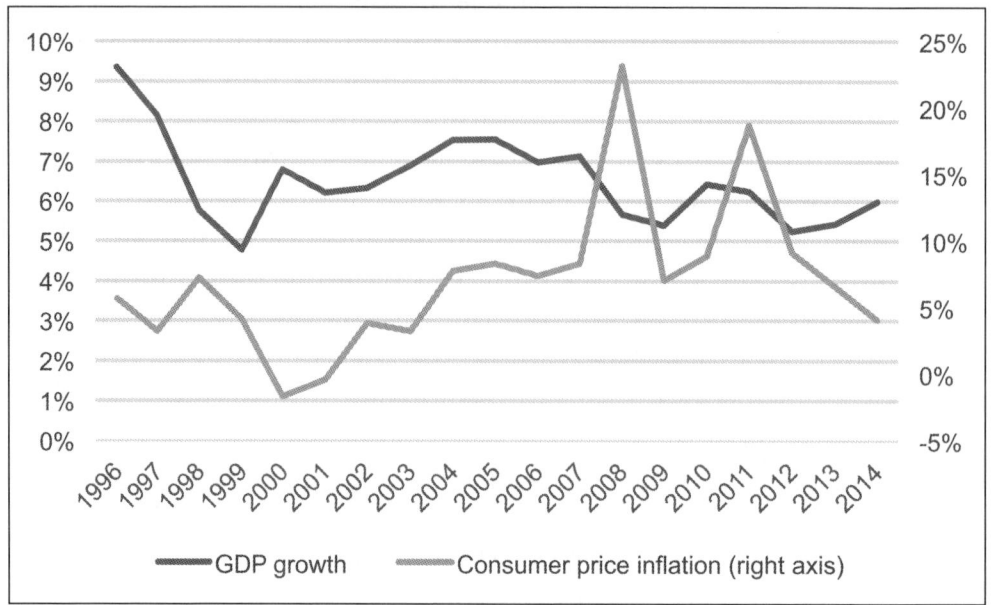

Source: World Development Indicators.

FIGURE 4
Foreign Direct and Portfolio Investment, Net as Percentage of GDP

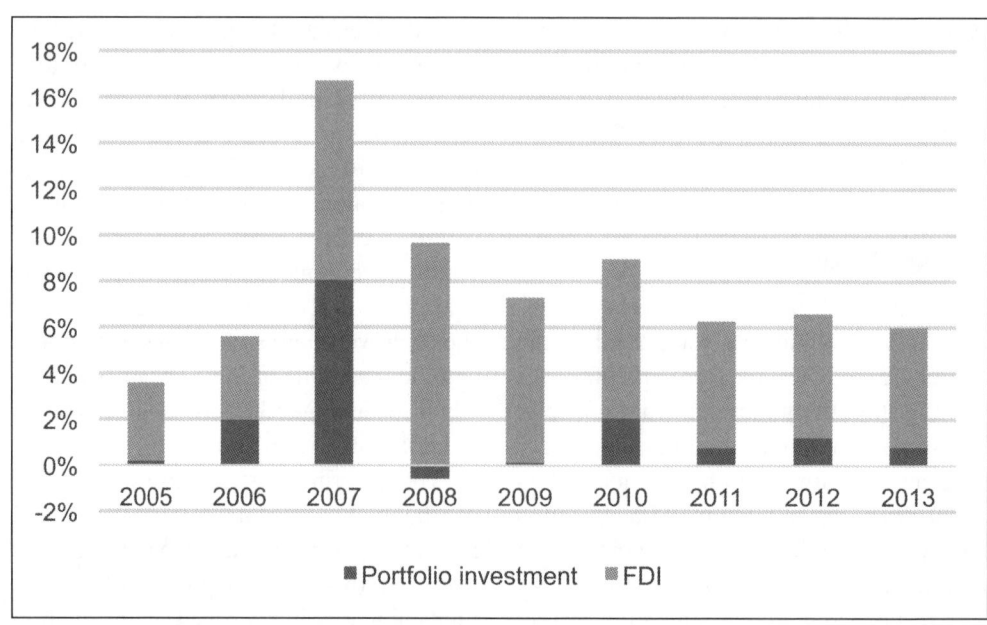

Source: World Development Indicators.

Vietnam was coming to grips with this first domestic crisis, a far more severe global shock was emerging on the horizon. As the gravity of America's sub-prime mortgage crisis became apparent, the government was forced to execute a 180-degree turn to stimulate domestic demand as global trade contracted and exports fell.

Like other export-oriented countries in the region, the main policy question facing the government in 2008–9 was not whether a domestic stimulus package was required, but what form the stimulus should take. Given Vietnam's infrastructure backlog, the most sensible option was to boost public investment in roads, railways, irrigation, drainage, water supply, sanitation and other projects that would support productivity growth and improve quality of life over the medium term, and would create jobs for thousands of low- or semi-skilled workers in the short term. This was the path taken by China, which financed infrastructure investment on a scale that not only sustained domestic growth but also global commodity prices as demand for steel and other inputs soared.

For various reasons the Vietnamese government decided that infrastructure investment would not deliver jobs in sufficient numbers within the timeframe required. The leadership opted instead to undertake a massive monetary stimulus conducted through the banking sector. The government subsidized borrowing undertaken by state and private enterprises in labour-intensive industries and provided additional loans to state enterprises through the state-owned commercial banks. Credit growth accelerated again, with the credit-to-GDP ratio reaching a new peak in 2010 (Figure 2). Lending was supported through 2010, but the government, eager to sustain growth through the Party Congress in January 2011, left the stimulus in place for too long. Inflation once again accelerated in 2011, forcing the government into another retreat and precipitating the third crisis in the series — this time a home-grown crash originating in the domestic banking sector.

Sharply falling asset prices and weak domestic demand triggered a rise in non-performing loans (NPLs). Major state economic groups collapsed and had to be bailed out by government injections of cash and loan forgiveness. The largest state lender, Agribank, was hit by a series of scandals and according to SBV accounted for a quarter of all NPLs in the system. Although official NPL rates did not rise much, bank officials and independent experts estimated that they were in fact as high as 15 per cent in some state-owned commercial and joint-stock banks. Connected ownership, connected lending and cross-shareholdings in the banking sector were rife, complicating efforts to isolate bad debt and failing financial institutions. The government was reluctant to take decisive action against undercapitalized banks, preferring instead to encourage mergers and restructuring with state assistance. Several small joint-stock banks were effectively insolvent by 2013, and three were eventually taken over by SBV. Credit became difficult to obtain as banks moved to strengthen their balance sheets, with the loan-to-GDP ratio actually falling in 2011 and 2012 (Figure 2).

High levels of debt and credit contraction forced the state and private business sectors and households to focus on deleveraging since 2011. This is apparent in Figure 5, which presents net lending for three sectors: the government, households and businesses, and the rest of the world (as reflected in the current account balance). By definition, net lending across these

FIGURE 5
Net Lending as Percentage of GDP

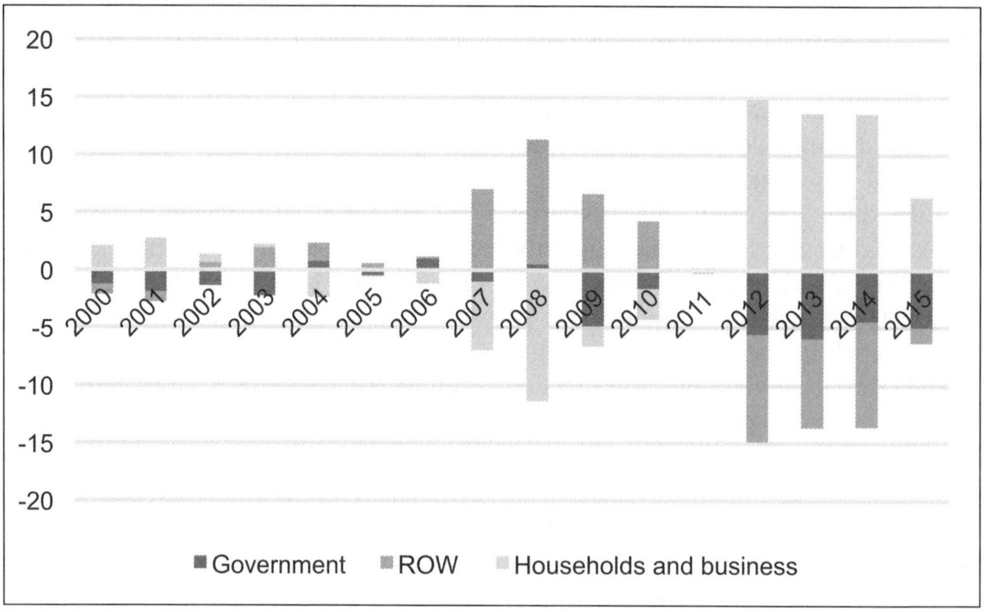

■ Government   ■ ROW   ■ Households and business

Source: IMF International Financial Statistics.

sectors must sum to zero, since all borrowing is balanced by an equal amount of lending. Unfortunately, flow-of-funds statistics from Vietnam do not yet permit us to separate the domestic corporate and household sectors.

Nevertheless, the results reveal the impact of the long crisis on Vietnam's growth model. Prior to 2007 the household/business sector was either a marginal net borrower or net lender, depending on the year. It is probably fair to conclude that households were net lenders and corporations net borrowers in most years, with the difference in demand for credit met by some combination of borrowing from abroad and government fiscal deficits. In any case, net borrowing was small relative to GDP, and no single sector sustained high levels of borrowing over consecutive years.

The big changes arrived in 2007 with WTO accession and the large capital inflows of 2007 and 2008. Suddenly the rest of the world was a large net lender to Vietnamese households and businesses, which borrowed massively over the period 2007 to 2010. This also covers the period of the monetary stimulus of 2009 to 2010, when both households and businesses acquired liabilities at historic rates. Borrowing on this scale fed asset bubbles that encouraged even more speculation, more borrowing and ultimately more non-performing loans in the banking system. The household and business sectors accumulated debt at an unsustainable rate, setting the scene for the lean years that followed.

By 2012 the process of deleveraging was in full swing, with households and businesses emerging as net lenders on a large scale to both government — which is running large fiscal deficits — and the rest of the world. Essentially the Vietnamese economy has been exporting its way out of its domestic debt overhang, suppressing domestic consumption, increasing exports and saving the surplus.

Domestic deleveraging has taken a large toll on economic growth by suppressing both domestic investment and consumption. This comes out clearly in Figure 6, which decomposes GDP growth since 1997. During the heyday of the *doi moi* model, growth was largely driven by domestic consumption. Exports grew rapidly in tandem with imports, but the main positive effect of vent-for-surplus growth was the creation of millions of jobs and other income-earning opportunities. Rising incomes in both cities and villages fuelled domestic consumption and investment. As noted earlier, investment assumes a greater role after 2000 with the increase in credit growth and diversification among state-owned enterprises. Investment and consumption soar during the triple crisis, first driven by capital inflows and then by the government's monetary stimulus. However, net exports become a drag on growth as the country records large trade deficits, which are merely the flipside of massive capital inflows.

Figure 6 also illustrates the impact of deleveraging on economic growth. Domestic consumption fell sharply after 2009 and did not recover even in 2014. This conclusion is supported by anecdotal evidence of continuing distress in the retail sector as consumers tighten their

FIGURE 6
Decomposition of GDP Growth

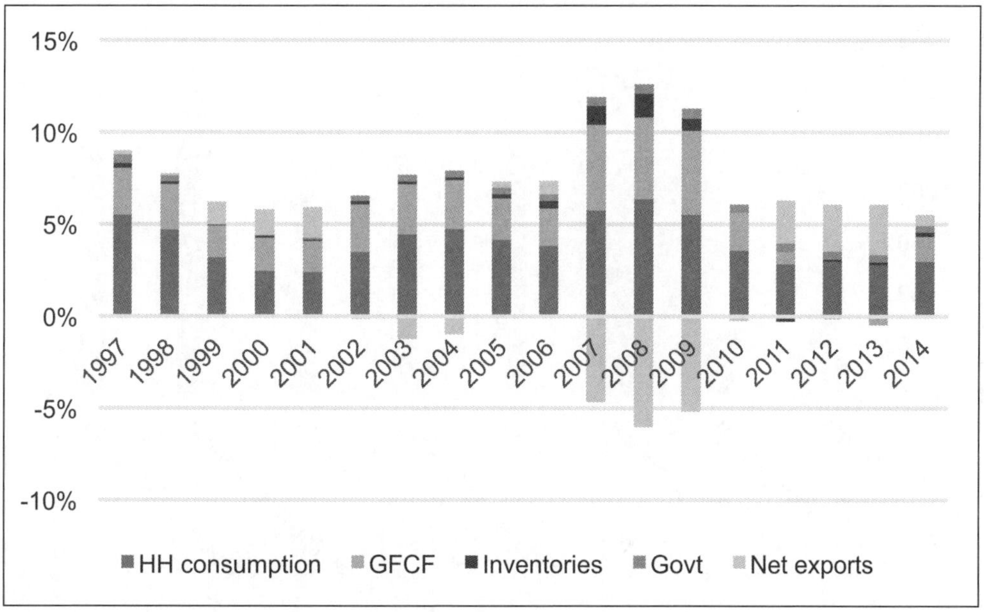

Source: World Development Indicators.

belts. Meanwhile, investment collapsed from 2011 to 2014 (see also Figure 2) as both non-state and private firms struggled with falling asset prices, high levels of debt and tight credit conditions. The only bright spot is net exports, which sustained growth from 2011 to 2013 and probably once again in 2015.

The Search for a New Growth Model

Donor reports and academic studies routinely urge the government to take steps to avoid the "middle-income trap", a problem that is thought to afflict countries that have exhausted opportunities for labour-intensive growth but are not yet able to move into higher value-added industries.[13] Because success in these industries requires educational, judicial and regulatory institutions that develop slowly over many decades, growth rates could decline as the country loses its comparative advantage in cheap and plentiful labour, but still lacks the institutional infrastructure to support capital- and technology-intensive industries such as machinery, electronics and chemicals.

While building the institutions required to support a modern economy is important, we should not lose sight of the fact that Vietnam is still a relatively poor country, where wages are low and underemployment still widespread. Measured in U.S. dollar terms, minimum wages are still low relative to most competitors (Figure 7). In international dollars (purchasing power parity dollars calculated by the World Bank), income per capita in Vietnam

FIGURE 7
Minimum Wages in Selected Asian Countries and Cities, November 2015

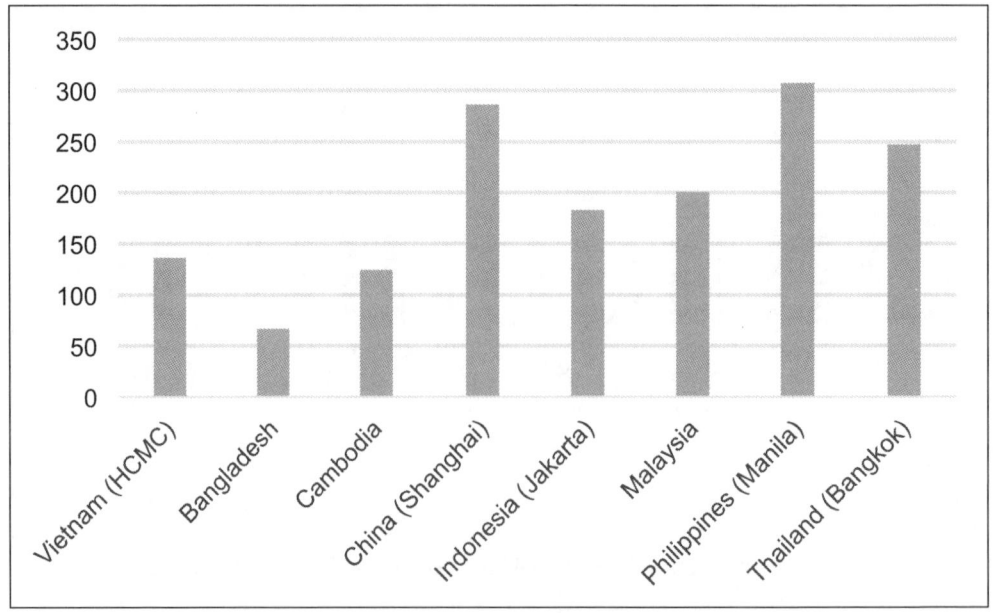

Source: Philippine National Wages and Productivity Commission.

is still one half of that in China and Indonesia and one-fifth of Malaysia's level. According to official statistics, two-thirds of the population live in rural areas and about half of the labour force is employed in agriculture (Figure 8). These indicators suggest that in Vietnam there is still plenty of scope for vent-for-surplus growth, boosting exports to create demand for labour and hence raise domestic incomes.

As wages have risen in China, labour-intensive industries have relocated to Vietnam. Garment exports as a share of GDP have risen consistently over the past decade, creating thousands of jobs and generating billions of dollars in foreign exchange (Figure 9). Given a realistic exchange rate, it is unlikely that Vietnamese labour will be priced out of these markets very soon. There are certainly countries with lower average wages, like Bangladesh and Cambodia, but other costs in these locations are higher. For example, the large number of strikes in Bangladesh effectively increases the cost of labour by increasing the number of workdays in which machines are left idle.

The challenge facing Vietnam is not necessarily moving out of garments and footwear, but instead moving backwards up the supply chain to capture a larger share of value added from exports. For example, Figure 9 compares net exports of garments to net inputs of fibre and yarn — inputs into garment and textile making that are largely imported from China. Vietnam consistently runs deficits in these inputs despite the country's growing importance to the world garment industry. Production of textiles, yarn and fibre are more techno-

FIGURE 8
Agriculture as a Percentage of Total Employment

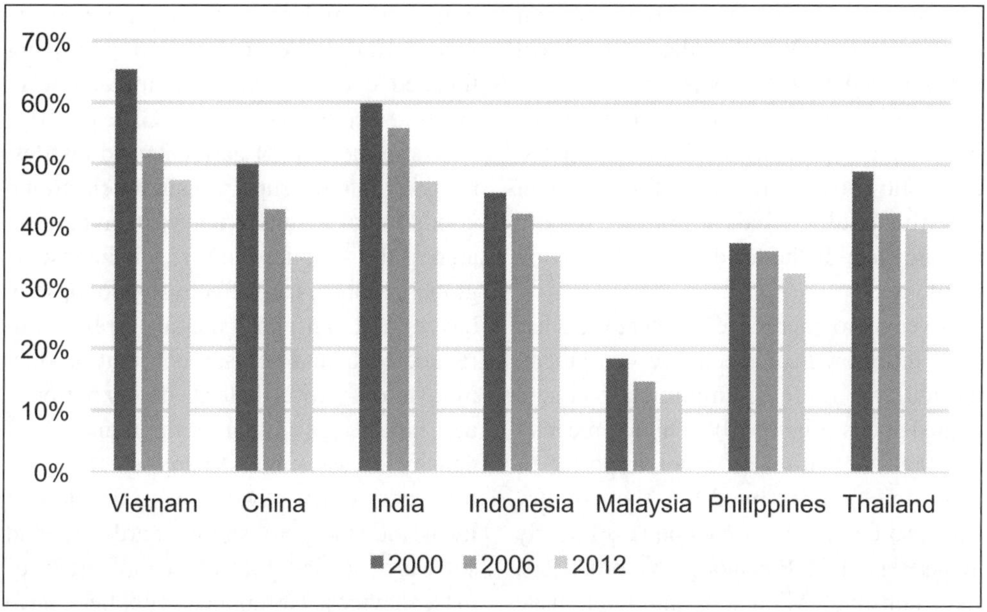

Source: World Development Indicators.

FIGURE 9
Net Exports of Garments and Inputs in Garment Manufacturing

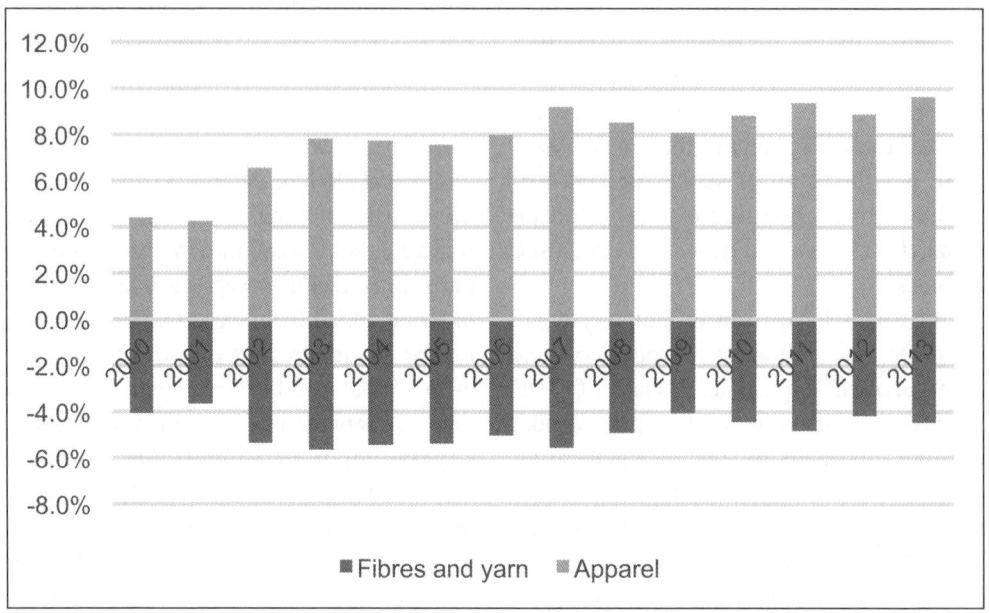

Source: UN Comtrade.

logically sophisticated industries in which economies of scale and scope play an important role. Vinatex, the state-owned garment and textile group, does produce inputs, but not of a quality and at a price that can compete with Chinese imports. Domestic private firms are still too small and financially weak to invest in and operate state-of-the-art dying and weaving facilities.

Even more impressive in recent years has been the growth of electronic equipment, particularly in telecommunications and related goods (Figure 10). While as recently as 2009 Vietnam was a net importer of electronic goods, by 2014 the country had recorded a net surplus equal to nearly 10 per cent of GDP. Major global producers, like Samsung, Microsoft and Intel, have built production facilities in Vietnam, and the trend looks set to continue. These are largely assemblers, importing components from around the region and exporting finished goods. Component imports were equal to about 7 per cent of GDP in 2014.

As in the case of garments and textiles, breaking into the supply chain for electronic goods is not a simple matter. Competition among the supplier industries is intense as global producers are effectively monopsony buyers and can apply massive pressure to reduce costs and demand constant product innovation. Nevertheless, the experience of China suggests that as the number and density of assemblers increases there are tremendous cost advantages to developing local industries to supply hardware and software needed for the manufacture of these devices. Component suppliers have a strong incentive to follow assemblers

**FIGURE 10
Net Exports of Electronics and Electronic Components**

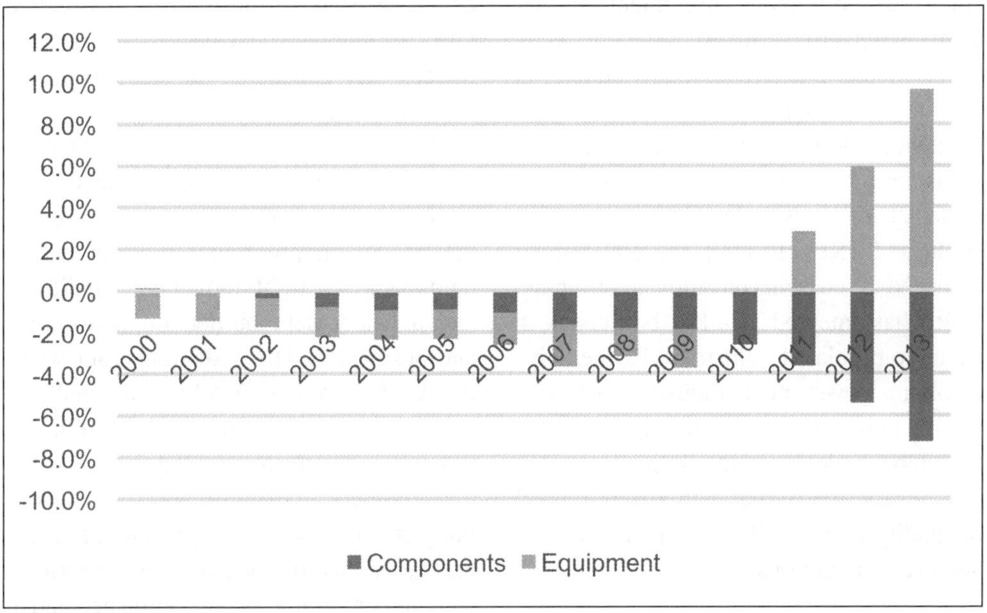

Source: UN Comtrade.

to reduce logistics costs and facilitate the flow of information from assembly operations to suppliers. An increasing proportion of the "inputs" into the production of electronic goods consists of the development, improvement, testing and application of software.

Vietnam's participation in the Trans-Pacific Partnership (TPP), a twelve-country trade deal that includes the United States, Australia and Japan but excludes China, Thailand and Cambodia, could help exports and also promote backward linkages, as supplier firms relocate to Vietnam to comply with the rules of origin provisions of the treaty. The experience of Mexico's automobile industry under the North American Free Trade Agreement suggests that access to the U.S. market can attract significant investment in upstream suppliers in the presence of other supporting factors. Moreover, the TPP, along with a new trade deal with the European Union, would require the government to rein in preferential treatment for state-owned companies. Much will depend on how these provisions are monitored and enforced. Ratification of the treaty, which is expected to take as long as two years, depends largely on the ability of the Obama administration to steer the deal through Congress with support of the Republicans and against the objections of many members of the president's own party.

With or without the TPP, creating the space for the development of supplier industries will require breaking the grip of the state on domestic markets. The government will need to transform itself from a gatekeeper, channelling lucrative domestic market opportunities to state and state-related companies, into a facilitator for domestic and foreign investment. Rather than restrict private firms' access to land, credit and permits, government agencies at all levels will need to work with assemblers to identify domestic and foreign supplier firms and formulate policies to reduce obstacles to investment. Beyond permits, credit and access to land, the government will need to focus on education and training, which has emerged as a key bottleneck in technology-related industries. Partnerships involving government, industry, local and foreign universities and colleges are needed to establish degree and diploma courses in relevant fields that can offer a level of quality that is still missing from most domestic institutions.

Conclusion

The *doi moi* growth model served Vietnam reasonably well for more than two decades. Vent-for-surplus growth created millions of jobs in agriculture and light manufacturing and generated billions of dollars in foreign exchange. Agricultural and manufactured exports were for the most part produced by small farms and workshops and foreign-invested enterprises. Export success produced the jobs and incomes needed to boost domestic consumption, which was the motor of the domestic economy. The state retained control over the commanding heights of the economy, including natural resources, distribution, finance, telecommunications and utilities. State and state-related companies benefited from close relationships to powerful government agencies and in addition enjoyed privileged access to land and capital. The absence of a genuinely independent commercial class reduced pressure on government to impose discipline on state firms. Over time these firms diversified into lucrative side businesses and became increasingly dependent on credit from the banking sector.

Three successive crises have brought the *doi moi* era to an end. While labour-intensive exports continue to expand, domestic consumption and investment are held back by tight monetary conditions and a heavy debt burden on households and businesses. The essential weakness of the *doi moi* growth model was the inability of the government to impose discipline on state-owned and state-related firms. Rather than compete on export markets or work to integrate into global supply chains, these firms used their privileged access to permits, land and credit to diversify into speculative ventures that promised higher returns but imposed huge risks on the economy. When the collapse came, the government lacked the capacity or political will to engineer a timely resolution of the bad debt problem weighing down the banking sector. As a result, domestic investment and consumption have remained depressed as businesses and households attempt to crawl out from under the wreckage of the crisis years.

Vietnam needs a new growth model, one that achieves closer integration between the successful export sector and the state-led domestic economy. In place of the "weird dualism" described by David Dapice more than a decade ago, Vietnam must find ways to capitalize on the presence of foreign firms to develop competitive domestic supplier industries and other firms servicing exporters.[14] Greater competition in domestic markets would favour more efficient firms and generate higher income and employment multiplier effects from investment and consumption. At the same time, long overdue banking reforms are needed to increase transparency and accountability among financial institutions, reduce connected lending, and channel credit to more efficient firms.

Building a political coalition in support of a new growth model will not be easy. The absence of established commercial groups that are independent from the state has left the country without an organized interest group pressing for deeper reforms. External pressure, for example from the partner countries of the TPP, while helpful, is not a replacement for a domestic constituency committed to change. As long as commercial advantage comes from relationships with government agencies and individuals, it is difficult to see how these groups will emerge. That the prolonged crisis from 2008 to the present had not generated more pressure for reform is a cause for concern.

Notes

1. Brian Van Arkadie and Raymond Mallon, *Viet Nam: A Transition Tiger?* (Canberra: Asia Pacific Press at the Australian National University, 2003); and Benedict J. Kerkvliet, *The Power of Everyday Politics: How Vietnamese Peasants Transformed National Policy* (Ithaca, NY: Cornell University Press, 2005).
2. U Hla Myint, *Southeast Asia's Economy: Development Policies in the 1970s* (Harmondsworth: Penguin, 1972).
3. Jonathan London, "Viet Nam and the Making of Market-Leninism", *Pacific Review* 22, no. 3 (2009): 375–99.
4. Martin Gainsborough, *Changing Political Economy of Vietnam: The Case of Ho Chi Minh City* (London: Routledge Curzon, 2003), p. 24.
5. Markus Taussig, Chi Hieu Nguyen, and Thuy Linh Nguyen, "Time for Real SOE Reform in Vietnam?" (Singapore: Center for Governance, Institutions and Organizations, NUS Business School, 2015), p. 21.
6. Martin Gainsborough, "Privatisation as State Advance: Private Indirect Government in Vietnam", *New Political Economy* 14, no. 2 (2009): 257–74.
7. Katariina Nilsson Hakkala and Ari Kokko, "The State and the Private Sector in Vietnam", Working Paper Series no. 236 (Stockholm: European Institute of Japan Studies, 2007) <http://www.researchgate.net/publication/5094556_The_State_And_The_Private_Sector_In_Vietnam>.
8. E.J. Malesky and M. Taussig, "Where Is Credit Due? Legal Institutions, Connections, and the Efficiency of Bank Lending in Vietnam", *Journal of Law, Economics, and Organization* 25 (June 2008): 535–78.
9. Cuong Nguyen and Quan Le, "Institutional Constraints and Private Sector Development: The Textile and Garment Industry in Vietnam", *ASEAN Economic Bulletin* 22 no. 3 (2005): 307.
10. Thuy Thu Nguyen and Mathijs A. van Dijk, "Corruption, Growth, and Governance: Private vs. State-owned Firms in Vietnam", *Journal of Banking & Finance* 36, no. 11 (2012): 2935–48.
11. Scott Cheshier and Jonathan Pincus, "Minsky Au Vietnam: State Corporations, Financial Instability and Industrialization", In *Minsky, Crisis and Development*, edited by Daniela Tavasci and Jan Toporowski (Basingstoke: Palgrave Macmillan, 2010), pp. 188–206.
12. Vu Minh Khuong, "Can Vietnam Achieve More Robust Economic Growth? Insights from a Comparative Analysis of Economic Reforms in Vietnam and China", *Southeast Asian Economies* 32, no. 1 (2015): 52.

13. Kenichi Ohno, "Avoiding the Middle-Income Trap: Renovating Industrial Policy Formulation in Vietnam", *ASEAN Economic Bulletin* 26, no. 1 (2009): 25–43.
14. David Dapice, "Vietnam's Economy: Success Story or Weird Dualism?", United Nations Development Program, 2003 <http://www.undp.org/content/dam/vietnam/docs/Publications/3977_Weird_Dualism_paper.pdf>.